CLYMER™

EVINRUDE/JOHNSON

OUTBOARD SHOP MANUAL
2-300 HP • 1991-1994 (Includes Jet Drives and Sea Drives)

The world's finest publisher of mechanical how-to manuals

INTERTEC PUBLISHING

P.O. Box 12901, Overland Park, KS 66282-2901

Copyright ©1994 Intertec Publishing Corporation

FIRST EDITION
First Printing October, 1994
Second Printing January, 1996

Printed in U.S.A.

ISBN: 0-89287-620-4

Library of Congress: 94-75184

Tools shown in Chapter Two courtesy of Thorsen Tool, Dallas, Texas. Test equipment shown in Chapter Two courtesy of Dixson, Inc., Grand Junction, Colorado.

Technical illustrations by Steve Amos, Diana Kirkland and Bob Caldwell.

COVER: Photo courtesy of Outboard Marine Corporation.

General Information   1

Tools and Techniques   2

Troubleshooting   3

Lubrication, Maintenance and Tune-up   4

Engine Synchronization and Linkage Adjustments   5

Fuel System   6

Ignition and Electrical Systems   7

Power Head   8

Gearcase   9

Power Trim and Tilt Systems   10

Oil Injection Systems   11

Automatic Rewind Starters   12

Sea Drives   13

Jet Drives   14

Index   15

Wiring Diagrams   16

The following books and guides are published by Intertec Publishing.

CLYMER™ SHOP MANUALS
Boat Motors and Drives
Motorcycles and ATVs
Snowmobiles
Personal Watercraft

**ABOS®/INTERTEC BLUE BOOKS®
AND TRADE-IN GUIDES**
Recreational Vehicles
Outdoor Power Equipment
Agricultural Tractors
Lawn and Garden Tractors
Motorcycles and ATVs
Snowmobiles and Personal Watercraft
Boats and Motors

AIRCRAFT BLUEBOOK-PRICE DIGEST®
Airplanes
Helicopters

AC-U-KWIK® DIRECTORIES
The Corporate Pilot's Airport/FBO Directory
International Manager's Edition
Jet Book

I&T SHOP SERVICE™ MANUALS
Tractors

INTERTEC SERVICE MANUALS
Snowmobiles
Outdoor Power Equipment
Personal Watercraft
Gasoline and Diesel Engines
Recreational Vehicles
Boat Motors and Drives
Motorcycles
Lawn and Garden Tractors

Contents

QUICK REFERENCE DATA IX

CHAPTER ONE
GENERAL INFORMATION 1
Manual organization 1
Notes, cautions and warnings 1
Torque specifications. 2
Engine operation 2
Fasteners 2
Lubricants 8
Gasket sealant 10
Galvanic corrosion 11
Protection from galvanic corrision 13
Propellers. 14

CHAPTER TWO
TOOLS AND TECHNIQUES. 21
Safety first 21
Basic hand tools. 21
Test equipment. 26
Service hints 28
Special tips. 30
Mechanic's techniques 31

CHAPTER THREE
TROUBLESHOOTING 33
Operating requirements 34
Starting system 34
AC (alternating current) lighting coil 50
Battery charging system 50
Ignition system 58
Breaker-point ignition testing (1-cylinder models). . . 63
Capacitor discharge ignition (CDI) troubleshooting. . . 65
CD2U (under flywheel) ignition troubleshooting. . . . 65
Capacitor discharge ignition system troubleshooting
(1991-on 3 and 4 hp models) 71
CD2 ignition system troubleshooting
(1993-on 6-30 hp models) 76
CD2 ignition troubleshooting (1992-on 35 Jet,
40 and 50 hp [except 48 hp] equipped with
12 amp charging system) 85
CD3 ignition troubleshooting (3-cylinder models). . . . 94
CD4 ignition system troubleshooting 108
CD4 ignition system troubleshooting (V4 loop
charge models—120 and 140 hp; 2.0 Sea Drive). . . 116
CD6 Ignition system troubleshooting
(1991 V6 cross flow models—
105 Jet, 150 and 175 hp). 129
CD6 ignition system troubleshooting
(1991-on V6 loop charge models—
200 and 225 hp; 3.0 Sea Drive) 149
CD6 OIS ignition system troubleshooting
(60° 150 and 175 hp models) 168
CD8 ignition system troubleshooting (1991-on
V8 loop charged models—250 and 300 hp;
4.0 Sea Drive models) 179
Key and neutral start switch 198
Fuel system 199
Engine temperature and overheating. 201
Engine 203

CHAPTER FOUR

LUBRICATION, MAINTENANCE AND TUNE-UP 215

Lubrication................................... 215
Storage...................................... 220
Complete submersion 224
Anticorrosion maintenance 225
Engine flushing 226
Tune-up 227

CHAPTER FIVE

ENGINE SYNCHRONIZATION AND LINKAGE ADJUSTMENTS 243

Engine timing and synchronization.............. 243
Required equipment........................... 243
3 and 4 (2-cylinder models)..................... 245
4 Deluxe models.............................. 246
6 and 8 hp (2-cylinder models) 247
1991 and 1992 9.9 and 15 hp (2-cylinder models) ... 249
1993-on 9.9 and 15 hp (2-cylinder models) 251
20, 25, 28 and 30 hp (2-cylinder models)......... 253
35 Jet, 40, 48 and 50 hp (2-cylinder models) 257
1991 and 1992 60 and 70 hp (3-cylinder models) ... 263
1993-on 60 and 70 hp (3-cylinder models
  equipped with tiller handle) 270
1993-on 60 and 70 hp (3-cylinder models
  equipped with remote control) 274
65 Jet, 80 Jet, 1.6 Sea Drive and 85-115 hp
  (90° V4 cross flow models) 278
2.0 Sea Drive, 120 and 140 hp (90° V4 loop
  charged models) 285
1991 105 Jet, 150 and 175 hp
  (90° V6 cross flow models) 288
1992-on 105 Jet, 1991-on 150 and 175 hp
  (60° V6 models) 290
3.0 Sea Drive, 1991 and 1992 200 and 225 hp
  (90° V6 loop charged models) 296
1993-on 200 and 225 hp (90° V6 loop
  charged models); 4.0 Sea Drive, 250
  and 300 hp (90° V8 loop charged models)........ 301

CHAPTER SIX

FUEL SYSTEM 307

Fuel pump 307
Carburetors 310
Carburetor (2, 2.3 and 3.3 hp)................. 313
Carburetor 3 and 4 hp; 4 Deluxe................ 316
Carburetor (6-20 hp models) 321
TR and SV carburetor (25-70 hp models)......... 327
Top feed carburetor (V4 and V6 cross flow models) . 337
Minlon carburetors (V4 and V6
  loop charged models) 342
Electric fuel primer pump (V8 models) 351
Manual fuel primer 352
Electric fuel primer solenoid................... 354
Fuel module and vapor separator (60° V6 models) .. 356
Fuel line and primer bulb 362

CHAPTER SEVEN

IGNITION AND ELECTRICAL SYSTEMS.. 363

Battery 363
Battery charging system 371
Electric starting system 376
Starter motor 376
Neutral start switch 388
Ignition system 390
Magneto breaker point ignition system service 391
CD2U ignition............................... 392
CD ignition................................. 396
CD ignition (all models except CD2U,
  3 and 4 hp and 60° V6 models) 398
Optical ignition system (60° V6 models) 406

CHAPTER EIGHT

POWER HEAD 416

Engine serial number......................... 417
Fasteners and torque 418
Gaskets and sealants 418
Flywheel 419
Power head 425
Leaf valves................................. 523
Thermostat................................. 530

CHAPTER NINE
GEARCASE **543**
Service precautions 543
Propeller. 545
Water pump 546
Gearcase 556
Pinion gear depth (40-70 hp, V4, V6
   and V8 models) 623

CHAPTER TEN
POWER TRIM AND TILT SYSTEMS **630**
Touch-trim 630
Trim/tilt motor testing 640
Power trim/tilt assembly removal/installation
   (40-50 hp) 641
Conventional power trim and tilt system 642
Trim/tilt motor testing 650
Power trim/tilt system removal/installation
   (conventional trim/tilt) 652
Fastrak power trim/tilt system. 653
Trim/tilt motor testing 661

CHAPTER ELEVEN
OIL INJECTION SYSTEMS. **665**
Accumix oil injection 665
OMC variable ratio oiling (VRO) system. 666

CHAPTER TWELVE
AUTOMATIC REWIND STARTERS. **673**
Rewind starter (2.0, 2.3 and 3.3 hp) 673
Rewind starter (3 and 4 [except 4 Deluxe] hp) 675
Rewind starter (4 Deluxe models). 678
Rewind starter (6 and 8 hp; 1993-on 9.9 and 15 hp). . 681
Rewind starter (1991-92 9.9 and 15 hp) 684
Rewind starter (20-30 hp) 687
Rewind starter (40 hp). 690

CHAPTER THIRTEEN
SEA DRIVES **693**
Selectrim (1.6 Sea Drive) 693
Selectrim/tilt (2.0, 3.0 and 4.0 Sea Drives) 700

CHAPTER FOURTEEN
JET DRIVES **706**
Maintenance. 706
Water pump 711
Jet drive 711
Bearing housing. 715
Intake housing liner. 719

INDEX. **720**

WIRING DIAGRAMS **723**

Quick Reference Data

TEST WHEEL RECOMMENDATIONS

Model	Test wheel (part No.)	Minimum test speed (rpm)
2 hp	_[1]	4500
2.3 hp	_[1]	4800
3.3 hp	115306	5000
3 hp, 4 hp	317738	4400
4 Deluxe	390123	5100
6 hp	390239	4800
8 hp	390239	5300
9.9 hp		
1991-1992	386537	4800
1993-on	435750	5200
15 hp		
1991-1992	386537	6100
1993-on	435750	5800
20 hp	386891	4550
25 hp	434505	4800
28 hp	398948	4800
30 hp	434505	5400
40 hp	432968	4900
48 hp, 50 hp	432968	5200
60 hp	386665	5000
70 hp	386665	5700
85 hp, 88 hp, 90 hp, 100, 115 hp	382861	4800
120 hp		
1991-1992	386246	5300
1993-on	433068	5200
120TXETF, 120TXATF	396277	5200
140TL		
1991-1992	386246	5500
1993-on	433068	5300
140TX		
1991-1992	387388	5500
1993-on	396277	5300
140CX		
1991-1992	398673	5500
1993-on	398673	5300
150 hp (149.4 cid)	387388	4500
175 hp (160.3 cid)	387388	4800
60° V6		
150 (158 cid)	387388[2]	4500
60° V6		
175 (158 cid)	387388[2]	4800
200XP, 200GT, 200STL		
1991-1992	387388	5700
200STL		
1993-on	436080	5700
200TX		
1991-1992	387388	5500
1993-on	436080	5500

(continued)

TEST WHEEL RECOMMENDATIONS (continued)

Model	Test wheel (part No.)	Minimum test speed (rpm)
200CX		
1991-1992	398673	5500
1993-on	436081	5500
225 hp		
1991-1992	387388	5700
1993-on	436080	5700
225CX		
1991-1992	388673	5700
1993-on	436081	5700
250 hp, 300 hp	396277	5500
250CX, 300CX	398674	5500

1. A test wheel is not used on 2 and 2.3 hp models. Use the standard propeller (part No. 115208) when running motor in a test tank.
2. On counter rotating (CX) models, use test wheel (part No. 398673).

RECOMMENDED SPARK PLUGS

Model	Champion plug type	Gap (in.)
2, 2.3, 3.3 hp		
1991-1992	QL77JC4	0.030
1993-on	L78YC	0.030
3-30 hp	QL77JC4[1]	0.030
40, 48, 50 hp	QL78C[1]	0.030
60-115 hp	QL77JC4[1]	0.030
120, 140 hp	QL77JC4[2]	0.030
150-300 hp	QL77JC4[1]	0.030
1.6-4.0 Sea Drive	QL77JC4[1]	0.030

1. The manufacturer recommends using Champion QL16V surface gap spark plug if operated at sustained high speed.
2. The manufacturer recommends using Champion QL78V (1991 and 1992 models) or QL16V (1993-on models) surface gap spark plugs if operated at sustained high speed.

GENERAL ENGINE SPECIFICATIONS

Model	Displacement cu. in. (cc)	Type
2, 2.3, 3.3	4.47 (77.8)	1-cylinder loop charged
3, 4, 4 Deluxe	5.29 (86.4)	2-cylinder cross flow
6, 8	10.0 (164)	2-cylinder cross flow
9.9, 15		
1991-92	13.2 (216)	2-cylinder cross flow
1993-on	15.6 (255)	2-cylinder cross flow
20, 25, 28, 30	31.8 (521.2)	2-cylinder cross flow
35 Jet, 40, 48, 50	44.99 (737.4)	2-cylinder loop charged
60, 70	56.1 (920)	3-cylinder loop charged

(continued)

GENERAL ENGINE SPECIFICATIONS (continued)

Model	Displacement cu. in. (cc)	Type
65 Jet, 80 Jet, 85, 88, 90, 115, 115	99.6 (1632)	90° V4 cross flow
120, 140	122 (2000)	90° V4 loop charged
105 Jet, 150 [1]	149.4 (2448)	90° V6 cross flow
60° V6 150/175	158 (2589)	60° V6 loop charged
175 [1]	160.3 (2626)	90° V6 cross flow
200, 225	183 (3000)	90° V6 loop charged
250, 300	244 (4000)	90° V8 loop charged
1.6 Sea Drive	99.6 (1632)	90° V4 cross flow
2.0 Sea Drive	122 (2000)	90° V4 loop charged
3.0 Sea Drive	183 (3000)	90° V6 loop charged
4.0 Sea Drive	244 (4000)	90° V6 loop charged

1. The 90° V6 cross flow power head was discontinued after the 1991 model year. The 105 Jet, 150 and 175 hp models for 1992-on are 60° loop charged V6 series engines.

BATTERY CAPACITY (HOURS)

Accessory draw	80 Amp-hour battery provides continuous power for:	Approximate recharge time
5 amps	13.5 hours	16 hours
15 amps	3.5 hours	13 hours
25 amps	1.8 hours	12 hours

Accessory draw	105 Amp-hour battery provides continuous power for:	Approximate recharge time
5 amps	15.8 hours	16 hours
15 amps	4.2 hours	13 hours
25 amps	2.4 hours	12 hours

APPROXIMATE STATE OF BATTERY CHARGE

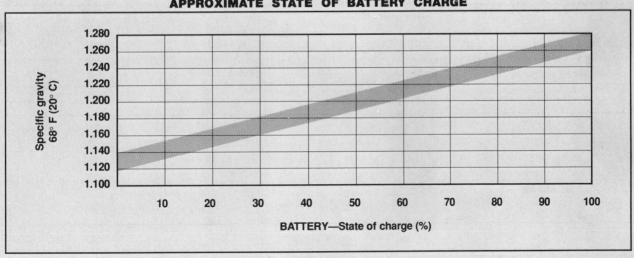

MINIMUM BATTERY RECOMMENDATIONS

Model	Minimum battery cold cranking amps (CCA) and reserve capacity
9.9-30 hp	350 CCA and 100 minutes reserve
40-140 hp	360 CCA and 115 minutes reserve
150-300 hp	500 CCA and 99 minutes reserve

GEARCASE GEAR RATIO, LUBRICANT CAPACITY AND RECOMMENDED LUBRICANT

Model	Recommended gear ratio	Lubricant capacity	Lubricant
2, 2.3, 3 hp	13:24	3 oz. (90 mL)	1
3, 4 hp	12:25	2.7 oz. (80 mL)	1
4 Deluxe	13:29	11 oz. (325 mL)	2
6, 8 hp	13:29	11 oz. (325 mL)	1
9.9, 15 hp	12:29	9 oz. (260 mL)	1
20, 25, 30 hp	13:28	11 oz. (325 mL)	1
28 hp	12:21	8 oz. (245 mL)	1
40, 48, 50 hp	12:29	16.4 oz. (485 mL)	1
60, 70 hp	12:29	22 oz. (650 mL)	1
85, 88, 90, 100, 115 hp	13:26	26 oz. (800 mL)	1
120, 140 hp	13:26	26 oz. (800 mL)	1
120TXETF, 120TXATF, 140CX	12:27	33 oz. (980 mL)	1
150, 175 hp	14:26	33 oz. (980 mL)	1
200, 275 hp	14:26	33 oz. (980 mL)	1
250, 300 hp	17:30	71 oz. (2100 mL)	1

1. OMC Hi-Vis Gearcase Lubricant.
2. OMC Premium Blend Gearcase Lubricant

ENGINE SPEED SPECIFICATIONS

Model	Idle speed[1] (rpm)	Full throttle speed (rpm)
2 hp	1100-1300	4000-5000
2.3 hp	1100-1300	4200-5200
3.3 hp	1100-1300	4300-5000
3, 4 hp	700-800	4500-5500
4 Deluxe	600-750	4500-5500
6 hp	650-700	4500-5500
8 hp	650-700	5000-6000
9.9, 15 hp	650-700	5000-6000
20, 25, 28 hp	650-700	4500-5500
30 hp	650-700	5200-5800
40, 48, 50 hp	725-775	4500-5500
60, 70 hp	600-700[2]	5000-6000
85, 90, 100, 115 hp	625-675	4500-5500
120, 140 hp	600-700[2]	5000-6000
150 hp (90°)	625-675	4500-5500

(continued)

ENGINE SPEED SPECIFICATIONS (continued)

Model	Idle speed[1] (rpm)	Full throttle speed (rpm)
175 hp (90°)	625-675	4750-5750
150, 175 hp (60°)	600-700[2]	4500-5500
200, 225 hp	600-700[2]	5000-6000
250 hp	550-650	4500-5500
300 hp	650-750	5000-6000

1. Idle speed should be checked with the boat in the water with the correct propeller installed, idling in forward gear with boat movement unrestrained.
2. Idle speed is adjusted by setting the idle timing. See Chapter Five.

Introduction

This Clymer shop manual covers service and repair of all 2-300 hp Evinrude/Johnson outboard motors designed for recreational use from 1991-1994. Coverage is also provided for 35-105 hp Jet drives and 1.6-4.0 Sea Drive models. It does not cover similar displacement engines designed expressly for racing, sailing or commercial use. The 90° V6 cross flow engine was discontinued after the 1991 model year. For 1992-on, the 105 Jet, 150 and 175 hp models are the 60° loop charged series engines.

Step-by-step instructions and hundreds of illustrations guide you through jobs ranging from simple maintenance to complete overhaul.

This manual can be used by anyone from a first time owner/amateur to a professional mechanic. Easy to read type, detailed drawings and clear photographs give you all the information you need to do the work right.

Having a well-maintained engine will increase your enjoyment of your boat as well as assuring your safety offshore. Keep this shop manual handy and use it often. It can save you hundreds of dollars in maintenance and repair bills and make yours a reliable, top-performing boat.

Chapter One

General Information

This detailed, comprehensive manual contains complete information on maintenance, tune-up, repair and overhaul. Hundreds of photos and drawings guide you through every step-by-step procedure.

Troubleshooting, tune-up, maintenance and repair are not difficult if you know what tools and equipment to use and what to do. Anyone not afraid to get their hands dirty, of average intelligence and with some mechanical ability, can perform most of the procedures in this book. See Chapter Two for more information on tools and techniques.

A shop manual is a reference. You want to be able to find information fast. Clymer books are designed with you in mind. All chapters are thumb tabbed and important items are indexed at the end of the book. All procedures, tables, photos, etc., in this manual assume that the reader may be working on the machine or using this manual for the first time.

Keep this book handy in your tool box. It will help you to better understand how your machine runs, lower repair and maintenance costs and generally increase your enjoyment of your marine equipment.

MANUAL ORGANIZATION

This chapter provides general information useful to marine owners and mechanics.

Chapter Two discusses the tools and techniques for preventive maintenance, troubleshooting and repair.

Chapter Three describes typical equipment problems and provides logical troubleshooting procedures.

Following chapters describe specific systems, providing disassembly, repair, assembly and adjustment procedures in simple step-by-step form. Specifications concerning a specific system are included at the end of the appropriate chapter.

NOTES, CAUTIONS AND WARNINGS

The terms NOTE, CAUTION and WARNING have specific meanings in this manual. A NOTE provides additional information to make a step or procedure easier or clearer. Disregarding a NOTE could cause inconvenience, but would not cause damage or personal injury.

A CAUTION emphasizes areas where equipment damage could result. Disregarding a CAUTION could cause permanent mechanical damage; however, personal injury is unlikely.

A WARNING emphasizes areas where personal injury or even death could result from negligence. Mechanical damage may also occur. WARNINGS *are to be taken seriously*. In some cases, serious injury or death has resulted from disregarding similar warnings.

TORQUE SPECIFICATIONS

Torque specifications throughout this manual are given in foot-pounds (ft.-lb.) and either Newton meters (N·m) or meter-kilograms (mkg). Newton meters are being adopted in place of meter-kilograms in accordance with the International Modernized Metric System. Existing torque wrenches calibrated in meter-kilograms can be used by performing a simple conversion: move the decimal point one place to the right. For example, 4.7 mkg = 47 N·m. This conversion is accurate enough for mechanics' use even though the exact mathematical conversion is 3.5 mkg = 34.3 N·m.

ENGINE OPERATION

All marine engines, whether 2- or 4-stroke, gasoline or diesel, operate on the Otto cycle of intake, compression, power and exhaust phases.

4-stroke Cycle

A 4-stroke engine requires two crankshaft revolutions (4 strokes of the piston) to complete the Otto cycle. **Figure 1** shows gasoline 4-stroke engine operation. **Figure 2** shows diesel 4-stroke engine operation.

2-stroke Cycle

A 2-stroke engine requires only 1 crankshaft revolution (2 strokes of the piston) to complete the Otto cycle. **Figure 3** shows gasoline 2-stroke engine operation. Although diesel 2-strokes exist, they are not commonly used in light marine applications.

FASTENERS

The material and design of the various fasteners used on marine equipment are not arrived at by chance or accident. Fastener design determines the type of tool required to work with the fastener. Fastener material is carefully selected to decrease the possibility of physical failure or corrosion. See *Galvanic Corrosion* in this chapter for more information on marine materials.

Threads

Nuts, bolts and screws are manufactured in a wide range of thread patterns. To join a nut and bolt, the diameter of the bolt and the diameter of the hole in the nut must be the same. It is just as important that the threads on both be properly matched.

The best way to determine if the threads on two fasteners are matched is to turn the nut on the bolt (or the bolt into the threaded hole in a piece of equipment) with fingers only. Be sure both pieces are clean. If much force is required, check the thread condition on each fastener. If the thread condition is good but the fasteners jam, the threads are not compatible.

Four important specifications describe every thread:
 a. Diameter.
 b. Threads per inch.
 c. Thread pattern.
 d. Thread direction.

Figure 4 shows the first two specifications. Thread pattern is more subtle. Italian and British

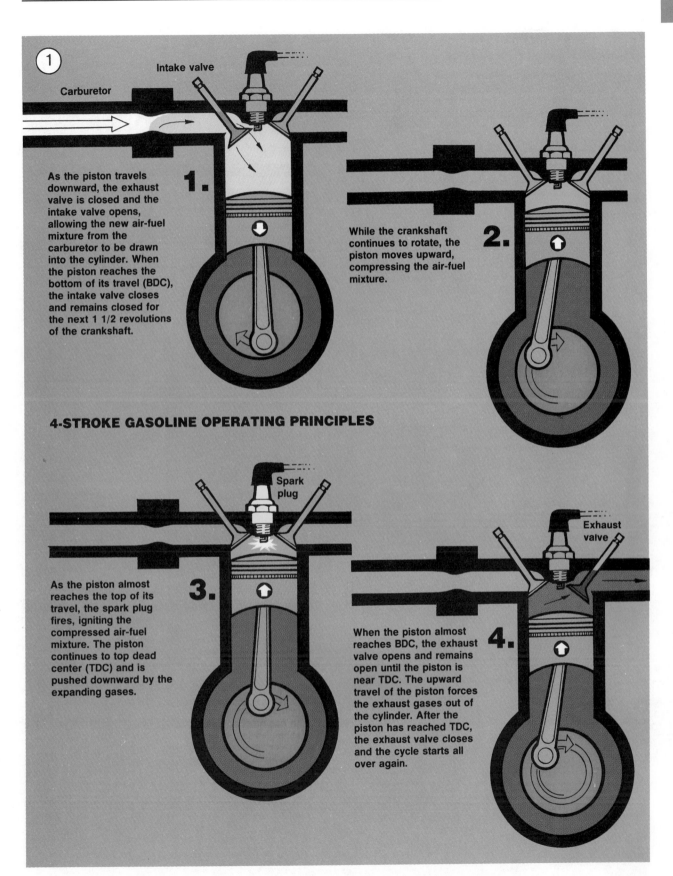

① Intake valve

Carburetor

As the piston travels downward, the exhaust valve is closed and the intake valve opens, allowing the new air-fuel mixture from the carburetor to be drawn into the cylinder. When the piston reaches the bottom of its travel (BDC), the intake valve closes and remains closed for the next 1 1/2 revolutions of the crankshaft.

1.

While the crankshaft continues to rotate, the piston moves upward, compressing the air-fuel mixture.

2.

4-STROKE GASOLINE OPERATING PRINCIPLES

Spark plug

As the piston almost reaches the top of its travel, the spark plug fires, igniting the compressed air-fuel mixture. The piston continues to top dead center (TDC) and is pushed downward by the expanding gases.

3.

Exhaust valve

When the piston almost reaches BDC, the exhaust valve opens and remains open until the piston is near TDC. The upward travel of the piston forces the exhaust gases out of the cylinder. After the piston has reached TDC, the exhaust valve closes and the cycle starts all over again.

4.

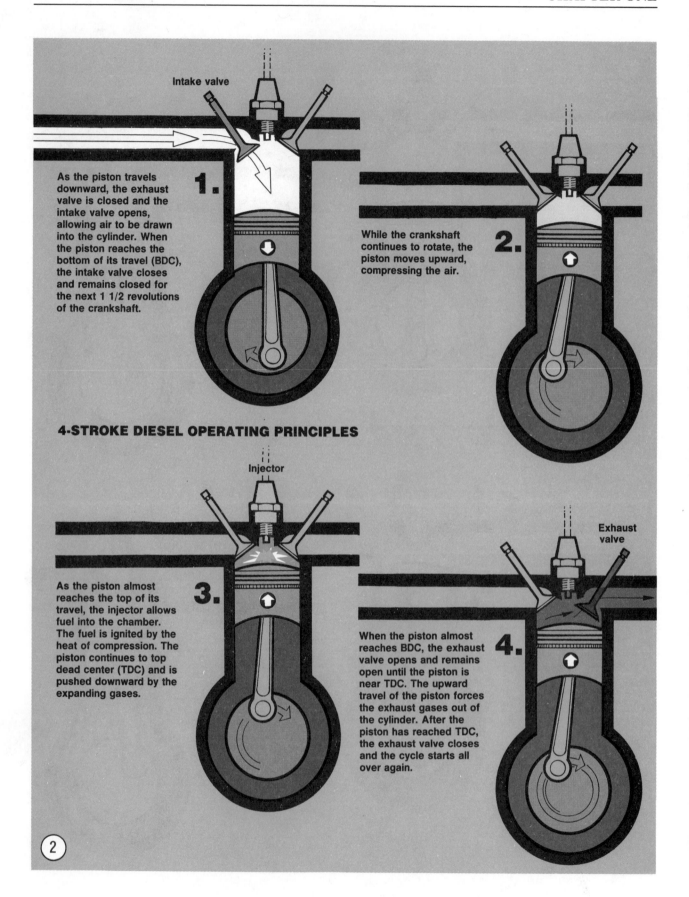

Intake valve

As the piston travels downward, the exhaust valve is closed and the intake valve opens, allowing air to be drawn into the cylinder. When the piston reaches the bottom of its travel (BDC), the intake valve closes and remains closed for the next 1 1/2 revolutions of the crankshaft.

1.

While the crankshaft continues to rotate, the piston moves upward, compressing the air.

2.

4-STROKE DIESEL OPERATING PRINCIPLES

Injector

As the piston almost reaches the top of its travel, the injector allows fuel into the chamber. The fuel is ignited by the heat of compression. The piston continues to top dead center (TDC) and is pushed downward by the expanding gases.

3.

Exhaust valve

When the piston almost reaches BDC, the exhaust valve opens and remains open until the piston is near TDC. The upward travel of the piston forces the exhaust gases out of the cylinder. After the piston has reached TDC, the exhaust valve closes and the cycle starts all over again.

4.

② 2

As the piston travels downward, it uncovers the exhaust port (A) allowing the exhaust gases to leave the cylinder. A fresh air-fuel charge, which has been compressed slightly in the crankcase, enters the cylinder through the transfer port (B). Since this charge enters under pressure, it also helps to push out the exhaust gases.

While the crankshaft continues to rotate, the piston moves upward, covering the transfer (B) and exhaust (A) ports. The piston compresses the new air-fuel mixture and creates a low-pressure area in the crankcase at the same time. As the piston continues to travel, it uncovers the intake port (C). A fresh air-fuel charge from the carburetor (D) is drawn into the crankcase through the intake port.

2-STROKE OPERATING PRINCIPLES

As the piston almost reaches the top of its travel, the spark plug fires, igniting the compressed air-fuel mixture. The piston continues to top dead center (TDC) and is pushed downward by the expanding gases.

As the piston travels down, the exhaust gases leave the cylinder and the complete cycle starts all over again.

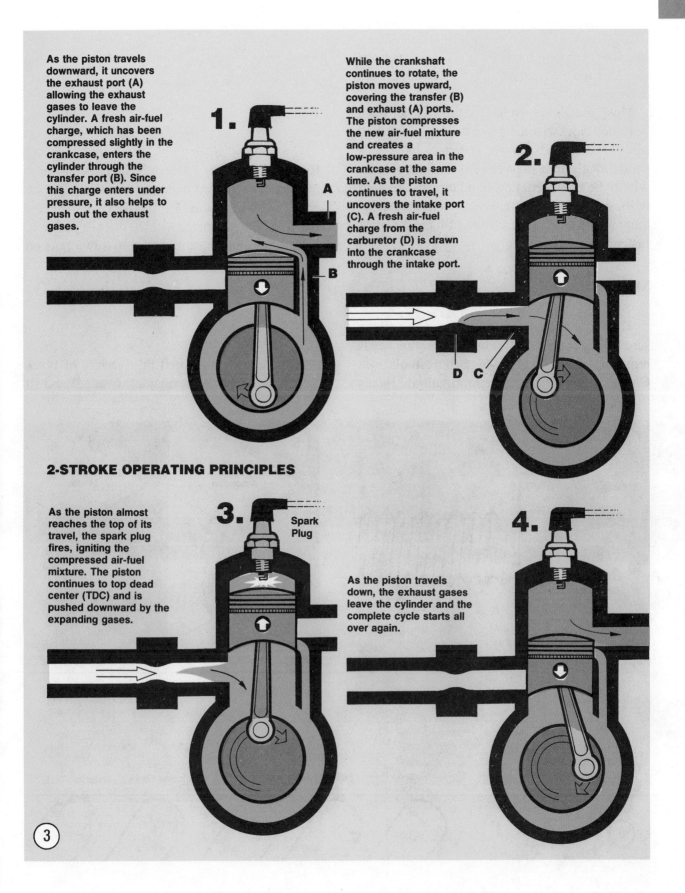

standards exist, but the most commonly used by marine equipment manufacturers are American standard and metric standard. The threads are cut differently as shown in **Figure 5**.

Most threads are cut so that the fastener must be turned clockwise to tighten it. These are called right-hand threads. Some fasteners have left-hand threads; they must be turned counterclockwise to be tightened. Left-hand threads are used in locations where normal rotation of the equipment would tend to loosen a right-hand threaded fastener.

Machine Screws

There are many different types of machine screws. **Figure 6** shows a number of screw heads requiring different types of turning tools (see Chapter Two for detailed information). Heads

are also designed to protrude above the metal (round) or to be slightly recessed in the metal (flat) (**Figure 7**).

Bolts

Commonly called bolts, the technical name for these fasteners is cap screw. They are normally described by diameter, threads per inch and length. For example, 1/4-20 × 1 indicates a bolt 1/4 in. in diameter with 20 threads per inch, 1 in. long. The measurement across two flats on the head of the bolt indicates the proper wrench size to be used.

Nuts

Nuts are manufactured in a variety of types and sizes. Most are hexagonal (6-sided) and fit

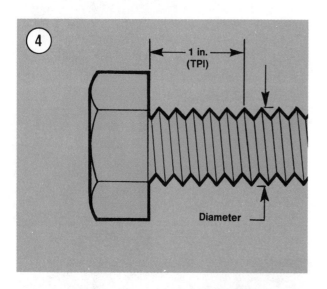
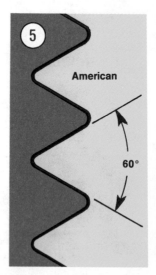
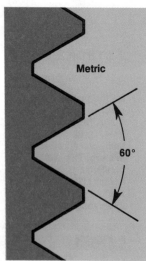
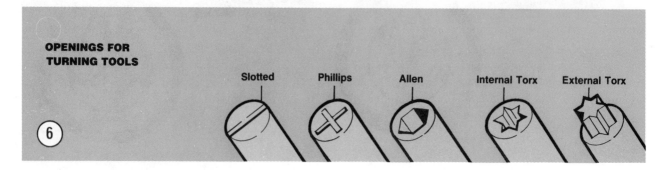

on bolts, screws and studs with the same diameter and threads per inch.

Figure 8 shows several types of nuts. The common nut is usually used with a lockwasher. Self-locking nuts have a nylon insert that prevents the nut from loosening; no lockwasher is required. Wing nuts are designed for fast removal by hand. Wing nuts are used for convenience in non-critical locations.

To indicate the size of a nut, manufacturers specify the diameter of the opening and the threads per inch. This is similar to bolt specification, but without the length dimension. The measurement across two flats on the nut indicates the proper wrench size to be used.

Washers

There are two basic types of washers: flat washers and lockwashers. Flat washers are simple discs with a hole to fit a screw or bolt. Lockwashers are designed to prevent a fastener from working loose due to vibration, expansion and contraction. **Figure 9** shows several types of lockwashers. Note that flat washers are often used between a lockwasher and a fastener to provide a smooth bearing surface. This allows the fastener to be turned easily with a tool.

Cotter Pins

Cotter pins (**Figure 10**) are used to secure special kinds of fasteners. The threaded stud

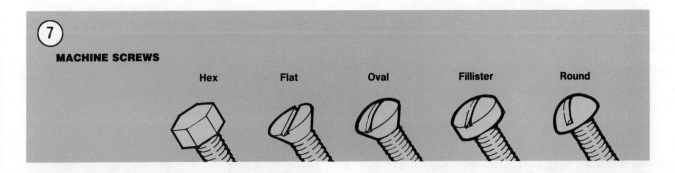

⑦ MACHINE SCREWS

Hex   Flat   Oval   Fillister   Round

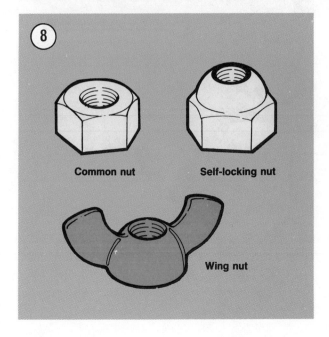

⑧

Common nut   Self-locking nut

Wing nut

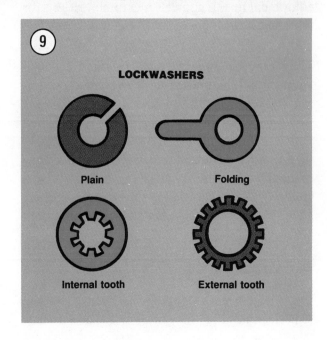

⑨ LOCKWASHERS

Plain   Folding

Internal tooth   External tooth

must have a hole in it; the nut or nut lock piece has projections that the cotter pin fits between. This type of nut is called a "Castellated nut." Cotter pins should not be reused after removal.

Snap Rings

Snap rings can be of an internal or external design. They are used to retain items on shafts (external type) or within tubes (internal type). Snap rings can be reused if they are not distorted during removal. In some applications, snap rings of varying thickness can be selected to control the end play of parts assemblies.

LUBRICANTS

Periodic lubrication ensures long service life for any type of equipment. It is especially important to marine equipment because it is exposed to salt or brackish water and other harsh environments. The *type* of lubricant used is just as important as the lubrication service itself; although, in an emergency, the wrong type of lubricant is better than none at all. The following paragraphs describe the types of lubricants most often used on marine equipment. Be sure to follow the equipment manufacturer's recommendations for lubricant types.

Generally, all liquid lubricants are called "oil." They may be mineral-based (including petroleum bases), natural-based (vegetable and animal bases), synthetic-based or emulsions (mixtures). "Grease" is an oil which is thickened with a metallic "soap." The resulting material is then usually enhanced with anticorrosion, antioxidant and extreme pressure (EP) additives. Grease is often classified by the type of thickener added; lithium and calcium soap are commonly used.

4-stroke Engine Oil

Oil for 4-stroke engines is graded by the American Petroleum Institute (API) and the So-

ciety of Automotive Engineers (SAE) in several categories. Oil containers display these ratings on the top or label (**Figure 11**).

API oil grade is indicated by letters, oils for gasoline engines are identified by an "S" and oils for diesel engines are identified by a "C." Most modern gasoline engines require SF or SG graded oil. Automotive and marine diesel engines use CC or CD graded oil.

Viscosity is an indication of the oil's thickness, or resistance to flow. The SAE uses numbers to indicate viscosity; thin oils have low numbers and thick oils have high numbers. A "W" after the number indicates that the viscosity testing was done at low temperature to simulate cold weather operation. Engine oils fall into the 5W-20W and 20-50 range.

Multi-grade oils (for example, 10W-40) are less viscous (thinner) at low temperatures and more viscous (thicker) at high temperatures. This allows the oil to perform efficiently across a wide range of engine operating temperatures.

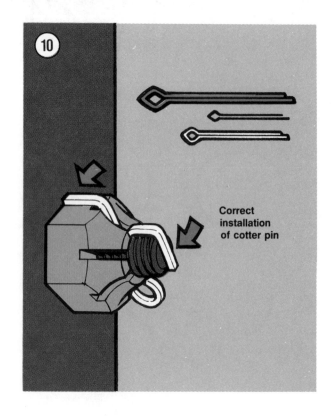

Correct installation of cotter pin

2-stroke Engine Oil

Lubrication for a 2-stroke engine is provided by oil mixed with the incoming fuel-air mixture. Some of the oil mist settles out in the crankcase, lubricating the crankshaft and lower end of the connecting rods. The rest of the oil enters the combustion chamber to lubricate the piston, rings and cylinder wall. This oil is then burned along with the fuel-air mixture during the combustion process.

Engine oil must have several special qualities to work well in a 2-stroke engine. It must mix easily and stay in suspension in gasoline. When burned, it can't leave behind excessive deposits. It must also be able to withstand the high temperatures associated with 2-stroke engines.

The National Marine Manufacturer's Association (NMMA) has set standards for oil used in 2-stroke, water-cooled engines. This is the NMMA TC-W (two-cycle, water-cooled) grade (**Figure 12**). The oil's performance in the following areas is evaluated:

a. Lubrication (prevention of wear and scuffing).
b. Spark plug fouling.
c. Preignition.
d. Piston ring sticking.
e. Piston varnish.
f. General engine condition (including deposits).
g. Exhaust port blockage.
h. Rust prevention.
i. Mixing ability with gasoline.

In addition to oil grade, manufacturers specify the ratio of gasoline to oil required during break-in and normal engine operation.

Gear Oil

Gear lubricants are assigned SAE viscosity numbers under the same system as 4-stroke engine oil. Gear lubricant falls into the SAE 72-250 range (**Figure 13**). Some gear lubricants are multi-grade; for example, SAE 85W-90.

Three types of marine gear lubricant are generally available: SAE 90 hypoid gear lubricant is designed for older manual-shift units; Type C gear lubricant contains additives designed for electric shift mechanisms; High viscosity gear lubricant is a heavier oil designed to withstand the shock loading of high-performance engines or units subjected to severe duty use. Always use a gear lubricant of the type specified by the unit's manufacturer.

Grease

Greases are graded by the National Lubricating Grease Institute (NLGI). Greases are graded by number according to the consistency of the grease; these ratings range from No. 000 to No. 6, with No. 6 being the most solid. A typical multipurpose grease is NLGI No. 2 (**Figure 14**). For specific applications, equipment manufacturers may require grease with an additive such as molybdenum disulfide (MOS^2).

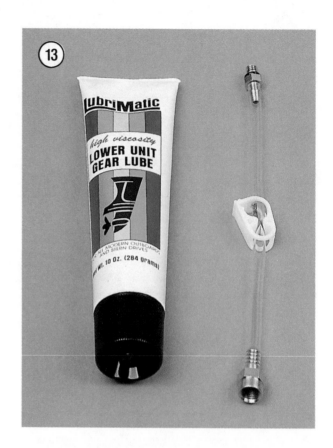

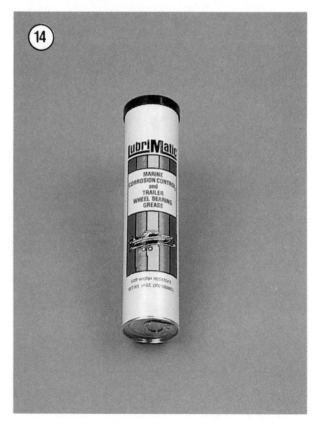

GASKET SEALANT

Gasket sealant is used instead of pre-formed gaskets on some applications, or as a gasket dressing on others. Two types of gasket sealant are commonly used: room temperature vulcanizing (RTV) and anaerobic. Because these two materials have different sealing properties, they cannot be used interchangeably.

RTV Sealant

This is a silicone gel supplied in tubes (**Figure 15**). Moisture in the air causes RTV to cure. Always place the cap on the tube as soon as possible when using RTV. RTV has a shelf life of one year and will not cure properly when the shelf life has expired. Check the expiration date on RTV tubes before using and keep partially used tubes tightly sealed. RTV sealant can generally fill gaps up to 1/4 in. (6.3 mm) and works well on slightly flexible surfaces.

Applying RTV Sealant

Clean all gasket residue from mating surfaces. Surfaces should be clean and free of oil and dirt. Remove all RTV gasket material from blind attaching holes because it can create a "hydraulic" effect and affect bolt torque.

Apply RTV sealant in a continuous bead 2-3 mm (0.08-0.12 in.) thick. Circle all mounting holes unless otherwise specified. Torque mating parts within 10 minutes after application.

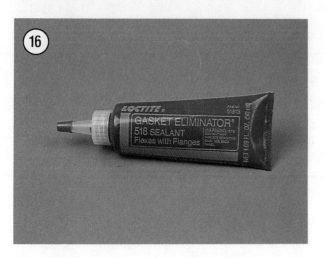

Anaerobic Sealant

This is a gel supplied in tubes (**Figure 16**). It cures only in the absence of air, as when squeezed tightly between two machined mating surfaces. For this reason, it will not spoil if the cap is left off the tube. It should not be used if one mating surface is flexible. Anaerobic sealant is able to fill gaps up to 0.030 in. (0.8 mm) and generally works best on rigid, machined flanges or surfaces.

Applying Anaerobic Sealant

Clean all gasket residue from mating surfaces. Surfaces must be clean and free of oil and dirt. Remove all gasket material from blind attaching holes, as it can cause a "hydraulic" effect and affect bolt torque.

Apply anaerobic sealant in a 1 mm or less (0.04 in.) bead to one sealing surface. Circle all mounting holes. Torque mating parts within 15 minutes after application.

GALVANIC CORROSION

A chemical reaction occurs whenever two different types of metal are joined by an electrical conductor and immersed in an electrolyte. Electrons transfer from one metal to the other through the electrolyte and return through the conductor.

The hardware on a boat is made of many different types of metal. The boat hull acts as a conductor between the metals. Even if the hull is wooden or fiberglass, the slightest film of water (electrolyte) within the hull provides conductivity. This combination creates a good environment for electron flow (**Figure 17**). Unfortunately, this electron flow results in galvanic corrosion of the metal involved, causing one of the metals to be corroded or eaten away by the process. The amount of electron flow (and, therefore, the amount of corrosion) depends on several factors:

a. The types of metal involved.

b. The efficiency of the conductor.

c. The strength of the electrolyte.

Metals

The chemical composition of the metals used in marine equipment has a significant effect on the amount and speed of galvanic corrosion. Certain metals are more resistant to corrosion than others. These electrically negative metals are commonly called "noble;" they act as the cathode in any reaction. Metals that are more subject to corrosion are electrically positive; they act as the anode in a reaction. The more noble metals include titanium, 18-8 stainless steel and nickel. Less noble metals include zinc, aluminum and magnesium. Galvanic corrosion becomes more severe as the difference in electrical potential between the two metals increases.

In some cases, galvanic corrosion can occur within a single piece of metal. Common brass is a mixture of zinc and copper, and, when immersed in an electrolyte, the zinc portion of the mixture will corrode away as reaction occurs between the zinc and the copper particles.

Conductors

The hull of the boat often acts as the conductor between different types of metal. Marine equipment, such as an outboard motor or stern drive unit, can also act as the conductor. Large masses of metal, firmly connected together, are more efficient conductors than water. Rubber mountings and vinyl-based paint can act as insulators between pieces of metal.

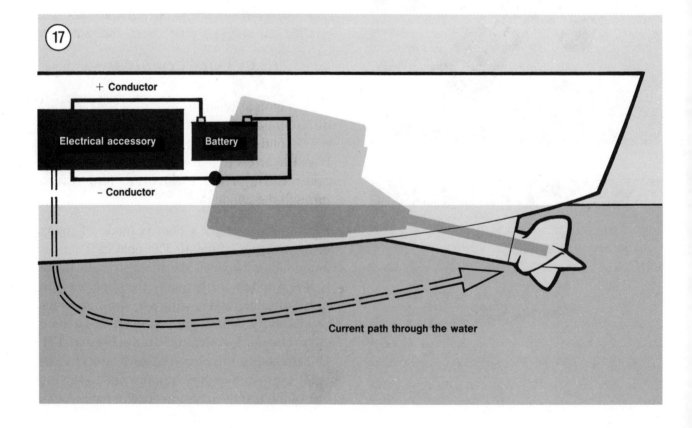

Current path through the water

Electrolyte

The water in which a boat operates acts as the electrolyte for the galvanic corrosion process. The better a conductor the electrolyte is, the more severe and rapid the corrosion.

Cold, clean freshwater is the poorest electrolyte. As water temperature increases, its conductivity increases. Pollutants will increase conductivity; brackish or saltwater is also an efficient electrolyte. This is one of the reasons that most manufacturers recommend a freshwater flush for marine equipment after operation in saltwater, polluted or brackish water.

PROTECTION FROM GALVANIC CORROSION

Because of the environment in which marine equipment must operate, it is practically impossible to totally prevent galvanic corrosion. There are several ways by which the process can be slowed. After taking these precautions, the next step is to "fool" the process into occurring only where *you* want it to occur. This is the role of sacrificial anodes and impressed current systems.

Slowing Corrosion

Some simple precautions can help reduce the amount of corrosion taking place outside the hull. These are *not* a substitute for the corrosion protection methods discussed under *Sacrificial Anodes* and *Impressed Current Systems* in this chapter, but they can help these protection methods do their job.

Use fasteners of a metal more noble than the part they are fastening. If corrosion occurs, the larger equipment will suffer but the fastener will be protected. Because fasteners are usually very small in comparison to the equipment being fastened, the equipment can survive the loss of

material. If the fastener were to corrode instead of the equipment, major problems could arise.

Keep all painted surfaces in good condition. If paint is scraped off and bare metal exposed, corrosion will rapidly increase. Use a vinyl- or plastic-based paint, which acts as an electrical insulator.

Be careful when using metal-based antifouling paints. These should not be applied to metal parts of the boat, outboard motor or stern drive unit or they will actually react with the equipment, causing corrosion between the equipment and the layer of paint. Organic-based paints are available for use on metal surfaces.

Where a corrosion protection device is used, remember that it must be immersed in the electrolyte along with the rest of the boat to have any effect. If you raise the power unit out of the water when the boat is docked, any anodes on the power unit will be removed from the corrosion cycle and will not protect the rest of the equipment that is still immersed. Also, such corrosion protection devices must not be painted because this would insulate them from the corrosion process.

Any change in the boat's equipment, such as the installation of a new stainless steel propeller, will change the electrical potential and could cause increased corrosion. Keep in mind that when you add new equipment or change materials, you should review your corrosion protection system to be sure it is up to the job.

Sacrificial Anodes

Anodes are usually made of zinc, a far from noble metal. Sacrificial anodes are specially designed to do nothing but corrode. Properly fastening such pieces to the boat will cause them to act as the anode in *any* galvanic reaction that occurs; any other metal present will act as the cathode and will not be damaged.

Anodes must be used properly to be effective. Simply fastening pieces of zinc to your boat in random locations won't do the job.

You must determine how much anode surface area is required to adequately protect the equipment's surface area. A good starting point is provided by Military Specification MIL-A-818001, which states that one square inch of new anode will protect either:

a. 800 square inches of freshly painted steel.
b. 250 square inches of bare steel or bare aluminum alloy.
c. 100 square inches of copper or copper alloy.

This rule is for a boat at rest. When underway, more anode area is required to protect the same equipment surface area.

The anode must be fastened so that it has good electrical contact with the metal to be protected. If possible, the anode can be attached directly to the other metal. If that is not possible, the entire network of metal parts in the boat should be electrically bonded together so that all pieces are protected.

Good quality anodes have inserts of some other metal around the fastener holes. Otherwise, the anode could erode away around the fastener. The anode can then become loose or even fall off, removing all protection.

Another Military Specification (MIL-A-18001) defines the type of alloy preferred that will corrode at a uniform rate without forming a crust that could reduce its efficiency after a time.

Impressed Current Systems

An impressed current system can be installed on any boat that has a battery. The system consists of an anode, a control box and a sensor. The anode in this system is coated with a very noble metal, such as platinum, so that it is almost corrosion-free and will last indefinitely. The sensor, under the boat's waterline, monitors the potential for corrosion. When it senses that corrosion could be occurring, it transmits this information to the control box.

The control box connects the boat's battery to the anode. When the sensor signals the need, the control box applies positive battery voltage to the anode. Current from the battery flows from the anode to all other metal parts of the boat, no matter how noble or non-noble these parts may be. This battery current takes the place of any galvanic current flow.

Only a very small amount of battery current is needed to counteract galvanic corrosion. Manufacturers estimate that it would take two or three months of constant use to drain a typical marine battery, assuming the battery is never recharged.

An impressed current system is more expensive to install than simple anodes but, considering its low maintenance requirements and the excellent protection it provides, the long-term cost may actually be lower.

PROPELLERS

The propeller is the final link between the boat's drive system and the water. A perfectly

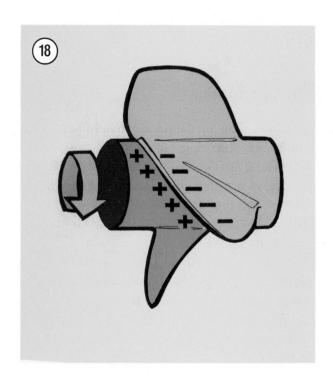

maintained engine and hull are useless if the propeller is the wrong type or has been allowed to deteriorate. Although propeller selection for a specific situation is beyond the scope of this book, the following information on propeller construction and design will allow you to discuss the subject intelligently with your marine dealer.

How a Propeller Works

As the curved blades of a propeller rotate through the water, a high-pressure area is created on one side of the blade and a low-pressure area exists on the other side of the blade (**Figure 18**). The propeller moves toward the low-pressure area, carrying the boat with it.

Propeller Parts

Although a propeller may be a one-piece unit, it is made up of several different parts (**Figure 19**). Variations in the design of these parts make different propellers suitable for different jobs.

The blade tip is the point on the blade farthest from the center of the propeller hub. The blade

tip separates the leading edge from the trailing edge.

The leading edge is the edge of the blade nearest to the boat. During normal rotation, this is the area of the blade that first cuts through the water.

The trailing edge is the edge of the blade farthest from the boat.

The blade face is the surface of the blade that faces away from the boat. During normal rotation, high pressure exists on this side of the blade.

The blade back is the surface of the blade that faces toward the boat. During normal rotation, low pressure exists on this side of the blade.

The cup is a small curve or lip on the trailing edge of the blade.

The hub is the central portion of the propeller. It connects the blades to the propeller shaft (part of the boat's drive system). On some drive systems, engine exhaust is routed through the hub; in this case, the hub is made up of an outer and an inner portion, connected by ribs.

The diffuser ring is used on through-hub exhaust models to prevent exhaust gases from entering the blade area.

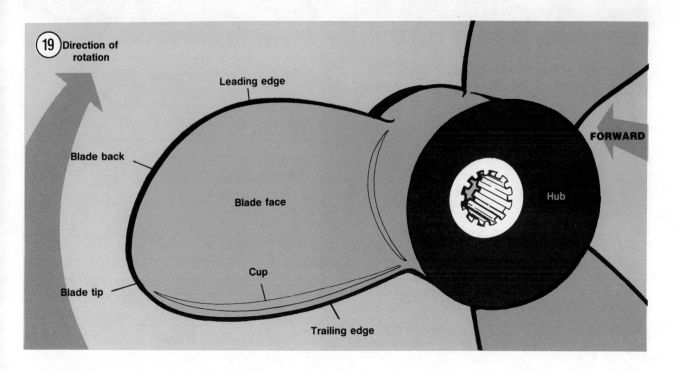

19 Direction of rotation

Leading edge

Blade back

Blade face

Blade tip

Cup

Trailing edge

FORWARD

Hub

Propeller Design

Changes in length, angle, thickness and material of propeller parts make different propellers suitable for different situations.

Diameter

Propeller diameter is the distance from the center of the hub to the blade tip, multiplied by

2. That is, it is the diameter of the circle formed by the blade tips during propeller rotation (**Figure 20**).

Pitch and rake

Propeller pitch and rake describe the placement of the blade in relation to the hub (**Figure 21**).

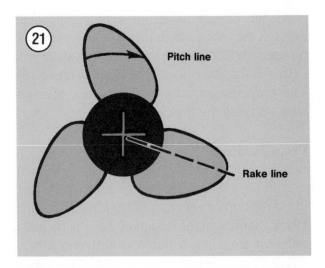

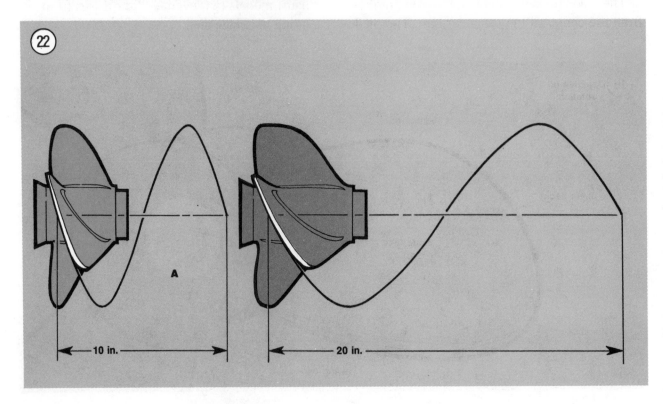

Pitch is expressed by the theoretical distance that the propeller would travel in one revolution. In A, **Figure 22**, the propeller would travel 10 inches in one revolution. In B, **Figure 22**, the propeller would travel 20 inches in one revolution. This distance is only theoretical; during actual operation, the propeller achieves about 80% of its rated travel.

Propeller blades can be constructed with constant pitch (**Figure 23**) or progressive pitch (**Figure 24**). Progressive pitch starts low at the leading edge and increases toward to trailing edge. The propeller pitch specification is the average of the pitch across the entire blade.

Blade rake is specified in degrees and is measured along a line from the center of the hub to the blade tip. A blade that is perpendicular to the hub (A, **Figure 25**) has 0° of rake. A blade that is angled from perpendicular (B, **Figure 25**) has a rake expressed by its difference from perpen-

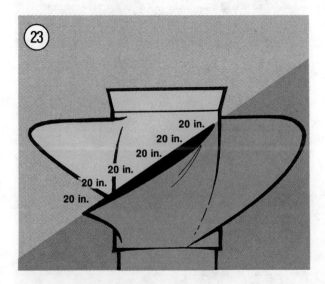

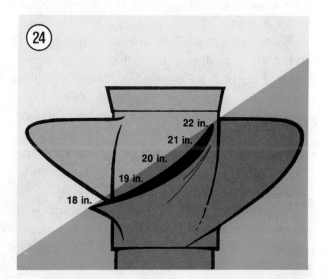

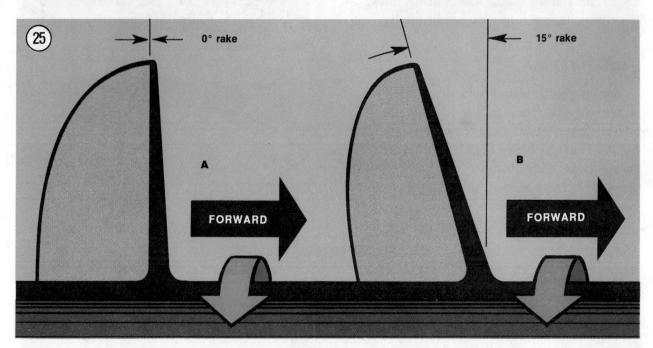

dicular. Most propellers have rakes ranging from 0-20°.

Blade thickness

Blade thickness is not uniform at all points along the blade. For efficiency, blades should be as thin as possible at all points while retaining enough strength to move the boat. Blades tend to be thicker where they meet the hub and thinner at the blade tip (**Figure 26**). This is to support the heavier loads at the hub section of the blade. This thickness is dependent on the strength of the material used.

When cut along a line from the leading edge to the trailing edge in the central portion of the blade (**Figure 27**), the propeller blade resembles an airplane wing. The blade face, where high pressure exists during normal rotation, is almost flat. The blade back, where low pressure exists during normal rotation, is curved, with the thinnest portions at the edges and the thickest portion at the center.

Propellers that run only partially submerged, as in racing applications, may have a wedge-shaped cross-section (**Figure 28**). The leading edge is very thin; the blade thickness increases toward the trailing edge, where it is the thickest. If a propeller such as this is run totally submerged, it is very inefficient.

Number of blades

The number of blades used on a propeller is a compromise between efficiency and vibration. A one-blade propeller would be the most efficient, but it would also create high levels of vibration. As blades are added, efficiency decreases, but so do vibration levels. Most propellers have three blades, representing the most practical trade-off between efficiency and vibration.

Material

Propeller materials are chosen for strength, corrosion resistance and economy. Stainless steel, aluminum and bronze are the most commonly used materials. Bronze is quite strong but

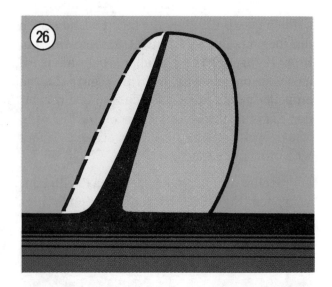

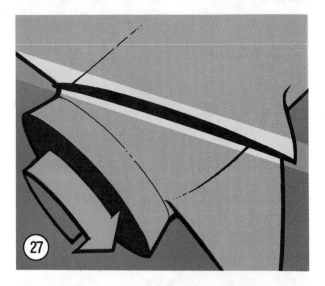

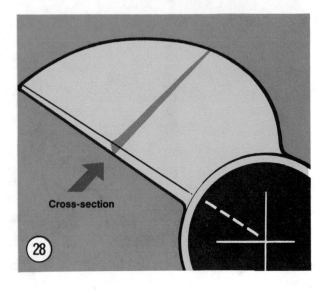

Cross-section

rather expensive. Stainless steel is more common than bronze because of its combination of strength and lower cost. Aluminum alloys are the least expensive but usually lack the strength of steel. Plastic propellers may be used in some low horsepower applications.

Direction of rotation

Propellers are made for both right-hand and left-hand rotation although right-hand is the most commonly used. When seen from behind the boat in forward motion, a right-hand propeller turns clockwise and a left-hand propeller turns counterclockwise. Off the boat, you can tell the difference by observing the angle of the blades (**Figure 29**). A right-hand propeller's blades slant from the upper left to the lower right; a left-hand propeller's blades are the opposite.

Cavitation and Ventilation

Cavitation and ventilation are *not* interchangeable terms; they refer to two distinct problems encountered during propeller operation.

To understand cavitation, you must first understand the relationship between pressure and the boiling point of water. At sea level, water will boil at 212° F. As pressure increases, such as within an engine's closed cooling system, the boiling point of water increases—it will boil at some temperature higher than 212° F. The opposite is also true. As pressure decreases, water will boil at a temperature lower than 212° F. If pressure drops low enough, water will boil at typical ambient temperatures of 50-60° F.

We have said that, during normal propeller operation, low-pressure exists on the blade back. Normally, the pressure does not drop low enough for boiling to occur. However, poor blade design

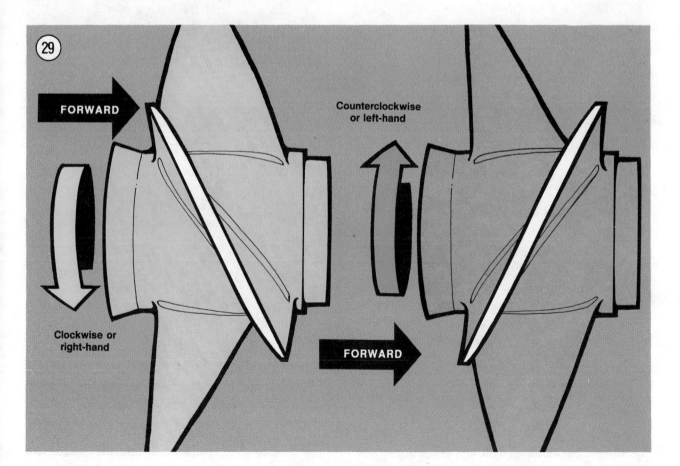

FORWARD

Counterclockwise or left-hand

Clockwise or right-hand

FORWARD

or selection, or blade damage can cause an unusual pressure drop on a small area of the blade (**Figure 30**). Boiling can occur in this small area. As the water boils, air bubbles form. As the boiling water passes to a higher pressure area of the blade, the boiling stops and the bubbles collapse. The collapsing bubbles release enough energy to erode the surface of the blade.

This entire process of pressure drop, boiling and bubble collapse is called "cavitation." The damage caused by the collapsing bubbles is called a "cavitation burn." It is important to remember that cavitation is caused by a decrease in pressure, *not* an increase in temperature.

Ventilation is not as complex a process as cavitation. Ventilation refers to air entering the blade area, either from above the surface of the water or from a through-hub exhaust system. As the blades meet the air, the propeller momentarily over-revs, losing most of its thrust. An added complication is that as the propeller over-revs, pressure on the blade back decreases and massive cavitation can occur.

Most pieces of marine equipment have a plate above the propeller area designed to keep surface air from entering the blade area (**Figure 31**). This plate is correctly called an "antiventilation plate," although you will often *see* it called an "anticavitation plate." Through hub exhaust systems also have specially designed hubs to keep exhaust gases from entering the blade area.

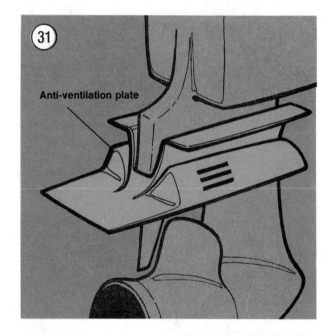

Anti-ventilation plate

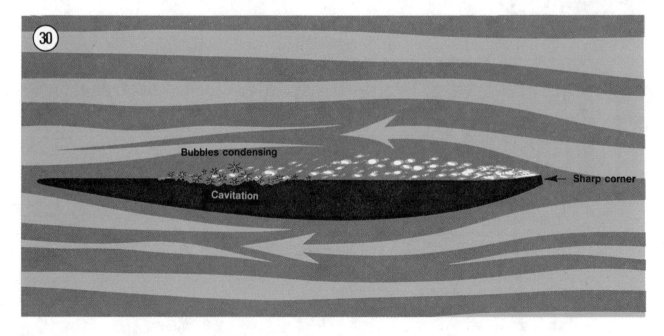

Bubbles condensing

Cavitation

Sharp corner

Chapter Two

Tools and Techniques

This chapter describes the common tools required for marine equipment repairs and troubleshooting. Techniques that will make your work easier and more effective are also described. Some of the procedures in this book require special skills or expertise; in some cases, you are better off entrusting the job to a dealer or qualified specialist.

SAFETY FIRST

Professional mechanics can work for years and never suffer a serious injury. If you follow a few rules of common sense and safety, you too can enjoy many safe hours servicing your marine equipment. If you ignore these rules, you can hurt yourself or damage the equipment.

1. Never use gasoline as a cleaning solvent.
2. Never smoke or use a torch near flammable liquids, such as cleaning solvent. If you are working in your home garage, remember that your home gas appliances have pilot lights.
3. Never smoke or use a torch in an area where batteries are being charged. Highly explosive hydrogen gas is formed during the charging process.

4. Use the proper size wrenches to avoid damage to fasteners and injury to yourself.
5. When loosening a tight or stuck fastener, think of what would happen if the wrench should slip. Protect yourself accordingly.
6. Keep your work area clean, uncluttered and well lighted.
7. Wear safety goggles during all operations involving drilling, grinding or the use of a cold chisel.
8. Never use worn tools.
9. Keep a Coast Guard approved fire extinguisher handy. Be sure it is rated for gasoline (Class B) and electrical (Class C) fires.

BASIC HAND TOOLS

A number of tools are required to maintain marine equipment. You may already have some of these tools for home or car repairs. There are also tools made especially for marine equipment repairs; these you will have to purchase. In any case, a wide variety of quality tools will make repairs easier and more effective.

Keep your tools clean and in a tool box. Keep them organized with the sockets and related drives together, the open end and box wrenches together, etc. After using a tool, wipe off dirt and grease with a clean cloth and place the tool in its correct place.

The following tools are required to perform virtually any repair job. Each tool is described and the recommended size given for starting a tool collection. Additional tools and some duplications may be added as you become more familiar with the equipment. You may need all standard U.S. size tools, all metric size tools or a mixture of both.

Screwdrivers

The screwdriver is a very basic tool, but if used improperly, it will do more damage than good. The slot on a screw has a definite dimension and shape. A screwdriver must be selected to conform with that shape. Use a small screwdriver for small screws and a large one for large screws or the screw head will be damaged.

Two types of screwdriver are commonly required: a common (flat-blade) screwdriver (**Figure 1**) and Phillips screwdrivers (**Figure 2**).

Screwdrivers are available in sets, which often include an assortment of common and Phillips blades. If you buy them individually, buy at least the following:

  a. Common screwdriver—5/16 × 6 in. blade.
  b. Common screwdriver—3/8 × 12 in. blade.
  c. Phillips screwdriver—size 2 tip, 6 in. blade.

Use screwdrivers only for driving screws. Never use a screwdriver for prying or chiseling. Do not try to remove a Phillips or Allen head screw with a common screwdriver; you can damage the head so that the proper tool will be unable to remove it.

Keep screwdrivers in the proper condition and they will last longer and perform better. Always keep the tip of a common screwdriver in good condition. **Figure 3** shows how to grind the tip to the proper shape if it becomes damaged. Note the parallel sides of the tip.

Pliers

Pliers come in a wide range of types and sizes. Pliers are useful for cutting, bending and crimping. They should never be used to cut hardened objects or to turn bolts or nuts. **Figure 4** shows several types of pliers.

Each type of pliers has a specialized function. General purpose pliers are used mainly for holding things and for bending. Locking pliers are used as pliers or to hold objects very tightly, like a vise. Needlenose pliers are used to hold or bend small objects. Adjustable or slip-joint pliers can

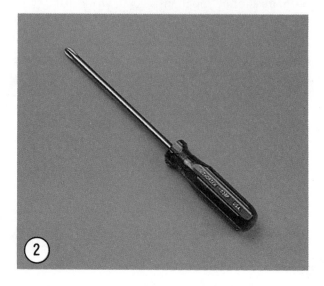

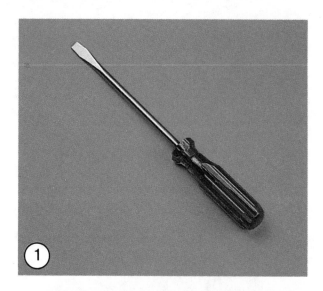

2

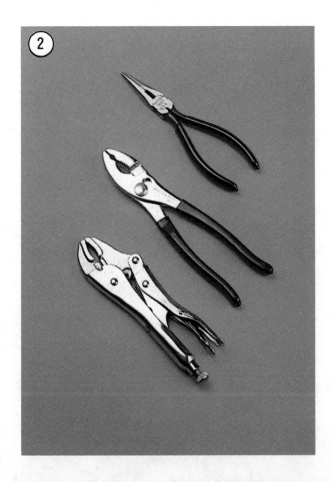

be adjusted to hold various sizes of objects; the jaws remain parallel to grip around objects such as pipe or tubing. There are many more types of pliers. The ones described here are the most commonly used.

Box and Open-end Wrenches

Box and open-end wrenches are available in sets or separately in a variety of sizes. See **Figure 5** and **Figure 6**. The number stamped near the end refers to the distance between two parallel flats on the hex head bolt or nut.

Box wrenches are usually superior to open-end wrenches. An open-end wrench grips the nut on only two flats. Unless it fits well, it may slip and round off the points on the nut. The box wrench grips all 6 flats. Both 6-point and 12-point openings on box wrenches are available. The 6-point gives superior holding power; the 12-point allows a shorter swing.

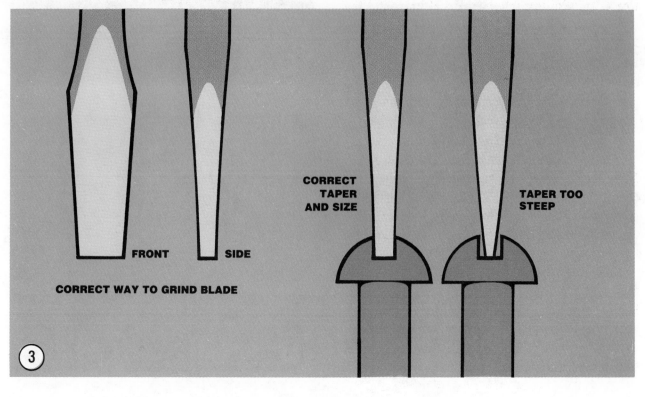

FRONT SIDE

CORRECT WAY TO GRIND BLADE

CORRECT TAPER AND SIZE

TAPER TOO STEEP

Combination wrenches, which are open on one side and boxed on the other, are also available. Both ends are the same size.

Adjustable Wrenches

An adjustable wrench can be adjusted to fit nearly any nut or bolt head. See **Figure 7**. However, it can loosen and slip, causing damage to the nut and maybe to your knuckles. Use an adjustable wrench only when other wrenches are not available.

Adjustable wrenches come in sizes ranging from 4-18 in. overall. A 6 or 8 in. wrench is recommended as an all-purpose wrench.

Socket Wrenches

This type is undoubtedly the fastest, safest and most convenient to use. See **Figure 8**. Sockets, which attach to a suitable handle, are available with 6-point or 12-point openings and use 1/4, 3/8 and 3/4 inch drives. The drive size indicates

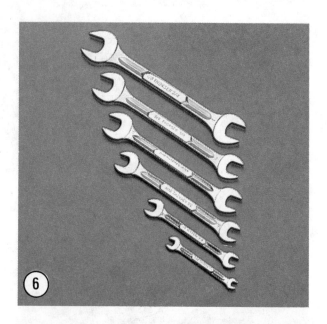

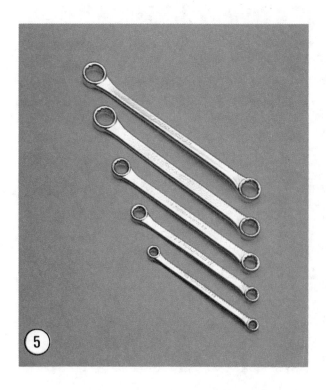

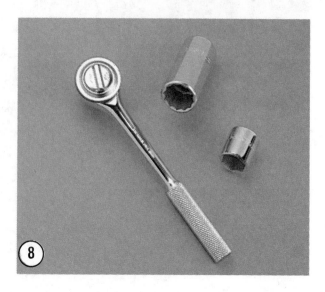

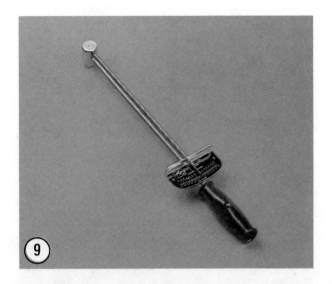

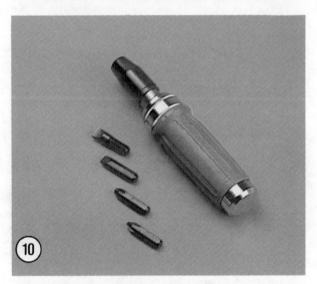

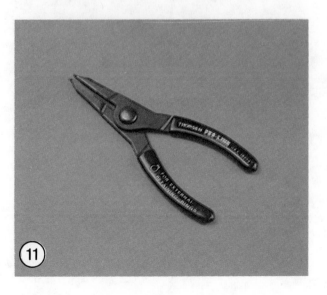

the size of the square hole that mates with the ratchet or flex handle.

Torque Wrench

A torque wrench (**Figure 9**) is used with a socket to measure how tight a nut or bolt is installed. They come in a wide price range and with either 3/8 or 1/2 in. square drive. The drive size indicates the size of the square drive that mates with the socket. Purchase one that measures up to 150 ft.-lb. (203 N·m).

Impact Driver

This tool (**Figure 10**) makes removal of tight fasteners easy and eliminates damage to bolts and screw slots. Impact drivers and interchangeable bits are available at most large hardware and auto parts stores.

Circlip Pliers

Circlip pliers (sometimes referred to as snap-ring pliers) are necessary to remove circlips. See **Figure 11**. Circlip pliers usually come with several different size tips; many designs can be switched from internal type to external type.

Hammers

The correct hammer is necessary for repairs. Use only a hammer with a face (or head) of rubber or plastic or the soft-faced type that is filled with buckshot (**Figure 12**). These are sometimes necessary in engine tear-downs. *Never* use a metal-faced hammer as severe damage will result in most cases. You can always produce the same amount of force with a soft-faced hammer.

Feeler Gauge

This tool has either flat or wire measuring gauges (**Figure 13**). Wire gauges are used to measure spark plug gap; flat gauges are used for all other measurements. A non-magnetic (brass) gauge may be specified when working around magnetized parts.

Other Special Tools

Some procedures require special tools; these are identified in the appropriate chapter. Unless otherwise specified, the part number used in this book to identify a special tool is the marine equipment manufacturer's part number.

Special tools can usually be purchased through your marine equipment dealer. Some can be made locally by a machinist, often at a much lower price. You may find certain special tools at tool rental dealers. Don't use makeshift tools if you can't locate the correct special tool; you will probably cause more damage than good.

TEST EQUIPMENT

Multimeter

This instrument (**Figure 14**) is invaluable for electrical system troubleshooting and service. It combines a voltmeter, an ohmmeter and an ammeter into one unit, so it is often called a VOM.

Two types of multimeter are available, analog and digital. Analog meters have a moving needle with marked bands indicating the volt, ohm and amperage scales. The digital meter (DVOM) is ideally suited for troubleshooting because it is easy to read, more accurate than analog, contains internal overload protection, is auto-ranging (analog meters must be recalibrated each time the scale is changed) and has automatic polarity compensation.

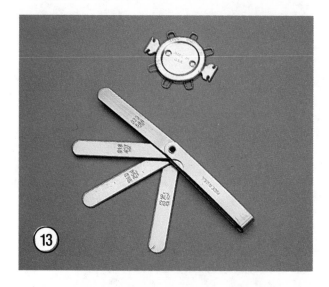

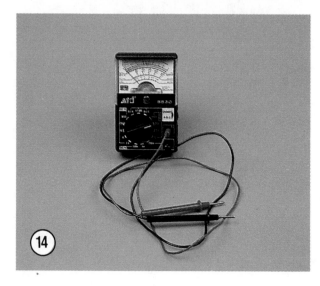

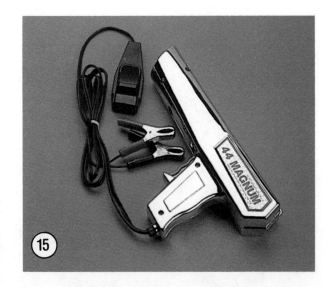

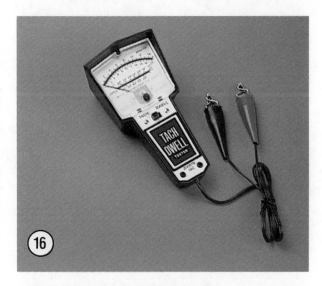

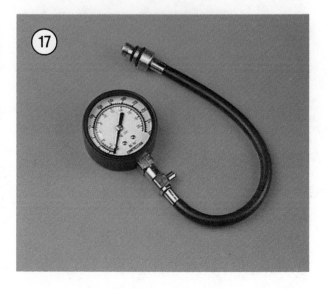

Strobe Timing Light

This instrument is necessary for dynamic tuning (setting ignition timing while the engine is running). By flashing a light at the precise instant the spark plug fires, the position of the timing mark can be seen. The flashing light makes a moving mark appear to stand still opposite a stationary mark.

Suitable lights range from inexpensive neon bulb types to powerful xenon strobe lights. See **Figure 15**. A light with an inductive pickup is best because it eliminates any possible damage to ignition wiring.

Tachometer/Dwell Meter

A portable tachometer is necessary for tuning. See **Figure 16**. Ignition timing and carburetor adjustments must be performed at the specified idle speed. The best instrument for this purpose is one with a low range of 0-1000 or 0-2000 rpm and a high range of 0-6000 rpm. Extended range (0-6000 or 0-8000 rpm) instruments lack accuracy at lower speeds. The instrument should be capable of detecting changes of 25 rpm on the low range.

A dwell meter is often combined with a tachometer. Dwell meters are used with breaker point ignition systems to measure the amount of time the points remain closed during engine operation.

Compression Gauge

This tool (**Figure 17**) measures the amount of pressure present in the engine's combustion chamber during the compression stroke. This indicates general engine condition. Compression readings can be interpreted along with vacuum gauge readings to pinpoint specific engine mechanical problems.

The easiest type to use has screw-in adapters that fit into the spark plug holes. Press-in rubber-tipped types are also available.

Vacuum Gauge

The vacuum gauge (**Figure 18**) measures the intake manifold vacuum created by the engine's intake stroke. Manifold and valve problems (on 4-stroke engines) can be identified by interpreting the readings. When combined with compression gauge readings, other engine problems can be diagnosed.

Some vacuum gauges can also be used as fuel pressure gauges to trace fuel system problems.

Hydrometer

Battery electrolyte specific gravity is measured with a hydrometer (**Figure 19**). The specific gravity of the electrolyte indicates the battery's state of charge. The best type has automatic temperature compensation; otherwise, you must calculate the compensation yourself.

Precision Measuring Tools

Various tools are needed to make precision measurements. A dial indicator (**Figure 20**), for example, is used to determine run-out of rotating parts and end play of parts assemblies. A dial indicator can also be used to precisely measure piston position in relation to top dead center; some engines require this measurement for ignition timing adjustment.

Vernier calipers (**Figure 21**) and micrometers (**Figure 22**) are other precision measuring tools used to determine the size of parts (such as piston diameter).

Precision measuring equipment must be stored, handled and used carefully or it will not remain accurate.

SERVICE HINTS

Most of the service procedures covered in this manual are straightforward and can be performed by anyone reasonably handy with tools.

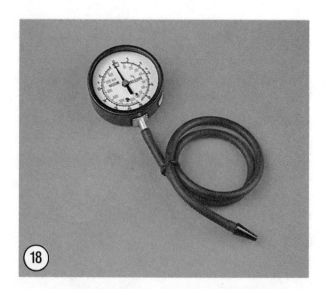

18

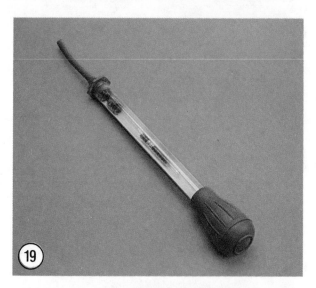

19

20

It is suggested, however, that you consider your own skills and toolbox carefully before attempting any operation involving major disassembly of the engine or gearcase.

Some operations, for example, require the use of a press. It would be wiser to have these performed by a shop equipped for such work, rather than trying to do the job yourself with makeshift equipment. Other procedures require precise measurements. Unless you have the skills and equipment required, it would be better to have a qualified repair shop make the measurements for you.

Preparation for Disassembly

Repairs go much faster and easier if the equipment is clean before you begin work. There are special cleaners, such as Gunk or Bel-Ray Degreaser, for washing the engine and related parts. Just spray or brush on the cleaning solution, let it stand, then rinse away with a garden hose. Clean all oily or greasy parts with cleaning solvent as you remove them.

> *WARNING*
> *Never use gasoline as a cleaning agent. It presents an extreme fire hazard. Be sure to work in a well-ventilated area when using cleaning solvent. Keep a Coast Guard approved fire extinguisher, rated for gasoline fires, handy in any case.*

Much of the labor charged for repairs made by dealers is for the removal and disassembly of other parts to reach the defective unit. It is frequently possible to perform the preliminary operations yourself and then take the defective unit in to the dealer for repair.

If you decide to tackle the job yourself, read the entire section in this manual that pertains to it, making sure you have identified the proper one. Study the illustrations and text until you have a good idea of what is involved in completing the job satisfactorily. If special tools or replacement parts are required, make arrangements to get them before you start. It is frustrating and time-consuming to get partly into a job and then be unable to complete it.

Disassembly Precautions

During disassembly of parts, keep a few general precautions in mind. Force is rarely needed to get things apart. If parts are a tight fit, such as

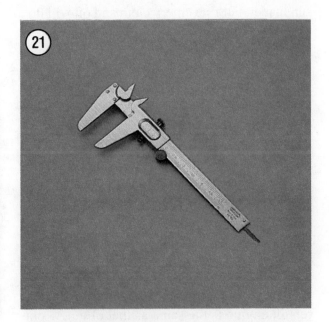

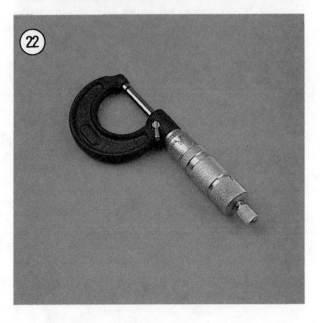

a bearing in a case, there is usually a tool designed to separate them. Never use a screwdriver to pry apart parts with machined surfaces (such as cylinder heads and crankcases). You will mar the surfaces and end up with leaks.

Make diagrams (or take an instant picture) wherever similar-appearing parts are found. For example, head and crankcase bolts are often not the same length. You may think you can remember where everything came from, but mistakes are costly. There is also the possibility you may be sidetracked and not return to work for days or even weeks. In the interval, carefully laid out parts may have been disturbed.

Cover all openings after removing parts to keep small parts, dirt or other contamination from entering.

Tag all similar internal parts for location and direction. All internal components should be reinstalled in the same location and direction from which removed. Record the number and thickness of any shims as they are removed. Small parts, such as bolts, can be identified by placing them in plastic sandwich bags. Seal and label them with masking tape.

Wiring should be tagged with masking tape and marked as each wire is removed. Again, do not rely on memory alone.

Protect finished surfaces from physical damage or corrosion. Keep gasoline off painted surfaces.

Assembly Precautions

No parts, except those assembled with a press fit, require unusual force during assembly. If a part is hard to remove or install, find out why before proceeding.

When assembling two parts, start all fasteners, then tighten evenly in an alternating or crossing pattern if no specific tightening sequence is given.

When assembling parts, be sure all shims and washers are installed exactly as they came out.

Whenever a rotating part butts against a stationary part, look for a shim or washer. Use new gaskets if there is any doubt about the condition of the old ones. Unless otherwise specified, a thin coat of oil on gaskets may help them seal effectively.

Heavy grease can be used to hold small parts in place if they tend to fall out during assembly. However, keep grease and oil away from electrical components.

High spots may be sanded off a piston with sandpaper, but fine emery cloth and oil will do a much more professional job.

Carbon can be removed from the cylinder head, the piston crown and the exhaust port with a dull screwdriver. *Do not* scratch either surface. Wipe off the surface with a clean cloth when finished.

The carburetor is best cleaned by disassembling it and soaking the parts in a commercial carburetor cleaner. Never soak gaskets and rubber parts in these cleaners. Never use wire to clean out jets and air passages; they are easily damaged. Use compressed air to blow out the carburetor *after* the float has been removed.

Take your time and do the job right. Do not forget that the break-in procedure on a newly rebuilt engine is the same as that of a new one. Use the break-in oil recommendations and follow other instructions given in your owner's manual.

SPECIAL TIPS

Because of the extreme demands placed on marine equipment, several points should be kept in mind when performing service and repair. The following items are general suggestions that may improve the overall life of the machine and help avoid costly failures.

1. Unless otherwise specified, use a locking compound, such as Loctite Threadlocker, on all bolts and nuts, even if they are secured with lockwashers. Be sure to use the specified grade

of thread locking compound. A screw or bolt lost from an engine cover or bearing retainer could easily cause serious and expensive damage before its loss is noticed.

When applying thread locking compound, use a small amount. If too much is used, it can work its way down the threads and stick parts together that were not meant to be stuck together.

Keep a tube of thread locking compound in your tool box; when used properly, it is cheap insurance.

2. Use a hammer-driven impact tool to remove and install screws and bolts. These tools help prevent the rounding off of bolt heads and screw slots and ensure a tight installation.

3. When straightening the fold-over type lockwasher, use a wide-blade chisel, such as an old and dull wood chisel. Such a tool provides a better purchase on the folded tab, making straightening easier.

4. When installing the fold-over type lockwasher, always use a new washer if possible. If a new washer is not available, always fold over a part of the washer that has not been previously folded. Reusing the same fold may cause the washer to break, resulting in the loss of its locking ability and a loose piece of metal adrift in the engine.

When folding the washer, start the fold with a screwdriver and finish it with a pair of pliers. If a punch is used to make the fold, the fold may be too sharp, thereby increasing the chances of the washer breaking under stress.

These washers are relatively inexpensive and it is suggested that you keep several of each size in your tool box for repairs.

5. When replacing missing or broken fasteners (bolts, nuts and screws), always use authorized replacement parts. They are specially hardened for each application. The wrong 50-cent bolt could easily cause serious and expensive damage.

6. When installing gaskets, always use authorized replacement gaskets *without* sealer, unless designated. Many gaskets are designed to swell when they come in contact with oil. Gasket sealer will prevent the gaskets from swelling as intended and can result in oil leaks. Authorized replacement gaskets are cut from material of the precise thickness needed. Installation of a too thick or too thin gasket in a critical area could cause equipment damage.

MECHANIC'S TECHNIQUES

Removing Frozen Fasteners

When a fastener rusts and cannot be removed, several methods may be used to loosen it. First, apply penetrating oil, such as Liquid Wrench or WD-40 (available at any hardware or auto supply store). Apply it liberally and allow it penetrate for 10-15 minutes. Tap the fastener several times with a small hammer; do not hit it hard enough to cause damage. Reapply the penetrating oil if necessary.

For frozen screws, apply penetrating oil as described, then insert a screwdriver in the slot and tap the top of the screwdriver with a hammer. This loosens the rust so the screw can be removed in the normal way. If the screw head is too chewed up to use a screwdriver, grip the head with locking pliers and twist the screw out.

Avoid applying heat unless specifically instructed because it may melt, warp or remove the temper from parts.

Remedying Stripped Threads

Occasionally, threads are stripped through carelessness or impact damage. Often the threads can be cleaned up by running a tap (for internal threads on nuts) or die (for external threads on bolts) through threads. See **Figure 23**.

Removing Broken Screws or Bolts

When the head breaks off a screw or bolt, several methods are available for removing the remaining portion.

If a large portion of the remainder projects out, try gripping it with vise-grip pliers. If the projecting portion is too small, file it to fit a wrench or cut a slot in it to fit a screwdriver. See **Figure 24**.

If the head breaks off flush, use a screw extractor. To do this, centerpunch the remaining portion of the screw or bolt. Drill a small hole in the screw and tap the extractor into the hole. Back the screw out with a wrench on the extractor. See **Figure 25**.

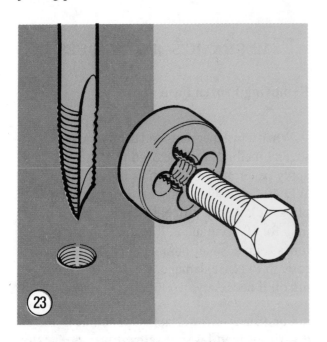

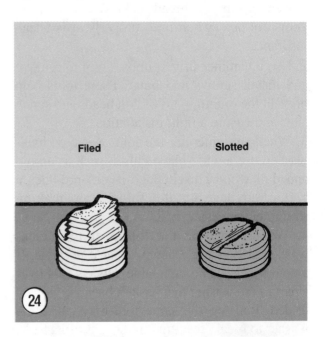

Filed   Slotted

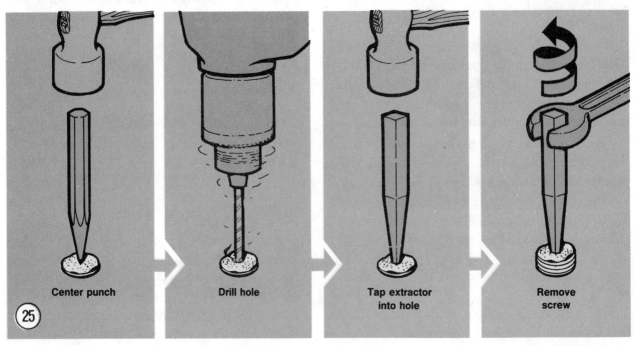

Center punch   Drill hole   Tap extractor into hole   Remove screw

Chapter Three

Troubleshooting

Troubleshooting is a relatively simple matter when it is done logically and systematically. The first step in any troubleshooting procedure is to define the symptoms as fully as possible and then localize the problem. Subsequent steps involve testing and analyzing those areas which could cause the symptoms. A haphazard approach may eventually solve the problem, but it can be very costly in terms of wasted time and unnecessary parts replacement.

Never assume anything. Do not overlook the obvious. If the engine suddenly quits when running, check the easiest and most accessible areas first. Make sure there is fuel in the tank, the fuel valve is in the ON position, the spark plug wires are properly connected and the wiring harnesses are properly connected.

If a quick visual check does not turn up the cause of the problem, look a little further. Learning to recognize and describe symptoms accurately will make repairs easier for you or a mechanic at the shop. Saying that it won't run isn't the same as saying it quit at high speed and won't restart.

Gather as many symptoms together as possible to aid in diagnosis. Note whether the engine lost power gradually or all at once, what color smoke (if any) came from the exhaust and so on. Remember, the more complicated an engine is, the easier it is to troubleshoot because symptoms point to specific problems.

After the symptoms are defined, areas which could cause the problems should be tested and analyzed. You don't need sophisticated test equipment to determine whether repairs can be attempted at home. A few simple checks can save a large repair bill and time lost while the engine sits at a repair shop.

On the other hand, be realistic and don't attempt repairs beyond your abilities. Service departments tend to charge heavily for putting together a disassembled engine that may have been abused. Some won't even take on such a job—so use common sense and don't get in over your head.

Proper lubrication, maintenance and periodic tune up as described in Chapter Four will reduce the necessity for troubleshooting. Even with the best of care, however, an outboard motor is prone to problems which will eventually require troubleshooting.

This chapter contains brief descriptions of each operating system and troubleshooting procedures to be used. **Tables 1-3** at the end of the chapter present typical starting, ignition and fuel system problems with their probable causes and solutions.

OPERATING REQUIREMENTS

Every outboard motor requires 3 basic things to run properly: an uninterrupted supply of fuel and air in the correct proportions, proper ignition at the right time and adequate compression. If any of these requirements are missing, the motor will not run.

The electrical system is generally the weakest link in the chain. More problems result from electrical malfunctions than from any other source. Keep this in mind before blaming the fuel system and making unnecessary carburetor adjustments or repairs.

If a motor has been sitting for any length of time and refuses to start, first check and clean the spark plugs. Then, check the condition of the battery (if so equipped) to make sure it has an adequate charge. If these are good, then look to the fuel delivery system. This includes the fuel tank, fuel pump, fuel lines and carburetor(s). Rust may have formed in the tank, restricting fuel flow. Gasoline deposits may have gummed up carburetor jets and air passages. Gasoline tends to lose its potency after standing for long periods. In addition, the fuel may be contaminated with water from condensation. Drain the old fuel and try starting with a fresh tankful.

Starting Difficulties

Occasionally, an older (high-hours) outboard motor may be plagued by hard starting and generally poor running for which there seems to be no good cause. Carburetion and ignition are satisfactory and a compression test indicates the pistons, rings and cylinders are in good condition.

What a compression test does not show, however, is a lack of primary compression. The crankcase of a 2-stroke engine must be alternately under pressure and vacuum. After the piston closes the intake port, further downward movement of the piston causes the trapped fuel and air charge to be pressurized so it can rush quickly into the cylinder when the scavenging or transfer ports are opened. Then, upward piston movement creates a vacuum in the crankcase, enabling a new fuel and air mixture to be drawn into the crankcase from the carburetor.

If the crankshaft seals or crankcase gaskets leak, the crankcase cannot hold pressure or vacuum and proper engine operation becomes impossible. Any other source of leakage, such as defective cylinder base gaskets or porous or cracked crankcase castings, will result in the same conditions.

Engines suffering from hard starting should be checked for pressure leaks using a small brush and water and soap solution. The following is a list of possible leakage points in a typical 2-stroke engine.

  a. Crankshaft seals.
  b. Spark plug threads.
  c. Cylinder head joint.
  d. Cylinder base joint.
  e. Carburetor mounting flange(s).
  f. Crankcase joint.

STARTING SYSTEM

Description

Johnson/Evinrude 9.9 hp and larger models may be equipped with electric start systems. See **Figure 1** for a typical starter motor installation. The motor is mounted vertically on the engine. When battery current is supplied to the starter motor, its pinion gear is thrust upward to engage the teeth on the engine flywheel. Once the engine starts, the pinion gear disengages from the fly-wheel. This process is similar to that used to crank an automotive engine.

The starting system requires a fully charged battery to provide the large amount of electrical current required to operate the starter motor. Electric start models are equipped with an alternator to charge the battery during operation.

Starting Circuit (9.9 and 15 hp)

The electric starting system on 9.9 and 15 hp models consists of the battery, starter motor, starter switch button, neutral start switch and related wiring.

Depressing the starter switch button completes the circuit between the battery and starter motor when the shift lever is in NEUTRAL. The neutral start switch prevents starter operation if the shift control lever is not in NEUTRAL.

Starting Circuit (20-300 hp)

The electric starting system on 20-300 hp models consists of the battery, starter motor, starter switch button (tiller handle models) or key switch (remote control models), neutral start

switch, a fuse (remote control) and related wiring.

Depressing the starter switch button or turning the key switch to the START position allows current to flow through the solenoid coil causing the solenoid contacts to close. This allows current to flow from the battery through the solenoid to the starter motor. The neutral start switch is designed to close when the shift control lever or remote control is in the NEUTRAL position only. If the shift lever or remote control is not in NEUTRAL, the switch opens, preventing starter operation.

Troubleshooting Preparation (All Models)

Before troubleshooting the starting system, make sure of the following:
a. The battery is in acceptable condition and fully charged.
b. The shift control or remote control lever is in NEUTRAL.
c. All electrical connections are clean and tight.
d. The wiring harness is in good condition, with no worn or frayed insulation.
e. Battery cables are the proper size and length. See **Table 6** for recommended cable sizes. Replace undersize cables or relocate the battery to shorten the distance between the battery and starter solenoid.
f. The fuse installed in the red wire between the starter solenoid and the ignition switch B terminal is good (remote control models).
g. The fuel system is filled with an adequate supply of fresh gasoline properly mixed with the recommended two-stroke engine oil. See Chapter Four.

Required Tools/Equipment

In addition to the normal hand tools necessary for disassembly and assembly, the following test equipment is required for troubleshooting the starting system:

 a. Voltmeter.
 b. Continuity tester.
 c. Ammeter (0-50 amps).
 d. Vibration tachometer (Frahm Reed Tachometer).

A multimeter is generally the most efficient and inexpensive instrument for checking voltage, resistance and current. Two types of multimeter are available, analog and digital.

The analog volt-ohmmeter (VOM) has a moving needle with marked bands indicating the volt, ohm and amperage scales. The digital multimeter (DVOM) is ideally suited for troubleshooting work because it is easy to read, contains internal overload protection, is autoranging (analog meters must be recalibrated each time the scale is changed) and has automatic polarity compensation.

An ammeter capable of reading up to 50 amps is necessary to check starter motor current draw. The ammeter used in a multimeter is generally only capable of measuring small amounts of current, and will be damaged if connected to a starter motor or other component with high current draw.

A continuity tester is used to test the integrity of a specific circuit. A typical continuity tester is battery-powered and uses a lamp or buzzer (or both) which activates when continuity is present. An ohmmeter can also be used to check continuity. When using an ohmmeter, continuity is indicated by low resistance. Keep in mind however, that a very low reading (zero ohm) can also indicate a short circuit. No continuity is indicated by very high resistance or infinity. When checking a circuit for continuity, the circuit must be isolated (disconnected) from any other circuits, especially battery power. An ohmmeter will be damaged or destroyed if connected to a circuit in which battery voltage is present.

A vibration tachometer is used to check the rpm of the starter motor. The vibration tachome-

ter is held against the starter frame while the starter is running and indicates the approximate speed of the motor.

Starting System Troubleshooting (9.9 and 15 hp [1991 and 1992])

If the starting system fails to operate, use the following troubleshooting procedure to determine the cause. Prior to troubleshooting, make sure the battery is fully charged and the battery

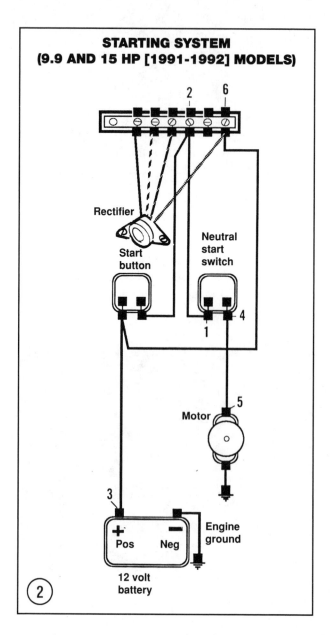

STARTING SYSTEM (9.9 AND 15 HP [1991-1992] MODELS)

Rectifier

Start button

Neutral start switch

Motor

Pos   Neg

Engine ground

12 volt battery

②

terminals are clean and tight. Refer to **Figure 2** for this procedure.

1. To prevent accidental starting, disconnect the spark plug leads from the spark plugs. Securely ground the spark plug leads to the power head.

2. Place the shift lever in NEUTRAL.

3. Remove the fuel pump (Chapter Six) to expose the neutral start switch terminals.

4. Connect a suitable voltmeter between a good engine ground and the neutral start switch at point 1, **Figure 2**.

5. Depress the start switch button and note the voltmeter. Battery voltage should be noted.

6. If no voltage is noted, move the positive voltmeter lead to the terminal board at point 2, **Figure 2**. Press the starter button and note the voltmeter.

7. If battery voltage is now noted, an open circuit is present in the wire between the neutral start switch (point 1, **Figure 2**) and the terminal board (point 2, **Figure 2**). Repair or replace the wire as necessary.

8. If battery voltage is not noted in Step 6, disconnect the starter button from the battery (point 3, **Figure 2**) and the terminal board at point 2 and point 6. Using an ohmmeter, check the starter button and wires as follows:

    a. Connect one ohmmeter lead to the wire disconnected from the neutral starter switch (point 1). Connect the remaining ohmmeter lead to the disconnected wire at point 2. Depress the starter button while noting the ohmmeter. Continuity should be noted. If not, an open circuit is present in the starter button or starter button wires. Replace the starter button assembly.

    b. Move one ohmmeter lead to the disconnected wire at point 3, **Figure 2**. Depress the starter button while noting the ohmmeter. Continuity should be noted. If not, replace the starter button assembly.

9. Reconnect the starter button wires to the battery and terminal board.

10. Connect the voltmeter between a good engine ground and point 4, **Figure 2**. Depress the starter button while noting the voltmeter. Battery voltage should be noted.

    a. If battery voltage is not noted, hold down on the starter button and manually depress the neutral start switch. If battery voltage is now noted, adjust the neutral start switch as described in Chapter Seven.

    b. If battery voltage is still not noted (after properly adjusting neutral start switch), replace the neutral start switch.

11. Move the positive voltmeter lead to the starter motor (point 5, **Figure 2**). Depress the starter button and note the voltmeter.

    a. If battery voltage is noted, the starter motor has failed and must be replaced or repaired.

    b. If no voltage is noted, an open circuit is present in the wire between the starter motor (point 5, **Figure 2**) and the neutral start switch (point 4, **Figure 2**). Repair or replace the wire as necessary.

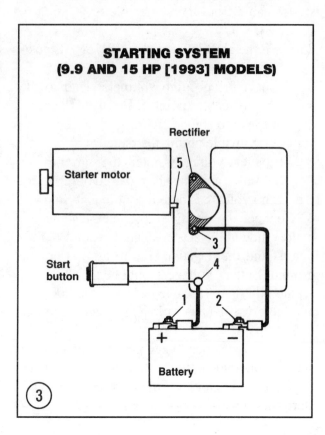

**STARTING SYSTEM
(9.9 AND 15 HP [1993] MODELS)**

Rectifier

Starter motor

Start button

Battery

3

Starting System Troubleshooting (9.9 and 15 hp [1993-on] Models)

If the starting system fails to operate, use the following troubleshooting procedure to determine the cause. Prior to troubleshooting, make sure the battery is fully charged and the battery terminals are clean and tight. Refer to **Figure 3** for this procedure.

1. To prevent accidental starter engagement during the following test procedure, disconnect the starter cable from the starter motor at point 5, **Figure 3**.

2. Place the shift lever in the NEUTRAL position.

3. Using a suitable voltmeter, check battery voltage between point 1, **Figure 3**, and point 2. If battery voltage is not at least 12 volts, charge and test the battery as described in Chapter Seven.

4. Connect the negative voltmeter lead to the ground connection at the rectifier (point 3, **Figure 3**). Connect the positive voltmeter lead to the positive battery terminal (point 1, **Figure 3**). If battery voltage is not noted, inspect the negative battery cable for loose or corroded connections or other defects. If battery voltage is noted, continue at Step 5.

5. Move the positive voltmeter lead to the battery cable connection at point 4, **Figure 3**, and note the voltmeter. If battery voltage is not noted, inspect the positive battery cable for loose or corroded connections or other defects. If battery voltage is noted, continue at Step 6.

6. Connect the voltmeter between a good engine ground and the battery cable connection at point 4. If battery voltage is noted, continue at Step 7. If not, check the negative battery cable connection at point 3, **Figure 3** for a loose or corroded connection. Clean and tighten as necessary.

7. Connect the voltmeter between a good engine ground and the starter motor cable at point 5, **Figure 3**. Depress the starter button while noting the voltmeter. If battery voltage is noted, continue at Step 8. If not, check the starter button as described in this chapter. Check the starter button wires and positive battery cable for loose or corroded connections, breaks, open circuits or other defects.

8. Reattach the cable to the starter motor at point 5. Depress the starter button and check starter motor operation. If the motor is inoperative, the starter motor has failed and must be repaired or replaced.

Starting System Troubleshooting (20-30 hp with Tiller Handle)

If the starting system fails to operate, use the following troubleshooting procedure to determine the cause. Prior to troubleshooting, make sure the battery is fully charged and the battery terminals are clean and tight. The shift lever must be in the NEUTRAL position throughout the entire test procedure. Refer to **Figure 4**.

1. To prevent accidental starter engagement during the following test procedure, disconnect the starter cable from the starter motor at point 6, **Figure 4**.

2. Place the shift lever in the NEUTRAL position.

3. Connect the positive voltmeter lead to the starter motor cable (point 6, **Figure 4**) and the negative lead to a good engine ground. Push the start button while noting the meter.

   a. If battery voltage is noted, the starter motor has failed and must be repaired or replaced.

   b. If no voltage is noted, continue at Step 4.

4. Connect the positive voltmeter lead to the battery side of the starter solenoid (point 4, **Figure 4**) and the negative lead to a good engine ground. Battery voltage should be noted. If not, replace the battery cable between the solenoid and battery. If battery voltage is noted, continue at Step 5.

5. Connect the positive voltmeter lead to the starter solenoid at point 3, **Figure 4** and the negative lead to a good engine ground. Push the start button while noting the meter.

a. If no voltage is noted, test the start button and connecting wiring.

b. If battery voltage is noted, continue at Step 6.

6. Disconnect the yellow/red wire from the neutral start switch. Connect the voltmeter between the disconnected wire and engine ground. Push the start button while noting the meter.

a. If no voltage is noted, replace the starter solenoid or the wire connecting the neutral start switch to the solenoid.

b. If battery voltage is noted, test the neutral start switch as described in Chapter Seven.

Replace the switch as necessary. If the switch is good, reconnect the yellow/red wire and continue at Step 7.

7. Connect the positive voltmeter lead to the starter solenoid at point 5, **Figure 4** and the negative lead to engine ground. Push the start button while noting the meter.

a. If the meter indicates no voltage, replace the starter solenoid.

b. If the meter indicates battery voltage, replace the cable between the solenoid and starter motor.

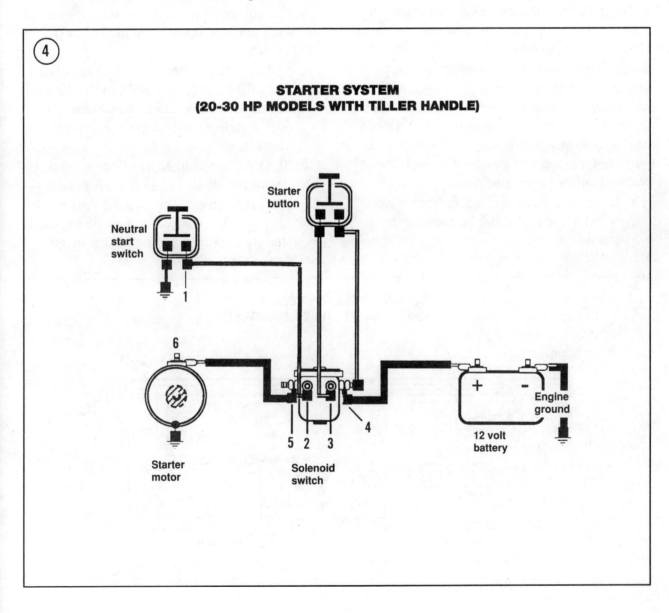

④

**STARTER SYSTEM
(20-30 HP MODELS WITH TILLER HANDLE)**

Starting System Troubleshooting (40-50 hp with Tiller Handle)

If the starting system fails to operate, use the following troubleshooting procedure to determine the cause. Prior to troubleshooting, make sure the battery is fully charged and the battery terminals are clean and tight. The shift lever must be in the NEUTRAL position throughout the entire test procedure. Refer to **Figure 5** for models without a key switch and **Figure 6** for models with a key switch.

1. To prevent accidental starter engagement during the following test procedure, disconnect the starter cable from the starter motor (point 1, **Figure 5** or **Figure 6**).

2. Place the shift lever in the NEUTRAL position.

3. Connect a voltmeter between the starter cable at point 1, **Figure 5** or **Figure 6** and a good engine ground. Turn the key switch to the ON position on models so equipped. Push the start button while noting the meter.

   a. If battery voltage is noted, the starter motor is defective and must be repaired or replaced.

   b. If no voltage is indicated, continue at Step 4A or 4B as required.

4A. *Models without key switch (**Figure 5**)*— Connect the voltmeter between the starter solenoid at point 2, **Figure 5** and engine ground.

   a. If no voltage is indicated, check the battery cable between the solenoid (point 2, **Figure 5**) and the battery for an open circuit or loose or corroded connections. Repair or replace the cable as necessary.

   b. If battery voltage is noted, continue at Step 5A.

4B. *Models with key switch (**Figure 6**)*—Connect the voltmeter between the starter solenoid at point 2 and engine ground. With the key switch ON, push the start button.

   a. If the meter indicates battery voltage, check the cable between the solenoid and starter motor for an open circuit or loose or corroded connections. Repair or replace the cable as necessary.

   b. If no voltage is noted, continue at Step 5B.

5A. *Models without key switch (**Figure 5**)*— Connect the voltmeter between the starter solenoid at point 3, **Figure 5** and engine ground. Push the start button while noting the meter.

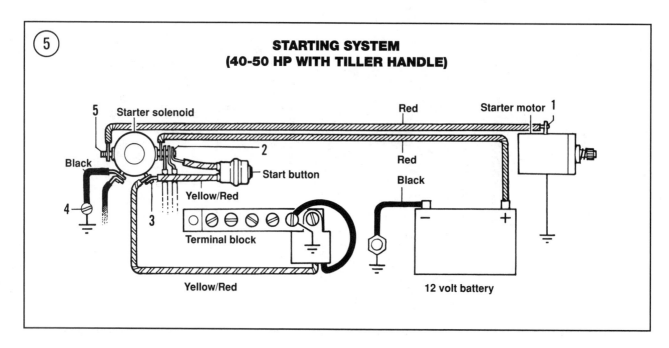

STARTING SYSTEM (40-50 HP WITH TILLER HANDLE)

a. If no voltage is noted, test the start button as described in this chapter.

b. If the meter indicates battery voltage, continue at Step 6A.

5B. *Models with key switch (**Figure 6**)*—Connect the voltmeter between the starter solenoid at point 3, **Figure 6** and engine ground.

a. If no voltage is indicated, check the positive battery cable for an open circuit, loose or corroded connections. Repair or replace the battery cable as necessary.

b. If battery voltage is indicated, continue at Step 6B.

6A. *Models without key switch (**Figure 5**)*—Disconnect the starter solenoid ground wire from the engine at point 4, **Figure 5**. Connect the voltmeter between the disconnected ground wire and the solenoid at point 3, **Figure 5**. Push the start button while noting the meter.

a. If no voltage is indicated, check the solenoid ground wire for an open circuit, loose or corroded connections. If the ground wire

and connections are acceptable, the solenoid is defective and must be replaced.

b. If battery voltage is indicated, reconnect the solenoid ground wire (point 4, **Figure 5**) and continue at Step 7A.

6B. *Models with key switch (**Figure 6**)*—Connect the voltmeter between the starter solenoid at point 4 and engine ground. With the key switch ON, push the start button while noting the meter.

a. If battery voltage is indicated, continue at Step 9.

b. If no voltage is indicated, continue at Step 7B.

7A. *Models without key switch (**Figure 5**)*—Connect the voltmeter between the starter solenoid at point 5, **Figure 5** and engine ground. Push the start button while noting the meter.

a. If the meter indicates battery voltage, check the starter cable for an open circuit or loose or corroded connections. Repair or replace the cable as necessary.

b. If no voltage is indicated, replace the starter solenoid.

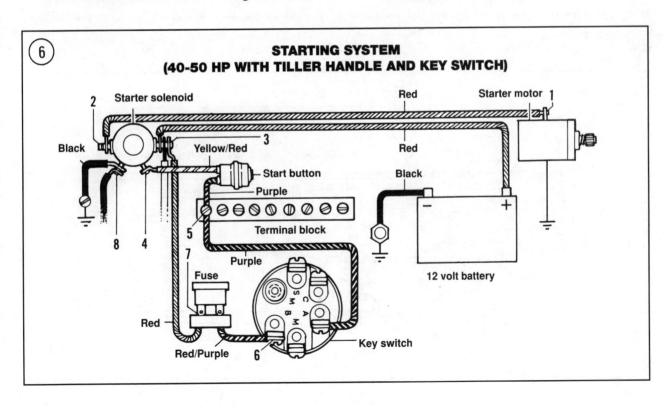

STARTING SYSTEM (40-50 HP WITH TILLER HANDLE AND KEY SWITCH)

7B. *Models with key switch (**Figure 6**)*—Connect the voltmeter between the purple wire connection at the terminal block (point 5, **Figure 6**) and engine ground. With the key switch in the ON position, note the voltmeter.

   a. If battery voltage is noted, check the start button wire between the button and terminal block for an open circuit. If the wire is good, replace the start button.

   b. If no voltage is noted, connect the voltmeter between the key switch at point 6, **Figure 6** and ground. If battery voltage is indicated, test the key switch as described in this chapter. Make sure the purple wire between the key switch and terminal block is in acceptable condition. If no voltage is indicated, continue at Step 8.

8. *Models with key switch (**Figure 6**)*—Check the voltage at the fuse (point 7). If battery voltage is noted at point 7, **Figure 6**, but not at point 6, the fuse is blown and must be replaced. If no voltage is noted at point 7, **Figure 6**, repair or replace the open circuit in the wire between the starter solenoid and the fuse at point 7.

9. *Models with key switch (**Figure 6**)*—Disconnect the solenoid ground wires from the solenoid at point 8, **Figure 6**. Connect the voltmeter between the solenoid ground terminal (point 8, **Figure 6**) and engine ground. With the key switch ON, push the start button.

   a. If the meter indicates battery voltage, check the solenoid ground wire for an open circuit or loose or corroded connections. Repair or replace the ground circuit as necessary.

   b. If no voltage is indicated, test the solenoid as described in this chapter.

Starting System Troubleshooting (60-85 hp with Tiller Handle)

If the starting system fails to operate, use the following troubleshooting procedure to determine the cause. Prior to troubleshooting, make sure the battery is fully charged and the battery terminals are clean and tight. The shift lever must

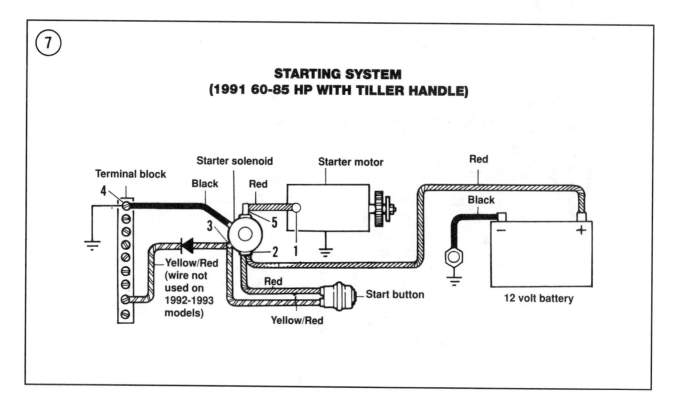

(7)

**STARTING SYSTEM
(1991 60-85 HP WITH TILLER HANDLE)**

be in the NEUTRAL position throughout the entire test procedure. Refer to **Figure 7**.

1. To prevent accidental starter engagement during the following test procedure, disconnect the cable from the starter motor terminal at point 1, **Figure 7**.

2. Place the shift lever in the NEUTRAL position.

3. Connect the voltmeter between the starter cable at point 1 and engine ground. Place the key switch to ON (models so equipped). Push the start button and note the voltmeter.

   a. If battery voltage is indicated, the starter motor is defective and must repaired or replaced.

   b. If no voltage is indicated, continue at Step 4.

4. Connect the voltmeter between the starter solenoid at point 2, **Figure 7** and engine ground.

   a. If no voltage is indicated, check the battery cables for an open circuit or loose or corroded connections. Repair or replace the cable(s) as necessary.

   b. If battery voltage is noted, continue at Step 5.

5. Connect the voltmeter to the starter solenoid at point 3, **Figure 7** and engine ground. Push the start button while noting the meter.

   a. If no voltage is indicated, check the start button wiring for open circuits or loose or corroded connections. If the wiring is in acceptable condition, test the start button as described in this chapter.

   b. If battery voltage is noted, continue at Step 6.

6. Disconnect the starter solenoid black ground wire from the engine or terminal block (point 4, **Figure 7**).

7A. *1991 models*—Connect the voltmeter between the disconnected solenoid ground wire and the solenoid at point 3, **Figure 7**. Push the start button while noting the meter.

7B. *1992-on models*—Connect the voltmeter between the disconnected solenoid ground wire

and engine ground. Push the start button while noting the meter.

   a. If no voltage is indicated, check the solenoid ground wire for an open circuit or loose or corroded connections. If the ground wire is in acceptable condition, replace the starter solenoid.

   b. If battery voltage is indicated, reconnect the solenoid ground wire and continue at Step 8.

8. Connect the voltmeter between the solenoid at point 5, **Figure 7** and engine ground. Push the start button and note the meter.

   a. If battery voltage is noted, check the cable between the solenoid and starter motor for an open circuit or loose or corroded connections. Repair or replace the cable as necessary.

   b. If no voltage is indicated, replace the starter solenoid.

Starting System Troubleshooting (20-300 hp Equipped with Remote Control)

If the starting system fails to operate, use the following troubleshooting procedure to determine the cause. Prior to troubleshooting, make sure the battery is fully charged and the battery terminals are clean and tight. The remote control lever must be in the NEUTRAL position throughout the entire test procedure. Refer to **Figure 8**.

1. To prevent accidental starter engagement, disconnect the starter cable from the solenoid at point 7, **Figure 8**.

2. Place the remote control lever in the NEUTRAL position.

CAUTION
Place the key switch in the OFF position prior to connecting or disconnecting the voltmeter in the following steps.

3. Disconnect the black solenoid wire at point 1. Connect the voltmeter between the end of the black wire (point 1, **Figure 8**) and a good engine

ground. Turn the key switch to the START position while noting the meter.

   a. If battery voltage is indicated, reconnect the black wire and continue at Step 9.

   b. If no voltage is indicated, turn the key switch to OFF and continue at Step 4.

4. Connect the voltmeter between a good engine ground and the solenoid at point 2, **Figure 8**. Turn the key to START and note meter.

   a. If battery voltage is noted, check the solenoid ground wire (black) between points 1 and 2, **Figure 8**, for an open circuit or loose or corroded connections. Repair or replace the wire as necessary.

   b. If no voltage is indicated, reattach the black solenoid ground wire to ground. Turn the key switch to OFF and continue at Step 5.

5. Connect the voltmeter between the solenoid at point 3, **Figure 8** and engine ground. Turn the key switch to START and note the meter.

   a. If battery voltage is noted, the solenoid is defective and must be replaced.

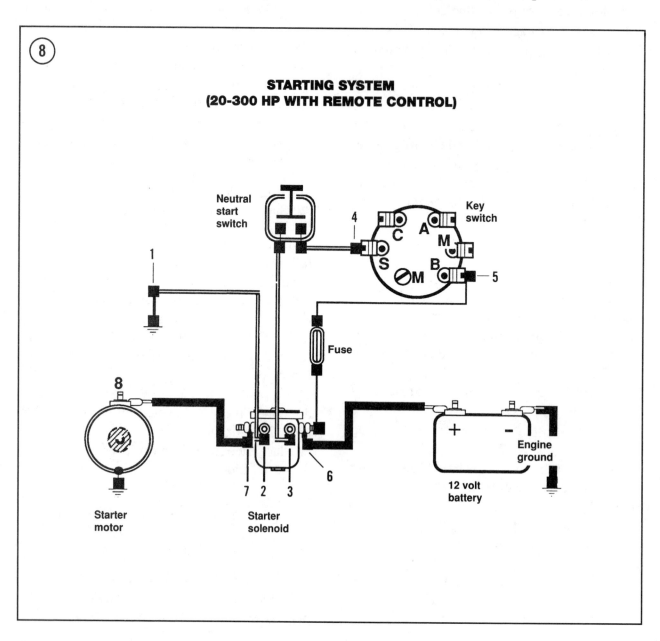

⑧

STARTING SYSTEM
(20-300 HP WITH REMOTE CONTROL)

b. If no voltage is indicated, turn the key switch to OFF and continue at Step 6.

6. Connect the voltmeter between the key switch S terminal (point 4, **Figure 8**) and engine ground. Turn the key switch to START and note the meter.

   a. If battery voltage is noted, check the wires between the neutral start switch and the solenoid, and the neutral start switch and the key switch for an open circuit, or loose or corroded connections. If the wires are good, the neutral switch is defective and must be replaced.

   b. If no voltage is indicated, turn the key switch to OFF and continue at Step 7.

7. Connect the voltmeter between the key switch B terminal (point 5, **Figure 8**) and engine ground. The key switch should be OFF.

   a. If battery voltage is indicated, test the key switch as described in this chapter.

   b. If no voltage is indicated, check the wire and fuse between the solenoid and the key switch B terminal for an open circuit, or loose or corroded connections. Replace the fuse if blown. If the wire and fuse are good, continue at Step 8.

8. Connect the meter between the solenoid at point 6, **Figure 8** and engine ground.

   a. If no voltage is indicated, check the positive battery cable for an open circuit, or loose or corroded connections. Repair or replace the cable as necessary.

   b. If battery voltage is noted, continue at Step 9.

9. Connect the voltmeter between the solenoid terminal at point 7, **Figure 8** and engine ground. Turn the key switch to START and note the meter.

   a. If no voltage is indicated, the solenoid is defective and must be replaced.

   b. If battery voltage is noted, and the solenoid clicks, turn the key switch OFF and continue at Step 10.

10. Reconnect the starter cable (disconnected in Step 1) to the solenoid at point 7, **Figure 8**. Connect the voltmeter between the starter terminal at point 8, **Figure 8** and engine ground. Turn the key switch to START and note the meter.

   a. If no voltage is indicated, check the starter cable for an open circuit between the solenoid and starter motor, or loose or corroded connections. Repair or replace the cable as necessary.

   b. If battery voltage is noted, but the starter motor does not turn, the starter motor has failed and must be repaired or replaced. See Chapter Seven.

Starting System Voltage Drop Test

Excessive voltage drop caused by a defective component, or loose or corroded connections can result in hard starting, slow cranking and excessive heat buildup in the starting circuit.

Use the following test to locate any component or connection with sufficient resistance to cause excessive voltage drop. To help locate an intermittent connection, pull, bend and flex wires and connections while noting the voltmeter during the test. A sudden change in the voltmeter reading indicates a poor connection has been located.

Refer to **Figures 9-12** for this procedure. Clean, tighten or replace any connection or component with excessive voltage drop.

1. Disconnect the spark plug leads from the spark plugs to prevent accidental starting.

2. Connect the positive voltmeter lead to the positive battery terminal. Connect the negative voltmeter lead to the positive solenoid terminal. See **Figure 9**.

3. Crank the engine with the electric starter while noting the voltmeter. If the meter indicates more than 0.3 volt, excessive voltage drop is present between the battery positive terminal and the starter solenoid. Clean and tighten the battery cable connections or replace the cable.

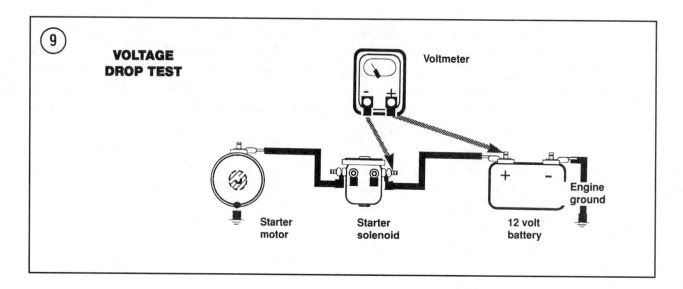

(9)

VOLTAGE DROP TEST

Voltmeter

Starter motor

Starter solenoid

12 volt battery

Engine ground

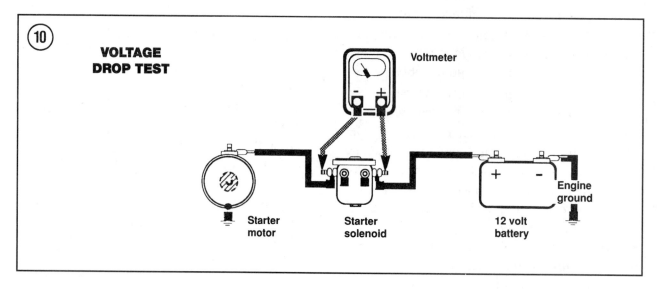

(10)

VOLTAGE DROP TEST

Voltmeter

Starter motor

Starter solenoid

12 volt battery

Engine ground

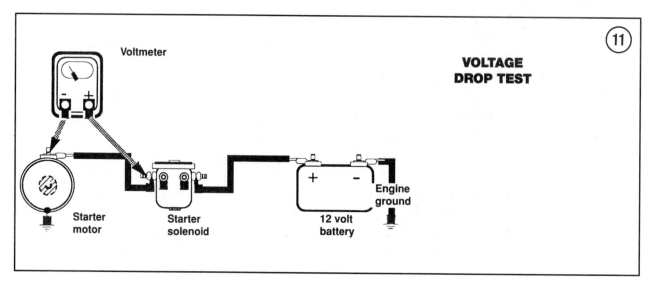

(11)

Voltmeter

VOLTAGE DROP TEST

Starter motor

Starter solenoid

12 volt battery

Engine ground

CAUTION
Do not connect the positive voltmeter lead in Step 4 until after the engine begins cranking, or damage to the voltmeter can result. In addition, be sure to disconnect the voltmeter before stopping cranking.

4. Connect the negative voltmeter lead to the starter side of the solenoid (**Figure 10**). Crank the engine with the electric starter. While cranking the engine, touch the positive voltmeter lead to the opposite solenoid terminal (**Figure 10**), note the meter reading, then remove the voltmeter lead and discontinue cranking. If the voltage drop exceeds 0.2 volt, the starter solenoid has excessive internal resistance and should be replaced.

5. Connect the positive voltmeter lead to the starter side of the solenoid (**Figure 11**). Connect the negative voltmeter lead to the starter motor terminal (**Figure 11**). Crank the engine with the electric starter while noting the meter. Voltage drop should not exceed 0.2 volt. If the reading is more than 0.2 volt, excessive resistance is present in the cable or connections between the solenoid and starter.

6. Connect the positive voltmeter lead to the common power head ground connection (**Figure 12**). Connect the positive voltmeter lead to the negative battery terminal (**Figure 12**). Crank the engine while noting the meter. If the meter indicates more than 0.3 volt, excessive resistance is present in the battery ground cable or connections.

Start Button Test
(Models Equipped with Tiller Handle)

1. Disconnect the start button wires from the starter solenoid.
2. Connect an ohmmeter between the start button wires.
3. Push the start button, note the meter then release the button.
4. Continuity should be indicated when the button is depressed and no continuity when the button is released.
5. Replace the start button if the results are not as specified.

Key (Ignition) Switch Test

Use a suitable ohmmeter or self-powered continuity tester to test the key switch. Refer to **Figure 13** for this procedure.

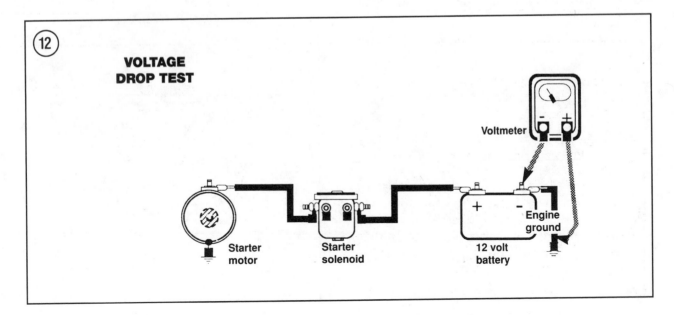

(12) **VOLTAGE DROP TEST**

Voltmeter

Starter motor

Starter solenoid

12 volt battery

Engine ground

1. Disconnect the battery cables from the battery.

2. Disconnect the wires from the key switch.

3. Connect a suitable continuity tester or ohmmeter betweeen the switch terminals marked BATT and A (or IGN). With the switch in the OFF position, no continuity should be noted.

4. Turn the switch to ON. Continuity should now be noted.

5. Turn the switch to START. Continuity should be noted.

6. Hold the switch in the START position and move one test lead from terminal A to terminal S. Continuity should be noted.

7. Turn the switch to OFF. Move the test leads to the 2 terminals marked M. Continuity should be noted.

8. While noting the meter or continuity tester, turn the switch first to START, then to ON. No continuity should be noted with the switch in either position.

9. Turn the switch OFF. Move the test leads to terminal B and terminal C. Turn the switch ON. No continuity should be noted. If equipped with a choke primer system, push the key inward while noting the meter or tester. Continuity should be noted when the key is depressed.

10. Repeat Step 8 with the key in the START position. Continuity should again be noted when the key is depressed.

11. Replace the key switch if it does not perform as specified.

Neutral Start Switch Test

Refer to Chapter Seven for neutral start switch test and adjustment procedures.

Starter Solenoid Test

Use the following test procedure to determine if the starter solenoid is functioning properly.

1. Disconnect all wires from the solenoid. If necessary, remove the solenoid from the motor.

2. Calibrate the ohmmeter on the appropriate scale.

3. Connect the ohmmeter to the large solenoid terminals as shown in **Figure 14**. The ohmmeter should indicate high (infinity) resistance. If a low reading (continuity) is indicated, replace the solenoid.

> *WARNING*
> *Make the final connections in Step 4 at the starter solenoid. DO NOT create any sparks at or near the battery or a serious explosion could occur.*

4. Next, attach a 12-volt battery to the small solenoid terminals using suitable jumper wires. See **Figure 14**. The solenoid should produce an audible click when the battery is connected.

5. The ohmmeter should now indicate low resistance (continuity). If high resistance (or infinity) is indicated, replace the solenoid.

6. After reinstallation of the solenoid, coat all terminal connections (except the positive battery connection) with OMC Black Neoprene Dip.

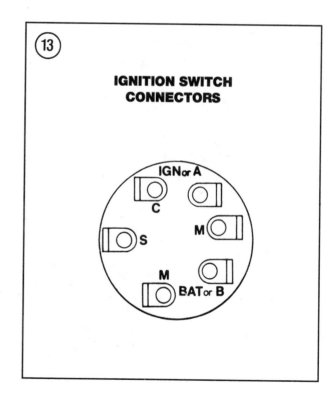

(13)

IGNITION SWITCH CONNECTORS

Starter Motor No-Load Current Draw

NOTE
On gear-reduction starter motors, the driven gear and pinion shaft must be removed from the motor before performing the no-load test. See Chapter Seven.

If starter system troubleshooting indicates that additional starter motor tests are necessary, use the starter no-load current draw test to determine if the motor is in acceptable condition.

An ammeter capable of measuring 0-50 amps, voltmeter, a vibration tachometer and a fully charged 12-volt battery of the correct capacity are necessary to perform the test.

1. Remove the starter motor from the power head. Securely fasten the motor in a vise or other suitable holding fixture.

2. Obtain a fully charged 12-volt battery of the correct minimum capacity. Minimum required cold cranking amps (CCA) are as follows:

   a. *9.9-30 hp*—350 CCA.

   b. *40 hp through V4 models*—360 CCA.

   c. *V6 and V8 models*—500 CCA.

3. Using a heavy gauge jumper cable, connect the ammeter in series with the positive battery and starter motor terminals. See **Figure 15**. Connect a voltmeter to the battery as shown in **Figure 15**.

4. If available, hold a vibration-type tachometer (such as a Frahm Reed Tachometer) against the starter frame.

WARNING
Make the last battery connection at the starter frame in Step 5. DO NOT create any sparks at or near the battery or a serious explosion could occur.

5. Connect a heavy gauge jumper cable to the negative battery terminal. Then, attach the jumper cable to the starter motor frame. See **Figure 15**. Note the starter rpm, current draw and battery voltage while the motor is running, then disconnect the jumper cable from the starter frame.

6. If the starter motor does not perform within specification (**Table 5**), the motor must be repaired or replaced. See Chapter Seven. Refer to **Table 1** for additional starting system and starter motor symptoms, causes and remedies.

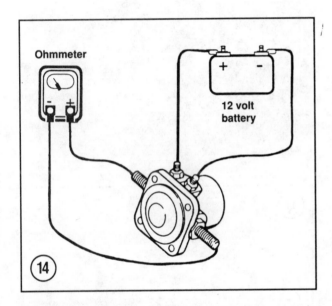

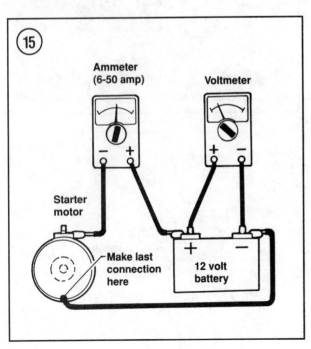

AC (ALTERNATING CURRENT) LIGHTING COIL

Rope start models may be equipped with a 4 amp lighting coil designed to provide AC current for the operation of lights or other accessories. The lighting coil is located under the flywheel, but flywheel removal is not necessary for testing purposes. Test the lighting coil using a suitable ohmmeter.

1. Disconnect the yellow/gray, yellow/blue and yellow lighting coil wires at their bullet connectors.

2. Calibrate the ohmmeter on the low-ohms or R × 1 scale.

3. Connect the meter between the yellow/gray and yellow wires. Resistance should be 0.81-0.91 ohms. Replace the lighting coil if resistance is not as specified.

4. Next, connect the meter between the yellow/gray and yellow/blue wires. Resistance should be 1.19-1.23 ohms. Replace the lighting coil if resistance is not as specified.

5. Calibrate the ohmmeter on the high-ohms or R × 1000 scale.

6. Connect the ohmmeter between a good engine ground and alternately to each lighting coil wire. Note the meter at each connection. No continuity should be indicated. If any continuity is noted, the lighting coil or one (or more) of the coil wires is shorted to ground. Repair the wire(s) or replace the lighting coil as necessary.

BATTERY CHARGING SYSTEM

Description

The 4 and 6 amp charging systems (without voltage regulator) consist of the flywheel (**Figure 16**), stator (B, **Figure 17**), rectifier (**Figure 18**), starter solenoid and battery.

Permanent magnets located in the rim of the flywheel induce alternating current (AC) into the stator coil windings as the flywheel rotates. The

rectifier converts (rectifies) the AC current to direct current (DC) for storage in the battery. The 4 and 6 amp nonregulated charging system is used on the following models equipped with electric start:

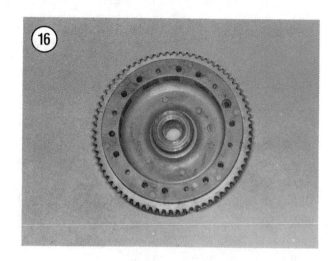

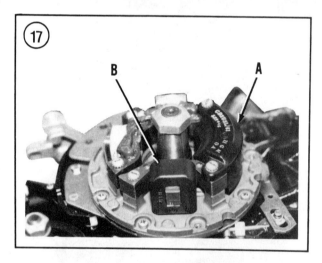

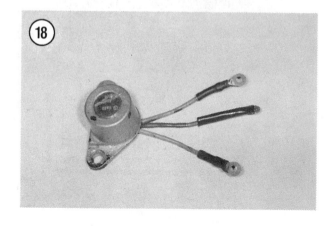

a. *4 amp*—1991 and 1992 6-50 hp and 1993-on 6-48 hp models.

b. *6 amp*—1991 and 1992 60, 70 and 88 hp models.

Some rope start models may be equipped with a 4 amp accessory charging system. Refer to the outboard motor owner's manual if necessary to determine the charging system used.

Because a nonregulated charging system has the potential to overcharge the battery during long periods of wide-open throttle operation,

always use a vented battery of the correct capacity (**Table 7**). *Do not* use maintenance-free batteries with a nonregulated charging system.

The regulated charging system consists of a flywheel (**Figure 16**), stator assembly (**Figure 19**), terminal block (**Figure 20**, typical), voltage regulator/rectifier, starter solenoid and battery. AC current is induced into the stator coil windings as the flywheel magnets rotate. The current is then rectified by the voltage regulator/rectifier for storage in the battery. The voltage regulator/rectifier also provides the signal for tachometer operation.

On 60° V6 models and 1993-on 200 and 225 hp models, the voltage regulator/rectifier assembly is equipped with a thermal cutout switch designed to prevent regulator/rectifier damage if the engine overheats. Should engine temperature exceed 190° F (87° C), the thermal switch opens, disabling the charging system, thereby preventing regulator/rectifier damage.

The following charging systems are used on models covered in this manual:

a. *6 amp*—1991 90 and 115 hp models with manual tilt; 1992-on 90 and 115 hp models with long shaft and manual tilt; 1993-on 60 and 70 hp models.

b. *3/9 amp*—1991 65 Jet, 80 Jet, 85, 90, 100, 115, 1.6 Sea Drive, 120, 140, 2.0 Sea Drive, 105 Jet and 150 hp; 1992 65 Jet, 80 Jet, 90, 115, 100XP, 120 and 140 hp models; 1993-on 65 Jet, 80 Jet, 90, 115, 100, 120 and 140 hp.

c. *5/10 amp*—1992-on 85 hp backtroller models.

d. *4/12 amp*—1991-92 Some 60 and 70 hp models.

e. *35 amp*—1991 150-300 hp 3.0 and 4.0 Sea Drive models; 1992-on 105 Jet, 150-300 hp models.

Some models are equipped with variations of the manufacturer's accessory package; refer to the outboard motor owner's manual for the specific charging system used.

3

The dual amperage charging systems are designed to charge the battery at the lower amperage rate during slow speed operation and the high amperage rate at cruising speeds.

A malfunction in the battery charging system generally causes the battery to be undercharged or discharged. Because the stator assembly is protected by its location under the flywheel, charging system malfunctions are often caused by battery, rectifier, voltage regulator/rectifier or related wiring problems. Note that the following conditions will cause rectifier or voltage regulator/rectifier damage:

a. Battery cables reversed.
b. Disconnecting battery cables while engine is running.
c. Broken or loose connection resulting in intermittent or open circuits.

Troubleshooting Preparation

Before attempting to troubleshoot the charging system, visually check the following points.

1. Make sure the positive (red) battery cable is connected to the positive battery terminal. If battery polarity is reversed, check for a defective rectifier or regulator rectifier.

NOTE
A damaged rectifier is often discolored or has a burned appearance.

2. Check all wiring for loose or corroded connections. Clean and tighten connections as necessary. Seal connections with OMC Black Neoprene Dip as necessary.
3. Check battery condition. Charge the battery as necessary. See Chapter Seven.
4. Check the wiring harness between the ignition plate and battery for damaged or deteriorated insulation and corroded, loose or faulty connections. Repair or replace the harness as necessary.

5. Check the fuse on regulated charging systems. Replace the fuse if blown, then determine and repair the cause.

Alternator Output Test (Nonregulated Charging Systems)

It is necessary to run the outboard at wide-open throttle during the alternator output test. Therefore, the outboard must be in a test tank or mounted on a boat in the water. *Do not* attempt to run the outboard at wide-open throttle on a flushing device.

An ammeter capable of measuring up to 10 amperes is necessary to perform the following test. For accurate results, the battery should be slightly discharged at the beginning of this test.

1. With the key switch in the OFF position, check battery voltage. If battery voltage is less than 12.5 volts, continue at Step 3. If battery voltage is 12.5 volts or more, continue at Step 2.

CAUTION
Do not crank the engine continuously for more than 10 seconds, or the starter motor may overheat. Allow the starter motor to cool for 2 minutes before cranking.

2. Separate the charge coil connector(s) to disable the ignition system. Crank the engine in short intervals until battery voltage is less than 12.5 volts measured with the key switch OFF.
3. Disconnect the battery cables from the battery.
4. Disconnect the red rectifier wire from the terminal block.
5. Connect a suitable ammeter in series with the rectifier red wire and the wiring harness red wire.

CAUTION
Do not allow the ammeter test leads or any red wire or terminals to contact ground during this test.

6. Reconnect the battery cables to the battery.

7. Start the engine and slowly advance the throttle to approximately 5500 rpm while noting the ammeter.

8. Alternator output should be as follows:

   a. *4 amp models*—Output should be approximately 0.5-0.75 amp at 1500 rpm and 4.0-4.5 amps at 5500 rpm.

   b. *6 amp models*—Output should be approximately 4.0-4.25 amps at 1500 rpm and 6 amps at 3500 rpm and above.

9. If low or no output is noted, check the stator resistance and perform the rectifier ohmmeter test as described in this chapter.

Stator Resistance Test
(Nonregulated Charging Systems)

Use a suitable ohmmeter to check the stator for the correct resistance and for shorted or open windings.

1. Disconnect the battery cables from the battery.

2. Disconnect the yellow/gray, yellow/blue and yellow stator wires from the terminal block. See **Figure 20**.

3. Calibrate the ohmmeter on the R × 1 or low-ohms scale.

4. Connect the red ohmmeter lead to the yellow stator wire and the black ohmmeter lead to the yellow/blue stator wire. Resistance should be 0.5-0.6 ohm.

5. Move the red ohmmeter lead to the yellow/gray stator wire. Resistance should be 0.5-0.6 ohm.

6. Replace the stator (Chapter Seven) if resistance is not as specified.

7. Next, check the stator for shorts to ground. Disconnect the ohmmeter leads. Calibrate the meter on the high-ohms scale, then connect the ohmmeter between a good engine ground and alternately to the yellow, yellow/gray and yellow/blue wires. No continuity should be present between engine ground and any stator wire.

8. If a low reading (continuity) is noted, check the stator for bare wires, damaged insulation or other damage. Repair the stator wires as necessary or replace the stator as described in Chapter Seven.

Rectifier Test
(Nonregulated Charging Systems)

The rectifier (**Figure 18**) is constructed of a series of diodes arranged to convert (rectify) the AC current produced by the stator to the DC current that's required to charge the battery. If one or more rectifier diodes become shorted or open, the charging system will not function properly.

A diode is essentially a one-way check valve for electricity. A good diode will allow current to pass through it in one direction, but not the other. A shorted diode will allow current to pass through it in both directions, and an open diode will not allow current to pass in either direction.

Test the rectifier using a suitable ohmmeter. Connect the ohmmeter leads to the diode, note the reading, then reverse the leads. A high reading (or no continuity) at one connection and a low reading (continuity) at the other indicates a good diode (current passing in one direction only). Test each rectifier diode individually as described in the following test procedure. If one or more diodes are defective, the rectifier must be replaced.

1. Disconnect the battery cables from the battery.

2. Disconnect the rectifier wires from the terminal block. See **Figure 20**.

3. Calibrate the ohmmeter on the R × 1000 or the high-ohms scale.

4. Connect the ohmmeter between a good engine ground (or the rectifier case) and the yellow/gray rectifier wire. Note the meter reading, then reverse the ohmmeter leads and again note the meter. A high reading in one direction and a low reading in the other should be noted. If two

high or two low readings are noted, the diode is defective and the rectifier must be replaced.

5. Repeat Step 4 with the ohmmeter connected between ground and the yellow rectifier wire, then the yellow/blue rectifier wire. The results should be the same as those in Step 4.

6. Next, connect the ohmmeter between the rectifier red and yellow/gray wires. Note the meter, then reverse the ohmmeter leads. One high and one low reading should be noted.

7. Repeat Step 6 at the rectifier red and yellow wires.

8. Repeat Step 6 at the red and yellow/blue wires.

9. The results should be the same as those of Step 6. If not, the rectifier is defective and must be replaced.

Alternator Output Test (Regulated Charging Systems)

It is necessary to run the outboard at wide-open throttle during the alternator output test. Therefore, the outboard must be in a test tank or mounted on a boat in the water. *Do not* attempt to run the outboard at wide-open throttle on a flushing device.

An ammeter capable of measuring up to 40 amperes is necessary to perform the following test.

For accurate results, the battery should be slightly discharged at the beginning of this test.

1. With the key switch in the OFF position, check battery voltage. If battery voltage is less than 12.5 volts, continue at Step 3. If battery voltage is 12.5 volts or more, continue at Step 2.

CAUTION
Do not crank the engine continuously for more than 10 seconds, or the starter motor may overheat. Allow the starter motor to cool for 2 minutes before cranking.

2. Separate the charge coil connector(s) to disable the ignition system. Crank the engine in short intervals until battery voltage is less than 12.5 volts measured with the key switch OFF.

3. Disconnect the battery cables from the battery.

4. Disconnect the red regulator/rectifier wire from the terminal block or the battery side of the starter solenoid.

5. Connect the ammeter in series with the red regulator/rectifier wire and the battery side of the starter solenoid.

CAUTION
Do not allow the ammeter test leads or any red wire or terminals to contact ground during this test.

6. Reconnect the battery cables to the battery. Start the engine and slowly advance the throttle to full throttle while noting the ammeter.

7. Alternator output should be as follows:

   a. *6 amp system*—Output should be approximately 4 amps at 1500 rpm and 6 amps at 4500 rpm and above.

   b. *9 amp system*—Output should be approximately 7.5 amps at 1500 rpm and 9-9.5 amps at 3500 rpm and above.

   c. *10 amp system*—Output should be approximately 7 amps at 1500 rpm and 10 amps at 4500 rpm and above.

   d. *35 amp system*—Output should be approximately 30 amps at 1500 rpm and 35-39 amps at 5500 rpm and above.

8. If alternator output is not as specified, or if no output is noted, check all wiring and terminals for loose or corroded connections and repair as necessary. If all wiring and connections are in acceptable condition, check the stator resistance as described in this chapter. If the stator resistance is within specification, test the voltage regulator/rectifier as described in this chapter.

Stator Resistance Test
(Regulated Charging System)

Use a suitable ohmmeter to check the resistance of the stator windings.

1. Disconnect the battery cables from the battery.

2. On 60° V6 models and 1993-on V8 models, disconnect the stator yellow and yellow/gray wire connector from the voltage regulator/rectifier. On all other models, disconnect the yellow and yellow/gray stator wires from the terminal block.

3. Calibrate the ohmmeter on the R × 1 or the low-ohms scale.

4. Connect the ohmmeter between the yellow and yellow/gray stator wires and note the meter.

5. Compare the resistance reading with the specifications in **Table 4**. Replace the stator/charge coil assembly if the resistance is not as specified.

6. Next, calibrate the ohmmeter on the high-ohms scale.

7. Connect the ohmmeter between a good engine ground and alternately to the yellow and yellow/gray wires. Note the meter at each connection. No continuity should be noted.

8. If continuity or a low reading is noted in Step 7, inspect the stator wires for damaged insulation or other damage causing a short to ground and repair as necessary. If the stator wires are in acceptable condition, the stator assembly is shorted and must be replaced. See Chapter Seven.

NOTE
Be sure the ignition timing maximum spark advance is correctly adjusted and functioning properly after replacing the stator/charge coil assembly. See Chapter Five.

Voltage Regulator/Rectifier Test

It is necessary to run the outboard at wide-open throttle during the voltage regulator/rectifier test. Therefore, the outboard must be in a test tank or mounted on a boat in the water. *Do not attempt to run the outboard at wide-open throttle on a flushing device.*

An ammeter capable of measuring up to 40 amperes is necessary to perform the following test. For accurate results, the battery should be slightly discharged at the beginning of this test.

NOTE
The voltage regulator/rectifier requires battery voltage from the purple wire to operate. Make sure battery voltage is present at the regulator/rectifier purple wire when the key switch is in the ON position.

1. With the key switch in the OFF position, check battery voltage. If battery voltage is less than 12.5 volts, continue at Step 3. If battery voltage is 12.5 volts or more, continue at Step 2.

CAUTION
Do not crank the engine continuously for more than 10 seconds, or the starter motor may overheat. Allow the starter motor to cool for 2 minutes before cranking.

2. Separate the charge coil connector(s) to disable the ignition system. Crank the engine in short intervals until battery voltage is less than 12.5 volts measured with the key switch OFF.

3. Disconnect the battery cables from the battery.

4. Disconnect the red voltage regulator/rectifier wire from the terminal block or the battery side of the starter solenoid.

5. Connect an ammeter in series with the red regulator/rectifier wire and the battery side of the starter solenoid. See **Figure 21**.

6. Reconnect the battery cables to the battery. Connect a suitable voltmeter across the battery terminals.

7. Reconnect the charge coil connector(s).

8. Start the engine and run at wide-open throttle while noting the ammeter and voltmeter.

9. The ammeter should indicate nearly full output:

   a. *6 amp system*—Output should be approximately 6 amps.

   b. *9 amp system*—Output should be approximately 9 amps.

   c. *10 amp system*—Output should be approximately 10 amps.

   d. *12 amp system*—Output should be approximately 12 amps.

   e. *35 amp system*—Output should be approximately 35 amps.

10. As the engine continues to run at wide-open throttle, the regulated voltage should begin to stabilize at approximately 14.5 volts and the alternator output should begin to decrease.

11. If the test results are not as specified, check all wiring and terminals for loose or corroded connections. If all wiring connections are in acceptable condition, check the stator resistance as described in this chapter. If stator resistance is within specifications, replace the voltage regulator/rectifier assembly and repeat this test.

Voltage Regulator/Rectifier Tachometer Circuit Test

If false NO OIL warning signals are noted, or if the tachometer fails to operate properly, the voltage regulator/rectifier may be defective. However, *be certain* the warning signals are false—the warning system is designed to alert the operator of possible oil injection (VRO) system malfunctions. To prevent serious power head failure, make sure the oil injection system, including all warning circuits, is functioning properly. See *Warning Horn Test* in this chapter.

A peak reading voltmeter (PRV) is required to check the tachometer circuit voltage. A conventional voltmeter will not work. A suitable PRV is available from the following vendors:

   a. *Stevens Model CD-77 Peak Reading Voltmeter:*
Stevens Instruments Company
P.O. Box 193
Waukegan, IL 60087

   b. *Merc-O-Tronic Model 781 Peak Reading Voltmeter:*
Merc-O-Tronic Instruments Corporation
3965 North Mill Street
Dryden, MI 48428

NOTE
The following test is based on the use of a Stevens Model CD-77 Peak Reading Voltmeter. If using another manufacturer's meter, follow the instructions provided with the meter.

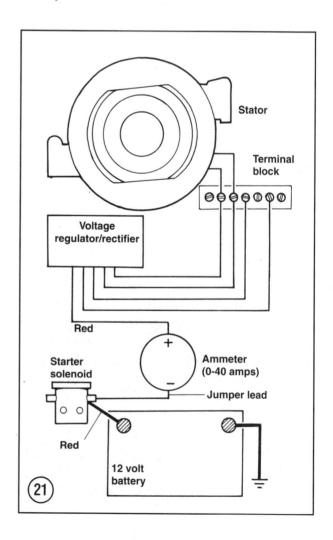

The outboard must be in a test tank, on a boat in the water, or be connected to a suitable flushing device while running. Prior to testing the tachometer circuit, make sure all connections are clean and tight. Test the circuit as follows:

1. Set the PRV polarity switch to POS and the voltage switch to 50.

2. Connect the PRV black lead to a good clean engine ground. Connect the red lead to the gray regulator/rectifier wire at the terminal block.

3. Start the engine and run at 1000 rpm while noting the meter. The meter should indicate 8 volts or more.

   a. If no voltage is noted, replace the regulator/rectifier assembly and repeat this test.

   b. If the meter indicates some voltage, but less than 8 volts, continue at Step 4.

   c. If the meter indicates 8 volts or more, continue at Step 5.

4. While the engine is running at 1000 rpm, disconnect the tachometer while observing the meter. The voltage should increase approximately 1 volt. Next, disconnect the 4-pin connector from the VRO pump (**Figure 22**) while observing the meter. The voltage should increase approximately 2 volts. Stop the engine after reading the meter.

   a. If the voltage increase is more than specified (Step 4) on both components, replace the regulator/rectifier assembly.

   b. If the voltage increase is more than specified on one component only, replace that component.

5. Place the key switch in the ON position (engine not running) and note the meter.

   a. If no voltage is indicated, the tachometer circuit is good. The warning horn system may be malfunctioning.

   b. If the meter indicates voltage, continue at Step 6.

6. Disconnect the gray regulator/rectifier wire from the terminal block. Move the red PRV test lead to the gray wire. With the key switch in the ON position (engine not running), note the meter.

   a. If the meter indicates voltage, the regulator/rectifier is defective and must be replaced.

   b. If no voltage is indicated, continue at Step 7.

7. Move the red PRV lead to the gray tachometer wire in the engine wiring harness. With the key switch in the ON position (engine not running), disconnect the tachometer while noting the meter. Then, disconnect the VRO pump 4-pin connector while observing the meter.

   a. If the voltage falls to zero volts after disconnecting a component, replace that component.

   b. If voltage is still indicated after disconnecting both components, either the remote control wiring harness or the engine wiring harness is damaged or defective. Substitute a known-good remote control wiring harness and repeat Step 7. If voltage is still indicated, the engine wiring harness is damaged or defective. Repair or replace the harness as necessary.

Warning Horn Test

The warning horn system is designed to alert the operator of oil injection or cooling system malfunctions. To prevent possible power head damage, the warning horn should be tested at the beginning of each boating season and periodically during the season. Also, refer to *Temperature Switch Test* in this chapter.

> *NOTE*
> *The temperature switch is located at the top of the cylinder head on inline models. Two temperature switches are used on V4, V6 and V8 models, and are located at the top of each cylinder head.*

1. Disconnect the tan temperature switch wire from the engine harness.
2. Turn the key switch to the ON position.
3. Touch the engine harness end of the tan wire to a good clean engine ground. The warning horn should sound when the tan wire is grounded.
4. If the horn does not sound, but all other electrical components function properly, the horn or horn wiring is defective or damaged. Repair or replace as necessary.

IGNITION SYSTEM

The wiring harness used between the ignition switch and engine is adequate to handle the electrical requirements of the outboard motor; however, it *will not* handle the electrical needs of accessories that may be installed. Whenever an accessory is added, run new wiring between the battery and the accessory, installing a separate fuse panel on the instrument panel.

If the ignition (key) switch should fail, *never* install an automotive type switch. A marine-grade switch must always be used.

Description

A breaker-point ignition system is used on 2, 2.3 and 3.3 hp (1-cylinder) models. All other models covered in this manual are equipped with a magneto-powered capacitor discharge ignition (CDI) system. The ignition systems and their respective outboard models are as follows:

a. *CD2U*—1991-92 2-cylinder models (except 3 and 4 hp and models with 12 amp charging system) 1993-on 4 Deluxe and 48 hp.
b. *CD2*—1992 2-cylinder models with 12 amp charging system and 1993-on 2-cylinder models (except 3 hp, 4 hp, 4 Deluxe and 48 hp).
c. *Capacitor discharge ignition*—1991-on 3 and 4 hp models.
d. *CD3*—60 and 70 hp 3-cylinder models.
e. *CD4*—65 Jet, 80 Jet and 85-140 hp V4 models.
f. *CD6*—105 Jet and 150-225 hp V6 models.
g. *CD6 Optical Ignition System*—60° 150 and 175 hp V6 models.
h. *CD8*—250-300 hp V8 models.

Refer to Chapter Seven for complete ignition system descriptions. Variations of each ignition system are used which contain different components and require different troubleshooting and service procedures. Be sure to refer to the appropriate procedure in this chapter. General troubleshooting procedures are provided in **Table 2**. **Figure 23** is a diagram of a typical 3-cylinder (CD3) ignition system showing the major components common to all models.

Troubleshooting Precautions

Several precautions should be strictly observed to avoid damaging the ignition system.
1. Do not reverse the battery connections. Reversing battery polarity will destroy the rectifier, voltage regulator/rectifier and power pack.
2. *Never* spark the battery terminals with the battery cable connections to check polarity. Any sparks or open flame near the battery can create a serious explosion.
3. Do not disconnect the battery cables while the engine is running.
4. Do not crank the engine if the power pack unit is not grounded to the power head.

5. Do not touch or disconnect any ignition component while the engine is running, while the key switch is ON or while the battery cables are connected.

6. If an outboard equipped with capacitor discharge ignition must be run without the battery connected, disconnect the charging system rectifier or voltage regulator/rectifier leads at the terminal block. Tape each wire separately to prevent contact with each other or engine ground.

Troubleshooting Preparation

1. Check the wiring harness and all plug-in connectors to make sure all connectors are tight, free of corrosion and the wiring insulation is in good condition.

2. Check all electrical components grounded to the engine for good clean connections.

3. Make sure that all ground wires are properly connected and the connections are clean and tight.

3

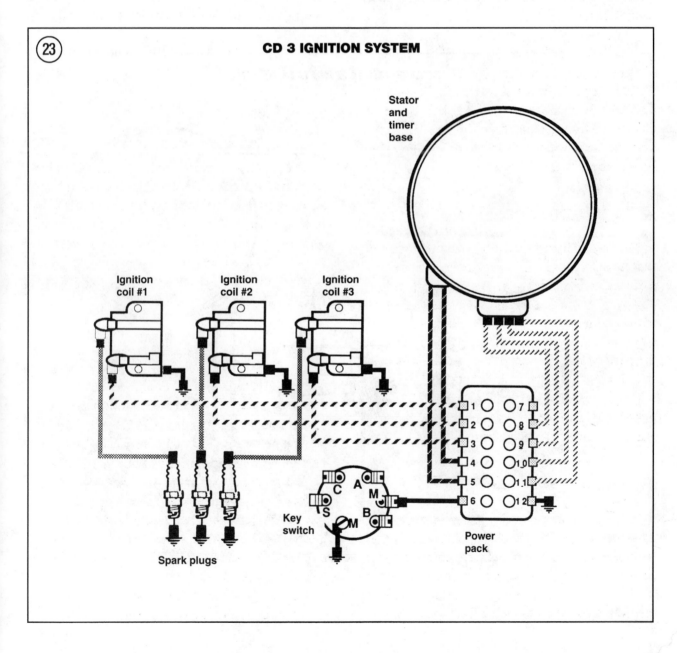

4. Check the remainder of the wiring for disconnected wires and shorts or open circuits.

5. Make sure an adequate supply of fresh fuel is available to the engine. Make sure the oil and gasoline is properly mixed in the correct proportions on models without oil injection.

6. Check the battery condition on electric start models. Clean the terminals and recharge the battery if necessary.

7. Check spark plug cable routing. Make sure the cables are properly connected to their spark plugs.

8. Remove all spark plugs, keeping them in the order removed.

WARNING
To prevent fire or explosion, do not create sparks at or near an open spark plug hole in Step 9 or Step 10.

9. Install a spark tester (**Figure 24**) between the spark plug wires and a good engine ground. Adjust the spark tester air gap to 1/2 in. (12.7 mm). Crank the engine while observing the spark tester. If a good crisp spark jumps at each

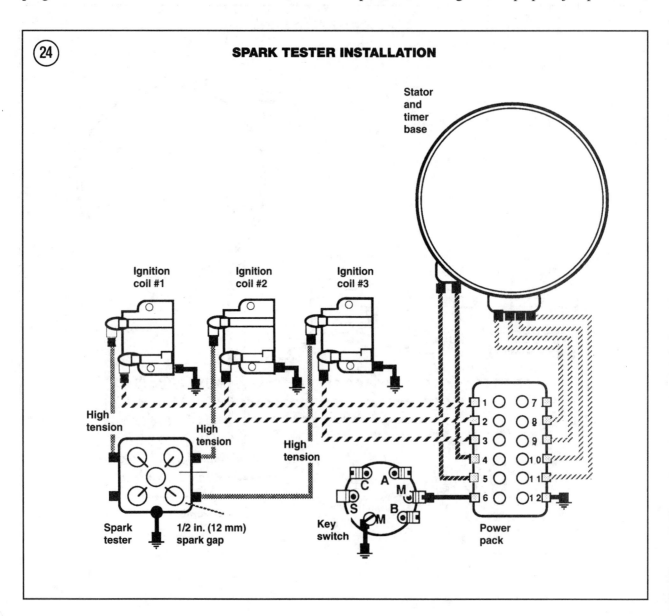

SPARK TESTER INSTALLATION

spark gap, the ignition system is functioning properly. If weak or no spark is noted, an ignition system malfunction is likely.

10. If a spark tester is not available, remove each spark plug and reconnect the proper plug cable to one plug. Lay the plug against the cylinder head so its base makes a good ground connection, then crank the engine while noting the spark gap. If a good crisp spark is noted, the ignition system is functioning properly. If weak or no spark is noted, an ignition system malfunction is likely.

Required Equipment (Breaker-Point Ignition)

To prevent unnecessary component replacement, a suitable ignition analyzer should be used to test the ignition system components. The manufacturer recommends using one of the following analyzers:

a. Merc-O-Tronic Model 98 Ignition Analyzer
Merc-O-Tronic Instruments Corporation
3965 North Mill Street
Dryden, MI 48428

b. Stevens Model ST-75 Ignition Analyzer
Stevens Instruments Company
P.O. Box 193
Waukegan, IL 60087

Each analyzer includes detailed instructions for component testing as well as specifications according to outboard model and year of manufacture. The procedures in this chapter are general in nature to acquaint you with component testing. Refer to the instructions provided with the particular analyzer to be used for the exact procedure.

In addition to an ignition analyzer, a suitable ohmmeter may be used to test the ignition coil, breaker points and driver coil. A multimeter is generally the most efficient and inexpensive instrument for checking resistance, in addition to voltage and current. Two types of multimeter are available, analog and digital.

The analog volt-ohmmeter (VOM) has a moving needle with marked bands indicating the volt, ohm and amperage scales. The digital multimeter (DVOM) is ideally suited for troubleshooting work because it is easy to read, contains internal overload protection, is auto-ranging (analog meters must be recalibrated each time the scale is changed) and has automatic polarity compensation.

An ohmmeter, although useful, is not always a good indicator of ignition system condition. This is primarily because resistance tests do not simulate actual operating conditions. For example, the power source in most ohmmeters is only 6-9 volts. A CDI charge coil, however, commonly produces 100-300 volts during normal operation. Such high voltage can cause coil insulation leakage that can not be detected with an ohmmeter.

Because resistance generally increases with temperature, perform resistance tests with the engine cold (room temperature). Resistance tests on hot components will indicate increased resistance and may result in unnecessary parts replacement without solving the basic problem.

Required Equipment (Capacitor Discharge Ignition [CDI])

The following test equipment is necessary to test CD ignition components and to prevent unnecessary parts replacement.

1. *Peak Reading Voltmeter (PRV)*—The manufacturer recommends using one of the following units:

a. Merc-O-Tronic Model 781
Merc-O-Tronic Instruments Corporation
3965 North Mill Street
Dryden, MI 48428

b. Stevens Model CD-77
Stevens Instruments Company
P.O. Box 193
Waukegan, IL 60087

c. Electro-Specialties Model PRV-1
Electronic-Specialties Inc.
3148 South Chrysler
Tucson, AZ 85713

NOTE
*A conventional voltmeter **can not** be used in place of a meter capable of reading peak volts.*

A typical PRV is equipped with 2 test leads, one red and one black. The test leads have a probe-type end that can be slipped under the connector sleeves or directly into an open connector. A plug-in clip connector is also provided with the tester for attaching a test lead onto an engine ground. The tester has 3 voltage scales: 0-5 volts, 0-50 volts and 0-500 volts. The voltage range is selected by turning the voltage knob on the meter. The PRV is also equipped with a polarity selector knob to select the sensor polarity of the voltage to be measured.

During testing, if the meter needle swings hard against the right-hand side of the scale, *immediately* disconnect the test leads or discontinue the test to prevent damage to the PRV. Recheck the meter switch settings or the test connections.

Slow cranking speed, caused by a weak battery, faulty starter motor or other starting system problem can result in invalid peak output readings. Make sure the battery is fully charged and the starting system is operating properly. Prior to performing peak output tests, make sure the spark plugs are installed and properly torqued.

2. *Breakout (junction) box*—A breakout box connects to a particular circuit and allows voltage measurements to be taken while the circuit remains intact. This will enable voltage output to be measured while the engine is running. Two commonly used breakout boxes are: Stevens Model SA-6 and Merc-O-Tronic Model 55-861.

3. *A suitable ohmmeter capable of measuring low and high ranges*—A multimeter is generally the most efficient and inexpensive instrument for checking resistance, in addition to voltage and current. Two types of multimeter are available, analog and digital.

The analog volt-ohmmeter (VOM) has a moving needle with marked bands indicating the volt, ohm and amperage scales. The digital multimeter (DVOM) is ideally suited for troubleshooting work because it is easy to read, contains internal overload protection, is autoranging (analog meters must be recalibrated each time the scale is changed) and has automatic polarity compensation.

An ohmmeter, although useful, is not always a good indicator of ignition system condition. This is primarily because resistance tests do not simulate actual operating conditions. For example, the power source in most ohmmeters is only 6-9 volts. A CDI charge coil, however, commonly produces 100-300 volts during normal operation. Such high voltage can cause coil insulation leakage that can not be detected with an ohmmeter.

Because resistance generally increases with temperature, perform resistance tests with the engine cold (room temperature). Resistance increases approximately 10 ohms per each degree of temperature increase. Therefore, resistance tests on hot components will indicate increased

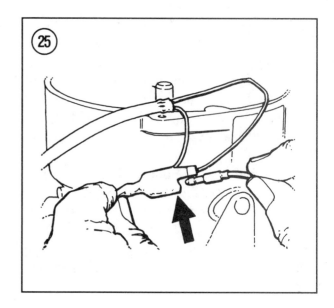

resistance and may result in unnecessary parts replacement without solving the basic problem.

4. *Stevens Ignition Module Load Adapter, part No. PL-88*—The PL-88 is required to test power pack output. If a PL-88 is not available, it can be fabricated using a 10 ohm, 10 watt resistor (Radio Shack part No. 271-132, or equivalent).

5. *Stevens Ignition Coil Terminals Extenders, part No. TS-77*—The terminal extenders are installed between the ignition coil primary terminals and primary wires, and are used to provide a meter connection to the primary circuit during the test procedure.

6. *Jumper wires for Amphenol connectors (4 are needed)*—Can be fabricated using 8 in. lengths of 16-gauge wire. Connect a pin (OMC part No. 511469) to one end of a wire and a socket (OMC part No. 581656) to the other end. Insulate both ends with heat shrink tubing (OMC part No. 510628.

7. *Spark Tester*—Stevens part No. S21, S13C or S48, or Merc-O-Tronic part No. 55-4S or 55-6S. The spark tester is connected between the spark plug leads and engine ground to check for spark output from the ignition system.

8. *The correct test wheel*—See **Table 8**. It is necessary to run the outboard under load during the power pack running output test.

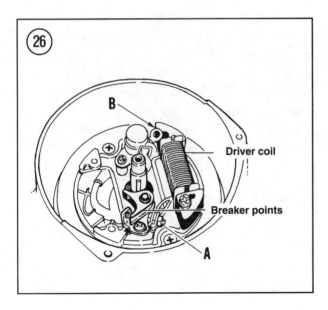

BREAKER-POINT IGNITION TESTING (1-CYLINDER MODELS)

Breaker Point Cleaning and Inspection

If an ignition system malfunction is evident, remove the flywheel (Chapter Eight) and inspect the breaker points for excessive or unusual wear, contamination or corrosion. Check the breaker point arm for freedom of movement and correct spring action. *Always* replace breaker points in questionable condition. Refer to Chapter Seven for breaker point removal/installation and adjustment. Note that breaker point adjustment can be performed without flywheel removal.

Any contamination, including oils and acids from a person's hands, can cause excessive resistance across the breaker point contacts. Any oil or grease on the contacts will cause the points to burn in a short time. Clean the breaker point contacts using alcohol and a suitable strip of clean cloth. If the breaker contacts can not be sufficiently cleaned, replace the points. *Never* file the breaker points to clean the contacts.

Breaker Points Resistance Test

Test breaker point contact resistance using a suitable ohmmeter as follows:

1. Rotate the flywheel until the breaker points are fully closed, then remove the flywheel as described in Chapter Eight.

2. Disconnect the stop button wire and ignition coil primary wire from the breaker plate output connector. See **Figure 25**.

3. Calibrate the ohmmeter on R × 1 or low-ohms scale.

4. Connect the positive ohmmeter lead to the breaker point terminal screw (A, **Figure 26**) and the black ohmmeter lead to a good clean ground.

5. Without disturbing the position of the driver coil, carefully remove the mounting screw (B, **Figure 26**), then lift the driver coil ground wire away from the coil. Make sure the ground wire

is not contacting the coil and note the meter. The ohmmeter should indicate very low resistance (zero ohm) with the points closed.

6. Using a small screwdriver or similar tool, open the points slightly while noting the meter. The ohmmeter should indicate no continuity with the points opened.

7. If test results are not as specified, clean the breaker point contacts surfaces as described in this chapter, then repeat this test. If the correct results are still not obtained, replace the breaker points (Chapter Seven). Do not file the breaker contacts.

8. Reconnect all circuits disconnected during this test. Reinstall the flywheel as described in Chapter Eight.

Driver Coil Resistance Test

Test the driver coil resistance using an ohmmeter as follows.

1. Disconnect the stop button and ignition coil primary wires from the breaker plate output connector. See **Figure 25**.

2. Remove the flywheel as described in Chapter Eight.

3. Calibrate the ohmmeter on the R × 1 or low-ohms scale.

4. Hold the breaker points open by inserting a clean match book or piece of paper between the breaker contacts.

5. Connect the ohmmeter positive lead to the breaker point terminal screw (A, **Figure 26**). Connect the black ohmmeter lead to a good clean breaker point ground.

6. Driver coil resistance should be 1.7-2.7 ohms. If not, replace the driver coil as described in Chapter Seven.

Condenser Tests

Using a suitable ignition analyzer, test the condenser for leakage, excessive resistance and capacity as follows:

1. Remove the flywheel. See Chapter Eight.

2. Disconnect the condenser wire from the breaker points. If necessary, unsolder the condenser wire from the breaker plate output wire.

3. Connect one analyzer test lead to the condenser lead. Connect the remaining test lead to the breaker plate.

WARNING
High voltage is involved in a condenser leakage test. Handle the analyzer leads carefully and turn the analyzer switch to DISCHARGE before disconnecting it from the condenser.

4. Set the analyzer controls according to its manufacturer's instructions. Check the condenser for leakage, excessive resistance and capacity.

5. Compare the results in Step 4 with the specifications provided by the analyzer manufacturer. Condenser capacity should be 0.22-0.26 mfd. Replace the condenser if it fails any of the 3 tests.

Ignition Coil Power/Surface Leakage Tests

1. Remove the ignition coil from the power head. See Chapter Seven. Place the coil on a wooden or insulated bench surface.

2. Connect an ignition analyzer according to its manufacturer's instructions.

3. Check the coil for continuity, power and surface leakage according to the analyzer manufacturer's instructions. Do not exceed the coil maximum operating amperage during testing. The maximum operating amperage is 1.3 amps if using a Merc-O-Tronic analyzer, or 1.8 amps if using a Stevens analyzer.

Ignition Coil Resistance Tests

Check the ignition coil primary and secondary windings for the proper resistance using an ohmmeter as follows. Coil resistance can be checked without removing the coil.

1. Remove the spark plug lead from the ignition coil. Disconnect the primary wire from the coil.
2. Calibrate the ohmmeter on R × 1 or the low-ohms scale.
3. Connect the positive ohmmeter lead to the coil primary terminal. Connect the negative ohmmeter lead to a good engine ground, or the coil ground bushing, if the coil is removed. Note the meter reading.
4. Primary winding resistance should be 1.26-1.54 ohms.
5. Next, connect the positive ohmmeter lead to the coil primary terminal and the black lead to the spark plug terminal. Note the meter reading.
6. Secondary winding resistance should be 4490-5990 ohms.
7. Replace the ignition coil if primary or secondary winding resistance is not as specified.

CAPACITOR DISCHARGE IGNITION (CDI) TROUBLESHOOTING

Several variations of the CD ignition system are used on outboards covered in this manual. Each variation may contain different components and require different troubleshooting and

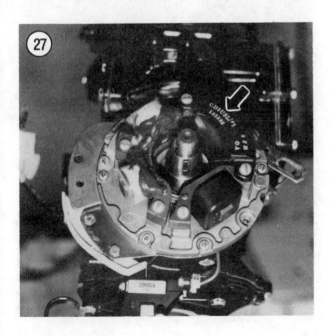

service procedures. Be sure to refer to the appropriate procedure in this chapter. See **Figure 23** for a diagram of a typical 3-cylinder (CD3) ignition system showing the major components common to all models.

CD2U (UNDER FLYWHEEL) IGNITION TROUBLESHOOTING

The CD2U ignition system is used on the 1991 2-cylinder models (except 3 and 4 hp), 1992 2-cylinder models (except 3 and 4 hp and 12 amp charging system) and 1993-on 4 Deluxe and 48 hp models.

NOTE
As a running change in 1992, the charging and ignition systems were changed on some 2-cylinder models. Two-cylinder outboards whose model numbers end with M, are equipped with a 4 amp charging system and under-flywheel ignition (CD2U). Two-cylinder outboards whose model numbers end with J, are equipped with a 12 amp charging system and CD2 (external) ignition.

The major components of the CD2U ignition system include the flywheel, ignition module, charge coil, ignition coils, spark plugs and related wiring. The power pack and sensor coil are contained in the 1-piece ignition module (**Figure 27**) which, along with the charge coil, is located under the flywheel.

The ignition system model number is printed on top of the ignition module (**Figure 27**) and is broken down as follows: CD—capacitor discharge; 2—two cylinders; U—under the flywheel; S—contains S.L.O.W. (speed limiting overheat warning) function; L—uses a speed limiting ignition module to prevent engine overspeed. Note that only 20-50 hp models incorporate the S.L.O.W. (S) and speed limiting (L) functions.

If the outboard motor is very hard or impossible to start, begin the troubleshooting procedure at *Total Output Test*. If an ignition malfunction is causing an intermittent high-speed miss or erratic running above cranking speed, begin at *Indexing Flywheel*. Unless specified otherwise, perform the following ignition system tests in the sequence given. Skipping tests or jumping around the troubleshooting procedure can result in misleading results and unnecessary parts replacement. Test the entire ignition system—more than one component may be defective.

Indexing Flywheel

If the outboard motor runs erratically, or if a high speed miss is noted, the ignition module may be defective. Internal module malfunctions can cause the module to double fire or fire erratically or continuously. Perform the following procedure to ensure the module is firing at the correct time.

1. Remove the spark plugs.

2. Position the No. 1 piston at TDC by rotating the flywheel clockwise. Insert a pencil or similar tool into the No. 1 spark plug hole while rotating the flywheel to ensure the piston is at TDC.

3. With the No. 1 piston at TDC, place a mark on the flywheel directly across from the timing pointer or starter pivot screw. Label the mark No. 1.

4. Repeat Step 2 and Step 3 on the No. 2 cylinder. Label this mark No. 2.

5. Reinstall the spark plugs and connect the plug leads.

> *CAUTION*
> *The outboard motor must be supplied with adequate cooling water while running. Install the motor in a test tank or on a boat in the water. Do not attempt to run the motor at high speed while connected to a flushing device.*

6. Start the motor and run it at the speed at which the problem is evident.

7. Alternately, connect a timing light to each cylinder. The timing light should indicate the cylinder number the timing light is connected to. For example, if the timing light is connected to the No. 1 spark plug wire, the No. 1 mark should be visible. In addition, the number should only appear near the timing pointer or starter pivot bolt.

8. If a different cylinder number appears, or if the number jumps around or appears at other than the timing pointer or starter pivot bolt, first make sure the primary ignition wires are properly connected. The orange/blue primary wire must be connected to the No. 1 (top) ignition coil. If the primary wires are correctly connected, replace the ignition module and repeat this test.

Total Output Test

> *NOTE*
> *If acceptable spark is noted at each spark gap during the total output test, but the engine pops or backfires during starting or running, the ignition system may be out of time. Be sure the orange/blue primary ignition wire is connected to the No. 1 (top) ignition coil, the spark plug leads are properly connected, the flywheel is properly located on the crankshaft and the timing and throttle linkage are properly synchronized.*

The total output test will determine if the ignition system is capable of delivering adequate spark to the spark plugs. Perform the output test with the spark plugs installed and properly tightened.

1. Disconnect the spark plug leads from the spark plugs.

2. Mount a suitable spark tester on the engine and connect the spark plug leads to the tester. See **Figure 28**. Make sure the spark tester mounting clip is secured to a good clean engine ground.

3. Connect the cutoff clip and lanyard to the emergency stop switch, if so equipped.

4. Adjust the spark tester spark gap to 1/2 in. (12.7 mm).

5. Crank the engine while observing the spark tester.

  a. If acceptable spark is noted at each spark gap, continue testing at *Running Output Test* in this chapter.

  b. If acceptable spark is noted at one spark gap, continue testing at *Ignition Plate Output Test* in this chapter.

  c. If no spark is noted at either spark gap, continue testing at *Stop Circuit Test* in this chapter.

Stop Circuit Test

The following test eliminates the stop circuit as a potential cause of an ignition malfunction. The stop button, key switch and lanyard emergency stop switch are connected to the ignition module through the engine wiring harness. Activating the stop circuit shorts ignition module output to ground, which disables the ignition system and stops the engine.

1. Connect a spark tester as described under *Total Output Test*.

NOTE
The stop circuit connector is a 1-pin Amphenol connector. Although the location of the connector may vary, the appearance is the same for all models.

2. Disconnect the 1-pin stop circuit connector. See **Figure 29**.

3. Crank the engine while observing the spark tester.

  a. If no spark is noted at one or both spark gaps, continue at *Ignition Plate Output Test*.

  b. If good spark is now noted at both spark gaps, continue at *Stop Button Ohmmeter Test* or *Key Switch Ohmmeter Test* as appropriate.

Stop button ohmmeter test

The tiller handle on most models contains a combination stop button/emergency stop switch. The emergency switch consists of a clip and lanyard which connects to the stop button. When the clip and lanyard are installed, the stop circuit is in the RUN mode; when the clip and lanyard are not installed, the ignition is disabled and the engine will not start. Test the stop button using an ohmmeter. The ohmmeter test must be performed with the engine NOT running.

1. Make sure the emergency switch clip and lanyard are properly installed.

2. Calibrate the ohmmeter on R × 100 or the low-ohm scale.

3. Disconnect the 1-pin stop circuit connector. See **Figure 29**.

4. Connect the ohmmeter between the stop button side of the 1-pin connector and a good engine ground. The meter should indicate no continuity. If continuity is noted, inspect the stop circuit wiring for a short to ground, and if not found, replace the stop button assembly.

5. Depress the stop button while observing the ohmmeter. The meter should indicate continuity. If no continuity is noted, inspect the stop circuit wiring for an open circuit, and if not found, replace the stop button assembly.

6. While observing the ohmmeter, remove the emergency clip and lanyard. The meter should indicate continuity. If no continuity is noted, inspect the stop circuit wiring for an open circuit, and if not found, replace the stop button assembly.

7. Reconnect any circuits disconnected during this test procedure.

Key switch ohmmeter test

If the engine fails to stop when the key switch is turned to OFF, an open circuit is present in the black/yellow engine harness wire, or the key switch or ignition module is defective. Test the key switch using an ohmmeter. Perform the ohmmeter test with the engine NOT running.

1. Make sure the clip and lanyard are properly installed on the emergency switch.

2. Calibrate the ohmmeter on the R × 100 or low ohm scale.

3. Connect the ohmmeter between the engine harness black/yellow wire (to key switch M terminal) and a good engine ground.

 a. With the key switch OFF, the meter should indicate continuity (low resistance).

 b. With the key switch ON, the meter should indicate no continuity (high resistance). If

continuity is noted with the key switch ON, continue at Step 4.

4. Disconnect the black/yellow wire(s) from the key switch M terminal. With the ohmmeter connected to the black/yellow wire, note the meter reading. If the meter indicates no continuity (or high resistance), test the key switch as described in this chapter.

5. Disconnect the emergency stop switch wire from the engine harness black/yellow wire at the key switch and note the meter.

 a. If the meter indicates no continuity, test the emergency stop switch as previously described.

 b. If the meter indicates continuity, test the engine wiring harness for damaged insulation, short circuits or other damage. Repair or replace the harness as necessary.

Ignition Plate Output Test

> *WARNING*
> *To prevent accidental starting, remove the spark plug leads from the spark plugs. Securely ground the plug leads to the power head.*

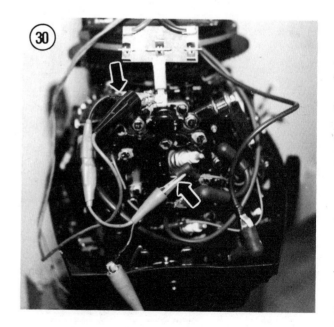

A suitable peak reading voltmeter (PRV) and a Stevens load adapter part No. PL-88 are necessary to test ignition plate output.

1. Disconnect the primary ignition wires from both ignition coils.

2. Connect the No. 1 ignition coil primary wire to the PL-88 red lead. Connect the PL-88 black lead to a good engine ground. See **Figure 30**.

3. Connect the red PRV test lead to the PL-88 red lead. Connect the black PRV test lead to a good engine ground. Set the PRV selector switches to POS and 500.

4. Crank the engine while observing the meter.

5. Repeat Steps 2-4 on the No. 2 ignition coil primary wire.

6. Ignition plate output should be 175 volts or more at each coil.

   a. If output is 175 volts or more at both coil primary wires, refer to *Ignition Coil Resistance Tests* in this chapter.

   b. If no output is noted at both primary wires, continue at *Charge Coil Test* in this chapter.

   c. If no output is noted at one primary wire, replace the ignition module as described in Chapter Seven.

7. Reconnect the ignition coil primary wires. Make sure the orange/blue wire is connected to the No. 1 (top) coil.

Charge Coil Resistance Test

Because resistance generally increases with temperature, perform resistance tests with the engine cold (room temperature). Resistance tests on hot components will indicate increased resistance and may result in unnecessary parts replacement without solving the basic problem.

1. Remove the rewind starter as described in Chapter Twelve.

2. Remove the flywheel as described in Chapter Eight.

3. Remove the 2 ignition module mounting screws and lift the module to expose the brown and brown/yellow charge coil wires. See **Figure 31**. Disconnect the brown and brown/yellow wires at their bullet connectors.

4. Calibrate the ohmmeter on the $R \times 100$ or low ohm scale.

5. Connect the ohmmeter between the brown and brown/yellow charge coil wires. Charge coil resistance should be 800-1000 ohms. If not, replace the charge coil as described in Chapter Seven.

6. Next, calibrate the ohmmeter on the $R \times 1000$ or high ohm scale.

7. Connect the black ohmmeter lead to a good engine ground. Then alternately connect the red lead to the brown and brown/yellow charge coil wires.

   a. The meter should show no continuity at each connection. If continuity is noted, the charge coil or charge coil wire(s) is shorted to ground. Repair the wire(s) or replace the charge coil as necessary.

   b. If charge coil resistance is within specification, the ignition module is defective and must be replaced. See Chapter Seven.

8. Reconnect the charge coil wires.

9. Clean the ignition module screws using clean solvent, then apply OMC Ultra Lock or a suitable equivalent thread locking compound to the threads. Install the screws and tighten to 30-40

in.-lb. (3.4-4.5 N.m). Reinstall the flywheel and rewind starter.

10. If removed, reconnect the primary wires to the ignition coils. Make sure the orange/blue wire is connected to the No. 1 (top) coil.

Running Output Test

> *CAUTION*
> *The outboard motor must be supplied with adequate cooling water while running. Install the motor in a test tank or on a boat in the water. Do not attempt to run the motor at high speed while connected to a flushing device.*

Use the running output test to determine the cause of an intermittent or high-speed ignition malfunction. A peak reading voltmeter (PRV) and 2 Stevens terminal extenders (part No. TS-77, or equivalent) are necessary to perform the test. Remove the propeller and install the correct test wheel (**Table 8**) prior to testing.

1. Remove the primary wires from both ignition coils.

2. Install the terminal extenders (part No. TS-77) on the ignition coil primary terminals, then install the primary wires on the terminal extenders. Make sure the orange/blue primary wire is connected to the No. 1 (top) coil.

3. Set the PRV selector switches to POS and 500.

4. Connect the red PRV lead to the No. 1 coil terminal extender. Connect the black PRV lead to a good engine ground.

5. Start the engine. While observing the meter, run it at the speed the malfunction is evident. Running output should be 200 volts or more.

6. Repeat Steps 4 and 5 at the No. 2 ignition coil.

7. If output is less than 200 volts at either cylinder, test the charge coil resistance as described in this chapter. If the charge coil resistance is within specification, replace the ignition module.

8. If testing is complete, remove the terminal extenders and reconnect the coil primary wires. Make sure the orange/blue primary wire is connected to the No. 1 (top) coil.

Ignition Coil Resistance Test

Because resistance generally increases with temperature, perform resistance tests with the engine at room temperature (70° F [21° C]). Resistance tests on hot components will indicate increased resistance and may result in unnecessary parts replacement without solving the basic problem. Ignition coil resistance can be checked without coil removal.

1. Remove the primary wire and the spark plug wire from the ignition coil.

2. Calibrate the ohmmeter on the R × 1 or low-ohm scale.

3. To check primary winding resistance, connect the black ohmmeter lead to a good engine ground or to the coil ground tab if the coil is removed. Connect the red ohmmeter lead to the coil primary terminal.

4. Primary resistance should be 0.05-0.15 ohm.

5. To check secondary winding resistance, calibrate the ohmmeter on the R × 100 or high-ohm scale. Connect the red ohmmeter lead to the coil primary terminal and the black lead to the spark plug terminal.

6. Secondary resistance should be 225-325 ohms.

7. Replace the coil if resistance is not as specified.

8. To check the spark plug leads, calibrate the ohmmeter on R × 1 or low-ohm scale. Connect the ohmmeter to each end of the lead and note the meter. The resistance should be nearly zero ohm.

S.L.O.W. Operation and Testing (20-50 hp Models)

Some 20-50 hp models are equipped with the speed limiting overheat warning (S.L.O.W.) system. The system is designed to limit engine speed to approximately 2000 rpm if engine temperature exceeds 180° F (82° C) on 20-30 hp or 203° F (95° C) on 35 Jet and 40-50 hp models. To deactivate S.L.O.W., the engine must be throttled back to idle, and allowed to cool to 155° F (68° C) on 20-30 hp or 162° F (72° C) on 35 Jet and 40-50 hp models.

On models equipped with remote electric start, a blocking diode located in the engine wiring harness is used to isolate the S.L.O.W. warning system from the other warning systems. Should the blocking diode become shorted, the S.L.O.W. function will remain activated regardless of engine temperature.

The S.L.O.W. system is activated by input from the engine temperature switch. The temperature switch is located in the top of the cylinder head. Test the temperature switch and S.L.O.W. system as follows.

1. Install the outboard motor in a test tank with the correct test wheel installed. See **Table 8**.
2. Connect an accurate tachometer according to the manufacturer's instructions.

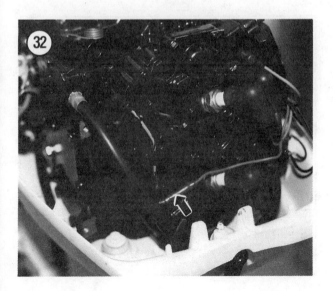

3. Disconnect the tan or tan/red temperature switch wire (**Figure 32**) at its bullet connector.
4. Start the engine and run at approximately 3500 rpm.
5. Connect the engine harness end of the tan or tan/red wire to a clean engine ground and note the engine speed.
6. Engine speed should reduce to approximately 2000 rpm when the wire is grounded. If not, check the engine wiring for an open circuit, and if not found, replace the ignition module. Refer to Chapter Seven. If the engine speed does reduce as specified (but S.L.O.W. function is inoperative), test the temperature switch as described in this chapter.
7. *Remote Electric Start Models*—Calibrate an ohmmeter to the R × 100 scale. Disconnect the red engine wiring harness connector. Connect one ohmmeter lead to the engine harness tan or tan/red temperature switch wire and the other lead to the tan or tan/red wire terminal in the red engine harness connector. Note the ohmmeter reading, then reverse the leads. Continuity (near zero resistance) should be noted in one direction and no continuity (infinity) should be noted in the other direction. If not, replace the blocking diode in the engine wiring harness.

RPM Limiting Power Pack

The outboard motor may be equipped with an RPM limiting power pack designed to prevent power head damage from overspeeding. On models so equipped, the power pack interrupts ignition if engine speed exceeds 6100 rpm. Be certain the correct power pack is used if replacement is necessary.

CAPACITOR DISCHARGE IGNITION SYSTEM TROUBLESHOOTING (1991-ON 3 AND 4 HP MODELS)

The major components used on 3 and 4 hp models include the flywheel, sensor coil, ignition module, ignition coil, spark plugs and related wiring. The ignition module contains an internal charge coil and a capacitor to store charge coil voltage. The ignition coil contains 2 separate coils molded into one assembly.

If the outboard motor is very hard or impossible to start, begin the troubleshooting procedure at *Total Output Test*. If an ignition malfunction is causing an intermittent high-speed miss or erratic running above cranking speed, begin at *Indexing Flywheel*. Unless specified otherwise, perform the following ignition system tests in the sequence given. Skipping tests or jumping around the troubleshooting procedure can result in misleading results and unnecessary parts replacement. Test the entire ignition system—more than one component may be defective.

Indexing Flywheel

If the outboard motor runs erratically, or if a high speed miss is noted, the ignition module may be defective. Internal module malfunctions can cause the module to double fire or fire erratically or continuously. Perform the following procedure to ensure the module is firing at the correct time.

1. Remove the spark plugs.
2. Position the No. 1 piston at TDC by rotating the flywheel clockwise. Insert a pencil or similar tool into the No. 1 spark plug hole while rotating the flywheel to ensure the piston is at TDC.
3. With the No. 1 piston at TDC, place a mark on the flywheel directly across from the timing pointer or starter pivot screw. Label the mark No. 1.
4. Repeat Step 2 and Step 3 on the No. 2 cylinder. Label this mark No. 2.
5. Reinstall the spark plugs and connect the plug leads.

CAUTION
The outboard motor must be supplied with adequate cooling water while running. Install the motor in a test tank or

on a boat in the water. Do not attempt to run the motor at high speed while connected to a flushing device.

6. Start the motor and run it at the speed at which the problem is evident.
7. Alternately, connect a timing light to each spark plug wire. The timing light should indicate the cylinder number the timing light is connected to. For example, if the timing light is connected to the No. 1 spark plug wire, the No. 1 mark should be visible. In addition, the number should only appear near the timing pointer or starter pivot bolt.
8. If a different cylinder number appears, or if the number jumps around or appears at other than the timing pointer or starter pivot bolt, first make sure the primary ignition wires are properly connected. The orange/blue primary wire must be connected to the No. 1 ignition coil. If the primary wires are correctly connected, replace the ignition module and repeat this test.

Total Output Test

NOTE
If acceptable spark is noted at each spark gap during the total output test, but the engine pops or backfires during starting or running, the ignition system

(33)

may be out of time. Be sure the orange/blue primary ignition wire is connected to the No. 1 ignition coil, the spark plug leads are properly connected, the flywheel is properly located on the crankshaft and the timing and throttle linkage are properly synchronized.

The total output test will determine if the ignition system is capable of delivering adequate spark to the spark plugs. Perform the output test with the spark plugs installed and properly tightened.

1. Disconnect the spark plug leads from the spark plugs.

2. Mount a suitable spark tester on the engine and connect the spark plug leads to the tester. See **Figure 28**. Make sure the spark tester mounting clip is secured to a good clean engine ground.

3. Connect the cutoff clip and lanyard to the emergency stop switch, if so equipped.

4. Adjust the spark tester spark gap to 3/8 in. (9.5 mm).

5. Crank the engine while observing the spark tester.

6. If a good crisp spark is noted at both spark gaps, continue at *Ignition Module Running Test* in this chapter. If weak or no spark is noted, continue at *Stop Circuit Elimination Test*.

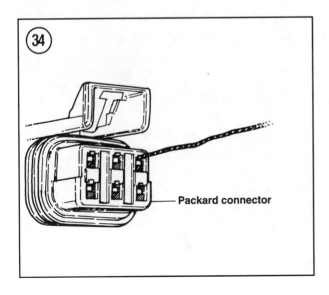

Packard connector

Stop Circuit Elimination Test

The following test eliminates the stop circuit as a potential cause of an ignition malfunction. The stop switch is connected to the ignition module through the engine wiring harness. Activating the stop circuit shorts ignition module output to ground, which disables the ignition system and stops the engine.

1. Connect a spark tester as described under *Total Output Test*.

2. Disconnect the 6-pin Packard connector from the ignition module. See **Figure 33**.

3. Carefully insert a paper clip or similar tool into terminal E (black/yellow wire) of the Packard connector. See **Figure 34**. Depress the terminal locking tab, then pull the black/yellow wire and terminal from the connector body. Tape the terminal of the wire to prevent contact with the power head.

4. Reconnect the 6-pin Packard connector to the ignition module (**Figure 33**).

5. Crank the engine while observing the spark tester.

   a. If good spark is now noted at both spark gaps, continue at *Stop Circuit Ohmmeter Test* in this chapter.

   b. If no spark is noted at one or both spark gaps, continue at *Sensor Coil Output Test* in this chapter.

6. Reinstall the black/yellow wire terminal into the Packard connector body. If necessary, carefully bend the terminal locking tab upward to ensure it will securely lock in the connector body.

Stop Circuit Ohmmeter Test

Test the stop circuit using an ohmmeter. Note that the engine must *not* be running when performing the ohmmeter test.

1. Disconnect the 6-pin Packard connector from the ignition module. See **Figure 33**.

2. Connect the ohmmeter between the black/yellow wire terminal (terminal E) and a good engine ground. The meter should indicate no continuity. If not, the stop button is defective or the black/yellow stop circuit wire is shorted to ground. Repair the wiring or replace the stop button as necessary.

3. Depress the stop button while observing the meter. The meter should indicate continuity when the button is depressed. If not, the stop button is defective or an open circuit is present in the black/yellow stop circuit wire. Repair the wire or replace the stop button as necessary.

4. If test is complete, reconnect the 6-pin connector to the ignition module.

Sensor Coil Tests

A suitable peak reading voltmeter (PRV) is necessary to test the sensor coil. In addition, jumper leads, such as contained in the 6-pin Packard test adapter from the OMC Ignition Test Kit (part No. 434017), are necessary. If the Packard test adapter is not available, the jumper leads can be fabricated using locally available materials. The sensor coil test involves 3 separate tests: ground test, output test and ohmmeter test. Be sure to perform the procedure in the sequence given.

Ground test

1. Disconnect the 6-pin Packard connector from the ignition module. See **Figure 33**.

2. Attach the Packard test adapter, or suitable jumper leads to the 6-pin connector.

3. Set the PRV selector switches to POS and 5. If using a Stevens Model CD-77, set the switches to SEN and 5.

4. Connect one meter lead to a good engine ground. Connect the remaining lead to terminal C (blue/white wire), then crank the engine and note the meter. Move the test lead from terminal C to terminal D (white wire), crank the engine and note the meter.

5. Any voltage output at either connection in Step 4 indicates the sensor coil or sensor coil wires are shorted to ground. Inspect the sensor coil wires for damaged insulation and repair as necessary. If the wires are good, the sensor coil is defective and must be replaced as described in Chapter Seven.

6. If no output is noted in Step 4, continue at *Output test.*

Output test

1. Connect one PRV test lead to terminal C (blue/white wire) and the remaining test lead to terminal D (white wire) in the 6-pin connector.

2. Set the PRV selector switches to POS and 5 or SEN and 5 if using a Stevens Model CD-77.

3. Crank the engine while noting the meter.

4. Sensor coil output should be 4 volts or more.

5. If less than 4 volts, inspect the condition of the sensor coil wiring and connectors and repair or replace as necessary. If the wiring and connectors are in acceptable condition, continue at *Ohmmeter test.*

6. If the meter indicates 4 volts or more in Step 4, continue at *Ignition Module Cranking Output Test* in this chapter.

Ohmmeter test

1. Calibrate the ohmmeter on the R × 100 or low-ohm scale.

2. Connect the ohmmeter between terminals C and D in the 6-pin connector (white/blue and white wires).

3. Sensor coil resistance should be 85-115 ohms.

4. Next, calibrate the ohmmeter on the R × 1000 or high-ohm scale. Connect the ohmmeter between a good engine ground and alternately to each sensor coil wire. No continuity should be present between either sensor coil wire and ground.

5. If continuity is noted, inspect the sensor coil wires for damaged insulation or shorts to ground.

If the wiring is in acceptable condition, the sensor coil is shorted and must be replaced as described in Chapter Seven.

6. If testing is complete, remove the test adaptor or jumper leads from the 6-pin connector, then reconnect it to the ignition module.

Ignition Module Cranking Output Test

> *WARNING*
> *To prevent accidental starting, remove the spark plug wires from the spark plugs. Connect the spark plug wires to a suitable spark tester.*

The ignition module cranking output test is used to determine if the module is capable of producing sufficient voltage to the ignition coil assembly.

1. Disconnect the orange/blue and orange/green primary wires from the ignition coil assembly.
2. Install Stevens terminal extenders (part No. TS-77) on the coil primary terminals, then attach the primary wires to the terminal extenders. Make sure the orange/blue wire is attached to the No. 1 coil.
3. Set the PRV selector switches to NEG and 500.
4. To check ignition module output to the No. 1 coil, connect the black meter lead to a good engine ground and the red meter lead to the terminal extender at the No. 1 ignition coil. Crank the engine while noting the meter.
5. Ignition module output should be 125 volts or more. If output is less than 125 volts, remove the No. 1 (orange/blue) primary wire from the terminal extender. Connect the red PRV lead to the primary wire, then crank the engine while noting the meter.
   a. If output is now 125 volts or more, test the ignition coil as described under *Ignition Coil Resistance Test* in this chapter.
   b. If output is still below 125 volts, inspect the condition of the orange/blue primary wire and its terminal and repair as necessary. If

the wire and terminal are in acceptable condition, replace the ignition module.

6. Test ignition module output to the No. 2 coil (orange/green primary wire) by repeating Steps 4 and 5.
7. If testing is complete, remove the terminal extenders and reconnect the primary wires to the ignition coil assembly. Make sure the orange/blue wire is attached to the No. 1 coil.

Ignition Module Running Output Test

> *CAUTION*
> *The outboard motor must be supplied with adequate cooling water while running. Install the motor in a test tank or on a boat in the water. Do not attempt to run the motor at high speed while connected to a flushing device.*

Use the running output test to determine the cause of an intermittent or high-speed ignition malfunction. Remove the propeller and install the correct test wheel (**Table 8**) prior to testing.

1. Disconnect the ignition coil primary wires from the coil assembly. Connect Stevens terminal extenders (part No. TS-77) to the ignition coil primary terminals. Then, connect the ignition coil primary wires to the terminal extenders, making sure the orange/blue wire is attached to the No. 1 coil.
2. Set the PRV selector switches to NEG and 500.
3. Connect the black PRV lead to a good engine ground and the red lead to the terminal extender connected to the No. 1 coil.
4. Start the engine and run at the speed the malfunction is evident, while observing the meter.

> *NOTE*
> *The voltage noted in Step 6 must be steady at a constant engine speed.*

5. The meter should indicate a continuous 150 volts or more. If the output is less than 150 volts,

stop the engine and remove the orange/blue primary wire from the terminal extender. Attach the red PRV lead to the wire. Crank the engine while noting the meter.

    a. If the output at cranking speed is now 125 volts or more, test ignition coil as described under *Ignition Coil Resistance Test* in this chapter.

    b. If output is still less than 125 volts, replace the ignition module. See Chapter Seven.

6. Test ignition module running output to the No. 2 ignition coil by repeating Steps 4-6 at the orange/green primary wire.

7. If testing is complete, remove the terminal extenders and reconnect the ignition coil primary wires. Make sure the orange/blue wire is connected to the No. 1 coil.

Ignition Coil Resistance Test

Because resistance generally increases with temperature, perform resistance tests with the engine at room temperature (70° F [21° C]). Resistance tests on hot components will indicate increased resistance and may result in unnecessary parts replacement without solving the basic problem. Ignition coil resistance can be checked without coil removal. Both coils on 3 and 4 hp models are molded into one coil assembly.

1. Remove the primary wires and the spark plug wires from the ignition coil assembly.

2. Calibrate the ohmmeter on the R × 1 or low-ohm scale.

3. To check primary winding resistance, connect the black ohmmeter lead to a good engine ground or to the coil ground tab if the coil is removed. Connect the red ohmmeter lead to the coil primary terminal.

4. Primary resistance should be 0.05-0.15 ohm.

5. To check secondary winding resistance, calibrate the ohmmeter on the R × 100 or high-ohm scale. Connect the red ohmmeter lead to the coil primary terminal and the black lead to the spark plug terminal.

6. Secondary resistance should be 225-325 ohms.

7. Repeat Steps 3-6 on the remaining coil.

8. Replace the coil if resistance is not as specified.

9. To check the spark plug leads, calibrate the ohmmeter on R × 1 or low-ohm scale. Connect the ohmmeter to each end of the lead and note the meter. The resistance should be nearly zero ohm.

CD2 IGNITION SYSTEM TROUBLESHOOTING (1993-ON 6-30 HP MODELS)

The major components of the CD2 ignition system used on 6-30 hp (1993-on) models include the flywheel, charge coil, sensor coil, power pack, ignition coils, temperature switch and related wiring.

If the outboard motor is very hard or impossible to start, begin the troubleshooting procedure at *Total Output Test*. If an ignition malfunction is causing an intermittent high-speed miss or erratic running above cranking speed, begin at *Indexing Flywheel*. Unless specified otherwise, perform the following ignition system tests in the sequence given. Skipping tests or jumping around the troubleshooting procedure can result in misleading results and unnecessary parts replacement. Test the entire ignition system—more than one component may be defective.

Indexing Flywheel

If the outboard motor runs erratically, or if a high speed miss is noted, the power pack may be defective. Internal module malfunctions can cause the power pack to double fire or fire erratically or continuously. Perform the following procedure to ensure the power pack is firing at the correct time.

1. Remove the spark plugs.

2. Position the No. 1 piston at TDC by rotating the flywheel clockwise. Insert a pencil or similar tool into the No. 1 spark plug hole while rotating the flywheel to ensure the piston is at TDC.

3. With the No.1 piston at TDC, place a mark on the flywheel directly across from the timing pointer or starter pivot screw. Label the mark No. 1.

4. Repeat Step 2 and Step 3 on the No. 2 cylinder. Label this mark No. 2.

5. Reinstall the spark plugs and connect the plug leads.

CAUTION
The outboard motor must be supplied with adequate cooling water while running. Install the motor in a test tank or on a boat in the water. Do not attempt to run the motor at high speed while connected to a flushing device.

6. Start the motor and run it at the speed at which the problem is evident.

7. Alternately, connect a timing light to each cylinder. The timing light should indicate the cylinder number the timing light is connected to. For example, if the timing light is connected to the No. 1 spark plug wire, the No. 1 mark should be visible. In addition, the number should only appear near the timing pointer or starter pivot bolt.

8. If a different cylinder number appears, or if the number jumps around or appears at other than the timing pointer or starter pivot bolt, first make sure the primary ignition wires are properly connected. The orange/blue primary wire must be connected to the No. 1 (top) ignition coil. If the primary wires are correctly connected, replace the ignition module and repeat this test.

Total Output Test

NOTE
If acceptable spark is noted at each spark gap during the total output test, but the engine pops or backfires during starting or running, the ignition system may be out of time. Be sure the orange/blue primary ignition wire is connected to the No. 1 (top) ignition coil, the spark plug leads are properly connected, the flywheel is properly located on the crankshaft and the timing and throttle linkage are properly synchronized.

The total output test will determine if the ignition system is capable of delivering adequate spark to the spark plugs. Perform the output test with the spark plugs installed and properly tightened.

1. Disconnect the spark plug leads from the spark plugs.

2. Mount a suitable spark tester on the engine and connect the spark plug leads to the tester. See **Figure 28**. Make sure the spark tester mounting clip is secured to a good clean engine ground.

3. Connect the cutoff clip and lanyard to the emergency stop switch, if so equipped.

4. Adjust the spark tester spark gap to 1/2 in. (12.7 mm).

5. Crank the engine while observing the spark tester.

   a. If acceptable spark is noted at each spark gap, continue testing at *Running Output Test* in this chapter.

   b. If acceptable spark is noted at only one spark gap, continue testing at *Power Pack Output Test* in this chapter.

   c. If no spark is noted at either spark gap, continue testing at *Stop Circuit Test* in this chapter.

Stop Circuit Test

The following test eliminates the stop circuit as a potential cause of an ignition malfunction. The stop button, key switch and lanyard emergency stop switch are connected to the power pack through the engine wiring harness. Activating the stop circuit shorts power pack output to ground, which disables the ignition system and stops the engine.

1. Connect a spark tester as described under *Total Output Test*.

2. Separate the power pack-to-ignition plate 5-pin connector. See **Figure 35**.

3. Insert jumper leads between terminals A, B, C and D in each connector half (**Figure 35**).

4. Crank the engine while observing the spark tester.

   a. If good spark is now noted at both gaps, the problem is in the stop circuit. Test the stop button or key switch as described in this chapter.

   b. If no spark is noted at either gap, test the charge coil as described in this chapter.

   c. If spark is noted at only one gap, continue at *Power Pack Output Test* in this chapter.

5. If testing is complete, remove the jumper leads and reconnect the 5-pin connector.

Stop button ohmmeter test

The tiller handle on most models contains a combination stop button/emergency stop switch. The emergency switch consists of a clip and lanyard which connects to the stop button. When the clip and lanyard are installed, the stop circuit is in the RUN mode; when the clip and lanyard are not installed, the ignition is disabled and the engine will not start. Test the stop button using an ohmmeter. The ohmmeter test must be performed with the engine *not* running.

1. Make sure the emergency switch clip and lanyard are properly installed.

2. Calibrate the ohmmeter on R × 100 or the low-ohm scale.

3. Separate the ignition plate-to-power pack 5-pin connector.

4. Insert a suitable jumper lead into the E terminal of the ignition plate end of the 5-pin connector. See **Figure 36**.

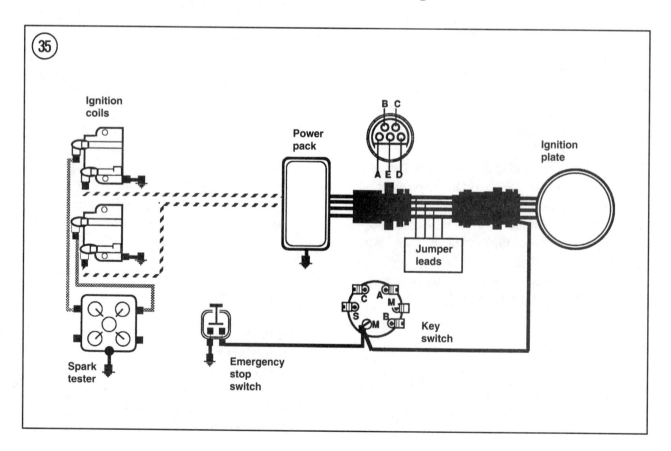

5. Connect the ohmmeter between the jumper lead and a good engine ground. The meter should indicate no continuity. If continuity is noted, the stop button or wiring is shorted to ground.

6. Depress the stop button while observing the ohmmeter. The meter should indicate continuity when the button is pressed. If not, the button is defective or an open circuit is present in the stop circuit wiring.

7. Remove the emergency switch clip and lanyard. The meter should indicate continuity. If not, replace the emergency switch.

8. If testing is complete, reconnect the 5-pin connector.

Key switch ohmmeter test

1. Separate the ignition plate-to-power pack 5-pin connector.

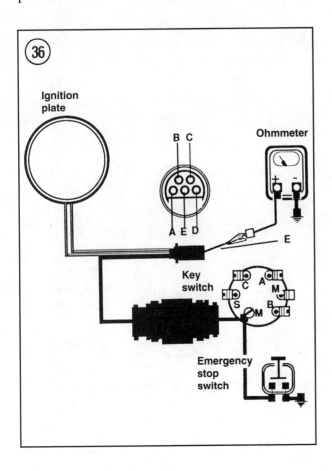

2. Make sure the emergency stop switch clip and lanyard are properly installed.

3. Insert a suitable jumper lead into terminal E of the ignition plate end of the 5-pin connector See **Figure 36**.

4. Connect the ohmmeter between the jumper lead and a good engine ground and note the meter.

   a. With the key switch OFF, the meter should indicate continuity.

   b. With the key switch ON, the meter should indicate no continuity.

5. If continuity is noted with the key switch ON, disconnect the engine harness black/yellow wires from the key switch M terminal.

6. If the meter indicates no continuity with the black/yellow wires disconnected, test the key switch. If continuity is still noted, continue at Step 7.

7. Separate the emergency switch wire from the wiring harness black/yellow wire at the key switch and note the meter.

   a. If the ohmmeter indicates no continuity, replace the emergency stop switch.

   b. If the ohmmeter indicates continuity, check for a defect in the black/yellow wire between the key switch and the 5-pin connector. Repair or replace as necessary.

8. If testing is complete, remove the jumper lead and reconnect the 5-pin connector.

Charge Coil Output Test

Perform the following test to ensure the charge coil is capable of producing sufficient voltage to charge the capacitor in the power pack and to make sure the charge coil or charge coil wiring is not shorted to ground. A peak reading voltmeter (PRV) is necessary to perform this test.

Refer to **Figure 37** for this procedure.

1. Disconnect the 5-pin Amphenol connector between the ignition plate and power pack.

2A. *1993-on 20-30 hp*—Set the PRV selector switches to POS and 500.

2B. *All others*—Set the PRV selector switches to NEG and 500.

3. Connect the black PRV test lead to a good engine ground. Connect the red test lead to the A terminal of the 5-pin connector.

4. Crank the engine while observing the meter, then move the red test lead to the D terminal. Again, crank the engine and note the meter.

5. Any voltage reading at either connection indicates the charge coil or charge coil wire(s) is grounded. Locate and repair the grounded wire(s) or replace the charge coil as described in Chapter Seven. If no voltage reading is noted, continue at Step 6.

6. Connect the black PRV test lead to the A terminal in the 5-pin connector. Connect the red test lead to the D terminal.

7. Crank the engine while noting the meter. Charge coil output should be 230 volts or more.

   a. If the meter indicates 230 volts or more, continue at *Sensor Coil Output Test* in this chapter.

   b. If output is less than 230 volts, inspect the condition of the charge coil wiring and connectors and repair as necessary. If the wiring and connectors are in acceptable condition, check charge coil resistance as described under *Charge Coil Resistance Test* in this chapter. If charge coil resistance is not as specified, the charge coil must be replaced.

8. If testing is complete, remove any jumper leads and reconnect the ignition plate-to-power pack 5-pin connector.

Charge Coil Resistance Test

Because resistance generally increases with temperature, perform resistance tests with the engine cold (room temperature). Resistance tests on hot components will indicate increased resistance and may result in unnecessary parts replacement without solving the basic problem.

1. Calibrate the ohmmeter on the appropriate scale.

2. With the 5-pin connector separated, insert jumper leads into terminals A and D. Connect the ohmmeter between the jumper leads. See **Figure 38**.

3. Charge coil resistance should be as follows:

   a. *800-1000 ohms*—6-8 hp, 9.9-15 hp rope start models and 20-30 hp.

   b. *680-840 ohms*—9.9-15 hp electric start models.

4. Replace the charge coil (Chapter Seven) if resistance is not as specified.

5. Next, calibrate the ohmmeter on the R × 1000 or high-ohm scale. Connect the ohmmeter alternately between each jumper lead and a good engine ground. See **Figure 39**. No continuity should be indicated at each connection.

   a. Any continuity between either charge coil wire and ground indicates the charge coil or charge coil wire(s) is grounded. Locate and repair the grounded wire(s).

   b. If the charge coil wires are in acceptable condition, replace the charge coil as described in Chapter Seven.

6. If testing is complete, remove any jumper leads and reconnect the ignition plate-to-power pack 5-pin connector.

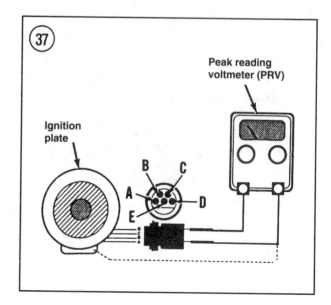

Sensor Coil Output Test

The sensor coil provides a voltage signal to the power pack which triggers power pack output to be directed to the correct ignition coil primary circuit. Perform this test to determine if the sensor coil is capable of producing sufficient voltage and to ensure the sensor coil or sensor coil wiring is not shorted to ground. A peak reading voltmeter (PRV) is necessary to perform this test.

1A. *6-15 hp*—Set the PRV selector switches to NEG and 5, or if using a Stevens CD-77, SEN and 5.

1B. *20-30 hp*—Set the PRV selector switches to POS and 5 or SEN and 5 if using a Stevens CD-77.

2. Insert suitable jumper leads into terminals B and C in the 5-pin ignition plate connector.

3. Connect one PRV test lead to a good engine ground. Alternately, connect the remaining test lead to terminals B and C. See **Figure 40**. Crank the engine at each connection and note the meter.

   a. Any voltage reading at either connection indicates the sensor coil or sensor coil wiring is shorted to ground. Locate and repair any short circuits, or replace the sensor coil as necessary.

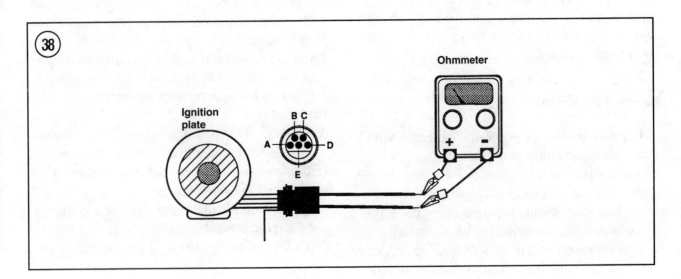

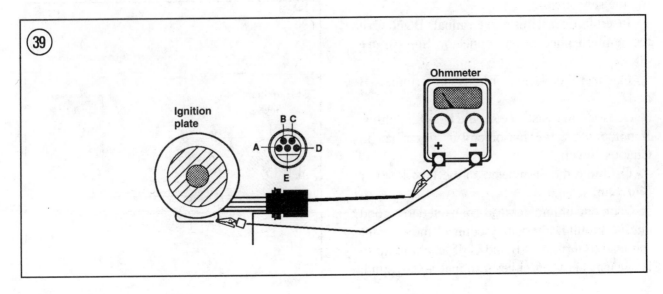

b. If no voltage reading is noted, continue at Step 4.

4. Connect the black PRV test lead to terminal C and the red test lead to terminal B. See **Figure 40**.

5. Crank the engine while observing the meter. Sensor coil output should be 1.5 volts or more.

   a. If the meter indicates 1.5 volts or more, continue at *Power Pack Output Test* in this chapter.

   b. If output is less than 1.5 volts, inspect the sensor coil wiring and connectors and repair as necessary. If the wiring and connectors are in acceptable condition, continue at *Sensor Coil Resistance Test* in this chapter.

6. If testing is complete, remove any jumper wires and reconnect the ignition plate-to-power pack 5-pin connector.

Sensor Coil Resistance Test

Because resistance generally increases with temperature, perform resistance tests with the engine cold (room temperature). Resistance tests on hot components will indicate increased resistance and may result in unnecessary parts replacement without solving the basic problem.

If sensor coil output is less than specified, perform the following resistance test before failing the sensor coil.

1. Insert jumper wires into terminals B and C of the ignition plate 5-pin connector. See **Figure 40**.

2. Connect the ohmmeter between terminals B and C.

3. Sensor coil resistance should be 30-50 ohms. If not, replace the sensor coil as described in Chapter Seven.

4. Calibrate the ohmmeter on the R × 1000 or high ohm scale.

5. With one ohmmeter lead connected to a good engine ground, alternately connect the remaining lead to terminals B and C. If any continuity is present between either terminal and ground,

the sensor coil or coil wires are shorted to ground. Locate and repair the short or replace the sensor coil as necessary. See Chapter Seven.

Power Pack Output Test

> *WARNING*
> *To prevent accidental starting, remove the spark plug leads from the spark plugs. Securely ground the plug leads to the power head, or connect the leads to a spark tester.*

A peak reading voltmeter (PRV) and Stevens load adapter (part No. PL-88) are necessary to test power pack output.

1. Disconnect the primary ignition wires from both ignition coils.

2A. *6-15 hp*—Set the PRV selector switches to NEG and 500.

2B. *20-30 hp*—Set the PRV selector switches to POS and 500.

3. Connect the No. 1 ignition coil primary wire to the PL-88 red lead. Connect the PL-88 black lead to a good engine ground. See **Figure 41**.

4. Connect the red PRV test lead to the PL-88 red lead. Connect the black PRV test lead to a good engine ground.

5. Crank the engine while observing the meter.

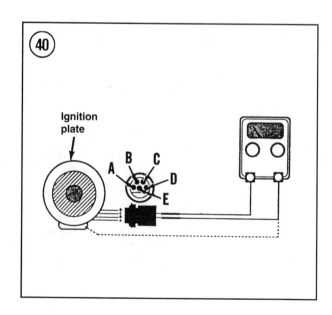

Ignition plate

6. Repeat Steps 2-5 on the No. 2 ignition coil primary wire.

7. Power pack output should be 175 volts or more at each primary wire.

   a. If output is 175 volts or more at both coil primary wires, refer to *Ignition Coil Resistance Tests* in this chapter.

   b. If no output is noted at both primary wires, test the charge coil as described in this chapter. If the charge coil tests good, replace the power pack. See Chapter Seven.

   c. If no output is noted at one primary wire, replace the power pack as described in Chapter Seven.

8. If testing is complete, reconnect the ignition coil primary wires. Make sure the orange/blue wire is connected to the No. 1 (top) coil. If an intermittent or high-speed malfunction is evident, continue at *Running Output Test*.

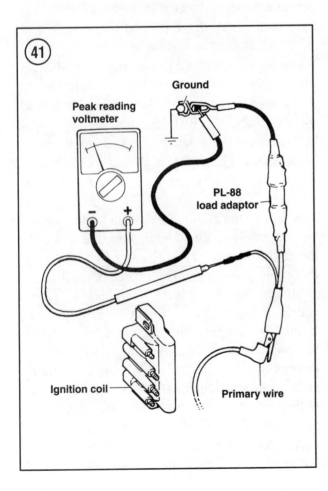

Running Output Test

A peak reading voltmeter (PRV) and Stevens Terminal Extenders (part No. TS-77) are necessary to perform the running output test. The running test is necessary to locate the cause of an intermittent malfunction or high-speed miss, especially if good spark is noted during the *Total Output Test*. Remove the propeller and install the correct test wheel (**Table 8**) prior to performing the test.

> *CAUTION*
> *The outboard motor must be supplied with adequate cooling water while running under load. Install the motor in a test tank or on a boat in the water. Do not attempt to run the motor at high speed while connected to a flushing device.*

1. Remove the primary wires from each ignition coil.

2. Install a Stevens Terminal Extender (part No. TS-77) on each coil primary terminal. Connect the primary wires to the terminal extenders. Make sure the orange/blue primary wire is attached to the No. 1 ignition coil.

3A. *6-15 hp*—Set the PRV selector switches to NEG and 500.

3B. *20-30 hp*—Set the PRV selector switches to POS and 500.

4. Connect the red PRV test lead to the terminal extender attached to the No. 1 ignition coil. Connect the black test lead to a good engine ground.

5. Start the engine and run at the speed the malfunction is evident while observing the meter. Power pack running output must be a consistent 200 volts or more.

6. Repeat Steps 4 and 5 on the No. 2 ignition coil.

7. If output is less than 200 volts at either coil, test the charge coil as described in this chapter. If the charge coil tests good, replace the power pack as described in Chapter Seven.

8. Remove the terminal extenders and reconnect the primary wires to the ignition coil(s). Make sure the orange/blue primary wire is attached to the No. 1 coil.

Ignition Coil Resistance Test

Because resistance generally increases with temperature, perform resistance tests with the engine at room temperature (70° F [21° C]). Resistance tests on hot components will indicate increased resistance and may result in unnecessary parts replacement without solving the basic problem. Ignition coil resistance can be checked without coil removal. Both coils on 6 and 8 hp models are molded into one coil assembly.

1. Remove the primary wires and the spark plug wires from the ignition coil assembly.
2. Calibrate the ohmmeter on the R × 1 or low-ohm scale.
3. To check primary winding resistance, connect the black ohmmeter lead to a good engine ground or to the coil ground tab if the coil is removed. Connect the red ohmmeter lead to the coil primary terminal.
4. Primary resistance should be 0.05-0.15 ohm.
5. To check secondary winding resistance, calibrate the ohmmeter on the R × 100 or high-ohm scale. Connect the red ohmmeter lead to the coil primary terminal and the black lead to the spark plug terminal.
6. Secondary resistance should be 225-325 ohms.
7. Repeat Steps 3-6 on the remaining coil.
8. Replace the coil if resistance is not as specified.
9. To check the spark plug leads, calibrate the ohmmeter on R × 1 or low-ohm scale. Connect the ohmmeter to each end of the lead and note the meter. The resistance should be nearly zero ohm.

S.L.O.W. Operation and Testing (20-30 hp Models)

Some 20-30 hp models are equipped with the speed limiting overheat warning (S.L.O.W.) system. The system is designed to limit engine speed to approximately 2000 rpm if engine temperature exceeds 180° F (82° C). To deactivate S.L.O.W., the engine must be throttled back to idle, and allowed to cool to 155° F (68° C).

On models equipped with remote electric start, a blocking diode located in the engine wiring harness is used to isolate the S.L.O.W. warning system from the other warning systems. Should the blocking diode become shorted, the S.L.O.W. function will remain activated regardless of engine temperature.

The S.L.O.W. system is activated by input from the engine temperature switch. The temperature switch is located in the top of the cylinder head. Test the temperature switch and S.L.O.W. system as follows.

1. Install the outboard motor in a test tank with the correct test wheel installed. See **Table 8**.
2. Connect an accurate tachometer according to the manufacturer's instructions.
3. Disconnect the tan or tan/red temperature switch wire (**Figure 32**) at its bullet connector.
4. Start the engine and run at approximately 3500 rpm.
5. Connect the engine harness end of the tan or tan/red wire to a clean engine ground and note the engine speed.
6. Engine speed should reduce to approximately 2000 rpm when the wire is grounded. If not, check the engine wiring for an open circuit, and if not found, replace the ignition module. Refer to Chapter Seven. If the engine speed does reduce as specified (but S.L.O.W. function is inoperative), test the temperature switch as described in this chapter.
7. *Remote Electric Start Models*—Calibrate an ohmmeter to the R × 100 scale. Disconnect the red engine wiring harness connector. Connect

one ohmmeter lead to the engine harness tan or tan/red temperature switch wire and the other lead to the tan or tan/red wire connector in the red engine harness connector. Note the ohmmeter reading, then reverse the leads. Continuity (near zero resistance) should be noted in one direction and no continuity (infinity) should be noted on the other direction. If not, replace the blocking diode in the engine wiring harness.

RPM Limiting Power Pack

The outboard motor (20-30 hp) may be equipped with an RPM limiting power pack designed to prevent power head damage from overspeeding. On models so equipped, the power pack interrupts ignition if engine speed exceeds 6100 rpm. Be certain the correct power pack is used if replacement is necessary.

CD2 IGNITION TROUBLESHOOTING (1992-ON 35 JET, 40 AND 50 HP [EXCEPT 48 HP] EQUIPPED WITH 12 AMP CHARGING SYSTEM)

NOTE
As a running change in 1992, the charging and ignition systems were changed on some 2-cylinder models. Two-cylinder outboards whose model numbers end with M, are equipped with a 4 amp charging system and under-flywheel ignition (CD2U). Two-cylinder outboards whose model numbers end with J, are equipped with a 12 amp charging system and CD2 (external) ignition. Be sure to refer to the appropriate section when troubleshooting the ignition system.

The major components of the CD2 ignition system used on late 40 and 50 hp models (equipped with 12 amp charging system) include the flywheel, charge coil, power coil, 2 sensor coils, power pack, 2 ignition coils, temperature switch and related wiring.

If the outboard motor is very hard or impossible to start, begin the troubleshooting procedure at *Total Output Test*. If an ignition malfunction is causing an intermittent high-speed miss or erratic running above cranking speed, begin at *Indexing Flywheel*. Unless specified otherwise, perform the following ignition system tests in the sequence given. Skipping tests or jumping around the troubleshooting procedure can result in misleading results and unnecessary parts replacement. Test the entire ignition system—more than one component may be defective.

Indexing Flywheel

If the outboard motor runs erratically, or if a high speed miss is noted, the power pack may be defective. Internal power pack malfunctions can cause the power pack to double fire or fire erratically or continuously. Perform the following procedure to ensure the power pack is firing at the correct time.

1. Remove the spark plugs.
2. Position the No. 1 piston at TDC by rotating the flywheel clockwise. Insert a pencil or similar tool into the No. 1 spark plug hole while rotating the flywheel to ensure the piston is at TDC.
3. With the No. 1 piston at TDC, place a mark on the flywheel directly across from the timing pointer. Label the mark No. 1.
4. Repeat Step 2 and Step 3 on the No. 2 cylinder. Label this mark No. 2.
5. Reinstall the spark plugs and connect the plug leads.

CAUTION
The outboard motor must be supplied with adequate cooling water while running. Install the motor in a test tank or on a boat in the water. Do not attempt to run the motor at high speed while connected to a flushing device.

6. Start the motor and run it at the speed at which the problem is evident.

7. Alternately, connect a timing light to each cylinder. The timing light should indicate the cylinder number the timing light is connected to. For example, if the timing light is connected to the No. 1 spark plug wire, the No. 1 mark should be visible. In addition, the number should only appear near the timing pointer.

8. If a different cylinder number appears, or if the number jumps around or appears at other than the timing pointer, first make sure the primary ignition wires are properly connected. The orange/blue primary wire must be connected to the No. 1 (top) ignition coil. If the primary wires are correctly connected, replace the ignition module and repeat this test.

Total Output Test

> *NOTE*
> *If acceptable spark is noted at each spark gap during the total output test, but the engine pops or backfires during starting or running, the ignition system may be out of time. Be sure the orange/blue primary ignition wire is connected to the No. 1 (top) ignition coil, the spark plug leads are properly connected, the flywheel is properly located on the crankshaft and the timing and throttle linkage are properly synchronized.*

The total output test will determine if the ignition system is capable of delivering adequate spark to the spark plugs. Perform the output test with the spark plugs installed and properly tightened.

1. Disconnect the spark plug leads from the spark plugs.

2. Mount a suitable spark tester on the engine and connect the spark plug leads to the tester. See **Figure 42**. Make sure the spark tester mounting clip is secured to a good clean engine ground.

3. Connect the cutoff clip and lanyard to the emergency stop switch, if so equipped.

4. Adjust the spark tester spark gap to 1/2 in. (12.7 mm).

5. Crank the engine while observing the spark tester.

   a. If acceptable spark is noted at each spark gap, continue testing at *Running Output Test* in this chapter.

   b. If acceptable spark is noted at only one spark gap, continue testing at *Power Pack Output Test* in this chapter.

   c. If no spark is noted at either spark gap, continue testing at *Stop Circuit Test* in this chapter.

Stop Circuit Test

The following test eliminates the stop circuit as a potential cause of an ignition malfunction. The stop button, key switch and lanyard emergency stop switch are connected to the power pack through the engine wiring harness. Activating the stop circuit shorts power pack output to ground, which disables the ignition system and stops the engine.

1. Connect a spark tester as described under *Total Output Test*.

2. Separate the power pack-to-ignition plate 5-pin connector. See **Figure 43**.

3. Insert jumper leads between the terminals A, B, C and D in both connector halves (**Figure 43**).

4. Crank the engine while observing the spark tester.

   a. If good spark is now noted at both gaps, the problem is in the stop circuit. Test the stop button or key switch as described in this chapter.

   b. If no spark is noted at either gap, test the charge coil as described in this chapter.

   c. If spark is noted at only one gap, continue at *Power Pack Output Test* in this chapter.

5. If testing is complete, remove any jumper leads and reconnect the 5-pin connector.

Stop button ohmmeter test

The tiller handle on most models contains a combination stop button/emergency stop switch. The emergency switch consists of a clip and lanyard which connects to the stop button. When the clip and lanyard are installed, the stop circuit is in the RUN mode; when the clip and lanyard are not installed, the ignition is disabled and the engine will not start. Test the stop button using an ohmmeter. The ohmmeter test must be performed with the engine NOT running.

1. Make sure the emergency switch clip and lanyard are properly installed.

2. Calibrate the ohmmeter on R × 100 or the low-ohm scale.

3. Separate the ignition plate-to-power pack 5-pin connector.

4. Insert a suitable jumper lead into the E terminal of the ignition plate end of the 5-pin connector. See **Figure 44**.

5. Connect the ohmmeter between the jumper lead and a good engine ground. The meter should indicate no continuity. If continuity is noted, the stop button or wiring is shorted to ground.

6. Depress the stop button while observing the ohmmeter. The meter should indicate continuity when the button is pressed. If not, the button is defective or an open circuit is present in the stop circuit wiring.

7. Remove the emergency switch clip and lanyard. The meter should indicate continuity. If not, replace the emergency switch.

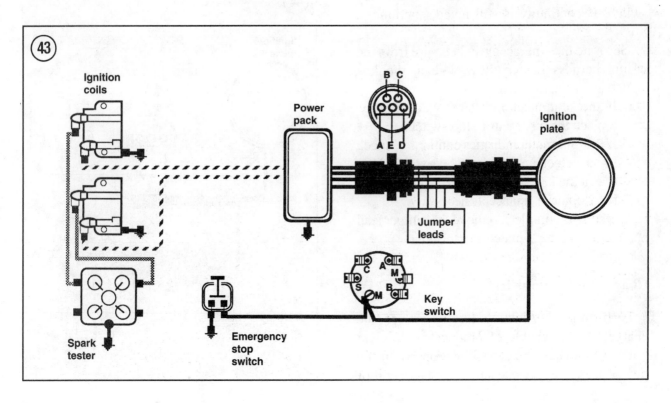

8. If testing is complete, remove the jumper wire and reconnect the 5-pin connector.

Key switch ohmmeter test

1. Separate the ignition plate-to-power pack 5-pin connector.

2. Make sure the emergency stop switch clip and lanyard are properly installed.

3. Insert a suitable jumper lead into terminal E of the ignition plate end of the 5-pin connector. See **Figure 44**.

4. Connect the ohmmeter between the jumper lead and a good engine ground and note the meter.

   a. With the key switch OFF, the meter should indicate continuity.

   b. With the key switch ON, the meter should indicate no continuity.

5. If continuity is noted with the key switch ON, disconnect the engine harness black/yellow wires from the key switch M terminal.

6. If the meter indicates no continuity with the black/yellow wires disconnected, test the key switch. If continuity is still noted, continue at Step 7.

7. Separate the emergency switch wire from the wiring harness black/yellow wire at the key switch and note the meter.

   a. If the ohmmeter indicates no continuity, replace the emergency stop switch.

   b. If the ohmmeter indicates continuity, check for a defect in the black/yellow wire between the key switch and the 5-pin connector. Repair or replace as necessary.

8. If testing is complete, remove the jumper lead and reconnect the 5-pin connector.

Charge Coil Output Test

Perform the following test to ensure the charge coil is capable of producing sufficient voltage to charge the capacitor properly in the power pack and to make sure the charge coil or charge coil wiring is not shorted to ground. A peak reading voltmeter (PRV) is necessary to perform this test.

1. Disconnect the ignition plate-to-power pack 5-pin Amphenol connector.

2A. *1992 models*—Set the PRV selector switches to NEG and 500.

2B. *1993-on models*—Set the PRV selector switches to POS and 500.

3. Connect one PRV test lead to a good engine ground. Alternately, connect the remaining test lead to the charge coil terminals A and B. See **Figure 45**. Crank the engine at each connection and note the meter.

   a. Any voltage reading at either terminal indicates a grounded charge coil or charge coil wire(s). Locate and repair grounded wire(s) or replace the charge coil as necessary.

   b. If no voltage reading is noted, continue at Step 4.

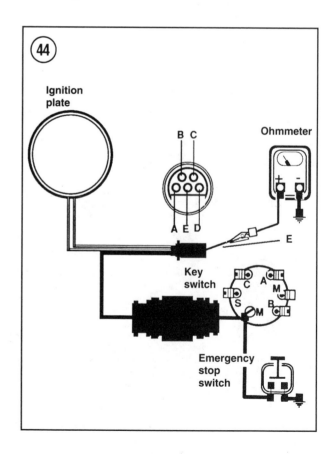

4. Connect the black PRV test lead to terminal A of the ignition plate 5-pin connector. Connect the red test lead to terminal B. See **Figure 45**.

5. Crank the engine while noting the meter. Charge coil output should be 230 volts or more.

   a. If charge coil output is 230 volts or more, continue at *Sensor Coil Output Test* in this chapter.

   b. If output is less than 230 volts, first inspect the charge coil wiring and connectors. If the wiring and connectors are in acceptable condition, continue at *Charge Coil Resistance Test* in this chapter.

6. If testing is complete, remove any jumper leads and reconnect the 5-pin connector.

Charge Coil Resistance Test

Because resistance generally increases with temperature, perform resistance tests with the engine cold (room temperature). Resistance tests on hot components will indicate increased resistance and may result in unnecessary parts replacement without solving the basic problem.

1. If necessary, disconnect the ignition plate-to-power pack 5-pin Amphenol connector.

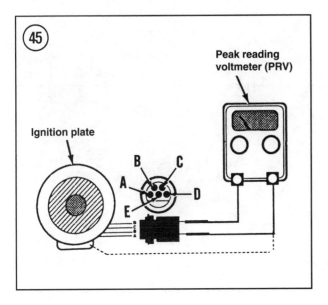

(45) Ignition plate — Peak reading voltmeter (PRV)

2. Connect the ohmmeter between terminals A and B of the ignition plate 5-pin connector.

3. Charge coil resistance should be 800-1000 ohms on rope start models and 750-950 ohms on electric start models. If not, replace the charge coil as described in Chapter Seven.

4. Next, connect one ohmmeter lead to a good engine ground. Then, alternately connect the remaining lead to terminals A and B. No continuity should be present between the charge coil terminals A and B and ground. If continuity is noted, either the charge coil or charge coil wire(s) is shorted to ground. locate and repair the grounded charge coil wire(s) or replace the charge coil as necessary.

5. If testing is complete, remove any jumper wires and reconnect the 5-pin connector.

Sensor Coil Output Test

The sensor coil provides a voltage signal to the power pack which triggers power pack output to be directed to the correct ignition coil primary circuit. Perform this test to determine if the sensor coil is capable of producing sufficient voltage and to ensure the sensor coil or sensor coil wiring is not shorted to ground. A peak reading voltmeter (PRV) is necessary to perform this test.

1. Disconnect the 3-pin Amphenol connector between the ignition plate and power pack.

2A. *1992 models*—Set the PRV selector switches to NEG and 5, or SEN and 5 if using a Stevens CD-77.

2B. *1993-on models*—Set the PRV selector switches to POS and 5, or SEN and 5 if using a Stevens CD-77.

3. Connect one PRV test lead to a good engine ground. Then, connect the remaining test lead to one sensor coil terminal in the ignition plate 3-pin connector. See **Figure 46**.

4. Crank the engine while noting the meter.

5. Repeat Steps 3 and 4 at the 2 remaining sensor coil terminals (**Figure 46**).

a. Any voltage reading at any sensor coil terminal indicates a shorted sensor or sensor wire(s). Locate and repair the shorted wire(s) or replace the sensor coil as necessary. See Chapter Seven.

b. If no voltage reading is noted, continue at Step 6A or 6B as appropriate.

6A. *1992 models*—Connect the black PRV test lead to terminal C in the ignition plate 3-pin connector. Connect the red test lead to terminal A (**Figure 47**).

6B. *1993-on models*—Connect the black PRV test lead to terminal B in the ignition plate 3-pin connector (**Figure 47**). Connect the red test lead to terminal A.

7. Crank the engine while observing the meter.

8A. *1992 models*—Move the red test lead to terminal B (**Figure 47**).

8B. *1993-on models*—Move the red test lead to terminal C (**Figure 47**).

9. Crank the engine while observing the meter. Sensor coil output should be 0.5 volt or more at each connection.

a. If output is 0.5 volt or more, continue at *Power Pack Output Test* in this chapter.

b. If output is less than 0.5 volt, inspect the sensor coil wiring and connectors and repair any damage as necessary. If the wiring and connectors are in acceptable condition, continue at *Sensor Coil Resistance Test* in this chapter.

10. If testing is complete, remove any jumper leads and reconnect the 3-pin connector.

Sensor Coil Resistance Test

Because resistance generally increases with temperature, perform resistance tests with the engine cold (room temperature). Resistance tests on hot components will indicate increased resistance and may result in unnecessary parts replacement without solving the basic problem.

If sensor coil output is less than specified, perform the following resistance test before replacing the sensor coil.

1. Disconnect the 3-pin Amphenol connector between the ignition plate and power pack. See **Figure 47**.

2. Connect the ohmmeter between terminals A and B and note the meter.

3. Next, connect ohmmeter between terminals C and B and note the meter.

4. Sensor coil resistance should be 13-17 ohms at both connections. If not, replace the sensor coil as described in Chapter Seven.

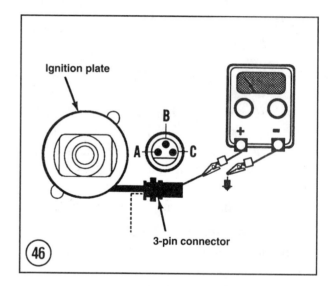

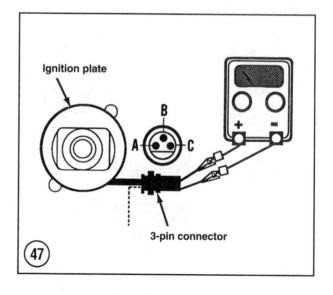

5. With the ohmmeter calibrated on the $R \times 1000$ or high-ohm scale, connect the leads between a good engine ground and each of the 3 sensor coil terminals. No continuity should be present between ground and any wire in the connector. If continuity is noted, the sensor coil or sensor coil wire(s) is shorted to ground. Locate and repair the shorted wire(s) or replace the sensor coil as described in Chapter Seven.

6. If testing is complete, remove any jumper leads and reconnect the ignition plate-to-power pack 3-pin Amphenol connector.

Power Pack Output Test

WARNING
To prevent accidental starting, remove the spark plug leads from the spark plugs. Securely ground the plug leads to the power head, or connect the leads to a spark tester.

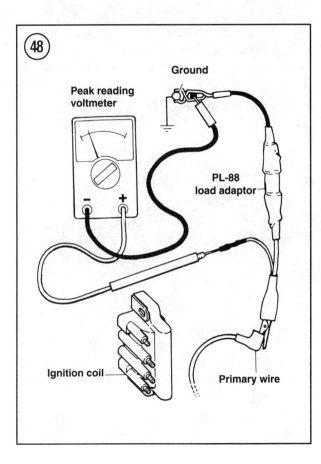

A peak reading voltmeter (PRV) and Stevens load adapter (part No. PL-88) are necessary to test power pack output.

1. Disconnect the primary ignition wires from both ignition coils.

2. Connect the primary wire from the No. 1 coil to the red lead of the PL-88 load adapter. Connect the black load adapter lead to a good engine ground. See **Figure 48**.

3A. *1992 models*—Set the PRV selector switches to NEG and 500.

3B. *1993-on models*—Set the PRV selector switches to POS and 500.

4. Connect the red PRV test lead to the red load adapter red lead. Connect the black PRV test lead to a good engine ground. See **Figure 48**.

5. Crank the engine while observing the meter. Power pack output should be 200 volts or more on 1992 models or 230 volts or more on 1993-on models.

6. Repeat Steps 2-5 on the No. 2 ignition coil.
   a. If power pack output is as specified at both ignition coils, continue at *Ignition Coil Resistance*.
   b. If power pack output is less than specified at one ignition coil, replace the power pack. See Chapter Seven.
   c. If power pack output is less than specified at both ignition coils, either the charge coil or the power pack is defective. Refer to *Charge Coil Resistance Test* in this chapter. If the charge coil is good, replace the power pack.

7. If testing is complete, remove the load adapter and reconnect the ignition coil primary wires. Make sure the orange/blue wire is connected to the No. 1 coil.

Running Output Test

A peak reading voltmeter (PRV) and Stevens Terminal Extenders (part No. TS-77) are necessary to perform the running output test. Running the outboard under load is necessary to locate the cause of an intermittent malfunction or high-speed miss, especially if good spark is noted during the *Total Output Test*. Remove the propeller and install the correct test wheel (**Table 8**) prior to performing the test.

> *CAUTION*
> *The outboard motor must be supplied with adequate cooling water while running. Install the motor in a test tank or on a boat in the water. Do not attempt to run the motor at high speed while connected to a flushing device.*

1. Remove the primary wires from each ignition coil.
2. Install a Stevens Terminal Extender (part No. TS-77) on each coil primary terminal. Connect the primary wires to the terminal extenders. Make sure the orange/blue primary wire is attached to the No. 1 ignition coil.
3A. *1992 models*—Set the PRV selector switches to NEG and 500.
3B. *1993-on models*—Set the PRV selector switches to POS and 500.
4. Connect the red PRV test lead to the terminal extender attached to the No. 1 ignition coil. Connect the black test lead to a good engine ground.
5. Start the motor and run under load at the speed at which the malfunction is evident. The running output should be 230 volts or more on 1992 models or 250 volts or more on 1993-on models.
6. Repeat Steps 4 and 5 on the No. 2 ignition coil.
7. If running output is less than specified on one or both coils, either the charge coil or the power pack is defective. If the charge coil tests good, replace the power pack as described in Chapter Seven.
8. Remove the terminal extenders and reconnect the primary wires to the ignition coils. Make sure the orange/blue primary wire is connected to the No. 1 coil.

Ignition Coil Resistance Test

Because resistance generally increases with temperature, perform resistance tests with the engine at room temperature (70° F [21° C]). Resistance tests on hot components will indicate increased resistance and may result in unnecessary parts replacement without solving the basic problem. Ignition coil resistance can be checked without coil removal. Both coils are molded into one coil assembly.

1. Remove the primary wires and the spark plug wires from the ignition coil assembly.
2. Calibrate the ohmmeter on the R × 1 or low-ohm scale.
3. To check primary winding resistance, connect the black ohmmeter lead to a good engine ground or to the coil ground tab if the coil is removed. Connect the red ohmmeter lead to the coil primary terminal.
4. Primary resistance should be 0.05-0.15 ohm.
5. To check secondary winding resistance, calibrate the ohmmeter on the R × 100 or high-ohm scale. Connect the red ohmmeter lead to the coil primary terminal and the black lead to the spark plug terminal.
6. Secondary resistance should be 225-325 ohms.
7. Repeat Steps 3-6 on the remaining coil.
8. Replace the coil if resistance is not as specified.
9. To check the spark plug leads, calibrate the ohmmeter on R × 1 or low-ohm scale. Connect the ohmmeter to each end of the lead and note the meter. The resistance should be nearly zero ohm.

S.L.O.W. Operation and Testing

Some models are equipped with the speed limiting overheat warning (S.L.O.W.) system. The system is designed to limit engine speed to approximately 2500 rpm if engine temperature exceeds 203° F (95° C). To deactivate S.L.O.W., the engine must be throttled back to idle, and allowed to cool to approximately 162° F (72° C). On models equipped with a 12 amp charging system, the engine must also be stopped in addition to the above requirements to deactivate the S.L.O.W. function.

On models equipped with remote electric start, a blocking diode located in the engine wiring harness is used to isolate the S.L.O.W. warning system from the other warning systems. Should the blocking diode become shorted, the S.L.O.W. function will remain activated regardless of engine temperature.

The S.L.O.W. system is activated by input from the engine temperature switch. The temperature switch is located in the top of the cylinder head.

The following conditions will cause the S.L.O.W. function to remain activated:

   a. Engine overheated.
   b. Engine temperature switch or switch wire shorted to ground.
   c. Blocking diode shorted to ground.
   d. Defective power pack.

The following conditions will prevent the S.L.O.W. function from operating:

   a. Engine temperature switch or switch wire open.
   b. Defective power pack.
   c. Defective power coil.

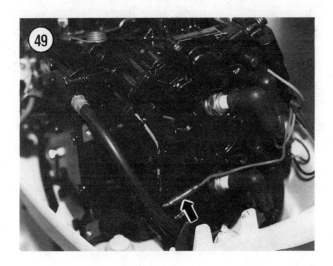

Test the temperature switch and S.L.O.W. system as follows.

1. Install the outboard motor in a test tank with the correct test wheel installed. See **Table 8**.
2. Connect an accurate tachometer according to the manufacturer's instructions.
3. Disconnect the tan or tan/red temperature switch wire (**Figure 49**) at its bullet connector.
4. Start the engine and run at approximately 3500 rpm.
5. Connect the engine harness end of the tan or tan/red wire to a clean engine ground and note the engine speed. Engine speed should reduce to approximately 2500 rpm when the wire is grounded.

   a. If the engine speed does reduce as specified, but the S.L.O.W. function is inoperative, test the temperature switch as described in this chapter.
   b. If engine speed does not reduce as specified, continue at Step 6.

6. Separate the ignition plate-to-power pack 5-pin Amphenol connector.
7. Connect an ohmmeter between a good engine ground and alternately to terminals C and D. No continuity should be noted. If continuity is present, repair the shorted stator wire(s) or replace the stator as described in Chapter Seven.
8. Connect the ohmmeter between terminals C and D. Resistance should be 360-440 ohms.

   a. If the resistance is not as specified, the power pack is defective and must be replaced.
   b. If the resistance is as specified, replace the stator.

RPM Limiting Power Pack

The outboard motor may be equipped with an RPM limiting power pack designed to prevent power head damage from overspeeding. On models so equipped, the power pack interrupts ignition if engine speed exceeds 6700 rpm on 1993-on 40-50 hp models or 6100 rpm on all other models. Be certain the correct power pack is used if replacement is necessary.

CD3 IGNITION TROUBLESHOOTING (3-CYLINDER MODELS)

The major components of the CD3 ignition system used on 1991 and 1992 models include the flywheel, charge coil, power coil (supplies voltage for S.L.O.W. operation), 3 sensor coils, power pack, 3 ignition coils, temperature switch and related wiring. On 1993-on models, the ignition system includes the flywheel, charge coil, power coil (supplies voltage for QuikStart and S.L.O.W. operation), 6 sensor coils (3 for ignition, 3 for QuikStart), power pack, 3 ignition coils, temperature switch and related wiring. The sensor coils are contained in a 1-piece timer base assembly. The power coil and charge coil are contained inside the stator assembly and are not serviced separately.

On 1993-on models, QuikStart electronic starting system is used. QuikStart automatically advances the ignition timing during engine starting, to aid starting and engine warm-up. Refer to *QuikStart Operation and Testing* in this chapter.

If the outboard motor is very hard or impossible to start, begin the troubleshooting procedure at *Total Output Test*. If an ignition malfunction is causing an intermittent high-speed miss or erratic running above cranking speed, refer to *Indexing Flywheel* and *Running Output Test*. Unless specified otherwise, perform the following ignition system tests in the sequence given. Skipping tests or jumping around the troubleshooting procedure can result in misleading results and unnecessary parts replacement. Test the entire ignition system—more than one component may be defective.

Indexing Flywheel

If the outboard motor runs erratically, or if a high speed miss is noted, the power pack may be defective. Internal power pack malfunctions can cause erratic ignition system operation. Perform the following procedure to ensure the power pack is firing at the correct time.

1. Remove the spark plugs.
2. Position the No. 2 piston at TDC by rotating the flywheel clockwise. Insert a pencil or similar tool into the No. 2 spark plug hole while rotating the flywheel to ensure the piston is at TDC.
3. With the No. 2 piston at TDC, place a mark on the flywheel directly across from the timing pointer. Label the mark No. 2.
4. Repeat Step 2 and Step 3 on the remaining cylinders.
5. Reinstall the spark plugs and connect the plug leads.

> *CAUTION*
> *The outboard motor must be supplied with adequate cooling water while running. Place the motor in a test tank or on a boat in the water. Do not attempt to run the motor at high speed while connected to a flushing device.*

6. Start the motor and run it at the speed at which the problem is evident.
7. Alternately connect a timing light to each cylinder. The timing light should indicate the cylinder number the timing light is connected to. For example, if the timing light is connected to the No. 2 spark plug wire, the No. 2 mark should be visible. In addition, the number should only appear near the timing pointer.
8. If a different cylinder number appears, or if the number jumps around or appears at other than the timing pointer, first make sure the primary ignition wires are properly connected. The primary wires must be connected as follows:

   a. *No. 1 coil*—orange/blue wire.

   b. *No. 2 coil*—orange/purple wire.

   c. *No. 3 coil*—orange/green wire.

If the primary wires are properly connected, verify wire and pin location on all timer base and power pack connectors. See wiring diagrams at end of the manual. If wire and pin location are correct, replace the power pack.

Total Output Test

> *NOTE*
> *If acceptable spark is noted at each spark gap during the total output test, but the engine pops or backfires during starting or running, the ignition system may be out of time. Be sure the orange/blue primary ignition wire is connected to the No. 1 (top) ignition coil, the orange/purple wire is connected to the No. 2 coil and the orange/green wire is connected to the No. 3 coil. Make sure the spark plug leads are properly connected, the flywheel is properly located on the crankshaft and the timing and throttle linkage are properly synchronized.*

The total output test will determine if the ignition system is capable of delivering adequate spark to the spark plugs. Perform the output test with the spark plugs installed and properly tightened.

1. Disconnect the spark plug leads from the spark plugs.
2. Mount a suitable spark tester on the engine and connect the spark plug leads to the tester. See

Figure 50. Make sure the spark tester mounting clip is secured to a good clean engine ground.
3. Connect the cutoff clip and lanyard to the emergency stop switch, if so equipped.
4. Adjust the spark tester spark gap to 1/2 in. (12.7 mm).
5. Crank the engine while observing the spark tester.
  a. If acceptable spark is noted at each spark gap, continue testing at *Running Output Test* in this chapter.
  b. If acceptable spark is noted on at least one spark gap, continue testing at *Sensor Coil Output Test* in this chapter.
  c. If no spark is noted at either spark gap, continue testing at *Stop Circuit Test* in this chapter.

Stop Circuit Test

The following test eliminates the stop circuit as a potential cause of an ignition malfunction. The stop button, key switch and lanyard emergency stop switch are connected to the power pack through the engine wiring harness. Activating the stop circuit shorts power pack output to ground, which disables the ignition system and stops the engine.

1. Connect a spark tester as described under *Total Output Test*.
2. Disconnect the 5-pin Amphenol connector between the stator assembly and power pack. See **Figure 51**.
3. Insert jumper leads between terminals A, B, C and D (**Figure 51**). Do not connect terminal E (stop circuit).
4. Crank the engine while observing the spark tester.
  a. If good spark is now noted at all gaps, the problem is in the stop circuit. Test the stop button or key switch as described in this chapter.
  b. If no spark is noted at any gap, test the charge coil as described in this chapter.

c. If spark is noted on at least one gap, continue at *Sensor Coil Output Test* in this chapter.

5. If testing is complete, remove the jumper leads and reconnect the 5-pin connector.

Stop button ohmmeter test

The tiller handle on models so equipped, contains a combination stop button/emergency stop switch. The emergency switch consists of a clip and lanyard which connect to the stop button. When the clip and lanyard are installed, the stop circuit is in the RUN mode; when the clip and lanyard are not installed, the ignition is disabled and the engine will not start. Test the stop button using an ohmmeter. The ohmmeter test must be performed with the engine NOT running.

1. Make sure the emergency stop switch clip and lanyard are properly installed.

2. Calibrate the ohmmeter on R × 100 or the low-ohm scale.

3. Separate the stator assembly-to-power pack 5-pin Amphenol connector.

4. Insert a suitable jumper lead into the E terminal of the stator end of the 5-pin connector. See **Figure 52**.

5. Connect the ohmmeter between the jumper lead and a good engine ground. The meter should indicate no continuity. If continuity is noted, the stop button or wiring is shorted to ground.

6. Depress the stop button while observing the ohmmeter. The meter should indicate continuity

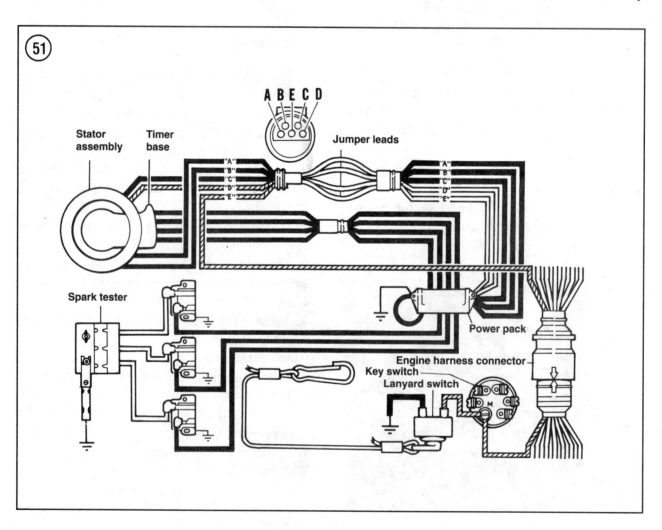

when the button is pressed. If not, the button is defective or an open circuit is present in the stop circuit wiring.

7. Remove the emergency stop switch clip and lanyard. The meter should indicate continuity. If not, replace the emergency switch.

8. If testing is complete, remove the jumper wire and reconnect the 5-pin connector.

Key switch ohmmeter test

1. Separate the stator-to-power pack 5-pin Amphenol connector.

2. Make sure the emergency stop switch clip and lanyard are properly installed.

3. Insert a suitable jumper lead into terminal E of the stator end of the 5-pin connector See **Figure 52**.

4. Connect the ohmmeter between the jumper lead and a good engine ground and note the meter.

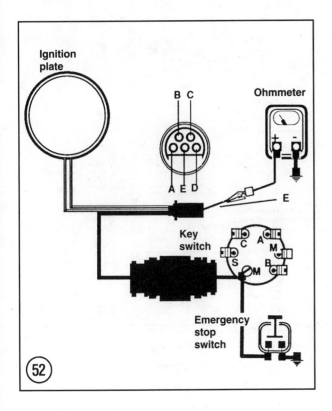

a. With the key switch OFF, the meter should indicate continuity.

b. With the key switch ON, the meter should indicate no continuity.

5. If continuity is noted with the key switch ON, disconnect the engine harness black/yellow wires from the key switch M terminal.

6. If the meter indicates no continuity with the black/yellow wires disconnected, test the key switch. If continuity is still noted, continue at Step 7.

7. Separate the emergency switch wire from the wiring harness black/yellow wire at the key switch and note the meter.

a. If the ohmmeter indicates no continuity, replace the emergency stop switch.

b. If the ohmmeter indicates continuity, check for a defect in the black/yellow wire between the key switch and the 5-pin connector. Repair or replace as necessary.

8. If testing is complete, remove the jumper lead and reconnect the 5-pin connector.

Charge Coil Output Test

Perform the following test to ensure the charge coil is capable of producing sufficient voltage to charge the capacitor in the power pack and to make sure the charge coil or charge coil wiring is not shorted to ground. A peak reading voltmeter (PRV) is necessary to perform this test.

1. Disconnect the 5-pin Amphenol connector between the stator assembly and power pack.

2. Set the PRV selector switches to POS and 500.

3. Connect one PRV test lead to a good engine ground. Connect the remaining test lead to terminal A in the stator connector. Crank the engine and note the meter. Move the test lead from terminal A to terminal B, crank the engine and note the meter.

a. Any voltage reading at either connection indicates a grounded charge coil or charge coil wire(s). Locate and repair the grounded wire(s) or replace the charge coil (Chapter Seven).

   b. If no voltage reading is noted, continue at Step 4.

4. Connect the black PRV test lead to terminal A in the stator 5-pin connector. Connect the red test lead to terminal B. See **Figure 53**.

5. Crank the engine while observing the meter. Charge coil output should be 250 volts or more.

   a. If output is 250 volts or more, continue at *Sensor Coil Output Test* in this chapter.

   b. If output is less than 250 volts, inspect the stator wiring and connectors and repair as necessary. If the wiring and connectors are in acceptable condition, continue at *Charge Coil Resistance Test*. Do not reconnect the 5-pin Amphenol connector.

6. If testing is complete, remove any jumper leads and reconnect the 5-pin Amphenol connector.

Charge Coil Resistance Test

Because resistance generally increases with temperature, perform resistance tests with the engine cold (room temperature). Resistance tests on hot components will indicate increased resistance and may result in unnecessary parts replacement without solving the basic problem.

1. Connect an ohmmeter between the stator connector terminals A and B. See **Figure 54**. Resistance should be as follows:

   a. *1991 models—430-530 ohms.*

   b. *1992-on models with 6 amp charging system—360-440 ohms.*

   c. *1992-on models with 12 amp charging system—750-950 ohms.*

2. Replace the stator assembly if charge coil resistance is not as specified. See Chapter Seven.

3. To check for a shorted charge coil, calibrate the ohmmeter on the R × 1000 or high-ohm scale. Connect the ohmmeter between a good engine ground and alternately to terminals A and B in the stator connector. See **Figure 55**.

4. Any continuity between engine ground and either terminal indicates a shorted charge coil or charge coil wire(s). Inspect the charge coil wires for damaged insulation and repair as necessary. If the charge coil wires are in acceptable condition, the charge coil is grounded. Replace the stator assembly as described in Chapter Seven.

5. If testing is complete, remove any jumper leads and reconnect the 5-pin Amphenol connector.

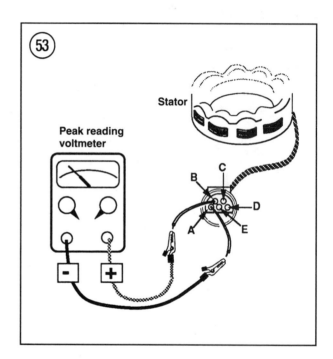

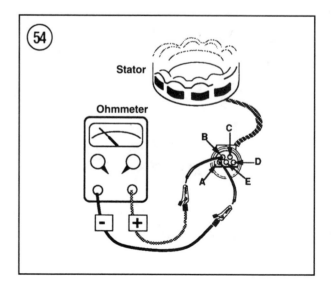

Sensor Coil Output Test

The sensor coil provides a voltage signal to the power pack which triggers power pack output to be directed to the correct ignition coil primary circuit. Perform this test to determine if the sensor coil is capable of producing a sufficient voltage signal, and to ensure the sensor coil or sensor coil wiring is not shorted to ground. A peak reading voltmeter (PRV) is necessary to perform this test.

3

1991 and 1992 models

1. Disconnect the 4-pin Amphenol connector between the timer base and power pack.
2. Set the PRV selector switches to POS and 5 (SEN and 5 on Stevens CD-77).
3. Connect one PRV test lead to a good engine ground. See **Figure 56**. Connect the remaining test lead to one timer base terminal. Crank the engine while observing the meter.
4. Repeat Step 3 at each remaining timer base terminal (**Figure 56**).
   a. Any voltage reading indicates sensor coil or sensor coil wire(s) is grounded. Locate and repair grounded wire(s) or replace the timer base assembly as necessary.
   b. If no voltage reading is noted, continue at Step 5.
5. Connect the black PRV test lead to the timer base terminal D. Connect the red test lead to timer base terminal A. See **Figure 57**.
6. Crank the engine while observing the meter.
7. Move the red test lead to timer base terminal B (**Figure 57**), crank the engine and note the

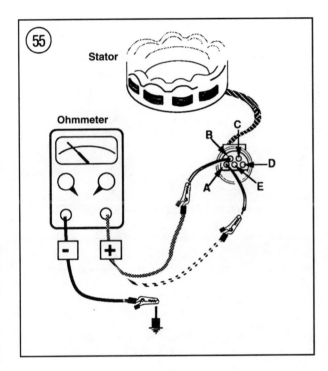

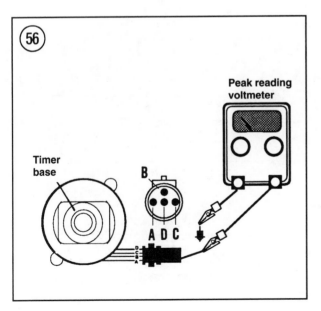

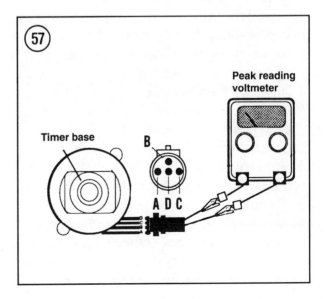

meter, then move the red test lead to timer base terminal C (**Figure 57**). Crank the engine and note the meter.

8. Sensor coil output should be 0.3 volt or more at each connection.

    a. If output is 0.3 volt or more, continue at *Power Pack Output Test* in this chapter.

    b. If output is less than 0.3 volt, inspect the timer base wires and connectors. If the wires and connectors are in acceptable condition, continue at *Sensor Coil Resistance Test* in this chapter.

1993-on models (equipped with QuikStart)

1. Disconnect the 5-pin Amphenol connector between the timer base and power pack.

2. Set the PRV selector switches to POS and 5 (Sen and 5 on Stevens CD-77).

3. Connect one PRV test lead to a good engine ground. Alternately, connect the remaining test lead to each timer base terminal (**Figure 58**), cranking the engine at each connection.

    a. Any voltage reading indicates shorted sensor coil(s) or sensor coil wire(s). Locate and repair grounded wire(s) or replace the timer base assembly as necessary.

    b. If no voltage is noted, continue at Step 4.

4. Connect the black PRV test lead to timer base terminal E. Connect the red test lead to timer base terminal A. See **Figure 59**.

5. Crank the engine while observing the meter.

6. Move the red test lead to timer base terminal B and repeat Step 5 (**Figure 59**).

7. Move the red test lead to timer base terminal C and repeat Step 5 (**Figure 59**).

8. Sensor coil output should be 1.5 volts or more at each connection.

    a. If output is 1.5 volts or more, continue at Step 9.

    b. If output is less than 1.5 volts, inspect condition of the timer base wiring and connections and repair as necessary. If the wiring and connections are in acceptable condi-

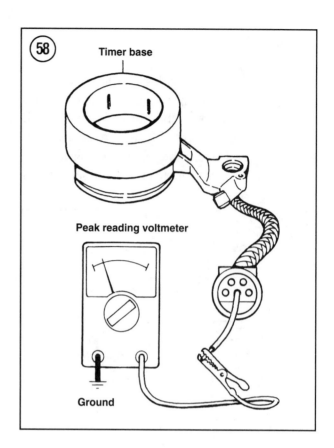

Timer base

Peak reading voltmeter

Ground

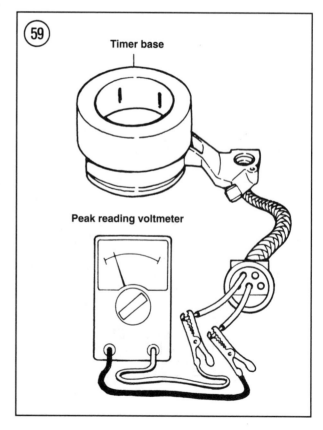

Timer base

Peak reading voltmeter

tion, continue at *Sensor Coil Resistance Test* in this chapter.

9. Connect terminals D and E in each connector half together by inserting jumper leads into the separated connectors. See **Figure 60**.

10. Connect the black PRV test lead to a good engine ground. Alternately, connect the red test lead to terminals A, B and C. Crank the engine and note the meter at each connection.

11. Output should be 1.5 volts or more.

   a. If output is 1.5 volts or more, continue at *Power Pack Output Test* in this chapter.

   b. If output is less than 1.5 volts, inspect the timer base wiring and connectors and repair as necessary. If the wiring and connectors are in acceptable condition, replace the timer base assembly. See Chapter Seven.

Sensor Coil Resistance Test

Because resistance generally increases with temperature, perform resistance tests with the engine cold (room temperature). Resistance tests on hot components will indicate increased resistance and may result in unnecessary parts replacement without solving the basic problem. The ohmmeter should be calibrated on the R × 1000 or high-ohm scale when checking for a grounded condition.

1991 and 1992 models

1. Connect the black ohmmeter lead to timer base terminal D (**Figure 61**).

2. Connect the red ohmmeter lead alternately to each remaining timer base terminal in the 4-pin connector. Note the meter at each connection.

3. Sensor coil resistance at each connection should be 8-14 ohms. If not, replace the timer base assembly as described in Chapter Seven.

4. If sensor coil resistance is within specification, check for continuity between a good engine ground and each timer base terminal in the 4-pin connector. No continuity should be present between any terminal and ground. If continuity is noted, check the timer base wiring for grounds and repair as necessary. If the wiring is in acceptable condition, replace the timer base assembly as described in Chapter Seven.

5. If testing is complete, remove all jumper leads and reconnect the 4-pin connector.

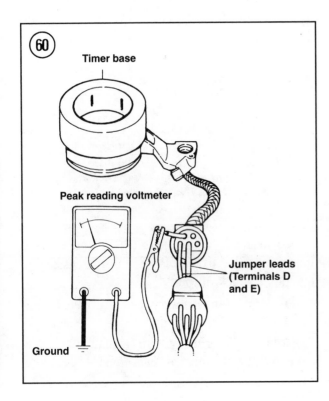

(60)

Timer base

Peak reading voltmeter

Jumper leads (Terminals D and E)

Ground

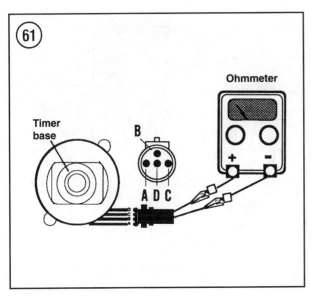

(61)

Timer base

B

Ohmmeter

A D C

1993-on models (equipped with QuikStart)

NOTE
*Ohmmeter polarity must be determined before proceeding with this test. To do so, calibrate the meter on the R × 100 or low-ohm scale. Connect the leads to a known-good diode as shown in **Figure 62**, then reverse the leads. If the first connection indicated very low resistance (zero ohm), and the second connection indicated very high resistance (infinity), the ohmmeter red lead is positive (+). If the opposite result is noted, reverse the ohmmeter leads so the red lead is positive (+).*

1. Connect the red (positive) ohmmeter lead to the timer base terminal E.

2. Alternately, connect the black ohmmeter lead to terminals A, B and C.

NOTE
The sensor coil resistance specifications in Step 3 and Step 5 are based on the use of a Stevens Model AT-101 or a Merc-O-Tronic Model M-700 ohmmeter. Resistance measured with an ohmmeter of another manufacturer may be different. Internal timer base components may cause sensor coil resistance readings to vary depending on individual ohmmeter impedance. Resistance readings may be higher or lower, however, they should be consistent.

3. If using a Stevens Model AT-101 ohmmeter, sensor coil resistance should be 270-330 ohms. If using a Merc-O-Tronic Model M-700 ohmmeter, sensor coil resistance should be 630-770 ohms.

4. Connect the red (positive) ohmmeter lead to the timer base terminal E. Connect the black lead to terminal D.

5. If using a Stevens Model AT-101 ohmmeter, resistance should be 405-495 ohms. If using a Merc-O-Tronic Model M-700 ohmmeter, resistance should be 450-550 ohms.

6. Next, connect the ohmmeter between a good engine ground and alternately to each timer base terminal in the 5-pin connector.

7. No continuity should be noted at each connection. If continuity is noted, locate and repair the grounded timer base wire(s) or replace the timer base assembly as necessary. See Chapter Seven.

8. If testing is complete, remove all jumper leads and reconnect the 5-pin connector.

Power Pack Output Test

WARNING
To prevent accidental starting, remove the spark plug leads from the spark plugs. Securely ground the plug leads to the power head, or connect the leads to a spark tester.

A peak reading voltmeter (PRV) and Stevens load adapter (part No. PL-88) are necessary to test power pack output.

1. Disconnect the primary wires from each ignition coil.

2. Connect the primary wire from the No. 1 coil (orange/blue) to the red lead of the PL-88 load

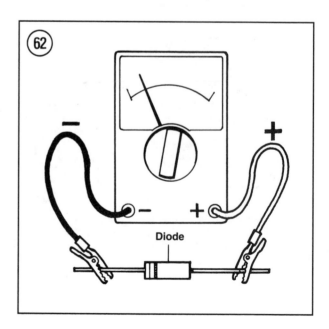

adapter. Connect the black load adapter lead to a good engine ground. See **Figure 63**.

3. Set the PRV selector switches to POS and 500.

4. Connect the red PRV test lead to the red load adapter lead. Connect the black PRV test lead to a good engine ground.

5. Crank the engine while observing the meter. Power pack output should be 230 volts or more on 1991 models or 190 volts or more on 1992-on models.

6. Repeat Steps 2-5 on the No. 2 primary wire (orange/purple), then the No. 3 primary wire (orange/green).

   a. If output is as specified (Step 5) at each primary wire, check ignition coil resistance as described in this chapter.

   b. If output is less than specified at one or more primary wires, replace the power pack. See Chapter Seven.

7. Remove the load adapter and reconnect the primary wires to the ignition coils. Make sure the

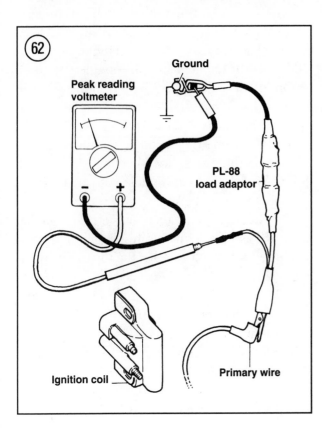

orange/blue wire is connected to the No. 1 coil, the orange/purple wire is connected to the No. 2 coil and the orange/green wire is connected to the No. 3 coil.

Running Output Test

A peak reading voltmeter (PRV) and Stevens Terminal Extenders (part No. TS-77) are necessary to perform the running output test. Running the outboard under load is necessary to locate the cause of an intermittent malfunction or high-speed miss, especially if good spark is noted during the *Total Output Test*. Remove the propeller and install the correct test wheel (**Table 8**) prior to performing the test.

> *CAUTION*
> *The outboard motor must be supplied with adequate cooling water while running. Install the motor in a test tank or on a boat in the water. Do not attempt to run the motor at high speed while connected to a flushing device.*

1. Remove the primary wires from each ignition coil.

2. Install a Stevens Terminal Extender (part No. TS-77) on each coil primary terminal. Connect the primary wires to the terminal extenders. Make sure the orange/blue primary wire is attached to the No. 1 ignition coil, the orange/purple wire is attached to the No. 2 ignition coil and the orange/green wire is attached to the No. 3 ignition coil.

3. Set the PRV selector switches to POS and 500.

4. Connect the red PRV test lead to the terminal extender attached to the No. 1 ignition coil. Connect the black test lead to a good engine ground.

5. Start the engine and run at the speed at which the malfunction is evident while observing the meter. Running output should be 250 volts or

more on 1991 models or 220 volts or more on 1992-on models.

6. Move the red PRV lead to the terminal extender attached to the No. 2 ignition coil and repeat Step 5. Note the meter reading.

7. Move the red PRV lead to the terminal extender attached to the No. 3 ignition coil. Repeat Step 5 while noting the meter.

   a. If output is less than specified (Step 5) on one or more ignition coils, test charge coil as described in this chapter. If the charge coil is in acceptable condition, replace the power pack.

   b. If no output is noted at one or more ignition coils, test the sensor coils as described in this chapter. If the sensor coils are in acceptable condition, replace the power pack.

8. If testing is complete, remove the terminal extenders and reconnect the primary wires to their respective ignition coils. Make sure the orange/blue wire is attached to the No. 1 coil, the orange/purple wire is attached to the No. 2 coil and the orange/green wire is attached to the No. 3 coil.

Ignition Coil Resistance Test

Because resistance generally increases with temperature, perform resistance tests with the engine at room temperature (70° F [21° C]). Resistance tests on hot components will indicate increased resistance and may result in unnecessary parts replacement without solving the basic problem. Ignition coil resistance can be checked without coil removal.

1. Remove the primary wires and the spark plug wires from the ignition coil assembly.

2. Calibrate the ohmmeter on the R × 1 or low-ohm scale.

3. To check primary winding resistance, connect the black ohmmeter lead to a good engine ground or to the coil ground tab if the coil is removed. Connect the red ohmmeter lead to the coil primary terminal.

4. Primary resistance should be 0.05-0.15 ohm.

5. To check secondary winding resistance, calibrate the ohmmeter on the R × 100 or high-ohm scale. Connect the red ohmmeter lead to the coil primary terminal and the black lead to the spark plug terminal.

6. Secondary resistance should be 225-325 ohms.

7. Repeat Steps 3-6 on each remaining coil.

8. Replace the coil if resistance is not as specified.

9. To check the spark plug leads, calibrate the ohmmeter on R × 1 or low-ohm scale. Connect the ohmmeter to each end of the lead and note the meter. The resistance should be nearly zero ohm.

S.L.O.W. Operation and Testing

All models are equipped with the speed limiting overheat warning (S.L.O.W.) system. The system is designed to limit engine speed to approximately 2500 rpm if engine temperature exceeds 240° F (114° C). To deactivate S.L.O.W., throttle back to idle, allow the engine to cool to 207° F (110° C), then stop the engine.

On models equipped with remote electric start, a blocking diode located in the engine wiring harness is used to isolate the S.L.O.W. warning system from the other warning systems. Should the blocking diode become shorted, the S.L.O.W. function will remain activated regardless of engine temperature.

The S.L.O.W. function is activated by a signal from the engine temperature switch. The temperature switch is located in the top of the cylinder head.

The following conditions will cause the S.L.O.W. function to remain activated:

   a. Engine overheated.

   b. Engine temperature switch or switch wire shorted to ground.

   c. Blocking diode closed or shorted to ground.

   d. Defective power pack.

The following conditions will prevent the S.L.O.W. function from operating:

a. Engine temperature switch or switch wire open.

b. Defective power pack.

c. Defective power coil.

If the S.L.O.W function is inoperative, test the temperature switch and S.L.O.W. system as follows.

1. Install the outboard motor in a test tank with the correct test wheel installed. See **Table 8**.

2. Connect an accurate tachometer according to the manufacturer's instructions.

3. Disconnect the tan/blue temperature switch wire from the tan engine harness wire.

4. Start the engine and run at approximately 3500 rpm.

5. Connect the engine harness end of the tan wire to a clean engine ground and note the engine speed. If the S.L.O.W. function is operating properly, the engine speed will reduce to approximately 2500 rpm when the wire is grounded.

a. If the engine speed does reduce when the tan wire is grounded but the S.L.O.W. system is still inoperative, test the temperature switch as described in this chapter.

b. If engine speed does not reduce as specified, continue at Step 6.

6. Separate the stator assembly-to-power pack 5-pin Amphenol connector.

7. Connect an ohmmeter between a good engine ground and alternately to terminals C and D. No continuity should be noted. If continuity is present, repair the shorted stator wire(s) or replace the stator as described in Chapter Seven.

8. Connect the ohmmeter between terminals C and D. Resistance should be 430-530 ohms on 1991 models or 360-440 ohms on 1992-on models.

a. If the resistance is as specified, the power pack is defective and must be replaced.

b. If the resistance is not as specified, replace the stator.

Blocking Diode Test (Electric Start Models)

A blocking diode is used to prevent the S.L.O.W. function from being activated by other engine warning horn systems. The blocking diode is located in the engine wiring harness.

If the S.L.O.W function is activated by the no oil, low oil or fuel vacuum warning signal, test the engine harness blocking diode as follows:

1. Disconnect the red engine harness connector.

2. Disconnect the temperature switch tan/blue wire from the engine harness tan wire.

3. Calibrate the ohmmeter on the R × 1000 or high-ohm scale.

4. Connect the ohmmeter between the tan wire (engine harness side) and the tan wire terminal in the red engine harness connector. See **Figure 64**.

5. Note the ohmmeter reading, then reverse the leads.

(64)

Engine harness connector

Tan or Tan/Blue wire (temperature switch)

6. A high reading (no continuity) in one direction and a low reading (continuity) in the other should be noted. If both readings are low, the diode is shorted (closed) and must be replaced. If both readings are high, the diode is open and must be replaced.

QuikStart Operation and Testing

The 1993-on models are equipped with QuikStart electronic starting system. The QuikStart circuit automatically advances the ignition timing when the engine temperature is less than 105° F (41° C) to improve engine warm-up. The ignition timing remains advanced until engine temperature exceeds approximately 105° F (41° C). In addition, QuikStart also advances the ignition timing for approximately 10 seconds each time the engine is started, regardless of engine temperature. To prevent power head damage due to detonation, the power pack disables QuikStart at engine speeds exceeding approximately 1100 rpm, regardless of engine temperature.

To determine if QuikStart is functioning properly, proceed as follows:

1. Remove the propeller and install the correct test wheel (**Table 8**).
2. Place the outboard motor in a suitable test tank. Start the engine and warm it to normal operating temperature. Engine temperature must be above 105° F (41° C) before running this test.

NOTE
Make sure engine synchronization and linkage adjustments are correctly set as outlined in Chapter Five.

3. Place temporary marks on the flywheel indicating TDC for all cylinders.
4. Disconnect the white/black wire at its bullet connector between the power pack and temperature switch. See **Figure 65**.
5. Attach an accurate tachometer to the power head according to the manufacturer's instructions.

6. Attach a timing light to the No. 1 cylinder according to the manufacturer's instructions.
7. Start the engine and shift into forward gear. Idle speed *must not* exceed 900 rpm in gear during this test. Adjust idle speed if necessary.
8. Observe the flywheel with the timing light. The timing pointer should be near 10° BTDC, indicating QuikStart is functioning.
9. While observing the timing marks, momentarily connect the white/black temperature switch wire. The timing should retard to approximately 2° ATDC when the wire is connected, indicating the timing has been released to the normal setting.

NOTE
*The engine **must** be stopped before testing each remaining cylinder to reset the QuikStart circuit.*

10. Stop the engine. Repeat Steps 6-9 for each remaining cylinder.
   a. If one or two cylinders do not react as specified (Step 9), replace the timer base assembly. See Chapter Seven.
   b. If no cylinders react as specified (Step 9), refer to *QuikStart inoperative* in this chapter.
   c. If all cylinders react as specified in Step 9, the QuikStart circuit is functioning properly.

QuikStart inoperative

The following conditions will cause the QuikStart circuit to be inoperative:
   a. Defective power coil.
   b. Defective power pack.
   c. Defective timer base (sensor coil[s]).
   d. An open circuit in the yellow/red wire between the power pack and starter solenoid or key switch.

A peak reading voltmeter (PRV) and a suitable breakout box are necessary to complete this test. Two commonly used breakout boxes are Stevens

Model SA-6 and Merc-O-Tronic Model 55-861. The breakout box is connected inline with the timer base circuit and allows voltage measurements while the circuit remains intact.

Troubleshoot the QuikStart circuit as follows:

1. Disconnect the white/black wire between the temperature switch and power pack (**Figure 65**).

2. Calibrate the ohmmeter on the R × 1000 or high-ohm scale.

NOTE
Engine temperature must be less than 89° F (32° C) in Step 3.

3. Connect the ohmmeter between the temperature switch white/black wire and a good engine ground. The ohmmeter should indicate high resistance (infinity) with engine temperature less than 89° F (32° C).

   a. If the meter indicates low resistance (continuity) in Step 3, test the temperature switch as described in this chapter.

   b. If the meter indicates high resistance (infinity) in Step 3, continue at Step 4.

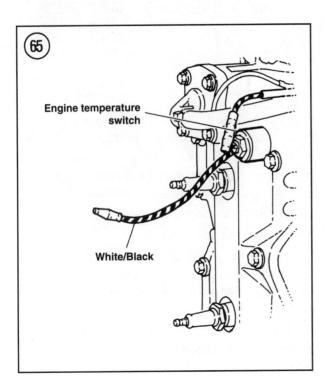

Engine temperature switch

White/Black

4. Disconnect the timer base 5-pin Amphenol connector. Attach each connector to the breakout box. Place all breakout box switches to the ON position.

5. Set PRV selector switches to POS and 500. Connect the black PRV test lead to a good engine ground. Connect the red test lead to the timer base black/white wire terminal D in the breakout box.

CAUTION
Do not run the engine with the timer base wires disconnected or the power pack will be destroyed. Be certain the breakout box is correctly installed and that all breakout box switches are in the ON position.

6. Remove the propeller and install the correct test wheel (**Table 8**). Place the outboard motor in a test tank.

7. Start the engine and run at 900 rpm in FORWARD gear while observing the PRV meter. Voltage should be 8-12 volts.

   a. If the meter indicates 8-12 volts, one or more sensor coils are defective. Replace the timer base assembly as outlined in Chapter Seven.

   b. If the meter does not indicate 8-12 volts, continue at Step 8.

8. Disconnect the 5-pin Amphenol connector between the stator and power pack.

9. Connect an ohmmeter between a good engine ground and alternately to the power coil terminals C and D in the stator connector. No continuity should be present at both connections. If continuity is noted, the power coil or power coil wire(s) is shorted to ground. Repair the wire(s) or replace the stator assembly as necessary.

10. Next, connect the ohmmeter between the power coil terminals C and D in the stator connector. Resistance should be 360-440 ohms.

   a. If power coil resistance is within 360-440 ohms, the power pack is defective and must be replaced. See Chapter Seven.

3

b. If power coil resistance is not within 360-440 ohms, the power coil is defective. Replace the stator assembly as described in Chapter Seven.

QuikStart always on

The following conditions can cause the Quik-Start circuit to remain on constantly:

a. Engine overcooling (not warming up to operating temperature).
b. Defective temperature switch.
c. Defective power pack.
d. Defective starter solenoid or key switch.

If QuikStart remains on constantly when the engine is operated *above* 1100 rpm, the power pack is defective and must be replaced. If Quik-Start remains on constantly regardless of time on and engine temperature, when the engine is operated *below* 1100 rpm, continue as follows:

1. Check for a defective starter solenoid or key switch which may cause a small voltage to bleed into the yellow/red wire leading to the power pack. This small voltage can activate the Quik-Start circuit.
2. Check for a defective or damaged engine temperature switch as described in this chapter.
3. Check for an open circuit or loose or corroded connections in the white/black power pack wire.
4. Check the engine for an overcooling condition as described in this chapter.
5. If no other problems are noted in Steps 1-4, replace the power pack. See Chapter Seven.

RPM Limiting Power Pack

Power packs marked "CDL" are equipped with an internal rpm limiting device designed to prevent power head damage from overspeeding. On models so equipped, the power pack interrupts ignition if engine speed exceeds 6700 rpm. Be certain the correct power pack is used if replacement is necessary.

CD4 IGNITION SYSTEM TROUBLESHOOTING

The CD4 ignition system is used on the V4 cross flow models (65 Jet, 80 Jet, 85, 88, 90, 100 and 115 hp; 1.6 Sea Drive).

The major components of the CD4 ignition system used on 4-cylinder cross-flow models include the flywheel, charge coil, 4 sensor coils, power pack, 4 ignition coils and related wiring. The charge coil is contained inside the stator assembly and is not serviced separately. The 4 sensor coils are contained in the 1-piece timer base assembly.

If the outboard motor is very hard or impossible to start, begin the troubleshooting procedure at *Total Output Test*. If an ignition malfunction is causing an intermittent high-speed miss or erratic operation, refer to *Indexing Flywheel* and *Running Output Test*. Unless specified otherwise, perform the following ignition system tests in the sequence given. Skipping tests or jumping around the troubleshooting procedure can result in misleading results and unnecessary parts replacement. Test the entire ignition system— more than one component may be defective.

Indexing Flywheel

If the outboard motor runs erratically, or if a high speed miss is noted, the power pack may be defective. Internal power pack malfunctions can cause erratic ignition system operation. Perform the following procedure to ensure the power pack is firing at the correct time.

1. Remove the spark plugs.
2. Position the No. 2 piston at TDC by rotating the flywheel clockwise. Insert a pencil or similar tool into the No. 2 spark plug hole while rotating the flywheel to ensure the piston is at TDC.
3. With the No. 2 piston at TDC, place a mark on the flywheel directly across from the timing pointer. Label the mark No. 2.

4. Repeat Step 2 and Step 3 on the remaining cylinders.

5. Reinstall the spark plugs and connect the plug leads.

CAUTION
The outboard motor must be supplied with adequate cooling water while running. Place the motor in a test tank or on a boat in the water. Do not attempt to run the motor at high speed while connected to a flushing device.

6. Start the motor and run it at the speed at which the problem is evident.

7. Alternately, connect a timing light to each cylinder. The timing light should indicate the cylinder number the timing light is connected to. For example, if the timing light is connected to the No. 2 spark plug wire, the No. 2 mark should be visible. In addition, the number should only appear near the timing pointer.

8. If a different cylinder number appears, or if the number jumps around or appears at other than the timing pointer, first make sure the primary ignition wires are properly connected. The primary wires must be connected as follows:

   a. *No. 1 coil*—orange/blue wire.
   b. *No. 2 coil*—orange/purple wire.
   c. *No. 3 coil*—orange/green wire.
   d. *No. 4 coil*—orange/pink wire.

If the primary wires are properly connected, verify wire and pin location on all timer base and power pack connectors. See wiring diagrams at end of manual. If wire and pin location are correct, replace the power pack.

Total Output Test

NOTE
If acceptable spark is noted at each spark gap during the total output test, but the engine pops or backfires during starting or running, the ignition system may be out of time. Be sure the orange/blue primary ignition wire is connected to the No. 1 (top starboard) ignition coil, the orange/purple wire is connected to the No. 2 coil (top port), the orange/green wire is connected to the No. 3 coil (bottom starboard) and the orange/pink wire is connected to the No. 4 coil (bottom port). Make sure the spark plug leads are properly connected, the flywheel is properly located on the crankshaft and the timing and throttle linkage are properly synchronized.

The total output test will determine if the ignition system is capable of delivering adequate spark to the spark plugs. Perform the output test with the spark plugs installed and properly tightened.

1. Disconnect the spark plug leads from the spark plugs.

2. Mount a suitable spark tester on the engine and connect the spark plug leads to the tester. See **Figure 66**. Make sure the spark tester mounting clip is secured to a good clean engine ground.

3. Connect the cutoff clip and lanyard to the emergency stop switch, if so equipped.

4. Adjust the spark tester spark gap to 1/2 in. (12.7 mm).

5. Crank the engine while observing the spark tester.

   a. If acceptable spark is noted at each spark gap, continue testing at *Running Output Test* in this chapter.

b. If acceptable spark is noted on at least one spark gap, continue testing at *Sensor Coil Output Test* in this chapter.

c. If no spark is noted at any spark gap, continue testing at *Stop Circuit Test* in this chapter.

Stop Circuit Test

The following test eliminates the stop circuit as a potential cause of an ignition malfunction. The stop button, key switch and lanyard emergency stop switch are connected to the power pack through the engine wiring harness. Activating the stop circuit shorts power pack output to ground, which disables the ignition system and stops the engine.

1. Connect a spark tester as described under *Total Output Test*.
2. Disconnect the wire 1-pin Amphenol stop circuit connector (black/yellow wire) between the key switch and power pack. See **Figure 67**.
3. Crank the engine while noting the spark tester.

a. If good spark is now noted at all gaps, the problem is in the stop circuit. Test the stop button or key switch as described in this chapter.

b. If no spark is noted at any gap, test the charge coil as described in this chapter.

c. If spark is noted on at least one gap, continue at *Sensor Coil Output Test* in this chapter.

4. If testing is complete, reconnect the 1-pin stop circuit connector.

Key Switch Ohmmeter Test

If the engine does not stop when the key switch is turned to OFF, an open circuit is present in the black/yellow stop circuit wire, the key switch is defective or the power pack is defective.

1. Install the cap and lanyard assembly on the emergency stop switch.
2. Disconnect the black/yellow 1-pin stop circuit connector (**Figure 68**).
3. Calibrate the ohmmeter on the R × 1000 or high-ohm scale.
4. Insert a suitable jumper lead into the key switch end of the stop circuit connector (**Figure 68**).
5. Connect the ohmmeter between a good engine ground and the jumper lead.

a. With the key switch in the OFF position, the ohmmeter should indicate low resistance (continuity). If not, an open circuit is present in the black/yellow wire between the

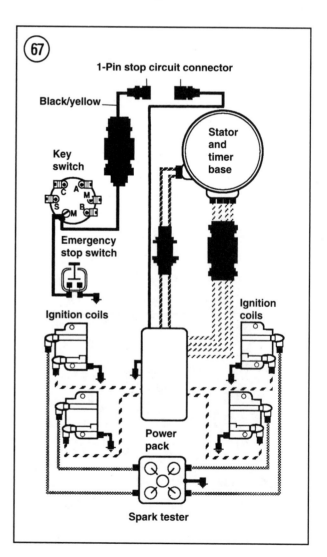

(67)

stop circuit connector and key switch, or the key switch is defective.

b. With the key switch in the ON position, the ohmmeter should indicate high resistance (no continuity). If low resistance (continuity) is noted, continue at Step 6.

6. Disconnect the black/yellow stop circuit wires from the key switch M terminal. See **Figure 68**.

a. If the meter now indicates high resistance (no continuity), the key switch is defective and must be replaced.

b. If low resistance (continuity) is still present, continue at Step 7.

7. Separate the emergency stop switch wire from the wiring harness black/yellow wire at the key switch.

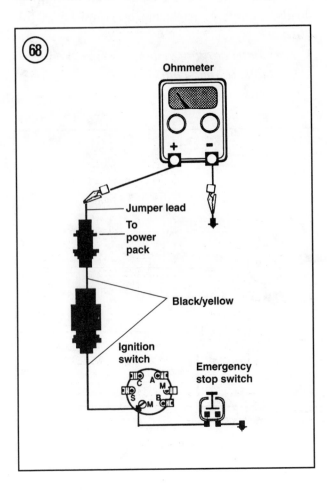

a. If high resistance (no continuity) is now noted, the emergency stop switch is defective and must be replaced.

b. If low resistance (continuity) is still present, check the black/yellow wire for a short to ground and repair as necessary.

8. If testing is complete, remove any jumper leads and reconnect the stop circuit connector.

Stop Button Ohmmeter Test (Tiller Handle Models)

If the engine does not stop when the stop button is depressed, an open circuit is present in the black/yellow stop circuit wire from the power pack or the black wire from the stop button.

1. Disconnect the black/yellow 1-pin stop circuit connector between the stop button and power pack.

2. Calibrate the ohmmeter on the R × 1000 or high-ohm scale.

3. Connect the red ohmmeter lead to the stop button end of the stop circuit connector. Connect the black ohmmeter lead to a good engine ground.

4. The ohmmeter should indicate high resistance (no continuity) with the stop button not pushed and low resistance (continuity) when the button is pushed.

5. If not, the stop button or stop button wire is defective.

Charge Coil Output Test

Perform the following test to ensure the charge coil is capable of producing sufficient voltage to charge the capacitor properly in the power pack and to make sure the charge coil or charge coil wiring is not shorted to ground. A peak reading voltmeter (PRV) is necessary to perform this test.

1. Disconnect the brown and brown/yellow wire 2-pin Amphenol connector between the stator assembly and power pack. See **Figure 69**.

2. Set the PRV selector switches to POS and 500.

3. Connect the PRV between a good engine ground and alternately to the A and B terminals in the stator end of the 2-pin connector. Crank the engine and note the meter at each connection.

    a. Any voltage reading at either terminal indicates the charge coil or charge coil wires are shorted to ground. Repair the short or replace the stator assembly as necessary.

    b. If no voltage is noted, continue at Step 4.

4. Connect the black PRV test lead to terminal A in the 2-pin stator connector. Connect the red test lead to terminal B.

5. Crank the engine while noting the meter. Charge coil output should be 150 volts or more.

    a. If output is 150 volts or more, reconnect the 2-pin connector and continue at *Sensor Coil Output Test*.

    b. If output is less than 150 volts, first inspect the condition of the charge coil wires and connectors, and repair as necessary. If the wiring and connectors are in acceptable condition, check charge coil resistance as outlined under *Charge Coil Resistance Test* in this chapter.

Charge Coil Resistance Test

Because resistance generally increases with temperature, perform resistance tests with the engine cold (room temperature). Resistance tests on hot components will indicate increased resistance and may result in unnecessary parts replacement without solving the basic problem.

1. Insert suitable jumper leads into the A and B terminals in the stator 2-pin connector.

2. Calibrate the ohmmeter on the appropriate scale.

3. Connect the ohmmeter between the jumper leads. Charge coil resistance should be as follows:

    a. *6 amp charging system—500-620 ohms.*

    b. *9 and 10 amp charging systems—430-530 ohms.*

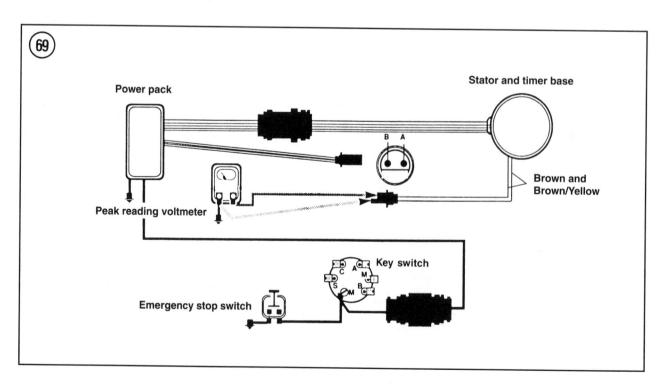

(69)

Power pack

Stator and timer base

B A

Brown and Brown/Yellow

Peak reading voltmeter

Key switch

Emergency stop switch

4. Replace the stator assembly if charge coil resistance is not as specified.

5. Next, check the charge coil and wires for shorts to ground. Calibrate the ohmmeter on the R × 1000 or high-ohm scale.

6. Connect the ohmmeter between a good engine ground and alternately to the A and B terminals in the stator 2-pin connector. Any continuity between ground and either terminal indicates the charge coil or charge coil wire(s) is shorted to ground. Locate and repair the grounded wire(s) or replace the stator assembly as necessary. See Chapter Seven.

7. If testing is complete, remove any jumper leads and reconnect the 2-pin connector.

Sensor Coil Output Test

The sensor coil provides a voltage signal to the power pack which triggers power pack output to be directed to the correct ignition coil primary circuit. Perform this test to determine if the sensor coil is capable of producing a sufficient voltage signal, and to ensure the sensor coil or sensor coil wiring is not shorted to ground. A peak reading voltmeter (PRV) is necessary to perform this test.

1. Disconnect the 5-pin Amphenol connector between the timer base and power pack. See **Figure 70**.

2. Set the PRV selector switches to POS and 5 (or SEN and 5 if using Stevens CD-77).

3. Connect the black PRV test lead to a good engine ground. Alternately, connect the red PRV test lead to each timer base terminal in the 5-pin connector. Crank the engine and note the meter at each connection.

   a. Any voltage reading indicates a shorted sensor coil or sensor coil wire(s). Repair the shorted wire(s) as necessary or replace the timer base assembly.

   b. If no voltage reading is noted, continue at Step 4.

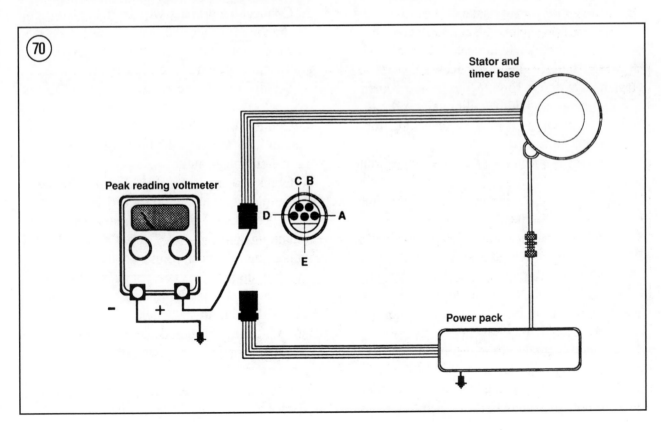

4. Connect the black PRV test lead to the timer base connector terminal E. Connect the red test lead to terminal A.

5. Crank the engine while observing the meter.

6. Alternately connect the red test lead to each remaining sensor coil terminal in the timer base connector. Crank the engine and note the meter at each connection. Sensor coil output at each terminal should be 0.3 volt or more.

    a. If output is 0.3 volt or more, reconnect the timer base 5-pin connector and continue at *Power Pack Output Test.*

    b. If output is less than 0.3 volt, check the condition of the timer base wiring and connectors and repair as necessary. If the wiring and connectors are in acceptable condition, check sensor coil resistance as outlined under *Sensor Coil Resistance Test.*

Sensor Coil Resistance Test

Because resistance generally increases with temperature, perform resistance tests with the engine cold (room temperature). Resistance tests on hot components will indicate increased resistance and may result in unnecessary parts replacement without solving the basic problem. The ohmmeter should be calibrated on the R × 1000 or high-ohm scale when checking for a grounded condition.

1. Calibrate the ohmmeter on the appropriate scale.

2. Connect the black ohmmeter lead to the timer base terminal E in the 5-pin connector.

3. Alternately, connect the red ohmmeter lead to each remaining timer base terminal in the 5-pin connector. Note the meter at each connection.

4. Sensor coil resistance should be 30-50 ohms at each connection. If not, replace the timer base assembly. See Chapter Seven.

5. Next, calibrate the ohmmeter on the R × 1000 or high-ohm scale.

6. Connect the ohmmeter between a good engine ground and alternately to each timer base

terminal in the 5-pin connector. Any continuity between ground and any timer base terminal indicates a short to ground. Inspect the condition of the timer base wires and repair as necessary, or replace the timer base assembly. See Chapter Seven.

7. If testing is complete, remove any jumper leads and reconnect the 5-pin connector.

Power Pack Output Test

WARNING
To prevent accidental starting, remove the spark plug leads from the spark plugs. Securely ground the plug leads to the power head, or connect the leads to a spark tester.

A peak reading voltmeter (PRV) and Stevens load adapter (part No. PL-88) are necessary to test power pack output.

1. Disconnect the primary wires from each ignition coil.

2. Connect the primary wire from the No. 1 coil (orange/blue) to the red lead of the PL-88 load adapter. Connect the black load adapter lead to a good engine ground. See **Figure 71**.

3. Set the PRV selector switches to POS and 500.

4. Connect the red PRV test lead to the red load adapter lead. Connect the black PRV test lead to a good engine ground.

5. Crank the engine while observing the meter. Power pack output should be 150 volts or more.

6. Repeat Steps 2-5 on the primary wire to each remaining ignition coil. Output should be 150 volts or more at each primary wire.

    a. If output is 150 volts or more at each primary wire, test ignition coil resistance as outlined in this chapter.

    b. If no output is noted at one or more primary wires, replace the power pack. See Chapter Seven.

7. If testing is complete, remove the PL-88 load adapter and reconnect the primary wires to the

ignition coils. Make sure the orange/blue wire is attached to the No. 1 coil, the orange/purple wire is attached to the No. 2 coil, the orange/green wire is attached to the No. 3 coil and the orange/pink wire is attached to the No. 4 coil.

Running Output Test

A peak reading voltmeter (PRV) and Stevens Terminal Extenders (part No. TS-77) are necessary to perform the running output test. Running the outboard under load is often necessary to locate the cause of an intermittent malfunction or high-speed miss, especially if good spark is noted during the *Total Output Test*. Remove the propeller and install the correct test wheel (**Table 8**) prior to performing the test.

CAUTION
The outboard motor must be supplied with adequate cooling water while running. Install the motor in a test tank or on a boat in the water. Do not attempt to

run the motor at high speed while connected to a flushing device.

1. Remove the primary wires from each ignition coil.
2. Install a Stevens Terminal Extender (part No. TS-77) on each coil primary terminal. Connect the primary wires to the terminal extenders. Make sure the orange/blue primary wire is attached to the No. 1 ignition coil, the orange/purple wire is attached to the No. 2 ignition coil, the orange/green wire is attached to the No. 3 ignition coil and the orange/pink wire is attached to the No. 4 ignition coil.
3. Set the PRV selector switches to POS and 500.
4. Connect the red PRV test lead to the terminal extender attached to the No. 1 ignition coil. Connect the black test lead to a good engine ground.
5. Start the engine and run at the speed at which the malfunction is evident while observing the meter. Running output should be 230 volts or more.
6. Move the red PRV lead to the terminal extender attached to the No. 2 ignition coil and repeat Step 5. Note the meter reading.
7. Move the red PRV lead to the terminal extender attached to the No. 3 ignition coil. Repeat Step 5 while noting the meter.
8. Move the red PRV test lead to the terminal extender attached to the No. 4 ignition coil. Repeat Step 5 while noting the meter.
   a. If output is less than specified (Step 5) on one or more ignition coils, test the charge coil as described in this chapter. If the charge coil is in acceptable condition, replace the power pack.
   b. If no output is noted at one or more ignition coils, test the sensor coils as described in this chapter. If the sensor coils are in acceptable condition, replace the power pack.
9. If testing is complete, remove the terminal extenders and reconnect the primary wires to their respective ignition coils. Make sure the

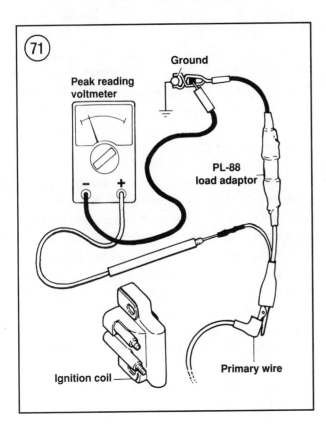

(71)

Peak reading voltmeter

Ground

PL-88 load adaptor

Primary wire

Ignition coil

orange/blue wire is attached to the No. 1 coil, the orange/purple wire is attached to the No. 2 coil, the orange/green wire is attached to the No. 3 coil and the orange/pink wire is attached to the No. 4 coil.

Ignition Coil Resistance Test

Because resistance generally increases with temperature, perform resistance tests with the engine at room temperature (70° F [21° C]). Resistance tests on hot components will indicate increased resistance and may result in unnecessary parts replacement without solving the basic problem. Ignition coil resistance can be checked without coil removal.

1. Remove the primary wires and the spark plug wires from the ignition coil assembly.
2. Calibrate the ohmmeter on the R × 1 or low-ohm scale.
3. To check primary winding resistance, connect the black ohmmeter lead to a good engine ground or to the coil ground tab if the coil is removed. Connect the red ohmmeter lead to the coil primary terminal.
4. Primary resistance should be 0.05-0.15 ohm.
5. To check secondary winding resistance, calibrate the ohmmeter on the R × 100 or high-ohm scale. Connect the red ohmmeter lead to the coil primary terminal and the black lead to the spark plug terminal.
6. Secondary resistance should be 225-325 ohms.
7. Repeat Steps 3-6 on each remaining coil.
8. Replace the coil if resistance is not as specified.
9. To check the spark plug leads, calibrate the ohmmeter on R × 1 or low-ohm scale. Connect the ohmmeter to each end of the lead and note the meter. The resistance should be nearly zero ohm.

RPM Limiting Power Pack

Power packs marked "CDL" are equipped with an internal rpm limiting device designed to prevent power head damage from overspeeding. On models so equipped, the power pack interrupts ignition if engine speed exceeds 6800 rpm. Be certain the correct power pack is used if replacement is necessary.

CD4 IGNITION SYSTEM TROUBLESHOOTING (V4 LOOP CHARGE MODELS—120 AND 140 HP; 2.0 SEA DRIVE)

The major components of the CD 4 ignition system used on V4 loop charged models include the flywheel, charge coil, power coil, 8 sensor coils, power pack, 4 ignition coils, 2 temperature switches and related wiring.

The charge coil and power coil are contained inside the stator assembly and are not serviced separately. The power coil is used to provide voltage for QuikStart and S.L.O.W. operation. The 8 sensor coils are contained in a 1-piece timer base assembly and are not serviced separately. Four sensor coils are used for QuikStart operation and 4 are used for ignition.

If the outboard motor is very hard or impossible to start, begin the troubleshooting procedure at *Total Output Test* in this chapter. If an ignition malfunction is causing an intermittent high-speed miss or erratic operation, refer to *Indexing Flywheel* and *Running Output Test* in this chapter. Unless specified otherwise, perform the following ignition system tests in the sequence given. Skipping tests or jumping around the troubleshooting procedure can result in misleading results and unnecessary parts replacement. Test the entire ignition system—more than one component may be defective.

Indexing Flywheel

If the outboard motor runs erratically, or if a high speed miss is noted, the power pack may be defective. Internal power pack malfunctions can cause erratic ignition system operation. Perform the following procedure to ensure the power pack is firing at the correct time.

1. Remove the spark plugs.
2. Position the No. 2 piston at TDC by rotating the flywheel clockwise. Insert a pencil or similar tool into the No. 2 spark plug hole while rotating the flywheel to ensure the piston is at TDC.
3. With the No. 2 piston at TDC, place a mark on the flywheel directly across from the timing pointer. Label the mark No. 2.
4. Repeat Step 2 and Step 3 on the remaining cylinders.
5. Reinstall the spark plugs and connect the plug leads.

CAUTION
The outboard motor must be supplied with adequate cooling water while running. Place the motor in a test tank or on a boat in the water. Do not attempt to run the motor at high speed while connected to a flushing device.

6. Start the motor and run it at the speed at which the problem is evident.
7. Alternately, connect a timing light to each cylinder. The timing light should indicate the cylinder number the timing light is connected to. For example, if the timing light is connected to the No. 2 spark plug wire, the No. 2 mark should be visible. In addition, the number should only appear near the timing pointer.
8. If a different cylinder number appears, or if the number jumps around or appears at other than the timing pointer, first make sure the primary ignition wires are properly connected. The primary wires must be connected as follows:

   a. *No. 1 coil*—orange/blue wire.
   b. *No. 2 coil*—orange/purple wire.
   c. *No. 3 coil*—orange/green wire.

   d. *No. 4 coil*—orange/pink wire.

If the primary wires are properly connected, verify wire and pin location on all timer base and power pack connectors. See wiring diagrams at end of manual. If wire and pin location are correct, replace the power pack.

Total Output Test

NOTE
If acceptable spark is noted at each spark gap during the total output test, but the engine pops or backfires during starting or running, the ignition system may be out of time. Be sure the orange/blue primary ignition wire is connected to the No. 1 (top) ignition coil, the orange/purple wire is connected to the No. 2 coil, the orange/green wire is connected to the No. 3 coil and the orange/pink wire is connected to the No. 4 coil. Make sure the spark plug leads are properly connected, the flywheel is properly located on the crankshaft and the timing and throttle linkage are properly synchronized.

The total output test will determine if the ignition system is capable of delivering adequate spark to the spark plugs. Perform the output test with the spark plugs installed and properly tightened.

1. Disconnect the spark plug leads from the spark plugs.
2. Mount a suitable spark tester on the engine and connect the spark plug leads to the tester. See **Figure 66**. Make sure the spark tester mounting clip is secured to a good clean engine ground.
3. Connect the cutoff clip and lanyard to the emergency stop switch, if so equipped.
4. Adjust the spark tester spark gap to 7/16 in. (11.1 mm).
5. Crank the engine while observing the spark tester.

   a. If acceptable spark is noted at each spark gap, continue testing at *Running Output Test* in this chapter.

b. If acceptable spark is noted on at least one spark gap, continue testing at *Sensor Coil Output Test* in this chapter.

c. If no spark is noted at any spark gap, continue testing at *Stop Circuit Test* in this chapter.

Stop Circuit Test

The following test eliminates the stop circuit as a potential cause of an ignition malfunction. The stop button, key switch and lanyard emergency stop switch are connected to the power pack through the engine wiring harness. Activating the stop circuit shorts power pack output to ground, which disables the ignition system and stops the engine.

1. Connect a spark tester as described under *Total Output Test*.
2. Disconnect the black/yellow wire 1-pin Amphenol stop circuit connector between the key switch and power pack. See **Figure 72**.
3. Crank the engine while noting the spark tester.

a. If good spark is now noted at all gaps, the problem is in the stop circuit. Test the key switch as described in this chapter.

b. If no spark is noted at any gap, test the charge coil as described in this chapter.

c. If spark is noted on at least one gap, continue at *Sensor Coil Output Test* in this chapter.

4. If testing is complete, reconnect the 1-pin stop circuit connector.

Key Switch Ohmmeter Test

If the engine does not stop when the key switch is turned to OFF, an open circuit is present in the black/yellow stop circuit wire, the key switch is defective or the power pack is defective.

1. Install the cap and lanyard assembly on the emergency stop switch.

2. Disconnect the black/yellow 1-pin stop circuit connector (**Figure 73**).
3. Calibrate the ohmmeter on the R × 1000 or high-ohm scale.
4. Insert a suitable jumper lead into the key switch end of the stop circuit connector (**Figure 73**).
5. Connect the ohmmeter between a good engine ground and the jumper lead.

a. With the key switch in the OFF position, the ohmmeter should indicate low resistance (continuity). If not, an open circuit is pre-

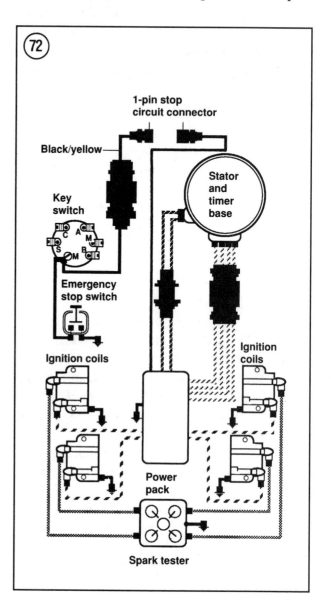

sent in the black/yellow wire between the stop circuit connector and key switch, or the key switch is defective.

b. With the key switch in the ON position, the ohmmeter should indicate high resistance (no continuity). If the meter indicates continuity (low resistance), continue at Step 6.

6. Disconnect the black/yellow stop circuit wires from the key switch M terminal. See **Figure 73**.

   a. If the meter now indicates no continuity, the key switch is defective and must be replaced.

   b. If continuity is still present, continue at Step 7.

7. Separate the emergency stop switch wire from the wiring harness black/yellow wire at the key switch.

   a. If no continuity is now noted, the emergency stop switch is defective and must be replaced.

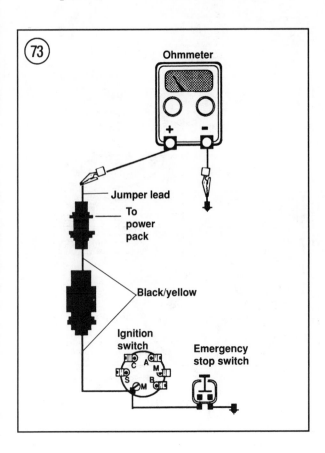

b. If continuity is still present, check the black/yellow wire for a short to ground and repair as necessary.

8. If testing is complete, remove any jumper leads and reconnect the stop circuit connector.

Charge Coil Output Test

Perform the following test to ensure the charge coil is capable of producing sufficient voltage to charge the capacitor properly in the power pack and to make sure the charge coil or charge coil wiring is not shorted to ground. A peak reading voltmeter (PRV) is necessary to perform this test.

1. Disconnect the brown and brown/yellow wire 2-pin Amphenol connector between the stator assembly and power pack.

2. Set the PRV selector switches to POS and 500.

3. Connect the PRV between a good engine ground and alternately to the A and B terminals in the stator end of the 2-pin connector. See **Figure 74**. Crank the engine and note the meter at each connection.

   a. Any voltage reading at either terminal indicates the charge coil or charge coil wires are shorted to ground. Repair the short or replace the stator assembly as necessary.

   b. If no voltage reading is noted, continue at Step 4.

4. Connect the black PRV test lead to terminal A in the 2-pin stator connector. Connect the red test lead to terminal B. See **Figure 75**.

5. Crank the engine while noting the meter. Charge coil output should be 175 volts or more.

   a. If output is 175 volts or more, reconnect the 2-pin connector and continue at *Sensor Coil Output Test*.

   b. If output is less than 175 volts, inspect the condition of the charge coil wires and connectors. If the wiring and connectors are in acceptable condition, check charge coil resistance as outlined under *Charge Coil Resistance Test* in this chapter.

Charge Coil Resistance Test

Because resistance generally increases with temperature, perform resistance tests with the engine cold (room temperature). Resistance tests on hot components will indicate increased resistance and may result in unnecessary parts replacement without solving the basic problem.

1. Insert suitable jumper leads into the A and B terminals in the stator 2-pin connector.

2. Calibrate the ohmmeter on the appropriate scale.

3. Connect the ohmmeter between terminals A and B in the 2-pin connector. See **Figure 76**. Charge coil resistance should be 430-530 ohms.

4. Replace the stator assembly if charge coil resistance is not as specified.

5. Next, check the charge coil and wires for shorts to ground. Calibrate the ohmmeter on the R × 1000 or high-ohm scale.

6. Connect the ohmmeter between a good engine ground and alternately to the A and B terminals in the stator 2-pin connector. See **Figure 77**. Any continuity between ground and either terminal indicates the charge coil or charge coil wire(s) are shorted to ground. Locate and repair the grounded wire(s) or replace the stator assembly as necessary. See Chapter Seven.

7. If testing is complete, remove any jumper leads and reconnect the 2-pin connector.

Sensor Coil Output Test

The sensor coil provides a voltage signal to the power pack which triggers power pack output to be directed to the correct ignition coil primary circuit. Perform this test to determine if the sensor coil is capable of producing a sufficient voltage signal, and to ensure the sensor coil or sensor coil wiring is not shorted to ground. A

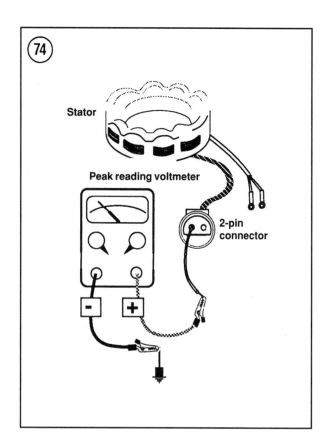

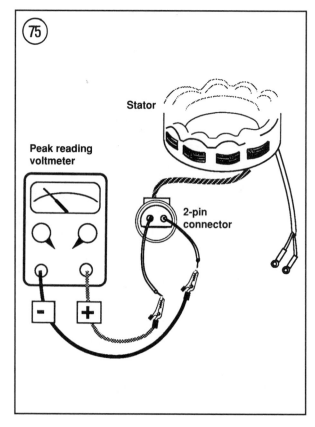

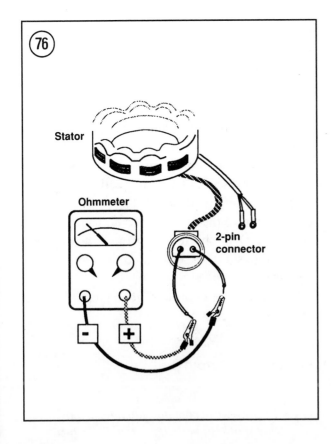

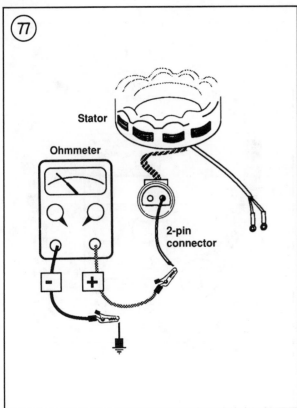

peak reading voltmeter (PRV) is necessary to perform this test.

1. Disconnect the 5-pin and 4-pin connectors between the timer base and power pack.

2. Set the PRV selector switches to POS and 5 (SEN and 5 if using Stevens CD-77).

3. Connect the PRV test leads between a good engine ground and alternately to each timer base terminal in the 5-pin (port) and 4-pin (starboard) connectors. See **Figure 78**.

4. Crank the engine and note the meter at each connection.

   a. Any voltage reading at any connection indicates sensor coil(s) or sensor coil wire(s) is shorted to ground. Locate and repair the short or replace the timer base assembly as necessary.

   b. If no voltage reading is noted at any connection, continue at Step 5.

5. Connect the black PRV test lead to terminal E in the 5-pin connector (port side). Connect the red test lead to one timer base terminal in the 4-pin connector (starboard side). See **Figure 79**.

6. Crank the engine while noting the meter. Sensor coil output should be 0.5 volt or more.

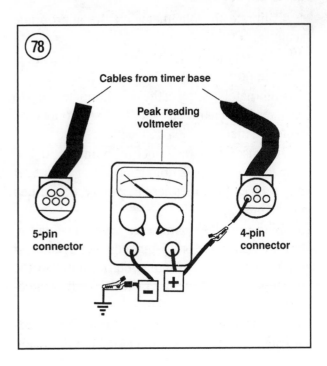

3

7. Alternately connect the red test lead to each remaining timer base terminal in the 4-pin connector, then the 5-pin connector. Crank the engine and note the meter at each connection.

  a. If output is 0.5 volt or more at each connection, continue at *Power Pack Output Test* in this chapter.

  b. If output is less than 0.5 volt at any connection, first inspect the condition of the timer base wiring and connectors. If the wiring and connectors are in acceptable condition, continue at *Sensor Coil Resistance Test* in this chapter.

Sensor Coil Resistance Test

Because resistance generally increases with temperature, perform resistance tests with the engine cold (room temperature). Resistance tests on hot components will indicate increased resistance and may result in unnecessary parts replacement without solving the basic problem. The ohmmeter should be calibrated on the R × 1000 or high-ohm scale when checking for a grounded condition.

1. Calibrate the ohmmeter on the appropriate scale.

2. Connect the black ohmmeter lead to terminal E in the port timer base connector (5-pin).

3. Alternately, connect the red ohmmeter lead to each terminal in the starboard (4-pin) connector. Note the meter at each connection.

4. If sensor coil resistance is within 130-160 ohms at each connection, continue at Step 5. If not, replace the timer base assembly as outlined in Chapter Seven.

5. With the black ohmmeter lead connected to terminal E in the port (5-pin) connector, connect the red lead to each remaining terminal in the port connector. Note the meter at each connection.

6. If sensor coil resistance is within 35-55 ohms at each connection, continue at Step 7. If not,

replace the timer base assembly as outlined in Chapter Seven.

7. Calibrate the ohmmeter on the R × 1000 or high-ohm scale.

8. Connect the ohmmeter between a good engine ground and alternately to each timer base terminal in the port (5-pin) and starboard (4-pin) connectors. No continuity (high resistance) should be present at each connection.

9. If continuity is present between any terminal and ground, either the sensor coil(s) or sensor coil wire(s) is shorted to ground. Locate and repair the short or replace the timer base as necessary.

10. If testing is complete, reconnect the timer base connectors.

Power Pack Output Test

> *WARNING*
> *To prevent accidental starting, remove the spark plug leads from the spark*

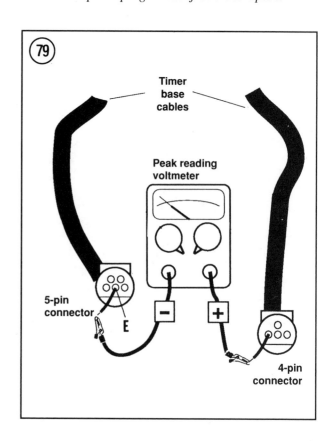

plugs. Securely ground the plug leads to the power head, or connect the leads to a spark tester.

A peak reading voltmeter (PRV) and Stevens load adapter (part No. PL-88) are necessary to test power pack output.

1. Disconnect the primary wires from each ignition coil.

2. Connect the primary wire from the No. 1 coil (orange/blue) to the red lead of the PL-88 load adapter. Connect the black load adapter lead to a good engine ground. See **Figure 80**.

3. Set the PRV selector switches to POS and 500.

4. Connect the red PRV test lead to the red load adapter lead. Connect the black PRV test lead to a good engine ground.

5. Crank the engine while observing the meter. Power pack output should be 150 volts or more.

6. Repeat Steps 2-5 on the primary wire to each remaining ignition coil. Output should be 150 volts or more at each primary wire.

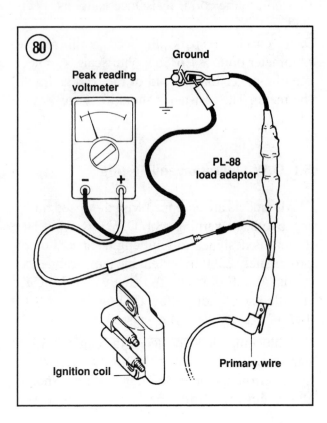

(80) Peak reading voltmeter

Ground

PL-88 load adaptor

Ignition coil

Primary wire

a. If output is 150 volts or more at each primary wire, test ignition coil resistance as outlined in this chapter.

b. If no output is noted at one or more primary wire, replace the power pack. See Chapter Seven.

7. If testing is complete, remove the PL-88 load adapter and reconnect the primary wires to the ignition coils. Make sure the orange/blue wire is attached to the No. 1 coil, the orange/purple wire is attached to the No. 2 coil, the orange/green wire is attached to the No. 3 coil and the orange/pink wire is attached to the No. 4 coil.

Running Output Test

A peak reading voltmeter (PRV) and Stevens Terminal Extenders (part No. TS-77) are necessary to perform the running output test. Running the outboard under load is often necessary to locate the cause of an intermittent malfunction or high-speed miss, especially if good spark is noted during the *Total Output Test*. Remove the propeller and install the correct test wheel (**Table 8**) prior to performing the test.

> *CAUTION*
> *The outboard motor must be supplied with adequate cooling water while running. Install the motor in a test tank or on a boat in the water. Do not attempt to run the motor at high speed while connected to a flushing device.*

1. Remove the primary wires from each ignition coil.

2. Install a Stevens Terminal Extender (part No. TS-77) on each coil primary terminal. Connect the primary wires to the terminal extenders. Make sure the orange/blue primary wire is attached to the No. 1 ignition coil, the orange/purple wire is attached to the No. 2 ignition coil, the orange/green wire is attached to the No. 3 ignition coil and the orange/pink wire is attached to the No. 4 ignition coil.

3. Set the PRV selector switches to POS and 500.

4. Connect the red PRV test lead to the terminal extender attached to the No. 1 ignition coil. Connect the black test lead to a good engine ground.

5. Start the engine and run at the speed at which the malfunction is evident while observing the meter. Running output should be 180 volts or more.

6. Move the red PRV lead to the terminal extender attached to the No. 2 ignition coil and repeat Step 5. Note the meter reading.

7. Move the red PRV lead to the terminal extender attached to the No. 3 ignition coil. Repeat Step 5 while noting the meter.

8. Move the red PRV test lead to the terminal extender attached to the No. 4 ignition coil. Repeat Step 5 while noting the meter.

   a. If output is less than 180 volts on one or more ignition coil(s), test the charge coil as described in this chapter. If the charge coil is in acceptable condition, replace the power pack.

   b. If no output (zero volt) is noted at one or more ignition coil(s), test the sensor coils as described in this chapter. If the sensor coils are in acceptable condition, replace the power pack.

9. If testing is complete, remove the terminal extenders and reconnect the primary wires to their respective ignition coils. Make sure the orange/blue wire is attached to the No. 1 coil, the orange/purple wire is attached to the No. 2 coil, the orange/green wire is attached to the No. 3 coil and the orange/pink wire is attached to the No. 4 coil.

Ignition Coil Resistance Test

Because resistance generally increases with temperature, perform resistance tests with the engine at room temperature (70° F [21° C]). Resistance tests on hot components will indicate increased resistance and may result in unnecessary parts replacement without solving the basic problem. Ignition coil resistance can be checked without coil removal.

1. Remove the primary wires and the spark plug wires from the ignition coil assembly.

2. Calibrate the ohmmeter on the R × 1 or low-ohm scale.

3. To check primary winding resistance, connect the black ohmmeter lead to a good engine ground or to the coil ground tab if the coil is removed. Connect the red ohmmeter lead to the coil primary terminal.

4. Primary resistance should be 0.05-0.15 ohm.

5. To check secondary winding resistance, calibrate the ohmmeter on the R × 100 or high-ohm scale. Connect the red ohmmeter lead to the coil primary terminal and the black lead to the spark plug terminal.

6. Secondary resistance should be 225-325 ohms.

7. Repeat Steps 3-6 on each remaining coil.

8. Replace the coil if resistance is not as specified.

9. To check the spark plug leads, calibrate the ohmmeter on R × 1 or low-ohm scale. Connect the ohmmeter to each end of the lead and note the meter. The resistance should be nearly zero ohm.

S.L.O.W. Operation and Testing

All models are equipped with the speed limiting overheat warning (S.L.O.W.) system. The system is designed to limit engine speed to approximately 2500 rpm if engine temperature exceeds 203° F (95° C). To deactivate S.L.O.W., throttle back to idle, allow the engine to cool to 147-177° F (64-81° C), then stop the engine.

A blocking diode located in the engine wiring harness is used to isolate the S.L.O.W. warning system from the other warning systems. Should the blocking diode become shorted, the

S.L.O.W. function will remain activated regardless of engine temperature.

The S.L.O.W. function is activated by a signal from the port or starboard engine temperature switch. The temperature switches are located in the top of each cylinder head.

The following conditions will cause the S.L.O.W. function to remain activated:

a. Engine overheated.

b. Engine temperature switch or switch wire shorted to ground.

c. Blocking diode closed or shorted to ground.

d. Defective power pack.

The following conditions will prevent the S.L.O.W. function from operating:

a. Engine temperature switch or switch wire open.

b. Defective power pack.

c. Defective power coil.

If the S.L.O.W function is inoperative, test the temperature switches and S.L.O.W. system as follows.

1. Install the outboard motor in a test tank with the correct test wheel installed. See **Table 8**.

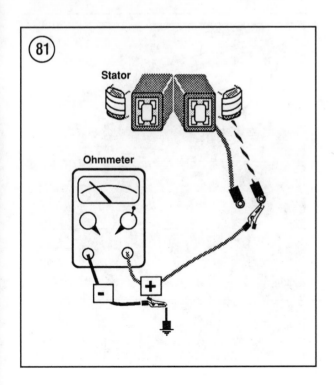

2. Connect an accurate tachometer according to the manufacturer's instructions.

3. Disconnect the tan port and starboard temperature switch wires from the engine harness wire.

4. Start the engine and run at approximately 3500 rpm.

5. Connect the engine harness end of the port tan wire to a clean engine ground and note the engine speed.

6. Throttle back to idle speed, then stop the engine.

7. Repeat Step 4 and 5 using the starboard tan wire.

a. If engine speed reduces to approximately 2500 rpm when each tan wire is grounded, test the temperature switch as described in this chapter.

b. If engine speed reduces when one temperature switch tan wire is grounded, but not the other, check the engine wiring harness and connectors and repair as necessary.

c. If engine speed does not reduce as specified when either tan wire is grounded, continue at Step 8.

8. Loosen the power pack and disconnect the orange and orange/black power coil wires from the terminal block.

9. Calibrate an ohmmeter on the R × 1000 or high-ohm scale.

10. Connect the ohmmeter between a good engine ground and alternately to each power coil wire (orange and orange/black). See **Figure 81**.

11. No continuity should be present between ground and either power coil wire.

a. If continuity is noted, either the power coil or power coil wire(s) is shorted to ground. Locate and repair the shorted wire(s) or replace the stator assembly as necessary.

b. If no continuity is noted, continue at Step 12.

12. Calibrate the ohmmeter on the appropriate scale.

13. Connect the ohmmeter between the orange and orange/black power coil wires. See **Figure 82**.

    a. If power coil resistance is within 86-106 ohms, replace the power pack.

    b. If power coil resistance is not within 86-106 ohms, replace the stator assembly. See Chapter Seven.

CAUTION
Do not start the engine with the orange and orange/black power coil wires disconnected.

14. If testing is complete, reconnect the orange and orange/black power coil wires to the terminal block. Reinstall the power pack.

Blocking Diode Test

A blocking diode is used to prevent the S.L.O.W. function from being activated by other engine warning horn systems. The blocking diode is located in the engine wiring harness.

If the S.L.O.W function is activated by the no oil, low oil or fuel vacuum warning signal, test the engine harness blocking diode as follows:

1. Disconnect the red engine harness connector.

2. Disconnect the port and starboard temperature switches from the engine harness (**Figure 83**, typical).

3. Calibrate the ohmmeter on the R × 1000 or high-ohm scale.

4. Connect the ohmmeter between either temperature switch tan wire (engine harness side) and the tan wire terminal in the red engine harness connector. See **Figure 84**.

5. Note the ohmmeter reading, then reverse the leads.

6. A high reading (no continuity) in one direction and a low reading (continuity) in the other should be noted. If both readings are low, the diode is shorted (closed) and must be replaced. If both readings are high, the diode is open and must be replaced.

QuikStart Operation and Testing

All models are equipped with QuikStart electronic starting system. The QuikStart circuit automatically advances the ignition timing when the engine temperature is less than 96° F (36° C) to improve engine warm-up. The ignition timing remains advanced until engine temperature exceeds approximately 96° F (36° C). In addition,

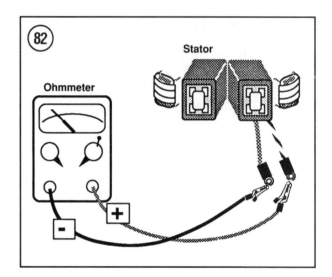

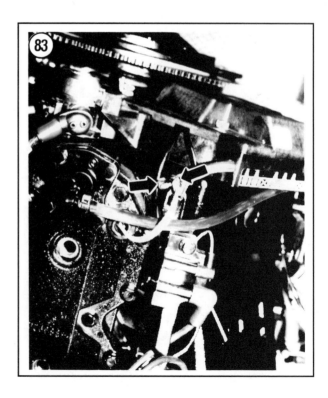

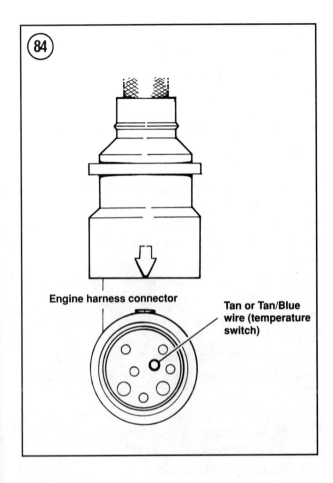

Engine harness connector

Tan or Tan/Blue wire (temperature switch)

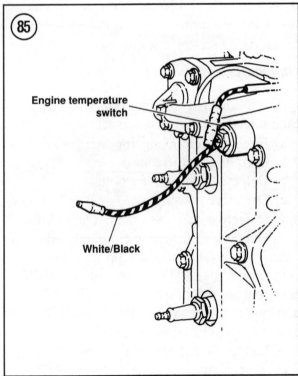

Engine temperature switch

White/Black

QuikStart also advances the ignition timing for approximately 5 seconds each time the engine is started, regardless of engine temperature. To prevent power head damage due to detonation, the power pack disables QuikStart at engine speeds exceeding approximately 1100 rpm, regardless of engine temperature.

To determine if QuikStart is functioning properly, proceed as follows:

1. Remove the propeller and install the correct test wheel (**Table 8**).

2. Place the outboard motor in a suitable test tank. Start the engine and warm it to normal operating temperature. Engine temperature must be above 96° F (36° C) before running this test.

NOTE
Make sure engine synchronization and linkage adjustments are correctly set as outlined in Chapter Five.

3. Place temporary marks on the flywheel indicating TDC for all cylinders.

4. Disconnect the white/black temperature switch wire between the power pack and the port temperature switch. See **Figure 85**, typical.

5. Attach an accurate tachometer to the power head according to the manufacturer's instructions.

6. Attach a timing light to the No. 1 cylinder according to the manufacturer's instructions.

7. Start the engine and shift into forward gear. Idle speed *must not* exceed 900 rpm in gear during this test. Adjust idle speed if necessary.

8. Observe the flywheel with the timing light. The No. 1 cylinder TDC mark should be near the timing pointer, indicating QuikStart is functioning.

9. While observing the timing marks, momentarily connect the white/black temperature switch wire. The timing mark should shift to the left approximately 1 in. (25.4 mm) when the wire is connected, indicating that QuikStart has returned the timing to the normal setting.

NOTE
*The engine **must** be stopped before testing each remaining cylinder to reset the QuikStart circuit.*

10. Stop the engine. Repeat Steps 6-9 for each remaining cylinder.
 a. If one or more cylinders do not react as specified (Step 9), replace the timer base assembly. See Chapter Seven.
 b. If no cylinders react as specified (Step 9), refer to *QuikStart inoperative* in this chapter.
 c. If all cylinders react as specified in Step 9, the QuikStart circuit is functioning properly.

QuikStart inoperative

The following conditions will cause the Quik-Start circuit to be inoperative:
 a. Defective power coil.
 b. Defective power pack.
 c. Defective timer base (sensor coil[s]).
 d. An open circuit in the yellow/red wire between the power pack and starter solenoid or key switch.
Troubleshoot the QuikStart circuit as follows:
1. Disconnect the white/black wire between the port temperature switch and power pack (**Figure 85**, typical).
2. Calibrate the ohmmeter on the R × 1000 or high-ohm scale.

NOTE
Engine temperature must be less than 89° F (32° C) in Step 3.

3. Connect the ohmmeter between the temperature switch white/black wire and a good engine ground. The ohmmeter should indicate high resistance (infinity) with engine temperature less than 89° F (32° C).
 a. If the meter indicates low resistance (continuity) in Step 3, test the temperature switch as described in this chapter.

 b. If the meter indicates high resistance in Step 3, continue at Step 4.
4. Loosen the power pack and disconnect the orange and orange/black power coil wires from the terminal block.
5. Calibrate the ohmmeter on the R × 1000 or high-ohm scale.
6. Connect the ohmmeter between a good engine ground and alternately to the power coil orange and orange/black wires. See **Figure 81**. No continuity should be present between either power coil wire and ground. If continuity is noted, repair the shorted power coil wire or replace the stator assembly as necessary. See Chapter Seven.
7. Calibrate the ohmmeter on the appropriate scale.
8. Connect the ohmmeter between the power coil orange and orange/black wires. See **Figure 82**.
 a. If power coil resistance is within 86-106 ohms, replace the power pack.
 b. If power coil is not within 86-106 ohms, replace the stator assembly.
9. If testing is complete, reconnect all circuits disconnected during this procedure.

QuikStart always on

The following conditions can cause the Quik-Start circuit to remain on constantly:
 a. Engine overcooling (not warming up to operating temperature).
 b. Defective temperature switch.
 c. Defective power pack.
 d. Defective starter solenoid or key switch.
If QuikStart remains on constantly when the engine is operated above 1100 rpm, the power pack is defective and must be replaced. If Quik-Start remains on constantly regardless of time on and engine temperature, when the engine is operated *below* 1100 rpm, continue as follows:
1. Check for a defective starter solenoid or key switch, which may cause a small voltage to bleed

into the yellow/red wire leading to the power pack. This small voltage can activate the Quik-Start circuit.

2. Check for a defective or damaged port side engine temperature switch as described in this chapter.

3. Check for an open circuit or loose or corroded connections in the white/black power pack wire.

4. Check the engine for an overcooling condition as described in this chapter.

5. If no other problems are noted in Steps 1-4, replace the power pack. See Chapter Seven.

RPM Limiting Power Pack

Power packs marked "CDL" are equipped with an internal rpm limiting device designed to prevent power head damage from overspeeding. On models so equipped, the power pack interrupts ignition if engine speed exceeds 6700 rpm. Be certain the correct power pack is used if replacement is necessary.

CD6 IGNITION SYSTEM TROUBLESHOOTING (1991 V6 CROSS FLOW MODELS—105 JET, 150 AND 175 HP)

The major components on models equipped with a 9 amp charging system include the flywheel, 2 charge coils, 6 sensor coils, 2 power packs, 6 ignition coils and related wiring. The charge coils are contained inside the stator assembly and are not serviced separately. The 6 sensor coils are contained in a 1-piece timer base assembly. The 2 power packs are contained in a 1-piece assembly and are not serviced separately.

The major components on models equipped with a 35 amp charging system include the flywheel, 2 charge coils, power coil, 6 double-wound sensor coils, 2 power packs, 6 ignition coils, 2 temperature switches and related wiring. The charge coils and power coil are contained inside the stator assembly and are not serviced

separately. The power coil supplies voltage to operate the QuikStart and S.L.O.W. systems. The 6 sensor coils are a double-wound design; 6 are used for ignition and 6 for QuikStart operation. The sensor coils are contained in a 1-piece timer base assembly. The 2 power packs are contained in a 1-piece assembly and are not serviced separately.

If the outboard motor is very hard or impossible to start, begin the troubleshooting procedure at *Total Output Test* in this chapter. If an ignition malfunction is causing an intermittent high-speed miss or erratic operation, refer to *Indexing Flywheel* and *Running Output Test* in this chapter. Unless specified otherwise, perform the following ignition system tests in the sequence given. Skipping tests or jumping around the troubleshooting procedure can result in misleading results and unnecessary parts replacement. Test the entire ignition system—more than one component may be defective.

Indexing Flywheel

If the outboard motor runs erratically, or if a high speed miss is noted, the power pack may be defective. Internal power pack malfunctions can cause erratic ignition system operation. Perform the following procedure to ensure the power pack is firing at the correct time.

1. Remove the spark plugs.

2. Position the No. 2 piston at TDC by rotating the flywheel clockwise. Insert a pencil or similar tool into the No. 2 spark plug hole while rotating the flywheel to ensure the piston is at TDC.

3. With the No. 2 piston at TDC, place a mark on the flywheel directly across from the timing pointer. Label the mark No. 2.

4. Repeat Step 2 and Step 3 on the remaining cylinders.

5. Reinstall the spark plugs and connect the plug leads.

CAUTION
The outboard motor must be supplied with adequate cooling water while running. Place the motor in a test tank or on a boat in the water. Do not attempt to run the motor at high speed while connected to a flushing device.

6. Start the motor and run it at the speed at which the problem is evident.

7. Alternately, connect a timing light to each cylinder. The timing light should indicate the cylinder number the timing light is connected to. For example, if the timing light is connected to the No. 2 spark plug wire, the No. 2 mark should be visible. In addition, the number should only appear near the timing pointer.

8. If a different cylinder number appears, or if the number jumps around or appears at other than the timing pointer, first make sure the primary ignition wires are properly connected. The primary wires must be connected as follows:

    a. *Orange/blue wires*—top ignition coils.

    b. *Orange wires*—center ignition coils.

    c. *Orange/green wires*—bottom ignition coils.

If the primary wires are properly connected, verify wire and pin location on all timer base and power pack connectors. See wiring diagrams at end of manual. If wire and pin location are correct, replace the power pack.

Total Output Test

NOTE
If acceptable spark is noted at each spark gap during the total output test, but the engine pops or backfires during starting or running, the ignition system may be out of time. Be sure the orange/blue primary ignition wires are connected to the top ignition coils, the orange wires are connected to the center ignition coils and the orange/green wires are connected to the bottom ignition coils. Make sure the spark plug leads are properly connected, the flywheel is prop-

erly located on the crankshaft and the timing and throttle linkage are properly synchronized.

The total output test will determine if the ignition system is capable of delivering adequate spark to the spark plugs. Perform the output test with the spark plugs installed and properly tightened.

1. Disconnect the spark plug leads from the spark plugs.

2. Mount a suitable spark tester on the engine and connect the spark plug leads to the tester. See **Figure 86**. Make sure the spark tester mounting clip is secured to a good clean engine ground.

3. *35 amp charging system:*

    a. Disconnect the 5-pin Amphenol connector between the power pack and engine wiring harness.

    b. Insert jumper leads into terminals A and D in both halves of the 5-pin connector. See **Figure 87**.

    c. Insert a jumper lead into terminal E in the power pack side of the 5-pin terminal. Connect the jumper lead to a good engine ground. See **Figure 87**.

4. Connect the cutoff clip and lanyard to the emergency stop switch, if so equipped.

5. Adjust the spark tester spark gap to 7/16 in. (11.1 mm).

6. Crank the engine while observing the spark tester.

   a. If acceptable spark is noted at each spark gap, continue testing at *Running Output Test* in this chapter.

   b. If acceptable spark is noted on at least one spark gap, continue testing at *Charge Coil Output Test* in this chapter.

   c. If no spark is noted at any spark gap, continue testing at *Stop Circuit Test* in this chapter.

7. *35 amp charging system*—Remove all jumper leads and reconnect the power pack-to-engine harness 5-pin connector.

Stop Circuit Test

The following test eliminates the stop circuit as a potential cause of an ignition malfunction. The stop button, key switch and lanyard emergency stop switch are connected to the power pack through the engine wiring harness. Activating the stop circuit shorts power pack output to ground, which disables the ignition system and stops the engine.

1. Connect a spark tester as described under *Total Output Test*.

2A. *9 amp charging system*—Disconnect the black/yellow wire 1-pin Amphenol stop circuit connector between the key switch and power pack. See A, **Figure 88**.

2B. *35 amp charging system*—Separate the 5-pin Amphenol connector between the power pack and engine wiring harness. Install a jumper lead into terminal E of the power pack connector. Connect the jumper lead to a good engine ground. See **Figure 89**.

3. Crank the engine while noting the spark tester.

   a. If good spark is now noted at all gaps, the problem is in the stop circuit. Test the key switch as described in this chapter.

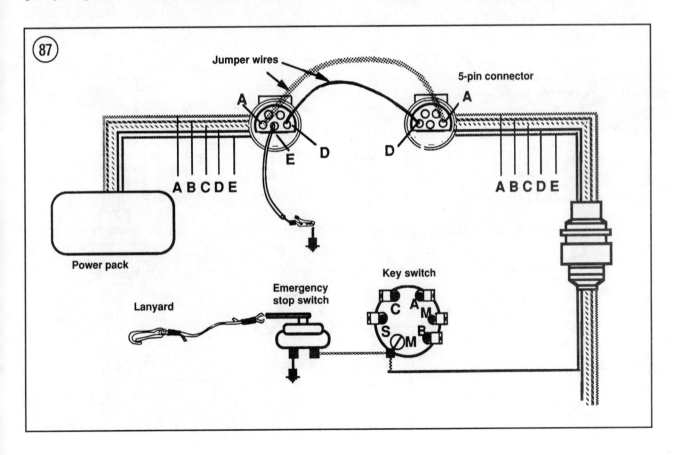

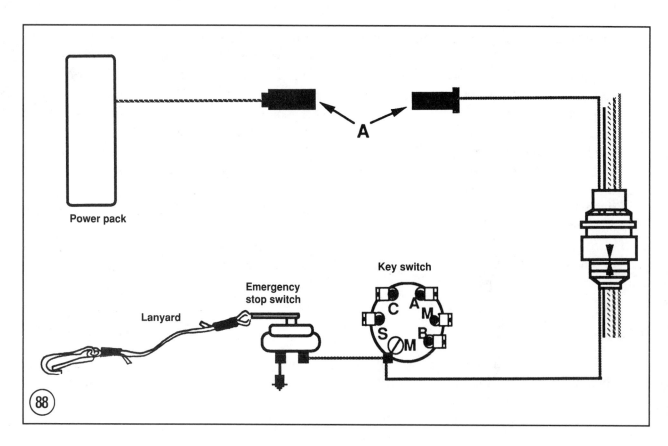

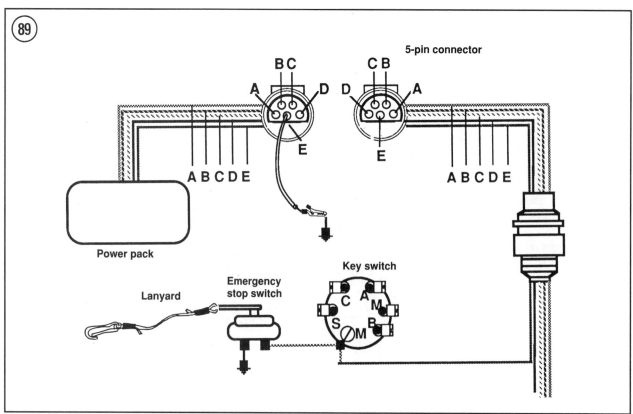

b. If no spark is noted at any gap, test the charge coil as described in this chapter.

c. If spark is noted on at least one gap, continue at *Sensor Coil Output Test* in this chapter.

4. If testing is complete, remove any jumper leads and reconnect the 1-pin (9 amp charging system) or 5-pin (35 amp charging system) connector.

Key Switch Ohmmeter Test

If the engine does not stop when the key switch is turned to OFF, an open circuit is present in the black/yellow stop circuit wire, the key switch is defective or the power pack is defective.

9 amp charging system

1. Install the cap and lanyard assembly on the emergency stop switch.

2. Disconnect the black/yellow 1-pin stop circuit connector (A, **Figure 90**).

3. Calibrate the ohmmeter on the R × 1000 or high-ohm scale.

4. Insert a suitable jumper lead into the key switch end of the stop circuit connector (**Figure 90**).

5. Connect the ohmmeter between a good engine ground and the jumper lead.

a. With the key switch in the OFF position, the ohmmeter should indicate low resistance (continuity). If not, an open circuit is pre-

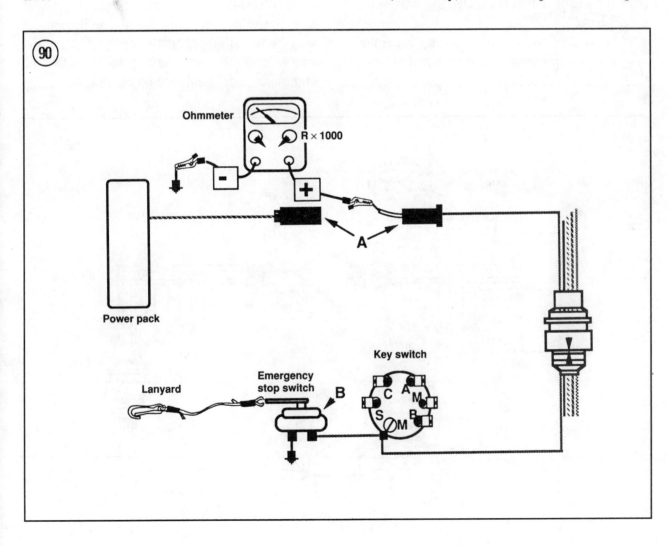

sent in the black/yellow wire between the stop circuit connector and key switch, or the key switch is defective.

b. With the key switch in the ON position, the ohmmeter should indicate high resistance (no continuity). If the meter indicates continuity (low resistance), continue at Step 6.

6. Disconnect the black/yellow stop circuit wires from the key switch M terminal. See **Figure 90**.

   a. If the meter now indicates no continuity, the key switch is defective and must be replaced.

   b. If continuity is still present, continue at Step 7.

7. Separate the emergency stop switch wire from the wiring harness black/yellow wire at the key switch.

   a. If no continuity is now noted, the emergency stop switch is defective and must be replaced.

b. If continuity is still present, check the black/yellow wire for a short to ground and repair as necessary.

8. If testing is complete, remove any jumper leads and reconnect the stop circuit connector.

35 amp charging system

1. Separate the 5-pin Amphenol connector between the power pack and engine wiring harness.

2. Install the emergency stop switch cap and lanyard, if so equipped.

3. Install a jumper lead into terminal A of the engine wiring harness connector. See **Figure 91**.

4. Calibrate the ohmmeter on the R × 1000 or high-ohm scale.

5. Connect the red ohmmeter lead to the jumper lead (terminal A) and the black lead to a good engine ground. Turn the key switch ON. the ohmmeter should indicate no continuity.

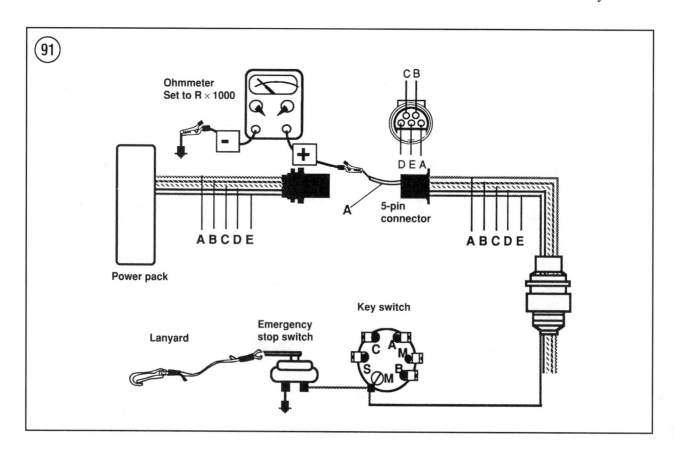

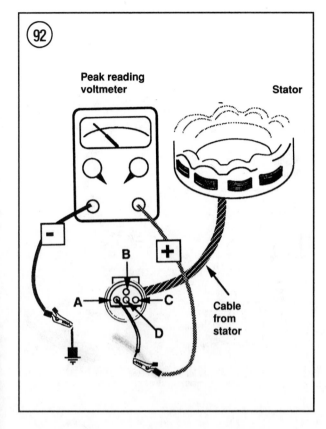

Peak reading voltmeter

Stator

B

A   C

Cable from stator

D

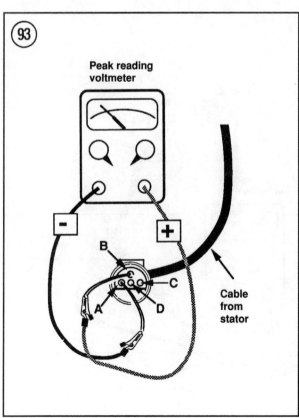

Peak reading voltmeter

B

A   C

Cable from stator

D

6. If any continuity is noted in Step 5, disconnect the black/yellow wire at the key switch M terminal (meter connected as described in Step 5). Note the meter.

    a. If the meter indicates no continuity, replace the emergency stop switch.

    b. If the ohmmeter indicates continuity, check for a defect (short) in the black/yellow wire between the key switch and 1-pin connector. Repair or replace as necessary.

7. Remove jumper leads and reconnect the power pack-to-engine harness connector.

Charge Coil Output Test

Perform the following test to ensure the charge coil is capable of producing sufficient voltage to charge the capacitor properly in the power pack and to make sure the charge coil or charge coil wiring is not shorted to ground. A peak reading voltmeter (PRV) is necessary to perform this test.

9 amp charging system

1. Disconnect the 4-pin Amphenol connector between the stator and power pack.

2. Set the PRV selector switches to POS and 500.

3. Connect the PRV test leads between a good engine ground and alternately to terminals A, B, C and D in the stator connector. See **Figure 92**. Crank the engine and note the meter at each connection.

    a. Any voltage reading indicates the charge coil(s) or charge coil wire(s) is shorted to ground. Locate and repair the shorted wire(s) or replace the stator assembly as outlined in Chapter Seven.

    b. If no voltage reading is noted, continue at Step 4.

4. Connect the black PRV test lead to terminal A in the stator connector. Connect the red test lead to terminal B. See **Figure 93**.

3

5. Crank the engine while observing the meter. Charge coil output should be 200 volts or more.

6. Connect the black PRV test lead to terminal C in the stator connector. Connect the red test lead to terminal D.

7. Repeat Step 5.

   a. If charge coil output is 200 volts or more, reconnect the 4-pin Amphenol connector and continue at *Sensor Coil Output Test*.

   b. If charge coil output is less than 200 volts, inspect the charge coil wiring and connectors and repair as necessary. If the wiring and connectors are in acceptable condition, check charge coil resistance as described under *Charge Coil Resistance Test*.

35 amp charging system

1. Disconnect the 6-pin Amphenol connector between the stator and power pack.

2. Set the PRV selector switches to POS and 500.

3. Connect the PRV test leads between a good engine ground and alternately to terminals A, B, C and D in the stator 6-pin connector. See **Figure 94**.

4. Crank the engine while observing the meter at each connection.

   a. Any voltage reading at any connection indicates the charge coil(s) or charge coil wire(s) is shorted to ground. Locate and repair the shorted wire(s) or replace the stator assembly as outlined in Chapter Seven.

   b. If no voltage is noted, continue at Step 5.

5. Connect the black PRV test lead to terminal A in the stator 6-pin connector. Connect the red test lead to terminal B. See **Figure 95**.

6. Crank the engine while observing the meter. Charge coil output should be 200 volts or more.

7. Connect the black PRV test lead to terminal C and the red test lead to terminal D in the stator connector (**Figure 95**).

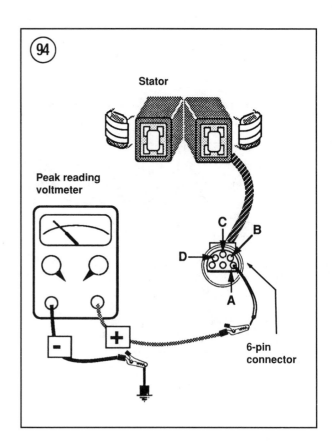

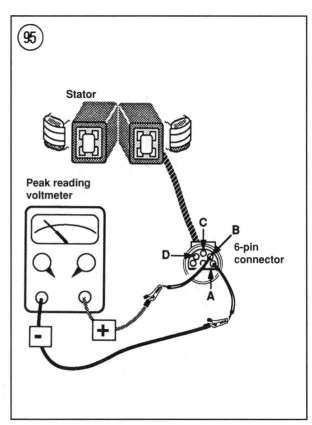

8. Repeat Step 6. Charge coil output should be 200 volts or more.

a. If output is 200 volts or more at each connection, continue at *Sensor Coil Output Test*.

b. If output is less than 200 volts, inspect charge coil wiring and connectors and repair as necessary. If the wiring and connectors are in acceptable condition, continue at *Charge Coil Resistance Test*.

Charge Coil Resistance Test

Because resistance generally increases with temperature, perform resistance tests with the engine cold (room temperature). Resistance tests on hot components will indicate increased resistance and may result in unnecessary parts replacement without solving the basic problem.

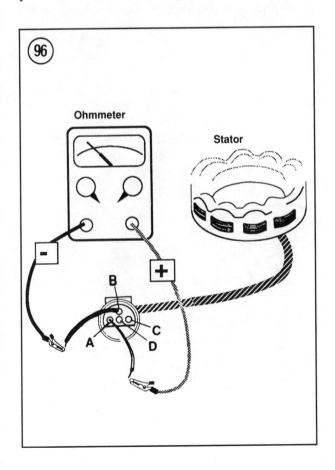

9 amp charging system

1. Install jumper leads into terminals A and B in the stator 4-pin connector.

2. Calibrate the ohmmeter on the appropriate scale. Connect the ohmmeter between the jumper leads (terminals A and B). See **Figure 96**.

3. Move the jumper leads to terminals C and D in the stator connector. Connect the ohmmeter to the jumper leads (terminals C and D).

4. If charge coil resistance is not within 455-505 ohms, replace the stator assembly (Chapter Seven).

5. Next, calibrate the ohmmeter on the R × 1000 or high-ohm scale.

6. Connect the ohmmeter between a good engine ground and alternately to each terminal in the 4-pin connector. See **Figure 97**. If no continuity is noted, remove jumper leads, reconnect the 4-pin stator-to-power pack connector and continue at *Sensor Coil Output Test*. If continuity is noted, the charge coil(s) or charge coil wire(s) is shorted to ground. Locate and repair the shorted wire(s) or replace the stator assembly as necessary.

35 amp charging system

1. Install jumper leads into terminals A and B in the stator 6-pin connector.

2. Calibrate the ohmmeter on the appropriate scale.

3. Connect the ohmmeter between the jumper leads (terminals A and B). See **Figure 98**.

a. Charge coil resistance should be within 765-935 ohms. If not, replace the stator assembly (Chapter Seven).

b. If resistance is within specification, continue at Step 4.

4. Install the jumper leads into terminals C and D in the stator 6-pin connector.

5. Connect the ohmmeter between the jumper leads (terminals C and D). See **Figure 98**.

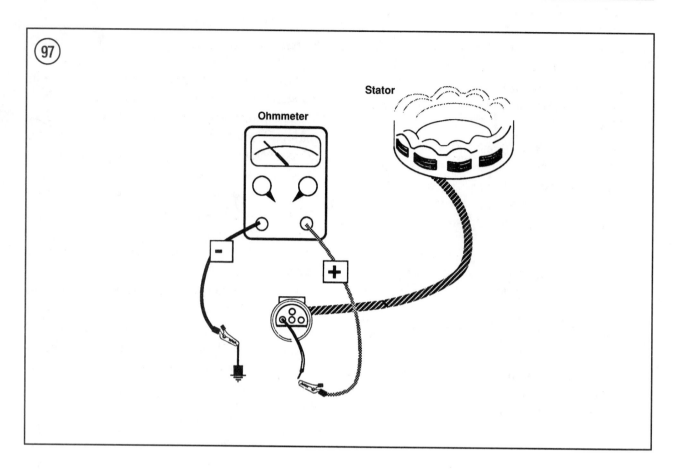

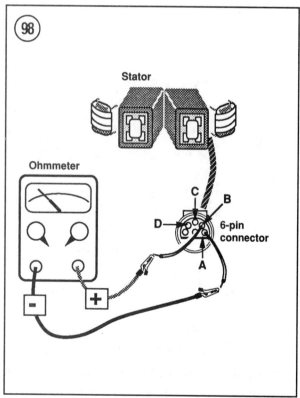

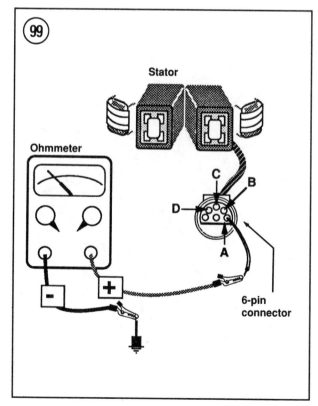

6. Charge coil resistance should be within 765-935 ohms. If not, replace the stator assembly (Chapter Seven).

7. Calibrate the ohmmeter on the R × 1000 or high-ohm scale.

8. Connect the ohmmeter between a good engine ground and alternately to terminal A, B, C and D in the stator 6-pin connector. See **Figure 99**.

    a. If no continuity is noted at each connection, remove any jumper leads, reconnect the stator-to-power pack 6-pin connector and continue at *Sensor Coil Output Test*.

    b. If continuity is indicated, the charge coil(s) or charge coil wire(s) is shorted to ground. Locate and repair the shorted wire(s) or replace the stator assembly as necessary.

Sensor Coil Output Test

The sensor coil provides a voltage signal to the power pack which triggers power pack output to be directed to the correct ignition coil primary circuit. Perform this test to determine if the sensor coil is capable of producing a sufficient voltage signal, and to ensure the sensor coil or sensor coil wiring is not shorted to ground. A peak reading voltmeter (PRV) is necessary to perform this test.

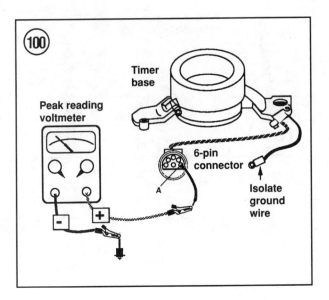

9 amp charging system

1. Disconnect the 6-pin Amphenol connector between the timer base and power pack.

2. Disconnect the timer base ground wire from the power head. Isolate the ground wire.

3. Set the PRV selector switches to POS and 5 (SEN and 5 if using CD-77).

4. Connect the PRV test leads between a good engine ground and alternately to each sensor coil terminal in the timer base connector. See **Figure 100**. Crank the engine while observing the meter at each connection.

    a. If any voltage reading is noted, the sensor coil(s) or sensor coil wire(s) is shorted to ground. Locate and repair the shorted wire(s) or replace the timer base as necessary. See Chapter Seven.

    b. If no voltage is indicated at any connection, continue at Step 5.

5. Connect the black PRV test lead to the timer base ground wire. Connect the red test lead to terminal A in the timer base connector. See **Figure 101**.

6. Crank the engine while observing the meter. Output should be 0.2 volt or more.

7. Alternately connect the red test lead to each remaining sensor coil terminal in the timer base connector. Crank the engine while observing the meter at each connection. Output should be 0.2 volt or more.

    a. If output is 0.2 volt or more, continue at *Power Pack Output Test*.

    b. If output is less than 0.2 volt, inspect the timer base wiring and connectors and repair as necessary. If the timer wiring and connectors are in acceptable condition, continue at *Sensor Coil Resistance Test*.

35 amp charging system

1. Disconnect both 4-pin Amphenol connectors between the timer base and power pack.

2. Set the PRV selector switches to POS and 5 (SEN and 5 if using CD-77).

3. Connect the PRV test leads between a good engine ground and each sensor coil terminal in both timer base 4-pin connectors. See **Figure 102**. Crank the engine while observing the meter at each connection.

    a. Any voltage reading indicates sensor coil(s) or sensor coil wire(s) is shorted to ground. Locate and repair the shorted wire(s) or replace the timer base assembly as outlined in Chapter Seven.

    b. If no voltage reading is noted, continue at Step 4.

4. Connect the black PRV test lead to terminal D in the port timer base connector. See **Figure 103**. Alternately, connect the red test lead to terminals A, B and C in the starboard timer base connector, then to terminals A, B and C in the port timer base terminal (**Figure 103**). Crank the engine while observing the meter at each connection. Sensor coil output should be 0.2 volt or more at each connection.

    a. If output is 0.2 volt or more, continue at Step 5.

    b. If output is less than 0.2 volt, inspect the timer base wiring and connection and repair as necessary. If the wiring and connectors are in acceptable condition, continue at *Sensor Coil Resistance Test*.

5. Connect the D terminal in the port timer base terminal to the D terminal in the port engine harness connector using a jumper lead. See **Figure 104**.

6. Connect the D terminal in the starboard timer base terminal to the D terminal in the starboard engine harness connector using a jumper lead. See **Figure 104**.

7. Connect the black PRV test lead to a good engine ground. Alternately, connect the red test lead to terminals A, B and C in the starboard timer base connector, then terminals A, B, C in the port timer base terminal. Crank the engine while observing the meter at each connection.

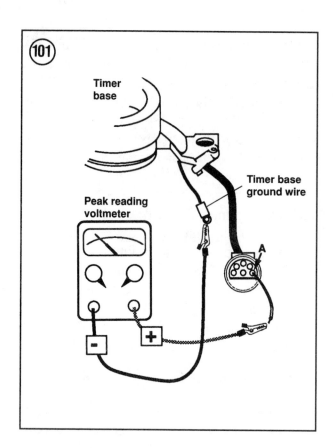

(101)

Timer base

Peak reading voltmeter

Timer base ground wire

A

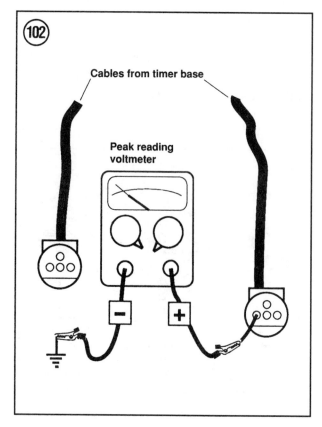

(102)

Cables from timer base

Peak reading voltmeter

a. If output is 1.2 volts or more, continue at *Power Pack Output Test*.

b. If output is less than 1.2 volts, inspect the timer base wiring and connectors and repair as necessary. If the wiring and connectors are in acceptable condition, continue at *Sensor Coil Resistance Test*.

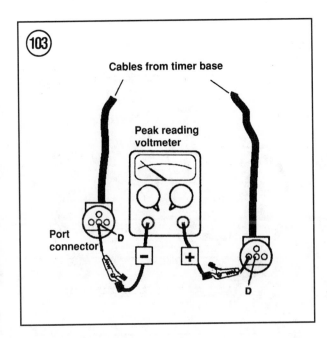

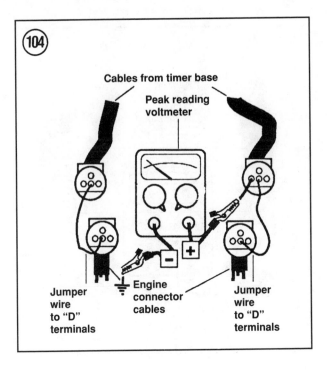

Sensor Coil Resistance Test

Because resistance generally increases with temperature, perform resistance tests with the engine cold (room temperature). Resistance tests on hot components will indicate increased resistance and may result in unnecessary parts replacement without solving the basic problem. The ohmmeter should be calibrated on the R × 1000 or high-ohm scale when checking for a grounded condition.

9 amp charging system

1. Disconnect the timer base ground wire from the power head. See **Figure 100**.

2. Calibrate the ohmmeter on the appropriate scale.

3. Connect the black ohmmeter lead to the timer base ground wire.

4. Alternately connect the red ohmmeter lead to each sensor coil terminal in the 6-pin timer base connector.

    a. If resistance at each connection is not within 30-50 ohms, replace the timer base assembly. See Chapter Seven.

    b. If resistance at each connection is within 30-50 ohms, continue at Step 5.

5. Connect the black ohmmeter lead to a good engine ground. Make sure the timer base ground wire disconnected in Step 1 is not contacting the power head or any other grounds.

6. Alternately connect the red ohmmeter lead to each sensor coil terminal in the 6-pin timer base connector. No continuity should be present between ground and any sensor coil terminal. If continuity is noted, the sensor coil(s) or sensor coil wire(s) is shorted to ground. Locate and repair shorted wire(s) or replace the timer base assembly as described in Chapter Seven.

7. Reconnect the timer base ground wire to the power head. Reconnect the timer base 6-pin connector.

35 amp charging system

NOTE
*Ohmmeter polarity must be determined before proceeding with this test. To do so, calibrate the meter on the R × 100 or low-ohm scale. Connect the leads to a known-good diode as shown in **Figure 105**, then reverse the leads. If the first connection indicated very low resistance (zero ohm), and the second connection indicated very high resistance (infinity), the ohmmeter red lead is positive (+). If the opposite result is noted, reverse the ohmmeter leads so the red lead is positive (+).*

1. Calibrate the ohmmeter on the appropriate scale.
2. Connect the red (positive) ohmmeter lead to terminal D in the port timer base connector. See **Figure 106**.
3. Alternately, connect the black ohmmeter lead to terminals A, B and C in the port timer base terminal, then terminals A, B and C in the starboard timer base terminal. Note the meter at each connection.

NOTE
The sensor coil resistance specifications in Step 4 and Step 6 are based on the use of a Stevens Model AT-101 or a Merc-O-Tronic Model M-700 ohmmeter. Resistance measured with an ohmmeter of another manufacturer may be different. Internal timer base components may cause sensor coil resistance readings to vary depending on individual ohmmeter impedance. Resistance readings may be higher or lower, however, they should be consistent.

4. If using a Stevens Model AT-101 ohmmeter, sensor coil resistance should be 330-390 ohms. If using a Merc-O-Tronic Model M-700 ohmmeter, sensor coil resistance should be 870-1070 ohms. If resistance is not as specified, replace the timer base assembly as outlined in Chapter Seven.

5. Next, connect the red ohmmeter lead to terminal D in the port timer base connector. Connect the black ohmmeter lead to terminal D in the starboard timer base connector. See **Figure 107**.

6. Resistance should be 200-260 ohms. If not, replace the timer base assembly as outlined in Chapter Seven.

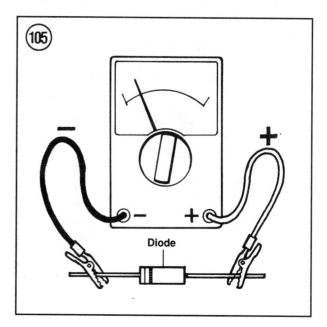

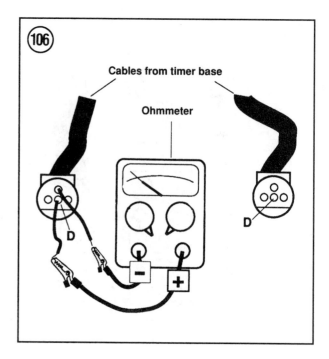

7. Next, connect the ohmmeter between a good engine ground and alternately to each sensor coil terminal in the port and starboard timer base connector.

8. No continuity should be noted at each connection. If continuity is noted, locate and repair the grounded timer base wire(s) or replace the

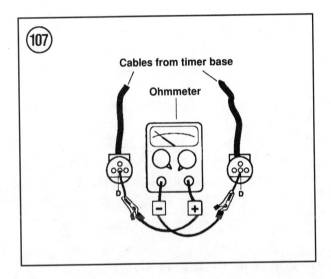

Cables from timer base

Ohmmeter

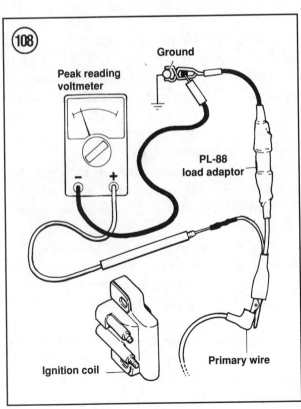

Peak reading voltmeter

Ground

PL-88 load adaptor

Ignition coil

Primary wire

timer base assembly as necessary. See Chapter Seven.

9. If testing is complete, reconnect the timer base terminals.

3

Power Pack Output Test

> *WARNING*
> *To prevent accidental starting, remove the spark plug leads from the spark plugs. Securely ground the plug leads to the power head, or connect the leads to a spark tester.*

A peak reading voltmeter (PRV) and Stevens load adapter (part No. PL-88) are necessary to test power pack output.

1. Disconnect the primary wires from each ignition coil.

2. Connect the primary wire from the No. 1 coil to the red lead of the PL-88 load adapter. Connect the black load adapter lead to a good engine ground. See **Figure 108**.

3. Set the PRV selector switches to POS and 500.

4. Connect the red PRV test lead to the red load adapter lead. Connect the black PRV test lead to a good engine ground.

5. Crank the engine while observing the meter. Power pack output should be 175 volts or more.

6. Repeat Steps 2-5 on the primary wire to each remaining ignition coil. Output should be 175 volts or more at each primary wire.

    a. If output is 175 volts or more at each primary wire, test ignition coil resistance as outlined in this chapter.

    b. If no output is noted at one primary wire, replace the power pack. See Chapter Seven.

7. If testing is complete, remove the PL-88 load adapter and reconnect the primary wires to the ignition coils. Make sure the orange/blue primary wires are attached to the top ignition coils, the orange primary wires are attached to the center ignition coils and the orange/green pri-

mary wires are attached to the bottom ignition coils.

Running Output Test

A peak reading voltmeter (PRV) and Stevens Terminal Extenders (part No. TS-77) are necessary to perform the running output test. Running the outboard under load is often necessary to locate the cause of an intermittent malfunction or high-speed miss, especially if good spark is noted during the *Total Output Test*. Remove the propeller and install the correct test wheel (**Table 8**) prior to performing the test.

CAUTION
The outboard motor must be supplied with adequate cooling water while running. Install the motor in a test tank or on a boat in the water. Do not attempt to run the motor at high speed while connected to a flushing device.

1. Remove the primary wires from each ignition coil.

2. Install a Stevens Terminal Extender (part No. TS-77) on each coil primary terminal. Connect the primary wires to the terminal extenders. Make sure the orange/blue primary wires are connected to the top ignition coils, the orange primary wires are attached to the center ignition coils and the orange/green primary wires are attached to the bottom ignition coils.

3. Set the PRV selector switches to POS and 500.

4. Connect the red PRV test lead to the terminal extender attached to the No. 1 ignition coil. Connect the black test lead to a good engine ground.

5. Start the engine and run at the speed at which the malfunction is evident while observing the meter. Running output should be 250 volts or more.

6. Repeat Steps 4 and 5 with the red PRV test lead connected to the terminal extender on each remaining ignition coil.

   a. If output is less than 250 volts on one or more ignition coil, test charge coil as described in this chapter. If the charge coil is in acceptable condition, replace the power pack.

   b. If no output (zero volt) is noted at one or more ignition coil, test the sensor coils as described in this chapter. If the sensor coils are in acceptable condition, replace the power pack.

7. If testing is complete, remove the terminal extenders and reconnect the primary wires to their respective ignition coils. Make sure the orange/blue wires are attached to the top coils, the orange wires are attached to the center coils and the orange/green wires are attached to the bottom coils.

Ignition Coil Resistance Test

Because resistance generally increases with temperature, perform resistance tests with the engine at room temperature (70° F [21° C]). Resistance tests on hot components will indicate increased resistance and may result in unnecessary parts replacement without solving the basic problem. Ignition coil resistance can be checked without coil removal.

1. Remove the primary wires and the spark plug wires from the ignition coil assembly.

2. Calibrate the ohmmeter on the R × 1 or low-ohm scale.

3. To check primary winding resistance, connect the black ohmmeter lead to a good engine ground or to the coil ground tab if the coil is removed. Connect the red ohmmeter lead to the coil primary terminal.

4. Primary resistance should be 0.05-0.15 ohm.

5. To check secondary winding resistance, calibrate the ohmmeter on the R × 100 or high-ohm scale. Connect the red ohmmeter lead to the coil

primary terminal and the black lead to the spark plug terminal.

6. Secondary resistance should be 225-325 ohms.

7. Repeat Steps 3-6 on each remaining coil.

8. Replace the coil if resistance is not as specified.

9. To check the spark plug leads, calibrate the ohmmeter on R × 1 or low-ohm scale. Connect the ohmmeter to each end of the lead and note the meter. The resistance should be nearly zero ohm.

S.L.O.W. Operation and Testing (35 Amp Charging System)

V6 models equipped with 35 amp charging systems are equipped with the speed limiting overheat warning (S.L.O.W.) system. The system is designed to limit engine speed to approximately 2500 rpm if engine temperature exceeds 203° F (95° C). To deactivate S.L.O.W., throttle back to idle, allow the engine to cool to 162° F (72° C), then stop the engine.

A blocking diode located in the engine wiring harness is used to isolate the S.L.O.W. warning system from the other warning systems. Should the blocking diode become shorted, the S.L.O.W. function will remain activated regardless of engine temperature.

The S.L.O.W. function is activated by a signal from the port or starboard engine temperature switch. The temperature switches are located in the top of each cylinder head.

The following conditions will cause the S.L.O.W. function to remain activated:

  a. Engine overheated.

  b. Engine temperature switch or switch wire shorted to ground.

  c. Blocking diode closed or shorted to ground.

  d. Defective power pack.

The following conditions will prevent the S.L.O.W. function from operating:

  a. Engine temperature switch or switch wire open.

  b. Defective power pack.

  c. Defective power coil.

If the S.L.O.W function is inoperative, test the temperature switches and S.L.O.W. system as follows.

1. Install the outboard motor in a test tank with the correct test wheel installed. See **Table 8**.

2. Connect an accurate tachometer according to the manufacturer's instructions.

3. Disconnect the tan port and starboard temperature switch wires from the engine harness wire.

4. Start the engine and run at approximately 3500 rpm.

5. Connect the engine harness end of the port tan wire to a clean engine ground and note the engine speed.

6. Throttle back to idle speed, then stop the engine.

7. Repeat Step 4 and Step 5 using the starboard tan wire.

  a. If engine speed reduces to approximately 2500 rpm when each tan wire is grounded, test the temperature switch as described in this chapter.

  b. If engine speed reduces when one temperature switch tan wire is grounded, but not the other, check the engine wiring harness and connectors and repair as necessary.

  c. If engine speed does not reduce as specified when either tan wire is grounded, continue at Step 8.

8. Disconnect the 6-pin Amphenol connector between the stator and power pack.

9. Calibrate an ohmmeter on the R × 1000 or high-ohm scale.

10. Connect the ohmmeter between a good engine ground and alternately to terminals E and F in the stator 6-pin connector. See **Figure 109**. No continuity should be present between ground and either terminal.

a. If continuity is noted, either the power coil or power coil wire(s) is shorted to ground. Locate and repair the shorted wire(s) or replace the stator assembly as necessary.

b. If no continuity is noted, continue at Step 11.

11. Calibrate the ohmmeter on the appropriate scale.

12. Connect the ohmmeter between terminals E and F in the stator 6-pin connector. See **Figure 110**.

a. If resistance is within 86-106 ohms, replace the power pack.

b. If resistance is not within 86-106 ohms, replace the stator assembly. See Chapter Seven.

CAUTION
Do not start the engine with the 6-pin connector unplugged.

13. If testing is complete, reconnect the 6-pin stator-to-power pack connector.

Blocking Diode Test
(35 Amp Charging System)

A blocking diode is used to prevent the S.L.O.W. function from being activated by other engine warning horn systems. The blocking diode is located in the engine wiring harness.

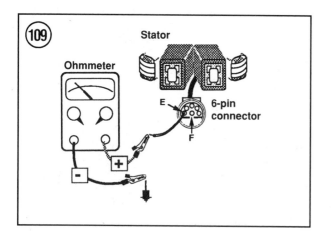

If the S.L.O.W function is activated by the no oil, low oil or fuel vacuum warning signal, test the engine harness blocking diode as follows:

1. Disconnect the red engine harness connector.

2. Disconnect the port and starboard temperature switches from the engine harness (**Figure 111**, typical).

3. Calibrate the ohmmeter on the R × 1000 or high-ohm scale.

4. Connect the ohmmeter between either temperature switch tan wire (engine harness side)

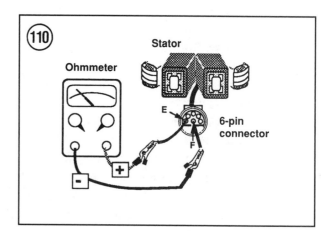

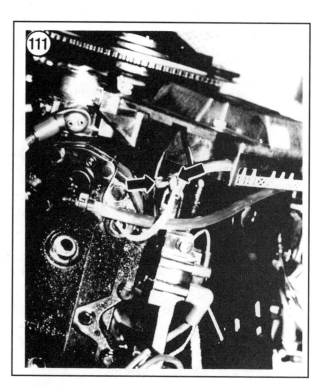

and the tan wire terminal in the red engine harness connector. See **Figure 112**.

5. Note the ohmmeter reading, then reverse the leads.

6. A high reading (no continuity) in one direction and a low reading (continuity) in the other should be noted. If both readings are low, the diode is shorted (closed) and must be replaced. If both readings are high, the diode is open and must be replaced.

QuikStart Operation and Testing (35 Amp Charging System)

V6 models equipped with 35 amp charging systems are equipped with QuikStart electronic starting system. The QuikStart circuit automatically advances the ignition timing when the engine temperature is less than 96° F (36° C) to improve engine warm-up. The ignition timing remains advanced until engine temperature exceeds approximately 96° F (36° C). In addition, QuikStart also advances the ignition timing for

approximately 5 seconds each time the engine is started, regardless of engine temperature. To prevent power head damage due to detonation, the power pack disables QuikStart at engine speeds exceeding approximately 1100 rpm, regardless of engine temperature.

To determine if QuikStart is functioning properly, proceed as follows:

1. Remove the propeller and install the correct test wheel (**Table 8**).

2. Place the outboard motor in a suitable test tank. Start the engine and warm it to normal operating temperature. Engine temperature must be above 96° F (36° C) before running this test.

NOTE
Make sure engine synchronization and linkage adjustments are correctly set as outlined in Chapter Five.

3. Place temporary marks on the flywheel indicating TDC for all cylinders.

4. Disconnect the white/black temperature switch wire between the power pack and the starboard temperature switch. See **Figure 113**, typical.

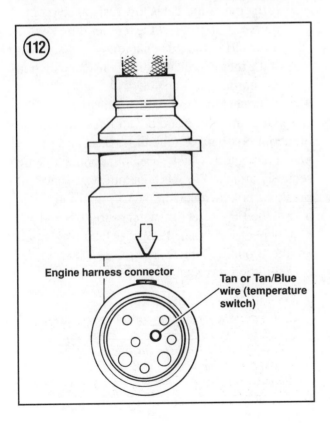

Engine harness connector

Tan or Tan/Blue wire (temperature switch)

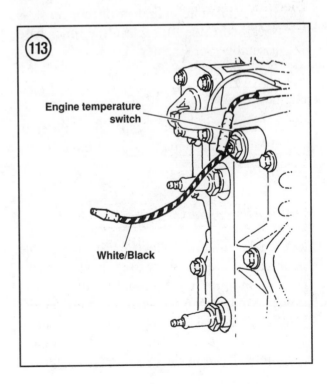

Engine temperature switch

White/Black

5. Attach an accurate tachometer to the power head according to the manufacturer's instructions.

6. Attach a timing light to the No. 1 cylinder according to the manufacturer's instructions.

7. Start the engine and shift into forward gear. Idle speed *must not* exceed 900 rpm in gear during this test. Adjust idle speed if necessary.

8. Observe the flywheel with the timing light. The No. 1 cylinder TDC mark should be near the timing pointer, indicating QuikStart is functioning.

9. While observing the timing marks, momentarily connect the white/black temperature switch wire. The timing mark should shift to the left approximately 1 in. (25.4 mm) when the wire is connected, indicating that QuikStart has returned the timing to the normal setting.

NOTE
*The engine **must** be stopped before testing each remaining cylinder to reset the QuikStart circuit.*

10. Stop the engine. Repeat Steps 6-9 for each remaining cylinder.

    a. If one or more cylinders do not react as specified (Step 9), replace the timer base assembly. See Chapter Seven.

    b. If no cylinders react as specified (Step 9), refer to *QuikStart inoperative* in this chapter.

    c. If all cylinders react as specified in Step 9, the QuikStart circuit is functioning properly.

QuikStart inoperative

A peak reading voltmeter (PRV) and a suitable breakout box are necessary to complete this test. Two commonly used breakout boxes are: Stevens Model SA-6 and Merc-O-Tronic Model 55-861. The breakout box is connected inline with the timer base circuit and allows voltage measurements while the circuit remains intact.

The following conditions will cause the Quik-Start circuit to be inoperative:

    a. Defective power coil.

    b. Defective power pack.

    c. Defective timer base (sensor coil[s]).

    d. An open circuit in the yellow/red wire between the power pack and starter solenoid or key switch.

Troubleshoot the QuikStart circuit as follows:

1. Disconnect the white/black wire between the starboard temperature switch and power pack (**Figure 113**, typical).

2. Calibrate the ohmmeter on the R × 1000 or high-ohm scale.

NOTE
Engine temperature must be less than 89° F (32° C) in Step 3.

3. Connect the ohmmeter between the temperature switch white/black wire and a good engine ground. The ohmmeter should indicate high resistance (infinity) with engine temperature less than 89° F (32° C).

    a. If the meter indicates low resistance (continuity) in Step 3, test the temperature switch as described in this chapter.

    b. If the meter indicates high resistance in Step 3, continue at Step 4.

4. Disconnect the starboard 4-pin connector between the timer base and power pack. Install the breakout box between the timer base and power pack connectors. Make sure both connectors are securely attached to the breakout box. Place all breakout box switches in the ON position.

5. Set the PRV selector switches to POS and 50.

6. Connect the black PRV test lead to a good engine ground. Connect the red test lead to the breakout box terminal D.

CAUTION
Do not run the engine with the timer base wires disconnected or the power pack will be destroyed. Be certain the breakout box is correctly installed and that all breakout box switches are in the ON position.

7. Remove the propeller and install the correct test wheel (**Table 8**). Place the outboard motor in a test tank.

8. Start the engine and run at 900 rpm in FORWARD gear while observing the meter. The meter will indicate 8-12 volts if the power pack is in acceptable condition.

   a. If the meter indicates 8-12 volts, replace the timer base.

   b. If the voltage is not within 8-12 volts, stop the engine and continue at Step 9.

9. Disconnect the 6-pin Amphenol connector between the stator and power pack.

10. Calibrate the ohmmeter on the R × 1000 or high-ohm scale.

11. Connect the ohmmeter between a good engine ground and alternately to terminals E and F in the stator 6-pin connector. No continuity should be noted.

12. Calibrate the ohmmeter on the appropriate scale.

13. Connect the ohmmeter between terminals E and F in the stator 6-pin connector.

   a. If resistance is within 86-106 ohms, replace the power pack as outlined in Chapter Seven.

   b. If resistance is not within 86-106 ohms, the power coil is defective. Replace the stator assembly as outlined in Chapter Seven.

14. Reconnect the stator-to-power pack 6-pin connector. Remove the breakout box and reconnect the starboard 4-pin timer base terminal. Do not attempt to start the outboard with any connectors unplugged or the power pack will be damaged.

QuikStart always on

The following conditions can cause the QuikStart circuit to remain on constantly:

   a. Engine overcooling (not warming up to operating temperature).

   b. Defective temperature switch.

   c. Defective power pack.

   d. Defective starter solenoid or key switch.

If QuikStart remains on constantly when the engine is operated *above* 1100 rpm, the power pack is defective and must be replaced. If QuikStart remains on constantly regardless of time on and engine temperature, when the engine is operated *below* 1100 rpm, continue as follows:

1. Check for a defective starter solenoid or key switch, which may cause a small voltage to bleed into the yellow/red wire leading to the power pack. This small voltage can activate the QuikStart circuit.

2. Check for a defective or damaged port side engine temperature switch as described in this chapter.

3. Check for an open circuit or loose or corroded connections in the white/black power pack wire.

4. Check the engine for an overcooling condition as described in this chapter.

5. If no other problems are noted in Steps 1-4, replace the power pack. See Chapter Seven.

RPM Limiting Power Pack

Power packs marked "CDL" are equipped with an internal rpm limiting device designed to prevent power head damage from overspeeding. On models so equipped, the power pack interrupts ignition if engine speed exceeds 5800 rpm. Be certain the correct power pack is used if replacement is necessary.

CD6 IGNITION SYSTEM TROUBLESHOOTING (1991-ON V6 LOOP CHARGE MODELS—200 AND 225 HP; 3.0 SEA DRIVE)

The major components of the CD6 ignition system used on 1991-on 200 and 225 hp models include the flywheel, 2 charge coils, power coil, 6 double-wound sensor coils, 2 power packs, 6 ignition coils, shift switch, 2 temperature switches and related wiring.

The charge coils and power coil are contained in the stator assembly and are not serviced separately. The power coil provides voltage for operation of the S.L.O.W. and QuikStart systems. The 6 sensor coils (1 per cylinder) are a double-wound design; 1 coil provides a trigger signal for ignition and 1 coil provides a timing signal for QuikStart operation. The sensor coils are contained in the timer base assembly and are not serviced separately. The 2 power packs are contained in a 1-piece assembly and are not serviced separately.

If the outboard motor is very hard or impossible to start, begin the troubleshooting procedure at *Total Output Test*. If an ignition malfunction is causing an intermittent high-speed miss or erratic operation, refer to *Indexing Flywheel* and *Running Output Test*. Unless specified otherwise, perform the following ignition system tests in the sequence given. Skipping tests or jumping around the troubleshooting procedure can result in misleading results and unnecessary parts replacement. Test the entire ignition system—more than one component may be defective.

Indexing Flywheel

If the outboard motor runs erratically, or if a high speed miss is noted, the power pack may be defective. Internal power pack malfunctions can cause erratic ignition system operation. Perform the following procedure to ensure the power pack is firing at the correct time.

1. Remove the spark plugs.
2. Position the No. 2 piston at TDC by rotating the flywheel clockwise. Insert a pencil or similar tool into the No. 2 spark plug hole while rotating the flywheel to ensure the piston is at TDC.
3. With the No. 2 piston at TDC, place a mark on the flywheel directly across from the timing pointer. Label the mark No. 2.
4. Repeat Step 2 and Step 3 on the remaining cylinders.

5. Reinstall the spark plugs and connect the plug leads.

> *CAUTION*
> *The outboard motor must be supplied with adequate cooling water while running. Place the motor in a test tank or on a boat in the water. Do not attempt to run the motor at high speed while connected to a flushing device.*

6. Start the motor and run it at the speed at which the problem is evident.
7. Alternately, connect a timing light to each cylinder. The timing light should indicate the cylinder number the timing light is connected to. For example, if the timing light is connected to the No. 2 spark plug wire, the No. 2 mark should be visible. In addition, the number should only appear near the timing pointer.
8. If a different cylinder number appears, or if the number jumps around or appears at other than the timing pointer, first make sure the primary ignition wires are properly connected. The primary wires must be connected as follows:
   a. *Orange/blue wires*—top ignition coils.
   b. *Orange wires*—center ignition coils.
   c. *Orange/green wires*—bottom ignition coils.

If the primary wires are properly connected, verify wire and pin location on all timer base and

power pack connectors. See wiring diagrams at end of manual. If wire and pin location are correct, replace the power pack.

Total Output Test

> *NOTE*
> *If acceptable spark is noted at each spark gap during the total output test, but the engine pops or backfires during starting or running, the ignition system may be out of time. Be sure the orange/blue primary ignition wires are connected to the top ignition coils, the orange wires are connected to the center ignition coils and the orange/green wires are connected to the bottom ignition coils. Make sure the spark plug leads are properly connected, the flywheel is properly located on the crankshaft and the timing and throttle linkage are properly synchronized.*

The total output test will determine if the ignition system is capable of delivering adequate spark to the spark plugs. Perform the output test with the spark plugs installed and properly tightened.

1. Disconnect the spark plug leads from the spark plugs.
2. Mount a suitable spark tester on the engine and connect the spark plug leads to the tester. See **Figure 114**. Make sure the spark tester mounting clip is secured to a good clean engine ground.
3. Adjust the spark tester spark gap to 7/16 in. (11.1 mm).
4. Connect the cutoff clip and lanyard to the emergency stop switch, if so equipped.
5. Crank the engine while observing the spark tester.
   a. If acceptable spark is noted at each spark gap, continue testing at *Running Output Test* in this chapter.
   b. If no spark is noted at cylinders 1, 3 and 5, continue at *Shift Switch Test* in this chapter.

   c. If acceptable spark is noted on at least one spark gap, continue testing at *Charge Coil Output Test* in this chapter.
   d. If no spark is noted at any spark gap, continue testing at *Stop Circuit Test* in this chapter.

Stop Circuit Test

The following test eliminates the stop circuit as a potential cause of an ignition malfunction. The key switch and lanyard emergency stop switch are connected to the power pack through the engine wiring harness. Activating the stop circuit shorts power pack output to ground, which disables the ignition system and stops the engine.

1A. *1991 and 1992 models*—Disconnect the two, 1-pin Amphenol connectors between the power pack and key switch. See A, **Figure 115**.
1B. *1993-on models*—Disconnect the 1-pin Amphenol connector between the engine wiring harness and shift switch. See A, **Figure 116**.
2. Crank the engine while observing the spark tester.
3A. *1991 and 1992 models:*
   a. If good spark is now noted at each spark gap, the problem is in the stop circuit. Continue at *Key Switch Ohmmeter Test*.
   b. If no spark is noted, continue at *Charge Coil Output Test*.
3B. *1993-on models:*
   a. If good spark is now noted at each spark gap, the problem is in the shift switch circuit. Continue at *Shift Switch Test*.
   b. If no spark is noted, disconnect the 2-pin stop circuit connector (B, **Figure 116**) and repeat Step 2. If good spark is now noted, the problem is in the stop circuit. Continue at *Key Switch Ohmmeter Test*. If there is still no spark, continue at *Charge Coil Output Test*.

Key Switch Ohmmeter Test

If the engine will not shut off when the key switch is turned OFF, test the key switch as outlined in this chapter.

If the engine will not shut off when the clip is removed from the emergency stop switch, replace the emergency stop switch.

If the engine will not shut off when the key switch is turned OFF and the clip is removed from the emergency stop switch, check for an open circuit in the black/yellow, black/orange and black wires between the power pack and key switch.

1991 and 1992 models

1. Install the emergency stop switch clip and lanyard.

2. Disconnect both 1-pin Amphenol connectors between the power pack and key switch. See A, **Figure 115**.

3. Calibrate the ohmmeter on the appropriate scale.

4. Connect the black ohmmeter lead to a good engine ground. Connect the red ohmmeter lead to either engine harness black/yellow wire. See A, **Figure 117**.

   a. With the key switch in the OFF position, the ohmmeter should indicate continuity (low resistance).

   b. With the key switch in the ON position, the ohmmeter should indicate no continuity (high resistance).

5. Move the red ohmmeter lead to the remaining engine harness black/yellow wire. The results should be the same as in Steps 4a and 4b.

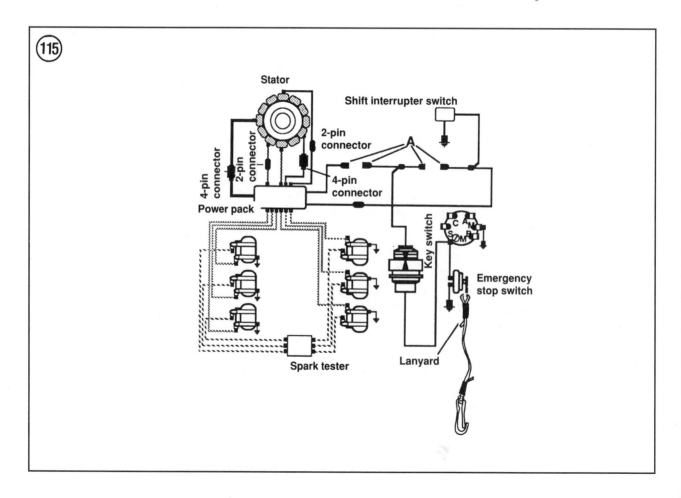

NOTE
If both black/yellow wires test good (Steps 4 and 5), but the stop circuit does not operate properly, the blocking diode in the power pack is defective. Replace the power pack as outlined in Chapter Seven.

6. If continuity is noted in Steps 4 and 5 when the key switch is ON, disconnect the engine harness black/yellow wires from the key switch M terminal.

   a. If the ohmmeter now indicates no continuity, replace the key switch.

   b. If continuity is still noted, continue at Step 7.

7. Disconnect the emergency stop switch wire from the engine harness black/yellow wire at the key switch.

   a. If the ohmmeter now indicates no continuity, replace the emergency stop switch.

   b. If continuity is still noted, the stop circuit wiring in the engine harness is defective. Repair or replace as required.

8. Reconnect the 1-pin Amphenol connectors.

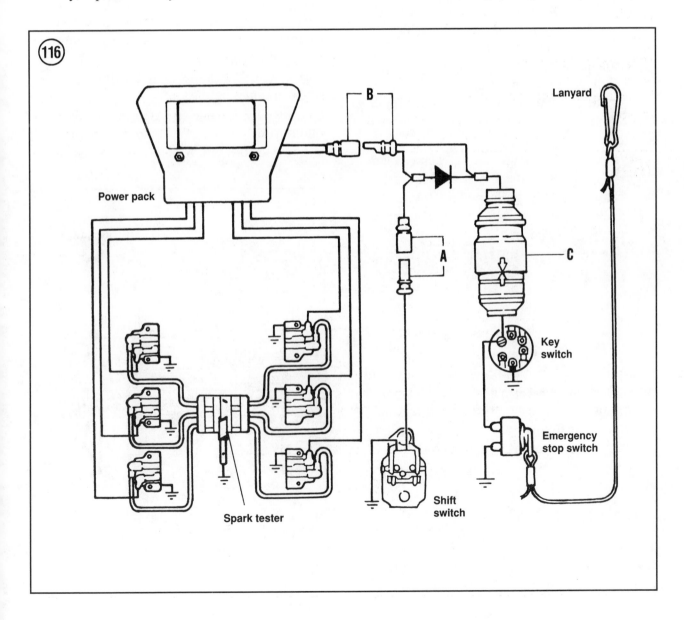

1993-on models

1. Install the emergency stop switch clip and lanyard.

2. Disconnect the 1-pin Amphenol connector between the engine wiring harness and shift switch (A, **Figure 116**).

3. Disconnect the 2-pin Amphenol connector between the power pack and key switch (B, **Figure 116**).

4. Connect the black ohmmeter lead to a good engine ground. Connect the red ohmmeter lead to terminal B (black/yellow wire) in the engine harness 2-pin connector.

    a. With the key switch in the OFF position, the ohmmeter should indicate continuity (low resistance).

    b. With the key switch in the ON position, the ohmmeter should indicate no continuity (high resistance). If continuity is noted, continue at Step 5.

5. Disconnect the engine wiring harness connector (C, **Figure 116**) and note the ohmmeter.

    a. If no continuity is now present, test the key switch, emergency stop switch and remote control wiring harness.

    b. If continuity is still present, repair or replace the engine wiring harness.

Shift Switch Test

The shift switch momentarily interrupts ignition to cylinders 1, 3 and 5 when the outboard motor is shifted into or out of gear. This power interruption causes the outboard to shift easier.

Perform the following test if no spark is noted on cylinders 1, 3 and 5 during the *Total Output Test*.

1991 and 1992 models

1. Install a spark tester as described under *Total Output Test* in this chapter. Adjust the spark gap to 7/16 in. (11.1 mm).

2. Disconnect both 1-pin Amphenol connectors between the shift switch and the power pack. See **Figure 118**.

3. Crank the engine while observing the spark tester.

    a. If cylinders 1, 3 and 5 now have good spark, continue at Step 4.

    b. If cylinders 1, 3 and 5 still do not have spark, continue at *Charge Coil Output Test*.

4. Calibrate the ohmmeter on the R × 1000 or high-ohm scale.

5. Connect the ohmmeter between a good engine ground and the power pack end of the shift switch harness. See **Figure 119**. No continuity (high resistance) should be noted. If continuity is present, replace the shift switch and wire harness.

6. Push down on the shift cable pin to activate the shift switch while observing the meter. Continuity (low resistance) should now be noted. If not, replace the shift switch and wire harness.

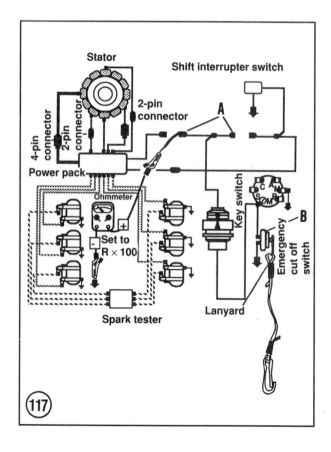

7. Connect the ohmmeter between both engine harness 1-pin connectors. Note the meter reading, then reverse the ohmmeter leads and note the second reading. One reading should be infinity (no continuity) and the other should be continuity (near zero ohm). If both readings are infinity, or if both readings are zero ohm, the blocking diode in the switch harness is defective. Replace the shift switch and harness.

1993-on models

1. Install a spark tester as described under *Total Output Test* in this chapter. Adjust the spark gap to 7/16 in. (11.1 mm).
2. Disconnect the 1-pin Amphenol connector between the engine wiring harness and the shift switch. See A, **Figure 116**.
3. Crank the engine while observing the spark tester.

   a. If spark is now noted at cylinders 1, 3 and 5, continue at Step 4.

b. If cylinders 1, 3 and 5 still do not have spark, continue at *Charge Coil Output Test*.
4. Calibrate the ohmmeter on the R × 1000 or high-ohm scale.
5. Connect the ohmmeter between a good engine ground and the shift switch connector. No continuity (infinity) should be noted. If continuity is present, replace the shift switch and wire harness.
6. Push down on the shift cable pin to activate the shift switch while observing the ohmmeter. Continuity should be noted when the switch is closed. If not, replace the shift switch and harness.
7. Disconnect the 1-pin Amphenol connector between the engine wiring harness and shift switch. See A, **Figure 116**. Disconnect the 2-pin Amphenol connector between the power pack and key switch. See B, **Figure 116**. Disconnect the engine wiring harness connector. See C, **Figure 116**.
8. Connect the red ohmmeter lead to the black/yellow wire terminal in the engine wiring harness. Connect the black ohmmeter lead to terminal A in the 2-pin Amphenol connector. See **Figure 120**. Note the meter reading, then reverse the ohmmeter leads. Note the meter reading.

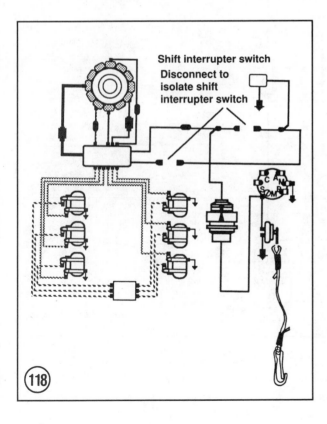

Shift interrupter switch
Disconnect to isolate shift interrupter switch

(118)

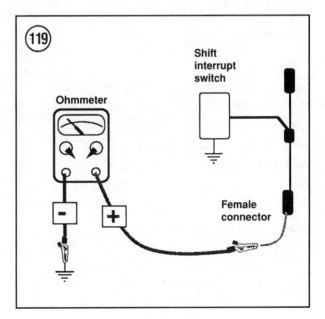

(119)

Ohmmeter

Shift interrupt switch

Female connector

a. One reading should be infinity and the other should be near zero ohm.

b. If both readings are infinity, or if both are near zero ohm, replace the blocking diode or repair or replace the engine wiring harness as necessary.

9. With the red ohmmeter lead connected to the black/yellow wire terminal in the engine harness connector (**Figure 120**), connect the black meter lead to terminal B (black/yellow) in the engine harness 2-pin connector (**Figure 120**). The meter should indicate low resistance. If not, repair or replace the engine wiring harness as necessary.

10. With the red ohmmeter lead connected to the black/yellow wire terminal in the engine harness connector (**Figure 120**), connect the black ohmmeter lead to the engine harness end of the 1-pin shift switch connector. Note the meter reading, reverse the ohmmeter leads and note reading. One reading should be infinity and the other reading should be near zero. If not, repair or replace the engine wiring harness as necessary.

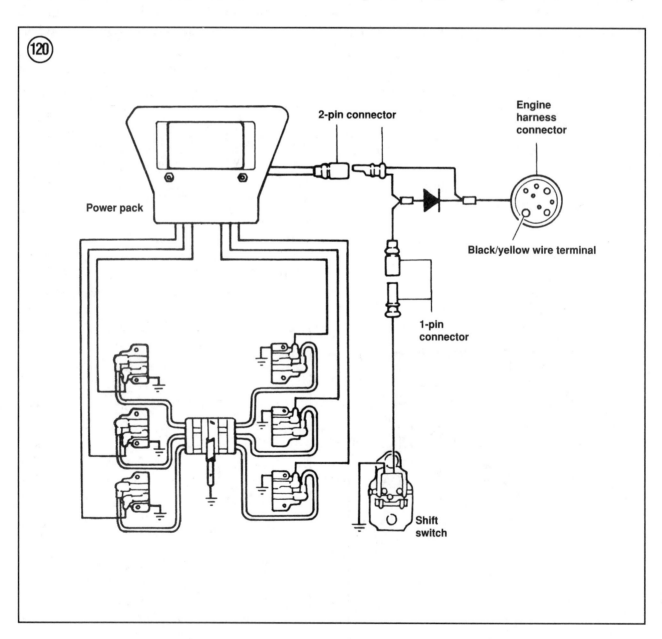

Charge Coil Output Test

Perform the following test to ensure the charge coil is capable of producing sufficient voltage to charge the capacitor properly in the power pack and to make sure the charge coil or charge coil wiring is not shorted to ground. A peak reading voltmeter (PRV) is necessary to perform this test.

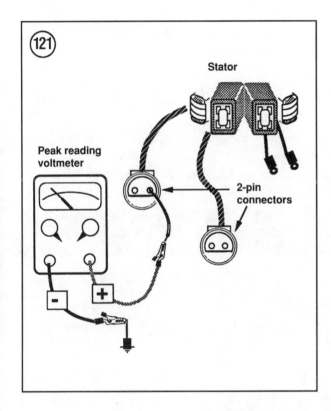

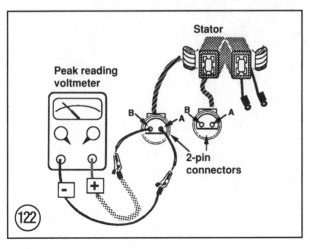

1. Disconnect the fore and aft 2-pin Amphenol connectors between the stator and power pack.

2. Set the PRV selector switches to POS and 500.

3. Connect one PRV test lead to a good engine ground. Alternately connect the remaining test lead to terminals A and B in the forward 2-pin stator connector. See **Figure 121**.

4. Crank the engine and note the meter at each connection.

   a. Any voltage reading indicates a shorted charge coil or charge coil wire(s). Locate and repair the shorted wire(s) or replace the stator assembly as outlined in Chapter Seven.

   b. If no voltage is noted, continue at Step 5.

5. Repeat Steps 3 and 4 with the PRV connected between ground and terminal A, then terminal B in the rear 2-pin stator connector.

   a. Any voltage reading indicates a shorted charge coil or charge coil wire(s). Locate and repair the shorted wire(s) or replace the stator assembly as outlined in Chapter Seven.

   b. If no voltage is noted, continue at Step 6.

6. Connect the black PRV test lead to terminal A in the forward 2-pin stator connector. See **Figure 122**. Connect the red test lead to terminal B in the forward 2-pin connector.

7. Crank the engine while observing the meter. Charge coil output should be 130 volts or more.

8. Connect the black PRV test lead to terminal A in the rear 2-pin stator connector. Connect the red test lead to terminal B in the rear connector.

9. Crank the engine while observing the meter. Charge coil output should be 130 volts or more.

   a. If output at both connectors is 130 volts or more, reconnect the 2-pin connectors and continue at *Sensor Coil Output Test*.

   b. If output is less than 130 volts at either connector, inspect the condition of the charge coil wiring and connectors. If the wiring and connectors are in acceptable condition, continue at *Charge Coil Resistance Test*.

Charge Coil Resistance Test

Because resistance generally increases with temperature, perform resistance tests with the engine cold (room temperature). Resistance tests on hot components will indicate increased resistance and may result in unnecessary parts replacement without solving the basic problem.

1. Calibrate the ohmmeter on the appropriate scale.

2. Connect the ohmmeter between terminals A and B in the forward 2-pin stator connector. See **Figure 123**. Resistance should be 765-935 ohms.

3. Connect the ohmmeter between terminals A and B in the rear 2-pin connector. Resistance should be 765-935 ohms.

4. If resistance is not as specified in Steps 2 and 3, replace the stator assembly as outlined in Chapter Seven.

5. Calibrate the ohmmeter on the R × 1000 or high-ohm scale.

6. Connect the ohmmeter between a good engine ground and alternately to each terminal in both 2-pin connectors. See **Figure 124**. Note the meter reading at each connection.

    a. No continuity (infinity) should be noted at each connection.

    b. Continuity between any terminal and ground indicates a shorted charge coil or charge coil wire(s). Locate and repair the shorted wire(s) or replace the stator assembly as outlined in Chapter Seven.

7. Reconnect the stator-to-power pack 2-pin connectors.

Sensor Coil Output Test

The sensor coil provides a voltage signal to the power pack which triggers power pack output to be directed to the correct ignition coil primary circuit. Perform this test to determine if the sensor coil is capable of producing a sufficient voltage signal, and to ensure the sensor coil or sensor coil wiring is not shorted to ground. A peak reading voltmeter (PRV) is necessary to perform this test.

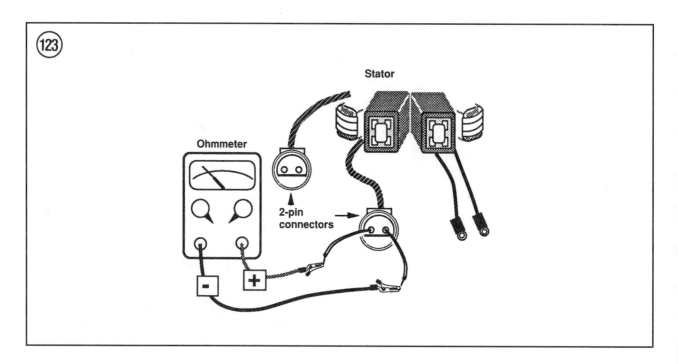

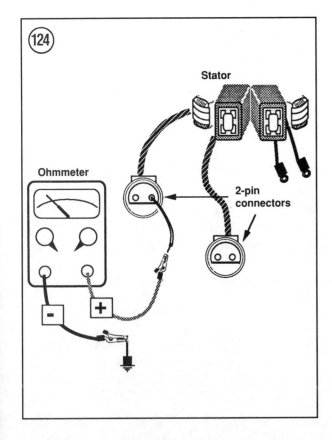

124

Stator

Ohmmeter

2-pin connectors

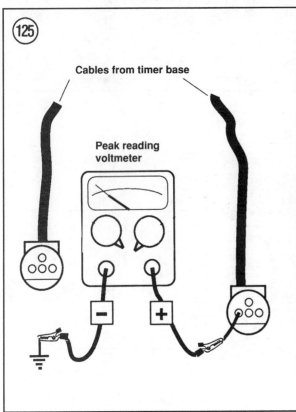

125

Cables from timer base

Peak reading voltmeter

1. Disconnect both 4-pin Amphenol connectors betweeen the timer base and power pack.

2. Set the PRV selector switches to POS and 5 (SEN and 5 if using Stevens CD-77).

3. Connect one PRV test lead to a good engine ground. Alternately connect the remaining test lead to each timer base terminal. See **Figure 125**.

4. Crank the engine while observing the meter at each connection.

   a. Any voltage reading indicates a shorted sensor coil or sensor coil wire(s). Locate and repair the shorted wire(s) or replace the timer base assembly as outlined in Chapter Seven.

   b. If no voltage is noted, continue at Step 5.

5. Connect the black PRV test lead to terminal D in the port timer base connector. Alternately connect the red test lead to terminals A, B and C in the port timer base connector, then terminals A, B and C in the starboard timer base connector. See **Figure 126**.

6. Crank the engine while observing the meter at each connection. Sensor coil output should be 0.2 volt or more.

   a. If output is 0.2 volt at each connection, continue at Step 7.

   b. If output is less than 0.2 volt, inspect the timer base wiring and connections and repair as necessary. If the wiring and connec-

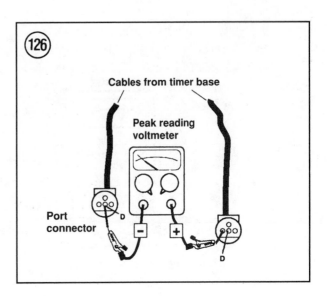

126

Cables from timer base

Peak reading voltmeter

Port connector

tors are in acceptable condition, continue at *Sensor Coil Resistance Test*.

7. Connect the D terminal in the port timer base terminal to the D terminal in the port engine harness connector using a jumper lead. See **Figure 127**.

8. Connect the D terminal in the starboard timer base terminal to the D terminal in the starboard engine harness connector using a jumper lead. See **Figure 127**.

9. Connect the black PRV test lead to a good engine ground. Alternately, connect the red test lead to terminals A, B and C in the starboard timer base connector, then terminals A, B, C in the port timer base terminal. Crank the engine while observing the meter at each connection.

   a. If output is 1.2 volts or more, continue at *Power Pack Output Test*.

   b. If output is less than 1.2 volts, inspect the timer base wiring and connectors and repair as necessary. If the wiring and connectors are in acceptable condition, continue at *Sensor Coil Resistance Test*.

Sensor Coil Resistance Test

Because resistance generally increases with temperature, perform resistance tests with the engine cold (room temperature). Resistance tests on hot components will indicate increased resistance and may result in unnecessary parts replacement without solving the basic problem. The ohmmeter should be calibrated on the R × 1000 or high-ohm scale when checking for a grounded condition.

NOTE
*Ohmmeter polarity must be determined before proceeding with this test. To do so, calibrate the meter on the R × 100 or low-ohm scale. Connect the leads to a known-good diode as shown in **Figure 128**, then reverse the leads. If the first connection indicated very low resistance (zero ohm), and the second connection indicated very high resistance (infinity),*

the ohmmeter red lead is positive (+). If the opposite result is noted, reverse the ohmmeter leads so the red lead is positive (+).

1. Calibrate the ohmmeter on the appropriate scale.

2. Connect the red (positive) ohmmeter lead to terminal D in the port timer base connector. See **Figure 129**.

3. Alternately, connect the black ohmmeter lead to terminals A, B and C in the port timer base terminal, then terminals A, B and C in the star-

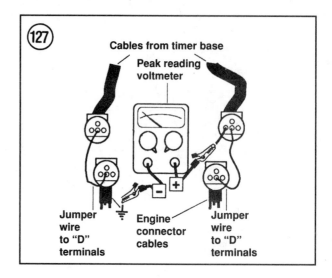

Cables from timer base
Peak reading voltmeter
Jumper wire to "D" terminals
Engine connector cables
Jumper wire to "D" terminals

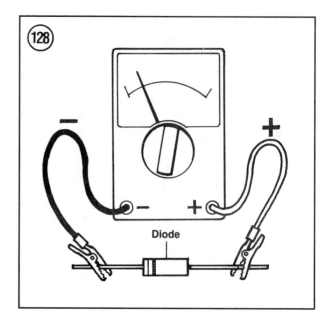

Diode

board timer base terminal. Note the meter at each connection.

NOTE
The sensor coil resistance specifications in Step 4 and Step 6 are based on the use of a Stevens Model AT-101 or a Merc-O-Tronic Model M-700 ohmmeter. Resistance measured with an ohmmeter of another manufacturer may be different. Internal timer base components may cause sensor coil resistance readings to vary depending on individual ohmmeter impedance. Resistance readings may be higher or lower, however, they should be consistent.

4. If using a Stevens Model AT-101 ohmmeter, sensor coil resistance should be 330-390 ohms. If using a Merc-O-Tronic Model M-700 ohmmeter, sensor coil resistance should be 870-1070 ohms. If resistance is not as specified, replace the timer base assembly as outlined in Chapter Seven.

5. Next, connect the red ohmmeter lead to terminal D in the port timer base connector. Connect the black ohmmeter lead to terminal D in

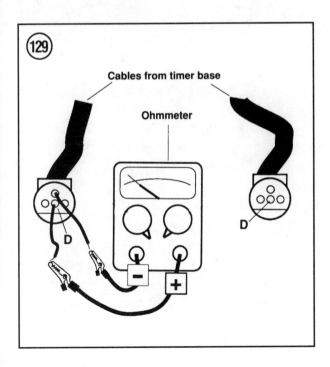

the starboard timer base connector. See **Figure 129**.

6. Resistance should be 200-260 ohms. If not, replace the timer base assembly as outlined in Chapter Seven.

7. Next, connect the ohmmeter between a good engine ground and alternately to each sensor coil terminal in the port and starboard timer base connector.

8. No continuity should be noted at each connection. If continuity is noted, locate and repair the grounded timer base wire(s) or replace the timer base assembly as necessary. See Chapter Seven.

9. If testing is complete, reconnect the timer base terminals.

Power Pack Output Test

WARNING
To prevent accidental starting, remove the spark plug leads from the spark plugs. Securely ground the plug leads to the power head, or connect the leads to a spark tester.

A peak reading voltmeter (PRV) and Stevens load adapter (part No. PL-88) are necessary to test power pack output.

1. Disconnect the primary wires from each ignition coil.

2. Connect the primary wire from the No. 1 coil to the red lead of the PL-88 load adapter. Connect the black load adapter lead to a good engine ground. See **Figure 130**.

3. Set the PRV selector switches to POS and 500.

4. Connect the red PRV test lead to the red load adapter lead. Connect the black PRV test lead to a good engine ground.

5. Crank the engine while observing the meter. Power pack output should be 100 volts or more.

6. Repeat Steps 2-5 on the primary wire to each remaining ignition coil. Output should be 100 volts or more at each primary wire.

---

(129)

Cables from timer base

Ohmmeter

D

D

a. If output is 100 volts or more at each primary wire, test ignition coil resistance as outlined in this chapter.

b. If no output is noted at one primary wire, replace the power pack. See Chapter Seven.

7. If testing is complete, remove the PL-88 load adapter and reconnect the primary wires to the ignition coils. Make sure the orange/blue primary wires are attached to the top ignition coils, the orange primary wires are attached to the center ignition coils and the orange/green primary wires are attached to the bottom ignition coils.

Running Output Test

A peak reading voltmeter (PRV) and Stevens Terminal Extenders (part No. TS-77) are necessary to perform the running output test. Running the outboard under load is often necessary to locate the cause of an intermittent malfunction or high-speed miss, especially if good spark is noted during the *Total Output Test*. Remove the propeller and install the correct test wheel (**Table 8**) prior to performing the test.

> *CAUTION*
> *The outboard motor must be supplied with adequate cooling water while running. Install the motor in a test tank or on a boat in the water. Do not attempt to run the motor at high speed while connected to a flushing device.*

1. Remove the primary wires from each ignition coil.

2. Install a Stevens Terminal Extender (part No. TS-77) on each coil primary terminal. Connect the primary wires to the terminal extenders. Make sure the orange/blue primary wires are connected to the top ignition coils, the orange primary wires are attached to the center ignition coils and the orange/green primary wires are attached to the bottom ignition coils.

3. Set the PRV selector switches to POS and 500.

4. Connect the red PRV test lead to the terminal extender attached to the No. 1 ignition coil. Connect the black test lead to a good engine ground.

5. Start the engine and run at the speed at which the malfunction is evident while observing the meter. Running output should be 130 volts or more.

6. Repeat Step 4 and Step 5 with the red PRV test lead connected to the terminal extender on each remaining ignition coil.

a. If output is less than 130 volts on one or more ignition coil, test charge coil as described in this chapter. If the charge coil is in acceptable condition, replace the power pack.

b. If no output (zero volt) is noted at one or more ignition coil, test the sensor coils as described in this chapter. If the sensor coils

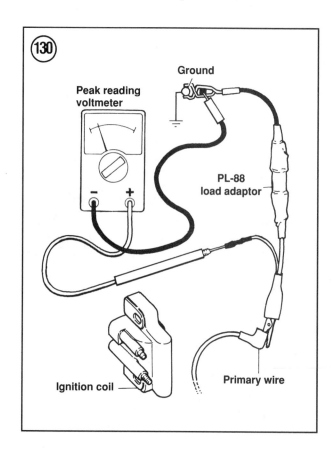

are in acceptable condition, replace the power pack.

7. If testing is complete, remove the terminal extenders and reconnect the primary wires to their respective ignition coils. Make sure the orange/blue wires are attached to the top coils, the orange wires are attached to the center coils and the orange/green wires are attached to the bottom coils.

Ignition Coil Resistance Test

Because resistance generally increases with temperature, perform resistance tests with the engine at room temperature (70° F [21° C]). Resistance tests on hot components will indicate increased resistance and may result in unnecessary parts replacement without solving the basic problem. Ignition coil resistance can be checked without coil removal.

1. Remove the primary wires and the spark plug wires from the ignition coil assembly.

2. Calibrate the ohmmeter on the R × 1 or low-ohm scale.

3. To check primary winding resistance, connect the black ohmmeter lead to a good engine ground or to the coil ground tab if the coil is removed. Connect the red ohmmeter lead to the coil primary terminal.

4. Primary resistance should be 0.05-0.15 ohm.

5. To check secondary winding resistance, calibrate the ohmmeter on the R × 100 or high-ohm scale. Connect the red ohmmeter lead to the coil primary terminal and the black lead to the spark plug terminal.

6. Secondary resistance should be 225-325 ohms.

7. Repeat Steps 3-6 on each remaining coil.

8. Replace the coil if resistance is not as specified.

9. To check the spark plug leads, calibrate the ohmmeter on R × 1 or low-ohm scale. Connect the ohmmeter to each end of the lead and note

the meter. The resistance should be nearly zero ohm.

S.L.O.W. Operation and Testing

All models are equipped with the speed limiting overheat warning (S.L.O.W.) system. The system is designed to limit engine speed to approximately 2500 rpm if engine temperature exceeds 203° F (95° C). To deactivate S.L.O.W., throttle back to idle, allow the engine to cool to 162° F (72° C), then stop the engine.

A blocking diode located in the engine wiring harness is used to isolate the S.L.O.W. warning system from the other warning systems. Should the blocking diode become shorted, the S.L.O.W. function will remain activated regardless of engine temperature.

The S.L.O.W. function is activated by a signal from the port or starboard engine temperature switch. The temperature switches are located in the top of each cylinder head.

The following conditions will cause the S.L.O.W. function to remain activated:

  a. Engine overheated.
  b. Engine temperature switch or switch wire shorted to ground.
  c. Blocking diode closed or shorted to ground.
  d. Defective power pack.

The following conditions will prevent the S.L.O.W. function from operating:

  a. Engine temperature switch or switch wire open.
  b. Defective power pack.
  c. Defective power coil.

If the S.L.O.W function is inoperative, test the temperature switches and S.L.O.W. system as follows.

1. Install the outboard motor in a test tank with the correct test wheel installed. See **Table 8**.

2. Connect an accurate tachometer according to the manufacturer's instructions.

3. Disconnect the port and starboard tan/green temperature switch wires from the engine harness tan wires.

4. Start the engine and run at approximately 3500 rpm.

5. Connect the engine harness end of the port tan wire to a clean engine ground and note the engine speed.

6. Throttle back to idle speed, then stop the engine.

7. Repeat Step 4 and Step 5 using the starboard tan wire.

   a. If engine speed reduces to approximately 2500 rpm when each tan wire is grounded, test the temperature switch as described in this chapter.

   b. If engine speed reduces when one temperature switch tan wire is grounded, but not the other, check the engine wiring harness and connectors and repair as necessary.

   c. If engine speed does not reduce as specified when either tan wire is grounded, continue at Step 8.

8. Loosen the power pack and disconnect the orange and orange/black power coil wires from the terminal block.

9. Calibrate an ohmmeter on the R × 1000 or high-ohm scale.

10. Connect the ohmmeter between a good engine ground and alternately to each power coil wire (orange and orange/black). See **Figure 131**.

11. No continuity should be present between ground and either power coil wire.

   a. If continuity is noted, either the power coil or power coil wire(s) is shorted to ground. Locate and repair the shorted wire(s) or replace the stator assembly as necessary.

   b. If no continuity is noted, continue at Step 12.

12. Calibrate the ohmmeter on the appropriate scale.

13. Connect the ohmmeter between the orange and orange/black power coil wires. See **Figure 132**.

   a. If power coil resistance is within 86-106 ohms, replace the power pack.

   b. If power coil resistance is not within 86-106 ohms, replace the stator assembly. See Chapter Seven.

CAUTION
Do not start the engine with the orange and orange/black power coil wires disconnected.

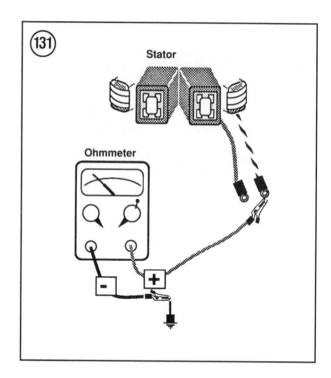

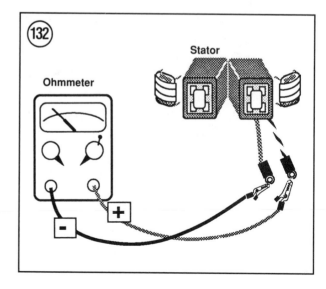

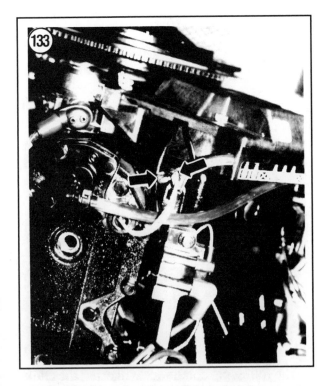

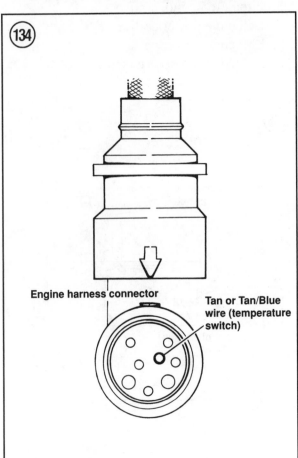

Engine harness connector

Tan or Tan/Blue wire (temperature switch)

14. If testing is complete, reconnect the orange and orange/black power coil wires to the terminal block. Reinstall the power pack.

Blocking Diode Test

A blocking diode is used to prevent the S.L.O.W. function from being activated by other engine warning horn systems. The blocking diode is located in the engine wiring harness.

If the S.L.O.W function is activated by the no oil, low oil or fuel vacuum warning signal, test the engine harness blocking diode as follows.

1. Disconnect the red engine harness connector.
2. Disconnect the port and starboard temperature switches from the engine harness (**Figure 133**, typical).
3. Calibrate the ohmmeter on the R × 1000 or high-ohm scale.
4. Connect the ohmmeter between either temperature switch tan wire (engine harness side) and the tan wire terminal in the red engine harness connector. See **Figure 134**.
5. Note the ohmmeter reading, then reverse the leads.
6. A high reading (no continuity) in one direction and a low reading (continuity) in the other should be noted. If both readings are low, the diode is shorted (closed) and must be replaced. If both readings are high, the diode is open and must be replaced.

QuikStart Operation and Testing

All models are equipped with QuikStart electronic starting system. The QuikStart circuit automatically advances the ignition timing when the engine temperature is less than 93-99° F (34-37° C) to improve engine warm-up. The ignition timing remains advanced until engine temperature exceeds approximately 93-99° F (34-37° C). In addition, QuikStart also advances the ignition timing for approximately 5 seconds each time the engine is started, regardless of engine temperature. To prevent power head damage due to detonation, the power pack disables QuikStart at engine speeds exceeding approximately 1100 rpm, regardless of engine temperature.

To determine if QuikStart is functioning properly, proceed as follows:

1. Remove the propeller and install the correct test wheel (**Table 8**).

2. Place the outboard motor in a suitable test tank. Start the engine and warm it to normal operating temperature. Engine temperature must be above 96° F (36° C) before running this test.

NOTE
Make sure engine synchronization and linkage adjustments are correctly set as outlined in Chapter Five.

3. Place temporary marks on the flywheel indicating TDC for all cylinders.

4. Disconnect the white/black temperature switch wire between the power pack and the port temperature switch. See **Figure 135**, typical.

5. Attach an accurate tachometer to the power head according to the manufacturer's instructions.

6. Attach a timing light to the No. 1 cylinder according to the manufacturer's instructions.

7. Start the engine and shift into forward gear. Idle speed *must not* exceed 900 rpm in gear during this test. Adjust idle speed if necessary.

8. Observe the flywheel with the timing light. The No. 1 cylinder TDC mark should be near the timing pointer, indicating QuikStart is functioning.

9. While observing the timing marks, momentarily connect the white/black temperature switch wire. The timing mark should shift to the left approximately 1 in. (25.4 mm) when the wire is connected, indicating that QuikStart has returned the timing to the normal setting.

NOTE
*The engine **must** be stopped before testing each remaining cylinder to reset the QuikStart circuit.*

10. Stop the engine. Repeat Steps 6-9 for each remaining cylinder.
   a. If one or more cylinders do not react as specified (Step 9), replace the timer base assembly. See Chapter Seven.
   b. If no cylinders react as specified (Step 9), refer to *QuikStart inoperative* in this chapter.
   c. If all cylinders react as specified (Step 9), the QuikStart circuit is functioning properly.

QuikStart inoperative

The following conditions will cause the QuikStart circuit to be inoperative:
   a. Defective power coil.
   b. Defective power pack.
   c. Defective timer base (sensor coil[s]).

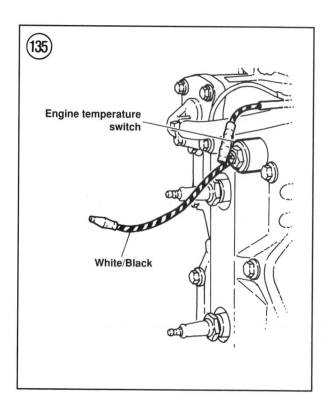

Engine temperature switch

White/Black

d. An open circuit in the yellow/red wire between the power pack and starter solenoid or key switch.

Troubleshoot the QuikStart circuit as follows:

1. Disconnect the white/black wire between the port temperature switch and power pack (**Figure 135**, typical).

2. Calibrate the ohmmeter on the R × 1000 or high-ohm scale.

NOTE
Engine temperature must be less than 89° F (32° C) in Step 3.

3. Connect the ohmmeter between the temperature switch white/black wire and a good engine ground. The ohmmeter should indicate high resistance (infinity) with engine temperature less than 89° F (32° C).

a. If the meter indicates low resistance (continuity) in Step 3, test the temperature switch as described in this chapter.

b. If the meter indicates high resistance in Step 3, continue at Step 4.

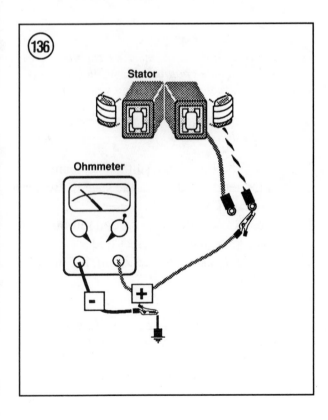

4. Loosen the power pack and disconnect the orange and orange/black power coil wires from the terminal block.

5. Calibrate the ohmmeter on the R × 1000 or high-ohm scale.

6. Connect the ohmmeter between a good engine ground and alternately to the power coil orange and orange/black wires. See **Figure 136**. No continuity should be present between either power coil wire and ground. If continuity is noted, repair the shorted power coil wire or replace the stator assembly as necessary. See Chapter Seven.

7. Calibrate the ohmmeter on the appropriate scale.

8. Connect the ohmmeter between the power coil orange and orange/black wires. See **Figure 132**.

a. If power coil resistance is within 86-106 ohms, replace the power pack.

b. If power coil resistance is not within 86-106 ohms, replace the stator assembly.

9. If testing is complete, reconnect all circuits disconnected during this procedure.

QuikStart always on

The following conditions can cause the QuikStart circuit to remain on constantly:

a. Engine overcooling (not warming up to operating temperature).

b. Defective temperature switch.

c. Defective power pack.

d. Defective starter solenoid or key switch.

If QuikStart remains on constantly when the engine is operated above 1100 rpm, the power pack is defective and must be replaced. If QuikStart remains on constantly regardless of time on and engine temperature, when the engine is operated *below* 1100 rpm, continue as follows:

1. Check for a defective starter solenoid or key switch, which may cause a small voltage to bleed into the yellow/red wire leading to the power

pack. This small voltage can activate the Quik-Start circuit.

2. Check for a defective or damaged port side engine temperature switch as described in this chapter.

3. Check for an open circuit or loose or corroded connections in the white/black power pack wire.

4. Check the engine for an overcooling condition as described in this chapter.

5. If no other problems are noted in Steps 1-4, replace the power pack. See Chapter Seven.

RPM Limiting Power Pack

Power packs marked "CDL" are equipped with an internal rpm limiting device designed to prevent power head damage from overspeeding. On models so equipped, the power pack interrupts ignition if engine speed exceeds 6700 rpm. Be certain the correct power pack is used if replacement is necessary.

CD6 OIS IGNITION SYSTEM TROUBLESHOOTING (60° 150 AND 175 HP MODELS)

The major components of the CD6 OIS (optical ignition system) used on 60° V6 models include the flywheel, 2 charge coils, power coil, optical timing sensor, timing wheel, 2 power packs, 3 dual-ignition coils, 2 temperature switches, shift switch and related wiring.

The charge coils and power coil are contained in the stator assembly and are not serviced separately. The power coil provides voltage for the operation of QuikStart, S.L.O.W., the timing sensor and other ignition functions. The timing sensor consists of 2 separate sensors. One sensor provides a signal for each revolution of the flywheel and is used to determine crankshaft position. The other sensor provides 6 supplemental timing signals and 1 additional signal to prevent the engine from running in reverse rotation. Both

power packs are contained in a 1-piece assembly and are not serviced separately.

If the outboard motor is very hard or impossible to start, begin the troubleshooting procedure at *Total Output Test*. If an ignition malfunction is causing an intermittent high-speed miss or erratic operation, refer to *Indexing Flywheel* and *Running Output Test*. Unless specified otherwise, perform the following ignition system tests in the sequence given. Skipping tests or jumping around the troubleshooting procedure can result in misleading results and unnecessary parts replacement. Test the entire ignition system—more than one component may be defective.

Indexing Flywheel

If the outboard motor runs erratically, or if a high speed miss is noted, the power pack may be defective. Internal power pack malfunctions can cause erratic ignition system operation. Perform the following procedure to ensure the power pack is firing at the correct time.

1. Remove the propeller and install the correct test wheel (**Table 8**).

CAUTION
The outboard motor must be supplied with adequate cooling water while running. Place the motor in a test tank or on a boat in the water. Do not attempt to run the motor at high speed while connected to a flushing device.

2. Place the outboard in a suitable test tank.

3. Start the motor and run at the speed at which the malfunction is evident.

4. Alternately connect an induction timing light to the spark plug wire to each cylinder. Note the timing marks adjacent to the timing pointer (A, **Figure 137**).

NOTE
*The cylinder numbers 2-6 are embossed in the timing wheel (B, **Figure 137**) along its outer periphery. The TDC mark on the timing grid represents the No. 1 cylinder.*

5. The timing light should indicate the cylinder number the timing light is connected to. For example, if the timing light is connected to the No. 2 spark plug wire, the No. 2 mark should be visible. In addition, the number should only appear near the timing pointer.

6. If a different cylinder number appears, or if the number jumps around or appears at other than the timing pointer, first make sure the primary ignition wires and spark plug wires are properly connected. The primary wires must be connected as follows:

a. Orange/blue wires—top ignition coil assembly.

b. Orange wires—center ignition coil assembly.

c. Orange/green wires—bottom ignition coil assembly.

If the primary wires and spark plug wires are properly connected, replace the power pack.

Total Output Test

The total output test will determine if the ignition system is capable of delivering adequate spark to the spark plugs. Perform the output test with the spark plugs installed and properly tightened.

1. Disconnect the spark plug leads from the spark plugs.

2. Mount a suitable spark tester on the engine and connect the spark plug leads to the tester. See **Figure 114**. Make sure the spark tester mounting clip is secured to a good clean engine ground.

3. Adjust the spark tester spark gap to 7/16 in. (11.1 mm).

4. Connect the cutoff clip and lanyard to the emergency stop switch, if so equipped.

> *NOTE*
> *If acceptable spark is noted at each spark gap during the total output test, but the engine pops or backfires during starting or running, the ignition system may be out of time. Be sure the orange/blue primary ignition wires are connected to the top ignition coils, the orange wires are connected to the center ignition coils and the orange/green wires are connected to the bottom ignition coils. Make sure the spark plug leads are routed correctly. Make sure the timing wheel is correctly located, the timing sensor is operating properly and the timing sensor cover is properly located. Make sure the timing and throttle linkage are properly synchronized.*

5. Crank the engine while observing the spark tester.

a. If acceptable spark is noted at each spark gap and the outboard runs good, the problem is not in the ignition system. Check the fuel and fuel delivery systems.

b. If acceptable spark is noted at each spark gap, but the outboard has a high-speed miss, continue at *Running Output Test*.

c. If acceptable spark is noted at each spark gap, but the outboard does not start, continue at *Power Coil Output Test*.

d. If no spark is noted at one spark gap, continue at *Power Pack Output Test*.

e. If no spark is noted at 3 spark gaps (1991 models), continue at *Charge Coil Output Test*.

f. If no spark is noted at cylinders 1, 3 and 5 (1992-on models), continue at *Shift Switch Test*.

g. If no spark is noted at all spark gaps, continue at *Stop Circuit Test*. Do not remove the spark tester.

Stop Circuit Test

The following test eliminates the stop circuit as a potential cause of an ignition malfunction. The key switch and lanyard emergency stop switch are connected to the power pack through the engine wiring harness. Activating the stop circuit shorts power pack output to ground, which disables the ignition system and stops the engine.

1. Disconnect the 5-pin Packard connector between the power pack and key switch. See **Figure 138**.
2. Crank the engine while observing the spark tester.
   a. If spark is now noted at each spark gap, the problem is in the stop circuit. Continue at *Key Switch Ohmmeter Test*.
   b. If no spark is noted at all spark gaps, continue at *Timing Sensor Test*.
3. Remove the spark tester. Reconnect the spark plug wires to the spark plugs.
4. Reconnect the 5-pin Packard connector.

Key Switch Ohmmeter Test

If the engine will not stop when the key switch is turned OFF, test the key switch as outlined in this chapter.

If the engine will not stop when the clip is removed from the emergency stop switch, replace the emergency stop switch.

If the engine will not stop when the key switch is turned OFF and the clip is removed from the emergency stop switch, check for an open circuit in the black/yellow, black/orange and black wires between the power pack and key switch.

1. Disconnect the 5-pin Packard connector (**Figure 138**) between the power pack and key switch.

2. Connect the 5-pin Packard test adapter from OMC Ignition Test Kit (part No. 434017) to the engine wiring harness connector. If the test adapter is not available, insert suitable jumper leads into the black/yellow wire terminals in the engine harness connector.

3. Install the emergency stop switch clip and lanyard, if so equipped.

4. Calibrate the ohmmeter on the R × 1000 or high-ohm scale.

5. Connect the ohmmeter between a good engine ground and one of the two black/yellow engine harness wires.

   a. With the key switch OFF, the ohmmeter should indicate continuity (low resistance).

   b. With the key switch ON, the ohmmeter should indicate no continuity (high resistance).

6. Repeat Step 5 with the ohmmeter connected to the remaining black/yellow wire.

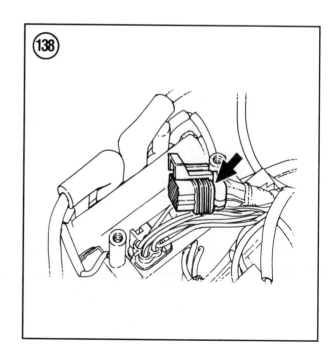
(138)

NOTE
If both ohmmeter tests are good, the blocking diode in the power pack is shorted. Replace the power pack as described in Chapter Seven.

7. If continuity (low resistance) is noted during the key ON test (Steps 4 and 5), disconnect the wiring harness black/yellow wires from the key switch M terminal and note the meter.

a. If the ohmmeter now indicates no continuity, replace the key switch assembly.

b. If continuity is still present, continue at Step 8.

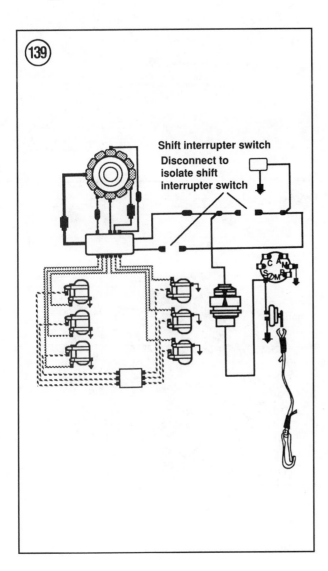

8. Disconnect the emergency stop switch wire from the engine harness black/yellow wire at the key switch and note the meter.

a. If the ohmmeter now indicates no continuity, replace the emergency stop switch.

b. If continuity is still present, check the engine wiring harness for a short in the stop circuit.

9. Remove the 5-pin Packard test adapter. Reconnect the 5-pin connector and all other circuits disconnected during this test.

Shift Switch Test

The shift switch momentarily interrupts ignition to cylinders 1, 3 and 5 when the outboard motor is shifted into or out of gear. This power interruption causes the outboard to shift easier.

Perform the following test if no spark is noted on cylinders 1, 3 and 5 during the *Total Output Test.*

1. Connect a spark tester as outlined under *Total Output Test.*

2. Isolate the shift switch by disconnecting the black/yellow wire at the two connectors between the power pack and shift switch. See **Figure 139**.

3. Crank the engine while observing the spark tester.

a. If cylinders 1, 3 and 5 now have good spark, continue at Step 4.

b. If cylinders 1, 3 and 5 still do not have spark, continue at *Charge Coil Output Test.*

4. Calibrate an ohmmeter on the R × 1000 or high-ohm scale.

5. Connect the ohmmeter between the shift switch black/yellow wire (A, **Figure 140**) and a good engine ground. The ohmmeter should indicate no continuity (high resistance). If not, replace the shift switch and wiring harness.

6. Activate the shift switch by pushing downward on the shift cable pin and note the meter. The ohmmeter should now indicate continuity (low resistance). If not, replace the shift switch and wiring harness.

7. Next, connect the ohmmeter between both shift switch 1-pin terminals (A and B, **Figure 140**). Note the meter, then reverse the ohmmeter leads. No continuity (high resistance) should be noted in one reading and continuity (low resistance) should be noted in the other. If continuity, or no continuity is noted in both readings, the blocking diode in the wiring harness is defective. Replace the shift switch and harness assembly.

8. If the shift switch tests good, reconnect the 1-pin connectors and continue at *Charge Coil Output Test*.

Power Coil Output Test

The power coil provides voltage to operate QuikStart, S.L.O.W., the timing sensor and other ignition functions. Should the power coil fail, the outboard motor will not start.

A peak-reading voltmeter (PRV) is necessary to perform this test.

1. Disconnect the 6-pin Packard connector (**Figure 141**) between the stator and power pack.

2. Connect the 6-pin Packard test adapter from OMC Ignition Test Kit (part No. 434017) to the 6-pin stator connector. If the test adapter is not available, insert suitable jumper leads into the orange and orange/black wire terminals in the stator connector.

3. Set the PRV selector switches to POS and 500.

4. Connect one PRV test lead to a good engine ground. Alternately connect the remaining test lead to the orange and orange/black stator wires in the 6-pin stator connector.

5. Crank the engine at each connection and note the meter.

   a. Any voltage reading indicates the power coil or power coil wire(s) is shorted to ground. Locate and repair the shorted wire(s) or replace the stator assembly as outlined in Chapter Seven.

   b. If no voltage is noted, continue at Step 6.

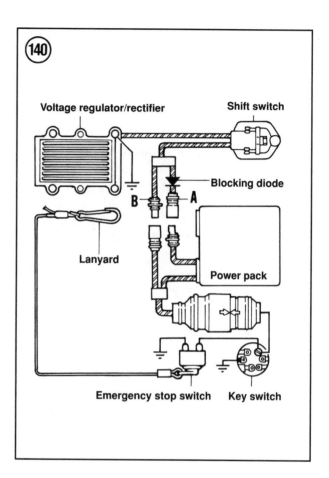

(140)

Voltage regulator/rectifier   Shift switch

Blocking diode

B   A

Lanyard

Power pack

Emergency stop switch   Key switch

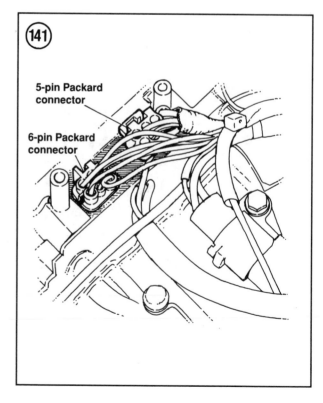

(141)

5-pin Packard connector

6-pin Packard connector

6. Connect the black PRV test lead to the orange stator wire. Connect the red test lead to the orange/black stator wire.

7. Crank the engine while observing the meter. Power coil output should be 50 volts or more.

a. If output is 50 volts or more, remove the 6-pin Packard test adapter and reconnect the 6-pin connector. Continue at *Timing Sensor Test*.

b. If output is less than 50 volts, inspect the stator wiring and connectors and repair as necessary. If the wiring and connectors are in acceptable condition, continue at *Power Coil Resistance Test*.

Power Coil Resistance Test

Because resistance generally increases with temperature, perform resistance tests with the

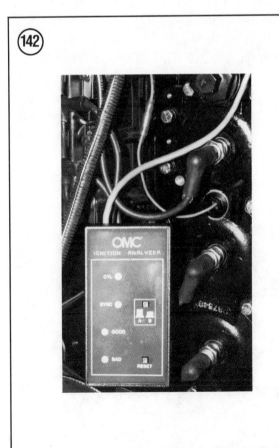

engine cold (room temperature). Resistance tests on hot components will indicate increased resistance and may result in unnecessary parts replacement without solving the basic problem. The ohmmeter should be calibrated on the R × 1000 or high-ohm scale when checking for a grounded condition.

1. Calibrate an ohmmeter on the appropriate scale.

2. Connect the ohmmeter between the orange and orange/black wire terminals in the 6-pin stator connector.

3. Resistance should be 90-110 ohms. If not, replace the stator assembly as outlined in Chapter Seven.

4. Next, connect the ohmmeter between a good engine ground and alternately to the orange and orange/black stator terminals.

5. Any continuity between ground and either stator wire indicates the power coil or power coil wire(s) is shorted to ground. Locate and repair the shorted wire(s) or replace the stator assembly as outlined in Chapter Seven.

6. Remove the test adapter or jumper leads and reconnect the 6-pin stator-to-power pack connector.

Timing Sensor Test

NOTE
Bright light can disrupt the operation of the optical timing sensor. Avoid running the outboard in bright sunlight with the timing wheel cover removed. Do not aim a timing light directly at the timing sensor.

OMC Ignition Analyzer part No. 434017 (**Figure 142**) is necessary to test the optical timing sensor. The sensor can not be tested using conventional test equipment. If the ignition analyzer is not available, have the timing sensor tested by an OMC dealership or other qualified marine specialist.

1. Remove the voltage regulator/rectifier cover.

2. Disconnect the timing sensor connector (**Figure 143**) from the timing sensor.

3. Attach the ignition analyzer (part No. 434017) to the timing sensor (**Figure 144**).

4. Place the analyzer switch to position A.

5. Press the analyzer RESET button.

6. Crank the engine a minimum of 3 revolutions while observing the meter.

   a. If the GOOD indicator light flashes while the engine is being cranked, continue at *Power Pack Output Test*.

   b. If the BAD indicator light flashes while the engine is being cranked, inspect the condition of the timing wheel. If the timing wheel is good, replace the timing sensor as outlined in Chapter Seven.

7. Remove the ignition analyzer and reconnect the wiring harness to the timing sensor. Reinstall the voltage regulator/rectifier cover.

Charge Coil Output Test

Perform the following test to ensure the charge coil is capable of producing sufficient voltage to charge the capacitor properly in the power pack and to make sure the charge coil or charge coil wiring is not shorted to ground. A peak reading voltmeter (PRV) is necessary to perform this test.

1. Disconnect the 6-pin Packard connector between the stator and power pack. See **Figure 141**.

2. Connect the 6-pin Packard test adapter from the OMC Test Kit (part No. 434017) to the 6-pin stator connector. If the test adapter is not available, insert suitable jumper leads into the brown and brown/yellow terminals in the stator connector.

3. Set the PRV selector switches to POS and 500.

4. Connect one PRV test lead to a good engine ground. Alternately connect the remaining test lead to the brown and brown/yellow stator wires.

Crank the engine while observing the meter at each connection.

5. Move the jumper leads to the brown/black and brown/white terminals in the stator connector.

6. Connect the PRV test leads between a good engine ground and alternately to the brown/black and brown/white stator wires. Crank the engine while observing the meter at each connection.

   a. Any voltage reading indicates the charge coil or charge coil wire(s) is shorted to ground. Locate and repair the short as necessary or replace the stator assembly as outlined in Chapter Seven.

   b. If no voltage reading is noted, continue at Step 7.

7. Connect the black PRV test lead to the brown stator wire. Connect the red test lead to the brown/yellow stator wire.

8. Crank the engine while observing the meter. Charge coil output should be 150 volts or more.

9. Move the black PRV test lead to the brown/black stator wire and the red test lead to the brown/white stator wire.

10. Crank the engine while observing the meter. Charge coil output should be 150 volts or more.

   a. If output is 150 volts or more, remove the 6-pin Packard adapter (or jumper leads),

reconnect the stator connector and continue at *Power Pack Output Test* in this chapter.

b. If output is less than 150 volts, inspect the stator wiring and connector and repair as necessary. If the wires and connector are in acceptable condition, continue at *Charge Coil Resistance Test.*

Charge Coil Resistance Test

Because resistance generally increases with temperature, perform resistance tests with the engine cold (room temperature). Resistance tests on hot components will indicate increased resistance and may result in unnecessary parts replacement without solving the basic problem.

1. Calibrate an ohmmeter on the appropriate scale.
2. Connect the ohmmeter between the brown and brown/yellow terminals in the stator 6-pin connector.
3. Resistance should be 495-605 ohms. If not, replace the stator assembly (Chapter Seven).
4. Connect the ohmmeter between the brown/black and brown/white terminals in the stator connector.

5. Resistance should be 495-605 ohms. If not, replace the stator assembly (Chapter Seven).
6. Next, calibrate the ohmmeter on the R × 1000 or high-ohm scale.
7. Connect the ohmmeter between a good engine ground and alternately to the brown, brown/yellow, brown/black and brown/white terminals in the stator connector.

a. No continuity should be present between ground and any stator terminals.

b. If continuity is present, the charge coil(s) or charge coil wire(s) is shorted to ground. Locate and repair the shorted wire(s) or replace the stator assembly (Chapter Seven) as necessary.

8. Remove the 6-pin Packard test adapter (or jumper leads) and reconnect the stator-to-power pack connector.

Power Pack Output Test

WARNING
To prevent accidental starting, remove the spark plug leads from the spark plugs. Securely ground the plug leads to the power head, or connect the leads to a spark tester.

A peak reading voltmeter (PRV) and Stevens load adapter (part No. PL-88) are necessary to test power pack output.

1. Remove the ignition cover and disconnect the primary wires from each ignition coil.
2. Connect the primary wire from the No. 1 coil to the red lead of the PL-88 load adapter. Connect the black load adapter lead to a good engine ground. See **Figure 130**.
3. Set the PRV selector switches to POS and 500.
4. Connect the red PRV test lead to the red load adapter lead. Connect the black PRV test lead to a good engine ground.
5. Crank the engine while observing the meter. Power pack output should be 100 volts or more.

6. Repeat Steps 2-5 on the primary wire to each remaining ignition coil. Output should be 100 volts or more at each primary wire.

  a. If output is 100 volts or more at each primary wire, test ignition coil resistance as outlined in this chapter.

  b. If no output is noted at one primary wire, replace the power pack. See Chapter Seven.

7. If testing is complete, remove the PL-88 load adapter and reconnect the primary wires to the ignition coils. Make sure the orange/blue primary wires are attached to the top ignition coils, the orange primary wires are attached to the center ignition coils and the orange/green primary wires are attached to the bottom ignition coils. Reinstall the ignition cover.

Running Output Test

A peak reading voltmeter (PRV) and Stevens Terminal Extenders (part No. TS-77) are necessary to perform the running output test. Running the outboard under load is often necessary to locate the cause of an intermittent malfunction or high-speed miss, especially if good spark is noted during the *Total Output Test*. Remove the propeller and install the correct test wheel (**Table 8**) prior to performing the test.

CAUTION
The outboard motor must be supplied with adequate cooling water while running. Install the motor in a test tank or on a boat in the water. Do not attempt to run the motor at high speed while connected to a flushing device.

1. Remove the ignition cover and remove the primary wires from each ignition coil.
2. Install a Stevens Terminal Extender (part No. TS-77) on each coil primary terminal. Connect the primary wires to the terminal extenders. Make sure the orange/blue primary wires are connected to the top ignition coils, the orange primary wires are attached to the center ignition

coils and the orange/green primary wires are attached to the bottom ignition coils.
3. Set the PRV selector switches to POS and 500.
4. Connect the red PRV test lead to the terminal extender attached to the No. 1 ignition coil. Connect the black test lead to a good engine ground.
5. Start the engine and run at the speed at which the malfunction is evident while observing the meter. Running output should be 130 volts or more.
6. Repeat Steps 4 and 5 with the red PRV test lead connected to the terminal extender on each remaining ignition coil.

  a. If output is less than 130 volts on one or more ignition coil, test charge coils as described in this chapter.

  b. If no output (zero volt) is noted at one or more ignition coil, test the power pack output as outlined in this chapter.

9. If testing is complete, remove the terminal extenders and reconnect the primary wires to their respective ignition coils. Make sure the orange/blue wires are attached to the top coils, the orange wires are attached to the center coils and the orange/green wires are attached to the bottom coils. Reinstall the ignition cover.

Ignition Coil Resistance Test

Because resistance generally increases with temperature, perform resistance tests with the engine at room temperature (70° F [21° C]). Resistance tests on hot components will indicate increased resistance and may result in unnecessary parts replacement without solving the basic problem. Ignition coil resistance can be checked without coil removal. Note that each ignition coil assembly contains 2 separate coils.
1. Remove the primary wires and the spark plug wires from the ignition coil assembly.
2. Calibrate the ohmmeter on the R × 1 or low-ohm scale.

3. To check primary winding resistance, connect the black ohmmeter lead to a good engine ground or to the coil ground tab if the coil is removed. Connect the red ohmmeter lead to the coil primary terminal.

4. Primary resistance should be 0.05-0.15 ohm.

5. To check secondary winding resistance, calibrate the ohmmeter on the R × 100 or high-ohm scale. Connect the red ohmmeter lead to the coil primary terminal and the black lead to the spark plug terminal.

6. Secondary resistance should be 225-325 ohms.

7. Repeat Steps 3-6 on each remaining coil.

8. Replace the coil if resistance is not as specified.

9. To check the spark plug leads, calibrate the ohmmeter on R × 1 or low-ohm scale. Connect the ohmmeter to each end of the lead and note the meter. The resistance should be nearly zero ohm.

S.L.O.W. Operation and Testing

All models are equipped with the speed limiting overheat warning (S.L.O.W.) system. The system is designed to limit engine speed to approximately 2500 rpm if engine temperature exceeds 240° F (114° C). To deactivate S.L.O.W., throttle back to idle, allow the engine to cool to 207° F (110° C), then stop the engine.

A blocking diode located in the engine wiring harness is used to isolate the S.L.O.W. warning system from the other warning systems. Should the blocking diode become shorted, the S.L.O.W. function will remain activated regardless of engine temperature.

The S.L.O.W. function is activated by a signal from the port or starboard engine temperature switch. The temperature switches are located in the top of each cylinder head.

The following conditions will cause the S.L.O.W. function to remain activated:

   a. Engine overheated.

   b. Engine temperature switch or switch wire shorted to ground.

   c. Blocking diode closed or shorted to ground.

   d. Defective power pack.

The following conditions will prevent the S.L.O.W. function from operating:

   a. Engine temperature switch or switch wire open.

   b. Defective power pack.

   c. Defective power coil.

If the S.L.O.W function is inoperative, test the temperature switches and S.L.O.W. system as follows.

1. Install the outboard motor in a test tank with the correct test wheel installed. See **Table 8**.

2. Connect an accurate tachometer according to the manufacturer's instructions.

3. Disconnect the port and starboard tan/blue temperature switch wires from the engine harness tan wires.

4. Start the engine and run at approximately 3500 rpm.

5. Connect the engine harness end of the port tan wire to a clean engine ground and note the engine speed.

6. Throttle back to idle speed, then stop the engine.

7. Repeat Step 4 and 5 using the starboard tan wire.

   a. If engine speed reduces to approximately 2500 rpm when each tan wire is grounded, test the temperature switches as described in this chapter.

   b. If engine speed reduces when one temperature switch tan wire is grounded, but not the other, check the engine wiring harness and connectors and repair as necessary.

   c. If engine speed does not reduce as specified when either tan wire is grounded, inspect the temperature switch wires and connectors and power pack wires and connectors and repair as necessary. If all wires and connectors are in acceptable condition, replace the power pack (Chapter Seven).

Blocking Diode Test

A blocking diode is used to prevent the S.L.O.W. function from being activated by other engine warning horn systems. The blocking diode is located in the engine wiring harness.

If the S.L.O.W function is activated by the no oil, low oil or fuel vacuum warning signal, test the engine harness blocking diode as follows:

1. Disconnect the red engine harness connector.

2. Disconnect the port and starboard temperature switches from the engine harness (**Figure 145**, typical).

3. Calibrate the ohmmeter on the R × 1000 or high-ohm scale.

4. Connect the ohmmeter between either temperature switch tan or tan/blue wire (engine harness side) and the tan wire terminal in the red engine harness connector. See **Figure 146**.

5. Note the ohmmeter reading, then reverse the leads.

6. A high reading (no continuity) in one direction and a low reading (continuity) in the other should be noted. If both readings are low, the diode is shorted (closed) and must be replaced. If both readings are high, the diode is open and must be replaced.

QuikStart Operation and Testing

All models are equipped with QuikStart electronic starting system. The QuikStart circuit automatically advances the ignition timing when the engine temperature is less than 105° F (41° C) to improve engine warm-up. The ignition timing remains advanced until engine temperature exceeds approximately 105° F (41° C). In addition, QuikStart also advances the ignition timing for approximately 5 seconds each time the engine is started, regardless of engine temperature. To prevent power head damage due to detonation, the power pack disables QuikStart at engine speeds exceeding approximately 1100 rpm, regardless of engine temperature.

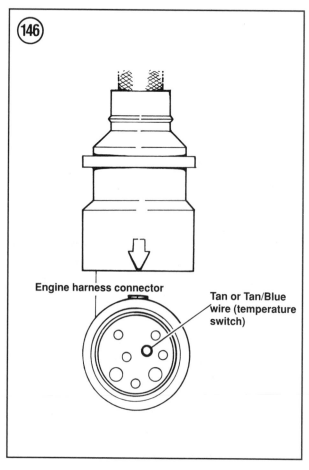

Engine harness connector

Tan or Tan/Blue wire (temperature switch)

To determine if QuikStart is functioning properly, proceed as follows.

1. Remove the propeller and install the correct test wheel (**Table 8**).

2. Place the outboard motor in a suitable test tank. Start the engine and warm it to normal operating temperature. Engine temperature must be above 105° F (41° C) before running this test.

NOTE
Make sure engine synchronization and linkage adjustments are correctly set as outlined in Chapter Five.

3. Remove the engine harness bracket.

4. Disconnect the white/black wire between the power pack and port temperature switch. See **Figure 147**, typical.

5. Attach an accurate tachometer to the power head according to the manufacturer's instructions.

6. Attach a timing light to the No. 1 cylinder according to the manufacturer's instructions.

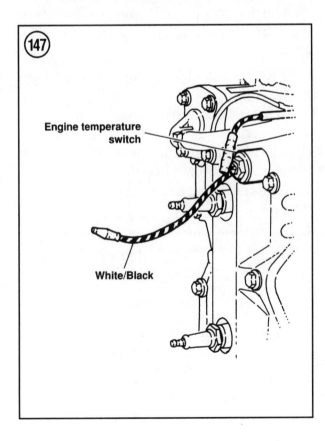

Engine temperature switch

White/Black

7. Start the engine and shift into forward gear. Idle speed *must not* exceed 900 rpm in gear during this test. Adjust idle speed if necessary.

8. Observe the timing wheel with the timing light. The timing pointer should be near 4° BTDC, indicating QuikStart is functioning. If QuikStart fails to advance the ignition timing, check for proper operation of the power pack and timing wheel.

9. While observing the timing marks, momentarily connect the white/black temperature switch wire. The timing should retard to approximately 6° ATDC when the wire is connected, indicating that QuikStart has returned the timing to the normal setting. If the timing does not retard as specified, check the temperature switch, power pack and related wiring and connectors.

CD8 IGNITION SYSTEM TROUBLESHOOTING (1991-ON V8 LOOP CHARGED MODELS—250 AND 300 HP; 4.0 SEA DRIVE MODELS)

The major components of the CD8 ignition system include the flywheel, 2 charge coils, power coil, 8 double-wound sensor coils, power pack, 8 ignition coils, shift switch, 2 temperature switches and related wiring.

The charge coil and power coil are contained inside the stator assembly and are not serviced separately. The power coil is used to provide voltage for QuikStart and S.L.O.W. operation. The 8 sensor coils are a double-wound design and are contained in a 1-piece timer base assembly. Eight sensor coils are used for QuikStart operation and 8 are used for ignition.

If the outboard motor is very hard or impossible to start, begin the troubleshooting procedure at *Total Output Test*. If an ignition malfunction is causing an intermittent high-speed miss or erratic operation, refer to *Indexing Flywheel* and *Running Output Test*. Unless specified otherwise, perform the following ignition system tests in the sequence given. Skipping tests or jumping around the troubleshooting procedure can result in misleading results and unnecessary parts replacement. Test the entire ignition system—more than one component may be defective.

Indexing Flywheel

If the outboard motor runs erratically, or if a high speed miss is noted, the power pack may be defective. Internal power pack malfunctions can cause erratic ignition system operation. Perform the following procedure to ensure the power pack is firing at the correct time.

1. Remove the spark plugs.

2. Position the No. 2 piston at TDC by rotating the flywheel clockwise. Insert a pencil or similar tool into the No. 2 spark plug hole while rotating the flywheel to ensure the piston is at TDC.

3. With the No. 2 piston at TDC, place a mark on the flywheel directly across from the timing pointer. Label the mark No. 2.

4. Repeat Step 2 and Step 3 on the remaining cylinders.

5. Reinstall the spark plugs and connect the plug leads.

> *CAUTION*
> *The outboard motor must be supplied with adequate cooling water while running. Place the motor in a test tank or on a boat in the water. Do not attempt to run the motor at high speed while connected to a flushing device.*

6. Start the motor and run it at the speed at which the problem is evident.

7. Alternately, connect a timing light to each cylinder. The timing light should indicate the cylinder number the timing light is connected to. For example, if the timing light is connected to the No. 2 spark plug wire, the No. 2 mark should be visible. In addition, the number should only appear near the timing pointer.

8. If a different cylinder number appears, or if the number jumps around or appears at other than the timing pointer, first make sure the primary ignition wires are properly connected. The primary wires must be connected as follows:

   a. *No. 1 coil*—orange/blue wire.
   b. *No. 2 coil*—orange/purple wire.
   c. *No. 3 coil*—orange/green wire.
   d. *No. 4 coil*—orange/pink wire.
   e. *No. 5 coil*—orange/blue/white wire.
   f. *No. 6 coil*—orange/purple/white wire.
   g. *No. 7 coil*—orange/green/white wire.
   h. *No. 8 coil*—orange/pink/white wire.

If the primary wires are properly connected, verify wire and pin location on all timer base and power pack connectors. See wiring diagrams at end of manual. If wire and pin location are correct, replace the power pack.

Total Output Test

The total output test will determine if the ignition system is capable of delivering adequate spark to the spark plugs. Perform the output test with the spark plugs installed and properly tightened.

1. Disconnect the spark plug leads from the spark plugs.

2. Mount a suitable spark tester on the engine and connect the spark plug leads to the tester. See **Figure 114**. Make sure the spark tester mounting clip is secured to a good clean engine ground.

3. Adjust the spark tester spark gap to 7/16 in. (11.1 mm).

4. Connect the cutoff clip and lanyard to the emergency stop switch, if so equipped.

> *NOTE*
> *If acceptable spark is noted at each spark gap during the total output test, but the engine pops or backfires during starting or running, the ignition system may be out of time. Be sure the primary ignition wires are properly connected. See **Indexing the Flywheel**. Make sure the spark plug leads are routed correctly.*

Make sure the timing and throttle linkage are properly synchronized.

5. Crank the engine while observing the spark tester.

a. If acceptable spark is noted at each spark gap, but the engine will not stop after starting, continue at *Stop Circuit Test*.

b. If acceptable spark is noted at each spark gap, but the outboard has a high-speed miss, continue at *Power Pack Output Test* and *Running Output Test*.

c. If acceptable spark is noted at each spark gap, but the outboard does not start, first verify that the QuikStart system is functioning as outlined under *QuikStart Operation and Testing*. If QuikStart is functioning properly, then make sure the timing pointer is properly located as outlined in Chapter Five, then check charge coil output as outlined in this chapter.

d. If good spark is noted on at least one spark gap, continue at *Charge Coil Output Test*.

e. If no spark is noted at any one spark gap, continue at *Sensor Coil Output Test*.

f. If no spark is noted at cylinders 5-8, continue at *Shift Switch Test*.

g. If no spark is noted at all spark gaps, continue at *Stop Circuit Test*.

Stop Circuit Test

The following test eliminates the stop circuit as a potential cause of an ignition malfunction. The key switch and lanyard emergency stop switch are connected to the power pack through the engine wiring harness. Activating the stop circuit shorts power pack output to ground, which disables the ignition system and stops the engine.

Perform this test if no spark is noted at all spark gaps during the previous total output test.

1. Connect a spark tester as outlined under *Total Output Test*.

2A. *1991 and 1992 models*—Disconnect the two, 1-pin Amphenol connectors between the power pack and key switch. See A, **Figure 148**.

2B. *1993-on models*—Disconnect the 1-pin Amphenol connector between the engine wiring harness and shift switch. See B, **Figure 149**.

3. Crank the engine while observing the spark tester.

4A. *1991 and 1992 models:*

a. If good spark is now noted at each spark gap, the problem is in the stop circuit. Continue at *Key Switch Ohmmeter Test*.

b. If no spark is noted, continue at *Charge Coil Output Test*.

4B. *1993-on models:*

a. If good spark is now noted at each spark gap, the problem is in the shift switch circuit. Continue at *Shift Switch Test*.

b. If no spark is noted, disconnect the 2-pin stop circuit connector (A, **Figure 149**) between the power pack and key switch and repeat Step 2. If good spark is now noted, the problem is in the stop circuit. Continue at *Key Switch Ohmmeter Test*. If there is still no spark, continue at *Charge Coil Output Test*. If both charge coils test good, replace the power pack (Chapter Seven).

Key Switch Ohmmeter Test

If the engine will not shut off when the key switch is turned OFF, test the key switch as outlined in this chapter.

If the engine will not shut off when the clip is removed from the emergency stop switch, replace the emergency stop switch.

If the engine will not shut off when the key switch is turned OFF and the clip is removed from the emergency stop switch, check for an open circuit in the black/yellow, black/orange and black wires between the power pack and key switch.

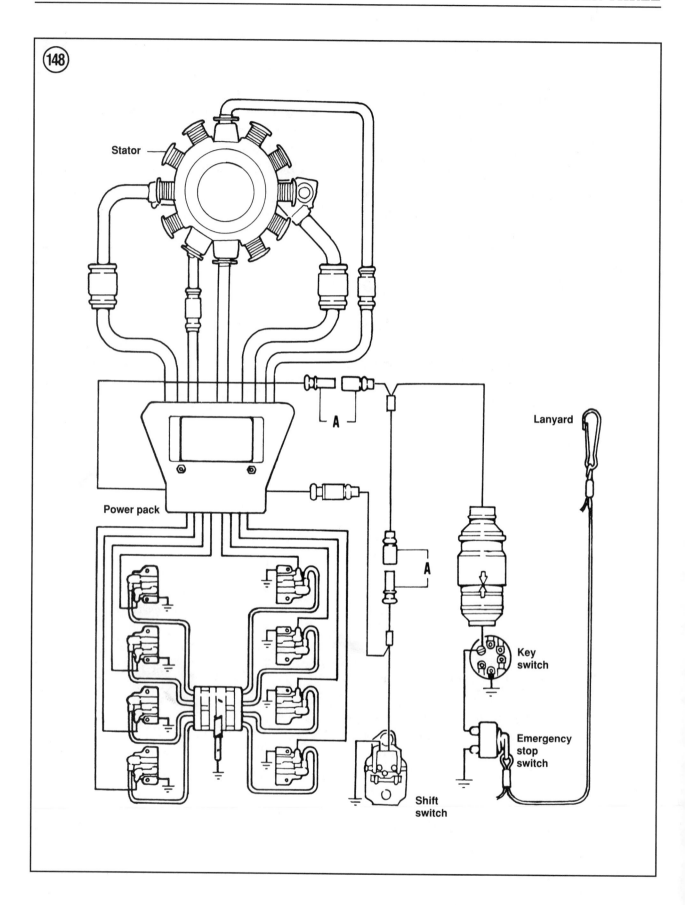

Stator

Power pack

A

Lanyard

Key switch

Emergency stop switch

Shift switch

1991 and 1992 models

1. Install the emergency stop switch clip and lanyard.

2. Disconnect both 1-pin Amphenol connectors between the power pack and key switch. See A, **Figure 148**.

3. Calibrate the ohmmeter on the appropriate scale.

4. Connect the black ohmmeter lead to a good engine ground. Connect the red ohmmeter lead to either engine harness black/yellow wire.

  a. With the key switch in the OFF position, the ohmmeter should indicate continuity (low resistance).

  b. With the key switch in the ON position, the ohmmeter should indicate no continuity (high resistance).

3

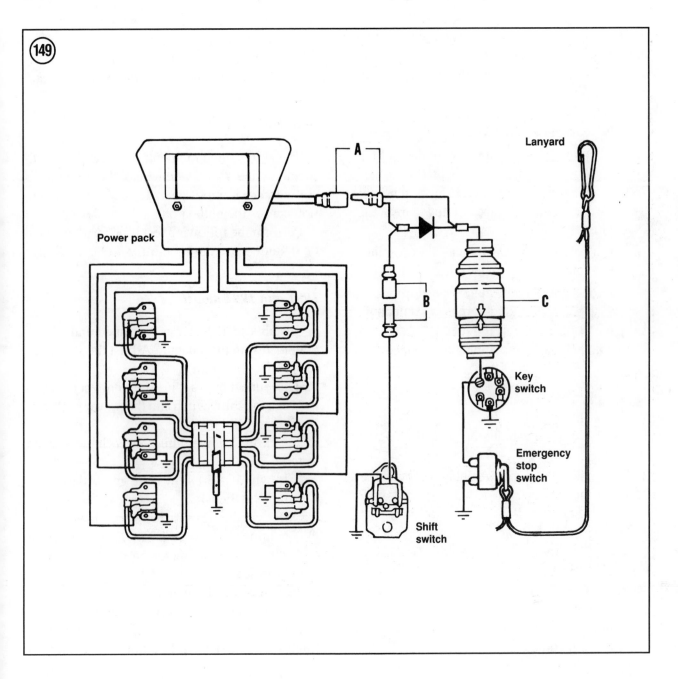

5. Move the red ohmmeter lead to the remaining engine harness black/yellow wire. The results should be the same as in Steps 4a and 4b.

> *NOTE*
> *If both black/yellow wires test good (Steps 4 and 5), but the stop circuit does not operate properly, the blocking diode in the power pack is defective. Replace the power pack as outlined in Chapter Seven.*

6. If continuity is noted in Steps 4 and 5 when the key switch is ON, disconnect the engine harness black/yellow wires from the key switch M terminal.

a. If the ohmmeter now indicates no continuity, replace the key switch.

b. If continuity is still noted, continue at Step 7.

7. Disconnect the emergency stop switch wire from the engine harness black/yellow wire at the key switch.

a. If the ohmmeter now indicates no continuity, replace the emergency stop switch.

b. If continuity is still noted, the stop circuit wiring in the engine harness is defective. Repair or replace as required.

8. Reconnect the 1-pin Amphenol connectors.

1993-on models

1. Install the emergency stop switch clip and lanyard.

2. Disconnect the 1-pin Amphenol connector between the engine wiring harness and shift switch (B, **Figure 149**).

3. Disconnect the 2-pin Amphenol connector between the power pack and key switch (A, **Figure 149**).

4. Connect the black ohmmeter lead to a good engine ground. Connect the red ohmmeter lead to terminal B (black/yellow wire) in the engine harness 2-pin connector.

a. With the key switch in the OFF position, the ohmmeter should indicate continuity (low resistance).

b. With the key switch in the ON position, the ohmmeter should indicate no continuity (high resistance). If continuity is noted, continue at Step 5.

5. Disconnect the engine wiring harness connector (C, **Figure 149**) and note the ohmmeter.

a. If no continuity is now present, test the key switch, emergency stop switch and remote control wiring harness.

b. If continuity is still present, repair or replace the engine wiring harness.

Shift Switch Test

The shift switch momentarily interrupts ignition to cylinders 5-8 when the outboard motor is shifted into or out of gear. This power interruption causes the outboard to shift easier.

Perform the following test if no spark is noted on cylinders 5-8 during the *Total Output Test*.

1991 and 1992 models

1. Install a spark tester as described under *Total Output Test* in this chapter. Adjust the spark gap to 7/16 in. (11.1 mm).

2. Disconnect both 1-pin Amphenol connectors between the shift switch and the power pack. See A, **Figure 148**.

3. Crank the engine while observing the spark tester.

a. If cylinders 5-8 now have good spark, continue at Step 4.

b. If cylinders 5-8 still do not have spark, continue at *Charge Coil Output Test*.

4. Calibrate the ohmmeter on the R × 1000 or high-ohm scale.

5. Connect the ohmmeter between a good engine ground and the power pack end of the shift switch harness. See **Figure 150**. No continuity (high resistance) should be noted. If continuity

is present, replace the shift switch and wire harness.

6. Push down on the shift cable pin to activate the shift switch while observing the meter. Continuity (low resistance) should now be noted. If not, replace the shift switch and wire harness.

7. Connect the ohmmeter between both engine harness 1-pin connectors. Note the meter reading, then reverse the ohmmeter leads and note the second reading. One reading should be infinity (no continuity) and the other should be continuity (near zero ohm). If both readings are infinity, or if both readings are zero ohm, the blocking diode in the switch harness is defective. Replace the shift switch and harness.

1993-on models

1. Install a spark tester as described under *Total Output Test* in this chapter. Adjust the spark gap to 7/16 in. (11.1 mm).

2. Disconnect the 1-pin Amphenol connector (black/yellow wire) between the engine wiring harness and the shift switch. See B, **Figure 149**.

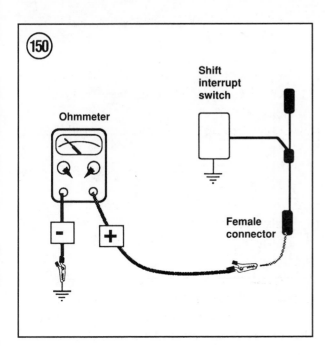

3. Crank the engine while observing the spark tester.
   a. If spark is now noted at cylinders 5-8, continue at Step 4.
   b. If cylinders 5-8 still do not have spark, continue at *Charge Coil Output Test*.

4. Calibrate the ohmmeter on the R × 1000 or high-ohm scale.

5. Connect the ohmmeter between a good engine ground and the shift switch connector. No continuity (infinity) should be noted. If continuity is present, replace the shift switch and wire harness.

6. Push down on the shift cable pin to activate the shift pin while observing the ohmmeter. Continuity should be noted when the switch is closed. If not, replace the shift switch and harness.

7. Disconnect the 2-pin Amphenol connector between the power pack and key switch. See A, **Figure 149**. Disconnect the engine wiring harness connector (C, **Figure 149**).

8. Connect the red ohmmeter lead to the black/yellow wire terminal in the engine wiring harness connector. Connect the black ohmmeter lead to terminal A in the 2-pin Amphenol connector (black/orange wire). See **Figure 151**. Note the meter reading, then reverse the ohmmeter leads. Note the meter reading.
   a. One reading should be infinity and the other should be near zero ohm.
   b. If both readings are infinity, or if both are near zero ohm, replace the blocking diode or repair or replace the engine wiring harness as necessary.

9. With the red ohmmeter lead connected to the black/yellow wire terminal in the engine harness connector (**Figure 151**), connect the black meter lead to terminal B (black/yellow) in the engine harness 2-pin connector (**Figure 151**). The meter should indicate low resistance. If not, repair or replace the engine wiring harness as necessary.

10. With the red ohmmeter lead connected to the black/yellow wire terminal in the engine harness

connector (**Figure 151**), connect the black ohmmeter lead to the engine harness end of the 1-pin shift switch connector. Note the meter reading, reverse the ohmmeter leads and note reading. One reading should be infinity and the other reading should be near zero. If not, repair or replace the engine wiring harness as necessary.

Charge Coil Output Test

Perform the following test to ensure the charge coil is capable of producing sufficient voltage to charge the capacitor properly in the power pack and to make sure the charge coil or charge coil wiring is not shorted to ground. A peak reading voltmeter (PRV) is necessary to perform this test.

1. Disconnect the forward and rear 2-pin Amphenol connectors from the power pack.

2. Set the PRV selector switches to POS and 500.

3. Connect one PRV test lead to a good engine ground. Alternately connect the remaining test lead to terminals A and B in the forward 2-pin stator connector. See **Figure 152**.

4. Crank the engine and note the meter at each connection.

    a. Any voltage reading indicates a shorted charge coil or charge coil wire(s). Locate and repair the shorted wire(s) or replace the

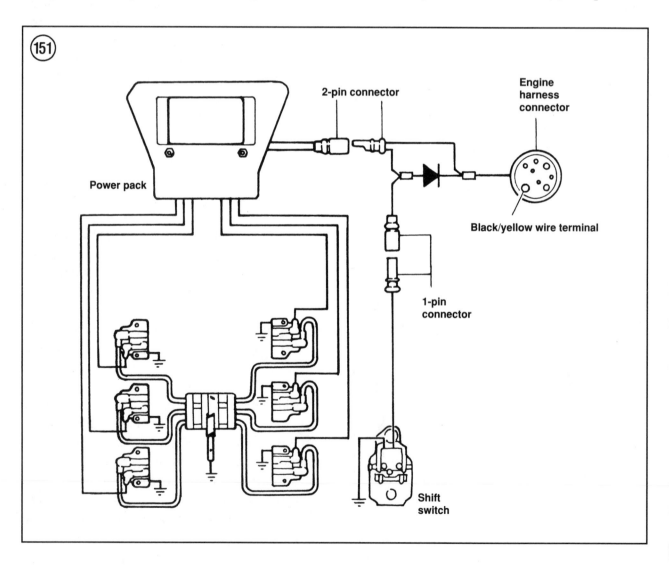

stator assembly as outlined in Chapter Seven.

b. If no voltage is noted, continue at Step 5.

5. Repeat Steps 3 and 4 with the PRV connected between ground and terminals A and B in the rear 2-pin stator connector.

a. Any voltage reading indicates a shorted charge coil or charge coil wire(s). Locate and repair the shorted wire(s) or replace the stator assembly as outlined in Chapter Seven.

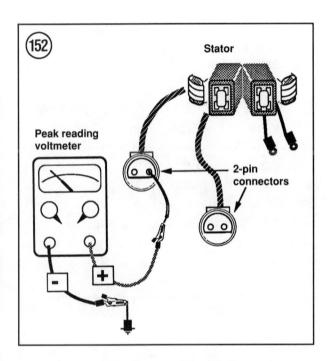

b. If no voltage is noted, continue at Step 6.

6. Connect the black PRV test lead to terminal A in the forward 2-pin stator connector. See **Figure 153**. Connect the red test lead to terminal B in the forward 2-pin connector.

7. Crank the engine while observing the meter. Charge coil output should be 130 volts or more.

8. Connect the black PRV test lead to terminal A in the rear 2-pin stator connector. Connect the red test lead to terminal B in the rear connector.

9. Crank the engine while observing the meter. Charge coil output should be 130 volts or more.

a. If output at both connectors is 130 volts or more, reconnect the 2-pin connectors and continue at *Sensor Coil Output Test*.

b. If output is less than 130 volts at either connector, inspect the condition of the charge coil wiring and connectors. If the wiring and connectors are in acceptable condition, continue at *Charge Coil Resistance Test*.

Charge Coil Resistance Test

Because resistance generally increases with temperature, perform resistance tests with the engine cold (room temperature). Resistance tests on hot components will indicate increased resistance and may result in unnecessary parts replacement without solving the basic problem.

1. Calibrate the ohmmeter on the appropriate scale.

2. Connect the ohmmeter between terminals A and B in the forward 2-pin stator connector. See **Figure 154**. Resistance should be 765-935 ohms.

3. Connect the ohmmeter between terminals A and B in the rear 2-pin connector. Resistance should be 765-935 ohms.

4. If resistance is not as specified in Steps 2 and 3, replace the stator assembly as outlined in Chapter Seven.

5. Calibrate the ohmmeter on the R × 1000 or high-ohm scale.

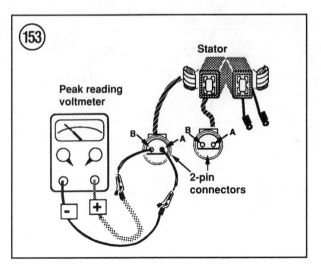

6. Connect the ohmmeter between a good engine ground and alternately to each terminal in both 2-pin connectors. See **Figure 155**. Note the meter reading at each connection.

   a. No continuity (infinity) should be noted at each connection.

   b. Continuity between any terminal and ground indicates a shorted charge coil or charge coil wire(s). Locate and repair the shorted wire(s) or replace the stator assembly as outlined in Chapter Seven.

7. Reconnect the stator-to-power pack 2-pin connectors.

Sensor Coil Output Test

The sensor coil provides a voltage signal to the power pack which triggers power pack output to be directed to the correct ignition coil primary circuit. Perform this test to determine if the sensor coil is capable of producing a sufficient voltage signal, and to ensure the sensor coil or sensor coil wiring is not shorted to ground. A peak reading voltmeter (PRV) is necessary to perform this test.

1. Disconnect both 5-pin Amphenol connectors between the timer base and power pack.

2. Set the PRV selector switches to POS and 5 (SEN and 5 if using Stevens CD-77).

3. Connect one PRV test lead to a good engine ground. Alternately connect the remaining test lead to each terminal in both timer base connectors. See **Figure 156**.

4. Crank the engine while observing the meter at each connection.

   a. Any voltage reading indicates a shorted sensor coil or sensor coil wire(s). Locate and repair the shorted wire(s) or replace the timer base assembly as outlined in Chapter Seven.

   b. If no voltage is noted, continue at Step 5.

5. Connect the black PRV test lead to terminal E in the port timer base connector. Alternately connect the red test lead to terminals A, B, C and D in the starboard timer base connector, then terminals A, B, C and D in the port timer base connector. See **Figure 157**.

6. Crank the engine while observing the meter at each connection. Sensor coil output should be 0.2 volt or more.

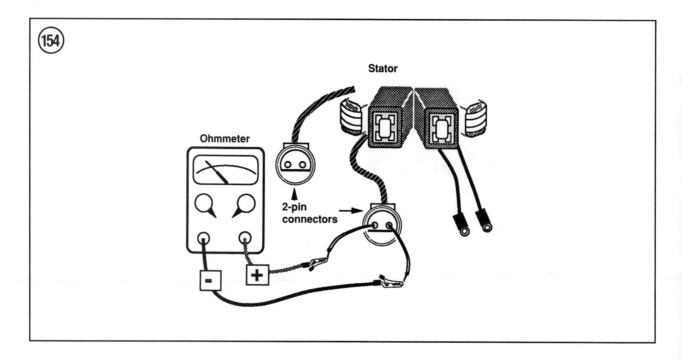

(154)

Stator

Ohmmeter

2-pin
connectors

−

+

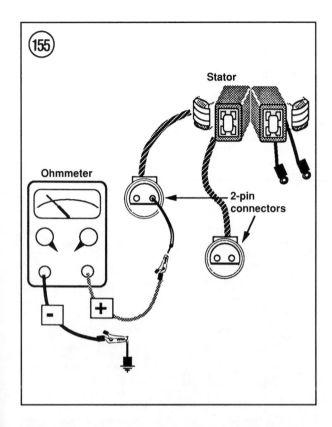

155

Stator

Ohmmeter

2-pin
connectors

− +

a. If output is 0.2 volt at each connection, continue at Step 7.

b. If output is less than 0.2 volt, inspect the timer base wiring and connectors and repair as necessary. If the wiring and connectors are in acceptable condition, continue at *Sensor Coil Resistance Test*.

7. Connect the E terminal in the port timer base terminal to the E terminal in the port engine harness connector using a jumper lead. See **Figure 158**.

8. Connect the E terminal in the starboard timer base terminal to the E terminal in the starboard engine harness connector using a jumper lead. See **Figure 158**.

9. Connect the black PRV test lead to a good engine ground. Alternately, connect the red test lead to terminals A, B, C and D in the starboard timer base connector, then terminals A, B, C and D in the port timer base terminal. Crank the engine while observing the meter at each connection.

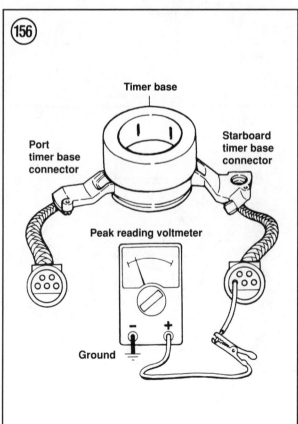

156

Timer base

Port
timer base
connector

Starboard
timer base
connector

Peak reading voltmeter

− +

Ground

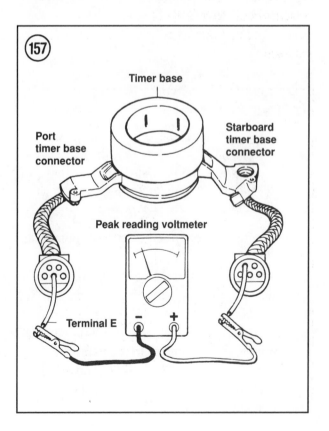

157

Timer base

Port
timer base
connector

Starboard
timer base
connector

Peak reading voltmeter

Terminal E

− +

3

a. If output is 1.2 volts or more, continue at *Power Pack Output Test*.

b. If output is less than 1.2 volts, inspect the timer base wiring and connectors and repair as necessary. If the wiring and connectors are in acceptable condition, replace the timer base assembly as outlined in Chapter Seven.

Sensor Coil Resistance Test

Because resistance generally increases with temperature, perform resistance tests with the engine cold (room temperature). Resistance tests on hot components will indicate increased resistance and may result in unnecessary parts replacement without solving the basic problem. The ohmmeter should be calibrated on the R × 1000 or high-ohm scale when checking for a grounded condition.

NOTE
Ohmmeter polarity must be determined before proceeding with this test. To do so, calibrate the meter on the R × 100 or low-ohm scale. Connect the leads to a known-good diode as shown in **Figure 159**, *then reverse the leads. If the first connection indicated very low resistance (zero ohm), and the second connection indicated very high resistance (infinity), the ohmmeter red lead is positive (+). If the opposite result is noted, reverse the ohmmeter leads so the red lead is positive (+).*

1. Calibrate the ohmmeter on the appropriate scale.

2. Connect the red (positive) ohmmeter lead to terminal E in the port timer base connector. See **Figure 160**.

3. Alternately, connect the black ohmmeter lead to terminals A, B, C and D in the port timer base terminal, then terminals A, B, C and D in the starboard timer base terminal. Note the meter at each connection.

NOTE
The sensor coil resistance specifications in Step 4 and Step 6 are based on the use of a Stevens Model AT-101 or a Merc-O-Tronic Model M-700 ohmmeter. Resistance measured with an ohmmeter of

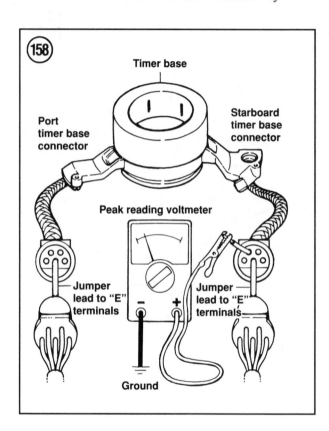

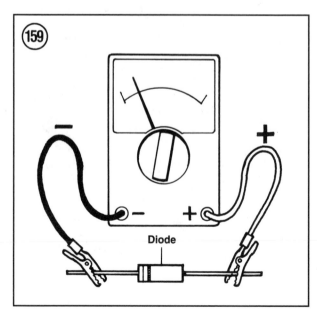

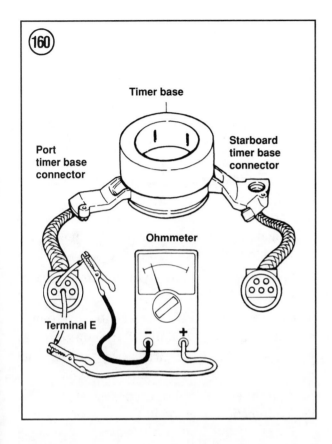

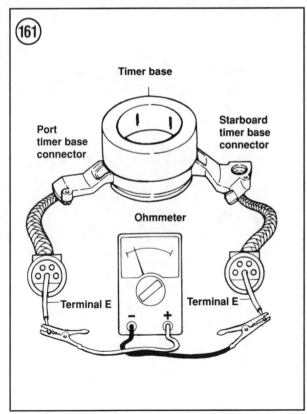

another manufacturer may be different. Internal timer base components may cause sensor coil resistance readings to vary depending on individual ohmmeter impedance. Resistance readings may be higher or lower, however, they should be consistent.

4. If using a Stevens Model AT-101 ohmmeter, sensor coil resistance should be 330-390 ohms. If using a Merc-O-Tronic Model M-700 ohmmeter, sensor coil resistance should be 870-1070 ohms. If resistance is not as specified, replace the timer base assembly as outlined in Chapter Seven.

5. Next, connect the red ohmmeter lead to terminal E in the port timer base connector. Connect the black ohmmeter lead to terminal E in the starboard timer base connector. See **Figure 161**.

6. Resistance should be 140-180 ohms. If not, replace the timer base assembly as outlined in Chapter Seven.

7. Next, connect the ohmmeter between a good engine ground and alternately to each sensor coil terminal in the port and starboard timer base connector.

8. No continuity should be noted at each connection. If continuity is noted, locate and repair the grounded timer base wire(s) or replace the timer base assembly as necessary. See Chapter Seven.

9. If testing is complete, reconnect the timer base terminals.

Power Pack Output Test

WARNING
To prevent accidental starting, remove the spark plug leads from the spark plugs. Securely ground the plug leads to the power head, or connect the leads to a spark tester.

A peak reading voltmeter (PRV) and Stevens load adapter (part No. PL-88) are necessary to test power pack output.

1. Disconnect the primary wires from each ignition coil.

2. Connect the primary wire from the No. 1 coil to the red lead of the PL-88 load adapter. Connect the black load adapter lead to a good engine ground. See **Figure 162**.

3. Set the PRV selector switches to POS and 500.

4. Connect the red PRV test lead to the red load adapter lead. Connect the black PRV test lead to a good engine ground.

5. Crank the engine while observing the meter. Power pack output should be 100 volts or more.

6. Repeat Steps 2-5 on the primary wire to each remaining ignition coil. Output should be 100 volts or more at each primary wire.

   a. If output is 100 volts or more at each primary wire, test ignition coil resistance as outlined in this chapter.

   b. If no output is noted at one primary wire, replace the power pack. See Chapter Seven.

7. If testing is complete, remove the PL-88 load adapter and reconnect the primary wires to the ignition coils. Make sure the primary ignition wires are connected to the correct ignition coils. See *Indexing Flywheel*.

Running Output Test

A peak reading voltmeter (PRV) and Stevens Terminal Extenders (part No. TS-77) are necessary to perform the running output test. Running the outboard under load is often necessary to locate the cause of an intermittent malfunction or high-speed miss, especially if good spark is noted during the *Total Output Test*. Remove the propeller and install the correct test wheel (**Table 8**) prior to performing the test.

CAUTION
The outboard motor must be supplied with adequate cooling water while running. Install the motor in a test tank or on a boat in the water. Do not attempt to

run the motor at high speed while connected to a flushing device.

1. Remove the primary wires from each ignition coil.

2. Install a Stevens Terminal Extender (part No. TS-77) on each coil primary terminal. Connect the primary wires to the terminal extenders. Make sure the orange/blue primary wires are connected to the top ignition coils, the orange primary wires are attached to the center ignition coils and the orange/green primary wires are attached to the bottom ignition coils.

3. Set the PRV selector switches to POS and 500.

4. Connect the red PRV test lead to the terminal extender attached to the No. 1 ignition coil. Connect the black test lead to a good engine ground.

5. Start the engine and run at the speed at which the malfunction is evident while observing the

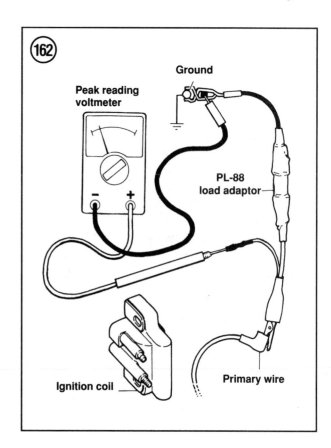

(162)

Ground

Peak reading voltmeter

PL-88 load adaptor

Ignition coil

Primary wire

meter. Running output should be 130 volts or more.

6. Repeat Steps 4 and 5 with the red PRV test lead connected to the terminal extender on each remaining ignition coil.

　a. If output is less than 130 volts on one or more ignition coil, test charge coil as described in this chapter.

　b. If no output (zero volt) is noted at one or more ignition coil, test the sensor coils as described in this chapter.

7. If testing is complete, remove the terminal extenders and reconnect the primary wires to their respective ignition coils. Make sure the primary wires are attached to the correct coils. See *Indexing Flywheel*.

Ignition Coil Resistance Test

Because resistance generally increases with temperature, perform resistance tests with the engine at room temperature (70° F [21° C]). Resistance tests on hot components will indicate increased resistance and may result in unnecessary parts replacement without solving the basic problem. Ignition coil resistance can be checked without coil removal.

1. Remove the primary wires and the spark plug wires from the ignition coil assembly.

2. Calibrate the ohmmeter on the R × 1 or low-ohm scale.

3. To check primary winding resistance, connect the black ohmmeter lead to a good engine ground or to the coil ground tab if the coil is removed. Connect the red ohmmeter lead to the coil primary terminal.

4. Primary resistance should be 0.05-0.15 ohm.

5. To check secondary winding resistance, calibrate the ohmmeter on the R × 100 or high-ohm scale. Connect the red ohmmeter lead to the coil primary terminal and the black lead to the spark plug terminal.

6. Secondary resistance should be 225-325 ohms.

7. Repeat Steps 3-6 on each remaining coil.

8. Replace the coil if resistance is not as specified.

9. To check the spark plug leads, calibrate the ohmmeter on R × 1 or low-ohm scale. Connect the ohmmeter to each end of the lead and note the meter. The resistance should be nearly zero ohm.

S.L.O.W. Operation and Testing

All models are equipped with the speed limiting overheat warning (S.L.O.W.) system. The system is designed to limit engine speed to approximately 2500 rpm if engine temperature exceeds 203° F (95° C). To deactivate S.L.O.W., throttle back to idle, allow the engine to cool to 162° F (72° C), then stop the engine.

A blocking diode located in the engine wiring harness is used to isolate the S.L.O.W. warning system from the other warning systems. Should the blocking diode become shorted, the S.L.O.W. function will remain activated regardless of engine temperature.

The S.L.O.W. function is activated by a signal from the port or starboard engine temperature switch. The temperature switches are located in the top of each cylinder head.

The following conditions will cause the S.L.O.W. function to remain activated:

　a. Engine overheated.

　b. Engine temperature switch or switch wire shorted to ground.

　c. Blocking diode closed or shorted to ground.

　d. Defective power pack.

The following conditions will prevent the S.L.O.W. function from operating:

　a. Engine temperature switch or switch wire open.

　b. Defective power pack.

　c. Defective power coil.

If the S.L.O.W function is inoperative, test the temperature switches and S.L.O.W. system as follows.

1. Install the outboard motor in a test tank with the correct test wheel installed. See **Table 8**.

2. Connect an accurate tachometer according to the manufacturer's instructions.

3. Disconnect the port and starboard tan/green temperature switch wires from the engine harness tan wires.

4. Start the engine and run at approximately 3500 rpm.

5. Connect the engine harness end of the port tan wire to a clean engine ground and note the engine speed.

6. Throttle back to idle speed, then stop the engine.

7. Repeat Step 4 and 5 using the starboard tan wire.

   a. If engine speed reduces to approximately 2500 rpm when each tan wire is grounded, test the temperature switch as described in this chapter.

   b. If engine speed reduces when one temperature switch tan wire is grounded, but not the other, check the engine wiring harness and connectors and repair as necessary.

   c. If engine speed does not reduce as specified when either tan wire is grounded, continue at Step 8.

8. Loosen the power pack and disconnect the orange and orange/black power coil wires from the terminal block.

9. Calibrate an ohmmeter on the R × 1000 or high-ohm scale.

10. Connect the ohmmeter between a good engine ground and alternately to each power coil wire (orange and orange/black). See **Figure 163**.

11. No continuity should be present between ground and either power coil wire.

   a. If continuity is noted, either the power coil or power coil wire(s) is shorted to ground. Locate and repair the shorted wire(s) or replace the stator assembly as necessary.

   b. If no continuity is noted, continue at Step 12.

12. Calibrate the ohmmeter on the appropriate scale.

13. Connect the ohmmeter between the orange and orange/black power coil wires. See **Figure 164**.

   a. If power coil resistance is within 86-106 ohms, replace the power pack.

   b. If power coil resistance is not within 86-106 ohms, replace the stator assembly. See Chapter Seven.

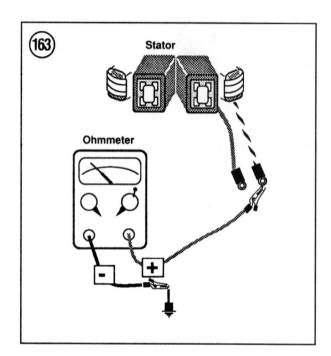

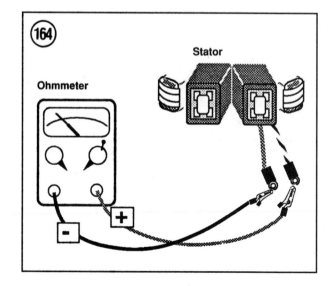

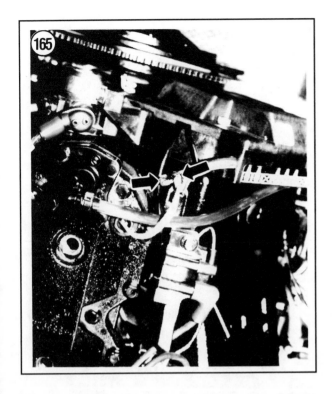

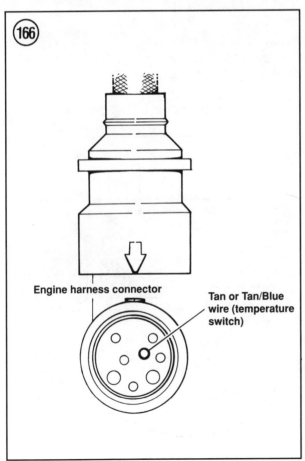

Engine harness connector

Tan or Tan/Blue
wire (temperature
switch)

CAUTION
*Do not start the engine with the orange
and orange/black power coil wires disconnected.*

14. If testing is complete, reconnect the orange
and orange/black power coil wires to the terminal block. Reinstall the power pack.

Blocking Diode Test

A blocking diode is used to prevent the
S.L.O.W. function from being activated by other
engine warning horn systems. The blocking diode is located in the engine wiring harness.

If the S.L.O.W function is activated by the no
oil, low oil or fuel vacuum warning signal, test
the engine harness blocking diode as follows:

1. Disconnect the red engine harness connector.
2. Disconnect the port and starboard temperature switches from the engine harness (**Figure
165**, typical).
3. Calibrate the ohmmeter on the R × 1000 or
high-ohm scale.
4. Connect the ohmmeter between either temperature switch tan wire (engine harness side)
and the tan wire terminal in the red engine harness connector. See **Figure 166**.
5. Note the ohmmeter reading, then reverse the
leads.
6. A high reading (no continuity) in one direction and a low reading (continuity) in the other
should be noted. If both readings are low, the
diode is shorted (closed) and must be replaced.
If both readings are high, the diode is open and
must be replaced.

QuikStart Operation and Testing

All models are equipped with QuikStart electronic starting system. The QuikStart circuit
automatically advances the ignition timing when
the engine temperature is less than 93-99° F
(34-37° C) to improve engine warm-up. The

ignition timing remains advanced until engine temperature exceeds approximately 93-99° F (34-37° C). In addition, QuikStart also advances the ignition timing for approximately 5 seconds each time the engine is started, regardless of engine temperature. To prevent power head damage due to detonation, the power pack disables QuikStart at engine speeds exceeding approximately 1100 rpm, regardless of engine temperature.

To determine if QuikStart is functioning properly, proceed as follows:

1. Remove the propeller and install the correct test wheel (**Table 8**).

2. Place the outboard motor in a suitable test tank. Start the engine and warm it to normal operating temperature. Engine temperature must be above 96° F (36° C) before running this test.

NOTE
Make sure engine synchronization and linkage adjustments are correctly set as outlined in Chapter Five.

3. Place temporary marks on the flywheel indicating TDC for all cylinders.

4. Disconnect the white/black temperature switch wire between the power pack and the port temperature switch. See **Figure 167**, typical.

5. Attach an accurate tachometer to the power head according to the manufacturer's instructions.

6. Attach a timing light to the No. 1 cylinder according to the manufacturer's instructions.

7. Start the engine and shift into forward gear. Idle speed *must not* exceed 900 rpm in gear during this test. Adjust idle speed if necessary.

8. Observe the flywheel with the timing light. The No. 1 cylinder TDC mark should be near the timing pointer, indicating QuikStart is functioning.

9. While observing the timing marks, momentarily connect the white/black temperature switch wire. The timing mark should shift to the left approximately 1 in. (25.4 mm) when the wire

is connected, indicating that QuikStart has returned the timing to the normal setting.

NOTE
*The engine **must** be stopped before testing each remaining cylinder to reset the QuikStart circuit.*

10. Stop the engine. Repeat Steps 6-9 for each remaining cylinder.

a. If one or more cylinders do not react as specified (Step 9), replace the timer base assembly. See Chapter Seven.

b. If no cylinders react as specified (Step 9), refer to *QuikStart inoperative* in this chapter.

c. If all cylinders react as specified (Step 9), the QuikStart circuit is functioning properly.

QuikStart inoperative

The following conditions will cause the QuikStart circuit to be inoperative:

a. Defective power coil.

b. Defective power pack.

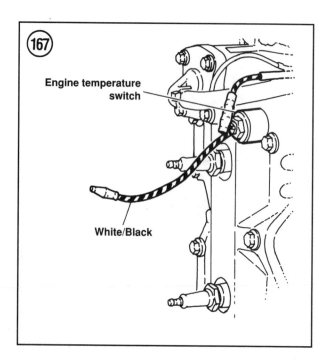

Engine temperature switch

White/Black

c. Defective timer base (sensor coil[s]).

d. An open circuit in the yellow/red wire between the power pack and starter solenoid or key switch.

Troubleshoot the QuikStart circuit as follows.

1. Disconnect the white/black wire between the port temperature switch and power pack (**Figure 167**, typical).

2. Calibrate the ohmmeter on the R × 1000 or high-ohm scale.

NOTE
Engine temperature must be less than 89° F (32° C) in Step 3.

3. Connect the ohmmeter between the temperature switch white/black wire and a good engine ground. The ohmmeter should indicate high resistance (infinity) with engine temperature less than 89° F (32° C).

a. If the meter indicates low resistance (continuity) in Step 3, test the temperature switch as described in this chapter.

b. If the meter indicates high resistance in Step 3, continue at Step 4.

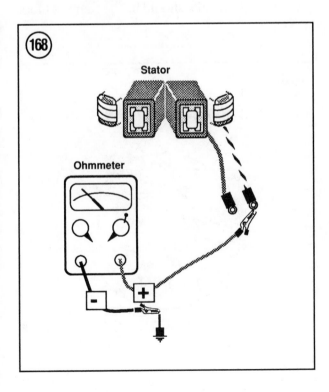

4. Loosen the power pack and disconnect the orange and orange/black power coil wires from the terminal block.

5. Calibrate the ohmmeter on the R × 1000 or high-ohm scale.

6. Connect the ohmmeter between a good engine ground and alternately to the power coil orange and orange/black wires. See **Figure 168**. No continuity should be present between either power coil wire and ground. If continuity is noted, repair the shorted power coil wire or replace the stator assembly as necessary. See Chapter Seven.

7. Calibrate the ohmmeter on the appropriate scale.

8. Connect the ohmmeter between the power coil orange and orange/black wires. See **Figure 164**.

a. If power coil resistance is within 86-106 ohms, replace the power pack.

b. If power coil resistance is not within 86-106 ohms, replace the stator assembly.

9. If testing is complete, reconnect all circuits disconnected during this procedure.

QuikStart always on

The following conditions can cause the Quik-Start circuit to remain on constantly:

a. Engine overcooling (not warming up to operating temperature).

b. Defective temperature switch.

c. Defective power pack.

d. Defective starter solenoid or key switch.

If QuikStart remains on constantly when the engine is operated above 1100 rpm, the power pack is defective and must be replaced. If Quik-Start remains on constantly regardless of time on and engine temperature, when the engine is operated *below* 1100 rpm, continue as follows:

1. Check for a defective starter solenoid or key switch, which may cause a small voltage to bleed into the yellow/red wire leading to the power

pack. This small voltage can activate the Quik-Start circuit.

2. Check for a defective or damaged port side engine temperature switch as described in this chapter.

3. Check for an open circuit or loose or corroded connections in the white/black power pack wire.

4. Check the engine for an overcooling condition as described in this chapter.

5. If no other problems are noted in Steps 1-4, replace the power pack. See Chapter Seven.

RPM Limiting Power Pack

Power packs marked "CDL" are equipped with an internal rpm limiting device designed to prevent power head damage from overspeeding. On models so equipped, the power pack interrupts ignition if engine speed exceeds 6700 rpm. Be certain the correct power pack is used if replacement is necessary.

KEY AND
NEUTRAL START SWITCH

The key (ignition) and neutral start switches can be tested with a self-powered test lamp or an ohmmeter. If defective, replace the key switch with a marine switch. Do not use an automotive switch.

Key Switch Test

Refer to **Figure 169** for this procedure.

1. Disconnect the negative battery cable from the battery. Disconnect the positive battery cable, then disconnect the key switch wires from the switch.

2. Connect a test lamp or ohmmeter leads between the switch terminals marked BATT and A. With the switch in the OFF position, no continuity should be noted.

3. Turn the switch to the ON position. The test lamp should light or the meter should show continuity.

4. Turn the switch to the START position. The test lamp should light or the meter should show continuity.

5. Hold the switch key in the START position and move the test lead from terminal A to terminal S. The lamp should light or the meter show continuity.

6. Turn the switch to OFF. Move the test leads to the 2 terminals marked M. The test lamp should light or the meter show continuity.

7. Turn the switch first to the START, then to the ON position. There should be no continuity in either position.

8. Turn the switch OFF. Move the test leads to terminal B and terminal C. Turn the switch ON. There should be no continuity. If equipped with a choke primer system, push inward on the key and the test lamp should light or the meter show continuity.

9. Repeat Step 8 with the switch in the START position. The results should be the same as those in Step 8.

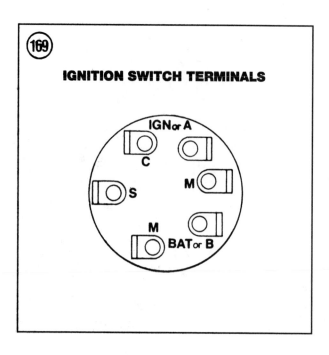

IGNITION SWITCH TERMINALS

NOTE
It is possible that the switch may pass an ohmmeter test but still have an internal short. If the switch passes but does not function properly, have a high-voltage leakage test performed by a qualified marine specialist, using a condenser tester.

10. Replace the switch if it fails any of the steps in this procedure.

Neutral Start Switch

The throttle cam or remote control box neutral start switch is not adjustable. If it does not prevent the motor from starting when the throttle is advanced beyond the START position, replace it.

To check the neutral start switch, disconnect the negative battery cable and connect an ohmmeter between the switch wires. There should be continuity only when the engine control is in NEUTRAL. If continuity is shown with the engine control in FORWARD or REVERSE or if the engine cranks in either gear, replace the switch.

FUEL SYSTEM

Outboard motor owners often assume the carburetor(s) is at fault when the engine does not run properly. While fuel system problems are not uncommon, carburetor adjustment is seldom the answer. In many cases, adjusting the carburetor only compounds the problem by making the engine run worse.

NOTE
Never attempt to adjust the carburetor(s) until the following conditions are ensured:

a. The ignition timing is correctly adjusted.
b. The engine throttle and ignition linkage have been correctly synchronized and adjusted.
c. The engine is running at normal operating temperature.
d. The outboard is in the water, running in forward gear with the correct propeller installed.

Fuel system troubleshooting should start at the fuel tank and work through the entire fuel delivery system, reserving the carburetors as the final point. The majority of fuel system problems result from an empty fuel tank, sour fuel, a plugged fuel filter or a malfunctioning fuel pump. **Table 3** provides a series of symptoms and causes that can be useful in localizing fuel system problems.

Troubleshooting

When troubleshooting the fuel system, first check the fuel flow. Remove the fuel tank cap and look into the tank. If fuel is present, disconnect and ground the spark plug leads to prevent starting. Disconnect the fuel hose at the carburetor (**Figure 170**, typical) and place it in a suitable container to catch discharged fuel. Determine if fuel flows freely from the hose when the primer bulb is squeezed.

If no fuel flows from the hose, the fuel valve at the tank may be shut off or blocked by rust or other foreign material. The hose may be plugged or kinked or a primer bulb check valve may be

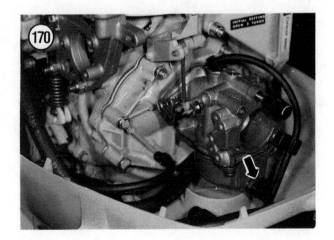

defective. To determine if a restriction is present in the fuel hose between the fuel pump and tank, connect a suitable vacuum gauge into the fuel delivery hose near (before) the fuel pump. Connect the vacuum gauge using a length of clear plastic hose. Start the outboard (in the water) and run at wide-open throttle while observing the vacuum gauge. If the gauge indicates more than 4 in. of vacuum, a restriction is present in the fuel line. If bubbles are present in the clear plastic hose, an air leak is present in the hose between the fuel tank and vacuum gauge.

If a good fuel flow from the fuel hose is present, crank the engine 10-12 revolutions to check fuel pump operation. A good, constant flow of fuel from the hose will result if the pump is operating properly. If the fuel flow varies from pulse to pulse, the pump may be failing. See Chapter Six for fuel pump testing and service procedures.

Carburetor choke valves can also present problems. If the choke valve sticks open, the outboard will start hard when cold; if the choke sticks closed, the engine will run excessively rich, stall and foul spark plugs.

During a hot engine shut-down, the fuel bowl temperature can rise above 200° F, causing the fuel inside to boil. While outboard carburetors are vented to the atmosphere to prevent this problem, there is a possibility some fuel will percolate over the high-speed nozzle.

A leaking inlet valve or a defective float will allow an excessive amount of fuel into the carburetor and intake manifold. Pressure in the fuel line after the engine is shut down forces fuel past the leaking inlet valve. This raises the fuel level, allowing fuel to overflow carburetor float bowl.

Excessive fuel consumption may not necessarily mean an engine or fuel system problem. Marine growth on the boat's hull, a bent or otherwise damaged propeller or fuel leak can cause an increase in fuel consumption. These areas should all be checked *before* servicing the carburetor.

Electric Primer System

A primer solenoid is used on electric start models. See **Figure 171**. When the key switch is pushed inward, the solenoid opens electrically and allows fuel to pass from the fuel pump directly into the intake manifold in sufficient quantity to start the engine.

The primer solenoid operation can be checked by running the engine at approximately 2000 rpm and depressing the ignition key. If the solenoid is functioning properly, the engine will run rich and drop about 1000 rpm until the key is

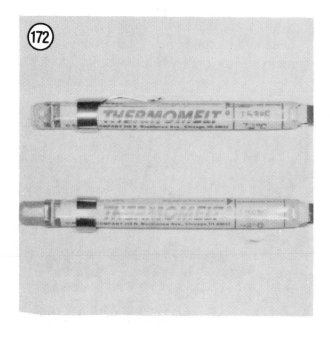

released. If the solenoid is suspected of not operating properly, shut the engine down and disconnect the purple/white wire at the terminal
block. Connect an ohmmeter between the pur-
ple/white wire and the black primer solenoid
ground wire. The ohmmeter should indicate 4-7
ohms. If the solenoid does not perform as specified, repair or replace the primer solenoid as
necessary.

ENGINE TEMPERATURE AND OVERHEATING

Proper engine temperature is critical to good
engine operation. Internal engine damage will
occur if the engine overheats. An outboard motor
that runs too cool will experience the following
conditions:

  a. Fouled spark plugs.
  b. Poor/rough idle operation.
  c. Loss of wide-open throttle speed.
  d. Excessive fuel consumption.
  e. Excessive carbon deposits in the combus-
     tion chamber.

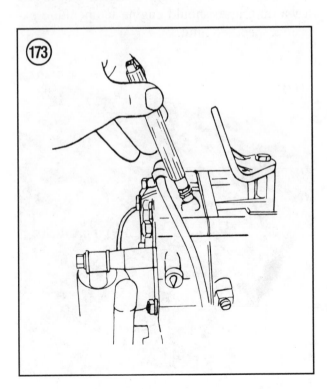

A variety of problems can cause an engine to
overheat. Some of the most common are a defective thermostat, defective water pump or damaged or mislocated water passage restrictors.

Troubleshooting

Engine temperature can be checked with the
use of Markal Thermomelt Stiks available at
your Johnson or Evinrude Dealer. This heat-sen-
sitive stick looks like a large crayon (**Figure 172**)
and is designed to melt at a specific temperature.

A much more accurate and convenient method
for checking engine temperature is by using a
pyrometer. A pyrometer is basically a thermometer which is capable of measuring high temperatures. Temperature adapters are available for
some digital multimeters which effectively convert the meter into a pyrometer.

Engine temperature check— Thermomelt Stik procedure

At least 2 Thermomelt Stiks are necessary to
check engine temperature. A 100° F (38° C) and
a 163° F (73° C) are necessary to check 2-8 hp
models. A 125° F (52° C) and a 163° F (73° C)
are necessary to check engine temperature on
9.9-300 hp models.

To be accurate, the cooling water inlet temperature should be within 60-80° F (18-24° C).
Remove the propeller and install the correct test
wheel (**Table 8**). Place the outboard motor in a
suitable test tank.

NOTE
*The Thermomelt Stik should not be ap-
plied to the center of the cylinder head,
as this area is normally hotter than 163°
F (73° C).*

1. Mark the top of the cylinder block near the
cylinder head with each Thermomelt Stik. See
Figure 173. The mark should appear similar to

a chalk mark. Make sure sufficient material is applied to the metal surface.

2. With the engine at normal operating temperature, running at 900 rpm in forward gear, the 100° F mark (2-8 hp) or the 125° F mark (9.9-300 hp) should melt. If not, the engine is running too cool. On thermostat equipped outboards, the thermostat may be stuck in the open position, causing the engine to overcool.

3. With the engine at normal operating temperature, running at 900 rpm in forward gear, the 163° F mark should not melt. If it does, the engine is overheating. Check for a defective water pump or plugged or leaking cooling system. On thermostat-equipped models, the thermostat may be stuck closed.

4. Increase engine speed to 5000 rpm. The 163° F mark should still not melt. If it does, the engine is overheating. Check for a defective water pump, leaking cooling system, damaged, missing or mislocated water passage restrictors.

Engine temperature check—pyrometer procedure

For accurate results during the following procedure, the cooling water inlet temperature should be within 60-80° F (18-24° C). Remove the propeller and install the correct test wheel (**Table 8**), then place the outboard motor in a suitable test tank.

1. Start the engine and run at 3000 rpm for at least 5 minutes to make sure the engine is at operating temperature.

2. Reduce engine speed and run at 900 rpm for 5 minutes. After 5 minutes, hold the pyrometer probe against the top of the cylinder head and note the meter reading. The temperature should be within 125-155° F (52-68° C).

   a. If temperature is below the specified temperature, check for the cause of overcooling. On thermostat equipped models, the thermostat may be stuck open.

   b. If temperature is above the specified temperature, the engine is overheating. Check for a defective water pump, plugged or leaking cooling system, damaged or missing restrictor plugs (under cylinder head) or sticking thermostat (closed) on models so equipped.

3. Increase engine speed to 5000 rpm and note the meter. Engine temperature must not exceed 120° F (49° C) on 35 Jet, 40-50 hp, 120 and 140 hp and 250-300 hp models, 155° F (68° C) on 200 and 225 hp models and 160° F (71° C) on all other models. If the temperature exceeds the specified amount, check for a defective water pump, plugged or leaking cooling system, damaged, missing or mislocated water passage restrictor plugs (under cylinder heads) or a thermostat sticking closed.

Engine Temperature Switches

The engine temperature switch is installed in the cylinder head(s) and is designed to activate a warning horn should engine temperature exceed a specified limit.

To test switch operation, disconnect the bullet connector, unscrew the switch cover and remove the switch from the cylinder head. See **Figure 174**, typical.

> *WARNING*
> *To prevent fire or explosion when testing temperature switch, be sure to use a suitable container to heat the oil. Use oil with a flash point above 300° F (150° C), such as OMC Cobra 4-Cycle Motor Oil. Never use an open flame to heat the oil.*

1. Connect a continuity lamp or ohmmeter between the temperature switch wire and the metal body of the switch.

2. Place the switch and an accurate thermometer in a container of engine oil. See **Figure 175**. Slowly increase the temperature of the oil using a suitable heat source (hot plate). *Do not* use open flame to heat the oil.

> *NOTE*
> *If using a self-powered continuity tester, the tester lamp should light when the switch closes and go out when the switch opens. If using an ohmmeter, the meter should indicate continuity when the switch closes and no continuity when the switch opens.*

3. While heating the oil, note the color of the switch wire and observe the following switch closing temperatures. Then, allow the oil to cool and observe the following switch opening temperatures:

   a. *Tan wire*—Close at 197-209° F (92-98° C); open at 155-185° F (70-84° C).
   b. *Tan/red wire*—Close at 174-186° F (79-85° C); open at 150-160° F (62-74° C).
   c. *Tan/blue wire*—Close at 234-246° F (110-118° C); open at 192-222° F (103-117° C).
   d. *Tan/green wire*—Close at 221-233° F (123-129° C); open at 155-185° F (70-84° C).
   e. *White/black wire (except 60° V6 and 1993-on 60-70 hp models)*—Close at 93-99° F (34-38° C); open at 86-92° F (30-34° C).
   f. *White/black wire (60° V6 and 1993-on 60-70 hp)*—Close at 102-108° F (39-43° C); open at 87-93° F (30-34° C).

4. If the switch fails to react as specified, replace it.

ENGINE

Engine problems are generally symptoms of something wrong in another system, such as ignition, fuel or starting. If properly maintained and serviced, the engine should experience no problems other than those caused by age and wear.

Overheating and Lack of Lubrication

Overheating and lack of lubrication cause the majority of engine mechanical problems. Outboard motors create a great deal of heat and are not designed to operate at a standstill for any length of time. Using a spark plug of the wrong heat range (too hot) can burn a piston. Incorrect

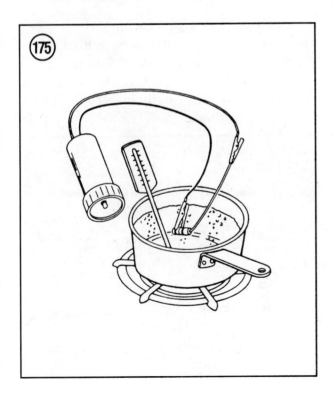

ignition timing, a defective water pump or thermostat, a propeller with excessive pitch or diameter or an excessively lean fuel mixture can also cause the engine to overheat.

Preignition

Preignition is the premature burning of the fuel charge and is caused by hot spots in the combustion chamber (**Figure 176**). The fuel actually ignites prior to ignition by the spark plug. Glowing deposits in the combustion chamber, inadequate cooling or overheated spark plugs can all cause preignition. Preignition is first noticed in the form of a power loss but will eventually result in extensive damage to the pistons and other internal engine components due to the higher combustion temperature and pressure.

Detonation

Commonly called "spark knock," detonation is the violent explosion of fuel in the combustion chamber instead of controlled burn that should normally take place. See **Figure 177**. Severe engine damage can result from detonation. Use of low octane gasoline is a common cause of detonation.

Even when high octane gasoline is used, detonation can still occur if the ignition timing is over advanced. Other causes are lean fuel mixture at or near full throttle, inadequate engine cooling, cross-firing spark plugs, excessive accumulation of deposits on the piston and combustion chamber or the use of a propeller with too much pitch or diameter (overpropped).

Since outboard motors are noisy, engine knock or detonation is likely to go unnoticed by the operator, especially at high engine speed when wind noise is also present. Such inaudible detonation may be the cause when engine damage occurs for no apparent reason.

Poor Idle

Some common causes of poor idle are improper carburetor adjustment, crankcase or vacuum leakage, incorrect ignition timing or ignition system malfunction.

Misfiring

Common causes of misfiring are a weak spark, dirty, contaminated or fouled spark plug(s) or excessively worn or defective spark plug(s). Check for chipped, cracked or broken reed valves. If misfiring only occurs under a

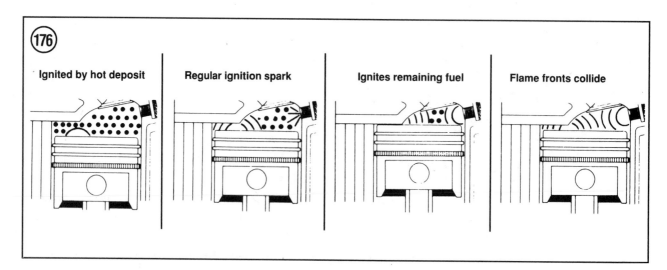

(176)

| Ignited by hot deposit | Regular ignition spark | Ignites remaining fuel | Flame fronts collide |

heavy load, as when accelerating, it is usually caused by a defective spark plug or plug wire. Run the motor at night to check for spark leaks along the plug wire(s) and under the spark plug boot(s).

> *WARNING*
> *Never run the engine in a dark garage to check for spark leakage. There is considerable danger of carbon monoxide poisoning.*

Water Leakage in Cylinder

The fastest and easiest method to check for water leakage into a cylinder is to check the spark plugs. Water inside the combustion chamber during combustion will turn to steam and thoroughly clean the spark plug and combustion chamber. If one spark plug on a multicylinder engine is very clean, and the other plugs show normal deposits, water ingestion is possibly taking place on the cylinder with the clean plug.

Water ingestion can be verified by installing used spark plugs with normal deposits into each cylinder. Run the engine in a test tank or on a boat in the water for 5-10 minutes. Stop the engine allow it to cool. Remove and inspect the spark plugs. If one or more spark plugs are thoroughly clean, water leakage is probably occurring.

Flat Spots

If the engine seems to die momentarily when the throttle is opened and then recovers, check for a dirty or restricted main jet in the carburetor, water in the fuel or an excessively lean fuel mixture. Also check for vacuum leaks at the carburetor-to-intake manifold joint, intake manifold or crankcase mating surfaces.

Power Loss

Several factors can cause a lack of power and speed. Look for air leaks in the fuel pump and fuel delivery system, chipped cracked or broken reed valves or a choke/throttle valve that operated improperly. Check ignition timing adjustment.

A piston or cylinder that is galling, incorrect piston clearance or a worn/sticky piston ring may be responsible. Look for loose bolts, defective gaskets or leaking mating surfaces on the cylinder head, cylinder or crankcase. Also check the crankshaft seals; worn seals can result in pressure or vacuum leaks.

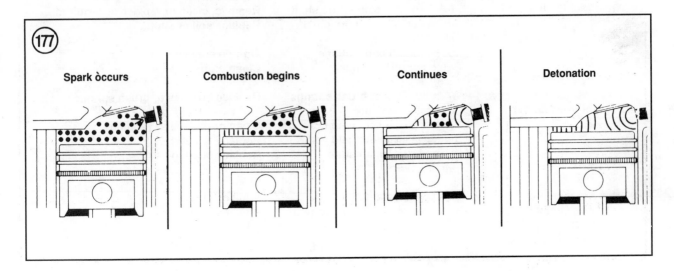

(177)

| Spark occurs | Combustion begins | Continues | Detonation |

To determine if the engine is capable of producing the necessary output, remove the propeller and install the correct test wheel. Connect an accurate tachometer to the power head according to its manufacturer's instructions. Place the outboard in a test tank, warm to normal operating temperature, then run at wide-open throttle while noting the tachometer. The engine power output can be considered acceptable if it will run up to or over the minimum test speed with the correct test wheel installed. See **Table 8**. If the engine will not reach minimum test wheel rpm, power output is insufficient and repair is necessary.

Excessive Vibration

Excessive vibration may be caused by loose motor mounts, worn rubber bushings, worn bearings, bent or damaged propeller or a generally poor running motor.

Engine Noises

Experience is needed to diagnose engine noises accurately. Noises are difficult to differentiate and even harder to describe. A deep knocking noise usually indicates main bearing failure. A slapping noise generally indicates excessive piston-to-cylinder clearance. A light knocking noise during acceleration may be a worn connecting rod bearing. Pinging (detonation) should be corrected immediately or damage to the piston(s) will result. A compression leak at the cylinder head mating surface will sound like a rapid on-off squeal.

Table 1 STARTER TROUBLESHOOTING

Trouble	Cause	Remedy
Pinion does not move when starter is turned on	Blown fuse	Replace fuse.
	Pinion rusted to armature shaft	Remove, clean or replace as required.
	Series coil or shunt broken or shorted	Replace coil or shunt.
	Loose switch connections	Tighten connections.
	Rusted or dirty plunger	Clean plunger.
Pinion meshes with ring gear but starter does not run	Worn brushes or brush springs touching armature	Replace brushes or brush springs.
	Dirty or burned commutator	Clean or replace as required.
	Defective armature field coil	Replace armature.
	Worn or rusted armature shaft bearing	Replace bearing.
Starter motor runs at full speed before pinion meshes with ring gear	Worn pinion sleeve	Replace sleeve.
	Pinion does not stop in correct position	Replace pinion.

(continued)

Table 1 STARTER TROUBLESHOOTING (continued)

Trouble	Cause	Remedy
Pinion meshes with gear and motor starts but engine does not crank	Defective overrunning clutch	Replace overrunning clutch.
Starter motor does not stop when turned off after engine has started	Rusted or dirty plunger	Clean or replace plunger.
Low starter motor speed with high current draw	Armature may be dragging on pole shoes from bent shaft, worn bearings or loose pole shoes	Replace shaft or bearings and/or tighten pole shoes.
	Tight or dirty bearings	Loosen or clean bearings.
High current draw with no armature rotation	A direct ground at switch, terminal or at brushes or field connections	Replace defective parts.
	Frozen shaft bearings which prevent armature from rotating	Loosen, clean or replace bearings.
Starter motor has grounded armature or field winding	Field and/or armature is burned or solder is thrown out of commutator due to excess heat	Raise grounded brushes from commutator and insulate them with cardboard. Use an ignition analyzer to check resistance between insulated terminal on starter motor and starter motor frame (remove ground connection of shunt coils on motors with this feature). If analyzer shows resistance (meter needle moves to right), there is a ground. Raise other brushes from armature and check armature and fields separately to locate ground.
Starter motor has grounded armature or field winding	Current passes through armature first, then to ground field windings	Disconnect grounded leads, then locate any abnormal grounds in starter motor.
	Wiring or key switch corroded	Coat with sealer to protect against further corrosion.
	Starter solenoid	Check for resistance between: (a) positive (+) terminal of battery and large input terminal of starter solenoid, (b) large wire at top of starter motor and negative (−) terminal of battery, and (c) small terminal or starter solenoid and positive battery terminal. Key switch must be in START position. Repair all defective parts.
	Starter motor	With a fully charged battery, connect a negative (−) jumper wire to upper terminal on side of starter motor and a positive (+) jumper to large lower terminal of starter motor. If motor still does not operate, remove for overhaul or replacement.

(continued)

3

Table 1 STARTER TROUBLESHOOTING (continued)

Trouble	Cause	Remedy
Starter turns over too slowly	Low battery or poor contact at battery terminal	See "Starter does not operate."
	Poor contact at starter solenoid or starter motor	Check all terminals for looseness and tighten all nuts securely.
Starter motor fails to operate and draws no current and/or high resistance	Open circuit in fields or armature, at connections or brushes or between brushes and commutator	Repair or adjust broken or weak brush springs, worn brushes, high insulation between commutator bars or a dirty, gummy or oily commutator.
High resistance in starter motor	Low no-load speed and a low current draw and low developed torque	Closed "open" field winding on unit which has 2 or 3 circuits in starter motor (unit in which current divides as it enters, taking 2 or 3 parallel paths).
High free speed and high current draw	Shorted fields in starter motor	Install new fields and check for improved performance. Fields normally have very low resistance, thus it is difficult to detect shorted fields, since difference in current draw between normal starter motor field windings would not be very great.
Excessive voltage drop	Cables too small	Install larger cables to accommodate high current draw.
High circuit resistance	Dirty connections	Clean connections.
Starter does not operate	Run-down battery	Check battery with hydrometer. If reading is below 1.230, recharge or replace battery.
	Poor contact at terminals	Remove terminal clamps. Scrape terminals and clamps clean and tighten bolts securely.
	Starter mechanism	Disconnect positive (+) battery terminal. Rotate pinion gear in disengaged position. Pinion gear and motor should run freely by hand. If motor does not turn over easily, clean starter and replace all defective parts.
Starter spins freely but does not engage engine	Low battery or poor contact at battery terminal	See "Starter does not operate."
	Poor contact at starter solenoid or starter motor	See "Starter does not operate."
	Dirty or corroded pinion drive	Clean thoroughly and lubricate the spline underneath the pinion with Lubriplate 777.
Starter does not engage freely	Pinion or flywheel gear	Inspect mating gears for excessive wear. Replace all defective parts.

(continued)

Table 1 STARTER TROUBLESHOOTING (continued)

Trouble	Cause	Remedy
	Small anti-drift spring	If drive pinion interferes with flywheel gear after engine has started, inspect anti-drift spring located under pinion gear. Replace all defective parts. NOTE: If drive pinion tends to stay engaged in flywheel gear when starter motor is in idle position, start motor at 1/4 throttle to allow starter pinion gear to release flywheel ring gear instantly.
Starter keeps on spinning after key is turned ON	Key not fully returned	Check that key has returned to normal ON position from START position. Replace switch if key constantly stays in START position.
	Starter solenoid	Inspect starter solenoid to see if contacts have become stuck in closed position. If starter does not stop running with small yellow lead disconnected from from starter solenoid, replace starter solenoid.
	Wiring or key switch	Inspect all wires for defects. Open remote control box and inspect wiring at switches. Repair or replace all defective parts.
Wires overheat	Battery terminals improperly connected	Check that negative marking on harness matches that of battery. If battery is connected improperly, red wire to rectifier will overheat.
	Short circuit in system	Inspect all wiring connections and wires for looseness or defects. Open remote control box and inspect wiring at switches.
	Short circuit in choke solenoid	Repair or replace all defective parts. Check for high resistance. If blue choke wire heats rapidly when choke is used, choke solenoid may have internal short. Replace if defective.
	Short circuit in starter solenoid	If yellow starter solenoid lead overheats, there may be internal short (resistance) in starter solenoid. Replace if defective.
	Low battery voltage	Battery voltage is checked with an ampere-volt test when battery is under a starting load. Battery must be recharged if it registers under 9.5 volts. If battery is below specified hydrometer reading of 1.230, it will not turn engine fast enough to start it.

3

Table 2 IGNITION TROUBLESHOOTING

Symptom	Probable cause
Engine won't start, but fuel and spark are good	Defective or dirty spark plugs. Spark plug gap set too wide. Improper spark timing. Shorted stop button. Air leaks into fuel pump. Broken piston ring(s). Cylinder head, crankcase or cylinder sealing faulty. Worn crankcase oil seal.
Engine misses at idle	Incorrect spark plug gap. Defective, dirty or loose spark plugs. Spark plugs of incorrect heat range. Leaking or broken high tension wires. Weak armature magnets. Defective coil or condenser. Defective ignition switch. Spark timing out of adjustment.
Engine misses at high speed	See "Engine misses at idle." Coil breaks down. Coil shorts through insulation. Spark plug gap too wide. Wrong type spark plugs. Too much spark advance.
Engine backfires	Cracked spark plug insulator. Improper timing. Crossed spark plug wires. Improper ignition timing.
Engine preignition	Spark advanced too far. Incorrect type spark plug. Burned spark plug electrodes.
Engine noises (knocking at power head)	Spark timing advanced too far.
Ignition coil fails	Extremely high voltage. Moisture formation. Excessive heat from engine.
Spark plugs burn and foul	Incorrect type plug. Fuel mixture too rich. Inferior grade of gasoline. Overheated engine. Excessive carbon in combustion chambers.
Ignition causing high fuel consumption	Incorrect spark timing. Leaking high tension wires. Incorrect spark plug gap. Fouled spark plugs. Incorrect spark advance. Weak ignition coil. Preignition.

3

Table 3 FUEL SYSTEM TROUBLESHOOTING

Symptom	Probable cause
No fuel at carburetor	No gas in tank. Air vent in gas cap not open. Air vent in gas cap clogged. Fuel tank sitting on fuel line. Fuel line fittings not properly connected to engine or fuel tank Air leak at fuel connection. Fuel pickup clogged. Defective fuel pump.
Flooding at carburetor	Choke out of adjustment. High float level. Float stuck. Excessive fuel pump pressure. Float saturated beyond buoyancy.
Rough operation	Dirt or water in fuel. Reed valve open or broken. Incorrect fuel level in carburetor bowl. Carburetor loose at mounting flange. Throttle shutter not closing completely. Throttle shutter valve installed incorrectly.
Carburetor spit-back at idle	Chipped or broken reed valve(s).
Engine misfires at high speed	Dirty carburetor. Lean carburetor adjustment. Restriction in fuel system. Low fuel pump pressure.
Engine backfires	Poor quality fuel. Air-fuel mixture too rich or too lean. Improperly adjusted carburetor.
Engine preignition	Excessive oil in fuel. Inferior grade of gasoline. Lean carburetor mixture.
Spark plugs burn and foul	Fuel mixture too rich or inferior grade of gasoline.
High gas consumption: Flooding or leaking	Cracked carburetor casting. Leaks at line connections. Defective carburetor bowl gasket. High float level. Plugged vent hole in cover. Loose needle and seat. Defective needle valve seat gasket. Worn needle valve and seat. Float binding in bowl. High fuel pump pressure.

(continued)

Table 3 FUEL SYSTEM TROUBLESHOOTING (continued)

Symptom	Probable cause
High gas consumption: (continued)	
Overrich mixture	Choke lever stuck.
	High float level.
	High fuel pump pressure.
Abnormal speeds	Carburetor out of adjustment.
	Too much oil in fuel.

Table 4 STATOR RESISTANCE VALUES

Model	Amperage	Resistance (ohms)
9.9-30 hp	4 amp	0.50-0.60
35 Jet, 40-50 hp	4 amp	0.50-0.60
60-70 hp	6 amp	1.3-1.5
	12 amp	0.4-0.6
65 Jet, 80 Jet, 85,		
90, 100, 115 hp	6 amp	1.2-1.4
	8 & 10 amp	0.65-0.75
150 & 175 hp (90°)	35 amp	0.11-0.21
150 & 175 hp (60°)		
1991	35 amp	0.067-0.167
1992-93	35 amp	0.05-0.19
120 & 140 hp	9 amp	0.65-0.75
200, 225, 250 & 300 hp	35 amp	0.11-0.21

Table 5 STARTER MOTOR NO-LOAD SPECIFICATIONS

Model	Volts	Max. amperage	Speed (rpm)
9.9-15 hp	12-12.4	7	7000-9200
20-30 hp	12-12.4	30	6500-7500
35 Jet, 40-50 hp	12-12.4	32	5700-8000
60-70 hp	12-12.4	32	5750-8000
65 Jet, 80 Jet, 85,			
90, 100, 115 hp	12-12.4	36	5350 (min.)
150 & 175 hp (90°)	12-12.4	25	6000-7000
150 & 175 hp (90°)*	12-12.4	30	10,500 (min.)
120 & 140 hp	12-12.4	36	5350 (min.)
200, 225, 250, 300 hp*	12-12.4	30	10,500 (min.)

* On gear reduction starters, the driven gear and pinion shaft must be removed from the motor when performing no-load test.

Table 6 MINIMUM BATTERY CABLE GAUGE SIZES

Model	Battery cables minimum gauge		
	1-10 ft.	11-15 ft.	16-20 ft.
9.9-15 hp	10	8	6
20-30 hp	6	4	3
	(continued)		

Table 6 MINIMUM BATTERY CABLE GAUGE SIZES (continued)

| Model | Battery cables minimum gauge | | |
	1-10 ft.	11-15 ft.	16-20 ft.
40-50 hp	6	4	3
60-70 hp, V4	4	3	1
V6	4	2	1
V8	4	2	1

Table 7 MINIMUM BATTERY RECOMMENDATIONS

Model	Minimum battery cold cranking amps (CCA) and reserve capacity at 80° F (27° C)
9.9-15 hp	350 CCA and 100 minutes reserve
20-30 hp	350 CCA and 100 minutes reserve
40-50 hp	360 CCA and 115 minutes reserve
60-70 hp, V4	360 CCA and 115 minutes reserve
V6 & V8	500 CCA and 99 minutes reserve

Table 8 TEST WHEEL RECOMMENDATIONS

Model	Test wheel (part No.)	Minimum test speed (rpm)
2 hp	1	4500
2.3 hp	1	4800
3.3 hp	115306	5000
3 hp, 4 hp	317738	4400
4 Deluxe	390123	5100
6 hp	390239	4800
8 hp	390239	5300
9.9 hp		
1991-1992	386537	4800
1993	435750	5200
15 hp		
1991-1992	386537	6100
1993	435750	5800
20 hp	386891	4550
25 hp	434505	4800
28 hp	398948	4800
30 hp	434505	5400
40 hp	432968	4900
48 hp, 50 hp	432968	5200
60 hp	386665	5000
70 hp	386665	5700
85 hp, 88 hp, 90 hp, 100, 115 hp	382861	4800
120 hp		
1991-1992	386246	5300
1993	433068	5200
120TXETF, 120TXATF	396277	5200
140TL		
1991-1992	386246	5500
1993	433068	5300
	(continued)	

3

Table 8 TEST WHEEL RECOMMENDATIONS (continued)

Model	Test wheel (part No.)	Minimum test speed (rpm)
140TX		
1991-1992	387388	5500
1993	396277	5300
140CX		
1991-1992	398673	5500
1993	398673	5300
150 hp (90°) (149.4 cid)	387388	4500
175 hp (90°) (160.3 cid)	387388	4800
150 hp (60°) (158 cid)	387388[2]	4500
175 hp (60°) (158 cid)	387388[2]	4800
200XP, 200GT, 200STL		
1991-1992	387388	5700
200STL		
1993	436080	5700
200TX		
1991-1992	387388	5500
1993	436080	5500
200CX		
1991-1992	398673	5500
1993	436081	5500
225 hp		
1991-1992	387388	5700
1993	436080	5700
225CX		
1991-1992	388673	5700
1993	436081	5700
250 hp, 300 hp	396277	5500
250CX, 300CX	398674	5500

1. A test wheel is not used on 2 and 2.3 hp models. Use the standard propeller (part No. 115208) when running motor in a test tank.
2. On counter rotating (CX) models, use test wheel (part No. 398673).

Chapter Four

Lubrication, Maintenance and Tune-up

The modern outboard motor delivers more power and performance than ever before, with higher compression ratios, new and improved electrical systems and other design advances. Proper lubrication, maintenance and tune-up have thus become increasingly important as ways in which you can maintain a high level of performance, extend engine life and extract the maximum economy of operation.

You can do your own lubrication, maintenance and tune-up if you follow the correct procedures and use common sense. The following information is based on recommendations from Johnson and Evinrude that will help you keep your outboard motor operating at its peak performance level. **Tables 1-5** are located at the end of this chapter.

LUBRICATION

Proper Fuel Selection

Two-stroke engines are lubricated by mixing oil with the fuel. The internal components of the engine are lubricated as the fuel-oil mixture passes through the crankcase and cylinders.

Since outboard fuel serves the dual function of producing combustion and distributing the lubrication, the use of low octane marine white gasoline or any other fuel not intended for use in modern gasoline-powered engines should be avoided. Among other problems, such fuel has a tendency to cause piston ring sticking and exhaust port plugging.

The recommended fuel is regular or premium unleaded gasoline with a *minimum* pump octane rating of 67 on 2-30 hp or 87 on all other models. For optimum performance and maximum engine life, gasoline with an octane rating of 89 or higher is recommended. Premium grade gasoline produced by a national brand refinery is specifically recommended. Premium grade gasolines (91-93 octane) contain a high concentration of detergent and dispersant additives that prevent carbon deposits on pistons and rings.

The use of alcohol extended gasoline is not recommended. However, gasoline containing not more than 10 percent ethanol alcohol or 5 percent methanol alcohol with 5 percent cosolvents may be used if it meets the minimum octane requirements. If alcohol extended gasoline is frequently used, the fuel system should be carefully inspected at regular intervals. Replace fuel system components if deterioration, corrosion or leakage is noted.

Sour Fuel

Gasoline should not be stored for more than 60 days (under ideal conditions). Gasoline forms gum and varnish deposits as it ages. Such fuel will cause starting problems, carburetor plugging and poor performance. A fuel additive such as OMC 2+4 Fuel Conditioner should be used in the fuel during storage or periods of nonuse. Always use fresh gasoline when mixing fuel for your outboard.

Alcohol Extended Gasoline

Some gasoline sold for marine use contains alcohol, although this fact may not be advertised. Although the manufacturer *does not* recommend using alcohol extended gasoline, testing to date has found that it causes no major deterioration of fuel system components when consumed *immediately* after purchase.

Gasoline with alcohol slowly absorbs moisture from the atmosphere. When the moisture content of the fuel reaches approximately one half of one percent, it combines with the alcohol and separates (phase separation) from the gasoline. This separation does not normally occur in an automobile, as the fuel is generally consumed within a few days after purchase; however, because boats often remain idle for days or even weeks, the problem does occur in marine use.

Moisture and alcohol become very corrosive when mixed and will cause corrosion of metal components and deterioration of rubber and plastic fuel system components. In addition, the alcohol and water mixture will settle to the bottom of the fuel tank. If this mixture enters the engine, it will wash off the oil film and may result in corrosion and damage to the cylinder walls and other internal engine components. It will be necessary to drain the fuel tank, flush out the fuel system with clean gasoline, and if necessary, remove and clean the spark plugs before the motor can be started.

The following is an accepted and widely used field procedure for detecting alcohol in gasoline. Note that the gasoline should be checked prior to mixing with the oil. Use any small transparent bottle or tube that can be capped and can be provided with graduations or a mark at approximately 1/3 full. A pencil mark on a piece of adhesive tape is sufficient.

1. Fill the container with water to the 1/3 full mark.
2. Add gasoline until the container is almost full. Leave a small air space at the top.
3. Shake the container vigorously, then allow it to set for 3-5 minutes. If the volume of water appears to have increased, alcohol is present. If the dividing line between the water and gasoline becomes cloudy, reference from the center of the cloudy band.

This procedure can not differentiate between types of alcohol (ethanol or methanol), nor is it considered to be absolutely accurate from a scientific standpoint, but it is accurate enough to determine if sufficient alcohol is present to cause the user to take precautions.

Recommended Fuel Mixture

NOTE
If the outboard is equipped with Oil Injection, read this chapter then refer to Chapter Eleven.

The recommended oil is Evinrude or Johnson Outboard Lubricant, Evinrude or Johnson XP Outboard Lubricant or OMC 2-Cycle Motor Oil.

CAUTION
Do not, under any circumstances, use multigrade or other high detergent automotive oil or oil containing metallic additives. Such oil is harmful to 2-stroke engines, and may result in piston scoring, bearing failure or other engine damage.

If Evinrude, Johnson or OMC oil is not available, use a good quality oil with the NMMA certification TCW-3. TCW-2 oil may be used on 30 hp and smaller models; however, if using TCW-2 engine oil, the manufacturer recommends adding OMC Carbon Guard fuel additive to the gasoline and the application of OMC Engine Tuner at 50 hour intervals to prevent excessive carbon, gum and varnish deposits on pistons and rings.

NOTE
The manufacturer specifically recommends using NMMA certified TCW-3 oil on 40 hp and larger models.

Models without oil injection

The fuel-oil ratio for normal service is 50:1. Mix 8 fl. oz. (236 mL) of a recommended oil for each 3 gallons (11.4 L) of gasoline. To provide the additional lubricant required during the break-in period (first 12 gallons of fuel), of a new or rebuilt power head, a 25:1 fuel-oil ratio should be used. Mix 16 fl. oz. (473 mL) of a recommended oil with each 3 gallons (11.4 L) of gasoline. After the first 12 gallons of fuel have been consumed (break-in period), switch to a 50:1 mixture.

Models equipped with oil injection

To provide the additional lubricant required during the break-in period (first 10 hours of operation) of a new or rebuilt power head, a 50:1 fuel-oil mixture should be used in the fuel tank in addition to the normal oil injection system.

After the first 10 hours of operation, first be certain the oil injection system is functioning (oil level in reservoir dropping), then switch to straight gasoline in the fuel tank.

CAUTION
If the oil injection system is disabled and not used, a 25:1 fuel-oil mixture must be used during the break-in period and a 50:1 mixture during normal service.

Correct Fuel Mixing

WARNING
Gasoline is an extreme fire hazard. Never use gasoline near heat, sparks or flame. Do not smoke while mixing fuel.

Mix the fuel and oil outdoors or in a well-ventilated indoor location. Using less than the specified amount of oil can result in insufficient lubrication and serious engine damage. Using more oil than specified causes spark plug fouling, erratic carburetor operation, excessive smoking and rapid carbon accumulation.

Cleanliness is of prime importance. Even a very small particle of dirt can cause carburetor problems. Always use fresh gasoline. Gum and varnish deposits tend to form in gasoline stored for any length of time. Use of sour fuel can result in carburetor plugging, spark plug fouling and poor performance.

Consistent Fuel Mixtures

The carburetor idle adjustment is sensitive to fuel mixture variations which result from the use of different oils and gasolines or from inaccurate measuring and mixing. This could result in readjustment of the idle needle to compensate for variations in the fuel-oil mixture. To prevent the necessity for constant readjustment of the carburetor from one batch of fuel to the next, always be consistent. Prepare each batch of fuel exactly the same as the previous one.

Pre-mixed fuel sold at some marinas is not recommended for use. The quality and consistency of pre-mixed fuel can vary greatly. The possibility of engine damage resulting from using an incorrect fuel mixture far outweighs the convenience offered by pre-mixed fuel. This is especially true if the marina uses alcohol or other additives in its fuel.

Lower Unit Lubrication

The lower unit lubricant should be replaced after the first 20 hours of operation and every 100 hours of operation thereafter. Check the lubricant level every 50 hours of operation and fill as necessary.

The recommended lubricant for all models except 4 Deluxe is OMC Hi-Vis gearcase lube. The recommended lubricant for 4 Deluxe models is OMC Premium Blend gearcase lube. If Hi-Vis gearcase lube is not available, OMC Premium Blend is an acceptable substitute for all models except 4 Deluxe, 60° 150 and 175 hp and 200-300 hp models. Alternate gearcase lubricants should not be used on these models.

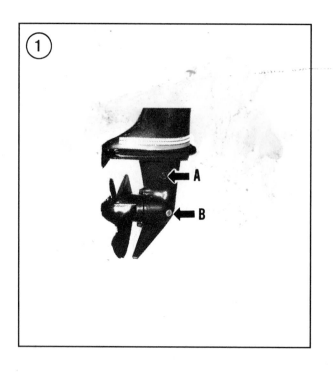

> *CAUTION*
> *Do not use regular automotive gear lube in the lower drive unit. Its expansion and foam characteristics are not suitable for marine use.*

Proceed as follows to drain and refill the lower unit lubricant.

1. Disconnect all spark plug wires to prevent accidental starting.

2. Position the outboard motor in the normal operating position. Place a suitable container under the gearcase.

> *CAUTION*
> *Do not attempt to fill the gearcase without first removing the oil level plug. The*

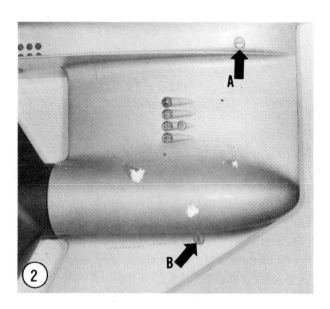

gearcase cannot be completely filled without removing the plug.

3. Locate and remove the oil level plug and gasket. See A, **Figure 1** or **Figure 2**, typical.

NOTE
The gearcase on 9.9-50 hp models has a Phillips head screw located near the drain/fill plug. See Figure 3. The Phillips head screw is the shift rod pivot screw, and if removed, it will be necessary to disassemble the gearcase completely to reinstall it. Do not remove the shift rod pivot screw by mistake.

4. Locate and remove the drain/fill plug and gasket. See B, **Figure 1** or **Figure 2**, typical.

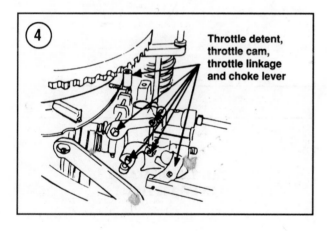

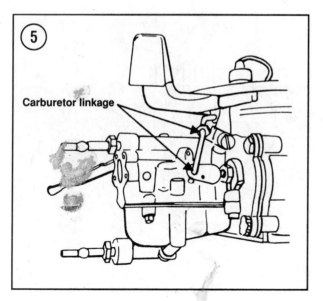

NOTE
If the lubricant is creamy in color (water contamination) or if metallic particles are found, the gearcase must be completely disassembled and repaired before returning the unit to service.

5. Allow the gearcase lubricant to drain completely.

6. To refill, inject the recommended lubricant into the drain/fill hole until the oil is even with the level plug hole. Without removing the lubricant tube or nozzle, install the level plug and gasket and tighten securely.

7. Remove the lubricant tube or nozzle and quickly install the drain/fill plug and gasket. Tighten both plugs to 30-40 in.-lb. (3.4-4.5 N•m) on 2.3 and 3.3 hp models, 40-50 in.-lb. (4.5-5.6 N•m) on 3 and 4 hp models and 60-84 in.-lb. (6.8-9.5 N•m) on all other models.

Other Lubrication Points

Refer to **Figures 4-19**, typical and **Table 1** for additional lubrication points, frequency of lubrication and the recommended lubricant to use.

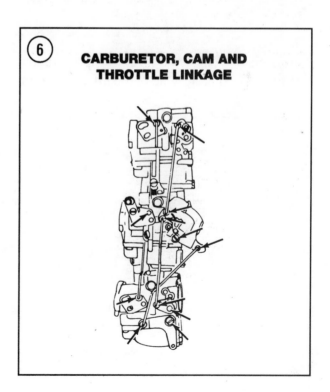

CAUTION
When lubricating the steering cable on models so equipped, make sure its core is fully retracted into the cable housing. Lubricating the cable while extended can cause a hydraulic lock to occur.

Saltwater Corrosion of Gearcase Housing and Propeller Shaft Bearing Housing/Nut

Corrosion that is allowed to accumulate between the gearcase housing and propeller shaft bearing housing can eventually split the housing and destroy the lower unit assembly. If the motor is used in saltwater, remove the propeller and bearing housing at least once per year after the initial 20-hour inspection. Refer to Chapter Nine. Clean all corrosion deposits and dried lubricant from the gearcase and bearing housing assemblies (**Figure 20**). Lubricate the bearing housing, O-rings and screw threads with OMC Gasket Sealing Compound. Install the bearing housing and tighten the screws to specification (Chapter Nine).

STORAGE

The major consideration during preparation for storage is to protect the outboard motor from

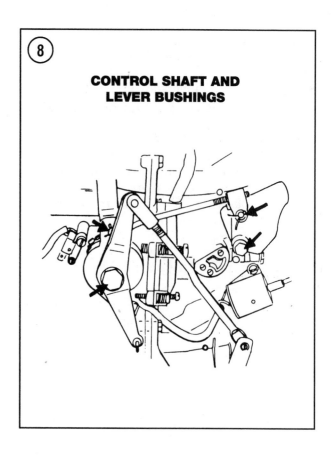

CONTROL SHAFT AND LEVER BUSHINGS

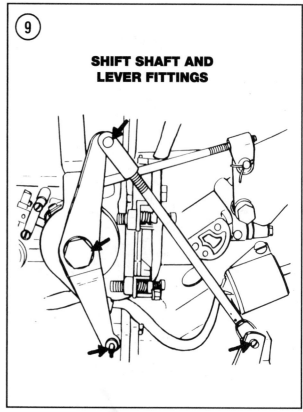

SHIFT SHAFT AND LEVER FITTINGS

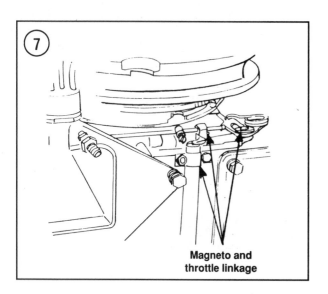

Magneto and throttle linkage

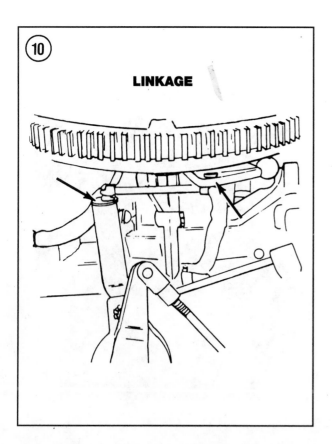

rust, corrosion and dirt or other contamination. The manufacturer recommends the following procedure.

1. If the boat is equipped with a built-in fuel tank, add one ounce of OMC 2+4 Fuel Condi-

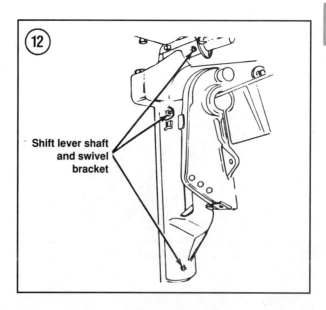

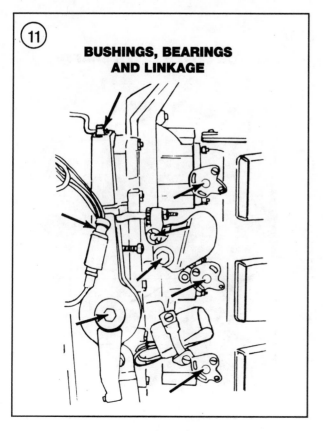

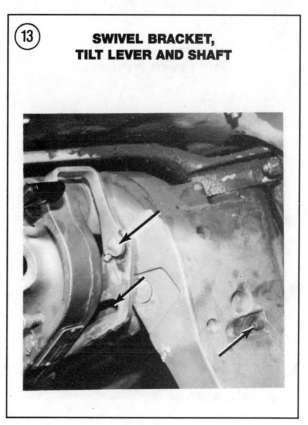

SWIVEL BRACKET, TILT/TRIM LOCK, TILT/RUN LEVER AND REVERSE LOCK

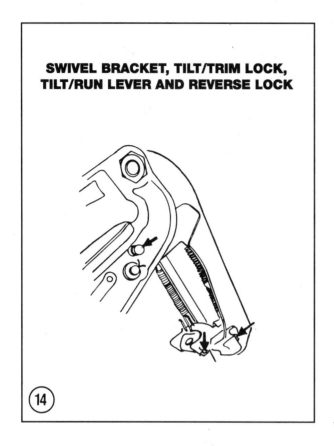

(14)

(16)   **TILT TUBE SHAFT**

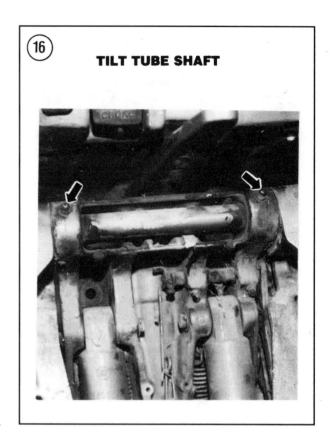

(15)   **SHIFT SHAFT AND LEVER FITTING**

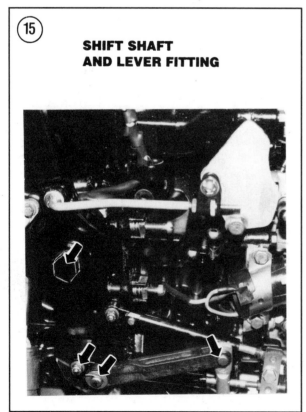

(17)   **MOTOR COVER LEVER SHAFTS**

tioner to the fuel tank for each gallon of fuel tank capacity. Then, fill the tank with a recommended fuel.

2. Operate the motor in a test tank, on the boat in the water or with a flushing device connected to the lower unit. Start the engine and run it at

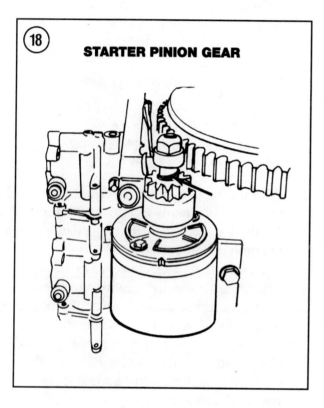

STARTER PINION GEAR

⑱

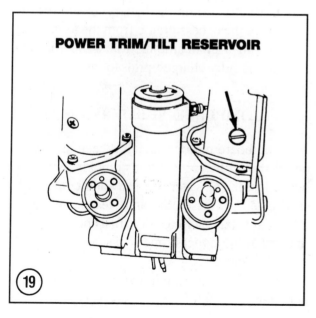

POWER TRIM/TILT RESERVOIR

⑲

idle speed to allow the stabilized fuel to circulate into the engine and carburetor(s).

3. Stop the engine after approximately five minutes.

4. Using a 6 gallon remote fuel tank, prepare the following storage mixture:

    a. Add 5 gallons of a recommended fuel.

    b. Add 2 quarts of OMC Storage Fogging Oil.

    c. Add 1 pint of Evinrude or Johnson Outboard Lubricant.

    d. Add 1 pint of OMC 2+4 Fuel Conditioner.

5. Thoroughly blend the mixture in the remote fuel tank.

6. Connect the remote fuel tank to the outboard motor.

7. With the motor in a test tank, in the water or connected to a flushing device, start the engine and run at 1500 rpm for 5 minutes to be sure the fuel delivery system and carburetor(s) contain stabilized fuel.

NOTE
*On models equipped with variable ratio oiling (VRO) **do not** disconnect the fuel hose with the engine running in an attempt to run the carburetors dry. When a low amount of gasoline is supplied to*

⑳

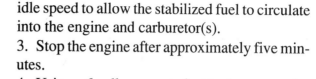

the VRO pump, a fuel mixture with a high oil-to-gasoline ratio is created. The resulting mixture will cause excessive oil consumption and difficulty restarting.

8. Stop the engine and disconnect the remote fuel tank.

9. Remove the spark plugs as described in this chapter.

10. Spray a liberal amount of OMC Storage Fogging Oil through the spark plug holes into each cylinder.

11. Rotate the flywheel (or timing wheel) clockwise to distribute the fogging oil throughout the cylinder(s).

12. Remove the flushing device or remove the outboard motor from the test tank or water. Rotate the flywheel or timing wheel clockwise several revolutions to drain any water from the water pump.

13. Clean and regap, or replace the spark plugs. Do not reconnect the spark plug leads.

14. If the storage fuel mixture is not to be used on any other outboard motors, *safely* drain and clean the remote fuel tank.

15. Drain and refill the gearcase as described in this chapter. Check the condition of the level and drain/fill plug gaskets and replace as necessary.

16. Refer to **Figures 4-19** and **Table 1** as appropriate and lubricate the motor at all specified points.

17. Remove and check the propeller condition. On models so equipped, remove any burrs from the drive pin hole and replace the drive pin if worn or bent. Look for propeller shaft seal damage from fishing line. Clean and lubricate the propeller shaft with OMC Triple-Guard grease. Reinstall the propeller with a new cotter pin or locking tab washer.

18. Clean all external parts of the motor with OMC All-Purpose Marine Cleaner and apply a good quality marine polish.

19. Store the outboard motor in an upright position in a dry and well-ventilated location.

20. Service the battery as follows:

a. Disconnect the battery cables from the battery, first the negative then the positive cable.

b. Remove all grease, corrosion or other contamination from the battery surface.

c. Check the electrolyte level in each cell and fill with distilled water as necessary. The electrolyte level in each cell should not be higher than 3/16 in. (4.8 mm) above the perforated baffles.

d. Lubricate the terminal bolts with grease or petroleum jelly.

CAUTION
A discharged battery can be damaged by freezing.

e. With the battery in a fully-charged condition (specific gravity at 1.260-1.275), store in a dry location where the temperature will not drop below freezing.

f. Recharge the battery every 45 days or whenever the specific gravity drops below 1.230. Before charging, cover the plates with distilled water, but not more than 3/16 in. (4.8 mm) above the battery baffles. The charge rate should not exceed 6 amps. Discontinue charging when the specific gravity reaches 1.260 at 80° F (27° C).

g. Before returning the battery to service, remove the excess grease from the terminals, leaving a small amount. Make sure the battery is fully charged prior to installation.

COMPLETE SUBMERSION

An outboard motor which has been lost overboard should be recovered as quickly as possible. If lost in saltwater or freshwater containing sand or silt, disassemble and clean it immediately—any delay will result in rust and corrosion of internal components once it has been removed from the water.

If the motor was running when it was lost, do not attempt to start it until it has been disassembled and checked. Internal components may be bent or out of alignment and running the motor may cause permanent damage.

The following emergency steps should be accomplished immediately if the motor is lost in freshwater.

CAUTION
If is not possible to disassemble and clean the motor immediately, resubmerge it in freshwater to prevent rust and corrosion formation until such time as it can be properly serviced.

1. Remove the engine cover.
2. Remove the spark plugs as described in this chapter.
3. Unplug the ignition connectors between the stator assembly and power pack.
4. Disconnect, drain and clean all fuel hoses.
5. Remove the carburetor float bowl drain screw(s) if so equipped. See Chapter Six.
6. Remove, drain and clean the VRO oil reservoir. Drain and clean all contaminated oil hoses.
7. Wash the outside of the motor with clean water to remove weeds, mud and other debris.

CAUTION
If sand or silt has entered the power head or gearcase, do not try to start the motor or severe internal damage may occur.

8. Drain as much water as possible from the power head by placing the motor in a horizontal position. Use the starter rope or rotate the flywheel or timing wheel by hand with the spark plug holes facing downward.

CAUTION
Do not force the motor if it does not turn over freely. This may be an indication of internal damage such as a bent connecting rod or broken piston.

9. Pour a recommended engine oil into the cylinders through the spark plug holes.
10. Remove and disassemble the carburetors as outlined in Chapter Six.

11. Disassemble the electric starter motor, if so equipped, and disconnect all electrical connections. Wash with clean freshwater. Spray all electrical components and connections with a water displacing electrical spray and allow to dry. Reassemble the starter motor, if so equipped, and reconnect all electrical connections.
12. Reinstall the spark plug(s) and carburetor(s).
13. Mix a fresh tank of fuel at the ratio recommended for the break-in period as outlined in this chapter.
14. Try to start the motor. If the motor will start, allow it to run at least 30 minutes.
15. If the motor will not start in Step 11, try to diagnose the cause as fuel, electrical or mechanical, then repair as necessary. If the engine cannot be started within 3 hours, disassemble, clean and thoroughly oil all parts.

ANTICORROSION MAINTENANCE

1. Flush the cooling system with freshwater as described in this chapter after each use in saltwater. Wash exterior with freshwater.

2. Dry exterior of the motor and apply primer over any paint nicks and scratches. Do not use antifouling paints containing mercury or copper. Do not paint sacrificial anodes or the trim tab.

3. Apply OMC Black Neoprene Dip to all exposed electrical connections except the positive terminal on the starter solenoid.

4. Check sacrificial anodes and replace any that are less than two-thirds their original size. To test for proper anode installation, proceed as follows:

   a. Calibrate an ohmmeter on the R × 1000 or high-ohm scale.

   b. Connect one ohmmeter lead to a good engine ground and the remaining lead to the anode. If necessary, clean the anode to ensure a good contact. Low resistance should be noted.

c. If high resistance is noted, remove the anode and thoroughly clean the mounting surfaces of the anode and motor and the threads of the mounting screws.

d. Reinstall the anode and retest as previously described. If high resistance is still noted between the anode and motor, replace the anode.

5. If the outboard is operated consistently in saltwater, polluted or brackish water, reduce the lubrication intervals stated in **Table 1** by one-half.

ENGINE FLUSHING

Periodic engine flushing will prevent salt, sand or silt deposits from accumulating in the water passageways. This procedure should also be performed whenever an outboard motor is operated in polluted, brackish or saltwater.

Position the outboard motor in its normal operating position during and after the flushing process. This prevents water from passing into the power head through the drive shaft housing and exhaust ports during the flushing procedure. It also eliminates the possibility of residual water being trapped in the drive shaft housing or other passageways.

> *WARNING*
> *When running the outboard motor on a flushing device, always remove the propeller to prevent serious personal injury from contact with the moving propeller.*

On 2, 2.3 and 3.3 hp models, the cooling water intake is located in the propeller shaft bearing head at the rear of the gearcase (**Figure 21**), directly in front of the propeller. On 4 Deluxe, 6 and 8 hp models, the cooling water intake is located on the exhaust port (**Figure 22**). These models require a special type of flushing device. See an Evinrude/Johnson Dealer for the correct flushing device.

On some V6 and V8 models and all 60° V6 models, a flushing port (**Figure 23**) is located on the rear of the engine. On models so equipped, remove the water pump indicator plug and attach a garden hose to the flushing port. Models equipped with a flushing port can be flushed without starting the engine; however, do not exceed 45 psi (310 kPa) water pressure.

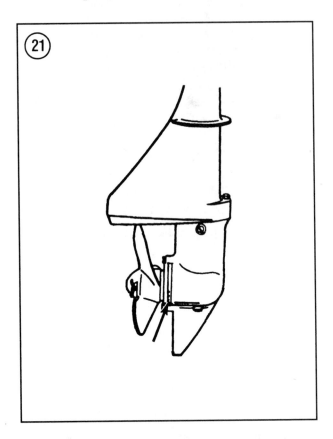

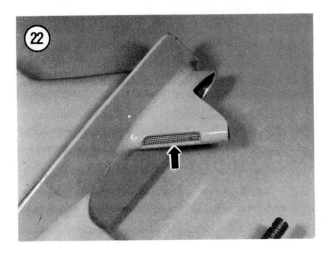

1A. *Models so equipped*—Remove the water pump indicator plug from the flushing port (**Figure 23**). Attach a suitable garden hose to the flushing port.

1B. *All others*—Attach the flushing device according to its manufacturer's instructions. See

Figure 24, typical. Attach a suitable garden hose to the flushing device.

2. Open the water tap partially—do not use full pressure.

3. Start the motor and run at approximately 1500 rpm.

4. Adjust the water flow so a slight loss of water around the rubber cups of the flushing device is noted (except flushing port models).

5. Check the motor to make sure water is being discharged from the "tell tale" nozzle. If no water is being discharged, stop the motor immediately then determine the cause of the problem.

CAUTION
Flush the motor for at least 5 minutes if
used in saltwater.

6. Flush the motor until the discharged water is clear, then stop the motor.

7. After stopping the motor, close the water tap and remove the flushing device or disconnect the hose from the flushing port.

TUNE-UP

A tune-up consists of a series of inspections, adjustments and parts replacement to compensate for normal wear and deterioration of outboard motor components. Regular tune-up is important to maintain sufficient power, performance and economy. The manufacturer recommends tune-up service be performed every 6 months or 50 hours of operation, whichever comes first. If subjected to limited use, the engine should be tuned at least once per year.

Since proper outboard motor operation depends on a number of interrelated system functions, a tune-up consisting of only one or two corrections will seldom give satisfactory results. For best results, a thorough and systematic procedure of analysis and correction is necessary.

Prior to performing a tune-up, flush the outboard motor as described in this chapter to check for satisfactory water pump operation.

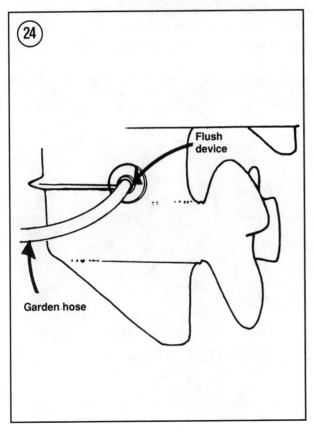

Flush device

Garden hose

The tune-up process recommended by the manufacturer includes the following:

a. Compression test.
b. Spark plug service.
c. Lower unit and water pump check.
d. Fuel system service.
e. Remove carbon deposits from combustion chamber(s).
f. Ignition system service.
g. Battery, starter motor and solenoid check, if so equipped.
h. Inspect wiring harness.
i. Engine synchronization and adjustment.
j. On-the-water performance test.

Any time the fuel or ignition systems are adjusted or require parts replacement, the engine timing, synchronization and linkage adjustment *must* be checked. These procedures are described in Chapter Five. Perform the synchronization and linkage adjustment procedure *before* running the performance test.

Compression Test

An accurate compression test gives an indication of the condition of the basic working parts of the engine. It is also an important first step in any tune-up, as a motor with low or uneven compression between cylinders *cannot* be satisfactorily tuned. Any compression problem discovered during the test must be corrected before continuing with the tune-up procedure.

1. Start the engine and warm to normal operating temperature.
2. Remove all spark plugs as described in this chapter.
3. Connect a compression tester to the top spark plug hole according to its manufacturer's instructions. See **Figure 25**.
4. Make sure the throttle is in the wide-open position, then crank the engine through at least 4 compression strokes. Record the gauge reading.

5. Repeat Step 3 and Step 4 on each remaining cylinder.

While minimum cylinder compression should not be less than 100 psi (689 kPa), the actual readings are not as important as the differences in readings between cylinders when interpreting the results. A variation of more than 15 psi (103.4 kPa) indicates a problem with the lower reading cylinder, such as defective head gasket, worn or sticking piston rings and/or scored pistons or cylinder walls. On V4 and V6 cross flow motors, compare compression readings from cylinders on the same bank, not cylinders on opposite banks.

If unequal or low compression is noted, pour a tablespoon of engine oil into the suspect cylinder and repeat Steps 3 and 4. If the compression is raised significantly (10 psi [69 kPa] or more) the piston rings are worn and should be replaced.

If evidence of overheating is noted (discolored or scorched paint), but the compression test is normal, check the cylinder(s) visually through the transfer ports for possible scoring. A cylinder can be slightly scored and still deliver a relatively

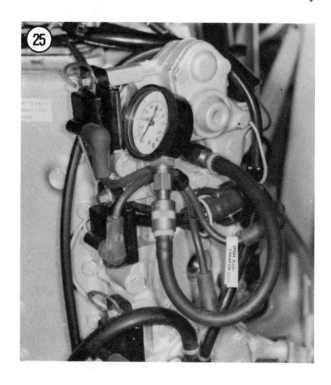

good compression reading. In such a case, it is also good practice to recheck the water pump and cooling system for possible causes of overheating.

If the outboard runs normally and the compression test is acceptable, continue the tune-up procedure.

Spark Plug Selection

> *NOTE*
> *The manufacturer recommends using surface gap spark plugs if the outboard motor is subjected to sustained high-speed operation.*

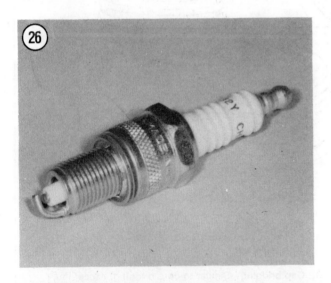

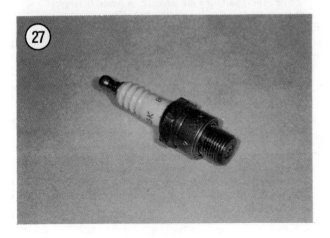

Evinrude and Johnson outboard motors are equipped with Champion or AC spark plugs selected for average use conditions. Under severe operating conditions, the recommended spark plug may foul or overheat. In such cases, check the ignition and carburetion systems to be sure they are operating correctly. If no defect is found, replace the spark plug with one of a hotter or colder heat range as required. **Table 3** shows the recommended spark plugs for all models covered in this manual.

> *CAUTION*
> *On 60° 150 and 175 hp models (OIS ignition), the use of suppression spark plugs is specifically recommended. Using nonsuppression spark plugs will result in erratic ignition system operation.*

Spark Plug Removal

> *CAUTION*
> *When the spark plugs are removed, dirt surrounding the base of the plugs can fall into the cylinder, causing serious engine damage.*

1. Blow any foreign material from around the spark plugs using compressed air.

2. Disconnect the spark plug wires by twisting the wire boot back and forth while pulling outward. Pulling on the wire instead of the boot will cause internal damage to the wire.

3. Remove the spark plugs using an appropriate size spark plug wrench or socket. Arrange the plugs in the order removed, so you know which cylinder they were removed from.

4. Examine each spark plug. See **Figure 26** for a conventional spark plug and **Figure 27** for a surface gap plug. Compare plug condition with **Figure 28** (conventional) or **Figure 29** (surface gap). Spark plug condition can be an indicator of engine condition and warn of developing trouble.

**SPARK PLUG ANALYSIS
(CONVENTIONAL GAP SPARK PLUGS)**

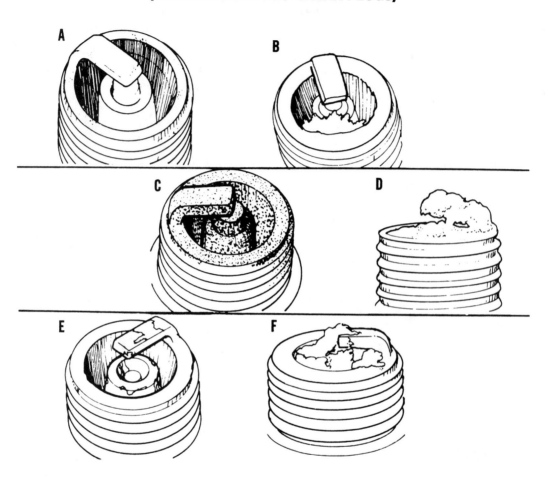

A. **Normal**—Light tan to gray color of insulator indicates correct heat range. Few deposits are present and the electrodes are not burned.

B. **Core bridging**—These defects are caused by excessive combustion chamber deposits striking and adhering to the firing end of the plug. In this case, they wedge or fuse between the electrode and core nose. They originate from the piston and cylinder head surfaces. Deposits are formed by one or more of the following:
  a. Excessive carbon in cylinder.
  b. Use of non-recommended oils.
  c. Immediate high-speed operation after prolonged trolling.
  d. Improper fuel-oil ratio.

C. **Wet fouling**—Damp or wet, black carbon coating over entire firing end of plug. Forms sludge in some engines. Caused by one or more of the following:
  a. Spark plug heat range too cold.
  b. Prolonged trolling.
  c. Low-speed carburetor adjustment too rich.

  d. Improper fuel-oil ratio.
  e. Induction manifold bleed-off passage obstructed.
  f. Worn or defective breaker points.

D. **Gap bridging**—Similar to core bridging, except the combustion particles are wedged or fused between the electrodes. Causes are the same.

E. **Overheating**—Badly worn electrodes and premature gap wear are indicative of this problem, along with a gray or white "blistered" appearance on the insulator. Caused by one or more of the following:
  a. Spark plug heat range too hot.
  b. Incorrect propeller usage, causing engine to lug.
  c. Worn or defective water pump.
  d. Restricted water intake or restriction somewhere in the cooling system.

F. **Ash deposits or lead fouling**—Ash deposits are light brown to white in color and result from use of fuel or oil additives. Lead fouling produces a yellowish brown discoloration and can be avoided by using unleaded fuels.

(29)

SURFACE GAP
SPARK PLUG ANALYSIS

A

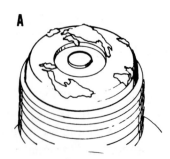

B

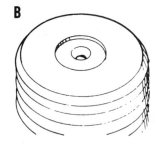

C

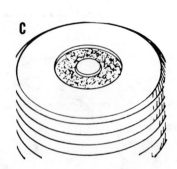

D

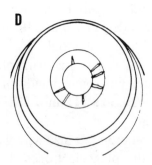

E

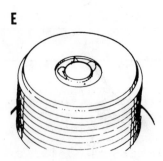

F

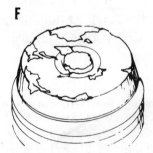

A. Normal—Light tan or gray colored deposits indicate that the engine/ignition system condition is good. Electrode wear indicates normal spark rotation.

B. Worn out—Excessive electrode wear can cause hard starting or a misfire during acceleration.

C. Cold fouled—Wet oil-fuel deposits are caused by "drowning" the plug with raw fuel mix during cranking, overrich carburetion or an improper fuel-oil ratio. Weak ignition will also contribute to this condition.

D. Carbon tracking—Electrically conductive deposits on the firing end provide a low-resistance path for the voltage. Carbon tracks form and can cause misfires.

E. Concentrated arc—Multi-colored appearance is normal. It is caused by electricity consistently following the same firing path. Arc path changes with deposit conductivity and gap erosion.

F. Aluminum throw-off—Caused by preignition. This is not a plug problem but the result of engine damage. Check engine to determine cause and extent of damage.

5. Check the make and heat range of each spark plug. All should be of the same make and heat range.

6. Discard the plugs. Although they could be cleaned and reused if in good condition, the best tune-up results will be obtained by installing new spark plugs.

Spark Plug Gapping (Conventional Gap Only)

New spark plugs should be carefully gapped to ensure reliable, consistent plug operation. Use a special spark plug tool with a wire gauge to measure electrode gap. **Figure 30** shows a common spark plug gapping tool.

1. If necessary, install the spark plug's gasket onto the plug. On some brands of plugs, the terminal end (**Figure 31**) must also be screwed onto the plug.

2. Insert the appropriate size wire gauge (**Table 3**) between the plug electrodes. If the gap is correct, a slight drag will be noted as the wire is pulled through. If no drag is noted, or if the wire gauge will not pull through, bend the side electrode with the gapping tool (**Figure 32**) to change the gap as necessary. Remeasure the gap after adjusting.

> *CAUTION*
> *Never close the electrode gap by tapping the plug on a solid surface. Doing so can damage the plug internally. Always use the gapping tool to open or close the gap.*

Spark Plug Installation

Improper installation is a common cause of poor spark plug performance in outboard motors. The gasket on the plug must be fully compressed against a clean plug seat for heat transfer to take place effectively. Therefore, the correct plug tightening procedure should be followed.

1. Inspect the spark plug threads in the cylinder head and clean with a thread chaser if necessary.

See **Figure 33**. Thoroughly clean the spark plug seating area in the cylinder head prior to installing new plugs.

2. Screw each spark plug into the cylinder head by hand, until seated. If force is necessary to turn the plug, it may be cross threaded. Remove the plug and try again.

3. Tighten the plugs using a suitable torque wrench to 17-20 ft.-lb. (23-27 N•m). If a torque wrench is not available, seat the plug finger-tight, then tighten an additional 1/4 turn with the appropriate size wrench.

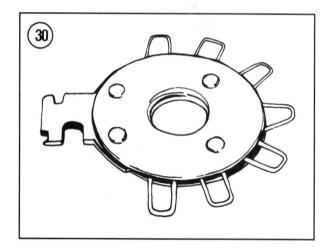

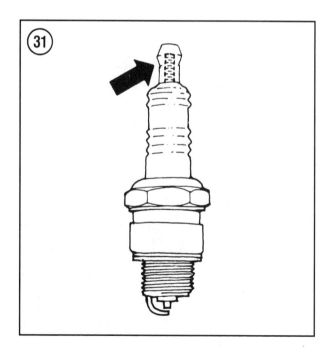

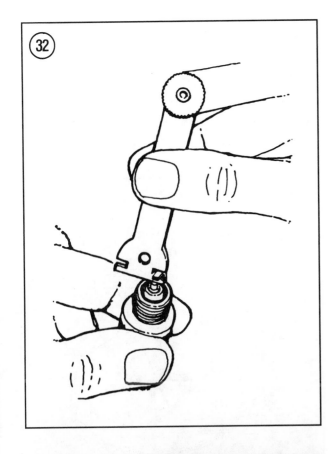

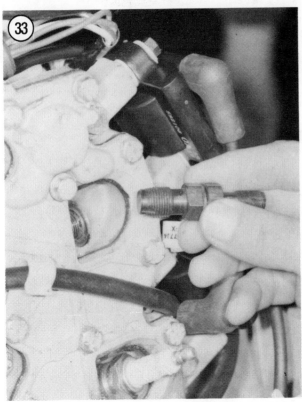

4. Inspect each spark plug wire before reconnecting it. If insulation is damaged or deteriorated, install a new wire. Apply a light coat of OMC Triple-Guard grease to the ribbed area of the plug ceramic insulator, then push the wire onto the plug. Make sure the wire terminal is fully seated on the plug.

Lower Unit and Water Pump

A faulty water pump or one that performs poorly can result in extensive engine damage from overheating. Therefore, it is good practice to replace the pump impeller, seals and gaskets once per year or anytime the lower unit is removed for service. See Chapter Nine.

Fuel Lines

1. Inspect all fuel hoses and lines for kinks, leaks, deterioration or other damage.
2. Disconnect the fuel lines and blow out with compressed air to dislodge any contamination or foreign material.
3. Coat fuel line fittings sparingly with OMC Gasket Sealing Compound then reconnect the lines.

Fuel Filter

A disposable, inline fuel filter is used on all models (except 60° V6 models). The filter is serviced as an assembly and should be replaced once per year or sooner if contaminated fuel is encountered. In addition to the inline fuel filter, a filter screen is used on all models equipped with a diaphragm fuel pump. The screen is located in the fuel pump, under the filter cover. On models equipped with an integral fuel tank (2, 2.3 and 3.3 hp), a filter screen is installed on the fuel shut-off valve attached to the fuel tank. On 60° 150 and 175 hp models, a cartridge type fuel filter is installed in the fuel components bracket.

The filter should be removed and cleaned once per year, or sooner if contaminated fuel is encountered.

Shut-off valve filter screen

Refer to **Figure 34** for this procedure.

1. Loosen the clamp securing the valve assembly to the fuel tank.
2. Remove the valve and filter assembly from the fuel tank.
3. Clean the filter using OMC Cleaning Solvent. Dry the filter using compressed air. If the filter is excessively plugged or damaged, replace the shut-off valve and filter as an assembly.
4. Installation is the reverse of removal.

Inline fuel filter

Refer to **Figure 35**, typical for this procedure.

1. Remove the clamps securing the fuel hoses to the filter.
2. Remove the hoses from the filter. Discard the filter.
3. Inspect the fuel hoses closely and replace as necessary.
4. Install the hoses on a new filter and clamp securely.

Fuel pump filter screen

1. Remove the screw securing the filter cover to the pump assembly (**Figure 36**).
2. Remove the filter screen from the filter cover (A, **Figure 37**) or pump housing (B).
3. Remove and discard the filter cover gasket.

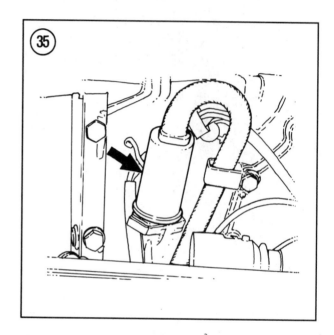

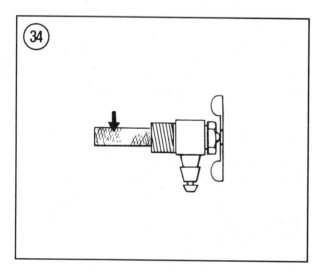

4. Clean the screen using OMC Cleaning Solvent. Discard the screen if it is excessively plugged.

5. Install the filter screen into the filter cover (A, **Figure 37**).

6. Reinstall the filter cover on the fuel pump, using a new gasket. Tighten the cover screw securely.

7. Prime the fuel system with the primer bulb and check the pump and fuel delivery system for leakage.

Cartridge fuel filter (60° 150 and 175 hp models)

1. Disconnect the 4 air silencer cover retaining straps, then lift the air silencer cover off the power head. See **Figure 38**.

2. Unscrew the fuel filter nut (**Figure 39**) and remove the filter element (C, **Figure 40**) from the vapor separator housing. If necessary, disconnect the fuel delivery hose from the filter fitting.

3. Inspect the filter element and clean using a mild aerosol solvent. Dry with compressed air.

FUEL FILTER ASSEMBLY (60° V6 MODELS)

4. Inspect the filter gasket (B, **Figure 40**) and O-ring (D) and replace if necessary.

5. Replace the filter element if excessive plugging or other damage is noted.

6. Lightly lubricate the filter O-ring with clean engine oil. Insert the filter element into the vapor separator housing and tighten the filter nut securely. Pressurize the fuel delivery system with the primary bulb to check for leakage.

7. Reinstall the air silencer cover.

Fuel Pump (Models without Variable Ratio Oil Injection)

The fuel pump does not normally require service during a routine tune-up; however, fuel pump diaphragms are fragile and a defective one often produces symptoms that are misleading. A common malfunction results from a tiny pinhole or crack in the diaphragm which allows fuel to enter the crankcase. The additional fuel wet-fouls the spark plug(s) at idle speed, causing hard starting and stalling at low speed. The problem may disappear at higher speeds because the fuel demand is greater at higher speeds.

Fuel Pump Pressure Test

Check fuel pump pressure by installing a pressure gauge in the fuel hose between the fuel pump and carburetor(s). See **Figure 41**. Perform the fuel pump test with the engine running in a test tank with the correct test wheel installed or on a boat in the water.

1. Loosen the fuel tank cap to relieve pressure inside the tank. Note that the fuel tank must not be more than 24 in. (61 cm) below the fuel pump.

2. Connect an accurate tachometer to the power head according to its manufacturer's instructions.

3. Start the engine and observe the pressure gauge and tachometer. Fuel pressure should be:

   a. 1 psi (6.895 kPa) at 600 rpm.

   b. 1.5 psi (10.3 kPa) at 2500-3000 rpm.

   c. 2.5 psi 17.2 kPa) at 4500 rpm.

4. If fuel pump pressure is low, first make sure the inline fuel filter and pump filter screen are clean. Disconnect the fuel hose between the fuel tank and pump and clean with compressed air. If the filters or fuel hoses are not restricted or

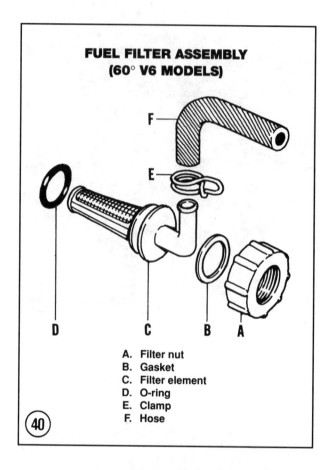

FUEL FILTER ASSEMBLY (60° V6 MODELS)

A. Filter nut
B. Gasket
C. Filter element
D. O-ring
E. Clamp
F. Hose

(40)

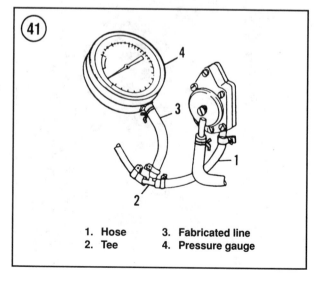

(41)

1. Hose
2. Tee
3. Fabricated line
4. Pressure gauge

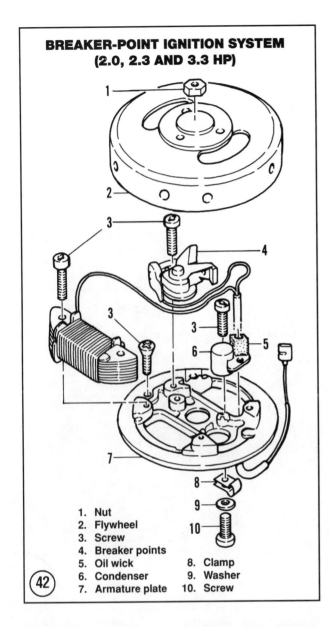

**BREAKER-POINT IGNITION SYSTEM
(2.0, 2.3 AND 3.3 HP)**

1. Nut
2. Flywheel
3. Screw
4. Breaker points
5. Oil wick
6. Condenser
7. Armature plate
8. Clamp
9. Washer
10. Screw

42

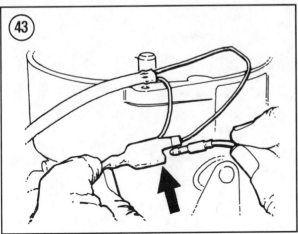

43

plugged, repair or replace the fuel pump. See Chapter Six.

Fuel Pump (Models Equipped with VRO [Variable Ratio Oiling] Oil Injection System)

The VRO oil injection system is a combination fuel and oil pump assembly and is operated by crankcase pulsations. See Chapter Eleven for testing and service on the oil injection system.

Breaker-Point Ignition Service (2.0, 2.3 and 3.3 hp)

The breaker points and condenser should be replaced during the tune-up procedure. Refer to **Figure 42** for an exploded view of the breaker-point ignition system. Proceed as follows to replace the points and condenser.

1. Disconnect the spark plug lead to prevent accidental starting.

2. Remove the rewind starter assembly. See Chapter Twelve.

3. Remove the flywheel. See Chapter Eight.

NOTE
The breaker points can be removed, installed and adjusted without removing the armature plate from the power head. The armature plate must be removed, however, for condenser replacement.

4. Remove the 2 screws securing the armature plate to the crankcase.

5. Disconnect the primary ignition and stop switch wires at the bullet connectors (**Figure 43**).

6. Remove the armature plate from the crankcase.

7. Disconnect the blue wire from the breaker points. Remove the points mounting screw and remove the points. Remove the condenser mounting screw and remove the condenser.

8. Install the points and condenser by reversing the removal procedure. Install a new oiler wick on the armature plate.

9. Reinstall the armature plate on the crankcase. Apply OMC Screw Lock (or equivalent) to the threads of the armature plate screws. Install the screws and tighten to 27-44 in.-lb. (3-5 N·m).

10. Reconnect the primary and stop switch wires (**Figure 43**).

11. Install the flywheel as described in Chapter Eight.

> *CAUTION*
> *Rotating the flywheel counterclockwise can damage the water pump impeller.*

12. Position the breaker point rubbing block on the high point of the breaker cam. Loosen the breaker point locking screw (**Figure 44**). Using a feeler gauge as shown in **Figure 44**, adjust the point gap to 0.008 in. (0.2 mm) on 2 hp models, 0.014 in. (0.35 mm) on 2.3 hp models and 0.020 in. (0.5 mm) on 3.3 hp models.

13. Securely tighten the breaker point locking screw, recheck the gap and readjust as necessary.

14. Reinstall the rewind starter as outlined in Chapter Twelve.

Battery and Starter Motor Check (Electric Start Models)

1. Check the battery state of charge. See Chapter Seven.

2. Connect a voltmeter between the starter motor positive terminal (**Figure 45**) and a good engine ground.

3. Crank the engine while noting the meter.

   a. If the meter indicates 9.5 volts or more but the starter motor is inoperative, troubleshoot the starting system as described in Chapter Three.

   b. If the voltage is less than 9.5 volts, recheck the battery and connections. Charge the battery if necessary and repeat this test procedure.

Starter Solenoid Check (Electric Start Models)

Test the starter solenoid as outlined in Chapter Three.

Internal Wiring Harness Check

1. Check the wiring harness for frayed or chafed insulation. Repair as necessary.

2. Check for loose connections between the wires and terminal ends.

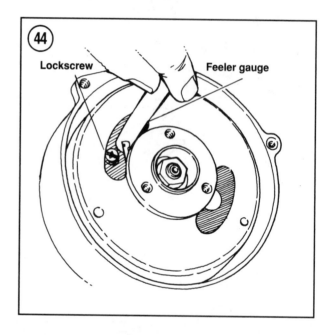

Lockscrew   Feeler gauge

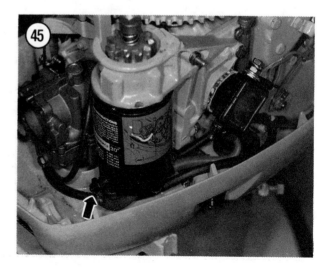

3. Check the harness connector for bent electrical pins.

4. Check the harness connector for corrosion. Clean as necessary.

5. If the harness is suspected of contributing to electrical malfunctions, check all wires for continuity and excessive resistance between the harness connector and terminal ends. Repair or replace the harness as necessary.

Removing Combustion Chamber Carbon

During operation, carbon deposits can accumulate on the piston(s), rings and exhaust ports causing decreased performance and stuck piston rings. To prevent the formation of excessive deposits, the manufacturer recommends adding OMC Carbon Guard to each tankful of fuel. If Carbon Guard is not used regularly, OMC Engine Tuner should be applied to the engine at 50 hour intervals. Follow the instructions on the Engine Tuner container.

Performance Test (On Boat)

Before performance testing the engine, make sure the boat bottom is cleaned of all marine growth and that excessive "hook" or "rocker" is not present in the hull. See **Figure 46**. Any of these conditions will reduce performance considerably.

The boat should be performance tested with an average load and with the motor tilted at an angle that will allow the boat to ride on an even keel. If equipped with an adjustable trim tab, it should be properly adjusted to allow the boat to steer in either direction with equal ease.

Check the engine rpm at wide-open throttle. If not within the maximum rpm range as specified in Chapter Five, check the propeller pitch. A propeller with excessive pitch will not allow the engine to reach the correct operating range; a propeller with insufficient pitch will allow the engine to overspeed.

For optimum results, adjust the idle mixture and idle speed with the outboard running at idle speed in forward gear, with the correct propeller installed and boat movement unrestrained.

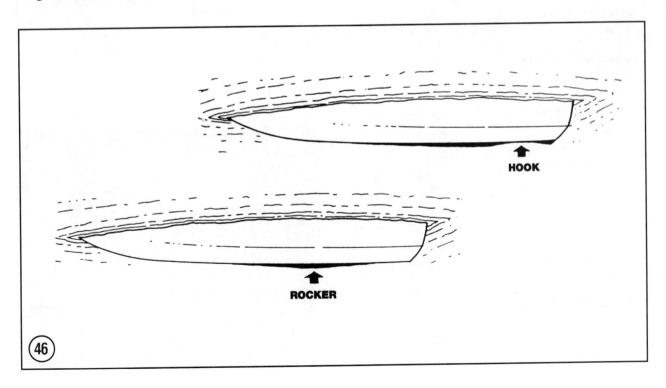

HOOK

ROCKER

46

Table 1 LUBRICATION AND MAINTENANCE[1] (2-30 HP MODELS)

Lubrication points	Figure
Throttle detent, cam, linkage and choke lever	4, 9
Choke linkage	5
Carburetor, cam and throttle linkage	6
Magneto and throttle linkage	7
Control shaft and control lever bushings	8
Shift, throttle, carburetor, choke linkage and springs; throttle cam, roller shaft, shift lever shaft and cover latch	10
Control shaft bushings, bearings and shift linkage	11
Shift lever shaft and swivel bracket	12
Swivel bracket, tilt lock lever, tilt lever link and shaft	13
Swivel bracket fitting and trail lock linkage	14
Shift shaft and lever fitting	15
Tilt tube shaft	16
Vertical throttle shaft and gears	17
Stater motor pinion gear[2]	18
Powr trim/tilt reservoir[3]	19

1. Complete list does not apply to all models. Perform only those tasks which apply to your model. Lubricate with OMC Triple-Guard Grease every 60 days (fresh water) or 30 days (saltwater) as required.
2. Use Lubriplate 777 grease.
3. Use OMC Power Trim/Tilt & Power Steering Fluid or Dexron II automatic transmission fluid.

Table 2 TEST WHEEL RECOMMENDATIONS

Model	Test wheel (part No.)	Minimum test speed (rpm)
2 hp	_[1]	4500
2.3 hp	_[1]	4800
3.3 hp	115306	5000
3 hp, 4 hp	317738	4400
4 Deluxe	390123	5100
6 hp	390239	4800
8 hp	390239	5300
9.9 hp		
1991-1992	386537	4800
1993	435750	5200
15 hp		
1991-1992	386537	6100
1993	435750	5800
20 hp	386891	4550
25 hp	434505	4800
28 hp	398948	4800
30 hp	434505	5400
40 hp	432968	4900
48 hp, 50 hp	432968	5200
60 hp	386665	5000
70 hp	386665	5700
85 hp, 88 hp, 90 hp, 100, 115 hp	382861	4800

(continued)

4

Table 2 TEST WHEEL RECOMMENDATIONS (continued)

Model	Test wheel (part No.)	Minimum test speed (rpm)
120 hp		
1991-1992	386246	5300
1993	433068	5200
120TXETF, 120TXATF	396277	5200
140TL		
1991-1992	386246	5500
1993	433068	5300
140TX		
1991-1992	387388	5500
1993	396277	5300
140CX		
1991-1992	398673	5500
1993	398673	5300
150 hp (90°) (149.4 cid)	387388	4500
175 hp (90°) (160.3 cid)	387388	4800
150 hp (60°) (158 cid)	387388[2]	4500
175 hp (60°) (158 cid)	387388[2]	4800
200XP, 200GT, 200STL		
1991-1992	387388	5700
200STL		
1993	436080	5700
200TX		
1991-1992	387388	5500
1993	436080	5500
200CX		
1991-1992	398673	5500
1993	436081	5500
225 hp		
1991-1992	387388	5700
1993	436080	5700
225CX		
1991-1992	388673	5700
1993	436081	5700
250 hp, 300 hp	396277	5500
250CX, 300CX	398674	5500

1. A test wheel is not used on 2 and 2.3 hp models. Use the standard propeller (part No. 115208) when running motor in a test tank.
2. On counter rotating (CX) models, use test wheel (part No. 398673).

Table 3 RECOMMENDED SPARK PLUGS

Model	Champion plug type	Gap (in.)
2, 2.3, 3.3 hp		
1991-1992	QL77JC4	0.030
1993	L78YC	0.030
3-30 hp	QL77JC4[1]	0.030
40, 48, 50 hp	QL78C[1]	0.030
60-115 hp	QL77JC4[1] (continued)	0.030

Table 3 RECOMMENDED SPARK PLUGS (continued)

Model	Champion plug type	Gap (in.)
120, 140 hp	QL77JC4[2]	0.030
150-300 hp	QL77JC4[1]	0.030
1.6-4.0 Sea Drive	QL77JC4[1]	0.030

1. The manufacturer recommends using Champion QL16V surface gap spark plug if operated at sustained high speed.
2. The manufacturer recommends using Champion QL78V (1991 and 1992 models) or QL16V (1993 models) surface gap spark plugs if operated at sustained high speed.

Table 4 GEARCASE GEAR RATIO,
LUBRICANT CAPACITY AND RECOMMENDED LUBRICANT

Model	Gear ratio	Lubricant capacity	Recommended lubricant
2, 2.3, 3 hp	13:24	3 oz. (90 mL)	1
3, 4 hp	12:25	2.7 oz. (80 mL)	1
4 Deluxe	13:29	11 oz. (325 mL)	2
6, 8 hp	13:29	11 oz. (325 mL)	1
9.9, 15 hp	12:29	9 oz. (260 mL)	1
20, 25, 30 hp	13:28	11 oz. (325 mL)	1
28 hp	12:21	8 oz. (245 mL)	1
40, 48, 50 hp	12:29	16.4 oz. (485 mL)	1
60, 70 hp	12:29	22 oz. (650 mL)	1
85, 88, 90, 100, 115 hp	13:26	26 oz. (800 mL)	1
120, 140 hp	13:26	26 oz. (800 mL)	1
120TXETF, 120TXATF, 140CX	12:27	33 oz. (980 mL)	1
150, 175 hp	14:26	33 oz. (980 mL)	1
200, 275 hp	14:26	33 oz. (980 mL)	1
250, 300 hp	17:30	71 oz. (2100 mL)	1

1. OMC Hi-Vis Gearcase Lubricant.
2. OMC Premium Blend Gearcase Lubricant

Chapter Five

Engine Synchronization and Linkage Adjustments

If an engine is to deliver its maximum efficiency and peak performance, the ignition must be correctly timed and the carburetor operation synchronized with the ignition. This procedure should always be the final step of tune-up. It must also be performed whenever the fuel or ignition systems are serviced or adjusted.

Procedures for engine synchronization and linkage adjustment on Johnson and Evinrude outboard motors differ according to model and ignition system. This chapter is divided into self-contained sections dealing with particular models/ignition systems for fast and easy reference.

Each section specifies the appropriate procedure and sequence to be followed and provides the necessary tune-up data. Read the general information at the beginning of the chapter and then select the section pertaining to your outboard. **Table 1** and **Table 2** are at the end of the chapter.

ENGINE TIMING AND SYNCHRONIZATION

Ignition timing advance and throttle opening must be synchronized to occur at the proper time for the engine to perform properly. Synchronizing is the process of timing the carburetor operation to the ignition spark advance.

REQUIRED EQUIPMENT

Dynamic engine timing adjustments require the use of a stroboscopic timing light connected to a spark plug wire. See **Figure 1**. As the engine is cranked or operated, the light flashes each time the spark plug fires. When the light is pointed at the moving flywheel, the mark on the flywheel appears to stand still. When the timing is correctly adjusted, the specified mark on the flywheel or timing wheel is aligned with the stationary timing pointer on the engine.

A simple tool, called a throttle shaft amplifier, can be made with an alligator clip and a length of stiff wire (a paper clip will do). This tool is designed to be attached to the throttle shaft and exaggerate throttle shaft movement. This makes it easier to determine the exact instant the throttle shaft begins to move. **Figure 2** shows the tool installed. The tool is especially useful on engines where the throttle cam and cam follower are partially hidden by the flywheel. To make the tool, enlarge the alligator clip's gripping surface by grinding out the front teeth on one side and secure the wire to the end of the clip. See **Figure 3**.

A an accurate shop tachometer (not the boat's tachometer) should be used to determine engine speed during idle and high-speed adjustments.

CAUTION
Never operate the engine without cooling water circulating through the gearcase to the power head. Running the motor without water will damage the water pump and cause the power head to overheat.

Some form of water supply is required whenever the motor is operated during the procedure. Using a test tank is the most convenient method,

although the procedures may be carried out with the boat in the water.

CAUTION
Do not use a flushing device to provide water during synchronization and linkage adjustment. Without the exhaust backpressure of a submerged engine, the engine will run lean. The proper test wheel must be used to apply a load on the propeller shaft or the power head can be damaged from excessive engine speed.

The step-by-step synchronizing and adjusting procedures must be followed in the exact se-

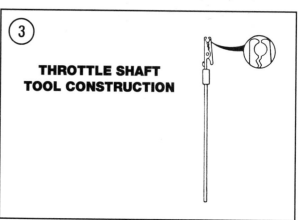

THROTTLE SHAFT TOOL CONSTRUCTION

quence given to produce smooth, consistent idle speeds and optimum performance throughout the engine speed range.

3 AND 4 HP (2-CYLINDER MODELS)

Ignition timing adjustment is not necessary on these models.

Cam Follower Pickup Point

1. Attach the throttle shaft amplifier to the end of the carburetor throttle shaft, opposite the cam follower linkage. See **Figure 2**, typical. Bend the tool wire upward at a 90° angle for easier viewing. See **Figure 4**.

2. Advance the throttle until the tip of the amplifier begins to move indicating the throttle valve is starting to open.

3. With the throttle in this position, the single mark on the throttle cam should be aligned with the center of the cam follower roller. See **Figure 5**.

4. If adjustment is necessary, back out the cam follower adjustment screw (4, **Figure 5**) until the throttle valve is fully closed. Then, turn the screw in until the throttle shaft just begins to move.

5. Repeat Step 2 to check adjustment and readjust as necessary.

Carburetor Adjustment

Start the outboard and allow to run in FORWARD gear at one-half throttle until warmed to normal operating temperature. For optimum results when adjusting low-speed mixture and idle speed, the outboard must be mounted on a boat in the water, running at normal operating temperature, in forward gear with boat movement unrestrained.

1. Stop the engine to prevent contact with the moving flywheel.

2. Loosen the 2 throttle cable retaining nuts (**Figure 6**).

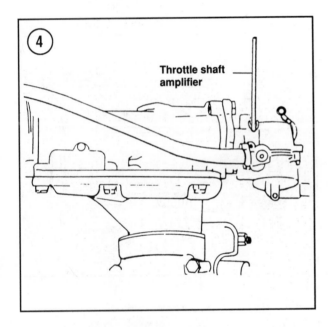

5

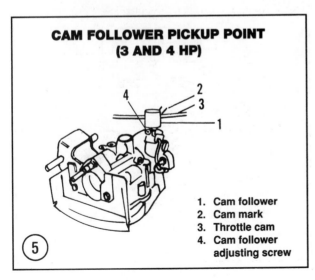

**CAM FOLLOWER PICKUP POINT
(3 AND 4 HP)**

1. Cam follower
2. Cam mark
3. Throttle cam
4. Cam follower adjusting screw

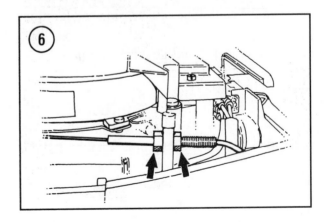

3. Back out the idle speed screw (**Figure 7**) until the ignition plate contacts its stop on the power head.

4. Start the motor and shift into FORWARD gear. Adjust the idle speed (**Figure 7**) to 700-800 rpm, then adjust the low-speed mixture (**Figure 8**) to obtain the highest consistent speed. Wait approximately 15 seconds between each low-speed mixture adjustment to allow the motor to respond. Once the highest speed is obtained, turn the low-speed mixture screw in (clockwise) 1/8 turn.

5. Readjust idle speed to 700-800 rpm in FORWARD gear.

6. Operate the motor at wide-open throttle for approximately 1 minute, then return to idle speed. The motor should idle smoothly.

7. If the motor stalls, backfires or idles poorly, the idle mixture may be too lean. Enrichen the mixture by turning the idle mixture screw counterclockwise. Turn the screw in 1/16 turn increments and wait after each adjustment to allow the motor to respond. Repeat Step 6 to be sure the mixture is correctly adjusted.

Throttle Cable Adjustment

1. Turn the tiller handle throttle control to the idle position.

2. With the ignition plate contacting the idle speed screw (**Figure 7**), adjust the throttle cable nuts (**Figure 6**) as necessary to remove any slack between the end of the cable casing and ignition plate.

3. Tighten the throttle cable nuts securely.

4 DELUXE MODELS

Ignition timing adjustment is not required on 4 Deluxe models. If all wires are correctly positioned in the harness connectors, the proper ignition timing will be maintained.

Cam Follower Pickup Point

1. Attach a throttle shaft amplifier to the end of the carburetor throttle shaft. See **Figure 9**, typical.

2. Advance the throttle until the tip of the amplifier begins to move, indicating the throttle valve is starting to open.

3. With the throttle in this position, the single mark on the throttle cam should be aligned with the center of the cam follower roller. See **Figure 5**.

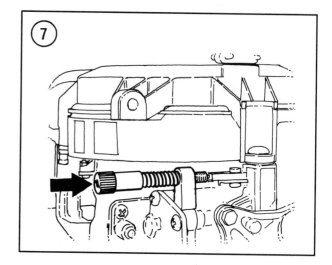

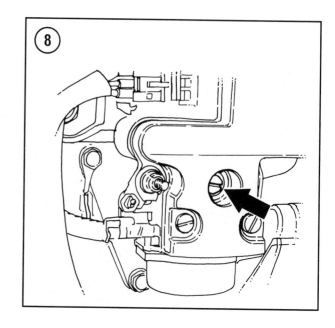

4. If adjustment is necessary, back out the cam follower adjustment screw (4, **Figure 5**) until the throttle valve is fully closed. Then, turn the screw in until the throttle shaft just begins to move.

5. Repeat Step 2 to check adjustment and readjust as necessary.

Carburetor Adjustment

Start the outboard and allow to run in FORWARD gear at one-half throttle until warmed to normal operating temperature. For optimum results when adjusting low-speed mixture and idle speed, the outboard should be mounted on a boat in the water, running at normal operating temperature, in forward gear, with the correct propeller installed and boat movement unrestrained.

1. Start the engine and run at 700-800 rpm.

2. Adjust the low-speed mixture screw until the highest consistent engine speed is obtained. Turn the screw in small increments and wait after each adjustment to allow the engine to respond.

3. After the highest idle speed is obtained, turn the mixture screw in (clockwise) 1/8 turn.

4. Adjust the idle speed to 600-650 rpm in FORWARD gear.

5. Operate the motor at wide-open throttle for 1 minute, then throttle back to idle and shift into NEUTRAL. The motor should idle smoothly.

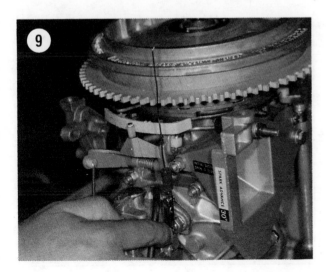

6. If the motor stalls, backfires or idles poorly, the idle mixture may be too lean. Enrichen the mixture by turning the idle mixture screw counterclockwise. Turn the screw in 1/16 turn increments and wait after each adjustment to allow the motor to respond. Repeat Step 5 to be sure the mixture is correctly adjusted.

6 AND 8 HP (2-CYLINDER MODELS)

Ignition timing adjustment is not required on 6 and 8 hp models. If all wires are correctly positioned in the harness connectors, the proper ignition timing will be maintained.

Throttle Cable Adjustment

1. Turn the idle speed adjustment knob on the tiller handle counterclockwise to the minimum idle speed position. Then, turn the tiller handle throttle control to the minimum throttle position. Make sure the throttle cam is contacting the idle stop.

2. Remove the throttle cable bracket-to-power head retaining screw.

3. After removing the throttle cable bracket retaining screw, adjust the bracket as necessary to align its mounting hole with the screw hole in the power head. Then, turn the bracket 1 turn toward the throttle lever to slightly preload the cable in the closed position.

4. Install the cable bracket-to-power head screw and tighten securely.

Carburetor Adjustment

Start the outboard and allow to run in FORWARD gear at one-half throttle until warmed to normal operating temperature. For optimum results when adjusting low-speed mixture and idle speed, the outboard must be mounted on a boat in the water, running at normal operating temperature, in forward gear, with the correct propeller installed and boat movement unrestrained.

> *NOTE*
> *If it is necessary to advance the throttle to access the throttle cam follower adjusting screw in Step 1, be sure to return the throttle to the minimum setting and confirm that the follower is not touching the throttle cam.*

1. Using a suitable ball-hex screwdriver (OMC part No. 327622), back out the throttle cam follower screw until the follower is not contacting the throttle cam. The cam follower screw can be reached by inserting the tool through the access hole in the air silencer as shown in **Figure 10**.

2. Turn the low-speed mixture screw (**Figure 11**) inward (clockwise) until *lightly* seated, then back it out 2-1/2 turns.

3. Loosen the idle speed screw (**Figure 12**) until the screw is not contacting the throttle link. Then, turn the screw inward (clockwise) until it just contacts the throttle link. After contact, turn the screw inward an additional 4 turns.

4. Connect an accurate tachometer according to its manufacturer's instructions.

5. Start the engine and run at fast idle until warmed to normal operating temperature.

6. Shift into FORWARD gear. Adjust the low-speed mixture screw (**Figure 11**) to obtain the highest consistent idle speed. Turn the screw in small increments and wait after each adjustment to allow the engine to respond. After the highest speed is obtained, turn the mixture screw counterclockwise 1/8 turn.

7. Adjust the idle speed to 650-700 rpm (**Figure 12**).

> *NOTE*
> *If the engine speed drops when the cam follower screw is adjusted into the cam in Step 8, the low-speed mixture is too lean. Turn the low-speed mixture screw 1/8 turn counterclockwise and repeat Steps 6 and 7.*

8. Using OMC ball-hex driver (part No. 327622), adjust the throttle cam follower screw (**Figure 10**) until the screw just contacts the throttle cam and engine speed begins to increase. Then, back off the screw 1/8 turn.

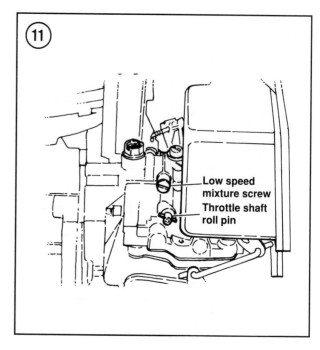

Wide-Open Throttle Stop

To prevent accidental contact with the moving flywheel, stop the engine prior to performing this procedure.

1. Turn the tiller handle throttle control to the wide-open position.

2. Check the position of the throttle shaft roll pin (**Figure 11**). The roll pin should be exactly vertical with the throttle wide open.

3. If adjustment is necessary, adjust the throttle cam (**Figure 10**) until the throttle shaft roll pin

is completely vertical with the throttle wide open.

1991 AND 1992 9.9 AND 15 HP (2-CYLINDER MODELS)

Ignition timing adjustment is not necessary on these models. If all wires are correctly positioned in the harness connectors, the proper ignition timing will be maintained.

Disconnect both remote control cables (if so equipped) from the power head.

Cam Follower Pickup Point

1. Attach a throttle shaft amplifier tool to the carburetor throttle shaft. See **Figure 13**.

2. Slowly advance the throttle until the tip of the amplifier begins to move. With the throttle in this position, the single mark on the throttle cam should be aligned with the center of the throttle cam follower. See **Figure 13**.

3. If adjustment is necessary, return the throttle to the idle position. Using OMC ball-hex driver (part No. 327622), turn the cam follower adjustment screw (**Figure 13**) counterclockwise until the throttle valve is fully closed. Then turn the adjusting screw clockwise until the throttle shaft just begins to move.

4. At this point the single mark on the throttle cam should be aligned with the center of the cam follower. If not, repeat Steps 2 and 3 as necessary.

Wide-Open Throttle Stop

Perform the wide-open throttle stop adjustment with the motor not running.

1. Shift the outboard into FORWARD gear.

2. Advance the throttle to the wide-open position and note the position of the throttle shaft roll pin. The roll pin should be exactly vertical.

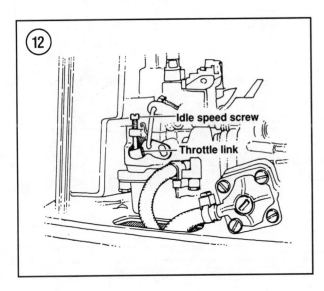

(12)
Idle speed screw
Throttle link

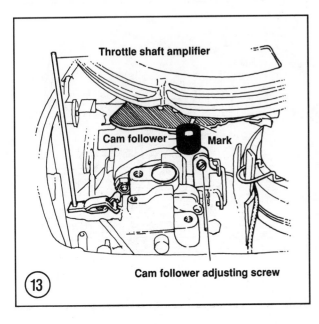

(13)
Throttle shaft amplifier
Cam follower — Mark
Cam follower adjusting screw

3. If adjustment is necessary, turn the throttle cam screw (**Figure 14**) to position the roll pin in the vertical position with the throttle wide open.

Carburetor Adjustment

Start the outboard and allow to run in FOR-WARD gear at one-half throttle until warmed to normal operating temperature. For optimum results when adjusting low-speed mixture and idle speed, the outboard must be mounted on a boat in the water, running at normal operating temperature, in forward gear, with the correct propeller installed and boat movement unrestrained.

Make sure the idle mixture is correctly set before adjusting the idle speed.

1. Connect an accurate tachometer according to its manufacturer's instructions.

2. Adjust the idle speed to 700-800 rpm in FOR-WARD gear.

3. Turn the low-speed mixture knob (adjacent to choke knob) to obtain the highest consistent idle speed. Turn the knob in small increments and wait approximately 15 seconds after each adjustment to allow the engine to respond.

4. After the highest idle speed is obtained, turn the idle mixture knob 1/8 turn counterclockwise. Without disturbing the mixture screw, remove the idle mixture knob and reposition it with its pointer facing down.

5. Adjust the idle speed to 650 rpm in FOR-WARD gear.

6. Operate the motor at wide-open throttle for 1 minute, then quickly throttle back to idle speed and shift into NEUTRAL. The motor should idle smoothly.

7. If the motor stalls, backfires or runs poorly, the idle mixture is too lean. Enrichen the mixture by turning the mixture knob counterclockwise 1/16 turn. Wait 15 seconds to allow the engine to respond. Repeat Step 6 to confirm correct adjustment.

8. On tiller handle models, turn the idle speed knob fully counterclockwise (slow).

9. With the engine running in FORWARD gear at normal operating temperature, idle speed should be 650-700 rpm.

10A. *Tiller handle*—Change position of the throttle cable mounting ball (**Figure 15**) as necessary to adjust idle speed.

10B. *Remote control*—Turn the idle speed screw (**Figure 16**) to adjust idle speed.

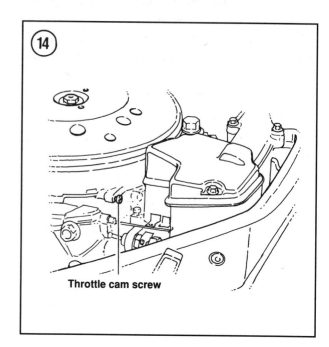

(14)

Throttle cam screw

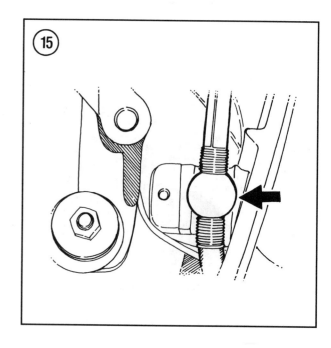

(15)

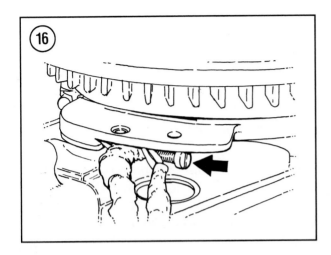

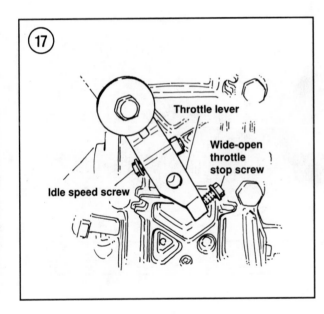

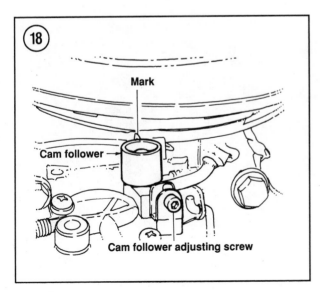

1993-ON 9.9 AND 15 HP (2-CYLINDER MODELS)

Ignition timing adjustment is not necessary on these models. If all wires are correctly positioned in the harness connectors, the proper ignition timing will be maintained.

Disconnect both remote control cables from the power head, if so equipped.

5

Cam Follower Pickup Point

1A. *Tiller handle*—Turn the idle speed knob on the tiller to the fully counterclockwise (slow) position.

1B. *Remote control*—Back out the idle speed screw (**Figure 17**) until the throttle lever contacts the power head.

2. Attach a throttle shaft amplifier to the carburetor throttle shaft.

3. Advance the throttle until the tip of the throttle shaft amplifier just begins to move. When the amplifier begins to move, the single mark on the throttle cam should be aligned with the center of the cam follower. See **Figure 18**.

4. Next, back out the cam follower adjusting screw (**Figure 18**) using OMC ball-hex driver (part No. 327622) until the throttle valve is fully closed. Then, turn the screw in (clockwise) until the throttle shaft just begins to move.

Wide-Open Throttle Stop

1. Adjust the wide-open throttle stop screw (**Figure 17**) so the tip of the screws extends through the throttle lever 1/8 in. (3.2 mm).

> *WARNING*
> *To prevent accidental starting, disconnect the spark plug wires from the plugs.*

2. While rotating the propeller shaft, shift the outboard into FORWARD gear.

3. Move the throttle to the wide-open position and note the position of the throttle shaft roll pin (**Figure 19**).

4. The roll pin should be in a vertical position. If not, adjust the throttle cam screw (**Figure 20**) as necessary to position the roll pin exactly vertical with the throttle wide-open.

Carburetor Adjustments

Start the outboard and run in FORWARD gear at one-half throttle until warmed to normal operating temperature. For optimum results when adjusting low-speed mixture and idle speed, the outboard must be mounted on a boat in the water, running at normal operating temperature, in forward gear, with the correct propeller installed and boat movement unrestrained.

Low-speed mixture adjustment

1. Connect an accurate tachometer according to its manufacturer's instructions.

2. On tiller handle models, turn the idle speed knob on the tiller to the fully counterclockwise (slow) position.

3. While running the outboard at 700-800 rpm in FORWARD gear, turn the low-speed mixture screw (**Figure 21**) to obtain the highest consistent idle speed. Turn the screw in small increments and wait approximately 15 seconds after each adjustment to allow the engine to respond.

4. After the highest idle speed is obtained, turn the idle mixture screw 1/8 turn counterclockwise.

5. Adjust the idle speed to 650 rpm in FORWARD gear.

6. Operate the motor at wide-open throttle for 1 minute, then quickly throttle back to idle speed and shift into NEUTRAL. The motor should idle smoothly.

7. If the motor stalls, backfires or runs poorly, the idle mixture is too lean. Enrichen the mixture by turning the mixture knob counterclockwise

1/16 turn. Wait 15 seconds to allow the engine to respond. Repeat Step 6 to confirm correct adjustment.

Idle speed adjustment

The low-speed mixture must be correctly set prior to adjusting the idle speed.

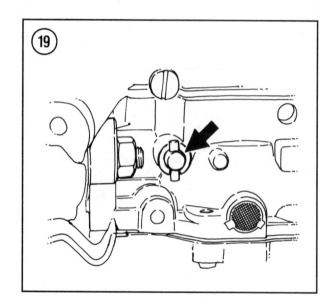

1. On tiller handle models, turn the idle speed knob on the tiller to the fully counterclockwise (slow) position.

2. With the engine running at normal operating temperature in FORWARD gear, idle speed should be 625-675 rpm.

3A. *Tiller handle*—To adjust idle speed, remove the screw securing the throttle cable bracket to the power head (**Figure 22**). Move the cable bracket as necessary to adjust idle speed. Reinstall the bracket and tighten the screw securely.

3B. *Remote control*—Turn the idle speed screw (**Figure 17**) as necessary to adjust idle speed.

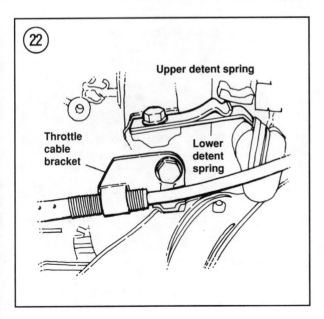

4. After adjustment, operate the outboard at wide-open throttle for 1 minute. Then, quickly throttle back to 700-800 rpm and shift into NEUTRAL. The motor should idle smoothly.

5. If the motor stalls, backfires or runs poorly, the idle mixture may be too lean. Readjust idle mixture as outlined under *Low-speed mixture adjustment* in this chapter.

Shift Lever Detent Adjustment

> *WARNING*
> *To prevent accidental starting, disconnect the spark plug wires from the plugs.*

1. While rotating the propeller shaft clockwise, shift the outboard into NEUTRAL.

2. With the outboard in NEUTRAL, the lower detent spring (**Figure 22**) should be centered in the notch in the shift lever.

3. If adjustment is necessary, loosen the screw securing the detent spring and move the spring as necessary. Securely retighten the screw.

20, 25, 28 AND 30 HP (2-CYLINDER MODELS)

Disconnect both remote control cables (if so equipped) from the power head.

Cam Follower Pickup Point

1. Connect a throttle shaft amplifier to the carburetor throttle shaft.

2A. *Tiller handle*—Turn the idle adjusting knob on the tiller to the fully counterclockwise (SLOW) position.

2B. *Remote control*—Back out the throttle arm stop screw until the arm contacts the stop screw mounting bracket.

3. Advance the throttle until the tip of the amplifier begins to move. Just as the amplifier moves, the cam follower should be centered

between the 2 marks on the throttle cam. See **Figure 23**.

4. If adjustment is necessary, loosen the adjusting lever screw (**Figure 24**) and move the lever as necessary. Retighten the adjusting screw securely.

Throttle Control Rod Adjustment (25-30 hp Only)

WARNING
To prevent accidental starting, disconnect the spark plug wires from the plugs.

1. While rotating the propeller shaft, shift the outboard into FORWARD gear.

2. Advance the throttle lever (C, **Figure 25**) until it contacts its stop on the power head.

3. Loosen the screw on the adjustment collar (A, **Figure 25**).

4. Move the throttle control rod to the fully open position (carburetor throttle valve horizontal).

5. Move the adjustment collar (A, **Figure 25**) back until it contacts the pivot block (B), then tighten the collar screw. Note that the offset on the pivot block must be facing toward the adjustment collar.

6. Move the throttle lever to the fully advanced position to check adjustment. If the carburetor throttle valve is not horizontal, repeat the adjustment procedure.

Maximum Spark Advance

NOTE
*To load the outboard motor properly when adjusting maximum spark advance, the outboard motor must be in a test tank or on a boat in the water with the correct test wheel installed (**Table 3**). Do not attempt to adjust the maximum timing with a propeller installed. **Do not** run the outboard at wide-open throttle while connected to a flushing device.*

1. Connect a timing light to the No. 1 (top) spark plug wire.

2. Start the motor and run at fast idle until warmed to normal operating temperature.

3. Shift into FORWARD gear.

4. Run the motor at wide-open throttle and note the timing marks with the timing light.

NOTE
Two timing scales are present on the flywheel. Use the grid marked "ELEC CD" on rope start models. On electric start models, use the grid marked "CD."

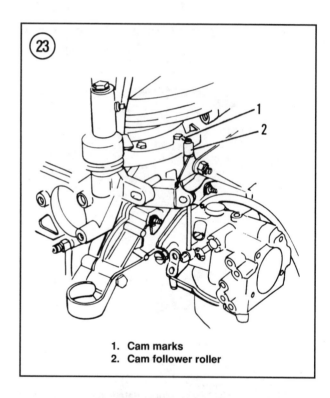

1. Cam marks
2. Cam follower roller

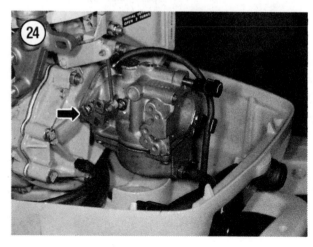

a. *Rope start*—The timing mark on the rewind starter housing should be aligned with the 33-35° BTDC (20 hp) or 29-31° BTDC (25-30 hp) mark on the flywheel. See **Figure 26**.

b. *Electric start*—The timing pointer on the starter motor bracket should be aligned with the 33-35° BTDC (20 hp) or 29-31° BTDC (25-30 hp) mark on the flywheel. See **Figure 27**.

> ### WARNING
> *To prevent accidental contact with the rotating flywheel, stop the motor prior to adjusting maximum spark advance.*

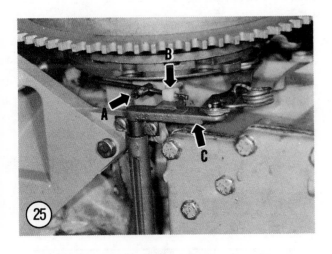

25

26

5. If adjustment is required, loosen the locknut on the maximum advance screw, then turn the screw as necessary. Turning the screw clockwise retards timing; turning the screw counterclockwise advances timing. Note that 1 turn of the screw equals approximately 1° timing change. Retighten the locknut securely, then repeat Step 4 to check adjustment.

5

Carburetor Adjustment

Start the outboard and run in FORWARD gear at one-half throttle until warmed to normal operating temperature. For optimum results when adjusting low-speed mixture and idle speed, the outboard must be mounted on a boat in the water, running at normal operating temperature, in forward gear, with the correct propeller installed and boat movement unrestrained.

Low-speed mixture (20 hp models)

1. Turn the idle adjusting knob to the fully SLOW position.

2. With the engine running at 700-800 rpm, turn the low-speed mixture screw (**Figure 28**) in small increments to obtain the highest consistent

27

idle speed. Wait approximately 15 seconds after each adjustment to allow the engine to respond.

3. After the highest idle speed is obtained, turn the mixture screw 1/8 turn counterclockwise.

4. Adjust idle speed to 650 rpm in FORWARD gear.

5. Operate the outboard at wide-open throttle for 1 minute. Then, quickly reduce engine speed to 700-800 rpm and shift into NEUTRAL. The motor should idle smoothly.

6. If the motor stalls, backfires or runs poorly, the mixture may be too lean. Turn the mixture screw counterclockwise 1/16 turn and wait for the motor to respond.

7. Repeat Step 5 to check adjustment. Repeat Step 6 if necessary.

8. If the motor does not respond to idle mixture adjustment, make sure:

   a. The engine is at normal operating temperature.

   b. The linkage is correctly adjusted.

   c. The external recirculation system is operating properly.

   d. Sufficient exhaust backpressure is present.

Idle mixture (25-30 hp models)

NOTE
*The low-speed mixture screw on 25, 28 and 30 hp models (**Figure 29**) is adjusted at the factory and should not require further adjustment. The following adjustment procedure should only be performed if the screw has been turned or removed.*

1. Turn the low-speed mixture screw (**Figure 28**) in until lightly seated. Then back out the screw 1-3/4 turns.

2. Place a reference mark on the mixture screw adapter sleeve (**Figure 29**) indicating the position of the screw.

3. Turn the idle adjusting knob to the fully SLOW position.

4. Start the motor and run at 700-800 rpm in FORWARD gear, until warmed to normal operating temperature.

   a. If the idle mixture is too lean, the motor will pop and backfire.

   b. If the idle mixture is too rich, the motor will idle roughly, load up and stall.

NOTE
Turning the idle mixture screw clockwise leans the mixture; turning the screw counterclockwise richens the mixture.

5. If adjustment is required, note the reference mark (Step 2) and turn the mixture screw in 1/12

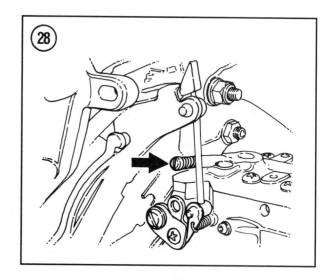

turn increments until the highest consistent idle speed is obtained. Wait 15 seconds after adjusting to allow the engine to respond.

6. After the highest consistent idle speed is obtained, operate the motor at wide-open throttle for 3 minutes (in FORWARD gear). Then throttle back to idle speed (in FORWARD gear). The motor should idle smoothly.

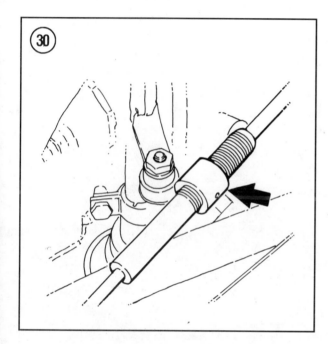

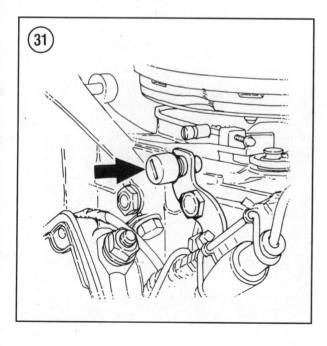

7. If the motor pops, backfires or runs poorly, repeat Step 5 as necessary. If the motor does not respond to adjustment, make sure:

a. The engine is at normal operating temperature.

b. The linkage is correctly adjusted.

c. The external recirculation system is operating properly.

d. Sufficient exhaust backpressure is present.

Idle speed (all models)

Make sure the idle mixture is properly set prior to adjusting the idle speed.

1. On tiller handle models, turn the idle speed adjusting knob on the tiller to the fully counterclockwise (SLOW) position.

2. Start the motor and shift into FORWARD gear. Run the motor until warmed to normal operating temperature.

3. Idle speed in FORWARD gear should be 650-700 rpm.

4A. *Tiller handle*—Move the throttle cable mounting bracket as necessary to adjust idle speed. See **Figure 30**.

4B. *Remote control*—Turn the throttle arm stop screw as necessary to adjust idle speed. See **Figure 31**.

5. Operate the motor at wide-open throttle for 1 minute (in FORWARD gear). Then throttle back to idle speed. The motor should idle smoothly.

6. If the motor pops, backfires, runs poorly or stalls, readjust the idle mixture as described in this chapter.

35 JET, 40, 48 AND 50 HP (2-CYLINDER MODELS)

Initial Linkage Adjustment

Adjust the length of the throttle and spark control rods as follows before performing the synchronization and adjustment procedure.

1. Disconnect the throttle cable from the throttle lever (8, **Figure 32**).

2. Measure the length of the throttle control rod. Measure from the center of each link rod connector. See A, **Figure 32**. The length should be:

    a. *7-13/16 in. (198 mm)*—All 1991 and 1992 models and 1993-on 40 hp rope start and 48 hp.

    b. *7-5/8 in. (193 mm)*—All 1993-on models except 40 hp rope start and 48 hp.

3. If adjustment is necessary, carefully pry the front control rod socket loose. Turn the socket as necessary to adjust.

4. Next, measure the length of the spark control rod (6, **Figure 32**). Measure from the center of each connector socket as shown at B, **Figure 32**. The length of the spark control rod should be:

    a. *2-1/16 in. (53 mm)*—All 1991 and 1992 models and 1993-on 40 hp rope start and 48 hp.

    b. *2-5/8 in. (67 mm)*—All 1993-on models except 40 hp rope start and 48 hp.

5. If adjustment is necessary, remove the rod by carefully prying the connector sockets loose. Turn the connector sockets as necessary to adjust, then reinstall the rod.

6A. *1991 and 1992 models*—Loosen the cam follower adjustment screw (3, **Figure 32**) and move the cam follower away from the throttle cam (1). Adjust the idle speed screw (5, **Figure 32**) until the spark lever cam follower (10) is centered between the 2 alignment marks.

6B. *1993-on models*—Loosen the locknut on the idle speed screw (5, **Figure 32**). Adjust the idle speed screw so 1/2 in. (12.7 mm) is present between the head of the screw and the spark control lever. See C, **Figure 32**. Tighten the idle speed screw locknut securely.

Throttle Valve Synchronization

Both carburetor throttle valves must be synchronized to open and close simultaneously. If the throttle valves do not open and close at exactly the same time, the motor will not idle or accelerate properly.

1. Loosen the throttle cam follower adjustment screw (3, **Figure 32**) and move the cam follower away from the throttle cam.

2. Loosen the throttle lever adjustment screw (A, **Figure 33**) on the upper carburetor.

3. Rotate the throttle shaft to partially open, then allow it to snap back to the closed position.

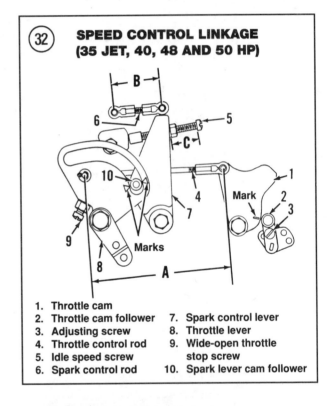

SPEED CONTROL LINKAGE (35 JET, 40, 48 AND 50 HP)

1. Throttle cam
2. Throttle cam follower
3. Adjusting screw
4. Throttle control rod
5. Idle speed screw
6. Spark control rod
7. Spark control lever
8. Throttle lever
9. Wide-open throttle stop screw
10. Spark lever cam follower

4. Gently rotate the upper carburetor throttle lever (B, **Figure 33**) counterclockwise (closed) and tighten the lever adjusting screw securely.

5. Operate the throttle shafts while observing the throttle valves. If the valves do not open and close at exactly the same time, repeat this adjustment procedure.

Cam Follower Pickup Point

1. Loosen the throttle cam follower adjustment screw (**Figure 34**).

2. Slowly push the throttle cam and cam follower together until they contact. With the cam and cam follower just touching and the carburetor throttle valves fully closed, align the mark on the throttle cam with the center of the cam follower, then tighten the adjustment screw securely. See **Figure 34**.

3. Next, push the idle speed screw (**Figure 35**) against its stop. With the idle speed screw against its stop, the spark lever cam follower should be centered between the alignment marks and a 0.010 in. (0.25 mm) clearance should be present

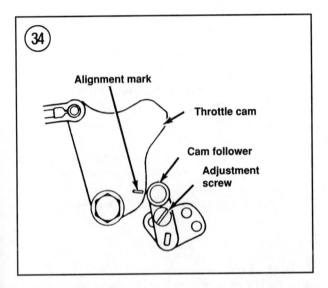

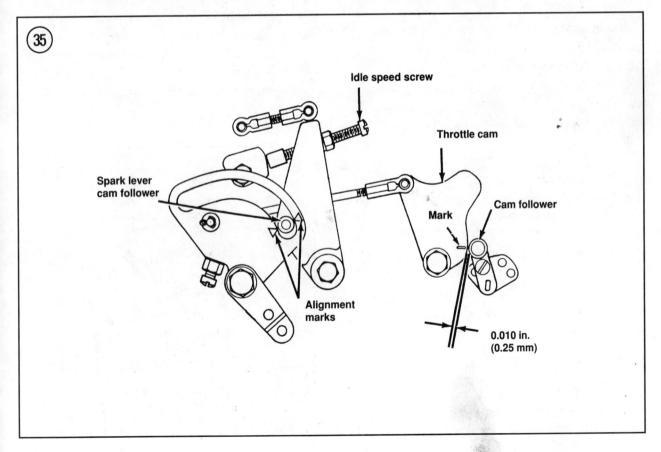

between the throttle cam and cam follower. See **Figure 35**.

4. If the cam follower clearance requires adjustment, proceed as follows:

   a. *1991 and 1992 models*—Carefully pry the throttle control rod (4, **Figure 32**) from the throttle cam. Rotate the control rod connector as necessary to obtain the 0.010 in. (0.25 mm) clearance between the throttle cam and follower (**Figure 35**). Reconnect the rod to the throttle cam and recheck clearance.

   b. *1993-on models*—While holding the idle speed screw against its stop, turn the screw as necessary to obtain the 0.010 in. (0.25 mm) clearance between the throttle cam and follower (**Figure 35**).

Wide-Open Throttle Stop

1. With the engine stopped, advance the throttle lever to the wide-open position.

2. With the throttle wide open, the carburetor throttle shaft roll pins should be in the vertical position (**Figure 36**).

3. If not, loosen the locknut and turn the wide-open throttle stop screw (9, **Figure 32**) as necessary to position the throttle shaft roll pins vertical with the throttle wide-open.

4. Securely tighten the locknut then recheck the position of the roll pins as described in Steps 1 and 2.

Maximum Spark Advance

> *NOTE*
> *To load the outboard motor properly when adjusting maximum spark advance, the outboard must be in a test tank or on a boat in the water with the correct test wheel installed (Table 3). Do not attempt to adjust the maximum timing with a propeller installed. Do not run the outboard at wide-open throttle while connected to a flushing device.*

1. Connect a timing light to the No. 1 (top) spark plug wire according to its manufacturer's instructions.

2. Connect a shop tachometer according to its manufacturer's instructions.

3. Start the motor and allow it to warm to normal operating temperature.

4. Shift the outboard into FORWARD gear. Advance the throttle to no less than 5000 rpm and note the timing with the timing light.

> *WARNING*
> *Do not attempt to adjust the maximum spark advance with the engine running in Step 5. Contact with the rotating flywheel could result in serious personal injury.*

5. Maximum spark advance should be 18-20° BTDC. If not, stop the engine and carefully pry the spark control rod (6, **Figure 32**) from the spark control lever (7). Turn the rod connector clockwise to advance timing or counterclockwise to retard timing. Note that 2 turns of the connector equal approximately 1° timing change.

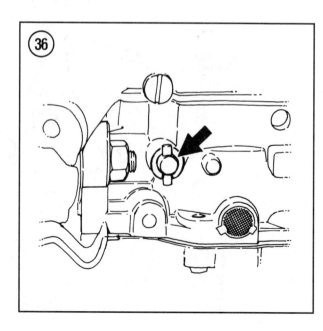

6. Reattach the spark control rod to the spark control lever. Verify the correct adjustment by repeating Steps 3 and 4.

Carburetor Adjustments

Start the outboard and run in FORWARD gear at one-half throttle until warmed to normal operating temperature. For optimum results when adjusting low-speed mixture and idle speed, the outboard must be mounted on a boat in the water, running at normal operating temperature, in forward gear, with the correct propeller installed and boat movement unrestrained.

Slow-speed mixture adjustment

NOTE
*The low-speed mixture screw on 35 Jet, 40, 48 and 50 hp models (**Figure 37**) is adjusted at the factory and should not require further adjustment. The following adjustment procedure should only be performed if the screw has been turned or removed.*

1. Turn the low-speed mixture screw (**Figure 28**, typical) in until lightly seated. Then back out the screw 2-1/4 turns on 40 hp and 2-3/4 turns on all other models.

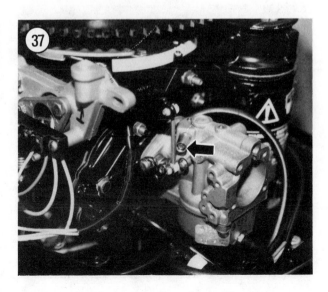

2. Place a reference mark on the mixture screw adapter sleeve (**Figure 37**) indicating the position of the screw.

3. Turn the idle adjusting knob to the fully SLOW position.

4. Start the motor and run at 700-800 rpm in FORWARD gear, until warmed to normal operating temperature.

   a. If the idle mixture is too lean, the motor will pop and backfire.

   b. If the idle mixture is too rich, the motor will idle roughly, load up and stall.

NOTE
Turning the idle mixture screw clockwise leans the mixture; turning the screw counterclockwise richens the mixture.

5. If adjustment is required, note the reference mark (Step 2) and turn the mixture screw in 1/12 turn increments until the highest consistent idle speed is obtained. Wait 15 seconds after adjusting to allow the engine to respond.

6. After the highest consistent idle speed is obtained, operate the motor at wide-open throttle for 3 minutes (in FORWARD gear). Then throttle back to idle speed (in FORWARD gear). The motor should idle smoothly.

7. If the motor pops, backfires or runs poorly, repeat Step 5 as necessary. If the motor does not respond to adjustment, make sure:

   a. The engine is at normal operating temperature.

   b. The linkage is correctly adjusted.

   c. The external recirculation system is operating properly.

   d. Sufficient exhaust backpressure is present.

Idle speed adjustment

1. Connect an accurate tachometer according to its manufacturer's instructions.

2. Start the motor and run at fast idle until warmed to normal operating temperature.

3. Shift the outboard into FORWARD gear and note the idle speed.

4. Idle speed with the outboard in FORWARD gear and the idle speed screw contacting its stop should be 725-775 rpm.

NOTE
*If adjustment of the idle speed screw is necessary, the 0.010 in. (0.25 mm) clearance between the throttle cam and cam follower must be reset. See **Throttle Cam Follower Pickup Point**.*

5. If idle speed requires adjustment, loosen the locknut and turn idle speed screw (5, **Figure 32**) as necessary. Retighten the locknut securely.

6. If the idle speed screw is turned, repeat the *Throttle Cam Follower Pickup Point* adjustment procedure in this chapter.

7. On 1991 and 1992 models, check idle timing after completing Steps 5 and 6. With the motor running at idle speed in FORWARD gear, the ignition timing should be 1-5° ATDC. If not, check the following:

   a. Make sure the engine is at normal operating temperature.

   b. The carburetor is properly calibrated and adjusted.

   c. The power head is in good mechanical condition.

   d. The flywheel is in good condition and the flywheel key is not sheared.

Throttle Cable Installation

Tiller handle models

1. Turn the idle speed knob on the tiller to the fully counterclockwise (SLOW) position.

2. Connect the throttle cable to the upper hole in the throttle lever (8, **Figure 32**) using the pin and cotter clip. Install the cotter clip so it is parallel to the embossed rib in the throttle lever.

3. While holding the tiller twist grip in the fully SLOW position (idle speed screw against its stop), pull on the throttle cable to remove any slack. Then rotate the cable mounting bracket to align with its mounting hole.

4. Rotate the cable mounting bracket 2 turns toward the end of the cable to obtain the correct preload. Install a flat washer between the bracket and intake manifold and install the bracket screw. Tighten the screw to 36 in.-lb. (4.1 N·m).

5. Open and close the throttle with the tiller twist grip to be certain the idle speed screw contacts its stop when the twist grip is in the SLOW position.

Remote control models

1. Place the fast idle lever on the remote control in the down position.

2. While rotating the propeller shaft, move the remote control handle from the NEUTRAL position to the FORWARD detent, then halfway back to the NEUTRAL position.

3. Push the throttle lever (A, **Figure 38**) until the idle speed screw (B) is contacting its stop.

4. Connect the throttle cable to the lower hole in the throttle lever using the pin and cotter clip. Install the cotter clip parallel to the embossed rib (C, **Figure 38**) on the throttle lever.

5. Pull on the throttle cable to remove any slack, then place the trunnion nut (D, **Figure 38**) into its anchor pocket.

6. Temporarily install the cable retainer and screw.

NOTE
If throttle cable adjustment is too loose, the idle speed may be excessive or inconsistent. If cable adjustment is too tight, throttle and shift control effort may be excessive.

7. Move the remote control handle to the FORWARD gear position, then pull it back slowly to NEUTRAL. Make sure the idle speed screw is against its stop. If not, remove cable backlash by adjusting the throttle cable trunnion nut (D, **Figure 38**).

1991 AND 1992 60 AND 70 HP (3-CYLINDER MODELS)

The following synchronizing and adjustment procedures should be followed in the sequence given. Some procedures, however, cover only tiller handle equipped models. These procedures will be specifically noted and must be skipped on remote control equipped outboards.

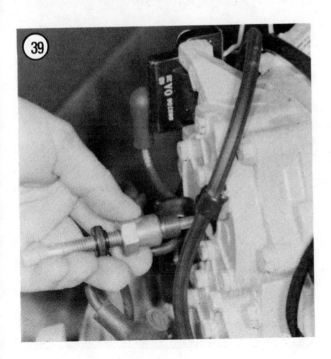

On models equipped with remote control, remove the throttle cable from the throttle control arm and anchor pocket before proceeding with the synchronizing and adjusting procedure.

Timing Pointer Alignment

Use the following procedure to check/adjust the alignment of the timing pointer with top dead center of the No. 1 (top) piston.

NOTE
Two timing grids are present on the flywheel. Be sure to reference the timing grid not marked "rope."

1. Disconnect the spark plug wires and remove the spark plugs.
2. Loosen the timing pointer mounting screw, move the pointer to the center of its adjustment slot and retighten the screw.
3. Turn the flywheel in a clockwise direction until the TDC mark on the flywheel is approximately 1-1/2 in. (38.1 mm) past the timing pointer.
4. Install OMC Piston Stop Tool (part No. 384887) into the No. 1 spark plug hole. Screw the tool into the plug hole until bottomed, then turn the tool plunger inward until it contacts the piston. Secure the plunger in place with the lockring. See **Figure 39**.
5. Hold the No. 1 piston firmly against the piston stop tool by turning the flywheel. While holding the flywheel, place a mark on the flywheel directly adjacent to the timing pointer. Label the mark "A." See **Figure 40**.
6. Rotate the flywheel in a clockwise direction until the No. 1 piston contacts the piston stop tool again. Hold the flywheel so the piston is against the tool, then place another mark on the flywheel adjacent to the timing pointer. Label this mark "B." See **Figure 40**.
7. Remove the piston stop tool.
8. Measure the distance between marks "A" and "B" using a flexible scale. Place a mark on the

flywheel at the mid-point between "A" and "B" and label this mark "C." See **Figure 40**.

9. If mark "C" is in alignment with the TDC mark cast in the flywheel, the timing pointer is properly adjusted. If not, turn the flywheel as necessary to align mark "C" with the timing pointer. While holding the flywheel in this position, loosen the timing pointer screw and move the pointer into alignment with the TDC mark cast in the flywheel. Tighten the pointer screw securely.

10. Reinstall the spark plugs.

Throttle Cable Adjustment (Tiller Handle Models Only)

1. Turn the idle speed knob on the tiller to the fully counterclockwise (SLOW) position.

2. Make sure the throttle cable mounting bracket is affixed to the forward mounting hole in the power head.

3. Back out the idle speed screw (B, **Figure 41**) and wide-open throttle stop screw (A) until the ends of the screws are flush with the anchor block.

4. Rotate the tiller handle twist grip to the wide-open throttle position.

5. Measure the gap between the spark control cam follower (roller) and the end of the slot in the spark control cam (**Figure 42**).

6. Rotate the tiller handle twist grip to the idle position and repeat Step 5 (**Figure 43**).

7. The gap should be approximately 1/4 in. (6.3 mm) at each end of the slot. If not, loosen the locknut (**Figure 43**) and turn the thumb wheel on the throttle cable as necessary. Retighten the locknut securely.

Throttle Valve Synchronization

Both carburetor throttle valves must be synchronized to open and close simultaneously. If the throttle valves do not open and close at exactly the same time, the motor will not idle or accelerate properly.

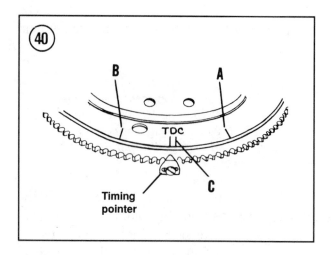

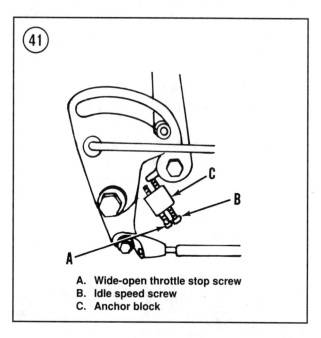

A. Wide-open throttle stop screw
B. Idle speed screw
C. Anchor block

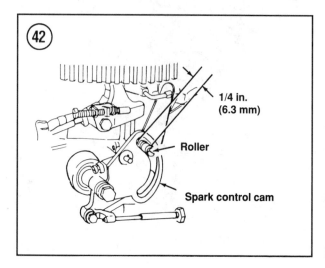

1. The throttle cam must not be in contact with the throttle cam follower during throttle valve synchronizing. Loosen the throttle cam follower adjustment screw (**Figure 44**) and move the follower away from the cam.

2. Loosen the upper and lower throttle lever adjusting screws at the top and bottom carburetors (A and B, **Figure 45**).

3. Confirm that the throttle valves are fully closed on all 3 carburetors.

4. Rotate the throttle levers lightly in a counterclockwise direction, then tighten the lower adjusting screw (B, **Figure 45**) then the upper (A).

5. Open and close the throttle while observing the throttle valves. Repeat this adjustment procedure if the valves do not open and close at exactly the same time.

Throttle Cam Follower Pickup Point

1. Attach a throttle shaft amplifier to the throttle lever on the top carburetor.

2. Disconnect the link rod from the throttle cam.

3. Push the throttle cam follower against the throttle cam, then move the throttle cam until the embossed mark on the cam intersects with the center of the cam follower (**Figure 46**). When the mark is aligned with the center of the follower, tighten the cam follower adjusting screw securely.

4. Next, slowly advance the throttle cam while observing the throttle shaft amplifier. When the amplifier just begins to move, the mark on the throttle cam should be aligned with the center of the cam follower. If not, repeat Step 3.

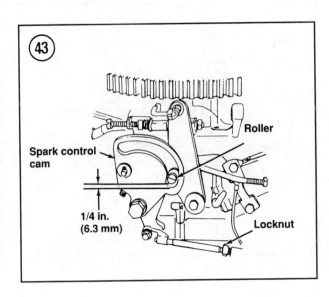

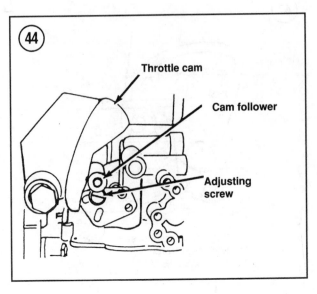

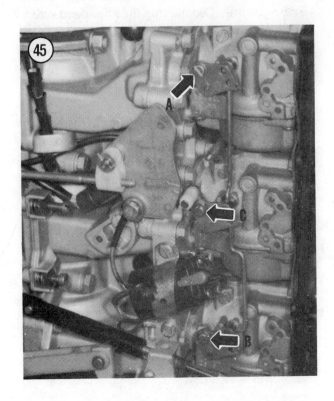

Throttle Cam Adjustment

1. On remote control equipped models, connect the throttle cable to the throttle arm as described in this chapter.

2A. *Tiller handle*—Confirm that the throttle arm is contacting the idle speed screw (B, **Figure 47**).

2B. *Remote control*—Confirm that the throttle arm is firmly contacting its idle stop screw (**Figure 48**).

3. Reconnect the link rod to the throttle cam coupler ball. See **Figure 49**. Then rotate the throttle cam and check the clearance (C, **Figure 49**) between the throttle cam and cam follower. The adjustment is correct if the clearance (C) is less than 0.010 in. (0.25 mm), but not touching.

4. If throttle cam adjustment is necessary, disconnect the link rod from the throttle cam and turn the link rod connector as necessary to obtain the specified clearance.

5. Reattach the link rod to the throttle cam. Slowly advance the throttle to fast-idle, then throttle back to the idle position. Confirm that the throttle arm is contacting the idle speed screw and approximately 0.010 in. (0.25 mm) is present between the throttle cam and cam follower. If not, repeat the adjustment procedure.

Wide-Open Throttle Stop Adjustment

1. With the motor *not* running, advance the throttle to the wide-open position.

> *CAUTION*
> *If the roll pins travel past the vertical position in Step 2, carburetor and/or throttle linkage damage can result.*

2. With the throttle wide open, adjust the wide-open throttle stop screw (**Figure 47** [tiller handle] or **Figure 48** [remote control]) so the throttle shaft roll pins are exactly vertical. See **Figure 50**.

Idle Timing (Remote Control Models)

The following idle timing procedure should provide the optimum idle quality within a range of 600-700 rpm (in gear), depending on the propeller used. But, if idle speed is too high after adjusting the timing, check the induction system for air leaks and repair as necessary. If idle speed is too slow, advance idle timing in small increments until the desired idle speed is obtained.

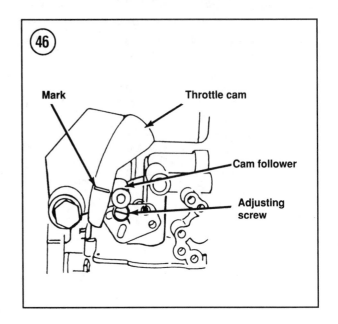

46

Mark

Throttle cam

Cam follower

Adjusting screw

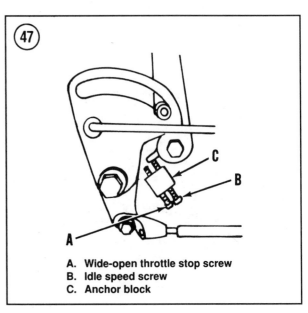

47

A. Wide-open throttle stop screw
B. Idle speed screw
C. Anchor block

1. Connect a timing light to the No. 1 (top) spark plug wire.

2. Start the motor and allow it to warm to normal operating temperature.

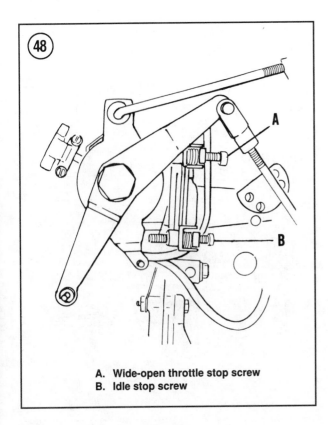

A. Wide-open throttle stop screw
B. Idle stop screw

3. Shift into FORWARD gear.

4. Make sure the throttle arm is contacting the idle speed screw.

5. Note the timing with the timing light. Idle timing should be 1-3° ATDC on 60 hp models or 3-5° ATDC on 70 hp models.

> *WARNING*
> *Do not attempt to adjust the ignition timing with the motor running in Step 6. Contact with the rotating flywheel can cause serious personal injury.*

6. If adjustment is necessary, stop the motor. Turn the idle timing screw (**Figure 51**) clockwise to advance timing or counterclockwise to retard timing.

7. Repeat Steps 3-5 to check adjustment.

Maximum Spark Advance

> *NOTE*
> *To load the outboard motor properly when adjusting maximum spark advance, the outboard must be in a test tank or on a boat in the water with the correct test wheel installed (**Table 3**). Do not attempt to adjust the maximum timing with a propeller installed. **Do not** run the*

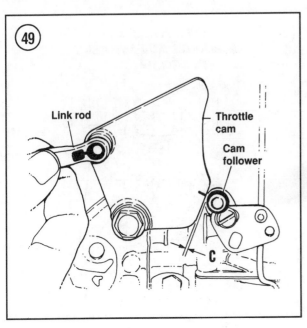

Link rod

Throttle cam

Cam follower

C

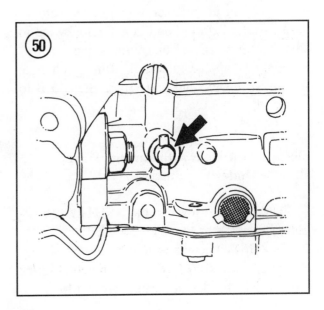

outboard at wide-open throttle while connected to a flushing device.

1. Connect a timing light to the No. 1 (top) spark plug wire.
2. Connect an accurate tachometer to the motor according to its manufacturer's instructions.
3. Start the motor and warm to normal operating temperature.
4. Shift into FORWARD gear. Advance the throttle to 5000 rpm (minimum) and note the timing with the timing light.
5. Maximum spark advance should be 18-20° BTDC.

> *WARNING*
> *Do not attempt to adjust the ignition timing with the motor running in Step 6. Contact with the rotating flywheel can cause serious personal injury.*

6A. *Tiller handle*—If adjustment is necessary, stop the motor. Remove the spark advance rod (**Figure 52**). Shorten the rod by bending its ends together to advance the timing; lengthen it by expanding the ends to retard the timing. Reinstall the spark advance rod and Repeat Steps 3-5 to check adjustment.

6B. *Remote control*—If adjustment is necessary, stop the motor. Loosen the locknut and turn the maximum advance screw (**Figure 53**) clockwise to retard timing and counterclockwise to advance timing. Note that turning the screw 1 turn equals approximately 1° timing change. Retighten the locknut and repeat Steps 3-5 to check adjustment.

Shift Lever Detent Adjustment (Tiller Handle Models)

1. Place the shift lever in the NEUTRAL position.
2. If the lower detent spring is not completely engaged in the shift lever detent notch (**Figure 54**), loosen the detent spring screw. Move the

spring until it fully engages the notch, then tighten the screw securely.

Slow-Speed Mixture Adjustment

The slow-speed mixture screw is adjusted at the factory and should not require further adjust-

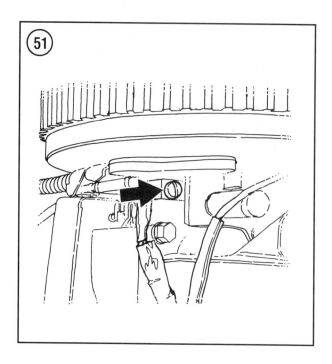

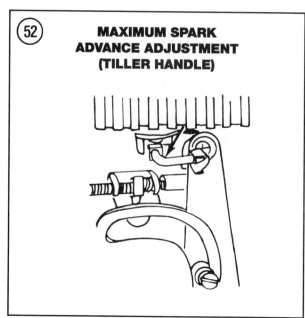

MAXIMUM SPARK ADVANCE ADJUSTMENT (TILLER HANDLE)

ment. If however, the screw is removed for cleaning purposes, adjustment may be necessary. Refer to the appropriate section in Chapter Six for the correct adjustment procedure.

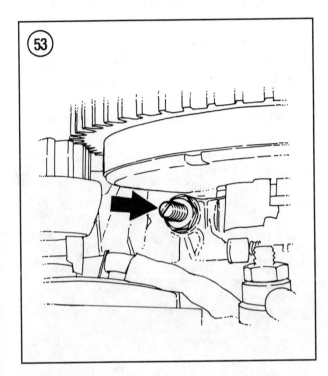

Idle Speed Adjustment (Tiller Handle Models)

For optimum results, adjust idle speed with the outboard mounted on a boat in the water, running at normal operating temperature in FORWARD gear, with the correct propeller installed and the boat's movement unrestrained.

1. Connect an accurate tachometer according to its manufacturer's instructions.
2. Start the motor and warm to normal operating temperature.
3. Shift into FORWARD gear and note the idle speed.
4. Idle speed should be 700-750 rpm in FORWARD gear.
5. If necessary, turn the idle speed screw (**Figure 47**) as required to obtain the specified idle speed.

Throttle Cable Installation/Adjustment (Remote Control Models)

1. Place the fast idle lever on the remote control in the down position.
2. While rotating the propeller shaft, move the remote control handle from the NEUTRAL position to the FORWARD detent, then halfway back to the NEUTRAL position.
3. Push the throttle lever firmly against the idle stop screw (**Figure 48**).
4. Connect the throttle cable to the throttle lever using the washer and locknut. Tighten the locknut securely.
5. Pull on the throttle cable to remove any slack, then place the trunnion nut into its anchor pocket.
6. Temporarily install the cable retainer and screw.

NOTE
If throttle cable adjustment is too loose, the idle speed may be excessive or inconsistent. If cable adjustment is too tight, throttle and shift control effort may be excessive.

5

7. Move the remote control handle to the FOR-WARD gear position, then pull it back slowly to NEUTRAL. Make sure the idle speed screw is against its stop. If not, remove cable backlash by adjusting the throttle cable trunnion nut (B, **Figure 55**).

1993-ON 60 AND 70 HP (3-CYLINDER MODELS EQUIPPED WITH TILLER HANDLE)

Timing Pointer Alignment

Use the following procedure to check/adjust the alignment of the timing pointer with top dead center of the No. 1 (top) piston.

> *NOTE*
> *Two timing grids are present on the fly-wheel. Be sure to reference the second timing grid when viewing the flywheel rotating in a clockwise direction.*

1. Disconnect the spark plug wires and remove the spark plugs.
2. Loosen the timing pointer mounting screw, move the pointer to the center of its adjustment slot and retighten the screw.
3. Turn the flywheel in a clockwise direction until the T mark on the flywheel is approximately 1-1/2 in. (38.1 mm) past the timing pointer.
4. Install OMC Piston Stop Tool (part No. 384887) into the No. 1 spark plug hole. Screw the tool into the plug hole until bottomed, then turn the tool plunger inward until it contacts the piston. Secure the plunger in place with the lockring. See **Figure 56**.
5. Hold the No. 1 piston firmly against the piston stop tool by turning the flywheel. While holding the flywheel, place a mark on the fly-wheel directly adjacent to the timing pointer. Label the mark "A." See **Figure 57**.
6. Rotate the flywheel in a clockwise direction until the No. 1 piston contacts the piston stop tool again. Hold the flywheel so the piston is against

the tool, then place another mark on the flywheel adjacent to the timing pointer. Label this mark "B." See **Figure 57**.
7. Remove the piston stop tool.
8. Measure the distance between marks "A" and "B" using a flexible scale. Place a mark on the flywheel at the mid-point between "A" and "B" and label this mark "C." See **Figure 57**.
9. If mark "C" is in alignment with the T mark cast in the flywheel, the timing pointer is prop-erly adjusted. If not, turn the flywheel as neces-

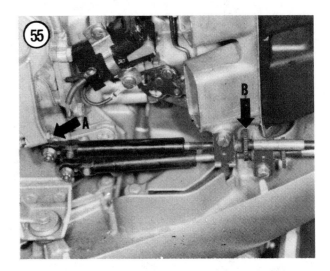

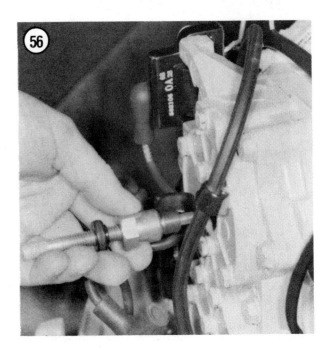

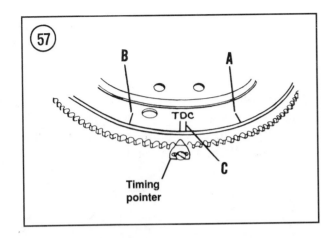

Timing pointer

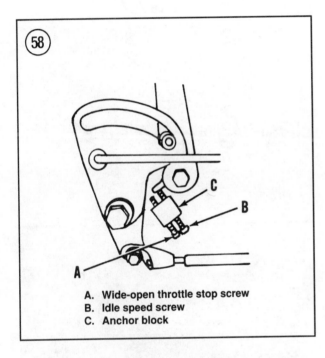

A. Wide-open throttle stop screw
B. Idle speed screw
C. Anchor block

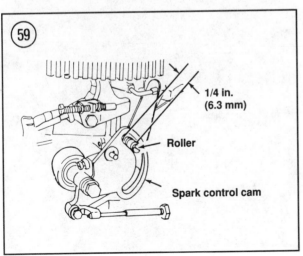

1/4 in.
(6.3 mm)

Roller

Spark control cam

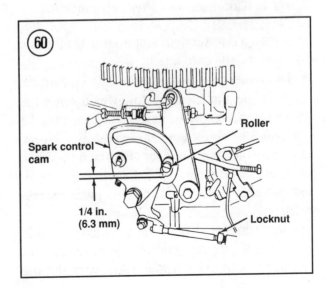

Roller

Spark control cam

1/4 in.
(6.3 mm)

Locknut

sary to align mark "C" with the timing pointer. While holding the flywheel in this position, loosen the timing pointer screw and move the pointer into alignment with the T mark cast in the flywheel. Tighten the pointer screw securely.

10. Reinstall the spark plugs.

Throttle Cable Adjustment

1. Turn the idle speed knob on the tiller to the fully counterclockwise (SLOW) position.

2. Make sure the throttle cable mounting bracket is affixed to the forward mounting hole in the power head.

3. Back out the idle speed screw and wide-open throttle stop screw (**Figure 58**) until the ends of the screws are flush with the anchor block.

4. Rotate the tiller handle twist grip to the wide-open throttle position.

5. Measure the gap between the spark control cam follower (roller) and the end of the slot in the spark control cam (**Figure 59**).

6. Rotate the tiller handle twist grip to the idle position and repeat Step 5 (**Figure 60**).

7. The gap should be approximately 1/4 in. (6.3 mm) at each end of the slot. If not, loosen the locknut (**Figure 60**) and turn the thumb wheel

5

on the throttle cable as necessary. Retighten the locknut securely.

Throttle Valve Synchronization

Both carburetor throttle valves must be synchronized to open and close simultaneously. If the throttle valves do not open and close at exactly the same time, the motor will not idle or accelerate properly.

1. The throttle cam must not be in contact with the throttle cam follower during throttle valve synchronizing. Loosen the throttle cam follower adjustment screw (**Figure 61**) and move the follower away from the cam.

2. Loosen the upper and lower throttle lever adjusting screws at the top and bottom carburetors (A and B, **Figure 62**).

3. Confirm that the throttle valves are fully closed on all 3 carburetors.

4. Rotate the throttle levers lightly in a counterclockwise direction, then tighten the lower adjusting screw (B, **Figure 62**) then the upper (A).

5. Open and close the throttle while observing the carburetor throttle valves. Repeat this adjustment procedure if the valves do not open and close at exactly the same time.

Throttle Cam Follower Pickup Point

1. Attach a throttle shaft amplifier to the throttle lever on the top carburetor.

2. Disconnect the link rod from the throttle cam.

3. Push the throttle cam follower against the throttle cam, then move the throttle cam until the embossed mark on the cam intersects with the center of the cam follower (**Figure 63**). When the mark is aligned with the center of the follower, tighten the cam follower adjusting screw securely.

4. Next, slowly advance the throttle cam while observing the throttle amplifier. When the amplifier just begins to move, the mark on the throttle

cam should be aligned with the center of the cam follower. If not, repeat Step 3.

Idle Timing

The following idle timing procedure should provide the optimum idle quality within a range

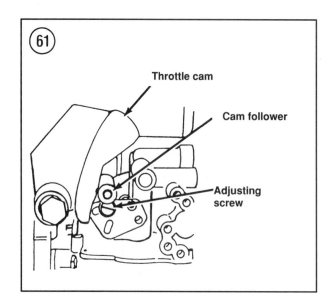

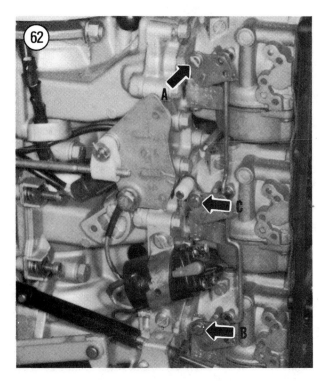

of 750-850 rpm (in gear), depending on the propeller used. But, if idle speed is too high after adjusting the timing, check the induction system for air leaks and repair as necessary. If idle speed is too slow, advance idle timing in small increments until the desired idle speed is obtained.

The slow-speed mixture screw is adjusted at the factory and should not require further adjustment. However, if the screw is removed for cleaning, it will require adjustment. See the appropriate section in Chapter Six for adjustment procedures.

1. Connect a timing light to the No. 1 (top) spark plug wire.

2. Start the motor and allow it to warm to normal operating temperature.

3. Shift into FORWARD gear.

4. Make sure the throttle arm is contacting the idle speed screw.

5. Note the timing with the timing light. Idle timing should be 1-3° ATDC.

WARNING
Do not attempt to adjust the ignition timing with the motor running in Step 6. Contact with the rotating flywheel can cause serious personal injury.

6. If adjustment is necessary, stop the motor. Turn the idle timing screw (**Figure 58**) clockwise to advance timing or counterclockwise to retard timing.

7. Repeat Steps 3-5 to check adjustment.

Throttle Cam Adjustment

1. Make sure the throttle arm is firmly contacting the idle speed screw (**Figure 58**).

2. Reconnect the link rod to the throttle cam coupler ball. See **Figure 64**. Then rotate the throttle cam and check the clearance (C, **Figure 64**) between the throttle cam and cam follower. The adjustment is correct if the clearance (C) is less than 0.010 in. (0.25 mm), but not touching.

3. If throttle cam adjustment is necessary, disconnect the link rod from the throttle cam and turn the link rod connector as necessary to obtain the specified clearance.

4. Reattach the link rod to the throttle cam. Slowly advance the throttle to fast-idle, then throttle back to the idle position. Confirm that the throttle arm is contacting the idle speed screw and approximately 0.010 in. (0.25 mm) is present between the throttle cam and cam follower. If not, repeat the adjustment procedure.

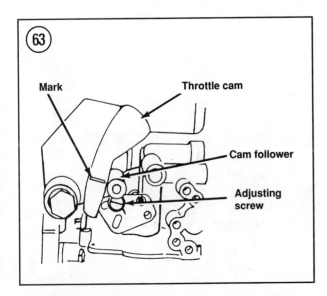

63

Mark — Throttle cam — Cam follower — Adjusting screw

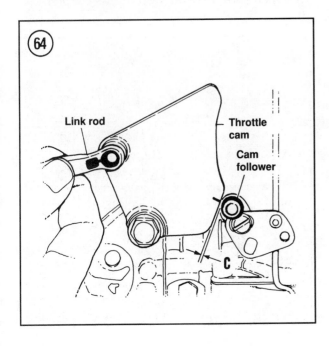

64

Link rod — Throttle cam — Cam follower — C

5

Wide-Open Throttle Stop Adjustment

1. With the motor *not* running, advance the throttle to the wide-open position.

CAUTION
If the roll pins travel past the vertical position in Step 2, carburetor and/or throttle linkage damage can result.

2. With the throttle wide open, adjust the wide-open throttle stop screw (**Figure 58**) so the throttle shaft roll pins are exactly vertical. See **Figure 50**.

Maximum Spark Advance

NOTE
*To load the outboard motor properly when adjusting maximum spark advance, the outboard must be in a test tank or on a boat in the water with the correct test wheel installed (**Table 3**). Do not attempt to adjust the maximum timing with a propeller installed. **Do not** run the outboard at wide-open throttle while connected to a flushing device.*

1. Connect a timing light to the No. 1 (top) spark plug wire.
2. Connect an accurate tachometer according to its manufacturer's instructions.
3. Start the motor and run at fast idle until warmed to normal operating temperature.
4. Shift into FORWARD gear. Advance the throttle to at least 5000 rpm and note the timing marks with the timing light. Maximum spark advance should be 18-20° BTDC.

WARNING
Do not attempt to adjust the timing with the engine running. Contact with the rotating flywheel can result in serious personal injury.

5. If adjustment is necessary, stop the engine. Loosen the cam roller screw (**Figure 65**), and turn the adjusting nut as necessary. Tighten the

screw securely and repeat Step 5 to check adjustment.

Shift Lever Detent Adjustment

1. Place the shift lever in the NEUTRAL position.
2. If the lower detent spring is not completely engaged in the shift lever detent notch (**Figure 66**), loosen the detent sparing screw. Move the spring until it fully engages the notch, then tighten the screw securely.

1993-ON 60 AND 70 HP (3-CYLINDER MODELS EQUIPPED WITH REMOTE CONTROL)

For optimum results, the synchronization and adjusting procedures should be followed in the sequence given.

Timing Pointer Alignment

Refer to *Timing Pointer Alignment* under *1993-on 60 and 70 hp (3-cylinder models equipped with tiller handle)* in this chapter.

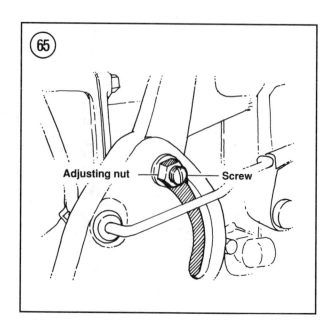
Adjusting nut — Screw

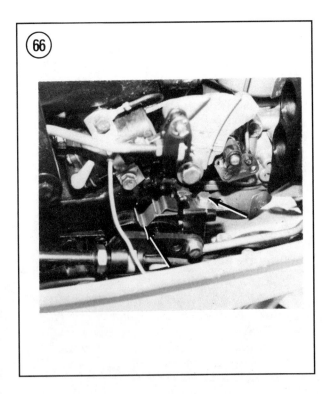

Throttle Valve Synchronization

Refer to *Throttle Valve Synchronization* under *60 and 70 hp (3-cylinder models equipped with tiller handle)* in this chapter.

Throttle Cam Follower Pickup Point

Refer to *Throttle Cam Follower Pickup Point* under *1993-on 60 and 70 hp (3-cylinder models equipped with tiller handle)* in this chapter.

Throttle Cam Adjustment

1. Connect the throttle cable to the throttle arm as described in this chapter.
2. Confirm that the throttle arm is firmly contacting idle stop screw (**Figure 67**).
3. Reconnect the link rod to the throttle cam coupler ball. See **Figure 68**. Then rotate the throttle cam and check the clearance (C, **Figure 68**) between the throttle cam and cam follower. The adjustment is correct if the clearance (C) is less than 0.010 in. (0.25 mm), but not touching.
4. If throttle cam adjustment is necessary, disconnect the link rod from the throttle cam and

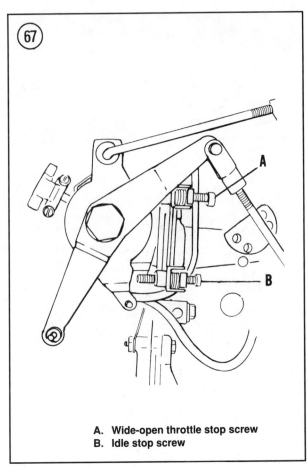

A. Wide-open throttle stop screw
B. Idle stop screw

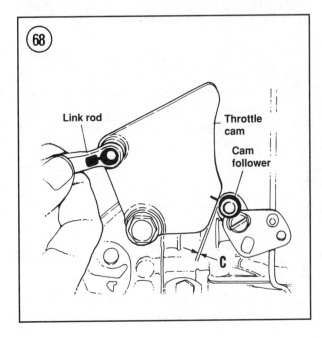

Link rod

Throttle cam

Cam follower

turn the link rod connector as necessary to obtain the specified clearance.

5. Reattach the link rod to the throttle cam. Slowly lift the fast idle lever on the remote control, then lower it back to the RUN position. Confirm that the throttle arm is contacting the idle speed screw and approximately 0.010 in. (0.25 mm) is present between the throttle cam and cam follower. If not, repeat the adjustment procedure.

Wide-Open Throttle Stop Adjustment

1. With the motor *not* running, advance the throttle to the wide-open position.

> *CAUTION*
> *If the roll pins travel past the vertical position in Step 2, carburetor and/or throttle linkage damage can result.*

2. With the throttle wide open, adjust the wide-open throttle stop screw (**Figure 67**) so the throttle shaft roll pins are exactly vertical. See **Figure 50**.

Idle Timing

The following idle timing procedure should provide the optimum idle quality within a range of 600-700 rpm (in gear), depending on the propeller used. But, if idle speed is too high after adjusting the timing, check the induction system for air leaks and repair as necessary. If idle speed is too slow, advance idle timing in small increments until the desired idle speed is obtained.

1. Connect a timing light to the No. 1 (top) spark plug wire.

2. Start the motor and allow it to warm to normal operating temperature.

3. Shift into FORWARD gear.

4. Make sure the throttle arm is contacting the idle speed screw.

5. Note the timing with the timing light. Idle timing should be 1-3° ATDC.

> *WARNING*
> *Do not attempt to adjust the ignition timing with the motor running in Step 6. Contact with the rotating flywheel can cause serious personal injury.*

6. If adjustment is necessary, stop the motor. Turn the idle timing screw (**Figure 69**) clockwise to advance timing or counterclockwise to retard timing.

7. Repeat Steps 3-5 to check adjustment.

Maximum Spark Advance

> *NOTE*
> *To load the outboard motor properly when adjusting maximum spark advance, the outboard must be in a test tank or on a boat in the water with the correct test wheel installed (**Table 3**). Do not attempt to adjust the maximum timing with a propeller installed. **Do not** run the outboard at wide-open throttle while connected to a flushing device.*

1. Connect a timing light to the No. 1 (top) spark plug wire.

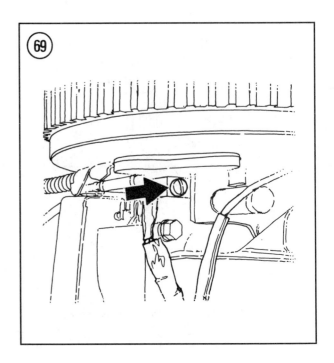

2. Connect an accurate tachometer to the motor according to its manufacturer's instructions.

3. Start the motor and warm to normal operating temperature.

4. Shift into FORWARD gear. Advance the throttle to 5000 rpm minimum and note the timing with the timing light.

5. Maximum spark advance should be 18-20° BTDC.

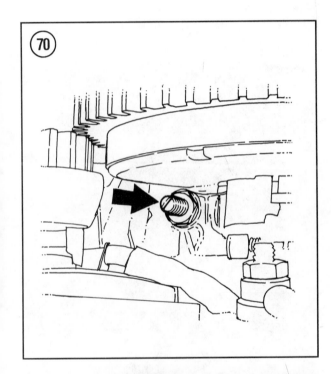

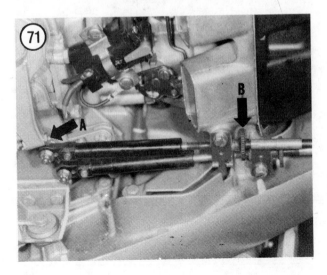

WARNING
Do not attempt to adjust the ignition timing with the motor running in Step 6. Contact with the rotating flywheel can cause serious personal injury.

6. If adjustment is necessary, stop the motor. Loosen the locknut and turn the maximum advance screw (**Figure 70**) clockwise to retard timing and counterclockwise to advance timing. Note that turning the screw 1 turn equals approximately 1° timing change. Retighten the locknut and repeat Steps 3-5 to check adjustment.

Throttle Cable Installation/Adjustment

1. Place the fast idle lever in the down position.
2. While rotating the propeller shaft, move the remote control handle from the NEUTRAL position to the FORWARD detent, then halfway back to the NEUTRAL position.
3. Push the throttle lever firmly against the idle stop screw (**Figure 67**).
4. Connect the throttle cable to the throttle lever using the washer and locknut. Tighten the locknut securely.
5. Pull on the throttle cable to remove any slack, then place the trunnion nut into its anchor pocket.
6. Temporarily install the cable retainer and screw.

NOTE
If throttle cable adjustment is too loose, the idle speed may be excessive or inconsistent. If cable adjustment is too tight, throttle and shift control effort may be excessive.

7. Move the remote control handle to the FORWARD gear position, then pull it back slowly to NEUTRAL. Make sure the idle speed screw is against its stop. If not, remove cable backlash by adjusting the throttle cable trunnion nut (B, **Figure 71**).

5

65 JET, 80 JET, 1.6 SEA DRIVE AND 85-115 HP (90° V4 CROSS FLOW MODELS)

For optimum results, the following procedures must be followed in the sequence given.

Disconnect both remote control cables (except tiller handle models) prior to continuing with synchronizing and adjusting procedure.

Timing Pointer Alignment

Use the following procedure to check/adjust the alignment of the timing pointer with top dead center of the No. 1 (top) piston.

1. Disconnect the spark plug wires and remove the spark plugs.

2. Loosen the timing pointer mounting screw, move the pointer to the center of its adjustment slot and retighten the screw.

3. Turn the flywheel in a clockwise direction until the TDC mark on the flywheel is approximately 1-1/2 in. (38.1 mm) past the timing pointer.

4. Install OMC Piston Stop Tool (part No. 384887) into the No. 1 spark plug hole. Screw the tool into the plug hole until bottomed, then turn the tool plunger inward until it contacts the piston. Secure the plunger in place with the lockring. See **Figure 72**.

5. Hold the No. 1 piston firmly against the piston stop tool by turning the flywheel. While holding the flywheel, place a mark on the flywheel directly adjacent to the timing pointer. Label the mark "A." See **Figure 73**.

6. Rotate the flywheel in a clockwise direction until the No. 1 piston contacts the piston stop tool again. Hold the flywheel so the piston is against the tool, then place another mark on the flywheel adjacent to the timing pointer. Label this mark "B." See **Figure 73**.

7. Remove the piston stop tool.

8. Measure the distance between marks "A" and "B" using a flexible scale. Place a mark on the flywheel at the mid-point between "A" and "B" and label this mark "C." See **Figure 73**.

9. If mark "C" is in alignment with the TDC mark cast in the flywheel, the timing pointer is properly adjusted. If not, turn the flywheel as necessary to align mark "C" with the timing pointer. While holding the flywheel in this position, loosen the timing pointer screw and move the pointer into alignment with the TDC mark cast in the flywheel. Tighten the pointer screw securely.

10. Reinstall the spark plugs.

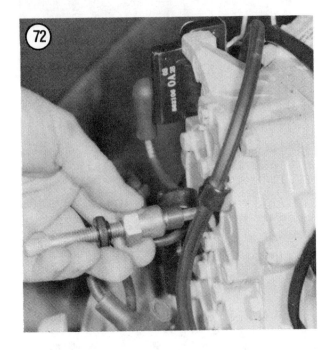

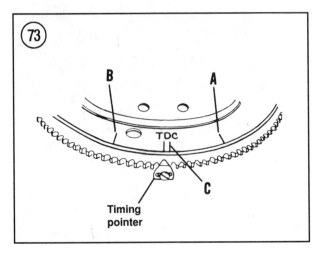

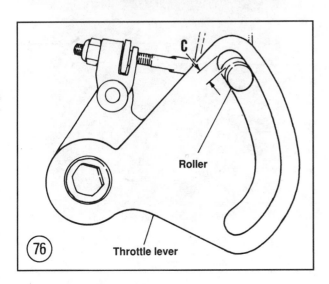

Locknut   Wide-open throttle stop screw

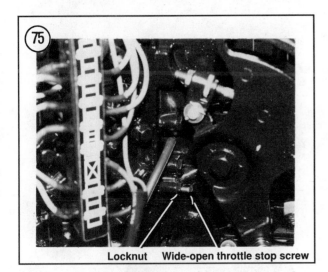

Roller

Throttle lever

Throttle Cable Adjustment
(Tiller Handle Models)

1. Turn the idle speed control knob on the tiller handle to the fully counterclockwise (SLOW) position.

2. Make sure the throttle cable mounting bracket is affixed to the power head in the front mounting hole.

3. Back out the idle speed screw (**Figure 74**) and the wide-open stop screw (**Figure 75**).

4. Turn the tiller twist grip to the wide-open throttle position and check the clearance (C, **Figure 76**) between the roller and the end of the slot in the throttle lever. Clearance (C) should be approximately 1/4 in. (6.3 mm).

5. Turn the tiller twist grip to the idle position and check the clearance (C, **Figure 77**) between the roller and the other end of the slot in the throttle lever. Clearance (C) should be approximately 1/4 in. (6.3 mm).

6. To adjust the clearance, loosen the locknut and turn the thumb wheel on the throttle cable as necessary to obtain the specified clearance. See **Figure 78**.

5

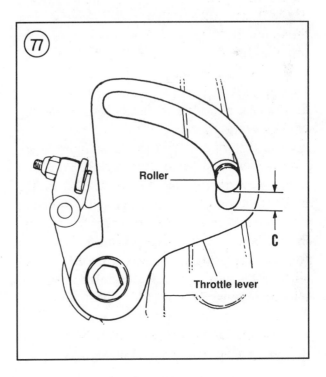

Roller

Throttle lever

7. Repeat Steps 4 and 5 to check adjustment.

Throttle Valve Synchronization

The carburetor throttle valves must be synchronized to open and close simultaneously. The engine will idle poorly if all throttle valves are not fully closed at idle.

1. Remove the air silencer cover.

> *NOTE*
> *The throttle cam must not be in contact with the cam follower during this procedure.*

2. Loosen the throttle cam follower adjustment screw (1, **Figure 79**). Move the cam follower away from the throttle cam.

3. Loosen the adjusting lever screw (2, **Figure 79**) on the lower carburetor. Rotate the throttle shafts partially open, then allow them to snap back to the closed position. Apply a slight downward pressure on the adjusting link tab to remove any backlash and tighten the adjustment screw.

4. Move the cam follower while watching the throttle valves. If the throttle valves do not start to move at exactly the same time, repeat Steps 2-4.

Cam Follower Pickup

1. Connect a throttle shaft amplifier to the top carburetor throttle shaft.

2. While observing the throttle shaft amplifier, slowly rotate the throttle cam. As the amplifier just begins to move, the embossed mark on the cam (1, **Figure 80**) should align with the center of the cam follower (2, **Figure 80**).

3. If adjustment is necessary loosen the cam follower adjustment screw (**Figure 81**). Make sure the throttle valves are fully closed, then hold the cam follower in contact with the throttle cam, in alignment with the embossed mark, and retighten the cam follower screw (**Figure 81**).

4. Repeat Step 2 to check adjustment.

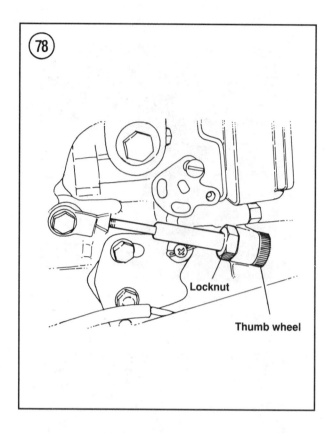

Maximum Spark Advance

NOTE
*To load the outboard motor properly when adjusting maximum spark advance, the outboard must be in a test tank or on a boat in the water with the correct test wheel installed (**Table 3**). Do not attempt to adjust the maximum timing with a propeller installed. **Do not** run the outboard at wide-open throttle while connected to a flushing device.*

1. If removed, install the spark plugs as described in Chapter Four.
2. Connect a timing light to the No. 1 (top starboard) spark plug wire.
3. Connect an accurate tachometer according to its manufacturer's instructions.
4. Start the engine and warm to normal operating temperature.
5. Shift into FORWARD gear, then run the motor at a minimum of 5000 rpm with the timer base fully advanced.
6. Check the timing mark position with the timing light. Maximum advance timing should be within 27-29° BTDC.
7. If adjustment is necessary, loosen the locknut at the front of the spark control rod retainer (**Figure 82**, typical). Rotate the thumb wheel at the retainer as necessary to obtain the specified timing. Turning the top of the thumb wheel toward the power head advances the timing; turning the top of the thumb wheel away from the power head retards the timing.
8. Tighten the locknut and repeat Steps 4-6 to check adjustment.

Cam Follower Pickup Timing

1. Connect a timing light to the No. 1 (top starboard) spark plug wire.
2. Start the motor.
3. Move the spark advance lever until the embossed mark on the throttle cam is aligned with

the center of the cam follower. At this point, the timing light should indicate 3-5° BTDC.

4. If adjustment is necessary, loosen the locknut (**Figure 83**) and turn the thumb wheel as necessary to obtain the specified pickup timing. Turn the top of the thumb wheel toward the power head to retard pickup timing and away from the power head to advance pickup timing.

5. Tighten the locknut securely and repeat Step 3 to check adjustment.

Wide-Open Throttle Stop

1. With the motor not running, open the throttle to the wide-open position. With the throttle wide open, the carburetor throttle shaft roll pins should be exactly vertical.

2. If the roll pins are not vertical, loosen the wide-open stop screw locknut and adjust the stop screw (**Figure 84**) as required to position the roll pins vertical when the throttle is wide open.

3. Tighten the locknut securely and repeat Step 1 to check adjustment.

Idle Speed Adjustment

Adjust idle speed with the outboard mounted on a boat in the water, running at normal operating temperature in FORWARD gear, with the correct propeller installed and the boat's movement unrestrained.

1. Connect an accurate tachometer according to its manufacturer's instructions.

2. Start the outboard and warm to normal operating temperature.

Locknut   Thumbwheel   ⑧⑶

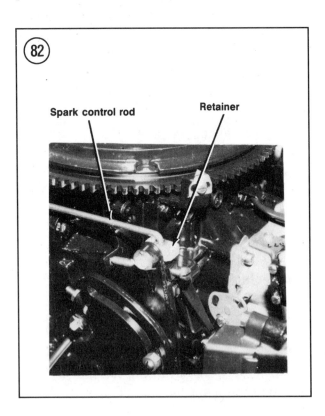

Spark control rod   Retainer

⑻⑵

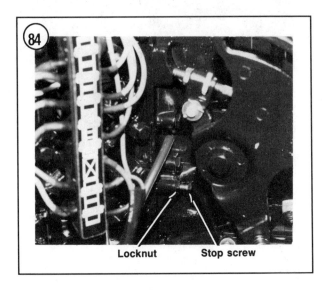

⑻⑷

Locknut   Stop screw

3. Shift into FORWARD gear and note idle speed. Idle speed should 600-700 rpm)in gear).

WARNING
Do not attempt to adjust idle speed with the motor running. Contact with the rotating flywheel can result in serious personal injury.

4. If adjustment is necessary, stop the motor and turn the idle speed screw (**Figure 85**) clockwise

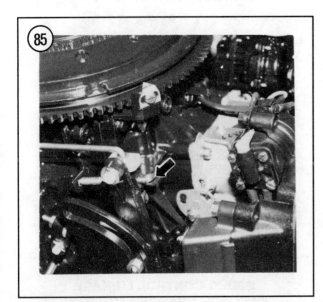

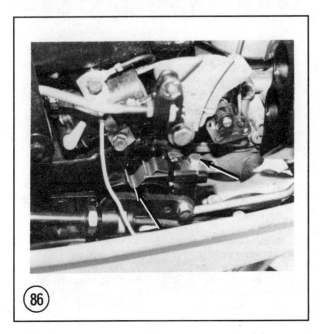

to increase rpm or counterclockwise to decrease rpm.

5. Start the engine and repeat Step 3 to check adjustment.

6. Install the remote control cables (except tiller handle models) as described in this chapter.

Shift Lever Detent (Tiller Handle Models)

1. Place the shift lever in the NEUTRAL position.

2. If the lower detent spring is not completely engaged in the shift lever detent notch (**Figure 86**), loosen the detent spring screw. Move the spring until it fully engages the notch, then tighten the screw securely.

Install/Adjust Remote Control Cables

Throttle cable

1. Extend the throttle cable and lubricate it with OMC Triple-Guard Grease. Apply Triple-Guard to both cable anchor pockets on the power head.

2. Make sure the fast idle lever on the remote control assembly is in the down position.

3. While rotating the propeller shaft, move the remote control handle from the NEUTRAL position to the FORWARD detent, then halfway back to the NEUTRAL position.

4. Push the throttle lever firmly against its stop.

5. Connect the throttle cable casing guide to the throttle lever using the washer and locknut. Tighten the locknut securely.

6. Pull on the throttle cable to remove any slack, then place the trunnion nut into its anchor pocket.

7. Temporarily install the anchor pocket cover and screw.

NOTE
If throttle cable adjustment is too loose, the idle speed may be excessive or inconsistent. If cable adjustment is too tight, throttle and shift control effort may be excessive.

5

8. Move the remote control handle to the FOR-WARD gear position, then pull it back slowly to NEUTRAL. Make sure the idle speed screw is against its stop. If not, remove cable backlash by adjusting the throttle cable trunnion nut (**Figure 87**).

Shift cable

1. Extend the shift cable and lubricate with OMC Triple-Guard Grease.

2. Make sure the fast idle lever on the remote control assembly is in the down position.

3. Place the remote control lever in the NEU-TRAL position, then move the lever to the FOR-WARD gear position.

4. While rotating the propeller shaft, shift the gearcase into FORWARD gear.

5. Install the shift cable onto the shift lever pin and secure with the washer and nut. Tighten the nut securely.

> *NOTE*
> *If insufficient threads are present for adjustment in Step 6, check shift rod height as outlined in Chapter Nine.*

6. Pull the cable firmly to remove any slack, then adjust the cable trunnion to fit into the cable anchor pocket.

7. Install the cable trunnion into the anchor pocket. Install the anchor pocket cover and screw. Tighten the screw to 60-84 in.-lb. (7-9 N.m)

8. Shift the remote control to the NEUTRAL position.

9. Temporarily remove the shift cable and confirm that the gearcase is still in its NEUTRAL detent. If the gearcase is in NEUTRAL, reattach the shift cable to the shift lever. Secure the cable using the washer and nut.

10. If the gearcase is not completely in the NEU-TRAL detent, repeat Step 6 as necessary.

> *WARNING*
> *Be certain the remote control cables are attached to the correct levers. To check, lift the fast idle lever on the remote control while observing the throttle lever on the power head. If the cables are correctly installed, the throttle cable and lever on the power head will move when the fast idle lever is lifted.*

TRUNNION ADJUSTMENT NUT

(87)

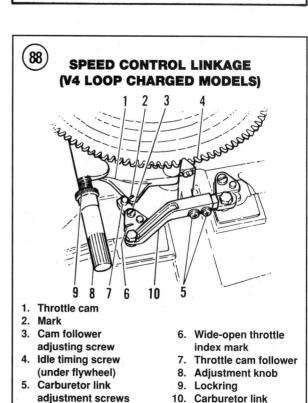

SPEED CONTROL LINKAGE (V4 LOOP CHARGED MODELS)

1. Throttle cam
2. Mark
3. Cam follower adjusting screw
4. Idle timing screw (under flywheel)
5. Carburetor link adjustment screws
6. Wide-open throttle index mark
7. Throttle cam follower
8. Adjustment knob
9. Lockring
10. Carburetor link

2.0 SEA DRIVE, 120 AND 140 HP (90° V4 LOOP CHARGED MODELS)

Timing Pointer Alignment

Use the following procedure to check/adjust the alignment of the timing pointer with top dead center of the No. 1 (top) piston.

Refer to *Timing Pointer Alignment* under *65 Jet, 80 Jet, 1.6 Sea Drive and 85-115 hp (90° V4 cross flow models)* in this chapter.

Throttle Valve Synchronization

The carburetor throttle valves must be synchronized to open and close simultaneously. The engine will idle poorly if all throttle valves are not fully closed at idle.

NOTE
The throttle cam and the throttle cam follower must not be touching during this procedure.

1. Loosen the throttle cam follower adjusting screw (3, **Figure 88**) and move the cam follower away from the throttle cam.
2. Back out the carburetor link stop screw (**Figure 89**) 4 full turns.

3. Loosen the 2 carburetor link adjustment screws (5, **Figure 88**) *not more* than 1/2 turn.
4. Next, turn the carburetor link stop screw (**Figure 89**) clockwise until the throttle valves on the port side carburetors just start to open. Then back out the screw just enough to close the throttle valves. Lightly press on the throttle valves to ensure they are closed.
5. While holding the carburetor link (10, **Figure 88**) against the stop screw, securely tighten the 2 link adjustment screws (5).
6. Open and close the throttle while observing the carburetor throttle valves. The port and starboard throttle valves *must* open and close at exactly the same time.
7. If adjustment is required, loosen the 2 carburetor link adjustment screws (5, **Figure 88**) *not more* than 1/2 turn. Turn the carburetor link stop screw (**Figure 89**) in or out as necessary. Then repeat Steps 5 and 6.
8. Do not tighten the throttle cam follower adjusting screw (3, **Figure 88**) at this point.

Throttle Cam Follower Pickup Point

Refer to **Figure 88** for this procedure.
1. Make sure the throttle cam follower adjusting screw is loose.
2. Loosen the lockring (9, **Figure 88**) and rotate the adjustment knob (8) counterclockwise until no internal spring tension is noted.
3. Move the throttle cam follower (7, **Figure 88**) into contact with the throttle cam (1).
4. While holding the cam follower against the cam, adjust the throttle arm stop screw (A, **Figure 90**) until the mark (2, **Figure 88**) on the cam is aligned with the center of the cam follower roller. Securely tighten the cam follower adjustment screw when the proper alignment is obtained.
5. Next, turn the throttle arm stop screw (A, **Figure 90**) 1 full turn counterclockwise to create the correct clearance between the throttle cam and cam follower.

5

Wide-Open Throttle Stop Adjustment

1. Loosen the locknut securing the wide-open throttle stop screw.

2. With the engine not running, advance the throttle to the wide-open position.

3. With the throttle wide-open, adjust the wide-open throttle stop screw B, (**Figure 90**) so the index mark (6, **Figure 88**) on the throttle cam is facing directly forward and is perpendicular to the air silencer base.

4. Retighten the locknut securely while holding the stop screw.

Throttle Cable Installation and Adjustment

NOTE
If throttle cable adjustment is too loose, the idle speed may be excessive or inconsistent. If cable adjustment is too tight, throttle and shift control effort may be excessive.

1. Extend the throttle cable and lubricate it with OMC Triple-Guard Grease. Apply Triple-Guard to both cable anchor pockets on the power head.

2. Make sure the fast idle lever on the remote control assembly is in the down position.

3. While rotating the propeller shaft, move the remote control handle from the NEUTRAL position to the FORWARD detent, then halfway back to the NEUTRAL position.

4. Push the throttle lever firmly against its stop.

5. Connect the throttle cable casing guide to the throttle lever using the washer and locknut. Tighten the locknut securely.

6. Pull on the throttle cable to remove any slack, then place the trunnion nut into its anchor pocket.

7. Install the cable retainer and screw. Tighten the screw to 60-84 in.-lb. (7-9 N•m).

8. Move the remote control handle to the FORWARD gear position, then pull it back slowly to NEUTRAL. Make sure the idle speed screw is against its stop. If not, remove cable backlash by adjusting the throttle cable trunnion nut.

Maximum Spark Advance

NOTE
*To load the outboard motor properly when adjusting maximum spark advance, the outboard must be in a test tank or on a boat in the water with the correct test wheel installed (**Table 3**). Do not attempt to adjust the maximum timing with a propeller installed. **Do not** run the outboard at wide-open throttle while connected to a flushing device.*

1. Connect a timing light to the No. 1 spark plug wire.

2. Connect an accurate tachometer to the motor according to its manufacturer's instructions.

3. Start the motor and warm to normal operating temperature.

4. Shift into FORWARD gear and advance the throttle to 4500-5000 rpm.

5. Check the timing mark position with the timing light. Maximum spark advance should be 17-19° BTDC.

WARNING
Do not attempt to adjust the spark advance with the motor running in Step 6. Contact with the rotating flywheel can result in serious personal injury.

6. If adjustment is necessary, stop the motor. Loosen the locknut and turn the maximum advance screw (C, **Figure 90**) clockwise to retard or counterclockwise to advance timing as necessary. One full turn of the screw equals approximately 1° of timing change.

7. Repeat Steps 4 and 5 to check adjustment.

Idle Timing Adjustment

The following idle timing procedure should provide the optimum idle quality within a range of 575-700 rpm (in gear), depending on the propeller used. But, if idle speed is too high after adjusting the timing, check the induction system for air leaks and repair as necessary. If idle speed is too slow, advance idle timing in small increments until the desired idle speed is obtained.

CAUTION
*Perform the following procedure with the outboard motor in a test tank with the correct test wheel installed (**Table 3**), or mounted on a boat in the water with the correct propeller installed. **Do not** attempt the idle timing adjustments with the outboard running on a flushing device.*

1. Connect a timing light to the No. 1 spark plug wire.

2. Connect an accurate tachometer according to its manufacturer's instructions.

3. Loosen the lockring (9, **Figure 88**). Then turn the lockring and adjustment knob (8) clockwise until fully bottomed.

4. Start the motor and warm to normal operating temperature. Engine temperature must be above 96° F (35.6° C), to perform this procedure.

5. Shift into FORWARD gear. With the motor at idle speed, in FORWARD gear, check the timing with the timing light.

6. Idle timing should be 8° ATDC.

WARNING
Do not attempt to adjust ignition timing with the motor running in Step 7. Contact with the moving flywheel can result in serious personal injury.

7. If adjustment is necessary, stop the engine. Turn the idle timing screw (**Figure 91**) clockwise to advance or counterclockwise to retard idle timing.

8. Next, start the motor and place the remote control lever into the FORWARD detent position.

9. Adjust the throttle arm stop screw (A, **Figure 90**) to obtain 950 rpm.

10. Without moving the throttle arm position, stop the motor and turn the adjustment knob (8, **Figure 88**) counterclockwise until the timer base just begins to move. Tighten the lockring (9, **Figure 88**) securely against the adjustment knob.

11. With the throttle arm stop screw (A, **Figure 90**) seated against the crankcase, rotate the stop screw counterclockwise until the throttle cam index mark (2, **Figure 88**) intersects the center of the cam follower roller (7). Continue to turn the stop screw (A, **Figure 90**) 1 complete turn counterclockwise from this point.

NOTE
After performing the previous adjustments, the outboard motor should idle between 575-700 rpm in FORWARD gear and the throttle cam follower roller should not touch the throttle cam when the remote control is in the NEUTRAL position. Refer to **Throttle Cam Pickup Point** *in this chapter if incorrect adjustment is noted.*

1991 105 JET, 150 AND 175 HP (90° V6 CROSS FLOW MODELS)

Timing Pointer Alignment

Use the following procedure to check/adjust the alignment of the timing pointer with top dead center of the No. 1 (top) piston.

Refer to *Timing Pointer Alignment* under *65 Jet, 80 Jet, 1.6 Sea Drive and 85-115 hp (90° V4 cross flow models)* in this chapter.

Throttle Valve Synchronization

NOTE
The throttle cam must not be in contact with the cam follower roller during the following procedure.

The carburetor throttle valves must be synchronized to open and close simultaneously. The engine will idle poorly if all throttle valves are not fully closed at idle.

1. Remove the air silencer cover.
2. Loosen the throttle cam follower adjustment screw (**Figure 92**). Move the cam follower away from the cam.
3. Loosen the upper and lower carburetor throttle lever screws (**Figure 93**), allowing the throttle return springs to close the throttle valves completely.
4. Rotate the throttle shafts partially open, then allow them to snap back to the closed position. Apply a slight downward pressure on the lower

adjusting link tab to remove any backlash then tighten the adjusting screw. Repeat this step to tighten the upper link screw.
5. Open and close the throttle while observing the throttle valves. Repeat Steps 3 and 4 if the throttle valves do not open and close at exactly the same time.

Throttle Cam Follower Pickup Point

1. Attach a throttle shaft amplifier to the top carburetor throttle shaft.

NOTE
Two marks are present on the throttle cam. Be sure to reference the short mark when checking the throttle cam pickup point.

2. While observing the throttle shaft amplifier, slowly rotate the throttle cam. As the end of the amplifier just starts to move, the short embossed mark on the throttle cam should be aligned with the center of the cam follower roller.
3. If adjustment is necessary, loosen the cam follower adjusting screw (**Figure 92**) and make sure the carburetor throttle valves are fully closed.

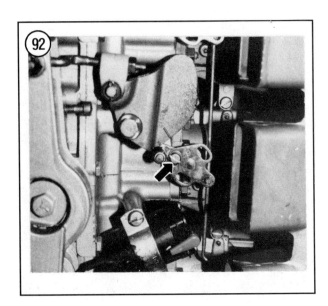

4. Then, while holding the cam follower against the cam, align the short mark on the cam with the center of the cam follower roller. When the mark and the follower are properly aligned, securely tighten the cam follower screw (**Figure 92**).

5. Repeat Step 2 to check adjustment.

Cam Follower Pickup Timing

1. Connect a timing light to the No. 1 spark plug wire.

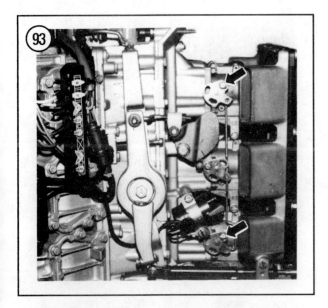

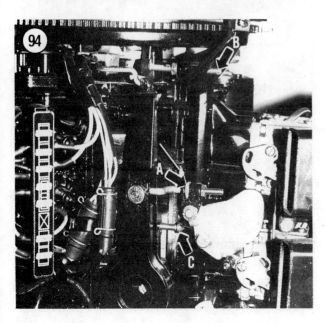

2. Attach the throttle shaft amplifier to the throttle shaft on the top carburetor.

3. Rotate the throttle cam until the throttle shaft amplifier just starts to move. Remove the amplifier, but do not change throttle position.

4. Start the motor and observe the timing marks with the timing light. Pickup timing should be 6-8° BTDC.

5. If adjustment is necessary, loosen the locknut on the link rod connecting the throttle cam to the throttle arm. Rotate the thumb wheel (A, **Figure 94**) as necessary to obtain the specified pickup timing. Turn the top of the thumb wheel away from the crankcase to retard or toward the crankcase to advance timing.

6. Tighten the locknut and repeat Steps 2-4 to check adjustment.

Wide-Open Throttle Stop

1. With the motor not running, advance the throttle to the wide-open position.

2. Note the position of the roll pins on the carburetor throttle shafts. The roll pins should be exactly vertical with the throttle wide open.

> *CAUTION*
> *If the roll pins travel past the vertical position in Step 3, carburetor and/or throttle linkage damage can result.*

3. If adjustment is necessary, turn the wide-open throttle stop screw (**Figure 95**) so the roll pins are positioned exactly vertical.

Maximum Spark Advance

> *NOTE*
> *To load the outboard motor properly when adjusting maximum spark advance, the outboard must be in a test tank or on a boat in the water with the correct test wheel installed (**Table 3**). Do not attempt to adjust the maximum timing with a propeller installed. **Do not** run the*

5

outboard at wide-open throttle while connected to a flushing device.

1. Connect a timing light to the No. 1 spark plug wire.

2. Connect a tachometer according to its manufacturer's instructions.

3. Loosen the locknut on the maximum advance screw (B, **Figure 94**) and adjust the screw to an initial length of 3/8 to 7/16 in. (9-11 mm) beyond the timing pointer bracket.

4. Start the motor and warm to normal operating temperature.

5. Shift into FORWARD gear. Run the motor at a minimum of 5000 rpm and note the timing marks on the No. 1 cylinder timing grid.

6. Throttle back to idle and stop the engine. Move the timing light to the No. 2 cylinder spark plug wire.

7. Start the motor and shift into FORWARD gear. Run the motor at a minimum of 5000 rpm and note the timing on the No. 2 cylinder timing grid.

WARNING
Do not attempt to adjust the maximum spark advance with the motor running. Contact with the moving flywheel can result in serious personal injury.

8. Select the cylinder with the most timing advance as the reference cylinder.

9. Stop the motor and loosen the maximum spark advance screw locknut. Turn the maximum spark advance screw (B, **Figure 94**) clockwise to retard or counterclockwise to advance the timing. One full turn in either direction changes timing approximately 1°.

10. Tighten the locknut and repeat Steps 5-7 to check adjustment.

Idle Speed

Adjust idle speed with the outboard mounted on a boat in the water, running at normal operating temperature in FORWARD gear, with the correct propeller installed and the boat's movement unrestrained.

1. Connect an accurate tachometer according to its manufacturer's instructions.

2. Start the motor and warm to normal operating temperature.

3. Shift into FORWARD gear and note the idle speed. Idle speed in FORWARD gear should be 600-700 rpm.

4. If necessary, stop the motor and adjust the idle speed screw (C, **Figure 94**) to the specified rpm.

5. Start the motor and repeat Step 3 to check adjustment.

1992-ON 105 JET, 1991-ON 150 AND 175 HP (60° V6 MODELS)

Disconnect the throttle cable from the throttle arm and remove the cable from the trunnion pocket prior to beginning the synchronizing and adjustment procedure.

Wide-open throttle stop screw   **Locknut**   (95)

Timing Pointer Alignment

Use the following procedure to check/adjust the alignment of the timing pointer with top dead center of the No. 1 (top) piston.

1. Disconnect the spark plug wires and remove the spark plugs.

2. Remove the 3 screws holding the timing wheel cover. Lift the cover off the power head.

3. Loosen the timing pointer (A, **Figure 96**) mounting screw. Move the pointer to the center of its adjustment slot then retighten the mounting screw.

CAUTION
Rotate the crankshaft in a clockwise directly only. Counterclockwise rotation may damage the water pump impeller.

4. Rotate the crankshaft clockwise until the TDC mark on the timing wheel is approximately 1 in. (25.4 mm) past the timing pointer. Rotate the crankshaft by turning the timing wheel (B, **Figure 96**) using an appropriate size wrench or socket as shown in **Figure 97**.

5. Install OMC Piston Stop Tool (part No. 384887) into the No. 1 spark plug hole. Screw the tool into the plug hole until bottomed, then turn the tool plunger inward until it contacts the piston. Secure the plunger in place with the lockring. See **Figure 98**, typical.

6. Hold the No. 1 piston firmly against the piston stop tool by turning the timing wheel. While holding the timing wheel, place a mark on the timing wheel directly adjacent to the timing

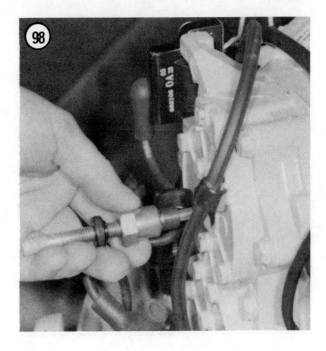

5

pointer. Label the mark "A." See **Figure 99**, typical.

7. Continue turning the crankshaft in a clockwise direction until the No. 1 piston contacts the piston stop tool again. Hold the timing wheel so the piston is against the tool, then place another mark on the timing wheel adjacent to the timing pointer. Label this mark "B." See **Figure 99**, typical.

8. Remove the piston stop tool.

9. Using the timing marks molded in the timing wheel, determine the mid point between marks "A" and "B." Place a mark on the timing wheel at the mid-point between "A" and "B" and label this mark "C." See **Figure 99**, typical.

10. If mark "C" is in alignment with the TDC mark cast in the timing wheel, the timing pointer is properly adjusted. If not, turn the timing wheel clockwise to align mark "C" with the timing pointer. While holding the timing wheel in this position, loosen the timing pointer screw and move the pointer into alignment with the TDC mark cast in the timing wheel. Tighten the pointer screw securely.

11. Reinstall the spark plugs.

Throttle Valve Synchronization

The carburetor throttle valves must be synchronized to open and close simultaneously. The engine will idle poorly if all throttle valves are not fully closed at idle.

1. Disconnect the 4 air silencer retaining straps (**Figure 100**) and slide the air silencer off the power head.

2. Loosen (but do not remove) the spark lever screw (B, **Figure 101**).

3. Push the spark lever roller (C, **Figure 101**) rearward.

4. Make sure the throttle cam (E, **Figure 101** and cam follower (F) are not touching.

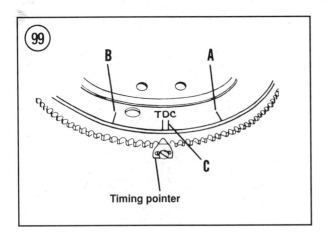

5. Loosen (but do not remove) the carburetor link screw (**Figure 102**).

6. Loosen the 4 throttle shaft connector screws (2 each side) using a 9/64 in. hex-head (Allen) wrench. *Do not* remove the screws from the connectors. See **Figure 103** (port) and **Figure 104** (starboard).

7. Looking into the carburetors, make sure all throttle valves are fully closed. Apply light pressure to the throttle valves to ensure they are fully closed, then tighten the throttle shaft connector screws (**Figures 103 and 104**).

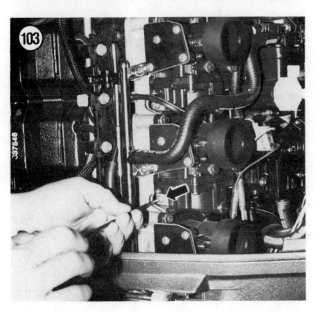

8. While holding the throttle linkage in position, securely tighten the carburetor link screw (Figure 102).

9. Do not retighten the spark lever screw (B, **Figure 101**) at this point.

Idle Timing

The following idle timing procedure should provide the optimum idle quality within a range of 600-700 rpm (in gear), depending on the propeller used. But, if idle speed is too high after adjusting the timing, check the induction system for air leaks and repair as necessary. If idle speed is too slow, advance idle timing in small increments until the desired idle speed is obtained.

OMC Ignition Analyzer (**Figure 105**) from the OMC Test Kit (part No. 434017) is required to perform timing adjustments on the 60° V6 motors.

1. Remove the voltage regulator/rectifier cover.

2. Disconnect the timing sensor connector (**Figure 105**) from the sensor.

3. Connect OMC Ignition Analyzer to the timing sensor. Move the analyzer selector switch to position A and connect the analyzer to a fully charged 12-volt battery.

4. Loosen the timer base detent screw (**Figure 107**).

5. Move theouter (A, **Figure 108**) and inner (B) detent tabs completely to the front of the detent plate. Make sure the timer base lever is contacting its stop on the flywheel cover.

6. Rotate the crankshaft clockwise until the timing pointer is aligned with the 6 ± 1° ATDC mark on the timing wheel. Hold the timing wheel in this position.

7. Hold the inner detent plate in position against the stop and move the detent plate forward until the "CYL" light on the analyzer goes off.

8. Mark the location of the inner detent tab on the detent plate.

9. Do not tighten the timer base detent screw or spark lever screw at this time. Do not disconnect the OMC Ignition Analyzer from the timing sensor.

Maximum Spark Advance

1. Make sure the spark lever screw (B, **Figure 101**) is loose.

2. Move the spark lever roller (C, **Figure 101**) to the wide-open throttle position.

3. Rotate the crankshaft clockwise until the timing pointer is aligned with 20° ±1° BTDC mark on the timing wheel. Hold the timing wheel in this position.

4. Move the outer detent tab (A, **Figure 108**) rearward on the detent plate until the "CYL" light on the analyzer goes off. Make sure the inner detent tab (B, **Figure 108**) is still aligned with the mark (made previously), then securely tighten the timer base detent screw (**Figure 107**).

5. Move the spark lever back to the idle position.

6. Disconnect the ignition analyzer from the timing sensor. Reconnect the timing sensor connector to the sensor. Reinstall the voltage regulator/rectifier cover.

Throttle Pickup Point

1. Make sure the spark lever screw (B, **Figure 101**) is loose.

2. Move the spark lever (A, **Figure 109**) and throttle linkage (B) toward the rear of the motor.

3. Slowly move the spark lever (A, **Figure 109**) forward until the roller (C) just contacts the spark cam (D). Hold the spark lever in this position.

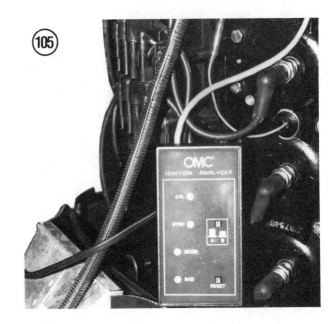

4. Next, slowly move the throttle linkage forward until the throttle cam (E, **Figure 101**) just contacts the throttle cam follower (F).

5. Securely tighten the spark lever screw (B, **Figure 101**) without disturbing the position of any linkage.

6. Move the linkage rearward, then forward to check adjustment. The timer base and carburetor linkage should start to move at exactly the same time. If not, repeat Steps 1-5.

7. Install the timing wheel cover and the air silencer.

8. Install the spark plugs.

9. Install the throttle cable as outlined in this chapter.

Throttle Cable Installation/Adjustment

NOTE
If throttle cable adjustment is too loose, the idle speed may be excessive or inconsistent. If cable adjustment is too tight, throttle and shift control effort may be excessive.

1. Extend the throttle cable and lubricate it with OMC Triple-Guard Grease. Apply Triple-Guard to both cable anchor pockets on the power head.

2. Make sure the fast idle lever on the remote control assembly is in the down position.

3. While rotating the propeller shaft, move the remote control handle from the NEUTRAL position to the FORWARD detent, then halfway back to the NEUTRAL position.

4. Remove the timing wheel cover. Make sure the timer base lever is contacting the flywheel cover stop.

5. Connect the throttle cable casing guide to the throttle lever using the washer and cotter clip.

6. Pull on the throttle cable to remove any slack, then place the trunnion nut into its anchor pocket.

7. Install the cable retainer and screw. Tighten the screw to 60-84 in.-lb. (7-9 N•m).

8. Move the remote control handle to the FORWARD gear position, then pull it back slowly to

NEUTRAL. Make sure the timer base lever contacts its stop on the flywheel cover. If not, remove backlash by adjusting the throttle cable trunnion nut.

3.0 SEA DRIVE, 1991 AND 1992 200 AND 225 HP (90° V6 LOOP CHARGED MODELS)

Remove the throttle cable from the throttle arm and cable trunnion pocket before proceeding with the synchronizing and adjusting procedure.

Timing Pointer Alignment

Use the following procedure to check/adjust the alignment of the timing pointer with top dead center of the No. 1 (top) piston.

Refer to *Timing Pointer Alignment* under *65 Jet, 80 Jet, 1.6 Sea Drive and 85-115 hp (90° V4 cross flow models)* in this chapter.

Throttle Valve Synchronization

The carburetor throttle valves must be synchronized to open and close simultaneously. The engine will idle poorly if all throttle valves are not fully closed at idle.

1. Remove the air silencer cover and baffle.
2. Loosen the cam follower screw (C, **Figure 110**) and move the cam follower away from the throttle cam. The cam and follower must not be touching during this procedure.
3. Loosen the 2 carburetor link adjustment screws (S, **Figure 111**) no more than one-half turn.
4. Loosen (but do not remove) the bottom screw on the port throttle shaft connector (E, **Figure 110**) and the top screw on the starboard throttle shaft connector (F).
5. Apply light pressure to the carburetor throttle valves to ensure they are fully closed. Tighten

the starboard throttle shaft connector screw, then the port throttle shaft connector screw.
6. Tighten the 2 carburetor link adjustment screws (S, **Figure 111**) while supporting the rear of the carburetor link. Do not tighten the throttle cam follower screw.

Throttle Cam Pickup Point

Refer to **Figure 110** and **Figure 111** for this procedure.
1. Make sure the throttle cam follower adjustment screw is loose and the cam follower is not touching the cam.

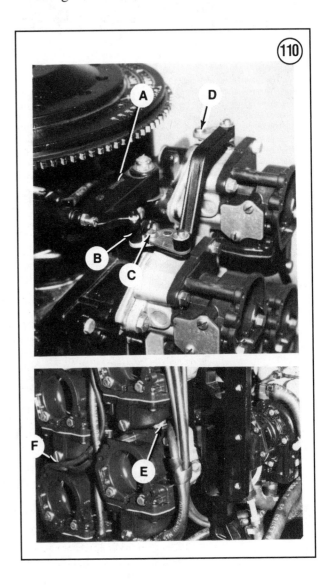

2. Loosen the expansion link lock and rotate the adjustment knob counterclockwise until no internal spring pressure is noted (Figure 111).

3. Hold the cam follower against the throttle cam and adjust the throttle arm stop screw (**Figure 112**) until the cam and follower contact the center of the cam follower roller intersecting the index line (I, **Figure 111**) on the cam.

4. When the cam index line intersects the center of the cam follower roller, tighten the cam follower screw.

5. After the pickup point is correctly adjusted, turn the throttle arm stop screw (**Figure 112**) 1 full turn counterclockwise to provide the required gap between the cam and follower.

Wide-Open Throttle Stop

Refer to **Figure 113** for this procedure.

1. Move the throttle arm and linkage toward the wide-open throttle position and loosen the locknut.

2. Adjust the wide-open throttle stop screw (1, **Figure 113**) until the carburetor throttle valves are fully open (horizontal).

3. Continue adjusting the stop screw (1, **Figure 113**) until the cam follower WOT index line faces directly forward and is perpendicular with the air silencer base. Hold the screw from moving and tighten the locknut.

Throttle Cable Installation and Adjustment

NOTE
If throttle cable adjustment is too loose, the idle speed may be excessive or inconsistent. If cable adjustment is too tight, throttle and shift control effort may be excessive.

5

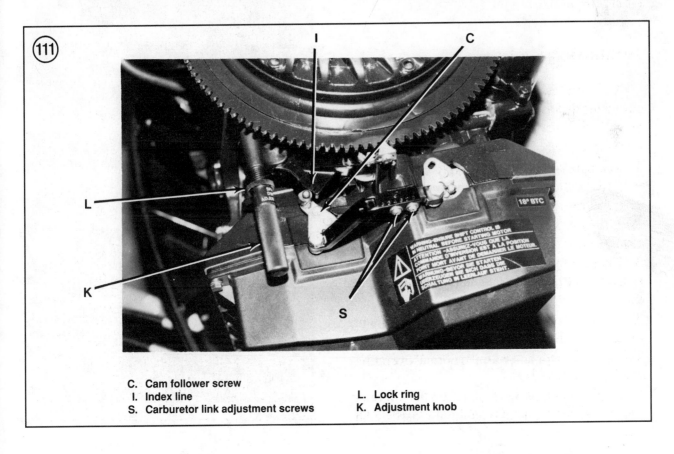

C. Cam follower screw
I. Index line
S. Carburetor link adjustment screws
L. Lock ring
K. Adjustment knob

1. Extend the throttle cable and lubricate it with OMC Triple-Guard Grease. Apply Triple-Guard to both cable anchor pockets on the power head.

2. Make sure the fast idle lever on the remote control assembly is in the down position.

3. While rotating the propeller shaft, move the remote control handle from the NEUTRAL position to the FORWARD detent, then halfway back to the NEUTRAL position.

4. Push the throttle lever firmly against its stop.

5. Connect the throttle cable casing guide to the throttle lever using the washer and locknut. Tighten the locknut securely.

6. Pull on the throttle cable to remove any slack, then place the trunnion nut into its anchor pocket.

7. Install the cable retainer and screw. Tighten the screw to 60-84 in.-lb. (7-9 N•m).

8. Move the remote control handle to the FORWARD gear position, then pull it back slowly to NEUTRAL. Make sure the idle speed screw is against its stop. If not, remove cable backlash by adjusting the throttle cable trunnion nut (2, **Figure 113**).

Maximum Spark Advance

NOTE
*To load the outboard motor properly when adjusting maximum spark advance, the outboard must be in a test tank or on a boat in the water with the correct test wheel installed (**Table 3**). Do not attempt to adjust the maximum timing with a propeller installed. **Do not** run the outboard at wide-open throttle while connected to a flushing device.*

Refer to **Figure 114** for this procedure.

1. Connect a timing light to the No. 1 spark plug wire.

2. Connect an accurate tachometer according to its manufacturer's instructions.

3. Start the motor and warm to normal operating temperature.

4. Shift into FORWARD gear. Run the motor at 4500-5000 rpm and note the timing marks with the timing light. Maximum spark advance should be 17-19° BTDC.

WARNING
Do not attempt to adjust maximum spark advance with the motor running. Contact with the moving flywheel can result in serious personal injury.

5. If adjustment is necessary, stop the motor. Loosen the maximum advance screw locknut and turn the screw clockwise to retard or counterclockwise to advance timing. One full turn in either direction changes timing approximately 1°.

6. Tighten the locknut and repeat Steps 3 and 4 to check adjustment.

MAXIMUM SPARK ADVANCE ADJUSTMENT

A. Timing pointer
B. Locknut
C. Full advance timing screw
D. Idle speed screw

5

Idle Timing

The following idle timing procedure should provide the optimum idle quality within a range of 575-700 rpm (in gear), depending on the propeller used. But, if idle speed is too high after adjusting the timing, check the induction system for air leaks and repair as necessary. If idle speed is too slow, advance idle timing in small increments until the desired idle speed is obtained.

> *CAUTION*
> *Perform the following procedure with the outboard motor in a test tank with the correct test wheel installed (**Table 3**), or mounted on a boat in the water with the correct propeller installed. **Do not** attempt the idle timing adjustments with the outboard running on a flushing device.*

1. Connect a timing light to the No. 1 spark plug wire.
2. Connect an accurate tachometer according to its manufacturer's instructions.
3. Loosen the lockring (L, **Figure 111**). Then turn the lock ring and adjustment knob clockwise until fully bottomed.
4. Start the motor and warm to normal operating temperature. Engine temperature must be above 96° F (35.6° C), to perform this procedure.
5. Shift into FORWARD gear. With the motor at idle speed, in FORWARD gear, check the timing with the timing light.
6. Idle timing should be 6° ATDC.

> *WARNING*
> *Do not attempt to adjust ignition timing with the motor running in Step 7. Contact with the moving flywheel can result in serious personal injury.*

7. If adjustment is necessary, stop the engine. Turn the idle timing screw (**Figure 115**) clockwise to advance or counterclockwise to retard idle timing.

8. Next, start the motor and place the remote control lever into the FORWARD detent position.
9. Adjust the throttle arm stop screw (**Figure 112**) to obtain 950 rpm.
10. Without moving the throttle arm position, stop the motor and turn the adjustment knob (K, **Figure 111**) counterclockwise until the timer base just begins to move. Tighten the lockring (L, **Figure 111**) securely against the adjustment knob.
11. With the throttle arm stop screw (**Figure 112**) seated against the crankcase, rotate the stop screw counterclockwise until the throttle cam index mark (I, **Figure 111**) intersects the center

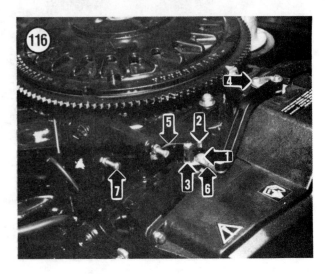

of the cam follower roller. Continue to turn the stop screw 1 complete turn counterclockwise from this point.

NOTE
*After performing the previous adjust-ments, the outboard motor should idle between 575-700 rpm in FORWARD gear and the throttle cam follower roller should not touch the throttle cam when the remote control is in the NEUTRAL position. Refer to **Throttle Cam Pickup Point** in this chapter if incorrect adjust-ment is noted.*

1993-ON 200 AND 225 HP (90° V6 LOOP CHARGED MODELS); 4.0 SEA DRIVE, 250 AND 300 HP (90° V8 LOOP CHARGED MODELS)

Disconnect the throttle cable from the throttle arm and remove from the trunnion pocket before proceeding with the synchronizing and adjusting procedure.

Timing Pointer Alignment

Use the following procedure to check/adjust the alignment of the timing pointer with top dead center of the No. 1 (top) piston.

Refer to *Timing Pointer Alignment* under *65 Jet, 80 Jet, 1.6 Sea Drive and 85-115 hp (90° V4 cross flow models)* in this chapter.

Throttle Valve Synchronization

The carburetor throttle valves must be syn-chronized to open and close simultaneously. The engine will idle poorly if all throttle valves are not fully closed at idle.

1. Loosen the throttle cam follower screw (1, **Figure 116**, typical) and move the cam follower (3) away from the cam. The cam (2) and follower (3) must not be touching during this procedure.

2. Turn the carburetor link stop screw (**Figure 117**) counterclockwise 4 full turns.

3. Loosen the 2 carburetor link adjustment screws (**Figure 118**) no more than one-half turn.

4. Remove the air silencer cover and baffle.

5. Loosen (but do not remove) the bottom screw on the port throttle shaft connector (E, **Figure 110**) and the top screw on the starboard throttle shaft connector (F, **Figure 110**).

6. Apply light pressure to the carburetor throttle valves to ensure they are fully closed. Tighten the starboard throttle shaft connector screw, then the port throttle shaft connector screw.

7. Make sure all throttle valves are fully closed, then tighten the starboard throttle shaft connec-

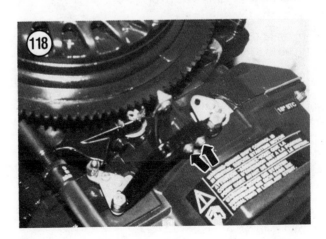

tor screw, then the port throttle shaft connector screw.

8. Turn the carburetor link stop screw (**Figure 117**) clockwise until the throttle valves on the port carburetors just begin to open, then back out the screw just enough to close the throttle valves.

9. While holding the carburetor link against the link stop screw, tighten the 2 link adjustment screws (**Figure 118**).

10. Open and close the throttle while observing the throttle valves. All carburetor throttle valves must open and close at exactly the same time. If not, loosen the carburetor link adjustment screws (**Figure 118**) one-half turn maximum. Then turn the carburetor link stop screw (**Figure 117**) in or out as necessary.

Throttle Cam Pickup Point

1. Make sure the throttle cam follower screw (1, **Figure 116**) is loose.

2. Hold the throttle cam follower against the throttle cam and adjust the throttle arm stop screw (7, **Figure 116**) until the mark on the throttle cam (5) is aligned with the center of the cam follower roller. Once the center of the roller is aligned with the mark, tighten the cam follower screw (1, **Figure 116**).

3. With the throttle arm in the idle position, a 0.005 in. (0.13 mm) clearance must be present between the throttle cam and the cam follower.

Wide-Open Throttle Stop

1. With the motor not running, advance the throttle to the wide-open position.

2. Loosen the locknut on the wide-open throttle stop screw (**Figure 119**). Adjust the wide-open throttle stop screw until the carburetor throttle valves are fully open (horizontal).

3. Continue adjusting the stop screw until the cam follower WOT index line (6, **Figure 116**) faces directly forward and is perpendicular with the air silencer base. Hold the screw from moving and tighten the locknut.

Throttle Cable Installation and Adjustment

NOTE
If throttle cable adjustment is too loose, the idle speed may be excessive or inconsistent. If cable adjustment is too tight, throttle and shift control effort may be excessive.

1. Extend the throttle cable and lubricate it with OMC Triple-Guard Grease. Apply Triple-Guard to both cable anchor pockets on the power head.

2. Make sure the fast idle lever on the remote control assembly is in the down position.

3. While rotating the propeller shaft, move the remote control handle from the NEUTRAL position to the FORWARD detent, then halfway back to the NEUTRAL position.

4. Push the throttle lever firmly against its stop.

5. Connect the throttle cable casing guide to the throttle lever using the washer and locknut. Tighten the locknut securely.

6. Pull on the throttle cable to remove any slack, then place the trunnion nut into its anchor pocket.

7. Install the cable retainer and screw. Tighten the screw to 60-84 in.-lb. (7-9 N•m).

8. Move the remote control handle to the FORWARD gear position, then pull it back slowly to NEUTRAL. Make sure the idle speed screw is against its stop. If not, remove cable backlash by

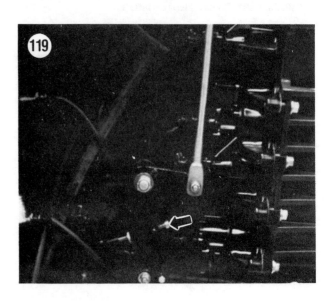

adjusting the throttle cable trunnion nut (2, **Figure 113**).

Maximum Spark Advance

NOTE
*To load the outboard motor properly when adjusting maximum spark advance, the outboard must be in a test tank or on a boat in the water with the correct test wheel installed (**Table 3**). Do not attempt to adjust the maximum timing with a propeller installed. **Do not** run the outboard at wide-open throttle while connected to a flushing device.*

1. Connect a timing light to the No. 1 spark plug wire.
2. Connect an accurate tachometer according to its manufacturer's instructions.
3. Start the motor and warm to normal operating temperature.
4. Shift into FORWARD gear. Run the motor at 4500-5000 rpm and note the timing marks with the timing light. Maximum spark advance should be 17-19° BTDC on 200, 225 and 250 hp models and 15-17° BTDC on 300 hp models.

WARNING
Do not attempt to adjust maximum spark advance with the motor running. Con-tact with the moving flywheel can result in serious personal injury.

5. If adjustment is necessary, stop the motor. Loosen the maximum advance screw locknut and turn the screw (A, **Figure 120**) clockwise to retard or counterclockwise to advance timing. One full turn in either direction changes timing approximately 1°.
6. Tighten the locknut and repeat Steps 3 and 4 to check adjustment.

Idle Speed

NOTE
The air silencer cover and baffle must be installed before the idle speed can be accurately adjusted.

Adjust idle speed with the outboard mounted on a boat in the water, running at normal operating temperature in FORWARD gear, with the correct propeller installed and the boat's movement unrestrained.

1. Connect a timing light to the No. 1 spark plug wire.
2. Connect an accurate tachometer according to its manufacturer's instructions.
3. Start the motor and warm to normal operating temperature.
4. Shift into FORWARD gear and note idle speed. Idle speed in FORWARD gear should be 650-750 rpm on 200, 225 and 300 hp models and 550-650 rpm on 250 hp models.

WARNING
Do not attempt to adjust idle speed with the motor running. Contact with the moving flywheel can result in serious personal injury.

5. If adjustment is necessary, stop the motor. Loosen the locknut on the idle timing screw (B, **Figure 120**). Turn the screw clockwise to decrease and counterclockwise to increase idle speed.

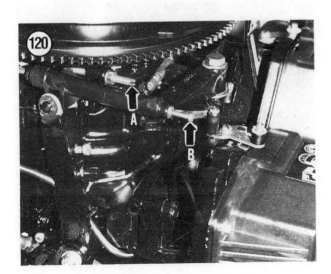

6. Tighten the locknut and repeat Steps 3 and 4 to check adjustment.

7. With the motor running at the specified idle speed in FORWARD gear, check idle timing. Idle timing should be as follows:

    a. *200 and 225 hp*—4-8° ATDC at 650-750 rpm.

    b. *250 hp*—2° ATDC-2° BTDC at 550-650 rpm.

    c. *300 hp*—6-10° ATDC at 650-750 rpm.

8. If the idle timing is not as correct at the specified rpm, recheck all linkage adjustments and repair as required.

Table 1 TIMING SPECIFICATIONS

Model	Idle timing	Pickup timing	Maximum spark advance
20 hp	–	–	33-35° BTDC
25-30 hp	–	–	29-31° BTDC
35 Jet, 40-50 hp	–	–	18-20° BTDC
60-70 hp	1-3° ATDC	–	18-20° BTDC
65 Jet, 80 Jet, 85-115 hp	–	3-5° BTDC	27-29° BTDC
120-140 hp	8° ATDC	–	17-19° BTDC
105 Jet, 150 hp (1991)	–	6-8° BTDC	31-33° BTDC
175 hp (1991)	–	6-8° BTDC	27-29° BTDC
60° 150-175 hp	5-7° ATDC	–	19-21° BTDC
200-225 hp	4-8° ATDC	–	17-19° BTDC
250 hp	2° BTDC-2° ATDC	–	17-19° BTDC
300 hp	6-10° ATDC	–	15-17° BTDC

Table 2 ENGINE SPEED SPECIFICATIONS

Model	Idle speed[1] (rpm)	Full throttle speed (rpm)
2 hp	1100-1300	4000-5000
2.3 hp	1100-1300	4200-5200
3.3 hp	1100-1300	4300-5000
3, 4 hp	700-800	4500-5500
4 Deluxe	600-750	4500-5500
6 hp	650-700	4500-5500
8 hp	650-700	5000-6000
9.9, 15 hp	650-700	5000-6000
20, 25, 28 hp	650-700	4500-5500
30 hp	650-700	5200-5800
40, 48, 50 hp	725-775	4500-5500
60, 70 hp	600-700[2]	5000-6000
85, 90, 100, 115 hp	625-675	4500-5500
120, 140 hp	600-700[2]	5000-6000
	(continued)	

Table 2 ENGINE SPEED SPECIFICATIONS (continued)

Model	Idle speed[1] (rpm)	Full throttle speed (rpm)
150 hp (90°)	625-675	4500-5500
175 hp (90°)	625-675	4750-5750
150, 175 hp (60°)	600-700[2]	4500-5500
200, 225 hp	600-700[2]	5000-6000
250 hp	550-650	4500-5500
300 hp	650-750	5000-6000

1. Idle speed should be checked with the boat in the water with the correct propeller installed, idling in forward gear with boat movement unrestrained.
2. Idle speed is adjusted by setting the idle timing. See Chapter Five.

Table 3 TEST WHEEL RECOMMENDATIONS

Model	Test wheel (part No.)	Minimum test speed (rpm)
2 hp	_[1]	4500
2.3 hp	_[1]	4800
3.3 hp	115306	5000
3 hp, 4 hp	317738	4400
4 Deluxe	390123	5100
6 hp	390239	4800
8 hp	390239	5300
9.9 hp		
1991-1992	386537	4800
1993	435750	5200
15 hp		
1991-1992	386537	6100
1993	435750	5800
20 hp	386891	4550
25 hp	434505	4800
28 hp	398948	4800
30 hp	434505	5400
40 hp	432968	4900
48 hp, 50 hp	432968	5200
60 hp	386665	5000
70 hp	386665	5700
85 hp, 88 hp, 90 hp, 100, 115 hp	382861	4800
120 hp		
1991-1992	386246	5300
1993	433068	5200
120TXETF, 120TXATF	396277	5200
140TL		
1991-1992	386246	5500
1993	433068	5300
140TX		
1991-1992	387388	5500
1993	396277	5300
140CX		
1991-1992	398673	5500
1993	398673	5300

(continued)

5

Table 3 TEST WHEEL RECOMMENDATIONS (continued)

Model	Test wheel (part No.)	Minimum test speed (rpm)
150 hp (90°) (149.4 cid)	387388	4500
175 hp (90°) (160.3 cid)	387388	4800
150 hp (60°) (158 cid)	387388[2]	4500
175 hp (60°) (158 cid)	387388[2]	4800
200XP, 200GT, 200STL		
1991-1992	387388	5700
200STL		
1993	436080	5700
200TX		
1991-1992	387388	5500
1993	436080	5500
200CX		
1991-1992	398673	5500
1993	436081	5500
225 hp		
1991-1992	387388	5700
1993	436080	5700
225CX		
1991-1992	388673	5700
1993	436081	5700
250 hp, 300 hp	396277	5500
250CX, 300CX	398674	5500

1. A test wheel is not used on 2 and 2.3 hp models. Use the standard propeller (part No. 115208) when running motor in a test tank.

2. On counter rotating (CX) models, use test wheel (part No. 398673).

Chapter Six

Fuel System

This chapter contains removal, overhaul, installation and adjustment procedures for fuel pumps, carburetors, choke and primer solenoids, fuel tanks and fuel delivery lines used on outboard motors covered in this manual.

FUEL PUMP

Evinrude and Johnson outboard motors equipped with an integral fuel tank use a gravity-flow fuel delivery system. Models so equipped do not require a fuel pump.

On 40 hp and larger motors (including 35 Jet), a variable ratio oil injection (VRO) system is used. The oil injection unit is a combination fuel and oil pump, which is operated by crankcase pressure/vacuum pulsations. See Chapter Eleven for coverage of the oil injection system.

Evinrude and Johnson outboard motors use a diaphragm-type fuel pump. See **Figure 1** (4 Deluxe-8 hp) and **Figure 2** (9.9-up). The pump is operated by crankcase pressure/vacuum pulsations. This type of fuel pump is not capable of creating sufficient vacuum to draw fuel from the tank at cranking speed, therefore, fuel is trans-

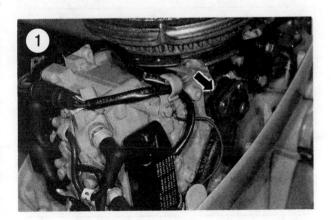

ferred to the carburetor for starting by operating the primer bulb installed in the fuel hose.

Pressure pulsations created by movement of the pistons reach the fuel pump through a passage between the crankcase and fuel pump. Upward piston motion creates a low pressure on the pump diaphragm. This low pressure opens the inlet check valve in the pump, drawing fuel from the line into the pump. At the same time, the low pressure draws the fuel-air mixture from the carburetor into the crankcase. Downward piston motion creates a high pressure on the pump diaphragm. This pressure closes the inlet check valve and opens the outlet check valve, forcing the fuel into the carburetor and drawing the fuel-air mixture from the crankcase into the cylinder for combustion. **Figure 3** shows the operational sequence of a typical diaphragm-type fuel pump.

Fuel pumps used on Evinrude and Johnson outboard motors are self-contained, remote assemblies. Fuel pump design is extremely simple and reliable in operation. Diaphragm failures are generally the most common problem, although the use of contaminated or improper fuel-oil mixtures can cause check valve problems. Repair kits are available to overhaul a defective pump assembly.

On a motor used on a boat equipped with a permanent fuel tank installed by the manufacturer, flow restrictions may be caused by the anti-siphon valve, primer, selector valves or other such devices that are part of the built-in fuel delivery system. Since low fuel flow can seriously damage an outboard motor, the fuel delivery system should be periodically checked for possible flow restrictions.

Fuel Line Restriction Test

Use the following procedure to determine if a restriction is present in the fuel line between the tank and fuel pump. Perform fuel pump tests with the motor mounted on a boat in the water or in a test tank. Prior to testing, remove the fuel tank fill cap to release any pressure that may be present.

1. Disconnect the fuel inlet hose from the fuel pump.

2. Connect a suitable vacuum gauge into the fuel hose using a "T" fitting and length of clear plastic hose. Connect the gauge as close (before) to the fuel pump as possible. Securely clamp all connections to prevent leakage.

3. Start the motor, shift into FORWARD gear and run at wide-open throttle while observing the gauge and clear hose.

4. If the gauge indicates more than 4 in. of vacuum, a restriction is present in the fuel line between the tank and fuel pump. Check for a

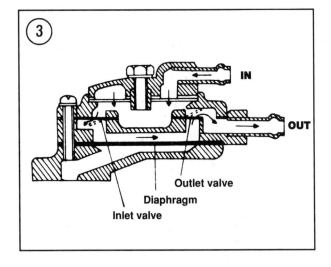

Outlet valve
Diaphragm
Inlet valve

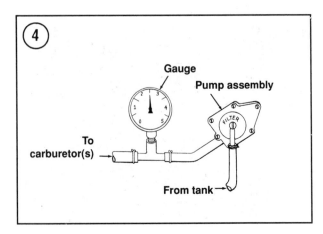

Gauge
Pump assembly
To carburetor(s) →
From tank →

partially closed fuel valve, plugged or kinked fuel hose or a defective primer bulb check valve.

5. If air bubbles are present in the clear plastic hose while running, an air leak is present in the hose between fuel tank and pump. Check for loose connections, cracked or broken fuel hose or other damage.

Fuel Pump Output Test

If fuel starvation is suspected, first remove the fuel hose from the fuel tank. Make sure the hose is clear by blowing through it with compressed air. Then, remove and clean the pump filter screen with clean solvent. See Chapter Four. Reinstall the filter screen with its lip facing the

pump cover gasket. If fuel delivery is still insufficient, test the pump as follows.

Perform fuel pump tests with the motor mounted on a boat in the water or in a test tank. Prior to testing, remove the fuel tank fill cap to release any pressure that may be present. The fuel tank must not be more than 24 in. (61 cm) below the fuel pump. The pump is not capable of lifting the fuel farther than 24 in. (61 cm).

1. Remove the fuel pump discharge hose at the carburetor.

2. Using a "T" fitting, connect a suitable fuel pressure gauge between the pump and carburetor. See **Figure 4**. Securely clamp all connections to prevent leakage.

3. Start the motor and observe the pressure gauge. Pump pressure should be as follows:

    a. 1 psi (7 kPa) at 600 rpm.

    b. 1.5 psi (10.3 kPa) at 2500-3000 rpm.

    c. 2.5 psi (17.2 kPa) at 4500 rpm.

4. If the fuel pump does not perform as specified, it should be repaired or replaced as outlined in this chapter.

Removal/Installation

1. Unscrew and remove the filter cover and screen (**Figure 5**, typical).

2. Remove the screws holding the pump to the power head (**Figure 6**, typical).

3. Carefully cut the clamp straps securing the fuel hoses to the pump. Then disconnect the fuel hoses from the pump.

4. Remove the pump and gasket from the engine. Discard the gasket.

5. Clean all gasket material from the power head mounting pad. Use caution to avoid gouging or damaging the mounting surface.

6. Clean the filter screen using a suitable solvent, then dry with compressed air. Replace the screen if extremely contaminated or damaged.

7. Installation is the reverse of removal. Use new gaskets and clamp straps. Apply OMC Nut Lock to the threads of the pump mounting screws

and tighten the screws to 24-36 in.-lb. (2.7-4.0 N.m).

Disassembly/Assembly

Refer to **Figure 7** (4 Deluxe-8 hp) or **Figure 8** (9.9 hp-larger) for this procedure.
1. Remove the screws holding the pump body together.
2. Separate the pump body. Remove and discard the diaphragm, check valves and gaskets.
3. Assembly is the reverse of disassembly. Install new diaphragm, check valves and gaskets during reassembly. Apply OMC Nut Lock to the threads of the pump body screws.

CARBURETORS

Various carburetors are used on Johnson and Evinrude outboard motors covered in this manual. All operate essentially the same, but housing shape and design varies according the model it's used on.

On all models (except 2, 2.3 and 3.3 hp), the intermediate- and high-speed fuel mixture is metered by fixed jets, which do not normally require adjustment. However, extreme changes in temperature, humidity or elevation may make recalibration (rejetting) necessary.

High-Elevation Modification

If the outboard motor is used primarily at high-altitude, the carburetor must be rejetted to lean the fuel mixture due to the reduction in air density.

The propeller used must allow the motor to run within the recommended speed range. The correct propeller should place full throttle speed in the middle of the recommended operating range. Changing the propeller for operation at high altitude will recover only that engine power

lost by not operating within the proper rpm range.

Always rejet and prop the outboard for the lowest elevation at which the boat will be operated to prevent the possibility of power head damage from an excessively lean mixture. If the boat is to be used at both high and low elevations,

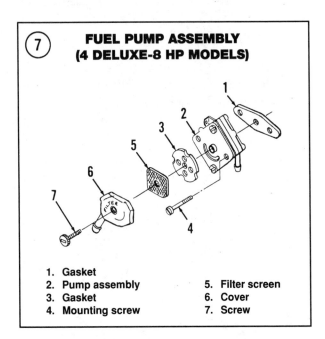

(7) **FUEL PUMP ASSEMBLY (4 DELUXE-8 HP MODELS)**

1. Gasket
2. Pump assembly
3. Gasket
4. Mounting screw
5. Filter screen
6. Cover
7. Screw

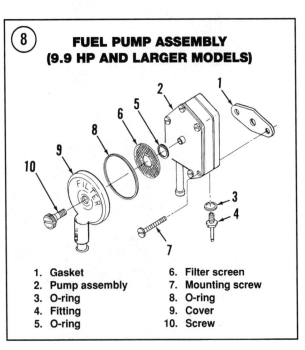

(8) **FUEL PUMP ASSEMBLY (9.9 HP AND LARGER MODELS)**

1. Gasket
2. Pump assembly
3. O-ring
4. Fitting
5. O-ring
6. Filter screen
7. Mounting screw
8. O-ring
9. Cover
10. Screw

you should have 2 sets of jets, 2 propellers and a fixed jet screwdriver (part No. 317002) for jet removal/installation.

NOTE
If the jet is visible from outside of the carburetor (without removing a plug), the jet is an air control jet. If the jet is not visible from outside of the carburetor, or if a plug must be removed to see the jet, the jet is a fuel control jet.

When rejetting the carburetor, change air control jets in 0.004 in. increments and fuel control jets in 0.001 in. increments.

Cleaning and Inspection

Before removing and disassembling the carburetor, be sure the proper overhaul kit, the proper tools and a sufficient quantity of cleaning solvent is available. Work slowly and carefully. Follow the disassembly procedures, referring to the exploded drawing of the carburetor when necessary. Do not apply excessive force at any time.

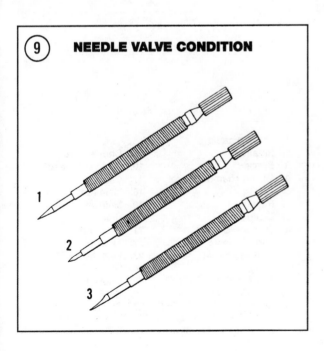

⑨ NEEDLE VALVE CONDITION

It is not necessary to disassemble the carburetor linkage or remove the throttle cam or other external components. Wipe the carburetor casting and linkage with a cloth moistened with solvent to remove any contamination and oil film. Clean the carburetor castings with an aerosol-type carburetor cleaner and brush. Do not submerge them in a hot tank or carburetor cleaner. A sealing compound is used around the metering tubes and on the castings to eliminate porosity problems. A hot tank or submersion in carburetor cleaner will remove this sealing compound.

Spray the cleaner on the casting and scrub off any gum or varnish with a small bristle brush. Spray the cleaner through all metering passages in the casting. Never clean passages with a wire or drill as you may enlarge the passage and change the carburetor calibration. Dry the castings using compressed air.

Check for excessive throttle shaft play and throttle valve misalignment. In most cases, the throttle shaft is not available separately from the carburetor body; if excessive wear or damage is noted, the carburetor body must be replaced.

Check all drillings and passages in the carburetor body for leakage using a hypodermic syringe filled with rubbing alcohol. Inject the alcohol into the passage while observing core plugs and lead shot plugs for leakage.

Check the float for fuel absorption. Check the float arm for wear in the hinge pin and needle valve contacts areas. Replace as necessary.

Check the mixture screw tip for grooving, nicks, scratches or excessive wear. **Figure 9** shows a good tip (1), a valve tip damaged from excessive pressure when seating (2) and one with wear on one side caused by vibration resulting from the use of a damaged propeller (3).

Check the throttle and choke shafts for excessive wear or play. The throttle and choke valves must move freely without binding. Replace the carburetor if any of these defects are noted.

6

Clean all gasket material from mating surfaces and remove any nicks, scratches or slight distortion with a surface plate and emery cloth.

Core Plugs and Lead Shot

Certain passages in the carburetor casting are covered with a core plug or have a lead shot installed. These usually require service only if the openings are leaking.

Core Plug Service

1. If leakage is noted, secure the carburetor in a vise with protective jaws.
2. Hold a flat end punch in the center of the core plug and tap sharply with a hammer to flatten the plug. Cover the plug area with Gasoila Sealant or fingernail polish.

CAUTION
Do not drill more than 1/16 in. (1.6 mm) below the core plug in Step 3 or the carburetor casting will be damaged.

3. If this does not solve the leakage problem or if the low-speed orifices are completely plugged, carefully drill a 1/8 in. (3.2 mm) hole through the center of the plug and pry it from the casting with a punch or similar tool.
4. Clean all residue from the core plug hole in the casting. If the hole is out-of-round, replace the casting.
5. If the low-speed passages are plugged, clean with a brush and an aerosol carburetor cleaner.
6. Coat the outer edge of a new core plug with Gasoila sealant and position it in the casting opening with its convex side facing up.
7. Hold a flat punch in the center of the core plug and tap sharply with a hammer to flatten the plug.
8. Check for leakage using a hypodermic syringe filled with rubbing alcohol.
9. Wipe the oil from the core plug and coat with Gasoila sealant or fingernail polish.

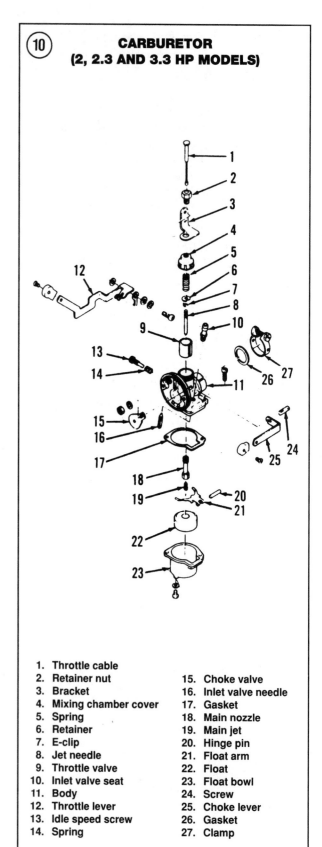

(10) CARBURETOR (2, 2.3 AND 3.3 HP MODELS)

1. Throttle cable
2. Retainer nut
3. Bracket
4. Mixing chamber cover
5. Spring
6. Retainer
7. E-clip
8. Jet needle
9. Throttle valve
10. Inlet valve seat
11. Body
12. Throttle lever
13. Idle speed screw
14. Spring
15. Choke valve
16. Inlet valve needle
17. Gasket
18. Main nozzle
19. Main jet
20. Hinge pin
21. Float arm
22. Float
23. Float bowl
24. Screw
25. Choke lever
26. Gasket
27. Clamp

Lead Shot Service

1. If leakage is noted, secure the carburetor in a vise with protective jaws.

2. Tap the center of the lead shot sharply with a small hammer and appropriate size punch.

3. If leakage remains, carefully pry the lead shot from its opening with a suitable knife, awl or other sharp instrument.

4. Thoroughly clean the lead shot opening in the casting.

5. Install a new lead shot in the opening and flatten out with a hammer and appropriate size punch.

6. Check for leakage using a hypodermic syringe filled with rubbing alcohol.

7. Clean the oil from the casting and coat the area with Gasoila sealant or fingernail polish.

CARBURETOR (2, 2.3 AND 3.3 HP)

Removal/Installation

1. Remove the engine covers.

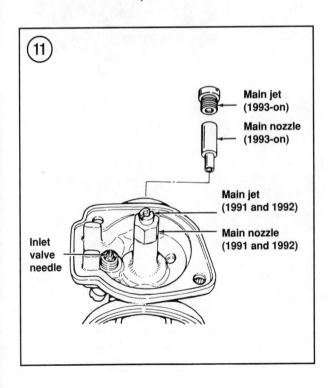

2. Remove the knobs from the throttle and choke levers.

3. Remove the air silencer from the carburetor.

4. Close the fuel shut-off valve.

5. Cut the tie strap from the fuel delivery hose at the carburetor. Disconnect the hose from the carburetor.

6. Loosen the carburetor mounting clamp and remove the carburetor.

7. To install the carburetor, place a new carburetor-to-power head gasket into the throat of the carburetor. Make sure the gasket is properly located.

8. Install the carburetor and securely tighten the mounting clamp.

9. Reconnect the fuel delivery hose. Clamp the hose using a new tie strap.

10. Complete installation by reinstalling the air silencer, choke and throttle lever knobs and engine covers.

Disassembly

Refer to **Figure 10** for this procedure.

1. Remove the 2 float bowl attaching screws. Separate the float bowl from the carburetor body. Remove and discard the float bowl gasket.

2. Invert the carburetor and lift off the float.

3. Remove the float hinge pin and the float arm.

4. Remove the inlet valve needle (**Figure 11**). Remove the inlet valve seat.

NOTE
On 1991 and 1992 models, the main nozzle is screwed into the carburetor body. On 1993-on models, the main nozzle is held in the carburetor body by the main jet. See Figure 11.

5A. *1991 and 1992 models*—Remove the main jet using a wide-blade screwdriver. Remove the main nozzle using an appropriate size wrench. See **Figure 11**.

5B. *1993-on models*—Remove the main jet using a wide-blade screwdriver, then extract the main nozzle from the carburetor body.

6. Remove the throttle lever.

7. Loosen the retainer nut several turns, then unscrew the carburetor body cover. Lift the throttle valve assembly (**Figure 12**) out of the carburetor body.

8. Compress the throttle valve spring and disconnect the throttle cable from the throttle valve. See **Figure 13**.

9. Remove the jet needle and the jet retainer from the throttle valve. See **Figure 13**. Do not lose the jet needle E-clip.

10. Lightly seat the idle speed screw, counting the turns required for reference during reassembly. Remove the idle speed screw and spring.

Cleaning and Inspection

1. Thoroughly clean all components using a suitable aerosol carburetor cleaner. Use a clean bristle brush to remove accumulated gum or varnish. Dry with compressed air. Thoroughly blow out all orifices, nozzles and passages.

2. Closely inspect the inlet valve needle and seat for grooves, nicks scratches or other damage. The inlet needle and seat must be replaced as a set.

3. Inspect the float for fuel absorption or deterioration. Replace float as necessary.

4. Inspect the jet needle for nicks, scratches, grooves or other damage. Replace the needle if any defects are noted.

5. Closely inspect the carburetor body for cracks, stripped threads or other damage.

Reassembly

Refer to **Figure 10** during this procedure. Replace all gaskets, O-rings and sealing washers during reassembly. Compare all new gaskets and other parts to be sure they match the old parts.

1. Slide the spring onto the idle speed screw. Install the screw into the carburetor body until lightly seated, then back out the number of turns noted during disassembly.

2. Insert the jet needle into the throttle valve. Place the needle retainer into the throttle valve over the needle E-clip. Align the retainer slot with the slot in the throttle valve. See **Figure 14**.

3. Reassemble the throttle valve components as follows:

   a. Place the throttle valve spring over the throttle cable.

   b. Compress the spring, then slide the throttle valve anchor through the slot and into position in the throttle valve. See **Figure 15**.

4. Align the slot in the throttle valve with the alignment pin in the carburetor body. Insert the throttle valve assembly into the body and tighten

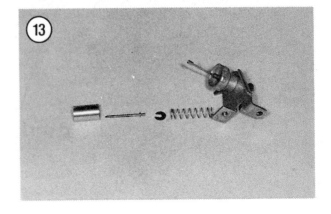

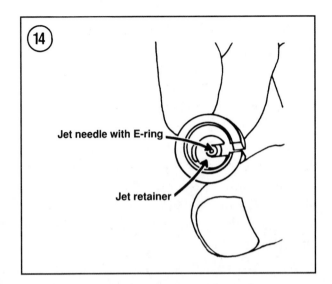

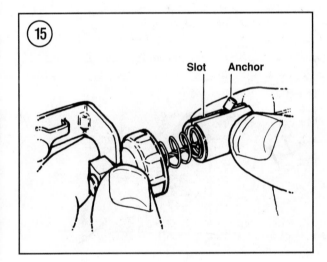

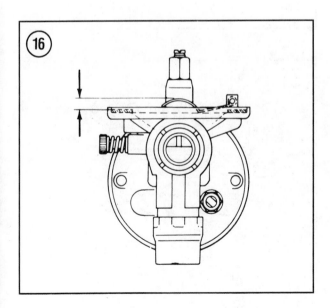

the carburetor body cover. Tighten the cover retainer nut securely.

5. Reinstall the throttle lever.

6. Install the main nozzle and main jet (**Figure 11**).

7. Install the inlet valve seat and needle.

8. Install the float arm and hinge pin. Check float level adjustment as described in this chapter.

9. Install the float.

10. Install the float bowl with a new gasket. Tighten the float bowl screws securely.

Carburetor Adjustments

Float level

1. With the float bowl removed, invert the carburetor and measure from the mating surface of the carburetor body (gasket installed) to the float arm as shown in **Figure 16**. The distance should be 0.090 in. (2.3 mm).

2. If adjustment is necessary, bend the float arms evenly to obtain the specified measurement.

High-speed mixture

High-speed mixture is controlled by the fixed main jet and is not adjustable.

Throttle jet needle (mid-range mixture)

The position of the E-clip on the jet needle determines the proper mixture between 1/4 and 3/4 throttle opening. See **Figure 17**. The E-clip should normally be located in the third groove from the top. This setting should be acceptable for most operating conditions.

If an excessively rich or lean condition results from extreme changes in elevation, temperature or humidity, the E-clip location can be changed. The mixture becomes leaner as the E-clip is moved to the upper grooves (**Figure 17**). Note

6

that it is always better to run a slightly rich mixture as opposed to one that is too lean.

1. Remove the carburetor as described in this chapter.

2. Remove and disassemble the throttle valve assembly as described in this chapter.

3. Relocate the E-clip as necessary, then reassemble and install the carburetor as described in this chapter.

Idle speed

For optimum results, adjust idle speed with the motor mounted on a boat in the water.

1. Start the motor and warm to normal operating temperature.

2. Place the throttle lever in the slowest position.

3. Adjust the idle speed screw to obtain 1100-1300 rpm.

CARBURETOR 3 AND 4 HP; 4 DELUXE

Removal/Installation (3 and 4 hp)

To prevent accidental starting, disconnect the spark plug wires from the spark plugs.

1. Remove the top engine cover.

2. Remove the choke knob. Pull the knob straight back and off the choke/fuel shut-off shaft.

3. Remove the stop button mounting nut.

4. Remove the upper and lower screws retaining the lower motor cover. Remove the rear lower cover.

5. Remove the tie strap clamp securing the fuel hose to the connector in the front lower cover. Disconnect the fuel hose then remove the front lower cover.

6. Remove the 2 screws securing the air silencer to the carburetor. Remove the air silencer.

7. Disconnect the choke and fuel shut-off valve linkage.

8. Using a pair of side-cutter pliers, remove the roll pin that holds the fuel shut-off valve in the float bowl. See **Figure 18**. Remove the shut-off valve from the carburetor.

9. Disconnect the fuel hose(s) from the carburetor.

10. Remove the shoulder screw (9, **Figure 19**), throttle cam follower (7) and cam follower link (10).

11. Remove the 2 carburetor mounting nuts, then remove the carburetor. Remove and discard the carburetor gasket.

NOTE
Do not use gasket sealant on the carburetor-to-intake manifold gasket.

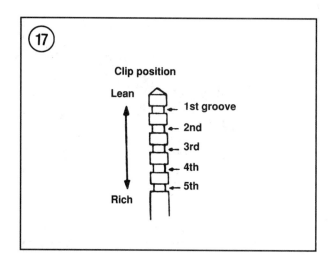

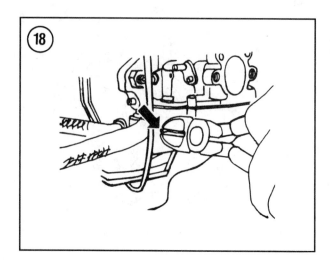

12. To reinstall the carburetor, first install a new gasket on the carburetor mounting studs.

13. Install the carburetor and mounting nuts. Tighten the nuts securely.

14. Connect the fuel hose(s) to the carburetor. Clamp the hoses with new tie straps.

15. Install the throttle cam follower, cam follower link and shoulder screw.

16. Make sure both O-rings are properly located on the fuel shut-off valve. Lightly lubricate the O-rings with clean engine oil. To prevent damaging the O-rings, install the valve into the float

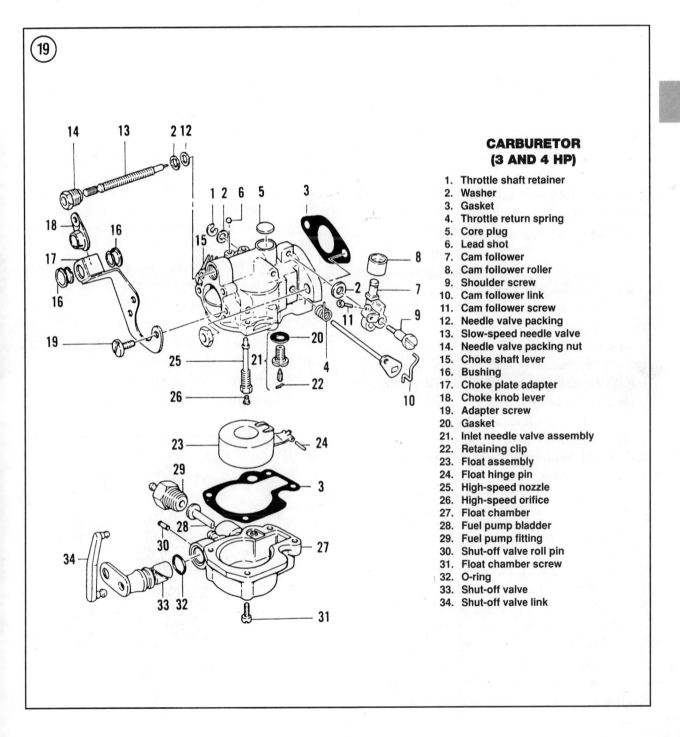

**CARBURETOR
(3 AND 4 HP)**

1. Throttle shaft retainer
2. Washer
3. Gasket
4. Throttle return spring
5. Core plug
6. Lead shot
7. Cam follower
8. Cam follower roller
9. Shoulder screw
10. Cam follower link
11. Cam follower screw
12. Needle valve packing
13. Slow-speed needle valve
14. Needle valve packing nut
15. Choke shaft lever
16. Bushing
17. Choke plate adapter
18. Choke knob lever
19. Adapter screw
20. Gasket
21. Inlet needle valve assembly
22. Retaining clip
23. Float assembly
24. Float hinge pin
25. High-speed nozzle
26. High-speed orifice
27. Float chamber
28. Fuel pump bladder
29. Fuel pump fitting
30. Shut-off valve roll pin
31. Float chamber screw
32. O-ring
33. Shut-off valve
34. Shut-off valve link

6

bowl with a turning motion. Secure the valve using a new roll pin.

17. Reattach the choke and fuel shut-off valve linkage.

18. Install the air silencer base and cover.

19. Install the front lower cover and connect the fuel hose to the connector in the cover. Clamp the hose using a new tie strap.

20. Install the rear lower cover.

21. Install the stop button nut and choke knob.

22. Perform synchronization and linkage adjustments as outlined in Chapter Five.

Removal/Installation
(4 Deluxe)

1. To prevent accidental starting, disconnect the spark plug wires from the spark plugs.

2. Remove the low-speed adjusting knob by pulling it straight off the adjustment screw.

3. Remove the clip securing the choke knob to the choke shaft (**Figure 20**) using needlenose pliers. Then pull the choke knob out of the lower motor cover.

4. Remove the screw (9, **Figure 21**) securing the throttle cam follower assembly to the carburetor body. Remove the cam follower (7) and follower link (10).

5. Disconnect the fuel hose from the carburetor.

6. Remove the 2 carburetor mounting nuts, then remove the carburetor. Remove and discard the carburetor gasket.

> *NOTE*
> *Do not use gasket sealant on the carburetor-to-intake manifold gasket.*

7. To reinstall the carburetor, first install a new gasket on the carburetor mounting studs.

8. Install the carburetor on the mounting studs. Install the 2 mounting nuts and tighten securely.

9. Connect the fuel hose to the carburetor. Securely clamp the hose using a new tie strap.

10. Install the throttle cam follower and link.

11. Install the choke knob and retaining clip.

12. Install the low-speed adjusting knob.

13. Perform synchronization and linkage adjustment as outlined in Chapter Five.

Disassembly
(4 Deluxe, 3 and 4 hp)

Refer to **Figure 19** (3 and 4 hp) or **Figure 21** (4 Deluxe) for this procedure.

1. Remove the 4 float bowl screws and separate the float bowl from the carburetor body. Remove and discard the float bowl gasket.

2. Unscrew the slow-speed needle valve packing nut, then remove the slow-speed needle valve.

3. Using a small seal pick or similar tool, carefully remove the washer and needle valve packing from the carburetor body. Do not damage the packing nut threads.

4. *3 and 4 hp*—Unscrew the fuel pump fitting. Remove the fitting and fuel pump bladder.

5. Using needlenose pliers, remove the float pin. Remove the float, retaining clip and inlet valve needle. Unscrew and remove the inlet valve seat using a wide-blade screwdriver.

6. Remove the high-speed orifice.

7. Remove the high-speed nozzle.

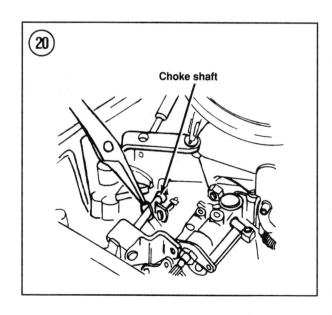

Choke shaft

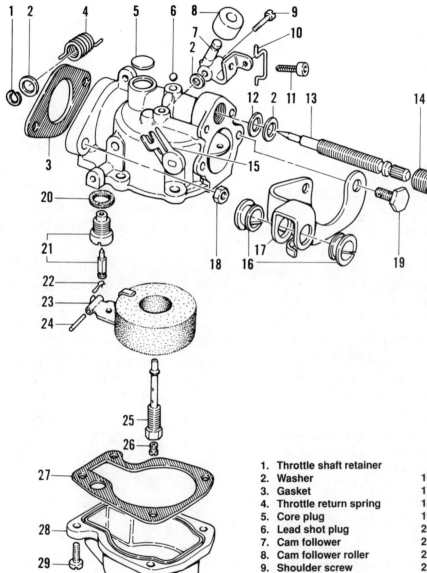

CARBURETOR
(4 DELUXE)

1. Throttle shaft retainer
2. Washer
3. Gasket
4. Throttle return spring
5. Core plug
6. Lead shot plug
7. Cam follower
8. Cam follower roller
9. Shoulder screw
10. Cam follower link
11. Cam follower screw
12. Needle valve packing
13. Slow-speed needle valve
14. Needle valve packing nut
15. Choke shaft lever
16. Bushing
17. Choke plate adapter
18. Nut
19. Adapter screw
20. Gasket
21. Inlet valve assembly
22. Retaining clip
23. Float
24. Float pin
25. High-speed nozzle
26. High-speed orifice
27. Float bowl gasket
28. Float bowl
29. Float bowl screw

6

Cleaning and Inspection
(4 Deluxe, 3 and 4 hp)

1. Thoroughly clean all components using a suitable aerosol carburetor cleaner. Use a clean bristle brush to remove accumulated gum or varnish. Dry with compressed air. Thoroughly blow out all orifices, nozzles and passages.

2. Closely inspect the inlet valve needle and seat for grooves, nicks scratches or other damage. The inlet needle and seat must be replaced as a set.

3. Inspect the float for fuel absorption or deterioration. Replace float as necessary.

4. Inspect the mixture screw for nicks, scratches, grooves or other damage. Replace the screw if any defects are noted.

5. Closely inspect the carburetor body for cracks, stripped threads or other damage.

Reassembly
(4 Deluxe, 3 and 4 hp)

Refer to **Figure 19** (3 and 4 hp) or **Figure 21** (4 Deluxe) for this procedure. Replace all gaskets, O-rings and sealing washers during reassembly. Compare all new gaskets and other parts to be sure they match the original parts.

1. Install the high-speed nozzle into the carburetor body and tighten securely. Install the high-speed orifice into the nozzle and tighten securely.

2. Place a new gasket on the inlet valve seat and install the seat into the carburetor body. Tighten the seat securely using a wide-blade screwdriver.

3. Install the inlet valve needle, retaining clip, float and float pin.

4. Check the float level and float drop adjustments as described in this chapter.

5. *3 and 4 hp*—Install the fuel pump bladder and fuel pump fitting.

6. Place a new gasket on the float bowl. Install the bowl and 4 screws. Tighten the float bowl screws alternately, in a crossing pattern, to 15-22 in.-lb. (1.7-2.2 N·m).

7. Install the cam follower and linkage.

8. Insert a new slow-speed needle valve packing into the carburetor body. Install the packing washer, then install (but do not tighten) the packing nut into the carburetor body.

9. Install the slow-speed needle valve. Carefully screw the needle valve into the carburetor body until *lightly* seated. Then back out the needle valve 1 full turn. Tighten the packing nut until the needle valve can just be turned using the fingers.

Carburetor Adjustments

Float level

The correct float level is necessary for proper carburetor operation. If the float level is too low, an excessively lean fuel mixture and/or fuel starvation at high speed can result. If the float level is too high, an excessively rich fuel mixture and/or carburetor flooding can result.

1. Invert the carburetor so the float is facing upward. Allow the weight of the float to close the inlet valve assembly.

2. Referring to **Figure 22**, check the float level as follows:

   a. Place OMC Float Gauge (part No. 324891) with the side marked "2 THRU 6 HP" over the float. Make sure the float gauge is rest-

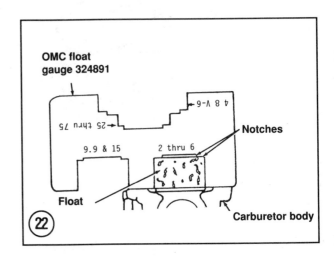

ing on the float bowl gasket surface (gasket not installed).

b. The top of the float should be located between the notches as shown. Make sure the float gauge is not pushing downward on the float.

c. If adjustment is necessary, carefully bend the float arm as required to position the float as shown. Do not force the inlet valve needle into the seat. Check the adjustment with the float gauge and readjust as necessary.

Float drop

The correct float drop adjustment is necessary to ensure the inlet valve opens fully. Fuel starvation at high speed can result if the float drop is insufficient. The inlet valve needle can become cocked in its seat and cause severe carburetor flooding if the float drop is excessive.

Refer to **Figure 23** for this procedure.

1. Hold the carburetor in the upright position with the float hanging by its own weight.

2. Measure the distance (D, **Figure 23**) from the float bowl gasket surface (gasket not installed) to the bottom of the float as shown. The distance (D) should be 1-1/8 to 1-1/2 in. (28-38 mm).

3. If adjustment is necessary, carefully bend the float arm tab (T, **Figure 23**) as necessary.

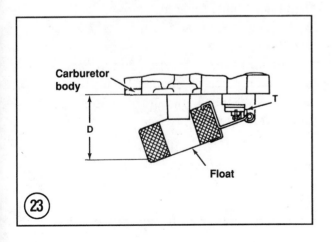

Carburetor body

T

D

Float

(23)

Slow-speed mixture

Refer to the appropriate section in Chapter Five for slow-speed mixture adjustment procedure.

Idle speed

Refer to the appropriate section in Chapter Five the idle speed adjustment procedure.

CARBURETOR
(6-20 HP MODELS)

A single, modular carburetor is used on 6-20 hp models. The term "modular" is used because the float bowl and body cover are constructed of a nonmetallic Minlon material while the carburetor body is made of aluminum. The low-speed mixture is controlled by an adjustable mixture screw located at the front of the carburetor body cover on 1991 and 1992 9.9-15 hp models or on the side of the body cover on all other models. Fuel enrichment for starting is provided by a choke valve on 6 and 8 hp models, a manual primer valve on 20 hp models equipped with rope start or tiller handle and an electric primer solenoid on 20 hp models equipped with remote control.

Removal/Installation
(6 and 8 hp)

To prevent accidental starting, disconnect the spark plug wires from the spark plugs.

1. Remove the manual rewind starter assembly as outlined in Chapter Twelve.

2. Remove the air silencer.

3. Remove the shoulder screw securing the choke linkage bellcrank to the carburetor. Disconnect the choke link from the choke lever.

4. Disconnect the fuel hose(s) from the carburetor.

5. Remove the 2 carburetor mounting nuts then remove the carburetor. Remove and discard the carburetor-to-intake manifold gasket.

6

NOTE
Do not apply gasket sealant to the carburetor-to-intake manifold gasket.

6. Install the carburetor using a new gasket. Install the carburetor mounting nuts and tighten securely.

7. Connect the fuel hose to the carburetor. Clamp the hose securely using a new tie strap.

8. Reconnect the choke link. Install the shoulder screw and bellcrank.

9. Install the air silencer.

10. Perform synchronization and linkage adjustments as outlined in Chapter Five.

Removal/Installation
(9.9 and 15 hp)

To prevent accidental starting, disconnect the spark plug wires from the spark plugs.

1. Remove the rewind starter as outlined in Chapter Twelve.

2. Remove the 2 air silencer mounting screws. Remove the air silencer.

3. Disconnect the choke link and remove the choke lever.

4. Remove the carburetor mounting nuts. Remove the carburetor, then cut the tie strap clamp securing the fuel delivery hose to the carburetor. Disconnect the fuel hose. Remove and discard the carburetor gasket.

NOTE
Do not apply gasket sealant to the carburetor-to-intake manifold gasket.

5. To install the carburetor, first place a new gasket on the carburetor mounting studs.

6. Attach the fuel delivery hose to the carburetor. Securely clamp the hose using a new tie strap.

7. Install the carburetor on the mounting studs. Install the carburetor mounting nuts and tighten securely.

8. Install the choke lever and reconnect the choke link.

9. Perform synchronization and linkage adjustment as outlined in Chapter Five. If necessary, adjust slow-speed mixture and idle speed as outlined in Chapter Five.

Removal/Installation
(20 hp)

To prevent accidental starting, disconnect the spark plug wires from the spark plugs.

1. Disconnect the cam follower link from the carburetor.

2. Remove the carburetor mounting nuts and slide the carburetor off the studs.

3. Cut the tie strap clamps and disconnect the large primer hose, fuel delivery hose and small primer hose from the carburetor. Remove the carburetor.

4. Remove and discard the carburetor gasket.

NOTE
Do not apply gasket sealant to the carburetor-to-intake manifold gasket.

5. To install the carburetor, first place a new carburetor-to-intake manifold gasket on the mounting studs.

6. Connect the fuel delivery hose and small primer hose to the carburetor. Securely clamp the hoses using new tie straps. Connect the large primer hose and clamp securely with a new tie strap.

7. Install the carburetor and mounting nuts. Tighten the nuts securely.

8. Connect the throttle cam link to the carburetor.

9. Perform synchronization and linkage adjustment as outlined in Chapter Five. If necessary, adjust slow-speed mixture and idle speed as outlined in Chapter Five.

Disassembly
(6-20 hp)

Refer to **Figure 24** for this procedure.

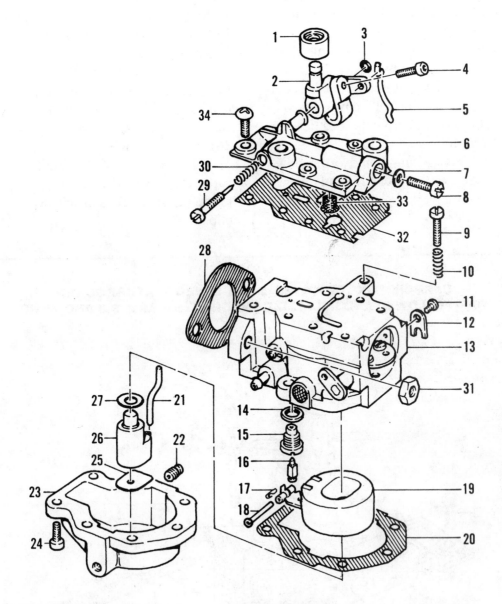

㉔

**MODULAR CARBURETOR
(6-20 HP)**

6

1. Cam follower roller (except 20 hp)	12. Choke shaft retainer clip	24. Screw
2. Cam follower (except 20 hp)	13. Carburetor body	25. Gasket
3. O-ring (except 20 hp)	14. Gasket	26. Nozzle well
4. Cam follower adjustment screw (except 20 hp)	15. Inlet valve seat	27. Gasket
5. Cam follower link (except 20 hp)	16. Inlet valve needle	28. Gasket
6. Body cover	17. Clip	29. Slow-speed mixture screw
7. Washer	18. Float pin	30. Spring
8. Plug	19. Float	31. Nut
9. Idle speed screw	20. Gasket	32. Gasket
10. Spring	21. Idle lift tube	33. Vent screen
11. Screw	22. High-speed orifice	24. Screw
	23. Float bowl	

1A. *Early models (except 20 hp)*—Remove the shoulder screw (3, **Figure 25**) securing the throttle cam follower assembly to the body cover. Disconnect the cam follower link from the throttle lever and remove the cam follower.

1B. *Late models (except 20 hp)*—Using a seal pick or similar tool, carefully remove the O-ring (3, **Figure 24**) holding the throttle cam follower assembly to the carburetor body cover. Disconnect the cam follower link from the throttle lever and remove cam follower.

2A. *Early 9.9 and 15 hp*—Remove the slow-speed mixture screw (9, **Figure 25**) and retainer (8) from the body cover.

2B. *Late 9.9-15 and all other models*—Remove the low-speed mixture screw (29, **Figure 24**) and spring (30).

3. Remove the 5 carburetor body cover screws. Lift the cover and gasket off the carburetor body. Discard the gasket.

4. Remove 7 float bowl screws. Separate the float bowl from the carburetor body. Remove and discard the float bowl gasket (A, **Figure 26**). Remove the nozzle well lower gasket (B, **Figure 26**) from the float bowl.

5. Push the float pin (A, **Figure 27**) from the carburetor body using a suitable tool, then remove the float (B) and inlet valve needle and clip.

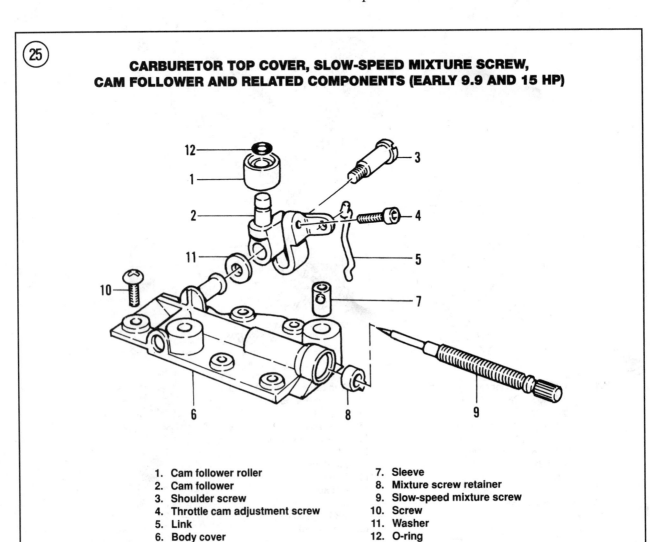

(25) CARBURETOR TOP COVER, SLOW-SPEED MIXTURE SCREW, CAM FOLLOWER AND RELATED COMPONENTS (EARLY 9.9 AND 15 HP)

1. Cam follower roller
2. Cam follower
3. Shoulder screw
4. Throttle cam adjustment screw
5. Link
6. Body cover
7. Sleeve
8. Mixture screw retainer
9. Slow-speed mixture screw
10. Screw
11. Washer
12. O-ring

6. Using a wide-blade screwdriver, unscrew and remove the inlet valve seat (A, **Figure 28**). Remove and discard the seat gasket.

7. Carefully cut the idle lift tube (B, **Figure 28**) at each end. Remove and discard the tube.

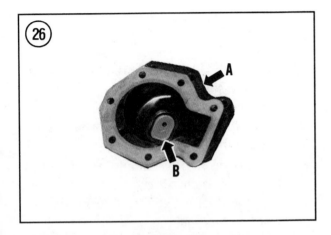

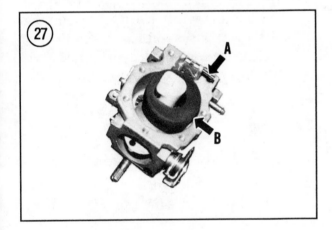

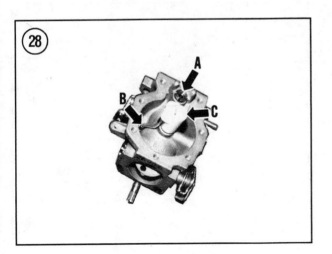

8. Remove the high-speed orifice (**Figure 29**). Remove the nozzle well (C, **Figure 28**) and nozzle well upper gasket.

Cleaning and Inspection

1. Thoroughly clean all components using a suitable aerosol carburetor cleaner. Use a clean bristle brush to remove accumulated gum or varnish. Dry with compressed air. Thoroughly blow out all orifices, nozzles and passages.

2. Closely inspect the inlet valve needle and seat for grooves, nicks scratches or other damage. The inlet needle and seat must be replaced as a set.

3. Inspect the float for fuel absorption or deterioration. Replace float as necessary.

4. Inspect the mixture screw for nicks, scratches grooves or other damage. Replace the screw if any defects are noted.

5. Closely inspect the carburetor body for cracks, stripped threads or other damage.

Reassembly
(6-20 hp)

Refer to **Figure 24** and **Figure 25** for this procedure. Replace all gaskets, O-rings and sealing washers during reassembly. Compare all new gaskets and other parts to be sure they match the original parts.

6

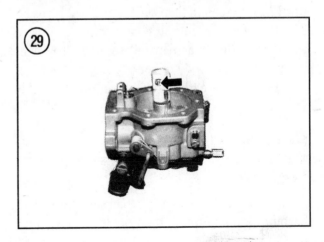

1. Install a new nozzle well upper gasket in place on the carburetor body.

2. Install the high-speed orifice into the nozzle well then install the nozzle well on the carburetor body.

3. Install a new idle lift tube. Make sure the tube is securely connected to the carburetor body and nozzle well.

4. Install the inlet valve seat using a new gasket. Tighten the seat securely using a wide-blade screwdriver.

5. Install the inlet valve needle, float and float pin.

6. Adjust the float level and float drop as outlined in this chapter.

7. Place the nozzle well lower gasket (B, **Figure 26**) in place in the float bowl. Install the float bowl using a new gasket. Tighten the 7 float bowl screws in the sequence embossed on the float bowl to 8-10 in.-lb. (0.8-1.2 N•m).

8. Install a new body cover gasket. Install the body cover and tighten the cover screws in the sequence embossed in the cover to 8-10 in.-lb. (0.8-1.2 N•m).

9A. *Early 9.9-15 hp*—Install the slow-speed mixture screw retainer (8, **Figure 25**) into the body cover. Install the mixture screw, turning it clockwise until *lightly* seated. Then, back out the screw 2-1/2 turns.

9B. *Late 9.9-15 hp and all other models*—Install the slow-speed mixture screw and spring into the body cover. Turn the screw clockwise until *lightly* seated, then back out 2-1/2 turns.

10. Reconnect the throttle cam follower link to the throttle lever and install the cam follower assembly to the body cover (except 20 hp).

11. Install the carburetor as outlined in this chapter.

Carburetor Adjustment

Float level

The correct float level is necessary for proper carburetor operation. If the float level is too low,

an excessively lean fuel mixture and/or fuel starvation at high speed can result. If the float level is too high, an excessively rich fuel mixture and/or carburetor flooding can result.

1. Invert the carburetor so the float is facing upward. Allow the weight of the float to close the inlet valve assembly.

2. Referring to **Figure 30**, check the float level as follows:

   a. Place OMC Float Gauge (part No. 324891) with the side marked "9.9 & 15 HP" over the float. Make sure the float gauge is resting on the float bowl gasket surface (gasket not installed).

   b. The top of the float should be located between the notches in the float gauge. Make sure the float gauge is not pushing downward on the float.

   c. If adjustment is necessary, carefully bend the float arm as required to position the float as shown. Do not force the inlet valve needle into the seat. Check the adjustment with the float gauge and readjust as necessary.

Float drop

The correct float drop adjustment is necessary to ensure the inlet valve opens fully. Fuel starvation at high speed can result if the float drop is

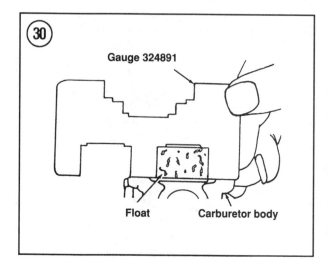

Gauge 324891

Float   Carburetor body

insufficient. The inlet valve needle can become cocked in its seat and cause severe carburetor flooding if the float drop is excessive.

Refer to **Figure 31** for this procedure.

1. Hold the carburetor in the upright position with the float hanging by its own weight.

2. Measure the distance (D, **Figure 31**) from the float bowl gasket surface (gasket not installed) to the bottom of the float as shown. The distance (D) should be 1 to 1-3/8 in. (25.4-35 mm).

3. If adjustment is necessary, carefully bend the float arm tab (T, **Figure 31**) as necessary.

Slow-speed mixture

Refer to the appropriate section in Chapter Five for slow-speed mixture adjustment procedure.

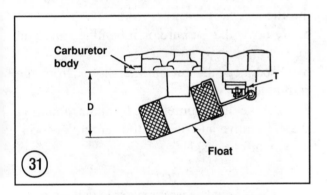

Idle speed

Refer to the appropriate section in Chapter Five the idle speed adjustment procedure.

TR AND SV CARBURETOR (25-70 HP MODELS)

Early (1991 and 1992) 25-70 hp models are equipped with TR carburetors. Late (1992-1/2-on) 25-70 hp models are equipped with SV carburetors. The TR and SV carburetors are similar, with the SV carburetor identified by its Minlon (nonmetallic) top body cover.

All models are equipped with a slow-speed mixture screw which is set at the factory and should not require additional adjustment. If, however, the removal of the mixture screw is necessary for carburetor cleaning, adjust the slow-speed mixture as outlined in this chapter and Chapter Five. Off idle and high-speed fuel mixtures are controlled by fixed jets.

Removal/Installation (25-30 hp)

To prevent accidental starting, disconnect the spark plug wires from the spark plugs.

> *CAUTION*
> *To prevent breakage, do not attempt to pull fuel hoses off Minlon (nonmetallic) fittings. Always push the hose off using the fingers, a screwdriver or other blunt tool. If pushing the hose will not easily separate the hose and fitting, carefully cut the hose along the side and peel it away from the fitting.*

1. Cut the tie strap clamp and disconnect the fuel primer hose (**Figure 32**) from the fitting at the top of the carburetor.

2. If equipped with electric start, remove the starter motor bracket and place it aside. See Chapter Seven.

3. Disconnect the throttle link from the cam follower (**Figure 33**).

4. Remove the screw securing the fuel primer solenoid (if so equipped) and lay the solenoid aside.

5. Remove the 2 carburetor mounting nuts and slide the carburetor off the mounting studs. Remove and discard the carburetor-to-intake manifold gasket.

6. Cut the tie strap clamps and disconnect the remaining fuel hoses.

NOTE
Do not apply gasket sealant to the carburetor-to-intake manifold gasket.

7. To install the carburetor, place a new carburetor-to-intake manifold gasket on the mounting studs.

8. Connect the fuel hoses to the carburetor. Securely clamp the hoses using new tie straps.

9. Install the carburetor on the mounting studs. Install the mounting nuts and tighten securely.

10. Install the electric primer solenoid (if so equipped).

11. Install the electric starter motor bracket (if so equipped).

12. Connect the primer hose to the fitting at the top of the carburetor. Clamp the hose using a new tie strap.

13. Perform synchronization and adjustment as outlined in Chapter Five.

Removal/Installation
(35 Jet, 40-50 hp)

To prevent accidental starting, disconnect the spark plug wires from the spark plugs.

CAUTION
To prevent breakage, do not attempt to pull fuel hoses off Minlon (nonmetallic) fittings. Always push the hose off using a screwdriver or other blunt tool. If pushing the hose will not easily separate the hose and fitting, carefully cut the hose
along the side and peel it away from the fitting.

The following procedure describes the removal/installation of both carburetors. The carburetors can be removed/installed individually, if necessary. Refer to **Figure 34**.

1. Remove the screws securing the air silencer cover. Remove the cover. Remove and discard the cover gasket.

2. Remove the air silencer base screws. Disconnect the drain hose, then remove the air silencer base and gasket. Discard the air silencer base gasket (5, **Figure 34**) and screws (4). New screws and gasket must be used during installation.

3. Cut the tie strap clamps and disconnect the fuel hoses.

4. Disconnect the throttle linkage from the throttle levers.

5. Remove the carburetor mounting nuts and lockwashers.

6. Disconnect the fuel primer hoses from the carburetor(s).

7. Remove the carburetor(s) from the mounting studs. Remove and discard the carburetor-to-intake manifold gaskets.

NOTE
Do not apply gasket sealant to the carburetor-to-intake manifold gaskets.

34

**CARBURETORS, AIR SILENCER ASSEMBLY AND RELATED COMPONENTS
(35 JET AND 40-50 HP WITH ELECTRIC START
[ROPE START MODELS ARE SIMILAR])**

6

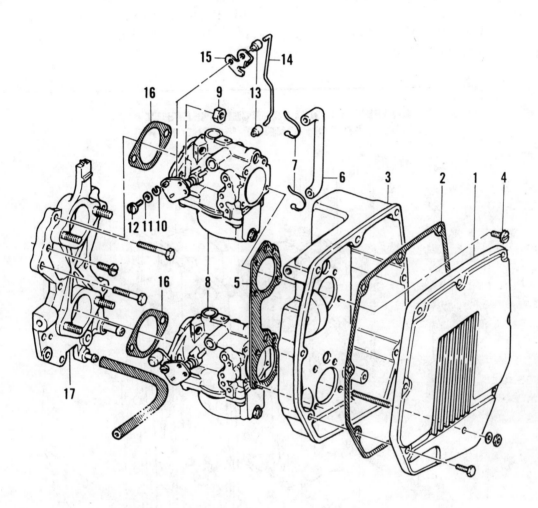

1. Air silencer cover
2. Gasket
3. Air silencer base
4. Base screws
5. Base-to-carburetors gasket
6. Pulse equalization hose
7. Tie strap
8. Carburetors
9. Carburetor mounting nuts
10. Lockwasher
11. Washer
12. Screw
13. Linkage retainer
14. Throttle linkage
15. Throttle lever
16. Carburetor-to-intake
    manifold gaskets
17. Intake manifold

8. Place new carburetor flange gaskets on the mounting studs.

9. Install the fuel primer hoses to the carburetor fittings.

10. Install the carburetors on the mounting studs. Install the lockwashers and nuts. Tighten the nuts securely.

11. Install the fuel hoses to the carburetors. Securely clamp with new tie straps.

12. Connect the throttle linkage to the throttle levers.

13. Connect the drain hose to the air silencer base. Install the air silencer base using a new gasket (5, **Figure 34**) and new screws (4). Install the air silencer cover using a new gasket.

14. If the slow-speed mixture screw was removed or disturbed, adjust as outlined in Chapter Five.

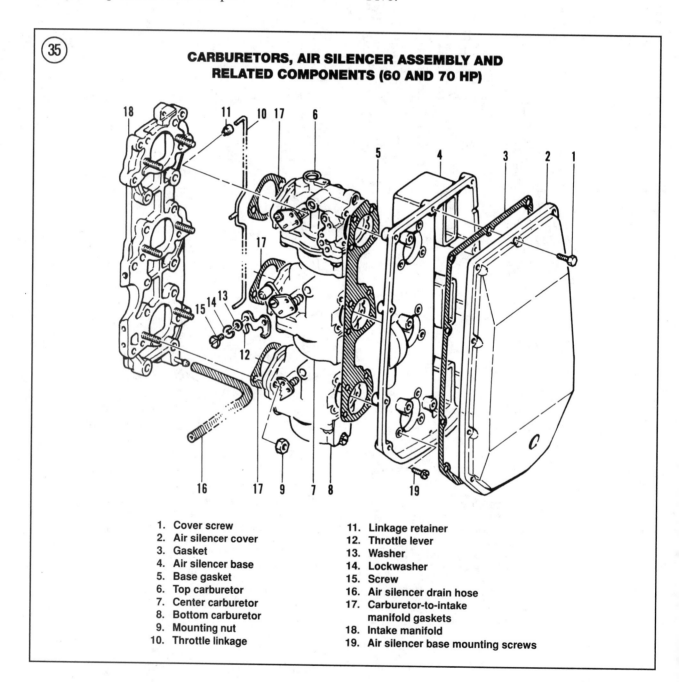

35

CARBURETORS, AIR SILENCER ASSEMBLY AND RELATED COMPONENTS (60 AND 70 HP)

1. Cover screw
2. Air silencer cover
3. Gasket
4. Air silencer base
5. Base gasket
6. Top carburetor
7. Center carburetor
8. Bottom carburetor
9. Mounting nut
10. Throttle linkage
11. Linkage retainer
12. Throttle lever
13. Washer
14. Lockwasher
15. Screw
16. Air silencer drain hose
17. Carburetor-to-intake manifold gaskets
18. Intake manifold
19. Air silencer base mounting screws

15. Perform synchronization and linkage adjustment as outlined in Chapter Five.

Removal/Installation
(60 and 70 hp)

To prevent accidental starting, disconnect the spark plug wires from the spark plugs.

> *CAUTION*
> *To prevent breakage, do not attempt to pull fuel hoses off Minlon (nonmetallic) fittings. Always push the hose off using the fingers, a screwdriver or other blunt tool. If pushing the hose will not easily separate the hose and fitting, carefully cut the hose along the side and peel it away from the fitting.*

The following procedure describes the removal/installation of all carburetors. The carburetors can be removed/installed individually if necessary. Refer to **Figure 35** for this procedure.

1. Remove the screws securing the air silencer cover. Remove the cover and gasket. Discard the gasket.

2. Remove the air silencer base screws (19, **Figure 35**). Disconnect the air silencer drain hose and remove the silencer base from the carburetors. Discard the air silencer gasket (5, **Figure 35**) and screws (19). New screws and gasket should be used during installation.

3. Cut the tie strap clamps and remove fuel hoses from the carburetors.

4. Disconnect the throttle linkage from the carburetor throttle levers.

5. Remove the carburetor mounting nuts and lockwashers. Slide the carburetors off the mounting studs and disconnect the fuel primer hoses from the carburetor fittings.

6. Remove and discard the carburetor-to-intake manifold gaskets.

> *NOTE*
> *Do not apply gasket sealant to the carburetor-to-intake manifold gaskets.*

7. To reinstall the carburetors, place new carburetor-to-intake manifold gaskets on the mounting studs.

8. Connect the fuel primer hoses to the carburetors.

9. Install the carburetors on the mounting studs. Install the lockwashers and carburetor mounting nuts. Tighten the nuts securely.

10. Install the fuel delivery hoses and clamp securely using new tie straps.

11. Install the throttle linkage to the throttle levers.

12. Perform synchronization and adjustment procedures as outlined in Chapter Five.

13. Connect the air silencer drain hose to the silencer base.

14. Install the air silencer base to the carburetors using a new gasket (5, **Figure 35**) and new screws (19). Tighten the screws to 24-36 in.-lb. (2.7-4.1 N•m).

15. Install the air silencer cover using a new gasket. Install the cover screws and tighten to 24-36 in.-lb. (2.7-4.1 N•m).

16. If the slow-speed mixture screw was removed or its position disturbed, adjust the slow-speed mixture as outlined in this chapter.

Disassembly
(TR and SV Carburetors)

Refer to **Figure 36** (TR) or **Figure 37** (SV) for this procedure.

1. Remove the drain plug or fuel hose fitting from the float bowl. Allow the fuel in the bowl to drain into a suitable container. Remove and discard the gasket on the plug or fitting.

2. Using OMC Orifice Driver (part No. 317002), remove the high-speed orifice.

3A. *2-cylinder models*—Remove the intermediate air bleed orifice (27, **Figure 36** or **Figure 37**).

3B. *3-cylinder models with TR carburetor*—Remove the plug (28, **Figure 36**) and gasket

6

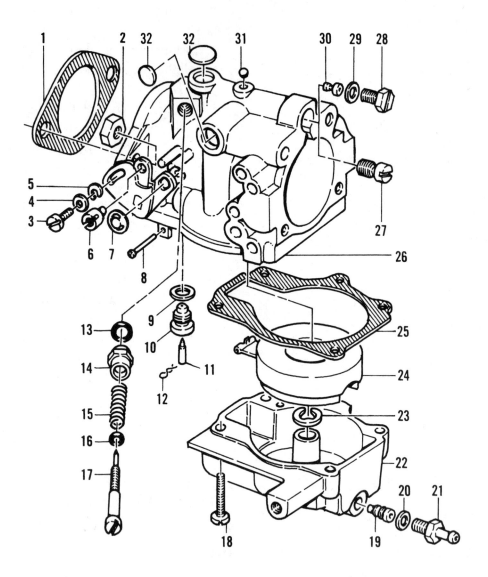

**TR CARBURETOR
(1991 AND 1992 25-70 HP)**

1. Carburetor-to-intake
   manifold gasket
2. Mounting nut
3. Throttle lever screw
4. Washer
5. Lockwasher
6. Linkage retainer
7. Push nut
8. Float pin
9. Gasket
10. Inlet valve seat
11. Inlet valve needle
12. Wire retainer
13. O-ring
14. Mixture screw
    adapter
15. Spring
16. O-ring
17. Slow-speed
    mixture screw
18. Screw
19. High-speed orifice
20. Gasket
21. Fitting
22. Float bowl
23. Nozzle well gasket
24. Float
25. Gasket
26. Carburetor body
27. Intermediate air
    bleed orifice
    (2-cylinder models)
28. Plug
29. Gasket
30. Intermediate fuel orifice
    (3-cylinder models)
31. Lead shot plug
32. Core plug

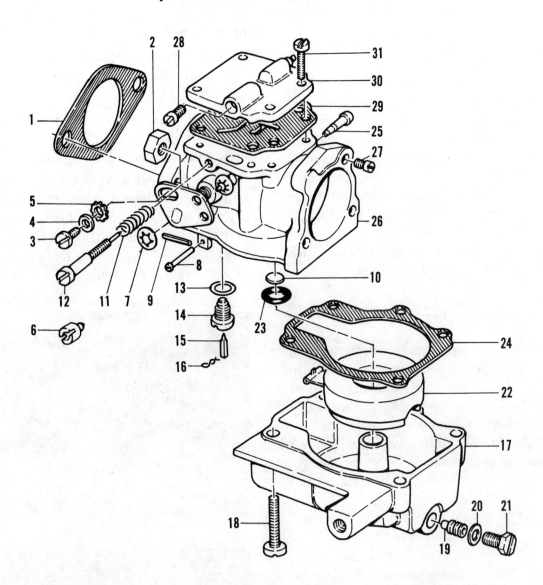

**SV CARBURETOR
(1992-1/2 AND LATER 25-70 HP)**

1. Carburetor-to-intake manifold gasket
2. Mounting nut
3. Throttle lever screw
4. Washer
5. Lockwasher
6. Linkage retainer
7. Push nut
8. Float pin
9. Roll pin
10. Core plug
11. Spring
12. Slow-speed mixture screw
13. Gasket
14. Inlet valve seat
15. Inlet valve needle
16. Wire retainer
17. Float bowl
18. Screw
19. High-speed orifice
20. Gasket
21. Plug
22. Float
23. Nozzle well gasket
24. Gasket
25. Fitting
26. Carburetor body
27. Intermediate air bleed orifice (2-cylinder models)
28. Intermediate air bleed orifice (3-cylinder models)
29. Gasket
30. Body cover
31. Screw

6

(29), then remove the intermediate fuel orifice (30).

3C. *3-cylinder models with SV carburetor*—Remove the intermediate air bleed orifice (28, **Figure 37**).

4. Remove the 4 float bowl screws. Remove the float bowl and gasket (**Figure 38**).

5. Remove the float pin, float and inlet needle valve (**Figure 39**). Remove the inlet valve seat (**Figure 40**) using a wide-blade screwdriver.

6. Remove and discard the nozzle well gasket.

7. Remove the slow-speed mixture screw and spring. On TR carburetors, remove the adapter sleeve and O-ring. Remove the O-ring from the head of the mixture screw. Discard the O-rings.

8. *SV carburetor*—Remove the 4 screws securing the carburetor body top cover. Remove the cover and gasket. Discard the gasket.

Cleaning and Inspection

1. Thoroughly clean all components using a suitable aerosol carburetor cleaner. Use a clean bristle brush to remove accumulated gum or varnish. Dry with compressed air. Thoroughly blow out all orifices, nozzles and passages.

2. Closely inspect the inlet valve needle and seat for grooves, nicks, scratches or other damage. The inlet needle and seat must be replaced as a set.

3. Inspect the float for fuel absorption or deterioration. Replace float as necessary.

4. Inspect the mixture screw for nicks, scratches, grooves or other damage. Replace the screw if any defects are noted.

5. Closely inspect the carburetor body for cracks, stripped threads or other damage.

Reassembly

Refer to **Figure 36** (TR carburetor) and **Figure 37** (SV carburetor) for this procedure. Replace all gaskets, O-rings and sealing washers during reassembly. Compare all new gaskets and other parts to be sure they match the original parts.

1. Place a new gasket on the inlet valve seat. Install the seat and tighten securely using a wide-blade screwdriver.

2. Install the wire retainer on the inlet valve needle. Clip the retainer to the float, then install the float and float pin.

3. Adjust the float level and float drop as described in this chapter.

4. Install a new nozzle well gasket.

5. Clean the float bowl attaching screws using OMC Locquic primer. Allow the primer to air dry then apply OMC Screw Lock to the threads of the screws. Install the float bowl using a new gasket, install the attaching screws and tighten in a crossing pattern to 12-16 in.-lb. (1.3-1.8

N•m) on TR carburetors or 25-35 in.-lb. (2.8-3.9 N•m) on SV carburetors.

6. *SV carburetor*—Install the carburetor body top cover using a new gasket. Tighten the cover attaching screws in a crossing pattern to 15-22 in.-lb. (1.6-2.4 N•m).

7. Install the intermediate orifice.

8. Install the high-speed orifice. Install the plug or fitting (21, **Figure 36** or **Figure 37**) using a new gasket (20).

9. *TR carburetor*—Install the slow-speed mixture screw adapter as follows:

   a. Install a new O-ring on the threaded end of the adapter sleeve.

   b. Lubricate the remaining O-ring using clean engine oil. Install the O-ring into the groove in the head of the mixture screw.

c. Install the adapter sleeve into the carburetor body. Tighten the sleeve to 30-35 in.-lb. (3.4-3.9 N•m).

10. Install the low-speed mixture screw and spring. Slowly turn the screw inward (clockwise) until lightly seated, then back the screw out as follows:

   a. *1 turn out*—1991 and 1992 70 hp.

   b. *1 3/4 turns out*—1991 and 1992 25-30 hp.

   c. *2 turns out*—1992-on 35 Jet, 40-50 hp; 1992 60 hp with remote control.

   d. *2 1/4 turns out*—1991 35 Jet, 40-50 hp; 1992 60 hp with tiller handle.

   e. *2 1/2 turns out*—1991 60 hp; 1993-on 25-30 hp and 48-70 hp.

   f. *2 3/4 turns out*—1991 48-50 hp.

Carburetor Adjustment

Float level

The correct float level is necessary for proper carburetor calibration and operation. If the float level is too low, an excessively lean fuel mixture and/or fuel starvation at high speed can result. If the float level is too high, an excessively rich fuel mixture and/or carburetor flooding can result.

1. Invert the carburetor so the float is facing upward. Allow the weight of the float to close the inlet valve assembly.

2. Referring to **Figure 41**, check the float level as follows:

   a. Place OMC Float Gauge (part No. 324891) with the side marked "25 THRU 75 HP" over the float. Make sure the float gauge is resting on the float bowl gasket surface (gasket not installed).

   b. The top of the float should be located between the notches in the float gauge. Make sure the float gauge is not pushing downward on the float.

   c. If adjustment is necessary, carefully bend the float arm as required to position the float as shown. Do not force the inlet valve nee-

6

dle into the seat. Check the adjustment with the float gauge and readjust as necessary.

Float drop

The correct float drop adjustment is necessary to ensure the inlet valve opens fully. Fuel starvation at high speed can result if the float drop is insufficient. The inlet valve needle can become cocked in its seat and cause severe carburetor flooding if the float drop is excessive.

Refer to **Figure 42** for this procedure.

1. Hold the carburetor in the upright position with the float hanging by its own weight.
2. Measure the distance (D, **Figure 42**) from the float bowl gasket surface (gasket not installed) to the bottom of the float as shown. The distance (D, **Figure 42**) should be 1-1/8 to 1-5/8 in. (28.6-41.3 mm).
3. If adjustment is necessary, carefully bend the float arm tab (T, **Figure 42**) as necessary.

Slow-speed mixture

The outboard motor must be installed in a test tank or mounted on a boat in the water during the following mixture adjustment procedure. Never operate the outboard at wide-open throttle with a flushing device attached.

On 25-50 hp models, adjust the slow-speed mixture as described in the appropriate section in Chapter Five. On 60 and 70 hp models, adjust the slow-speed mixture as follows.

1. Set the slow-speed mixture screw at its initial adjustment as outlined under *Reassembly* in this chapter.
2. Place a reference mark on the carburetor body or adapter sleeve that indicates mixture screw position.
3. On tiller handle models, turn the idle speed adjustment knob on the tiller counterclockwise to the fully SLOW position.

4. Start the motor and warm to normal operating temperature. Shift into FORWARD gear and run the outboard for 3 minutes at idle speed.

   a. If popping and backfiring are noted, the mixture is too lean.

   b. If the engine smokes excessively, runs roughly and stalls, the mixture is too rich.

> *NOTE*
> *Turn the slow-speed mixture screw clockwise to lean the mixture or counterclockwise to richen the fuel mixture.*

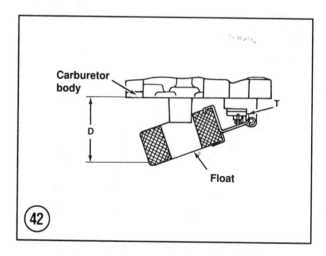

Carburetor body

D

T

Float

42

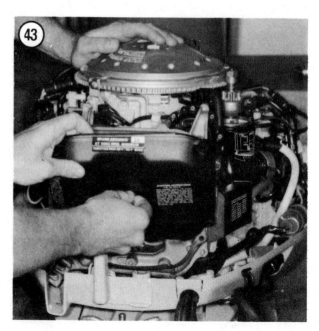

43

5. If adjustment is necessary, turn the mixture screw in 1/12 turn increments as necessary, noting the reference mark made in Step 2. Continue adjusting in 1/12 turn increments until the highest consistent idle speed is noted. Wait 15 seconds between each adjustment to allow the motor to stabilize.

6. Repeat Steps 2-5 as necessary for each remaining carburetor.

7. Run the outboard at wide-open throttle for 3 minutes, then quickly throttle back to idle speed. The motor will idle smoothly if the mixture is correctly set. If the motor is unresponsive to mixture adjustment, make sure the engine is at normal operating temperature, the linkage is properly synchronized and adjusted, the external recirculation system is operating properly and that sufficient exhaust backpressure is present.

> *NOTE*
> *The motor must be in the water or a test tank for sufficient exhaust backpressure to be present. Operating the outboard motor while connected to a flushing device does not provide sufficient backpressure or propeller load for idle mixture to be correctly adjusted.*

Idle speed

On 25-50 hp models, adjust the idle speed as described in the appropriate section in Chapter Five. On 60 and 70 hp models, the idle speed is adjusted by correctly setting the idle timing. See Chapter Five.

TOP FEED CARBURETOR (V4 AND V6 CROSS FLOW MODELS)

Top feed carburetors are used on 65 Jet, 80 Jet, 1.6 Sea Drive, 85, 88, 90, 100 and 115 hp models.

The top feed carburetor is a 2-barrel design with a Minlon (nonmetallic) float bowl. V4 models are equipped with 2 carburetors and V6 models are equipped with 3 carburetors.

Removal/Installation

To prevent accidental starting, disconnect the spark plug wires from the spark plugs.

> *CAUTION*
> *To prevent breakage, do not attempt to pull fuel hoses off the fittings. Always push the hose off using the fingers, a screwdriver or other blunt tool. If pushing the hose will not easily separate the hose and fitting, carefully cut the hose along the side and peel it away from the fitting.*

1. Remove the air silencer cover and gasket. See **Figure 43** (typical, V4 models; V6 is similar). Discard the gasket.

2. Remove the screws securing the air silencer base. See **Figure 44** for V4 models; V6 is similar. Disconnect the air silencer drain hose and remove the base and gasket. Discard the gasket.

3. On V4 models, remove the oil injection pump (VRO) attaching screws without disconnecting oil or fuel hoses. Lay the pump assembly aside.

4. Disconnect the throttle linkage between the carburetors.

5. Remove the carburetor mounting screws.

6. Cut the tie strap clamps from the fuel delivery and primer hoses. Disconnect the primer hoses from the carburetor fittings, then remove the carburetors. Remove and discard the carburetor-to-intake manifold gaskets.

NOTE
Do not apply gasket sealant to the carburetor-to-intake manifold gaskets.

7. To install the carburetors, first install new carburetor-to-intake manifold gaskets. Be sure the gaskets are provided with a hole for the fuel primer fitting.

8. Install the fuel delivery and primer hoses. Clamp the hoses securely using new tie straps.

9. Install the carburetors and mounting screws. Tighten the screws securely.

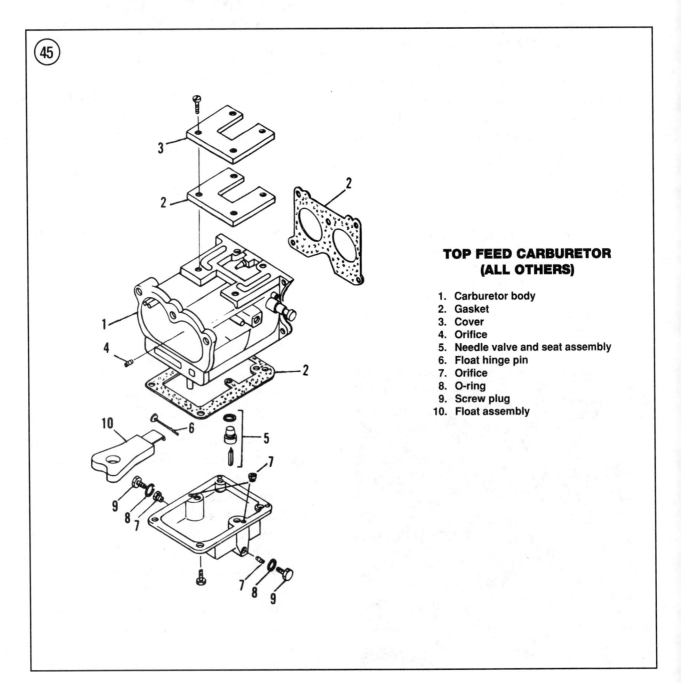

TOP FEED CARBURETOR (ALL OTHERS)

1. Carburetor body
2. Gasket
3. Cover
4. Orifice
5. Needle valve and seat assembly
6. Float hinge pin
7. Orifice
8. O-ring
9. Screw plug
10. Float assembly

10. Install the throttle linkage to the carburetors. Perform synchronization and linkage adjustment as outlined in Chapter Five.

11. *V4 models*—Install the oil injection pump (VRO) assembly to the air silencer base, if removed. Tighten the pump mounting screws to 18-24 in.-lb. (2.0-2.7 N.m).

12. Connect the air silencer drain hose to the air silencer base. Install the air silencer base using a new gasket. Apply OMC Screw Lock to the threads of the base mounting screws. Install the screws and tighten to 35-60 in.-lb. (4.0-6.8 N.m).

13. Pressurize the fuel system using the primer bulb to check for fuel leaks. Repair any fuel leakage as necessary before proceeding.

14. Install the air silencer cover using a new gasket. Tighten the cover screws securely.

Disassembly

Refer to **Figure 45** for this procedure.

1. Invert the carburetor and drain any fuel remaining in the float bowl into a suitable container.

2. Remove the drain plugs and O-rings from the float bowl. Remove and discard the O-rings.

3. Using OMC Orifice Driver (part No. 317002), remove the high-speed orifices. Note the number stamped in each orifice for reference during reassembly. **Figure 46** shows both float bowl drain plugs and high-speed orifices removed.

4. Remove the idle air bleed orifices (**Figure 47**). Note the number stamped in each orifice for reference during reassembly.

5. Remove the 4 float bowl attaching screws. Remove the float bowl and gasket (**Figure 48**). Discard the gasket.

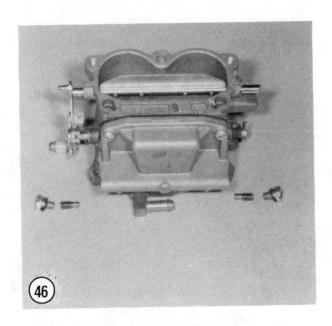

46

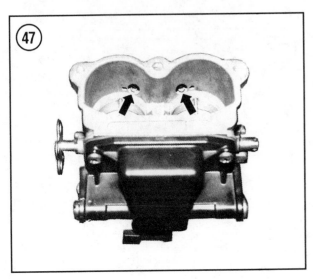

47

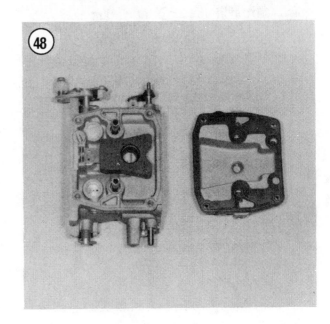

48

6. Remove the float pin, float and inlet valve needle (**Figure 49**).

7. Remove the inlet valve seat using a wide-blade screwdriver (**Figure 50**). Remove and discard the seat gasket.

8. Remove the intermediate fuel orifices (**Figure 51**) using OMC Orifice Driver (part No. 317002). Note the number stamped in the orifices for reference during reassembly.

9. Remove the idle chamber cover (**Figure 52**) and gasket. Discard the gasket.

Cleaning and Inspection

1. Thoroughly clean all components using a suitable aerosol carburetor cleaner. Use a clean bristle brush to remove accumulated gum or varnish. Dry with compressed air. Thoroughly blow out all orifices, nozzles and passages.

2. Closely inspect the inlet valve needle and seat for grooves, nicks, scratches or other damage. The inlet needle and seat must be replaced as a set.

3. Inspect the float for fuel absorption or deterioration. Replace float as necessary.

4. Closely inspect the carburetor body for cracks, stripped threads or other damage.

5. Invert the carburetor and fill the idle circuit with isopropyl alcohol. Check for leakage between the emulsion pickup tubes and the carburetor body. If alcohol leakage is noted, dry the area with compressed air and apply a drop of OMC Ultra Lock at the arrows.

Reassembly

Refer to **Figure 45** for this procedure. Replace all gaskets, O-rings and sealing washers during

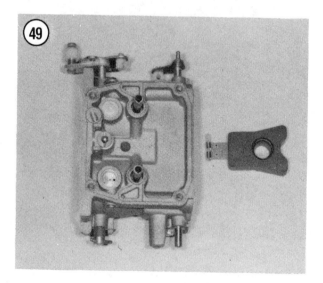

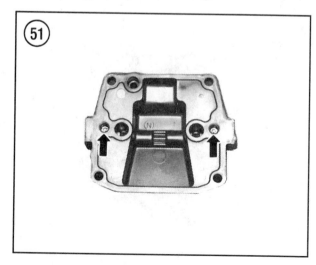

reassembly. Compare all new gaskets and other parts to be sure they match the original parts.

NOTE
After a period of time, the idle chamber cover gasket can be sucked down into the L-shaped idle passage in the carburetor body, restricting idle fuel flow. To prevent this from occurring, carefully cut out a L-shaped portion of the gasket corresponding to the idle passage in the body.

1. Install the idle chamber cover using a new gasket. Tighten the 4 screws securely.

2. Install the inlet valve seat using a new gasket. Tighten the seat securely using a wide-blade screwdriver.

3. Install the inlet valve needle, float and float pin.

4. Adjust float level and float drop as described in this chapter.

5. Install the intermediate fuel orifices into the float bowl. Securely tighten the orifices using OMC Orifice Driver (part No. 317002).

6. Install the float bowl using a new gasket. Apply OMC Screw Lock to the threads of the 4 float bowl screws. Install the screws and tighten in a crossing pattern to 24-36 in.-lb. (2.7-4.1 N•m).

7. Install the idle air bleed orifices. Tighten the orifices securely.

8. Install the high-speed orifices. Tighten the orifices securely.

9. Install the float bowl drain plugs with new O-rings. Tighten the plugs securely.

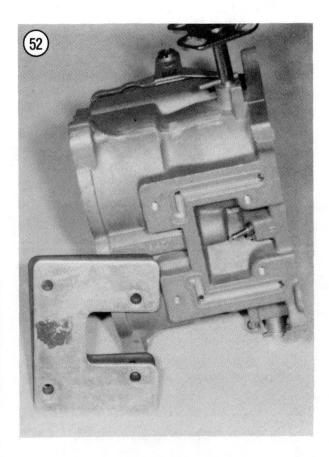

Carburetor Adjustment

Float level

The correct float level is necessary for proper carburetor calibration and operation. If the float level is too low, an excessively lean fuel mixture and/or fuel starvation at high speed can result. If the float level is too high, an excessively rich fuel mixture and/or carburetor flooding can result.

1. Invert the carburetor body with its float bowl gasket surface horizontal.

2. Place float gauge (part No. 324891) on the gasket surface and hold it next to the float (**Fig-**

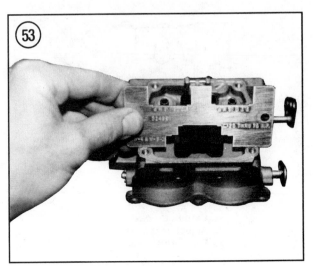

ure 53). Do not allow the gauge to push down on the float.

3. If the top of the float is not between the gauge notches (**Figure 53**), carefully bend the metal float arm as necessary to position the float as specified. Do not force the inlet needle valve into the seat.

Float drop

The correct float drop adjustment is necessary to ensure the inlet valve opens fully. Fuel starvation at high speed can result if the float drop is insufficient. The inlet valve needle can become cocked in its seat and cause severe carburetor flooding if the float drop is excessive.

1. Hold the carburetor in the upright position, with the float hanging by its own weight.

2. Measure the distance between the carburetor body and the bottom of the float as shown in **Figure 54**.

3. The float drop should be 7/8 to 1-1/8 in. (22-28 mm).

4. If adjustment is necessary, carefully bend the adjustment tang as necessary.

Idle speed

Refer to the appropriate section in Chapter Five for idle speed adjustment procedures.

Fuel mixture

Idle, off idle and high-speed fuel mixtures are controlled by fixed orifices and under normal circumstances, should not require additional adjustment. See *High Elevation Modification* in this chapter. Make certain that all other systems are functioning properly *before* rejetting the carburetors to correct a performance problem.

MINLON CARBURETORS (V4 AND V6 LOOP CHARGED MODELS)

Minlon carburetors are used on 2.0 Sea Drive, 120 and 140 hp (V4 models), 3.0 and 4.0 Sea Drive, 200, 225 hp, 60° 150 and 175 (V6 models), 250 and 300 hp (V8 models).

On V4 models, two 2-barrel type carburetors are used. Each carburetor assembly has a common throttle body (A, **Figure 55**) with separate main body assemblies (B).

On V6 models (except 60° V6 models), two 2-barrel and two 1-barrel carburetors are used. The 2-barrel carburetors (upper) share a common throttle body with separate main body assemblies. The 1-barrel carburetors (lower) each consist of 1 main body and 1 throttle body.

On 60° V6 models, each carburetor assembly consists of 6 main body assemblies which share a common throttle body.

On V8 models, four 2-barrel type carburetors are used. Each carburetor assembly consists of a common throttle body assembly (A, **Figure 55**) with separate main body assemblies (B).

Each main body assembly is equipped with its own float, inlet valve and fuel metering circuits.

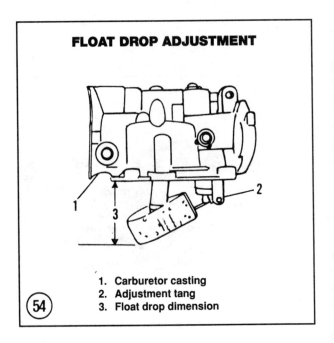

FLOAT DROP ADJUSTMENT

54

1. **Carburetor casting**
2. **Adjustment tang**
3. **Float drop dimension**

The idle mixture is controlled by the idle air bleed orifice (D, **Figure 55**). Some late models may be equipped with a slow-speed mixture screw in addition to the idle air bleed orifice. Intermediate (off idle) fuel mixture is controlled by the intermediate air bleed orifice (C, **Figure 55**). High-speed mixture is controlled by the high-speed fuel orifice behind the float bowl plugs (E, **Figure 55**). Carburetor calibration can be changed without removing the carburetors or main body assemblies from the power head.

The carburetor main body assemblies are constructed of a nonmetallic Minlon material. Care must be used when working with the main body assembly. *Do not* overtighten any screws that thread into the main body. Tighten each screw in small increments in a crossing pattern to prevent damage to the carburetor body.

The main bodies on each carburetor can be removed individually for service or cleaning without disconnecting the throttle linkage or re-moving the throttle body. When overhauling the power head, the carburetors are removed as assemblies. Because of their special construction, observe the cleaning and inspection procedures and tightening sequence and values.

Main Body Removal/Installation (All Models Except 60° V6 Models [150 and 175 hp])

> *CAUTION*
> *To prevent breakage, do not attempt to pull fuel hoses off plastic or Minlon fittings. Always push the hose off using the fingers, a screwdriver or other blunt tool. If pushing the hose will not easily separate the hose and fitting, carefully cut the hose along the side and peel it away from the fitting.*

1. Remove the power steering hose support bracket, if so equipped.

2. Loosen the screws holding the port and starboard lower engine covers. Remove the covers.

3. Remove the air silencer assembly.

4. Remove the 4 mounting screws holding the main body to the throttle body.

5. Remove the main body assembly. Remove and discard the carburetor body O-ring seal.

6. Cut the tie strap(s) and disconnect the fuel inlet hose(s) at the carburetor(s).

7. Use a new main body-to-throttle body O-ring seal during reinstallation.

8. Place the carburetor main body in position and reconnect the fuel hose(s). Clamp the hose(s) with new tie straps.

9. Install the main body and 4 mounting screws. Tighten the screws in a crossing pattern to 45-55 in.-lb. (5.1-6.2 N•m).

10. Check the fuel delivery system for leakage by squeezing the primer bulb. Repair any fuel leakage noted.

11. Perform synchronization and linkage adjustment as outlined in Chapter Five.

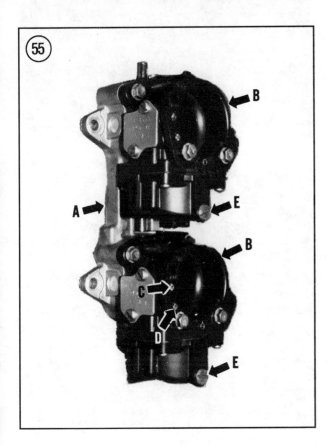

12. Install the air silencer using a new gasket. Tighten the silencer mounting screws to 60-84 in.-lb. (6.8-9.5 N·m).

13. Install the power steering support bracket (if so equipped) and lower motor covers.

Main Body Removal/Installation (60° V6 Models)

> *CAUTION*
> *To prevent breakage, do not attempt to pull fuel hoses off plastic or Minlon fittings. Always push the hose off using the fingers, a screwdriver or other blunt tool. If pushing the hose will not easily separate the hose and fitting, carefully cut the hose along the side and peel it away from the fitting.*

1. Disconnect the air silencer retaining straps (**Figure 56**) and remove the silencer assembly.

2. Cut the tie strap clamp securing the main fuel delivery hoses (A, **Figure 57**) to the carburetor fuel manifolds (B). Push the hoses off the fittings.

3. Disconnect the balance hoses (C, **Figure 57**) from the balance tube manifolds (D).

4. Disconnect the fuel primer hoses (E, **Figure 57**) from the intake manifold.

5. If removal of the top carburetor on the port side is necessary, cut the tie strap holding the trim/tilt relays bracket to the carburetor.

6. Remove the screws securing the carburetor main body to the throttle body (**Figure 58**). If all main body assemblies are to be removed, remove the top carburetor first, then install a suitable screw in the throttle body to hold the throttle body assembly and gasket to the intake manifold. Remove and discard the main body-to-throttle body O-ring seal.

7. Use a new carburetor main body-to-throttle body O-ring seal during installation.

8. Attach the main body to the throttle body. Make certain the O-ring seal is in position, then install the mounting screws and tighten in a crossing pattern to 45-55 in.-lb. (5.1-6.2 N·m).

9. Complete the remaining installation by reversing the removal procedure. Securely clamp fuel hoses using new tie straps.

10. Perform synchronization and linkage adjustment as outlined in Chapter Five.

Carburetor Assembly Removal/Installation (All Models Except 60° V6 Models)

> *CAUTION*
> *To prevent breakage, do not attempt to pull fuel hoses off plastic or Minlon fit-*

tings. Always push the hose off using the fingers, a screwdriver or other blunt tool. If pushing the hose will not easily separate the hose and fitting, carefully cut the hose along the side and peel it away from the fitting.

1. Remove the power steering hose support bracket, if so equipped.

2. Loosen the retaining screws holding the port and starboard lower motor covers. Remove the covers.

3. Remove the air silencer cover.

4. Cut the tie strap holding the main body fuel delivery hose. Carefully disconnect the hose to prevent damaging the fitting.

5. Loosen the throttle shaft link at one or both ends.

6. Cut the tie strap(s) and disconnect the fuel delivery hose at the carburetors.

7. Cut the primer hose tie strap and disconnect the hose from the fuel manifold.

8. Cut the oil injection (VRO) pump outlet tie strap and disconnect the hose.

9. Note the primer hose routing over the top of the carburetors, then remove the hoses from the intake manifold fittings.

10. Remove the 2 nuts and 2 screws for each carburetor assembly to be removed.

11. Remove the carburetor assembly from the intake manifold, slowly drawing the fuel supply hose through the intake manifold grommet.

12. Remove and discard the carburetor flange gaskets.

13. Use new gaskets (without sealant) during installation.

14. Connect all fuel hoses and clamp with new tie straps.

15. Place the carburetor assembly in position and engage the throttle shaft connector links.

16. Install 2 nuts and 2 screws at each carburetor assembly. Tighten the fasteners in a crossing pattern to 120-144 in.-lb. (13.6-16.3 N•m).

17. Pressurize the fuel system by squeezing the primer bulb (except V8 models) or activating the electric fuel primer pump (V8 models) to check for leakage. Repair any fuel leakage prior to returning the unit to service.

18. Perform synchronization and linkage adjustment as outlined in Chapter Five.

19. Install the air silencer using a new gasket. Tighten the silencer screws to 60-84 in.-lb. (6.8-9.5 N•m).

20. Complete the remaining installation by reversing the removal procedure.

Carburetor Assembly Removal/Installation (60° V6 Models)

CAUTION
To prevent breakage, do not attempt to pull fuel hoses off plastic or Minlon fittings. Always push the hose off using the fingers, a screwdriver or other blunt tool. If pushing the hose will not easily separate the hose and fitting, carefully cut the hose along the side and peel it away from the fitting.

1. Disconnect the air silencer retaining straps (**Figure 56**) and remove the silencer assembly.

(58)

6

2. Cut the tie strap clamp securing the main fuel delivery hoses (A, **Figure 57**) to the carburetor fuel manifolds (B). Push the hoses off the fittings.

3. Disconnect the balance hoses (C, **Figure 57**) from the balance tube manifolds (D).

4. Disconnect the fuel primer hoses (E, **Figure 57**) from the intake manifold.

5. Cut the tie strap holding the trim/tilt relays bracket to the upper port carburetor. Place the bracket and relays aside.

6. Remove the carburetor link screw from the upper port carburetor. See **Figure 59**.

7. Remove 8 screws securing the carburetor assemblies. Remove the carburetor/throttle body assemblies from the intake manifold.

8. Remove and discard the throttle body-to-intake manifold ring seals.

9. Install a new throttle body-to-intake manifold O-ring seal onto the intake manifold.

10. Install the carburetor assemblies on the intake manifold, then install the 8 mounting screws. Tighten the screws in a crossing pattern to 45-55 in.-lb. (5.1-6.2 N•m).

11. Install the carburetor link screw (**Figure 59**) finger tight.

12. Install the fuel primer hose (E, **Figure 57**) to the intake manifold.

13. Install the balance hose (C, **Figure 57**) to the balance manifold (D).

14. Install the main fuel delivery hose (A, **Figure 57**) to the carburetor fuel manifold (B) and clamp using a new tie strap.

15. Pressurize the fuel system by squeezing the primer bulb to check for leakage. Repair any fuel leakage prior to returning the unit to service.

16. Perform synchronization and linkage adjustment as outlined in Chapter Five.

17. Complete the remaining installation by reversing the removal procedure.

Disassembly

Keep all components from each carburetor separate from each other during disassembly.

Refer to **Figure 60** (except 60° V6 models) or **Figure 61** (60° V6 models).

1. Remove the main body attaching screws. Separate the main body assembly from the throttle body. Remove and discard the main body-to-throttle body O-ring seal.

2. Remove the float bowl screws. Separate the float bowl from the main body. Remove and discard the float bowl gasket.

3. Remove the float pin anchor screw. See A, **Figure 62** (except 60° V6 models) or A, **Figure 63** (60° V6 models). Remove the float, float pin and inlet valve needle. Remove and discard the nozzle well gasket on 60° V6 models.

4. Remove the inlet valve seat using a wide-blade screwdriver. Remove and discard the gasket.

5. Remove the high-speed orifice plug from the float bowl.

6. Remove the high-speed fuel orifice using OMC Orifice Driver (part No. 317002). See B, **Figure 62**.

7. Remove the side cover and gasket. Discard the gasket.

8. Remove the idle and intermediate air bleed orifices using OMC Orifice Driver (part No. 317002). See **Figure 64**. Remove the slow-speed mixture screw and spring on models so equipped. See 36 and 37, **Figure 60**.

CARBURETOR MAIN BODY/THROTTLE BODY ASSEMBLY
(V4 AND V6 LOOP CHARGED MODELS EXCEPT 60° V6)

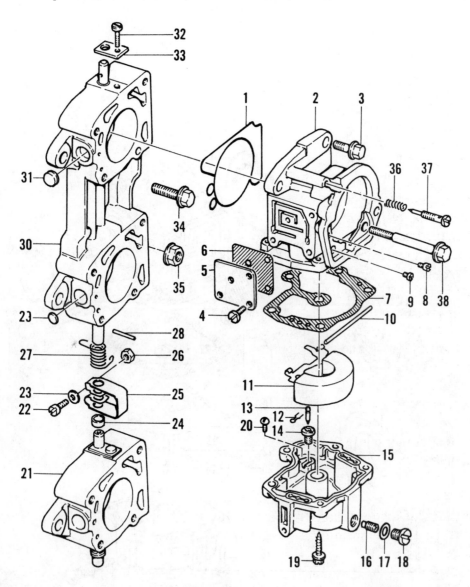

6

1. O-ring seal
2. Main body
3. Screw
4. Screw
5. Side cover
6. Side cover gasket
7. Float bowl gasket
8. Intermediate air bleed orifice
9. Idle air bleed orifice
10. Float pin
11. Float
12. Spring clip
13. Inlet valve needle

14. Inlet valve seat
15. Float bowl
16. High-speed fuel orifice
17. O-ring
18. Plug
19. Screw
20. Float pin anchor screw
21. Lower throttle
    body assembly
22. Screw
23. Washer
24. Sleeve
25. Throttle shaft connector

26. Nut
27. Throttle return spring
28. Roll pin
29. Core plug
30. Upper throttle body assembly
31. Core plug
32. Screw
33. Clip
34. Screw
35. Nut
36. Spring (some models)
37. Slow-speed mixture screw
    (some models)

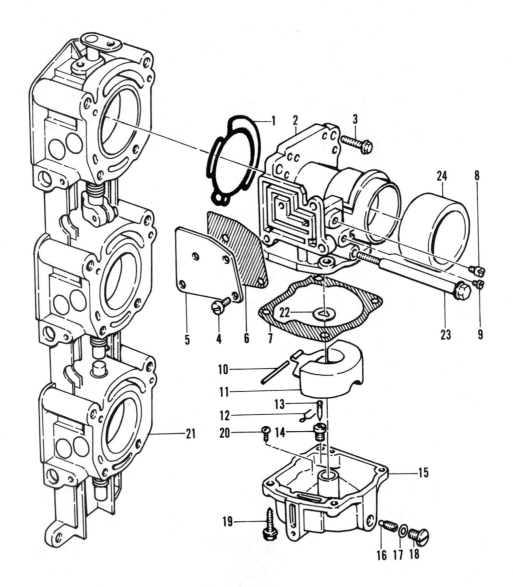

**CARBURETOR/THROTTLE BODY ASSEMBLY
(60° V6 MODELS)**

1. O-ring seal
2. Main body
3. Screw
4. Screw
5. Side cover
6. Side cover gasket
7. Float bowl gasket
8. Intermediate air bleed orifice

9. Idle air bleed orifice
10. Float pin
11. Float
12. Spring clip
13. Inlet valve needle
14. Inlet valve seat
15. Float bowl

16. High-speed fuel orifice
17. O-ring
18. Plug
19. Screw
20. Float pin anchor screw
21. Throttle body assembly
22. Nozzle well gasket

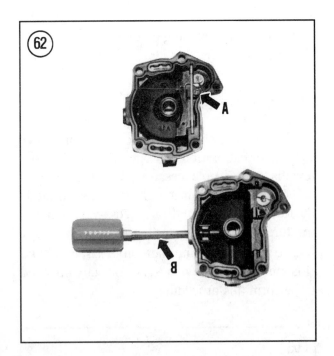

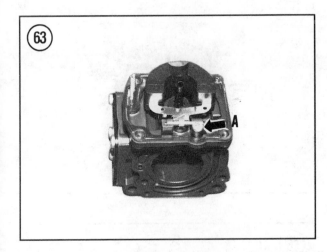

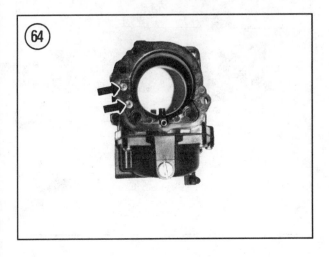

Cleaning and Inspection

1. Clean all components using a mild aerosol solvent. Do not submerge carburetor components in a hot tank or strong automotive carburetor cleaner.

2. Flush all holes and passages with a syringe containing isopropyl alcohol. Blow all holes and passages dry with compressed air. For best results, direct the compressed air in the opposite direction to the normal flow of fuel or air.

3. Inspect the inlet valve needle and seat for distortion, excessive wear or other damage. Replace the needle and seat as an assembly if any defects are noted.

4. Inspect the throttle body assembly and shaft for excessive wear or other damage. Make certain the throttle valve retaining screws are tight and that the valves seat properly in the throttle body casting. Maximum allowable clearance between the edge of the throttle valves and the throttle body casting is 0.002 in. (0.05 mm).

5. Make sure all gasket mating surfaces are smooth and flat.

Assembly

Refer to **Figure 60** (except 60° V6 models) or **Figure 61** (60° V6 models) as necessary during this procedure. Replace all gaskets, seals and O-rings. During assembly, compare all new gaskets to the old ones to make sure all holes are properly punched.

1. If removed, install new core plugs in the throttle body. Position the plugs with their convex side facing up, then seat firmly using a suitable flat punch. Seal the area around the rim of the plug with Gasoila sealant or fingernail polish. See *Core Plug and Lead Shot* in this chapter.

2. On models so equipped, install the slow-speed mixture screw and spring. Turn the screw clockwise until lightly seated, then back out 2 full turns.

3. Install the idle and intermediate air bleed orifices using OMC Orifice Driver (part No. 317002). Tighten the orifices securely.

4. Install the main body side cover using a new gasket. Tighten the cover screws to 18-24 in.-lb. (2.0-2.7 N·m).

5. Install a new float bowl gasket on the main body. On 60° V6 models, install a new nozzle well gasket.

6. Install the inlet valve seat using a new gasket.

7A. *Except 60° V6 models*—Attach the spring clip to the inlet valve needle, then attach the clip to the float. The clip must face toward the port side of the float bowl. Insert the float pin into the float arm, then install the float, inlet valve needle and float pin into the float bowl as an assembly. Install the float pin anchor screw and tighten securely.

7B. *60° V6 models*—Attach the spring clip to the inlet valve needle then attach the clip to the float arm. Insert the float pin into the float arm, then install the float, inlet valve needle and float pin on the main body as an assembly. Install the float pin anchor screw and tighten securely.

8. Adjust the float level as outlined in this chapter.

9. Install the high-speed fuel orifice into the float bowl using OMC Orifice Driver (part No. 317002). Tighten the orifice securely, then install the float bowl plug using a new O-ring. Tighten the plug to 30-35 in.-lb. (3.4-4.0 N·m)

10. Install the float bowl and retaining screws on the main body. Make sure the screws engage their original threads in the main body.

11A. *Except 60° V6*—Tighten the float bowl screws to 18-24 in.-lb. (2.0-2.7 N·m) in the sequence shown in **Figure 65**.

11B. *60° V6 models*—Tighten the float bowl screws in a crossing pattern to 18-24 in.-lb. (2.0-2.7 N·m).

12. Install a new O-ring seal between the main body and throttle body. Install the main body on the throttle body making sure the O-ring seal is properly located. Install the main body screws

and tighten in a crossing pattern to 45-55 in.-lb. (5.1-6.2 N·m).

Float Adjustment

The correct float level is necessary for proper carburetor calibration and operation. If the float level is too low, an excessively lean fuel mixture and/or fuel starvation at high speed can result. If the float level is too high, an excessively rich fuel mixture and/or carburetor flooding can result.

The float, float pin, inlet valve assembly and float pin anchor screw must be correctly installed to perform this procedure.

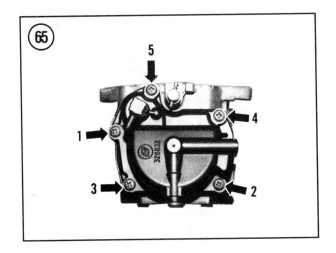

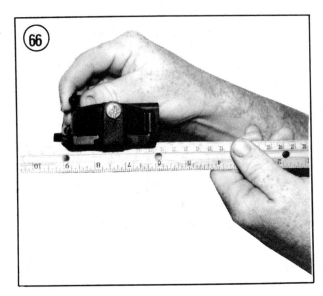

All models except 60° V6 models

1. Invert the float bowl so its gasket mating surface is horizontal.

2. Place a suitable straightedge against the float bowl mating surface as shown in **Figure 66**.

3. The float should be level with the float bowl mating surface to within 1/32 in. (0.8 mm). If adjustment is necessary, carefully bend the float arm as necessary. Do not force the inlet valve needle into the seat.

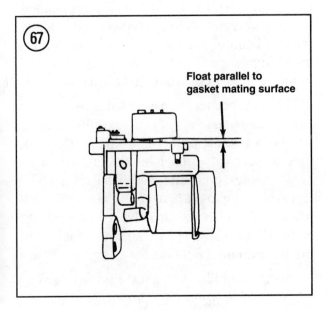

Float parallel to gasket mating surface

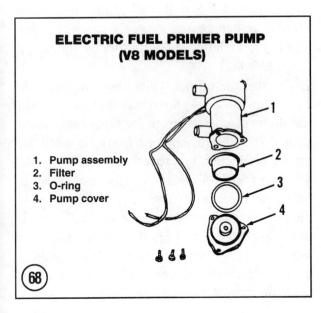

ELECTRIC FUEL PRIMER PUMP (V8 MODELS)

1. Pump assembly
2. Filter
3. O-ring
4. Pump cover

60° V6 models

1. Invert the carburetor so the float bowl gasket surface is horizontal and facing upward.

2. The float should be parallel with the float bowl mating surface to within 1/32 in. (0.8 mm). See **Figure 67**.

3. If adjustment is necessary, carefully bend the float arm as necessary. Do not force the inlet needle into the seat.

4. Next, hold the carburetor upright. Measure the distance between the float bowl mating surface and the bottom of the float. The distance should be 11/16 to 1-1/8 in. (17-28 mm). If not, carefully bend the tang on the float arm as necessary to obtain the specified float drop.

Idle Speed

The idle speed is adjusted by correctly setting the idle timing. Refer to the appropriate section in Chapter Five.

Fuel Mixture

Idle, off idle and high-speed fuel mixtures are controlled by fixed orifices and under normal circumstances should not require additional adjustment. See to *High Elevation Modification* in this chapter. Make certain that all other systems are functioning properly *before* rejetting the carburetors to correct a performance problem.

ELECTRIC FUEL PRIMER PUMP (V8 MODELS)

V8 models are equipped with an electric fuel primer pump. When actuated by a spring-loaded toggle switch, the primer pump pressurizes the fuel delivery system.

6

NOTE
Do not use a fuel line primer bulb on V8 models equipped with an electric fuel primer pump.

Refer to **Figure 68** and proceed as follows to determine if the pump is functioning properly.

1. Disconnect the primer pump outlet hose (top) from the pump. Plug the hose to prevent leakage.
2. Install a suitable 0-15 psi (0-103 kPa) fuel pressure gauge to the pump outlet fitting. Securely clamp the gauge to the fitting.

NOTE
The electric primer pump circuit is protected by an inline 5 amp fuse located near the pump switch. If the pump does not operate when activated, check the fuse first.

3. Turn the key switch to the ON position. Momentarily actuate the pump with the toggle switch and note the pressure gauge. The pump should be capable of delivering a minimum of 4.5 psi (31 kPa) fuel pressure. If not, first make sure the battery is in acceptable condition and fully charged. If output pressure is still not as specified, replace the primer pump assembly.

Electric Primer Pump Filter Service

Use the following procedure to clean, inspect or replace the electric fuel primer pump filter. See **Figure 68**.

1. Disconnect all fuel hoses and pipe fittings from the pump assembly. Remove the pump from its mounting bracket.
2. Remove the pump bracket then carefully pry both metal end caps from the pump.
3. Remove the 3 cover screws, then remove the cover, O-ring and filter. Clean the filter using mild solvent then dry with compressed air. Replace the filter if excessively contaminated.
4. Install a new cover O-ring during reassembly. Tighten the 3 cover screws to 60-84 in.-lb. (6.8-

9.5 N•m). Complete remaining assembly by reversing the disassembly procedure.
5. After assembly and installation, pressurize the fuel system by actuating the pump to check for leakage. Repair any fuel leaks prior to returning the unit to service.

MANUAL FUEL PRIMER

A plunger-type fuel primer valve is used on 20-50 hp models equipped with rope start or electric start with a tiller handle. When operated, the primer valve delivers fuel into the intake manifold through a fitting near the carburetor mounting flange. This fuel provides mixture enrichment to ease cold starts and engine warm up.

When the primer knob is pulled, a check valve in the plunger assembly opens and allows fuel to be drawn into the primer housing. At the same time, a check valve under the outlet fitting (small nipple) closes, preventing fuel in the primer hose from returning to the housing. When the knob is pushed, the inlet check valve closes and the outlet check valve opens, allowing fuel to be discharged into the primer hose.

Proceed as follows to test the primer valve.

1. Disconnect the primer outlet hose at the carburetor fitting. Place the end of the hose into a suitable container.
2. Fill the carburetor(s) with fuel by squeezing the primer bulb.
3. Operate the primer while observing the disconnected hose. Approximately 1 cc of fuel should be discharged from the primer with each stroke. If fuel is discharged from the hose, the primer is functioning properly.
4. If no fuel is discharged, remove the primer hose from the primer valve outlet fitting. Operate the primer while observing the fitting. If fuel is now discharged, inspect the primer hose for kinks, plugging or restrictions. If the hose is in acceptable condition, remove and repair or replace the primer valve assembly.

Primer Valve Removal/Installation

1. Cut the tie strap clamps securing the inlet and outlet fuel hoses to the primer valve. Disconnect the hoses from the primer by pushing instead of pulling. If the hoses do not separate easily from the primer, carefully cut the hose along the side and peel it away from the fitting.

2. Remove the screw (13, **Figure 69**) securing the primer knob, then remove the knob. Remove the nut (11, **Figure 69**) to complete removal.

3. Install the primer valve by reversing the removal procedure. Tighten the mounting nut securely. Clamp all fuel hoses using new tie straps.

Primer Valve Disassembly/Assembly

1. Remove the retainer (4, **Figure 69**) from the valve using needlenose pliers.

2. Pull the plunger assembly (5, **Figure 69**) from the housing (1).

3. Remove and discard the plunger O-rings.

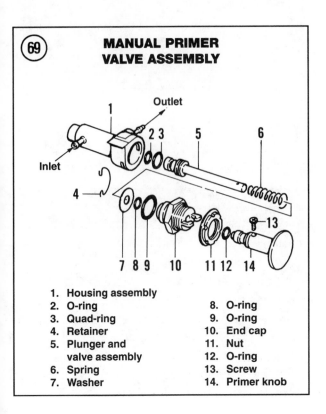

MANUAL PRIMER VALVE ASSEMBLY

Outlet

Inlet

1. Housing assembly
2. O-ring
3. Quad-ring
4. Retainer
5. Plunger and valve assembly
6. Spring
7. Washer
8. O-ring
9. O-ring
10. End cap
11. Nut
12. O-ring
13. Screw
14. Primer knob

NOTE
The primer O-rings are made of a special material to prevent deterioration and leakage. Be sure to install the correct O-rings during reassembly.

4. Install new O-rings and Quad-ring on the plunger shaft.

5. Place the spring and washer on the plunger shaft.

6. Install a new O-ring into the end cap and slide the end cap onto the plunger shaft.

7. Insert the plunger shaft into the primer housing. Then, push the end cap into the housing and install the retainer.

Inspection

1. Inspect the plunger shaft for nicks, scratches or other damage. Remove small scratches using crocus cloth. Replace the plunger if deep scratches, nicks or burrs are noted.

2. To check the primer outlet fitting check valve, connect a suitable squeeze bottle to the outlet fitting (small nipple) with a clear plastic hose. Fill the squeeze bottle with isopropyl alcohol. Squeeze the bottle while observing the primer housing.

   a. If alcohol enters the housing in a steady stream, the check valve is defective. Replace the primer housing assembly.

   b. If the check valve blocks the flow of alcohol (a few drops are acceptable), the check valve is functioning properly.

3. Next, connect the squeeze bottle to the primer inlet fitting (large nipple).

NOTE
*O-ring (2, **Figure 69**) and Quad-ring (3) must be installed on the plunger to test the inlet check valve in Step 4.*

4. While holding the plunger in the housing, squeeze the bottle of alcohol. Alcohol should flow freely from the primer outlet fitting. If not,

the inlet check valve is defective. Replace the plunger assembly.

ELECTRIC FUEL PRIMER SOLENOID

An electric fuel primer solenoid is used on all electric start models with remote control. The solenoid is actuated by pushing the key switch IN and diverts fuel directly to the intake manifolds to provide mixture enrichment to ease cold starting.

Proceed as follows to determine if the primer is functioning properly.

1. Start the motor and warm it to normal operating temperature.

2. While the outboard is running at fast idle, push the key IN.

3. The engine speed should drop approximately 1000 rpm and the engine should run roughly, indicating that mixture enrichment has occurred.

4. If not, check primer hoses for kinks, plugging or restrictions. Check primer fittings for plugging or restrictions. If the hoses and fittings are in acceptable condition, test the solenoid as outlined in this chapter.

Primer Solenoid Removal/Installation

Figure 70 shows a typical primer solenoid installation (except 60° V6 models). The primer solenoid used on 60° V6 models is shown at A, **Figure 71**.

1A. *Except 60° V6 models*—Disconnect the solenoid purple/white wire at the terminal board or bullet connector.

1B. *60° V6 models*—Disconnect the purple/white and black wires at their bullet connectors.

2A. *Except 60° V6 models*—Remove the screws securing the solenoid bracket. Carefully disconnect the 3 fuel hoses and remove the solenoid.

2B. *60° V6 models*—Remove the 2 screws securing the primer solenoid to the fuel component

bracket. Carefully disconnect the 2 fuel hoses and remove the solenoid.

3. Installation is the reverse of removal.

   a. *Except 60° V6 models*—Install the 3 fuel hoses and clamp the large hose with a new tie strap. Be sure to reinstall the ground wire under the mounting clamp.

   b. *60° V6 models*—Connect the 2 fuel hoses to the primer solenoid. Tighten the solenoid mounting screws to 18-24 in.-lb. (2.0-2.7 N•m) and reconnect the solenoid wires at their bullet connectors.

Primer Solenoid Test

The solenoid plunger must be free of dirt, corrosion or any contamination that might prevent it from moving freely.

Connect an ohmmeter between the purple/white wire and the black ground wire. Primer solenoid resistance should be 4-7 ohms. If not, replace the solenoid.

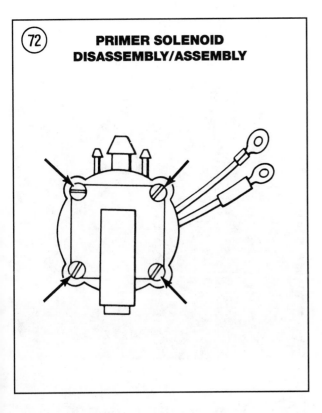

Primer Solenoid Disassembly/Assembly

1. Remove the cover screws (**Figure 72**). Remove the cover and gasket. Discard the gasket.
2. Remove the valve seat, filter, valve, plunger and both springs. See **Figure 73**.
3. Clean or replace the filter as necessary.
4. Clean the plunger to remove any contamination or corrosion.
5. Assembly is the reverse of disassembly. Install a new valve seat and use a new cover gasket.

Vacuum Switch

V6 and V8 loop charged models are equipped with a vacuum sensitive switch designed to activate the warning horn should a restriction in the boat's fuel system occur. See B, **Figure 71** (60° V6 models) or **Figure 74** (V6 [except 60° V6] and V8 models) for typical vacuum switch installations.

Proceed as follows to determine if the vacuum switch is functioning properly. Make sure the battery and all other electrical circuits are connected.

6

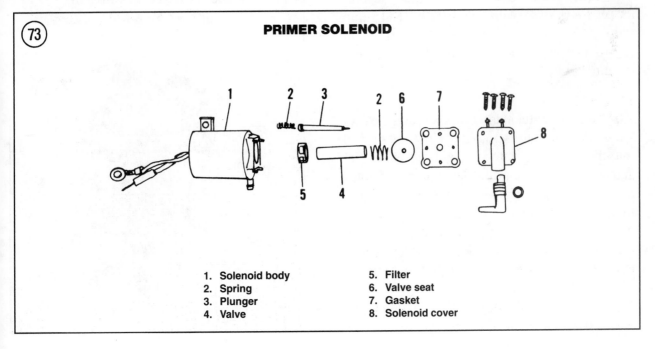

PRIMER SOLENOID

1. Solenoid body
2. Spring
3. Plunger
4. Valve
5. Filter
6. Valve seat
7. Gasket
8. Solenoid cover

1. Remove the vacuum switch hose from the fuel manifold (except 60° V6 models) or the vapor separator assembly (60° V6 models).

2. Connect a suitable vacuum pump to the hose. A gearcase vacuum tester works well for this test.

3. Turn the key switch to the ON position.

4. Slowly draw a vacuum on the switch. The warning horn should sound continuously when the vacuum on the switch is within 6.5-7.5 in. Hg.

5. If the warning horn does not activate, inspect the warning horn circuit for broken or disconnected wires or other damage. If the circuit is acceptable, replace the vacuum switch. Note that on 60° V6 models, the fuel module must be removed as outlined in this chapter to replace the vacuum switch.

FUEL MODULE AND VAPOR SEPARATOR (60° V6 MODELS)

The fuel module consists of the vapor separator (A, **Figure 75**), vapor pump (B), VRO pump (C), vacuum switch (D), fuel primer solenoid (E), fuel filter (F) and related bracket, hoses and circuitry.

Fuel from the fuel tank flows through the fuel filter into the vapor separator. The flow of fuel into the vapor separator is regulated by a float and inlet valve assembly. The vapor separator allows the fuel vapor to separate from the liquid fuel. The liquid fuel is then delivered to the oil injection pump (VRO). Refer to Chapter Eleven for a description of the oil injection (VRO) system. The diaphragm-type vapor pump is actuated by crankcase pulsations and designed to remove fuel vapor from the separator and pump the vapor to the air silencer.

Fuel Module Removal

CAUTION
To prevent breakage, do not attempt to pull fuel hoses off plastic or Minlon fittings. Always push the hose off using the fingers, a screwdriver or other blunt

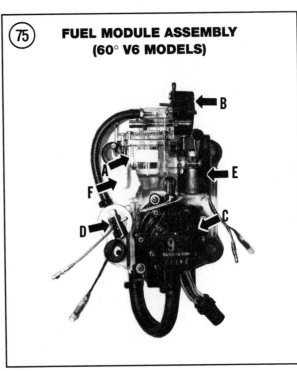

FUEL MODULE ASSEMBLY (60° V6 MODELS)

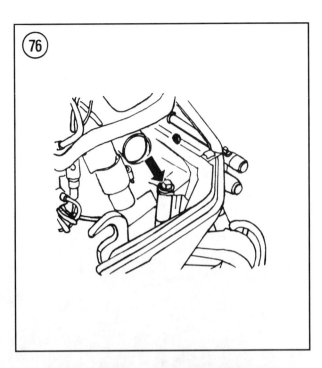

tool. If pushing the hose will not easily separate the hose and fitting, carefully cut the hose along the side and peel it away from the fitting.

1. Remove the air silencer.
2. Remove the cover from the fuel and oil fitting bracket.

NOTE
Label all fuel and oil hoses during removal for reference during installation.

3. Disconnect the fuel and oil hoses from the fuel module. Remove the screw (**Figure 76**) securing the fuel and oil fitting bracket to the motor lower cover. Remove the bracket.
4. Cut the tie strap clamp from the main fuel delivery hose (A, **Figure 77**) at the starboard fuel manifold. Disconnect the hose from the manifold. Next, cut the tie strap clamp from the main fuel delivery hose (B, **Figure 77**) at the port fuel manifold. Disconnect the hose from the manifold.
5. Disconnect the pulse hose (A, **Figure 78**) and the recirculation hose(B) from the vapor pump.
6. Disconnect the tan and black vacuum switch wires at their bullet connectors.
7. Disconnect the purple/white and black primer solenoid wires at their bullet connectors.
8. Disconnect the pulse hose from the oil injection (VRO) pump. The pulse hose is the innermost hose on the bottom of the pump assembly. See **Figure 79**.
9. Disconnect the oil injection pump wiring harness at the Amphenol connector.
10. Remove the 4 fuel module mounting screws (**Figure 80**). Support the fuel module to prevent it from falling when the last screw is removed.
11. Disconnect the 2 fuel primer hoses from the back side of the primer solenoid.

Fuel Module Disassembly

Refer to **Figure 81** for this procedure.

6

1. Remove the 2 screws securing the fuel primer solenoid to the fuel module bracket. Remove the solenoid.

2. Remove the screws securing the oil injection (VRO) pump assembly to the fuel module bracket. Remove the pump assembly.

NOTE
The push clip securing the vacuum switch to the fuel module bracket must be replaced if removed. Therefore, do not remove the vacuum switch in Step 3 unless replacement is necessary.

3. If necessary, remove the vacuum switch from the fuel module bracket.

4. Remove the fuel filter assembly.

5. Remove the vapor pump assembly.

6. Remove the screws holding the vapor separator cover to the fuel module bracket. Lift the cover along with the float and inlet valve off the bracket.

Cleaning and Inspection

1. Clean the fuel filter in clean solvent and dry with compressed air. Direct the air in the opposite direction of normal fuel flow. Replace the filter if excessive contamination is noted.

2. Remove the float pin anchor screw. Slide the float pin out of its bracket, then remove the float and inlet valve needle. Remove the inlet valve seat using a wide-blade screwdriver. Inspect the inlet needle and seat for excessive wear, distortion or other damage. Replace the needle and seat as a set if any defects are noted.

3. Inspect all hoses and fittings for cracking, deterioration or other damage. Replace as necessary.

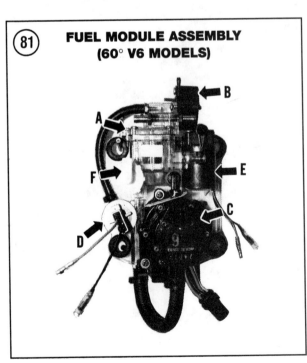

**FUEL MODULE ASSEMBLY
(60° V6 MODELS)**

Fuel Module Assembly

Refer to **Figure 81** and **Figure 82** for this procedure.

1. Using a new gasket, install the inlet valve seat into the vapor separator cover. Tighten the seat securely using a wide-blade screwdriver.

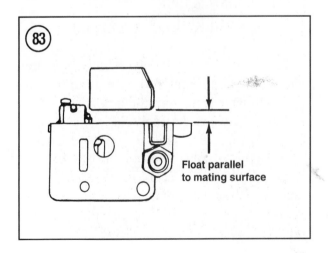

FUEL MODULE BRACKET, VAPOR SEPARATOR COVER, AND RELATED COMPONENTS

1. Vapor separator cover
2. Gasket
3. Float
4. Float pin
5. Float pin anchor screw
6. Spring clip
7. Inlet valve needle
8. Inlet valve seat
9. Fuel module bracket assembly

(82)

2. Attach the spring clip to the inlet valve needle, then connect the needle and clip to the float arm.

3. Install the float and inlet needle. Install the float pin and secure with the anchor screw.

   a. Invert the vapor separator cover and position the cover mating surface horizontal. The float should be parallel with the mating surface as shown in **Figure 83**. If not, carefully bend the float arm as necessary to adjust.

   b. Next, position the cover upright and allow the float to hang by its own weight. Measure the distance from the cover mating surface to the bottom of the float at the end. The distance should be 1-1/4 to 1-11/32 in. (32-34 mm). If not, bend the tang on the float arm as necessary to obtain the specified float drop.

4. Install a new gasket on the vapor separator cover. Install the cover assembly on the fuel module bracket. Install the cover screws and tighten in a crossing pattern to 18-24 in.-lb. (2.0-2.7 N·m).

5. Install the vapor pump to the vapor separator. Tighten the mounting screws to 18-24 in.-lb (2.0-2.7 N·m).

6. Install the fuel filter using new O-rings. Tighten the filter cover securely.

7. Install the vacuum switch to the fuel module bracket. Secure the switch using a new push clip.

(83)

Float parallel to mating surface

8. Install the oil injection (VRO) pump assembly to the fuel module bracket. Tighten the mounting screws to 18-24 in.-lb. (2.0-2.7 N•m).

9. Install the fuel primer solenoid to the fuel module bracket.

Fuel Module Installation

1. Connect the 2 fuel primer hoses to the rear side of the primer solenoid. Place the fuel module in position, then install the 4 bracket mounting screws and washers (**Figure 80**). Tighten the screws to 18-24 in.-lb. (2.0-2.7 N•m).

2. Connect the oil injection (VRO) harness Amphenol connector.

3. Connect the pulse hose to the oil injection unit. See **Figure 79**. Securely clamp the hose with a ratchet hose clamp.

4. Connect the fuel primer solenoid and vacuum switch at their bullet connectors.

5. Install the vapor pump pulse hose (A, **Figure 78**). Clamp the hose with a ratchet clamp. Connect the recirculation hose (B, **Figure 78**) to the vapor pump.

6. Connect the main fuel delivery hoses to the port and starboard fuel manifolds. See A and B, **Figure 77**.

7. Install the fuel connector bracket in the motor lower cover. Tighten the attaching screw securely.

8. Install the fuel connector bracket cover.

ANTI-SIPHON DEVICES

In accordance with industry safety standards, late model boats equipped with a built-in fuel tank will have some form of anti-siphon device installed between the fuel tank outlet and the outboard fuel inlet. This device is designed to shut the fuel supply off in case the boat capsizes or is involved in an accident. Quite often, the malfunction of anti-siphon devices leads the operator to replace the fuel pump in the belief that it is defective.

Anti-siphon devices can malfunction in one of the following ways:

  a. Anti-siphon valve: orifice in the valve is too small or clogs easily; valve sticks in the closed or partially closed position; valve fluctuates between open and closed position; thread sealant, metal filings or dirt/debris clogs the orifice or lodges in the relief spring.

  b. Solenoid-operated fuel shut-off valve: the solenoid fails with the valve in the closed position; solenoid malfunctions, leaving the valve in the partially closed position.

  c. Manually-operated fuel shut-off valve: valve is left in the completely closed position; valve is not full opened.

The easiest way to determine if an anti-siphon valve is defective is to bypass it by operating the engine with a remote fuel supply. If a fuel system problem is suspected, check the fuel filter first. If the filter is not clogged or restricted, bypass the anti-siphon device. If the engine runs properly with the anti-siphon device bypassed, contact the boat manufacturer for replacement of the device.

FUEL TANK

Integral Fuel Tank

Models 2.0-3.3 hp, are equipped with an integral fuel tank. On 2.0, 2.3 and 3.3 hp models, the

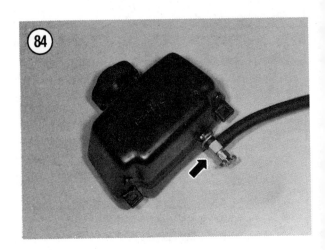

tank is equipped with a fuel shut-off valve located at the tank outlet. See **Figure 84**. An inline fuel filter is located on the inlet side of the shut-off valve. The valve and filter are serviced as an assembly only.

On 3.0 hp models, the shut-off valve is contained in the carburetor. On models equipped with an integral fuel tank, the fuel is gravity-fed to the carburetor.

The integral fuel tank should be drained and flushed at least once per year and during each tune-up or major repair procedure.

Inspect the fuel tank and shut-off valve for fuel leakage. Replace the tank or valve as necessary if any leakage is noted. Inspect the fill cap and gasket for damage or leakage. Replace the cap and/or gasket as necessary.

Remote Fuel Tank

Figure 85 shows a typical portable, remote fuel tank including the primer bulb assembly.

To remove any dirt or water that may have entered the fuel tank, clean the inside of the tank once per season by flushing with clean gasoline or kerosene.

6

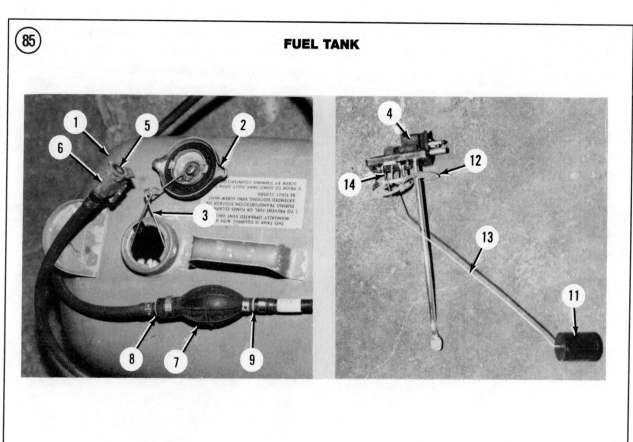

FUEL TANK

1. Fuel tank
2. Cap
3. Cap anchor
4. Upper housing assembly
5. O-ring
6. Connector assembly
7. Primer bulb
8. Outlet valve
9. Inlet valve
11. Indicator float
12. Housing gasket
13. Indicator arm
14. Indicator support

Check the inside and outside of the tank for rust, leakage or corrosion. Replace as necessary. Do not attempt to patch the tank with automotive fuel tank repair materials. Portable marine fuel tanks are subject to much greater pressure and vacuum conditions than automotive fuel tanks.

To check the fuel tank filter for restrictions, unscrew the fuel pickup nipple and withdraw the pickup tube and filter assembly from the tank. The filter on the end of the pickup tube can be cleaned with OMC Cleaning Solvent.

Alcohol blended with gasoline may cause a gradual deterioration of the indicator lens in some portable fuel tanks. The use of a tank with an alcohol-resistant lens is recommended if alcohol extended gasoline is used frequently.

FUEL LINE AND PRIMER BULB

CAUTION
*V8 models are equipped with an electric fuel primer pump and do not require a primer bulb for priming the carburetors. If a fuel line containing a primer bulb must be used, **do not** use the primer bulb to prime the fuel system.*

When priming the engine, the primer bulb should gradually become firm. If it does not become firm or if it stays firm even when disconnected, a check valve inside the primer bulb is malfunctioning.

The line should be checked periodically for cracks, breaks, restrictions and chafing. The bulb should be checked periodically for proper operation. Make sure all fuel line connections are tight and securely clamped.

Chapter Seven

Ignition and Electrical Systems

This chapter provides service procedures for the battery, starter motor, charging and ignition systems used on models covered in this manual. Wiring diagrams are located at the end of the manual. **Tables 1-6** are located at the end of this chapter.

BATTERY

Batteries used in marine applications endure far more rigorous treatment than those used in automotive electrical systems. Therefore, marine batteries have a thicker exterior case to cushion the plates during tight turns and rough water operation. Thicker plates are also used, with each plate individually fastened within the case to prevent premature failure. Spill-proof caps on the battery cells prevent electrolyte from spilling into the bilge.

Automotive batteries should be used in a boat *only* during an emergency situation when a suitable marine battery is not available.

> *CAUTION*
> *Sealed or maintenance-free batteries are* ***not*** *recommended for use with the un-regulated charging systems used on* some outboard motors. Excessive charging during continued high-speed operation will cause the electrolyte to overheat and evaporate, resulting in its loss. Since water cannot be added to such batteries, the battery will be ruined. Sealed batteries can be used satisfactorily, however, on models equipped with a voltage regulator/rectifier.

A separate battery (deep cycle) may be used to provide power for accessories such as lighting, fish finders and depth finders. To determine the required capacity of such batteries, calculate the accessory current (amperage) draw rate of the accessory and refer to **Table 1**.

> *NOTE*
> *The cranking battery should be dedicated to the engine only. A separate battery should be used for accessories such as depth finders, fish finders and trolling motors.*

Two batteries may be connected in parallel to double battery capacity while maintaining the required 12 volts. **Figure 1** shows 2 batteries connected in parallel. For accessories which require 24 volts, the batteries may be connected in series (**Figure 2**), but only accessories specifically requiring 24 volts should be connected to the system. If charging becomes necessary, batteries connected in a parallel or series circuit should be disconnected and charged individually.

Battery Rating Methods

The battery industry has developed specifications and performance standards to evaluate batteries and their energy potential. Several rating methods are available to provide meaningful information on battery selection. Refer to **Table 3** for the recommended batteries for use on outboard motors covered in this manual.

Ampere-Hour Rating

> *NOTE*
> *The ampere-hour method of rating batteries has been largely discontinued by the battery industry. Cold cranking amps and reserve capacity are now the most common battery rating methods.*

The ampere-hour rating describes the consistent current flow the battery can deliver for 20 hours at 80° F (26.7° C) without falling below 1.75 volts per cell, or 10.5 volts total for a 12-volt battery. For example, a battery that is capable of delivering a constant 3 amps for 20 hours at 80° F (26.7° C) is rated as a 60 ampere-hour battery.

Cold Cranking Amps (CCA) and Marine Cranking Amps (MCA)

Cold cranking amps (CCA) describes the current a fully charged battery is capable of delivering for 30 seconds at 0° F (-17.8° C) without falling below 1.2 volts per cell, or 7.2 volts total for a 12-volt battery. The higher the battery rating, the more amperage that is available for engine cranking. Marine cranking amps (MCA) is rated exactly the same, but, because pleasure

boats are not normally operated at such low temperatures, is based at 32° F (0° C) instead of 0° F (-17.6° C).

Reserve Capacity

Reserve capacity describes the time (in minutes) that a fully charged battery, at 80° F (26.7° C), can deliver 25 amps without falling below 1.75 volts per cell or 10.5 volts total for a 12-volt battery. Therefore, reserve capacity is the length of time a boat can be operated should the charging system fail. The higher the reserve capacity rating, the longer the battery can deliver current for powering ignition, lighting and other accessories.

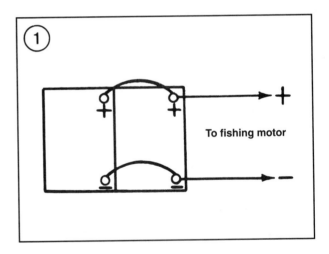

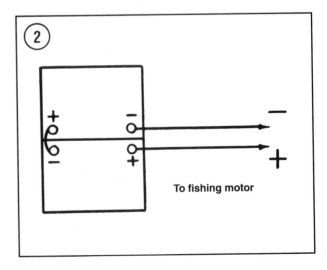

Battery Installation in Aluminum Boats

If the battery is not properly secured and grounded when installed in an aluminum boat, it may contact the hull and short circuit to ground.

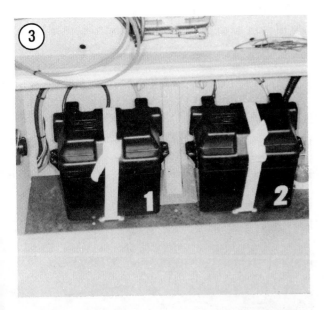

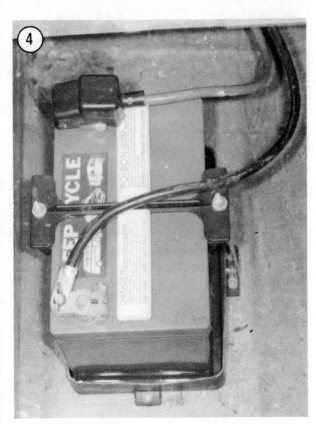

This will burn out remote control cables, tiller handle cables or wiring harnesses.

The following preventive steps should be carefully observed when installing a battery in any boat, especially a metal boat.

1. Choose a location as far as practical from the fuel tank while providing access for maintenance.

2. Install the battery in a plastic battery box with a cover and tie-down strap.

3. If a covered battery box is not used, cover the positive battery terminal with a nonconductive shield or boot.

4. Make sure the battery is secured inside the battery box and the box is fastened in position with a suitable tie-down strap or fixture.

7

Care and Inspection

1. Remove the battery tray or container cover. See **Figure 3** for a typical installation.

2. Disconnect the negative battery cable first, then the positive cable. See **Figure 4**.

NOTE
Some batteries have a built-in carry strap (Figure 5) for use in Step 3.

3. Attach a suitable battery carry strap to the terminal posts. Remove the battery from the battery tray or container.

4. Check the exterior battery case for cracks, holes or other damage.

5. Inspect the battery tray or container for corrosion and clean if necessary with a solution of baking soda and water.

NOTE
Do not allow the baking soda cleaning solution to enter the battery cells in Step 6 or the electrolyte will be severely weakened.

6. Clean the top of the battery with a stiff bristle brush using the baking soda and water solution

(**Figure 6**). Rinse the battery case with clear water and wipe dry with a clean cloth or paper towel.

7. Position the battery in the battery tray or container.

8. Clean the battery cable terminals and clamps using a wire brush or a suitable tool made for this purpose. See **Figure 7** and **Figure 8**.

9. Reconnect the positive battery cable first, then the negative cable.

> *CAUTION*
> *Be sure the battery cables are connected to their proper terminals. Reversing the battery polarity will result in rectifier and ignition system damage.*

10. Securely tighten the battery connections. Coat the connections with petroleum jelly or a light grease to inhibit corrosion.

> *NOTE*
> *Do not overfill the battery cells in Step 11. The electrolyte expands due to heat generated during charging and will overflow if the level is more than 3/16 in. (4.8 mm) above the battery plates.*

11. Remove the fill caps and check the electrolyte level. Add distilled water, if necessary, to bring the level up to 3/16 in. (4.8 mm) above the plates in the battery case. See **Figure 9**.

Testing

On batteries with removable fill caps, checking the specific gravity of the electrolyte using a

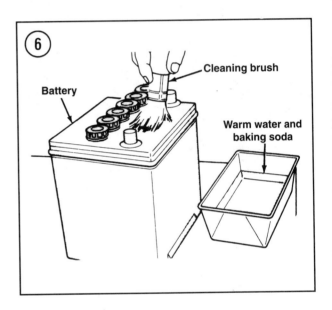

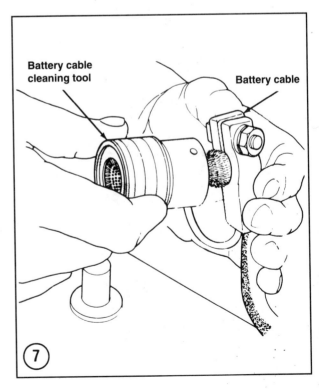

hydrometer is the best method to check the battery's state of charge. Use a hydrometer with numbered graduations from 1.100-1.300 points rather than one with color-coded bands. To use the hydrometer, squeeze the rubber bulb, insert the tip into a cell, then release the bulb to fill the hydrometer. See **Figure 10**.

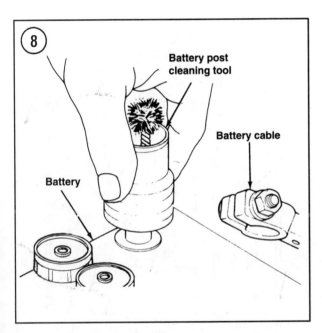

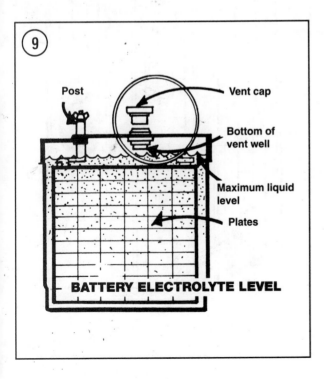

NOTE
Do not test specific gravity immediately after adding water to the battery cells, as the water will dilute the electrolyte and lower the specific gravity. To obtain accurate hydrometer readings, the battery must be charged after adding water.

Draw sufficient electrolyte to raise the float inside the hydrometer. When using a temperature-compensated hydrometer, discharge the electrolyte back into the battery cell and repeat the process several times to adjust the temperature of the hydrometer to that of the electrolyte.

Hold the hydrometer upright and note the number on the float that is even with the surface of the electrolyte (**Figure 11**). This number is the

7

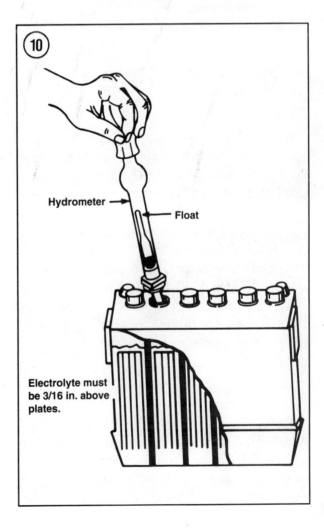

specific gravity for the cell. Discharge the electrolyte back into the cell from which it came.

The specific gravity of a cell is the indicator of the cell's state of charge. A fully charged cell will read 1.260 or more at 80° F (26.7° C). A cell that is 75 percent charged will read from 1.220-1.230 while a cell with a 50 percent charge will read from 1.1700-1.180. Any cell reading 1.120 or less should be considered discharged. All cells should be within 30 points specific gravity of each other. If over 30 points variation is noted, the battery condition is questionable. Charge the battery and recheck the specific gravity. If 30 points or more variation remains between cells after charging, the battery has failed and should be replaced.

NOTE
If a temperature-compensated hydrometer is not used, add 4 points specific gravity to the actual reading for every 10° above 80° F (26.7° C). Subtract 4 points specific gravity for every 10° below 80° (26.7° C).

On sealed or closed-cell batteries (fill caps not removable), the only way to check state of charge accurately is measure the open-circuit (no load) voltage of the battery. Use a digital voltmeter to check battery's open-circuit voltage. For the most accurate results, allow the battery to set at rest for at least 30 minutes to allow the battery to stabilize. Then, observing the correct polarity, connect the voltmeter to the battery and note the voltage. If open-circuit voltage is 12.7 volts or more, the battery can be considered fully charged. Refer to **Table 2** for open-circuit voltage and state of charge relationship.

Battery Storage

Wet cell batteries slowly discharge when stored. They discharge faster when warm than when cold. Before storing a battery, clean the case with a solution of baking soda and water. Rinse with clear water and wipe dry. The battery

should be fully charged and then stored in a cool, dry location. Check electrolyte level and state of charge frequently (every 6-8 weeks) during storage. If battery state of charge falls below 75 percent (**Table 2**), recharge the battery.

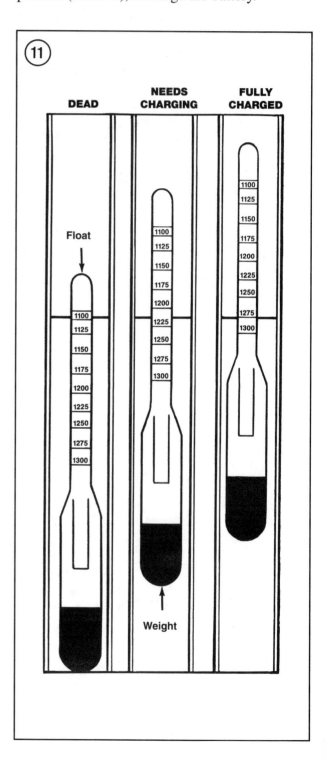

Battery Charging

A good state of charge should be maintained in batteries used for starting. Check the battery with a voltmeter as shown in **Figure 12**. Any battery that cannot deliver at least 9.6 volts under starting load should be charged. If, after charging, the battery is still unable to deliver at least 9.6 volts while cranking the engine, it should be replaced.

The battery does not have to be removed from the boat for charging, but it is a recommended safety procedure, since a charging battery releases highly explosive hydrogen gas. In many boats, the area around the battery is not well ventilated and the gas may remain in the area for hours after the charging process has been completed. Sparks or flames occurring near the battery can cause it to explode, spraying battery acid over a wide area. For this reason, it is important to observe the following precautions:

a. Never smoke around batteries that are charging, or that have been recently charged.

b. Do not disconnect a live circuit at the battery creating a spark that can ignite any hydrogen gas that may be present.

Disconnect the negative battery cable first, then the positive cable. Make sure the electrolyte is at the proper level.

Connect the charger to the battery, negative charger lead to the negative battery terminal and positive charger lead to the positive battery terminal. If the charger output is variable, select a 4 ampere setting. Set the voltage switch to 12 volts and switch the charger on.

> *WARNING*
> *Be extremely careful not to create any sparks around the battery when connecting the battery charger leads.*

If the battery is severely discharged, allow it to charge for at least 8 hours. Check the charging process with a hydrometer of voltmeter. The battery can be considered fully charged when the specific gravity of all cells does not increase when checked 3 times at 1 hour intervals, and all cells are gassing freely.

7

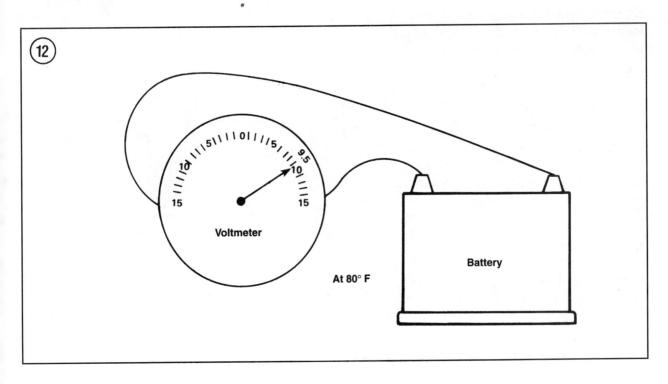

(12) Voltmeter — At 80° F — Battery

Jump Starting

If the battery becomes severely discharged, it is possible to "jump start" the engine from another battery. If the proper procedure is not followed, however, jump starting can be dangerous. Check the electrolyte level of the discharged battery before attempting the jump start. If the electrolyte is not visible or if it appears to be frozen, do not jump start the discharged battery.

WARNING
*Use extreme caution when connecting a booster battery to one that is discharged to avoid personal injury or damage to the system. **Be certain** the jumper cables are connected in the correct polarity.*

1. Connect the jumper cables in the order and sequence shown in **Figure 13**.

WARNING
An electrical arc may occur when the final connection is made. This could cause an explosion if it occurs near the battery. For this reason, the final connection should be made to a good engine ground, away from the battery and not to the battery itself.

2. Check that all jumper cables are out of the way of moving engine parts.

3. Start the engine. Once it starts, run it at a moderate speed.

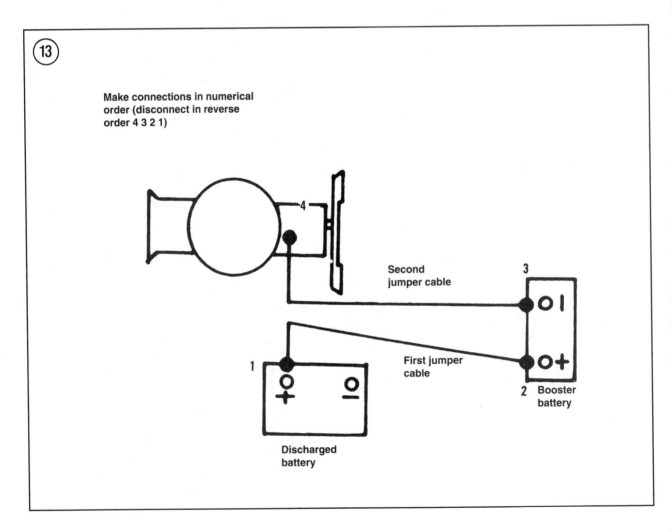

Make connections in numerical order (disconnect in reverse order 4 3 2 1)

Second jumper cable

First jumper cable

Discharged battery

Booster battery

CAUTION
Running the engine at high speed with a discharged battery can damage the charging system.

4. Remove the jumper cables in the exact reverse of the order shown in **Figure 13**. Remove the cable at point 4, then 3, 2 and 1.

BATTERY CHARGING SYSTEM

A battery charging system is standard equipment on all electric start models.

The nonregulated charging system consists of the flywheel, stator, rectifier, starter solenoid and battery. See **Figure 14**, typical.

The regulated charging system consists of the flywheel, stator, terminal block, regulator/rectifier assembly, fuse or circuit breaker, starter solenoid and battery. See **Figure 15**, typical. The following models are equipped with a regulated charging system:

    a. *1991*—65 Jet, 80 Jet and 85 hp and larger models.

    b. *1992*—60 hp and larger models.

    c. *1993-on*—40 hp and larger models.

The flywheel (**Figure 16**) contains permanent magnets which induce alternating current into the stator windings (**Figure 17** or **Figure 18**) as the flywheel rotates. The alternating current (AC) from the stator windings is converted (rectified) into direct current (DC) by the rectifier

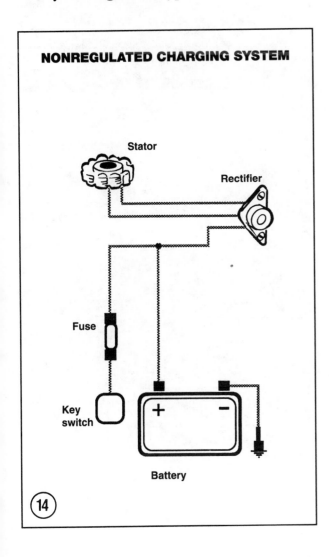

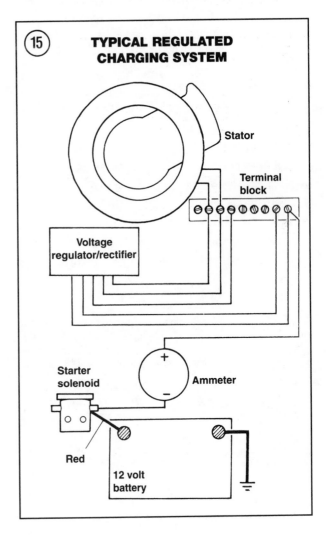

(**Figure 19**) for storage in the battery. The voltage regulator/rectifier assembly (**Figure 20**) on models so equipped, performs full-wave rectification and regulates the voltage output of the alternator. The regulator/rectifier also contains a gray wire which provides a tachometer signal. Therefore, an inoperative tachometer can indicate that the regulator/rectifier has failed. Refer to Chapter Three for troubleshooting procedures.

A malfunction in a nonregulated charging system generally results in an undercharged battery. The regulated charging system may produce too little (undercharge) or too much (overcharge) current. Perform the following inspection to determine the cause of the problem. If the inspection proves satisfactory, test the stator coils and rectifier. With regulated systems, also check the voltage regulator/rectifier. See Chapter Three.

1. Make sure the battery cables are connected properly. The red cable must be connected to the positive battery terminal. If polarity is reversed, the rectifier or the regulator/rectifier will be damaged.

2. Inspect the battery terminals for loose or corroded connections. Tighten or clean as required.

3. Inspect the physical condition of the battery. Look for bulges or cracks in the case, leaking electrolyte or excessive corrosion.

4. Carefully check the wiring between the stator coils and battery for chafing, deterioration or other damage.

5. Check the circuit wiring for loose or corroded connections, shorted or open circuits or other defects. Clean, tighten or reconnect wires as necessary.

NOTE
The cranking battery should be dedicated to the engine only. A separate bat-

tery should be used for operating any accessories such as depth finders, fish finders and trolling motors.

6. Determine if the electrical load on the battery from accessories is greater than the battery capacity.

7. Check the fuse on regulated charging systems. Replace the fuse as necessary.

Stator and Charge Coil Replacement

Refer to the appropriate section under *Armature Plate Disassembly/Assembly* in this chapter.

Rectifier Removal/Installation

1. Disconnect the negative battery cable from the battery, on models so equipped.

2. Disconnect the red, yellow, yellow/gray and yellow/blue rectifier leads at the terminal board. Some models will also use a yellow/blue wire that should be disconnected.

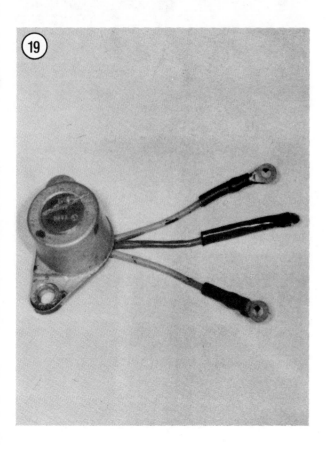

3. If necessary, remove the 2 screws (B, **Figure 21**) retaining the terminal block and place the terminal block out of the way.

4. Remove the 2 rectifier mounting screws. Remove the rectifier. See A, **Figure 21** or arrow, **Figure 22**.

5. Installation is the reverse of removal. Coat the terminal board mounting screw threads with OMC Screw Lock, or equivalent. Coat the rectifier lead connections with OMC Black Neoprene Dip.

Voltage Regulator/Rectifier Removal/Installation (Inline Models)

1. Disconnect the battery cables from the battery.

2. Disconnect the voltage regulator/rectifier wires from the terminal block.

3. Remove the 2 regulator/rectifier mounting screws and remove the regulator/rectifier from the power head.

4. To install, place the regulator/rectifier in position on the power head and install the mounting

7

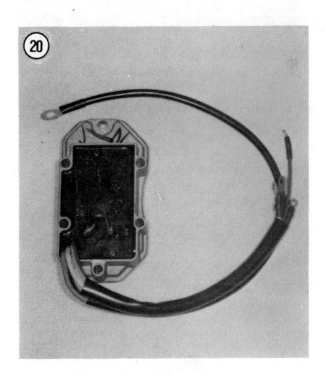

screws. Tighten the screws to 60-84 in.-lb. (6.8-9.5 N.m).

5. Connect the regulator/rectifier wires to the terminal block. Coat the terminal block connections with OMC Black Neoprene Dip.

6. Connect the battery cables to the battery.

Voltage Regulator/Rectifier Removal/Installation (V4 and V6 Cross Flow Models)

1. Disconnect the battery cables from the battery.

2. Disconnect the yellow, yellow/gray, gray and purple regulator/rectifier wires from the terminal block.

3. Disconnect the red regulator/rectifier wire from the starter solenoid.

4. Remove the flywheel as described in Chapter Eight.

5. Remove the stator assembly as described in this chapter.

6. Remove the 6 mounting screws then remove the regulator/rectifier assembly to the power head. Remove and discard the regulator/rectifier gasket.

7. To install, apply OMC Gasket Sealing Compound the both sides of a new regulator/rectifier gasket. Place the gasket into position on the power head.

8. Install the regulator/rectifier assembly on the power head.

9. Apply OMC Gasket Sealing Compound to the threads of the 6 regulator/rectifier mounting screws. Install the screws and tighten to 60-84 in.-lb. (6.8-9.5 N.m).

10. Install the stator as described in this chapter. Install the flywheel as described in Chapter Eight.

11. Connect the red regulator/rectifier wire to the battery side of the starter solenoid. Connect the yellow, gray, yellow/gray and purple regulator/rectifier wires to the terminal block, as indi-

cated on the terminal block decal. Reconnect the battery cables to complete installation.

Voltage Regulator/Rectifier Removal/Installation (V4, V6 [Except 60° V6 Models] and V8 Loop Charged Models)

1. Disconnect the battery cables from the battery.

2. Remove the power pack assembly. See **Figure 23**.

3. Place the electrical component bracket aside to expose the voltage regulator/rectifier assembly. See **Figure 24**.

4. Disconnect the regulator/rectifier-to-power pack electrical connections. Disconnect the red regulator/rectifier wire from the starter solenoid.

5. Remove the 6 regulator/rectifier mounting screws. Remove the regulator/rectifier from the

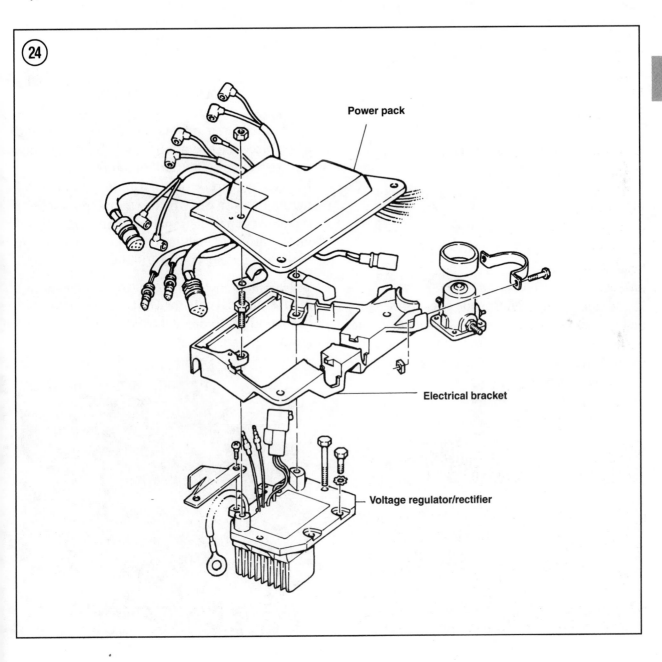

24

Power pack

Electrical bracket

Voltage regulator/rectifier

7

power head. Remove and discard the regulator/rectifier gasket.

6. To install, apply OMC Gasket Sealing Compound to both sides of a new regulator/rectifier gasket.

7. Install the regulator/rectifier and new gasket on the power head.

8. Apply OMC Gasket Sealing Compound to the threads of the regulator/rectifier mounting screws. Install the star-type washers on the front center screws. Install the screws and tighten to 36-84 in.-lb. (4.1-9.5 N·m).

9. Connect the regulator/rectifier electrical connections. Install the electrical component bracket and power pack.

10. Reconnect the battery cables to complete installation.

Voltage Regulator/Rectifier Removal/Installation (60° V6 Models)

1. Disconnect the battery cables from the battery.

2. Remove the regulator/rectifier cover.

3. Disconnect the yellow and yellow/gray regulator/rectifier-to-stator wires. Disconnect the purple and gray wires at their bullet connectors.

4. Remove the red regulator/rectifier wire from the starter solenoid.

5. Remove the 4 regulator/rectifier mounting screws. Remove the regulator/rectifier assembly from the power head. See **Figure 25**.

6. Inspect the regulator/rectifier seal. The seal can be reused if in acceptable condition. If not, replace the seal.

7. To install, apply a light coat of OMC Gasket Sealing Compound to the regulator/rectifier seal. Install the seal into its groove in the regulator/rectifier.

8. Place the regulator/rectifier into position on the power head. Install the 4 mounting screws and tighten to 60-84 in.-lb. (6.8-9.5 N·m).

9. Reconnect all regulator/rectifier circuits. Coat the red wire connection at the starter solenoid with OMC Black Neoprene Dip.

10. Install the regulator/rectifier cover and reconnect the battery cables.

ELECTRIC STARTING SYSTEM

The electrical starting system consists of the battery, starter solenoid (except early 9.9 and 15 hp), starter motor, neutral start switch, key switch and related circuitry.

STARTER MOTOR

Marine starter motors are similar in design, appearance and operation to those found on automotive engines. The starter motors used on outboards covered in this manual have an inertia-type drive in which external spiral splines on the armature shaft mate with internal splines on the drive assembly. A gear-reduction starter motor is used on V6 and V8 models.

The starter motor is capable of producing very high torque, but only for a brief time, due to rapid heat buildup. To prevent overheating, never operate the starter motor continuously for more

than 10 seconds. Allow the motor to cool for at least 2 minutes before further operation.

If the starter motor does not crank the engine, check the battery and all connecting wiring for loose or corroded connections, shorted or open circuits, or other defects. If this inspection does not determine the problem, test the starting system as described in Chapter Three.

Starter Motor Removal/Installation (9.9 and 15 hp)

1. Disconnect the negative battery cable from the battery.
2. Remove the engine cover.
3. Remove the 2 screws holding the starter motor to the by-pass cover. Remove the starter.
4. Disconnect the starter motor cable at the bottom of the starter.
5. On late models, remove the rectifier from the starter motor bracket.
6. Installation is the reverse of removal. Tighten the mounting screws to 10-12 ft.-lb. (13.6-16.3 N·m). Apply OMC Black Neoprene Dip to the starter motor cable terminal.

> *CAUTION*
> *When attaching the cable to the starter motor, be certain the cable terminal does not turn and contact the starter motor or lower engine cover.*

Starter Motor Removal/Installation (20-30 hp)

1. Disconnect the negative battery cable from the battery.
2. Remove the starter solenoid from the starter bracket.
3. Remove the screws (A, **Figure 26**) securing the vertical throttle shaft clamp (B) to the power head. Remove the clamp.
4. Disconnect the red cable from the starter motor.
5. Remove the screws and locknut securing the starter motor bracket to the power head. Lift the starter and bracket off the power head.
6. To install, place the solenoid in the starter bracket and secure the clamp with 2 screws. Make sure the rubber sleeve is properly installed around the solenoid.
7. Place the starter bracket on the power head and install the 2 screws and 1 locknut. Make sure the ground wire and lockwashers are installed under the lower screw. Securely tighten the screws and locknut.
8. Install the vertical throttle shaft on the power head. Install the vertical shaft clamp (B, **Figure 26**) and 2 screws (A). Tighten the screws securely. See **Figure 26**.
9. Attach all wires to the starter solenoid. Apply OMC Black Neoprene Dip to all electrical connections except the positive battery cable terminal.
10. Reconnect the negative battery cable to the battery.

Starter Motor Removal/Installation (35 Jet and 40-70 hp)

1. Disconnect the negative battery cable from the battery.
2. Remove the carburetor air silencer assembly.
3. Disconnect the starter cable from the starter motor.

4. Remove the 3 screws securing the starter motor to the power head. Lift the motor off the power head.

5. Apply OMC Nut Lock to the threads of the starter motor mounting screws.

6. Position the starter motor on the power head and install the mounting screws. Tighten the front screw first, then the remaining screws to 14-16 ft.-lb. (19-22 N·m).

7. Connect the starter cable to the motor. Apply OMC Black Neoprene Dip to the cable connection.

8. Install the air silencer assembly using new screws.

9. Reconnect the negative battery cable to the battery.

Starter Motor Removal/Installation (V4, V6 [Except 60° V6 Models] and V8 Models)

1. Disconnect the negative battery cable from the battery.

2. Disconnect the starter cable (A, **Figure 27**) from the starter motor. On V6 models, disconnect the negative battery cable (B, **Figure 27**) from the starter motor mounting flange.

3. Remove the air silencer assembly if necessary for improved clearance.

4. Remove the starter solenoid.

5A. *200-300 hp*—Remove the 4 starter motor mounting screws and remove the motor.

5B. *All other models*—Remove the 3 starter motor mounting screws and remove the starter.

6. To install, clean the starter motor mounting screws using OMC Locquic Primer and allow to air dry. Then, apply OMC Nut Lock to the threads of the mounting screws. Position the starter motor in place on the power head and install the mounting screws.

7A. *200-300 hp*—Tighten the starter mounting screws to 14-16 ft.-lb. (19-22 N·m). Tighten the top 2 screws first, then the bottom screws.

7B. *All other models*—Starting with the front screw, tighten the starter motor mounting screws to 14-16 ft.-lb. (19-22 N·m).

8. Install the starter solenoid.

9. Connect the starter cable to the starter motor. On V6 models, connect the ground cable to the motor. See **Figure 27**. Apply OMC Black Neoprene Dip to the connections.

10. Install the air silencer to the carburetors using new screws.

11. Connect the negative battery cable to the battery.

Starter Motor Removal/Installation (60° V6 Models)

1. Disconnect the negative battery cable from the battery.

2. Disconnect the battery ground cable (B, **Figure 28**) from the starter motor.

3. Disconnect the positive battery cable from the starter solenoid.

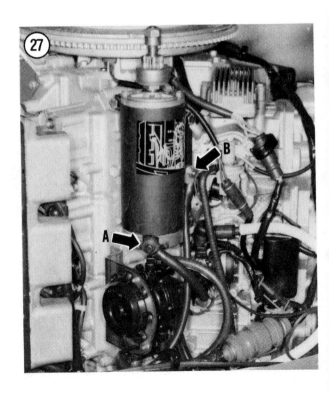

4. Disconnect the power trim and VRO ground wires from the bottom of the starter motor.

5. Disconnect the red regulator/rectifier, engine cable and power trim wires from the large solenoid terminal post.

6. Disconnect the yellow/red neutral start switch wire from the bottom solenoid terminal post.

7. Disconnect the ground wire from the bottom solenoid terminal post.

8. Remove the 2 starter motor mounting screws (C, **Figure 28**) and remove the motor from the power head.

9. To install, clean the starter motor mounting screws using OMC Locquic Primer and allow to air dry. Apply OMC Nut Lock to the threads of the mounting screws.

10. Place the starter motor into position on the power head, then install the mounting screws. Tighten the screws to 14-16 ft.-lb. (19-22 N·m).

11. Connect the ground wire and the yellow/red neutral start switch wire to the small terminals posts on the bottom of the starter solenoid. Tighten the nuts securely.

12. Connect the red regulator/rectifier, engine cable and power trim wires to the large solenoid terminal post. Tighten the nut securely.

13. Connect the power trim and VRO ground wires to the starter motor.

14. Connect the negative battery cable to the starter motor. Tighten the nut to 14-16 ft.-lb. (19-22 N·m). Connect the positive battery cable to the starter solenoid.

15. Apply OMC Black Neoprene Dip to all electrical connections.

16. Connect the negative battery cable to the battery.

**Starter Motor Disassembly
(9.9-15 hp)**

Always replace brushes in complete sets. Refer to **Figure 29** for this procedure.

1. Remove the starter motor as outlined in this chapter.

2. Remove the 2 through-bolts, then remove the drive end cap and armature from the housing.

3. Remove the brush plate from the housing.

4. While securely holding the drive gear with a pair of pliers, remove the armature nut. Then slide the spacer (2, **Figure 29**), spring (3) and drive assembly (4) off the armature shaft. Remove the drive end cap from the armature shaft.

5. If necessary, remove the screw holding each brush. Remove the brush from the brush plate.

Cleaning and Inspection

1. Inspect the brushes. Replace both brushes if either is oil soaked, pitted or worn to 3/8 in. (9.5 mm) or less.

2. Clean the commutator using 300 grade emery cloth. The commutator should be trued on an armature lathe if the commutator is pitted, out-of-round or unevenly worn.

3. Clean all oil, metal dust or other contamination from the armature, housing, drive end cap and brush plate.

4. Inspect the drive gear for chipped, broken or excessively worn teeth. Replace the drive assembly as necessary.

Starter Motor Assembly (9.9-15 hp)

Refer to **Figure 29** for this procedure.

1. Lubricate the bearing surfaces of the armature with one drop of SAE 10 engine oil. Lubricate the spiral splines on the armature shaft with OMC Starter Pinion Lube (part No. 337016).
2. Place a new gasket on the brush plate. Install the brushes into the brush plate.
3. While keeping the brushes recessed in the brush holders, install the brush plate onto the housing. Make sure the housing and brush plate match marks are aligned.
4. Install thrust washer (6, **Figure 29**) onto the armature shaft.
5. Install a new gasket onto the drive end cap.
6. Install the drive end cap, making sure the end cap and housing match marks are aligned.
7. Lightly lubricate the through-bolt threads with clean engine oil. Install the through-bolts and tighten to 30-40 in.-lb. (3.4-4.5 N•m).
8. Apply OMC Black Neoprene Dip to the drive end cap and brush plate-to-housing seams.
9. Install the drive assembly, spring, spacer and nut onto the armature shaft. Tighten the nut to 150-170 in.-lb. (16.9-19.2 N•m).
10. Install the starter motor as outlined in this chapter.

Starter Motor Disassembly (20-140 hp, 1.6 Sea Drive, 2.0 Sea Drive and V6 Cross Flow [1991 105 Jet, 150 and 175 hp] Models)

Always replace starter brushes in complete sets. Refer to **Figure 30** for this procedure.

1. Remove the starter motor as outlined in this chapter.

NOTE
The 4 brush springs are loose when the commutator end cap is removed. Remove the end cap carefully to prevent the loss of any springs.

2. Carefully tap the commutator end cap from the starter frame.
3. Remove the brushes and springs from the brush holder. Remove the brush holder from the end cap.

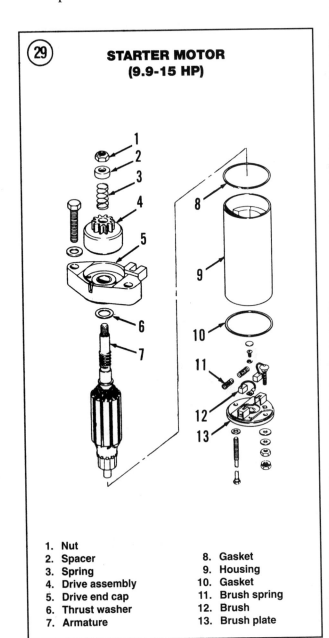

(29)

STARTER MOTOR (9.9-15 HP)

1. Nut
2. Spacer
3. Spring
4. Drive assembly
5. Drive end cap
6. Thrust washer
7. Armature
8. Gasket
9. Housing
10. Gasket
11. Brush spring
12. Brush
13. Brush plate

4. Carefully tap the drive end cap to dislodge it from the frame. Remove the drive end cap and armature from the frame as an assembly.

5. If necessary, remove the drive assembly as follows:

   a. Hold the armature assembly from turning using a suitable strap wrench.

   b. Remove and discard the drive assembly locknut. Remove the spacer, spring, drive

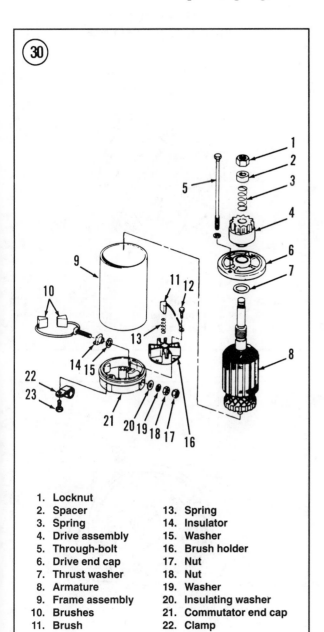

1. Locknut
2. Spacer
3. Spring
4. Drive assembly
5. Through-bolt
6. Drive end cap
7. Thrust washer
8. Armature
9. Frame assembly
10. Brushes
11. Brush
12. Screw
13. Spring
14. Insulator
15. Washer
16. Brush holder
17. Nut
18. Nut
19. Washer
20. Insulating washer
21. Commutator end cap
22. Clamp
23. Screw

assembly, drive end cap and thrust washer from the armature shaft.

Cleaning and Inspection

1. Inspect the brushes. Replace all brushes if any are oil soaked, pitted or worn to 3/8 in. (9.5 mm) or less. Replace brush springs if weak, broken or damaged.

2. Clean the commutator using 300 grade emery cloth. The commutator should be trued on an armature lathe if the commutator is pitted, out-of-round or unevenly worn.

3. Clean all oil, metal dust or other contamination from the armature, housing, drive end cap and brush plate.

4. Inspect the drive gear for chipped, broken or excessively worn teeth. Replace the drive assembly as necessary.

Starter Motor Assembly
(20-140 hp, 1.6 Sea Drive, 2.0 Sea Drive and V6 Cross Flow [1991 105 Jet, 150 and 175 hp] Models)

Refer to **Figure 30** for this procedure.

1. Lubricate the bearing surfaces of the armature with one drop of SAE 10 engine oil. Lubricate the spiral splines on the armature shaft with OMC Starter Pinion Lube (part No. 337016).

2. If removed, install the thrust washer, drive end cap, drive assembly, spring and spacer on the armature shaft. Hold the armature using a suitable strap wrench and install a *new* drive assembly locknut. Tighten the nut to 20-25 ft.-lb. (27-34 N.m).

3. Install the armature into the frame assembly. Align the drive end cap and frame match marks.

4. Install the insulated brush and terminal set into the commutator end cap as shown in **Figure 31**.

5. Install the brush holder into the commutator end cap. Install the brush springs into the holder.

Insert the brushes and tighten the brush lead screws to the holder.

6. Fit the ground brushes into the holder slots. **Figure 32** shows the reassembled brush holder.

7. Align the commutator and drive end cap match marks (or notch and rib). Hold the brushes in place and assemble the end cap to the frame. A putty knife with a 1 × 1/2 in. slot cut in its end makes a suitable tool for keeping the brushes in place during this step. See **Figure 33**.

8. Lightly lubricate the through-bolt threads with clean engine oil. Install the through-bolts and tighten to 95-100 in.-lb. (11-12 N·m).

9. Seal each end cap-to-frame joint with OMC Black Neoprene Dip.

10. Install the starter motor as outlined in this chapter.

Gear Reduction Starter Motor Disassembly (200-300 hp, 3.0 and 4.0 Sea Drive)

Always replace starter brushes as complete sets. Refer to **Figure 34** for this procedure.

1. Remove the starter motor as described in this chapter.

2. Remove the through-bolt nuts holding the bracket to the starter frame. Remove the bracket and washers.

3. Remove the 3 drive end housing screws. Remove the drive end housing.

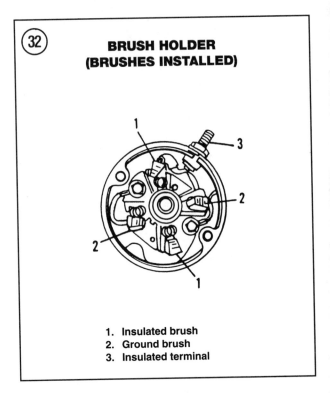

(32) **BRUSH HOLDER (BRUSHES INSTALLED)**

1. Insulated brush
2. Ground brush
3. Insulated terminal

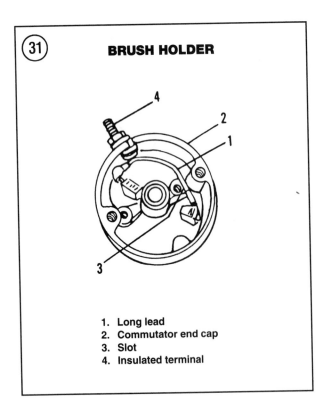

(31) **BRUSH HOLDER**

1. Long lead
2. Commutator end cap
3. Slot
4. Insulated terminal

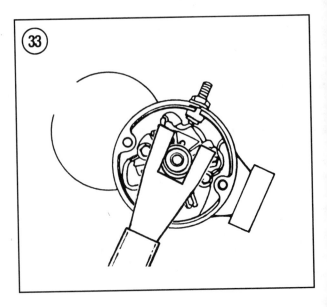

(33)

**GEAR REDUCTION STARTER MOTOR
(200-300 HP)**

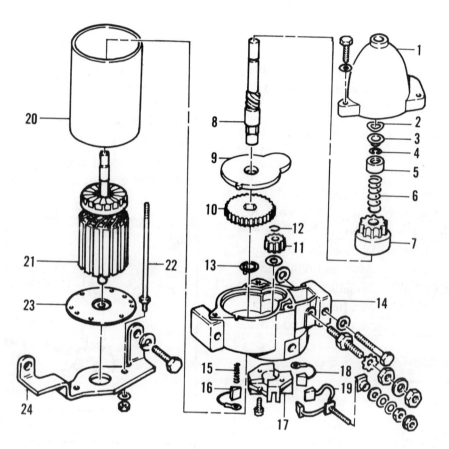

1. Drive end housing
2. Wave washer
3. Bushing
4. Retaining ring
5. Spacer
6. Spring
7. Drive assembly
8. Pinion shaft
9. Weather cover
10. Driven gear
11. Drive gear
12. Retaining ring
13. Thrust washer
14. Gear housing
15. Spring
16. Ground brush
17. Brush holder
18. Ground brush
19. Insulated brushes
20. Frame
21. Armature
22. Through-bolt
23. End cap
24. Bracket

4. Remove the wave washer and spacer from the armature shaft. See **Figure 35**.

5. Place an appropriate size deep socket over the armature shaft as shown in **Figure 36**. Lightly tap the socket to lower the spacer and expose the drive assembly retaining ring.

6. Remove the retaining ring and slide the spacer, spring and drive assembly off the pinion shaft.

7. Remove the plastic weather cover and pinion shaft. Remove the driven gear and thrust washer (located under gear). See **Figure 37**.

8. Using suitable snap ring pliers, remove the drive gear retaining ring and drive gear from the armature shaft.

9. Place match marks on the end cap and frame assembly for reference during reassembly. Remove the 2 through-bolts, then gently tap the end cap with a soft-face mallet to dislodge the end cap. Remove the end cap. After removing the end cap, check the end of the armature, or inside the end cap for the insulator cap. Inspect the insulator cap for excessive wear or damage and replace as necessary.

10. While holding the armature in place, slide the frame away from the gear housing and off the armature.

11. Slide the armature out of the gear housing. Remove the thrust washer from the armature. See **Figure 38**.

Cleaning and Inspection

1. Inspect the brushes. Replace all brushes if any are oil soaked, pitted or worn to 3/8 in. (9.5 mm) or less. Replace brush springs if weak, broken or damaged.

2. Clean the commutator using 300 grade emery cloth. The commutator should be trued on an

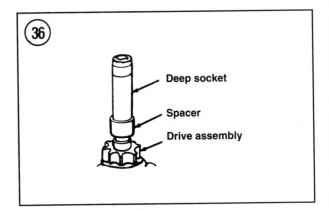

(36)

Deep socket
Spacer
Drive assembly

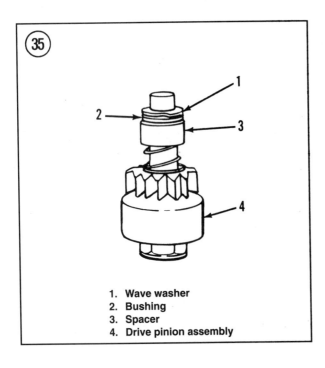

(35)

1. Wave washer
2. Bushing
3. Spacer
4. Drive pinion assembly

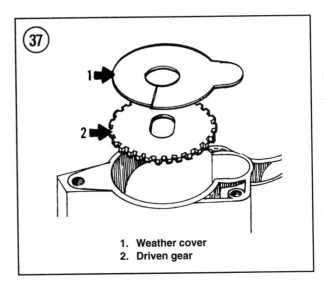

(37)

1. Weather cover
2. Driven gear

armature lathe if the commutator is pitted, out-of-round or unevenly worn.

3. Clean all oil, metal dust or other contamination from the armature, housing, drive end cap and brush plate.

4. Inspect the drive gear for chipped, broken or excessively worn teeth. Replace the drive assembly as necessary.

Starter Motor Assembly
(200-300 hp, 3.0 and 4.0 Sea Drive)

Refer to **Figure 34** for this procedure.

1. If removed, clean the brush holder screws using OMC Locquic Primer and allow to air dry.

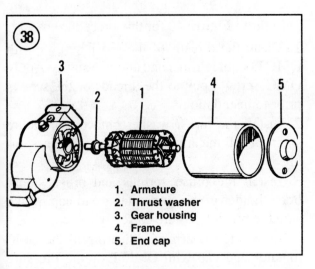

1. Armature
2. Thrust washer
3. Gear housing
4. Frame
5. End cap

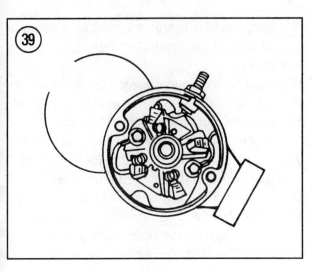

Apply OMC Screw Lock to the threads of the brush screws prior to installation.

2. Make sure the brush leads are correctly routed (**Figure 39**) then install the springs and brushes.

3. Apply OMC Extreme Pressure Grease to the armature bearing in the gear housing. Use a putty knife with a $1 \times 1/2$ in. slot cut in its end to hold the brushes and springs in place. See **Figure 33**. Install the thrust washer on the armature, then install the armature into the gear housing while holding the brushes with the modified putty knife.

4. Install the frame assembly, making sure the long match mark on the frame is aligned with the positive terminal stud on the gear housing.

5. Install the insulator cap on the end cap end of the armature shaft.

6. Lightly lubricate the end cap bearing with OMC Extreme Pressure Grease, then install the end cap.

7. Install the 2 through-bolts and tighten to 50-65 in.-lb. (5.6-7.3 N•m).

8. Lightly lubricate the drive gear with OMC Triple-Guard grease. Install the drive gear on the armature shaft. Install the drive gear retaining ring, with its flat side facing upward, using suitable snap ring pliers.

9. Lightly lubricate the driven gear with OMC Triple-Guard grease. Lubricate the gear housing with OMC Extreme Pressure Grease. Install the driven gear thrust washer and driven gear.

10. Install the plastic weather cover.

11. Lubricate the pinion shaft splines with OMC Starter Pinion Lube (part No. 337016). Install the drive assembly, spring and spacer (large diameter upward) on the pinion shaft. Install the retaining ring. Install the wave washer and bushing on the pinion shaft.

12. Without disturbing the position of the driven gear or thrust washer, carefully lower the pinion shaft and drive assembly into position.

13. Lightly lubricate the drive end housing bearing with OMC Starter Pinion Lube (part No. 337016). Install the housing and housing screws.

7

Tighten the screws to 60-84 in.-lb. (6.8-9.5 N.m).

14. Install the starter motor bracket. Apply OMC Nut Lock to the bracket mounting nuts, then install and tighten the nuts to 50-65 in.-lb. (5.6-7.3 N.m).

15. Install the starter motor as outlined in this chapter.

Starter Motor Disassembly (60° V6 Models)

Always replace starter brushes as complete sets. Refer to **Figure 40** for this procedure.

> *NOTE*
> *The flywheel cover must be removed from the power head to service the drive gear, pinion and shaft assembly (17-25, **Figure 40**).*

1. Remove the starter motor as outlined in this chapter.

2. Using snap ring pliers, remove the retaining ring securing the drive gear (2, **Figure 40**) to the armature shaft. Lift the drive gear off the shaft.

3. Remove the bracket and solenoid from the starter motor.

4. Place match marks on both end caps and the starter frame for alignment reference during assembly.

5. Remove the 2 through-bolts.

6. Remove the commutator end cap. Note that the brush springs are loose when the end cap is removed. Remove the end cap carefully to prevent the loss of any springs.

7. Remove the drive end cap. Remove the thrust washer from the armature shaft, then pull the armature out of the frame.

Cleaning and Inspection

1. Inspect the brushes. Replace all brushes if any are oil soaked, pitted or worn to 3/8 in. (9.5 mm)

or less. Replace brush springs if weak, broken or damaged.

2. Clean the commutator using 300 grade emery cloth. The commutator should be trued on an armature lathe if the commutator is pitted, out-of-round or unevenly worn.

3. Clean all oil, metal dust or other contamination from the armature, housing, drive end cap and brush plate.

4. Inspect the drive gear for chipped, broken or excessively worn teeth. Replace the drive assembly as necessary.

Starter Motor Assembly (60° V6 Models)

Refer to **Figure 40** for this procedure.

1. Clean the threads of the brush screws with OMC Locquic Primer and allow to air dry. Apply OMC Screw Lock to the threads of the screws prior to installation.

2. Install the thrust washer onto the armature shaft. Install the armature into the frame assembly.

3. Install the brush springs and brushes into brush holder in the commutator end cap. Make sure the brush leads are correctly routed.

4. Lubricate the armature bearing in the commutator end cap with OMC Extreme Pressure Grease.

5. Use a putty knife with a 1 × 1/2 in. slot cut in its end to hold the brushes and springs in place. See **Figure 33**.

6. Install the commutator end cap, making sure the end cap and frame match marks are aligned. Hold the end cap firmly against the armature and frame, then withdraw the modified putty knife.

7. Clean the through-bolt threads with OMC Locquic Primer and allow to air dry. Then, apply OMC Screw Lock to the through-bolt threads. Install the drive end cap, making sure the match marks are aligned. Install the through-bolts and tighten to 50-60 in.-lb. (5.6-6.8 N.m).

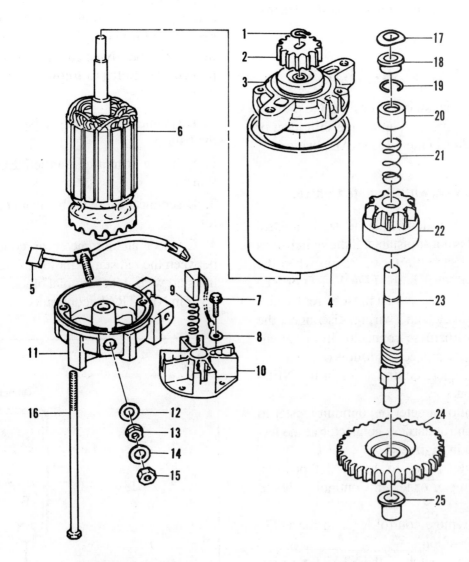

40

GEAR REDUCTION STARTER MOTOR
(60° V6 MODELS)

1. Retaining ring
2. Drive gear
3. Drive end cap
4. Frame assembly
5. Insulated brushes
6. Armature
7. Brush screw
8. Ground brushes
9. Brush spring
10. Brush holder
11. Commutator end cap
12. Insulating washer
13. Nut
14. Lockwasher
15. Nut
16. Through-bolt
17. Wave washer
18. Bushing
19. Retaining ring
20. Spacer
21. Spring
22. Drive pinion assembly
23. Pinion shaft
24. Driven gear
25. Pinion shaft-to-
    crankcase bushing

7

8. Lubricate the drive gear with OMC Triple-Guard grease. Install the drive gear and retaining ring.

9. Install the solenoid and bracket on the starter motor. Install the starter motor as outlined in this chapter.

NEUTRAL START SWITCH

The neutral start switch is designed to prevent electric starter operation unless the shift lever or remote control is in the NEUTRAL position.

Models Equipped with Remote Control

The switch is located inside the remote control assembly and is not adjustable. If the switch does not prevent electric starter operation when the remote control lever is the FORWARD or REVERSE position, the switch must be replaced.

To test the switch and wiring, disconnect the remote control harness connector from the engine harness and proceed as follows.

1. Place the remote control lever in the NEUTRAL position.

2. Connect an ohmmeter or continuity tester to the remote control harness connector at the terminals shown in **Figure 41**.

3. Turn the key switch to the START position and note the meter or tester. Continuity should be noted.

4. Place the remote control lever in the FORWARD gear position.

5. Turn the key switch to the START position and note the meter or tester. No continuity should be noted.

6. Move the remote control lever to the REVERSE gear position.

7. Turn the key switch to the START position. No continuity should be noted.

8. If the test results are not as specified, inspect the neutral start switch wiring for open or short circuits. If the wiring is in acceptable condition, the switch is defective and must be replaced.

Neutral Start Switch Test and Adjust (1991 and 1992 9.9 and 15 hp)

The correct neutral start switch adjustment can only be accomplished if the shift lever is properly adjusted. Refer to the appropriate section in Chapter Nine for shift lever adjustment procedures. Refer to **Figure 42** for this procedure.

1. Disconnect the negative battery cable from the battery.

2. Shift the gearcase into the NEUTRAL position.

3. Disconnect the red cable from the starter motor.

4. Connect an ohmmeter or continuity tester between the red starter motor cable and the neutral start wire at the terminal block. With the shift lever in NEUTRAL, continuity should be noted.

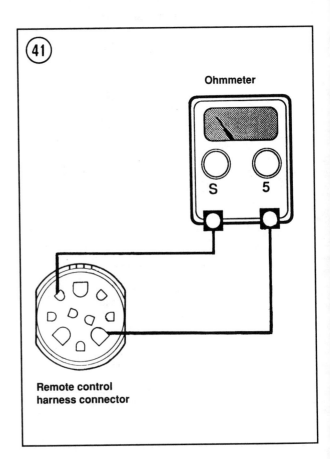

41

Ohmmeter

S   5

**Remote control
harness connector**

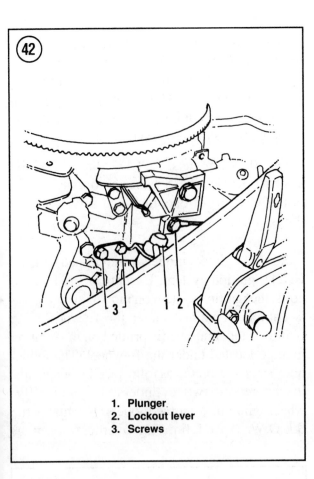

1. Plunger
2. Lockout lever
3. Screws

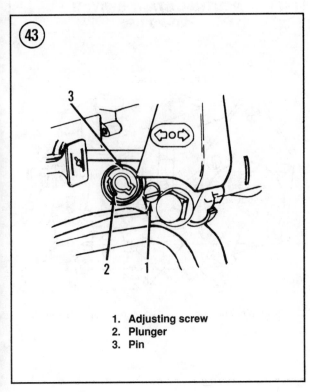

1. Adjusting screw
2. Plunger
3. Pin

5. Shift into FORWARD gear, note the meter or tester, then shift into REVERSE gear. No continuity should be noted with the shift lever in either gear.

6. If adjustment is necessary, remove the fuel pump from the power head. Place the pump to one side.

7. Loosen the neutral start switch mounting screws (3, **Figure 42**).

8. With the shift lever in NEUTRAL, center the switch plunger (1, **Figure 42**) with the lobe (2) on the lockout lever. Then, raise the neutral start switch until its plunger is depressed 3/32 to 5/32 in. (2.4-4.0 mm) and tighten the switch mounting screws securely.

9. Repeat Steps 2-5 to check switch operation. Replace the switch if it still does not function properly.

10. Reinstall the fuel pump. See Chapter Four. Connect the red cable to the starter motor and battery cable to the battery.

Neutral Start Switch Test and Adjust (1993-on 9.9 and 15 hp)

1. Disconnect the negative battery cable from the battery.

2. Disconnect the red cable from the starter motor.

3. Place the shift lever in NEUTRAL.

4. Connect an ohmmeter or continuity tester between the red starter cable and the neutral start wire at the electrical box. With the shift lever in NEUTRAL, continuity should be noted.

5. Place the shift lever into FORWARD, then REVERSE while noting the meter or tester. No continuity should be present with the gearcase in either gear.

6. If adjustment is necessary, loosen the neutral start switch adjusting screw (1, **Figure 43**).

7. Center the switch plunger (2, **Figure 43**) with the pin (3) on the switch, then retighten the screw (1).

8. Repeat Steps 4 and 5 to check switch operation. Replace the switch if it still does not function properly.

9. Reconnect the red cable to the starter motor and the negative battery cable to the battery.

Neutral Start Switch Test and Adjust (20-30 hp)

The correct neutral start switch adjustment can only be accomplished if the shift lever is properly adjusted. Refer to the appropriate section in Chapter Nine for shift lever adjustment procedures. Refer to **Figure 44** for this procedure.

1. Disconnect the negative battery cable from the battery.

2. Disconnect the yellow/red wire from the neutral start switch.

3. Place the shift lever in NEUTRAL.

4. Connect an ohmmeter or continuity tester between the yellow/red terminal on the neutral start switch and a good engine ground. With the shift lever in neutral, continuity should be noted.

5. Shift into FORWARD, then REVERSE while noting the meter or tester. No continuity should be present in either gear.

6. If adjustment is necessary, loosen the 2 neutral start switch mounting screws. Insert a 1/16 in. drill bit between the top of the plunger and the bottom of the switch. Move the switch until the switch and plunger contact the drill bit, then retighten the screws securely.

7. Repeat Steps 4 and 5 to check switch operation. Replace the switch if it still does not function properly.

IGNITION SYSTEM

One-cylinder models (2.0, 2.3 and 3.3 hp) are equipped with a conventional magneto breaker point ignition system. All other models are equipped with breakerless capacitor discharge (CD) ignition. The ignition system designation indicates the number of cylinders the particular model has. For example, 2-cylinder models are equipped with CD2 ignition, 3-cylinder models are equipped with CD3 ignition and V4, V6 and V8 models are equipped with CD4, CD6 and CD8 ignition systems, respectively.

On 60° V6 models, the CD6 Optical Ignition system (OIS) is used. See the appropriate section in this chapter for operation and service procedures.

Some 2-cylinder models are equipped with the CD2U ignition system. Except for the ignition coils, the ignition system on models so equipped is entirely contained under the flywheel. The ignition model number is printed on the ignition module located under the flywheel. The model number is interpreted as follows: CD—capacitor discharge; 2—two cylinders; U—under flywheel ignition; S (some models)—contains the S.L.O.W. (speed limiting overheat warning)

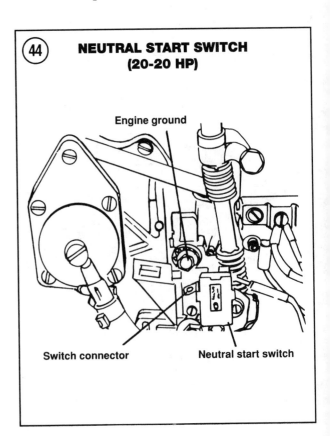

(44) NEUTRAL START SWITCH (20-20 HP)

Engine ground

Switch connector   Neutral start switch

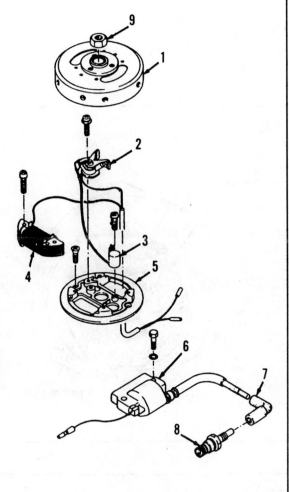

BREAKER POINT IGNITION SYSTEM (1-CYLINDER MODELS)

1. Flywheel
2. Breaker points
3. Condenser
4. Driver coil
5. Armature plate
6. Ignition coil
7. Spark plug boot
8. Spark plug
9. Flywheel nut

(45)

function; L (some models)—contains an engine speed limiter built into the module.

Refer to Chapter Three for troubleshooting and test procedures for all systems.

MAGNETO BREAKER POINT IGNITION SYSTEM SERVICE

The major components of the breaker point ignition system include the flywheel, breaker points, condenser, driver (primary) coil, ignition (secondary) coil, armature plate, spark plug and stop switch. See **Figure 45**.

Operation

As the flywheel rotates, permanent magnets situated around its inner diameter induce current through the closed breaker points into the driver (primary) coil windings. When the breaker cam opens the breaker points, the voltage in the driver coil collapses, inducing a high voltage in the secondary coil windings which provides the voltage necessary to fire the spark plug. The condenser absorbs excess voltage when the points open to prevent point arcing.

Breaker Points and Condenser Removal/Installation

Refer to the appropriate section in Chapter Four for breaker point removal, installation and adjustment procedures.

Armature Plate Removal/Installation

1. Disconnect the spark plug lead from the spark plug to prevent accidental starting.
2. Remove the rewind starter. See Chapter Twelve.
3. Remove the flywheel as described in Chapter Eight.

4. Remove the armature plate mounting screws (A, **Figure 46**).

5. Disconnect the ignition coil primary and stop switch wires at their bullet connectors (**Figure 47**).

6. Lift the armature plate assembly from the power head.

7. To install, place the armature plate assembly into position on the power head.

8. Apply OMC Screw Lock to the threads of the armature plate mounting screws (A, **Figure 46**). Install the screws and tighten to 27-44 in.-lb. (3.0-4.9 N·m).

9. Connect the stop switch and ignition primary wires (**Figure 47**).

10. Install the flywheel (Chapter Eight) and rewind starter (Chapter Twelve). Connect the spark plug wire to the spark plug.

Driver Coil Removal/Installation

1. Remove the armature plate as described in this chapter.

2. Remove the 2 screws securing the driver coil to the armature plate. Invert the armature plate and remove the screw clamping the primary ignition wire to the bottom of the armature plate.

3. To install, mount the driver coil on the armature plate. Make sure the ground wire is positioned under the coil mounting screws (**Figure 46**) and tighten the mounting screws securely.

4. Clamp the primary wire to the bottom of the armature plate.

5. Install the armature plate as described in this chapter.

Ignition (Secondary) Coil Removal/Installation

1. Disconnect the spark plug lead from the spark plug.

2. Disconnect the coil primary wire.

3. Remove the 2 screws securing the coil to the power head. Remove the coil assembly.

4. To install, reverse the removal procedure. Tighten the coil mounting screws to 62-89 in.-lb. (7-10 N·m).

CD2U IGNITION

The following models are equipped with CD2U ignition:

  a. *1991*—4 Deluxe, 6-50 hp (except 3 and 4 hp).

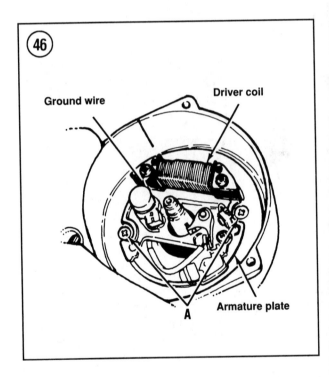

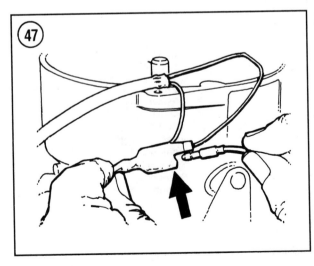

b. *1992*—4 Deluxe, 6-30 hp and 35 Jet- 50 hp equipped with 4 amp charging system.

c. *1993-on*—4 Deluxe and 48 hp.

The major components of the CD2U ignition system include the flywheel, charge coil, ignition module, ignition coils, spark plugs, stop circuit and related circuitry. The power pack and sensor coil are contained in the 1-piece ignition module (A, **Figure 48**).

Operation (CD2U)

As the crankshaft turns, permanent magnets located inside the flywheel induce alternating current into the charge coil (B, **Figure 48**) wind-ings. The alternating current created in the charge coil flows into the ignition module where it is rectified (converted to direct current) and stored inside a capacitor in the module. As the flywheel magnets rotate past the ignition module, a small current is induced into the internal sensor coil windings. The sensor coil voltage then closes an electronic switch (SCR) in the module which allows the stored voltage in the capacitor to discharge into the ignition coil primary windings. This voltage is induced into the coil secondary windings which creates the voltage necessary to fire the spark plugs. This sequence of events is repeated with each revolution of the crankshaft. When activated, the stop circuit disables the ignition system by shorting ignition module output to ground.

On some models, a power coil is located inside the ignition module. The power coil provides the voltage necessary to operate the S.L.O.W. and QuikStart systems.

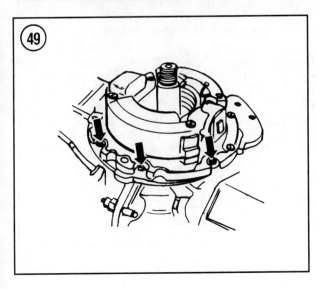

Armature Plate Removal/Installation (CD2U Ignition)

To prevent accidental starting, disconnect the spark plug leads from the spark plugs.

1. Disconnect the negative battery cable from the battery, if so equipped.

2. Remove the rewind starter, if so equipped.

3. Remove the flywheel. See Chapter Eight.

4. Disconnect the armature plate wire connectors.

5. Remove the 5 armature plate mounting screws (**Figure 49**). Remove the armature plate assembly from the power head.

6. Remove the 4 support plate mounting screws (**Figure 50**). Remove the retainer plate and support plate from the power head.

7. To install, place the retainer plate, then the support plate on the power head.

8. Apply OMC Nut Lock to the threads of the 4 support plate screws. Install the screws and tighten to 48-60 in.-lb. (5.4-6.8 N·m).

9. Lubricate the crankcase boss and the groove in the armature plate bearing (Delrin ring) with OMC Moly Lube, or equivalent. See **Figure 51**.

10. While installing the armature plate in position, compress the armature plate bearing using needlenose pliers inserted into the grooves (**Figure 52**) in the bearing.

11. Apply OMC Nut Lock to the threads of the 5 armature plate mounting screws. Align the armature plate and retainer plate screw holes, install the 5 screws and tighten to 25-35 in.-lb. (2.8-3.9 N•m)

12. Install the flywheel (Chapter Eight). Install the rewind starter if so equipped (Chapter Twelve).

13. Perform linkage adjustment and synchronization (Chapter Five).

Charge Coil, Ignition Module or Stator Coil Removal/Installation (CD2U Ignition)

1. Disconnect the spark plug leads from the spark plugs to prevent accidental starting.

2. Remove the armature plate as previously described in this chapter.

3. Remove the 2 screws holding the wire clamp in place. See **Figure 53**.

4. Invert the armature plate and remove the cover plate. See **Figure 54**.

5. Remove the screws securing the component being replaced. See **Figure 55**.

6. Pull the wires of the defective component(s) from the spiral wrap insulation sleeve. See *Connector Terminal Removal/Installation* in this chapter.

7. Remove the defective component(s) and wiring from the armature plate.

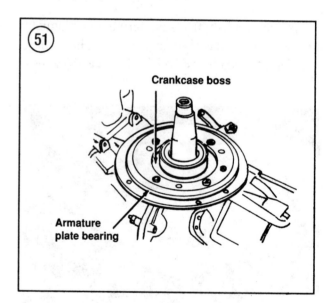

Crankcase boss

Armature plate bearing

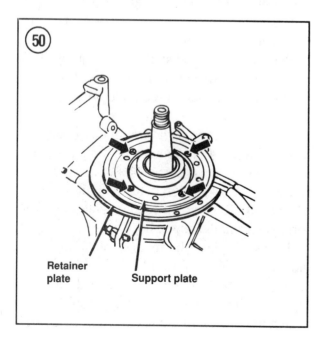

Retainer plate

Support plate

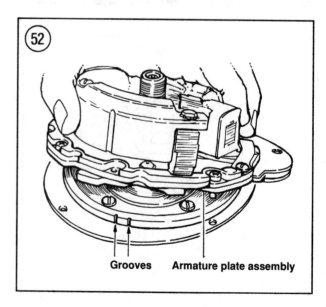

Grooves   Armature plate assembly

8. During installation, apply OMC Ultra Lock to the threads of the component mounting screws. Install the component on the armature plate. Loosely install the mounting screws.

CAUTION
Make sure all wires routed through the clamp and plate in Step 9 are not twisted or wrapped around each other. The wires must pass through the plate and clamp in one single layer.

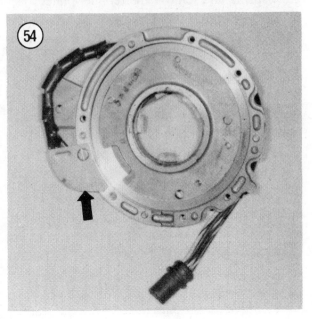

9. Correctly route all wiring, then install plate (**Figure 54**) and clamp (**Figure 53**). Tighten all screws securely. Insert wiring into the spiral wrap insulation sleeve.

NOTE
The outer edges of the charge coil, ignition module and stator coil must be flush with the machined surface of the armature plate to provide the proper clearance between each component and the flywheel magnets. The manufacturer recommends using OMC Locating Ring (part No. 334994) to simplify this process.

10. Place OMC Locating Ring (part No. 334994) over the machined bosses on the armature plate. See **Figure 55**. While holding the locating ring firmly in place, push the component(s) outward against the ring, then tighten the mounting screws to 30-40 in.-lb. (3.4-4.5 N•m).

11. Install the armature plate as described in this chapter.

12. Install the flywheel (Chapter Eight). Install the rewind starter (Chapter Twelve), if so equipped. Reconnect the negative cable to the battery, if so equipped.

13. Perform linkage adjustment and synchronization as outlined in Chapter Five.

7

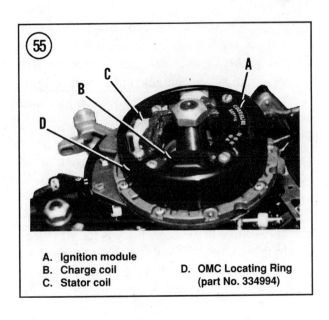

A. Ignition module
B. Charge coil
C. Stator coil
D. OMC Locating Ring (part No. 334994)

Ignition Coil Removal/Installation (CD2U Ignition)

1. Disconnect the spark plug leads and primary wires from the coil assembly.

2. Loosen the coil mounting screws, noting the orientation of the flat washers, fiber washers, ground wires/straps, clamps and star washers. Remove the screws and coil.

3. To install, make sure the washers, ground wires/straps and clamps are located in the same positions as removed. Install and tighten the mounting screws to 48-96 in.-lb. (5.4-10.8 N•m).

4. Apply a light coat of OMC Triple-Guard grease to the spark plug and primary wire boots. When connecting the primary wires, make sure the orange/blue wire is connected to the No. 1 ignition coil.

CD IGNITION

Operation (3 and 4 hp)

The major components of the ignition system used on 3 and 4 hp models include the flywheel, sensor coil, ignition module, ignition coil, stop switch, spark plugs and related circuitry. See **Figure 56**.

The sensor coil is located along the outer diameter of the flywheel and is part of the timer base assembly. The charge coil, capacitor and related circuitry are contained in a 1-piece ignition module. Ignition coils for both cylinders are contained in a 1-piece coil assembly.

As the crankshaft turns, permanent magnets located inside the flywheel induce alternating current in the charge coil windings located inside the ignition module. The ignition module then rectifies the alternating current into direct current for storage in the capacitor. As the flywheel continues to rotate, a small voltage is generated by the sensor coil. This voltage triggers an electronic switch (SCR) inside the ignition module

to close, which allows the stored voltage in the capacitor to discharge into the ignition coil primary windings. This voltage is induced into the coil secondary windings which produce the voltage necessary (up to 40,000 volts) to fire the spark plug. This sequence of events is repeated with each revolution of the crankshaft. When activated, the stop circuit stops the engine by shorting ignition module output to ground.

Ignition Plate Disassembly/Assembly

Refer to **Figure 56** for this procedure.

1. Remove the rewind starter as outlined in Chapter Twelve.

2. Remove the flywheel as outlined in Chapter Eight.

3. Remove the 3 screws securing the timer base assembly to the support plate. Disconnect the timer base spring, then lift the timer base from the power head.

4. Disconnect the throttle cable from the timer base.

5. If necessary, remove the screws securing the support plate and retainer plate. Lift the support plate off the power head. Disconnect the retainer plate spring and remove the retainer plate.

6. To reassemble the ignition plate, place the retainer plate on the power head and reconnect the spring.

7. Install the support plate on the power head.

8. Apply OMC Nut Lock to the threads of the support plate screws, then install the screws and tighten to 48-60 in.-lb. (5.4-6.8 N•m).

9. Lightly lubricate the groove of the timer base bearing with clean engine oil. Install the bearing on the support plate.

10. Lubricate the crankcase boss (timer base pilot) with OMC Moly Lube.

NOTE
The gap in the timer base bearing (Delrin ring) must be centered around the throttle cable connection.

11. Install the throttle cable in the timer base. Compress the timer base bearing and install the timer base. Apply OMC Screw Lock to the threads of the timer base screws, install the screws and tighten to 25-35 in.-lb. (2.8-3.9 N·m).

12. Install the flywheel (Chapter Eight) and rewind starter (Chapter Twelve).

13. Perform linkage adjustment and synchronization as outlined in Chapter Five.

Ignition Coil Removal/Installation (3 and 4 hp)

1. Disconnect the spark plug leads and primary wires from the coil assembly.

2. Loosen the coil mounting screws, noting the orientation of the flat washers, fiber washers and star-type lockwashers. Remove the screws and coil.

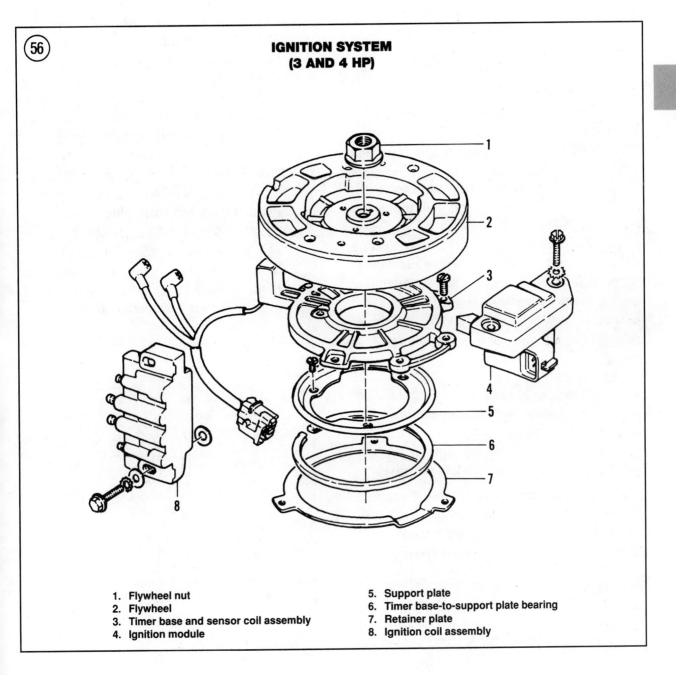

(56)

**IGNITION SYSTEM
(3 AND 4 HP)**

7

1. Flywheel nut
2. Flywheel
3. Timer base and sensor coil assembly
4. Ignition module
5. Support plate
6. Timer base-to-support plate bearing
7. Retainer plate
8. Ignition coil assembly

3. To install, make sure the washers are located in the same positions as removed. Install and tighten the mounting screws to 48-96 in.-lb. (5.4-10.8 N•m).

4. Apply a light coat OMC Triple-Guard grease to the spark plug and primary wire boots. When connecting the primary wires, make sure the orange/blue wire is connected to the No. 1 ignition coil.

5. Perform linkage adjustment and synchronization procedures as outlined in Chapter Five.

Ignition Module Removal/Installation (3 and 4 hp)

1. Disconnect the wire harness connector from the module.

2. Remove the module mounting screws and remove the module.

3. Clean the module mounting surfaces to ensure a good ground connection with the power head.

4. Apply a light coat of OMC Gasket Sealing Compound to the threads of the module mounting screws. Install the module and the mounting screws. Tighten the screws finger tight.

5. Using a suitable nonmetallic gauge, set the air gap between the ignition module and flywheel magnets to 0.013-0.017 in. (0.33-0.43 mm). See **Figure 57**.

6. When the correct air gap is established, tighten the module mounting screws to 60-84 in.-lb. (6.8-9.5 N•m).

7. Perform linkage adjustment and synchronization procedures as outlined in Chapter Five.

CD IGNITION
(ALL MODELS EXCEPT CD2U, 3 AND 4 HP AND 60° V6 MODELS)

Operation

Several different variations of the capacitor discharge (CD) ignition system are used; how-

ever, they all operate essentially the same. The ignition system designation indicates the number of cylinders the particular model has (except 3 and 4 hp). For example, 2-cylinder models are equipped with CD2 ignition, 3-cylinder models are equipped with CD3 ignition and V4, V6 and V8 models are equipped with CD4, CD6 and CD8 ignition systems, respectively.

The major components for each variation of the CD ignition system include:

a. *CD2 (except 40 and 50 hp)*—The flywheel, charge coil, sensor coil, power pack, 2 ignition coils and spark plugs.

b. *CD2 40-50 hp (except 48 hp)*—The flywheel, charge coil, power coil (supplies voltage for S.L.O.W.), 2 sensor coils, power pack, 2 ignition coils and spark plugs.

c. *CD3 (1990 and 1992)*—The flywheel, charge coil, power coil (supplies voltage for S.L.O.W.), 3 sensor coils, power pack, 3 ignition coils and spark plugs.

d. *CD3 (1993-on)*—The flywheel, charge coil, power coil (supplies voltage for Quik-Start and S.L.O.W.), 6 sensor coils (3 for ignition and 3 for QuikStart), power pack, 3 ignition coils and spark plugs.

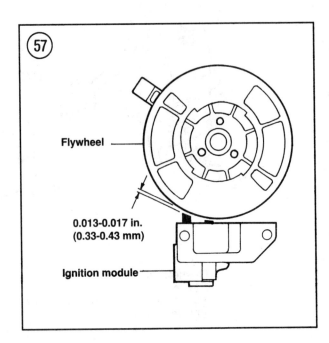

(57)

Flywheel

0.013-0.017 in.
(0.33-0.43 mm)

Ignition module

e. *CD4 cross flow models*—The flywheel, charge coil, 4 sensor coils, power pack, 4 ignition coils and spark plugs.

f. *CD4 loop charged models*—The flywheel, charge coil, power coil (supplies voltage for QuikStart and S.L.O.W.), 8 sensor coils (4 for ignition and 4 for QuikStart), power pack, 4 ignition coils and spark plugs.

g. *CD6 1990 and 1991 cross flow models (9 amp charging system)*—The flywheel, 2 charge coils, 6 sensor coils, 2 power packs (molded into 1 assembly), 6 ignition coils and spark plugs.

NOTE
Double-wound sensor coils are used on some models to conserve space under the flywheel. Each double-wound sensor coil contains 2 separate coils.

h. *CD6 1990 and 1991 cross flow models (35 amp charging system)*—The flywheel, 2 charge coils, power coil (supplies voltage for QuikStart and S.L.O.W.), 6 double-wound sensor coils (6 for ignition and 6 for QuikStart), 2 power packs (molded into 1 assembly), 6 ignition coils and spark plugs.

i. *CD6 loop charged models*—The flywheel, 2 charge coils, power coil (supplies voltage for QuikStart and S.L.O.W.), 6 double-wound sensor coils (6 for ignition and 6 for QuikStart), 2 power packs (molded into 1 assembly), 6 ignition coils and spark plugs.

j. *CD8*—The flywheel, 2 charge coils, power coil (supplies voltage for QuikStart and S.L.O.W.), 8 double-wound sensor coils (8 for ignition and 8 for QuikStart), 2 power packs (molded into 1 assembly), 8 ignition coils and spark plugs.

NOTE
Refer to Chapter Three for troubleshooting procedures on all systems and a description of the QuikStart and S.L.O.W. systems.

The charge coil (A, **Figure 58**) and sensor coil (B) are mounted on the armature plate on 6-30 hp and rope start 40 hp models. On all other models, the charge coil(s) and power coil (if so equipped) are contained in a 1-piece stator assembly (**Figure 59**) and the sensor coils are contained in a 1-piece timer base assembly (**Figure 60**).

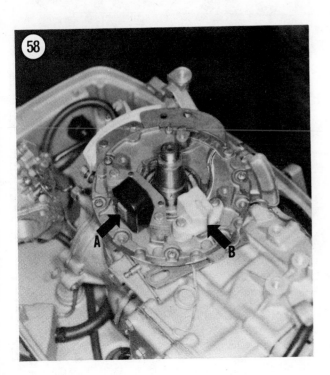

7

As the crankshaft rotates, the permanent magnets located in the outer rim of the flywheel create alternating current in the charge coil windings. The alternating current is rectified (converted) to direct current and stored in a capacitor located in the power pack(s).

As the crankshaft continues to rotate, permanent magnets located in the hub of the flywheel create a small voltage in the sensor coil windings. The voltage from the sensor coil closes an electronic switch (SCR) inside the power pack, which allows the stored voltage in the capacitor to release into the primary windings of the ignition coil. The primary voltage is induced into the ignition coil secondary windings, which create the voltage (up to 40,000 volts) necessary to fire the spark plugs. This process fires each spark plug in the correct firing order and repeats itself with each revolution of the flywheel.

Armature Plate Removal/Installation (1993-on 6-30 hp and 40 hp rope start)

1. Disconnect the negative battery cable from the battery, if so equipped.
2. Remove the rewind starter (Chapter Twelve), if so equipped.
3. Remove the flywheel. See Chapter Eight.
4. Disconnect the armature plate wires from their support clamps.
5. Disconnect the armature plate wire connectors and terminal block connections.
6. Remove the armature plate retaining screws (**Figure 61**). Remove the armature plate and cable assembly from the power head. See **Figure 62**, typical.
7. If necessary to remove the retainer and support plates, disconnect the armature plate-to-throttle lever link and remove the support plate screws. Remove the retainer and support plates (**Figure 63**).
8. Installation is the reverse of removal. Apply OMC Nut Lock to the threads of the support plate screws. Tighten the support plate screws to

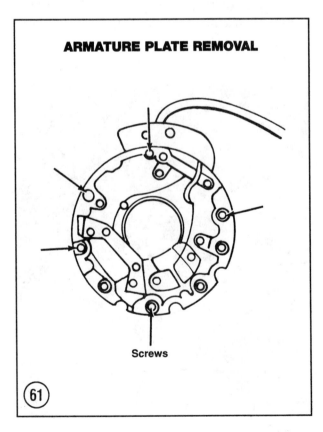

ARMATURE PLATE REMOVAL

Screws

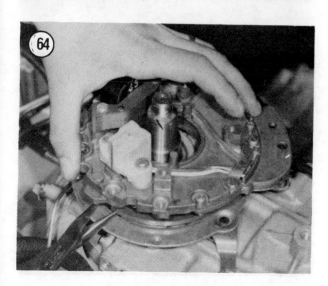

48-60 in.-lb. (5.4-6.8 N·m). Coat the crankcase pilot boss with OMC Moly Lube. Lubricate the armature plate bearing (Delrin ring) with clean engine oil Compress the armature plate bearing with needlenose pliers (**Figure 64**) and guide the armature plate into position. Tighten the armature plate screws to 25-35 in.-lb. (2.8-3.9 N·m).

9. Perform linkage adjustment and synchronization procedures as outlined in Chapter Five.

Charge Coil, Sensor Coil or Stator Removal/Installation (1993-on 6-30 hp and 40 hp Rope Start)

1. Remove the armature plate outlined in this chapter.

2. Invert the armature plate and remove the cover plate. See **Figure 65**, typical.

3. Remove the 2 screws holding the wiring clamp strap in place (**Figure 66**).

4. Remove the screws securing the component being removed. Disconnect the component wires, pull the wires from the insulation sleeve and remove the component.

5. During installation, apply OMC Ultra Lock to the threads of the component mounting

7

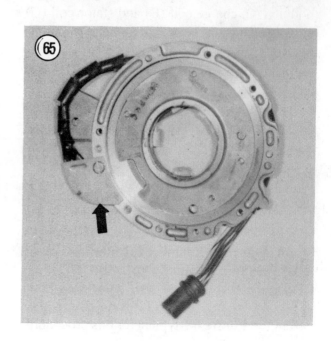

screws. Install the component on the armature plate. Loosely install the mounting screws.

> *CAUTION*
> *Make sure all wires routed through the clamp and plate in Step 6 are not twisted or wrapped around each other. The wires must pass through the plate and clamp in one single layer.*

6. Correctly route all wiring, then install plate (**Figure 65**) and clamp (**Figure 66**). Tighten all screws securely. Insert wiring into the spiral wrap insulation sleeve.

> *NOTE*
> *The outer edges of the sensor coil, charge coil and stator coil must be flush with the machined surface of the armature plate to provide the proper clearance between the component and the flywheel magnets. The manufacturer recommends using OMC Locating Ring (part No. 334994) to simplify this process.*

7. Place OMC Locating Ring (part No. 334994) over the machined bosses on the armature plate. See D, **Figure 67**, typical. While holding the locating ring firmly in place, push the ignition module (A), charge coil (B) and stator coil (C) outward against the ring, then tighten the mounting screws to 30-40 in.-lb. (3.4-4.5 N•m).

8. Install the armature plate as described in this chapter.

9. Install the flywheel (Chapter Eight). Install the rewind starter (Chapter Twelve), if so equipped. Reconnect the negative cable to the battery, if so equipped.

10. Perform linkage adjustment and synchronization as outlined in Chapter Five.

Stator Assembly Removal/Installation (CD2 [1993-on 40 and 50 hp], CD3, CD4, CD6 and CD8)

Refer to **Figure 68**, typical for this procedure.

1. Disconnect the negative battery cable from the battery.

2. Disconnect the spark plug leads from the spark plugs.

3. Remove the rewind starter, if so equipped. See Chapter Twelve.

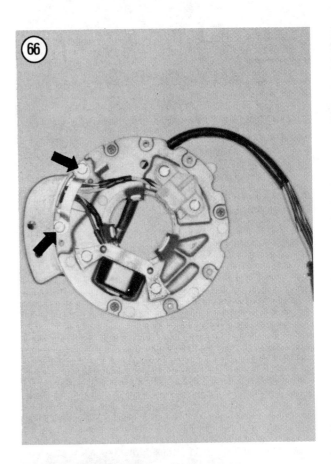

4. Remove the flywheel. See Chapter Eight.

5. Disconnect the stator yellow and yellow/gray wires from the terminal block.

6. Disconnect the stator harness connector(s).

7. On V4, V6 and V8 loop charged models, disconnect the power coil orange and orange/black wires from the terminal block.

8. On 40-70 hp models, remove the yellow/black stop circuit wire from the 5-pin Amphenol connector. See *Connector Terminal Removal/Installation* in this chapter.

9. Remove 3 or 4 stator mounting screws and remove the stator assembly from the power head.

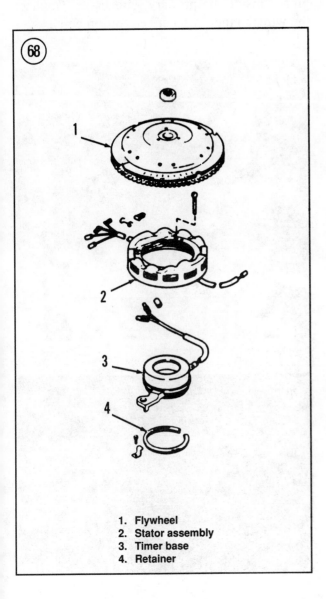

1. Flywheel
2. Stator assembly
3. Timer base
4. Retainer

10. Thoroughly clean any varnish or corrosion from the stator in the area of the mounting screw holes. A good clean metal-to-metal connection must be present between the stator, mounting screws and crankcase head.

CAUTION
*Patchlock screws that have lost their locking ability **must** be replaced.*

11A. *35 amp charging system*—Use only Patchlock screws to secure the stator assembly to the power head. Replace the screws if their locking ability is diminished.

11B. *All others*—Clean the stator mounting screws using OMC Locquic Primer and allow to air dry. Apply OMC Nut Lock to the threads of the stator mounting screws.

12. Install the stator assembly, making sure all wires are properly routed. Install the mounting screws and tighten to 120-144 in.-lb. (13.6-16.3 N•m).

13. Connect the stator yellow and yellow/gray wires to the terminal block. Coat the terminal block connections with OMC Black Neoprene Dip.

14. On 40-70 hp, insert the black/yellow wire into the 5-pin Amphenol connector. See *Connector Terminal Removal/Installation* in this chapter. Reconnect the stator and power coil harness connectors, making sure the wires are correctly routed.

15. Install the flywheel (Chapter Eight). Install the rewind starter (Chapter Twelve), if so equipped.

16. Perform linkage adjustment and synchronization procedures as outlined in Chapter Five.

**Timer Base Removal/Installation
(CD2 [1993-on 40 and 50 hp], CD3, CD4, CD6 and CD8)**

Refer to **Figure 68**, typical for this procedure.

1. Remove the stator assembly as outlined in this chapter.

2. Disconnect the timer base connector(s).

3. Remove the screws securing the timer base retaining clips. Remove the timer base from the power head.

4. Thoroughly clean the crankcase head and timer base bearing surfaces. Make sure the bearing surfaces are completely free of metal chips, corrosion or other contamination.

5. Lubricate the timer base bearing and crankcase head bearing surface with OMC Moly Lube.

6. Lubricate the groove in the retainer ring with clean engine oil.

7. Compress the timer base retainer while guiding the timer base into position. Connect the timer base connector(s), making sure the wires are correctly routed.

8. Install the timer base retaining clips and screws. Tighten the screws to 25-35 in.-lb. (2.8-3.9 N•m).

9. Install the stator assembly as outlined in this chapter. Perform linkage adjustment and synchronization procedures as outlined in Chapter Five.

Power Pack Removal/Installation (CD2 [1993-on 40 and 50 hp], CD3, CD4 [Cross Flow] and CD6 [Cross Flow] Models)

1. Disconnect the negative battery cable from the battery.

2. Separate the power pack connectors.

3. Disconnect the primary wires from the ignition coils.

4. Remove the power pack mounting screws while noting ground wire, washer, insulator and clamp locations. Remove the power pack from the power head or ignition bracket. See **Figures 69-71** for typical power pack mounting locations.

NOTE
A good ground connection between the power pack and engine or bracket is necessary. Be sure the power head or

mounting bracket and power pack mounting surfaces are clean.

5. Thoroughly clean the power pack and power head mounting surfaces to ensure a good, clean ground connection.

6. Install the power pack, making sure the washers, insulators, clamps and ground wires are in their original locations. Tighten the mounting screws to 60-84 in.-lb. (6.8-9.5 N•m).

7. Lubricate the Amphenol connectors with isopropyl alcohol. Connect the Amphenol connectors and secure with a wire retainer, where used.

8. Apply a light coat of OMC Triple-Guard grease inside the primary wire boots. Connect the wires to their respective ignition coils.

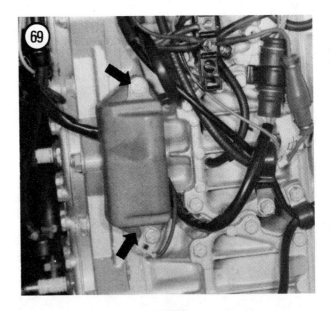

a. *Two-cylinder models*—Orange/blue wire to the No. 1 coil, orange/green wire to the No. 2 coil.

b. *Three-cylinder models*—Orange/blue wire to the No. 1 coil, orange/purple to the No. 2 coil and the orange/green wire to the No. 3 coil.

c. *V4 models*—Orange/blue wire to the No. 1 coil, orange/purple wire to the No. 2 coil,

orange/green wire to the No. 3 coil and orange/pink wire to the No. 4 coil.

d. *V6 models*—Orange/blue wires to the top coils, orange wires to the center coils and the orange/green wires to the bottom coils.

9. Check ignition timing advance as outlined in Chapter Five.

Power Pack Removal/Installation (CD4, CD6 and CD8 Loop Charged Models)

1. Disconnect the negative battery cable from the battery.

2. Disconnect the spark plug leads from the spark plugs.

3. Remove the 2 screws, 2 nuts and washers securing the power pack assembly to the mounting bracket. See **Figure 72**.

4. Lift the power pack assembly off the mounting bracket.

5. Disconnect the charge coil connectors, timer base connectors, key switch wire(s), yellow/red wire, tan wires, white/black wire and orange and orange/black wires. Disconnect the primary wires from the ignition coils. Remove the power pack assembly.

6. To install, make sure the power pack wiring is correctly routed under the electrical component mounting bracket, then place the power pack into position. Do not install the power pack mounting fasteners at this point.

7. Lubricate the Amphenol connectors with isopropyl alcohol. Connect the charge coil connector(s) then the timer base connectors. Place the charge coil and timer base connectors in the component bracket.

8. Reconnect all circuits and be certain of the proper wire harness routing. Install the ground wire (**Figure 72**) and the mounting nuts, screws and washers. Tighten the nuts and screws to 48-60 in.-lb. (5.4-6.8 N•m).

9. Apply a light coat of OMC Triple-Guard grease inside the primary wire boots. Connect

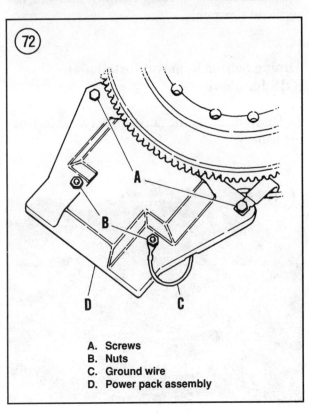

A. Screws
B. Nuts
C. Ground wire
D. Power pack assembly

7

the wires to their respective ignition coils as follows:

  a. *V4 models*—orange/blue wire to the No. 1 coil, orange/purple wire to the No. 2 coil, orange/green wire to the No. 3 coil and the orange/pink wire to the No. 4 coil.

  b. *V6 models*—Orange/blue wires to the top coils, orange wires to the center coils and orange/green wires to the bottom coils.

  c. *V8 models*—Orange/blue wire to the No. 1 coil, orange/purple wire to the No. 2 coil, Orange/green wire to the No. 3 coil, Orange/pink wire to the No. 4 coil, Orange/blue/white wire to the No. 5 coil, orange/purple/white wire to the No. 6 coil, orange/green/white wire to the No. 7 coil and the orange/pink/white wire to the No. 8 coil.

10. Check and/or adjust the ignition timing maximum spark advance as outlined in Chapter Five.

Ignition Coil Removal/Installation (All Models)

1. Disconnect the spark plug lead from the coil to be removed.

2. Disconnect the primary wire from the coil.

3. While noting the order of washers, insulators and clamps, remove the coil fasteners and remove the coil.

4. Installation is the reverse of removal. Make sure all washers, insulators and clamps are in their original locations. Tighten the coil fasteners to 48-96 in.-lb. (5.4-10.8 N•m). Apply a light coat of OMC Triple-Guard grease to the inside of the primary wire and spark plug boots. See *Power Pack Removal/Installation* in this chapter for the correct primary ignition wiring order.

OPTICAL IGNITION SYSTEM (60° V6 MODELS)

The major components of the CD6 OIS (optical ignition system) include the flywheel, 2 charge coils, power coil (supplies voltage for timing sensor, QuikStart and S.L.O.W.), optical timing sensor, timing wheel, 2 power packs (molded into 1 assembly), 3 dual ignition coils and spark plugs.

The charge coils and power coil are contained in the 1-piece stator assembly and are not serviced separately. The power coil provides voltage for the operation of QuikStart, S.L.O.W., the timing sensor and other ignition features. The infrared timing sensor consists of 2 separate sensors. One sensor provides a signal for each revolution of the flywheel and is used to determine crankshaft position. The other sensor provides 6 supplemental timing signals and 1 additional signal to prevent the engine from running in reverse rotation. Both power packs are contained in a 1-piece assembly and are not serviced separately.

Timing Sensor Removal/Installation (OIS Ignition)

1. Disconnect the negative battery cable from the battery.

2. Remove the timing sensor cover and the voltage regulator/rectifier cover.

3. Unplug the timing sensor connector (D, **Figure 73**).

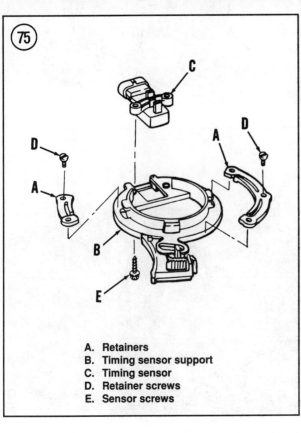

A. Retainers
B. Timing sensor support
C. Timing sensor
D. Retainer screws
E. Sensor screws

NOTE
Use the piston stop tool in Step 4 to prevent the crankshaft from turning while removing the timing wheel retaining screw.

4. Place an appropriate size wrench or socket on the timing wheel screw and rotate the crankshaft to approximately 30° ATDC. Remove the No. 1 spark plug and install OMC Piston Stop Tool (part No. 384887) into the spark plug hole. See **Figure 74**. Turn the piston stop tool in until it contacts the piston, then lock the tool with its lock ring.

5. With the No. 1 piston firmly against the piston stop tool, remove the timing wheel screw (A, **Figure 73**).

6. Remove the piston stop tool from the No. 1 spark plug hole. Lift the timing wheel (C, **Figure 73**) off the crankshaft. Be sure to retrieve the timing wheel key. Remove the timing pointer (B, **Figure 73**) if necessary for clearance.

7. Disconnect the sensor support return spring (E, **Figure 73**) from the post on the flywheel cover.

8. Remove the 5 screws securing the 2 sensor support retainers. See **Figure 75**. Remove the 2 retainers and lift the sensor support off the flywheel cover.

9. Invert the sensor support and remove the 2 screws (E, **Figure 75**) holding the timing sensor (C) to the sensor support (B).

10. To install the timing sensor, place the sensor in position on the sensor support. Install the 2 sensor mounting screws and tighten to 15-20 in.-lb. (1.7-2.3 N•m).

11. Lightly lubricate the contact surfaces of the sensor support, then install the support on the flywheel cover.

12. Install the 2 sensor support retainers. Install the 5 retainer screws and tighten securely.

13. Reconnect the sensor support return spring. Connect the timing sensor connector.

7

CAUTION
A strong light source can interfere with the optical ignition timing sensor, resulting in misfire or erratic ignition timing. Do not operate the motor in bright ambient light with the timing wheel removed. Do not operate the motor with a timing light pointing at the timing sensor.

14. If removed, install the timing wheel key into its slot in the crankshaft. Install the timing wheel. Clean the threads of the timing wheel screw with OMC Locquic Primer and allow to air dry. Apply OMC HT 400 to the threads of the screw, then install the screw and tighten to 120-140 in.-lb. (13.6-15.8 N·m).

15. Perform linkage adjustment and synchronization as outlined in Chapter Five.

Stator Assembly Removal/Installation (OIS Ignition)

1. Disconnect the negative battery cable from the battery.

2. Remove the flywheel cover and flywheel as outlined in Chapter Eight.

3. Remove the voltage regulator/rectifier cover.

4. Disconnect the stator connector from the regulator/rectifier.

5. Cut any tie straps securing the stator wiring to the engine harness. Disconnect the 6-pin Packard connector between the stator and power pack.

6. Remove the 4 stator mounting screws (**Figure 76**). Lift the stator assembly off the power head.

7. Thoroughly clean any varnish, corrosion or other contamination from both sides of the stator mounting screw holes. A clean metal-to-metal connection must be present between the stator, mounting screws and power head.

8. Route the stator wires through the hole in the cylinder block and install the stator, making sure the stator roll pin is properly aligned with its locating hole in the block. Firmly seat the stator

on the cylinder block and install the grommet in the hole in the block.

9. Thoroughly clean all thread locking compound from the threads of the stator mounting screws. Then, clean the threads with OMC Locquic Primer and allow to air dry.

10. Apply OMC Nut Lock to the threads of the stator screws. Install the screws and tighten to 120-140 in.-lb. (13.6-15.8 N·m).

11. Secure the stator wiring to the engine harness using new tie straps.

12. Connect all circuits disconnected during removal. Install the voltage regulator/rectifier cover. Install the flywheel and flywheel cover as outlined in Chapter Eight.

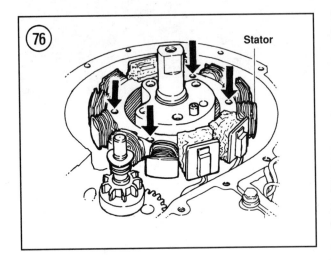

13. Perform linkage adjustment and synchronization procedures as outlined in Chapter Five.

Ignition Coils and Power Pack Removal/Installation (OIS Ignition)

1. Disconnect the negative battery cable from the battery.

2. Remove the timing sensor cover (A, **Figure 77**), voltage regulator/rectifier cover (B) and the power pack cover (C).

3. Unplug the timing sensor connector (D, **Figure 73**).

4. Disconnect the 5-pin and 6-pin Packard connectors from the power pack.

5. Disconnect the primary wire and spark plug lead from the top ignition coil assembly. Remove the top coil mounting screws and remove the coil assembly.

6. Repeat Step 5 on the center and bottom coil assemblies. The power pack can be removed after the bottom ignition coil is removed.

7. To install, place the power pack and bottom ignition coil in position on the power head. Install the lockwasher, flat washer and power pack ground wire on the port coil mounting screw and install the screw finger tight. Install the starboard coil mounting screw along with its lockwasher and flat washer, then tighten both screws to 50-95 in.-lb. (5.6-10.7 N·m).

8. Connect the primary wire and spark plug lead to the bottom ignition coil assembly.

9. Repeat Step 7 and Step 8 to install the remaining ignition coils.

10. Connect the power pack 5-pin and 6-pin connectors.

11. Connect the timing sensor connector. Install the power pack cover, voltage regulator/rectifier cover and the timing sensor cover. If the power pack has been replaced, be sure to check and/or adjust the ignition timing spark advance as outlined in Chapter Five.

Connector Terminal Removal/Installation

Waterproof plug-in connectors (Amphenol) are used on many models covered in this manual. Some connectors halves are secured by a retaining clamp which must be removed before they can be separated. See **Figure 79**, typical.

Whenever an ignition component is replaced on models so equipped, the component wires and

7

their plug terminals must be removed from the connector. A set of 3 special tools is available for quick and easy terminal removal/installation: insert tool part No. 322697, pin remover tool part No. 322698 and socket remover tool part No. 322699. Each tool has the appropriate tip for its intended use.

Connector terminals should be removed and installed according to this procedure. Use of tools or lubricant other than specified can result in high resistance connections, short circuits between terminals or damage to the connector material.

1. Lubricate the terminal pin or socket to be removed with rubbing alcohol (isopropyl) at both ends of the connector cavity.

2. Hold the connector against the edge of a flat surface, allowing sufficient clearance for terminal and socket removal.

3. Insert the proper removal tool in the connector end of the plug and carefully push the terminal or socket from the plug. See **Figure 80**.

4. If the pin or socket requires replacement, install a new one on the end of the wire. Make sure the insulation is stripped back far enough to allow the new pin or socket to make complete contact with the wire.

5. Crimp the new terminal onto the wire with crimping pliers (part No. 322696) or equivalent. If crimping pliers are not available, solder the wire in the pin or socket.

6. Lubricate the connector cavity with rubbing alcohol.

7. Place the insert tool against the pin or socket shoulder. Carefully guide the pin or socket into the rear of the connector plug cavity and press it in place until the insert tool shoulder rests against the connector plug. Withdraw the insert tool.

8. Reconnect the connector plug halves and install the retaining clamp.

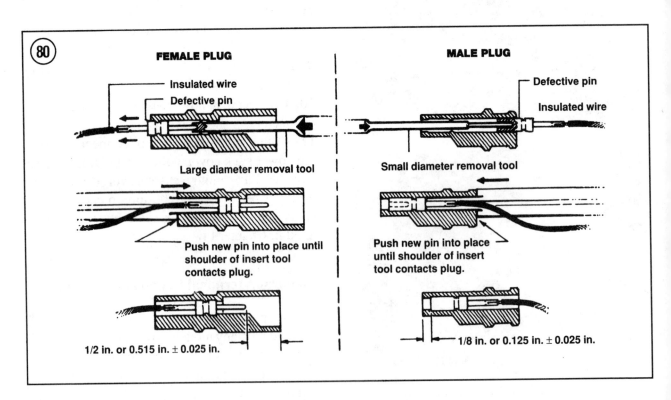

(80)

FEMALE PLUG

— Insulated wire
— Defective pin

Large diameter removal tool

Push new pin into place until shoulder of insert tool contacts plug.

1/2 in. or 0.515 in. ± 0.025 in.

MALE PLUG

— Defective pin

Insulated wire

Small diameter removal tool

Push new pin into place until shoulder of insert tool contacts plug.

1/8 in. or 0.125 in. ± 0.025 in.

Table 1 BATTERY CAPACITY (HOURS)

Accessory draw	80 Amp-hour battery provides continuous power for:	Approximate recharge time
5 amps	13.5 hours	16 hours
15 amps	3.5 hours	13 hours
25 amps	1.8 hours	12 hours

Accessory draw	105 Amp-hour battery provides continuous power for:	Approximate recharge time
5 amps	15.8 hours	16 hours
15 amps	4.2 hours	13 hours
25 amps	2.4 hours	12 hours

Table 2 APPROXIMATE STATE OF CHARGE

State of charge	Specific gravity	Open-circuit voltage (12-volt battery)
100%	1.265	12.7
75%	1.225	12.4
50%	1.190	12.2
25%	1.155	12.1

Readings are based on electrolyte temperature at 80° F (26.7° C)

Table 3 MINIMUM BATTERY RECOMMENDATION (CCA/RESERVE)

Model	Minimum battery cold cranking amps (CCA) and reserve capacity
9.9-30 hp	350 CCA and 100 minutes reserve
40-140 hp	360 CCA and 115 minutes reserve
150-300 hp	500 CCA and 99 minutes reserve

Table 4 MINIMUM BATTERY CABLE GAUGE SIZES

Model	Battery cables minimum gauge		
	1-10 ft.	11-15 ft.	16-20 ft.
9.9-15 hp	10	8	6
20-30 hp	6	4	3
40-50 hp	6	4	3
60-70 hp, V4	4	3	1
V6	4	2	1
V8	4	2	1

Specifications based on the use of stranded copper wire without splices. Do not use aluminum battery cables. Do not exceed 20 ft. (50 cm), regardless of cable diameter.

7

Table 5 TIGHTENING TORQUES

2-8 HP MODELS			
Fastener	**in.-lb.**	**ft.-lb.**	**N·m**
Armature plate screws			
2-3.3 hp	27-44		3.0-5.0
Charge coil screws			
3 hp, 4 hp, 4 Deluxe	30-40		3.4-4.5
6-8 hp	15-22		1.7-2.5
Flywheel nut			
2-3.3 hp		29-33	39-44
3 hp, 4 hp, 4 Deluxe		30-40	41-54
6-8 hp		40-50	54-68
Ignition coil screws			
2-3.3 hp	62-89		7-10
3-8 hp	48-96		5.4-10.8
Ignition module screws			
3 hp, 4 hp, 4 Deluxe	30-40		3.4-4.5
Ignition plate screws			
3-8 hp	25-35		2.8-3.9
Ignition support plate screws			
3-8 hp	48-60		5.4-6.8
Power pack			
6 & 8 hp	60-84		6.8-9.5
Sensor coil screws			
6 & 8 hp	15-22		1.7-2.5
Spark plug	216-240	18-20	24-27

9.9-30 HP MODELS			
Fastener	**in.-lb.**	**ft.-lb.**	**N·m**
Charge coil screws			
CD2	15-22		1.7-2.5
CD2U	30-40		3.4-4.5
Electrical components bracket screws			
9.9-15 hp	48-96		5.4-10.8
Flywheel nut			
9.9-15 hp		45-50	61-68
20-30 hp		100-105	136-142
Ignition coil screws	48-96		5.4-10.8
Ignition module (CD2U)	30-40		3.4-4.5
Ignition plate screws	25-35		2.8-3.9
Ignition support plate screws	48-60		5.4-6.8
Power pack screws (CD2)	60-84		6.8-9.5
Sensor coil screws (CD2)	15-22		1.7-2.5
Stator screws			
9.9-15 hp	25-35		2.8-3.9
20-30	30-40		3.4-4.5
Spark plug	216-240	18-21	24-27
Starter motor mounting screws			
9.9-15 hp		10-12	13.6-16.3
Starter motor			
pinion (drive) gear nut	150-170	13-14	17-19
	240-300	20-25	27-34

(continued)

Table 5 TIGHTENING TORQUES (continued)

Fastener	in.-lb.	ft.-lb.	N·m
9.9-30 HP MODELS (continued)			
Starter motor through-bolts			
9.9-15 hp	30-40		3.4-4.5
20-30 hp	95-100		10.7-11.3

Fastener	in.-lb.	ft.-lb.	N·m
35 JET, 40, 48 & 50 HP MODELS			
Charge coil screws			
CD2	15-22		1.7-2.5
CD2U	30-40		3.4-4.5
Flywheel nut		100-105	136-142
Ignition coil screws	48-96		5.4-10.8
Ignition module (CD2U)	30-40		3.4-4.5
Ignition plate screws	25-35		2.8-3.9
Ignition support plate screws	48-60		5.4-6.8
Power pack screws (CD2)	60-84		6.8-9.5
Sensor coil screws (CD2)	15-22		1.7-2.5
Spark plug	216-240	18-20	24-27
Starter motor mounting screws		14-16	19-22
Starter motor pinion (drive)			
gear nut	240-300	20-25	27-34
Starter motor through-bolts	95-110		10.7-12.4
Stator screws (CD2)	120-144		13.6-16.3
Timer base screws (CD2)	25-35		2.8-3.9

Fastener	in.lb.	ft.-lb.	N·m
60-70 HP MODELS			
Flywheel nut		100-105	136-142
Ignition coil screws	48-96		5.4-10.8
Power pack screws	60-84		6.8-9.5
Spark plug	216-240	18-20	24-27
Starter motor mounting screws	168-192	14-16	19-21
Starter motor pinion (drive)			
gear nut	240-300	20-25	27-34
Starter motor through-bolts	95-110		10.7-12.4

Fastener	in.-lb.	ft.-lb.	N·m
V4 AND V6 CROSS FLOW MODELS			
Flywheel nut			
V4		100-105	136-142
V6		140-145	190-196
Ignition coil screws	48-96		5.4-10.8
Power pack screws	60-84		6.8-9.5
Spark plug	216-240	18-20	24-27
Starter motor mounting screws	168-192	14-16	19-21
Starter motor pinion (drive)			
gear nut	240-300	20-25	27-34
Starter motor through-bolts	95-110		10.7-12.4
Timer base retainer screws	25-35		2.8-3.9

(continued)

7

Table 5 TIGHTENING TORQUES (continued)

V4, V6 (EXCEPT 60° MODELS) AND V8 LOOP CHARGED MODELS			
Fastener	**in.-lb.**	**ft.-lb.**	**N·m**
Flywheel nut		140-150	190-203
Ignition coil screws	48-96		5.4-10.8
Electrical bracket screws	48-60		5.4-6.8
Power pack screws	48-60		5.4-6.8
Power steering belt tensioning nut	96-120		10.8-13.5
Power steering pulley screws	60-84		6.8-9.5
Spark plugs	216-240	18-20	24-27
Starter motor mounting screws		14-16	19-21
Starter motor			
Pinion (drive) gear nut			
V4	240-300	20-25	27-34
Through-bolts			
V4	95-110		10.7-12.4
V6 & V8	50-65		5.6-7.3
Pinion housing screws			
V6 & V8	60-84		6.8-9.5

60° V6 SERIES (150-175 HP)			
Fastener	**in.-lb.**	**ft.-lb.**	**N·m**
Ignition coil screws	50-95		5.6-10.7
Flywheel screws	276-300	23-25	31-34
Flywheel cover screws	40-50		4.5-5.6
Power pack screws	50-95		5.6-10.7
Spark plug	216-240	18-20	24-27
Starter motor			
Mounting screws		14-16	19-21
Through-bolts	50-60		5.6-6.8

STANDARD SCREWS, BOLTS AND NUTS (ALL MODELS)			
Fastener	**in.-lb.**	**ft.-lb.**	**N·m**
No. 6	7-10		0.8-1.1
No. 8	15-22		1.7-2.5
No. 10	25-35		2.8-3.9
No. 12	35-40		3.9-4.5
1/4 in.	60-84	5-7	6.8-9.5
5/16 in.	120-144	10-12	13.5-16.3
3/8 in.		18-20	24-27
7/16 in.		28-30	38-41

Table 6 GENERAL ENGINE SPECIFICATIONS

Model	Displacement cu. in. (cc)	Type
2, 2.3, 3.3	4.47 (77.8)	1-cylinder loop charged
3, 4, 4 Deluxe	5.29 (86.4)	2-cylinder cross flow
6, 8	10.0 (164)	2-cylinder cross flow
(continued)		

Table 6 GENERAL ENGINE SPECIFICATIONS (continued)

Model	Displacement cu. in. (cc)	Type
9.9, 15		
1991-92	13.2 (216	2-cylinder cross flow
1993	15.6 (255)	2-cylinder cross flow
20, 25, 28, 30	31.8 (521.2)	2-cylinder cross flow
35 Jet, 40, 48, 50	44.99 (737.4)	2-cylinder loop charged
60, 70	56.1 (920)	3-cylinder loop charged
65 Jet, 80 Jet, 85, 88, 90, 115, 115	99.6 (1632)	90° V4 cross flow
120, 140	122 (2000)	90° V4 loop charged
105 Jet, 150*	149.4 (2448)	90° V6 cross flow
60° 150/175 hp	158 (2589)	60° V6 loop charged
175*	160.3 (2626)	90° V6 cross flow
200, 225	183 (3000)	90° V6 loop charged
250, 300	244 (4000)	90° V8 loop charged
1.6 Sea Drive	99.6 (1632)	90° V4 cross flow
2.0 Sea Drive	122 (2000)	90° V4 loop charged
3.0 Sea Drive	183 (3000)	90° V6 loop charged
4.0 Sea Drive	244 (4000)	90° V6 loop charged

* The 90° V6 cross flow power head was discontinued after the 1991 model year. The 105 Jet, 150 and 175 hp models for 1992-on are 60° loop charged engines.

7

Chapter Eight

Power Head

Basic repair of Johnson and Evinrude outboard power heads is similar from model to model, with minor differences. Some procedures require the use of special tools, which can be purchased from a Johnson/Evinrude or OMC dealer. Certain tools may be fabricated by a machinist, often at substantial savings. Power head stands are available from specialty shops such as Bob Kerr's Marine Tool Company, P.O. Box 771135, Winter Garden, Florida, 34777, or Specialty Motors Manufacturing, P.O. Box 157, Longview, Washington, 98632.

Power head repair requires considerable mechanical ability. Carefully consider your capabilities before attempting any operation involving major disassembly of the engine.

Much of the labor charge for dealer repairs involves the removal and disassembly of other parts to reach the defective component. Even if you decide not to attempt the entire power head overhaul after studying the text and illustrations in this chapter, it can be financially beneficial to perform the preliminary operations yourself and then take the power head to your dealer. Since many marine dealers have lengthy waiting lists for service (especially during the spring and summer seasons), this practice can reduce the time your unit is in the shop. If you have done much of the preliminary work, your repair can be scheduled and performed much quicker.

Repairs proceed much faster and easier if your motor is clean before starting work. There are special cleaners for washing the motor and related parts. Just spray or brush on the cleaning solution, allow it to stand, then rinse thoroughly with clean water. Clean all oily or greasy parts with fresh solvent as you remove them.

WARNING
Never use gasoline as a cleaning agent. Gasoline presents an extreme fire hazard. Be sure to work in a well-ventilated area when using cleaning solvents. Keep a fire extinguisher rated for gasoline and oil fires nearby in case of an emergency.

Once you have decided to do the job yourself, read this chapter thoroughly until you have a good idea of what is involved in completing the repair satisfactorily. Make arrangements to buy or rent any special tools necessary and obtain replacement parts before starting. It is frustrating and time consuming to start an overhaul and then be unable to finish because the necessary tools or parts are not at hand.

Before beginning the repair procedure, read Chapter Two of this manual again. You will do a better job with this information fresh in your mind.

Since this chapter covers a large range of models, the procedures are somewhat generalized to accommodate all models. Where individual differences occur, they are specifically pointed out. The power heads shown in the accompanying pictures are current designs. While it is possible that the components shown in the

pictures may not be identical with those being serviced, they are representative and the step-by-step procedures may be used with all models covered in this manual. **Tables 1-3** are located at the end of the chapter.

CAUTION
Whenever a power head is rebuilt, it should be treated as a new engine. On models without oil injection (or if VRO pump is disconnected), use a 25:1 fuel-oil mixture in the tank during the first 10 hours of operation. On models with oil injection, use a 50:1 fuel-oil mixture in the fuel tank in combination with the normal oil injection system. Refer to Chapter Four for complete engine break-in procedures.

8

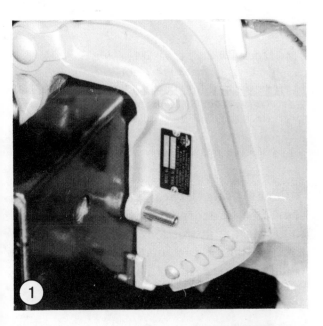

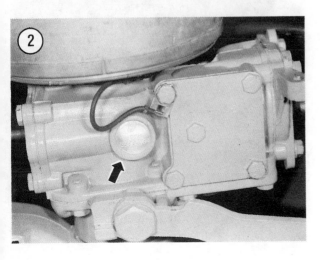

ENGINE SERIAL NUMBER

Johnson and Evinrude outboard motors are identified by a engine serial number. This number is stamped on a plate riveted to the transom clamp (**Figure 1**). It is also stamped into a core plug installed on the power head (**Figure 2**). Exact location of the transom clamp plate and core plug varies according to model.

The serial number identifies the outboard motor and indicates if there are unique parts or if changes have been made during the model year. The serial number should be used when ordering any replacement parts for the outboard.

The model year designation is contained in the outboard model number and is coded. The last 2 letters of the model code indicate the model year of the motor. To determine the year of a particular model, write the word "INTRODUCES." Below the word, number the letters 1-0. Match these numbers to the last 2 letters of the model code. For example, an outboard with the model code J60ELEI is a 1991 60 hp model (E=9 and I=1).

FASTENERS AND TORQUE

Always replace a worn or damaged fastener with one of the same size, type and torque requirement.

Power head tightening torques are given in **Table 2**. Where a specification is not provided for a given fastener, use the standard bolt and nut torque according to fastener size.

Where specified, clean fastener threads with OMC Locquic Primer, then apply the appropriate OMC (or equivalent) thread locking compound as required.

Power head fasteners should be tightened in 2 steps, unless instructed otherwise. Tighten to 50 percent of the torque value in the first step, then to 100 percent in the second step.

Retighten the cylinder head screws after the engine has been run at normal operating temperature, then allowed to cool.

To retighten the power head mounting fasteners properly, back them out one turn then retighten to specification.

When spark plugs are installed after an overhaul, tighten to the specified torque, warm the engine to normal operating temperature, then allow to cool and retighten the plugs to specification.

GASKETS AND SEALANTS

The following sealants are generally recommended for use during power head service: OMC Gasket Sealing Compound, Permatex No. 2 Sealant, OMC Adhesive M and OMC Gel Seal II. Unless otherwise specified, OMC Gasket Sealing Compound is used with gaskets. OMC Gel Seal II is an anaerobic-type sealant and is used to seal the crankcase cover to the cylinder block.

> *CAUTION*
> *OMC Gel Seal II has a shelf life of approximately 1 year. If the age of the Gel Seal II can not be determined, it should be replaced. Using Gel Seal that is too old can result in crankcase air leakage.*

Mating surfaces must be absolutely free of gasket material, sealant, dirt, oil, grease or other contamination. OMC Gel Seal and Gasket Remover, lacquer thinner, acetone, isopropyl alcohol or similar solvents work well for cleaning mating surfaces. Avoid using solvents with an oil, wax or petroleum base as they may not be compatible with some sealants. If scraping is necessary, use a broad, flat scraper or a somewhat dull putty knife. Avoid nicks, scratches or other damage to mating surfaces.

> *CAUTION*
> *The crankcase cover and cylinder block mating surfaces **must not** be scratched or damaged. The manufacturer specifically recommends using OMC Gel Seal and Gasket Remover and a **plastic** scraper to clean the cylinder block/crankcase cover mating surfaces.*

Prior to using Gel Seal II, the mating surfaces should be treated with OMC Locquic Primer, following the instructions on the container. If Locquic Primer is not used, the assembly should be allowed to set for 24 hours before returning the unit to service.

FLYWHEEL

The flywheel magnets must be of a particular strength to produce sufficient voltage to operate the ignition and charging systems. Weak magnets can cause misleading results during troubleshooting and testing, which can lead to unnecessary parts replacement.

If the magnets in the outer rim of the flywheel become loose, they can be glued back in place using a suitable epoxy-type adhesive. The magnets must be positioned exactly in their original locations and must not be broken.

The magnets in the flywheel hub (sensor coil magnets) can not be repaired. Should the magnets in the hub become loose, the flywheel must be replaced.

If oil is present under the flywheel, the upper crankshaft seal may be leaking. On 3-15 hp and 4 Deluxe models, the upper seal can be replaced without disassembling the crankcase assembly, if the proper special tools are used. See the appropriate section in this chapter for seal replacement procedures. On all other models, the power head must be removed and disassembled to replace the upper crankshaft seal. See the appropriate section in this chapter for disassembly/reassembly procedures.

Removal/Installation
(2.0, 2.3 and 3.3 hp Models; 3 and 4 hp and 4 Deluxe Models)

OMC universal puller kit (part No. 378103) is recommended for flywheel removal.

1. Disconnect the spark plug lead from the spark plug to prevent accidental starting.

2. Remove the rewind starter assembly. See Chapter Twelve.

3. *2.0-3.3 hp*—Remove the 3 screws securing the starter pulley to the flywheel. Remove the pulley.

4A. *2.0, 2.3 and 3.3 hp*—Hold the flywheel using OMC Flywheel Holder (part No. 115315).

4B. *3 and 4 hp*—Hold the flywheel using OMC Flywheel Holder (part No. 333827).

4C. *4 Deluxe*—Hold the flywheel using a suitable strap wrench.

5. Remove the flywheel nut using an appropriate size socket. See **Figure 3**, typical.

6. Install the puller on the flywheel with its flat side facing up. Lubricate the puller pressing screw with OMC Moly Lube.

7. Hold the puller body with the puller handle and tighten the pressing screw (**Figure 4**) until the flywheel releases from crankshaft. Then lift the flywheel off the crankshaft and retrieve the flywheel key.

8. Thoroughly clean the flywheel and crankshaft tapers using OMC Cleaning Solvent (or equivalent). Make sure the tapers are absolutely clean and dry.

9. To install, insert the flywheel key into its slot in the crankshaft. The key's outer edge should be parallel to the centerline of the crankshaft. See **Figure 5**.

10. Lower the flywheel onto the crankshaft, making sure the key slot in the flywheel is aligned with the key in the crankshaft.

11. Coat the crankshaft threads with OMC Gasket Sealing Compound (or equivalent). Install the flywheel nut. Hold the flywheel using the

appropriate flywheel holder and tighten the nut to:

  a. *2.0-2.3 and 3.3 hp*—29-33 ft.-lb. (39-45 N.m).

  b. *3 and 4 hp and 4 Deluxe*—30-40 ft.-lb. (41-54 N.m).

12. *2.0-3.3 hp*—Install the starter pulley and 3 mounting screws. Tighten the screws securely.

13. Reverse Steps 1 and 2 to complete flywheel installation.

Removal/Installation (6 and 8 hp)

1. Disconnect the spark plugs leads from the spark plugs to prevent accidental starting.

2. Remove the rewind starter as outlined in Chapter Twelve.

3. Remove the spark plug from the No. 1 (top) cylinder.

NOTE
The manufacturer recommends using the piston stop tool in Step 4 to prevent the engine from turning while loosening the flywheel nut. A strap wrench may be a suitable alternative.

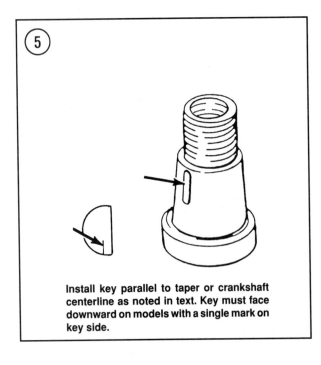

Install key parallel to taper or crankshaft centerline as noted in text. Key must face downward on models with a single mark on key side.

4. Rotate the flywheel clockwise until the No. 1 piston is at TDC. After the piston is at TDC, turn the flywheel an additional 2-3 in. (51-76 mm) clockwise.

5. Install OMC Piston Stop Tool (part No. 384887) into the No. 1 spark plug hole. See **Figure 6**. Lock the tool in place with the lock ring. Slowly, rotate the flywheel *counterclockwise* until the No. 1 piston contacts the piston stop tool.

6. Install the puller on the flywheel with its flat side facing up. Lubricate the puller pressing screw with OMC Moly Lube.

7. Hold the puller body with the puller handle and tighten the pressing screw (**Figure 4**) until the flywheel releases from crankshaft. Then lift the flywheel off the crankshaft and retrieve the flywheel key.

8. Thoroughly clean the flywheel and crankshaft tapers using OMC Cleaning Solvent (or equivalent). Make sure the tapers are absolutely clean and dry.

9. To install, insert the flywheel key into its slot in the crankshaft. The key's outer edge should be

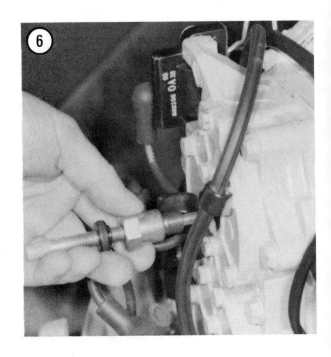

parallel to the centerline of the crankshaft. See **Figure 5**.

10. Lower the flywheel onto the crankshaft, making sure the key slot in the flywheel is aligned with the key in the crankshaft.

11. Coat the crankshaft threads with OMC Gasket Sealing Compound (or equivalent). Install the flywheel nut. Slowly rotate the crankshaft clockwise until the No. 1 piston contacts the piston stop tool, then tighten the nut to 40-50 ft.-lb. (54-68 N•m).

12. Remove the piston stop tool from the No. 1 spark plug hole. Reverse Steps 1 and 2 to complete flywheel installation.

Removal/Installation
(9.9-300 [Except 60° V6] hp Models)

Use a strap wrench or a flywheel holding tool to prevent the flywheel from turning while removing the flywheel nut. OMC Universal Puller Kit (part No. 378103) is recommended for flywheel removal.

1. Disconnect the spark plug leads from the spark plugs to prevent accidental starting.

2. Remove the rewind starter (Chapter Twelve), if so equipped.

3. Hold the flywheel with a suitable flywheel holding tool and remove the flywheel nut using an appropriate size socket. See **Figure 7**.

4. Install the puller on the flywheel with its flat side facing up. Lubricate the puller pressing screw with OMC Moly Lube (or equivalent).

5. Hold the puller body with the puller handle and tighten the pressing screw until the flywheel dislodges from the crankshaft. See **Figure 8**. Lift the flywheel off the crankshaft and retrieve the flywheel key.

6. Remove the puller from the flywheel.

7. Thoroughly clean the flywheel and crankshaft tapers with OMC Cleaning Solvent. The tapers must be absolutely clean and dry.

8. Install the flywheel key into its slot in the crankshaft as follows (**Figure 9**):

   a. *9.9-15 hp*—Install the key with its outer edge parallel to the taper of the crankshaft.

   b. *All other models*—Install the key with its outer edge parallel to the crankshaft centerline and the single mark on the key facing down.

9. Align the key slot in the flywheel with the key and place the flywheel on the crankshaft. Coat the threads of the flywheel nut with OMC Gasket Sealing Compound and tighten the nut to:

   a. *9.9-15 hp*—45-50 ft.-lb. (61-68 N•m).

8

b. *20-70 hp and V4 models*—100-105 ft.-lb. (135.6-142.4 N.m).

c. *V6 and V8 models*—140-150 ft.-lb. (190-203 N.m).

10. Reverse Steps 1 and 2 to complete flywheel installation.

Removal/Installation (60° V6 Models)

On 60° V6 models, the flywheel cover must be removed before removing the flywheel. Proceed as follows.

1. Disconnect the negative battery cable from the battery.

2. Disconnect the spark plug leads from the spark plugs to prevent accidental starting.

3. Remove the timing sensor cover (A, **Figure 10**) and voltage regulator/rectifier cover (B).

4. Unplug the timing sensor connector (D, **Figure 11**) from the timing sensor.

NOTE
Use the piston stop tool in Step 5 to prevent the crankshaft from turning while loosening the timing wheel retaining screw.

5. Place an appropriate size wrench or socket on the timing wheel screw and rotate the crankshaft to approximately 30° ATDC. Remove the No. 1 spark plug and install OMC Piston Stop Tool (part No. 384887) into the No. 1 spark plug hole. See **Figure 12**. Turn the piston stop tool inward until it contacts the piston, then lock the tool with its lock ring.

6. With the piston firmly against the piston stop tool, remove the timing wheel screw (A, **Figure 11**).

7. Lift the timing wheel (C, **Figure 11**) off the crankshaft. Be sure to retrieve the timing wheel key. Remove the timing pointer (B, **Figure 11**) if necessary for clearance.

8. Remove 17 flywheel cover mounting screws (F, **Figure 11**).

9. Remove the 2 screws (D, **Figure 13**) securing the spark lever retainer. Remove the retainer and lift the spark lever (A, **Figure 13**) off the throttle roller vertical shaft (B). Position the spark lever aside.

10. Next, lift the flywheel cover upward while tapping the vertical throttle shaft (C, **Figure 13**) out of the throttle arm. Remove the flywheel cover. Remove and discard the flywheel cover gasket.

11. Hold the flywheel using a suitable flywheel holder (Snap-on part No. A-144, or equivalent) and remove the 5 flywheel mounting screws. Discard the flywheel screws.

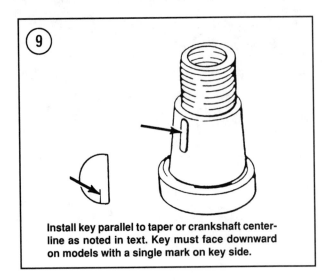

⑨ Install key parallel to taper or crankshaft center-line as noted in text. Key must face downward on models with a single mark on key side.

⑩

CAUTION
To prevent damage to the flywheel magnets, the manufacturer recommends using only OMC Flywheel Service Kit (part No. 434649) to remove the flywheel.

12. Secure the flywheel puller from OMC Flywheel Service Kit (part No. 434649) to the flywheel using the two 3/8-24 × 1 in. screws provided with the kit. Note that 2 of the five flywheel screw holes are threaded to accept the puller screws.

13. Remove the flywheel from the crankshaft by turning the puller center screw.

14. To install, insert the timing wheel key into its slot in the crankshaft. Position the key with its outer edge parallel to the crankshaft centerline.

15. Thoroughly clean any metal cuttings or other debris from the flywheel magnets. Install the flywheel on the crankshaft, making sure the roll pin in the crankshaft (**Figure 14**) is aligned with the hole in the flywheel.

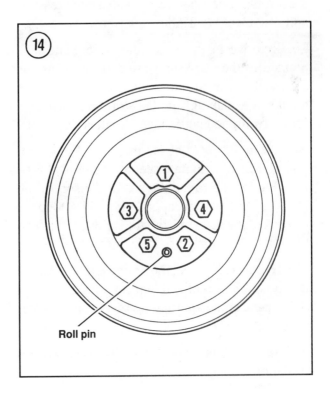

Roll pin

16. Install 5 *new* flywheel mounting screws. Tighten the screws to 25-35 ft.-lb. (34-47 N•m) in the sequence shown in **Figure 14**.

17. Apply OMC Gasket Sealing Compound to a new flywheel cover gasket and install the gasket on the power head.

> *CAUTION*
> *To prevent damage to the flywheel cover seal, apply a single layer of cellophane tape around the crankshaft. The bottom edge of the tape should be just below the flat surfaces of the crankshaft.*

18. Be sure the starter motor wave washer is properly positioned on the starter shaft. See **Figure 15**.

19. Install the flywheel cover while guiding the throttle shaft (C, **Figure 13**) into the throttle arm. Install the 17 flywheel cover screws and tighten in a crossing pattern to 40-50 in.-lb. (4.5-5.6 N•m). Install the spark lever (A, **Figure 13**) on the throttle roller shaft (B) and install the retainer and 2 screws (D). Tighten the screws securely.

20. Remove all traces of the cellophane tape applied to the crankshaft prior to installing the flywheel cover. Install the timing wheel on the crankshaft, making sure the slot in the wheel is properly aligned with the key in the crankshaft.

21. Clean all traces of old thread locking compound from the timing wheel screw. Apply OMC Locquic Primer to the threads of the screw and allow to air dry. Then, apply OMC HT 400 to the threads of the screw, install the screw and tighten to 120-140 in.-lb. (13.5-15.8 N•m).

22. If removed, install the timing pointer. Adjust the pointer as outlined under *Timing Pointer Alignment* in the appropriate section in Chapter Five.

23. Reverse Steps 1-4 to complete flywheel installation.

Upper Crankshaft Seal Replacement (3-15 hp)

The upper crankshaft seal can be replaced on 3-15 hp models without disassembling the crankcase assembly. OMC Seal Remover/Installer part No. 391060 is necessary to remove the seal.

1. Place the appropriate seal remover tip on the seal remover body. Use tip A on 3 and 4 hp and 4 Deluxe models, tip B on 6 and 8 hp and tip C on 9.9 and 15 hp models.

2. Remove the flywheel as outlined in this chapter.

3. Place the seal remover/installer assembly over the crankshaft. Thread the remover tip firmly into the seal.

4. Hold the remover/installer body and tighten the pressing screw to remove the seal.

5. Apply OMC Gasket Sealing Compound to the outer diameter of a new crankshaft seal. Lubricate the seal lip with clean engine oil. Install the seal, with its lip facing down, over the crankshaft.

6. Remove the remover tip and pressing screw from the seal remover/installer body. Place the body over the crankshaft. Tap the body with a

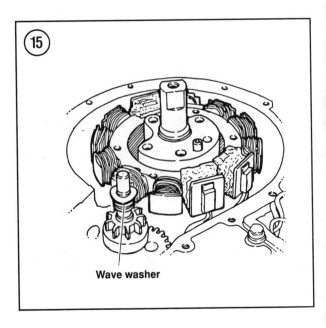

Wave washer

soft-face mallet to install the seal into the crankcase.

POWER HEAD

Before removing the power head assembly, it is a good idea to make a sketch or take an instant picture of the location, routing and positioning of wires, hoses and clamps for reference during reassembly. Note where wires, ground connections and washers are located so they can be reinstalled in their correct positions. Unless specified otherwise, install lockwashers on the engine side of ground connections to ensure a good connection.

Removal/Installation
(2.0, 2.3 and 3.3 hp)

1. Disconnect the spark plug lead and remove the spark plug.
2. Remove the engine covers.
3. Remove the fuel tank and carburetor.
4. Remove the rewind starter as outlined in Chapter Twelve.
5. Remove the flywheel and armature plate as outlined in Chapter Seven.
6. Remove the 6 screws securing the power head to the exhaust housing. Lift the power head off the exhaust housing and place on a clean bench or mount in a suitable holding fixture. Remove and discard the power head-to-exhaust housing gasket.
7. Thoroughly clean any gasket material from the exhaust housing and power head mating surfaces.
8. Apply OMC Moly Lube to the square end of the crankshaft.
9. Apply OMC Gasket Sealing Compound to both sides of a new power head gasket, then place the gasket on the exhaust housing.
10. Install the power head on the exhaust housing. Apply OMC Gasket Sealing Compound to the threads of the power head mounting screws.

Install the screws and tighten to specification (**Table 2**).
11. Install the ignition components as outlined in Chapter Seven. Install the flywheel as outlined in this chapter. Install the carburetor and fuel tank (Chapter Six). Install the rewind starter (Chapter Twelve) and engine covers.

Removal/Installation
(3 and 4 hp)

1. Disconnect the spark plug leads from the spark plugs.
2. On models so equipped, remove the integral fuel tank.
3. Remove the flywheel as outlined in this chapter.
4. Remove the ignition plate as outlined in Chapter Seven.
5. Remove the air silencer and carburetor as outlined in Chapter Six.
6. Remove the shield from the midsection. Remove the 6 screws securing the power head to the exhaust housing. Lift the power off the exhaust housing and place on a clean workbench or mount in a suitable holding fixture.
7. Thoroughly clean all gasket material from the power head and exhaust housing mounting surfaces.
8. Apply OMC Moly Lube to the drive shaft splines. Place a new power head gasket on the exhaust housing. Install the power head on the exhaust housing.
9. Apply OMC Gasket Sealing Compound to the threads of the power head mounting screws. Install the screws and tighten to specification (**Table 2**).
10. Install the carburetor and air silencer (Chapter Six). Install the ignition plate (Chapter Seven). Install the flywheel as outlined in this chapter. Install the integral fuel tank, if so equipped. Install the spark plugs, if removed, and connect the spark plug leads.

8

Removal/Installation
(4 Deluxe)

1. Disconnect the spark plug leads from the spark plugs.
2. Remove the fuel tank.
3. Remove the rewind starter (Chapter Twelve). Remove the ignition plate and ignition coils (Chapter Seven).
4. Remove the slow-speed mixture knob and choke knob. See Chapter Six.
5. Remove the 6 screws securing the power head to the exhaust housing. Lift the power head off the exhaust housing and place on a clean workbench. Remove the exhaust tube and gasket. Discard the gasket.
6. Remove the gearcase from the exhaust housing. See Chapter Nine.
7. Lubricate the end of the water tube with liquid soap. Install the water tube in position in the inner exhaust housing. Install the exhaust tube on the power head using a new gasket. Do not use gasket sealant on the gasket. Tighten the housing screws to 60-84 in.-lb. 6.8-9.5 N•m).
8. Install the power head on the exhaust housing. Tighten the power head mounting screws to specification (**Table 2**).

> *CAUTION*
> *Do not apply lubricant to the top of the drive shaft in Step 9. Grease on top of the drive shaft can cause a hydraulic lock to occur, preventing complete engagement of the drive shaft and crankshaft splines.*

9. Apply OMC Moly Lube to the drive shaft splines.
10. Install the gearcase to the exhaust housing (Chapter Nine). Make sure the water tube properly enters the water pump grommet. Apply OMC Gasket Sealing Compound to the threads of the gearcase mounting screws. Install the screws and tighten to 60-84 in.-lb. (6.8-9.5 N•m).
11. Install the ignition and fuel system components. Perform linkage adjustment and synchronization procedures as outlined in Chapter Five.

Removal/Installation
(6 and 8 hp)

1. Disconnect the spark plug leads from the spark plugs.
2. Remove the air silencer assembly.
3. Disconnect the throttle control screw and nut. Remove the throttle control.
4. Remove the water pump indicator hose.
5. Remove the flywheel as outlined in this chapter.
6. Remove the ignition plate as outlined in Chapter Seven.
7. Remove the ignition coil assembly.
8. Remove the rewind starter. See Chapter Twelve.
9. Disconnect the fuel hose and remove the carburetor and fuel pump.
10. Remove the motor lower cover.
11. Remove the 6 power head mounting screws.
12. Remove 3 screws attaching the adapter plate to the exhaust housing (**Figure 16**).
13. Lift the power head off the exhaust housing. Remove and discard the power head-to-exhaust housing gasket.

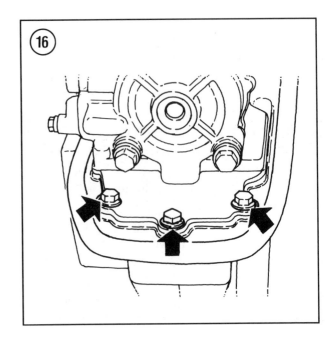

14. Remove the exhaust tube from the power head. Remove and discard the exhaust tube gasket. Remove the adapter plate from the power head. Mount the power head in a suitable holding fixture.

15. Thoroughly clean all gasket material from the adapter plate, exhaust housing, exhaust tube and power head mating surfaces.

16. Inspect the condition of the water tube upper grommet in the top side of the exhaust tube. Replace the grommet as required.

17. Using a new gasket, install the adapter plate on the power head. Install the water tube and grommet in the exhaust tube. Lubricate the grommet with liquid soap.

18. Install a new gasket on the exhaust tube (without sealant). Install the exhaust tube on the power head and tighten the screws to specification (**Table 2**).

CAUTION
Do not apply lubricant to the top of the drive shaft in Step 19. Grease on top of the drive shaft can cause a hydraulic lock to occur, preventing complete engagement of the drive shaft and crankshaft splines.

19. Apply OMC Moly Lube to the drive shaft splines. Install a new power head gasket on the exhaust housing, then install the power head. Install the power head mounting screws and tighten to specification (**Table 2**).

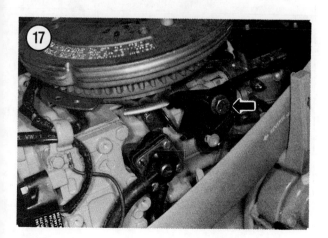

20. Complete installation by reversing the removal procedure. Perform linkage adjustment and synchronization procedures as outlined in Chapter Five.

Removal/Installation
(9.9 and 15 hp [1991 and 1992])

1. Disconnect the spark plug leads from the spark plugs. If necessary, remove the spark plugs.

2. Disconnect the battery cables from the battery, on models so equipped. Remove the battery cables from the outboard motor.

3. Remove the flywheel as outlined in this chapter. Remove the ignition plate as outlined in Chapter Seven.

4. Disconnect the fuel delivery hose from the fuel pump. Remove the carburetor and fuel pump. See Chapter Six.

5. Remove the shift lock lever screw (**Figure 17**). Swing the lever and rod out of the way, then remove the starter interlock screw.

6A. *Manual start*—Remove the rewind starter. See Chapter Twelve.

6B. *Electric start*—Remove the starter motor. See Chapter Seven.

7. Remove the ignition coils. See Chapter Seven. Note that the stop switch and ignition module ground wires are installed under one ignition coil mounting screw.

8. Disconnect the Amphenol 1-pin stop switch connector (black/yellow wire).

9. Remove the low-speed adjustment knob and the choke knob.

10. Remove the nuts and washers from the motor lower pan. Disconnect the water pump indicator hose from the fitting on the power head.

11. Remove 6 power head mounting screws. Lift the power head straight up and off the exhaust housing. Place the power head on a clean workbench and remove the exhaust and water tube assembly from the power head. Remove and discard the exhaust tube gasket. If further

disassembly is necessary, mount the power head on a suitable holding fixture.

12. To ensure the water tube is correctly installed in the water pump grommet, remove the gearcase from the exhaust housing as described in Chapter Nine.

13. Place a new power head gasket (without sealant) on the exhaust housing. See A, **Figure 18**.

14. Make sure the water pump grommets are properly located in the exhaust tube. Install the water tubes into the exhaust tube, making sure the tubes are centered in the grommets. Then, install the exhaust and water tube assembly to the power head. Tighten the mounting screws to 60-84 in.-lb. (6.8-9.5 N•m).

15. Thoroughly coat the machined surface of the lower crankcase head (C, **Figure 18**) with Permatex No. 2 gasket sealant.

16. Install a rubber band (B, **Figure 18**) as shown to hold the long water tube firmly against the exhaust tube. While slowly lowering the power head onto the exhaust housing, guide the long water tube into the water tube opening in the exhaust housing. Guide the small water tube into the opening at the rear of the exhaust housing. Guide the vertical control shaft into the control shaft gear.

17. Use an awl to align the rubber mount sleeves and washers with the lower motor cover mounting holes, if necessary. Install the mounting nuts with the power head ground wire under the rear stud. Tighten the screws securely.

18. Apply OMC Gasket Sealing Compound to the threads of the power head mounting screws. Install the 2 longer screws in the rear mounting holes, then install the remaining 4 screws. Make sure the ground wire is installed on the front screw, if so equipped. Tighten the power head mounting screws to specification (**Table 2**).

19. Install the gearcase as outlined in Chapter Nine.

20. Reverse Steps 1-10 to complete installation. Perform linkage adjustment and synchronization

as described in Chapter Five. Adjust the shift lever as described in appropriate section in Chapter Nine. Adjust the neutral start switch as described in Chapter Seven.

Removal/Installation
9.9 and 15 hp [1993-on])

1. Disconnect the spark plug leads from the spark plugs to prevent accidental starting.

2. On models so equipped, disconnect the battery cables from the battery. Remove the battery cables from the motor.

3. Remove the 2 screws and nuts from the upper rear of the lower motor cover. Remove the screw from the lower rear of the motor cover. Disconnect the water pump indicator hose.

4. Remove the 2 screws from the upper front of the lower motor cover and the screw and nut from the lower front of the lower motor cover.

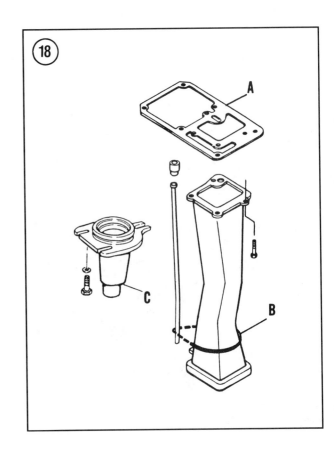

Separate, then remove the port and starboard lower motor cover halves.

5. Remove the electric starter motor, if so equipped, as described in Chapter Seven. Remove the rewind starter as described in Chapter Twelve. Remove the flywheel as described in this chapter. Remove the ignition plate and ignition coil as described in Chapter Seven.

6. Remove the air silencer and carburetor as described in Chapter Six.

7. On tiller handle models, disconnect the linkage rod from the shift handle. Remove the screw securing the shift handle. On remote control models, disconnect the shift and throttle cables from the power head.

8. Remove neutral start lockout rod.

9. Remove the choke lever and grommet and the shift rod, pin and grommet.

10. Remove the 6 power head mounting screws (3 on each side). Lift the power head straight up and off the exhaust housing. Remove and discard the power head-to-exhaust housing gasket. Mount the power head on a suitable holding fixture.

11. Remove the exhaust and water tube assembly from the power head. Remove and discard the gasket.

12. Thoroughly clean all gasket material from the power head, exhaust housing and exhaust tube mating surfaces.

13. Remove the gearcase (Chapter Nine) to ensure the water tube is properly inserted into the water pump grommet during power head installation.

14. Place a new power head gasket (without sealant) on the exhaust housing.

15. Make sure the water pump grommets are properly located in the exhaust tube. Install the water tubes into the exhaust tube, making sure the tubes are centered in the grommets. Then, install the exhaust and water tube assembly to the power head. Tighten the mounting screws to 60-84 in.-lb. (6.8-9.5 N·m).

16. Thoroughly coat the machined surface of the lower crankcase head with Permatex No. 2 gasket sealant.

17. Install a rubber band (B, **Figure 18**) as shown to hold the long water tube firmly against the exhaust tube. While slowly lowering the power head onto the exhaust housing, guide the long water tube into the water tube opening in the exhaust housing. Guide the small water tube into the opening at the rear of the exhaust housing. Guide the vertical control shaft into the control shaft gear.

18. Use an awl to align the rubber mount sleeves and washers with the lower motor cover mounting holes, if necessary. Install the mounting nuts with the power head ground wire under the rear stud. Tighten the nuts securely.

19. Apply OMC Gasket Sealing Compound to the threads of the power head mounting screws. Install the 2 longer screws in the rear mounting holes, then install the remaining 4 screws. Make sure the ground wire is installed on the front screw, if so equipped. Tighten the power head mounting screws to specification (**Table 2**).

20. Install the gearcase as outlined in Chapter Nine.

21. Reverse Steps 1-9 to complete installation. Perform linkage adjustment and synchronization as described in Chapter Five. Adjust the shift lever as described in appropriate section in Chapter Nine. Adjust the neutral start switch as described in Chapter Seven.

Removal/Installation
(20-30 hp)

1. Disconnect the spark plug leads from the spark plugs to prevent accidental starting. On electric start models, disconnect the battery cables from the battery and remove the cables from the motor.

2. Remove the rewind starter as described in Chapter Twelve.

3. Disengage the throttle arm spring (A, **Figure 19**) from the throttle arm. Remove the pin from

8

the end of the throttle control rod (B, **Figure 19**). Separate the ignition plate link from the throttle control lever.

4. Remove the screws and clamps holding the vertical throttle shaft. Lift the shaft from the throttle gear (**Figure 20**).

5. On electric start models, remove the starter motor and solenoid. See Chapter Seven.

6. Remove the air silencer.

7. Disconnect the throttle cam-to-cam follower link (A, **Figure 21**). Disconnect the recirculation hose (B, **Figure 21**), if so equipped.

8. Remove the fuel filter (**Figure 22**), then remove the fuel pump attaching screws (**Figure 23**). Place the fuel pump and filter assembly to one side.

9. Remove the carburetor mounting nuts. Pull the carburetor, gasket and choke bracket (if so equipped) from the intake manifold studs (**Figure 24**) while disengaging the choke shaft from the carburetor choke lever. Remove with the fuel pump assembly attached. Discard the carburetor gasket.

10. Remove the flywheel as described in this chapter.

11. On electric start models, disconnect all wires at the terminal block. Remove the terminal block.

12. On manual start models equipped with an actuator cam, install a piece of wire through the hole in the top of the shaft (A, **Figure 25**) to keep

the shaft from coming out of the bracket. Remove the cotter pin and washer holding the cam link to the cam (B, **Figure 25**).

13. Remove the cam bolt and the 2 bracket nuts. Remove the assembly (**Figure 26**).

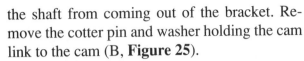

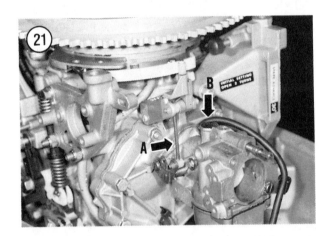

14. Disconnect the water pump indicator hose from the exhaust cover fitting (**Figure 27**). Slide the hose through the J-clamp and remove it from the motor.

15. Remove the ignition coils. Note that the stop switch ground wire is attached to one of the coil mounting screws.

16. On CD2 ignition (1993-on models), use the pin removal tool (part No. 322698) to remove the stop switch wire from the E terminal in the 5-pin Amphenol connector. On CD2U ignition (1991-92 models), disconnect the orange/black 1-pin stop switch connector.

17. Remove the ignition plate as described in Chapter Seven.

18. On CD2 ignition, remove the power pack assembly (**Figure 28**). Note the location of the power pack ground wire.

NOTE
At this point, there should be no hoses, wires or linkages connecting the power head to the exhaust housing. Recheck to be sure nothing will interfere with power head removal.

8

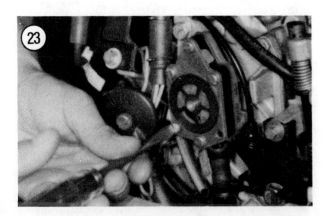

19. Remove the 4 power head mounting screws. Then locate the port and starboard power head retaining nuts and washers (**Figure 29**). Remove the nuts using OMC tool part No. 322700, or an offset 1/2 in. box wrench (**Figure 30**).

20. Rock the power head from side to side to break the gasket seal. Carefully lift the power head from the exhaust housing (**Figure 31**) and place it on a clean workbench.

21. Remove the inner exhaust tube attaching screws. Tap the end of the tube with a soft-face hammer (**Figure 32**) to break it loose. Remove the exhaust tube. Remove and discard the gasket.

22. Depress the water tube guide tab and pull the guide from the tube. Remove and discard the exhaust tube rubber grommet.

23. Install the power head on a suitable holding fixture.

24. Installation is the reverse of removal. Lubricate the drive shaft splines with OMC Moly Lube. Make sure the O-ring is in the end of the crankshaft. Apply Permatex No. 2 sealant to both sides of the power head-to-exhaust housing gasket in the area of the inner exhaust housing mounting surface. Lubricate the top of the water tube with liquid soap. Rotate the power head as required to align the crankshaft and drive shaft splines. Apply OMC Nut Lock to the port and starboard exhaust housing studs. Tighten fasteners to specification (**Table 2**). Use pin insert tool part No. 322697 to install the stop switch into terminal E (CD2 ignition) in the 5-pin Amphenol connector. Complete linkage adjustment and synchronization procedures as outlined in Chapter Five.

Removal/Installation (35 Jet, 40, 48 and 50 hp)

1. Disconnect the spark plug wires from the spark plugs to prevent accidental starting.

2. On electric start models, disconnect the battery cables from the battery and remove the cables from the motor.

3. Remove the screws securing the lower engine cover. Separate and remove the port and starboard lower motor cover halves.

4. Remove the shift rod screw (**Figure 33**).

5. Remove the nut at the rear of the power head.

6. Disconnect the fuel delivery hose from the fuel pump. Plug the hose to prevent leakage. On models equipped with oil injection, disconnect the oil delivery hose from the VRO pump assembly. Plug the hose to prevent leakage.

7. Remove 8 power head mounting screws (4 each side).

> *NOTE*
> *At this point, there should be no hoses, wires or linkage connecting the power head to the exhaust housing. Recheck to be sure nothing will interfere with power head removal.*

8. Install the body of OMC universal puller kit (part No. 378103) to the flywheel (flat side fac-

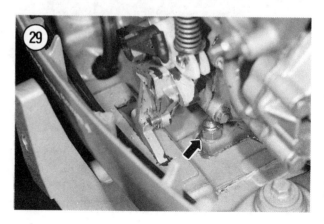

ing upward) with 3 appropriately sized screws and flat washers.

9. Thread OMC lifting eye part No. 321537 (or equivalent) into the puller body until its taper contacts the crankshaft taper. Tighten the lifting eye in place.

10. Attach a suitable hoist to the lifting eye. Remove the power head from the exhaust hous-

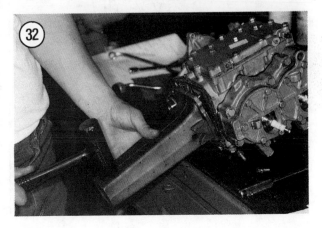

ing adapter with a hoist. Place the power head on a clean workbench or mount in a suitable holding fixture.

11. Remove the carburetors (Chapter Six). Remove the ignition plate (CD2U ignition), stator and timer base (CD2 ignition), ignition coils, power pack and starter motor (Chapter Seven).

12. Clean all gasket material from the power head and exhaust housing mating surfaces.

13. Place a new power head gasket (without sealant) on the exhaust housing.

CAUTION
Do not apply lubricant to the top of the drive shaft in Step 14. Grease on top of the drive shaft can cause a hydraulic lock to occur, preventing complete engagement of the drive shaft and crankshaft splines.

14. Lubricate the drive shaft splines with OMC Moly Lube.

15. Using the hoist, install the power head on the exhaust housing. Rotate the engine crankshaft as necessary to align the crankshaft and drive shaft splines.

16. Apply OMC Gasket Sealing Compound to the threads of the power head mounting screws.

Shift rod screw

8

Install the screws and tighten to 18-20 ft.-lb. (24-27 N.m).

17. Install the exhaust housing-to-power head nut at the rear of the power head. Tighten the nut 18-20 ft.-lb. (24-27 N.m).

18. Complete the remaining installation by reversing the removal procedure. Prior to connecting the oil delivery hose to the oil injection pump on models so equipped, squeeze the oil primer bulb until oil flows from the oil delivery hose to remove air or any contamination that may be present in the hose. Perform linkage adjustment and synchronization procedures as described in Chapter Five.

Removal/Installation
(60-70 hp)

1. Disconnect the spark plug leads from the spark plugs to prevent accidental starting.

2. Disconnect the battery cables from the battery, then remove the battery cables from the power head.

3. On tiller handle models, disconnect the throttle cable from the engine and remove the throttle cable bracket. Disconnect the shift lever link from the shift lever.

4. Disconnect the fuel delivery hose from the fuel pump (without oil injection) or fuel filter (with oil injection). Disconnect the oil hose from the VRO sight tube. Do not disconnect any hoses from the VRO pump unless the pump requires replacement.

5. Remove the stop switch ground wire. Remove the stop switch wire from terminal E in the 5-pin stator connector. Lubricate the terminal and connector using isopropyl alcohol, then remove the wire terminal using OMC Pin Remover part No. 322698.

6. Remove the shift rod screw (**Figure 34**, typical).

7. On models with oil injection, remove the hairpin clip from the shift rod through-shaft at the base of the power head, then push the through-shaft toward the power head and disconnect the shift rod from the shift lever.

8. Remove the 4 lower cover screws and remove the rear lower cover. Remove the 2 front lower cover screws and remove the front lower cover.

9. Disconnect the water pump indicator hose from the power head. Remove the port and starboard lower pan support screws.

10. Remove the nut and washer from the stud at the rear of the power head.

11. Disconnect the power trim/tilt connector, if so equipped. Disconnect the tilt limit switch wires at their bullet connectors. Disconnect the power trim/tilt switch at the bullet connectors.

12. Remove the 6 power head mounting screws.

NOTE
At this point, there should be no hoses, wires or linkage connecting the power head to the exhaust housing. Recheck to be sure nothing will interfere with power head removal.

13. Attach a suitable lifting fixture to the power head. The manufacturer recommends installing the puller body of OMC universal puller (part No. 378103) on the flywheel (flat side facing upward) using appropriately size screws and flat

(34)

**Shift clevis
attachment screw**

washers. Then thread OMC lifting eye part No. 321537 into the puller body until it contacts the crankshaft taper. Tighten the lifting eye firmly in place.

14. Attach a suitable hoist to the lifting eye and carefully lift the power head off the exhaust housing. Place the power head on a clean workbench or mount in a suitable holding fixture.

15. Clean all gasket material from the power head and exhaust adapter mating surfaces.

CAUTION
Do not apply lubricant to the top of the drive shaft in Step 16. Grease on top of the drive shaft can cause a hydraulic lock to occur, preventing complete engagement of the drive shaft and crankshaft splines.

16. Lubricate the drive shaft splines with OMC Moly Lube.

17. Install a new power head gasket (without sealant) on the exhaust adapter.

18. Carefully lower the power head into position on the exhaust adapter. Rotate the flywheel clockwise to align the crankshaft and drive shaft splines.

19. Apply OMC Gel Seal II to the threads of the power head mounting screws. Install the screws and tighten in 3 steps to 18-20 ft.-lb. (24-27 N•m). Install the exhaust adapter-to-power head nut and washer and tighten to 60-84 in.-lb. (6.8-9.5 N•m).

20. The remaining installation is the reverse of removal. Refer to the appropriate chapter during fuel and electrical component installation. Tighten the shift rod shoulder screw to 60-84 in.-lb. (6.8-9.5 N•m). Prior to connecting the oil delivery hose to the VRO sight tube, squeeze the oil system primer bulb until oil flows from the hose to remove air and any contamination that may be present in the hose. Perform linkage adjustment and synchronization procedures as described in Chapter Five.

Removal/Installation
(All V4 and V6 Cross Flow Models)

Carefully identify wiring leads and hoses as components are removed. Make accurate notes of lead and hose routing for reference during installation.

1. Disconnect the spark plug leads from the spark plugs.

2. Disconnect the negative battery cable from the battery. Remove the battery cables from the engine.

3. Disconnect the stator and timer base-to-power pack connections.

4. Remove the starter motor. See Chapter Seven.

5. Remove the air silencer cover and base assembly.

6. Disconnect the fuel delivery hose from the fuel pump, if so equipped. If equipped with oil injection, remove the VRO pump assembly and lay aside. Disconnect the VRO pump pulse hose from the power head.

7. Remove the flywheel as described in this chapter.

8. Remove the stator and timer base assemblies. See Chapter Seven.

9. *V4 models*—Remove the thermostat hoses from each cylinder head. See **Figure 35**. Disconnect the water pump indicator hose from the lower motor cover fitting.

10. Remove the ignition coils (**Figure 36**) and power pack (**Figure 37**) from each side of the power head. See Chapter Seven.

11. Disconnect all ground wires from the power head.

12. Remove the front rubber mount screws on each side of the power head.

13A. *V4 models*—Remove the shift rod retainer (**Figure 38**).

13B. *V6 models*—Remove the shift rod connector screw (**Figure 39**).

14. Remove the power head fasteners as follows:

8

a. 2 exhaust cover screws on each side of the power head.

b. 2 lower motor cover-to-rear exhaust housing cover screw on each side.

c. Front exhaust housing cover-to-lower motor cover screw on each side.

d. Power head-to-exhaust adapter housing nuts at the rear of the power head.

e. One screw and one nut at the front of the power head on each side.

f. 3 long screws on each side holding the power head to the adapter housing.

NOTE
At this point, there should be no hoses, wires or linkage connecting the power head to the exhaust housing. Recheck to be sure nothing will interfere with power head removal.

15. Temporarily reinstall the flywheel. Secure the body of OMC puller part No. 378103 (flat side facing up) to the flywheel with the 3 screws and flat washers. Thread lifting eye part No. 321537 into the puller until it contacts the crankshaft taper. Tighten the lifting eye firmly in place.

16. Attach a suitable hoist to the lifting eye and lift the power head from the exhaust housing adapter.

17. With the power head on the hoist, reinstall the nuts on the studs at the power head base until flush with the stud ends to protect the threads.

18. Lower the power head onto a clean workbench or mount in a suitable holding fixture.

19. Remove remaining components from the power head to gain access to the power head assembly fasteners.

20. Thoroughly clean all gasket material from the power head and exhaust housing adapter mating surfaces.

21. Remove the nuts from the power head adapter studs (installed in Step 17).

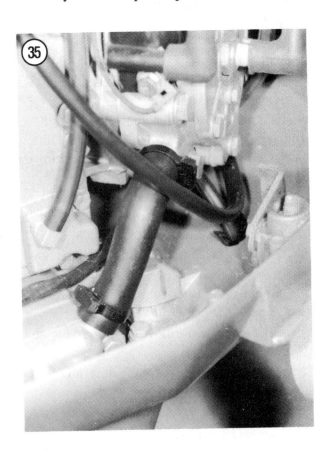

CAUTION
Do not apply lubricant to the top of the drive shaft in Step 22. Grease on top of the drive shaft can cause a hydraulic

lock to occur, preventing complete engagement of the drive shaft and crankshaft splines.

22. Install a new O-ring on the drive shaft. Lubricate the drive shaft splines with OMC Moly Lube.

23. Install a new power head gasket (without sealant) on the exhaust housing adapter.

24. Using the hoist, carefully lower the power head on the exhaust housing. If necessary, rotate the flywheel clockwise to align the crankshaft and drive shaft splines.

CAUTION
All power head to exhaust housing screws must be retightened to the correct torque after the outboard motor has been operated and allowed to cool.

25. Apply OMC Gel Seal II to the threads of the power head-to-exhaust housing screws. Install the screws and tighten in 3 steps to:
   a. V4—16-18 ft.-lb. (22-24 N•m).
   b. V6—18-20 ft.-lb. (24-27 N•m).

26. Apply OMC Gel Seal II to the threads of the exhaust adapter-to-power head screws and nuts. Install the screws and nuts and tighten to 120-145 in.-lb. (13.6-16.4 N•m).

27. Complete the remaining installation by reversing the removal procedure. On models equipped with oil injection, be sure to purge air from the injection system and verify proper injection system operation. See Chapter Eleven. Perform linkage adjustment and synchronization procedures as described in Chapter Five.

**Removal/Installation
(V4, V6 [Except 60° Models] and V8 Loop Charged Models)**

NOTE
If the outboard motor is not equipped with power steering, disregard the steps which refer to power steering in the following procedure.

8

Carefully identify wiring leads and hoses during power head removal. Make accurate notes and label lead and hose routing for reference during installation.

Many types and sizes of fasteners are used on these models. Therefore, to simplify reassembly, it is helpful to reinstall fasteners in their original locations after components are removed (if possible).

1. Disconnect the spark plug leads from the spark plugs.
2. Disconnect the negative battery cable from the battery. Remove the battery cables from the engine.
3. Remove the power steering hose support bracket from the starboard side lower motor cover.
4. Disconnect the water pump indicator hose. Loosen the lower motor cover screws, then remove the spring clips and lower cover halves.
5. Loosen the power steering belt adjusting nuts (D, **Figure 40**) to relieve tension on the belt.

Remove the 6 flywheel-to-pulley screws (A, **Figure 40**).

6. Remove the flywheel as described in this chapter.
7. Remove the screws holding the stator assembly to the power head. Tilt the stator and pulley to remove the screws holding the power steering reservoir to the power head. Remove the power steering assembly from the power head without disconnecting any hydraulic lines and place to one side out of the way.
8. Disconnect the power trim wiring harnesses at the power head.
9. Disconnect the shift rod screw (**Figure 41**, typical).
10. Disconnect the fuel and oil delivery hoses from the fuel pump or VRO pump assembly.
11. Remove the power head-to-exhaust housing fasteners. On V4 and V6 models, remove 4 screws and 1 nut from each side. On V8 models, remove 5 screws and 1 nut from each side.

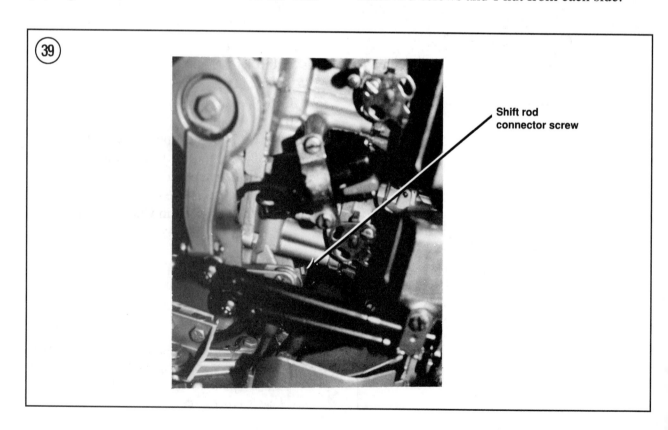

Shift rod connector screw

12. Remove the 2 screws and 1 nut holding the rear of the power head to the exhaust adapter.

13. Thread OMC lifting eye part No. 396748 (or equivalent) on the crankshaft.

NOTE
At this point, there should be no hoses, fasteners, wires or linkage connecting the power head to the exhaust housing. Recheck to be sure nothing will interfere with power head removal.

14. Attach a hoist to the lifting eye. Remove the power head from the exhaust housing adapter with the hoist.

15. Lower the power head onto a clean workbench with the crankcase side facing up, then remove the hoist from the lifting eye.

16. Remove the lifting eye. Remove the VRO injection pump, fuel and carburetion system and electrical components from outside the power head to provide access to the power head assembly fasteners.

17. Thoroughly clean all gasket material from the power head and exhaust housing adapter mating surfaces. Make sure the mating surfaces are clean and free of oil, grease or other contamination.

18. Install a new power head base gasket (without sealant) on the exhaust housing adapter.

CAUTION
Do not apply lubricant to the top of the drive shaft in Step 19. Grease on top of the drive shaft can cause a hydraulic lock to occur, preventing complete engagement of the drive shaft and crankshaft splines.

19. Lubricate the drive shaft splines with OMC Moly Lube. Install OMC lifting eye (part No. 396748) securely on the crankshaft and attach the hoist to the lifting eye.

20. Using the hoist, carefully lower the power head on the exhaust housing.

NOTE
The power head mounting fasteners must be retorqued after operating the motor. Allow the motor to cool, loosen each fastener 1/4 turn, then retighten to specification.

21. Apply OMC Locquic Primer to the threads of the power head-to-exhaust housing fasteners and allow to air dry. Then apply OMC Gel Seal II to the fastener threads. Install all fasteners finger tight, then tighten to 144-168 in.-lb. (16.3-19.0 N·m).

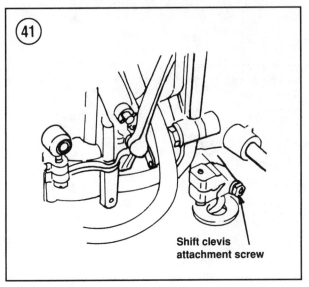

**Shift clevis
attachment screw**

22. Install the power head-to-exhaust adapter fasteners (2 screws and 1 nut) and tighten to 144-168 in.-lb. (16.3-19.0 N•m).

23. *Power steering*—Install the power steering system, making sure the hoses are routed in their original locations. Apply OMC Nut Lock to the power steering fasteners. Tighten the reservoir mounting screws to 18-20 ft.-lb. (24.4-27 N•m).

24. Install the stator assembly (Chapter Seven). Install the flywheel as described in this chapter.

25. Install the flywheel-to-power steering pulley screws and tighten to 60-84 in.-lb. (6.8-9.5 N•m).

26. Complete the remaining installation by reversing the removal procedure. Prior to connecting the oil delivery hose to the VRO sight tube, squeeze the oil system primer bulb until oil flows from the hose to remove air and any contamination that may be present in the hose. Perform linkage adjustment and synchronization procedures as described in Chapter Five.

27. Tension the power steering belt as follows:

  a. Make sure the idler housing screws (C, **Figure 40**) and adjustment nuts (D) are loose.

  b. Check belt tightness at the midpoint between the idler and flywheel pulleys. Use OMC Gauge part No. 984850, or a suitable belt tension gauge. Turn the belt adjusting nuts as necessary to obtain 25-30 lb. belt tension.

  c. Tighten the idler housing screws and adjusting nuts to 108-132 in.-lb. (12-15 N•m).

  d. Start the outboard motor and run at 800 rpm for approximately 2 minutes. Stop the motor and repeat substeps 27a-27c.

  e. Recheck belt tension after 10 hours of operation.

Removal/Installation
(60° V6 Models)

NOTE
If the outboard motor is not equipped with power steering, disregard the steps

which refer to power steering in the following procedure.

Carefully identify wiring leads and hoses during power head removal. Make accurate notes and label lead and hose routing for reference during installation.

Many types and sizes of fasteners are used on these models. Therefore, to simplify reassembly, it is helpful to reinstall fasteners in their original locations after components are removed (if possible).

1. Disconnect the spark plug leads from the spark plugs.

2. Disconnect the negative battery cable from the battery. Remove the battery cables from the power head.

3. Disconnect the fuel and oil hoses from the fuel/oil connector in the lower motor cover. Remove the fuel/oil connector bracket from the lower motor cover.

4. Remove the air silencer. See Chapter Six.

5. Disconnect the power trim/tilt connector.

6. Remove the motor lower cover screws. Remove the starboard lower cover half. Disconnect the lower cover mounted trim/tilt switch at its

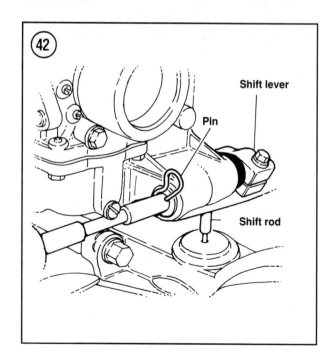

bullet connectors and remove the port lower cover half.

7. Disconnect the tilt limit switch (blue/white wires) at its bullet connectors.

8. Disconnect the trim sender at its 2-pin Amphenol connector and bullet connector.

9. Remove the pin (**Figure 42**) and disconnect the shift rod from the shift lever.

10. Remove the power head-to-exhaust housing and power head-to-steering arm bracket screws.

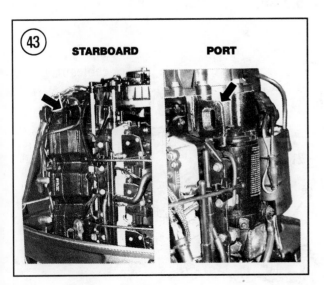

WARNING
The chain used to lift the power head in Step 11 must have a 500 lb. capacity and be at least 36 in. (91 cm) long.

11. Attach a suitable lifting chain to the power head lifting eyes (**Figure 43**). Make sure the chain is at least 18 in. (46 cm) long between each attachment point and the hoist to prevent damage to the power head.

12. Lift the power head using the hoist. If necessary, carefully pry the power head loose from the exhaust housing. Do not damage the power head and exhaust housing mating surfaces.

13. Place the power head on a clean workbench or mount in a suitable holding fixture. Remove the fuel (Chapter Six), electrical and ignition components (Chapter Seven) from the power head.

14. Thoroughly clean all gasket material, oil grease or other contamination from the power head and exhaust adapter mating surfaces.

15. Apply Permatex No. 2 gasket sealant to the inner exhaust housing flange (**Figure 44**). Apply OMC Gasket Sealing Compound to both sides of a new power head-to-exhaust adapter gasket (**Figure 44**). Install the gasket on the adapter.

CAUTION
Do not apply lubricant to the top of the drive shaft in Step 16. Grease on top of the drive shaft can cause a hydraulic lock to occur, preventing complete engagement of the drive shaft and crankshaft splines.

16. Lubricate the drive shaft splines with OMC Moly Lube.

17. Using the hoist, carefully install the power head on the exhaust housing. Install and tighten the steering arm-to-upper mount screws to 65-70 ft.-lb. (88-95 N·m).

NOTE
The power head mounting fasteners must be retorqued after the outboard motor is operated at normal operating temperature and allowed to cool. Loosen the

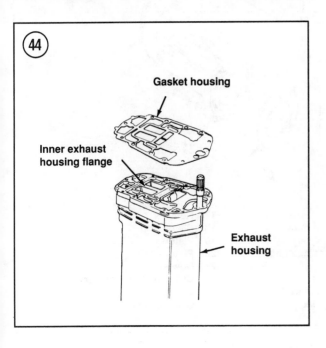

Gasket housing

Inner exhaust
housing flange

Exhaust
housing

fasteners 1/4 to 1/2 turn, then retighten to specification.

18. Apply OMC Gasket Sealing Compound to the threads of the power head-to-exhaust housing screws. Install the screws finger tight. Tighten the 6 large screws to 18-20 ft.-lb. (24-27 N•m). Tighten the 5 small screws to 60-84 in.-lb. (6.8-9.5 N•m).

19. Complete remaining installation by reversing the removal procedure. Prior to connecting the oil delivery hose to the VRO sight tube, squeeze the oil system primer bulb until oil flows from the hose to remove air and any contamination that may be present in the hose. Perform linkage adjustment and synchronization procedures as described in Chapter Five.

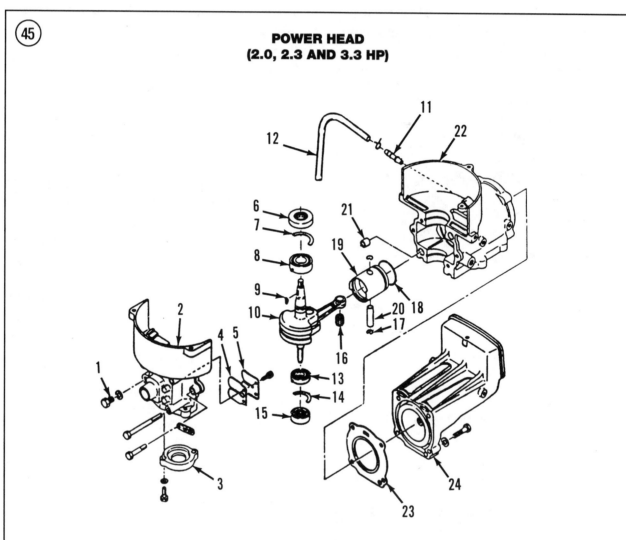

(45)

**POWER HEAD
(2.0, 2.3 AND 3.3 HP)**

1. Plug	9. Flywheel key	17. Retainer
2. Crankcase assembly	10. Crankshaft assembly	18. Piston ring
3. Lower crankcase head	11. Fitting	19. Piston
4. Leaf valve	12. Water pump indicator hose	20. Piston pin
5. Leaf stop	13. Main bearing	21. Dowel
6. Upper crankshaft seal	14. Bearing retainer	22. Cylinder block assembly
7. Bearing retainer	15. Lower crankshaft seal	23. Gasket
8. Main bearing	16. Piston pin bearing	24. Cylinder head

Disassembly
(2.0, 2.3 and 3.3 hp)

Refer to **Figure 45** for this procedure.

1. Remove the lower crankcase head.

2. Remove the cylinder head. Remove and discard the head gasket.

3. Remove the 6 crankcase cover screws and remove the crankcase cover from the cylinder block. If necessary, tap upward on the crankshaft with a soft-face mallet to separate the crankcase cover and cylinder block. *Do not* pry between the cylinder block and crankcase cover mating surfaces.

4. Remove the 2 screws securing the leaf stop and leaf valves to the crankcase cover. Remove the leaf valves and stop.

5. Remove the crankshaft, connecting rod and piston assembly from the cylinder block.

6. Slide the crankshaft seals and bearing retainers from each end of the crankshaft.

7. Remove the piston ring using a suitable piston ring expander tool.

8. Remove the piston pin retainers using needlenose pliers (**Figure 46**). Discard the retainers.

9. Remove the piston pin using a suitable tool, then separate the piston from the connecting rod.

NOTE
Main bearings are destroyed during removal. Do not remove the main bearings from the crankshaft unless replacement is necessary.

10. If necessary, remove the upper and lower main bearings from the crankshaft using OMC Crankshaft Bearing Puller (part No. 115316) or a suitable equivalent press plate.

Disassembly
(4 Deluxe and 3-8 hp)

NOTE
All components that are to be reused should be marked for original location and direction for reference during reassembly.

Refer to **Figure 47** (4 Deluxe, 3 and 4 hp) **Figure 48** (6 and 8 hp) and **Figure 49** (all models, typical) for this procedure.

1. Remove the intake manifold along with the leaf plate and valve assembly. Remove and discard the gaskets.

2. *6 and 8 hp*—Remove the thermostat cover, thermostat and related components from the cylinder head. Remove and discard the cover O-ring.

3. Remove the cylinder head. Remove and discard the cylinder head gasket.

4. Mark the cylinder number on each piston crown using an indelible marker.

5. Remove the exhaust cover. On 6 and 8 hp, remove the inner exhaust cover. Remove and discard the gasket(s).

6. Remove the lower crankcase head on 3 and 4 hp and 4 Deluxe.

7. Remove the bottom crankshaft seal. Using suitable snap ring pliers, remove the crankshaft retainer.

CAUTION
*The taper pin is used to position the crankcase cover and cylinder block in the correct alignment. **Do not** damage*

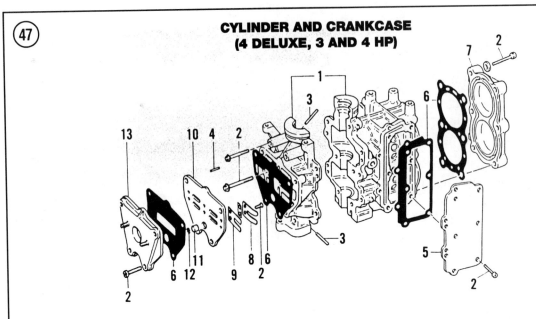

**CYLINDER AND CRANKCASE
(4 DELUXE, 3 AND 4 HP)**

1. Cylinder and crankcase assembly
2. Screw
3. Tube
4. Taper pin
5. Exhaust cover plate
6. Gasket
7. Cylinder head
8. Leaf stop
9. Leaf valve
10. Leaf plate
11. Check valve
12. Check valve screen
13. Intake manifold

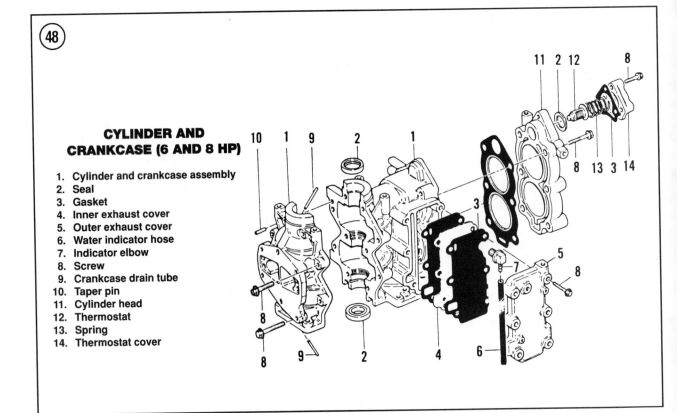

**CYLINDER AND
CRANKCASE (6 AND 8 HP)**

1. Cylinder and crankcase assembly
2. Seal
3. Gasket
4. Inner exhaust cover
5. Outer exhaust cover
6. Water indicator hose
7. Indicator elbow
8. Screw
9. Crankcase drain tube
10. Taper pin
11. Cylinder head
12. Thermostat
13. Spring
14. Thermostat cover

the taper pin bore during removal, or correct alignment may not be possible. During removal, always use a tool that is larger than the taper pin bore to prevent the tool from entering and damaging the bore.

8. Using a suitable punch or similar tool, remove the taper pin. Remove the pin by driving it toward the intake manifold side of the power head.

9. Remove the crankcase cover-to-cylinder block screws.

10. Reinstall the cylinder head and finger tighten the screws to prevent the pistons from falling out of the power head when the crankshaft is removed.

11. Position the power head with its intake manifold facing upward. Using a soft-face mallet, carefully tap the flywheel end of the crankshaft in an upward direction until the crankcase cover separates from the cylinder block. Lift the cover off the cylinder block. Use caution not to nick, scratch or damage the crankcase cover and cylinder block mating surfaces.

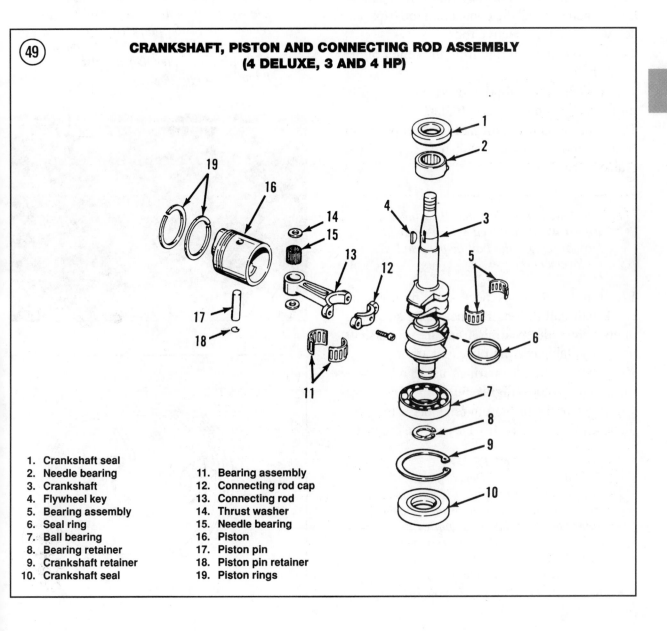

⁴⁹

CRANKSHAFT, PISTON AND CONNECTING ROD ASSEMBLY
(4 DELUXE, 3 AND 4 HP)

8

1. Crankshaft seal
2. Needle bearing
3. Crankshaft
4. Flywheel key
5. Bearing assembly
6. Seal ring
7. Ball bearing
8. Bearing retainer
9. Crankshaft retainer
10. Crankshaft seal
11. Bearing assembly
12. Connecting rod cap
13. Connecting rod
14. Thrust washer
15. Needle bearing
16. Piston
17. Piston pin
18. Piston pin retainer
19. Piston rings

CAUTION
Always store piston pins, piston pin bearings, locating washers, connecting rod bearings, rod caps and rod cap screws together with their respective piston and connecting rod so they can be reinstalled in their original locations.

12. Remove the center main bearing liner and 30 bearing rollers. Place the liner and bearing rollers in an appropriately labeled container.

13. Mark the cylinder number on the connecting rod caps. Remove the caps and connecting rod bearings. Lift the crankshaft out of the cylinder block, then reinstall the connecting rod caps and screws on their respective rods.

14. Remove the seal ring from the center of the crankshaft.

15. Remove the cylinder head and carefully push each piston from its cylinder.

16. Slide the upper crankshaft seal, upper main bearing and the lower crankshaft seal off the crankshaft.

NOTE
*The lower crankshaft ball bearing (7, **Figure 49**) is damaged during removal. Do not remove the ball bearing unless replacement is necessary.*

17. If replacement is necessary, remove the crankshaft ball bearing retainer using snap ring pliers. Press the bearing from the crankshaft using a suitable bearing plate and arbor press.

18. Remove the piston rings using a suitable ring expander tool (**Figure 50**).

19. Remove the piston pin retainers using needlenose pliers (**Figure 46**). Discard the retainers.

NOTE
*On 3 and 4 hp and 4 Deluxe models, the piston pin fit in the piston is a press-fit on one side and a loose fit on the opposite side. The loose side is identified by an "L" on the underside of the piston (**Figure 51**). To prevent piston damage, the piston pin must be removed from the piston toward the press-fit side. During*

installation, insert the pin into the loose side first.

20A. *4 Deluxe, 3 and 4 hp*—Place the piston into OMC Piston Cradle part No. 326572. See **Figure 52**. Make sure the "L" side of the piston is facing upward. Press the piston pin from the piston using OMC Wrist Pin Pressing Pin part No. 326624, or equivalent driver. Retrieve the 2 thrust washers and 21 loose needle bearing rollers as the pin is removed.

NOTE
On 6 and 8 hp models, the piston must be heated to 200-400° F (93-204° C) to remove the piston pin. Heat the piston using a suitable heat gun, heat lamp or by boiling in water. Do not use open flame to heat pistons.

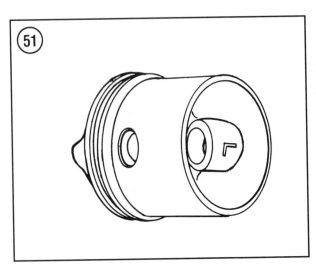

20B. *6 and 8 hp*—Place the piston on OMC Piston Cradle part No. 326573. See **Figure 52**. Press the piston pin from the piston using OMC Pressing Pin 333141. Be sure to retrieve the 2 thrust washers and loose needle bearing rollers as the pin is removed.

21. Repeat Steps 20A or 20B as appropriate to separate the remaining piston and connecting rod.

Disassembly (9.9 and 15 hp)

> *NOTE*
> *All components that are to be reused should be marked for original location and direction for reference during reassembly.*

Refer to **Figure 53** and **Figure 54** for this procedure.

1. Remove the crankcase head and discard the O-ring. Remove the seals from the crankcase head using a suitable punch and mallet.

2. Remove the exhaust cover screws and remove the inner and outer exhaust covers from the power head. If necessary, bump the edge of the cover with a soft-face mallet to dislodge the cover from the power head. Separate the inner and outer covers, then remove and discard the gaskets.

3. Remove the thermostat cover, thermostat and related components. Remove the temperature switch, if so equipped.

4. Remove the cylinder head and gasket. Discard the gasket. Mark the cylinder number on each piston crown.

5. Remove the bypass cover and gasket. Discard the gasket.

6. Remove the intake manifold, leaf valve assembly and gasket. Discard the gasket.

> *CAUTION*
> *The taper pin is used to position the crankcase cover and cylinder block in the correct alignment. **Do not** damage the taper pin bore during removal, or correct alignment may not be possible. During removal, always use a tool that is larger than the taper pin bore to prevent the tool from entering and damaging the bore.*

7. With the crankcase and cylinder block on a solid surface, drive out the taper pin from the cylinder side toward the intake side of the power head.

8. Remove the crankcase cover-to-cylinder block screws.

9. Tap the top of the crankshaft with a plastic mallet to separate the cylinder block and crankcase cover.

> *NOTE*
> *The connecting rod caps must be removed before the crankshaft can be removed from the cylinder block. Note that one side of the rod and cap has raised dots and that the corners are chamfered for proper rod/cap alignment. Caps are not interchangeable and cannot be turned.*

10. To prevent the pistons from falling out when the crankshaft is removed, reinstall the cylinder head with 2 screws tightened finger-tight. Mark

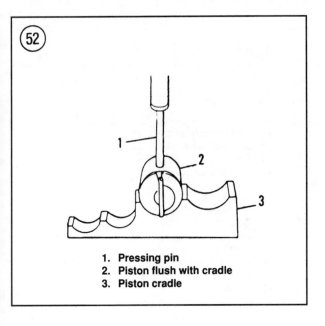

52

1. Pressing pin
2. Piston flush with cradle
3. Piston cradle

8

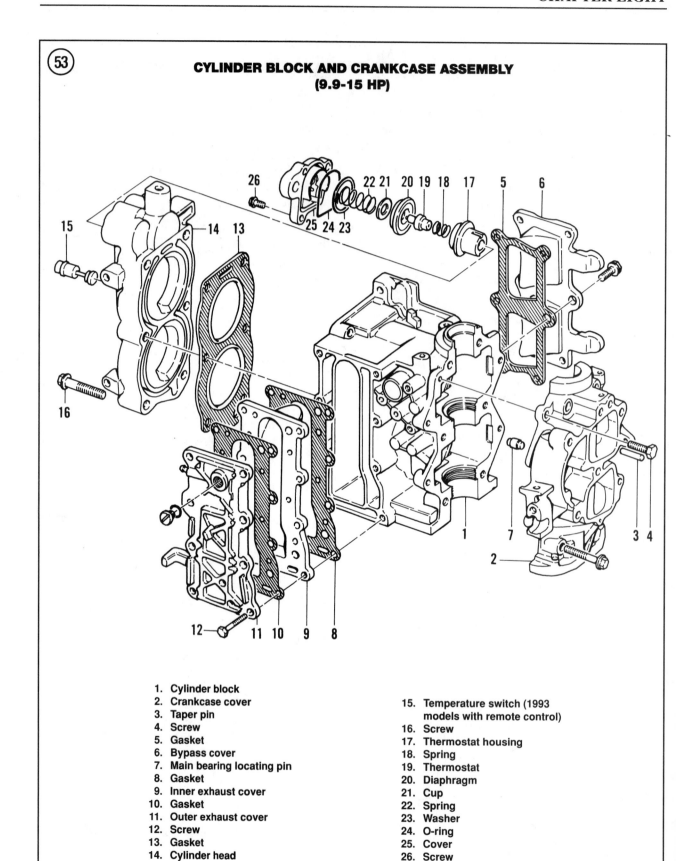

CYLINDER BLOCK AND CRANKCASE ASSEMBLY
(9.9-15 HP)

1. Cylinder block
2. Crankcase cover
3. Taper pin
4. Screw
5. Gasket
6. Bypass cover
7. Main bearing locating pin
8. Gasket
9. Inner exhaust cover
10. Gasket
11. Outer exhaust cover
12. Screw
13. Gasket
14. Cylinder head
15. Temperature switch (1993 models with remote control)
16. Screw
17. Thermostat housing
18. Spring
19. Thermostat
20. Diaphragm
21. Cup
22. Spring
23. Washer
24. O-ring
25. Cover
26. Screw

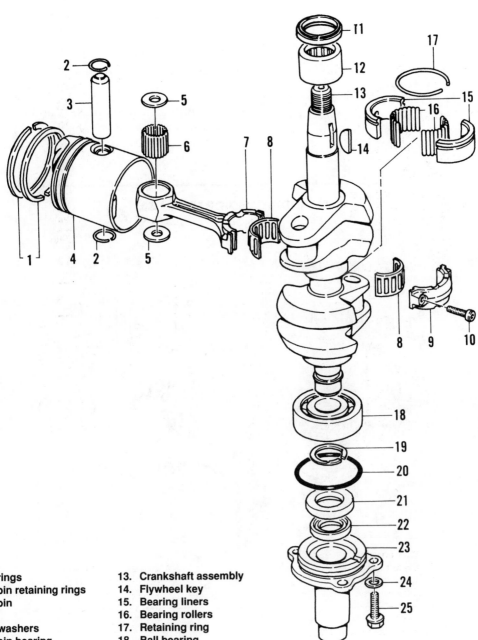

54 CRANKSHAFT, CONNECTING ROD, PISTON AND RELATED COMPONENTS
(9.9-15 HP)

8

1. Piston rings
2. Piston pin retaining rings
3. Piston pin
4. Piston
5. Thrust washers
6. Piston pin bearing
7. Connecting rod
8. Connecting rod
   bearing assembly
9. Connecting rod cap
10. Screw
11. Seal
12. Needle roller bearing
13. Crankshaft assembly
14. Flywheel key
15. Bearing liners
16. Bearing rollers
17. Retaining ring
18. Ball bearing
19. Snap ring
20. O-ring
21. Seal
22. Seal
23. Crankcase head
24. Washer
25. Screw

the cylinder number on each connecting rod and cap. Remove each connecting rod cap and bearing and place them in a clean container.

11. Remove the crankshaft from the cylinder block.

12. Remove the remaining connecting rod bearings and place in their respective container.

CAUTION
Always store piston pins, piston pin bearings, locating washers, connecting rod bearings, rod caps and rod cap screws together with their respective pis-

ton and connecting rod so they can be reinstalled in their original location.

13. Reinstall each rod cap on its respective connecting rod. Remove the piston and rod assemblies from their cylinders. Mark the cylinder number on the top of each piston with a felt-tipped marker.

14. Carefully pry the crankshaft center main bearing retaining ring from its groove. Slide the retaining ring to one side and remove the roller bearing assembly. Place the 23 bearing rollers in a clean container.

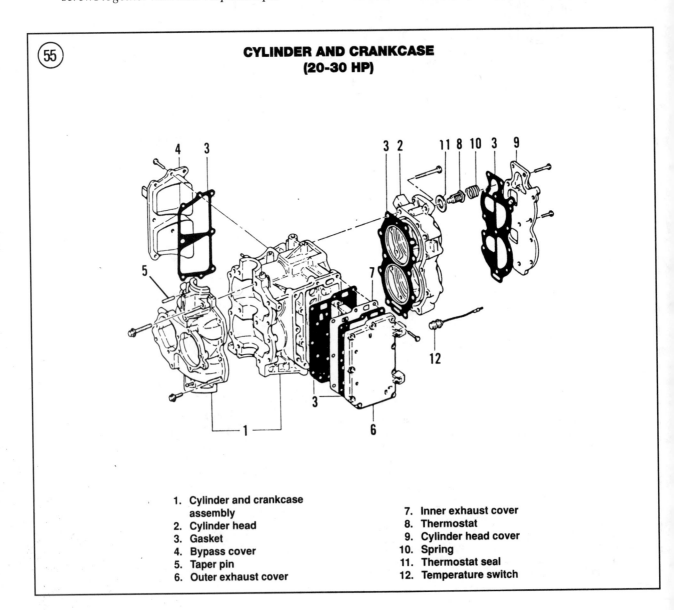

(55)

**CYLINDER AND CRANKCASE
(20-30 HP)**

1. Cylinder and crankcase
   assembly
2. Cylinder head
3. Gasket
4. Bypass cover
5. Taper pin
6. Outer exhaust cover
7. Inner exhaust cover
8. Thermostat
9. Cylinder head cover
10. Spring
11. Thermostat seal
12. Temperature switch

15. Slide the crankshaft upper seal and main bearing off the crankshaft.

NOTE
Do not remove the lower main bearing from the crankshaft unless the bearing requires replacement.

16. If the lower main bearing requires replacement, remove the snap ring and remove the bearing with an appropriate puller.

17. Remove the piston rings using a suitable ring expander.

18. If the pistons are to be removed from the connecting rods, remove the piston pin retaining rings using needlenose pliers. See **Figure 46**. Discard the retaining rings.

NOTE
The piston on 1991 and 1992 models must be heated to remove the piston pin

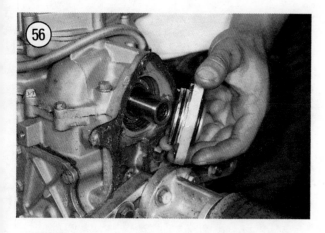

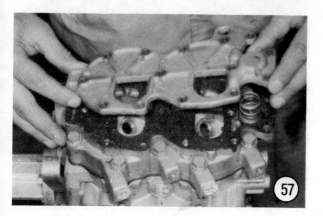

in Step 19. *Heat the piston using a heat gun, heat lamp or by boiling in water. Do not use open flame to heat the piston.*

19A. *1991-92 models*—Heat the piston to 200-400° F (93-204° C). Then place the piston on OMC Piston Cradle part No. 326573. See **Figure 52**. Press the piston pin out of the piston using OMC Pressing Pin part No. 392511, or equivalent, and an arbor press. Remove the piston from the connecting rod along with the 2 thrust washers and 22 loose bearing rollers. Repeat this procedure on the remaining piston/connecting rod.

19B. *1993-on models*—The piston pin is a slip-fit in both sides of the piston. Push the pin out of the piston, then remove the piston from the rod along with 22 loose bearing rollers and 2 thrust washers. Repeat this procedure on the remaining piston/connecting rod.

Disassembly
(20-30 hp)

NOTE
All components that are to be reused should be marked for original location and direction for reference during reassembly.

Refer to **Figure 55** for this procedure.

1. Remove the 3 screws securing the lower crankcase head. Dislodge the crankcase head by carefully prying on opposite sides of the crankcase head. See **Figure 56**. Remove and discard the 2 crankcase head O-rings. Drive the seal from the crankcase head using an appropriate size punch.

2. Remove the cylinder head cover and gasket. See **Figure 57**. If necessary, tap along the edge of the cover with a soft-face mallet to dislodge it. Remove and discard the gasket.

3. Remove the thermostat and related components. See **Figure 58**. Discard the thermostat seal.

8

4. Remove the cylinder head and gasket (**Figure 59**). Remove and discard the gasket. After removing the cylinder head, mark the cylinder number on each piston crown.

5. Remove the exhaust cover screws. Tap along the edge of the cover using a soft-face mallet to break the seal. Remove the outer cover and gasket (**Figure 60**). Discard the gasket.

6. Remove the inner exhaust cover and gasket (**Figure 61**). Remove and discard the gasket.

7. Remove the intake bypass cover and gasket (**Figure 62**). Discard the gasket.

8. Remove the 7 hex-head and 1 flat-head screws securing the intake manifold to the crankcase cover. Remove the intake manifold and gasket (**Figure 63**). Discard the gasket.

> *CAUTION*
> *The taper pin is used to position the crankcase cover and cylinder block in the correct alignment. **Do not** damage the taper pin bore during removal, or correct alignment may not be possible. During removal, always use a tool that is larger than the taper pin bore to prevent the tool from entering and damaging the bore.*

9. Using a suitable punch, drive the taper pin out of the crankcase assembly (**Figure 64**). Drive the pin from the cylinder side toward the intake side of the power head.

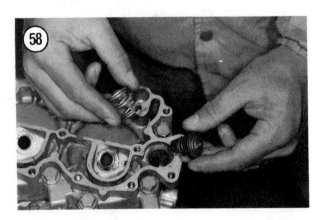

10. Remove the single Phillips-head screw securing the leaf valve assembly to the crankcase cover. See **Figure 65**.

11. Remove the crankcase cover-to-cylinder block screws. See **Figure 66**.

12. Position the power head so the cylinder side is facing down. Tap upward on the crankshaft

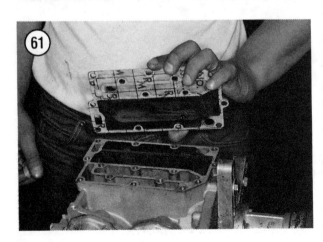

(flywheel end) with a soft-face mallet until the crankcase cover separates from the cylinder block. Then, lift the crankcase cover off the cylinder block. See **Figure 67**.

13. Temporarily, reinstall the cylinder head and secure with 2 screws installed finger tight, to prevent the pistons from falling out during crankshaft removal.

CAUTION
Always store piston pins, piston pin bearings, locating washers, connecting rod bearings, rod caps and rod cap screws together with their respective piston and connecting rod so they can be reinstalled in their original locations.

14. Mark the cylinder number on the connecting rods and caps. Note that one side of the rod and cap has raised dots for directional reference. Rod caps are not interchangeable and cannot be turned.

15. Remove the connecting rod screws using OMC Torque Socket part No. 331638, or an

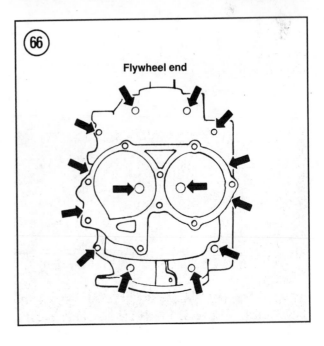

8

equivalent 5/16 in. 12-point socket. Remove each connecting rod cap and bearing assembly. See **Figure 68**.

16. Lift the crankshaft out of the cylinder block (**Figure 69**). Reinstall each rod cap and bearing on their respective connecting rod and install the rod cap screws finger tight. Remove the retaining ring securing the 2 center main bearing liners together. Remove the 2 liner halves and bearing and cage assembly. Place the bearing and liner assembly into a clean labeled container.

17. Remove the cylinder head, then remove the pistons from the cylinders.

18. Remove the flywheel key from the crankshaft, if installed. Slide the upper seal and bearing off the crankshaft. Discard the seal.

19A. *1991-92 models*—Remove and discard the O-ring (drive shaft seal) from inside the bottom of the crankshaft.

19B. *1993-on models*—Remove and discard the O-ring (drive shaft seal) from inside the sleeve installed on the bottom of the crankshaft. Inspect the sleeve and replace if necessary. Remove the sleeve using a suitable slide-hammer puller with internal jaws.

> *NOTE*
> *The crankshaft lower main bearing is destroyed during removal. Do not remove the bearing unless it requires replacement.*

20. If the crankshaft lower main bearing requires replacement, proceed as follows:

    a. Remove the snap ring under the bearing using snap ring pliers.

    b. Press the bearing off the crankshaft using a suitable bearing separator and arbor press. Discard the bearing.

21. Remove and discard the piston rings using suitable ring expanders. See **Figure 70**.

22. Remove the piston pin retaining rings using needlenose pliers. See **Figure 71**. Discard the retaining rings.

23. Push the piston pin through the piston. Separate the piston, along with 2 thrust washers and 28 loose bearing rollers, from the connecting rod. Repeat this procedure for the remaining piston/connecting rod.

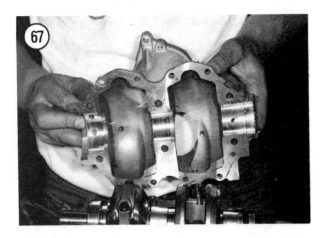

Disassembly
(35 Jet and 40-50 hp)

> *NOTE*
> *All components that are to be reused should be marked for original location and direction for reference during reassembly.*

Refer to **Figure 72** and **Figure 73** for this procedure.

On late models, 2 seals are installed in the crankcase head assembly (12, **Figure 72**), instead of one seal used on earlier models. The lower seal, on models so equipped, eliminates the crankshaft-to-drive shaft O-ring seal (11, **Figure 72**).

1. Remove the intake manifold and leaf valve assembly. Remove and discard the gasket.

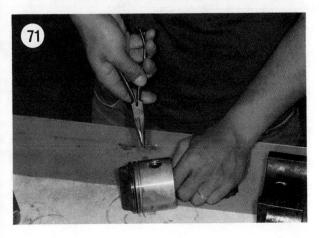

2. Remove the starboard side lower motor cover mounting bracket.

> *CAUTION*
> *The taper pin is used to position the crankcase cover and cylinder block in the correct alignment. **Do not** damage the taper pin bore during removal, or correct alignment may not be possible. During removal, always use a tool that is larger than the taper pin bore to prevent the tool from entering and damaging the bore.*

3. Using a suitable punch, drive the taper pin (9, **Figure 73**) out of the crankcase assembly. Drive the pin from the cylinder side toward the intake side of the power head.

4. Remove the crankcase head assembly. Remove and discard the O-ring. Remove both crankcase head seals using OMC Puller Bridge (part No. 432127) and OMC Puller (part No. 432131). Discard the seals.

5. Remove the exhaust cover. If necessary, bump the edge of the cover with a soft-face mallet to break the seal. Remove and discard the exhaust cover gasket.

6. Remove the 8 screws along the crankcase cover flange, then the 6 inner cover (main bearing) screws.

7. Position the power head so the cylinders are facing downward. Tap on the flywheel end of the crankshaft with a soft-face mallet to dislodge the crankcase cover from the cylinder block, then lift the cover off the cylinder block. See **Figure 74**.

> *CAUTION*
> *Always store piston pins, piston pin bearings, locating washers, connecting rod bearings, rod caps and rod cap screws together with their respective piston and connecting rod so they can be reinstalled in their original locations.*

8. Mark the cylinder number on each connecting rod and cap. Note that rod caps are not interchangeable and cannot be turned.

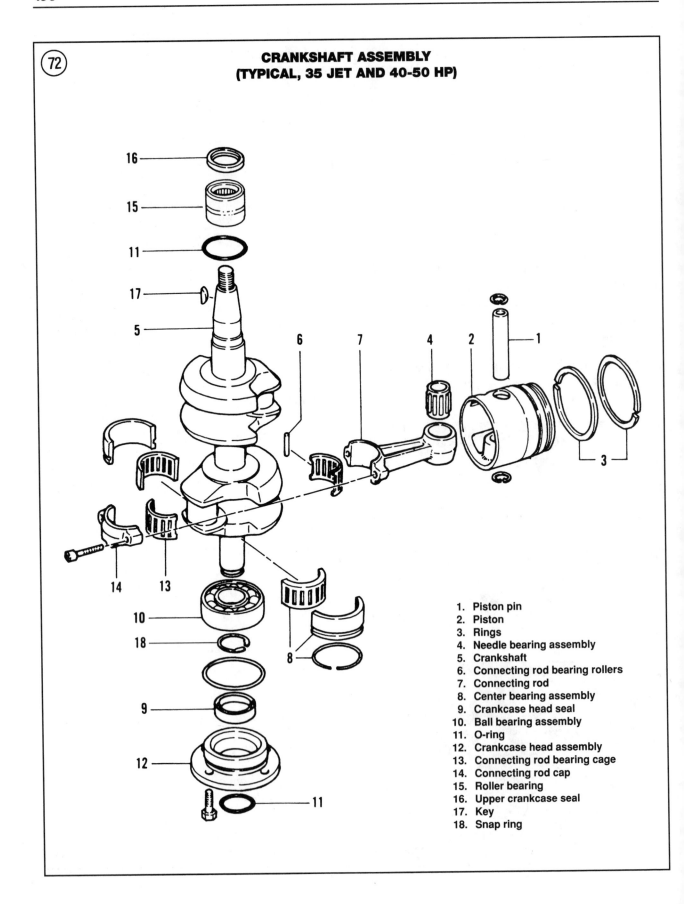

**CRANKSHAFT ASSEMBLY
(TYPICAL, 35 JET AND 40-50 HP)**

72

1. Piston pin
2. Piston
3. Rings
4. Needle bearing assembly
5. Crankshaft
6. Connecting rod bearing rollers
7. Connecting rod
8. Center bearing assembly
9. Crankcase head seal
10. Ball bearing assembly
11. O-ring
12. Crankcase head assembly
13. Connecting rod bearing cage
14. Connecting rod cap
15. Roller bearing
16. Upper crankcase seal
17. Key
18. Snap ring

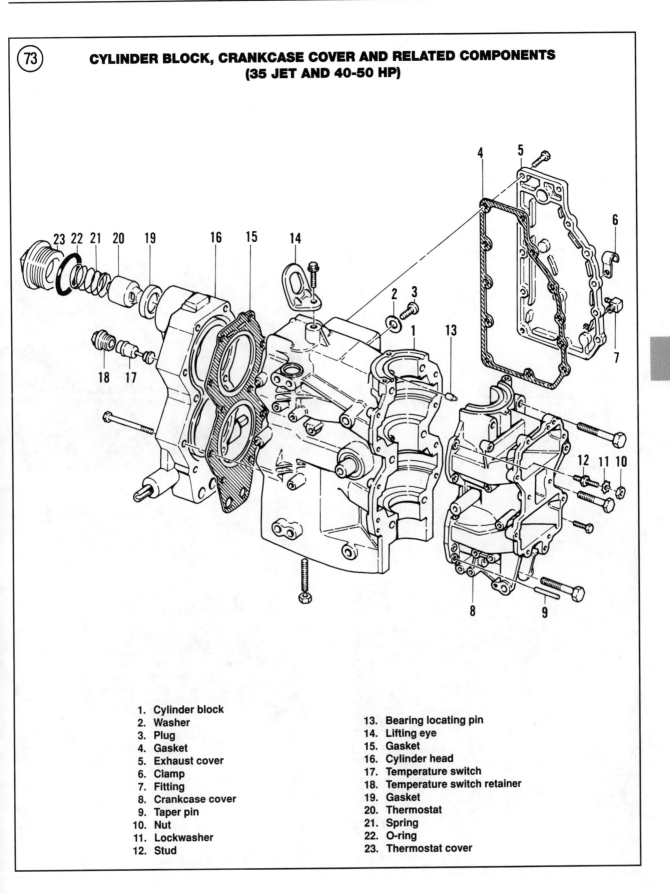

73

CYLINDER BLOCK, CRANKCASE COVER AND RELATED COMPONENTS
(35 JET AND 40-50 HP)

1. Cylinder block
2. Washer
3. Plug
4. Gasket
5. Exhaust cover
6. Clamp
7. Fitting
8. Crankcase cover
9. Taper pin
10. Nut
11. Lockwasher
12. Stud
13. Bearing locating pin
14. Lifting eye
15. Gasket
16. Cylinder head
17. Temperature switch
18. Temperature switch retainer
19. Gasket
20. Thermostat
21. Spring
22. O-ring
23. Thermostat cover

8

9. Remove the connecting rod screws using OMC Torque Socket part No. 331638, or an equivalent 5/16 in. 12-point socket. Remove each connecting rod cap and bearing assembly. See **Figure 75**.

10. Lift the crankshaft up and out of the cylinder block and place on a clean workbench (**Figure 76**). Reinstall the connecting rod caps on their respective connecting rods (**Figure 77**) and install the rod cap screws finger tight.

11. Slide the upper bearing and seal assembly off the crankshaft. Remove and discard the seal and O-ring.

12. Remove the retaining ring from the center main bearing. Remove the bearing liners and the 2 bearing halves.

> *CAUTION*
> *The lower main bearing is destroyed during removal. Do not remove the lower bearing unless it requires replacement.*

13. If the crankshaft lower bearing requires replacement, remove the snap ring under the bearing, using snap ring pliers. Then, using a bearing separator and arbor press, remove the bearing from the crankshaft.

14. Remove the thermostat cover, thermostat and related components from the cylinder head (**Figure 78**, typical). Remove and discard the O-ring from the thermostat cover.

15. If necessary, remove the temperature switch retainer and switch from the cylinder head. Remove the cylinder head. Remove and discard the gasket.

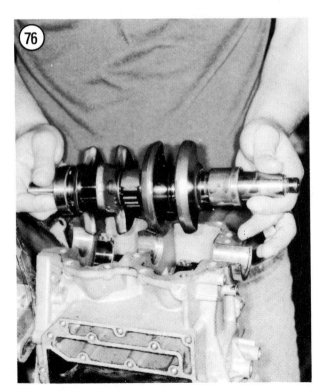

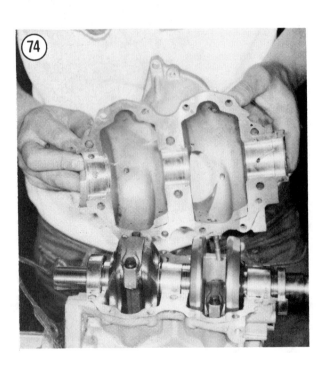

16. Mark the cylinder number on each piston crown, then push the pistons out of the cylinders.

17. Remove the piston rings using a suitable piston ring expander. Discard the rings.

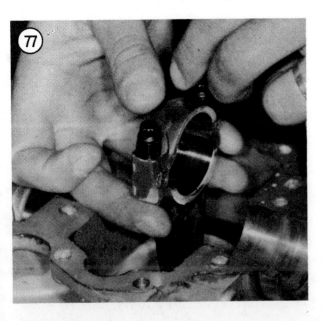

18. Remove the piston pin retaining rings using needlenose pliers. See **Figure 79**. Discard the retaining rings.

19. Push the piston pin through the piston. Separate the piston, along with 2 thrust washers and 28 loose bearing rollers, from the connecting rod. Repeat this procedure for the remaining piston/connecting rod. See **Figure 80**.

Disassembly
(60-70 hp)

> *NOTE*
> *All components that are to be reused should be marked for original location and direction for reference during reassembly.*

Refer to **Figure 81**, typical and **Figure 82** for this procedure. On late models, 2 seals are installed in the crankcase head assembly (12, **Fig-**

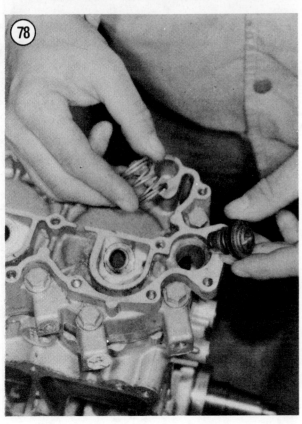

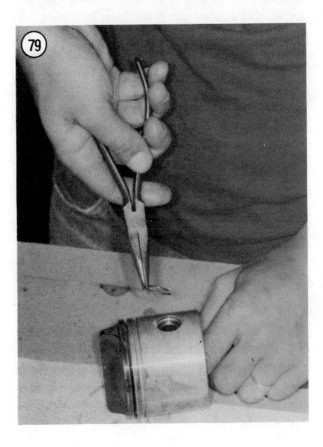

8

ure 81), instead of one seal used on earlier models. The lower seal eliminates the crankshaft-to-drive shaft O-ring seal (11, **Figure 81**).

1. Remove the flywheel as described in this chapter. Remove the stator, timer base, power pack and ignition coils as described in Chapter Seven.

2. Remove the carburetors, primer valve, fuel pump or VRO pump assembly, if so equipped.

3. Remove the intake manifold and leaf valve assembly. Remove and discard the manifold gasket.

4. If necessary, remove the thermostat cover, thermostat and related components. See 15-23, **Figure 82**. Discard the housing gasket.

5. Remove the cylinder head. Remove and discard the gasket.

6. Remove the exhaust cover. Remove and discard the gasket.

7. Remove the lower crankcase head. Remove and discard the crankcase head O-ring seal. Remove and discard the crankshaft lower seal on 1991-92 models. On 1993-on models, remove and discard the 2 seals in the crankcase head.

CAUTION
The taper pin is used to position the crankcase cover and cylinder block in the correct alignment. ***Do not*** *damage the taper pin bore during removal, or correct alignment may not be possible. During removal, always use a tool that is larger than the taper pin bore to prevent the tool from entering and damaging the bore.*

8. Using a suitable punch, drive the taper pin (3, **Figure 82**) out of the crankcase assembly. Drive the pin from the cylinder side toward the intake side of the power head.

9. Starting at the center, and working in a circular pattern, loosen the main bearing screws and nuts. After all screws and nuts are loose, remove them. Remove the crankcase cover-to-cylinder block flange screws.

10. Position the power head so the cylinders are facing downward. Tap upward on the flywheel end of the crankshaft with a soft-face mallet to loosen the crankcase cover. Lift the cover up and off the cylinder block.

CAUTION
Do not allow the pistons to fall out of the cylinder block when the connecting rod caps are removed.

11. Mark the cylinder number on each connecting rod and cap. Using OMC Torque Socket (part No. 331638), or equivalent 5/16 in. 12-point socket, loosen and remove the connecting rod cap screws to the top cylinder. Remove the connecting rod cap and bearing (**Figure 75**). Push the piston from the cylinder, then reinstall the rod cap. Tighten the cap screws finger-tight.

CAUTION
Always store piston pins, piston pin bearings, locating washers, connecting

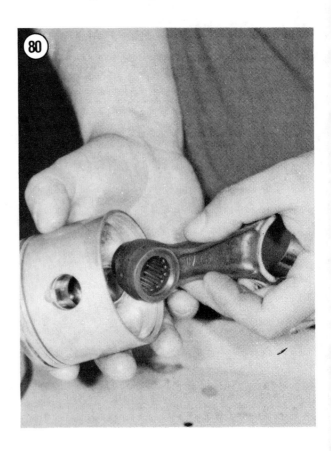

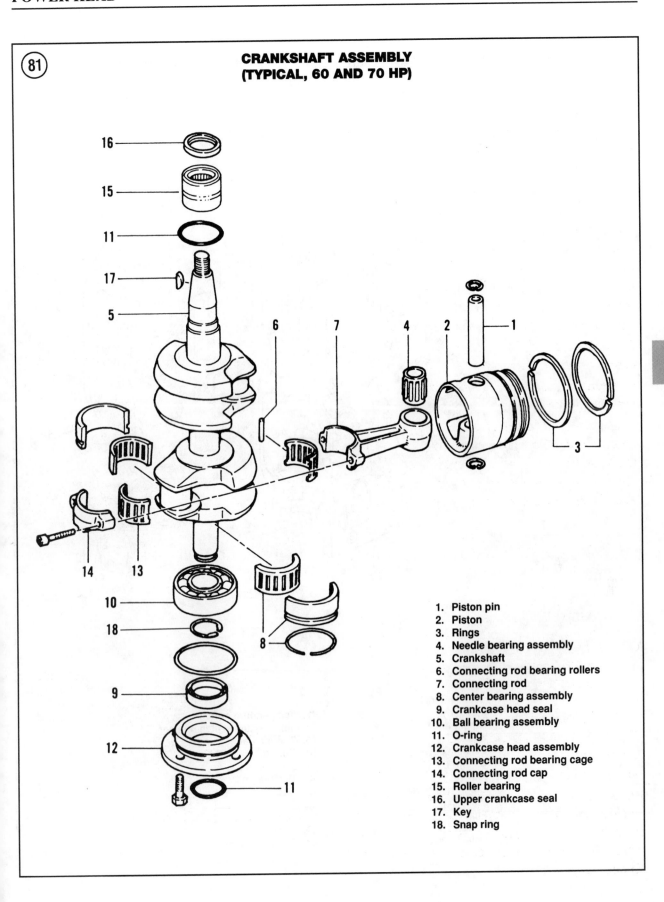

81

**CRANKSHAFT ASSEMBLY
(TYPICAL, 60 AND 70 HP)**

8

1. Piston pin
2. Piston
3. Rings
4. Needle bearing assembly
5. Crankshaft
6. Connecting rod bearing rollers
7. Connecting rod
8. Center bearing assembly
9. Crankcase head seal
10. Ball bearing assembly
11. O-ring
12. Crankcase head assembly
13. Connecting rod bearing cage
14. Connecting rod cap
15. Roller bearing
16. Upper crankcase seal
17. Key
18. Snap ring

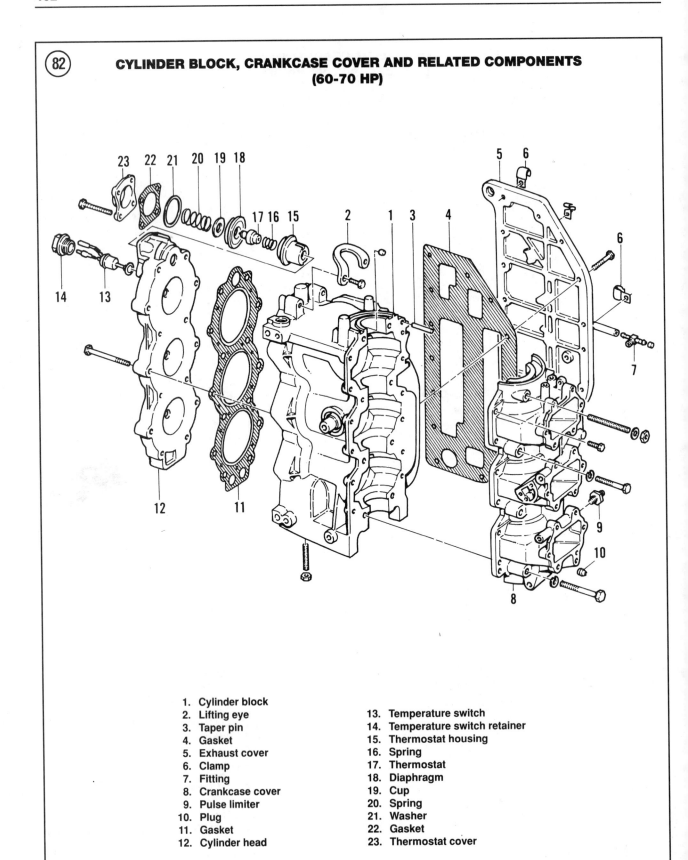

**CYLINDER BLOCK, CRANKCASE COVER AND RELATED COMPONENTS
(60-70 HP)**

1. Cylinder block
2. Lifting eye
3. Taper pin
4. Gasket
5. Exhaust cover
6. Clamp
7. Fitting
8. Crankcase cover
9. Pulse limiter
10. Plug
11. Gasket
12. Cylinder head
13. Temperature switch
14. Temperature switch retainer
15. Thermostat housing
16. Spring
17. Thermostat
18. Diaphragm
19. Cup
20. Spring
21. Washer
22. Gasket
23. Thermostat cover

rod bearings, rod caps and rod cap screws together with their respective piston and connecting rod so they can be reinstalled in their original locations.

12. Repeat Step 11 for each remaining cylinder.

13. Lift the crankshaft straight upward and out of the cylinder block.

14. Remove the crankshaft upper bearing and seal. Discard the O-ring. Pry the seal from the upper bearing. Discard the seal.

15. Remove the retaining rings from the center main bearings. Remove the bearing liners and roller bearings. Store the bearings, liners and retaining rings in a clean, appropriately labeled container.

CAUTION
The crankshaft lower bearing is destroyed during removal. Do not remove the bearing unless it requires replacement.

16. To remove the lower main bearing from the crankshaft, first remove the snap ring below the bearing using snap ring pliers. Then press the bearing from the crankshaft using a suitable bearing separator and arbor press.

17. Remove the piston rings from the pistons using a suitable ring expander. Discard the piston rings.

18. Remove the piston pin retaining rings using needlenose pliers. See **Figure 79**. Discard the retaining rings.

19. Push the piston pin through the piston. Separate the piston, along with 2 thrust washers and 28 loose needle bearing rollers from the connecting rod. See **Figure 80**. Repeat this step to disassemble the remaining piston/connecting rod assemblies.

Disassembly
(V4 and V6 Cross-Flow Models)

NOTE
All components that are to be reused should be marked for original location

and direction for reference during reassembly.

Refer to **Figure 83** and **Figure 84** for this procedure. The figures show the crankshaft and cylinder block assemblies for V4 models; however, V6 models are similar.

1. Remove the screws securing the intake manifold, then tap around its edge with a soft-face mallet to dislodge it from the crankcase cover. Do not pry between the mating surfaces to remove the manifold. On 4-cylinder models, disconnect the recirculation hose from the fitting on the cylinder block. Remove the intake manifold and leaf valve assembly. Remove and discard the gasket.

2. Remove the cylinder head covers. Remove and discard the cover gaskets. After removing the cylinder head covers, the temperature sending switch can be removed by carefully prying it out with a small screwdriver.

3. Remove the cylinder heads. Remove and discard the head gaskets.

4. Mark the cylinder number on the crown of each piston. If reused, the pistons must be reinstalled in their original cylinders.

5. Remove the exhaust cover screws, then remove the outer and inner exhaust covers. Separate the covers if necessary, then remove and discard the gaskets.

NOTE
Note the location and label the intake bypass covers, cover fasteners, fuel primer and recirculation hoses, clamps and hose connectors. The lower starboard bypass cover on V4 models and the covers on which the starter solenoid and the terminal block are mounted on V6 models are different from the other covers and must be reinstalled in their original locations.

6. Remove the intake bypass covers. Store each cover with its fasteners, clamps and hose connectors so they can be installed in their original locations.

8

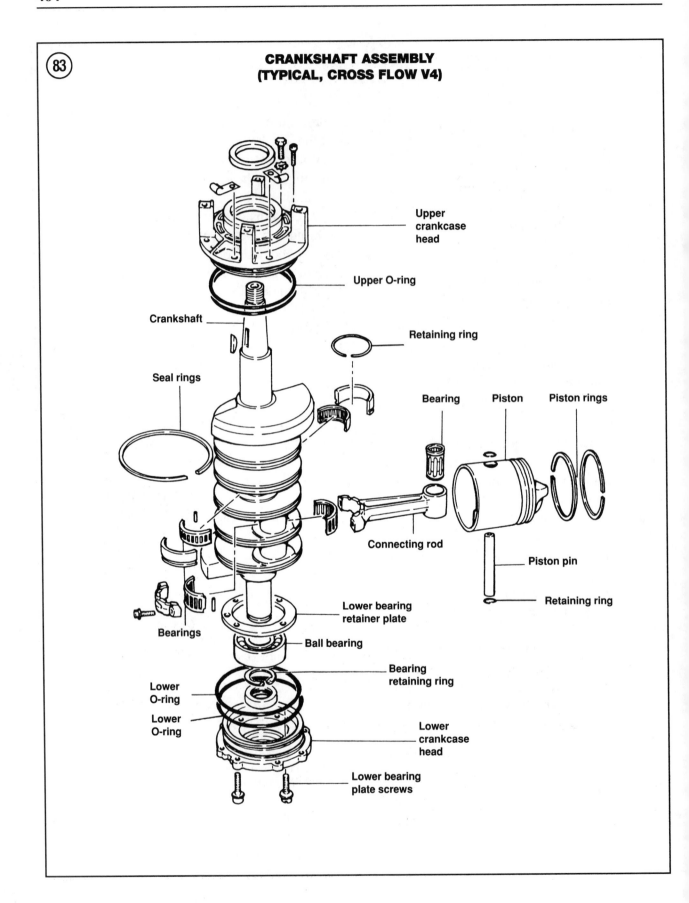

**CRANKSHAFT ASSEMBLY
(TYPICAL, CROSS FLOW V4)**

(83)

Upper crankcase head

Upper O-ring

Crankshaft

Retaining ring

Seal rings

Bearing

Piston

Piston rings

Connecting rod

Piston pin

Retaining ring

Lower bearing retainer plate

Bearings

Ball bearing

Bearing retaining ring

Lower O-ring

Lower O-ring

Lower crankcase head

Lower bearing plate screws

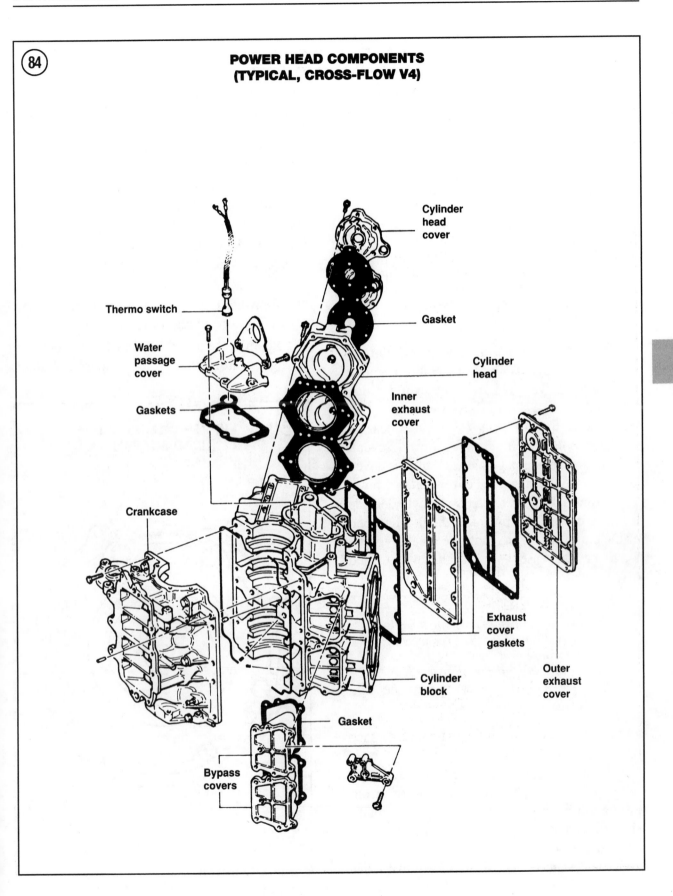

**POWER HEAD COMPONENTS
(TYPICAL, CROSS-FLOW V4)**

Thermo switch

Water passage cover

Gaskets

Crankcase

Cylinder head cover

Gasket

Cylinder head

Inner exhaust cover

Exhaust cover gaskets

Outer exhaust cover

Cylinder block

Gasket

Bypass covers

7. Remove the screws securing the upper (**Figure 85**) and lower (**Figure 86**) crankcase heads. Do not remove the crankcase heads yet. Loosen but do not remove the 4 screws holding the lower bearing retainer plate to the lower crankcase head (**Figure 86**).

> *CAUTION*
> *The taper pins are used to position the crankcase cover and cylinder block in the correct alignment. **Do not** damage the taper pin bores during removal, or correct alignment may not be possible. During removal, always use a tool that is larger than the taper pin bore to prevent the tool from entering and damaging the bore.*

8. Locate the taper pins at opposite ends of the crankcase and cylinder block assembly. Remove the pins by driving out from the cylinder side toward the intake side of the power head.

9. Remove 6 (V4) or 8 (V6) main bearing screws. Loosen each screw evenly in several steps to prevent warpage of the crankcase cover.

10. Remove the crankcase cover flange screws.

11. Position the power head so the cylinder side is facing down. Tap upward on the flywheel end of the crankshaft with a soft-face mallet to dislodge the crankcase cover. Lift the cover up and off the cylinder block.

> *CAUTION*
> *Always store piston pins, piston pin bearings, locating washers, connecting rod bearings, rod caps and rod cap screws together with their respective piston and connecting rod so they can be reinstalled in their original locations.*

12. Mark the cylinder and directional reference on each connecting rod and cap.

13. Temporarily reinstall the cylinder heads with 2 screws each, to prevent the pistons from falling out of the cylinder block during crankshaft removal.

14. Rotate the crankshaft to position the No. 1 and No. 2 connecting rods as shown in **Figure**

87. Remove the connecting rod cap screws using OMC Torque Socket part No. 331638, or an equivalent 5/16 in. 12-point socket. Remove the connecting rod caps, bearing rollers and cages. Note that each crankpin bearing consists of 18 loose rollers. Place the bearings and cages in individual containers marked with their respective cylinder number. Repeat this step on each remaining connecting rod cap.

15. Lift the crankshaft along with the upper and lower crankcase heads from the cylinder block. Place the crankshaft assembly on a clean workbench.

16. Reinstall the connecting rod caps on their respective connecting rods.

17. Position the power head so the cylinders are facing upward. Remove the cylinder heads, then

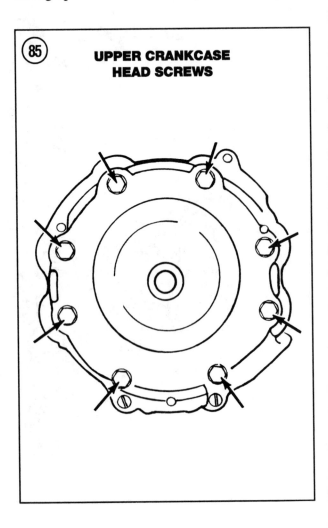

(85) **UPPER CRANKCASE HEAD SCREWS**

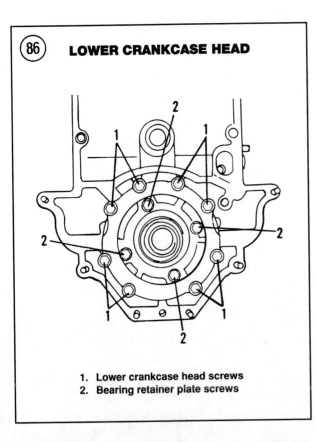

86 **LOWER CRANKCASE HEAD**

1. Lower crankcase head screws
2. Bearing retainer plate screws

87

push each piston assembly out of the cylinder block.

18. Slide the upper crankcase head off the crankshaft. Remove and discard the O-rings. Carefully drive the seal from the crankcase head with a punch inserted through the bottom of the bearing to engage the seal lip.

19. Remove and discard the 4 screws (loosened in Step 7) securing the lower bearing retainer plate to the lower crankcase head. See 2, **Figure 86**. Remove the lower crankcase head from the crankshaft. Remove and discard the O-rings. Carefully drive the seal from the crankcase head with a punch inserted through the bottom of the bearing to engage the seal lip. Discard the seal.

20. Remove the retaining rings holding the center main bearing outer races together. Separate the bearing outer races and remove the needle bearing halves.

CAUTION
The crankshaft lower main bearing is destroyed during removal. Do not remove the bearing unless it requires replacement.

21. If the lower main bearing requires replacement, remove the snap ring, then remove the bearing using a suitable puller or bearing separator and press.

22. Remove the piston rings using a suitable ring expander. If a ring expander is not available, pry each ring far enough from the piston to grip it with pliers, then break the rings off the piston. Discard the rings.

23. Remove the piston pin retaining rings using needlenose pliers. Discard the retaining rings.

24. Push the piston pin out of the piston. Separate the piston from the connecting rod along with 2 thrust washers and 28 loose needle bearing rollers. See **Figure 88**. Repeat Steps 22-24 on each remaining piston/connecting rod assembly.

8

Disassembly
(V4, V6 [Except 60° Models] and V8 Loop Charged Models)

> *NOTE*
> *All components that are to be reused should be marked for original location and direction for reference during reassembly.*

Refer to **Figure 89** and **Figure 90** for this procedure. Although the figures show the cylinder block/crankcase cover (**Figure 89**) and crankshaft assembly (**Figure 90**) used on V6 models, they are representative of V4 and V8 models. The O-ring (23, **Figure 90**) and crankshaft sleeve (24) are absent on V8 and early V4 and V6 models. The piston pin bearing (18, **Figure 90**) is a caged roller bearing on 1991 models. The thrust washers (13, **Figure 90**) are absent on models equipped with a caged bearing.

1. Note the position and label the crankcase recirculation hoses for reference during reassembly, then disconnect all recirculation hoses.

> *NOTE*
> *The nut securing the torsional damper on V8 models is tightened to 148-152 ft.-lb. (200-206 N•m) during assembly at the factory. Be sure to use appropriate tools to remove the nut. The manufacturer recommends using a 1/2 in. impact wrench to remove the nut.*

2. V8 models—Remove the nut securing the torsional damper to the bottom of the crankshaft, using a 1-3/4 in. socket. Attach OMC Universal Puller part No. 378103 (or equivalent) to the damper. Tighten the puller screw to remove the damper from the crankshaft.

3. Remove the screws around the crankcase cover flange.

4. Remove the screws securing the upper (**Figure 85**) and lower (**Figure 86**) crankcase heads. Do not remove the bearing retainer plate screws (2, **Figure 86**) from the lower crankcase head.

5. Loosen the main bearing screws evenly in several steps to prevent warpage. Note that the screw located in the upper intake port must be removed with a 3/8 in. Allen wrench.

> *CAUTION*
> *The taper pins are used to position the crankcase cover and cylinder block in the correct alignment.* **Do not** *damage the taper pin bores during removal, or correct alignment may not be possible. During removal, always use a tool that is larger than the taper pin bore to prevent the tool from entering and damaging the bore.*

6. Locate the taper pins at opposite ends of the crankcase cover and cylinder block assembly. Using a suitable punch, drive out the taper pins from the cylinder side toward the intake side of the power head.

7. Position the power head so the cylinders are facing downward. Then tap upward on the fly-

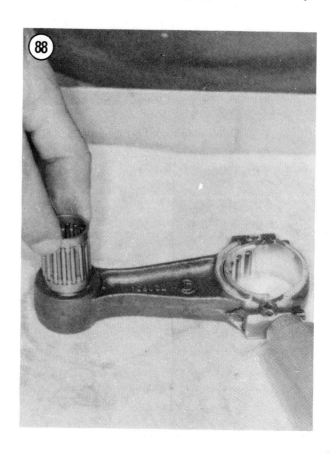

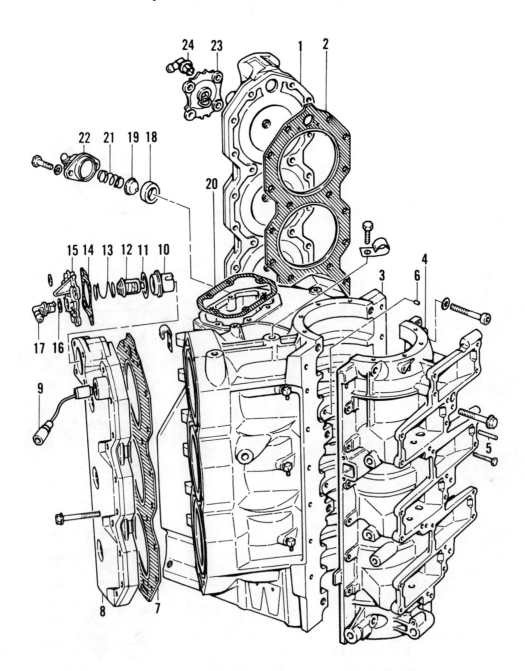

89 CYLINDER BLOCK, CRANKCASE COVER AND RELATED COMPONENTS
(V6 LOOP CHARGED MODELS)

1. Port cylinder head
2. Gasket
3. Cylinder block
4. Crankcase cover
5. Taper pin
6. Main bearing locating pin
7. Gasket
8. Starboard cylinder head
9. Temperature switch
10. Sleeve
11. Gasket
12. Thermostat
13. Spring
14. Gasket
15. Thermostat cover
16. O-ring
17. Fitting
18. Pressure release valve seal
19. Pressure release valve
20. Voltage regulator/rectifier gasket
21. Spring
22. Pressure release valve cover
23. Thermostat cover
24. Fitting

8

**CRANKSHAFT, PISTON, CONNECTING ROD AND RELATED COMPONENTS
(V6 LOOP CHARGED MODELS)**

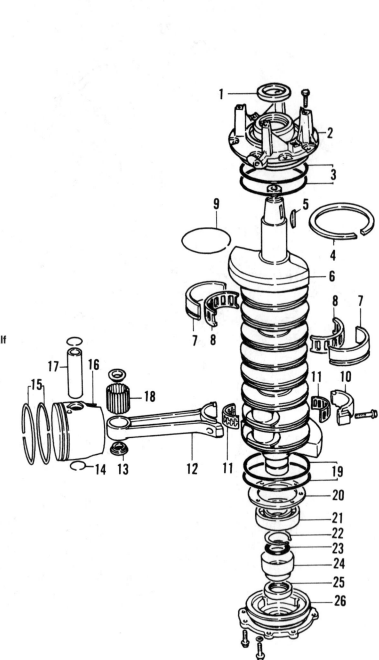

1. Seal
2. Upper crankcase head
3. O-rings
4. Crankshaft seal ring
5. Flywheel key
6. Crankshaft
7. Main bearing liner
8. Main bearing half
9. Retaining ring
10. Connecting rod cap
11. Connecting rod bearing half
12. Connecting rod
13. Thrust washer
14. Piston pin retaining ring
15. Piston rings
16. Piston
17. Piston pin
18. Piston pin
    bearing assembly
19. O-rings
20. Lower main bearing
    retaining plate
21. Lower main bearing
22. Snap ring
23. O-ring
24. Crankshaft sleeve
25. Seal
26. Lower crankcase head

wheel end of the crankshaft with a soft-face mallet until the crankcase cover separates from the cylinder block. Remove the crankcase cover.

8. Mark each connecting rod cap with its respective cylinder number.

CAUTION
Always store piston pins, piston pin bearings, locating washers, connecting rod bearings, rod caps and rod cap screws together with their respective piston and connecting rod so they can be reinstalled in their original locations.

9. Loosen the cylinder head retaining screws evenly in several stages, to prevent head warpage. Remove the screws and cylinder heads. Mark the crown of each piston with its respective cylinder number.

10. Rotate the crankshaft to position the No. 1 and No. 2 connecting rods as shown in **Figure 87**. Remove the connecting rod cap screws using OMC Torque Socket part No. 331638 or an equivalent 5/16 in. 12-point socket. Remove the rod caps and bearing assemblies, then push the pistons out of the cylinder block. Reinstall the bearings and rod caps to their respective connecting rods.

11. Repeat Step 10 to remove the remaining piston/connecting rod assemblies from the cylinder block.

12. After removing all piston/connecting rod assemblies, carefully lift the crankshaft, along with the upper and lower crankcase heads, straight up and out of the cylinder block.

13. Slide the upper crankcase head from the crankshaft. Remove and discard the O-rings. Carefully drive the seal from the crankcase head with a punch inserted through the bottom of the bearing to engage the seal lip.

14. Remove the 4 screws holding the lower bearing retainer plate to the lower crankcase head (**Figure 86**). Remove the lower crankcase head from the crankshaft. Remove and discard the O-rings. Remove the seals from the crankcase head with a punch placed from the outside

of the crankcase head onto the seals and then driving the seals into the inside.

15. Remove the center main bearing retaining rings from the bearing liners. Remove the liners and bearing assemblies.

16. *1993-on V4 and V6 models*—Using a suitable seal pick or similar hooked tool, extract the crankshaft-to-drive shaft O-ring seal (23, **Figure 90**) from the crankshaft sleeve (24). Discard the seal. If the crankshaft sleeve requires replacement, remove the sleeve using a suitable slide hammer puller with internal jaws.

NOTE
The lower main bearing is destroyed during removal. Do not remove the bearing from the crankshaft unless replacement is necessary.

17. If the lower main bearing requires replacement, remove the bearing retaining ring using snap ring pliers, then remove the bearing from the crankshaft using a suitable puller.

NOTE
If the crankshaft seal rings are to be reused, be sure to mark them for reinstallation in their original grooves.

18. Remove the crankshaft seal rings from the crankshaft.

19. Remove and discard the piston pin retaining rings using needlenose pliers. See **Figure 79**.

20. Place a piston in OMC Piston Cradle part No. 326572, then remove the piston pin using OMC Piston Pin Driver part No. 396747 (or equivalent).

21. Separate the piston, along with 2 thrust washers and 28 loose bearing rollers (1991-92 models) or 33 loose bearing rollers (1993-on models) from the connecting rod. See **Figure 88**. Place the piston, piston pin, connecting rod and bearing in a clean labeled container.

22. Repeat Steps 20 and 21 to disassemble the remaining piston/connecting rod assemblies.

8

Disassembly
(60° V6 Models)

NOTE
All components that are to be reused should be marked for original location and direction for reference during reassembly.

Refer to **Figure 91** (cylinder block/cover assembly) and **Figure 92** (crankshaft assembly) for this procedure.

1. Note the position and label the crankcase recirculation hoses for reference during reassembly, then disconnect all recirculation hoses.
2. Disconnect the shift link from the trunnion block. Remove the trunnion block from the crankcase.
3. Remove the 20 screws along the crankcase cover mating flange.
4. Loosen the 8 main bearing screws evenly, in several steps, to prevent the crankcase cover from warping.

CAUTION
*The taper pin is used to position the crankcase cover and cylinder block in the correct alignment. **Do not** damage the taper pin bore during removal, or correct alignment may not be possible. During removal, always use a tool that is larger than the taper pin bore to prevent the tool from entering and damaging the bore.*

5. Locate the taper pin at the upper corner (flywheel end) of the cylinder block/crankcase cover assembly. Using a suitable punch, drive out the taper pins from the cylinder side toward the intake side of the power head.
6. Lift the crankcase cover off the cylinder block. If necessary, bump the edge of the cover with a soft-face mallet to separate the cover from the block.
7. Remove and discard the crankshaft upper seal.

8. Loosen the cylinder head screws evenly, in several steps. Remove the screws and cylinder heads. Remove and discard the cylinder head O-ring seals.
9. Mark the cylinder number on each connecting rod cap.

CAUTION
Do not allow the piston(s) to fall out of the cylinder after the connecting rod cap screws are removed in Step 10.

10. Turn the crankshaft to position the No. 1 and No. 2 connecting rods as shown in **Figure 87**. Remove the connecting rod cap screws using OMC Torque Socket part No. 331638, or an equivalent 5/16 in. 12-point socket. Remove the rod cap and bearing half, then push the piston out of the cylinder block. Remove the remaining connecting rod bearing half, then reinstall the bearings, cap and screws to the connecting rod.
11. Repeat Step 10 to remove the remaining piston/connecting rod assemblies.
12. Lift the crankshaft assembly straight up and out of the cylinder block.
13. Slide the lower seal housing off the crankshaft. Remove and discard the housing O-ring. Tap the seal from the housing using a suitable punch.
14. *Except 1991 models*—Remove the drive shaft-to-crankshaft O-ring seal (20, **Figure 92**) from the crankshaft sleeve (21) using a seal pick or other hooked tool. Discard the O-ring.
15. If necessary, remove the crankshaft sleeve from the crankshaft using a suitable slide hammer puller with internal jaws.

NOTE
The lower main bearing is destroyed during removal. Do not remove the bearing from the crankshaft unless bearing replacement is necessary.

16. If lower main bearing replacement is necessary, remove the bearing retaining ring using snap ring pliers. Then, remove the bearing from the crankshaft using a suitable bearing separator

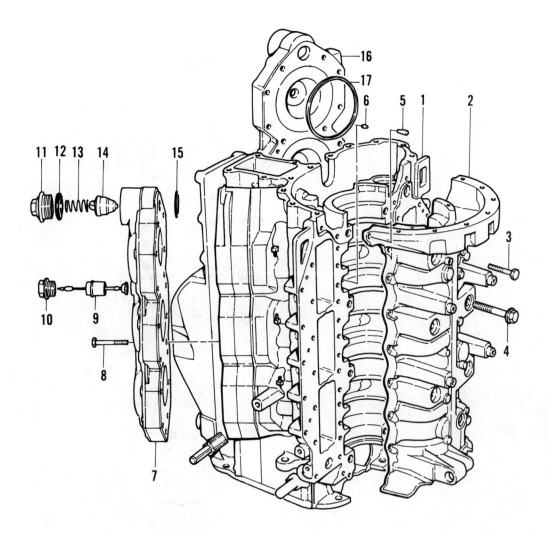

⑨¹

CYLINDER BLOCK AND CRANKCASE COVER ASSEMBLY
(60° V6 MODELS)

1. Cylinder block
2. Crankcase cover
3. Screw
4. Screw
5. Taper pin
6. Bearing locating pin
7. Cylinder head
8. Screw
9. Temperature switch
10. Temperature switch cover
11. Thermostat cover
12. O-ring
13. Spring
14. Thermostat
15. Thermostat seal
16. Cylinder head
17. O-ring

8

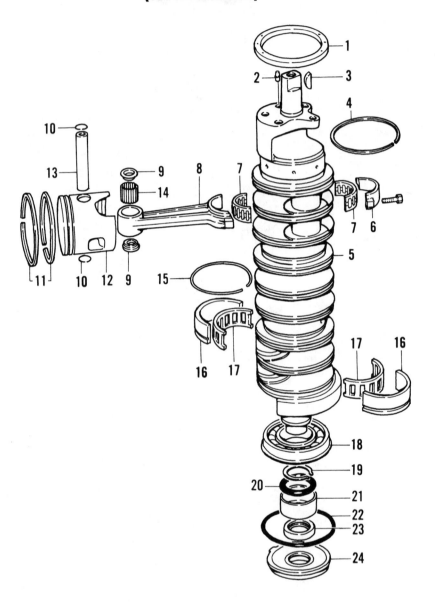

CRANKSHAFT ASSEMBLY AND RELATED COMPONENTS (60° V6 MODELS)

1. Upper seal
2. Flywheel locating pin
3. Flywheel key
4. Crankshaft seal ring
5. Crankshaft
6. Connecting rod cap
7. Connecting rod bearing half
8. Connecting rod
9. Thrust washer
10. Piston pin retaining ring
11. Piston rings
12. Piston
13. Piston pin
14. Piston pin bearing
15. Retaining ring
16. Main bearing liner
17. Main bearing half
18. Ball bearing
19. Retaining ring
20. O-ring (except 1991 models)
21. Crankshaft sleeve (except 1991 models)
22. Lower seal
23. O-ring
24. Seal housing

and arbor press. Be sure to support the crankshaft properly while pressing the bearing off.

17. Remove the crankshaft seal rings. If the rings are to be reused, be sure to mark them for installation in their original locations.

18. Remove the retaining rings securing the center main bearing outer liners. Separate the liners and remove the bearing halves. Place the bearings, liners and retaining rings in a labeled container.

19. Remove the piston rings from all pistons using a suitable ring expander. Discard the rings. Never reinstall used piston rings during reassembly.

20. Remove the piston pin retaining rings from one piston using needlenose pliers. Discard the retaining rings.

CAUTION
Always store piston pins, piston pin bearings, locating washers, connecting rod bearings, rod caps and rod cap screws together with their respective piston and connecting rod so they can be reinstalled in their original locations.

21. Push the piston pin through the piston. Separate the piston, along with 2 thrust washers and 28 loose bearing rollers from the connecting rod. Place the thrust washers, bearing rollers, piston and pin in a clean labeled container.

22. Repeat Steps 20 and 21 to disassemble the remaining piston/connecting rod assemblies.

Cylinder Block and Crankcase Cleaning and Inspection (All Models)

The cylinder block and crankcase cover are matched, align-bored assemblies. Therefore, do not attempt to assemble a power head with parts salvaged from other blocks. If inspection indicates that either the cylinder block or crankcase cover is damaged or excessively worn, replace both as an assembly.

WARNING
Wear hand and eye protection when working with OMC Gel Seal and Gasket Remover. In addition, you should remove your wrist watch or other jewelry. The substance is powerful enough to damage watches or jewelry, and will severely irritate the eyes and bare skin.

The cylinder block and crankcase cover mating surfaces must be absolutely free of old Gel Seal, dirt, oil, grease or other contamination. The manufacturer recommends using OMC Gel Seal and Gasket Remover to clean the old Gel Seal from the mating surfaces.

CAUTION
*The crankcase cover and cylinder block mating surfaces **must not** be scratched, nicked or damaged. The manufacturer specifically recommends using OMC Gel Seal and Gasket Remover and a **plastic** scraper to clean the mating surfaces. An ordinary household light switch or electrical outlet cover makes a good scraper for this purpose.*

Carefully remove all sealant and gasket material from the cylinder block and crankcase mating surfaces. Spray the area to be cleaned with OMC Gel Seal and Gasket Remover, allow the solvent to stand for 5-10 minutes, then clean with a plastic scraper. Clean the aluminum surfaces carefully to avoid scratches or nicks. After removing all traces of old Gel Seal, use OMC Cleaning Solvent, acetone or isopropyl alcohol to finish cleaning the mating surfaces. Do not use solvent with an oil, wax or petroleum base, as they are not compatible with OMC Gel Seal II.

After thoroughly cleaning the mating surfaces of the cylinder block, crankcase cover, cylinder head(s) and exhaust cover(s), place the mating surface of each component on a suitable surface plate or a large pane of glass. Apply uniform downward pressure on the component and check for warpage. The component should lay completely flat without rocking. Replace each component if more than a slight degree of warpage

8

exists. In cases where there is only a slight amount of warpage, it can often be eliminated by placing the mating surface of each component on a large sheet of 120 emery cloth. Apply a slight amount of pressure and move the component in a figure-8 pattern. See **Figure 93**. Remove the component and emery cloth and recheck flatness using the surface plate or pane of glass.

If warpage exists, the high spots will be dull while low areas will remain unchanged in appearance. It may be necessary to repeat this procedure until the entire mating surface has been polished. Do not remove more than a total of 0.010 in. (0.25 mm) from any component.

1. Thoroughly clean the cylinder block and crankcase cover with solvent and brush. Dry with compressed air, making sure all holes and passages are clean and open.

2. Carefully remove all sealant and gasket material from the mating surfaces of all components.

3. Check the cylinder head(s) and exhaust ports for excessive carbon deposits. Remove all carbon using a blunt instrument. Do not scratch, nick or damage combustion chambers or exhaust ports.

4. Check the cylinder block, crankcase cover and cylinder head(s) for cracks, fractures, stripped threads or other damage.

5. Check all mating surfaces for nicks, grooves, cracks or excessive distortion. Check cylinder heads for warpage using a suitable straightedge and feeler gauge. Cylinder head should be resurfaced at a machine shop if warpage exceeds 0.004 in. (0.10 mm)

6. Check all oil and water passages in the cylinder block and crankcase cover for obstructions. Make sure all plugs are properly tightened.

CAUTION
If metal particles are found in the cylinder block or crankcase cover, replace the recirculation system check valve(s) and make certain all recirculation hoses and fittings are clean and free of restrictions.

7. Make sure all water passage deflectors (if so equipped) are in good condition and properly installed. See **Figure 94** and **Figure 95**. Note that 3, 4 and 4 Deluxe models should have 2 deflectors; 20-30 hp models should have 3 deflectors; V4 models (except 120 and 140 hp) should have 2 deflectors in each cylinder blank; V6 models (except 60° models) should have 3 deflectors in each cylinder bank. To function properly, the water deflectors must extend slightly past the gasket surface of the cylinder block. Damaged, loose or missing deflectors will interfere with cooling water circulation and result in engine overheating.

8. Check the inner and outer exhaust covers (if so equipped) for warpage or signs of overheating. Replace the covers as necessary.

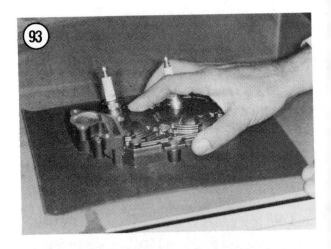

9. Check the crankcase recirculation check valve or orifice, if so equipped, and clean with OMC tool part No. 326623.

10. Check cylinder bore(s) for aluminum transfer from the pistons to the cylinder walls. Minor cylinder wall scoring can often be cleaned up by honing the cylinder.

11. Measure each cylinder bore diameter using an inside micrometer (**Figure 96**). Refer to **Table 3** for the standard cylinder bore diameters. Take 2 measurements at the top of piston ring travel, 90° apart. Then repeat the measurements at the bottom of piston ring travel. Compare the measurements to determine if the bore is out-of-round or tapered.

12. Maximum allowable cylinder bore out-of-round is:
   a. *2-70 hp*—0.003 in. (0.08 mm).
   b. *V4, V6 and V8 models*—0.004 in. (0.10 mm).

13. Maximum allowable cylinder bore taper is 0.002 in. (0.05 mm) on all models.

14. Maximum allowable cylinder bore wear is:
   a. *2-15 hp*—0.002 in. (0.05 mm).
   b. *20-70 hp*—0.003 in. (0.08 mm).
   c. *V4, V6 and V8 models*—0.004 in. (0.10 mm).

15. If any cylinders are excessively worn, tapered or out-of-round, the cylinder must be bored oversize. Note that pistons and rings are available in 0.020 in. oversize on 1993-on 9.9 and 15 hp and 0.030 in. on all other models. If the cylinder is damaged or worn beyond the available oversize, the cylinder block/crankcase cover assembly must be replaced.

NOTE
Overbore only the worn or damaged cylinder. Because oversize pistons weigh approximately the same as standard pistons, it is acceptable to have one or more oversize cylinders in a power head.

16. To determine the correct cylinder bore oversize dimension, add the piston oversize amount to the standard cylinder bore diameter (**Table 3**). The sum of the standard bore diameter plus 0.030 in. equals the finished diameter of the oversize cylinder.

CAUTION
The procedure for determining the correct oversize cylinder bore diameter (Step 16) is based on the use of pistons provided by the manufacturer. The manufacturer does not provide piston-

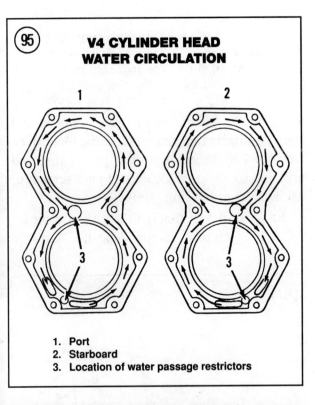

95

V4 CYLINDER HEAD WATER CIRCULATION

1   2

3   3

1. Port
2. Starboard
3. Location of water passage restrictors

96

to-cylinder clearance specifications for the models covered in this manual, therefore, use caution if installing aftermarket pistons. Make certain that sufficient piston clearance is present.

Crankshaft and Connecting Rod Bearings Cleaning and Inspection (All Models)

Bearings can be reused if they are in acceptable condition. It is always good practice, however, to replace all bearings once the power head is disassembled. New bearings are inexpensive compared to the cost of the entire overhaul, especially if a recently overhauled power head is destroyed by the use of marginal bearings.

1. Thoroughly clean all bearings with clean solvent, removing all grease, sludge or other contamination.

2. Dry bearings with compressed air. *Do not* spin bearings with the compressed air.

3. After cleaning, lubricate the bearings with a light coat of engine oil, then closely inspect for rust, wear, scuffed edges, heat discoloration or other damage.

4. If loose needle bearing rollers are to be reused, repeat Steps 1-3, cleaning one set at a time to prevent mixing bearings. Closely inspect all bearing rollers for rust, wear, scuffed surfaces, heat discoloration or other damage. If one roller is worn or damaged, replace the entire bearing assembly. In addition, if one bearing roller is lost, replace the entire bearing assembly. Never borrow a roller from another bearing.

5. Repeat Step 4 for any caged roller bearings.

6. If any piston pin bearings require replacement, replace the piston pin in addition to the bearings.

Piston Cleaning and Inspection (All Models)

1. Closely inspect the piston(s) for scoring, cracking, cracked or worn piston pin bores or other damage. Replace the piston and pin as an assembly, if any defects are noted.

2. Check piston ring grooves for distortion, loose ring locating pins, excessive wear or other damage.

CAUTION
Do not use an automotive piston ring groove cleaner to clean the ring grooves in Step 3. An automotive ring groove cleaner will damage the ring grooves.

3. Clean the piston crown, ring grooves and skirt. A suitable ring groove cleaning tool can be fabricated by breaking a used piston ring and grinding an angle on the end. *Do not* scratch or damage the piston ring grooves.

4. Immerse the piston(s) in a carbon removal solution to remove carbon deposits. A bristle

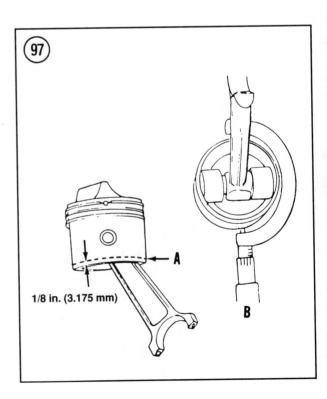

brush may be used to finish cleaning the pistons. Avoid burring or rounding the machined edges.

5. Using a micrometer, measure piston diameter to determine if the piston is out-of-round or excessively worn.

6A. *2-15 hp*—Refer to **Table 3** for standard piston diameter. Measure the piston(s) as follows:

a. Measure piston diameter at a point 1/8 in. (3.2 mm) up from the bottom of the piston skirt (A, **Figure 97**), and 90° to the piston pin bore (B).

b. Take a second measurement directly aligned with the piston pin bore (1/8 in. [3.2 mm] up from bottom). See **Figure 98**.

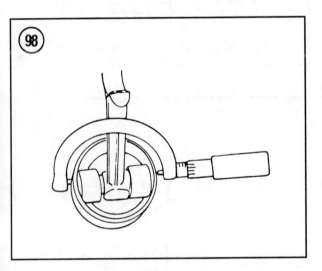

c. If the difference between the 2 measurements exceeds 0.002 in. (0.05 mm), the piston is out-of-round and must be replaced.

6B. *20-30 hp*—The pistons used on these models are a cam-ground design. Cam ground pistons are not round when cold, but become round as they heat up and expand.

NOTE
The pistons used on 20-30 hp models may be from 3 different piston vendors, Art, Rightway or Zollner. The pistons manufactured by Art and Rightway have slightly different dimensions than those produced by Zollner. Refer to Figure 99 to identify the pistons. Art and Rightway pistons have a semi-circle shape in the deflector on the piston crown, while the edge of the deflector is straight on Zollner pistons.

Refer to **Table 3** for standard piston diameter. To check cam-ground pistons, first measure the piston major diameter (A, **Figure 99**) at 90° to the piston pin bore. Then, measure the piston minor diameter (B, **Figure 99**) parallel to the piston pin bore. Subtract the minor diameter from the major diameter to obtain the piston cam dimension. The minor diameter must be smaller than the major diameter by the cam dimension, or the piston should be replaced. Measure the pistons as follows:

a. Measure piston diameter 1/8 to 1/4 in. (3.2-6.3 mm) up from the bottom of the piston skirt.

b. First, measure the piston major diameter (A, **Figure 99**) at 90° to the piston pin bore.

c. Next, measure the piston minor diameter (B, **Figure 99**) parallel to the piston pin bore.

d. Subtract the minor diameter from the major diameter. The minor diameter must be smaller than the major diameter by the cam dimension of 0.005-0.007 in. (0.13-0.18 mm) on Zollner pistons or 0.0015-0.0025 in. (0.038-0.063 mm) on Art or Rightway

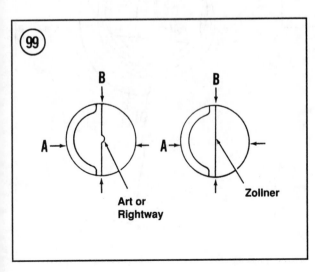

pistons. If not, replace the piston(s) and pin(s).

e. If the piston skirt grooves are worn smooth in the area 90° to the piston pin bore, replace the piston and pin.

6C. *35 Jet, 40-50 hp*—Check pistons as follows:

a. Measure the pistons at a point 1/8 in. (3.2 mm) up from the bottom of the skirt, directly aligned with the top piston ring locating pin. See **Figure 100**. This dimension is the piston major diameter.

b. The major diameter should be no less than 3.1831 in. (80.851 mm) on a standard piston or 3.2131 in. (81.6127 mm) on an oversize piston. Replace the piston and pin if the major diameter is less than specified.

c. Measure the piston in several locations around the skirt (1/8 in. [3.2 mm] up from

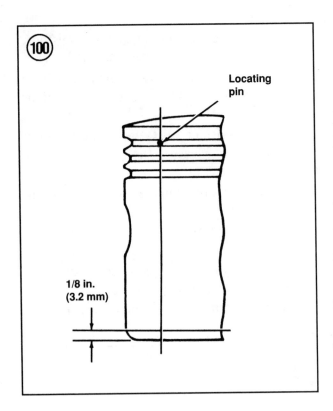

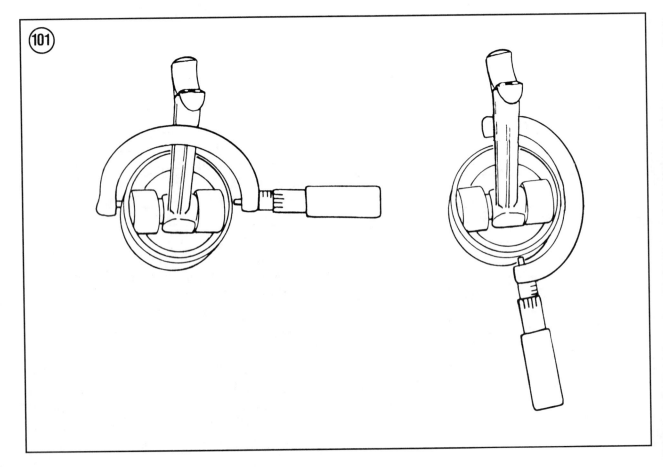

the bottom). Replace the piston and pin if any measurement is larger than the major diameter (substep b), or if any measurement is more than 0.004 in. (0.10 mm) smaller than the major diameter.

d. If the piston skirt grooves are worn smooth in the area 90° to the piston pin bore, replace the piston and pin.

6D. *60-300 hp*—Check pistons as follows:

a. Measure the piston diameter at a point 1/4 in. (6.3 mm) up from the bottom of the skirt, at 90° to the piston pin bore. Repeat the measurement at a point parallel to the pin bore. See **Figure 101**.

b. The difference between the measurements indicates piston out-of-round condition.

c. Replace the piston and pin if out-of-round more than 0.003 in. (0.08 mm) on 60-70 hp and 60° V6 models or 0.004 in. (0.10 mm) on all other V4, V6 and V8 models.

d. Replace the piston and pin assembly if the skirt grooves are worn smooth in the area 90° to the piston pin bore.

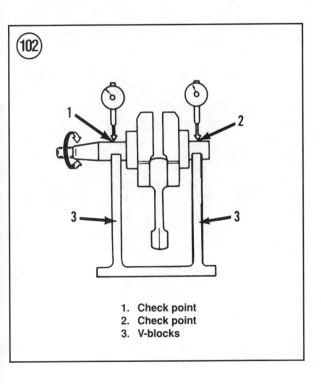

1. Check point
2. Check point
3. V-blocks

Crankshaft Cleaning and Inspection (2.0, 2.3 and 3.3 hp)

The crankshaft, connecting rod, crankpin and crankpin bearing are a pressed-together assembly. Individual crankshaft components are available; however, disassembly and reassembly of the crankshaft unit should only be attempted by a shop with the equipment and experience necessary to perform such work.

1. Thoroughly clean the crankshaft assembly using clean solvent. Dry the crankshaft with compressed air, then apply a light coat of clean engine oil.

2. Check the splines on the drive shaft end of the crankshaft for damage or excessive wear. Check the connecting rod for straightness.

3. Check the crankshaft bearing surfaces for grooves, pitting, scratches and evidence of overheating. Minor marks may be cleaned up with crocus cloth.

4. Clean the piston pin bore in the connecting rod using crocus cloth.

5. Grasp the outer race of the crankshaft ball bearings and attempt to work them back and forth. Replace the bearings if excessive play is noted.

6. Lubricate the ball bearings with a light oil and rotate the outer race. Replace the bearings if they sound or feel rough, or if they do not rotate smoothly.

7. Support the crankshaft assembly in V-blocks as shown in **Figure 102**. Mount a dial indicator at the check points shown, then rotate the crankshaft assembly and check runout. Replace the crankshaft assembly if runout exceeds 0.001 in. (0.025 mm).

8. Determine connecting rod, crankpin and crankpin bearing wear by checking the connecting rod small end play (A, **Figure 103**). Replace the crankshaft assembly if play is not within 0.022-0.056 in. (0.56-1.42 mm).

8

Crankshaft Cleaning and Inspection (3-300 hp)

1. Thoroughly clean the crankshaft with clean solvent and brush. Dry the crankshaft with compressed air, then lightly lubricate it with clean engine oil.

2. Check the crankshaft journals and crankpins for scratches, heat discoloration or other damage. See **Figure 104** (2-cylinder) or **Figure 105** (V4). Three-cylinder, V6 and V8 crankshafts are similar.

3. Measure the crankshaft journals and crankpins with a micrometer and compare to the appropriate table at the end of this chapter. Measure the bottom journal only if the ball bearing is removed from the crankshaft.

4. Check the drive shaft splines and flywheel taper threads for wear or damage. Replace the crankshaft as necessary.

5. If the lower crankshaft ball bearing has not been removed, grasp its outer race and attempt to work it back and forth. Replace the bearing if excessive play is noted.

6. Lubricate the ball bearing with clean engine oil and rotate its outer race. Replace the bearing if it sounds or feels rough or if it does not rotate smoothly.

> *NOTE*
> *If the crankshaft seal rings are reused, be sure to install them in their original locations.*

7. Check the crankshaft seal rings on V4, V6 and V8 models for excessive wear or damage. Replace the seal rings if they do not seal tightly around the crankshaft web. Carefully remove seal rings and inspect for grooves, chips or excessive wear. Replace any seal ring that is less than 0.154 in. (3.9 mm) thick. To install seal rings, carefully spread the end gap just enough to slip the ring over the crankshaft journal, then install the ring into its groove using a suitable piston ring expander.

Piston and Connecting Rod Reassembly (2.0, 2.3 and 3.3 hp)

1. Lubricate the piston pin with clean engine oil and insert it into the piston from either direction.

2. Lubricate the piston pin bearing with clean engine oil and place it into the connecting rod bore.

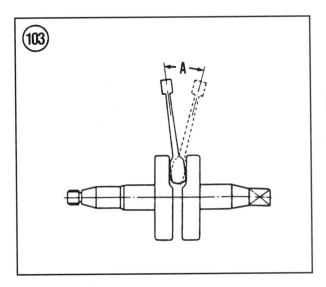

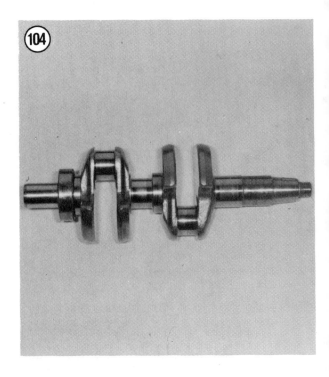

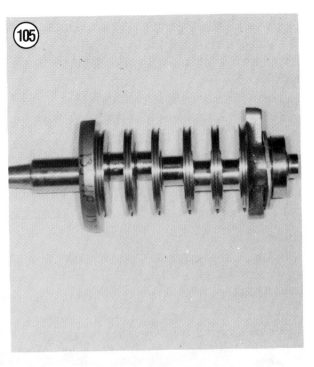

(105)

3. Place the piston on the connecting rod, making sure the arrow on the piston crown is facing the BOTTOM of the crankshaft.

4. Align the piston pin with the piston pin bearing and drive the pin through the piston and connecting rod.

5. Install *new* piston pin retaining rings.

6. Before installing the piston ring on the piston, place the new ring inside the cylinder. Push the ring into the cylinder with the piston to position the ring squarely in the cylinder. Then measure the piston ring end gap using a feeler gauge as shown in **Figure 106**. The end gap should be 0.006-0.013 in. (0.15-0.33 mm). If the gap is excessive, replace the ring or check the cylinder bore diameter. If the gap is insufficient, carefully file the ring ends until the specified gap is obtained.

7. Once the ring end gap is established, roll the ring around the piston ring groove to check for binding or tightness. See **Figure 107**.

8. Using a suitable ring expander, install the piston ring on the piston. Expand the ring only enough to fit over the piston crown (**Figure 108**) and into position in its groove. Make sure the ring end gap properly engages the piston ring locating pin inside the ring groove.

9. Using a feeler gauge, measure the clearance between the piston ring and the side of the ring

8

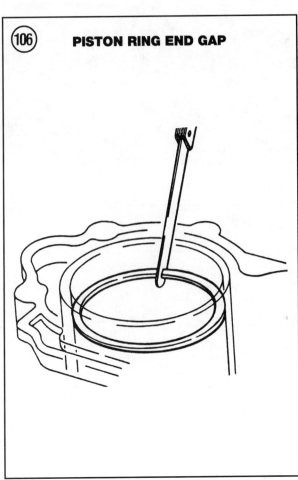

(106) **PISTON RING END GAP**

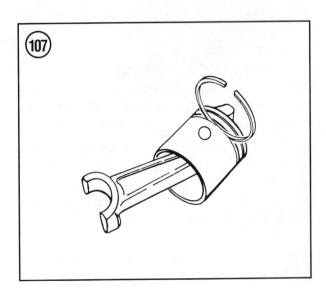

(107)

groove. The ring side clearance should not exceed 0.0026 in. (0.066 mm). If side clearance is excessive, replace the piston.

Piston and Connecting Rod Reassembly (4 Deluxe, 3 and 4 hp)

The piston pin fit in the piston is a press-fit on one side and a loose fit on the opposite side. The loose side is identified by an "L" on the underside of the piston (**Figure 109**). During installation, the piston pin must be inserted into the loose side first, to prevent piston damage.

The long sloping side of the piston crown must face the exhaust ports when installed. If the connecting rod has a single hole in the face of the rod, the oil hole must face upward. See **Figure 110**. If the connecting rod has 2 oil holes in the piston pin end (**Figure 110**), the rod can be installed with either side facing up, however, the connecting rod should always be installed in the same direction as removed.

1. Lubricate the piston pin with clean engine oil and insert it into the loose side of the piston. See **Figure 109**. Install the pin just past the inside edge of the piston pin bore.

2. Place one thrust washer on the piston pin (inside piston). Apply OMC Needle Bearing Assembly Grease to the connecting rod piston pin bore, then arrange the 21 loose needle bearing rollers inside the bore. Apply more grease as necessary to hold the rollers in position.

3. Making sure the connecting rod is correctly oriented on the piston, install the rod into the piston. Place the piston/rod assembly into OMC Piston Cradle part No. 326572 and press the piston pin through the rod, leaving just enough space to install the remaining thrust washer. Be certain that all 21 bearing rollers and the 2 thrust washers are still in position, then finish installing the piston pin.

4. Center the pin in the piston and install *new* piston pin retainers. Repeat Steps 1-4 to assemble the remaining piston and connecting rod.

5. Before installing the piston rings on the piston, place each ring inside its respective cylinder. Push the ring into the cylinder with the piston to position the ring squarely in the cylinder. Then measure the piston ring end gap using a feeler gauge as shown in **Figure 106**. The end gap should be 0.005-0.015 in. (0.13-0.38 mm) on both rings. If the gap is excessive, replace the ring or check the cylinder bore diameter. If the gap is insufficient, carefully file the ring ends until the specified gap is obtained.

6. Once the end gap for each ring is established, roll the rings around their respective ring grooves to check for binding or tightness. See **Figure 107**.

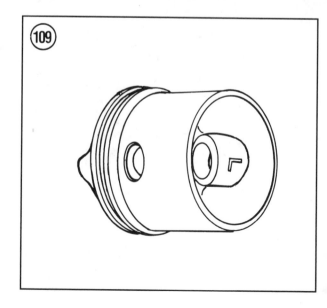

7. Using a suitable ring expander, install the piston rings on the piston. Expand the rings only enough to fit over the piston crown (**Figure 108**) and into position in their grooves. Make sure the ring end gaps properly engage the piston ring locating pin inside the ring groove. See **Figure 111**.

8. Using a feeler gauge, measure the clearance between the piston ring and the side of the ring

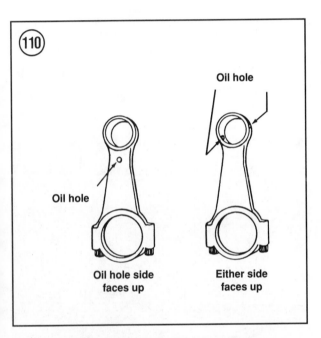

groove. The ring side clearance should not exceed 0.004 in. (0.10 mm). If side clearance is excessive, replace the piston.

Piston and Connecting Rod Reassembly (6-15 hp)

The long sloping side of the piston crown must face the exhaust ports when installed. If the connecting rod has a single hole in the face of the rod, the oil hole must face upward. See **Figure 110**. If the connecting rod has 2 oil holes in the piston pin end (**Figure 110**), the rod can be installed with either side facing up, however, if reused, the connecting rod should always be installed in the same direction as removed. Be certain the pistons and connecting rods are correctly oriented during assembly.

The piston pin is a press-fit on 6-8 hp and 1991 and 1992 9.9 and 15 hp models. On these models, the piston must be heated to 200-400° F (93-204° C) to install the piston pin. Heat the piston using a suitable heat gun, heat lamp, or by boiling the piston in water. Do not use open flame to heat pistons.

The piston must be properly supported while pressing in the piston pin to prevent damage to the piston. Place the piston into OMC Piston Cradle part No. 326573 (or equivalent). Press the piston pin using OMC Pressing Pin part No. 333141 (6-8 hp) or 392511 (9.9-15 hp), or a suitable equivalent. See **Figure 112**.

1. *6-8 hp*—If removed, press new piston pin bearing assemblies into the connecting rods using OMC Bearing Installer part No. 327645 (or equivalent).

   a. *Be certain* that the oil hole in the bearing is aligned with the oil hole in the connecting rod, and that the bearing enters the rod squarely.

   b. Lubricate the outer diameter of the bearing assembly with clean engine oil. Lubricate the bearing rollers with OMC Needle Bearing Assembly Grease.

2. Install a new piston pin retaining ring into one side of each piston. Position the retaining ring so its end gap will face down, opposite the cutout in the piston pin bore.

    a. *6-8 hp*—Use OMC Cone part No. 333142 and Driver part No. 333141 to install the retaining ring. See **Figure 113**, typical. Make sure the retaining ring is securely seated in its groove.

    b. *9.9-15 hp*—Use OMC Wrist Pin Retaining Ring Installer and Pressing Pin part No. 392511 to install the retaining ring. See **Figure 113**, typical. Make sure the retaining ring is securely seated in its groove.

WARNING
Use insulated gloves when handling the hot piston in the following procedure.

3A. *6-8 hp:*

    a. Heat the piston to 200-400° F (93-204° C) using a heat gun, heat lamp or by boiling in water.

    b. Place the piston into OMC Piston Cradle (part No. 326573), lubricate the piston pin with engine oil, then start it into the piston. Do not install the pin past the inner edge of the piston pin bore.

    c. Place the connecting rod into the piston making sure the piston and rod are correctly oriented. Using OMC Pressing Pin part No. 333141 (**Figure 112**), install the piston pin through the piston and rod until it contacts the piston pin retaining ring installed in Step 2.

    d. Install the remaining piston pin retaining ring as described in Step 2.

    e. Using a micrometer, measure the piston at a point 1/8 to 1/4 in. (3.2-6.3 mm) up from the bottom skirt. Take 2 measurements— one parallel to the piston pin bore and one 90° to the pin bore. If the difference between the measurements exceed 0.002 in. (0.05 mm), the piston was distorted during

the pin pressing procedure and must be replaced.

    f. Repeat this procedure on the remaining piston/connecting rod.

WARNING
Use insulated gloves when handling the hot piston in the following procedure.

3B. *1991-1992 9.9-15 hp:*

    a. Heat the piston to 200-400° F (93-204° C) using a heat gun, heat lamp or by boiling in water.

    b. Place the piston on OMC Piston Cradle (part No. 326573), lubricate the piston pin

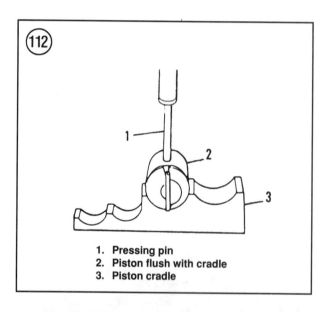

1. Pressing pin
2. Piston flush with cradle
3. Piston cradle

with engine oil and insert the pin into the piston on the opposite side of the retaining ring installed in Step 2. Do not install the pin past the inner edge of the pin bore.

NOTE

*A suitable bushing or sleeve can be placed inside the piston pin bore and used as shown in **Figure 114** to ease installation of the loose needle bearing rollers.*

c. Apply OMC Needle Bearing Assembly Grease to the connecting rod piston pin bore. Arrange the 22 loose piston pin bearing rollers in the bore, then place the thrust

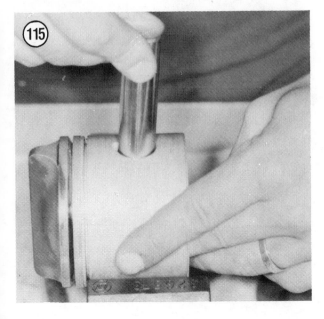

washers on each side of the connecting rod. Apply additional needle bearing assembly grease as necessary to hold the bearing rollers and thrust washers in place.

d. Carefully assemble the connecting rod to the piston, making sure the thrust washers and bearing rollers remain in position. Using OMC Pressing Pin (part No. 392511), press the piston pin through the piston until it contacts the retaining ring installed in Step 2. See **Figure 112**. If the thrust washers and bearing rollers are in place, install the remaining piston pin retaining ring as described in Step 2.

e. Using a micrometer, measure the piston at a point 1/8 to 1/4 in. (3.2-6.3 mm) up from the bottom skirt. Take 2 measurements— one parallel to the piston pin bore and one 90° to the pin bore. If the difference between the measurements exceed 0.002 in. (0.05 mm), the piston was distorted during the pin pressing procedure and must be replaced.

f. Repeat this procedure on the remaining piston/connecting rod.

3C. *1993-on 9.9-15 hp:*

a. Lubricate the piston pin with clean engine oil. Insert the pin into the piston on the opposite side of the retaining ring installed in Step 2. See **Figure 115**. Do not push the pin past the inner edge of its bore in the piston.

NOTE

*A suitable bushing or sleeve can be placed inside the piston pin bore and used as shown in **Figure 114** to ease installation of the loose needle bearing rollers.*

b. Apply OMC Needle Bearing Assembly Grease to the connecting rod piston pin bore. Arrange the 22 loose piston pin bearing rollers in the bore, then place the thrust washers on each side of the connecting rod. Apply additional needle bearing assembly

8

grease as necessary to hold the bearing rollers and thrust washers in place.

c. Carefully assemble the connecting rod to the piston, making sure the thrust washers and bearing rollers remain in position. Using OMC Pressing Pin (part No. 392511), press the piston pin through the piston until it contacts the retaining ring installed in Step 2. See **Figure 112**. If the thrust washers and bearing rollers are in place, install the remaining piston pin retaining ring as described in Step 2. Repeat this procedure to assemble the remaining piston/connecting rod assembly.

4. Before installing the piston rings on the pistons, place each ring, individually, inside its respective cylinder. Push the ring into the cylinder with the piston to position the ring squarely in the cylinder. Then measure the piston ring end gap using a feeler gauge as shown in **Figure 106**. The end gap should be 0.005-0.015 in. (0.13-0.38 mm) on the upper and lower rings. If the gap is excessive, repeat the measurement with the ring in another cylinder. If the gap is still excessive, discard the ring and replace it with a new ring. If the gap is insufficient, carefully file the ring ends until the specified gap is obtained.

5. Once the correct ring gap is established, roll the rings (lower ring only on 9.9-15 hp) around the piston ring groove to check for binding or tightness. See **Figure 107**.

6. Using a suitable ring expander, install the piston rings on the piston. Expand the rings only enough to fit over the piston crown (**Figure 108**) and into position in their grooves. Make sure the ring end gaps properly engage the piston ring locating pin inside the ring groove. See **Figure 111**.

NOTE
The upper ring on 9.9-15 hp models is a pressure-back design. Side clearance cannot be checked on pressure-back rings because of their tapered shape. To check pressure-back ring-to-groove fit,

*place a straightedge across the ring groove as shown in **Figure 116**. The straightedge should touch the piston on both sides of the ring. Perform several checks at different areas around of the piston. If the ring holds the straightedge away from the piston at any point, the ring groove is not sufficiently clean. Remove the ring and repeat the ring groove cleaning procedure.*

7. Using a feeler gauge, measure the clearance between the piston ring and the side of the ring groove. Ring side clearance should not exceed 0.004 in. (0.10 mm) on the upper and lower rings on 6-8 hp or the lower ring on 9.9-15 hp models. If side clearance is excessive, replace the piston.

Piston and Connecting Rod Reassembly (20-30 hp)

The long sloping side of the piston crown must face the exhaust ports when the pistons are installed. Although the connecting rods do not have any specific directional orientation, they should always be installed in the same direction as removed. Be certain the pistons and connecting rods are correctly oriented during assembly.

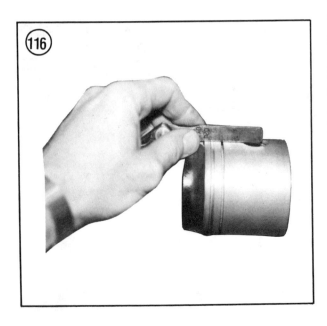
(116)

NOTE
*OMC Wrist Pin Bearing Tool part No. 336660 or a suitable bushing or sleeve can be placed inside the piston pin bore and used as shown in **Figure 114** to ease installation of the loose needle bearing rollers.*

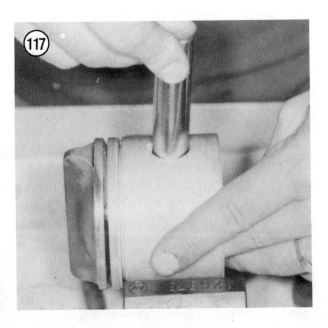

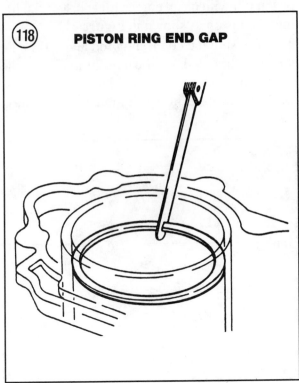

PISTON RING END GAP

1. Apply OMC Needle Bearing Assembly Grease to the connecting rod piston pin bore. Arrange the 28 loose piston pin bearing rollers in the bore, then place the thrust washers on each side of the connecting rod. The flat side of the thrust washers must face outward. Apply additional needle bearing assembly grease as necessary to hold the bearing rollers and thrust washers in place.

2. Place the piston in OMC Piston Cradle (part No. 326573) or a suitable support. Lubricate the piston pin with clean engine oil and start the pin into the piston as shown in **Figure 117**.

3. Make sure the connecting rod and piston are correctly oriented, then carefully assemble the connecting rod to the piston. Make sure the thrust washers and bearing rollers remain in position and push the piston pin through the piston and connecting rod.

4. Install new piston pin retaining rings on each side of the piston as follows:

   a. Insert the retaining ring into the tapered end of OMC Cone part No. 318600.

   b. Position the cone over the piston pin bore, making sure the retaining ring end gap is facing downward, away from the cutout in the piston.

   c. Insert OMC Driver (part No. 318599) into the cone and push the retaining ring into its groove.

   d. Turn the piston over and repeat this procedure to install the other retaining ring.

   e. Make sure both retaining rings are securely seated in their grooves.

5. Before installing the piston rings on the pistons, place each ring, individually, inside its respective cylinder. Push the ring into the cylinder with the piston to position the ring squarely in the cylinder. Then measure the piston ring end gap using a feeler gauge as shown in **Figure 118**. The end gap should be 0.007-0.017 in. (0.18-0.43 mm) on the upper and lower rings. If the gap is excessive, repeat the measurement with the ring in another cylinder. If the gap is still

excessive, discard the ring and replace it with a new ring. If the gap is insufficient, carefully file the ring ends until the specified gap is obtained.

6. Once the correct end gap is established for each ring, roll the lower ring around the piston ring groove to check for binding or tightness. See **Figure 119**.

7. Using a suitable ring expander, install the piston rings on the piston. Expand the rings only enough to fit over the piston crown (**Figure 120**) and into position in their grooves. Make sure the ring end gaps properly engage the piston ring locating pins inside the ring grooves. See **Figure 111**.

> *NOTE*
> *The upper piston ring is a pressure-back design. Side clearance cannot be checked on pressure-back rings because of their tapered shape. To check pressure-back ring-to-groove fit, place a straightedge across the ring groove as shown in **Figure 116**. The straightedge should touch the piston on both sides of the ring. Perform several checks at different areas around of the piston. If the ring holds the straightedge away from the piston at any point, the ring groove is not sufficiently clean. Remove the ring and repeat the ring groove cleaning procedure.*

8. Using a feeler gauge, measure the clearance between the lower piston ring and the side of the ring groove. The ring should be free to move in the groove but the side clearance should not exceed 0.004 in. (0.10 mm). If side clearance is excessive, replace the piston.

9. Repeat Steps 1-7 to assemble the remaining piston/connecting rod.

Piston and Connecting Rod Reassembly (35 Jet, 40-70 hp)

The "UP" mark on the piston crown must face the flywheel end of the power head when the pistons are installed. Although the connecting rods do not have any specific directional orientation, they should always be installed in the same direction as removed. Be certain the pistons and connecting rods are correctly oriented during assembly.

> *NOTE*
> *OMC Wrist Pin Bearing Tool part No. 336660 or a suitable bushing or sleeve can be placed inside the piston pin bore and used as shown in **Figure 114** to ease installation of the loose needle bearing rollers.*

1. Apply OMC Needle Bearing Assembly Grease to the connecting rod piston pin bore. Arrange the 28 loose piston pin bearing rollers in the bore, then place the thrust washers on each side of the connecting rod. The flat side of the thrust washers must face outward. Apply additional needle bearing assembly grease as necessary to hold the bearing rollers and thrust washers in place.

2. Place the piston in OMC Piston Cradle (part No. 326573) or a suitable support. Lubricate the piston pin with clean engine oil and start the pin into the piston as shown in **Figure 117**.

3. Make sure the connecting rod and piston are correctly oriented, then carefully assemble the connecting rod to the piston. Make sure the thrust washers and bearing rollers remain in position

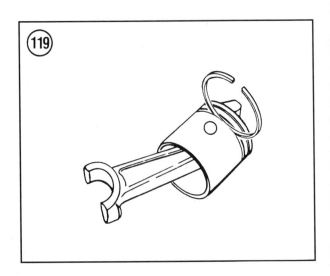

and push the piston pin through the piston and connecting rod.

4. Install new piston pin retaining rings on each side of the piston as follows:

  a. Insert the retaining ring into the tapered end of OMC Cone part No. 318600.

  b. Position the cone over the piston pin bore making sure the retaining ring end gap is facing downward, away from the cutout in the piston.

  c. Insert OMC Driver (part No. 318599) into the cone and push the retaining ring into its groove. See **Figure 113**.

  d. Turn the piston over and repeat this procedure to install the other retaining ring.

  e. Make sure both retaining rings are securely seated in their grooves.

5. Before installing the piston rings on the pistons, place each ring, individually, inside its respective cylinder. Push the ring into the cylinder with the piston to position the ring squarely in the cylinder. Then measure the piston ring end gap using a feeler gauge as shown in **Figure 118**. The end gap should be 0.007-0.017 in. (0.18-0.43 mm) on the upper and lower rings. If the gap is excessive, repeat the measurement with the ring in another cylinder. If the gap is still excessive, discard the ring and replace it with a new ring. If the gap is insufficient, carefully file the ring ends until the specified gap is obtained.

6. Once the correct end gap is established for each ring, roll the lower ring around the piston ring groove to check for binding or tightness. See **Figure 119**.

7. Using a suitable ring expander, install the piston rings on the piston. Expand the rings only enough to fit over the piston crown (**Figure 120**) and into position in their grooves. Make sure the ring end gaps properly engage the piston ring locating pin inside the ring groove. See **Figure 111**.

NOTE
The upper piston ring is a pressure-back design. Side clearance cannot be checked on pressure-back rings because of their tapered shape. To check pressure-back ring-to-groove fit, place a straightedge across the ring groove as shown in **Figure 116**. *The straightedge should touch the piston on both sides of the ring. Perform several checks at different areas around of the piston. If the ring holds the straightedge away from the piston at any point, the ring groove is not sufficiently clean. Remove the ring and repeat the ring groove cleaning procedure.*

8. Using a feeler gauge, measure the clearance between the lower piston ring and the side of the ring groove. The ring should be free to move in the groove but the side clearance should not exceed 0.004 in. (0.10 mm). If side clearance is excessive, replace the piston.

9. Repeat Steps 1-7 to assemble the remaining piston/connecting rods.

Piston and Connecting Rod Reassembly (V4 and V6 Cross Flow Models)

When installed, the long sloping side of the piston crown must face the exhaust ports. See **Figure 121**. In addition, the oil hole (**Figure 122**) in the connecting rod must face up when installed. Be certain the pistons and connecting rods are correctly oriented during assembly.

NOTE
*OMC Wrist Pin Bearing Tool part No. 336660 or a suitable bushing or sleeve can be placed inside the piston pin bore and used as shown in **Figure 123** to ease installation of the loose needle bearing rollers.*

1. Apply OMC Needle Bearing Assembly Grease to the connecting rod piston pin bore. Arrange the 28 loose piston pin bearing rollers in the bore, then place the thrust washers on each side of the connecting rod. The flat side of the thrust washers must face outward. Apply additional needle bearing assembly grease as necessary to hold the bearing rollers and thrust washers in place.

2. Place the piston in OMC Piston Cradle (part No. 326573) or a suitable support. Lubricate the piston pin with clean engine oil and start the pin into the piston as shown in **Figure 124**.

3. Make sure the connecting rod and piston are correctly oriented, then carefully assemble the connecting rod to the piston. Make sure the thrust washers and bearing rollers remain in position and push the piston pin through the piston and connecting rod.

4. Install new piston pin retaining rings on each side of the piston as follows:

   a. Insert the retaining ring into the tapered end of OMC Cone part No. 318600.

   b. Position the cone over the piston pin bore, making sure the retaining ring end gap is facing downward, away from the cutout in the piston.

   c. Insert OMC Driver (part No. 318599) into the cone and push the retaining ring into its groove. See **Figure 125**.

   d. Turn the piston over and repeat this procedure to install the other retaining ring.

---

(121)

**CORRECT PISTON INSTALLATION
(V4 AND V6 CROSS-FLOW ENGINE)**

1. Intake side of piston
2. Exhaust side of piston
3. Cylinder exhaust ports

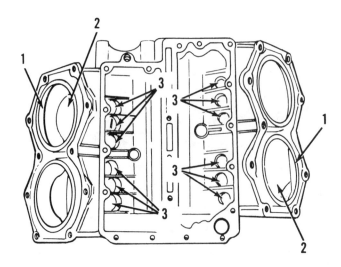

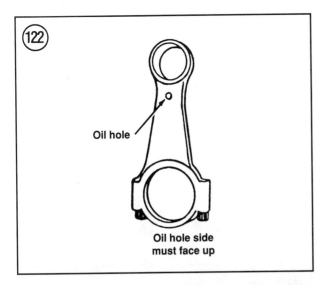

Oil hole

Oil hole side
must face up

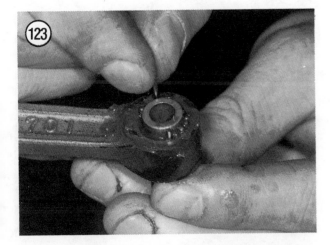

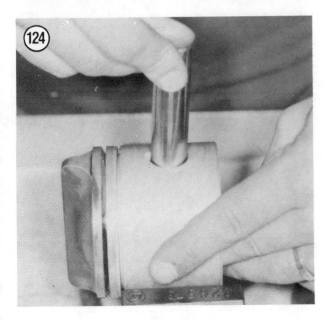

e. Make sure both retaining rings are securely seated in their grooves.

5. Before installing the piston rings on the pistons, place each ring, individually, inside its respective cylinder. Push the ring into the cylinder with the piston to position the ring squarely in the cylinder. Then measure the piston ring end gap using a feeler gauge as shown in **Figure 118**. The end gap for the upper and lower rings should be 0.019-0.031 in. (0.48-0.79 mm) on 85-150 hp or 0.020-0.033 in. (0.51-0.84 mm) on 175 hp models. If the gap is excessive, repeat the measurement with the ring in another cylinder. If the gap is still excessive, discard the ring and replace it with a new ring. If the gap is insufficient, carefully file the ring ends until the specified gap is obtained.

6. Once the correct end gap is established for each ring, roll the lower ring around the piston ring groove to check for binding or tightness. See **Figure 126**.

7. Using a suitable ring expander, install the piston rings on the piston. Expand the rings only enough to fit over the piston crown (**Figure 120**) and into position in their grooves. Make sure the ring end gaps properly engage the piston ring locating pin inside the ring groove. See **Figure 127**.

NOTE
The upper piston ring is a pressure-back design. Side clearance cannot be

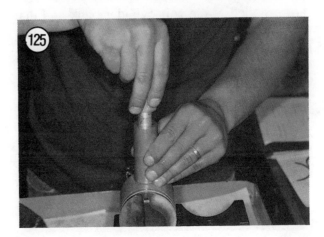

8

*checked on pressure-back rings because of their tapered shape. To check pressure-back ring-to-groove fit, place a straightedge across the ring groove as shown in **Figure 116**. The straightedge should touch the piston on both sides of the ring. Perform several checks at different areas around of the piston. If the ring holds the straightedge away from the piston at any point, the ring groove is not sufficiently clean. Remove the ring and repeat the ring groove cleaning procedure.*

8. Using a feeler gauge, measure the clearance between the lower piston ring and the side of the ring groove. The ring should be free to move in the groove, but the side clearance should not exceed 0.004 in. (0.10 mm). If side clearance is excessive, replace the piston.

9. Repeat Steps 1-7 to assemble the remaining piston/connecting rods.

Piston and Connecting Rod Reassembly (V4, V6 [Including 60° V6] and V8 Loop Charged Models)

On V4, V6 and V8 loop charged power heads, the pistons from each cylinder bank differ slightly. For this reason, the piston crowns are stamped "PORT" and "STBD," to indicate their respective cylinder banks. See **Figure 128**. In addition, the piston crowns are stamped "EXHAUST." Make sure pistons marked "PORT" are installed in the port cylinder bank and that pistons marked "STBD" are installed in the starboard cylinder bank. On all pistons, make sure the side marked "EXHAUST" is facing the cylinder exhaust ports when installed.

If the connecting rod has an oil hole drilled diagonally to the piston pin bore (**Figure 129**), the oil hole must face the flywheel end of the crankshaft. If the oil hole is drilled through the piston pin bore (**Figure 129**), the rod has no specific directional orientation; however, always reinstall the rod in the same direction as re-

moved. Be certain of the correct piston and connecting rod orientation before installing the piston pin.

1A. *1991 (except 60°) models*—Lubricate the piston pin bearing with clean engine oil. Insert the bearing into connecting rod piston pin bore.

NOTE
*OMC Wrist Pin Bearing Tool part No. 336660 or a suitable bushing or sleeve can be placed inside the piston pin bore and used as shown in **Figure 123** to ease*

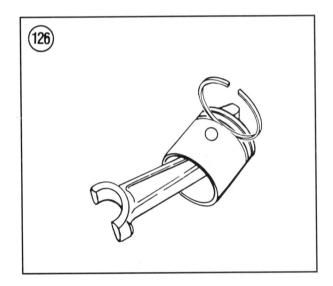

installation of the loose needle bearing rollers. The piston pin bearing consists of 28 loose rollers on 60° power heads and all other 1992 models. On 1993-on models (except 60°), the bearing consists of 33 loose rollers.

1B. *1992-1993 (including all 60°) models*— Apply OMC Needle Bearing Assembly Grease to the connecting rod piston pin bore. Arrange the loose piston pin bearing rollers in the bore, then place the thrust washers on each side of the connecting rod. The flat side of the thrust washers must face outward. Apply additional needle bearing assembly grease as necessary to hold the bearing rollers and thrust washers in place.

2. Place the piston in OMC Piston Cradle (part No. 326573) or a suitable support. Lubricate the piston pin with clean engine oil and start the pin into the piston as shown in **Figure 124**.

3. Make sure the connecting rod and piston are correctly oriented, then carefully assemble the connecting rod to the piston. On models so equipped, make sure the thrust washers and bearing rollers remain in position. Push the piston pin through the piston and connecting rod.

4. Install new piston pin retaining rings on each side of the piston as follows:

   a. Insert the retaining ring into the tapered end of OMC Cone part No. 331913.

   b. Position the cone over the piston pin bore, making sure the retaining ring end gap is facing downward, away from the cutout in the piston.

   c. Insert OMC Driver (part No. 396747) into the cone and push the retaining ring into its groove. See **Figure 125**.

   d. Turn the piston over and repeat this procedure to install the other retaining ring.

   e. Make sure both retaining rings are securely seated in their grooves.

5. Before installing the piston rings on the pistons, place each ring, individually, inside its re-

8

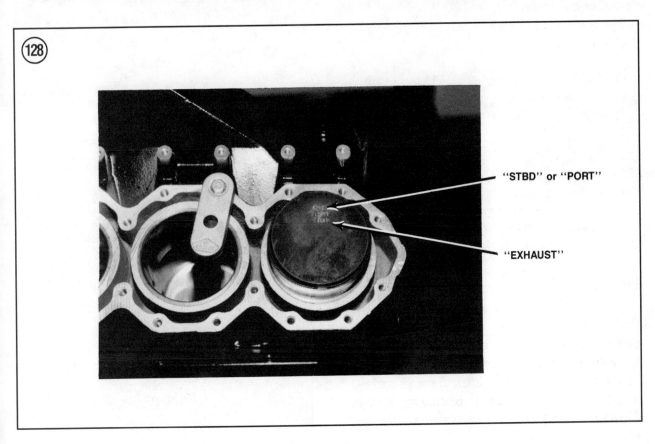

128

"STBD" or "PORT"

"EXHAUST"

spective cylinder. Push the ring into the cylinder with the piston to position the ring squarely in the cylinder. Then measure the piston ring end gap using a feeler gauge as shown in **Figure 118**. The end gap for the upper and lower rings should be 0.011-0.023 in. (0.28-0.58 mm) on 60° models and 0.019-0.031 in. (0.48-0.79 mm) on all other models. If the gap is excessive, repeat the measurement with the ring in another cylinder. If the gap is still excessive, discard the ring and replace it with a new ring. If the gap is insufficient, carefully file the ring ends until the specified gap is obtained.

6. Once the correct end gap is established for each ring, roll the lower ring around the piston ring groove to check for binding or tightness. See **Figure 126**.

7. Using a suitable ring expander, install the piston rings on the piston. Expand the rings only enough to fit over the piston crown (**Figure 120**) and into position in their grooves. Make sure the ring end gaps properly engage the piston ring locating pin inside the ring groove. See **Figure 127**.

> *NOTE*
> *The upper piston ring is a pressure-back design. Side clearance cannot be checked on pressure-back rings because of their tapered shape. To check pressure-back ring-to-groove fit, place a straightedge across the ring groove as shown in* **Figure 130**. *The straightedge should touch the piston on both sides of the ring. Perform several checks at different areas around of the piston. If the ring holds the straightedge away from the piston at any point, the ring groove is not sufficiently clean. Remove the ring and repeat the ring groove cleaning procedure.*

8. Using a feeler gauge, measure the clearance between the lower piston ring and the side of the ring groove. The ring should be free to move in the groove, but the side clearance should not

exceed 0.004 in. (0.10 mm). If side clearance is excessive, replace the piston.

9. Repeat Steps 1-7 to assemble the remaining piston/connecting rods.

Piston and Connecting Rod Installation (All Models Except 2.0, 2.3 and 3.3 hp)

> *NOTE*
> *If reused, pistons and connecting rods should always be installed in the same location and direction from which removed during disassembly.*

Piston/connecting rod assemblies must be installed into the cylinder block in the correct direction. The manufacturer uses 3 different methods for designating the correct piston installation direction:

   a. *All cross flow models*—Install the pistons with the long sloping side of the piston deflector facing the cylinder exhaust ports.

   b. *35 Jet and 40-70 hp*—Install the pistons with the "UP" mark stamped in the crown facing flywheel.

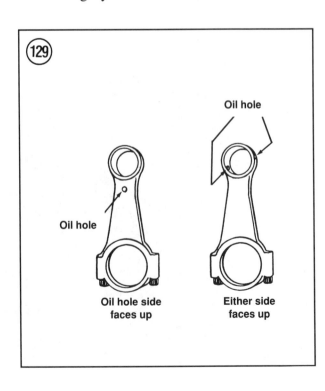

(129)

Oil hole

Oil hole

Oil hole side faces up

Either side faces up

c. *V4, V6 and V8 loop charged models*—Pistons are marked "PORT," "STBD" and "EXHAUST." Install the pistons in the specified cylinder bank with the "EXHAUST" mark stamped in the crown facing the cylinder exhaust ports.

Before installing piston into the cylinder block, check for the correct connecting rod-to-piston orientation as described under *Piston and Connecting Rod Reassembly* in this chapter.

1. Match the piston and connecting rod assembly to its correct cylinder (numbered during disassembly).

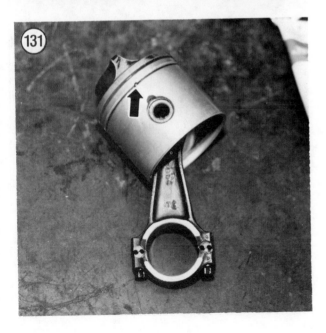

2. Orient the piston and connecting rod assembly in the correct direction according the stamped mark on the piston crown.

3. Lubricate the piston, rings and cylinder wall with clean engine oil.

4. Insert the piston into its cylinder bore. Make sure the ring end gap is properly located at the ring locating pin (**Figure 131**).

5. Install the correct OMC (or equivalent) piston ring compressor over the piston and rings. See **Figure 132**. OMC piston ring compressor part Nos. are as follows:

  a. *3 and 4 hp, 4 Deluxe*—327017.

  b. *6-8 hp*—326589.

  c. *9.9-15 hp*—Standard piston 339754; oversize piston 339755.

  d. *20-30 hp*—Standard piston 326591; oversize piston 330223.

  e. *35 Jet, 40-50 hp*—Standard piston 326592; oversize piston 330222.

8

f. *60-70 hp*—Standard piston 326592; oversize piston 330222.

g. *85-115 hp*—Standard piston 327018; oversize piston 330221.

h. *150 hp (except 60°)*—Standard piston 327018; oversize piston 330221.

i. 175 hp (except 60°)—Standard piston 326734; oversize piston 330220.

j. 150 and 175 hp (60°)—Standard piston 336314; oversize piston 336313.

k. 120-300 hp—Standard piston 334140; oversize piston 334141.

6. Hold the connecting rod end with one hand to prevent it from scraping or scratching the cylinder wall, then slowly push the piston into the cylinder. See **Figure 132**.

7. Remove the ring compressor and repeat Steps 5 and 6 to install the remaining piston/connecting rod assemblies.

8. Temporarily install the cylinder head(s) with 2 screws to prevent the pistons from slipping out of the cylinder block during crankshaft installation.

9. Reach through the exhaust port and lightly depress each piston ring with a small screwdriver or similar tool. See **Figure 133**. The ring should snap back when the pressure is released. If not, the ring was broken during piston installation. Remove the piston and replace the broken ring.

Crankshaft Assembly Installation (2.0, 2.3 and 3.3 hp)

1. Using an arbor press and OMC Bearing Installer (part No. 115309), press the crankshaft ball bearings onto the crankshaft. Note that the sides of the bearings with the alignment pins must face the bottom of the crankshaft. Press on the bearing inner race only.

2. Make sure the piston ring end gap is properly positioned at the ring locating pin. Lift the crankshaft assembly and position the piston at the cylinder bore. Compress the piston ring using a suitable tool, then push the piston into the cylinder.

3. Install the crankshaft on the cylinder block. Turn the ball bearings as necessary to position the locating pins in the notches in the cylinder block. Firmly seat the bearings and crankshaft assembly in the cylinder block.

4. Reach through the exhaust port and lightly depress each piston ring with a small screwdriver or similar tool. See **Figure 133**, typical. The ring should snap back when the pressure is released. If not, the ring was broken during piston instal-

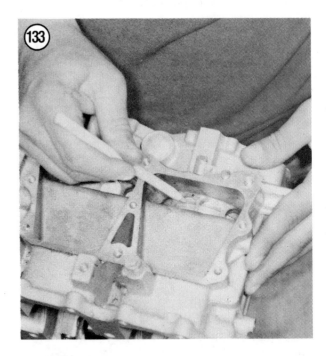

lation. Remove the piston and replace the broken ring.

5. Install the upper and lower ball bearing retainers in the cylinder block.

6. Lubricate the seal lips of the crankshaft upper and lower seals with OMC Needle Bearing Assembly Grease. Position the seals with their lips facing inward and install on the crankshaft. Use caution not to cut or damage the seal lips during installation.

Crankshaft Reassembly and Installation (3 and 4 hp and 4 Deluxe)

Use a recommended oil whenever a procedure specifies lubrication with engine oil. A torque wrench is essential for proper fastener tightening. Do not use any grease inside the power head that is not gasoline soluble. Always use new gaskets, seals and O-rings during reassembly.

1. *Except 1991 models*—Lubricate the inner diameter of a new crankshaft seal sleeve (if removed) with isopropyl alcohol. Then, while securely supporting the crankshaft between the lower counterweights, press the sleeve onto the bottom of the crankshaft.

2. Next, press a new lower main bearing (if removed) on the crankshaft. Make sure the crankshaft is securely supported on the lower counterweights during bearing installation. Press on the bearing inner race only.

3. Using snap ring pliers, install the lower main bearing retaining ring. Make sure the flat side of the ring is facing away from the bearing.

4. Lubricate the upper main bearing with clean engine oil. Slide the bearing on the top of the crankshaft. The lettered side of the bearing should face DOWN.

5. Coat the outer diameter of a new upper seal with OMC Gasket Sealing Compound. Lubricate the seal lip with clean engine oil then, with the lip facing DOWN, install the seal on the crankshaft.

6. Install a new seal ring on the crankshaft.

7. Install one main bearing liner (with hole) into position in the cylinder block. Make sure the hole in the liner properly engages the locating pin in the cylinder block.

8. Lubricate the bearing liner (in cylinder block) and the 30 center main bearing roller with OMC Needle Bearing Assembly Grease. Install 14 of the loose rollers into the cylinder block bearing liner. Apply additional needle bearing assembly grease as necessary to hold the rollers in place.

9. Lubricate the crankshaft with clean engine oil. Align the locating pin on the upper main bearing with its notch in the cylinder block (**Figure 134**, typical), then carefully install the crankshaft into the cylinder block. Check to make sure the 14 center main bearing rollers are still in place after the crankshaft is securely seated.

10. Pull one connecting rod up toward the crankshaft. Insert the crankpin bearing half into the connecting rod, mate the rod to the crankpin, then place the remaining bearing half on the crankpin. See **Figure 135**.

11. While holding the connecting rod against the crankpin, install the connecting rod cap (**Figure 136**), making sure it is correctly oriented. Lubricate the connecting rod cap screws with clean engine oil. Install the screws and tighten evenly, in 3 steps, to 60-70 in.-lb. (6.8-7.9 N•m).

12. Repeat Steps 10 and 11 for the remaining connecting rod.

8

13. Lubricate the remaining 16 center main bearing rollers with OMC Needle Bearing Assembly Grease. Carefully arrange the bearing rollers on the crankshaft center main journal, then install the remaining center main bearing liner, making sure the dovetailed ends of the liners are properly engaged.

14. Check to make sure the crankshaft assembly is properly seated in the cylinder block and that the connecting rod caps are correctly oriented with the rods. Refer to *Cylinder Block and Crankcase Cover Reassembly* in this chapter to complete reassembly.

Crankshaft Reassembly and Installation (6-8 hp)

Use a recommended oil whenever a procedure specifies lubrication with engine oil. A torque wrench is essential for proper fastener tightening. Do not use any grease inside the power head that is not gasoline soluble. Always use new gaskets, seals and O-rings during reassembly.

1. If removed, press a new seal sleeve on the lower end of the crankshaft. Lubricate the inside of the sleeve with isopropyl alcohol. Securely support the crankshaft between the lower counterweights during the pressing procedure.

2. If removed, press a new lower main bearing on the crankshaft as follows:

   a. Support the crankshaft between the lower counterweights.

   b. Lightly lubricate the inner diameter of a new bearing with clean engine oil.

   c. Press the bearing on the crankshaft until fully seated. Press against the bearing inner race only.

   d. Using snap ring pliers, install a new bearing retaining ring with its flat side facing away from the bearing. Make sure the retaining ring is firmly seated in the crankshaft groove.

3. Lubricate the upper main bearing with clean engine oil. Install the bearing on the crankshaft with its lettered side facing DOWNWARD.

4. Apply OMC Gasket Sealing Compound (or equivalent) to the outer diameter of a new crankshaft upper seal. Position the seal with its lip facing DOWN, then install the seal on the crankshaft.

5. Install the cylinder block half (with hole) of the center main bearing liner into the block.

6. Lubricate the 30 center main bearing rollers with OMC Needle Bearing Assembly Grease. Arrange 14 of the rollers in the cylinder block.

7. Lubricate the crankshaft assembly with clean engine oil. Install the crankshaft into the cylinder block. Make sure the 14 center main bearing rollers installed in Step 6 are still in position. Align the locating pin in the upper main bearing with its hole in the cylinder block. See **Figure 134**, typical.

8. Make sure the crankshaft is properly seated in the cylinder block, then install the remaining center main bearing rollers. Install the bearing liner, making sure the dovetailed ends are aligned.

NOTE
*The connecting rod caps must be correctly oriented to the connecting rod. When installing the caps, align the embossed dots (**Figure 137**) or the marks made during disassembly.*

9. Pull the connecting rods up close to their crankpins. Lubricate the crankpin bearing assemblies with OMC Needle Bearing Assembly Grease. Install one bearing half into each connecting rod, then pull the rods up firmly against the crankshaft.

10. Lubricate the rod cap screws with clean engine oil. Install the connecting rod caps on their respective connecting rods, making sure the embossed dots on the rod and cap are aligned. See **Figure 136**.

11. Tighten the rod cap screws evenly in 3 steps, to 60-70 in.-lb. (6.8-7.9 N·m).

12. Check to make sure the crankshaft assembly is properly seated in the cylinder block and that the connecting rod caps are correctly oriented with the rods. Refer to *Cylinder Block and Crankcase Cover Reassembly* in this chapter to complete reassembly.

Crankshaft Reassembly and Installation (9.9-15 hp)

Use a recommended oil whenever a procedure specifies lubrication with engine oil. A torque wrench is essential for proper fastener tightening. Do not use any grease inside the power head

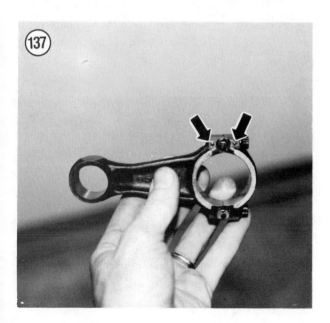

that is not gasoline soluble. Always use new gaskets, seals and O-rings during reassembly.

1. If removed, install a new lower main bearing on the crankshaft as follows:

   a. Support the crankshaft between the lower counterweights.

   b. Lightly lubricate the inner diameter of a new bearing with clean engine oil.

   c. Press the bearing on the crankshaft until fully seated. Press against the bearing inner race only.

   d. Using snap ring pliers, install a new bearing retaining ring with its flat side facing away from the bearing. Make sure the retaining ring is firmly seated in the crankshaft groove.

2. Lubricate the upper main bearing with clean engine oil. Install the bearing on the crankshaft with its lettered side facing the flywheel end of the crankshaft.

3. Lubricate the 23 center main bearing rollers with OMC Needle Bearing Assembly Grease. Position the crankshaft upright and arrange the 23 loose rollers around the center main crankshaft journal. Install the center main bearing liner halves around the bearing rollers, making sure the retaining ring groove is toward the flywheel end of the crankshaft. Install the liner retainer ring around the liners.

4. If installed, remove the rod caps from the connecting rods. Place one crankpin bearing half into each connecting rod. Lubricate the bearings with clean engine oil.

5. Place the crankshaft into the cylinder block while aligning the hole in the center main bearing with its locating pin in the cylinder block and the locating pin in the upper main bearing with its groove in the cylinder block.

6. Pull the connecting rods up against the crankpins. Lubricate and install the remaining crankpin bearing halves on their respective crankpins. See **Figure 135**.

7. Lubricate the threads of the connecting rod cap screws. Install the rod caps, making sure the

alignment dots on the rod caps are aligned with the dots on the rods. See **Figure 136**. Tighten the screws finger tight.

8. Tighten the connecting rod cap screws as follows:

 a. Run a pencil point, seal pick or similar tool over the rod and cap mating surfaces to check alignment. See **Figure 138**. The rod and cap must be aligned so the tool point will pass smoothly across the parting line on at least 3 of the 4 corners.

 b. If rod-to-cap alignment is not acceptable, gently tap the rod cap in the required direction using a soft-face mallet then recheck alignment. Repeat this procedure as many times as necessary to obtain the correct alignment.

 c. If the correct alignment cannot be obtained, the connecting rod and cap assembly must be replaced.

 d. If alignment is acceptable, tighten the rod cap screws evenly in 3 steps to 60-70 in.-lb. (6.8-7.9 N•m).

9. Check to make sure the crankshaft assembly is properly seated in the cylinder block and that the connecting rod caps are correctly oriented with the rods. Refer to *Cylinder Block and Crankcase Cover Reassembly* in this chapter to complete reassembly.

Crankshaft Reassembly and Installation (20-30 hp)

Use a recommended oil whenever a procedure specifies lubrication with engine oil. A torque wrench is essential for proper fastener tightening. Do not use any grease inside the power head that is not gasoline soluble. Always use new gaskets, seals and O-rings during reassembly.

1. If removed, install a new lower main bearing on the crankshaft as follows:

 a. Support the crankshaft between the lower counterweights.

 b. Lightly lubricate the inner diameter of a new bearing with clean engine oil.

 c. Press the bearing on the crankshaft until fully seated. Press against the lettered side of the bearing inner race only.

 d. Using snap ring pliers, install a new bearing retaining ring with its flat side facing away from the bearing. Make sure the retaining ring is firmly seated in the crankshaft groove.

2. *1993-on models*—If removed, install a new seal sleeve on the crankshaft as follows:

 a. Place the sleeve into OMC Crank-shaft/Bearing Sleeve Tool (part No. 339749).

 b. Lubricate the inner diameter of the sleeve with engine oil. Place the tool and sleeve on the bottom of the crankshaft.

 c. Drive the sleeve on the crankshaft until the tool contacts the lower main bearing.

 d. Carefully inspect the seal sleeve after installation. If the sleeve is distorted or damaged, it must be replaced.

3. Lubricate a new drive shaft O-ring seal with OMC Moly Lube. Install the O-ring into the bottom of the crankshaft on 1991-1992 models or into the seal sleeve on 1993-on models.

4. Lubricate the upper main bearing with engine oil. Slide the bearing onto the crankshaft with its lettered side facing the flywheel end of the crankshaft.

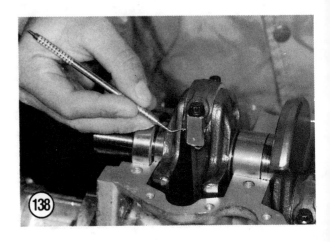

5. Apply OMC Gasket Sealing Compound to the outer diameter of a new crankshaft upper seal. Lubricate the seal lip with engine oil and slide the seal onto the crankshaft. Make sure the seal lip is facing DOWN.

6. Lubricate the center main bearing halves with engine oil. Place the bearing halves around the crankshaft center main journal. Install the center main bearing liner halves around the center bearing. Make sure the retaining ring groove in the liners is facing the bottom of the crankshaft (**Figure 139**), then install the retaining ring around the liners.

7. If installed, remove the rod caps from the connecting rods. Install one crankpin bearing half into each connecting rod. Lubricate the bearing halves with engine oil.

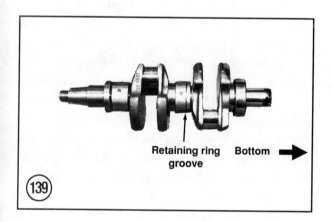

Retaining ring groove   Bottom ➡

⑬⑨

⑭⓪

8. Install the crankshaft into the cylinder block while aligning the center and upper bearings with their locating pins in the cylinder block. Firmly seat the crankshaft assembly in the cylinder block.

9. Pull the connecting rods up against the crankpins. Install the remaining crankpin bearing halves onto the crankpins. See **Figure 135**.

10. Lubricate the threads of the rod cap screws with engine oil then install each cap and screws (**Figure 136**). Make sure the alignment marks on the rod and cap are aligned, tighten the screws finger tight.

CAUTION
All models are equipped with precision-ground connecting rods. Precision-ground connecting rods require the use of OMC Rod Cap Alignment Fixture part No. 396749 to align the rod and cap correctly. The use of an incorrect procedure could result in serious or permanent damage to the connecting rod(s) and crankshaft.

11. Assemble OMC Rod Cap Alignment Fixture (part No. 396749) on the connecting rod following the instructions provided with the tool. See **Figure 140**.

CAUTION
If perfect connecting rod-to-cap alignment cannot be obtained, replace the connecting rod assembly.

12. Once the rod and cap are correctly aligned, use OMC Torque Socket (part No. 331638) or a suitable 5/16 in. 12-point socket to tighten the connecting rod cap screws. Tighten the screws evenly in 3 steps to 30-32 ft.-lb. (41-43 N•m). If using an extension on the torque wrench, keep its length to a minimum to maintain accurate torque readings.

13. Repeat Steps 11 and 12 on the remaining connecting rod.

8

Crankshaft Reassembly and Installation (35 Jet and 40-70 hp)

Use a recommended oil whenever a procedure specifies lubrication with engine oil. A torque wrench is essential for proper fastener tightening. Do not use any grease inside the power head that is not gasoline soluble. Always use new gaskets, seals and O-rings during reassembly.

1. If removed, install a new lower main bearing on the crankshaft as follows:

   a. Support the crankshaft between the lower counterweights.

   b. Lightly lubricate the inner diameter of a new bearing with clean engine oil.

   c. Press the bearing on the crankshaft until fully seated. Press against the lettered side of the bearing inner race only.

   d. Using snap ring pliers, install a new bearing retaining ring with its flat side facing away from the bearing. Make sure the retaining ring is firmly seated in the crankshaft groove.

2. Apply OMC Gasket Sealing Compound to the outer diameter of a new crankshaft upper seal. Install the seal into the upper main bearing (lip facing bearing) using OMC Seal Installer part No. 334500 (2-cylinder) or part No. 326567 (3-cylinder) or equivalent. Lubricate the seal lip with OMC Triple-Guard Grease and the bearing rollers with engine oil.

3. Slide the upper bearing and seal assembly on the crankshaft, making sure the seal is toward the top.

4. *1991-1992 3-cylinder models*—Lubricate a new drive shaft O-ring with OMC Moly Lube and install the O-ring into its bore in the bottom of the crankshaft.

5. Lubricate the center main crankshaft journal(s) with clean engine oil. Install the center main bearing halves around the crankshaft journal.

6. Install the center main bearing liner halves around the center main bearing. The retaining ring groove in the liners must face the bottom of the crankshaft. See **Figure 139**, typical. Install the liner retaining ring around the liners.

7. Install a new O-ring around the upper main bearing. Lubricate the bearing with OMC Triple-Guard Grease.

8. Position the cylinder block so the cylinder head side is facing DOWN. If installed, remove the connecting rod caps from the rods.

9. Install one crankpin bearing half into each connecting rod. Lubricate the bearing halves with engine oil.

10. Carefully install the crankshaft assembly into the cylinder block, making sure the upper main bearing O-ring is properly aligned with its groove and the holes in the main bearings are aligned with their locating pins. Firmly seat the crankshaft assembly in the cylinder block.

11. Make sure the crankpin bearing halves are correctly located in the connecting rods then pull the rods up against the crankpins. Install the remaining crankpin bearing halves on the crankpins (**Figure 135**). Lubricate the bearing halves with engine oil.

12. Lubricate the connecting rod cap screws with engine oil, then install the rod caps (**Figure 136**). Make sure the alignment marks on the rods and caps are correctly aligned and tighten the screws finger tight.

CAUTION
All models are equipped with precision-ground connecting rods. Precision-ground connecting rods require the use of OMC Rod Cap Alignment Fixture part No. 396749 to align the rod and cap correctly. The use of an incorrect procedure could result in serious or permanent damage to the connecting rod(s) and crankshaft.

13. Assemble OMC Rod Cap Alignment Fixture (part No. 396749) on the connecting rod following the instructions provided with the tool. See **Figure 140**.

*If perfect connecting rod-to-cap align-
ment cannot be obtained, replace the
connecting rod assembly.*

14. Check connecting rod and cap alignment by running a pencil point, seal pick or similar tool across the machined corners of the rod assembly as shown in **Figure 138**. The tool will pass across the rod-to-cap parting line smoothly and the line will be nearly invisible if alignment is correct.

15. Once the rod and cap are correctly aligned, use OMC Torque Socket (part No. 331638) or a suitable 5/16 in. 12-point socket to tighten the connecting rod cap screws. Tighten the screws evenly in 3 steps to 30-32 ft.-lb. (41-43 N•m). If using an extension on the torque wrench, keep its length to a minimum to maintain accurate torque readings.

16. Repeat Steps 13-15 on the remaining connecting rod(s).

Crankshaft Reassembly and Installation (V4, V6 [Except 60°] and V8 Models)

Use a recommended oil whenever a procedure specifies lubrication with engine oil. A torque wrench is essential for proper fastener tightening. Do not use any grease inside the power head that is not gasoline soluble. Always use new gaskets, seals and O-rings during reassembly.

Figure 141 shows the crankshaft assembly typical of all models.

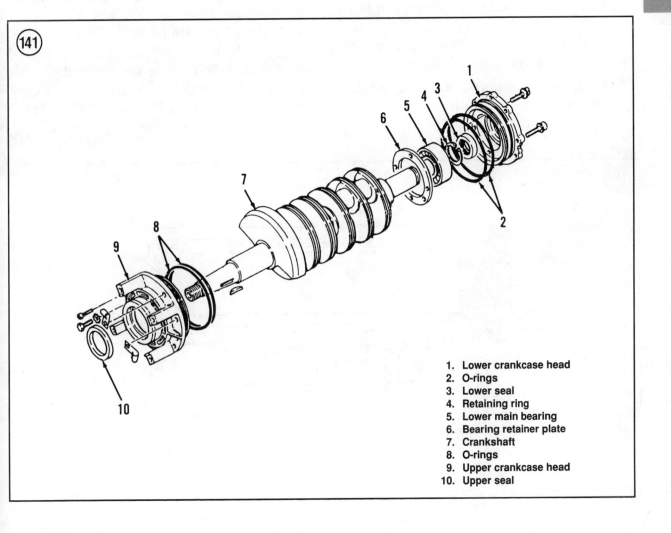

1. Lower crankcase head
2. O-rings
3. Lower seal
4. Retaining ring
5. Lower main bearing
6. Bearing retainer plate
7. Crankshaft
8. O-rings
9. Upper crankcase head
10. Upper seal

1. Lubricate the center main bearing assemblies with clean engine oil. Install the center bearing assemblies on their original crankshaft journals (if reusing bearings), then install the bearing liners around the bearings. The retaining ring groove in the liners must face toward the bottom of the crankshaft. Secure liners with the retaining rings.

2. Place the lower main bearing retainer plate on the crankshaft. The flat side of the plate must face toward the lower end of the crankshaft.

3. If removed, install a new lower main bearing on the crankshaft as follows:

   a. First, lubricate the bottom end of the crankshaft using clean engine oil.

   b. Place the bearing on the crankshaft (lettered side facing toward bottom of crankshaft).

   c. Using an appropriate driver and soft-face mallet, drive the bearing onto the crankshaft until fully seated. Note that the driver should contact the bearing inner race only.

   d. Using snap ring pliers, install the bearing retaining ring with its flat (sharp) side facing away from the bearing.

NOTE
The installation tool may stick to the seal sleeve after installation in Step 4. If so, remove the tool using a suitable puller (OMC Slide Hammer part No. 391008). Do not damage the seal sleeve.

4. *1992-on models (except V8)*—Install a new seal sleeve on the bottom of the crankshaft as follows:

   a. Using OMC Crankshaft Bearing/Sleeve Installer (part No. 338648), drive the sleeve onto the crankshaft until fully seated.

   b. After installation, carefully inspect the sleeve. If the sleeve is distorted or damaged during the installation procedure, it must be replaced.

   c. Lubricate a new drive shaft O-ring seal with OMC Moly Lube. Install the O-ring into the seal sleeve.

5. Apply a light coat of OMC Gasket Sealing Compound to the outer diameter of a new crankshaft lower seal. Position the seal in the lower crankcase head with the extended seal lip facing DOWN. See **Figure 142**. Using OMC Seal Installer part No. 326567 (cross flow models) or

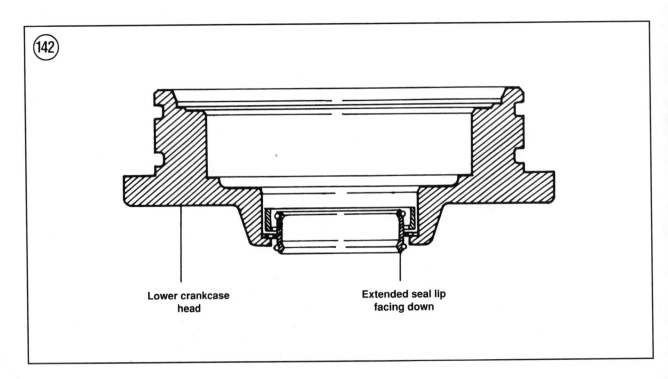

Lower crankcase
head

Extended seal lip
facing down

325453 (loop charged models), carefully drive the seal into the crankcase head until fully seated. Make certain the seal is not distorted or damaged during installation. Lubricate the seal lip with OMC Triple-Guard Grease.

6. Lubricate 2 new lower crankcase head O-rings with OMC Triple-Guard Grease. Install the O-rings in their grooves on the lower crankcase head.

7. Slide the lower crankcase head on the lower end of the crankshaft and fully engage it with the lower main bearing.

8. Apply OMC Nut Lock (or equivalent) to the threads of the crankcase head-to-bearing retainer plate screws (**Figure 143**). Align the bearing retainer plate and the crankcase head screw holes, install the screws and tighten evenly to 96-120 in.-lb. (10.8-13.6 N.m).

9. Apply a light coat of OMC Gasket Sealing Compound to the outer diameter of the crankshaft upper seal. Install the seal (lip facing DOWN) into the upper crankcase head using a suitable tool. Lubricate the seal lip with OMC Triple-Guard Grease.

10. Lubricate the 2 upper crankcase head O-rings with OMC Triple-Guard Grease. Install the O-rings on the upper crankcase head. Lubricate the upper main bearing (inside upper crankcase

head) with clean engine oil and slide the upper crankcase head on the crankshaft.

11. If removed, install the crankshaft seal rings in their original grooves.

12. Position the cylinder block assembly so the block-to-crankcase cover mating surface is facing upward. With the cylinder heads installed loosely, push all pistons to top dead center and remove all connecting rod caps. Make sure the caps are properly numbered for reference during reinstallation.

13. Tie each connecting rod toward the outside of the cylinder block using string or rubber bands.

14. Carefully install the crankshaft assembly into the cylinder block, making sure of the following:

   a. All crankshaft seal ring gaps are facing upward.

   b. Each center main bearing assembly properly engages its locating pin in the cylinder block and the crankshaft assembly is fully seated in the cylinder block.

15. Loosely secure the upper and lower crankcase heads to the cylinder block using 2 screws each.

16. Using a soft-face mallet, tap the crankshaft in an UPWARD direction to ensure the crankshaft and lower crankcase head are properly seated.

17. Lubricate the crankpin bearings, connecting rods and rod caps with clean engine oil.

18. Carefully, pull the No. 1 cylinder connecting rod up close to its crankpin. Do not nick the crankpin journal with the edge of the rod.

19. Install one crankpin bearing half into the No. 1 connecting rod. Pull the rod up against the crankpin.

20. Lubricate the threads of the connecting rod cap screws with engine oil, then install the No. 1 rod cap and screws. See **Figure 136**. Make sure the match marks on the rod and cap are aligned, then tighten the rod cap screws finger tight.

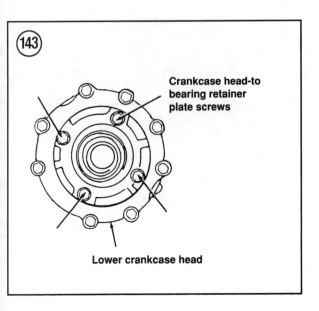

(143)

Crankcase head-to bearing retainer plate screws

Lower crankcase head

8

CAUTION
All models are equipped with precision-ground connecting rods. Precision-ground connecting rods require the use of OMC Rod Cap Alignment Fixture part No. 396749 to align the rod and cap correctly. The use of an incorrect procedure could result in serious or permanent damage to the connecting rod(s) and crankshaft.

21. Assemble OMC Rod Cap Alignment Fixture (part No. 396749) on the connecting rod following the instructions provided with the tool. See **Figure 144**.

CAUTION
If perfect connecting rod-to-cap alignment cannot be obtained, replace the connecting rod assembly.

22. Check connecting rod and cap alignment by running a pencil point, seal pick or similar tool across the machined corners of the rod assembly as shown in **Figure 138**. The tool will pass across the rod-to-cap parting line smoothly and the line will be nearly invisible if alignment is correct.

23. Once the rod and cap are correctly aligned, use OMC Torque Socket (part No. 331638) or an equivalent 5/16 in. 12-point socket to tighten the connecting rod cap screws. Tighten the screws evenly in 3 steps to 30-32 ft.-lb. (41-43 N·m) on cross flow models or 42-44 ft.-lb. (57-59 N·m) on loop charged models. If using an extension on the torque wrench, keep its length to a minimum to maintain accurate torque readings.

24. Repeat Steps 18-24 at each remaining connecting rod assembly.

Crankshaft Reassembly and Installation (60° V6 Models)

Use a recommended oil whenever a procedure specifies lubrication with engine oil. A torque wrench is essential for proper fastener tightening. Do not use any grease inside the power head

that is not gasoline soluble. Always use new gaskets, seals and O-rings during reassembly.

1. If removed, install a new lower main bearing as follows:

   a. Lubricate the bearing and the lower end of the crankshaft with engine oil.

   b. Position the bearing on the crankshaft with its lettered side facing away from the crankshaft.

   c. Using OMC Bearing Installer part No. 314426 (1991 models) or 338647 (1992-on), drive the bearing on the crankshaft

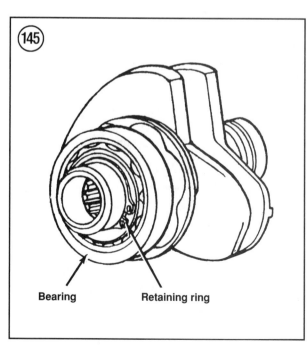

Bearing   **Retaining ring**

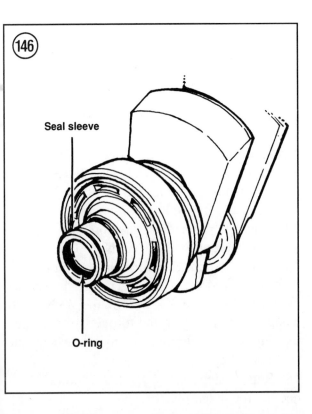

(146)

Seal sleeve

O-ring

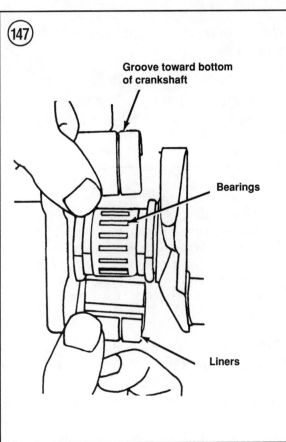

(147)

Groove toward bottom
of crankshaft

Bearings

Liners

until fully seated. See **Figure 145**. Make sure the installation tool contacts only the inner race of the bearing.

d. Using snap ring pliers, install a new bearing retaining ring on the crankshaft. See **Figure 145**. Make sure the flat side (sharp edge) of the retaining ring is facing away from the bearing.

NOTE
The bearing/sleeve installation tool may stick to the seal sleeve after installation. If so, remove the tool using a suitable puller (OMC Slide Hammer part No. 391008).

2. *1992-on*—Using OMC Bearing/Sleeve Installer part No. 338647 (or equivalent), drive a new seal sleeve (**Figure 146**) on the bottom of the crankshaft until fully seated. Carefully inspect the sleeve after installation. If the sleeve is distorted or damaged during the installation process, it must be replaced.

3. *1992-on*—Lubricate a new drive shaft O-ring seal with OMC Moly Lube. Install the O-ring into the seal sleeve (**Figure 146**).

4. Lubricate the center main bearing assemblies with clean engine oil. Install the center bearing assemblies on their original crankshaft journals (if reusing bearings), then install the bearing liners around the bearings. The retaining ring groove in the liners must face toward the bottom of the crankshaft. Secure liners with the retaining rings. See **Figure 147**.

5. Apply a light coat of OMC Gasket Sealing Compound to the outer diameter of a new lower housing seal. Press the seal into the lower housing. Lubricate the seal lip with OMC Triple-Guard Grease.

6. Lubricate a new lower housing O-ring seal with OMC Triple-Guard Grease and install the O-ring around the lower housing. Install the lower housing and seal assembly on the bottom of the crankshaft.

8

7. With the cylinder heads installed loosely with 2 screws each, position the cylinder block so the cylinders are facing DOWN.

8. Push all pistons to top dead center and remove the rod caps. Make sure the rod caps are properly identified for reference during assembly.

9. If removed, install the crankshaft seal rings in their original locations (if reusing rings).

10. Carefully install the crankshaft into the cylinder block. Make sure the crankshaft seal ring end gaps are facing UP, each center main bearing properly engages its locating pin in the cylinder block and the tab on the lower bearing/seal housing properly engages its notch in the cylinder block.

11. Lubricate the No. 1 cylinder crankpin bearing assembly with engine oil.

12. Carefully, pull the No. 1 cylinder connecting rod up close to its crankpin. Do not nick the crankpin journal with the edge of the rod.

13. Install one crankpin bearing half into the No. 1 connecting rod. Pull the rod up against the crankpin.

14. Lubricate the threads of the connecting rod cap screws with engine oil, then install the No. 1 rod cap and screws. See **Figure 136**. Make sure the match marks on the rod and cap are aligned, then tighten the rod cap screws finger tight.

CAUTION
All models are equipped with precision-ground connecting rods. Precision-ground connecting rods require the use of OMC Rod Cap Alignment Fixture part No. 396749 to align the rod and cap correctly. The use of an incorrect procedure could result in serious or permanent damage to the connecting rod(s) and crankshaft.

15. Assemble OMC Rod Cap Alignment Fixture (part No. 396749) on the connecting rod following the instructions provided with the tool. See **Figure 144**.

CAUTION
If perfect connecting rod-to-cap alignment cannot be obtained, replace the connecting rod assembly.

16. Check connecting rod and cap alignment by running a pencil point, seal pick or similar tool across the machined corners of the rod assembly as shown in **Figure 138**. The tool will pass across the rod-to-cap parting line smoothly and the line will be nearly invisible if alignment is correct.

17. Once the rod and cap are correctly aligned, use OMC Torque Socket (part No. 331638) or an equivalent 5/16 in. 12-point socket to tighten the connecting rod cap screws. Tighten the screws evenly in 3 steps to 30-32 ft.-lb. (41-43 N.m). If using an extension on the torque wrench, keep its length to a minimum to maintain accurate torque readings.

18. Repeat Steps 11-17 at each remaining connecting rod assembly.

Cylinder Block and Crankcase Assembly (General Procedures)

CAUTION
OMC Gel Seal II has a shelf life of approximately 1 year. If the age of the Gel Seal II can not be determined, it should be replaced. Using Gel Seal that is too old can result in crankcase air leakage.

WARNING
Wear hand and eye protection when working with OMC Gel Seal and Gasket Remover. In addition, you should remove your wrist watch or other jewelry. The substance is powerful enough to damage watches or jewelry, and will severely irritate the eyes and bare skin.

Mating surfaces must absolutely free of gasket material, sealant, dirt, oil, grease or other contamination. OMC Gel Seal and Gasket Remover, lacquer thinner, acetone, isopropyl alcohol or similar solvents work well for cleaning mating surfaces. Avoid using solvents with an oil, wax or petroleum base as they may not be compatible with some sealants. If scraping is necessary, use a broad, flat scraper or a somewhat dull putty knife. Avoid nicks scratches or other damage to mating surfaces.

CAUTION
*The crankcase cover and cylinder block mating surfaces **must not** be scratched or damaged. The manufacturer specifically recommends using OMC Gel Seal and Gasket Remover and a **plastic** scraper to clean the cylinder block/crankcase cover mating surfaces.*

Prior to using Gel Seal II, the mating surfaces should be treated with OMC Locquic Primer, following the instructions on the container. If Locquic Primer is not used, the assembly should be allowed to set for 24 hours before returning the unit to service.

Cylinder Block and Crankcase Cover Reassembly
(2.0, 2.3 and 3.3 hp)

1. Thoroughly clean the leaf valve and stop with solvent. Inspect the leaf valve for cracks, chips or evidence of fatigue.
2. Apply OMC Screw Lock to the threads of leaf valve retaining screws. Install the leaf valve and leaf valve stop into the crankcase cover. Install the screws and tighten to 27-35 in.-lb. (3-4 N•m).

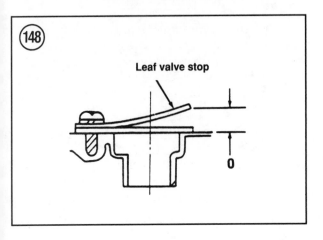

(148)

Leaf valve stop

O

3. Make sure the leaf valve is flush (or nearly flush) to the seat along its entire length. If not, replace the leaf valve assembly.
4. Measure the leaf stop opening (O, **Figure 148**). If the opening is not within 0.236-0.244 in. (6.0-6.2 mm), replace the leaf stop.
5. Thoroughly clean the crankcase cover and cylinder block mating surfaces with OMC Cleaning Solvent, acetone or isopropyl alcohol. Allow the solvent to air dry.
6. Spray the crankcase cover mating surface with OMC Locquic Primer and allow to air dry.
7. Apply a continuous bead of OMC Gel Seal II sealant to the cylinder block mating surface. Run the bead to the inside of all screw holes. Make sure the bead is continuous, but avoid excess application. Keep the sealant approximately 1/4 in. (6.3 mm) from bearings and seals to prevent contamination.
8. Install the crankcase cover on the cylinder block. Apply Gel Seal II to the threads of the 6 main bearing screws. Install the screws and tighten evenly to 90-120 in.-lb. (10-13 N•m).
9. Apply OMC Gasket Sealing Compound to the threads of the crankcase head screws. Install the crankcase head and screws. Tighten the screws to 60-84 in.-lb. (7-9 N•m).
10. Apply a light coat of OMC Gasket Sealing Compound to both sides of a new cylinder head gasket. Install the gasket and cylinder head. Tighten the fasteners to 60-84 in.-lb. (7-9 N•m).
11. Rotate the crankshaft to check for binding or unusual noise. If binding or noise is noted, the power head *must* be disassembled and repaired before proceeding with power head assembly.
12. Install the power head assembly as described in this chapter.

Cylinder Block and Crankcase Cover Reassembly
(4 Deluxe and 3-8 hp)

Replace all gaskets, seals and O-rings during reassembly.

8

1. Thoroughly clean the crankcase cover and cylinder block mating surfaces with OMC Cleaning Solvent, acetone or isopropyl alcohol. Make certain the mating surfaces are absolutely free of oil, grease or other contamination. Allow the solvent to air dry.

2. Spray the crankcase cover mating surface with OMC Locquic Primer and allow to air dry.

3. Apply a continuous bead of OMC Gel Seal II sealant to the cylinder block mating surface. Run the bead to the inside of all screw holes and make sure the bead is continuous, but avoid excess application. Keep the sealant approximately 1/4 in. (6.3 mm) from bearings and seals to prevent contamination.

4. Install the crankcase cover on the cylinder block. Apply Gel Seal II to the threads of the 6 main bearing screws, then install the screws finger tight.

5. Make sure the crankcase cover is fully seated, then install and firmly seat the taper pin.

6. Using a soft-face mallet, tap upward on the bottom of the crankshaft to seat the lower main bearing properly.

7. Tighten the 6 main bearing screws, evenly in 3 steps, to 144-168 in.-lb. (16.3-19.0 N.m). Start at the center screws and work outward in a circular pattern.

8. Rotate the crankshaft several turns to check for binding or unusual noise. If binding or noise is noted, the power head *must* be disassembled and repaired before proceeding.

9. Using snap ring pliers, install the lower main bearing retaining ring with its beveled side facing away from the bearing. The retaining ring *must not* block the oil hole at the front of the crankcase. Make sure its end gap is centered around the oil hole as shown in **Figure 149**.

10A. *4 Deluxe and 3 and 4 hp*—Apply OMC Gasket Sealing Compound to the outer diameter of a new crankshaft lower seal. Install the seal, with its lip facing away from the lower main bearing, until fully seated against the lower bearing retaining ring.

10B. *6 and 8 hp*—Apply OMC Gasket Sealing Compound to the outer diameter of a new crankshaft lower seal. Install the seal, with its lip facing toward the lower main bearing, until fully seated against the bearing retaining ring.

11. Install the lower crankcase head. Tighten the fasteners to 25-35 in.-lb. (2.8-3.9 N.m).

12. Apply a light coat of OMC Gasket Sealing Compound to both sides of a new cylinder head gasket. On 4 Deluxe, 3 and 4 hp models, install the gasket with the tab on one end facing up and the numbered side facing the cylinder block. Install the cylinder head and tighten the fasteners to 144-168 in.-lb. (16.3-19.0 N.m) in the sequence shown in **Figure 150**.

13. *6 and 8 hp*—Apply OMC Gasket Sealing Compound to a new thermostat cover gasket. Install the thermostat and related components.

14. Apply OMC Gasket Sealing Compound to a new exhaust cover gasket(s). Install the exhaust cover(s) and gasket(s). Tighten the screws to 25-35 in.-lb. (2.8-3.9 N.m) on 4 Deluxe, 3 and 4 hp or 60-84 in.-lb. (6.8-9.5 N.m) on 6 and 8 hp.

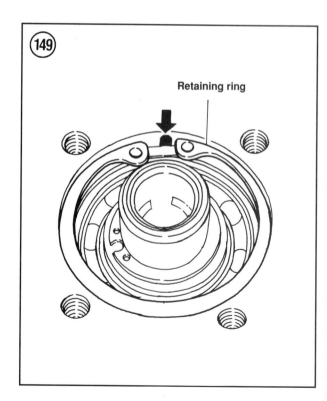

(149)

Retaining ring

15. Using a new gasket (without sealant), install the intake manifold and leaf valve plate. Tighten the fasteners to 60-84 in.-lb. (6.8-9.5 N•m).

16. Lubricate the water tube grommet, then install the grommet and water tube into the lower exhaust tube. Using a new gasket (without sealant), install the inner exhaust tube on the power head. Install the exhaust tube fasteners and tighten to 60-84 in.-lb. (6.8-9.5 N•m).

17. Install the power head as described in this chapter.

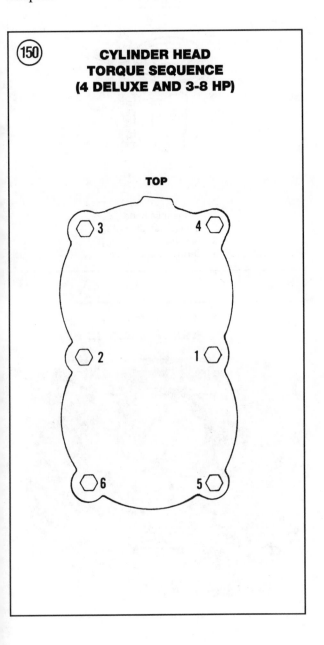

CYLINDER HEAD TORQUE SEQUENCE (4 DELUXE AND 3-8 HP)

Cylinder Block and Crankcase Cover Reassembly (9.9-15 hp)

Replace all gaskets, seals and O-rings during reassembly. All gaskets, unless instructed otherwise, should be lightly coated on both sides with OMC Gasket Sealing Compound prior to installation. In addition, the outer diameter of all seals, unless instructed otherwise, should be coated with OMC Gasket Sealing Compound.

1. Thoroughly clean the crankcase cover and cylinder block mating surfaces with OMC Cleaning Solvent, acetone or isopropyl alcohol. Make certain the mating surfaces are absolutely free of oil, grease or other contamination. Allow the solvent to air dry.

2. Spray the crankcase cover mating surface with OMC Locquic Primer and allow to air dry.

3. Apply a continuous bead of OMC Gel Seal II sealant to the cylinder block mating surface. Run the bead to the inside of all screw holes. Make sure the bead is continuous, but avoid excess application. Keep the sealant approximately 1/4 in. (6.3 mm) from bearings and seals to prevent contamination.

4. Install the crankcase cover into position on the cylinder block. Apply Gel Seal II to the threads of the 6 main bearing screws, then install the screws finger tight.

5. Be sure the crankcase cover is fully seated, then install and firmly seat the taper pin using a suitable punch and mallet.

6. Using a soft-face mallet, tap the bottom of the crankshaft to ensure the lower main bearing is properly seated.

7. Apply OMC Gasket Sealing Compound to the outer diameter of a new upper seal. Install the seal with its lip facing DOWN, using OMC Seal Installer part No. 391060, or equivalent.

8. Apply OMC Gasket Sealing Compound to the outer diameter of the 2 new crankcase head seals. See **Figure 151**. Place the small diameter seal on OMC Crankcase Head Installer part No.

8

330251 or 433391. The seal must be on the small-diameter end of the tool with its lip facing the center of the tool. Carefully drive the seal into the crankcase head until the installer tool contacts the crankcase head. Then, place the large diameter seal on the opposite end of the tool (large-diameter end) with its lip facing away from the center of the tool. Drive the seal into the crankcase head until the tool contacts the crankcase head. Note that when correctly installed, both seal lips face each other.

9. Lightly coat the crankcase head seals, and the area between the seals, with OMC Moly Lube.

10. Lubricate a new crankcase head O-ring (**Figure 151**) with engine oil and install the O-ring.

11. Apply OMC Gasket Sealing Compound to the threads of the crankcase head attaching screws. Install the crankcase head and tighten the screws finger tight.

12. Tighten the 6 main bearing screws to 144-168 in.-lb. (16.3-19.0 N•m). Tighten the screws in a circular pattern, starting at the center. Tighten the small crankcase cover screws to 60-84 in.-lb. (6.8-9.5 N•m).

13. Tighten the crankcase head attaching screws to 60-84 in.-lb. (6.8-9.5 N•m).

14. Apply a light coat of OMC Gasket Sealing Compound to both sides of a new cylinder head gasket. Install the head and gasket, then tighten the fasteners evenly, in 3 steps, to 216-240 in.-lb. (24.4-27.1 N•m). Follow the tightening sequence shown in **Figure 152**.

15. Install the thermostat, temperature switch (if so equipped) and related components into the cylinder head. Install the thermostat cover using a new O-ring.

16. Apply a light coat of OMC Gasket Sealing Compound to both sides of new exhaust cover gaskets. Install the inner and outer covers with the gaskets. Tighten the exhaust cover fasteners to 60-84 in.-lb. (6.8-9.5 N•m).

17. Install the intake manifold and leaf valve assembly using new gaskets (without sealant).

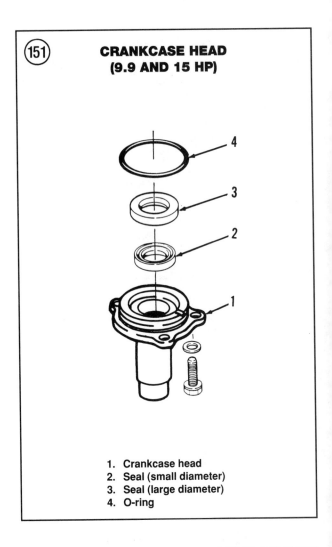

(151) CRANKCASE HEAD (9.9 AND 15 HP)

1. Crankcase head
2. Seal (small diameter)
3. Seal (large diameter)
4. O-ring

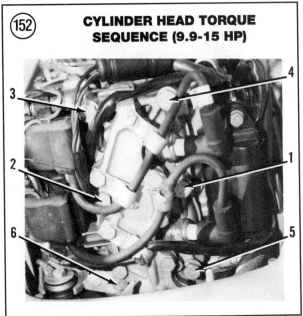

(152) CYLINDER HEAD TORQUE SEQUENCE (9.9-15 HP)

Tighten the fasteners to 60-84 in.-lb. (6.8-9.5 N.m).

18. Install the power head as described in this chapter.

Cylinder Block and Crankcase Cover Reassembly (20-30 hp)

Replace all gaskets, seals and O-rings during reassembly. All gaskets, unless instructed otherwise, should be lightly coated on both sides with OMC Gasket Sealing Compound prior to installation. In addition, the outer diameter of all seals, unless instructed otherwise, should be coated with OMC Gasket Sealing Compound.

1. If removed, install the 3 water deflectors into the cylinder block. See **Figure 153**. The deflectors should be flush, or nearly flush with the cylinder head gasket surface. Lubricate the deflectors with STP Oil Treatment to ease installation.

2. Apply OMC Gasket Sealing Compound to the outer diameter of a new lower seal. Press the seal into the lower crankcase head using OMC Installer part No. 333520 until the tool contacts the crankcase head. Note that the sharp edge of the seal metal case should be facing the installation tool during the pressing procedure. Lubricate the seal lip with OMC Triple-Guard grease.

3. Thoroughly clean the crankcase cover and cylinder block mating surfaces with OMC Cleaning Solvent, acetone or isopropyl alcohol. Make certain the mating surfaces are absolutely free of oil, grease or other contamination. Allow the solvent to air dry.

4. Spray the crankcase cover mating surface with OMC Locquic Primer and allow to air dry.

5. Apply a continuous bead of OMC Gel Seal II sealant to the cylinder block mating surface. Run the bead to the inside of all screw holes. Make sure the bead is continuous, but avoid excess application. Keep the sealant approximately 1/4 in. (6.3 mm) from bearings and labyrinth seals to prevent contamination.

6. Install the crankcase cover into position on the cylinder block. Apply Gel Seal II to the threads of the 6 main bearing screws, then install the screws finger tight.

7. Be sure the crankcase cover is fully seated, then install and firmly seat the taper pin using a suitable punch and mallet.

8. Using a soft-face mallet, tap the bottom of the crankshaft to ensure the lower main bearing is properly seated. Rotate the crankshaft several turns to check for binding or unusual noise. If binding or noise is noted, the power head must be disassembled and repaired before proceeding.

9. Apply a light coat of OMC Gasket Sealing Compound to the machined surface of the crankcase head. Lubricate a new crankcase head O-ring with OMC Triple-Guard, then install the O-ring on the crankcase head (**Figure 154**). Ap-

ply OMC Gasket Sealing Compound, install the crankcase head and install the fasteners (**Figure 155**) finger tight.

10. Tighten the 6 main bearing screws to 168-192 in.-lb. (19.0-21.7 N·m) and the remaining 8 crankcase cover screws to 60-84 in.-lb. (6.8-9.5 N·m). Tighten the center screws first, then work outward. Next, tighten the crankcase head screws to 60-84 in.-lb. (6.8-9.5 N·m).

11. Apply OMC Gasket Sealing Compound to the outer diameter of a new upper seal. Install the seal (lip facing DOWN) using OMC Seal Installer part No. 321539, or a suitable equivalent driver.

12. Apply a light coat of OMC Gasket Sealing Compound to both sides of a new cylinder head gasket. Install the gasket, cylinder head and fasteners. Tighten the fasteners to 216-240 in.-lb. (24.4-27.1 N·m) in the sequence shown in **Figure 156**.

13. Install the thermostat, a new thermostat seal and the thermostat spring into the cylinder head. Apply OMC Gasket Sealing Compound to both sides of a new cylinder head cover gasket. Install the gasket, cylinder head cover (**Figure 157**) and fasteners. Tighten the fasteners in a circular pattern to 60-84 in.-lb. (6.8-9.5 N·m).

14. Apply OMC Gasket Sealing Compound to both sides of the inner and outer exhaust cover gaskets. Install the covers and gaskets (**Figure 158**). Tighten the fasteners to 48-84 in.-lb. (5.4-9.5 N·m).

15. Apply a thin bead of OMC Adhesive M to both sides of a new bypass cover gasket. Install the gasket and bypass cover. See **Figure 159**. Tighten the screws to 60-84 in.-lb. (6.8-9.5 N·m).

16. Install a new leaf valve gasket, then install the leaf valve assembly. See **Figure 160**.

17. Install the intake manifold with a new gasket (**Figure 161**). Tighten the fasteners to 60-84 in.-lb. (6.8-9.5 N·m).

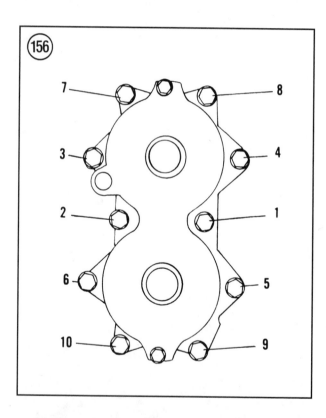

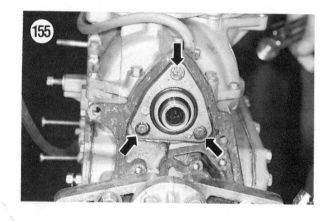

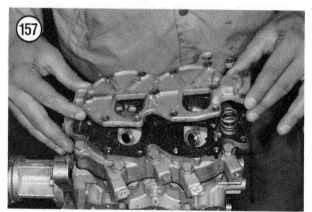

18. Install the inner exhaust housing (if necessary). Tighten the screws to 96-120 in.-lb. (10.8-13.5 N.m).

19. Install the power head as described in this chapter.

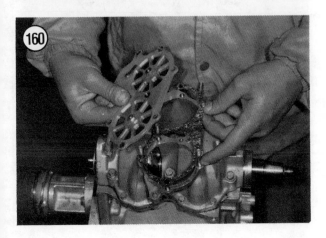

Cylinder Block and Crankcase Cover Reassembly
(35 Jet, 40-70 hp)

Replace all gaskets, seals and O-rings during reassembly. All gaskets, unless instructed otherwise, should be lightly coated on both sides with OMC Gasket Sealing Compound prior to installation. In addition, the outer diameter of all seals, unless instructed otherwise, should be coated with OMC Gasket Sealing Compound.

1. Apply OMC Gasket Sealing Compound to the outer diameter of the 2 lower crankshaft seals.

2. Install the small diameter seal into the crankcase head, then the large diameter seal. Use OMC Seal Installer part No. 334998 (1991-1992 2-cylinder models) or 339752 (1993-on 2-cylinder and all 3-cylinder models). Both seal lips should face UP. Lubricate the seal lips with OMC Moly Lube.

3. Thoroughly clean the crankcase cover and cylinder block mating surfaces with OMC Cleaning Solvent, acetone or isopropyl alcohol. Make certain the mating surfaces are absolutely free of oil, grease or other contamination. Allow the solvent to air dry.

4. Spray the crankcase cover mating surface with OMC Locquic Primer and allow to air dry.

5. Apply a continuous bead of OMC Gel Seal II sealant to the cylinder block mating surface. Run the bead to the inside of all screw holes. Make

sure the bead is continuous, but avoid excess application. Keep the sealant approximately 1/4 in. (6.3 mm) from bearings and labyrinth seals to prevent contamination.

6. While aligning the mounting holes and upper main bearing O-ring groove, install the crankcase cover on the cylinder block. Install the main bearing screws finger tight.

7. Make sure the crankcase cover is properly seated, then install the taper pin. Firmly seat the taper pin using a suitable punch and mallet.

8. Using a soft-face mallet, lightly tap the bottom of the crankshaft to ensure the lower main bearing is properly seated.

9. Install a new O-ring seal on the lower crankcase head. Lubricate the O-ring with OMC Triple-Guard grease. Apply a light coat of OMC Gasket Sealing Compound to the crankcase head mating flange. Install the crankcase head and install the attaching screws finger tight.

10. Tighten the main bearing screws, in 3 steps, to 18-20 ft.-lb. (24.4-27.1 N.m).

11. Turn the crankshaft several turns to check for binding or unusual noise. If binding or noise is noted, the power head must be disassembled before proceeding. If necessary, temporarily install the flywheel and key to ease crankshaft rotation.

12. Install the crankcase cover flange screws. Tighten the screws to 60-84 in.-lb. (6.8-9.5 N.m). Tighten the lower crankcase head screws to 60-84 in.-lb. (6.8-9.5 N.m) on 2-cylinder models or 96-120 in.-lb. (10.8-13.5 N.m) on 3-cylinder models.

13. Apply a light coat of OMC Gasket Sealing Compound to both sides of a new cylinder head gasket. Install the gasket, cylinder head and fasteners.

  a. On 2-cylinder models, tighten the cylinder head fasteners to 18-20 ft.-lb. (24.4-27.1 N.m) following the sequence shown in **Figure 162**.

  b. On 3-cylinder models, tighten the cylinder head fasteners to 18-20 ft.-lb. (24.4-27.1 N.m) following the sequence shown in **Figure 163**.

14. Apply OMC Gasket Sealing Compound to the outer diameter of the temperature sending switch. Install the switch and cover in the cylinder head.

15A. *2-cylinder models*—Install the thermostat and related components, then the thermostat spring into cylinder head. Install a new O-ring on the thermostat cover. Install and securely tighten the cover.

15B. *3-cylinder models*—Install the pin into the thermostat with its convex end facing outward, then install the thermostat into the thermostat seal. Place the retainer and spring into the thermostat housing and reassemble the halves. Install the thermostat assembly into the cylinder head. Make sure the pin side of the thermostat is facing OUT. Apply a light coat of OMC Gasket Sealing Compound to both sides of a new thermostat cover gasket, install the gasket and cover and tighten the cover fasteners to 60-84 in.-lb. (6.8-9.5 N.m).

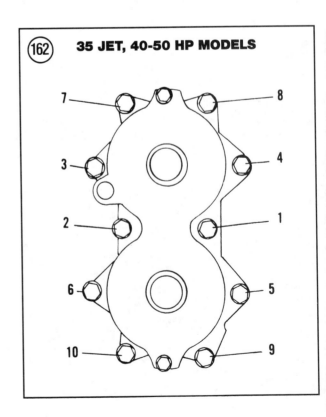

(162) **35 JET, 40-50 HP MODELS**

16. Apply a light coat of OMC Gasket Sealing Compound to both sides of a new exhaust cover gasket. Install the gasket, exhaust cover and fasteners. Tighten the fasteners in 3 steps to 60-84 in.-lb. (6.8-9.5 N•m).

17. Install the intake manifold and leaf valve assembly, using a new gasket (without sealant). Tighten the attaching screws to 60-84 in.-lb. (6.8-9.5 N•m).

18. Install the power head as described in this chapter.

Cylinder Block and Crankcase Cover Reassembly (V4 and V6 Cross Flow Models)

Replace all gaskets, seals and O-rings during reassembly. All gaskets, unless instructed other- wise, should be lightly coated on both sides with OMC Gasket Sealing Compound prior to instal- lation. In addition, the outer diameter of all seals, unless instructed otherwise, should be coated with OMC Gasket Sealing Compound.

1. *115 and 175 hp*—If removed, reinstall the filler blocks (**Figure 164**) into the cylinder block. Use brass screws and apply OMC Ultra Lock to the threads. Install locking tabs on the center and bottom screws on 115 hp models or the center screws on 175 hp models. Tighten the screws to 30-54 in.-lb. (3.4-6.1 N•m).

NOTE
The filler blocks must be flush with the cylinder head mating surface after in- stallation. If new blocks are installed, they must be machined flush with the mating surface by a machine shop.

2. Thoroughly clean the crankcase cover and cylinder block mating surfaces with OMC Cleaning Solvent, acetone or isopropyl alcohol. Make certain the mating surfaces are absolutely free of oil, grease or other contamination. Allow the solvent to air dry.

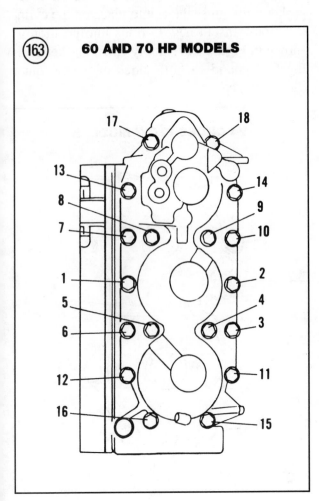

163 **60 AND 70 HP MODELS**

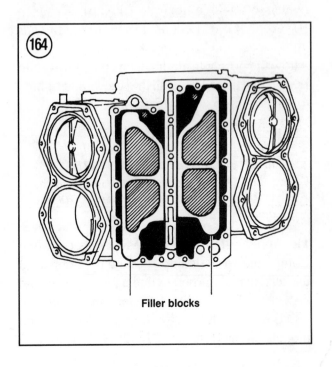

164

Filler blocks

3. Spray the crankcase cover mating surface with OMC Locquic Primer and allow to air dry.

4. Apply a continuous bead of OMC Gel Seal II sealant to the cylinder block mating surface. Run the bead to the inside of all screw holes. Make sure the bead is continuous, but avoid excess application. Keep the sealant approximately 1/4 in. (6.3 mm) from bearings and seals to prevent contamination.

5. While aligning the mounting holes and upper main bearing O-ring groove, install the crankcase cover on the cylinder block. Install the main bearing screws finger tight.

6. With the crankcase cover properly seated, install the taper pins. Firmly seat the taper pins, using a suitable punch and mallet.

7. Starting with the center screws, tighten the main bearing screws, in 3 steps, to 18-20 ft.-lb. (24.4-27.1 N·m) in a circular pattern.

8. Turn the crankshaft several turns to check for binding or unusual noise. Temporarily install the flywheel and key, if necessary, to ease crankshaft rotation. If noise or binding is noted, the power head must be disassembled and repaired before proceeding.

9. Install the crankcase cover flange screws and tighten to 60-84 in.-lb. (6.8-9.5 N·m).

10. Apply OMC Locquic Primer to the threads of the upper and lower crankcase head fasteners. Allow the primer to air dry, then apply OMC Nut Lock to the threads. Install the screws and tighten to 96-120 in.-lb. (10.8-13.5 N·m).

NOTE
On V6 cross flow models, the cylinder head gaskets are marked "HEAD SIDE." Install the head gaskets with the marked side facing away from the cylinder block.

11. Apply a light coat of OMC Gasket Sealing Compound to both sides of new cylinder head gaskets. Install the port cylinder head, gasket and fasteners. Tighten the fasteners in 3 steps to 18-20 ft.-lb. (24.4-27.1 N·m) on V4 and 150 hp models or 20-22 ft.-lb. (27.1-29.8 N·m) on 175

hp models. Follow the tightening sequence shown in **Figure 165** (V4) or **Figure 166** (V6).

12. Apply OMC Gasket Sealing Compound to the outer diameter of the temperature sending switches and both sides of new cylinder head cover gaskets. Install the switches into the cylinder heads, then install the cylinder head covers. Starting with the center screws, tighten the cover screws to 60-84 in.-lb. (6.8-9.5 N·m) in a circular pattern.

13A. *Except 175 hp*—Apply OMC Gasket Sealing Compound to both sides of new inner and outer exhaust cover gaskets. Install the inner and outer exhaust covers, with gaskets, on the cylinder block. Starting with the center screws, tighten the exhaust cover fasteners to 60-84 in.-lb. (6.8-9.5 N·m).

13B. *175 hp*—Install the inner exhaust cover gasket (without sealant) into place on the cylinder block. Install new O-rings into position as shown in **Figure 167**. Apply OMC Gasket Sealing Compound to both sides of a new outer

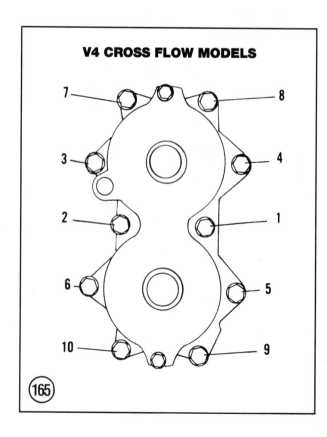

V4 CROSS FLOW MODELS

7 — 8
3 — 4
2 — 1
6 — 5
10 — 9

(165)

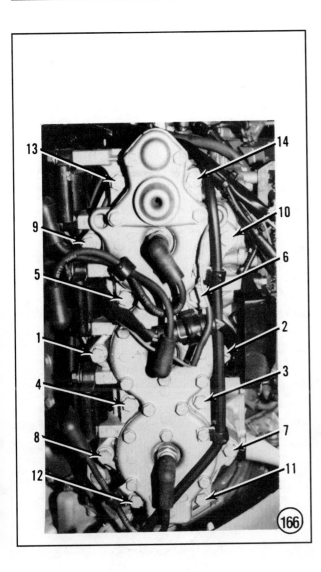

exhaust cover gasket, install the gasket, then the inner and outer exhaust covers.

14. Apply OMC Gasket Sealing Compound to both sides of the new bypass cover gaskets. Install the gaskets and bypass covers and tighten the attaching screws to 50-84 in.-lb. (5.6-9.5 N.m).

15. Install the intake manifold and leaf valve assemblies using a new gasket (without sealant).

16. Install the power head as described in this chapter.

Cylinder Block and Crankcase Cover Reassembly (V4, V6 [Except 60°], and V8 Models Loop Charged)

Replace all gaskets, seals and O-rings during reassembly. All gaskets, unless instructed otherwise, should be lightly coated on both sides with OMC Gasket Sealing Compound prior to installation. In addition, the outer diameter of all seals, unless instructed otherwise, should be coated with OMC Gasket Sealing Compound.

1. Thoroughly clean the crankcase cover and cylinder block mating surfaces with OMC Cleaning Solvent, acetone or isopropyl alcohol. Make certain the mating surfaces are absolutely free of oil, grease or other contamination. Allow the solvent to air dry.

2. Spray the crankcase cover mating surface with OMC Locquic Primer and allow to air dry.

3. Apply a continuous bead of OMC Gel Seal II sealant to the cylinder block mating surface. Run the bead to the inside of all screw holes. Make sure the bead is continuous, but avoid excess application. Keep the sealant approximately 1/4 in. (6.3 mm) from bearings and seals to prevent contamination.

4. While aligning the mounting holes and upper main bearing O-ring groove, install the crankcase cover on the cylinder block. Install the main bearing screws finger tight.

5. With the crankcase cover properly seated, install the taper pins. Firmly seat the taper pins using a suitable punch and mallet.

6. Starting with the center screws, tighten the main bearing screws, in 3 steps, to 26-30 ft.-lb. (35.3-40.7 N·m) following a circular pattern.

7. Install the crankcase cover flange screws. Tighten to 60-84 in.-lb. (6.8-9.5 N·m).

8. Apply OMC Locquic Primer to the threads of the upper and lower crankcase head screws. Allow the primer to air dry, then apply OMC Nut Lock to the screws. Install and tighten the screws to 72-96 in.-lb. (8.1-10.8 N·m).

9. Reconnect the recirculation hoses to their respective fittings (as noted during disassembly). Connect cooling hoses and securely clamp with new tie straps.

NOTE
On V8 models, the port cylinder head is equipped with one cooling hose fitting while the starboard head has 2 fittings.

10. Apply a light coat of OMC Gasket Sealing Compound to both sides of new cylinder head gasket. Install the gasket and port cylinder head with the thermostat end facing the flywheel. Tighten the fasteners to 18-20 ft.-lb. (24.4-27.1 N·m) following the sequence marked on the cylinder heads.

11. Repeat Step 10 for the starboard cylinder head.

12. Install the intake manifold(s) with new gasket(s). Do not use gasket sealant on intake manifold gaskets. On V6 and V8 models, install the upper manifold first, then the lower manifold. Tighten the manifold fasteners to 60-84 in.-lb. (6.8-9.5 N·m).

13. *V8 models*—Thoroughly clean the crankshaft and torsional damper tapers with OMC Cleaning Solvent, or equivalent. Apply OMC Gasket Sealing Compound to the threads of the damper attaching nut, then install the damper and nut. Tighten the nut to 148-152 ft.-lb. (200.7-206.1 N·m).

Cylinder Block and Crankcase Cover Reassembly (60° V6 Models)

Replace all gaskets, seals and O-rings during reassembly. All gaskets, unless instructed otherwise, should be lightly coated on both sides with OMC Gasket Sealing Compound prior to installation. In addition, the outer diameter of all seals, unless instructed otherwise, should be coated with OMC Gasket Sealing Compound.

1. Lubricate new cylinder head O-rings with OMC Triple-Guard grease. Install the O-rings into the grooves around each cylinder.

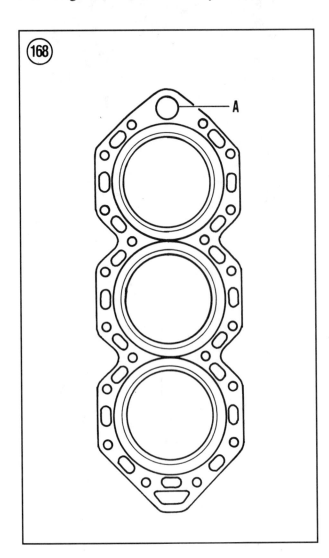

2. Apply a thin bead (1/16 in.) of RTV sealant around ALL cooling water passages in the cylinder block-to-head mating surface. Do not apply sealant around the thermostat seat area (A, **Figure 168**).

NOTE
The temperature switch installed in the port cylinder head has 2 wires; the switch in the starboard cylinder head has 1 wire.

3. Install one cylinder head and fasteners. Tighten the fasteners to 20-22 ft.-lb. (24.4-29.8 N•m) following the sequence marked on the cylinder head.

4. Repeat Steps 2 and 3 on the remaining cylinder head.

5. Position the cylinder block so the crankcase cover mating surface is facing upward.

6. Thoroughly clean the crankcase cover and cylinder block mating surfaces with OMC Cleaning Solvent, acetone or isopropyl alcohol. Make certain the mating surfaces are absolutely free of oil, grease or other contamination. Allow the solvent to air dry.

7. Spray the crankcase cover mating surface with OMC Locquic Primer and allow to air dry.

8. Apply a continuous bead of OMC Gel Seal II sealant to the cylinder block mating surface. Run the bead to the inside of all screw holes. Make sure the bead is continuous, but avoid excess application. Keep the sealant approximately 1/4 in. (6.3 mm) from bearings and seals to prevent contamination.

9. Make sure the upper seal area on the crankshaft is thoroughly clean and lubricated with engine oil. Install a new upper seal (without sealant) on the crankshaft.

10. Carefully install the crankcase cover into position on the cylinder block. Install the main bearing screws finger tight. Make sure the 2 shorter screws are installed on the bottom of the cover.

11. Make sure the crankcase cover is fully seated, then install the taper pin. Firmly seat the taper pin using a suitable punch and mallet.

12. After seating the taper pin, tighten the main bearing screws, in 3 steps, to 26-30 ft.-lb. (35.2-40.7 N•m). Tighten the center screws first, then work outward in a circular pattern.

13. If removed, attach the lower drain fitting.

14. Install and tighten the crankcase cover flange screws to 60-84 in.-lb. (6.8-9.5 N•m).

15. Connect the recirculation hoses to their respective fittings, as noted during disassembly.

16. Install the power head as described in this chapter.

LEAF VALVES

Leaf (reed) valves control the passage of air-fuel mixture into the crankcase by opening and closing as crankcase pressure changes. When crankcase pressure is high, the leaf valves maintain contact with their seats. As crankcase pressure drops on the compression stroke, the leaf valves move away from their seats and allow the air-fuel mixture to enter the crankcase. Leaf valve travel is limited by the leaf valve stop opening.

The leaf valve assembly on 1-cylinder models (2.0, 2.3 and 3.3 hp) is located inside the crankcase cover.

On all other models, the leaf valves are affixed to a leaf plate or block located between the intake manifold and the crankcase cover. See **Figure 169** (3-8 hp, typical), **Figure 170** (20-30 hp, typical) and **Figure 171** (typical, all other models).

The leaf valve should be centered over the leaf valve opening and seat lightly against the leaf plate or block throughout its entire length, with the least possible tension. The leaf valve should be smooth, flat and completely free of nicks, cracks or other damage.

Do not disassemble leaf valve assemblies unless replacement is necessary. Do not bend or

8

flex the leaf valves if they are distorted or do not make contact with their seats as designed. Never attempt to straighten or repair a bent or damaged leaf valve. Never turn a used leaf valve over for reuse.

The leaf valves should be inspected anytime the intake manifold is removed. Check the leaf plate or block for excessive gum, varnish and broken, chipped or distorted leaves. The seating area of the leaf plate or block should be smooth and flat.

Chipped, cracked or broken leaf valves will generally cause the motor to run roughly, pop or backfire through the carburetor, stall during acceleration and lose wide-open throttle speed. If a defective leaf valve is suspected, operate the motor while holding a piece of stiff paper or cardboard close to the carburetor inlet(s). If the paper quickly becomes wet with fuel, a defective leaf valve is likely.

> *CAUTION*
> *If a leaf valve breaks during operation, the broken piece will be ingested by the power head and can result in serious power head damage. If a broken leaf valve is noted during inspection, the broken piece must be located and removed before returning the unit to service. If necessary, disassemble the power head to locate the broken leaf valve.*

Removal/Installation (2.0, 2.3 and 3.3 hp)

The leaf valve assembly is located inside the crankcase cover on these models. Remove the crankcase cover as described in this chapter to access the leaf valve assembly. Refer to *Cylinder Block and Crankcase Cover Reassembly (2.0, 2.3 and 3.3 hp)* in this chapter for reassembly.

Removal/Installation (4 Deluxe, 3-8 hp)

1. Remove the carburetor. See Chapter Six.

2. Remove the 4 screws securing the intake manifold to the crankcase cover.

3. Separate the intake manifold and leaf valve plate from the crankcase cover.

4. Remove and discard the intake manifold and leaf plate gaskets.

5. To install the leaf valve assembly, reverse disassembly procedure. Use new gaskets (without sealant) on both sides of the leaf plate. Tighten the intake manifold screws to 60-84 in.-lb. (6.8-9.5 N•m).

Removal/Installation (9.9 and 15 hp)

1. Remove the power head as described in this chapter. Remove the carburetor as described in Chapter Six.

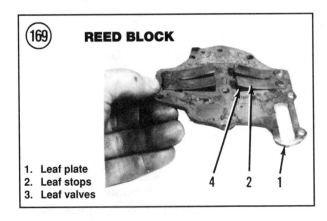

(169) **REED BLOCK**

1. Leaf plate
2. Leaf stops
3. Leaf valves

4   2   1

(170)

2. Remove the 6 screws attaching the intake manifold to the crankcase cover.

3. Remove the intake manifold and leaf plate from the crankcase cover.

4. Remove and discard the manifold and leaf plate gaskets.

5. To install, place new gaskets (without sealant) on each side of the leaf plate.

6. Install the intake manifold and attaching screws. Tighten the screws to 60-80 in.-lb. (6.8-9.0 N·m).

7. Complete the remaining installation by reversing the removal procedure. Perform linkage adjustment and synchronization as described in Chapter Five.

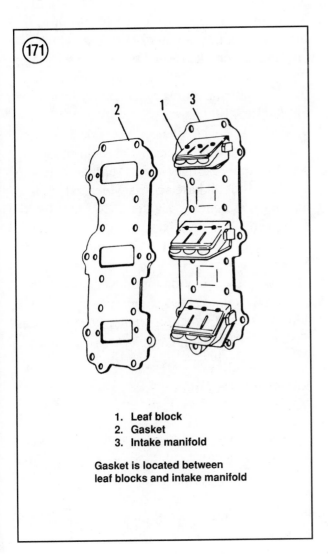

1. Leaf block
2. Gasket
3. Intake manifold

Gasket is located between leaf blocks and intake manifold

Removal/Installation (20-30 hp)

1. Remove the carburetor (Chapter Six).

2. Disconnect the throttle shaft from the vertical shaft.

3. Disconnect the oil recirculation hose from the intake manifold fitting.

4. Remove the intake manifold from the power head.

5. Remove the Phillips-head screw securing the leaf plate to the power head. See **Figure 170**. Remove the leaf plate.

6. Remove and discard the intake manifold and leaf plate gaskets.

7. To install, place a new leaf plate gasket (without sealant) on the power head, then install the leaf plate.

8. Apply OMC Gel Seal II to the threads of the leaf plate attaching screw (Phillips head). Loosely install the screw, align the leaf plate and gasket with the crankcase cover and tighten the Phillips screw securely.

9. Install the intake manifold using a new gasket (without sealant). Complete the remaining installation by reversing the removal procedure. Perform linkage adjustment and synchronization as described in Chapter Five.

Removal/Installation (35 Jet, 40-70 hp)

1. Remove the carburetors (Chapter Six).

2. Remove the intake manifold as described in this chapter.

3. Remove the leaf plate assembly.

4. Remove and discard the intake manifold and leaf plate gaskets.

5. To install, place a new plate gasket (without sealant) on the power head and install the leaf plate.

6. Install the intake manifold using a new gasket (without sealant).

8

7. Tighten the intake manifold screws to 60-84 in.-lb. (6.8-9.5 N.m).

8. Complete the remaining installation by reversing the removal procedure. Perform linkage adjustment and synchronization procedures as described in Chapter Five.

Removal/Installation
(V4 and V6 Cross Flow Models)

1. Remove the carburetors (Chapter Five).

2. Remove the fuel primer solenoid on V6 models.

3. Disconnect the throttle linkage.

4. Disconnect the recirculation hoses, while noting their location for reference during reassembly.

5. Remove the screws attaching the intake manifold to the power head. Remove the intake manifold and leaf plate assembly. Remove and discard the gaskets.

6. To install, place the leaf plate and intake manifold on the power head using new gaskets (without sealant).

7. Tighten the intake manifold screws to 60-84 in.-lb. (6.8-9.5 N.m).

8. Connect the recirculation hoses to their correct fittings as noted during disassembly. Securely clamp the hoses using new tie straps.

9. Complete the remaining installation by reversing the removal procedure. Perform linkage adjustment and synchronization procedures as described in Chapter Five.

Removal/Installation
(V4, V6 [Except 60°] and V8 Loop Charged Models)

1. Remove the carburetors and throttle valve assemblies (Chapter Six). It is not necessary to disconnect the throttle shaft links; remove the carburetors as an assembly.

2. Disconnect the fuel manifolds and remove the fuel system.

3. Disconnect the fuel primer solenoid purple/white wire. Remove the air silencer base screws, then remove the base.

4. Remove the intake manifold mounting screws and remove the manifolds. On V6 and V8 models, the lower manifold must be removed first.

5. If removing the upper manifold, remove the throttle cam nut and washer, then remove the cam.

6. To install, place new intake manifold gaskets (without sealant) on the power head.

7. On V6 and V8 models, the upper intake manifold must be installed first. Install the throttle cam, washer and nut on the manifold. Install the lower manifold.

8. Apply Permatex No. 2 gasket sealant to the threads of all intake manifold screws which extend into the crankcase cavity. Tighten the intake manifold screws to 60-84 in.-lb. (6.8-9.5 N.m), then tighten the throttle cam nut to 144-168 in.-lb. (16.3-19.0 N.m).

9. Install a new air silencer base gasket without sealant. Install the silencer base and mounting screws. Apply Permatex No. 2 gasket sealant to the threads of all base screws which extend into the crankcase cavity. Tighten the screws to 96-120 in.-lb. (10.8-13.5 N.m).

10. Install the carburetor assemblies (Chapter Six).

11. Complete the remaining installation by reversing the removal procedure. Perform linkage adjustment and synchronization procedures as described in Chapter Five.

Removal/Installation
(60° V6 Models)

1. Remove the carburetors (Chapter Six).

2. Remove the 2 clips holding the balance tube to the crankcase cover flange. Pull the balance tube from the intake manifold.

3. Remove the intake manifold mounting screws.

4. Remove the 2 screws securing the upper throttle shaft retainer to the starboard intake manifold. Remove the retainer.

5. Remove the intake manifolds from the crankcase cover.

NOTE
Do not disassemble the leaf valves. The leaf valve assemblies are not serviceable on 60° V6 models. The leaf valves must be replaced as assemblies.

6. To install, place new gaskets (without sealant) on the intake manifolds.

7. Install the intake manifolds on the power head. On the starboard manifold, install the upper throttle shaft and retainer. Tighten the retainer screws securely.

8. Install the intake manifold screws. Starting with the center screws, tighten the screws in 3 steps to 40-50 in.-lb. (4.5-5.6 N•m). Complete the remaining installation by reversing the removal procedure. Perform linkage adjustment

and synchronization procedures as described in Chapter Five.

**Cleaning and Inspection
(All Models)**

1. Check all leaf plate screws for looseness. Remove any loose screws and apply OMC Screw Lock to the threads, then reinstall and tighten to specification. See *Leaf Valve or Stop Replacement* in this chapter.

2. Check leaf valves for chips, cracks, breakage, distortion or other damage. Defective leaf valves must be replaced. Never attempt to straighten or repair a damaged leaf.

3. Check leaf valve stops for looseness, distortion or other damage and replace as necessary.

4. If so equipped, check the recirculation check valve and screen for excessive carbon or other damage. The check valve must be intact and free to move inside its housing. Clean or replace the check valve as necessary.

5. Using a suitable straight edge and feeler gauge, check the leaf plate and intake manifold for flatness. The leaf plate must be flat to within 0.003 in. (0.08 mm). The intake manifold must be flat to within 0.004 in. (0.10 mm).

6. Thoroughly clean the leaf valve assembly before reinstallation.

**Leaf Valve or Leaf Stop Replacement
(4 Deluxe, 3-15 hp Models)**

1. Remove the leaf valve plate as described in this chapter.

2. Remove the screws securing the leaf valves and stops to the plate. See **Figure 172** (typical, 4 Deluxe, 3-8 hp) or **Figure 173** (9.9-15 hp). Separate the leaf stops, valves and shims (if so equipped) from the plate. Keep all components separate for reference during reassembly.

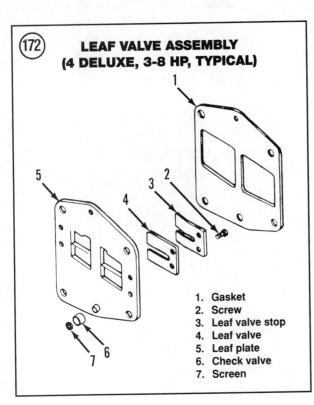

**(172) LEAF VALVE ASSEMBLY
(4 DELUXE, 3-8 HP, TYPICAL)**

1. Gasket
2. Screw
3. Leaf valve stop
4. Leaf valve
5. Leaf plate
6. Check valve
7. Screen

8

CAUTION
*Do not turn **used** leaf valves over for reuse.*

3. Place new leaf valves on the leaf plate. If the valves do not seat properly, turn the leaf valve over. If the leaf valve still does not seal properly, it should be replaced.

NOTE
It is acceptable for a leaf valve to stand open slightly if it can be closed with light pressure. If light pressure will not close the valve, inspect the seat area for burrs or high spots.

4. Apply OMC Screw Lock to the threads of the leaf valve mounting screws. Install the leaf valve, leaf stop and shim (if so equipped). Make sure the leaf valves are centered over the openings, then install and tighten the leaf valve mounting screws to 25-35 in.-lb. (3-4 N•m).

Leaf Valve or Leaf Valve Stop Replacement (20-30 hp)

Refer to **Figure 174** for this procedure.

1. Remove the leaf stop and valve assembly attaching screws.

2. Separate the leaf valves and stops from the leaf valve plate.

3. If reusing any components, arrange them for installation in their original locations.

4. Place the leaf valves on the plate.

5A. *Used leaf valve*—If the leaf valves do not seat properly on the plate, replace the valve assembly.

5B. *New leaf valve*—If the leaf valves do not seat properly on the plate, turn the valve over and recheck. If the valve still does not seat properly, replace the leaf valve assembly.

NOTE
It is acceptable for a leaf valve to stand open slightly if it can be closed with light pressure. If light pressure will not close

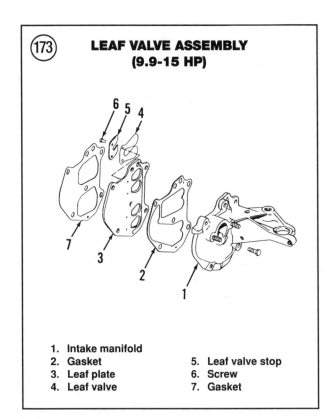

LEAF VALVE ASSEMBLY (9.9-15 HP)

1. Intake manifold
2. Gasket
3. Leaf plate
4. Leaf valve
5. Leaf valve stop
6. Screw
7. Gasket

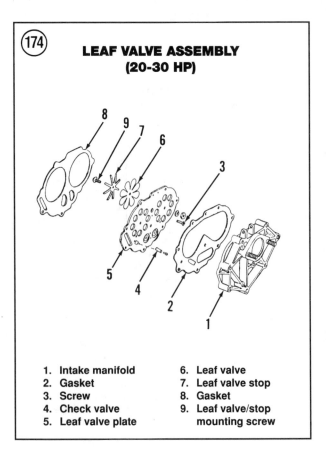

LEAF VALVE ASSEMBLY (20-30 HP)

1. Intake manifold
2. Gasket
3. Screw
4. Check valve
5. Leaf valve plate
6. Leaf valve
7. Leaf valve stop
8. Gasket
9. Leaf valve/stop mounting screw

the valve, inspect the seat area for burrs or high spots, or replace the valve.

6. While viewing the leaf plate from the leaf stop side, place the leaf valves on the plate so the alignment notches in the center of the valves are positioned as follows (**Figure 175**):

a. *Port side valve*—Alignment notch should face the 1 o'clock position.

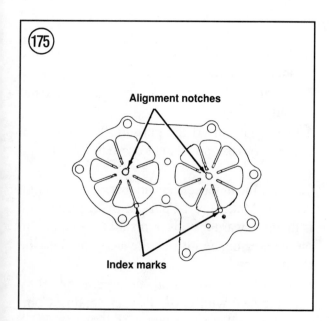

175

Alignment notches

Index marks

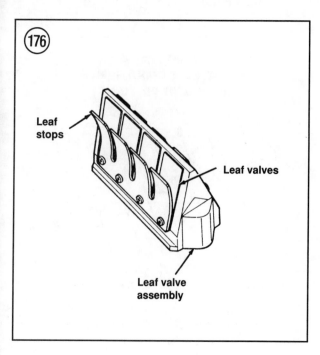

176

Leaf stops

Leaf valves

Leaf valve assembly

b. *Starboard side valve*—Alignment notch should face the 11 o'clock position.

7. Center the leaf valves on the plate according to the index marks (**Figure 175**), then install the leaf valve stops and mounting screws.

8. Center the leaf valve stops and tighten the mounting screws to 25-35 in.-lb. (3-4 N.m).

Leaf Valve or Leaf Stop Replacement (35 Jet, 40-70 hp, V4, V6 and V8 Models)

NOTE
Individual leaf valve components are not available on V4, V6 and V8 loop charged models. Replace the leaf valves as an assembly. On all other models, check component availability before disassembling the leaf valve assemblies. Individual components are not available on all models.

All models are equipped with one leaf valve assembly for each cylinder. The leaf valves are affixed to a leaf block assembly which is fastened directly to the intake manifold. See **Figure 171**, typical.

1. Remove the intake manifold(s) and leaf valve assemblies as described in this chapter.

2. Remove the 2 screws securing each leaf valve assembly to be removed. Separate the leaf valve assembly from the intake manifold. See **Figure 176**.

3. Remove the screws securing the leaf stops and valves to the leaf block (plate). Separate the valves and stops from the block. Keep all valves, stops, shims and screws together for installation in their original locations.

4. Place the leaf valves on the leaf block.

5A. *Used leaf valve*—If the leaf valves do not seat properly on the plate, replace the valve assembly.

5B. *New leaf valve*—If the leaf valves do not seat properly on the plate, turn the valve over and recheck. If the valve still does not seat properly, replace the leaf valve assembly.

8

NOTE
It is acceptable for a leaf valve to stand open slightly if it can be closed with light pressure. If light pressure will not close the valve, inspect the seat area for burrs or high spots, or replace the valve.

6. Apply OMC Locquic Primer to the threads of the leaf valve attaching screws and allow to air dry. Then, apply OMC Screw Lock to the screws.

7. Install the leaf valves, shims (if so equipped) and stops. Install 2 mounting screws loosely, near the center of the valves. Center the leaf valves over the openings in the seats, then install the remaining mounting screws. Check to be sure the valves are still centered, and if so, tighten all mounting screws to 25-35 in.-lb. (3-4 N.m).

8. Apply OMC Locquic Primer, then Screw Lock to the threads of the leaf valve assembly-to-intake manifold screws. Install the leaf valve assemblies to the manifold using new gaskets (without sealant) and tighten the screws to 25-35 in.-lb. (3-4 N.m).

THERMOSTAT

On 2- and 3-cylinder models (6 hp and larger, except 20-30 hp), the thermostat is located in the cylinder head, under the thermostat cover. On 20-30 hp models, the thermostat is located in the cylinder head, under the cylinder head cover. On cross flow V4 models, the thermostats and pressure valves are installed in the exhaust housing adapter. On cross flow V6 models, a thermostat and pressure valve is installed in each cylinder head. On loop charged V4, V6 and V8 models, a single unit thermostat and pressure valve is installed in each cylinder head. A temperature switch in each cylinder head is connected to a warning horn in the remote control assembly. Should engine cooling water temperature exceed the temperature switch rating, the warning horn will sound to alert the operator. The thermostats and pressure valves should be serviced whenever

the power head is removed or if engine overheating or overcooling is indicated.

Removal/Installation
(6-15 hp, 60 and 70 hp)

Refer to **Figure 177** for this procedure.

1. Remove the screws securing the thermostat cover. Remove the cover and spring. Remove the cover seal and discard.

2. Remove the thermostat, along with the washer, cup and diaphragm.

3. Remove the inner spring and thermostat housing.

4. To install, insert the pin into the thermostat with its convex end facing toward the thermostat cover.

5. Place the inner spring and thermostat into the housing. Make sure the pin side of the thermostat is facing toward the cover. Install the diaphragm on the housing and install the assembly into the cylinder head.

6. Install a new cover seal into the cover. Lightly coat the seal with OMC Gasket Sealing Compound. Install the relief spring into the cover.

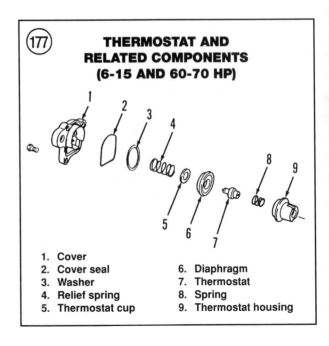

THERMOSTAT AND RELATED COMPONENTS (6-15 AND 60-70 HP)

1. Cover
2. Cover seal
3. Washer
4. Relief spring
5. Thermostat cup
6. Diaphragm
7. Thermostat
8. Spring
9. Thermostat housing

7. Install the cover and spring. Tighten the cover screws to 60-84 in.-lb. (6.8-9.5 N·m).

Removal/Installation
(35 Jet, 40-50 hp)

Refer to **Figure 178** for this procedure.

1. Unscrew the thermostat cover using an appropriate size wrench. Remove and discard the cover O-ring.

2. Remove the spring and thermostat from the cylinder head.

3. Inspect the thermostat seat inside the cylinder head. Remove the seat and replace if necessary.

4. To install, insert the thermostat seat (if removed) into the cylinder head.

5. Install the thermostat and spring into the head.

6. Place a new O-ring on the cover. Apply OMC Gasket Sealing Compound to the O-ring, install the cover and tighten securely.

7. Start and run the outboard in a test tank or in the water to check for leakage and proper operation.

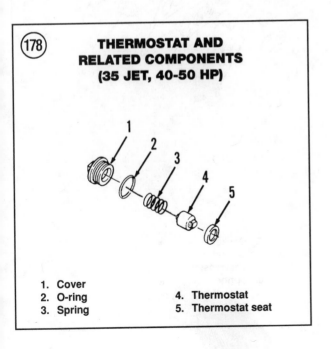

THERMOSTAT AND RELATED COMPONENTS (35 JET, 40-50 HP)

1. Cover
2. O-ring
3. Spring
4. Thermostat
5. Thermostat seat

Removal/Installation
(20-30 hp)

Remove and install the cylinder head cover, thermostat and related components as described under *Power Head Disassembly and Reassembly* in this chapter.

Cleaning and Inspection
(2- and 3-Cylinder Models)

1. Wash the thermostat and related components in clean water.

2. Test the thermostat if suspected of malfunctioning. See Chapter Three.

3. Check the thermostat, spring(s) and related components for corrosion or other damage and replace as required.

Removal/Installation
(V4 Cross Flow Models)

Refer to **Figure 179** for this procedure.

1. Remove the thermostat cover screws.

2. Tap the cover with a soft-face mallet to break the gasket seal, then remove the cover.

3. Remove the gaskets, thermostats, grommets, springs and pressure valves. Discard the gaskets and grommets.

4. Clean all gasket material from the exhaust housing adapter, valve body and thermostat cover mating surfaces.

5. Coat both sides of a new valve body-to-adapter gasket with OMC Gasket Sealing Compound. Install the gasket to the adapter.

6. Install the 2 relief valve springs.

7. Coat both sides of a new valve body-to-cover gasket with OMC Gasket Sealing Compound. Install the gasket on the thermostat cover.

8. Install the thermostats in the valve body. Install new gaskets on the thermostats.

9. Install the thermostat cover to the valve body.

8

10. Align the relief valves in the valve body with the springs in the adapter. Install the valve body and cover to the adapter.

11. Install the cover screws and tighten to 60-80 in.-lb. (6.8-9.0 N·m).

12. Start and run the outboard in a test tank or in the water to check for leakage and proper operation.

Removal/Installation (V6 Cross Flow Models)

Refer to **Figure 180** for this procedure.

1. Remove the 4 screws holding the thermostat housing to its cylinder head. (**Figure 181**).

2. Top the cover with a soft-face mallet to break the gasket seal, then remove the cover.

3. Remove the gasket, thermostat, O-ring, spring and pressure valve. Discard the gasket and O-ring.

4. Check the grommet under the cylinder head cover. If deteriorated, remove the cylinder head cover and gasket. Discard the grommet and gasket. Install a new grommet into the cylinder head and reinstall the cover with a new gasket.

5. Clean all gasket material and sealant from the thermostat cover and cylinder head cover mating surfaces.

6. Install the thermostat and pressure valve in the cylinder head with new O-rings.

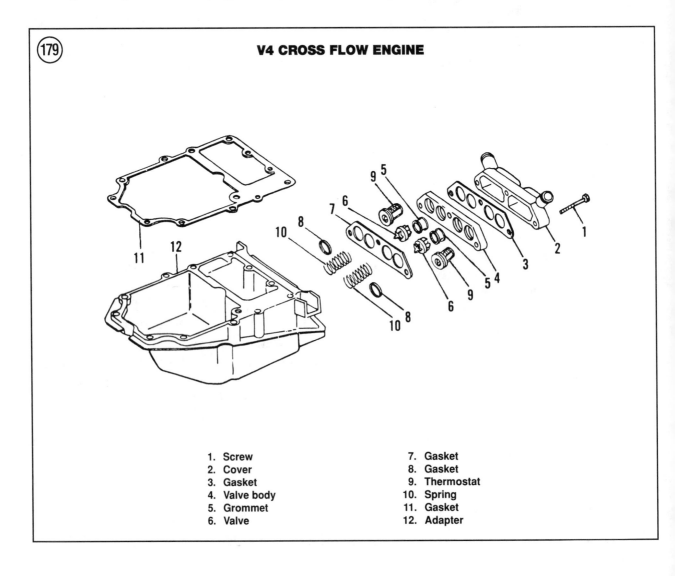

(179) **V4 CROSS FLOW ENGINE**

1. Screw	7. Gasket
2. Cover	8. Gasket
3. Gasket	9. Thermostat
4. Valve body	10. Spring
5. Grommet	11. Gasket
6. Valve	12. Adapter

7. Coat both sides of a new thermostat cover gasket with OMC Gasket Sealing Compound and install the gasket on the cover.

8. Fit the spring in the thermostat cover and install the cover on the cylinder head. Tighten the screws to 60-84 in.-lb. (6.8-9.5 N·m).

9. Start and run the outboard in a test tank or on the water to check for leakage and proper operation.

Cleaning and Inspection (All Cross Flow Models)

1. Remove the thermostat (A, **Figure 182**) as described in this chapter.

2. Discard the gasket or seal (B, **Figure 182**).

3. Thoroughly wash the thermostat in clean water.

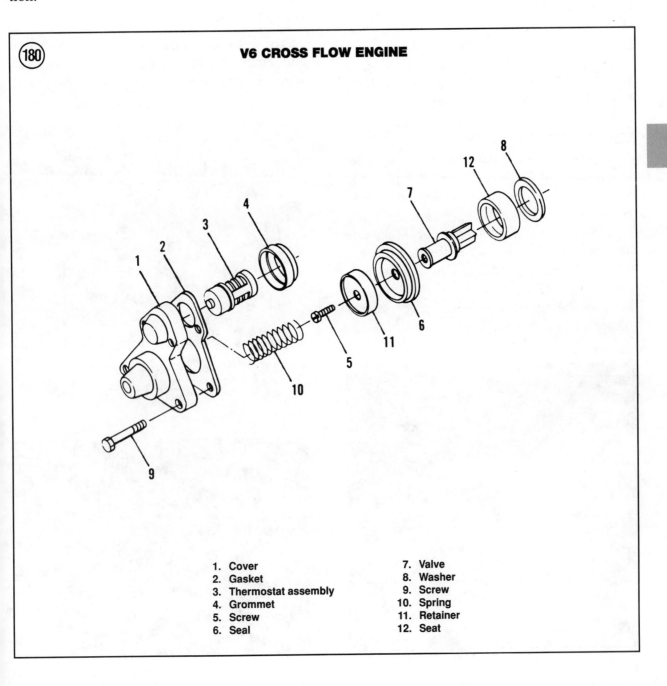

(180) **V6 CROSS FLOW ENGINE**

8

1. Cover	7. Valve
2. Gasket	8. Washer
3. Thermostat assembly	9. Screw
4. Grommet	10. Spring
5. Screw	11. Retainer
6. Seal	12. Seat

4. Test the thermostat if suspected of malfunctioning. See Chapter Three.

5. Check the thermostat spring (C, **Figure 182**) for loss of tension, distortion or corrosion. Replace the spring as necessary.

Removal/Installation
(V4, V6 [Except 60°] and V8 Loop Charged Models)

1. Remove the 4 screws holding the thermostat cover to its cylinder head (**Figure 183**).

2. Tap the cover with a soft-face mallet to break the cover loose, then remove the cover with the diaphragm and thermostat assembly.

3. Separate the cover from the diaphragm and thermostat assembly from the diaphragm.

4. Inspect the thermostat seal in the cylinder head passage. If the seal is damaged, replace the cup and seal. The lip on the cup must face toward the thermostat assembly.

5. Inspect the diaphragm for damage. Make sure the vent hole is not restricted. Replace the diaphragm if damage is noted or if the diaphragm's resilience is no longer present.

6. Clean the cylinder head and cover sealing surfaces.

7. Install the thermostat assembly in the diaphragm. Position the diaphragm and thermostat assembly on the cylinder head. Install the cover and tighten the retaining screws to 60-84 in.-lb. (6.8-9.5 N·m).

8. Start and run the outboard in a test tank or on the water to check for leakage and proper operation.

Removal/Installation
(60° V6 Models)

1. Using an appropriate size wrench, unscrew and remove the thermostat cover (**Figure 184**). Remove and discard the O-ring from the cover.

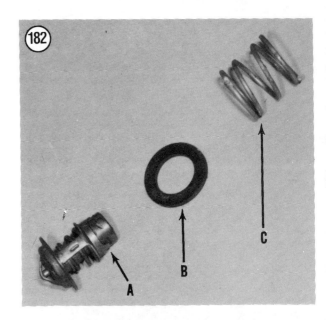

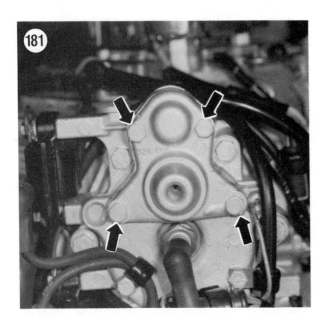

2. Remove the thermostat assembly and spring.

3. Inspect the thermostat seal inside the cylinder head. If the seal is damaged, replace the seal.

4. To install, insert the spring and thermostat assembly into the cylinder head.

5. Place a new O-ring on the thermostat cover. Apply a thin coat of OMC Gasket Sealing Compound to the O-ring.

6. Install the cover and tighten to 120-144 in.-lb. (10.8-16.3 N·m).

Cleaning and Inspection
(V4, V6 and V8 Loop Charged Models)

NOTE
The pressure relief valve is contained within the thermostat assembly.

1. Remove the thermostat assembly as described in this chapter.

2. Unscrew the 2 thermostat halves and remove the vernatherm and spring.

3. Inspect the thermostat housing for physical or heat damage. Replace the complete thermostat assembly if damage is noted.

4. Inspect the vernatherm and spring for corrosion, pitting or heat damage. Replace components if damage is noted.

5. Install the vernatherm and spring between the thermostat halves. Make sure the rounded end of the vernatherm pin protrudes from the end facing the thermostat cover.

6. Screw the 2 thermostat halves together, making sure the vernatherm and spring properly seat within the housings.

8

Table 1 GENERAL ENGINE SPECIFICATIONS

Model	Displacement cu. in. (cc)	Type
2, 2.3, 3.3	4.47 (77.8)	1-cylinder loop charged
3, 4, 4 Deluxe	5.29 (86.4)	2-cylinder cross flow
6, 8	10.0 (164)	2-cylinder cross flow
9.9, 15		
1991-92	13.2 (216)	2-cylinder cross flow
1993	15.6 (255)	2-cylinder cross flow
20, 25, 28, 30	31.8 (521.2)	2-cylinder cross flow
35 Jet, 40, 48, 50	44.99 (737.4)	2-cylinder loop charged
60, 70	56.1 (920)	3-cylinder loop charged
65 Jet, 80 Jet, 85, 88, 90,		
115, 115	99.6 (1632)	90° V4 cross flow
120, 140	122 (2000)	90° V4 loop charged
105 Jet, 150*	149.4 (2448)	90° V6 cross flow
60° 150/175 hp	158 (2589)	60° V6 loop charged

(continued)

Table 1 GENERAL ENGINE SPECIFICATIONS (continued)

Model	Displacement cu. in. (cc)	Type
175*	160.3 (2626)	90° V6 cross flow
200, 225	183 (3000)	90° V6 loop charged
250, 300	244 (4000)	90° V8 loop charged
1.6 Sea Drive	99.6 (1632)	90° V4 cross flow
2.0 Sea Drive	122 (2000)	90° V4 loop charged
3.0 Sea Drive	183 (3000)	90° V6 loop charged
4.0 Sea Drive	244 (4000)	90° V6 loop charged

* The 90° V6 cross flow power head was discontinued after the 1991 model year. The 105 Jet, 150 and 175 hp models for 1992-on are 60° loop charged engines.

Table 2 POWER HEAD TIGHTENING TORQUES

Fastener	2-30 HP in.-lb.	ft.-lb.	N·m
Bypass cover screws			
9.9-30 hp	60-84		6.8-9.5
Connecting rod screws			
3-15 hp	60-70		6.8-7.9
20-30 hp		30-32	40.7-43.4
Crankcase head screws	60-84		6.8-9.5
Cylinder head screws			
4 Deluxe, 2, 2.3, 3.3, 4 hp	60-84		6.8-9.5
6, 8 hp	144-168		16.3-19.0
9.9-30 hp	216-240	18-20	24.4-27.1
Cylinder head cover screws			
9.9-30 hp	60-84		6.8-9.5
Exhaust cover screws			
4 Deluxe, 3-8 hp	60-84		6.8-9.5
9.9, 15 hp	95-130		10.7-14.7
Flywheel			
2, 2.3, 3.3 hp		29-33	39.3-44.7
4 Deluxe, 3, 4 hp		30-40	40.7-54.2
6, 8 hp		40-50	54.2-67.8
9.9, 15 hp		45-50	61.0-67.8
20-30 hp		100-105	136-142
Inner exhaust tube screws			
4 Deluxe, 3-15 hp	60-84		6.8-9.5
20-30 hp	96-120		10.8-13.5
Intake manifold screws/nuts	60-84		6.8-9.5
Main bearing screws			
2, 2.3, 3.3 hp	96-120		10.8-13.5
4 Deluxe, 3-8 hp	60-84		6.8-9.5
9.9, 15 hp	144-168	12-14	16.3-19.0
20-30 hp	168-192	14-16	19.0-21.7
Power head mounting fasteners			
2-15 hp	60-84		6.8-9.5
20-30	192-216	16-18	21.7-24.4

(continued)

Table 2 POWER HEAD TIGHTENING TORQUES (continued)

Fastener	in.-lb.	ft.-lb.	N·m
35 JET, 40-70 HP			
Adapter-to-power head screws			
60, 70 hp		60-84	6.8-9.5
Connecting rod screws		30-32	41-43
Crankcase flange screws	60-84		6.8-9.5
Crankcase head screws	60-84		6.8-9.5
Cylinder head screws	216-240	18-20	24.4-27.1
Cylinder head cover screws	60-84		6.8-9.5
Exhaust cover screws	60-84		6.8-9.5
Exhaust housing screws			
60, 70 hp	216-240	18-20	24.4-27.1
Flywheel nut		100-105	136-142
Intake manifold screws	60-84		6.8-9.5
Main bearing screws	216-240	18-20	24.4-27.1
Power head mounting screws			
35 Jet, 40-50 hp	216-240	18-20	24.4-27.1
Spark plug	216-240	18-20	24.4-27.1
V4 AND V6 CROSS FLOW MODELS			
Bypass cover screws	60-84		6.8-9.5
Bearing retainer plate screws	96-120		10.8-13.5
Connecting rod screws		30-32	40.7-43.4
Crankcase head screws (upper & lower)	96-120		10.8-13.5
Cylinder head screws			
V4 & 150 hp		18-20	24.4-27.1
175 hp		20-22	24.4-29.8
Cylinder head cover screws	60-84		6.8-9.5
Exhaust adapter-to-power head screws/nuts	144-168	12-14	16.3-19.0
Exhaust cover screws	60-84		6.8-9.5
Exhaust housing-to-power head screws		16-18	21.7-24.4
Flywheel nut			
V4		100-105	136-140
V6		140-145	190-196
Intake manifold screws	60-84		6.8-9.5
Main bearing screws		18-20	24.4-27.1
V4, V6 [EXCEPT 60°] AND V8 LOOP CHARGED MODELS			
Air silencer base screws	96-120		10.8-13.5
Connecting rod screws		42-44	57-59
Crankcase cover flange screws	60-84		6.8-9.5
Cylinder head screws	240-264	20-22	27.1-29.8
Crankcase head screws (upper & lower)	72-96		8.1-10,8
Damper nut			
V8		148-152	200-206

(continued)

8

Table 2 POWER HEAD TIGHTENING TORQUES (continued)

Fastener	in.-lb.	ft.-lb.	N·m
V4, V6 [EXCEPT 60°] AND V8 LOOP CHARGED MODELS (continued)			
Flywheel nut		140-150	190-203
Lower bearing retainer plate screws	96-120		10.8-13.5
Main bearing screws		26-30	35.3-40.7
Power head mounting screws	144-168	12-14	16.3-19.0
Power pack mounting screws	48-60		5.4-6.8
Power steering pulley screws	60-84		6.8-9.5
Recirculation valve	78-85		8-9
Regulator/rectifier screws	60-84		6.8-9.5
Spark plug	216-240	18-20	24.4-27.1
Stator mounting screws	120-144	10-12	13.5-16.3
Timer base screws	25-35		2.8-3.9

Fastener	in.-lb.	ft.-lb.	N·m
60° V6 MODELS			
Connecting rod screws		30-32	40.7-43.4
Crankcase cover flange screws	40-50		4.5-5.6
Cylinder block-to-exhaust housing screws (small)	60-84		6.8-9.5
Cylinder head screws		20-22	27.1-29.8
Flywheel screws		23-25	31.2-33.9
Flywheel cover screws	40-50		4.5-5.6
Exhaust housing-to-cylinder block screws (large)		18-20	24.4-27.1
Main bearing screws	40-50		4.5-5.6
Steering arm-to-upper mount screws		65-70	88.1-95.0
Timing wheel screw	120-140		13.5-15.8

Fastener	in.-lb.	ft.-lb.	N·m
STANDARD FASTENERS			
No. 6	7-10		0.8-1.1
No. 8	15-22		1.7-2.5
No. 10	25-35		2.8-3.9
No. 12	35-45		3.9-5.1
1/4 in.	60-80		6.8-9.0
5/16 in.	120-140	10-12	13.6-15.8
3/8 in.	220-240	18-20	24.4-27.1
7/16 in.		28-30	38-41

Table 3 POWER HEAD SPECIFICATIONS

2.0, 2.3 & 3.3 HP	
Cylinders	1
Standard bore size	1.8890-1.8906 in. (47.981-48.021 mm)
Stroke	1.6929 in. (43mm)
Displacement	4.75 cu. in. (77.8 cc)

(continued)

Table 3 POWER HEAD SPECIFICATIONS (continued)

2.0, 2.3 & 3.3 HP (continued)	
Crankshaft journal diameter	
Top	0.7875-0.7878 in. (20.002-20.010 mm)
Bottom	0.5906-0.5910 in. (15.001-15.011 mm)
Crankpin	0.6299-0.6301 in. (16.00-16.005 mm)
Maximum crankshaft runout	0.001 in. (0.025 mm)
Standard piston diameter	1.8868-1.8873 in. (47.925-47.937 mm)
Piston ring end gap	0.0059-0.0138 in. (0.150-0.350 mm)
Piston ring side clearance	0.0026 in. max. (0.152 mm)

4 DELUXE, 3 AND 4 HP	
Cylinders	2
Standard bore size	1.5643-1.5650 in. (39.733-39.751 mm)
Stroke	1.374 in. (34.9 mm)
Displacement	5.28 cu. in. (87.0 cc)
Crankshaft journal diameter	
Top	0.7515-0.7520 in. (19.08-19.10 mm)
Center	0.6685-0.6690 in. (16.980-16.993 mm)
Bottom	0.6691-0.6695 in. (16.995-17.00 mm)
Crankpin	0.6695-0.6700 in. (17.005-17.018 mm)
Standard piston diameter	1.5625-1.5631 in. (39.687-39.703 mm)
Piston ring end gap	0.005-0.015 in. (0.13-0.38 mm)
Piston ring side clearance	0.004 in. max. (0.10 mm)

6 AND 8 HP	
Cylinders	2
Standard bore	1.9373-1.9380 in. (49.207-49.225 mm)
Stroke	1.700 in. (43.18 mm)
Displacement	10.0 cu. in. (164 cc)
Crankshaft journal diameter	
Top	0.8762-0.8767 in. (22.225-22.268 mm)
Center	0.8127-0.8132 in. (20.643-20.655 mm)
Bottom	0.6691-0.6700 in. (16.995-17.018 mm)
Crankpin	0.6695-0.6700 in. (17.005-17.018 mm)
Standard piston diameter	1.9345-1.9355 in. (49.136-49.162 mm)
Piston ring end gap	0.005-0.015 in. (0.13-0.38 mm)
Piston ring side clearance	0.004 in. max. (0.10 mm)

9.9 AND 15 HP	
Cylinders	2
Standard bore	
1991 & 1992	2.1875-2.1883 in. (55.562-55.583 mm)
1993	2.3745-2.3750 in. (60.312-60.325 mm)
Stroke	1.760 in. (44.70 mm)
Displacement	
1991 & 1992	13.2 cu. in. (216 cc)
1993	15.6 cu. in. (255 cc)
Crankshaft journal diameter	
Top	0.8757-0.8762 in. (22.243-22.255 mm)
Center	0.8120-0.8125 in. (20.625-20.637 mm)
Bottom	0.7870-0.7874 in. (19.990-20.00 mm)
Crankpin	0.8120-0.8125 in. (20.625-20.637 mm)

(continued)

8

Table 3 POWER HEAD SPECIFICATIONS (continued)

9.9 AND 15 HP (continued)	
Piston ring end gap	0.005-0.015 in. (0.13-0.38 mm)
Piston ring side clearance	
Bottom ring	0.004 in. max. (0.10 mm)

20-30 HP	
Cylinders	2
Standard bore	2.9995-3.0005 in. (76.187-76.213 mm)
Stroke	2.250 in. (57.15 mm)
Displacement	31.8 cu. in. (521 cc)
Crankshaft journal diameter	
Top	1.2510-1.2515 in. (31.775-31.788 mm)
Center	1.1833-1.1838 in. (30.056-30.068 mm)
Bottom	0.9842-0.9846 in. (24.999-25.009 mm)
Crankpin	1.1823-1.1828 in. (30.030-30.043 mm)
Standard piston diameter	See Chapter Eight
Piston ring end gap	0.007-0.017 in. (0.18-0.0.43 mm)
Piston ring side clearance	0.004 in. max. (0.10 mm)

40-50 HP	
Cylinders	2
Standard bore	3.1870-3.1880 in. (80.950-80.975 mm)
Stroke	2.820 in. (71.63 mm)
Displacement	45 cu. in. (737 cc)
Crankshaft journal diameter	
Top	1.4974-1.4979 in. (38.034-38.047 mm)
Center	1.3748-1.3752 in. (34.920-34.930 mm)
Bottom	1.1810-1.1815 in. (29.997-30.010 mm)
Crankpin	1.1823-1.1828 in. (29.997-30.043 mm)
Standard piston diameter	See Chapter Eight
Piston ring end gap	0.007-0.017 in. (0.18-0.38 mm)
Piston ring side clearance	
Bottom ring	0.004 in. max. (0.10 mm)

60 AND 70 HP	
Cylinders	3
Standard bore diameter	3.1870-3.1880 in. (80.950-80.975 mm)
Stroke	3.188 in. (80.975 mm)
Displacement	56.1 cu. in. (913 cc)
Crankshaft journal diameter	
Top	1.4974-1.4979 in. (38.034-38.047 mm)
Center (both)	1.3748-1.3752 in. (34.920-34.930 mm)
Bottom	1.1810-1.1815 in. (29.997-30.010 mm)
Crankpin	1.1823-1.1828 in. (30.030-30.043 mm)
Standard piston diameter	3.1806-3.1841 in. (80.787-80.876 mm)
Piston ring end gap	0.007-0.017 in. (0.18-0.38 mm)
Piston ring side clearance	
Bottom ring	0.004 in. max (0.10 mm)

(continued)

Table 3 POWER HEAD SPECIFICATIONS (continued)

V4 CROSS FLOW	
Cylinders	V4
Standard bore diameter	3.4995-3.5005 in. (88.887-88.913 mm)
Stroke	2.588 in. (65.73 mm)
Displacement	99.6 cu. in. (1632 cc)
Crankshaft journal diameter	
Top	1.6199-1.6204 in. (41.145-41.158 mm)
Center	2.1870-2.1875 in. (55.550-55.562 mm)
Bottom	1.3779-1.3784 in. (34.998-35.011 mm)
Crankpin	1.3757-1.3762 in. (34.943-34.955 mm)
Standard piston diameter	3.4930-3.4950 in. (88.722-88.773 mm)
Piston ring end gap	0.019-0.031 in. (0.48-0.79 mm)
Piston ring side clearance	
Bottom ring	0.004 in. max. (0.10 mm)

V6 CROSS FLOW	
Cylinders	V6
Standard bore diameter	
150 hp	3.4995-3.5005 in. (88.887-88.913 mm)
175 hp	3.6245-3.6255 in. (92.062-92.088 mm)
Stroke	2.588 in. (65.735 mm)
Displacement	
150 hp	149.4 cu. in. (2448 cc)
175 hp	160.3 cu. in. (2627 cc)
Crankshaft journal diameter	
Top	1.6199-1.6205 in. (41.145-41.161 mm)
Center	2.1870-2.1875 in. (55.550-55.562 mm)
Bottom	1.3779-1.3784 in. (34.999-35.011 mm)
Crankpin	1.3757-1.3762 in. (34.943-34.955 mm)
Standard piston diameter	
150 hp	3.4955-3.4965 in. (88.786-88.811 mm)
175 hp	3.6195-3.6205 in. (91.935-91.961 mm)
Piston ring end gap	
150 hp	0.019-0.031 in. (0.48-0.79 mm)
175 hp	0.020-0.033 in. (0.51-0.84 mm)
Piston ring side clearance	
Bottom ring	0.004 in. max. (0.10 mm)

V4 LOOP CHARGED MODELS	
Cylinders	4
Standard bore diameter	3.6845-3.6855 in. (93.586-93.612 mm)
Stroke	2.858 in. (72.593 mm)
Displacement	122 cu. in. (2000 cc)
Crankshaft journal diameter	
Top	1.6199-1.6204 in. (41.145-41.158 mm)
Center	2.1870-2.1875 in. (55.550-55.562 mm)
Bottom	1.5747-1.5752 in. (39.997-40.010 mm)
Crankpin	1.4995-1.5000 in. (38.087-38.100 mm)
Standard piston diameter	3.6803-3.6823 in. (93.480-93.530 mm)
Piston ring end gap	0.019-0.031 in. (0.48-0.79 mm)
Piston ring side clearance	
Bottom ring	0.004 in. max. (0.10 mm)

(continued)

8

Table 3 POWER HEAD SPECIFICATIONS (continued)

V6 (EXCEPT 60°) LOOP CHARGED MODELS

Cylinders	V6
Standard bore diameter	3.6845-3.6855 in. (93.586-93.612 mm)
Stroke	2.858 in. (72.593 mm)
Displacement	183 cu. in. (3000 cc)
Crankshaft journal diameter	
Top	1.6199-1.6204 in. (41.145-41.158 mm)
Center	2.1870-2.1875 in. (55.550-55.562 mm)
Bottom	1.5747-1.5752 in. (39.997-40.010 mm)
Crankpin	1.4995-1.5000 in. (38.087-38.100 mm)
Standard piston diameter	See chapter Eight
Piston ring end gap	0.019-0.031 in. (0.48-0.79 mm)

60° V6 LOOP CHARGED MODELS

Cylinders	V6
Standard bore diameter	3.5995-3.6005 in. (91.427-91.453 mm)
Stroke	2.588 in. (65.73 mm)
Displacement	158 cu. in. (2589 cc)
Crankshaft journal diameter	
Top	2.1870-2.1875 in. (55.550-55.562 mm)
Center	2.1870-2.1875 in. (55.550-55.562 mm)
Bottom	1.5747-1.5752 in. (39.997-40.010 mm)
Crankpin	1.3757-1.3762 in. (34.942-34.955 mm)
Standard bore diameter	See Chapter Eight
Piston ring end gap	0.011-0.023 in. (0.28-0.58 mm)
Piston ring side clearance	
Bottom ring	0.004 in. max. (0.10 mm)

Chapter Nine

Gearcase

Torque from the power head is transferred from the engine crankshaft to the gearcase by a drive shaft. A pinion gear on the drive shaft meshes with a drive gear in the gearcase to change the vertical power flow into a horizontal flow to the propeller shaft.

On models with shift capability, a sliding clutch engages a forward or reverse gear in the gearcase. This gear engagement creates a direct coupling that transfers the power flow from the pinion gear to the propeller shaft.

The gearcase used on 2.0, 2.3 and 3.3 hp models has forward gear only—neutral and reverse gear shifting capability is not provided. On 3 and 4 hp models, neutral and forward gear shift capability is provided, but not reverse. To reverse direction on these models, the outboard motor must be rotated 360° using the tiller handle. On 4 Deluxe and larger models, full forward-neutral-reverse shift capability is provided.

The gearcase can be removed without removing the entire outboard motor from the boat. This chapter contains gearcase removal, overhaul and installation, in addition to propeller and water pump service procedures. **Table 1** (tightening torques), **Table 2** (shift rod length dimensions)

and **Table 3** (gearcase lubricant capacity and type) are at the end of the chapter.

The gearcase assemblies covered in this chapter differ somewhat in design and construction, and thus require slightly different service procedures. The chapter is arranged in a normal disassembly/assembly sequence. When only a partial repair is necessary, follow the procedure(s) until you reach a point where the problem can be repaired, then reassemble the unit.

Since this chapter covers a wide range of models, the gearcase units shown in the accompanying pictures are the most common. While it is possible that the components shown in the pictures may not be identical with those being serviced, the step-by-step procedures may be used with all models covered in this manual.

SERVICE PRECAUTIONS

When working on an outboard motor, there are several procedures to keep in mind that will make your work easier, safer and more accurate.

1. Never use elastic stop nuts more than twice. It is good practice to replace such nuts each time

they are removed. Never use worn stop nuts or nonlocking nuts.

2. Use special tools where noted. In some cases, it may be possible to perform a procedure with makeshift tools, however, it is not recommended. The use of makeshift tools can damage the components and may cause serious personal injury.

3. Use a vise with protective jaws to hold housings or parts. If protective jaws are not available, insert blocks of wood or similar padding on each side of the part or assembly before clamping in the vise.

4. Remove and install pressed-on parts with an appropriate mandrel, support and hydraulic press. Do not attempt to pry or hammer press-fit components on or off.

5. Refer to the appropriate table at the end of the chapter for torque values, if not given in the text. Proper torque is essential to ensure long life and satisfactory service from outboard components.

6. Apply OMC Gasket Sealing Compound to the outer surfaces of all bearing carrier, retainer and housing mating surfaces, gaskets and the outer diameter of metal cased seals, unless specifically instructed otherwise. Do not allow the sealant to enter bearings or gear.

7. Discard all O-rings, seals and gaskets during disassembly. Apply OMC Triple-Guard grease to new O-rings and seal lips.

8. Record the location and thickness of all shims removed from the gear housing. As soon as the shims are removed, inspect them for damage and record their thickness and location. Wire the shims together for reassembly and place them in a safe place. Follow shimming instructions closely. If gear backlash is not properly adjusted, the unit will be noisy and suffer premature gear failure. Incorrect bearing preload will result in premature bearing failure.

9. Work in an area with good lighting and sufficient space for component storage. Keep an ample number of clean containers available for storing small parts. When not being worked on,

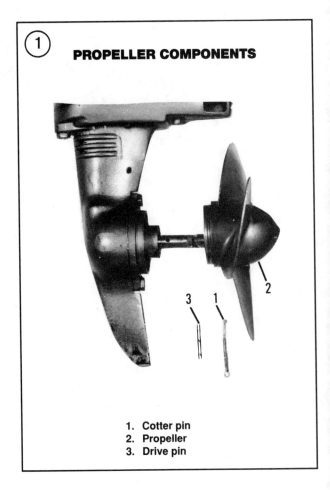

① PROPELLER COMPONENTS

1. Cotter pin
2. Propeller
3. Drive pin

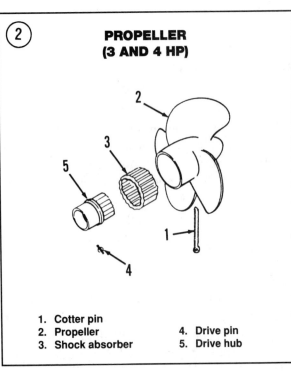

② PROPELLER (3 AND 4 HP)

1. Cotter pin
2. Propeller
3. Shock absorber
4. Drive pin
5. Drive hub

cover parts and assemblies with clean shop towels.

10. All moving or wearing components that will be reused should be reinstalled in their original locations and direction. During disassembly, mark the components for reference during reassembly.

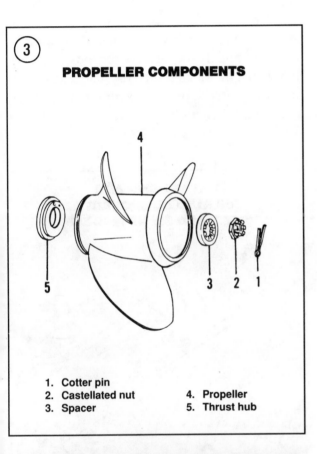

③

PROPELLER COMPONENTS

1. Cotter pin
2. Castellated nut
3. Spacer
4. Propeller
5. Thrust hub

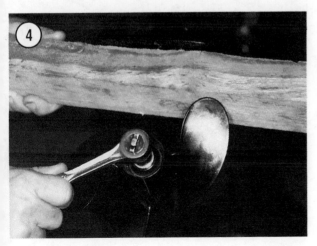

④

PROPELLER

WARNING
Avoid accidental starting when working around the propeller. Disconnect the spark plug wire(s) from the spark plug(s).

The outboard motors covered in this manual use variations of 2 propeller attachment designs. On 2-8 hp models, the propeller is fastened to the propeller shaft using a cotter pin. See **Figure 1**. On 3 and 4 hp, the propeller rides on a shock absorber which is driven by a drive hub and drive pin. See **Figure 2**. On 9.9 and larger outboards, the propeller is fastened to the propeller shaft with a castellated nut which is secured with a cotter pin. See **Figure 3**.

Removal/Installation (2-8 hp)

1. Remove and discard the cotter pin.
2. Pull the propeller off the propeller shaft.
3A. On 3 and 4 hp, slide the propeller shock absorber off the drive hub. Push the drive pin through the drive hub and propeller shaft, then pull the hub off the shaft. See **Figure 2**.
3B. Remove and discard the drive pin from the propeller shaft. Inspect the pin engagement slot in the propeller hub for wear or damage.
4. Installation is the reverse of removal. Lubricate the entire length of the propeller shaft with OMC Triple-Guard grease. Use a new drive pin and cotter pin.

Removal/Installation (9.9-Larger Models)

1. Remove and discard the cotter pin.
2. Remove the propeller nut using an appropriate size wrench. If necessary, place a block of wood between the propeller blades and antiventilation plate to prevent the propeller from turning. See **Figure 4**.

9

NOTE
*If the spacer (3, **Figure 3**) is made of
nylon, remove and discard it (Step 3).
Replace it with a brass spacer during
propeller installation.*

3. Remove the spacer, propeller and thrust hub
from the propeller shaft.

4. Thoroughly clean the propeller shaft.

5. Installation is the reverse of removal. Lubricate the entire propeller shaft with OMC Triple-
Guard grease. Tighten the propeller nut securely
on 9.9-30 hp models. Tighten the propeller nut
to 120 in.-lb. (13.5 N.m) on 40-70 hp and V4
models and 70-80 ft.-lb. (95-108 N.m) on V6 and
V8 models. Secure the propeller nut on all models with a new cotter pin.

WATER PUMP

On 2.0-2.3 and 3.3 hp models, the rubber
water pump impeller is located inside the gearcase housing. The impeller is mounted on and
driven by the propeller shaft. The water pump
can be serviced without gearcase removal.

On all other models, the water pump impeller
is secured to the drive shaft by a key or pin that
fits between a flat area on the drive shaft and
impeller hub. As the drive shaft rotates, the impeller rotates with it. Water between the impeller
blades and pump housing is pumped up to the
power head through the water tube.

All seals and gaskets should be replaced
whenever the water pump is removed. Since
proper water pump operation is critical to outboard operation, it is also good practice to install
a new impeller at the same time. The manufacturer recommends replacing the pump impeller
at least once per year, or any time the gearcase is
removed for service, regardless of its appearance.

If the original impeller must be reused, be
certain it is installed in the same rotational direction as removed to prevent premature failure.
Never turn a used impeller over and reuse it. The
impeller rotates in a clockwise direction with the
drive shaft and the impeller vanes gradually take
a "set" in that direction. Turning the impeller
over will cause the vanes to move in a direction
opposite to the "set" in the vanes. This will cause
the vanes to break off, causing water pump failure which can result in power head overheating
and possible damage.

If the outboard motor is started without an
adequate supply of cooling water, impeller failure can quickly occur (60 seconds or less).
Should the motor be started dry, the water pump
impeller should be removed for inspection
and/or replacement before returning the unit to
service.

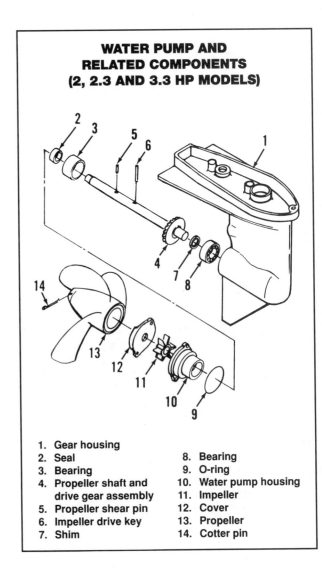

**WATER PUMP AND
RELATED COMPONENTS
(2, 2.3 AND 3.3 HP MODELS)**

1. Gear housing	
2. Seal	8. Bearing
3. Bearing	9. O-ring
4. Propeller shaft and	10. Water pump housing
drive gear assembly	11. Impeller
5. Propeller shear pin	12. Cover
6. Impeller drive key	13. Propeller
7. Shim	14. Cotter pin

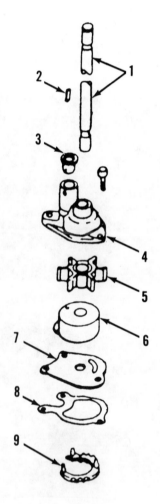

**WATER PUMP ASSEMBLY
(3 AND 4 HP)**

1. Drive shaft
2. Impeller drive key
3. Water tube grommet
4. Pump housing
5. Impeller
6. Liner
7. Impeller plate
8. Gasket
9. Water intake screen

Removal and Disassembly
(2.0, 2.3 and 3.3 hp)

1. Remove the propeller and drive pin as described in this chapter. Drain the gear housing lubricant. See Chapter Four.

2. Remove the 2 screws securing the pump housing cover (12, **Figure 5**). Separate the cover from the gear housing and slide it off the propeller shaft.

3. Inspect the impeller wear surface on the cover. Replace the cover if excessively worn.

4. Pry the impeller off the propeller shaft using a screwdriver or similar tool.

5. Inspect the impeller for cracked, worn or glazed blades. Inspect the impeller hub for separation from the rubber. Replace the impeller if any defects are noted.

6. Remove the impeller drive pin from the propeller shaft.

7. Remove the pump housing (10, **Figure 5**) from the gearcase housing. Inspect the impeller wear surface in the housing. Replace the housing if necessary.

8. Inspect the bearing inside the pump housing. Replace the bearing if it does not roll smoothly or if rust or other damage is noted. Remove the bearing from the housing using a suitable puller.

9. Place the pump housing on a bench and drive out the seal (2, **Figure 5**) from the housing using a suitable punch and hammer. Discard the seal. Remove and discard the O-ring seal around the housing.

Removal and Disassembly
(3 and 4 hp)

Refer to **Figure 6** for this procedure.

1. Remove the gearcase as described in this chapter.

2. Secure the gearcase in a suitable holding fixture.

9

NOTE
Hold the drive shaft in place (downward)
during Step 3 to prevent it from moving
up enough to disengage with the pinion
gear. Should this happen, it may be nec-
essary to disassemble the gearcase to
reinstall the drive shaft.

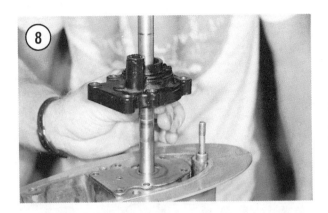

3. Remove the water pump housing screws.
While holding DOWN on the drive shaft, carefully pry the pump housing loose using 2 screwdrivers or similar tools placed at the fore and aft
ends of the housing. Slide the housing up and off
the drive shaft.

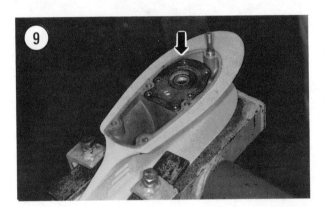

NOTE
In extreme cases, the impeller hub may
have to be split with a chisel to remove
it (Step 4).

4. If the impeller came off with the pump housing, proceed to Step 5. If the impeller remained
on the gearcase, lift it up and off the drive shaft
while holding the drive shaft in place.

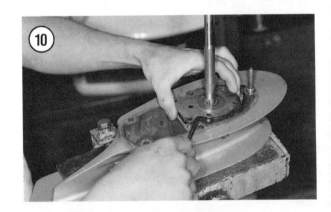

5. Dislodge the impeller plate using a screwdriver or similar tool. Lift the plate up and off the
drive shaft.

6. Remove the water intake screen from the
gearcase. Inspect the screen for plugging, breakage or other damage.

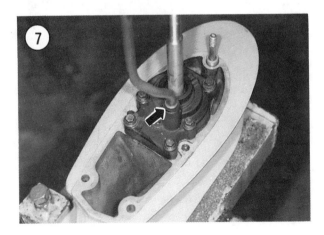

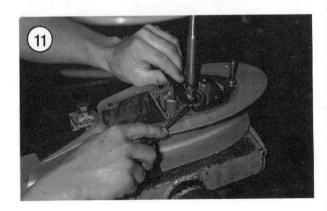

Removal and Disassembly
(All Other Models)

1. Remove the gearcase as described in this chapter. Secure the gearcase in a suitable holding fixture.

2. Remove the water tube from the pump housing. See **Figure 7**, typical.

3. Remove the impeller housing screws and washers. Insert screwdrivers at the fore and aft ends of the pump housing and carefully pry it loose.

4. Slide the pump housing up and off the drive shaft (**Figure 8**, typical).

NOTE
If the impeller is severely corroded to the drive shaft, it may be necessary to split the impeller hub with a chisel and hammer to remove it (Step 5).

5. If the impeller did not come off with the pump housing, carefully pry the impeller loose and lift it up and off the drive shaft. If the impeller came off with the housing, remove it from the housing.

6. Remove and discard the top impeller plate gasket, if loose. See **Figure 9**. If it is not loose, remove it in Step 7 along with the impeller plate.

7. Carefully pry the impeller plate loose with a screwdriver (**Figure 10**), then slide the plate and gasket (if used) up and off the drive shaft. Discard the gasket.

8. If the bottom impeller plate gasket did not come free with the impeller plate, carefully loosen it with a suitable tool. See **Figure 11**.

9. Remove the nylon water intake screen from the gearcase cavity (**Figure 12**), if so equipped.

10. Remove the impeller housing water tube grommet (A, **Figure 13**). Remove the impeller housing seal or grommet and O-ring. See B, **Figure 13** or A, **Figure 14**.

11. If necessary, remove the pump housing insert. See **Figure 15**.

12. Remove the shift rod O-ring seal (if so equipped). See B, **Figure 16**. Remove the housing seal (C, **Figure 16**) if so equipped.

9

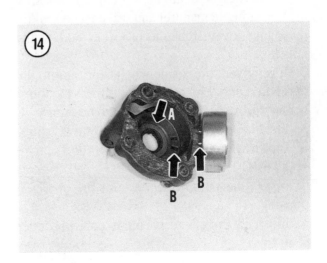

Cleaning and Inspection
(All Models)

When removing seals from the impeller housing, note and record the direction in which the lip of each seal faces for reference during reinstallation.

1. Check the pump housing for cracks, distortion damage from overheating. Replace the housing if necessary.
2. Clean all components with solvent and dry with compressed air.
3. Carefully remove all gasket material from the pump mating surfaces.
4. Check the impeller plate and insert for grooving or rough surfaces. Replace if any defects are noted.
5. If the original impeller is to be reused, check the bonding between the impeller hub and rubber vanes. See **Figure 17**. The impeller must be replaced if the hub is starting to separate from the vanes. Check the side seal surfaces of the impeller and vane ends for cracks, tears, wear or glazed or melted appearance. If any defects are noted, do *not* reuse the impeller.

Reassembly and Installation
(2.0, 2.3 and 3.3 hp)

Refer to **Figure 5** for this procedure.
1. Press a new seal into the water pump housing using a suitable mandrel and driver. The seal lip must face away from the propeller end of the housing.
2. If removed, press a new ball bearing into the pump housing. Press the bearing from the numbered side, until fully seated in the housing.
3. Install a new O-ring onto the pump housing.
4. Lubricate the ball bearing, O-ring and seal lip with OMC Triple-Guard grease.
5. Install the pump housing into the gearcase housing.
6. Insert the impeller drive pin into the propeller shaft.

7. Slide the impeller onto the propeller shaft. Install the impeller into the pump housing while rotating the impeller in a clockwise direction. Make sure the impeller properly engages the drive pin.
8. Apply OMC Gasket Sealing Compound to the threads of the pump housing screws. Install the screws and tighten to 60-84 in.-lb. (6.8-9.5 N.m).

Reassembly and Installation
(3 and 4 hp)

Refer to **Figure 6** for this procedure.

1. Install the water intake screen in the gearcase housing. Make sure the tabs on the screen are facing UP.
2. Apply OMC Gasket Sealing Compound to both sides of a new impeller plate gasket. Install the gasket and impeller plate over the drive shaft and into position on the gearcase housing.
3. Install the impeller drive pin into position on the drive shaft. Hold the pin in place with a suitable grease.
4. Install a new water tube grommet in the pump housing. Lightly lubricate the grommet with OMC Triple-Guard grease.
5. If removed, apply a light coat of OMC Gasket Sealing Compound to the outer diameter of the

(15)

housing liner. Install the liner in the pump housing.

6. Apply a light coat of engine oil to the impeller vanes, then install the impeller into the pump housing with a counterclockwise turning motion.

7. Install a new housing O-ring seal into the housing. Apply a light coat of OMC Triple-Guard grease to the O-ring.

8. Place the pump housing assembly over the drive shaft. Engage the drive pin with the impeller, then rotate the housing (counterclockwise only) as necessary to align the mounting screw holes.

9. After aligning the screw holes, apply OMC Gasket Sealing Compound to the threads of the housing screws. Make sure the pump housing is

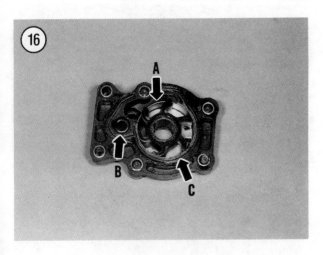

properly seated, then install the mounting screws and tighten to specification (**Table 1**).

10. Install the gearcase assembly as described in this chapter.

Reassembly and Installation (4 Deluxe, 6 and 8 hp)

1. Apply a light coat of OMC Gasket Sealing Compound to both sides of a new pump plate gasket. Install the gasket and plate on the gearcase housing.

2. Install a new water tube grommet into the pump housing. Lubricate the grommet with OMC Triple-Guard grease.

3. Place the impeller drive key into position on the drive shaft. Use a suitable grease to hold the key in place.

4. Apply a light coat of OMC Gasket Sealing Compound to the outer diameter of the pump housing liner. Install the liner into the pump housing.

> *CAUTION*
> *If the original impeller is to be reused, install it in the same rotational direction as removed to prevent water pump failure.*

5. Lightly lubricate the tips of the impeller vanes with light oil. Install the impeller into the pump housing by twisting it in a counterclockwise direction while pushing it into the housing.

6. Apply OMC Gasket Sealing Compound to the threads of the pump housing screws.

7. Place the pump housing assembly over the drive shaft. Engage the impeller with the drive key, then rotate the housing (counterclockwise only) as necessary to align the housing mounting screw holes. After aligning the screw holes, fully seat the housing and install the screws.

8. Tighten the 4 water pump screws to specification (**Table 1**).

9. Install the gearcase assembly as described in this chapter.

9

Reassembly and Installation (9.9-30 hp)

1A. *9.9 and 15 hp*—Apply OMC Gasket Sealing Compound to the outer diameter of a new pump housing seal. Using a suitable driver, install the seal into the upper side of the drive shaft bore in the pump housing so the seal lip faces the impeller side.

1B. *28 hp*—Apply OMC Gasket Sealing Compound to the outer diameter of a new pump housing seal. Using OMC Upper Drive shaft Seal Installer part No. 330655 (or equivalent), install the seal into the lower side of the drive shaft bore in the pump housing so the seal lip faces away from the impeller side.

1C. *20-30 (except 28) hp*—Lubricate the shift rod bushing with light oil and install it into the pump housing. Then, apply OMC Triple-Guard grease to the shift rod O-ring and install it into the housing against the shift rod bushing. See A, **Figure 18**. Next, lubricate the pump housing O-ring with Triple-Guard grease and install it into the housing. See B, **Figure 18**.

2A. *9.9-15 hp*—Apply OMC Adhesive M to the pump housing upper O-ring. Install the O-ring in the housing. See B, **Figure 19**. Apply Adhesive M to the outer diameter of a new water tube grommet and install it into the housing. See A, **Figure 19**. Lubricate the inner diameter of the grommet with OMC Triple-Guard grease.

2B. *20-30 hp (except 28 hp)*—Apply Scotch-Grip Rubber Adhesive 1300 to the outer diameter of a new water tube grommet. Install the grommet into the housing.

2C. *28 hp*—Lubricate a new water tube grommet with light oil. Install the grommet into the pump housing.

3. Apply a light coat of OMC Gasket Sealing Compound to the outer diameter of the pump housing liner. Install the liner into the pump housing while aligning the tabs on the liner with the locating cutouts in the housing. See B, **Fig-** ure 14. Make sure the liner is fully seated in the housing.

> *CAUTION*
> *If the original impeller must be reused, install it in the same rotational direction as removed to prevent water pump failure.*

4. Lubricate the tips of the impeller vanes and the inner diameter of the housing liner with light oil. With a counterclockwise twisting motion, install the impeller into the housing. The curl of

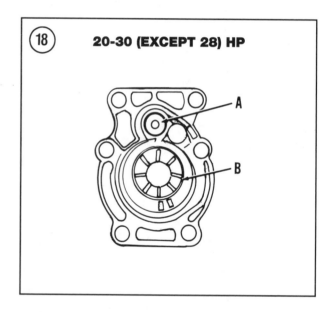

20-30 (EXCEPT 28) HP

the impeller vanes must be positioned as shown in **Figure 20**.

5A. *9.9 and 15 hp*—Apply a light coat of OMC Adhesive M to the machined area of the gearcase housing that contacts the pump plate. Then, install the plate over the drive shaft and seat it on the gearcase housing.

5B. *20-30 hp*—Apply OMC Gasket Sealing Compound to both sides of a new pump plate lower gasket. Place the gasket over the drive shaft and onto the gearcase housing. Install the pump plate on the gasket.

6A. *28 hp*—Apply a light coat of OMC Gasket Sealing Compound to both sides of a new pump plate upper gasket. Install the gasket on the plate.

6B. *20-30 hp (except 28)*—Apply a light bead of OMC Adhesive M to the pump housing seal groove. Install a new seal into the groove. See C, **Figure 16**.

> *NOTE*
> *On 20-30 hp models (except 28 hp), install the impeller drive key so its sharp edge is the leading edge as the drive shaft is rotated clockwise (as viewed from top).*

7. Apply OMC Triple-Guard grease to the impeller drive pin or key surface on the drive shaft. Install the pin or key into place on the drive shaft.

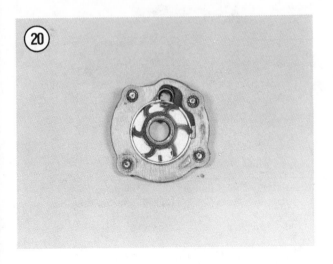

Apply additional grease as necessary to hold the pin or key in position.

8. *9.9 and 15 hp*—Apply a light coat of OMC Gasket Sealing Compound to the pump housing mating surface.

9. Install the pump housing assembly over the drive shaft and engage the impeller with the drive pin or key. Then rotate the housing in a counterclockwise direction until the housing mounting screw holes are aligned. Fully seat the housing.

10. Apply OMC Gasket Sealing Compound to the threads of the housing mounting screws. Install the screws and tighten evenly, in 3 steps, to the specification listed in **Table 1**.

11. Install the gearcase assembly as described in this chapter.

Reassembly and Installation (40-70 hp)

9

Refer to **Figure 21** for this procedure.

1. Install a new top plate into the pump housing, if removed. Make sure the index tab securely locks in plate in the housing.

2. Install the liner into the housing.

> *CAUTION*
> *If the original impeller must be used, install it in the same rotational direction as removed to prevent water pump failure.*

3. Lubricate the tips of the impeller vanes and the inner diameter of the liner with light oil. With a counterclockwise twisting motion, install the impeller into the housing. The curl of the impeller vanes must be positioned as shown in **Figure 20** and the drive cam cutout in the impeller hub must be facing outward.

4. Install the water tube grommet into the housing.

5. Apply OMC Adhesive M to the outer diameter of a new housing grommet, then install the grommet into the housing. Lubricate the inner

diameter of the grommet with OMC Triple-Guard grease.

6. Apply a thin bead of OMC Adhesive M into the pump housing seal groove, then install the O-ring seal (5, **Figure 21**).

7. Apply OMC Gasket Sealing Compound to both sides of a new plate gasket. Install the gasket and plate.

> *NOTE*
> *Install the impeller drive cam so its sharp edge is the leading edge as the drive shaft is rotated clockwise (as viewed from top).*

8. Apply OMC Needle Bearing Assembly Grease to the impeller drive cam flat on the drive shaft. Install the drive cam. Apply additional grease as necessary to hold the cam in place.

9. Place the pump housing assembly over the drive shaft and engage the impeller with the drive cam. Be sure the drive cam is still in position.

10. Rotate the housing assembly in a counter-clockwise direction to align the housing screw holes. Make certain the impeller is properly engaged with the drive cam, then seat the housing on the gearcase.

11. Apply OMC Gasket Sealing Compound to the threads of the pump housing mounting screws. Install the screws and tighten evenly to specification (**Table 1**).

Reassembly and Installation (V4, V6 and V8 Models)

Refer to **Figure 22** for this procedure.

> *CAUTION*
> *Do not allow adhesive in the pump housing air bleed groove (**Figure 23**) in Step 1. If the bleed hole is blocked, the pump may not function and could result in power head overheating.*

1. Apply a small drop of OMC Adhesive M to each of the 4 ribs inside the pump housing. See

Figure 23. Install the seal ring into its groove in the housing.

2. Apply a light coat of OMC Gasket Sealing Compound to the outer diameter of the pump housing liner. Install the liner into the housing.

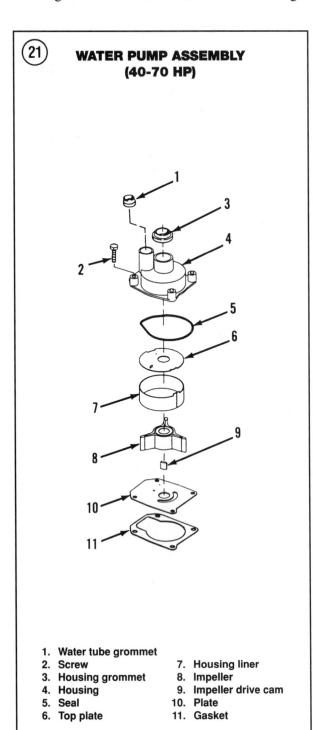

(21)   WATER PUMP ASSEMBLY (40-70 HP)

1. Water tube grommet
2. Screw
3. Housing grommet
4. Housing
5. Seal
6. Top plate
7. Housing liner
8. Impeller
9. Impeller drive cam
10. Plate
11. Gasket

3. Install the water tube grommet so its inside taper faces upward.

4. Install the housing cover and tighten the screw securely.

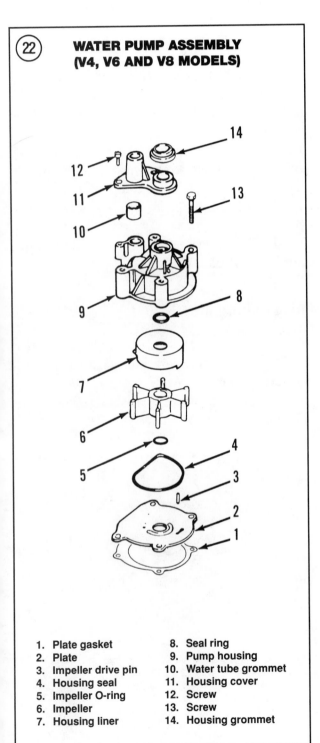

WATER PUMP ASSEMBLY (V4, V6 AND V8 MODELS)

1. Plate gasket
2. Plate
3. Impeller drive pin
4. Housing seal
5. Impeller O-ring
6. Impeller
7. Housing liner
8. Seal ring
9. Pump housing
10. Water tube grommet
11. Housing cover
12. Screw
13. Screw
14. Housing grommet

5. Apply a light coat of OMC Adhesive M to the flat side of the housing grommet. Install the grommet on the housing (flat side down).

CAUTION
If the original impeller must be used, install it in the same rotational direction as removed to prevent water pump failure.

6. Lubricate the tips of the impeller vanes and the inner diameter of the housing liner with light oil. With a counterclockwise twisting motion, install the impeller into the housing. The curl of the impeller vanes must be facing as shown in **Figure 20**.

7. Apply a light coat of OMC Adhesive M to the pump housing seal groove. Install the O-ring seal into the housing groove.

8. Apply a light coat of OMC Gasket Sealing Compound to both sides of a new plate gasket. Install the gasket and plate on the gearcase.

9. Apply OMC Triple-Guard grease to a new impeller O-ring, then install the O-ring over the drive shaft. Slide the O-ring down until it contacts the pump plate.

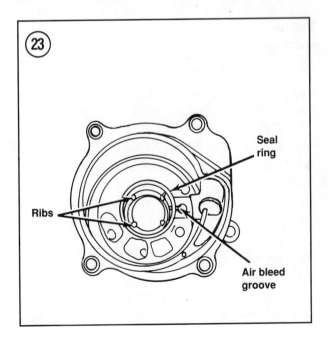

Seal ring

Ribs

Air bleed groove

10. Apply OMC Needle Bearing Assembly Grease to the impeller drive cam area of the drive shaft. Install the drive cam on the drive shaft so its sharp edge is the leading edge as the drive shaft rotates clockwise (as viewed from top). If necessary, apply additional grease to hold the drive cam in place.

11. Install the pump housing assembly over the drive shaft. Rotate the drive shaft clockwise to align the drive cam with the cam slot in the impeller hub. When the impeller properly engages the drive cam, seat the pump housing assembly on the gearcase. Make certain the drive cam and impeller are properly aligned and engaged.

12. Apply OMC Gasket Sealing Compound to the threads of the pump housing mounting screws. Install the screws and tighten evenly to specification (**Table 1**).

GEARCASE

Removal/Installation
(2.0, 2.3 and 3.3 hp)

1. Disconnect the spark plug lead from the spark plug to prevent accidental starting.

2. Remove the propeller as described in this chapter.

3. Close the fuel shut-off valve on the power head.

4. Tilt the outboard to the fully UP position.

5. Remove the 2 mounting screws and pull the gearcase assembly off the exhaust housing. Use caution not to damage the drive shaft or water tube.

6. Mount the gearcase in a suitable holding fixture. If necessary, drain the gearcase lubricant as described in Chapter Four.

7. Pull the upper drive shaft and drive shaft tube from the gearcase.

8. To install, apply OMC Moly Lube to the outside diameter of the tube (**Figure 24**), then

insert the tube into the drive shaft exhaust housing until fully seated.

9. Apply OMC Moly Lube to the inside diameter (both ends) of the upper drive shaft. Insert the shaft into the tube (**Figure 24**), then onto the engine crankshaft.

10. Lubricate the water tube grommet with light oil.

11. Install the gearcase while aligning the water tube and upper and lower drive shafts. Rotate the propeller shaft clockwise to engage the drive shafts.

12. Apply OMC Nut Lock to the threads of the gearcase mounting screws. Install the screws and tighten to specification (**Table 1**).

13. Install the propeller as described in this chapter.

14. Refill the gearcase with the recommended lubricant (**Table 3**).

Removal/Installation
(3 and 4 hp)

1. Disconnect the spark plug leads to prevent accidental starting.

2. Remove the propeller as described in this chapter.

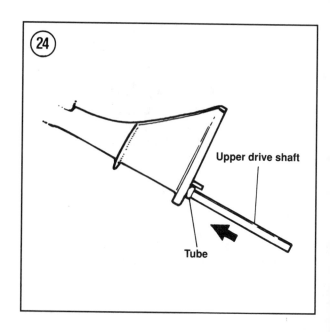

Upper drive shaft

Tube

3. If gearcase disassembly is necessary, drain the gearcase lubricant by removing the oil level and drain/fill plugs.

NOTE
If the lubricant is white or cream color, or if metal particles are found in Step 4, the gearcase should be disassembled to determine and repair the problem.

4. Rub a small amount of lubricant between a thumb and finger to check for the presence of metal particles or chips. A small amount of fine (powder-like) particles indicates normal wear. Note the color of the lubricant. A white or cream color indicates water contamination. Check the container for water separation from the lubricant.

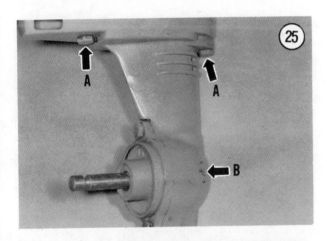

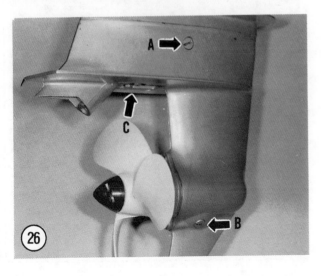

5. Remove the 2 screws holding the gearcase to the exhaust housing. See A, **Figure 25**.

6. Carefully separate the gearcase from the exhaust housing. Use care not to damage the water tube or drive shaft. Remove the gearcase assembly and mount in a suitable holding fixture.

7. If the water tube remained in the exhaust housing, remove it from the grommet.

8. To reinstall the gearcase, lubricate the water tube grommet in the exhaust housing with light oil or liquid soap.

CAUTION
Do not grease the top of the drive shaft in Step 9. Excess grease between the top of the drive shaft and the engine crankshaft can create a hydraulic lock, preventing the drive shaft from fully engaging the crankshaft.

9. Lubricate the drive shaft splines with OMC Moly Lube or an equivalent water-resistant grease.

10. Position the gearcase under the exhaust housing and align the water tube with its grommet, the drive shaft with the crankshaft and the shift rod with its bushing.

11. Apply OMC Nut Lock to the threads of the 2 gearcase mounting screws. Install the screws and tighten to specification (**Table 1**).

12. Install the propeller as described in this chapter.

13. Refill the gearcase with the recommended lubricant (**Table 3**).

**Removal/Installation
(4 Deluxe, 6-8 hp)**

1. Disconnect the spark plug leads to prevent accidental starting.

2. Remove the propeller as described in this chapter.

3. If gearcase disassembly is necessary, place a suitable container under the gearcase, remove the oil level plug (A, **Figure 26**), then the drain/fill plug (B). Allow the lubricant to drain.

9

NOTE
If the lubricant is white or cream color, or if metal particles are found in Step 4, the gearcase should be disassembled to determine and repair the problem.

4. Rub a small amount of lubricant between a thumb and finger to check for the presence of metal particles or chips. A small amount of fine (powder-like) particles indicates normal wear. Note the color of the lubricant. A white or cream color indicates water contamination. Check the container for water separation from the lubricant.

5. Place the shift lever into the FORWARD gear position while rotating the propeller shaft clockwise.

6. Remove the 2 mounting screws at the rear of the zinc anode cavity (C, **Figure 26**) and the screw just below the lower steering pivot point (**Figure 27**).

7. Remove the gearcase from the exhaust housing. Mount the gearcase in a suitable holding fixture.

8. Remove and discard the drive shaft O-ring, if so equipped.

9. To reinstall, install a new drive shaft O-ring (if so equipped) into its groove at the top of the shaft.

CAUTION
Do not grease the top of the drive shaft in Step 10. Excess grease between the top of the drive shaft and the engine crankshaft can create a hydraulic lock, preventing the drive shaft from fully engaging the crankshaft.

10. Lubricate the drive shaft splines with OMC Moly Lube or an equivalent water-resistant grease. Lubricate the water tube grommet in the water pump with OMC Triple-Guard grease.

11. Install the gearcase assembly into position under the exhaust housing. Align the water tube with its grommet in the water pump. Rotate the flywheel clockwise to align the crankshaft and drive splines and seat the gearcase on the exhaust housing.

12. Apply OMC Nut Lock to the threads of the gearcase mounting screws. Install the screws and tighten the 2 rear screws (**Figure 26**) to 60-84 in.-lb. (6.8-9.5 N•m) and the front screw (**Figure 27**) to 120-144 in.-lb. (13.5-16.3 N•m).

13. Install the propeller as described in this chapter. Refill the gearcase with the recommended lubricant (**Table 3**).

Removal/Installation (9.9 and 15 hp)

1. Disconnect the spark plug leads to prevent accidental starting.

2. Remove the propeller as described in this chapter.

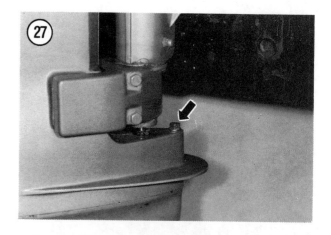

3. If gearcase disassembly is necessary, remove the oil level plug (A, **Figure 28**), then the drain/fill plug (B) and allow the lubricant to drain into a suitable container. *Do not* mistake the shift lever pivot pin (C, **Figure 28**) for the drain/fill plug.

NOTE
If the lubricant is white or cream color, or if metal particles are found in Step 4, the gearcase should be disassembled to determine and repair the problem.

4. Rub a small amount of lubricant between a thumb and finger to check for the presence of metal particles or chips. A small amount of fine (powder-like) particles indicates normal wear. Note the color of the lubricant. A white or cream color indicates water contamination. Check the container for water separation from the lubricant.

5. Remove the 6 screws securing the gearcase to the exhaust housing.

6. Separate the gearcase from the exhaust housing sufficiently to expose the shift rod connector (**Figure 29**). Remove the upper screw in the connector and remove the gearcase from the

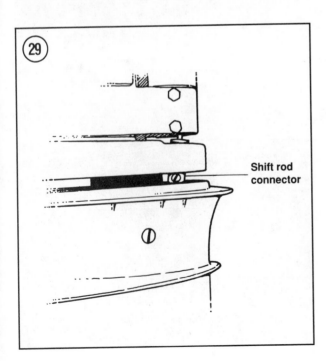

Shift rod connector

exhaust housing. Mount the gearcase in a suitable holding fixture.

CAUTION
Do not grease the top of the drive shaft in Step 7. Excess grease between the top of the drive shaft and the engine crankshaft can create a hydraulic lock, preventing the drive shaft from fully engaging the crankshaft.

7. Lubricate the drive shaft splines with OMC Moly Lube or an equivalent water-resistant grease. Lubricate the outer diameter of the bottom end of the water tube with OMC Triple-Guard grease.

8. Place the shift lever on the outboard motor in the REVERSE position. Shift the gearcase into REVERSE by pulling upward on the shift rod while rotating the propeller shaft counterclockwise.

9. Position the gearcase under the exhaust housing. Align the water tube with the water pump grommet, the drive shaft with the crankshaft and the shift rod with the shift rod connector. If necessary, rotate the flywheel clockwise to align the drive shaft and crankshaft splines.

10. Push the gearcase into position until the groove in the lower shift rod is aligned with the screw hole in the shift rod connector (**Figure 29**). Apply OMC Gasket Sealing Compound to the shift rod connector screw, install the screw and washer, then tighten to 60-84 in.-lb. (6.8-9.5 N.m).

11. Apply OMC Gasket Sealing Compound to the threads of the 6 gearcase mounting screws. Make sure the gearcase is fully mated to the exhaust housing, then install the mounting screws and tighten to specification (**Table 1**).

12. Refill the gearcase with the recommended lubricant (**Table 3**).

13. Install the propeller as described in this chapter.

9

Removal/Installation
(20-30 hp)

1. Disconnect the spark plug leads to prevent accidental starting.

2. Remove the propeller as described in this chapter.

3. If gearcase disassembly is necessary, remove the oil level plug, then remove the drain/fill plug. Do not remove the Phillips-head, shift lever pivot screw forward of the drain/fill plug. Allow the lubricant to drain into a suitable container.

> *NOTE*
> *If the lubricant is white or cream color, or if metal particles are found in Step 4, the gearcase should be disassembled to determine and repair the problem.*

4. Rub a small amount of lubricant between a thumb and finger to check for the presence of metal particles or chips. A small amount of fine (powder-like) particles indicates normal wear. Note the color of the lubricant. A white or cream color indicates water contamination. Check the container for water separation from the lubricant.

5. Place the shift lever into FORWARD gear position while rotating the propeller shaft.

6A. *28 hp*—Remove the exhaust housing cover plate and gasket to provide access to the shift rod connector screw. See **Figure 30**. Remove the bottom screw from the shift rod connector.

6B. *20-30 (except 28) hp*—Remove the water intake screen from each side of the gearcase to provide access to the shift rod connector. See **Figure 31**. Hold the lower connector nut with an appropriate size open-end wrench and turn the upper nut with another wrench. When the upper and lower shift rods disengage, remove and discard the plastic keeper between the shift rods.

7. Remove the 4 screws and 1 nut securing the gearcase to the exhaust housing. Separate the gearcase from the exhaust housing and place it in a suitable holding fixture.

8. The water pump housing spacer (**Figure 32**) may remain in the exhaust housing or come off

with the gearcase. Locate the spacer and remove it. Remove and discard the O-rings from each end of the spacer.

9. To reinstall the gearcase, place the shift lever on the outboard motor in the FORWARD gear position. Shift the gearcase into FORWARD gear by pulling upward on the lower shift rod while rotating the propeller shaft clockwise.

10. Apply OMC Triple-Guard grease to the 2 new pump housing spacer O-rings. Install one O-ring on each end of the spacer, then slide the spacer over the drive shaft and into position on the water pump housing. The tabs on the spacer should face the rear of the gearcase.

> *CAUTION*
> *Do not grease the top of the drive shaft in Step 11. Excess grease between the top of the drive shaft and the engine crank-*

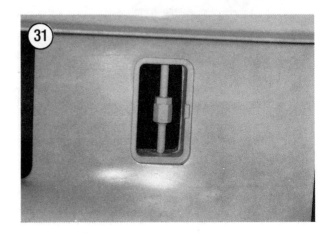

shaft can create a hydraulic lock, preventing the drive shaft from fully engaging the crankshaft.

11. Lubricate the drive shaft splines with OMC Moly Lube or an equivalent water-resistant grease.

12. If removed, lubricate the outer diameter of both ends of the water tube with OMC Triple-Guard grease. Install the water tube into the water pump housing grommet.

13. *20-30 (except 28) hp*—Coat the upper shift rod with OMC Triple-Guard grease, then temporarily install the upper shift rod connector on the lower shift rod.

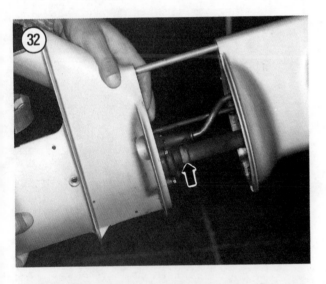

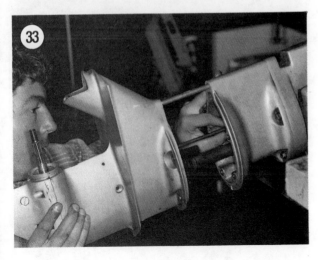

14. Position the gearcase under the exhaust housing. Align the water tube with the water pump grommet, the drive shaft with the crankshaft and the lower shift rod with the shift rod connector. See **Figure 33**, typical. If necessary, rotate the flywheel clockwise to align the crankshaft and drive shaft splines.

15A. *Except 28 hp*—Apply OMC Gasket Sealing Compound to the threads of the gearcase mounting fasteners. Install the 4 screws and 1 nut and tighten evenly to 16-18 ft.-lb. (22-24 N•m).

15B. *28 hp*—Apply OMC Gasket Sealing Compound to the threads of the 4 gearcase mounting screws. Apply OMC Locquic Primer to the threads of the mounting stud, allow to air dry, then apply OMC Nut Lock. Install the nut. Tighten the screws to 16-18 ft.-lb. (22-24 N•m) and the nut to 45-50 ft.-lb. (61-67 N•m).

16A. *Except 28 hp*—Slide the upper shift rod connector half upward onto the upper shift rod, then install the plastic keeper. Move the shift lever on the outboard motor until the upper shift rod engages the lower shift rod connector. Hold the lower connector with a suitable open-end wrench while tightening the upper connector with a second wrench.

16B. *28 hp*—Align the groove in the lower shift rod with the connector screw. Install the screw with the washer and tighten to 120-144 in.-lb. (14-16 N•m) Apply OMC Adhesive M to both sides of a new exhaust housing cover gasket. Install the cover plate and gasket. Tighten the screws securely.

17. Install the propeller as described in this chapter.

18. Refill the gearcase with the recommended lubricant (**Table 3**).

19. To adjust the shift lever, shift the outboard into NEUTRAL while rotating the propeller. Loosen both shift lever screws and move the shift actuator cam until the lockout lever detents (centers) into the cam notch. Tighten the shift lever screws to 60-84 in.-lb. (6.8-9.5 N•m).

9

Removal/Installation (40-50 hp)

1. Disconnect the spark plug leads to prevent accidental starting.

2. Remove the propeller as described in this chapter.

3. If gearcase disassembly is necessary, remove the level plug, then the drain/fill plug and allow the lubricant to drain into a suitable container.

NOTE
If the lubricant is white or cream color, or if metal particles are found in Step 4, the gearcase should be disassembled to determine and repair the problem.

4. Rub a small amount of lubricant between a thumb and finger to check for the presence of metal particles or chips. A small amount of fine (powder-like) particles indicates normal wear. Note the color of the lubricant. A white or cream color indicates water contamination. Check the container for water separation from the lubricant.

5. Remove the screw (**Figure 34**) securing the gearcase shift rod to the shift rod connector (located under carburetors on port side).

6. Remove the screw (B, **Figure 35**) forward of the trim tab using a thin-wall 5/8 in. socket.

7. Remove the 4 gearcase mounting screws (2 on each side). See A, **Figure 36**.

8. Separate and remove the gearcase from the exhaust housing. Do not bend the shift rod.

9. Mount the gearcase in a suitable holding fixture.

CAUTION
Do not grease the top of the drive shaft in Step 10. Excess grease between the top of the drive shaft and the engine crankshaft can create a hydraulic lock, preventing the drive shaft from fully engaging the crankshaft.

10. To reinstall the gearcase, lubricate the drive shaft splines with OMC Moly Lube.

11. Install the gearcase on the exhaust housing while making sure the water tube properly enters

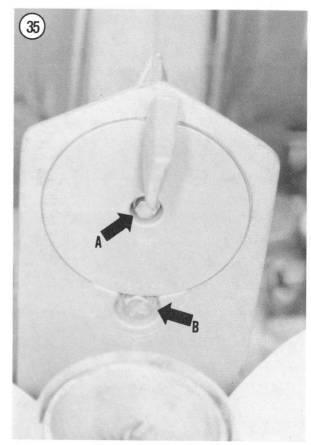

the water pump housing grommet. Rotate the flywheel clockwise as necessary to align the crankshaft and drive shaft splines.

12. Apply OMC Nut Lock to the threads of the gearcase mounting fasteners. Tighten the 3/8 in. screws (A, **Figure 36**) to 18-20 ft.-lb. (24-27

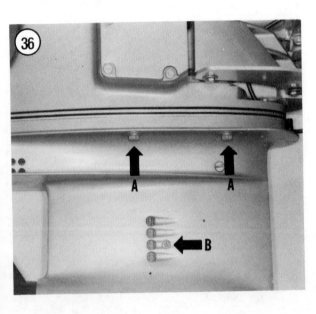

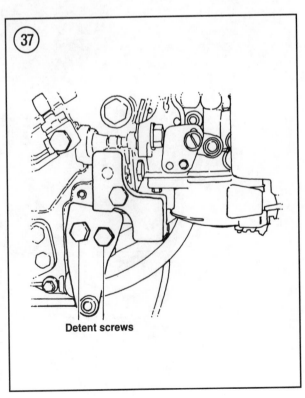

Detent screws

N.m). Tighten the 7/16 in. screw (B, **Figure 35**) to 28-30 ft.-lb. (38-40 N.m).

13. Connect the shift rod to the shift rod connector, then install the shift rod screw (**Figure 34**) and tighten securely.

14. To adjust the shift linkage, loosen the 2 shift detent screws on the power head (**Figure 37**). Make sure the gearcase is in NEUTRAL by rotating the propeller shaft. Then, place the outboard shift lever in the NEUTRAL position and tighten the detent screws (**Figure 37**) to 60-84 in.-lb. (6.8-9.5 N.m).

15. Refill the gearcase with the recommended lubricant (**Table 3**). Install the propeller as described in this chapter.

Removal/Installation (60 and 70 hp)

1. Disconnect the spark plug leads to prevent accidental starting.

2. Remove the propeller as described in this chapter.

3. If gearcase disassembly is necessary, remove the level plug, then the drain/fill plug and allow the lubricant to drain into a suitable container.

NOTE
If the lubricant is white or cream color, or if metal particles are found in Step 4, the gearcase should be disassembled to determine and repair the problem.

4. Rub a small amount of lubricant between a thumb and finger to check for the presence of metal particles or chips. A small amount of fine (powder-like) particles indicates normal wear. Note the color of the lubricant. A white or cream color indicates water contamination. Check the container for water separation from the lubricant.

5A. *If equipped with shift rod screw (2, **Figure 38**)*—Remove the shift rod screw (2, **Figure 38**) and disconnect the shift rod from the shift lever.

5B. *If equipped with shift rod retaining pin (**Figure 39**)*—Remove the shift rod retaining pin.

9

Push the shift lever toward the power head and disconnect the rod from the lever.

6. Mark the trim tab position relative to the gearcase housing for reference during reinstallation. Remove the trim tab screw (A, **Figure 40**) and trim tab.

7. Remove the countersunk screw forward of the trim tab (B, **Figure 40**) using a thin-wall 5/8 in. socket.

8. Remove the screw inside the trim tab cavity (**Figure 41**).

9. Remove the 4 (2 each side) remaining screws securing the gearcase to the exhaust housing. See (A, **Figure 36**).

10. Remove the gearcase from the exhaust housing, using caution not to bend the shift rod. Mount the gearcase in a suitable holding fixture.

CAUTION
Do not grease the top of the drive shaft in Step 11. Excess grease between the top of the drive shaft and the engine crankshaft can create a hydraulic lock, preventing the drive shaft from fully engaging the crankshaft.

11. Lubricate the drive shaft splines with OMC Moly Lube.

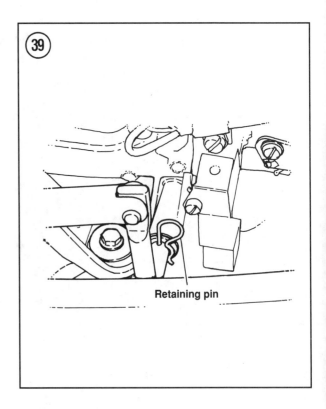

Retaining pin

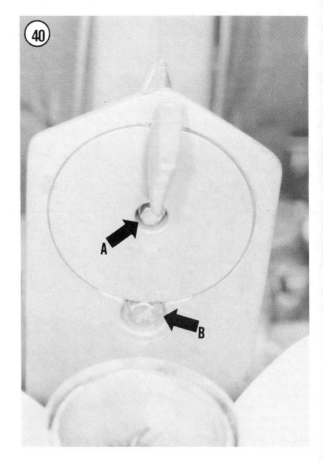

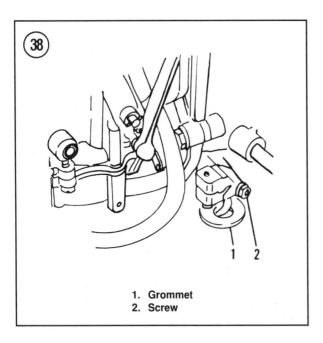

1. Grommet
2. Screw

12. Install the gearcase on the exhaust housing while aligning the drive shaft with the crankshaft and the water tube with the pump housing grommet.

13. Apply OMC Gasket Sealing Compound to the threads of the gearcase mounting screws and install the screws. Tighten the 3/8 in. screws to 18-20 ft.-lb. (24-27 N·m) and the 7/16 in. screw to 28-30 ft.-lb. (38-40 N·m).

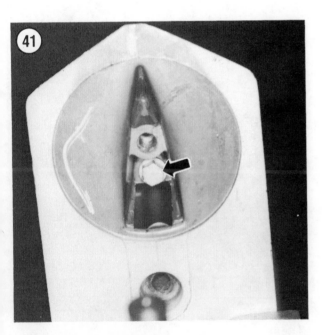

14. Apply OMC Gasket Sealing Compound to the trim tab screw, then install the trim tab and screw. Align the trim tab marks and tighten its mounting screw to 35-40 ft.-lb. (47-54 N·m).

15A. *If equipped with shift rod screw ((***Figure 38***)*—Connect the shift rod to the connector, install the screw and tighten securely.

15B. *If equipped with shift rod pin (***Figure 39***)*—Shift the gearcase into NEUTRAL and align the shift rod with the shift rod lever. Pull the lever away from the power head, connect the shift rod and install the retaining pin.

16. Refill the gearcase with the recommended lubricant (**Table 3**). Install the propeller as described in this chapter.

Removal/Installation (V4, V6 and V8 Models)

1. Disconnect the spark plug leads to prevent accidental starting.

2. Remove the propeller as described in this chapter.

3. If gearcase disassembly is necessary, remove the level plug (A, **Figure 42**), then the drain/fill plug (B) and allow the lubricant to drain into a suitable container.

> *NOTE*
> *If the lubricant is white or cream color, or if metal particles are found in Step 4, the gearcase should be disassembled to determine and repair the problem.*

4. Rub a small amount of lubricant between a thumb and finger to check for the presence of metal particles or chips. A small amount of fine (powder-like) particles indicates normal wear. Note the color of the lubricant. A white or cream color indicates water contamination. Check the container for water separation from the lubricant.

5A. *60° V6 models*—Shift the outboard into FORWARD gear while rotating the propeller shaft.

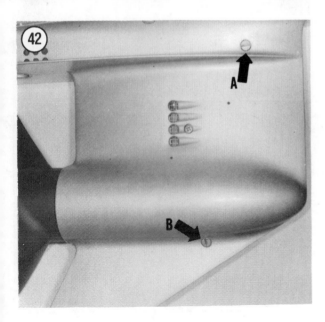

5B. *All other models*—Shift the outboard into REVERSE gear while rotating the propeller shaft.

6. Disconnect the shift rod from the shift lever as follows:

    a. *Loop charged models (except 60° V6)*— Remove the shift rod screw and disconnect the shift rod from the shift rod lever. See **Figure 43**.

    b. *V4 and late V6 cross flow*—Remove the shift rod retaining pin (**Figure 44**), then push the shift lever toward the power head and disconnect the shift rod.

    c. *Early V6 cross flow models*—Remove the shift rod retaining screw (**Figure 45**) and disconnect the shift rod from the shift lever.

    d. *60° V6 models*—Remove the shift rod retaining pin (**Figure 46**). Push the shift shaft/lever toward the power head (arrow, **Figure 46**) and disconnect the shift rod from the lever.

7. Note and record the index mark alignment on the trim tab and gearcase housing for reference during reinstallation. If index marks are not present, make match marks on the trim tab and gearcase with a pencil. Remove the trim tab screw (A, **Figure 40**) and trim tab. Note that some models may not be equipped with a trim tab.

8. Remove the screw forward of the trim tab (B, **Figure 40**) and the screw in the trim tab cavity (**Figure 41**).

WARNING
V4, V6 and especially V8 power heads are very heavy. The engine may suddenly fall to its fully trimmed out position when the gearcase is removed. To prevent personal injury, securely support the engine weight using a suitable hoist or trailering arms before removing the gearcase.

9. Remove the remaining 4 gearcase mounting screws (2 each side). See A, **Figure 36**. Remove the gearcase, being careful not to damage the shift rod. Mount the gearcase in a suitable hold-

ing fixture. Remove and discard the lower exhaust housing seals.

CAUTION
Do not grease the top of the drive shaft in Step 10. Excess grease between the top of the drive shaft and the engine crank-

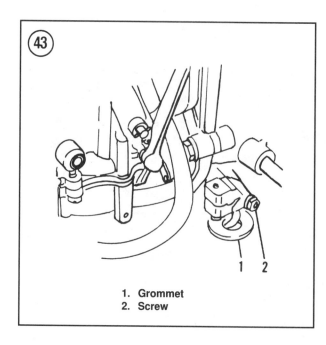

1. Grommet
2. Screw

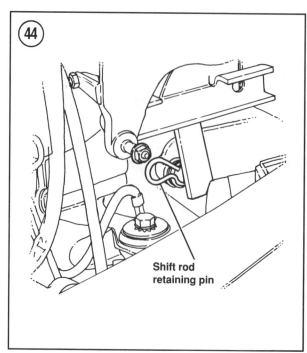

Shift rod retaining pin

shaft can create a hydraulic lock, preventing the drive shaft from fully engaging the crankshaft.

10. On models so equipped, install a new drive shaft O-ring into its groove on the drive shaft.

Shift rod retaining screw

(45)

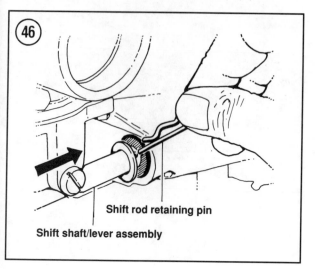

(46)

Shift rod retaining pin

Shift shaft/lever assembly

Apply OMC Moly Lube to the drive shaft splines (all models).

11. Apply OMC Adhesive M to the seal area of the lower exhaust housing. Install new seals on the lower exhaust housing. Apply OMC Triple-Guard grease to the outer surfaces of the seals. Place the housing in place on the gearcase.

12A. *60° V6 models*—Shift the gearcase into FORWARD gear by pulling up on the shift rod while rotating the propeller shaft.

12B. *All other models*—Shift the gearcase into REVERSE by pushing down on the shift rod while rotating the propeller shaft.

13. Position the gearcase under the exhaust housing. Align the water tube with the pump grommet, the drive shaft with the crankshaft and the shift rod with the shift rod seal. Seat the gearcase on the exhaust housing, making sure the lower exhaust housing does not fall out of position.

14. Apply OMC Gasket Sealing Compound to the threads of the gearcase mounting fasteners. Install the fasteners and tighten to specification (**Table 1**).

15. Install the trim tab (if so equipped) and screw. Align the trim tab index marks and tighten the fastener to 35-40 ft.-lb. (47-54 N•m).

16. Reconnect the shift rod to the shift lever and install the screw or retaining pin. See **Figures 43-46** as necessary.

NOTE
The gearcase lubricant on a new or overhauled gearcase should be changed after the initial 10-20 hours of operation.

17. Refill the gearcase with the recommended lubricant (**Table 3**). Install the propeller as described in this chapter.

Cleaning and Inspection (All Models)

1. Discard all seals, O-rings and gaskets during disassembly.

2. Clean all components using solvent. Dry with compressed air. Lightly lubricate internal components to prevent rusting.

3. Inspect the water pump components as described in this chapter.

4. Inspect all gears, bearings and other internal components for excessive wear, corrosion, pitting, chipping, galling, distortion or discoloration due to excessive heat or lack of lubrication.

5. Make sure the cooling water intake screen(s) is clean and free of contamination.

6. Inspect the threads and splines of the drive shaft and propeller shaft for excessive wear, cracks, chips or other damage. See A, **Figure 47**. Check bearing and gear contact surfaces for metal transfer, corrosion or discoloration. See B, **Figure 47**. Excessive or uneven spline wear usually indicates a distorted gearcase or exhaust housing due to impact with an underwater object. The housing(s) must be replaced if distorted.

7. Install V-blocks under the bearing surfaces at each end of the drive shaft. Slowly rotate the shaft while watching for runout or wobble. Replace the shaft if noticeable runout or wobble is noted. Repeat the procedure on the propeller shaft.

8. Replace any anodes which are eroded to 2/3 original size.

9. Thoroughly clean all gasket and sealant material from the gearcase housing. Make sure all threaded holes are free of corrosion, gasket sealant or other contamination. Be certain the upper drive shaft oil circulation passage is clean.

10. Thoroughly clean all thread locking compound from gearcase fasteners. If necessary, clean the threads using a wire brush.

11. Clean all roller bearings with solvent and dry with compressed air. Lightly lubricate bearings to prevent rusting. Replace any bearing if corrosion, flat spots or excessive wear is noted.

12. Inspect the bearing housing and needle bearing(s) for excessive wear or damage. See **Figure 48**, typical.

13. Check all shift components for excessive wear or damage. Check for excessive wear on the shift lever, cradle (A, **Figure 49**), shift shaft and clutch dog engagement surfaces (B, **Figure 49**).

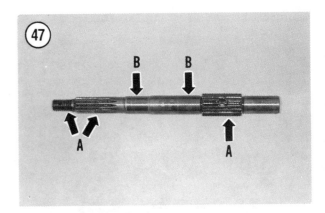

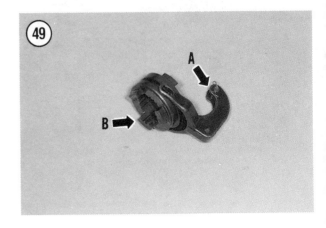

14. Check the pinion gear needle bearing and thrust washers for wear or damage (**Figure 50**, typical).

15. Check the forward, reverse and pinion gears for excessive wear or other damage. See **Figure 51**, typical. Check the clutch engagement dogs (**Figure 51**, typical). If the clutch dogs or teeth are pitted, chipped, broken or excessively worn, replace the gear or clutch.

16. Check the propeller for nicks, cracks or damaged blades. Minor nicks can be removed with a file, taking care to retain the shape of the propeller blade. Replace the propeller if any blades are bent, cracked or badly chipped.

Disassembly/Reassembly (2.0, 2.3 and 3.3 hp)

NOTE
Gearcase removal is not necessary to service the water pump on these models.

Record the location and thickness of all shims and thrust washers removed from the gear housing during disassembly. Refer to **Figure 52** for this procedure.

1. Remove the gearcase as described in this chapter. Remove the propeller as described in this chapter.

2. Remove the water pump, pump housing and related components as described in this chapter.

3. Using a screwdriver or similar tool, reach into the gear cavity and remove the clip securing the pinion gear to the lower drive shaft. Lift the drive shaft out the top of the gearcase, then remove the pinion gear from the gear cavity.

4. Pull the propeller shaft and drive gear assembly from the gearcase. Be sure to retrieve the thrust washer located on the end of the shaft. See 16, **Figure 52**.

5. Inspect the propeller shaft/drive gear assembly and replace it if the impeller drive pin hole or shear pin hole are elongated or excessively worn.

6. Remove and discard the water tube grommet from the gearcase.

NOTE
Inspect the ball bearings in the water pump housing and gearcase and replace if rusted, discolored or if they do not roll smoothly and freely. Do not remove the bearings unless replacement is necessary.

7. Remove the drive shaft seal (4, **Figure 52**) from the gearcase using a suitable seal puller.

8. Remove the snap ring (5, **Figure 52**) from the drive shaft bore using snap ring pliers.

9. Arrange OMC Puller Bridge part No. 432127, Backing Plate part No. 115312 and Puller part No. 432130 (or equivalent 2-jaw

9

puller) as shown in **Figure 53**. Remove the top drive shaft ball bearing using the puller arrangement.

10. After removing the ball bearing, lift the drive shaft spacer out of the gearcase.

11. Using OMC Puller Kit part No. 115307 (or equivalent), remove the lower drive shaft bearing (8, **Figure 52**) and the front propeller shaft bearing (15).

12. Remove the rear propeller shaft bearing (20, **Figure 52**) and seal (21) from the water pump housing/gearcase head assembly using a suitable puller.

13. Clean and inspect all components as described in this chapter.

NOTE
Lubricate all bearings, shafts and gears with OMC Hi-Vis gear lubricant during reassembly.

14. Lubricate the outer diameter of a new propeller shaft forward bearing with gear lube. Using a suitable driver, install the bearing into the gearcase housing until fully seated. The lettered side of the bearing should face the propeller end of the gearcase. Make sure the driver contacts only the outer race of the bearing during installation.

15. Install a new drive shaft lower bearing using OMC Bearing and Seal Installer (part No. 115310) along with OMC Collar (part No. 115314), or a suitable equivalent driver. The lettered side of the bearing should face up. Make sure the installing tool contacts only the outer race of the bearing during installation.

16. Install the drive shaft spacer, then the drive shaft upper bearing using OMC Bearing Installer (part No. 115310) or equivalent. Drive the bearing from its lettered side and make sure the tool contacts only the bearing outer race. Install the snap ring (5, **Figure 52**) using snap ring pliers. Make sure the flat side of the snap ring is facing UP.

17. Apply OMC Gasket Sealing Compound to the outer diameter of a new drive shaft upper seal. Install the seal with its lip facing DOWN using OMC Bearing Installer part No. 115310.

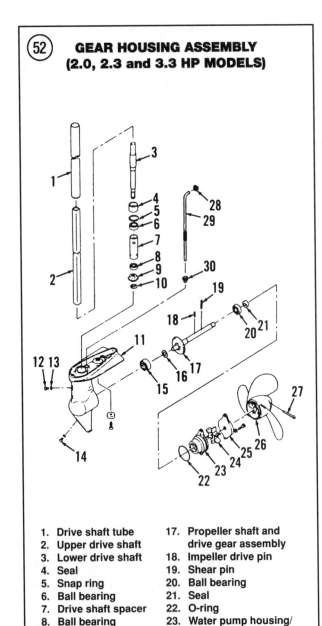

(52) GEAR HOUSING ASSEMBLY (2.0, 2.3 and 3.3 HP MODELS)

1. Drive shaft tube	17. Propeller shaft and
2. Upper drive shaft	drive gear assembly
3. Lower drive shaft	18. Impeller drive pin
4. Seal	19. Shear pin
5. Snap ring	20. Ball bearing
6. Ball bearing	21. Seal
7. Drive shaft spacer	22. O-ring
8. Ball bearing	23. Water pump housing/
9. Pinion gear	gearcase head assembly
10. Clip	24. Impeller
11. Gearcase housing	25. Cover
12. Vent (level) plug	26. Propeller
13. Gasket	27. Cotter pin
14. Drain/fill plug	28. Grommet
15. Ball bearing	29. Water tube
16. Thrust washer	30. Grommet

18. Apply Scotch-Grip Rubber Adhesive 1300 to the outer diameter of a new water tube grommet. Install the grommet into the gearcase housing.

19. Apply OMC Gasket Sealing Compound to the outer diameter of a new water pump housing seal. Install the seal into the water pump housing with its lip facing away from the propeller end. Lubricate the seal lip with OMC Triple-Guard grease.

20. Install a new bearing into the water pump housing. Drive the bearing into the housing using OMC Bearing Installer (part No. 115311), or equivalent, until fully seated. Make sure the driver contacts only the bearing outer race.

21. Install the thrust washer or original shim(s) on the front of the propeller shaft/drive gear assembly. Install the shaft into the gearcase housing.

22. Install the pinion gear into position in the gearcase housing, then install the drive shaft. Make sure the drive shaft and pinion gear are properly engaged and install the pinion gear

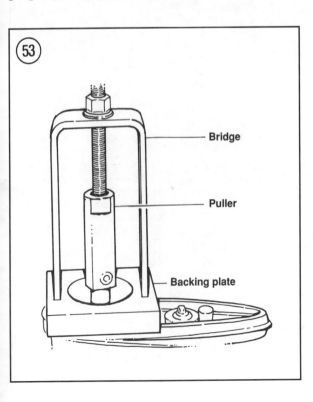

retaining clip. Make sure the sharp side of the clip faces away from the pinion gear.

23. Install a new O-ring on the water pump housing. Lubricate the O-ring with OMC Triple-Guard grease. Install the water pump housing. The slots in the housing should face the port side of the gearcase.

24. Install the impeller drive pin into the propeller shaft. With a clockwise twisting motion, install the water pump impeller into the water pump housing.

25. Apply OMC Gasket Sealing Compound to the threads of the water pump cover fasteners. Install the cover over the propeller shaft and up against the water pump housing. Install the cover fasteners and tighten to specification (**Table 1**).

26. Pressure and vacuum test the gearcase as outlined in this chapter.

27. Install the gearcase as outlined in this chapter.

Disassembly/Reassembly (3 and 4 hp)

Record the location and thickness of all shims and thrust washers removed from the gear housing during disassembly. Refer to **Figure 54** for this procedure. Lubricate all bearings, shafts and gears with OMC Hi-Vis gearcase lubricant during reassembly.

1. Remove the gearcase as described in this chapter.

2. Remove the water pump as described in this chapter.

3. Pull the drive shaft out the top of the gearcase.

4. Remove the 2 gearcase head mounting screws (**Figure 55**).

5. Tap the gearcase head ears with a soft-face mallet to break the seal, then rotate the head free of the gearcase and remove it with the propeller shaft and gear assembly. See **Figure 56**.

6. If the forward gear thrust washer and bearing assembly did not come out with the propeller shaft assembly, remove them from the gearcase. See A, **Figure 57**.

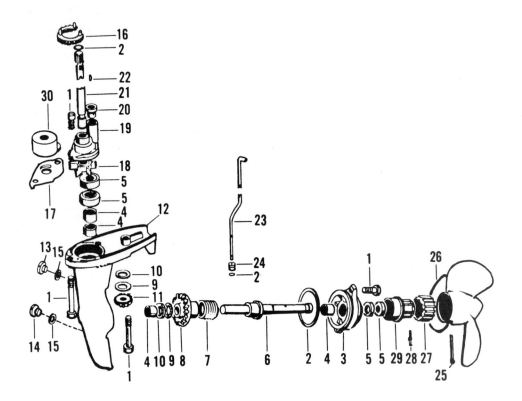

GEARCASE
(3 AND 4 HP)

54

1. Screw	11. Pinion gear	21. Drive shaft
2. O-ring	12. Gearcase housing	22. Impeller drive pin
3. Gearcase head	13. Oil level plug	23. Shift rod
4. Bearing	14. Oil drain plug	24. Shift rod bushing
5. Seal	15. Plug washer	25. Cotter pin
6. Propeller shaft	16. Water inlet screen	26. Propeller
7. Clutch	17. Water pump housing plate	27. Propeller shock absorber
8. Forward gear	18. Impeller	28. Propeller drive pin
9. Thrust bearing	19. Water pump housing	29. Propeller drive hub
10. Thrust washer	20. Water tube grommet	30. Water pump housing liner

7. Remove the pinion gear (B, **Figure 57**) and thrust washer/bearing assembly from the gearcase. Place the washer/bearing assembly in a separate container to prevent it from being mixed up with the forward gear washer/bearing assembly.

8. Inspect the propeller shaft, clutch spring and forward gear assembly. Do not disassemble unless necessary:

a. If inspection indicates further disassembly is necessary, insert an appropriate size

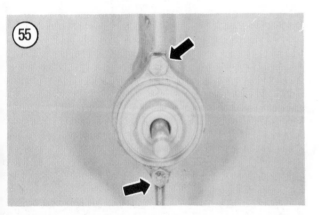

55

56

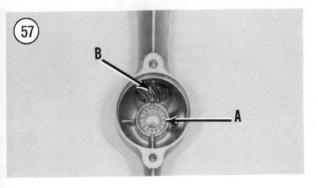

57

punch into the propeller shaft drive pin hole.

b. Hold the forward gear from moving and rotate the propeller shaft in a counterclockwise direction while pulling outward on it. The shaft and gear will separate (**Figure 58**).

c. Carefully remove the spring to prevent distorting its coils. If the coils do not touch each other at all points, replace the spring.

d. Reassemble the propeller shaft components by reversing Sub-steps a-c. The tanged end of the spring should face the gear.

e. Install the forward gear thrust bearing and thrust washer on the propeller shaft in that order.

9. Remove and discard the gearcase head seals (**Figure 59**).

10. Place the gearcase head on a flat surface and remove the needle bearing (A, **Figure 60**) with a suitable driver. Remove and discard the O-ring (B, **Figure 60**).

11. Clean and inspect all components as described in this chapter.

12. Coat the metal case of 2 new gearcase head seals with OMC Gasket Sealing Compound. Install the inner seal (lip facing inward) with in-

9

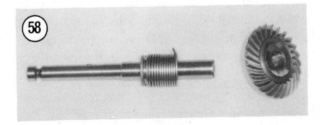

58

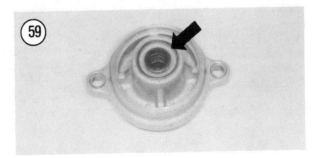

59

staller (part No. 327572), then install the outer seal (lip facing outward) with the same tool.

13. Pack the cavity between the 2 seals with OMC Triple-Guard grease.

14. Lubricate a new O-ring with OMC Hi-Vis Gear lubricant and install on the gearcase head.

15. Turn the gearcase head over and install a new bearing with tool part No. 392091. The lettered side of the bearing must face the installation tool to prevent bearing damage.

16. Remove the 2 drive shaft seals from the gearcase with tool part No. 391259.

17. If the upper and lower drive shaft bearings require removal, assemble the components of tool part No. 392092 as shown in **Figure 61**. Attach a slide hammer to the tool and remove the 2 bearings.

18. If the shift rod bushing requires removal, assemble the guide plate and rod from tool part No. 392092 as shown in **Figure 62**. Thread the rod into the bushing, attach a slide hammer and remove the bushing and O-ring.

19. If the forward gearcase bearing requires removal, assemble tool part No. 391259 with the puller jaws in a vertical position and remove the bearing.

20. If the shift rod bushing was removed, assemble tool part No. 392092 installer and rod. Fit a new bushing on the installer (O-ring facing down) and coat the outer diameter of the bushing with OMC Adhesive M. Drive the bushing into the gearcase with a mallet until fully seated.

21. If the gearcase forward bearing was removed, support the gearcase nose on a block of wood. Install a new bearing with tool part No.

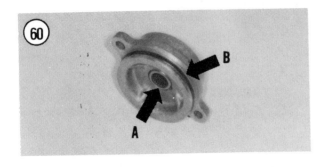

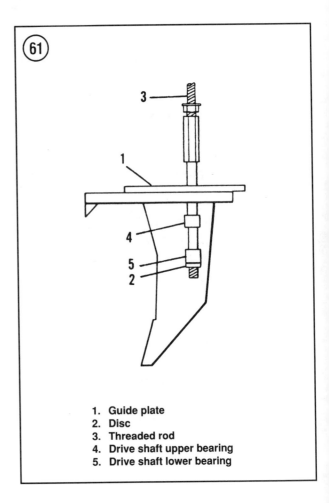

1. Guide plate
2. Disc
3. Threaded rod
4. Drive shaft upper bearing
5. Drive shaft lower bearing

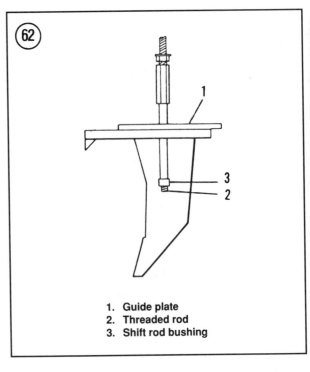

1. Guide plate
2. Threaded rod
3. Shift rod bushing

392091 and mallet. The lettered side of the bearing should face the tool to prevent bearing damage.

22. If the drive shaft upper and lower bearings were removed, install new bearings as follows:

  a. *Lower bearing*—Assemble tool (part No. 392092) components as shown in **Figure 63**. With the lettered side of the bearing facing the tool, drive it in place until the pin touches the guide plate.

  b. *Upper bearing*—Assemble tool (part No. 392092) components as shown in **Figure 64**. With the lettered side of the bearing facing the tool, drive it in place until firmly seated.

23. Coat the outer diameter of the 2 new drive shaft seals with OMC Gasket Sealing Compound. Install the inner seal (lip facing inward) with installer part No. 327431, then install the outer seal (lip facing outward) with the same tool. Pack the cavity between the 2 seals with OMC Triple-Guard grease.

24. Slant the gearcase in the holding fixture so that the pinion gear can be installed and will remain in place. Install the thrust washer, thrust bearing and pinion gear in that order.

25. Lubricate the drive shaft from the pinion gear end to the water pump drive key flat with OMC Hi-Vis gear lubricant. Install the drive shaft in the gearcase and rotate it until it is secured to the pinion gear.

26. Install the water pump as described in this chapter.

27. Install the propeller shaft and forward gear/bearing assembly in the gearcase.

28. Cover the groove in the propeller shaft with a single layer of cellophane tape to prevent it from damaging the gearcase head seals.

29. Lubricate the gearcase head O-ring with OMC Hi-Vis gearcase lubricant. Install the gearcase head over the propeller shaft and seat it in the gearcase. Remove the cellophane tape from the shaft.

30. Coat the gearcase head screw threads with OMC Gasket Sealing Compound. Install and tighten the screws to specification (**Table 1**).

31. Pressure and vacuum test the gearcase as described in this chapter.

32. Install the gearcase as described in this chapter. Fill the gearcase with the recommended lubricant (**Table 3**).

33. Check the gearcase lubricant level after a short water test. Change the gearcase lubricant after 10 hours of operation. See Chapter Four.

Disassembly and Reassembly (4 Deluxe, 6 and 8 hp)

Refer to **Figure 65** for this procedure. Record the location and thickness of all shims and thrust washers removed from the gear housing during

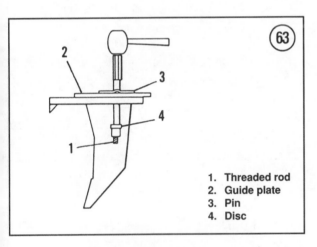

63

1. Threaded rod
2. Guide plate
3. Pin
4. Disc

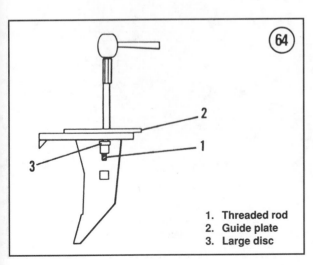

64

1. Threaded rod
2. Guide plate
3. Large disc

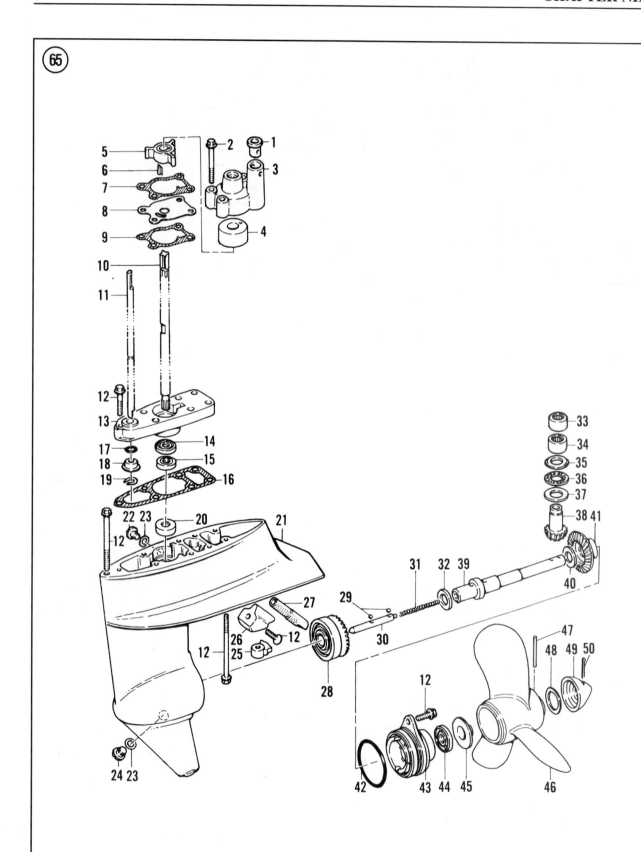

GEARCASE ASSEMBLY
(4 DELUXE, 6 AND 8 HP)

1. Water tube grommet
2. Screw
3. Water pump housing
4. Liner
5. Impeller
6. Impeller drive key
7. Gasket
8. Plate
9. Gasket
10. Drive shaft
11. Lower shift rod
12. Screw
13. Gearcase cover
14. Seal
15. Seal
16. Gasket
17. O-ring
18. Shift rod bushing
19. Retaining ring
20. Bearing and sleeve assembly
21. Gearcase housing
22. Level (vent) plug
23. Gasket
24. Drain/fill plug
25. Shift cam
26. Anode
27. Water intake screen
28. Forward gear and
    bearing assembly
29. Detent balls
30. Shift plunger
31. Spring
32. Thrust washer
33. Drive shaft upper bearing
34. Pinion gear bearing
35. Thrust washer
36. Thrust bearing
37. Thrust washer
38. Pinion gear
39. Propeller shaft
40. Thrust washer
41. Reverse gear
42. O-ring
43. Gearcase head assembly
44. Seal
45. Thrust hub
46. Propeller
47. Propeller drive pin
48. Thrust washer
49. Propeller cap
50. Cotter pin

disassembly. Lubricate all bearings, shafts and gears with OMC Premium Blend gear lubricant (4 Deluxe) or OMC Hi-Vis gearcase lubricant (6 and 8 hp) during reassembly.

1. Remove the gearcase as described in this chapter.

2. Remove the water pump as described in this chapter.

3. Remove the 3 gearcase cover screws (**Figure 66**). Lift the cover up and slide it off the drive shaft and shift rod. Remove and discard the gasket.

4. Pull the drive shaft and shift rod from the gearcase.

5. Remove the 2 gearcase head screws (**Figure 67**).

6. Rotate the gearcase head in the gearcase approximately 15° by tapping it with a soft-face mallet. Then, drive the head rearward by alter-

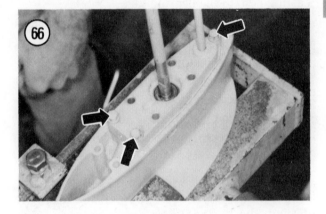

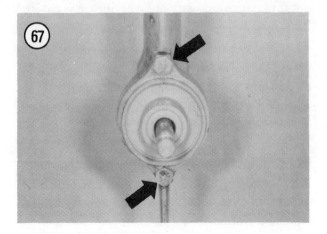

nately tapping on the mounting ears until the O-ring is exposed. Remove the gearcase head and propeller shaft as an assembly. See **Figure 68**.

7. Separate the gearcase head, reverse gear and thrust washer from the propeller shaft. Remove the plunger, spring and 4 detent balls from the propeller shaft (**Figure 69**).

8. Reach inside the housing and rotate the forward gear under the pinion gear to remove it.

9. Remove the shift cam by tilting the gearcase until the cam falls out.

10. Remove the pinion gear, 2 thrust washers and thrust bearing from the gearcase. See **Figure 70**.

11. If the forward gear bearing race requires replacement, remove it with OMC puller part No. 432131 and a slide hammer. Make sure the puller jaws fit into the grooves in the gearcase casting behind the bearing race.

12. If the drive shaft upper bearing and sleeve assembly requires replacement, remove the seals with an appropriate puller, then reverse the jaws of OMC Puller part No. 391012 so that their tips face inward. Stretch a stiff rubber band over the jaws to hold them in place. Remove the bearing and sleeve assembly with the puller and a slide hammer.

13. If the pinion bearing requires replacement, insert OMC Remover Tool part No. 319880 through the top of the gearcase and drive the pinion bearings downward into the gear cavity. Remove and discard the bearings.

14. Check the water intake screen on the gearcase. If clogged or damaged, carefully depress the tab and slide the screen from its cavity. If the tab breaks off during screen removal, install a new screen.

15. Check the zinc anode (26, **Figure 65**) fastened to the bottom of the antiventilation plate. If the anode is eroded to less than two-thirds of its original size, remove the attaching screw and replace the anode.

16. Remove the O-ring from the gearcase head. Temporarily reinstall the head in the gearcase with both screws. Install an appropriate puller and slide hammer and remove the 2 propeller shaft seals.

17. Remove the gearcase cover seals with OMC Puller Bridge part No. 432127 and OMC Small Puller part No. 432131.

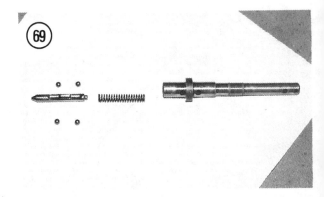

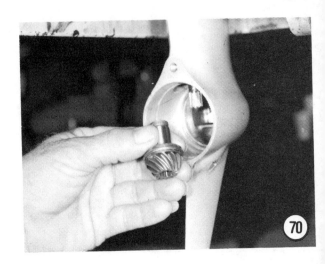

18. Use a punch or similar tool to pry the shift rod bushing from the gearcase cover. Remove and discard the O-ring.

19. Clean and inspect all components as described in this chapter.

20. Apply OMC Gasket Sealing Compound to the outer diameter of a new gearcase head seal. Install the seal (lip facing inward) with a suitable driver, until fully seated in the gearcase head. Lubricate the seal lip with OMC Triple-Guard grease.

21. Apply OMC Gasket Sealing Compound to the outer diameter of 2 new gearcase cover seals. Install the seals back-to-back with OMC Installer part No. 326547. Pack the cavity between the 2 seals with OMC Triple-Guard grease.

22. Lubricate a new shift rod O-ring with OMC Triple-Guard grease and install it in the gearcase cover.

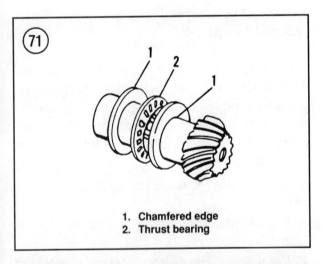

1. Chamfered edge
2. Thrust bearing

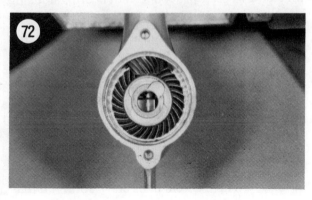

23. Apply a thin bead of OMC Adhesive M to a new shift rod bushing. Install the bushing in the gearcase cover. Allow the adhesive to dry.

24. Install the drive shaft upper bearing using OMC tool part No. 326575. Use a mallet and tap the driver to install the bearing into the gearcase bore until properly seated. The pinion bearing must be installed by pulling the bearing into position. Position the bearing through the propeller shaft opening and into the pinion bearing bore. Slide a 6-1/2 × 3/8 in. coarse-thread bolt with a wide washer through the upper drive shaft bearing and pinion bearing. Thread OMC Pinion Bearing Installer part No. 319878 onto the end of the bolt. Rotate the bolt to pull the pinion bearing into its properly seated position.

NOTE
If either the forward gear bearing or race requires replacement, install a new bearing and race as an assembly.

9

25. If the forward bearing race was removed, install a new race with OMC Installer Tool part No. 326025. Drive the race into the gearcase until fully seated.

26. To replace the forward gear bearing, separate the race from the bearing using a universal puller and arbor press. Install the bearing to the gear with an appropriate mandrel and arbor press.

27. Insert the shift cam into the gearcase housing with the side marked "UP" facing the top of the housing. Hold the cam in that position and slide the shift rod (retaining ring end first) into the gearcase. Rotate the shift rod as necessary to engage the cam.

28. Apply OMC Adhesive M to both sides of a new gearcase cover gasket. Install the cover and gasket. Apply OMC Nut Lock to the cover screws, then install and tighten the screws to specification (**Table 1**).

29. Place the pinion gear thrust bearing between the 2 thrust washers. The thrust washer with the chamfered inside diameter must face the pinion

gear. The thrust washer with the chamfered outer diameter must face away from the pinion gear. See **Figure 71**.

30. Invert the gearcase in the holding fixture and install the pinion gear/bearing assembly.

31. Insert the forward gear into the gearcase, then install the propeller shaft into the gear and pull up sharply on the shaft to snap the gear into its proper position. This will hold the pinion gear in place. See **Figure 72**. Remove the propeller shaft.

32. Install the reverse gear thrust washer onto the propeller shaft with its outer beveled side toward the propeller shaft shoulder. Slide the reverse gear onto the propeller shaft up to the detent ball openings.

33. Install the spring and shift plunger into the end of the propeller shaft.

34. Apply OMC Needle Bearing Assembly Grease on 2 of the detent balls. Depress the plunger to align the ramps in the plunger with the openings in the propeller shaft. Place the other thrust washer on the forward gear side of the propeller shaft. Install 2 detent balls in the openings adjacent to the reverse gear. Slide the reverse gear over the detent balls to retain the balls and plunger in the propeller shaft.

35. Apply OMC Needle Bearing Assembly Grease on the 2 remaining detent balls. Hold the reverse gear in position and install the detent balls in the forward gear openings of the propeller shaft.

36. While holding the reverse gear in position, install the propeller shaft into the gearcase housing. Make sure the detent balls are positioned 90° away from the drive lugs on the forward gear. Turn the propeller shaft to be sure the reverse gear is properly engaged with the pinion gear.

37. Apply OMC Gasket Sealing Compound to the O-ring flange area of the gearcase head and the gearcase head attaching screws. Apply OMC Triple-Guard grease to the gearcase head O-ring and seal lips. Install the O-ring on the gearcase

head. Install the gearcase head and tighten the screws to specification (**Table 1**).

38. Install the seal saver (if so equipped) on the propeller shaft. Make sure the seal saver lip is facing outward, then press it securely in place.

39. Lubricate the drive shaft seal lips with OMC Triple-Guard grease. Install the drive shaft into the gearcase with a rotating motion to engage the drive shaft with the pinion gear splines.

40. Install the water pump as described in this chapter.

41. Pressure and vacuum test the gearcase as described in this chapter.

42. Install the gearcase as described in this chapter. Fill the gearcase with the recommended lubricant (**Table 3**).

43. Check the gearcase lubricant level after a short water test. Change the lubricant after 10 hours of operation.

Disassembly/Reassembly (9.9 and 15 hp)

Refer to **Figure 73** for this procedure. Record the location and thickness of all shims and thrust washers removed from the gear housing during disassembly. Lubricate all bearings, shafts and gears with OMC Hi-Vis gearcase lubricant during reassembly.

1. Remove the gearcase as described in this chapter.

2. Remove the water pump as described in this chapter.

3. Remove the 2 propeller shaft bearing housing screws.

4. Install OMC Gearcase Bearing Housing Puller part No. 386631, using the propeller nut to hold the puller on the propeller shaft. Turn the nut until the puller loosens the bearing housing, then remove the puller. Slide the bearing housing off the propeller shaft and remove it from the gearcase.

5. Remove the propeller shaft and reverse gear assembly with 2 detent balls and a spring. It may

⑦③

**GEARCASE
(9.9 AND 15 HP)**

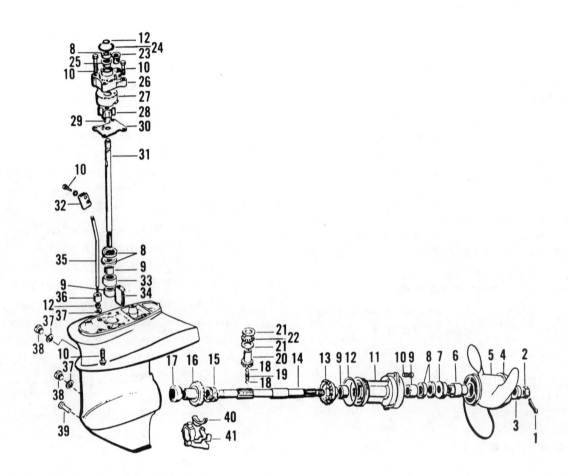

1. Cotter pin	14. Propeller shaft	28. Impeller
2. Castellated nut	15. Clutch dog	29. Impeller drive pin
3. Thrust washer	16. Forward gear	30. Impeller housing plate
4. Converging ring	17. Forward gear bearing	31. Drive shaft
5. Propeller	18. Detent balls	32. Shift rod connector
6. Propeller bushing	19. Detent spring	33. Drive shaft bearing sleeve
7. Thrust bushing	20. Pinion gear	34. Water intake screen
8. Seals	21. Thrust washer	35. Shift rod
9. Needle bearing	22. Needle thrust bearing	36. Shift rod bushing
10. Screw	23. Water tube grommet	37. Washer
11. Gearcase bearing	24. Impeller housing seal	38. Gearcase plug
housing assembly	25. Water restrictor	39. Pivot pin
12. O-ring	26. Impeller housing	40. Clutch dog cradle
13. Reverse gear	27. Impeller housing liner	41. Shift lever and yoke

9

be necessary to use a magnetic tool to locate and remove the detent balls and spring.

6. Remove the pivot pin from the gearcase. Remove and discard the pivot pin O-ring.

7. Pull the drive shaft up and out of the gearcase.

8. Unscrew the shift rod and remove it from the gearcase.

9. Reach into the propeller shaft bore with a pair of needlenose pliers and remove the clutch dog.

10. Remove the pinion gear and thrust bearing/washer assembly.

11. Reach into the propeller housing with a pair of needlenose pliers and grasp the shift lever. Move the lever back and forth and remove it with the forward gear and clutch dog yoke.

12. Slant the gearcase enough to remove the forward gear tapered roller bearing. If one or both detent balls failed to come out in Step 5, it will come out at this time.

13. To remove the shift rod bushing:

   a. Position the remover tool and handle (OMC part No. 327693) under the bushing.

   b. Insert a slide hammer adaptor through the bushing and thread it into the remover tool.

   c. Remove the handle from the remover tool and pull the bushing out with the slide hammer.

   d. Remove and discard the bushing O-ring. Examine the bushing for excessive wear or damage. Replace the bushing as necessary.

14. Using OMC Puller Bridge part No. 432127 and Puller Jaws part No. 432131, remove the 2 drive shaft seals. See **Figure 74**.

NOTE
The drive shaft and pinion gear bearings are destroyed during removal. Inspect the bearings while installed in the gearcase. Do not remove the bearings unless replacement is necessary.

15. Using OMC Puller Bridge part No. 432127 and Puller Jaws part No. 432131, remove the drive shaft upper bearing and sleeve from the gearcase. Discard the bearing.

16. Attach a slide hammer to OMC Bearing Puller part No. 432130. Insert the puller into the recess behind the forward bearing race and remove the race.

NOTE
One pinion gear bearing is used on 1991 and 1992 models. On 1993-on models, 2 pinion gear bearings are used.

17. Insert OMC Bearing Remover part No. 319880 into the drive shaft bore and drive the pinion gear bearing(s) downward into the propeller shaft cavity.

18. Secure the propeller shaft bearing housing in a vise with protective jaws. Remove and discard the bearing housing O-ring.

   a. *1991-1992 models*—Drive the 2 propeller shaft seals from the bearing housing assembly using OMC Bearing And Seal Remover part No. 391259. Remove the small propeller shaft bearing (aft end of housing) by driving it out using OMC Bearing And Seal Remover part No. 319880. Then, drive out the larger bearing (front) using OMC Bearing And Seal Remover part No. 391259.

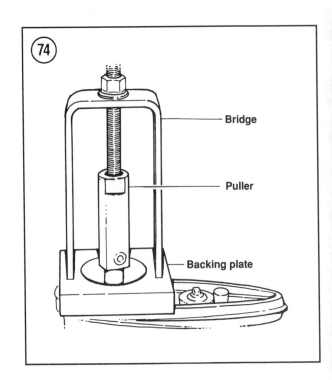

(74)

Bridge

Puller

Backing plate

b. *1993-on models*—Remove the 2 propeller shaft seals using OMC Puller Bridge part No. 432127 and Puller part No. 432131. Discard the seals. Next, drive the small propeller shaft bearing (aft end of housing) from the bearing housing using OMC Driver part No. 319880. Then, remove the large propeller shaft bearing (front) from the housing using Puller Bridge part No. 432130. Discard both bearings.

19. Clean and inspect all components as described in this chapter.

20A. *1991-92 models*—Lubricate the propeller shaft bearings with gear lube and install into the propeller shaft bearing housing as follows:

a. Install the large bearing first, into the forward end of the bearing housing using OMC Bearing Installer part No. 319876. Make sure the lettered side of the bearing is facing the tool during installation.

b. Next, install the small bearing into the aft end of the bearing housing, using OMC

Bearing Installer tool part No. 319875. Make sure the lettered side of the bearing is facing the tool during installation.

20B. *1993-on models*—Lubricate the propeller shaft bearings with gear lube and install into the propeller shaft bearing housing as follows:

a. Install the small bearing first, into the aft end of the bearing housing, using OMC Bearing Installer tool part No. 339751. Make sure the lettered side of the bearing is facing the tool during installation.

b. Then, install the large bearing into the forward end of the bearing housing, using OMC Bearing Installer tool part No. 339751. Make sure the lettered side of the bearing is facing the tool during installation.

21. Apply OMC Gasket Sealing Compound to the outer diameter of 2 new propeller shaft seals. Drive the inner seal into the propeller shaft bearing housing (lip facing inward) using OMC Seal Installer part No. 335822, until the tool contacts the housing. Drive the outer seal (lip facing outward) into the housing using the opposite end of the same installer tool, until the tool contacts the housing. Pack the cavity between the seals with OMC Triple-Guard grease.

22. Install a new O-ring on the bearing housing. Lubricate the O-ring with OMC Triple-Guard grease.

23. If removed, install a new forward gear bearing race. Remove the gearcase housing from the holding fixture, then place the nose of the housing on a wooden block on the floor. Drive the bearing race into the housing, until fully seated using OMC Race Installer part No. 319929, Handle part No. 311880 and a mallet.

CAUTION
*To ensure the correct pinion bearing position, the washer (2, **Figure 75**) must be flat and fasteners at each end of the installation tool must be securely tightened.*

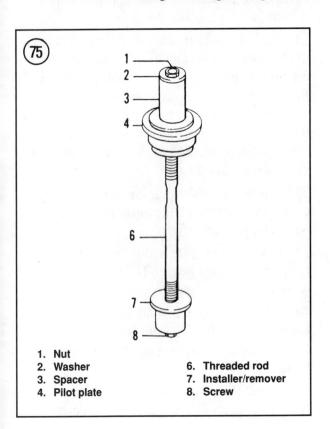

1. Nut
2. Washer
3. Spacer
4. Pilot plate
6. Threaded rod
7. Installer/remover
8. Screw

24A. *1991-92 models*—If removed, install a new pinion gear bearing as follows:

  a. Assemble the components of OMC universal pinion bearing tool part No. 391257 as shown in **Figure 75**.

  b. Lubricate the outer diameter of the bearing with gear lube.

  c. Place the bearing on the remover/installer, with its lettered side facing the tool. Coat the inner diameter of the bearing with OMC Needle Bearing Assembly Grease to hold the bearing on the tool.

  d. Insert the tool and bearing into the gearcase. Tap the bearing into the gearcase until the washer (2, **Figure 75**) contacts the spacer (3).

24B. *1993-on models*—If removed, install 2 new pinion gear bearings as follows:

  a. Assemble the components of OMC universal pinion bearing tool part No. 391257 as shown in **Figure 75**, using the short spacer (3, **Figure 75**) part No. 326585.

  b. Lubricate the outer diameter of the lower bearing with gear lube.

  c. Place the lower bearing on the remover/installer, with its lettered side facing the tool. Coat the inner diameter of the bearing with OMC Needle Bearing Assembly Grease to hold the bearing on the tool.

  d. Insert the tool and bearing into the gearcase. Tap the bearing into the gearcase until the washer (2, **Figure 75**) contacts the short spacer (3).

  e. Remove the tool from the gearcase. Reassemble the tool using the long spacer part No. 339753. Then repeat sub-steps b-d to install the upper pinion gear bearing.

25. If removed, install a new drive shaft bearing (lettered side facing up) in the bearing sleeve with an arbor press and OMC Bearing Installer part No. 319931.

26. Install the bearing and sleeve (lettered side up) into the gearcase with OMC Bearing Installer part No. 319931.

27. Apply OMC Gasket Sealing Compound to the outer diameter of 2 new drive shaft seals. Install the inner seal (lip facing toward gearcase) with OMC Seal Installer part No. 326554, then install the outer seal (lip facing away from gearcase) using the same tool. Pack the cavity between the seals with OMC Triple-Guard grease.

28. Lubricate a new shift rod bushing O-ring with OMC Triple-Guard grease. Install the O-ring into the shift rod bushing. Apply OMC Gasket Sealing Compound to the outer diameter of the shift rod bushing, then drive the bushing into place using a suitable driver and mallet.

29. Lubricate the forward gear bearing with gear lube and install in the forward gear bearing race.

30. Thread OMC yoke locator tool part No. 319991 through the shift rod bushing and into the shift yoke. Pull on the tool and guide the yoke/lever assembly into the gearcase. When properly located, the forward gear will rest against the forward bearing and the shift lever will fit in the gearcase slot.

31. Place the pinion gear thrust bearing between the 2 thrust washers and install the bearing/washers on the pinion gear. Note that on 1991-1992 models, the chamfer on the inside diameter of the small thrust washer must face the pinion gear and the chamfered outside diameter of the large thrust washer must face away from the pinion gear. See **Figure 71**.

32. Guide the pinion gear into place in the gearcase while pushing on the top of the forward gear with a long screwdriver.

33. Position the clutch dog with its grooves facing the forward gear and install it in the cradle with needlenose pliers.

34. Coat the propeller shaft spring and 2 detent balls with OMC Needle Bearing Assembly Grease. Install the spring and balls in the propeller shaft.

35. Install the propeller shaft in the clutch dog, forward gear and bearing. Align the detent balls

with the clutch dog lugs and slide the reverse gear on the propeller shaft.

36. Install the bearing housing in the gearcase. Apply OMC Gasket Sealing Compound to the threads of the housing screws. Install the screws and tighten to specification (**Table 1**).

37. Locate the shift yoke pin hole by probing through the pivot pin hole in the gearcase with an awl or similar tool. Align the shift yoke and gearcase holes. Apply a new O-ring on the pivot pin and coat the O-ring and pivot pin threads with OMC Gasket Sealing Compound. Install the pin and tighten to specification (**Table 1**).

38. Install the drive shaft with a rotating motion to engage the shaft and pinion gear splines.

39. Lubricate the shift rod threads with gear lube. Slide the shift rod through the shift rod bushing and thread it into the yoke.

NOTE
On models equipped with a gearcase extension, make the adjustment in Step 40 after installing the extension.

40. Shift the gearcase into NEUTRAL. Measure the distance between the top of the gearcase-to-exhaust housing mating surface and the highest point of the shift rod connector (32, **Figure 73**). The measurement should be between 13/32 and 7/16 in. (10.3 and 11.1 mm) with the flat surface of the shift rod connector facing the drive shaft. Rotate the shift rod as necessary to obtain the specified distance and position the flat side of the connector toward the drive shaft.

41. Install the water pump as described in this chapter.

42. Pressure and vacuum test the gearcase as described in this chapter.

43. Install the gearcase as described in this chapter. Fill the gearcase with the recommended lubricant (**Table 3**).

44. Check the gearcase lubricant level after a short water test. Change the lubricant after 10 hours of operation.

Disassembly/Reassembly (28 hp)

Refer to **Figure 76** for this procedure. Record the location and thickness of all shims and thrust washers removed from the gear housing during disassembly. Lubricate all bearings, shafts and gears with OMC Hi-Vis gearcase lubricant during reassembly.

1. Remove the gearcase as described in this chapter.

2. Remove the water pump assembly as described in this chapter.

3. Remove the drive shaft from the gearcase.

4. Invert the gearcase in the holding fixture. Remove the Phillips-head shift lever pivot pin. Remove and discard the pivot pin O-ring.

5. Remove the 6 screws holding the lower gearcase to the upper gearcase. Tap the skeg with a soft-face mallet to break the seal and remove the lower gearcase (**Figure 77**). Remove and discard the gearcase seal (**Figure 78**).

6. Pivot the shift lever to the rear and remove the shift cradle (**Figure 79**).

7. Slide the propeller shaft assembly straight up and to the side, then remove it from the gearcase. See **Figure 80**.

8. Remove the pinion gear, thrust washers/bearing assembly from the gearcase (**Figure 81**).

9. Examine the upper end of the shift rod for burrs. If necessary, remove burrs with No. 400 grit wet or dry sandpaper. Slide the shift rod out of the gearcase.

10. Slide all components (except the clutch dog) from the propeller shaft.

11. Slowly slide the clutch dog to the front of the propeller shaft, catching the spring and 2 detent balls as the clutch is removed.

12. Remove the 2 gearcase head seals using OMC Puller Bridge part No. 432127 and puller part No. 432131. Remove and discard the O-ring. See **Figure 82**.

9

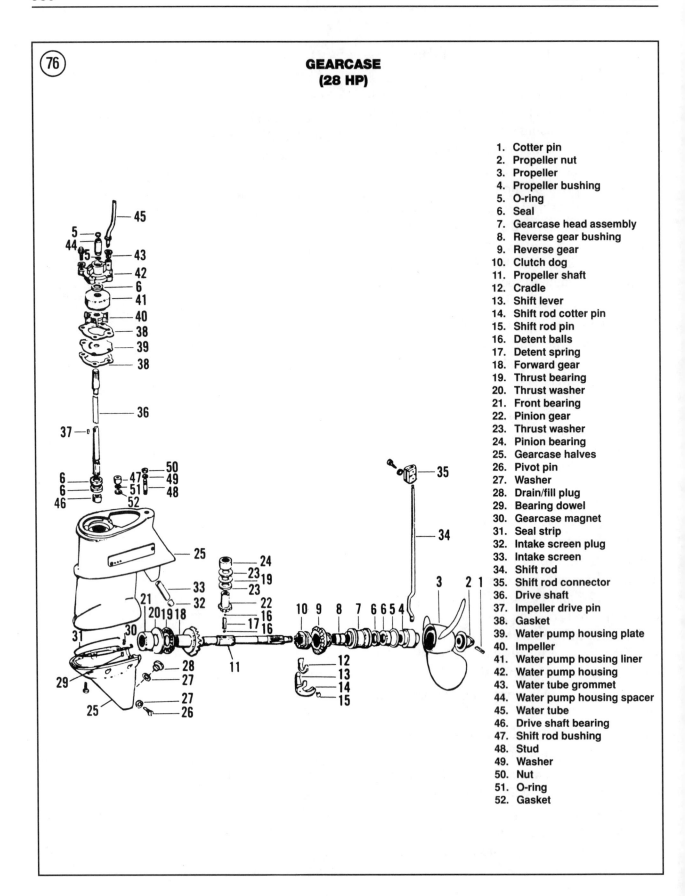

GEARCASE
(28 HP)

1. Cotter pin
2. Propeller nut
3. Propeller
4. Propeller bushing
5. O-ring
6. Seal
7. Gearcase head assembly
8. Reverse gear bushing
9. Reverse gear
10. Clutch dog
11. Propeller shaft
12. Cradle
13. Shift lever
14. Shift rod cotter pin
15. Shift rod pin
16. Detent balls
17. Detent spring
18. Forward gear
19. Thrust bearing
20. Thrust washer
21. Front bearing
22. Pinion gear
23. Thrust washer
24. Pinion bearing
25. Gearcase halves
26. Pivot pin
27. Washer
28. Drain/fill plug
29. Bearing dowel
30. Gearcase magnet
31. Seal strip
32. Intake screen plug
33. Intake screen
34. Shift rod
35. Shift rod connector
36. Drive shaft
37. Impeller drive pin
38. Gasket
39. Water pump housing plate
40. Impeller
41. Water pump housing liner
42. Water pump housing
43. Water tube grommet
44. Water pump housing spacer
45. Water tube
46. Drive shaft bearing
47. Shift rod bushing
48. Stud
49. Washer
50. Nut
51. O-ring
52. Gasket

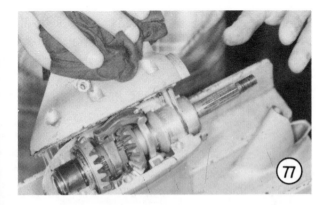

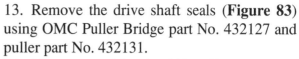

13. Remove the drive shaft seals (**Figure 83**) using OMC Puller Bridge part No. 432127 and puller part No. 432131.

14. If necessary, drive the shift rod bushing from the gearcase using a suitable punch.

NOTE
The drive shaft and pinion bearings are destroyed during removal. Inspect the bearings while still installed in the gear-

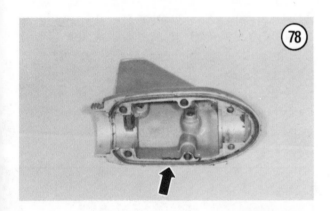

case; do not remove the bearings unless replacement is necessary. If the OMC special tools necessary for bearing installation are not available, note the exact position of the bearings for reference during reassembly.

15. If necessary, remove the drive shaft bearing by driving it downward, out of the gearcase using OMC Bearing Remover part No. 326570, or an equivalent punch.

16. If necessary, remove the pinion bearing using OMC Bearing Remover part No. 326571. Insert the tool into the pinion bearing (from top of gearcase), then drive the bearing from the gearcase.

17. Clean and inspect all components as described in this chapter.

18. Lubricate the shift rod O-ring with OMC Triple-Guard grease. Install the O-ring into the shift rod bushing.

19. Apply OMC Gasket Sealing Compound to the outer diameter of the shift rod bushing. Drive the bushing and O-ring into the shift rod bore until fully seated using OMC Bushing Installer part No. 304515.

20. If removed, lubricate a new drive shaft bearing with gear lube. Using OMC Drive Shaft Bearing Installer part No. 326564, press the bearing into the drive shaft bore until the tool contacts the gearcase. Make sure the lettered side of the bearing is facing the tool during installation.

21. Apply OMC Gasket Sealing Compound to the outer diameter of 2 new drive shaft seals. Using OMC Drive Shaft Seal Installer part No. 330655 and OMC Drive Handle part No. 378737, install the lower seal (lip facing gearcase) into the drive shaft bore. Using the same tool, install the upper seal (lip facing away from gearcase) until it contacts the lower seal. Lubricate the seal lips with OMC Triple-Guard grease.

22. Using OMC Pinion Bearing Installer part No. 326565, press a new pinion bearing into the gearcase (if removed) until the tool contacts the

gearcase. Make sure the lettered side of the bearing is facing the tool during installation.

23. Apply OMC Gasket Sealing Compound to the outer diameter of 2 new gearcase head (propeller shaft) seals. Using OMC Seal Installer part No. 326691, press the inner seal into the gearcase head with its lip facing away from the propeller end. Using the same tool, press the outer seal into the gearcase head with its lip facing the propeller end. Lubricate both seal lips with OMC Triple-Guard grease.

24. Lubricate a new gearcase head O-ring with OMC Triple-Guard grease. Install the O-ring into its groove on the head. See **Figure 82**.

25. Place the pinion gear thrust bearing between the 2 thrust washers. The thrust washer with the chamfered inside diameter (smaller washer) must be installed on the gear first, with the

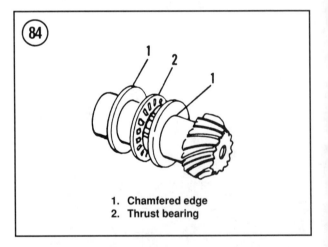

1. Chamfered edge
2. Thrust bearing

chamfered side facing the gear. The chamfered outer diameter of the remaining washer (larger washer) must face away from the gear. See **Figure 84**.

26. Lubricate the pinion gear and thrust washer/bearing assembly. Install the gear and bearing assembly into the gearcase (**Figure 85**).

27. Lubricate the end of the shift rod with OMC Triple-Guard grease. Insert the rod through the shift rod bushing and place the shift cradle on the shift lever (B, **Figure 86**).

28. Insert the spring into the propeller shaft. Position a detent ball on each side of the spring. While holding the spring and balls in place, slide the clutch dog into position. The chamfered and grooved lugs on the clutch dog must face the front of the propeller shaft.

29. Lubricate the remaining propeller shaft components with gear lube. Install the roller

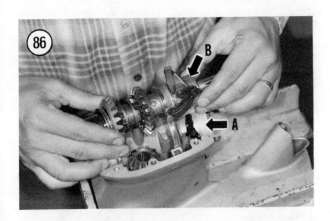

bearing (lettered end facing forward), thrust washer, thrust bearing and gear in that order.

30. Next, install the reverse gear, bushing and gearcase head in that order.

31. Apply a bead of OMC Adhesive M on the upper gearcase at point A, **Figure 86**.

32. Install the propeller shaft assembly into the upper gearcase (**Figure 86**). Make sure the hole in the gearcase head engages the locating pin in the gearcase. Pry the clutch dog forward into gear with a flat-blade screwdriver while rotating the propeller shaft, then position the shift cradle.

33. Install OMC Alignment Tool part No. 390880 on the propeller shaft (**Figure 87**) to seat the forward gear and thrust bearing against the gearcase and prevent them from cocking. Leave the tool in place until the other half of the gearcase is installed.

NOTE
The lower gearcase-to-upper gearcase seal strip is sold in bulk rolls. Obtain at least 13 in. (33 cm) for use in Step 34.

34. Coat the machined surfaces of both gearcase halves and the exposed area of the gearcase head with OMC Adhesive M. Place the seal strip in the lower gearcase groove, then cut the ends of the seal exactly flush with the end of the groove. Apply RTV sealant to each end of the seal for a distance of 1/2 in. (12.7 mm).

35. Apply OMC Gasket Sealing Compound to the threads of the 6 gearcase screws. Install the lower gearcase half and install the 2 front and 2 rear screws. Finger tighten the 4 screws alternately and evenly, until the gearcase halves are drawn together.

36. Install the remaining screws and finger tighten. Then, tighten all screws evenly, in several steps, alternating sides and working from front-to-rear. Tighten the screws to specification (**Table 1**) and remove the alignment tool.

37. Apply OMC Triple-Guard grease to a new pivot pin O-ring and install the O-ring on the pivot pin. Apply OMC Nut Lock to the threads

9

of the pivot pin. Install the pivot pin while moving the shift rod in and out to locate the pivot pin hole in the shift lever. Tighten the pivot pin to specification (**Table 1**).

38. Install the drive shaft with a rotating motion to engage the drive shaft and pinion gear splines.

39. Install the water pump as described in this chapter.

40. Pressure and vacuum test the gearcase assembly as described in this chapter.

41. Install the gearcase as described in this chapter. Fill with the recommended lubricant (**Table 3**).

42. Check the gearcase lubricant level after a short water test. Change the lubricant after 10 hours of operation.

Disassembly/Reassembly
(20, 25 and 30 hp)

Refer to **Figure 88** for this procedure. Record the location and thickness of all shims and thrust washers removed from the gear housing during disassembly. Lubricate all bearings, shafts and gears with the recommended gear lubricant (**Table 3**) during reassembly.

If the OMC special tools necessary for seal and bearing installation are not available, note the exact position of the seals and bearings for reference during reassembly.

1. Remove the gearcase as described in this chapter.

2. Remove the water pump assembly as described in this chapter. Remove the drive shaft along with the water pump.

3. Remove the 2 screws securing the propeller shaft bearing housing in the propeller shaft bore. See **Figure 89**.

4. Install puller part No. 378103 as shown in **Figure 90**. Tighten the puller screw to break the seal, then remove the bearing housing from the gearcase. See **Figure 91**.

GEARCASE ASSEMBLY
(20, 25 AND 30 HP)

1.	Water tube seal	
2.	Water tube	
3.	O-ring	
4.	Drive shaft spacer	
5.	Water tube grommet	
6.	Water pump housing	
7.	O-ring	
8.	Water pump housing liner	
9.	Impeller	
10.	Impeller drive key	
11.	Bushing	
12.	O-ring	
13.	Seal	
14.	Plate	
15.	Gasket	
16.	Drive shaft	
17.	Upper shift rod connector	
18.	Shift rod keeper	
19.	Lower shift rod	
20.	Lower shift rod connector	
21.	Lower shift rod bushing	
22.	O-ring	
23.	O-ring	
24.	Washer	
25.	Drive shaft seals	
26.	Drive shaft bearing	
27.	Bearing sleeve	
28.	Gearcase housing	
29.	Gasket	
30.	Level (vent) plug	
31.	O-ring	
32.	Shift lever pivot pin	
33.	Drain/fill plug	

34.	Pinion gear upper bearing	
35.	Bearing	
36.	Thrust washers	
37.	Thrust bearing	
38.	Pinion gear	
39.	Detent balls	
40.	Detent spring	
41.	Propeller shaft	
42.	Shift yoke and connector	
43.	Dog clutch	
44.	Forward gear	
45.	Forward gear bearing	
46.	Shift cradle	
47.	Shift lever	
48.	Pin and cotter pin	
49.	Reverse gear	
50.	Reverse gear bushing	
51.	Bearing housing retainer plate	
52.	Snap ring	
53.	Thrust washer	
54.	Bearing	
55.	O-ring	
56.	O-ring	
57.	Propeller shaft bearing housing	
58.	Screw	
59.	Bearing	
60.	Propeller shaft seals	
61.	Thrust hub	
62.	Propeller bushing	
63.	Propeller	
64.	Spacer	
65.	Nut	
66.	Cotter pin	

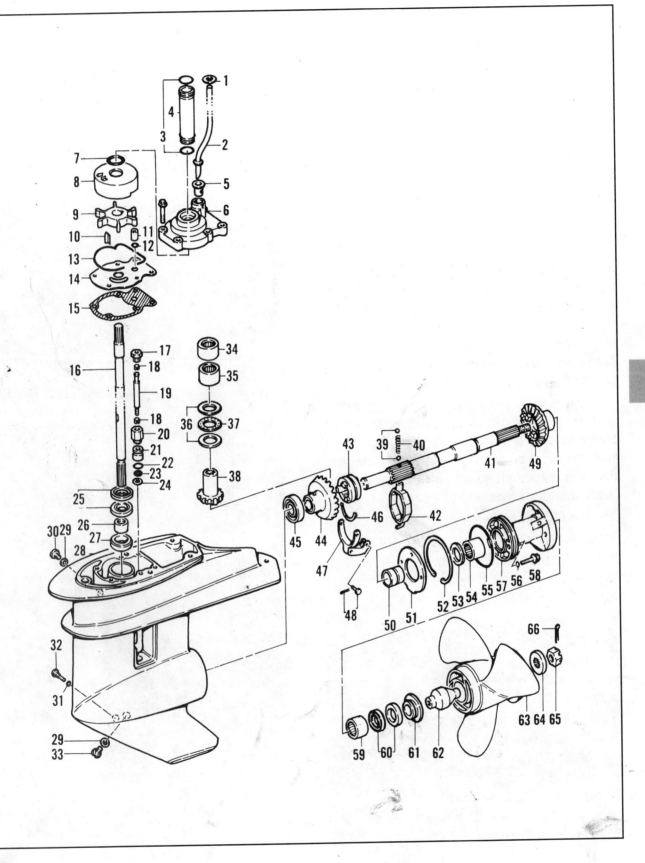

9

WARNING
*The snap ring (52, **Figure 88**) is under extreme pressure when compressed during removal. Wear suitable eye and hand protection when removing the snap ring.*

5. Remove the large snap ring from the gearcase using OMC Snap Ring Pliers part No. 331045, or equivalent. See **Figure 92**.

6. Remove the bearing housing retainer plate from the gearcase.

7. Turn the lower shift rod counterclockwise until it is free of the shift yoke, then remove it from the gearcase. Remove and discard the lower plastic keeper.

8. Reach into the gearcase with needlenose pliers and remove the shift yoke (**Figure 93**).

9. Remove the shift lever pivot pin (Phillips head). Remove and discard the pivot pin O-ring.

10. Remove the propeller shaft assembly along with the reverse gear. The 2 clutch dog detent balls will dislodge and drop into the gearcase. Remove the clutch dog and shift cradle using long needlenose pliers. Tilt the gearcase and catch the detent spring and balls or remove them with a magnetic tool.

11. Remove the forward gear and bearing assembly. Remove the pinion gear, pinion gear thrust bearing and 2 thrust washers. If necessary, use a right-angle tool to retrieve the pinion gear assembly. See **Figure 94**.

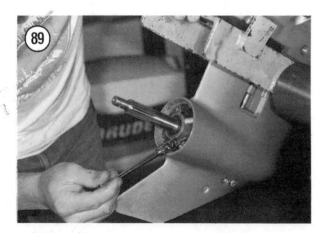

NOTE
Do not remove the forward gear race from the gearcase unless replacement is necessary. Always replace the forward gear bearing and race as a set.

12. Attach a slide hammer to a narrow 2-jaw puller (OMC part No. 432130). Insert the puller jaws into the grooves at each side of the gearcase

behind the forward gear bearing race. Remove the bearing race.

13. Using OMC Puller Bridge part No. 432127 and Small Puller part No. 432131, remove the drive shaft seals. See **Figure 95**.

> *NOTE*
> *The drive shaft and pinion bearings are destroyed during removal. Inspect the bearing while still installed and do not remove unless replacement is necessary.*

14. Using the same tools (Step 13), remove the drive shaft bearing and bearing sleeve (**Figure 95**, typical). Press the bearing from the sleeve. Discard the bearing.

15. To remove the pinion bearings, assemble the components of Universal Pinion Bearing Tool part No. 391257 as shown in **Figure 96**. Insert the tool into the drive shaft bore and slide the remover/installer into the top pinion bearing.

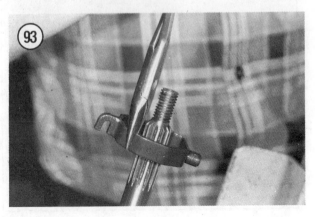

9

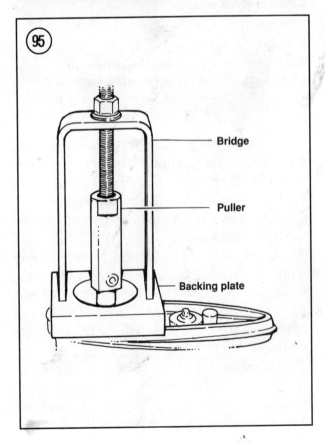

Using a soft-mallet, drive both bearings downward into the propeller shaft cavity. Discard the bearings.

16. To remove the shift rod bushing:
   a. Position OMC Shift Rod Bushing Remover part No. 327693 under the shift rod bushing.
   b. Insert a slide hammer adaptor through the bushing and thread it into the remover tool.
   c. Remove the handle from the remover tool and pull the bushing out with the slide hammer.
   d. Remove and discard the bushing O-rings and washer. Examine the bushing for excessive wear or damage. Replace the bushing as necessary.

17. Remove and discard the O-ring from the propeller shaft bearing housing.

18. Remove the propeller shaft seals from the bearing housing using OMC Puller Bridge part No. 432127 and Small Puller part No. 432131. Discard the seals.

NOTE
The propeller shaft bearings are destroyed during removal from the bearing housing. Inspect the bearing while still installed and do not remove unless replacement is necessary.

19. Remove the propeller shaft bearings from each end of the bearing housing using OMC Puller Bridge part No. 432127 and Small Puller part No. 432131. Discard the bearings.

20. Clean and inspect all components as described in this chapter.

21. Lubricate a new rear propeller shaft bearing with gear lube. Place the lettered end of the bearing against OMC Bearing Installer tool part No. 335820 and press the bearing into the aft end of the bearing housing until the tool contacts the housing.

22. Lubricate a new front propeller shaft bearing with gear lube. Place the lettered end of the bearing against OMC Bearing Installer tool part No. 321428 and press the bearing into the front end of the bearing housing until the tool contacts the housing.

23. Apply OMC Gasket Sealing Compound to the outer diameter of new propeller shaft seals. Using OMC Seal Installer tool part No. 335821, press the inner seal (lip facing bearing housing) into the bearing housing. Next, using the opposite end of the installer tool, press the outer seal (lip facing away from housing) into the bearing housing until it contacts the inner seal. Pack the cavity between the seals with OMC Triple-Guard grease.

24. Lubricate a new bearing housing O-ring with OMC Triple-Guard grease. Install the O-ring into its groove on the bearing housing.

25. Lubricate the forward gear bearing race with gear lube. Install the race into the gearcase housing using OMC Installer tool part No. 319929 and Driver Handle part No. 311880. Support the leading edge of the gearcase housing on a wooden block and drive the race into the housing until fully seated.

26. Lubricate a new shift rod O-ring and install it into the shift rod bushing. Apply OMC Gasket

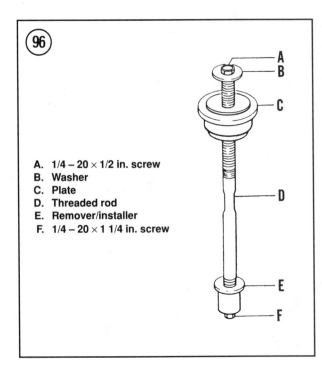

(96)

A. 1/4 – 20 × 1/2 in. screw
B. Washer
C. Plate
D. Threaded rod
E. Remover/installer
F. 1/4 – 20 × 1 1/4 in. screw

Sealing Compound to the outer diameter of the shift rod bushing. Install the remaining new O-ring around the bushing. Then, drive the bushing and washer into the gearcase using OMC Shift Rod Bushing Installer part No. 304515.

27. Lubricate the 2 new pinion bearings with gear lube. To install the pinion bearings, assemble the components of OMC Universal Pinion Bearing Remover and Installer part No. 391257 as shown in **Figure 97**. Proceed as follows:

a. First, assemble the tools using the short spacer part No. 330067 (3, **Figure 97**). Place the lower bearing on the installer tool with its lettered side facing the tool. Insert the tool and bearing into the drive shaft bore and drive the bearing into its bore until the washer (2, **Figure 97**) contacts the spacer (3).

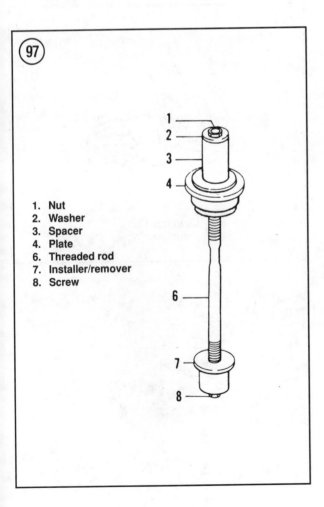

(97)

1 —
2 —
3 —
4 —

1. Nut
2. Washer
3. Spacer
4. Plate
6. Threaded rod
7. Installer/remover
8. Screw

6 —

7 —

8 —

b. Next, assemble the tools using the long spacer part No. 330068. Place the upper bearing on the installer tool with its lettered side facing the tool. Insert the tool and bearing into the drive shaft bore and drive the bearing into its bore until the washer (2, **Figure 97**) contacts the spacer (3).

28. Lubricate a new drive shaft bearing with gear lube. Install the bearing into the bearing sleeve (lettered side facing up) using OMC Bearing Installer part No. 322923. The bearing should be fully seated in the sleeve.

29. Using OMC iNstaller Tool part No. 322923 attached to Plate part No. 318122, install the drive shaft bearing and sleeve assembly (lettered side facing up) into the gearcase until the plate contacts the gearcase.

30. Apply OMC Gasket Sealing Compound to the outer diameter of the new drive shaft seals. Install the lower seal into the gearcase with its lip facing down and the upper seal with its lip facing up, using OMC Seal Installer part No. 326552.

31. Lubricate the forward gear bearing with gear lube and install it into the forward race.

32. Place the pinion gear thrust bearing between the 2 thrust washers. Make sure the small washer is installed first, with its chamfered inside diameter facing the gear. Make sure the large washer is installed last, with its chamfered outer diameter facing away from the gear. See **Figure 98**. Lubricate the thrust washers, bearing and pinion gear with gear lube.

33. Install the pinion gear and thrust bearing/washers into the gearcase (**Figure 94**).

34. Install the forward gear into the gearcase.

35. Place the shift cradle and lever assembly (A, **Figure 99**) on the clutch dog (B). The grooved end of the clutch must face the forward gear when installed. Apply a liberal coat of OMC Needle Bearing Assembly Grease to hold the cradle/lever assembly in place on the clutch.

36. Install the clutch assembly into the gearcase using long needlenose pliers.

9

37. Lubricate a new shift lever pivot pin O-ring with OMC Triple-Guard grease, then install it onto the pivot pin. Apply OMC Nut Lock to the threads of the pivot pin.

38. Align the shift lever hole with the hole in the gearcase and install the pivot pin. Tighten the pin to specification (**Table 1**).

39. Install OMC Shift Detent Tool part No. 328081 over the propeller shaft. Align the slot in the tool with the hole in the propeller shaft. See A, **Figure 100**. Insert 1 detent ball, then the spring and the remaining ball into the slot. Push downward on the second detent ball with your thumb and slide the tool back (B, **Figure 100**) until the balls engage the detent in the tool. Leave the tool in this position.

NOTE
Work slowly and carefully in Step 40. The detent balls and spring will not engage the clutch dog if the tool legs and clutch dog ramps are not aligned properly.

40. Insert the propeller shaft and detent tool into the gearcase (**Figure 101**). Make sure the propeller shaft enters the forward gear. Push the shaft forward, aligning the legs on the detent tool with the clutch dog ramps until the detent balls and spring enter the clutch dog. If necessary tap the propeller shaft with a soft mallet. Remove the detent tool.

41. Install the reverse gear onto the propeller shaft and into the gearcase. Lubricate the reverse gear bushing with gear lube. Slide the bushing onto the propeller shaft and into place in the reverse gear.

42. Grasp the shift yoke with needlenose pliers. Install the yoke into the gearcase, engaging its top in the upper gearcase cavity and locating its bottom hook on the shift lever clevis pin at the bottom of the gearcase cavity.

43. Lubricate the lower shift rod with gear lube. Install the rod and a new plastic keeper through the water intake opening until it engages the shift yoke. Thread the rod into the yoke until bottomed.

44. Position the bearing housing retainer plate on the propeller shaft with its tab facing the skeg. Slide the plate into position.

WARNING
The snap ring installed in Step 44 is under extreme pressure when compressed. Wear suitable eye and hand protection when installing the snap ring.

45. Install the retainer plate snap ring using OMC Snap Ring Pliers part No. 331045. See **Figure 92**. Make sure the sharp outer edge of the snap ring is facing outward and the ring is properly seated in its groove.

46. Thread guide pin (OMC part No. 383175) into the retainer plate holes.

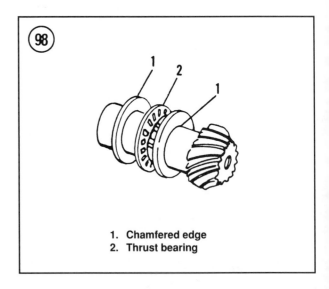

98

1. Chamfered edge
2. Thrust bearing

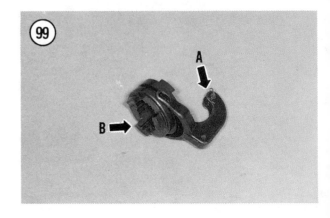

99

47. Apply OMC Needle Bearing Assembly Grease to the reverse gear thrust washer. Stick the washer to the aft end of the propeller shaft bearing housing using the grease.

48. Apply OMC Gasket Sealing Compound to the aft support flange of the bearing housing. Place the bearing housing on the guide pin, making sure the "UP" mark on the housing is facing the top.

49. Slide the bearing housing into the gearcase. Seat the bearing housing by tapping into place with a brass punch and mallet.

50. Install new O-rings on the bearing housing screws. Apply OMC Gasket Sealing Compound to the screw threads and O-rings.

51. Install 1 screw into the housing and finger tighten. Remove the guide pin, then install the remaining screws. Tighten the screws evenly to specification (**Table 1**).

52. Lubricate the drive shaft splines with gear lube. Install the shaft into the gearcase with a rotating motion to engage the pinion gear.

53. Install the water pump as described in this chapter.

54. Pressure and vacuum test the gearcase as described in this chapter.

55. Install the gearcase as described in this chapter. Fill the gearcase with the recommended lubricant (**Table 3**). Check the lubricant level after a short water test. Change the lubricant after 10 hours of operation.

Disassembly/Reassembly (40-50 hp)

Refer to **Figure 101** for this procedure. Record the location and thickness of all shims and thrust washers removed from the gear housing during disassembly. Lubricate all bearings, shafts and gears with the recommended gear lubricant (**Table 3**) during reassembly.

If the OMC special tools necessary for seal and bearing installation are not available, note the exact position of the seals and bearings for reference during reassembly.

1. Remove the gearcase and mount it in a suitable holding fixture as described in this chapter.

2. Remove the water pump as described in this chapter.

3. Remove the propeller shaft bearing housing anode retaining screws and remove the anode.

4. Remove the propeller shaft bearing housing retaining screws and retainers. See **Figure 102**.

5. Assemble flywheel puller (OMC part No. 378103) with two 1/4-20 × 8 in. cap screws and flat washers. Screw the cap screws into the threaded holes for the retaining screws in the propeller shaft bearing housing. Tighten the puller jackscrew until the bearing housing comes loose.

6. Remove the puller assembly from the bearing housing. Remove the bearing housing from the gearcase. Remove and discard the bearing housing O-ring. See **Figure 103**.

7. Remove the thrust washer (A, **Figure 104**) from the front end of the bearing housing.

8. Tilt the gearcase housing with the propeller shaft angled down and slide the reverse gear (C, **Figure 104**) and thrust bearing (B) off the propeller shaft. Reposition the gearcase housing with the antiventilation plate level.

9. Remove the shift lever pivot pin. See **Figure 105**. Remove and discard the pivot pin O-ring.

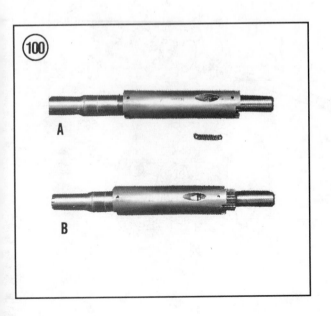

9

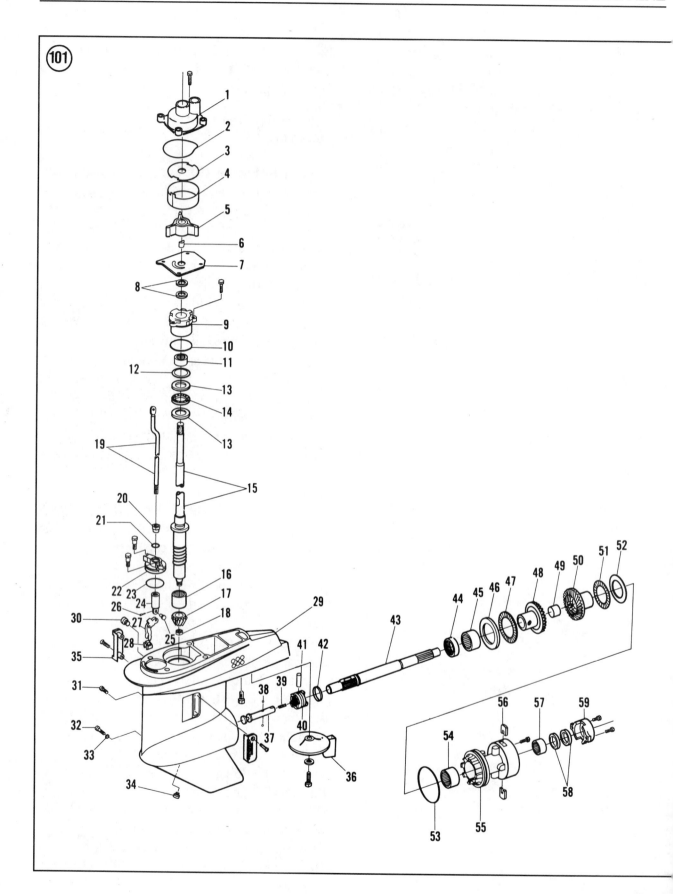

**GEARCASE
(40-50 HP)**

1. Water pump housing
2. Housing plate seal
3. Impeller plate
4. Impeller liner
5. Impeller
6. Impeller drive key
7. Water pump housing plate
8. Seals
9. Drive shaft bearing housing
10. O-ring
11. Bearing
12. Shim(s)
13. Thrust washers
14. Thrust bearing
15. Drive shaft
16. Bearing
17. Pinion gear
18. Nut
19. Shift rod
20. Bushing
21. O-ring
22. Shift rod cover
23. O-ring
24. Connector
25. Pin
26. Cotter pin
27. Shift lever
28. Cradle
29. Gearcase
30. Oil level plug
31. Bearing retaining screw
32. Shift lever pivot pin
33. O-ring
34. Drain/fill plug
35. Water intake screen
36. Trim tab
37. Shift shaft
38. Detent ball (3)
39. Spring
40. Clutch dog
41. Pin
42. Retaining spring
43. Propeller shaft
44. Bearing (short)
45. Bearing (long)
46. Thrust washer
47. Thrust bearing
48. Forward gear
49. Bushing
50. Reverse gear
51. Thrust bearing
52. Thrust washer
53. O-ring
54. Bearing
55. Propeller shaft bearing housing
56. Retainer (2)
57. Bearing
58. Seals
59. Anode

10. Remove the 2 shift rod cover retaining screws. See **Figure 106**.

11. Grasp the shift rod and lift the assembly from the gearcase.

12. Disassemble the shift rod and discard 2 O-rings. See **Figure 107**.

13. Remove the propeller shaft assembly (B, **Figure 108**) and cradle (A) from the gearcase.

14. Carefully lift one end of the clutch dog retaining spring and insert a screwdriver blade

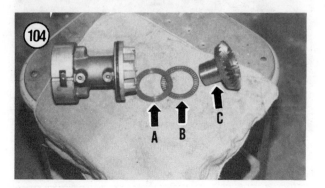

or the tip of an awl under it. Carefully pry the retaining spring from the dog clutch. See **Figure 109**.

15. Push the clutch dog cross pin from clutch and propeller shaft (**Figure 110**), then slide the clutch dog off the propeller shaft.

> *WARNING*
> *To prevent possible personal injury, eye protection is recommended prior to disassembly of shift detent.*

16. Remove the shift shaft, 3 detent balls and spring from the propeller shaft. See **Figure 111**.

17. Remove the 3 screws holding the drive shaft bearing housing.

18. Install OMC Drive Shaft Holding Socket, part No. 334995, on the drive shaft splines and connect a breaker bar.

19. Place a 11/16 in. wrench into the propeller shaft cavity and onto the pinion gear nut. Pad the

area around the wrench with shop towels to prevent damage to the gearcase housing.

20. While holding the pinion nut from turning, turn the drive shaft to break the pinion nut loose.

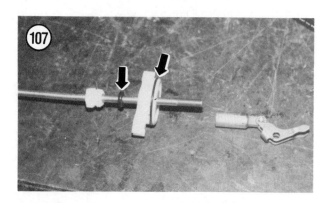

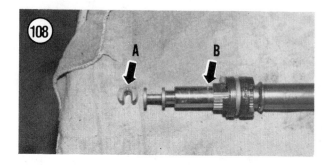

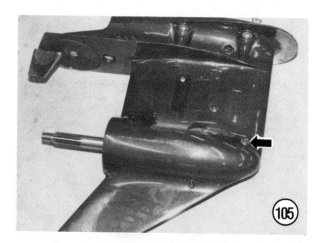

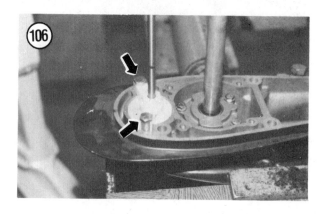

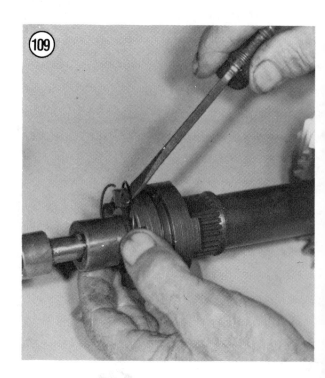

See **Figure 112**. Remove the pinion nut and drive shaft holding tool.

21. Remove the pinion nut and gear from the gearcase.

22. Pull the drive shaft and bearing housing from the gearcase. The drive shaft and pinion gear connection is a splined, tapered fit. If the drive shaft is difficult to remove, use OMC Puller part No. 387206 and Plate part No. 325867 to break loose the drive shaft.

23. Separate the bearing housing, shim(s), thrust washers and thrust bearing from the drive shaft. See **Figure 113**.

24. Remove the forward gear, thrust washer and thrust bearing from the gearcase.

NOTE
The pinion bearing is destroyed during removal. Inspect the bearing while still installed—do not remove the bearing unless replacement is necessary.

25. If the pinion gear bearing requires replacement, remove the bearing retaining screw (**Fig-**

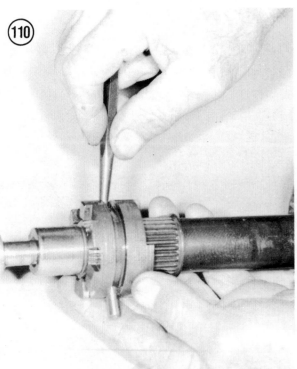
(110)

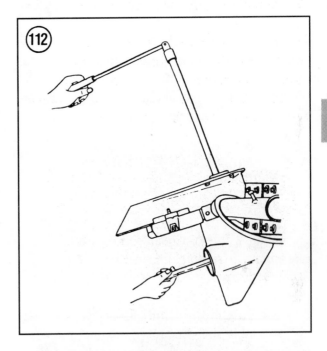
(112)

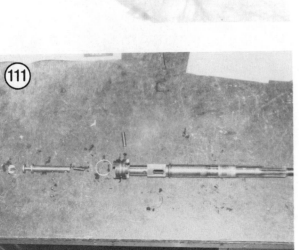
(111)

(113)

9

ure 114) from the gearcase. Remove and discard the O-ring on the screw.

26. Assemble the following components from OMC Pinion Bearing Remover/Installer Kit part No. 391257 and Pinion Service Kit part No. 433033 as shown in **Figure 115**:

 a. 1/4-20 × 1/2 in. cap screw (A, **Figure 115**).
 b. Flat washer (B, **Figure 115**).
 c. Guide plate part No. 334987 (C, **Figure 115**).
 d. Rod part No. 326582 (D, **Figure 115**).
 e. Pinion Bearing Remover/Installer part No. 326575 (E, **Figure 115**).
 f. 1/4-20 × 1-1/4 in. cap screw (F, **Figure 115**).

27. Install the assembled tool into the gearcase through the top of the drive shaft bore and into the pinion bearing. Using a mallet, drive the pinion bearing downward into the propeller shaft cavity. Discard the bearing.

NOTE
The forward gear bearings are destroyed during removal. Inspect the bearings while still installed—do not remove unless replacement is necessary.

28. If the 2 forward gear bearings require replacement, assemble OMC Forward Bearing Service Kit (part No. 433034) and remove the bearings from the gearcase.

29. Use OMC Bearing Puller (part No. 432130) and a suitable slide hammer to extract the bearings and oil seals from the propeller shaft bearing housing, if replacement is necessary.

30. Drive the oil seals from the drive shaft bearing housing using a suitable punch and mallet. Remove and discard the bearing housing outer O-ring.

NOTE
The drive shaft upper bearing and the drive shaft bearing housing are not available separately.

31. Clean and inspect all components as described in this chapter.

32. Reassemble the propeller shaft bearing housing as follows:

 a. Use OMC Bearing Installer (part No. 334997) and drive new fore and aft bearings into the bearing housing, with the lettered side of the bearing facing outward, until the tool contacts the bearing housing.

 b. Position the oil seals back-to-back (open sides facing away from each other). Apply OMC Gasket Sealing Compound on the

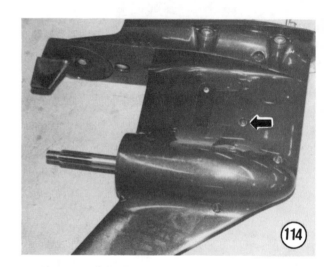

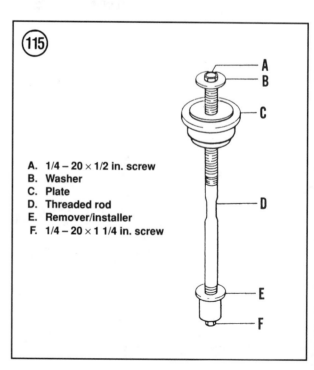

A. 1/4 – 20 × 1/2 in. screw
B. Washer
C. Plate
D. Threaded rod
E. Remover/installer
F. 1/4 – 20 × 1 1/4 in. screw

outer diameter of the seals. Using OMC Seal Installer (part No. 910585), drive the seals into the aft end of the bearing housing. Apply OMC Triple-Guard grease to the seal lips after installation.

c. Apply OMC Triple-Guard grease to the bearing outer O-ring. Install the O-ring into its groove around the bearing housing. See **Figure 103**.

33. Reassemble the drive shaft bearing housing as follows:

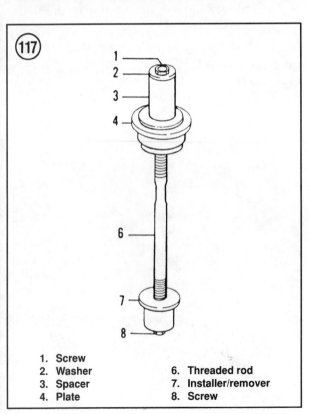

1. Screw
2. Washer
3. Spacer
4. Plate
6. Threaded rod
7. Installer/remover
8. Screw

NOTE
The drive shaft bearing is not available separately from the bearing housing. If the bearing requires replacement, replace the drive shaft bearing housing assembly.

a. Position the bearing housing seals back-to-back (open sides facing away from each other). Apply OMC Gasket Sealing Compound to the outer diameter of the seals. Using OMC Seal Installer (part No. 335823), drive the seals into the bearing housing. Apply OMC Triple-Guard grease to the seal lips after installation. See **Figure 116**.

b. Apply OMC Triple-Guard grease to the bearing housing O-ring, then install the O-ring around the housing.

34. If removed, install a new pinion gear bearing into the gearcase. Assemble the following components from OMC Pinion Bearing Remover/Installer Kit part No. 391257 and Pinion Service Kit part No. 433033 as shown in **Figure 117**:

a. 1/4-20 × 1/2 in. cap screw (1, **Figure 117**).

b. Flat washer (2, **Figure 117**).

c. OMC Spacer part No. 334986 (3, **Figure 117**).

d. OMC Guide Plate part No. 334987 (4, **Figure 117**).

e. OMC Rod part No. 326582 (6, **Figure 117**).

f. OMC Pinion Bearing Remover/Installer part No. 326575 (7, **Figure 117**).

g. 1/4-20 × 1-1/4 in. cap screw (8, **Figure 117**).

35. Apply OMC Needle Bearing Assembly Grease to the bearing rollers. Install the new pinion bearing on the installer tool, with its lettered side facing the tool. Use the grease to help hold the bearing on the installer tool.

36. Insert the tool and bearing into the drive shaft bore. Using a soft-face mallet, drive the bearing into its bore until the washer (2, **Figure 117**) contacts the spacer (3).

9

37. Install a new O-ring on the pinion bearing retaining screw. Apply OMC Nut Lock to the threads of the bearing retaining screw, install the screw (**Figure 114**) and tighten to specification (**Table 1**).

38. If removed, install new forward gear bearings as follows:

  a. Assemble OMC Forward Gear Bearing Service Kit (part No. 433034) and Drive Handle (part No. 311880).

  b. Support the leading edge of the gearcase on a wooden block.

  c. First, install the short bearing into the gearcase with its lettered side facing the installer tool. Drive the bearing into the gearcase, using a suitable mallet, until the installer tool contacts the gearcase. Then, install the long bearing following the same procedure. Note that one side of the installation tool is used to install the short bearing, then turned around, and the other side used to install the long bearing.

CAUTION
Pinion gear depth is a precision adjustment that is controlled by shim(s) located between the drive shaft bearing housing and the upper thrust washer. If pinion gear depth is not correctly adjusted, excessive noise and/or early gearcase failure could result. If the OMC special tools necessary for pinion depth adjustment are not available, it is strongly recommended to have the shim selection process performed by a qualified marine technician before proceeding with reassembly.

39. Perform the pinion gear shim selection process as described under *Pinion Gear Depth* in this chapter.

40. Position the clutch dog next to the propeller shaft with the end stamped "PROP END" facing the propeller end of the shaft. Align the clutch holes and propeller shaft slot, then install the clutch on the shaft.

WARNING
To prevent personal injury, eye protection is recommended prior to assembly of the shift detent.

41. Insert 2 detent balls into the detent hole in the side of the shift shaft, then install the remaining ball and detent spring (in that order) into the end of the shift shaft.

42. While holding the balls from falling out of the shaft, align the shift shaft holes and propeller shaft slot, then carefully slide the shift shaft into the propeller shaft. Push the shift shaft into the propeller shaft until the detent balls enter the detent groove in the propeller shaft.

NOTE
Wedge-shaped tool used in Step 43 should be 9/32 in. diameter and 2-5/8 in. long. The sharp end should be ground at 20°.

43. With the holes aligned, insert a suitable wedge-shaped tool through the holes to serve as a guide as shown in **Figure 118**. The angled side of the tool should be facing the front of the propeller shaft.

44. Push the wedge tool through the propeller shaft using the clutch dog cross pin as shown in **Figure 118**.

45. Install one end of a new clutch dog retaining spring over the clutch, then rotate the propeller

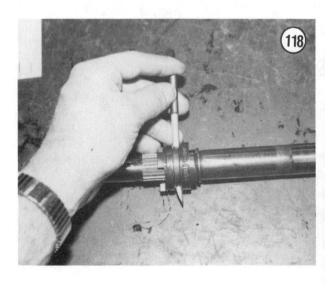

shaft to wind the spring into place. Make sure no coils overlap.

46. Install the forward gear thrust washer into the gearcase with the chamfered side facing toward the gearcase leading edge.

47. Apply OMC Needle Bearing Assembly Grease on the forward gear thrust bearing and assemble the bearing on the forward gear. Install the forward gear and thrust bearing assembly into the gearcase.

48. Assemble the thrust washers and thrust bearing onto the drive shaft. See **Figure 113**. Install the bottom thrust washer with the chamfered side facing down and the top thrust washer with the chamfered side facing up.

49. Lightly coat the drive shaft shim(s) with OMC Needle Bearing Assembly Grease and position them in the drive shaft bearing housing.

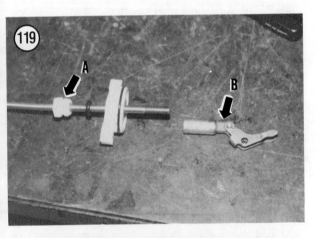

50. Slide the drive shaft bearing housing onto the drive shaft.

51. Apply a light coat of OMC Gasket Sealing Compound on the gearcase area where the drive shaft bearing housing mounting flange contacts.

52. Install the drive shaft and bearing housing assembly into the gearcase.

53. Install the pinion gear and nut onto the drive shaft.

54. Install OMC Drive Shaft Holding Socket, part No. 334995, on the drive shaft splines. Reaching into the propeller shaft cavity, hold the pinion nut with a 11/16 in. wrench. See **Figure 112**.

55. While holding the pinion nut from turning, turn the drive shaft to tighten the pinion nut to specification (**Table 1**).

56. Apply OMC Gasket Sealing Compound to the threads of the drive shaft bearing housing retaining screws and tighten to specification (**Table 1**).

57. Apply OMC Triple-Guard grease to the 2 shift rod cover O-rings. See **Figure 107**. Install the larger, thinner O-ring on the cover and the smaller, thicker O-ring on the shift rod.

58. Apply OMC Adhesive M to the threads of the shift rod cover bushing. See A, **Figure 119**. Screw the bushing into the cover and tighten to 48-60 in.-lb. (5.4-6.8 N•m).

59. Screw the shift lever and connector assembly (B, **Figure 119**) *nine* turns onto the shift rod.

60. Apply OMC Needle Bearing Assembly Grease to the shift shaft cradle and position the cradle on the shift shaft. See **Figure 120**. Make sure the part number on the cradle is facing up and use additional grease as necessary to hold the cradle in place.

61. Tilt the gearcase so the leading edge is facing down. Slide the propeller shaft assembly into the gearcase with the shift shaft cradle facing upward.

62. Install the shift rod assembly into the gearcase. Make sure the shift lever tangs engage the slots in the shift shaft cradle before proceeding.

9

63. Install a new O-ring on the shift lever pivot pin. Apply OMC Nut Lock on the threads of the pin. Install the pin (**Figure 105**) and tighten to specification (**Table 1**).

64. Apply OMC Gasket Sealing Compound to the threads of the shift rod cover retaining screws, install the screws (**Figure 106**) and tighten to specification (**Table 1**).

65. Apply OMC Needle Bearing Assembly Grease to the reverse gear thrust bearing and assemble the bearing on the reverse gear. Install the reverse gear and thrust bearing assembly into the gearcase.

66. Apply a light coat of OMC Gasket Sealing Compound to the O-ring flange and rear support flange on the propeller shaft bearing housing.

67. Apply OMC Needle Bearing Assembly Grease to the reverse gear thrust washer and position the washer onto the propeller shaft bearing housing. See **Figure 121**.

68. Position the propeller shaft bearing housing with the mounting screw holes in a vertical position and the drain slot on the bottom. Then slide the propeller shaft bearing housing into the gearcase.

69. Install the propeller shaft bearing housing retainers. Apply OMC Nut Lock to the threads of the bearing housing screws, then install the screws (**Figure 102**) and tighten to specification (**Table 1**).

70. Install the propeller shaft bearing housing anode and secure with the retaining screws. Tighten to specification (**Table 1**).

71. Place the shift rod in NEUTRAL. Position OMC Universal Shift Rod Gauge (part No. 389997) on the gearcase beside the vertical shift rod and align the gauge and shift rod holes. Insert the gauge pin in the gauge hole. See **Figure 122**, typical. Screw the shift rod in or out of the connector to obtain the correct shift rod height (**Table 2**).

72. Install the water pump as described in this chapter.

73. Pressure and vacuum test the gearcase as described in this chapter.

74. Install the gearcase as described in this chapter. Fill the gearcase with the recommended lubricant (**Table 3**). Check the lubricant level after a short water test. Change the lubricant after 10 hours of operation.

Disassembly
(60 and 70 hp, V4, V6 and V8 Models)

Refer to **Figure 123** for this procedure. Note that V4, V6 and V8 models may be equipped with a 2-piece drive shaft. Record the location and thickness of all shims and thrust washers removed from the gear housing during disassembly.

If the OMC special tools necessary for seal and bearing installation are not available, note the exact position of the seals and bearings for reference during reassembly.

1. Remove the gearcase as described in this chapter.

2. Remove the water pump as described in this chapter.

3A. *60 and 70 hp, V4 models*—Remove the 4 screws securing the propeller shaft bearing housing assembly. See **Figure 124**, typical.

3B. *V6 and V8 models*—Remove the 2 propeller shaft bearing housing screws and retainers (**Figure 124**, typical).

4A. *60 and 70 hp, V4 models*—Assemble fly-wheel puller part No. 378103 and 2 puller screws part No. 316982 (5/16-18 × 8 in.). Thread the puller screws into the bearing housing as shown in **Figure 125**. Tighten the puller center screw until the bearing housing breaks free of the gear-case.

4B. *V6 models*—Obtain 2 lengths of 5/16-18 threaded rod, each 11 in. long, 2 5/16 in. flat washers and 2 5/16-18 nuts from a local supplier. Screw the threaded rods into the bearing housing and connect OMC Flywheel Puller (part No. 378103) using the washers and nuts as shown in **Figure 125**. Tighten the puller center screw until the bearing housing breaks free of the gearcase.

4C. *V8 models*—Assemble OMC Puller Legs (part No. 330278) to the Flywheel Puller (part No. 378103). Connect the puller legs to the

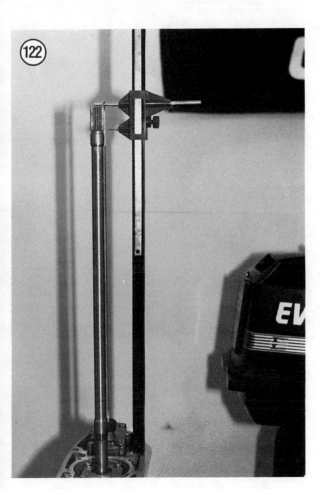

bearing housing, then tighten the puller center screw until the bearing housing breaks free of the gearcase.

5. Remove the puller assembly, then slide the bearing housing out of the gearcase and off the propeller shaft (**Figure 126**).

WARNING
*The snap rings (51, **Figure 123**) are under extreme pressure when com-pressed during removal. Wear suitable eye and hand protection when removing the snap rings to prevent personal injury.*

6. On models so equipped, remove the 2 large snap rings from inside the propeller shaft bore using OMC Snap Ring Pliers 331045, or equiva-lent. See **Figure 127**. Remove the bearing hous-ing retainer plate.

7. Next, remove the reverse gear along with the reverse gear thrust bearing and thrust washer. See **Figure 128**. If so equipped, slide the small thrust washer (forward of reverse gear) off the propeller shaft.

8. Remove the 4 screws securing the drive shaft bearing housing to the gearcase.

9. Shift the gearcase into FORWARD gear by pulling the lower shift rod upward.

10. Install OMC Drive Shaft Holding Socket part No. 334995 (60 and 70 hp) or 311875 (all others) on the drive shaft splines. Place an ap-propriate size socket with a breaker bar on the drive shaft holding socket.

11A. *60 and 70 hp*—Reach into the propeller shaft bore with an 11/16 in. wrench to hold the pinion gear nut. **Figure 129** shows the pinion gear and nut with the propeller shaft removed.

11B. *All others*—Reach into the propeller shaft bore with OMC Pinion Holder part No. 334455 (or equivalent) to hold the pinion gear nut. **Fig-ure 129** shows the pinion gear and nut with the propeller shaft removed.

12. While securely holding the pinion nut with the wrench or pinion holder, turn the drive shaft counterclockwise to loosen and remove the pin-ion gear nut. See **Figure 130**. Remove the drive

9

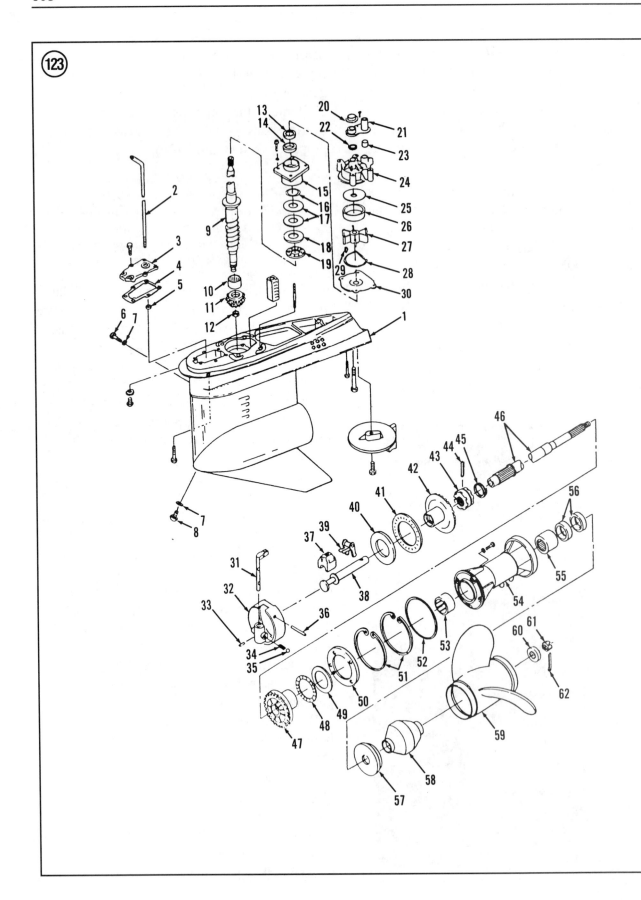

shaft holding socket and pinion holder or wrench.

13. Pull the drive shaft and bearing housing assembly, along with the shim(s), thrust washers and thrust bearing, from the gearcase. The drive shaft and pinion gear connection is a splined, tapered fit. If the drive shaft is difficult to re-

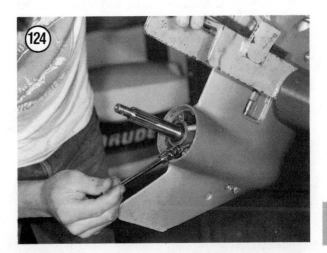

**GEARCASE
(60 AND 70 HP, V4, V6
AND V8 [TYPICAL] MODELS)**

1. Gearcase housing
2. Lower shift rod
3. Shift rod cover and seal assembly
4. Gasket
5. O-ring
6. Level (vent) plug
7. Gasket
8. Drain/fill plug
9. Drive shaft
10. Pinion bearing
11. Pinion gear
12. Nut
13. Drive shaft upper seal
14. Drive shaft lower seal
15. Drive shaft bearing housing
16. O-ring
17. Shims
18. Thrust washer
19. Thrust bearing
20. Grommet
21. Water pump housing cover
22. O-ring
23. Grommet
24. Water pump housing
25. Water pump housing plate
26. Water pump housing liner
27. Impeller
28. Seal
29. Impeller drive key
30. Plate
31. Shift detent
32. Bearing housing assembly
33. Pin
34. Spring
35. Detent ball
36. Pin
37. Shift cradle
38. Shift shaft
39. Shift lever
40. Thrust washer
41. Thrust bearing
42. Forward gear
43. Dog clutch
44. Cross pin
45. Retainer spring
46. Propeller shaft
47. Reverse gear
48. Thrust bearing
49. Thrust washer
50. Bearing housing retainer plate
51. Snap rings
52. O-ring
53. Propeller shaft bearing
54. Propeller shaft bearing housing
55. Propeller shaft bearing
56. Propeller shaft seals
57. Thrust hub
58. Propeller bushing
59. Propeller
60. Spacer
61. Propeller nut
62. Cotter pin

9

move, use OMC Puller part No. 387206 (60 and 70 hp) or 390706 (V4, V6 and V8) and Plate part No. 325867 to break loose the drive shaft from the pinion gear.

14. Reach into the propeller shaft bore and remove the pinion gear (**Figure 131**).

15. Reach into the propeller shaft bore and retrieve any loose needle bearing rollers (except 60 and 70 hp) that dropped out of position when the drive shaft was removed.

16. Push the shift rod downward to engage reverse gear, then unscrew the shift rod from the shift detent. Remove the shift rod cover screws and lift the shift rod and cover from the gearcase. Remove and discard the cover gasket, O-ring and the shift rod O-ring.

17. Remove the propeller shaft, forward gear and bearing housing from the gearcase as an assembly. See **Figure 132**. On V6 models, the

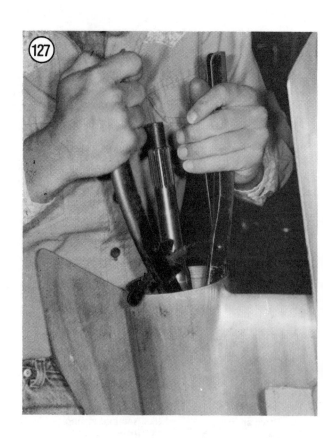

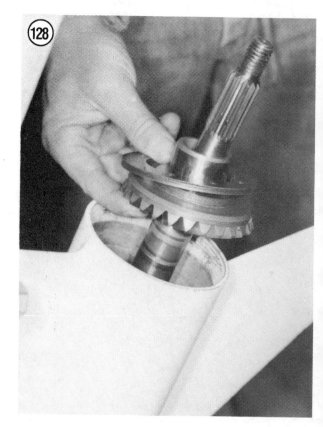

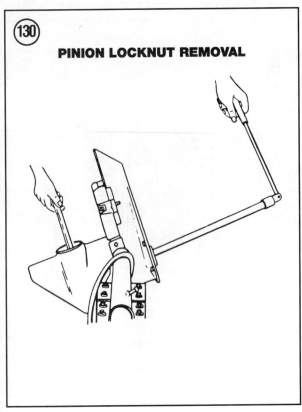

PINION LOCKNUT REMOVAL

forward gear needle bearings are loose and may drop out as the propeller shaft is removed.

18. Slip a small screwdriver under one end of the clutch dog retaining spring and remove it by unwrapping it from the clutch. Discard the spring.

19. Push the clutch dog retaining pin through the clutch and propeller shaft using a small punch or similar tool. Then remove the bearing housing assembly and clutch dog from the propeller shaft. Remove the forward gear, thrust washer and thrust bearing from the bearing housing. See **Figure 133**.

20A. *60 and 70 hp*—Disassemble the bearing housing as follows:

    a. Remove the shift lever pin (4, **Figure 134**) from the bearing housing using a suitable punch.

    b. Disconnect the shift lever from the shift shaft cradle, then remove the shaft, cradle and lever. See **Figure 134**.

9

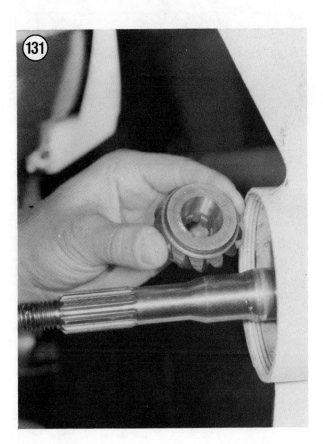

c. Depress the detent ball and spring by rotating the shift detent lever 90° in either direction.

> *WARNING*
> *The detent ball and spring can fly out of the bearing housing with considerable force. Wear hand and eye protection while removing the detent lever. Cover the bearing housing with a shop towel to prevent losing the ball and spring.*

d. Catch the detent ball and spring as the detent lever is removed from the bearing housing. See 2, **Figure 135**.

20B. *V4, V6 and V8 models*—Disassemble the bearing housing as follows:

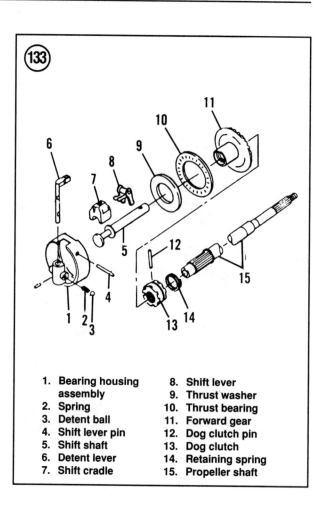

1. Bearing housing assembly
2. Spring
3. Detent ball
4. Shift lever pin
5. Shift shaft
6. Detent lever
7. Shift cradle
8. Shift lever
9. Thrust washer
10. Thrust bearing
11. Forward gear
12. Dog clutch pin
13. Dog clutch
14. Retaining spring
15. Propeller shaft

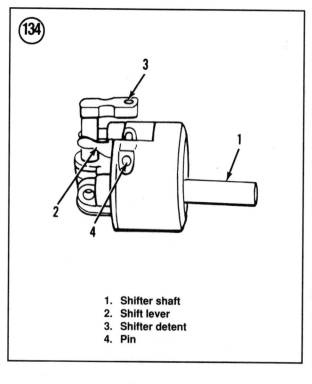

1. Shifter shaft
2. Shift lever
3. Shifter detent
4. Pin

a. Push the detent lever to its fully down position, then remove the shift shaft along with the shift cradle.

b. Next, pull upward on the detent lever to position it in the NEUTRAL detent. Push the shift lever pin out of the housing using a small punch, then reach into the housing and remove the shift lever.

c. Rotate the detent lever 90° in either direction, then pull the lever out of the housing.

WARNING
The detent ball and spring can fly out of the bearing housing with considerable force. Wear hand and eye protection while removing the detent lever. Cover

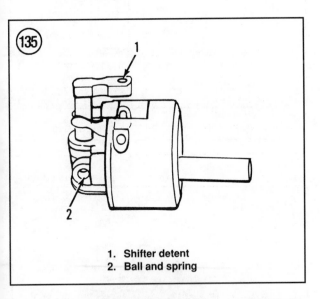

1. **Shifter detent**
2. **Ball and spring**

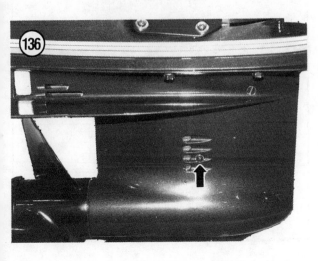

the bearing housing with a shop towel to prevent losing the ball and spring.

d. Catch the detent ball and spring as the detent lever is removed from the bearing housing. See 2, **Figure 135**.

e. Remove 25 loose bearing rollers from the bearing housing assembly.

NOTE
The forward gear bearing and the bearing housing are not available separately. If the bearing or the housing is worn or damaged, replace the bearing housing assembly.

NOTE
The pinion gear bearing is destroyed during removal. Inspect the bearing while still installed—do not remove unless replacement is necessary.

21A. *V6 cross flow (1991) and 1993-on 60° V6 models*—If the pinion bearing requires replacement, first remove the bearing retaining ring on the top side of the bearing.

21B. *All others*—If the pinion bearing requires replacement, first remove the bearing retaining screw (**Figure 136**). Remove and discard the retaining screw O-ring.

22A. *60 and 70 hp, V6 and V8 models*—Assemble the following components of OMC Pinion Bearing Remover/Installer part No. 391257 (**Figure 137**):

a. Flange nut part No. 326586 (1, **Figure 137**).

b. Plate part No. 391260 (2, **Figure 137**).

c. Rod part No. 326582 (3, **Figure 137**).

d. Remover part No. 326580 (60 and 70 hp) or 326579 (V6 and V8) (4, **Figure 137**).

22B. *V4 models*—Assemble the following components from OMC Pinion Bearing Remover/Installer part No. 391257 (**Figure 138**):

a. 1/4-20 × 1/2 in. hex-head screw (1, **Figure 138**).

b. Flat washer, 1 in. outside diameter (2, **Figure 138**).

9

c. Plate part No. 391260 (3, **Figure 138**).

d. Rod part No. 326582 (4, **Figure 138**).

e. Remover part No. 326574 (5, **Figure 138**).

f. 1/4-20 × 1-1/4 in hex-head screw (6, **Figure 138**).

NOTE
All loose needle bearing rollers (if so equipped) must be installed in the pinion bearing to provide a contact surface for the remover tool. Hold the rollers in position using OMC Needle Bearing Assembly Grease.

23A. *60 and 70 hp, V6 and V8 models*—With the pinion bearing tool properly assembled in the gearcase, hold the remover (4, **Figure 137**) with a wrench while tightening the upper nut until the bearing is drawn upward and out of its bore. Discard the bearing.

23B. *V4 models*—Install the assembled tool into the gearcase. Make sure the remover is securely engaged with the pinion bearing, then tap the top of the tool with a mallet to drive the bearing downward into the propeller shaft cavity. Discard the bearing.

24. Remove both propeller shaft seals from the bearing housing (**Figure 139**) using OMC Puller Bridge part No. 431257 and Puller Jaws part No. 432129. Discard the seals. Remove and discard the bearing housing O-ring.

NOTE
The propeller shaft bearings are destroyed during removal from the bearing housing. Inspect the bearings while still installed—do not remove unless replacement is necessary.

25. If necessary, drive the propeller shaft bearings from each end of the propeller shaft bearing housing (**Figure 139**) using a suitable driver and mallet. Discard the bearings.

NOTE
The drive shaft upper bearing is not available separately from the bearing housing. If the bearing is worn or dam-

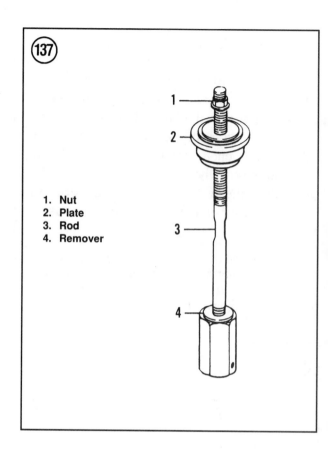

(137)

1. Nut
2. Plate
3. Rod
4. Remover

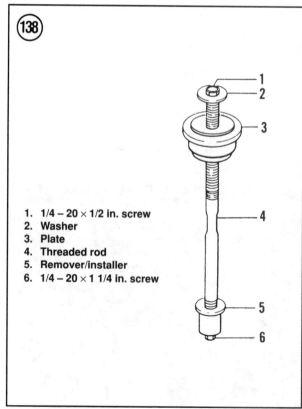

(138)

1. 1/4 – 20 × 1/2 in. screw
2. Washer
3. Plate
4. Threaded rod
5. Remover/installer
6. 1/4 – 20 × 1 1/4 in. screw

aged, replace the drive shaft bearing housing assembly.

26. Remove and discard the drive shaft bearing housing O-ring. Remove the drive shaft seals from the bearing housing using OMC Puller Bridge part No. 432127 and Puller Jaws part No. 432131. Discard the seals.

27. Clean and inspect all components as described in this chapter.

Drive shaft service (2-piece shaft)

A 2 piece drive shaft assembly is used on some V4, V6 and V8 models. Replace the upper or lower drive shaft if excessively worn or damaged. The upper and lower shafts are connected with a spring and roll pin on 1991 and 1992 models or a connector and roll pin on 1993-on models.

1. Support the drive shaft assembly on wooden blocks.

2. *1991 and 1992 models*—Compress the shaft slightly to relieve the tension on the spring located between the upper and lower shafts.

3. Using an appropriate size punch and mallet, drive the roll pin through the drive shaft assembly. Discard the roll pin.

4. Separate the upper and lower drive shafts.

5. To reassemble the drive shaft, start a new roll pin into the lower drive shaft.

6. On 1991 and 1992 models, place the spring into the lower drive shaft. On 1993-on models, install the drive shaft retainer on the upper drive shaft, making sure the roll pin hole is facing away from the shaft.

7. Align the roll pin holes and insert the upper shaft into the lower shaft.

8. On 1991 and 1992 models, compress the drive shaft spring sufficiently to align the roll pin holes.

9. Using a mallet and punch, drive the roll pin into the shafts to the following dimension (A, **Figure 140**):

   a. *All V4 models*—Install the pin flush with the outer surface of the lower shaft.

   b. *All V6 models except 1993-on 60° models*—Install the pin 0.110 in. (2.8 mm) below the outer surface of the lower shaft.

   c. *1991 and 1992 V8 models*—Install the pin 0.075 in. (1.9 mm) below the outer surface of the lower shaft.

   d. *1993-on 60° V6 models*—Install the pin 0.125 in. (3.2 mm) below the outer surface of the lower shaft.

   e. *1993-on V8 models*—Install the pin 0.062 in. below the outer surface of the lower shaft.

9

Reassembly
(60 and 70 hp, V4, V6 and V8 Models)

Refer to **Figure 123** for this procedure.

> *CAUTION*
> *Pinion gear depth is a precision adjustment that is controlled by shim(s) located between the drive shaft bearing housing and the thrust washer. If pinion gear depth is not correctly adjusted, excessive noise and/or early gearcase failure could result. If the OMC special tools necessary for pinion depth adjustment are not available, it is strongly recommended to have the shim selection process performed by a qualified marine technician before proceeding with reassembly.*

1. If any of the following components are replaced during reassembly, perform the pinion gear shim selection process as described under *Pinion Gear Depth* in this chapter.
    a. Drive shaft.
    b. Pinion gear.
    c. Drive shaft bearing housing.
    d. Drive shaft thrust bearing.
    e. Drive shaft thrust washer.
2. If removed, install a new pinion bearing into the gearcase. OMC Pinion Bearing Remover/Installer (part No. 391257) is necessary to install the pinion bearing.
3A. *60 and 70 hp*—Assemble the following components from OMC Pinion Bearing Remover/Installer Kit part No. 391257:
    a. 1/4-20 × 1/2 in. screw (1, **Figure 141**).
    b. Flat washer (2, **Figure 141**).
    c. Spacer part No. 326584 (3, **Figure 141**).
    d. Plate part No. 391260 (4, **Figure 141**).
    e. Rod part No. 326582 (5, **Figure 141**).
    f. Installer part No. 326575 (7, **Figure 141**).
    g. 1/4-20 × 1-1/4 screw (8, **Figure 141**).
3B. *V4 and V6 models*—Assemble the following components from OMC Pinion Bearing Remover/Installer Kit part No. 391257:
    a. 1/4-20 × 1/2 in. screw (1, **Figure 141**).

b. Flat washer (2, **Figure 141**).
    c. Spacer part No. 326585 (3, **Figure 141**).
    d. Plate part No. 391260 (4, **Figure 141**).
    e. Rod part No. 326582 (5, **Figure 141**).
    f. Washer (V6 only) part No. 326587 (6, **Figure 141**).
    g. Installer part No. 326575 (7, **Figure 141**).
    h. 1/4-20 × 1-1/4 screw (8, **Figure 141**).
3C. *V8 models*—Assemble the following components from OMC Pinion Bearing Remover/Installer Kit part No. 391257:
    a. 1/4-20 × 1/2 in. screw (1, **Figure 141**).
    b. Flat washer (2, **Figure 141**).
    c. Spacer part No. 326584 (3, **Figure 141**).
    d. Plate part No. 391260 (4, **Figure 141**).
    e. Rod part No. 326582 (5, **Figure 141**).
    f. Installer part No. 328828 (7, **Figure 141**).
    g. 1/4-20 × 1-1/4 screw (8, **Figure 141**).

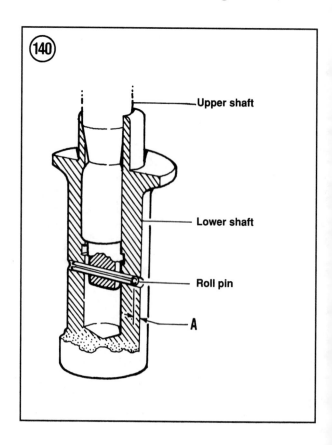

(140)
Upper shaft
Lower shaft
Roll pin
A

CAUTION
The lettered side of the pinion bearing ***must*** *be facing UP after installation in the gearcase.*

4A. *60 and 70 hp and V4 models*—Lubricate the pinion bearing with OMC Needle Bearing Assembly Grease.

  a. Place the bearing on the bearing installer (7, **Figure 141**). Make certain the lettered side of the bearing is facing the installer tool. Insert the tool and bearing into the gearcase.

  b. Drive the bearing into the gearcase until the washer (2, **Figure 141**) contacts the spacer (3). Remove the installation tool from the gearcase.

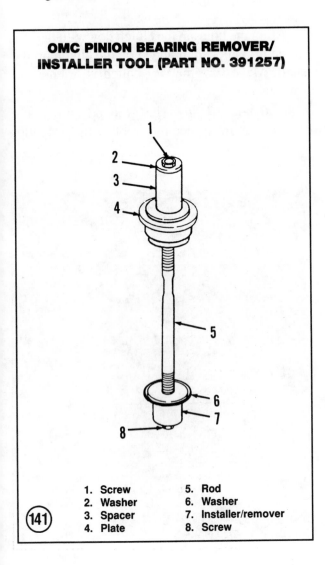

OMC PINION BEARING REMOVER/ INSTALLER TOOL (PART NO. 391257)

1. Screw	5. Rod
2. Washer	6. Washer
3. Spacer	7. Installer/remover
4. Plate	8. Screw

(141)

  c. Install a new O-ring on the pinion bearing retaining screw. Apply OMC Nut Lock to the threads of the screw, then install it (**Figure 136**) and tighten to 48-80 in.-lb. (5.4-9.0 N·m).

CAUTION
The lettered side of the pinion bearing ***must*** *be facing UP after installation in the gearcase.*

4B. *V6 and V8 models*—Apply OMC Needle Bearing Assembly Grease to the loose pinion bearing rollers. Install 18 (V6) or 19 (V8) loose bearing rollers into the bearing case. Hold the rollers in place with additional grease as necessary.

  a. Place the bearing on the installer tool (7, **Figure 141**). Make certain the lettered side of the bearing is facing the installer tool. Insert the tool and bearing into the gearcase.

  b. Drive the bearing into the gearcase until the washer (2, **Figure 141**) contacts the spacer (3). Remove the installation tool from the gearcase.

  c. If a bearing retaining ring is used, install the retaining ring into its groove at the top of the pinion bearing. Make sure the ring is fully seated in the groove.

  d. If a pinion bearing retaining screw is used, install a new O-ring on the screw then apply OMC Nut Lock to the threads. Install the screw and tighten to 48-80 in.-lb. (5.4-9.0 N·m).

5A. *60 and 70 hp*—Reassemble the forward gear bearing housing as follows:

  a. Coat the forward bearing housing detent spring and ball with OMC Needle Bearing Assembly Grease. Insert the spring and then the ball into the housing. See 2, **Figure 135**.

  b. Install the shift detent lever into the forward gear bearing housing. Depress the detent ball and spring with a suitable punch, then insert the detent lever into the housing. Face the lever toward either side of the housing and push it in until it clears the detent ball. Once the detent lever is past the ball, remove the punch and push the detent lever completely into the housing.

c. Coat the shift cradle with OMC Needle Bearing Assembly Grease and install the cradle on the shift shaft. Insert the cradle and shaft into the housing, engage the cradle with the shift lever and install the shift lever retaining pin (4, **Figure 134**).

5B. *V4, V6 and V8 models*—Reassemble the forward gear bearing housing as follows:

a. Coat the forward bearing housing detent spring and ball with OMC Needle Bearing Assembly Grease. Insert the spring and then the ball into the housing. See 2, **Figure 135**.

b. Insert the detent lever into the forward gear bearing housing. Depress the detent ball and spring with a suitable punch, then insert the detent lever into the housing. Face the lever toward either side of the housing and push it in until it clears the detent ball. Once the detent lever is past the ball, remove the punch, rotate the detent lever to face the rear of the housing, then position the lever in its NEUTRAL detent.

c. Apply OMC Needle Bearing Assembly Grease to the 25 loose bearing housing rollers. Install the rollers into the bearing housing and hold in place with additional grease as necessary.

d. Install the shift lever so its narrow arms are facing the detent lever, then attach it to the detent lever. Align the holes in the lever and housing and install the pin (4, **Figure 134**).

e. Push the detent lever into the bearing housing to its fully down position. Apply OMC Needle Bearing Assembly Grease to the shift cradle, then install the cradle on the shift shaft. Install the shift shaft and cradle making sure the wide arms on the shift lever properly engage the cradle. Pull the detent

lever up to its NEUTRAL detent to hold the shift shaft and cradle in place.

6. Apply OMC Needle Bearing Assembly Grease to the forward gear thrust bearing and thrust washer. Install the thrust bearing first, and then the thrust washer on the forward gear shoulder. See **Figure 142**.

7. Install the forward gear assembly into the forward gear bearing housing. Do not dislodge any loose bearing rollers on V6 and V8 models.

NOTE
The clutch dog is not symmetrical. Make certain the clutch is properly oriented on the propeller shaft in Step 8. If installed backward, clutch and forward gear failure will quickly result.

8. Align the holes in the clutch dog with the slot in the propeller shaft and slide the clutch on the shaft. Make sure the dog clutch is oriented as follows:

a. *60 and 70 hp*—The grooved end of the clutch must face the front of the propeller shaft.

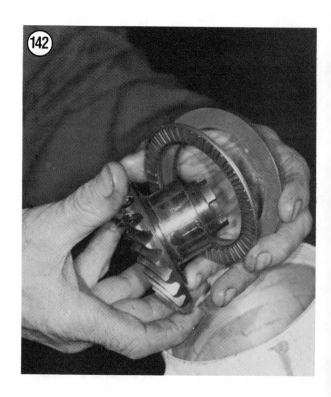

b. *V4 models*—The clutch dog lugs that do not have internal splines must facing the rear of the propeller shaft.

c. *V6 and V8 models*—The end of the clutch dog marked "PROP END" must face the rear of the propeller shaft.

9. Install the propeller shaft over the shift shaft. Align the holes in the shift shaft, propeller shaft and clutch dog, then install the clutch dog cross pin. Secure the pin with a *new* retaining spring. Make sure the ends of the spring do not overlap after installation.

10. Push the detent lever fully DOWN, to the REVERSE position.

11. Install the propeller shaft, bearing housing and forward gear into the gearcase. The detent lever must be facing UP and the locating pin on the bearing housing must engage the locating hole in the gearcase.

12. Lubricate new shift rod cover O-ring(s) with OMC Triple-Guard grease and install the O-ring(s) in the cover. Lubricate the threaded end of the shift rod with Triple-Guard and insert it through the cover bushing. To prevent damaging the cover O-ring(s), rotate the shift rod while pushing it through the bushing.

13. Apply OMC Gasket Sealing Compound to both sides of a new shift cover gasket. Install the gasket on the gearcase.

14. Install the shift rod and cover assembly into the gearcase. Screw the shift rod into the shift detent lever approximately 4 turns.

15. Push forward on the propeller shaft while moving the shift rod back and forth to ensure the locating pin in the forward gear bearing housing is properly engaged with the locating hole in the gearcase. Lightly tap the rear of the propeller shaft with a soft-face mallet to seat the bearing housing fully.

16. Apply OMC Gasket Sealing Compound to the shift rod cover screws, install the screws and tighten to 60-84 in.-lb. (6.8-9.5 N.m).

> *CAUTION*
> *Be sure to determine the correct pinion depth adjusting shims before installing the drive shaft into the gearcase. See **Pinion Depth Adjustment** in this chapter.*

17. Install the drive shaft thrust bearing, thrust washer and shim(s) (selected during pinion depth adjustment) on the drive shaft, in that order. See **Figure 143**. Lubricate the bearing and washer with gear lube.

18. Apply OMC Gasket Sealing Compound to the outer diameter of new drive shaft seals. Using OMC Seal Installer part No. 326545 (60 and 70 hp) or 330268 (V4, V6 and V8), press the lower seal (lip facing down) into the drive shaft bearing housing until the installer tool contacts the housing. Using the opposite end of the installer tool, press the upper seal into the drive shaft bearing

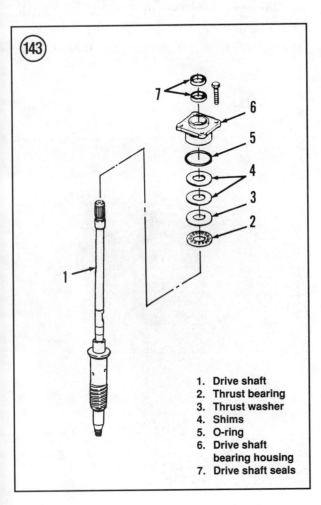

1. Drive shaft
2. Thrust bearing
3. Thrust washer
4. Shims
5. O-ring
6. Drive shaft bearing housing
7. Drive shaft seals

housing until the tool contacts the housing. See **Figure 144**.

19. Install a new O-ring around the drive shaft bearing housing (**Figure 145**). Lubricate the cavity between the drive shaft seals and the O-ring with OMC Triple-Guard grease.

20. Wrap the drive shaft splines with one layer of cellophane tape. Carefully slide the drive shaft bearing housing on the drive shaft, then remove the tape.

21. Apply a light coat of OMC Gasket Sealing Compound to the area of the drive shaft bearing housing flange that contacts the gearcase. *Do not* apply sealant to the bearing housing inner bore surface of the gearcase, just the flange area where the housing and gearcase make contact.

22. Shift the gearcase into FORWARD gear by pulling upward on the shift shaft.

23. Make sure the drive shaft and pinion gear tapers are absolutely free of grease, oil, corrosion or other contamination.

24. Install the pinion gear into the propeller shaft bore and mesh it with the forward gear teeth.

25. Install the drive shaft along with the thrust bearing, thrust washer, shim(s) and bearing housing into the gearcase. Turn the drive shaft as necessary to engage the drive shaft and pinion gear spines.

26. Lightly lubricate the pinion nut with gear lube. Hold the nut in position under the pinion gear and turn the drive shaft by hand to start the nut.

27. Install OMC Drive Shaft Holding Socket part No. 334995 (60 and 70 hp) or 311875 (all others) on the drive shaft splines. Place an appropriate size socket with a breaker bar on the drive shaft holding socket.

28A. *60 and 70 hp*—Reach into the propeller shaft bore with an 11/16 in. wrench to hold the pinion gear nut.

28B. *All others*—Reach into the propeller shaft bore with OMC Pinion Holder part No. 334455 (or equivalent) to hold the pinion gear nut.

29. While securely holding the pinion nut with the wrench or pinion holder, turn the drive shaft clockwise to tighten the pinion gear nut to specification (**Table 1**). See **Figure 146**.

30A. 60 and 70 hp—Position the drive shaft bearing housing with the mark "FRONT" facing the shift rod. Firmly seat the housing in the gearcase.

30B. All others—Firmly seat the drive shaft bearing housing in the gearcase.

31. Apply OMC Gasket Sealing Compound to the threads of the bearing housing screws. Install the screws and tighten evenly in 3 steps, to specification (**Table 1**).

32. Install the front thrust washer (if used) into its recess on the front side of the reverse gear. Hold the washer in place with OMC Needle Bearing Assembly Grease. Install the reverse gear thrust bearing, then the thrust washer on the back side of the reverse gear. Lubricate the thrust bearing and washer with gear lube, then slide the

gear assembly on the propeller shaft until it contacts the pinion gear.

33. If removed, press new propeller shaft bearings into each end of the propeller shaft bearing housing. Using OMC Bearing Installer part No. 326562 (60 and 70 hp and V4 models) or 339750 (V6 and V8 models), press the bearings into place in the housing. Press against the lettered side of the bearings only. Lubricate the bearings with OMC Needle Bearing Assembly Grease.

34. Next, install new propeller shaft seals into the bearing housing. Apply OMC Gasket Sealing Compound to the outer diameter of the seals.

Using OMC Seal Installer part No. 326551 (60 and 70 hp and V4 models) or 336311 (V6 and V8 models), press the inner seal into the bearing housing with its lip facing the front end of the housing. Then using the opposite end of the installer, press the outer seal into the bearing housing with its lip facing the propeller end of the housing. Lubricate the seal lips with OMC Triple-Guard grease. Lubricate a new bearing housing O-ring with Triple-Guard grease and install it around the housing.

> **WARNING**
> *The snap rings (51, **Figure 123**) are under extreme pressure when compressed during installation. Wear suitable eye and hand protection when installing the snap rings to prevent personal injury.*

35. Install the propeller shaft bearing housing retainer plate (if used) over the propeller shaft and into place in the gearcase. Then install the 2 snap rings into the gearcase using OMC Snap Ring Pliers part No. 331045. Make sure the snap rings are securely seated in their grooves.

9

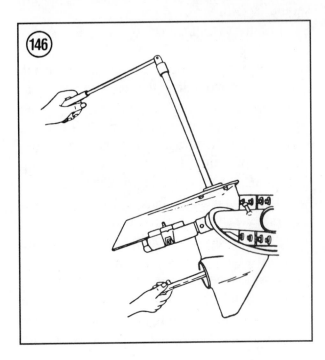

36. Apply OMC Gasket Sealing Compound to the O-ring flange and aft support flange of the propeller shaft bearing housing. *Do not* apply sealant to the propeller shaft seals or bearings.

37A. *Except V8 and 60° V6*—Install the propeller shaft bearing housing in the gearcase. Be sure the "UP" mark on the aft end of the housing is facing UP and the bearing housing and retainer plate screw holes are aligned. Push the housing into place then firmly seat it by tapping with a soft mallet.

37B. *V8 and 60° V6 models*—Install the propeller shaft bearing housing in the gearcase. Be sure the housing screw holes are in a vertical position and the anode is facing DOWN. Push the housing into place then firmly seat it by tapping with a soft mallet.

38A. *Except V8 and 60° V6*—Apply OMC Gasket Sealing Compound to the threads of the bearing housing screws. Install and tighten the screws evenly to specification (**Table 1**).

38B. *V8 and 60° V6*—Apply OMC Ultra Lock 271 to the threads of the bearing housing screws. Install the retainers, screws and washers. Tighten to specification (**Table 1**). If the retainers have rounded edges on one side, the rounded edges should face forward.

39. Install the trim tab (if so equipped). Apply OMC Gasket Sealing Compound to the threads of the trim tab retaining screw. Align the trim tab match marks and tighten the screw to specification (**Table 1**).

40. Adjust shift rod height using OMC Universal Shift Rod Gauge part No. 389997. Shift rod height is measured from the gearcase mating surface to the shift rod hole using the gauge.

   a. Place the gearcase in NEUTRAL and position the shift rod offset (top) facing the port side (60 and 70 hp) or forward (V4, V6 and V8).

   b. Position the shift rod gauge on the gearcase adjacent to the shift rod (**Figure 147**). Align the gauge and shift rod hole, then insert the gauge pin into the shift rod hole. Compare

the shift rod height to the specification in **Table 2**.

   c. Turn the shift rod up or down to obtain the specified shift rod height. After adjustment, the shift rod offset at the top must face the port side on 60 and 70 hp or forward on V4, V6 and V8 models.

41. Install the water pump as described in this chapter.

42. Pressure and vacuum test the gearcase as described in this chapter.

43. Install the gearcase as described in this chapter. Fill the gearcase with the recommended lubricant (**Table 3**). Check the lubricant level after a short water test. Change the lubricant after 10 hours of operation.

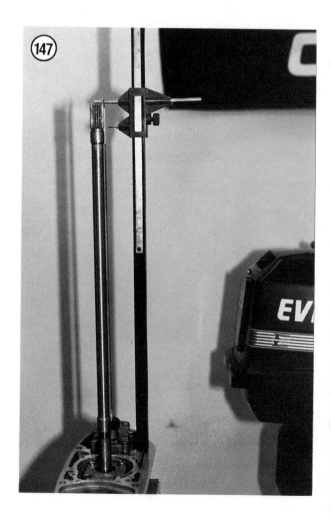

PINION GEAR DEPTH
(40-70 HP, V4, V6 AND V8 MODELS)

If a new drive shaft, pinion gear, drive shaft bearing housing, thrust bearing or thrust washer is installed, the pinion gear must be adjusted to mesh properly with the forward/reverse drive gears. Pinion gear depth is a precision adjustment that is controlled by shim(s) located between the drive shaft bearing housing and the thrust washer. If pinion gear depth is not correctly adjusted, excessive noise and/or early gearcase failure could result.

OMC Universal Shim Tool part No. 393185 is necessary to perform the shim selection procedure. If the special tools are not available, it is strongly recommended to have the shim selection process performed by a qualified marine technician before proceeding with reassembly.

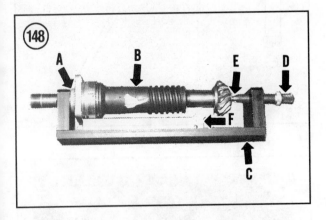

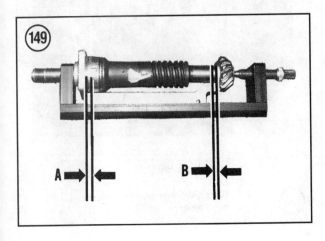

1. Thoroughly clean all oil, grease or other contamination from the drive shaft and pinion gear tapers. Dry with compressed air.
2. Install the pinion gear on the drive shaft, lubricate the pinion nut with light oil, then install and tighten the nut to: 40-45 ft.-lb. (54-61 N•m) on 40-70 hp; 70-80 ft.-lb. (95-108 N•m) on V4 and V6 models; 100-110 ft.-lb. (136-149 N•m) on V8 models.
3. Install the thrust bearing (2, **Figure 143**) and thrust washer (3) on the drive shaft (but not shims [4]).
4. Install the fully assembled drive shaft bearing housing on the drive shaft. Do not damage the drive shaft seals.
5. Next, place the shim collar (A, **Figure 148**) on the drive shaft, after the bearing housing. The shim collars are as follows:
   a. *40-50 hp*—Collar part No. 334985 (from OMC Service Kit part No. 433032).
   b. *60-70 hp*—Collar part No. 328363.
   c. *V4, V6 and V8*—Collar part No. 328362.
6. Place the drive shaft assembly (B, **Figure 148**) and collar into the shim tool base as shown. While rotating the drive shaft assembly, tighten the preload screw (D, **Figure 148**) until the line on the plunger (E) is flush with the end of the preload screw. Tighten the preload screw locknut.
7. Then place the appropriate shim gauge (F, **Figure 148**) onto the dowel pins on the tool base (1). The correct shim bars are as follows:
   a. *40-50 hp*—OMC Shim Gauge part No. 334984.
   b. *60 and 70 hp, V4*—OMC Shim Gauge part No. 328366.
   c. *V6*—OMC Shim Gauge part No. 328367.
   d. *V8*—OMC Shim Gauge part No. 330224.
8. Next, hold the shim gauge firmly against the pinion gear. Then measure the clearance (A, **Figure 149**) between the shim gauge and drive shaft bearing housing using a feeler gauge. Take 4 measurements, between each screw hole in the housing. If the difference between measure-

9

ments exceeds 0.004 in. (0.10 mm), the bearing housing is distorted and must be replaced.

9. Hold the shim gauge firmly against the drive shaft bearing housing (between screw holes). Then, using a feeler gauge, measure the clearance between the gauge bar and the pinion gear (B, **Figure 149**). Take 4 measurements while rotating the drive shaft and pinion gear, but not the bearing housing. Record the measurements. Replace the drive shaft or pinion gear (or both) if the difference between the measurements exceeds 0.002 in. (0.05 mm).

NOTE
*The gauge factor for **gold** colored shim gauges is 0.030 in. The gauge factor for all other shim gauges is 0.020 in.*

10. Determine the average clearance (B, **Figure 149**) from the measurements taken in Step 9. Subtract the average clearance from 0.030 in. on 40-50 hp and V8 models or 0.020 in. on all other models. The remainder is the thickness of the shim pack required to set the pinion depth properly.

11. Remove the drive shaft assembly from the shim tool. Remove the collar and bearing housing, add the required amount of shims between the bearing housing and thrust washer, then reinstall the housing on the drive shaft. Select the fewest number of shims that equal the required thickness determined in Step 10.

12. Check the shim selection by reassembling the drive shaft with the shim pack (determined in Step 10) and collar. Place the assembly in the shim tool (**Figure 148**) as described in Step 6 and recheck the clearance between the pinion gear and shim gauge. The shim pack is the correct thickness if the clearance (B, **Figure 149**) is exactly 0.030 in. (40-50 hp and V8) or 0.020 in. (all other models). Repeat the shim selection procedure as necessary.

PRESSURE AND VACUUM TEST

Whenever a gearcase is disassembled and reassembled, it should be pressure and vacuum tested to check for leakage before refilling it with gear lubricant. If the gearcase fails either the pressure or vacuum test, it must be disassembled and repaired before returning the unit to service. Failure to perform a pressure and vacuum test after gearcase service will result in either lubri-

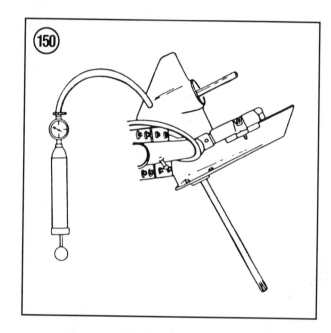

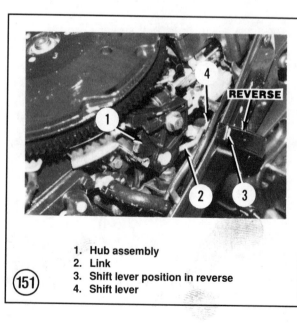

1. Hub assembly
2. Link
3. Shift lever position in reverse
4. Shift lever

cant leakage from the gearcase, or water leakage into the gearcase.

1. Thread a pressure test gauge into the drain/fill plug hole. See **Figure 150**, typical.

2. Pump the pressure tester to 3-6 psi (21-41 kPa). If the pressure holds steady, increase the pressure to 16-18 psi (110-124 kPa). Rotate, push, pull and wiggle all shafts while observing the pressure gauge.

3. If the pressure drops, submerge the gearcase in water and check for air bubbles to indicate the source of the leak.

4. If the pressure holds steady at 16-18 psi (110-124 kPa), release pressure and remove the pressure tester.

5. Install a vacuum tester into the drain/fill plug hole (**Figure 150**, typical).

6. Draw a 3-5 in.-Hg vacuum and note the vacuum gauge. If the vacuum holds steady, increase

to 15 in.-Hg. If the vacuum does not hold at this level, apply oil around the suspected area to determine if the leak stops.

7. If the vacuum holds steady at 15 in.-Hg, release the vacuum and remove the tester.

8. If the source of a leak can not be determined visually, disassemble the gearcase to locate the leak.

9. If no leakage is noted, fill the gearcase with the recommended lubricant (**Table 3**).

SHIFT LEVER ADJUSTMENT

1991 and 1992

9.9 and 15 hp

Refer to **Figure 151** for this procedure.

1. Disconnect the fuel hose at the carburetor.

2. Remove the cotter pin and washer from the shift lever link.

3. Move the shift lever and hub assembly to REVERSE.

4. Adjust the link to align with the shift lever hole without moving the shift lever.

5. When the link aligns with the shift lever hole, shorten it one turn. Apply a slight pressure to the shift lever and reinstall the link.

6. Install the washer and a new cotter pin, then reconnect the carburetor fuel hose to the carburetor.

7. Check and adjust the neutral start switch. See Chapter Three.

20-30 hp

Refer to **Figure 152** for this procedure.

1. Move the shift lever to REVERSE.

2. Loosen the adjustment and clamp screws.

3. Rotate the adjustment lever counterclockwise until full engagement of the clutch dog is felt in REVERSE gear.

4. Rotate the shift lever counterclockwise until the lever roller contacts the end of the shifter lock reverse detent.

5. Tighten the adjustment and clamp screws securely.

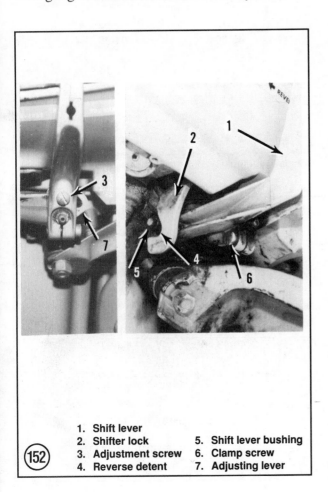

(152)

1. Shift lever	
2. Shifter lock	5. Shift lever bushing
3. Adjustment screw	6. Clamp screw
4. Reverse detent	7. Adjusting lever

9

Table 1 GEARCASE TIGHTENING TORQUES

Fastener	in.-lb.	ft.-lb.	N·m
2-8 hp			
Drain/fill/level plugs			
2.0, 2.3, 3.3 hp	31-40	–	3.5-4.5
3 & 4 hp	40-50	–	4.5-5.6
4 Deluxe, 6 & 8 hp	60-84	–	6.8-9.5
Gearcase head screws			
4 Deluxe, 3-8 hp	60-84	–	6.8-9.5
Gearcase mounting screws			
2.0, 2.3, 3.3 hp	89-115	–	10-13
3 & 4 hp	60-84	–	6.8-9.5
4 Deluxe, 6 & 8 hp	*		
Water pump screws			
2.0, 2.3, 3.3 hp	62-89	–	7-10
3 & 4 hp	25-35	–	2.8-3.9
4 Deluxe, 6 & 8 hp	60-84	–	6.8-9.5

Fastener	in.-lb.	ft.-lb.	N·m
9.9-30 hp			
Drain/fill/level plugs	60-80	–	6.8-9.0
Gearcase mounting nut			
20, 25 & 30 hp	–	16-18	22-24
28 hp	–	45-50	61-68
Gearcase mounting screws			
9.9-15 hp	96-120	–	11-13
20-30 hp	–	16-18	22-24
Lower gearcase half-to-upper gearcase half			
28 hp	60-80	–	6.8-9.0
Pivot pin	48-84	–	5.4-9.5
Propeller shaft bearing housing	60-80	–	6.8-9.0
Water pump screws	60-80	–	6.8-9.0

Fastener	in.-lb.	ft.-lb.	N·m
40-50 hp			
Anode screws	108-132	9-11	12-15
Drain/fill/level plugs	60-84	–	6.8-9.5
Gearcase mounting screws			
3/8 in.	–	18-20	24-27
7/16 in.	–	28-30	38-40
Drive shaft bearing housing screws	–	14-16	19-21
Pinion nut	–	40-45	54-67
Propeller shaft bearing housing screws	120-144	10-12	13.6-16.3
Shift rod cover screws	60-84	–	6.8-9.5
Trim tab screw	216-240	18-20	24-27
Water pump screws	60-84	–	6.8-9.5

(continued)

Table 1 GEARCASE TIGHTENING TORQUES (continued)

60 & 70 hp			
Fastener	in.-lb.	ft.-lb.	N·m
Drain/fill/level plugs	60-84	–	6.8-9.5
Drive shaft bearing housing screws	120-144	10-12	13.6-16.3
Gearcase mounting screws			
3/8 in.	–	18-20	24-27
7/16 in.	–	28-30	38-40
Pinion bearing retaining screw	48-80	–	5.4-9.0
Pinion nut	–	40-45	54-68
Propeller shaft bearing housing screws	120-144	10-12	13.6-16.3
Shift rod cover screws	60-84	–	6.8-9.5
Water pump screws	60-84	–	6.8-9.5

V4, V6 & V8			
Fastener	in.-lb.	ft.-lb.	N·m
Anode screws	84-108	–	9.5-12.2
Anode screws (patch lock)	108-132	–	12-15
Drain/fill/level plugs	60-84	–	6.8-9.5
Drive shaft bearing housing screws	–	14-16	19-22
Gearcase mounting screws			
3/8 in.			
V4	–	22-24	30-32
V6 & V8	–	26-28	35-38
7/16 in.			
V4	–	30-32	41-43
V6 (except cross flow) & V8	–	45-50	54-68
V6 cross flow	–	65-70	88-95
Pinion bearing retaining screw			
(if so equipped)	48-80	–	5.4-9.0
Pinion nut			
V4 & V6	–	70-80	95-108
V8	–	100-110	136-149
Propeller shaft bearing housing screws			
V4	120-144	10-12	13.6-16.3
V6 cross flow	–	18-20	24-27
V6 (except cross flow) & V8	–	20-24	27-32
Shift rod cover screws	60-84	–	6.8-9.5
Trim tab screw	–	35-40	47-54
Water pump screws	60-84	–	6.8-9.5

Standard screws and nuts			
No. 6	7-10	–	0.8-1.1
No. 8	15-22	–	1.7-2.5
No. 10	25-35	–	2.8-3.9
No. 12	35-40	–	3.9-4.5
1/4 in.	60-80	–	6.8-9.0
5/16 in.	120-140	10-12	13.6-15.8
3/8 in.	220-240	18-20	24-27
7/16 in.	–	28-30	38-40

* Tighten the front gearcase mounting screw to 120-144 in.-lb. (14-16 N·m) and the rear screw to 60-84 in.-lb. (6.8-9.5 N·m).

9

Table 2 SHIFT ROD HEIGHT
(USING OMC UNIVERSAL SHIFT ROD GAUGE PART NO. 389997)

Model	Shift rod dimension from gearcase to center of shift rod hole*
40, 48 & 50 hp	
Standard shaft	16-15/16 in. (430.21 mm)
Long shaft	21-15/16 in. (557.21 mm)
Extra long shaft	24-7/16 in. (620.71 mm)
60 & 70 hp	
Long shaft (20 in. transom)	21-23/32 in. (551.66 mm)
Long shaft 22.5 in. transom)	24-7/32 in. (615.16 mm)
Extra long shaft (25 in. transom)	26-23/32 in. (678.66 mm)
85-115 hp (V4 cross flow)	
Long shaft	21-27/32 in. (554.83 mm)
Extra long shaft	26-27/32 in. (681.83 mm)
120 & 140 hp (V4 loop charged)	
Long shaft (20 in.)	21-15/16 in. (557.21 mm)
Long shaft (22.5 in.)	24-7/16 in. (620.71 mm)
Extra long shaft (25 in.)	26-15/16 in. (684.21 mm)
1991 150 & 175 hp (V6 cross flow)	
Long shaft	22-1/16 in. (560.39 mm)
Extra long shaft	27-1/16 in. (687.39 mm)
150 & 175 hp (60° V6)	
1991	
Long shaft	21-5/16 in. (541.34 mm)
Extra long shaft	26-5/16 in. (668.34 mm)
1992-on	
Long shaft	21-1/4 in. (539.75 mm)
Extra long shaft	26-1/4 in. (666.75 mm)
200 & 225 hp (V6 loop charged)	
Long shaft (20 in.)	21-15/16 in. (557.21 mm)
Long shaft (25 in.	26-15/16 in. (684.21 mm)
Extra long shaft (30 in.)	31-15/16 in. (811.21 mm)
250 & 300 hp (V8 loop charged)	
Long shaft (20 in.)	22-13/16 in. (579.44 mm)
Long shaft (25 in.)	27-13/16 in. (706.44 mm)
Extra long shaft (30 in.)	32-13/16 in. (833.44 mm)

*All measurements are plus or minus 1/32 in. (0.794 mm)

Table 3 GEARCASE GEAR RATIO, LUBRICANT CAPACITY
AND RECOMMENDED LUBRICANT

Model	Recommended gear ratio	Lubricant capacity	Lubricant
2, 2.3, 3 hp	13:24	3 oz. (90 mL)	1
3, 4 hp	12:25	2.7 oz. (80 mL)	1
4 Deluxe	13:29	11 oz. (325 mL)	2
6, 8 hp	13:29	11 oz. (325 mL)	1
9.9, 15 hp	12:29	9 oz. (260 mL)	1
20, 25, 30 hp	13:28	11 oz. (325 mL)	1
28 hp	12:21	8 oz. (245 mL)	1

(continued)

**Table 3 GEARCASE GEAR RATIO, LUBRICANT CAPACITY
AND RECOMMENDED LUBRICANT (continued)**

Model	Recommended gear ratio	Lubricant capacity	Lubricant
40, 48, 50 hp	12:29	16.4 oz. (485 mL)	1
60, 70 hp	12:29	22 oz. (650 mL)	1
85, 88, 90, 100, 115 hp	13:26	26 oz. (800 mL)	1
120, 140 hp	13:26	26 oz. (800 mL)	1
120TXETF, 120TXATF, 140CX	12:27	33 oz. (980 mL)	1
150, 175 hp	14:26	33 oz. (980 mL)	1
200, 275 hp	14:26	33 oz. (980 mL)	1
250, 300 hp	17:30	71 oz. (2100 mL)	1

1. OMC Hi-Vis Gearcase Lubricant.
2. OMC Premium Blend Gearcase Lubricant

9

Chapter Ten

Power Trim and Tilt Systems

The usual method of raising and lowering the smaller outboards consists of a series of holes in the transom bracket. To trim the motor, an adjustment pin is removed from the bracket, the outboard is repositioned and the pin reinserted in the proper holes to hold the unit in place. With power trim and tilt, low-effort control of the outboard position is provided whether the boat is underway or at rest.

Four different trim and tilt systems are used on outboard motors covered in this manual:

   a. Touch-Trim system.
   b. 40 and 50 hp power trim/tilt system.
   c. Conventional power trim/tilt system.
   d. FasTrak power trim/tilt system.

The Touch-Trim system is used on some 40-50 hp models. Other 40 and 50 hp models are equipped with single-ram electric power trim/tilt unit. Sixty-225 hp (except 60°) models may be equipped with a conventional or FasTrak power trim/tilt system. FasTrak is used on 60° V6 models. V8 models (250 and 300 hp) are equipped with a conventional power trim/tilt system.

This chapter includes maintenance, troubleshooting procedures and trim/tilt system re-placement for each system. **Table 1** and **Table 2** are located at the end of this chapter.

TOUCH-TRIM

The Touch-Trim system consists of a pressurized tilt assist cylinder and a control lever and cable. When the control lever is moved to the tilt position, the motor can be easily tilted due to the pressurized tilt assist cylinder. When the lever is placed in the RUN position, the outboard is locked in its current position.

WARNING
The fluid and internal components of the Touch-Trim system are under extremely high pressure. To prevent personal injury, do not attempt to disassemble any part of the hydraulic system.

The Touch-Trim unit can only be serviced by replacing the complete cylinder assembly. The hydraulic fluid and internal components contained within the unit are under high pressure. Consequently, the unit should *not* be disassembled.

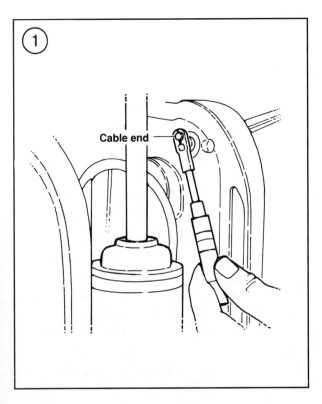

① Cable end

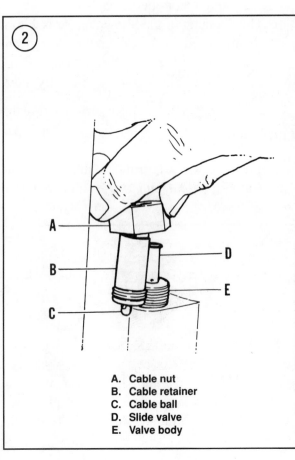

②

A. Cable nut
B. Cable retainer
C. Cable ball
D. Slide valve
E. Valve body

Touch-Trim Control Cable Replacement

1. Tilt the motor to its fully UP position. Engage the tilt support and lower the motor until the support contacts the stern brackets.

2. Remove the cable from its anchor then carefully pry the cable end (**Figure 1**) from the lever ball adjacent to the cylinder assembly or under the tiller handle.

> *WARNING*
> *If the valve body (E, **Figure 2**) unscrews as the cable nut (A) is removed, discontinue nut removal. Carefully screw the nut and valve body back into the Touch-Trim unit. If the cable must be replaced, remove and replace the cable and Touch-Trim cylinder as an assembly.*

3. Remove the cable nut (A, **Figure 2**) using an open-end wrench.

4. Lift the cable upward and disconnect the cable ball (C, **Figure 2**) from the slide valve (D).

5. *Tiller handle*—While holding the cable with pliers, unscrew the cable retainer (B, **Figure 2**) by turning it clockwise (left-hand threads). Remove the retainer, then slide the cable nut off the cable.

6. Remove the cable from the clamp on the stern bracket.

7. While closely noting its routing, remove the cable from the outboard motor. Retain the cable nut for use with the new control cable.

8. To install the new cable, first apply OMC Triple-Guard grease to the cable retainer cavity and cable ball.

9. Apply a light coat of Permatex No. 2 sealant to the valve body external threads.

10. *Tiller handle*—Place the cable nut on the cable. Lubricate the cable retainer O-ring with OMC Triple-Guard grease, then install the retainer on the cable (left-hand threads).

11. Connect the cable ball to the slide valve. While pushing down on the cable retainer, install the cable nut and tighten to 36-48 in.-lb. (4.1-5.4 N•m).

10

12. Route the cable as noted during removal and secure as necessary with new tie straps.

13. Thread the cable end (**Figure 1**) onto the cable so the cable can be just pulled into alignment with the anchor block while the cable end is held against the lever ball.

14. Snap the cable end onto the lever ball. Snap the cable retainer into the anchor block. Cycle the lever between TILT and RUN 10-12 times, then adjust the cable as described in this chapter.

Touch-Trim Control Cable Adjustment

If the control cable is adjusted too loosely, the outboard motor will be hard to tilt (no tilt assist). If the cable is too tight, the motor will leak down from the tilted position and the reverse lock may not function. The slide valve in the cylinder assembly must fully close before the control lever reaches the RUN position. To ensure that this happens, the lever must have some reserve movement after the valve closes.

1. Tilt the motor to the fully UP position and place the control lever in the UP position (A, **Figure 3**).

2. Slowly move the lever toward the RUN position (**Figure 3**). The motor will slowly tilt DOWN. When the motor stops moving, the control valve is closed (**Figure 3**). Stop moving the control lever and leave it in this position.

3. To ensure the valve is fully closed, push down hard on the gearcase. The outboard will hold its position if the valve is fully closed.

4. Next, move the lever from the valve closed position to the run position (**Figure 3**) while measuring the distance the lever moved (reserve movement) using a tape measure or similar scale.

5. The lever reserve movement should be approximately 1/8 in. (3.2 mm). If adjustment is necessary, disconnect the cable end from the lever ball and turn the cable end as required. Reconnect the cable and recheck reserve movement. If the reserve movement is excessive and the cable end runs out of threads before the

proper adjustment is obtained, the cable inner liner is worn. If so, the cable must be replaced.

40-50 HP POWER TRIM AND TILT SYSTEM

The power trim/tilt system used on 40-50 hp models consists of a manifold that contains the hydraulic pump, electric motor, oil reservoir, hydraulic cylinder and all valves. **Figure 4** shows the trim/tilt unit removed from the outboard. A trim/tilt switch, trim angle indicator gauge and related circuitry complete the system.

An electric motor manufactured by Bosch or Showa may be used on the 40-50 hp power trim/tilt system. The motors can be identified by motor diameter and the location of the motor wires.

  a. The diameter of the Bosch motor is 2.5 in. (63.5 mm) and the wires exit the motor from the commutator end.

  b. The diameter of the Showa motor is 2.4 in. (61 mm) and the wires exit the motor from the side (near the mounting base).

The Bosch and Showa motors are fully interchangeable.

Operation

Depressing the UP trim switch closes the pump motor circuit and causes the motor to

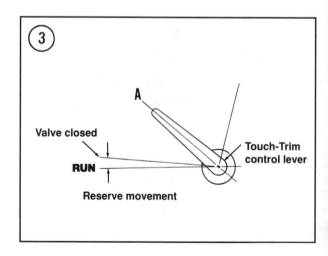

rotate the pump in a counterclockwise direction. Hydraulic fluid, under pressure, is directed to the bottom of the trim/tilt cylinder which causes the piston to move upward. As the piston moves upward, fluid displaced from the top of the cylinder passes through the DOWN check valve and is recirculated back to the pump. When the piston is completely extended, the UP relief valve located in the piston is mechanically opened to prevent excessively high pressure in the cylinder. The initial 15° of upward movement is considered the trim range as the swivel bracket is supported between the stern brackets. The remaining 50° of upward movement is the tilt range.

Depressing the DOWN trim button closes the pump motor circuit and causes the motor to rotate the pump in a clockwise direction. Hydraulic fluid, under pressure, is directed to the top of the hydraulic cylinder which causes the piston to move downward. As the piston moves downward, fluid displaced from the bottom of the cylinder passes through the UP check valve and is recirculated back to the pump. When the piston is completely retracted, the DOWN relief

valve located in the piston is mechanically opened to prevent excessively high pressure in the cylinder.

On early models, the outboard motor can be manually lowered from a tilted position by opening the manual release valve a minimum of 3 full turns. The slotted manual release valve is accessed through the port stern bracket thrust rod hole. The manual release valve must be tightened to 45-55 in.-lb. (5.1-6.2 N•m) to continue normal operation.

On late models (1993-1/2-on), the outboard motor can be manually raised or lowered by opening the manual release valve. The manual release valve is located on the back side of the power trim/tilt unit on late models. The manual valve must be tightened to 45-55 in.-lb. (5.1-6.2 N•m) to continue normal operation.

Hydraulic Fluid Check

The hydraulic reservoir fluid level should be checked at least once per season, or after every 100 hours of operation. The power trim/tilt system fluid capacity is 11.7 fl. oz. (345 mL). Insufficient fluid will result in erratic trim/tilt system operation. The recommended fluid is OMC Power Trim/Tilt and Power Steering Fluid. If the recommended fluid is not available, GM Dexron II automatic transmission fluid is a suitable substitute. To check the fluid level:

1. Tilt the outboard to its fully UP position and engage the tilt lock levers.

2. Remove the fill/level plug (**Figure 4**). The fluid should be even with the bottom of the fill/level plug hole.

NOTE
Do not overfill the trim/tilt reservoir.

3. If not, add the recommended fluid as necessary. Reinstall the plug and tighten to 45-55 in.-lb. (5.1-6.2 N•m).

4. Release the tilt lock levers, then run the system through 5 or more UP/DOWN cycles to

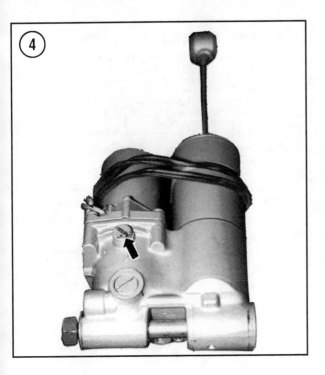

(4)

10

purge any air that may be present in the system. When cycling the system, hold the trim switch down for 5-10 seconds after the cylinder is completely extended or retracted. If the reservoir was nearly empty, it may be necessary to add more fluid during the air purging process. Make certain the cylinder is fully extended before removing the fill/level plug.

5. Inspect the entire system for leakage and repair as necessary.

Troubleshooting

Should a malfunction occur in the power trim/tilt system, the initial step is to determine if the problem is electrical or hydraulic. Electrical tests are given in this chapter. If the problem appears to be in the hydraulic system, refer it to a qualified specialist for repair.

The following preliminary checks should be performed prior to troubleshooting the electrical system:

1. Make sure the plug-in connectors are properly engaged and all terminals and wires are free of corrosion. Tighten and clean all connections as necessary.

2. Make sure the battery is fully charged and in acceptable condition. Charge or replace the battery as necessary.

3. Check the system fuse or circuit breaker, if so equipped.

4. Check the fluid level as described in this chapter.

5. Make sure the manual release valve is fully closed and properly tightened.

NOTE
The seating area of the manual release valve must be in perfect condition or leak-down or other operational problems may occur. Check the valve seat using a suitable magnifying glass. Replace the valve if any defects are noted.

Power Supply Tests
(1991 40-50 hp)

Perform the following test procedure to determine the condition of all power supply circuits.

1. Place the key switch in the OFF position. Remove the ignition cutoff switch clip and lanyard.

2. Make sure the battery is fully charged and in acceptable condition. Charge or replace the battery as required.

3. Connect a voltmeter black lead to a good clean engine ground.

4. Check for voltage at the battery side of the starter solenoid.

   a. If battery voltage is not noted, check the battery cables for clean tight connections and repair as necessary.

   b. If battery voltage is noted, continue at Step 5.

NOTE
*Check relay bracket voltages from the relay side of the bracket. See **Figure 5**.*

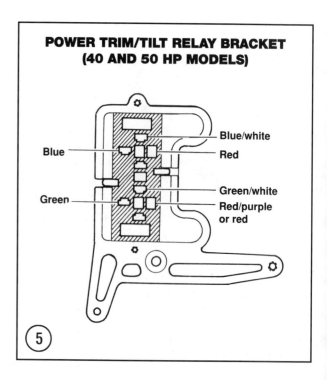

POWER TRIM/TILT RELAY BRACKET (40 AND 50 HP MODELS)

Blue/white
Blue
Red
Green/white
Green
Red/purple
or red

⑤

5. Remove the UP (top) and DOWN (bottom) relays from the relay bracket.

6. Check the voltage at the red and red/purple relay terminals in the bracket. See **Figure 5**.

   a. If battery voltage is noted, continue at Step 7.

   b. If no voltage is noted, inspect the condition of the red and red/purple wires between the relay bracket and terminal block. Repair or replace the wire(s) as necessary.

7. Check the voltage at the red/purple wires on the terminal block.

   a. If battery voltage is noted, continue at Step 8.

   b. If no voltage is noted, check the 20 amp fuse and the red/purple wire in the engine wiring harness. Repair the red/purple wire or replace the fuse as necessary.

8. Check the voltage at the green/white relay terminal (**Figure 5**) while depressing the DOWN trim button.

   a. If battery voltage is noted, continue at Step 9.

   b. If no voltage is noted, inspect the condition of the trim switch wiring between the relay bracket and switch. If the wiring is in acceptable condition, replace the trim switch.

9. Install the DOWN relay. Push the relay only halfway into the bracket so the relay terminals can be probed with the meter. Check the voltage at the M (green wire) relay terminal while depressing the DOWN button.

   a. If battery voltage is noted, continue at Step 10.

   b. If no voltage is noted, test the DOWN relay as described under *Relay Test* in this chapter.

10. Check the voltage at the green wire terminal in the trim motor harness connector while depressing the DOWN trim button.

   a. If battery voltage is noted, the trim motor is defective and must be repaired or replaced.

   b. If no voltage is noted, repair or replace the green wire in the trim system wiring harness.

11. Check the voltage at the blue/white relay terminal (**Figure 5**) while depressing the UP trim button.

   a. If battery voltage is noted, continue at Step 12.

   b. If no voltage is noted, check the condition of the UP circuit wiring between the trim switch and relay bracket. If the wiring is in acceptable condition, replace the trim switch.

12. Install the UP relay. Push the relay only halfway into the bracket so the relay terminals can be probed with the meter. Check the voltage at the M (blue) relay terminal while depressing the UP trim button.

   a. If battery voltage is noted, continue at Step 13.

   b. If no voltage is noted, test the UP relay as described under *Relay Test* in this chapter.

13. Check the voltage at the blue wire terminal in the trim motor harness connector while pushing the UP trim button.

   a. If battery voltage is noted, repair or replace the defective trim motor.

   b. If no voltage is noted, repair or replace the blue wire in the trim system wiring harness.

Power Supply Tests
(1992-on 40-50 hp)

Perform the following test procedure to determine the condition of all power supply circuits. Unless specified otherwise, make all voltage checks from the relay side of the trim/tilt relay bracket.

1. Place the key switch in the OFF position. Remove the ignition cutoff switch clip and lanyard.

2. Make sure the battery is fully charged and in acceptable condition. Charge or replace the battery as required.

10

3. Connect a voltmeter black lead to a good clean engine ground.

4. Check for voltage at the battery side of the starter solenoid.

   a. If battery voltage is not noted, check the battery cables for clean, tight connections and repair as necessary.

   b. If battery voltage is noted, continue at Step 5 (or Step 11 if problem is in DOWN circuit only).

5. Remove the UP (top) and DOWN (bottom) relays from the relay bracket.

6. Check the voltage at the red relay terminal (**Figure 5**).

   a. If battery voltage is noted, continue at Step 7.

   b. If no voltage is noted, check the voltage at the red wire terminal at the terminal block. If battery voltage is present at the terminal block, repair or replace the red wire between the terminal block and relay bracket.

7. Check the voltage at the blue/white relay terminal (**Figure 5**) while depressing the UP trim button.

   a. If battery voltage is noted, continue at Step 8.

   b. If no voltage is noted, check the condition of the red/purple wire and repair or replace as necessary. If the red/purple wire is in acceptable condition, replace the trim switch.

8. Install the UP (top) relay into the bracket. Push the relay only halfway into the relay bracket so the relay terminals can be probed with the voltmeter.

9. Check the voltage at the M relay (blue) terminal.

   a. If no voltage is noted, test the relay as described under *Relay Test* in this chapter.

   b. If battery voltage is noted, continue at Step 10.

10. Disconnect the green and blue wire connector from the trim/tilt motor. Check the voltage at the blue wire in the trim motor connector while depressing the UP trim button.

   a. If battery voltage is noted, first inspect the blue wire connector for looseness or corrosion. If the connector is in acceptable condition, replace the trim/tilt motor.

   b. If no voltage is noted, repair or replace the blue wire between the relay bracket and trim/tilt motor.

11. Remove the UP relay from the relay bracket.

12. Check the voltage at the red relay terminal (**Figure 5**).

   a. If battery voltage is noted, continue at Step 13.

   b. If no voltage is noted, check the voltage at the red wire at the terminal block. If battery voltage is noted, repair or replace the red wire between the terminal block and relay bracket.

13. Check the voltage at the green/white relay terminal (**Figure 5**) while depressing the DOWN trim button.

   a. If battery voltage is noted, continue at Step 14.

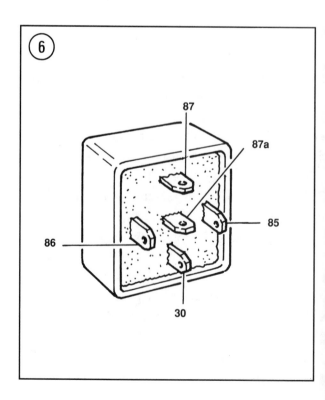

b. If no voltage is noted, check the red/purple wire to the trim switch. If the red/purple wire is in acceptable condition, replace the trim switch.

14. Install the DOWN (bottom) relay into the relay bracket. Push the relay only halfway into the bracket so the relay terminals can be probed with the voltmeter.

15. Check the voltage at the M (green) relay terminal.

a. If battery voltage is noted, continue at Step 16.

b. If no voltage is noted, test the relay as described under *Relay Test* in this chapter.

16. Disconnect the green and blue wire connector from the trim/tilt motor. Check the voltage at the green wire while depressing the DOWN trim button.

a. If battery voltage is noted, repair or replace the defective trim motor.

b. If no voltage is noted, repair or replace the green wire in the trim system wiring harness.

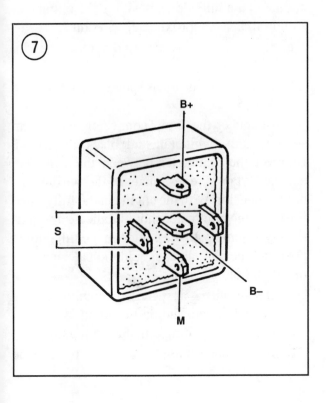

Relay Test
(1991 40-50 hp)

Use an ohmmeter to test the trim/tilt relays. Calibrate the meter on the high-ohm scale when checking for continuity.

1. Remove the relay to be tested from the relay bracket.

2. Connect the ohmmeter between relay terminals 87a and 30. See **Figure 6**. Continuity should be noted.

3. Connect the ohmmeter between relay terminals 87 and 30 (**Figure 6**). No continuity should be noted.

4. Calibrate the ohmmeter on the low-ohm scale. Connect the ohmmeter between relay terminals 85 and 86 (**Figure 6**). The ohmmeter should indicate 55-85 ohms.

5. Using jumper leads, connect the positive terminal of a 12-volt battery to relay terminal 85 and the negative terminal to relay terminal 86. Then connect the ohmmeter between relay terminals 87 and 30. With the 12-volt battery connected to the relay, the ohmmeter should indicate continuity.

6. With the 12-volt battery still connected to the relay, connect the ohmmeter between relay terminals 87a and 30 (**Figure 6**). The ohmmeter should indicate no continuity.

7. Replace the relay if test results are not as specified.

Relay Test
(1992-on 40-50 hp)

Use an ohmmeter to test the trim/tilt relays. Calibrate the meter on the high-ohm scale when checking for continuity.

The location and orientation of the trim/tilt relays will vary between models, however, the relay terminals are always connected as follows (**Figure 7**):

10

a. Relay S (switch) terminals are connected to the blue/white or green/white trim/tilt circuit.

b. Relay B+ (12-volt source) terminal is connected to the red trim/tilt circuit.

c. Relay B- terminal is connected to the black (ground) circuit.

d. Relay M (motor) terminal is connected to the blue or green circuit.

1. Remove the relay to be tested from the relay bracket.

2. Connect the ohmmeter between relay terminals B- and M (**Figure 7**). Continuity should be indicated.

3. Connect the ohmmeter between relay terminals B+ and M (**Figure 7**). No continuity should be noted.

4. Calibrate the ohmmeter on the low-ohm scale. Connect the meter between the S terminals (**Figure 7**). The meter should indicate 70-100 ohms.

5. Using jumper leads, connect a suitable 12-volt battery to the relay S terminals. Then calibrate the ohmmeter on the high-ohm scale and connect it between the B+ and M terminals (**Figure 7**). With the 12-volt source connected to the S terminals, continuity should be present between relay terminals B+ and M.

6. Next, with the battery still attached to the relay S terminals, connect the ohmmeter between terminals B- and M. No continuity should be present.

7. Replace the relay(s) if any test results are not as specified.

Trim Gauge and Circuit Test

1. Connect a voltmeter between trim gauge terminals I and G. Place the key switch in the ON position and note the voltmeter. If no voltage is noted, continue at Step 2. If voltage is present, continue at Step 4.

2. Connect the voltmeter between the trim gauge G terminal and terminal A in the 3-pin connector at the remote control assembly. See **Figure 8**. Turn the key switch to ON and note the voltmeter. If voltage is present, continue at Step 3. If no voltage is noted, repair or replace the purple wire between the trim gauge and remote control.

3. Connect the voltmeter between a good engine ground and the key switch terminal A (**Figure 8**). Turn the key switch ON and note the meter. If no voltage is noted, check the 20 amp fuse in the engine harness. If the fuse is good, replace the key switch. If voltage is noted, repair or replace the purple wire between the key switch and warning horn, or between the warning horn and the 3-pin trim gauge connector at the remote control.

4. Place the key switch in the OFF position. Disconnect the trim harness white/tan and black/tan wires from the gauge terminals S and G, respectively. Calibrate an ohmmeter on the low-ohm scale, then connect the ohmmeter between the white/tan and black/tan wires. With the engine in the fully tilted position, the ohmmeter should indicate approximately 1 ohm. With the engine in the fully down position, the ohmmeter should indicate approximately 88 ohms.

a. If resistance is as specified, replace the trim gauge.

b. If resistance is not as specified, continue at Step 5.

5. Disconnect the 2-pin connector at the trim sending unit (white/tan and black/tan wires). Connect the ohmmeter between the white/tan and black/tan wire terminals in the wiring harness connector. With the engine in the fully tilted position, the ohmmeter should indicate approximately 1 ohm. With the engine in the fully down position, the ohmmeter should indicate approximately 88 ohms.

a. If resistance is as specified, repair or replace the white/tan and/or black/tan wires between the sending unit and trim gauge.

b. If resistance is not as specified, replace the sending unit.

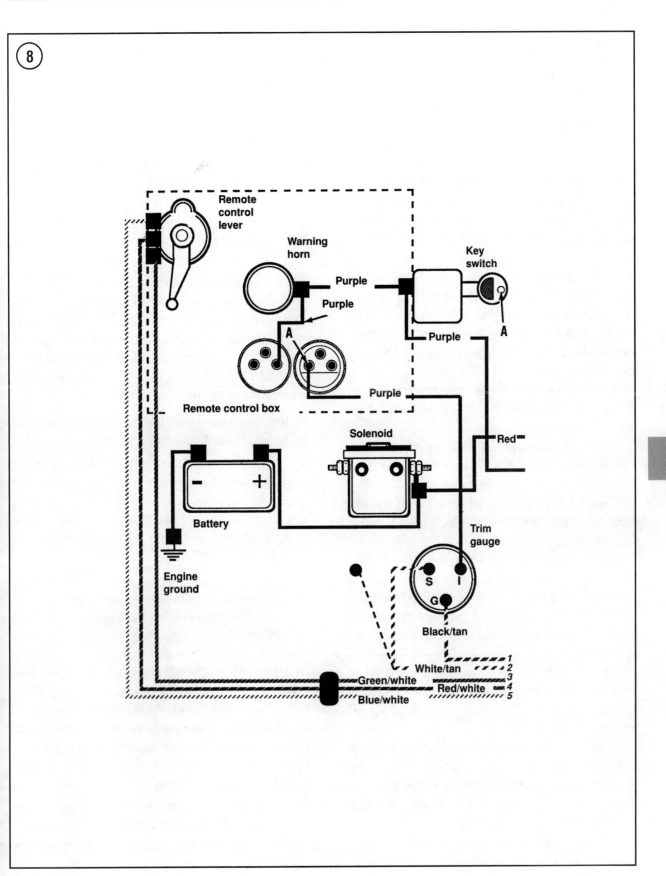

TRIM/TILT MOTOR TESTING

Amperage (Current Draw) Test

This test evaluates the condition of the hydraulic system by determining the current requirements of the pump motor. A suitable stop watch and DC ammeter capable of measuring up to 25 amps are necessary to perform the procedure. The battery must be fully charged and in acceptable condition for the following test to be valid.

An electric motor manufactured by Bosch or Showa may be used on the 40-50 hp power trim/tilt system. The motors can be identified by motor diameter and the location of the motor wires. The Bosch and Showa motors are fully interchangeable.

  a. The diameter of the Bosch motor is 2.5 in. (63.5 mm) and the wires exit the motor from the commutator end.
  b. The diameter of the Showa motor is 2.4 in. (61 mm) and the wires exit the motor from the side (near the mounting base).

1. Connect the ammeter in series with the red wire between the terminal block and trim/tilt relay bracket.
2. Tilt the outboard to the fully up position while observing the ammeter and stop watch. Record the current draw and the time required to reach full tilt. Depress the UP trim/tilt button with the tilt cylinder fully extended to check the up stall current draw.
3. Next, run the motor to the fully trimmed in position while observing the ammeter and stop watch. Again, stall the motor in the down position and note the ammeter.
4. Repeat Steps 3 and 4 through several cycles to ensure consistent test results. Compare the results with the specifications in **Table 1**.

  a. If the current draw is within specification, but a trim/tilt malfunction is evident, a defective pump control piston or malfunctioning check valves is indicated.

  b. Excessive current draw indicates the pump or motor is binding or defective. Perform the motor no-load current draw test as described in this chapter.
  c. Low current draw indicates a worn or defective pump assembly, leaking relief valve(s) or an internal leak in the pump or elsewhere in the hydraulic system.

No-Load Current Draw Test

The no-load current draw test is used to determine the condition of the electric motor. A DC ammeter capable of measuring up to 25 amps and a mechanical or vibration tachometer are necessary to perform the test. In addition, a fully charged 12-volt battery (360 cold cranking amps minimum) is required.

1. Remove the pump motor from the trim/tilt system as described in this chapter.
2. Mount the motor securely in a vise or other holding fixture.

> *NOTE*
> *If the positive battery terminal is connected to the motor's blue (UP) wire terminal, the motor should turn clockwise as viewed from the pump end. The motor should turn the opposite direction if connected to the green (DOWN) wire terminal.*

3. Using suitable jumper leads, connect the positive battery terminal, along with the ammeter (in series) to either of the motor terminals.
4. Then connect the negative battery terminal to the motor case. Attach a vibration or mechanical tachometer to the motor, then note the motor speed and amperage draw.
5. Compare the motor speed and current draw to the no-load specifications in **Table 2**. Repair or replace the motor if the results are not as specified.

POWER TRIM/TILT ASSEMBLY REMOVAL/INSTALLATION (40-50 HP)

1. Tilt the motor to the fully UP position and engage the tilt lock levers.

2. Disconnect the blue and green wire connector from the motor.

3. Remove the spring retainer clip from the cylinder end mounting pin. Remove the cylinder mounting pin.

4. Remove the 3/4 in. locknut from one side of the trim-in angle adjustment rod. Slide the rod out of the stern brackets and remove the trim/tilt unit far enough to disconnect the ground wire attached to one motor mounting screw. Disconnect the wire and remove the unit.

5. To install the trim/tilt unit, lubricate the cylinder end mounting pin and bushings with OMC Triple-Guard grease.

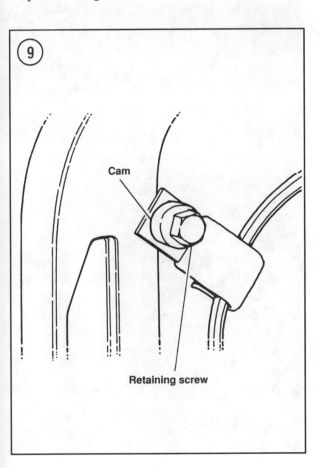

Cam

Retaining screw

6. Place the trim/tilt unit into position between the stern brackets and reattach the ground wire to the motor screw.

7. Lubricate the trim-in angle adjusting pin and bushings with OMC Triple-Guard grease. Install the pin through the stern brackets and trim/tilt unit. Install the locknut(s) and tighten to 20-25 ft.-lb. (27-34 N.m).

Motor Removal/Installation (40-50 hp)

1. Remove the power trim/tilt unit as described in this chapter.

2. Remove the 4 screws securing the motor to the power trim/tilt manifold assembly.

3. Remove the motor from the manifold. Be sure to retrieve the motor-to-pump drive coupling if it came off with the motor. Reinstall the drive coupling into position in the pump. Remove and discard the motor O-ring.

4. To install the motor, install a new O-ring on the motor.

5. Install the motor on the trim/tilt manifold. Make sure the motor properly engages the drive coupling.

6. Install the 4 mounting screws and tighten to 35-52 in.-lb. (4-6 N.m).

7. Install the power trim/tilt unit as described in this chapter.

Trim Indicator Sending Unit Adjustment

The trim gauge sending unit should be adjusted so the gauge needle is aligned with the correct mark as the DOWN/IN movement of the outboard stops.

1. Tilt the outboard to the fully UP position and engage the tilt lock levers.

2. Loosen the adjusting cam retaining screw (**Figure 9**) and rotate the cam as necessary to position the gauge needle at the appropriate mark (bottom).

10

3. Tighten the cam retaining screw securely. Tilt the motor up and down to check adjustment.

CONVENTIONAL POWER TRIM AND TILT SYSTEM

Components

The conventional power trim/tilt system consists of a manifold containing an electric motor, fluid reservoir, pump, valve body and 2 hydraulic trim cylinders. A combination hydraulic tilt cylinder and shock absorber is also attached to the manifold. See **Figure 10**. The complete trim/tilt system is contained entirely between and attached to the stern brackets. A trim/tilt switch, indicator gauge and the necessary wiring complete the system.

The pump motor may be manufactured by Prestolite, Bosch or Showa. In addition, 3 different Showa motors are used. The various motors are identified by the motor diameter and location of the motor wires. Note that the motors are all interchangeable as assemblies.

  a. *Prestolite*—3.0 in. (76.2 mm) in diameter and the wires exit from the commutator end of the motor.

  b. *Bosch*—2.5 in. (63.5 mm) in diameter and the wires exit from the commutator end of the motor.

  c. *Showa*—3.0 in. (76.2 mm) in diameter and the wires exit the commutator end of the motor.

  d. *Showa*—2.4 in. (61 mm) in diameter and the wires exit from the side of the motor at the pump end.

  e. *Showa*—2.9 in. (73.7 mm) in diameter and the wires exit from the side of the motor at the pump end.

Operation

Depressing the UP trim button closes the pump motor circuit and the motor drives the pump, forcing hydraulic fluid into the trim cylinders. The trim cylinder pistons push on the

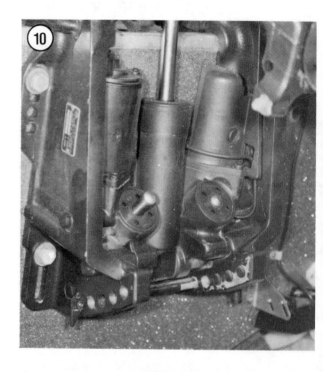

swivel bracket thrust pads to trim the outboard upward from 0° to 15°. At 15°, the trim cylinders are fully extended and the hydraulic fluid is diverted into the tilt cylinder, which moves the outboard through the final 50° of upward travel.

Depressing the DOWN trim button causes the motor to rotate in the opposite direction, forcing fluid into the tilt cylinders causing the outboard to move downward, back to the 15° position. At this point, the swivel brackets rest on the trim rods. The trim rods then lower the outboard to the fully down/in position.

The power tilt will temporarily maintain the outboard at any angle within its range to allow shallow water operation at slow speed, launching, beaching or trailering. At about 1500 rpm, however, an overload switch will automatically lower the outboard to its fully trimmed out (15°) position to prevent damage to the outboard motor.

A manual release valve with a slotted head permits manual raising and lowering of the outboard should the electrical system fail. See **Figure 11**. The manual release valve must be closed and tightened to 45-55 in.-lb. (5-6 N•m) before normal operation can be resumed.

A trim gauge sending unit is located on the inside of the port stern bracket (**Figure 12**). Access to the sending unit requires the outboard be fully tilted up.

A tilt lock is provided to relieve the pressure on the hydraulic system when trailering or during storage. To engage the tilt lock, tilt the outboard to the fully up position, move the locks into position, then lower the outboard so the locks contact the stern brackets.

Hydraulic Fluid Check

Check the hydraulic fluid level in the reservoir once per season or after every 100 hours of operation. The recommended fluid is OMC Power Trim and Tilt and Power Steering Fluid or GM Dexron II automatic transmission fluid. The system capacity is 25 fl. oz. (740 mL).

Low fluid level and/or air in the hydraulic system will result in erratic and noisy trim/tilt operation.

1. Tilt the outboard to the fully UP position.

2. If necessary, clean the area around the reservoir fill/level plug (**Figure 13**) to prevent contamination, then remove the plug using a screwdriver.

3. The fluid level should be even with the bottom of the fill/level plug hole. Add the recommended fluid as necessary.

NOTE
Do not overfill the trim/tilt reservoir.

4. If necessary to add a large amount of fluid because of leakage or service, bleed any air from the system as follows:

NOTE
Do not remove the reservoir fill/level plug unless the cylinders are fully extended (outboard UP).

a. Fill the reservoir as previously outlined.
b. Install the fill plug loosely, then cycle the outboard to fully UP and fully DOWN, checking and adding fluid as necessary.
c. Continue for at least 5 complete UP/DOWN cycles to purge air from the system. Recheck the fluid level and add as required. Then, install the reservoir plug and tighten securely.

Troubleshooting

If a malfunction develops in the power trim/tilt system, the initial step is to determine if the problem is electrical or hydraulic. Electrical tests are given in this chapter. If the problem appears to be in the hydraulic system, refer it to a qualified marine/hydraulic specialist for service.

To determine if the problem is electric or hydraulic, proceed as follows:

1. Make sure all connectors are clean and tight. Clean and tighten connections as necessary.
2. Make sure the battery is fully charged and in acceptable condition. A weak or undercharged battery will result in unsatisfactory trim/tilt operation.
3. Check the system fuse, if so equipped.
4. Make sure the reservoir is full of the recommended fluid and that no air is present in the system.

NOTE
The seating area of the manual release valve must be in perfect condition. Inspect the seat using a suitable magnifying glass. If excessively worn, nicked,

scratched or damaged, replace the valve.

5. Make sure the manual release valve is closed and properly tightened to 45-55 in.-lb. (5-6 N.m).

NOTE
The power trim/tilt assembly must be removed from the outboard motor to perform the remaining tests. Mount the unit in a suitable holding fixture (OMC Test Stand part No. 390008). A fully charged 12-volt battery and suitable jumper leads are necessary to perform the following tests.

6. Remove the power trim/tilt unit as described in this chapter.
7. Install the OMC Trim and Tilt Pressure Tester part No. 390010 (**Figure 14**) as follows:

a. Remove the manual release valve retaining ring using snap ring pliers.
b. Connect the battery to the trim/tilt motor green wire terminal and completely retract the cylinders.
c. Turn the manual release counterclockwise one full turn.

d. Momentarily operate the trim/tilt motor in the UP direction, then in the DOWN direction.

CAUTION
Residual hydraulic pressure may be present when manual release valve is removed. To prevent personal injury, wear suitable eye protection and cover the manual release valve with a shop towel during removal.

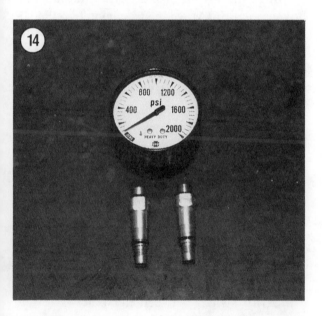

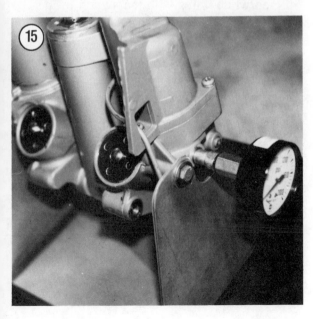

e. Slowly remove the manual release valve by turning it counterclockwise.

f. Screw the pressure gauge and the appropriate adapter together. Tighten the gauge and adapter securely. Adapter A is used to test the UP circuit and adapter B is used to test the DOWN circuit.

g. Install the pressure gauge and adapter A into the manual release valve passage and tighten to 5-10 in.-lb. (0.6-1.1 N•m). See **Figure 15**. Do not overtighten or the adapter O-ring may be damaged.

h. Using the battery and jumpers, operate the unit UP and DOWN several cycles, then check the reservoir fluid level. Add the recommended fluid as necessary.

8. With the trim/tilt cylinders fully retracted, operate the system in the UP direction while observing the pressure gauge. Run the motor for a short time after the cylinders are fully extended and the motor stalls.

a. The gauge should indicate approximately 200 psi (1379 kPa) as the cylinders are extending.

b. The gauge should indicate approximately 1500 psi (10,342 kPa) when the motor stalls.

c. The gauge should not drop by more than 200 psi (1379 kPa) after the motor is stopped.

9. Remove the pressure gauge and adapter A. Remove adapter A from the gauge, then install adapter B into the gauge. Screw the gauge and adapter into the manual release valve port and tighten to 5-10 in.-lb. See **Figure 15**. (0.6-1.1 N•m). Do not overtighten or the adapter O-ring may be damaged.

10. With the trim/tilt cylinders fully extended, operate the motor in the DOWN direction while observing the pressure gauge. Continue running the motor for a short time after the trim/tilt cylinders are fully retracted and the motor stalls.

10

a. The gauge should indicate approximately 800 psi (5516 kPa) as the cylinders are retracting.

b. The gauge should indicate approximately 900 psi (6206 kPa) when the motor stalls.

c. The gauge should not drop by more than 200 psi (1379 kPa) after the motor stops.

11. If the test results are not as specified, a problem in the hydraulic system is present. If the results are as specified, an electrical problem is indicated.

12. Remove the test gauge and adapter and install the manual release valve. Tighten to 45-55 in.-lb. (5-6 N•m). Install the manual release valve retaining ring, with its sharp edge facing outward.

Trim/Tilt Switch Circuit Test

Refer to **Figure 16** for this procedure.

1. With the key switch ON, connect the voltmeter red test lead to point E1 in the junction box. Connect the black test lead to point G in the junction box. Battery voltage should be noted.

2. If battery voltage is not indicated in Step 1, move the red test lead to point E2 on the starter solenoid. If battery voltage is present, check the red wire and connectors to the junction box, or the junction box fuse. If no voltage is noted, check for poor connections or an open circuit in the wiring between the junction box and battery.

3. Move the red test lead to point E3 in the junction box. Move the trim switch to the DOWN position. If battery voltage is noted, move the red test lead to points E4 and E5. With the trim switch in the DOWN position, battery voltage should be present at each point. If voltage is present, but the trim/tilt motor does not operate, probe connector C2 at the trim motor. If battery voltage is noted at connector C2, repair or replace the motor.

4. If no voltage is present at point E3 in Step 3, check connector C1 between the junction box and remote control assembly. If the connector is

in acceptable condition, check for an open circuit in the following circuits:

a. Green/white wire between the trim switch and junction box.

b. Trim switch between the green/white and red/white wires with the switch in the DOWN position.

c. Red/white wire between the trim switch and point E1 on the terminal block (disconnect connector C1).

5. Move the voltmeter red lead to the junction box at point E6. Move the trim switch to the UP position. If battery voltage is shown, move the red test lead to point E7 (trim switch DOWN) and ten point E8 (trim switch UP). If battery voltage is shown at each point, check connector C2 at the trim motor. If battery voltage is shown at the C2 connector, but the motor will not operate, repair or replace the motor.

6. If no voltage is noted at point E6, check connector C1 between the junction box and remote control assembly. If the connector is good, check for an open circuit in the following circuits:

a. Blue/white wire between the junction box and remote control assembly.

b. Trim switch between the blue/white and red/white wires with the switch in the UP position.

c. Red/white wire between the trim switch and point E1 on the terminal block (connector C1 disconnected).

Relay Test

Use an ohmmeter to test the trim/tilt relays. Calibrate the ohmmeter on the high-ohm scale when checking for continuity.

On early models, the relay terminals are labeled and identified as shown in **Figure 17**. Later models are labeled as shown in **Figure 18**. Identify the relay per **Figure 17** or **Figure 18** and refer to the appropriate test procedure.

The location and orientation of the trim/tilt relays will vary between models, however, the relay terminals are always connected as follows (**Figure 17** or **Figure 18**):

  a. Relay S (switch) or 85 and 86 terminals are connected to the blue/white or green/white trim/tilt circuits.
  b. Relay B+ or 87 terminal (12-volt source) is connected to the red trim/tilt circuit.
  c. Relay B- or 87a terminal is connected to the black (ground) circuit.
  d. Relay M or 30 (motor) terminal is connected to the blue or green motor circuit.

Early relay design

Refer to **Figure 17** for this procedure.
1. Remove the relay to be tested from the relay bracket.
2. Connect the ohmmeter between relay terminals 87a and 30. See **Figure 17**. No continuity should be noted.
3. Connect the ohmmeter between relay terminals 87 and 30 (**Figure 17**). No continuity should be noted.
4. Calibrate the ohmmeter on the low-ohm scale. Connect the ohmmeter between relay terminals 85 and 86 (**Figure 17**). The ohmmeter should indicate 55-85 ohms.
5. Using jumper leads, connect the positive terminal of a 12-volt battery to relay terminal 85 and the negative battery terminal to relay terminal 86. Then, calibrate the ohmmeter on the high-ohm scale and connect it between relay terminals 87 and 30. With the 12-volt battery connected to the relay, the ohmmeter should indicate continuity (high-ohm scale).
6. With the 12-volt battery still connected to the relay, connect the ohmmeter between relay terminals 87a and 30 (**Figure 17**). the ohmmeter should indicate no continuity.
7. Replace the relay if test results are not as specified.

Late relay design

Refer to **Figure 18** for this procedure.
1. Remove the relay to be tested from the relay bracket.
2. Connect the ohmmeter between relay terminals B- and M (**Figure 18**). Continuity should be noted.
3. Connect the ohmmeter between relay terminals B+ and M (**Figure 18**). No continuity should be noted.
4. Calibrate the ohmmeter on the low-ohm scale. Connect the meter between the S terminals (**Figure 18**). The ohmmeter should indicate 70-100 ohms.
5. Using jumper leads, connect a suitable 12-volt battery to the relay S terminals. Then calibrate the ohmmeter on the high-ohm scale and connect it between the B+ and M relay terminals (**Figure 18**). With the battery connected to the S terminals, continuity should be present between relay terminals B+ and M.
6. Next, with the battery still attached to the relay S terminals, connect the ohmmeter between terminals B- and M. No continuity should be present.
7. Replace the relay(s) if any test results are not as specified.

Trim Indicator Circuit Test

Refer to **Figure 16** for this procedure.
1. Place the key switch in the ON position.
2. Connect the voltmeter red lead to point E9 (terminal I) on the indicator gauge. Connect the black test lead to gauge terminal G. If battery voltage is indicated, continue at Step 5.
3. If no voltage is noted in Step 2, move the red test lead to point E10 (accessory plug). If battery voltage is indicated, check for an open circuit between the accessory plug and the trim indicator gauge.
4. If no voltage is noted in Step 3, move the red test lead to point E11 (key switch accessory

10

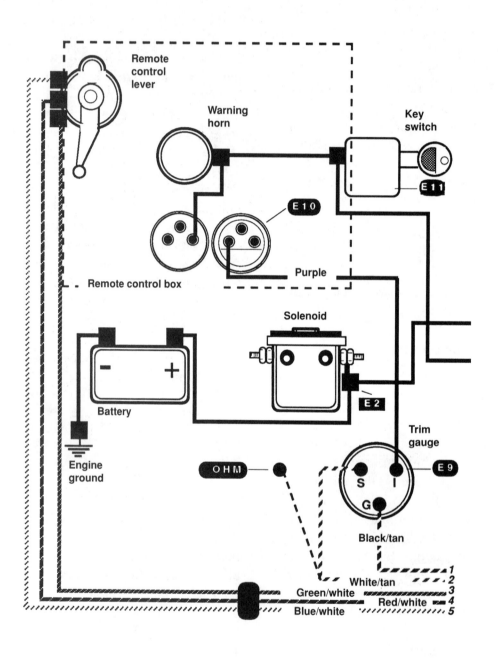

**REMOTE CONTROL LEVER AND SWITCH
(COMMON TO ALL MODELS)**

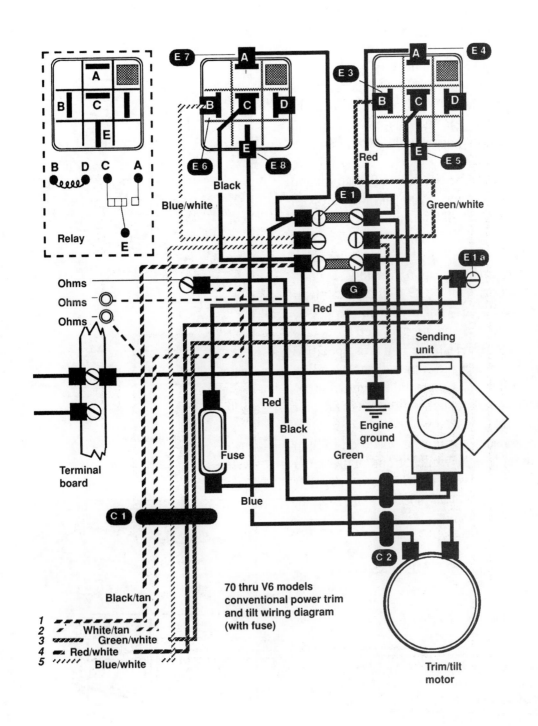

Relay

Ohms
Ohms
Ohms

Terminal
board

Black/tan
1
2   White/tan
3   Green/white
4   Red/white
5   Blue/white

E 7
E 3
E 4
E 6
E 8
E 5
E 1
E 1a
E 1

A
B   C   D
E

Black
Blue/white
Red
Green/white
Red
G
Red

Fuse

Red
Black
Blue

C 1

C 2

Green

Engine
ground

Sending
unit

Trim/tilt
motor

70 thru V6 models
conventional power trim
and tilt wiring diagram
(with fuse)

B   D   C   A
A
B   C
E

10

terminal). If no voltage is present at point E11, check for a blown or defective 20 amp fuse (or circuit breaker) or an open circuit in the key switch wiring. If the 20 amp fuse (or circuit breaker) and wiring are good, replace the key switch.

5. Place the key switch in the OFF position.

6. Disconnect the white/tan and black/tan wires from gauge terminals S and G, respectively. Calibrate an ohmmeter on the low-ohm scale and connect the meter between the white/tan and black/tan wires.

7. Tilt the outboard to the fully UP position and note the meter reading. Then, trim the outboard to the fully DOWN/IN position and note the meter.

8. With the outboard tilted fully UP, the ohmmeter should indicate approximately 1 ohm. With the outboard fully DOWN/IN, the meter should indicate approximately 88 ohms.

9. If resistance is as specified in Step 8, replace the trim gauge. If resistance is not as specified (Step 8), disconnect the trim indicator sending unit 2-pin connector. Connect the ohmmeter between the terminals in the sending unit connector half and repeat Step 7.

10. If the resistance is now as specified in Step 8, repair or replace the white/tan and/or black/tan wires between the sending unit and gauge. If resistance is still not as specified in Step 8, replace the sending unit.

TRIM/TILT MOTOR TESTING

Amperage (Current Draw) Test

> *WARNING*
> *Do not attempt to perform the following test on a moving boat. The specifications contained in **Table 2** are based on static hydraulic tests (boat at rest).*

This test evaluates the condition of the hydraulic system by determining the current re-

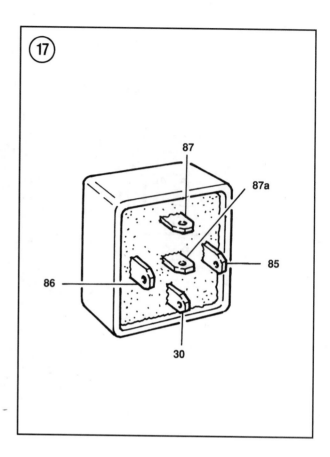

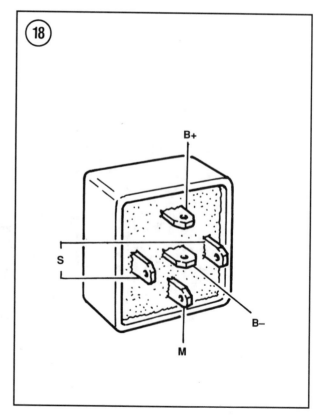

quirements of the pump motor. A suitable stop watch and DC ammeter capable of measuring up to 60 amps are necessary to perform the procedure. The battery must be fully charged and in acceptable condition for the following test to be valid.

1. Disconnect the red 14-gauge wire from the trim/tilt junction box from the battery side of the starter solenoid. Connect the ammeter in series with the solenoid and red wire. See **Figure 19**.

NOTE
The trim range is the initial 0-15° of motor travel. The tilt range is the remaining 16-65° of motor travel.

2. Operate the trim/tilt system through several full UP/DOWN cycles while observing the ammeter and stopwatch. Repeat this step as necessary to obtain consistent results, then compare the results with the specifications in **Table 1**.

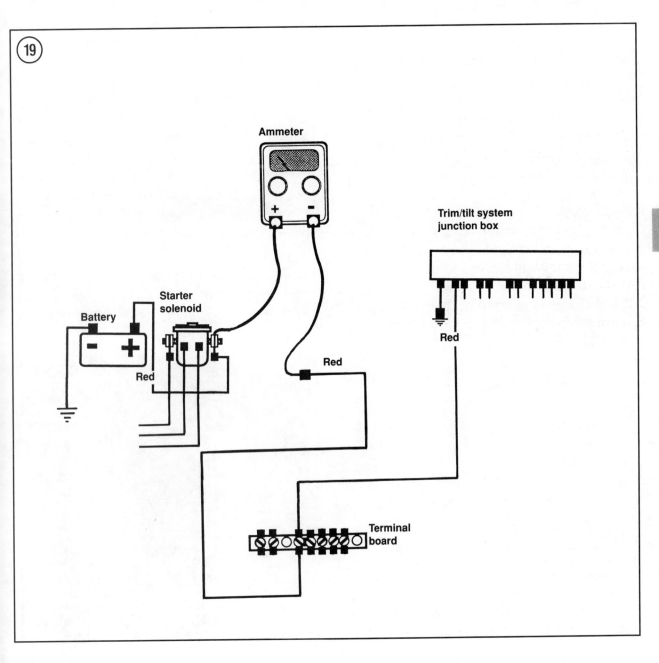

a. If the current draw is within specifications, but a trim/tilt malfunction is evident, a defective pump control piston or malfunctioning check valve is indicated.

b. Excessive current draw indicates the pump or motor is binding or defective. Perform the motor no-load current draw test as described in this chapter.

c. Low current draw indicates a worn or defective pump assembly, leaking relief valve(s) or an internal leak in the pump or elsewhere in the hydraulic system.

No-Load Current Draw Test

The no-load current draw test is used to determine the condition of the electric motor. A DC ammeter capable of measuring up to 50 amps and a mechanical or vibration tachometer are necessary to perform the test. In addition, a fully charged 12-volt battery (360 cold cranking amps minimum) is required.

1. Remove the pump motor from the trim/tilt system as described in this chapter.

2. Mount the motor securely in a vise or other holding fixture.

> *NOTE*
> *If the positive battery terminal is connected to the motor's blue (UP) wire terminal, the motor should turn clockwise as viewed from the pump end. The motor should turn the opposite direction if connected to the green (DOWN) wire terminal.*

3. Using suitable jumper leads, connect the positive battery terminal, along with the ammeter (in series) to either of the motor terminals.

4. Then connect the negative battery terminal to the motor case. Attach a vibration or mechanical tachometer to the motor, then note the motor speed and amperage draw.

5. Compare the motor speed and current draw to the no-load specifications in **Table 2**. Repair or replace the motor if the results are not as specified.

POWER TRIM/TILT SYSTEM REMOVAL/INSTALLATION (CONVENTIONAL TRIM/TILT)

The entire power trim/tilt system must be removed to service the electric motor or the trim/tilt cylinders or manifold.

1. Mark the trim-in angle rod location, then remove the rod.

2. Disconnect the electric cable from the motor.

3. Tilt the outboard to its fully UP position using a suitable hoist. Engage the tilt lock levers and lower the motor so the levers contact the stern brackets.

4. Remove the tilt cylinder pin spring retainer clip (**Figure 20**). Remove the tilt cylinder pin with a punch and mallet. Retract the cylinder manually.

5. Remove the screws (3 each side) holding the power trim/tilt manifold to the stern brackets.

6. Angle the power trim/tilt manifold down and out of the stern brackets, pulling the control cable through the bracket.

7. To install the unit, lubricate the tilt cylinder eye and pin with OMC Triple-Guard grease. Place the trim/tilt unit into position between the

stern brackets and install the tilt cylinder retaining pin. Install the spring retaining clip in the pin.

8. Route the electrical cable through the stern brackets.

9. Apply OMC Nut Lock to the threads of 6 *new* manifold-to-stern bracket screws. Install the screws and tighten to 18-20 ft.-lb. (24-27 N•m).

10. Reinstall the trim-in angle adjusting pin into the same hole as removed.

Electric Motor Removal/Installation

1. Remove the power trim/tilt unit as described in this chapter. Mount the unit in a suitable holding fixture.

2. Remove the 3 large screws securing the motor to the manifold. Lift the motor off the manifold. Remove the pump drive coupling and inspect the rubber cushion on the tang end. If the cushion is missing or damaged, replace the drive coupling.

3. Remove and discard the motor O-ring.

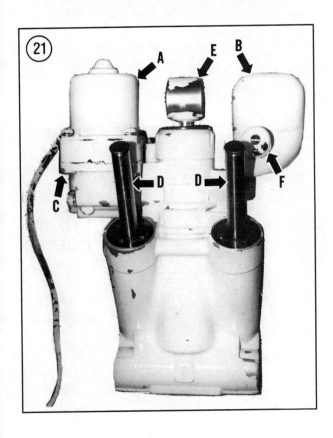

4. To install the motor, insert the drive coupling (tang end down) into the pump assembly.

5. Install a new O-ring on the motor base. Install the motor, making sure it properly engages the pump drive coupling.

6. Install the motor mounting screws and tighten evenly and securely.

FASTRAK POWER TRIM/TILT SYSTEM

The FasTrak power trim/tilt system was introduced in 1991 to be used on selected 60-225 hp models. The FasTrak system provides 4° more negative trim, 2° more positive trim and 10° more tilt up than the conventional trim/tilt system.

The FasTrak system is attached to and entirely contained between the stern brackets. The system consists of a manifold assembly that contains all valves, an electric motor (A, **Figure 21**), oil reservoir (B), oil pump (C), 2 trim cylinders (D) and a combination tilt/shock absorbing cylinder (E). A trim/tilt switch, indicator gauge, tilt limit switch and related relays and circuitry complete the system.

Operation

Depressing the UP trim/tilt switch closes the electric motor circuit which causes the motor to drive the fluid pump. The pump delivers fluid under pressure to the bottom of the trim cylinders and tilt cylinder. The trim cylinders move the outboard through the trim range (first 21° movement). At this point, the trim cylinders are fully extended and the tilt cylinder tilts the outboard the remaining 54° of travel (tilt range).

> *NOTE*
> *To prevent personal injury or damage to the outboard motor, the engine will only run at slow speed when the motor is positioned anywhere within the tilt range (22-75°).*

Depressing the DOWN trim/tilt switch causes the motor to reverse direction and the pump delivers fluid into the top of the tilt cylinder (but not trim cylinders). The mechanical force of the tilt cylinder moving down, propeller thrust and the weight of the outboard all contribute to the DOWN/IN movement of the motor.

A manual release valve is provided to allow the outboard to be manually raised or lowered throughout its entire trim/tilt range. The valve is accessed through the port stern bracket (**Figure 22**) and has a slotted head to accommodate a screwdriver. To raise or lower the motor, loosen the manual release valve approximately 3-1/2 turns (counterclockwise) or until it lightly contacts its retainer ring. The manual release valve must be closed and tightened to 45-55 in.-lb. (5-6 N•m) to maintain shock absorber protection, reverse thrust capability and all other normal trim/tilt functions.

WARNING
If manually raising the outboard to its full-tilt position, be sure to engage the trailering bracket or tilt lock lever to prevent the motor from suddenly falling down to the trim range after the manual release valve is tightened.

To prevent damage to the hydraulic components, a trailering bracket is provided to secure the outboard motor in its tilted position. The trailering bracket should be used anytime the outboard is trailered. Tilt the motor to the fully UP position, engage the trailering bracket, then lower the motor until the bracket is securely in place. In addition, a tilt lock lever is provided for mooring and storage. The tilt lock lever will support the outboard at 50° or 73° of its tilt angle. The tilt lock lever should not be used during trailering.

A tilt limit switch located on the tilt tube (between the stern brackets) is provided to adjust the upper tilt range. If the outboard motor contacts the hull or motor well during full tilt, adjust the tilt limit switch as described in this chapter to prevent damage to the outboard or boat.

Hydraulic Fluid Check

The reservoir fluid level should be checked at least once per season or after every 100 hours of operation. The recommended fluid is OMC Power Trim and Tilt and Power Steering Fluid or GM Dexron II automatic transmission fluid. The hydraulic system capacity is approximately 21 fl. oz. (622 mL).

Low fluid level and/or air in the hydraulic system will result in erratic and noisy trim/tilt operation.

1. Tilt the outboard to the fully UP position and engage the tilt lock support.

2. If necessary, clean the area around the reservoir fill cap (F, **Figure 21**) to prevent contamination, then remove the cap.

3. The fluid level should be even with the bottom of the fill cap hole. Add the recommended fluid as necessary.

NOTE
Do not overfill the trim/tilt reservoir.

4. If necessary to add a large amount of fluid because of leakage or service, bleed any air from the system as follows:

NOTE
Do not remove the reservoir fill/level plug unless the cylinders are fully extended (outboard UP).

a. Fill the reservoir as previously outlined.

b. Install the fill cap, then cycle the outboard to full UP and full DOWN, checking and adding fluid as necessary.

c. Continue for at least 5 complete UP/DOWN cycles to purge air from the system. Recheck the fluid level and add as required.

Troubleshooting

If a malfunction develops in the power trim/tilt system, the initial step is to determine if the problem is electrical or hydraulic. Electrical tests are given in this chapter. If the problem appears to be in the hydraulic system, refer it to a qualified marine/hydraulic specialist for service.

To determine if the problem is electric or hydraulic, proceed as follows:

1. Make sure all connectors are clean and tight. Clean and tighten connections as necessary.

2. Make sure the battery is fully charged and in acceptable condition. A weak or undercharged battery will result in unsatisfactory trim/tilt operation.

3. Check the system fuse, if so equipped.

4. Make sure the reservoir is full of the recommended fluid and that no air is present in the system.

NOTE
The seating area of the manual release valve must be in perfect condition. Inspect the seat using a suitable magnifying glass. If excessively worn, nicked, scratched or damaged, replace the valve.

5. Make sure the manual release valve is closed and properly tightened to 45-55 in.-lb. (5-6 N•m).

NOTE
The power trim/tilt assembly must be removed from the outboard motor to perform the remaining tests. Mount the unit in a suitable holding fixture (OMC Test Stand part No. 390008). A fully charged 12-volt battery and suitable jumper leads are necessary to perform the following tests.

6. Remove the power trim/tilt unit as described in this chapter.

7. Install the OMC Trim/Tilt Service Kit part No. 434524, along with the gauge from OMC Power Trim/Tilt Service Kit part No. 390010 (**Figure 23**) as follows:

a. Remove the manual release valve retaining ring using snap ring pliers.

b. Connect the battery to the trim/tilt motor green wire terminal and completely retract the cylinders.

c. Turn the manual release counterclockwise one full turn.

d. Momentarily operate the trim/tilt motor in the UP direction, then in the DOWN direction.

CAUTION
Residual hydraulic pressure may be present when manual release valve is removed. To prevent personal injury, wear suitable eye protection and cover the manual release valve with a shop towel during removal.

e. Slowly remove the manual release valve by turning it counterclockwise.

f. Screw the pressure gauge and the appropriate adapter together. Tighten the gauge and adapter securely. Adapter A is used to test the UP circuit and adapter B is used to test the DOWN circuit.

g. Install the OMC Pressure Gauge and Adapter A (part No. 336658) into the manual release valve passage and tighten to 5-10 in.-lb. (0.6-1.1 N.m). See **Figure 24**, typical. Do not overtighten or the adapter O-ring may be damaged.

h. Using the battery and jumpers, operate the unit UP and DOWN several cycles, then check the reservoir fluid level. Add the recommended fluid as necessary.

8. With the trim/tilt cylinders fully retracted, operate the system in the UP direction while observing the pressure gauge. Run the motor for a short time after the cylinders are fully extended and the motor stalls.

a. The gauge should indicate approximately 200 psi (1379 kPa) as the cylinders are extending.

b. The gauge should indicate approximately 1400-1600 psi (9653-11,032 kPa) when the motor stalls.

c. The gauge should not drop by more than 200 psi (1379 kPa) after the motor is stopped.

9. Remove the pressure gauge and adapter. Remove Adapter A from the gauge, then install adapter B (part No. 336659) into the gauge.

Screw the gauge and adapter into the manual release valve port and tighten to 5-10 in.-lb. See **Figure 24**. (0.6-1.1 N.m). Do not overtighten or the adapter O-ring may be damaged.

10. With the trim/tilt cylinders fully extended, operate the motor in the DOWN direction while observing the pressure gauge. Continue running the motor for a short time after the trim/tilt cylinders are fully retracted and the motor stalls.

a. The gauge should indicate approximately 0-200 psi (0-5516 kPa) as the cylinders are retracting.

b. The gauge should indicate approximately 800 psi (5516 kPa) when the motor stalls.

c. The gauge should not drop by more than 200 psi (1379 kPa) after the motor stops.

11. If the test results are not as specified, a problem in the hydraulic system is present. If the results are as specified, an electrical problem is indicated.

12. Remove the test gauge and adapter and install the manual release valve. Tighten to 45-55 in.-lb. (5-6 N.m). Install the manual release valve retaining ring using snap ring pliers. Make sure the sharp edge of the ring is facing outward.

Power Supply Test

Perform the following test procedure to determine the condition of all power supply circuits. Unless specified otherwise, make all voltage checks from the relay side of the trim/tilt relay bracket. Refer to **Figure 25** and to the appropriate wiring diagram at the end of the manual during this procedure.

1. Place the key switch in the OFF position. Remove the ignition cutoff switch clip and lanyard.

2. Make sure the battery is fully charged and in acceptable condition. Charge or replace the battery as required.

3. Connect a voltmeter black lead to a good clean engine ground.

4. Check for voltage at the battery side of the starter solenoid.

   a. If battery voltage is not noted, check the battery cables for clean tight connections and repair as necessary.

   b. If battery voltage is noted, continue at Step 5 (or Step 11 if problem is in DOWN circuit only).

5. Remove the UP and DOWN relays from the relay bracket.

6. Check the voltage at the red (UP relay) relay terminal (**Figure 25**).

   a. If battery voltage is noted, continue at Step 7.

   b. If no voltage is noted, repair or replace the red wire between the starter solenoid and trim/tilt relay bracket. terminal block and relay bracket.

7. Check the voltage at the blue/white relay terminal (**Figure 25**) while depressing the UP trim button.

   a. If battery voltage is noted, continue at Step 8.

   b. If no voltage is noted, check the condition of the red/purple wire and repair or replace as necessary. If the red/purple wire is in acceptable condition, replace the trim switch.

8. Install the UP relay into the bracket. Push the relay only halfway into the relay bracket so the relay terminals can be probed with the voltmeter.

9. Check the voltage at the M (blue wire) relay terminal.

   a. If no voltage is noted, test the relay as described under *Relay Test* in this chapter.

   b. If battery voltage is noted, continue at Step 10.

10. Disconnect the green and blue wire connector from the trim/tilt motor. Check the voltage at the blue wire in the trim motor connector while depressing the UP trim button.

   a. If battery voltage is noted, first inspect the blue wire connector for looseness or corrosion. If the connector is in acceptable condition, replace the trim/tilt motor.

   b. If no voltage is noted, repair or replace the blue wire between the relay bracket and trim/tilt motor.

11. Remove the UP relay from the relay bracket.

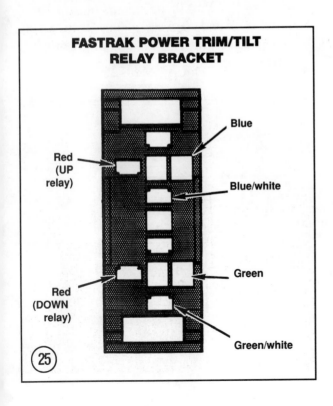

FASTRAK POWER TRIM/TILT RELAY BRACKET

Blue

Red (UP relay)

Blue/white

Green

Red (DOWN relay)

Green/white

(25)

12. Check the voltage at the red (DOWN) relay terminal (**Figure 25**).

    a. If battery voltage is noted, continue at Step 13.

    b. If no voltage is noted, repair or replace the red wire between the starter solenoid and trim/tilt relay bracket.

13. Check the voltage at the green/white relay terminal (**Figure 25**) while depressing the DOWN trim button.

    a. If battery voltage is noted, continue at Step 14.

    b. If no voltage is noted, check the red/purple wire to the trim switch. If the red/purple wire is in acceptable condition, replace the trim switch.

14. Install the DOWN relay into the relay bracket. Push the relay only halfway into the bracket so the relay terminals can be probed with the voltmeter.

15. Check the voltage at the relay M (green) terminal.

    a. If battery voltage is noted, continue at Step 16.

    b. If no voltage is noted, test the relay as described under *Relay Test* in this chapter.

16. Disconnect the green and blue wire connector from the trim/tilt motor. Check the voltage at the green wire while depressing the DOWN trim button.

    a. If battery voltage is noted, repair or replace the defective trim motor.

    b. If no voltage is noted, repair or replace the green wire in the trim system wiring harness.

Relay Test

Use an ohmmeter to test the trim/tilt relays. Calibrate the ohmmeter on the high-ohm scale when checking for continuity.

On early models, the relay terminals are labeled and identified as shown in **Figure 26**. Later models are labeled as shown in **Figure 27**. Identify the relay per **Figure 26** or **Figure 27** and refer to the appropriate test procedure.

The location and orientation of the trim/tilt relays will vary between models, however, the relay terminals are always connected as follows (**Figure 26** or **Figure 27**):

    a. Relay 85 and 86 or S (switch) terminals are connected to the blue/white or green/white trim/tilt circuits.

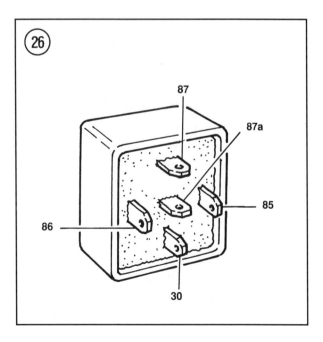

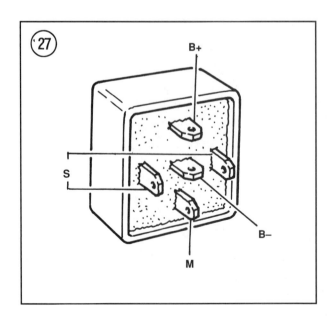

b. Relay 87 or B+ terminal (12-volt source) is connected to the red trim/tilt circuit.

c. Relay 87a or B- terminal is connected to the black (ground) circuit.

d. Relay 30 or M (motor) terminal is connected to the blue (UP) or green (DOWN) motor circuit.

Early relay design

Refer to **Figure 26** for this procedure.

1. Remove the relay to be tested from the relay bracket.

2. Connect the ohmmeter between relay terminals 87a and 30. See **Figure 26**. No continuity should be noted.

3. Connect the ohmmeter between relay terminals 87 and 30 (**Figure 26**). No continuity should be noted.

4. Calibrate the ohmmeter on the low-ohm scale. Connect the ohmmeter between relay terminals 85 and 86 (**Figure 26**). The ohmmeter should indicate 55-85 ohms.

5. Using jumper leads, connect the positive terminal of a 12-volt battery to relay terminal 85 and the negative battery terminal to relay terminal 86. Then, calibrate the ohmmeter on the high-ohm scale and connect it between relay terminals 87 and 30. With the 12-volt battery connected to the relay, the ohmmeter should indicate continuity (high-ohm scale).

6. With the 12-volt battery still connected to the relay, connect the ohmmeter between relay terminals 87a and 30 (**Figure 26**). the ohmmeter should indicate no continuity.

7. Replace the relay if test results are not as specified.

Late relay design

1. Remove the relay to be tested from the relay bracket.

2. Connect the ohmmeter between relay terminals B- and M (**Figure 27**). Continuity should be noted.

3. Connect the ohmmeter between relay terminals B+ and M (**Figure 27**). No continuity should be noted.

4. Calibrate the ohmmeter on the low-ohm scale. Connect the meter between the S terminals (**Figure 27**). The ohmmeter should indicate 70-100 ohms.

5. Using jumper leads, connect a suitable 12-volt battery to the relay S terminals. Then calibrate the ohmmeter on the high-ohm scale and connect it between the B + and M relay terminals (**Figure 27**). With the battery connected to the S terminals, continuity should be present between relay terminals B+ and M.

6. Next, with the battery still attached to the relay S terminals, connect the ohmmeter between terminals B- and M. No continuity should be present.

7. Replace the relay(s) if any test results are not as specified.

Trim Gauge and Circuit Test

1. Connect a voltmeter between trim gauge terminals I and G. Place the key switch in the ON position and note the voltmeter. If no voltage is noted, continue at Step 2. If voltage is present, continue at Step 4.

2. Connect the voltmeter between the trim gauge G terminal and terminal A in the 3-pin connector at the remote control assembly. See **Figure 28**. Turn the key switch to ON and note the voltmeter. If voltage is present, continue at Step 3. If no voltage is noted, repair or replace the purple wire between the trim gauge and remote control.

3. Connect the voltmeter between a good engine ground and the key switch terminal A (**Figure 28**). Turn the key switch ON and note the meter. If no voltage is noted, check the 20 amp fuse in the engine harness. If the fuse is good, replace the key switch. If voltage is noted, repair or replace the purple wire between the key switch and warning horn, or between the warning horn

10

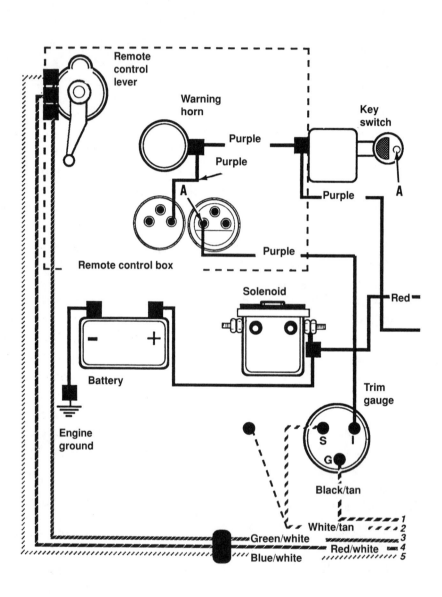

Remote control lever

Warning horn

Key switch

Purple

Purple

Purple

A

Remote control box

Purple

Solenoid

Red

Battery

Trim gauge

S   I

Engine ground

G

Black/tan

White/tan   1
             2
Green/white   3
Red/white   4
Blue/white   5

and the 3-pin trim gauge connector at the remote control.

4. Place the key switch in the OFF position. Disconnect the trim harness white/tan and black/tan wires from the gauge terminals S and G, respectively. Calibrate an ohmmeter on the low-ohm scale, then connect the ohmmeter between the white/tan and black/tan wires. With the engine in the fully tilted position, the ohmmeter should indicate approximately 1 ohm. With the engine in the fully down position, the ohmmeter should indicate approximately 88 ohms.

   a. If resistance is as specified, replace the trim gauge.

   b. If resistance is not as specified, continue at Step 5.

5. Disconnect the 2-pin connector at the trim sending unit (white/tan and black/tan wires). Connect the ohmmeter between the white/tan and black/tan sending unit wire terminals in the wiring harness connector. With the engine in the fully tilted position, the ohmmeter should indicate approximately 1 ohm. With the engine in the fully down position, the ohmmeter should indicate approximately 88 ohms.

   a. If resistance is as specified, repair or replace the white/tan and/or black/tan wires between the sending unit and trim gauge.

   b. If resistance is not as specified, replace the sending unit.

TRIM/TILT MOTOR TESTING

Amperage (Current Draw) Test

WARNING
*Do not attempt to perform the following test on a moving boat. The specifications contained in **Table 2** are based on static hydraulic tests (boat at rest).*

This test evaluates the condition of the hydraulic system by determining the current requirements of the pump motor. A suitable stop watch and DC ammeter capable of measuring up

to 100 amps are necessary to perform the procedure. The battery must be fully charged and in acceptable condition for the following test to be valid.

1. Disconnect the red 14-gauge wire from the trim/tilt junction box from the battery side of the starter solenoid. Connect the ammeter in series with the solenoid and red wire.

NOTE
The trim range is the initial 0-21° of motor travel. The tilt range is the remaining 22-75° of motor travel.

2. Operate the trim/tilt system through several full UP/DOWN cycles while observing the ammeter and stopwatch. Repeat this step as necessary to obtain consistent results, then compare the results with the specifications in **Table 1**.

   a. If the current draw is within specifications, but a trim/tilt malfunction is evident, a defective pump control piston or malfunctioning check valve is indicated.

   b. Excessive current draw indicates the pump or motor is binding or defective. Perform the motor no-load current draw test as described in this chapter.

   c. Low current draw indicates a worn or defective pump assembly, leaking relief valve(s) or an internal leak in the pump or elsewhere in the hydraulic system.

No-Load Current Draw Test

The no-load current draw test is used to determine the condition of the electric motor. A DC ammeter capable of measuring up to 50 amps and a mechanical or vibration tachometer are necessary to perform the test. In addition, a fully charged 12-volt battery (360 cold cranking amps minimum) is required.

1. Remove the pump motor from the trim/tilt system as described in this chapter.

2. Mount the motor securely in a vise or other holding fixture.

10

NOTE
If the positive battery terminal is connected to the motor's blue (UP) wire terminal, the motor should turn clockwise as viewed from the pump end. The motor should turn the opposite direction if connected to the green (DOWN) wire terminal.

3. Using suitable jumper leads, connect the positive battery terminal, along with the ammeter (in series) to either of the motor terminals.

4. Then connect the negative battery terminal to the motor case. Attach a vibration or mechanical tachometer to the motor, then note the motor speed and amperage draw.

5. Compare the motor speed and current draw to the no-load specifications in **Table 2**. Repair or replace the motor if the results are not as specified.

Tilt Limit Switch Adjustment

If the outboard motor contacts the boat hull or motor well when fully tilted, the tilt limit switch should be adjusted to limit the upward tilt range. The tilt limit switch is located between the stern brackets on the tilt tube.

1. Trim the outboard to the fully DOWN/IN position.

2. *1991 models*—Loosen the cam screws (**Figure 29**) using an appropriate size Allen wrench.

3. Rotate the cam upward to decrease trim range or downward to increase trim range. See **Figure 29** (1991) or **Figure 30** (1992-on).

4. *1991 models*—Tighten the cam screws securely.

5. Tilt the outboard to its fully UP position to check adjustment. Repeat adjustment as necessary.

POWER TRIM/TILT SYSTEM REMOVAL/INSTALLATION (FASTRAK SYSTEM)

1. Disconnect the negative battery cable from the battery.

2. Remove the air silencer assembly.

3. Disconnect the power trim/tilt harness connector. Remove the wire terminals from the connector. Depress the tab in the back of the connector using a small screwdriver, then pull the wires from the connector.

4. Remove the fuel/oil connector bracket from the lower motor cover. Remove the 4 screws securing the lower motor cover and remove the starboard and port lower covers.

5. Loosen the manual release valve, tilt the unit up and engage the trailering bracket.

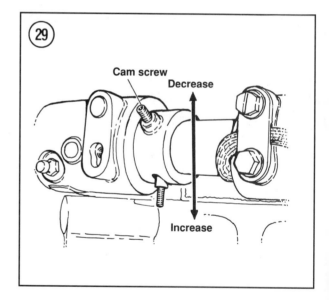

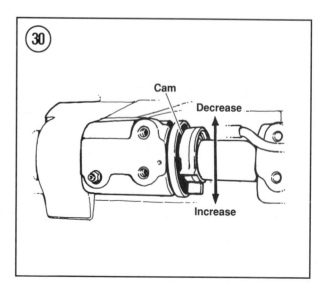

6. Disconnect the trim sender. Pull the trim sender wires, along with the braided outer cover, through the stern bracket. Disconnect the blue and green wire connector from the electric motor.

7. Using a No. 3 Pozi-Driv screwdriver, remove the ground wire from the electric motor retaining screw.

8. Remove the snap rings from the tilt cylinder upper mounting pin. Remove the pin using a suitable punch and mallet.

9. Loosen the manual release valve and push the trim cylinder to the fully retracted position.

10. Remove the snap rings from the lower mounting pin. While supporting the trim/tilt unit, remove the lower pin using a suitable punch and mallet.

11. Remove the power trim/tilt unit.

12. To install, first lubricate the upper and lower mounting pins with OMC Triple-Guard grease.

13. Place the trim/tilt into place between the stern brackets, install the lower pin, then extend the trim cylinder to align with its hole in the swivel bracket. Install the upper pin. Install the mounting pin snap rings with their sharp edges facing OUT.

14. Connect the ground wire to the electric motor mounting screw. Connect the motor connector to the motor. Route the trim sender wires through the stern bracket. Connect the trim sender wires.

15. Complete the remaining installation by reversing the removal procedure. Check the reservoir fluid level as described in this chapter.

Electric Motor Removal/Installation

1. Remove the trim/tilt unit as described in this chapter.

2. Remove the screw securing the wire clamp to the manifold. Remove the 4 screws securing the motor to the manifold assembly using a Pozi-Driv screwdriver.

3. Lift the motor off the manifold. Remove and discard the motor O-ring.

4. To install, lubricate a new motor O-ring with the recommended hydraulic fluid. Install the O-ring on the motor base.

5. Install the motor and the 4 Pozi-Driv screws. Tighten the screws to 35-52 in.-lb. (4-6 N·m). Reattach the motor wire clamp to the manifold and tighten the screw securely.

10

Table 1 CURRENT DRAW (AMPS) AND DURATION (SECONDS) UNDER LOAD

	40 and 50 hp Trim/Tilt System Current draw (amps)	
Unit movement	Bosch	Showa
Stall up	5-10	7-12
Stall down	10-15	15-20
Time (seconds)		
Full range up	13-19	13-19
Full range down	10-16	10-16
(continued)		

Table 1 CURRENT DRAW (AMPS) AND DURATION (SECONDS) UNDER LOAD (continued)

	Conventional Trim/Tilt System Current draw (amps)			
	Prestolite	**Bosch**	**Showa (3 in. dia.)**	**Showa (2.4 & 2.9 in. dia.)**
Trim up	11-15	7-10	5-8	7-9
Tilt up	11-15	7-10	8-10	9-12
Stall up	30-35	30-35	19-23	25-29
Stall down	21-25	18-32	14-18	12-17
	Time (seconds)			
Trim range	7-9	7-9	8-10	8-10
Tilt range	7-9	6-9	7-9	6-7
Full range up	15-20	15-20	16-18	15-17

FasTrak Trim/Tilt System	
Unit movement	**Current draw (amps)**
Trim out (trim range)	22
Trim in (trim range)	16
Tilt up (stall)	60-75
Trim in (stall)	35-45
Time (seconds)	
Trim out (trim range)	9
Trim in (trim range)	9

Table 2 TRIM/TILT MOTOR NO-LOAD CURRENT DRAW

40-50 hp Trim/Tilt System			
Motor	**Amps (min.)**	**Volts**	**Minimum speed (rpm)**
Bosch	4.5	12.5	5200
Showa	4.5	12.5	5000

Conventional Trim/Tilt System			
Motor	**Amps (min.)**	**Volts**	**Minimum speed (rpm)**
Prestolite	7	12.5	4700
Bosch	4.5	12.5	5450
Showa (2.4 in.)	4.5	12.5	5000
Showa (2.9 in.)	10	12.5	7000
Showa (3.0 in.)	4.5	12.5	5000

FasTrak Trim/Tilt System			
Motor	**Amps (min.)**	**Volts**	**Minimum speed (rpm)**
Showa	10	12.5	7000

Chapter Eleven

Oil Injection Systems

Two-stroke engines are lubricated by mixing oil with the gasoline. The various internal engine components are lubricated as the fuel and oil mixture passes through the crankcase and cylinders. The optimum fuel:oil ratio required by an outboard motor depends on engine demand. Without oil injection, the oil must be hand mixed with the gasoline at a predetermined ratio to ensure sufficient lubrication is provided at all engine speeds and load conditions. While this predetermined ratio is adequate for high-speed operation, it may contain more oil than necessary during idle and slow-speed operation. This often results in excessive smoking and can cause fouled spark plugs when operated at slow speed.

Oil injection eliminates the need to hand mix oil and gasoline together in the fuel tank. On models equipped with variable ratio oil injection (VRO) the amount of oil delivered to the engine can be varied instantly and accurately to supply the optimum fuel:oil ratio for all engine speeds and load conditions.

OMC AccuMix oil injection is available as an option on models under 40 hp. Variable ratio oiling (VRO) is available on 40 hp through V8 models.

ACCUMIX OIL INJECTION

AccuMix is an electro-mechanical oil injection system consisting of a fuel pump activated oil metering pump built into a portable fuel tank. See **Figure 1**. A similar metering pump design is available for boats with built-in fuel tanks.

The Accumix system delivers fuel:oil to the carburetor(s) at a constant 50:1 ratio. A low oil warning indicator is triggered if the oil in the reservoir reaches the 1/2 qt. (0.47 l) level. This allows the use of one full tank of gasoline before the reservoir requires refilling. Should the oil level drop to a critical level, the sensor will automatically shut down the motor to prevent damage.

Service to the AccuMix system is limited to draining and flushing the fuel tank at each tune-up or at least once per year. The AccuMix unit is serviced by replacement.

Removal/Installation

1. Remove the 8 screws holding the oil reservoir to the fuel tank. Lift the reservoir up and out of

the tank. Remove and discard the reservoir gasket.

2. Remove the cover from the reservoir. Discard the cover seal.

3. Wash the oil reservoir components with a mild cleaner and dry with compressed air.

4. Insert the pickup hose in the clip and position the reservoir on the fuel tank with a new gasket.

5. Fit a new cover seal in position and wipe the outer diameter of the fuel tube with a light coat of OMC Triple-Guard grease.

6. Fit the cover on the reservoir, making sure the fuel tube enters the cavity in the cover.

7. Insert the reservoir in the tank opening. Install the screws and washers, adding an extra washer under each tank bracket fastener. Tighten the screws to 10-12 in.-lb. (1.1-1.3 N•m).

OMC VARIABLE RATIO OILING (VRO) SYSTEM

Variable ratio oiling (VRO) is used on 40 hp and larger outboard motors (except 48 and 88 hp). The oil injection pump is a combination mechanical fuel and oil pump. The oil injection pump is actuated by crankcase pressure and vacuum pulsations. See **Figure 2** and **Figure 3** for typical installations. A remote mounted oil tank, warning horn and related hoses and circuitry complete the basic system.

Two oil injection pump assemblies are used on V8 models, each supplying fuel/oil to 4 cylinders. In addition, V8 models are equipped with a pressure-sensitive fuel manifold bypass valve. The valve is designed to open if it detects a reduction in fuel pressure, from either pump assembly. This allows the remaining pump to supply fuel and oil to both fuel manifolds. One pump, however, is not capable of delivering sufficient fuel/oil for full throttle operation.

Operation

The oil injection system is operated by crankcase pressure/vacuum pulsations, similar to a conventional diaphragm-type fuel pump. The injection pump draws fuel and oil from separate tanks and mixes them inside the pump assembly

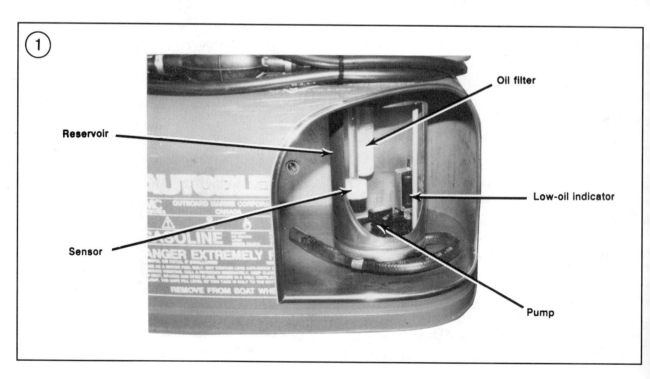

at a ratio varying from approximately 75:1 at idle to approximately 50:1 at wide-open throttle. If desired, the oil injection system can be disabled as described in Chapter Four. If so, the fuel tank must contain a 50:1 fuel and oil mixture.

Break-in Procedure

During break-in of a new or rebuilt power head, all models equipped with oil injection must be operated on a 50:1 fuel-oil mixture in the fuel tank, *in addition* to the normal oil injection system. This provides the 25:1 fuel-oil ratio required during break-in. Prior to switching to straight gasoline in the fuel tank, mark the oil level on the translucent remote oil tank and periodically check to make sure the oil injection system is operating (oil level dropping).

Pulse Limiter Fitting

A pulse limiter fitting is connected to the injection pump pulse hose fitting (2, **Figure 4**). The pulse limiter is screwed into the crankcase on V4 and 60° V6 models (A, **Figure 5**) and connected inline (B, **Figure 5**) with the pulse hose on all other models. The pulse limiter is equipped with an integral check valve which must be periodically inspected and cleaned.

> *CAUTION*
> *A plugged pulse limiter fitting will result in limited fuel and oil delivered to the power head which can cause extensive power head damage. If excessive carbon is found, replace the pulse limiter, then check the engine for the following causes of backfiring:*

a. Incorrect linkage adjustment and synchronization.
b. Power head overcooling.
c. Crankcase air leakage.
d. Carburetor malfunctions.

Clean and inspect the pulse limiter fitting as follows.

1. Remove the pulse limiter from the crankcase (V4 and 60° V6) or pulse hoses (all others).

2. Clean the pulse limiter by backflushing with aerosol carburetor cleaner. Dry with compressed

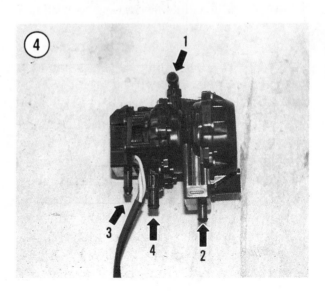

air. Inspect the pulse limiter for excessive carbon or other damage. Replace the pulse limiter as necessary.

3A. *V4 and 60° V6 models*—Thoroughly clean the threaded end of the pulse limiter and apply suitable pipe sealer to the threads. Install the fitting and connect the pulse hose.

3B. *All other models*—Install the fitting into the pulse hose with its blue fitting end facing the injection pump assembly.

NOTE
The current pulse limiter fitting has a blue fitting. If a fitting with a color other than blue is noted, it should be replaced with the current design. The pulse limiter fitting must always be installed so the blue colored fitting is facing the oil injection pump.

Warning Horn

A warning horn is installed in the accessory or remote control wiring harness. The warning horn has 3 functions: low-oil warning, no-oil warning and engine overheat warning.

The sending unit in the remote oil tank is connected to the warning horn on all models through the key switch and grounded to the power head. If the oil level in the tank drops below the 1/4 full point, the warning horn sounds for 1/2 second every 40 seconds to alert the operator to a low oil level. If the system runs completely out of oil or oil flow to the pump is obstructed, the warning horn sounds for 1/2 second every second.

A temperature sending unit is installed in the cylinder head(s) and is connected to the warning horn through the key switch to warn of an overheat condition. If the power head temperature exceeds 211° F (99.5° C), the horn sounds continuously. Backing off on the throttle will shut the horn off as soon as the power head temperature reaches 175° F (79.5° C), unless a restricted water intake is causing the overheat condition. If

the water pump indicator does not deliver a steady stream or if the horn continues sounding after 2 minutes, the engine should be shut off immediately to prevent power head damage.

CAUTION
If the engine overheats and the warning horn sounds, retorque the cylinder heads after the engine cools to minimize the possibility of power head damage from a blown head gasket.

A vacuum switch (V6 and V8 models) on the power head is connected to the warning horn through the key switch and is grounded to the power head. The switch is designed to monitor vacuum within the fuel delivery hose and activate the warning horn should the pressure drop to a predetermined level, indicating a restriction in the hose. The switch is connected to the fuel inlet side of the injection pump with a hose. If the vacuum in the fuel hose reaches 7 in. Hg, the

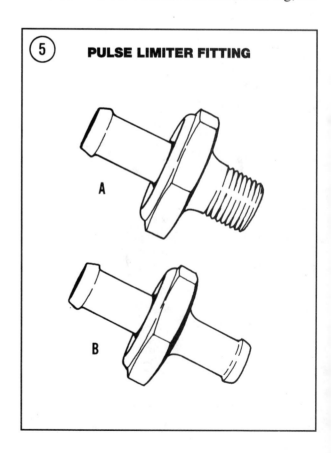

⑤ **PULSE LIMITER FITTING**

A

B

switch activates the warning horn to alert the user to a restricted fuel delivery hose.

Warning System Tests

The warning system is designed to alert the operator to conditions which may result in serious power head damage. For this reason, the warning horn system should be tested periodically to be certain the system is functioning properly.

Warning horn test

The horn should be tested at the beginning of each boating season or after each 100 hours of operation.

1. Disconnect the temperature switch-to-engine wiring harness connector.
2. Place the key switch in the ON position (engine not running).
3. Connect the tan engine harness wire to a good engine ground.
4. The horn should activate when the tan wire is grounded. If not, check the horn and tan wire. Repair the wire or replace the horn as necessary. Also see *Temperature Switch Test* in Chapter Three.

Low-oil and no-oil warning test

The low-oil warning is designed to alert the operator when the oil level in the remote tank drops to 1/4 full. The no-oil warning alerts the operator if the remote tank is empty or a complete oil injection failure occurs.

1. With the remote oil tank empty, turn the key switch ON (engine not running). The warning horn should activate for 1/2 second every 40 seconds.
2. With the remote oil tank 1/4 full, warning horn activation should stop.

3. Connect a remote fuel tank containing a 50:1 fuel and oil mixture to the outboard motor.
4. Disconnect the oil delivery hose from the injection pump inlet fitting (3, **Figure 4**).
5. Place the outboard in a test tank or in the water, mounted on a boat. Start the outboard, shift into FORWARD gear and run at 1000 rpm.
6. The no-oil warning horn should activate after all residual oil is consumed. The no-oil warning horn should activate for 1/2 second every second.
7. If the horn does not activate, connect a voltmeter between a good engine ground and the purple wire (D terminal) in the injection pump connector. Start the motor and note the voltmeter.
   a. If no voltage is present, check the purple wire for an open circuit.
   b. If battery voltage is noted, check the tachometer circuit as described under *Voltage Regulator/Rectifier Tachometer Circuit Test* in Chapter Three. If the tachometer circuit is good, replace the injection pump assembly.

Vacuum switch test (V6 and V8 models)

Insufficient fuel and oil delivered to the power head can result in extensive engine damage. The vacuum switch is designed to activate the warning horn should a restriction in the fuel delivery hose occur. Test the switch as follows:

1. Disconnect the vacuum switch hose from the fuel manifold.
2. Connect a gearcase vacuum tester or other suitable vacuum source to the vacuum switch hose.
3. Turn the key switch to the ON position.
4. Slowly draw a vacuum on the vacuum switch hose. The warning horn should sound continuously when the vacuum on the switch reaches 6.5-7.5 in. Hg.
5. If not, check the warning horn as described in this chapter. If the horn and circuit is good, replace the vacuum switch.

11

Troubleshooting

Although certain oil injection pump replacement parts are available, the pump assembly should generally be serviced by replacement, if defective. If the oil inlet hose is disconnected from the pump, it must be reinstalled with the same type of clamps as removed. The use of worm clamps will damage the vinyl hose while tie straps will not apply sufficient clamping pressure to seal the hose.

Fuel Pressure Test

Refer to **Figure 4** for inlet and outlet identification.

> *CAUTION*
> *The pump nipples are plastic and can be broken if excess pressure is used to remove hoses. Always push, not pull the hoses from the fittings to prevent breakage. If gentle pushing will not disconnect the hose, carefully cut the side of the hose and separate it from the fitting.*

1. Disconnect the fuel outlet hose from the injection pump. Install a tee fitting in the end of the hose and connect a 4 in. (101.6 mm) length of 5/16 in. hose to the tee fitting.

2. Lubricate the pump outlet fitting with a drop of oil and connect the hose and tee fitting assembly to the pump.

3. Connect a 0-15 psi (0-103 kPa) pressure gauge to the tee fitting.

4. Fasten all hose connections with tie straps or hose clamps.

> *CAUTION*
> *The motor must be supplied with adequate cooling water when running. Place the outboard in a test tank, attach a flushing device or mount the motor on a boat in the water.*

5. Start the motor and run at approximately 800 rpm in FORWARD gear. The pressure gauge should indicate *not less* than 3 psi (20.7 kPa).

6. If no pressure is shown in Step 5:

  a. Check for fuel in the tank.

  b. Check for a pinched, kinked or restricted fuel hose.

  c. Check for a pinched or leaking injection pump pulse hose.

  d. Check the pulse limiter fitting for plugging or other damage.

7. If low pressure is shown in Step 5:

  a. Check the fuel filter for restrictions.

  b. Check for a pinched or leaking injection pump pulse hose.

  c. Check for a pinched, kinked or restricted fuel hose.

  d. Check the pulse limiter fitting for restrictions or other damage.

  e. Squeeze the fuel primer bulb several times to clear any possible vapor lock condition in the hose.

8. If no pressure or low pressure is shown in Step 5 and the items in Step 6 and Step 7 are good, replace the injection pump assembly.

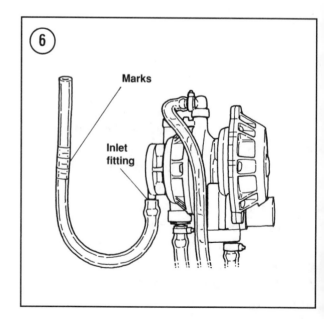

Oil Flow Test

Perform this test to verify the correct fuel-oil ratio and oil consumption.

1. Place the outboard motor in a test tank or mount on a boat in the water. Do not attempt this test with a flushing device providing cooling water to the outboard.

2. Start the motor and run in FORWARD gear until warmed to normal operation temperature.

CAUTION
The pump nipples are plastic and can be broken if excess pressure is used to remove hoses. Always push, not pull the hoses from the fittings to prevent breakage. If gentle pushing will not disconnect the hose, carefully cut the side of the hose and separate it from the fitting.

3. Disconnect the oil delivery hose from the injection pump fitting (3, **Figure 4**).

4. Obtain a 10 in. (254 mm) length of 1/4 in. clear vinyl hose. At one end of the hose, place marks every 1/2 in. (12.7 mm) for 3 in. (76.2). Measure carefully and make sure the marks are accurate.

5. Attach the unmarked end of the hose to the injection pump inlet fitting. See **Figure 6**.

6. Fill the vinyl hose with a recommended engine oil. Start the motor and run long enough to purge any air from the hose. Stop the motor and add or subtract oil from the vinyl hose as necessary to align the oil level with the highest mark.

7. Start the outboard and run at 800 rpm. While observing the oil in the vinyl hose, closely monitor the injection pump pulses by applying light finger pressure to the fuel outlet hose. The injection pump will click with each cycle. The oil level in the vinyl hose should drop 1 in. (25.4 mm) in approximately 5 pulses.

8. Repeat Step 7 while running the motor at wide-open throttle. The oil level in the hose should drop 1 in. (25.4 mm) in approximately 3 pulses.

9. If the injection pump performance is not as specified, check the condition of the pulse limiter fitting. Clean or replace the pulse limiter as necessary. If the pulse limiter is in acceptable condition, replace the injection pump assembly.

Excessive Engine Smoke

Check the fuel system and filters for restrictions. It is normal for a 2-stroke engine to smoke after cold starting. Also check the following if excessive oil consumption is evident:

    a. Fuel system air leakage.
    b. Incorrect antisiphon valve.
    c. Incorrect fuel fitting or hose diameters.

Check the following if oil ratio appears to be excessively lean:

    a. Plugged or restricted oil pickup screen.
    b. Oil system air leakage.
    c. Stuck or restricted check valves.
    d. Plugged or restricted pulse limiter fitting.

Pickup Unit and Filter Service

Other than filter replacement, the oil pickup unit is serviced as an assembly if it does not function properly.

1. Remove the oil pickup mounting screws with a No. 25 Torx driver. Remove the pickup unit from the tank and allow it to drain into a suitable container.

2. Note the position of the foam baffle (if so equipped) for reinstallation and remove it from the pickup unit.

3. Pull the plastic filter assembly from the end of the pickup tube with needlenose pliers.

4. Clean the filter in fresh solvent and dry with compressed air. Replace the filter if excessively plugged or damaged.

5. To reinstall the filter, insert it into the plastic cap from a felt-tip marker. The marker cap should be large enough to hold the filter but no larger than the outer diameter of the filter head.

11

6. Use the marker cap to press the filter into the pickup tube.

7. Reinstall the foam baffle (if so equipped) in the position noted in Step 2.

8. Reinstall the pickup unit into the oil tank and tighten the 4 retaining screws securely.

CAUTION
Failure to purge air from the system properly in Step 9 can result in serious power head damage from insufficient lubrication.

9. Disconnect the oil hose at the inlet fitting on the lower engine cover. Hold the hose in a suitable clean container and squeeze the oil primer bulb until all air is purged from the oil hose.

10. Reinstall the oil hose to the engine inlet fitting and tighten the clamp securely.

Chapter Twelve

Automatic Rewind Starters

Manual start 2-40 hp models are equipped with a rope-operated rewind starter assembly. The starter is mounted above the flywheel on all models except 4 Deluxe. Pulling the rope handle causes the starter rope pulley to rotate, engage the flywheel and turn the engine.

Rewind starters are relatively trouble free; a broken or frayed rope is the most common failure. This chapter covers starter removal, rope replacement, disassembly, cleaning and inspection, reassembly and installation.

REWIND STARTER
(2.0, 2.3 AND 3.3 HP)

Removal/Installation

Refer to **Figure 1** for this procedure.

1. Disconnect the spark plug lead to prevent accidental starting.
2. Remove the port and starboard motor covers.
3. Remove the 2 screws securing the fuel tank.
4. Remove the 2 screws securing the rewind starter assembly to the power head. Lift the starter off the power head.

5. To reinstall, lift the fuel tank up and place the starter onto the power head. If necessary, extend the rope slightly to engage the ratchet with the starter cup.
6. Install the starter mounting screws. Tighten the screws securely. Install the fuel tank mounting screws and tighten to 60-84 in.-lb. (6.8-9.5 N•m).

Disassembly/Reassembly

Refer to **Figure 1** for this procedure.

1. Remove the starter as described in this chapter. Untie the knot securing the rope handle to the rope. While securely holding the rope pulley from turning, remove the handle from the rope.
2. Slowly, allow the rope pulley to unwind, releasing the tension on the rewind spring.
3. Invert the starter and remove the clip (10, **Figure 1**), thrust washer (9) and friction plate (8).
4. Remove the return spring (7, **Figure 1**), cover (6) and friction spring (5).
5. Carefully lift the rope pulley approximately 1/2 in. (13 mm) out of the housing, then turn the

pulley back and forth to disengage the rewind spring from the pulley.

6. Remove the pulley from the housing. Remove the rope from the pulley.

NOTE
Do not remove the rewind spring from the starter housing unless replacement is necessary. Wear suitable hand and eye protection when removing or installing the rewind spring.

7. If rewind spring replacement is necessary, place the starter housing upright (rewind spring facing down) on a suitable bench. Tap the top of the housing until the rewind spring falls out and unwinds inside the housing.

8. Clean all components with solvent and dry with compressed air.

9. Inspect all components for excessive wear or other damage. Inspect the rope pulley for sharp or rough edges that could fray the new starter rope. If necessary, smooth rough edges with a file.

10. To reassemble the starter, lubricate the rewind spring area of the starter housing with OMC Triple-Guard or Lubriplate 777 grease.

11. The rewind spring must be installed into the housing in a counterclockwise direction, starting from the outer coil as shown in **Figure 2**. Make sure the hook in the outer coil of the spring is properly engaged with the catch in the housing as shown.

12. Cut a new length of starter rope 53 in. (135 cm) long.

13. Insert the rope through the hole in the pulley. Tie a suitable knot in the rope, then push the knot into the recess of the pulley.

14. Wind the starter rope onto the pulley in a clockwise direction as viewed from the rewind spring side of the pulley.

15. Install the pulley and rope assembly into the housing. Make sure the hook on the inner coil of the rewind spring properly engages the slot in the pulley.

16. Install the ratchet (4, **Figure 1**), friction spring (5) and cover (6) onto the starter housing center shaft.

17. Hook one end of the return spring into the friction plate and the other end of the spring into the ratchet. See **Figure 3**. Install the friction plate and return spring onto the center shaft. Install the thrust washer (9, **Figure 1**) and clip (10).

18. Place the rope into the notch (**Figure 4**) in the pulley. While holding the rope in the notch,

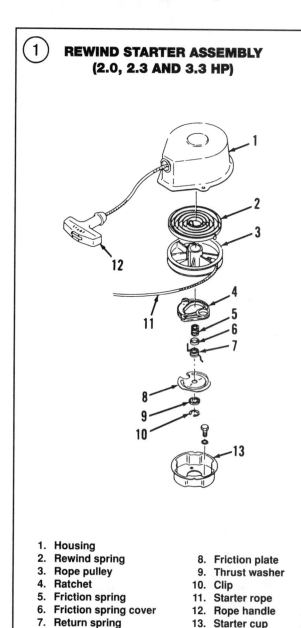

① **REWIND STARTER ASSEMBLY (2.0, 2.3 AND 3.3 HP)**

1. Housing
2. Rewind spring
3. Rope pulley
4. Ratchet
5. Friction spring
6. Friction spring cover
7. Return spring
8. Friction plate
9. Thrust washer
10. Clip
11. Starter rope
12. Rope handle
13. Starter cup

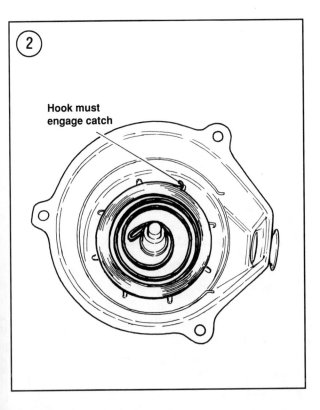

Hook must engage catch

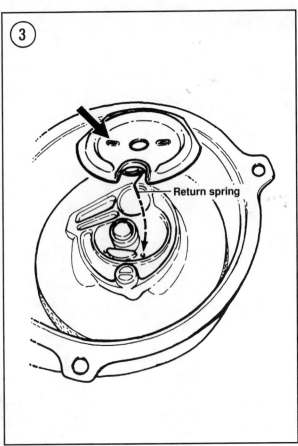

Return spring

rotate the rope pulley 3 turns counterclockwise to apply tension on the rewind spring.

19. Hold the rope securely, then pass the rope through the rope guide in the housing and into the rope handle. Fix the handle to the rope with a knot (**Figure 5**).

20. Install the starter assembly as described in this chapter.

REWIND STARTER
(3 AND 4 [EXCEPT 4 DELUXE] HP)

Removal/Installation

1. Remove the upper motor cover. Disconnect the spark plug leads to prevent accidental starting.

2. Remove the 3 screws securing the starter housing to the power head.

3. Lift the starter assembly off the power head.

4. To install, place the starter assembly on the power head, install the mounting screws and tighten to 60-84 in.-lb. (6.8-9.5 N•m).

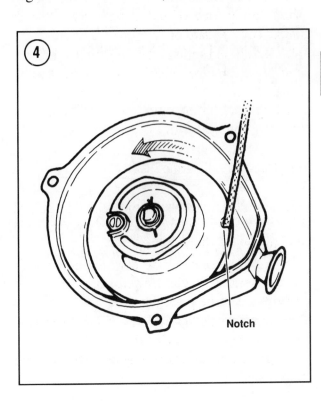

Notch

12

Starter Rope Replacement

1. Remove the starter assembly from the power head.

2. Extend the starter rope and tie a slip knot close to the housing. Allow the rope to retract into the housing up to the knot, to relieve tension on the rope. Then, untie the knot or cut the rope at the handle and remove the handle.

3. Completely extend the rope, hold the rope pulley firmly and remove the slip knot. Then, while holding the pulley from turning, remove the rope from the pulley by pulling on the knotted end.

4. After removing the rope, carefully allow the pulley to slowly unwind, relieving the rewind spring tension.

5. Cut a new rope to 59.5 in. (151 cm) long. Tie a suitable knot in one end.

6. Preload the rewind spring by turning the rope pulley 4-1/2 turns counterclockwise. Hold the pulley firmly in this position.

7. While holding the pulley, insert the rope through the hole in the pulley and insert it into the rope guide in the starter housing. Pull the rope to seat the knot in the pulley firmly.

8. Install the rope handle and secure with a knot (**Figure 5**). Then, carefully allow the rewind spring to retract the rope slowly.

9. Install the starter assembly as described in this chapter.

Disassembly

> *WARNING*
> *During starter disassembly, the rewind spring may unwind violently. Wear suitable hand and eye protection during starter service.*

Refer to **Figure 6** for this procedure.

1. Remove the starter as described in this chapter.

2. Remove the rope from the starter as described in this chapter.

3. Remove the retainer clip (15, **Figure 6**), pawl (14), friction spring (12) along with the friction spring links (13).

4. Remove the spindle screw while firmly holding the rope pulley in the housing. Invert the starter housing and lift out the spindle.

5. Carefully remove the rope pulley from the housing without disturbing the rewind spring.

6. If rewind spring removal is necessary, place the starter housing upright on a bench. Bump the housing against the bench to remove the spring. Allow the spring to unwind under the housing.

Cleaning and Inspection

1. Clean all components with solvent and dry with compressed air.

2. Inspect all components for excessive wear or other damage.

3. Closely inspect the rope pulley for rough or sharp edges which might damage the rope. Smooth any rough edges with a file.

Reassembly

> *WARNING*
> *During starter reassembly, the rewind spring may unwind violently. Wear suit-*

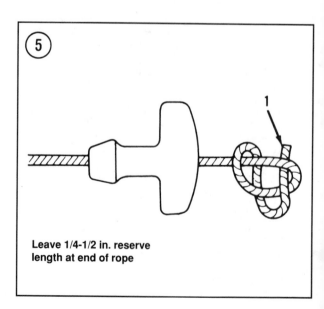

⑤

Leave 1/4-1/2 in. reserve
length at end of rope

able hand and eye protection during starter service.

Refer to **Figure 6** for this procedure.

1. Cut a new rope to 59-1/2 in. (151 cm) long.

2. Lubricate the rewind spring and spring area in the housing with OMC Triple-Guard or Lubriplate 777 grease.

3. Engage the hook in the inner coil of the rewind spring with the slot in the pulley as shown in **Figure 7**. Install the spindle into the pulley.

4. Install the pulley and spring into the housing with the spring passing through the opening in the housing.

5. Thoroughly clean all thread locking compound from the threads of the spindle screw.

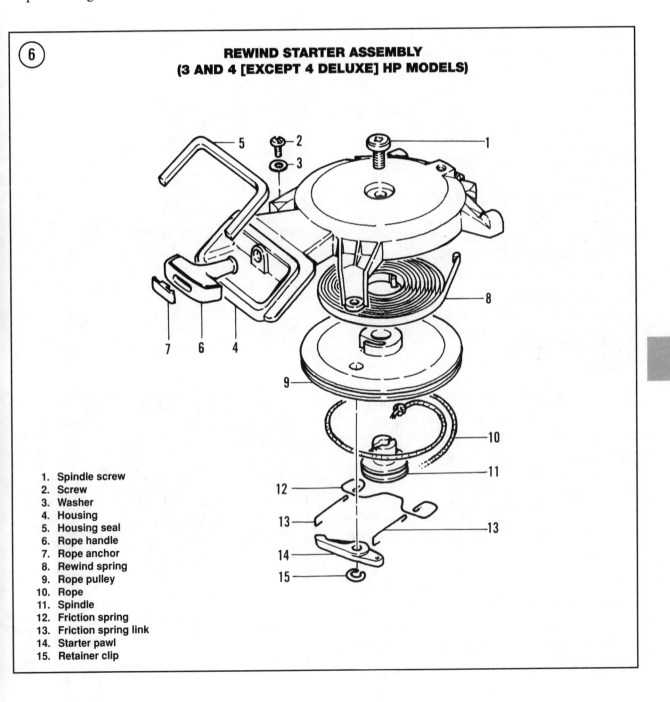

⑥ **REWIND STARTER ASSEMBLY (3 AND 4 [EXCEPT 4 DELUXE] HP MODELS)**

1. Spindle screw
2. Screw
3. Washer
4. Housing
5. Housing seal
6. Rope handle
7. Rope anchor
8. Rewind spring
9. Rope pulley
10. Rope
11. Spindle
12. Friction spring
13. Friction spring link
14. Starter pawl
15. Retainer clip

12

Apply OMC Locquic Primer to the threads of the screw and allow to air dry. Then apply OMC Nut Lock to the threads, install the screw and lockwasher and tighten to 60-84 in.-lb. (6.8-9.5 N.m).

6. Turn the rope pulley counterclockwise until the hook in the outer coil of the rewind spring engages the outer face of the spring cavity. See **Figure 8**.

7. Install the pawl, friction spring and friction spring links. Secure the pawl with the retainer clip. See **Figure 9**. Make sure the sharp edge of the retainer clip is facing away from the rope pulley.

8. Install the rope as described in this chapter. Install the starter assembly as described in this chapter.

REWIND STARTER
(4 DELUXE MODELS)

A swing-arm type rewind starter is used on 4 Deluxe models. The starter assembly must be partially disassembled to replace the rope.

Removal/Installation

1. Disconnect the spark plug leads to prevent accidental starting.

2. Pull the starter rope out enough to tie a slip knot behind the handle. Untie the knot holding the rope in the handle and remove the handle.

3. Release the slip knot and gradually allow the starter to unwind while holding the pulley.

4. Disconnect the starter spring at the cup and stop assembly and pull it out as far as possible to relieve spring tension.

5. Remove the port ignition coil from the power head.

6. Remove the shoulder screw (A, **Figure 10**) and the adjustment screw (B). Firmly hold the starter assembly together and remove it from the power head.

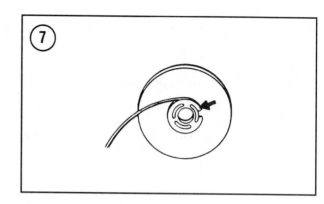

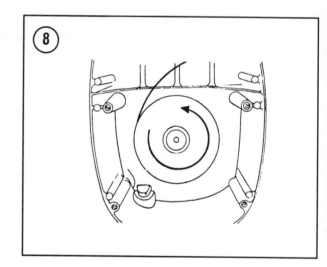

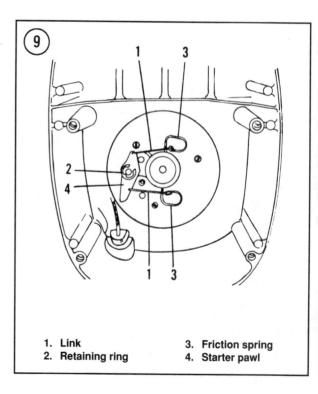

1. Link
2. Retaining ring
3. Friction spring
4. Starter pawl

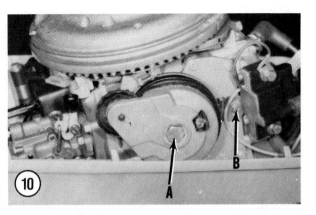

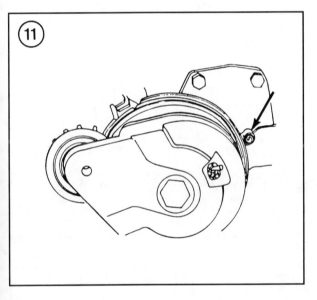

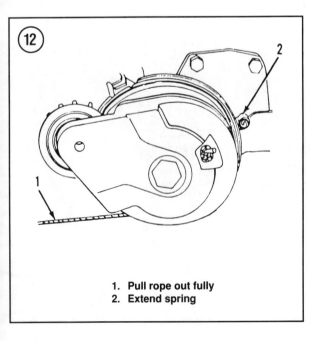

1. **Pull rope out fully**
2. **Extend spring**

7. Thoroughly clean all thread locking compound from the 2 screws. Apply OMC Locquic Primer to the screw threads.

8. Apply OMC Screw Lock to the threads of the shoulder screw. Make sure the idler gear arm is located between the 2 tabs of the cup and stop assembly. Position the starter assembly on the power head and install the shoulder and adjustment screws finger tight.

9. Coat the starter spring with a light coat of OMC Triple-Guard or Lubriplate 777 grease.

10. Install OMC tool part No. 383967 in the lower motor cover groove at the side of the idler arm. Rotate the tool thumbscrew as required to position it in the idler arm hole.

11. Make sure the idler gear engages the flywheel, then turn the flywheel clockwise and wind the starter spring into the cup and stop assembly until the spring loop touches the pulley slot. See **Figure 11**.

12. Hold the pulley from turning and remove the tool (part No. 383967), then allow the pulley to rotate slowly until the spring tension is relieved.

13. Reinstall the tool (part No. 383967) and turn the flywheel clockwise enough to rotate the starter pulley 1-1/2 turns to preload the spring. Hold the pulley and remove the tool.

14. Release the end of the rope and feed it through the lower motor cover hole, pulling it out as far as possible. Hold the rope fully extended and grasp the spring end loop. Pull the spring from the cup and stop assembly. See **Figure 12**. If the spring can be pulled out 8-18 in. (20-46 cm), the preload is satisfactory. If not, repeat Steps 11-14.

15. Install the rope handle assembly and tie a knot in the end of the rope.

16. Hold the idler gear arm stop against the cup stop. Make sure the idler gear teeth engage the flywheel properly, then tighten the adjustment screw.

17. Tighten the shoulder screw to 10-12 ft.-lb. (14-16 N•m).

18. Reinstall the port ignition coil.

12

Disassembly

1. Remove the idler gear arm, gear and gear arm spring from the starter assembly. See **Figure 13**.

2. Separate the pulley from the cup and stop assembly. Note the spring loop position and disconnect the spring from the pulley roll pin. See **Figure 14**.

3. Remove the rope from the pulley, then remove the rope bushing.

4. Remove the idler gear arm bushing. Remove the bushing from each side of the pulley.

Cleaning and Inspection

1. Clean all metal components in solvent and dry with compressed air.

2. Check all metal components for corrosion. Remove any corrosion and wipe parts with light oil.

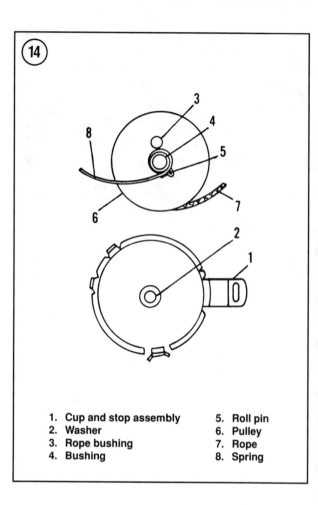

(14)

1. Cup and stop assembly
2. Washer
3. Rope bushing
4. Bushing
5. Roll pin
6. Pulley
7. Rope
8. Spring

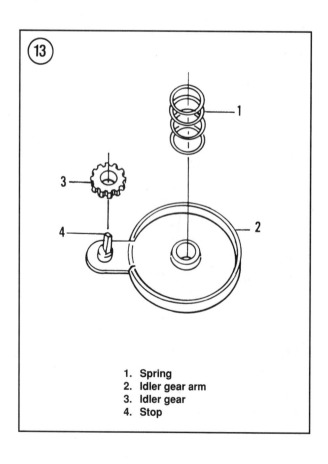

(13)

1. Spring
2. Idler gear arm
3. Idler gear
4. Stop

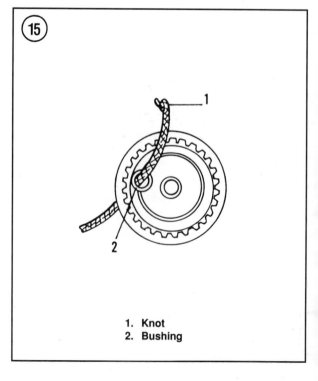

(15)

1. Knot
2. Bushing

3. Check the spring for wear or broken end loops. Replace the spring if necessary.

4. Check the rope for fraying or other damage. Replace the rope if necessary.

Reassembly

1. Insert the pulley bushing.

2. Tie a knot in one end of the rope. Insert the other end through the bushing rope hole. See **Figure 15**.

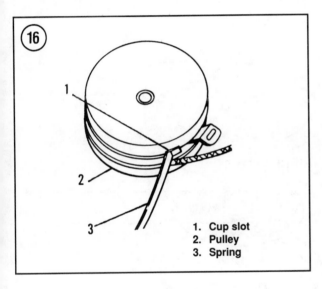

1. Cup slot
2. Pulley
3. Spring

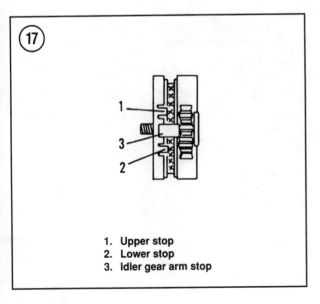

1. Upper stop
2. Lower stop
3. Idler gear arm stop

3. Pull the rope through until the knot seats in the pulley bushing. Hold the pulley with the knot facing you, then wind the pulley clockwise. Tape or install a rubber band to hold the rope in the pulley.

4. Apply OMC Triple-Guard or Lubriplate 777 grease to the bushings. Insert the bushings in the pulley and idler gear arm.

5. Install the washer into the cup and pulley assembly, hooking the spring end loop to the pulley roll pin. See **Figure 14**.

6. Sandwich the pulley and spring to the cup and stop assembly. The spring should extend through the cup slot. See **Figure 16**.

7. Assemble the idler gear with the shoulder resting against the gear arm, then install the arm and spring to the pulley and cup. Locate the idler gear shaft stop between the cup and stop assembly tabs without turning the pulley and disengaging the spring end. See **Figure 17**.

8. Install the starter assembly on the power head as described in this chapter.

REWIND STARTER (6 AND 8 HP; 1993-ON 9.9 AND 15 HP)

Removal/Installation

1. Disconnect the spark plug leads to prevent accidental starting.

2. Remove the 3 screws securing the starter housing to the power head. Lift the starter assembly from the power head. Do not lose the mounting screw spacers (6 and 8 hp).

3A. *6 and 8 hp*—Using a screwdriver, depress the locking tabs and remove the neutral start lockout cable and plunger from the starter housing.

3B. *9.9 and 15 hp*—Disconnect the neutral start lockout cable link from the lockout cam.

4. Remove the starter assembly.

5. To install, reconnect the neutral start lockout cable to the starter housing. On 6 and 8 hp, the locking tabs should be positioned on the sides.

12

6. Position the housing assembly on the power head. Install the mounting screws and spacers (6 and 8 hp). Tighten the mounting screws to 60-84 in.-lb. (6.8-9.5 N•m).

7. Pull the starter rope to check neutral start lockout operation. The starter should not operate if the gearcase is in FORWARD or REVERSE gear.

Disassembly

> *WARNING*
> *During starter disassembly, the rewind spring may unwind violently. Wear suitable hand and eye protection during starter service.*

Refer to **Figure 18** for this procedure.

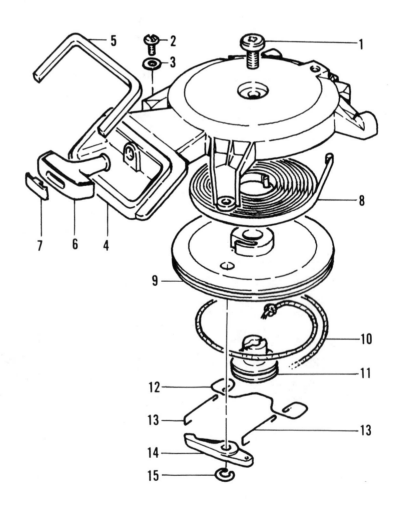

**REWIND STARTER ASSEMBLY
(6 AND 8 HP; 1993-ON 9.9 AND 15 HP MODELS)**

1. Spindle screw
2. Screw
3. Washer
4. Housing
5. Housing seal
6. Rope handle
7. Rope anchor
8. Rewind spring
9. Rope pulley
10. Rope
11. Spindle
12. Friction spring
13. Friction spring link
14. Starter pawl
15. Retainer clip

1. Remove the starter assembly as described in this chapter.

2. On 9.9 and 15 hp, pull out the lockout retaining pin (4, **Figure 19**) and remove the neutral start lockout plunger (5), spring (2), tappet (3) and cam (6) from the housing.

3. Remove retainer clip securing the starter pawl. Remove the pawl and friction spring and links as an assembly.

4. Extend the starter rope and tie a slip knot close to the housing. Pry the rope anchor out of the handle, cut or untie the knot and remove the handle.

5. Hold the rope pulley firmly and untie the slip knot. Carefully allow the pulley to unwind, relieving rewind spring tension.

6. Remove the spindle screw and locknut. Remove the spindle.

7. Place the starter housing upright on a bench and tap the housing on the bench to dislodge the rope pulley and rewind spring. Allow the spring to unwind *under* the housing.

8. Remove the pulley, rewind spring and shield from the housing.

Cleaning and Inspection

1. Thoroughly clean all components with solvent and dry with compressed air.

2. Inspect the rewind spring for cracks, broken loops or other damage.

3. Closely inspect the rope pulley for rough or sharp edges which could damage the rope. Smooth rough edges with a file.

4. Inspect the neutral lockout components for wear or damage. Replace components as necessary.

Reassembly

WARNING
During starter reassembly, the rewind spring may unwind violently. Wear suit-

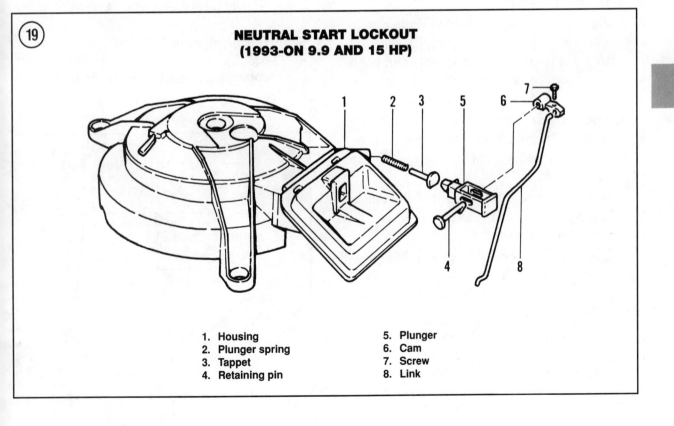

NEUTRAL START LOCKOUT (1993-ON 9.9 AND 15 HP)

1. Housing
2. Plunger spring
3. Tappet
4. Retaining pin
5. Plunger
6. Cam
7. Screw
8. Link

12

able hand and eye protection during starter service.

1. Cut a new rope to 59-1/2 in. (151 cm) long.

2. *9.9 and 15 hp models*—Tie a knot in one end of the rope, then feed it through the passage in the rope pulley. Wind the rope around the pulley in a counterclockwise direction.

3. Install the shield into the housing. Lubricate the shield and rewind spring with OMC Triple-Guard Grease.

4. Starting with the inner coil, wind the rewind spring into the housing in a clockwise direction.

5. Install the rope pulley, making sure the rewind spring is properly engaged with the pulley.

6. Thoroughly clean all thread locking compound from the spindle screw and locknut. Apply OMC Locquic Primer to the threads of the screw, allow to air dry and apply OMC Nut Lock to the threads. Install the spindle screw and locknut and tighten to 120-140 in.-lb. (14-16 N•m).

7A. *6 and 8 hp*—Install the rope and preload the rewind spring as follows:

  a. Note the location of the rope anchor point in the rope pulley. Then, turn the pulley 4 to 4 1/2 turns counterclockwise and position the rope anchor point direction adjacent to the rope guide in the housing.

  b. Insert a small screwdriver or similar tool through the hole in the pulley and housing to hold the pulley from turning. See **Figure 20**, typical.

  c. Insert the rope through the handle, attach the rope to the rope anchor and seat the anchor in the handle.

  d. Using a small hooked tool, thread the rope into the housing, through the rope guide and into the pulley. Secure the rope to the pulley with a suitable knot.

  e. While firmly holding the pulley, remove the tool securing the pulley (**Figure 20**). Carefully allow the rewind spring to wind the rope onto the pulley.

  f. Install the pawl, friction spring, friction spring links. Secure the pawl with the retainer ring. See **Figure 21**, typical.

7B. *9.9 and 15 hp*—Preload the rewind spring as follows:

  a. Turn the rope pulley 1/2 to 1-1/2 turns counterclockwise, then thread the rope through the hole in the pulley and through the rope guide in the starter housing.

  b. Next, turn the rope pulley counterclockwise until the rewind spring is tight. Then, tie a slip knot in the rope and allow the pulley to back off (clockwise) approximately 1/2 to 1 turn.

  c. Install the starter pawl, friction spring and friction spring links. Secure the pawl with the retainer clip. See **Figure 21**, typical.

  d. Install the rope handle, then remove the slip knot and allow the rewind spring to wind the rope around the pulley.

REWIND STARTER
(1991-92 9.9 AND 15 HP)

Removal/Installation

1. Disconnect the spark plug leads to prevent accidental starting.

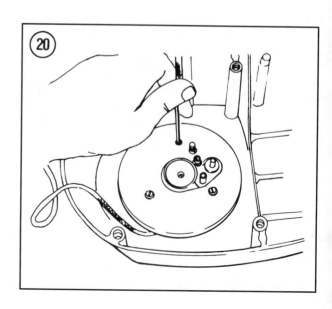

2. Extend the starter rope enough to tie a slip knot behind the handle. Untie the knot holding the rope in the handle and remove the handle.

3. Release the slip knot and gradually allow the pulley to slowly unwind, relieving tension on the rewind spring.

4. Remove the air silencer assembly from the power head.

5. Loosen the starter mounting screw. Hold the pulley and cup together to keep the spring in the cup and remove the mounting screw.

6. If the starter does not require disassembly, install a 3/8 × 16 nut on the mounting screw and finger-tighten to prevent the cup and pulley from coming apart.

7. To install, remove the 3/8 × 16 nut from the mounting screw (if installed).

8. Thoroughly clean all thread locking compound from the mounting screw threads. Apply OMC Locquic Primer, allow to air dry, then apply OMC Screw Lock to the mounting screw threads.

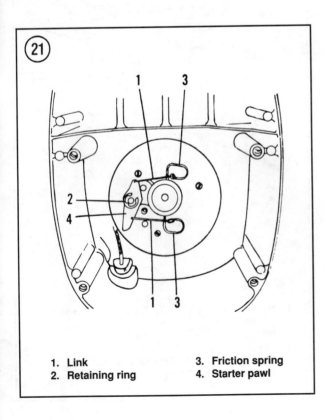

1. Link	**3. Friction spring**
2. Retaining ring	**4. Starter pawl**

9. While holding the pulley and rewind spring in the cup, install the starter assembly. Tighten the mounting screw to 24-26 ft.-lb. (32.5-35.2 N·m).

10. Complete the remaining installation by reversing the removal procedure.

Starter Rope Replacement

WARNING
During starter service, the rewind spring may unwind violently. Wear suitable hand and eye protection during starter service.

1. Remove the starter as described in this chapter.

2. Carefully secure the starter housing horizontally in a vise with protective jaws.

3. Remove the mounting screw and washer.

4. Unclip the pinion spring and remove it from the starter pulley with the pinion gear.

5. Insert a putty knife or similar tool between the pulley and cup to hold the spring in place. Remove the pulley from the cup.

6. Thread the new rope through the hole in the pulley. Tie a knot in the end of the rope and wind the rope onto the pulley in a counterclockwise direction.

7. Fit the pulley to the cup so that the spring loop will engage the pulley shaft cutout.

8. Install the pinion and pinion spring on the pulley.

9. Lubricate the mounting screw and washer with light oil. Install the screw through the pulley, cup washer and cup.

10. If the starter is not to be immediately installed on the power head, install a 3/8 × 16 nut on the mounting screw to hold the assembly together.

12

Disassembly

WARNING
During starter disassembly, the rewind spring may unwind violently. Wear suitable hand and eye protection during starter service.

Refer to **Figure 22** for this procedure.

1. Remove the starter as described in this chapter.

2. Carefully secure the starter assembly vertically in a vise with protective jaws.

3. Slip a flat screwdriver blade through the exposed spring loop and withdraw the spring from the cup.

4. Remove the starter from the vise. Remove the nut, mounting screw and washer.

5. Unclip the pinion spring and remove it from the starter pulley with the pinion gear.

6. Remove the pulley, spring, cup washer and spring retainer from the cup assembly.

7. Remove the rope from the pulley, if required.

Cleaning and Inspection

1. Thoroughly clean all components with solvent and dry with compressed air.

2. Inspect the rewind spring for cracks, broken loops or other damage.

3. Closely inspect the rope pulley for rough or sharp edges which could damage the rope. Smooth rough edges with a file.

4. Inspect the pinion and pulley for excessive wear and chipped or broken teeth.

5. Check the cup for corrosion or other damage. Clean or replace the cup as required.

Reassembly

Refer to **Figure 22** for this procedure.

1. Install the starter rope as described in this chapter.

2. Lubricate the spring surface in the cup with OMC Triple-Guard or Lubriplate 777 grease.

3. Install the spring and retainer in the cup as shown in **Figure 23**.

4. Position the cup washer and install the pulley with the spring loop engaging the pulley loop anchor (**Figure 23**).

5. Place the pinion on the pulley. Install the mounting screw and washer through the pulley, cup washer and cup.

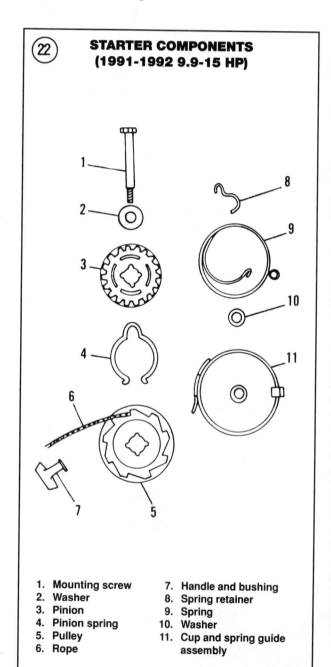

(22) **STARTER COMPONENTS**
(1991-1992 9.9-15 HP)

1. Mounting screw	7. Handle and bushing
2. Washer	8. Spring retainer
3. Pinion	9. Spring
4. Pinion spring	10. Washer
5. Pulley	11. Cup and spring guide
6. Rope	assembly

6. To hold the assembly together, install a 3/8 × 16 nut on the mounting screw.

7. Hold the cup in one hand and wind the spring into the cup by turning the pulley counterclockwise (as viewed from the top of the pulley). As the spring is wound and resistance felt, feed the spring into the cup through the slot to relieve tension.

8. When the spring is completely wound into the cup with the outer loop drawn up against the cup, wind the rope counterclockwise around the pulley and install the pinion spring.

9. Install the starter on the power head as described in the chapter.

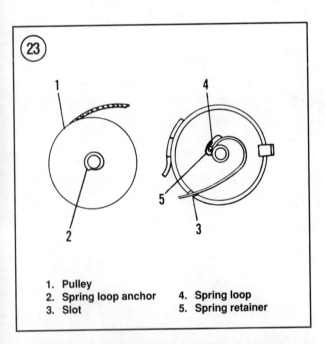

1. Pulley
2. Spring loop anchor
3. Slot
4. Spring loop
5. Spring retainer

10. Pull the rope out as far as possible, then pull out the spring loop end. It should extend at least 1/2 in. (12.7 mm) from the cup.

11. Make sure the starter lockout functions properly. The starter should lock when the throttle is opened beyond the START position.

REWIND STARTER (20-30 HP)

Removal/Installation

1. Disconnect the spark plug leads to prevent accidental starting.

2. Remove the 3 starter mounting screws. Lift the starter assembly from the power head.

3. From the lower side of the starter housing, depress the locking tab on the lockout cable (**Figure 24**), then pull the cable from the housing.

4. To install, place the starter lockout cable into the housing.

5. Place the starter assembly on the power head. Install the 3 mounting screws (short screw on port side). Tighten the screws to 48-72 in.-lb. (5.4-8.1 N·m).

Disassembly

WARNING
During starter disassembly, the rewind spring may unwind violently. Wear suitable hand and eye protection during starter service.

Refer to **Figure 25** for this procedure.

1. Extend the starter rope and tie a slip knot close to the housing. Then pry the rope anchor from the rope handle and remove the anchor and handle.

2. While firmly holding the rope pulley, remove the slip knot and carefully allow the pulley to unwind slowly, relieving rewind spring tension.

3. Remove the spindle nut (5, **Figure 25**). Invert the starter assembly and remove the spindle

12

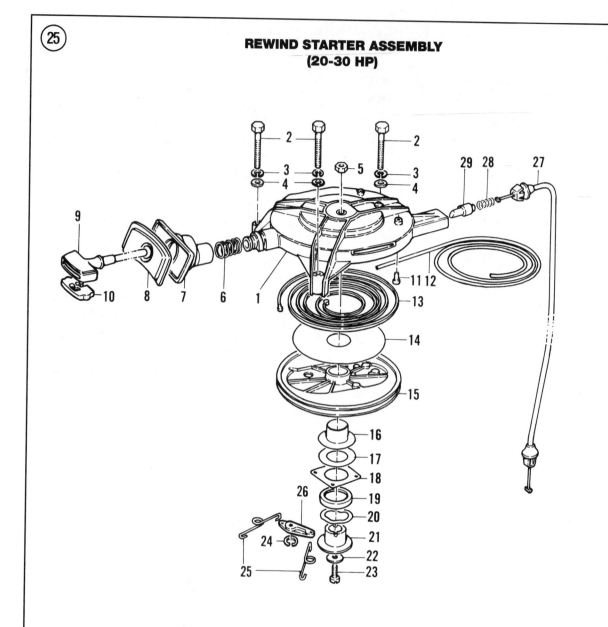

**REWIND STARTER ASSEMBLY
(20-30 HP)**

1. Housing
2. Mounting screw
3. Lockwasher
4. Flat washer
5. Spindle nut
6. Handle support spring
7. Grommet
8. Handle support plate
9. Handle
10. Rope anchor
11. Guide pin
12. Rope
13. Rewind spring
14. Shield
15. Rope pulley
16. Spindle bushing
17. Shim
18. Friction plate
19. Friction ring
20. Spring washer
21. Spindle
22. Washer
23. Spindle screw
24. Retaining ring
25. Pawl links
26. Pawl
27. Lockout cable
28. Spring
29. Lockout plunger

screw (23, **Figure 25**), washer (22), spring washer(s) (20) and friction ring (19).

4. Remove the 2 retaining rings (24, **Figure 25**), pawls (26), links (25) and spindle bushing (16) and shim (17).

5. Place the starter assembly upright on a bench and tap the housing assembly on the bench to dislodge the pulley and rewind spring. Allow the rewind spring to unwind under the housing.

Cleaning and Inspection

1. Thoroughly clean all components with solvent and dry with compressed air.

2. Inspect the rewind spring for cracks, broken loops or other damage.

3. Closely inspect the rope pulley for rough or sharp edges which could damage the rope. Smooth rough edges with a file.

4. Inspect the pinion and pulley for excessive wear and chipped or broken teeth.

5. Check the cup for corrosion or other damage. Clean or replace the cup as required.

Reassembly

> *WARNING*
> *During starter reassembly, the rewind spring may unwind violently. Wear suitable hand and eye protection during starter service.*

1. Lubricate the rewind spring and spring area in the housing with OMC Triple-Guard or Lubriplate 777 grease.

2. Place the outer spring loop over the pin in the housing cutout (**Figure 26**). Carefully wind the spring into the housing. See **Figure 26**.

3. Place the rewind spring shield onto the rope pulley.

4. Install the pulley into the housing, making sure the pin on the pulley engages the inner spring loop.

5. Lightly lubricate the spindle and spindle bushing with OMC Triple-Guard or Lubriplate 777 grease. Install the bushing (16, **Figure 25**) and shim (17) into the pulley.

6. Install the friction plate (18, **Figure 25**), links (25) and pawls (26). Secure the pawls with the retainer rings.

7. Install the spindle (21, **Figure 25**), friction ring (19) and spring washer(s) (20).

8. Thoroughly clean all thread locking compound from the spindle screw threads. Install the spindle screw and washer and tighten to 120-145 in.-lb. (14-16 N•m). Next, spray the exposed threads of the spindle screw with OMC Locquic Primer and allow to air dry. Then apply OMC Nut Lock to the threads of the spindle nut, install the nut and tighten to 120-145 in.-lb. (14-16 N•m).

9. Wind the pulley counterclockwise until the spring is tight, then back off the pulley 1/2 to 1 turn and align the pulley and housing holes (**Figure 27**). Insert a punch or similar tool into the holes to lock the pulley in place.

12

10. Cut a new starter rope 73-1/2 in. (187 cm) long. Tie a knot in the end of the rope. Insert the opposite end of the rope into the pulley hole and feed the rope until it comes out the side of the housing. Pull the rope through the pulley until the knot rests against it.

11. Lubricate the handle end of the rope with OMC Triple-Guard or Lubriplate 777 grease, then thread the rope through the handle.

12. Press the rope into the channel in the rope anchor with the end of the rope butted tightly against the channel. See **Figure 28**. Install the anchor into the handle.

13. Pull on the end of the rope to make sure the knot seats against the pulley, then while firmly holding the rope pulley, remove the punch locking the pulley. Allow the pulley to slowly wind the rope into the housing.

REWIND STARTER
(40 HP)

Removal/Installation

1. Disconnect the spark plug leads to prevent accidental starting.

2. Remove the screw holding the starter lockout cable clamp to the housing. See A, **Figure 29**.

3. Remove the lockout slide (B, **Figure 29**) from the housing.

4. Remove the 3 starter housing mounting screws along with their lockwashers and flat washers.

5. Remove the 2 screws holding the starter handle bracket to the power head. Remove the starter from the power head.

6. Installation is the reverse of removal, plus the following:

   a. Make sure the washers are installed between the rubber starter mounts and power head.

   b. Tighten the bracket screws to 60-84 in.-lb. (6.8-9.5 N·m) and housing mounting screws to 120-144 in.-lb. (14-16 N·m).

   c. Lubricate the lockout slide area on the housing with OMC Triple-Guard or Lubriplate 777 grease.

   d. Shift the outboard into NEUTRAL and adjust the lockout cable to center the lockout slide on the lockout lever. Tighten the cable clamp screw snugly.

Disassembly

> *WARNING*
> *During starter disassembly, the rewind spring may unwind violently. Wear suitable hand and eye protection during starter service.*

1. Pull the starter rope out enough to tie a slip knot behind the handle. Pry the rope anchor from the handle.

2. Remove the handle, untie the slip knot and gradually allow the starter to unwind while holding the pulley.

3. With the starter housing placed upright on a clean workbench, remove the lockout lever shoulder screw. Remove the lockout lever, spring and washer from the housing.

4. Remove the nut from the center of the housing holding the pawl retaining screw.

5. Carefully invert the starter housing and remove the pawl retaining screw, washer, pawl plate and return spring.

6. Remove the spring from the pawl screw cavity. Remove the pawl and spring washer.

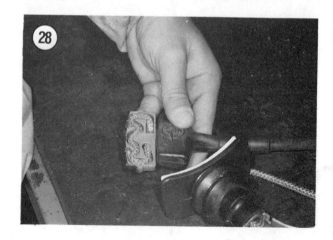

7. Carefully open the pulley lockring with a screwdriver and remove it from the housing.

8. Remove the friction plate and spring washer.

9. Hold the pulley in the housing while turning the housing upright on the bench or floor.

10. Release the pulley and rap the housing sharply to dislodge the pulley and spring. The spring should uncoil within the starter housing legs.

11. Lift the housing up and remove the spring and pulley.

12. Remove the bushing from the pulley. If necessary, remove the rope guide shoulder screw and guide from the housing.

Cleaning and Inspection

1. Thoroughly clean all components with solvent and dry with compressed air.

2. Inspect the rewind spring for cracks, broken loops or other damage.

3. Closely inspect the rope pulley for rough or sharp edges which could damage the rope. Smooth rough edges with a file.

4. Inspect the pinion and pulley for excessive wear and chipped or broken teeth.

5. Check the cup for corrosion or other damage. Clean or replace the cup as required.

Reassembly

WARNING
During starter reassembly, the rewind spring may unwind violently. Wear suitable hand and eye protection during starter service.

1. Lubricate the pulley bushing with OMC Triple-Guard or Lubriplate 777 grease.

2. Position the spring shield in the starter housing.

3. Inserting the open loop of the spring first, carefully coil the spring into the housing cutout.

4. Install the pulley bushing in the pulley and position the pulley shim on the pulley.

5. Install the pulley in the starter housing, making sure the outer loop of the spring engages the pin in the housing.

6. Position the friction plate spring washer and plate on the pulley hub, then install the lockring.

7. Coat the starter pawl boss with OMC Triple-Guard or Lubriplate 777 grease. Position the spring washer on the pawl boss and install the pawl into the pulley.

8. Install the spring into the retaining screw cavity.

9. Install the return spring on the pawl plate, press the other end of the spring on the pulley boss and position the pawl plate on the pulley.

10. Install the pawl plate retaining screw and washer. Tighten the screw to 10-12 ft.-lb. (14-16 N•m).

11. With the starter housing upright on the bench, spray the threads of the retaining screw and nut with OMC Locquic Primer and allow to air dry. Then, apply OMC Screw Lock to the threads of the nut. Install and tighten the nut securely.

12. If the rope guide shoulder screw and guide were removed, reinstall and tighten the screw snugly.

13. Tie a knot in the end of a new rope. Invert the starter housing on a workbench and wind the pulley counterclockwise as far as possible. Back

12

off the rewind spring until the pulley rope cavity aligns with the rope guide.

14. Insert a new rope through the pulley, rope guide and handle bracket outlet. Feed the rope until it comes out the side of the housing. Pull the rope through the pulley until the knot seats against it, then tie a slip knot in the rope to hold it in position.

15. Lubricate the handle end of the rope with OMC Triple-Guard or Lubriplate 777 grease. Thread the rope through the handle.

16. Press the rope into the channel in the rope anchor with the end of the rope butted tightly against the channel. See **Figure 28**. Install the anchor into the handle.

17. Pull on the end of the rope to make sure the knot seats against the pulley, then untie the slip knot and slowly allow the rope to wind around the pulley.

18. Pull the starter rope out and check pawl operation. Pawl should extend when the rope is pulled out and retract when the rope is released.

19. Pull the rope out and release it several times, then check to make sure the housing arrow aligns with the pulley mark. If not properly aligned, pull the rope out and release several more times. A new rope must lose some of its stiffness before the marks will properly align.

20. Position the starter lockout lever, spring and washer on the starter housing. Install the shoulder screw and tighten securely.

Chapter Thirteen

Sea Drives

Service on the outboard motor assembly of the Sea Drive is the same as a standard outboard motor. The Sea Drive units and their equivalent outboard models are as follows:

a. *1.6 Sea Drive*—V4 cross flow models (85-115 hp).

b. *2.0 Sea Drive*—V4 loop charged models (12- and 140 hp).

c. *3.0 Sea Drive*—V6 loop charged models (200 and 225 hp).

d. *4.0 Sea Drive*—V8 models (250 and 300 hp).

Only service that is unique to the Sea Drive is covered in this chapter. For service that is related to the power head or other areas related to the outboard motor, refer to the appropriate chapter. Note the model year, engine design and/or related outboard motor horsepower when determining maintenance of service information applicable to your year and model of Sea Drive.

SELECTRIM (1.6 SEA DRIVE)

Components

The unit consists of a valve body assembly, oil pump, electric motor, trim cylinder and combination tilt cylinder/shock absorber mounted on an anchor bracket. A rubber hose connects the anchor bracket reservoir to the remote reservoir.

Operation

Moving the trim/tilt switch to the UP position closes the pump motor circuit. The motor drives the oil pump, forcing oil into the UP side of the trim and tilt cylinders. Because of system design, the trim cylinder functions first and moves the outboard motor upward the first 0-17°. At 17°, the trim cylinder is fully extended and the hydraulic fluid is diverted into the tilt cylinder, which moves the motor through the final 45° of travel.

Moving the trim/tilt switch to the DOWN position also closes the motor circuit. The motor runs in the opposite direction, forcing oil into the tilt cylinder and bringing the outboard motor back to the 17° position, where the trim cylinder lowers the outboard motor the remainder of the way.

The power tilt will temporarily maintain the outboard at any angle within its range to allow shallow water operation at slow speed, launching, beaching or trailering. At approximately 3000 rpm, however, the trim-up relief valve opens, allowing the motor to automatically lower to its fully trimmed out (17°) position.

A manual release valve with a slotted head permits manual raising and lowering of the outboard motor through its tilt range (17-45°).

A trim gauge sending unit is mounted on a bracket located on the inside of the outboard motor mounting brackets. The sending unit uses a calibrated lever positioned against the trim cylinder to calculate trim angle. Access to the sending unit requires the outboard motor to be fully tilted UP.

Hydraulic Pump Fluid Check

1. Tilt the outboard motor to its fully UP position.
2. Check the fluid level in the remote reservoir (**Figure 1**, typical). The fluid should be level with the reservoir "FULL" mark.
3. If necessary, remove the remote reservoir fill cap and add OMC Power Trim/Tilt and Power Steering Fluid to obtain the proper level.

Hydraulic Pump Fluid Refill

Follow this procedure if a large amount of fluid is lost due to leakage or service to the unit.
1. Remove the remote reservoir (**Figure 1**, typical) fill cap and add OMC Power Trim/Tilt and Power Steering Fluid as necessary to bring the

level to the "FULL" mark. Make certain the cylinders are fully extended.

2. Loosen the oil pump bleed screw (**Figure 2**) and allow fluid to escape around the plug threads until no air bubbles are noted in the fluid. Then, tighten the plug securely.

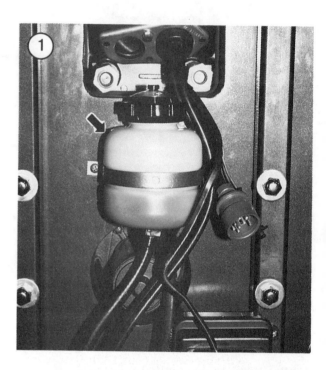

3. Recheck the fluid level in the reservoir and add as required.

4. Run the pump motor while rechecking the oil level. Add fluid as necessary. Run the unit fully UP and fully DOWN through at least 5 cycles, adding fluid as required when the cylinders are fully extended.

5. It may be necessary to charge the battery after this procedure. See Chapter Seven.

Troubleshooting

If a problem occurs in the power trim/tilt system, the initial step is to determine whether the problem is in the electric or hydraulic system. Electrical tests are covered in this chapter. If the

problem appears to be in the hydraulic system, refer it to a qualified marine specialist for repair.

To determine if the problem is in the electric or hydraulic system, proceed as follows:

1. Make sure the plug-in connectors are properly engaged and all terminals and wires are free of corrosion. Tighten and clean as necessary.

2. Make sure the battery is fully charged. Charge or replace as necessary.

3. Check the system fuse.

4. Check the fluid level as described in this chapter. Add fluid as necessary.

NOTE
The power trim/tilt mechanism does not need to be removed from the boat to perform the following tests.

5. Proceed as follows to install OMC Trim and Tilt Pressure Tester part No. 390010 (**Figure 3**):

   a. Remove the manual release valve retaining ring (**Figure 4**).

   b. Operate the trim/tilt motor to retract all cylinders completely.

   c. Turn the manual release valve 1 full turn counterclockwise.

   d. Place a drain pan under the manual release valve.

   e. Momentarily operate the trim/tilt motor in the UP direction and then in the DOWN direction

CAUTION
Residual hydraulic pressure may be present when the manual release valve is removed. To prevent personal injury, make sure suitable eye protection is worn. Cover the manual release valve with a shop towel during removal.

   f. Slowly rotate the manual release valve counterclockwise to remove.

   g. Securely screw pressure gauge and adapter together. Adapter "B" is used to test UP pressure and adapter "A" is used to check DOWN pressure.

13

h. Install the pressure gauge and adapter into the manual release valve passage and tighten to 5-10 in.-lb. (0.6-1.1 N.m). Do not overtighten the gauge/adapter assembly or the adapter O-ring can be damaged.

i. Operate the unit UP and DOWN several cycles, then recheck and add fluid to the reservoir as necessary.

6. Perform the following operations and note the pressure gauge:

a. Install the pressure gauge and adapter "B" into the manual release port.

b. Operate the trim/tilt motor to extend the cylinders (UP direction). Pressure gauge should indicate approximately 200 psi (1379 kPa) as the trim cylinder is extending and approximately 450 psi (3102 kPa) as the tilt cylinder is extending. The pressure gauge should indicate approximately 1250 psi (8619 kPa) when the unit stalls (fully extended). The pressure gauge should not drop by more than 200 psi (1379 kPa) from the stall reading when the trim/tilt motor is stopped.

c. Install the pressure gauge and adapter "A" into the manual release valve port.

d. Operate the trim/tilt motor to retract the cylinders (DOWN direction). The pressure gauge should indicate approximately 800 psi (5516 kPa) as the cylinders are retracting. The gauge should indicate approximately 800 psi (5516 kPa) as the unit stalls. The gauge should not drop by more than 200 psi (1379 kPa) when the trim/tilt motor is stopped.

7. If the system fails any part of Step 6, the problem is hydraulic. If the hydraulic system is in acceptable condition, the problem is in the electrical system.

Trim and Tilt Switch Circuit Test

Refer to **Figure 5** for this procedure.

1. With the key switch ON, connect the voltmeter red test lead to point E1 in the trim/tilt junction box. Connect the black test lead to point G in the trim/tilt junction box. The meter should indicate battery voltage.

2. If battery voltage is not shown in Step 1, move the red test lead to point J1 in the battery junction box. If battery voltage is shown, check the 50 amp fuse in the battery junction box. If the fuse is good, look for poor connections or an open circuit in the fuse holder and connecting wiring.

3. Move the red test lead to point E3 in the trim/tilt junction box. Move the trim/tilt switch to the DOWN position. If battery voltage is shown, move the red test lead to points E4 and E5. With the trim/tilt switch in the DOWN position, there should be voltage at each point. If voltage is shown and the trim motor does not run, probe connector C2 at the pump motor. If voltage is shown at the connector and the motor does not run, test the motor as described in this chapter.

4. If no voltage is noted at point E3 in Step 3, check connector C1 between the trim/tilt junction box and the trim/tilt switch. If the connector is good, check for an open circuit in the following:

a. Green/orange wire between the trim/tilt switch and trim/tilt junction box.

b. Trim/tilt switch between the green/orange and purple wires with the switch in the DOWN position.

5. Move the red test lead to point E6 in the trim/tilt junction box. Move the trim/tilt switch to the UP position. If battery voltage is indicated, move the red test lead to points E7 and E8. With the trim/tilt switch in the UP position, voltage should be noted at each point. If voltage is not present and the trim motor does not run, probe connector C2 at the pump motor. If voltage is present at the connector and the motor still does not run, test the motor as described in this chapter.

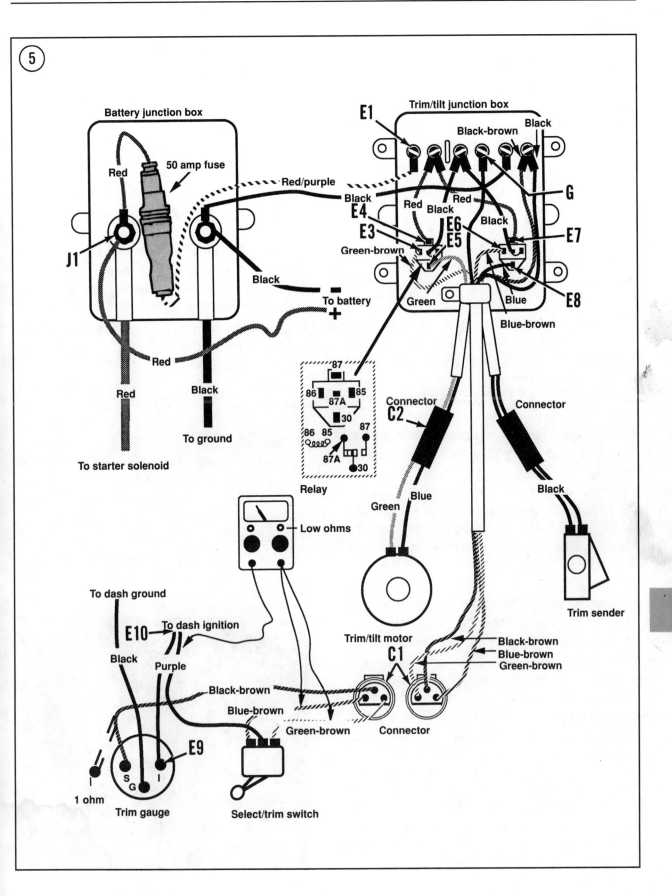

13

6. If no voltage is noted at point E6 in Step 5, check connector C1 between the trim/tilt junction box and trim/tilt switch. If the connector is good, check for an open circuit in the following:
   a. Blue/orange wire between the trim/tilt switch and trim/tilt junction box.
   b. Trim/tilt switch between the blue/orange and purple wires with the switch in the UP position.

Trim Indicator Circuit Test

Refer to **Figure 5** for this procedure.
1. Turn the key switch to the ON position.
2. Connect the voltmeter red test lead to point E9 on the indicator gauge. Connect the black test lead to the indicator gauge G terminal. If battery voltage is noted, continue at Step 5.
3. If battery voltage is not noted in Step 2, move the red test lead to point E10 (accessory plug). If battery voltage is noted, an open circuit is present between the accessory plug and the trim indicator gauge.
4. If no voltage is noted in Step 3, move the red test lead to the accessory terminal on the key switch. If no voltage is noted at the accessory terminal, look for a bad fuse or an open circuit in the key switch wiring. If the fuse and wiring are good, replace the switch.
5. Turn the key switch to the OFF position.
6. Disconnect the black/orange wire at the indicator gauge S terminal. With an ohmmeter on the low-ohm scale, connect the red test lead to the disconnected black/orange wire and the black test lead to the indicator gauge G terminal. With the outboard motor in the fully trimmed in (DOWN) position, the ohmmeter should indicate 82-88 ohms. With the outboard at full tilt (UP), the ohmmeter should indicate 0-10 ohms.
7. If the resistance readings are not as specified in Step 6, check for an open circuit in the ground wire between the indicator gauge and the trim/tilt junction box or in the black/orange wire disconnected from the indicator gauge S terminal.

8. If the wiring is good, disconnect the black sending unit wires at the terminal strip in the trim/tilt junction box. Connect an ohmmeter between the disconnected sender leads and check the resistance of the sending unit. If not within the specifications in Step 6, replace the sending unit (**Figure 6**).

Trim and Tilt Motor Amperage Test

This test evaluates the pump output pressure by determining the current requirements of the pump motor (**Figure 7**). Readings must be taken with the boat at rest.

1. Connect an ammeter between the positive battery terminal and the heavy red cable at the battery junction box.
2. Move the trim/tilt switch to the UP position and note the meter reading, then move the trim/tilt switch to the DOWN position and note the reading.
3. Compare the readings obtained in Step 2 to the specifications in **Table 1**.
   a. If the current draw is within specifications, the motor, hydraulic pump and relief valves are functioning properly.
   b. Low current draw indicates a malfunctioning pump, leaking valves, weak relief

valves or leaking O-rings on the valve bodies.

c. High current draw in either the UP or DOWN direction indicates a problem in the electric motor or hydraulic pump, or the relief valves are opening at too high pressure. With the motor separated from the hydraulic pump, perform a no-load current draw test as described in this chapter.

No-load Current Draw Test

1. Separate the electric motor (**Figure 7**) from the hydraulic pump.

2. Connect an ammeter in series with the motor and a fully charged battery. Connect the motor blue wire (UP) to the negative battery terminal and the motor green wire (DOWN) to the positive battery terminal. The motor shaft should rotate counterclockwise. Note the ammeter reading. Reverse the motor leads and note the ammeter reading.

3. Ammeter should read a current draw of 7 amps at a minimum of 6700 rpm.

4. If the current draw is not as specified, repair or replace the motor.

System Removal/Installation

1. Disconnect the battery cables from the battery terminals.

2. Remove the remote oil reservoir from the mounting bracket and pour the oil into a suitable container.

3. Disconnect the trim sender and electric motor wiring harnesses at the connectors located between the respective component and trim/tilt junction box.

4. Rotate the manual release valve counterclockwise 2 full turns.

5. Use a lifting device or physically tilt the outboard motor outward until the motor tilt lock arms (**Figure 8**) can be engaged to secure the motor at the highest tilt position.

6. Mark the sending unit bracket for correct repositioning on the anchor bracket, then loosen the sending unit bracket mounting screws.

7. Loosen the cylinder support mounting screws, then slide the support up on the slotted holes and retighten the screws.

8. Remove the transom bracket cover to expose the tilt cylinder upper mounting bracket.

13

9. Note the wire ties and the hoses each tie secures for correct reassembly, then use a suitable tool and remove the wire ties.

10. Remove the trailer lock rod spring by removing one end of the spring from the trailer lock rod and the other end of the spring from the anchor bracket.

11. Remove the 4 screws retaining the tilt cylinder upper mounting bracket to the port and starboard engine bracket assemblies.

12. Support the outboard motor to secure its tilt position, then release the tilt lock arms. Allow the outboard motor to lower until the tilt lock arms can be engaged in the lowest tilt lock position. Remove the pin from the tilt cylinder upper eyelet and upper mounting bracket. Remove the upper mounting bracket.

13. Remove the 4 screws securing the anchor bracket to the port and starboard transom bracket assembly. Pull the SelecTrim/Tilt assembly forward enough to allow the sending unit wiring harness and electric motor wiring harness to be pulled through the lower transom cutout.

14. Withdraw the SelecTrim//Tilt assembly while slowly guiding the remote reservoir through the lower transom cutout.

15. Installation is the reverse of removal. Note the following during installation:

    a. Apply Scotch-Grip Rubber Adhesive 1300 on the anchor bracket gasket.

    b. The 2 disc locks for each of the 4 anchor plate mounting screws must be installed on the screws with the interlocking (teethed) side of the discs facing each other. Tighten the screws to 45-50 ft.-lb. (61-68 N·m).

    c. Tighten the 4 screws retaining the tilt cylinder upper mounting brackets to 45-50 ft.-lb. (61-68 N·m).

    d. Use wire ties to secure the hoses as noted during the removal procedure.

    e. Apply terminal grease on the terminals in the connector C2 (**Figure 5**). Apply terminal grease on the back side of the connector ends after assembling the connector.

    f. Refill the hydraulic system as outlined under *Hydraulic Pump Fluid Refill* in this chapter.

SELECTRIM/TILT
(2.0, 3.0 AND 4.0 SEA DRIVES)

Components

The unit consists of a valve body assembly, oil pump, electric motor and combination trim and tilt cylinder/shock absorber mounted on an anchor bracket. A rubber hose connects the anchor bracket fluid reservoir to the remote reservoir.

Operation

Moving the trim/tilt switch to the UP position closes the pump motor circuit. The motor drives the oil pump, forcing oil into the UP side of the trim and tilt cylinders. Because of system design, the trim cylinder functions first and moves the outboard motor upward the first 0-17°. At 17°, the trim cylinder is fully extended and the hydraulic fluid is diverted into the tilt cylinder, which moves the motor through the final 45° of travel.

Moving the trim/tilt switch to the DOWN position also closes the motor circuit. The motor runs in the opposite direction, forcing oil into the tilt cylinder and bringing the outboard motor back to the 17° position, where the trim cylinder lowers the outboard motor the remainder of the way.

The power tilt will temporarily maintain the outboard at any angle within its range to allow shallow water operation at slow speed, launching, beaching or trailering. At approximately 3000 rpm, however, the trim-up relief valve opens, allowing the motor to automatically lower to its fully trimmed out (17°) position.

A manual release valve with a slotted head permits manual raising and lowering of the outboard motor through its tilt range (17-45°).

A trim gauge sending unit is mounted on a bracket located on the inside of the outboard motor mounting brackets. The sending unit uses a calibrated lever positioned against the trim cylinder to calculate trim angle. Access to the sending unit requires the outboard motor to be fully tilted UP.

Hydraulic Pump Fluid Check

1. Tilt the outboard motor to its fully UP position.
2. Check the fluid level in the remote reservoir (**Figure 1**, typical). The fluid should be level with the reservoir "FULL" mark.
3. If necessary, remove the remote reservoir fill cap and add OMC Power Trim/Tilt and Power Steering Fluid to obtain the proper level.

Hydraulic Pump Fluid Refill

Follow this procedure if a large amount of fluid is lost due to leakage or service to the unit.

1. Remove the remote reservoir (**Figure 1**, typical) fill cap and add OMC Power Trim/Tilt and Power Steering Fluid as necessary to bring the level to the "FULL" mark. Make certain the cylinders are fully extended.
2. Loosen the oil pump bleed screw (**Figure 2**) and allow fluid to escape around the plug threads until no air bubbles are noted in the fluid. Then, tighten the plug securely.
3. Recheck the fluid level in the reservoir and add as required.
4. Run the pump motor while rechecking the oil level. Add fluid as necessary. Run the unit fully UP and fully DOWN through at least 5 cycles, adding fluid as required when the cylinders are fully extended.
5. It may be necessary to charge the battery after this procedure. See Chapter Seven.

Troubleshooting

If a problem occurs in the power trim/tilt system, the initial step is to determine whether the problem is in the electric or hydraulic system. Electrical tests are covered in this chapter. If the problem appears to be in the hydraulic system, refer it to a qualified marine specialist for repair.

To determine if the problem is in the electric or hydraulic system, proceed as follows:

1. Remove the SelecTrim/Tilt assembly from the port and starboard transom bracket assembly as outlined in this chapter.
2. Mount the SelecTrim/Tilt assembly in a suitable holding fixture.
3. Make sure the plug-in connectors are properly engaged and all terminals and wires are free of corrosion. Clean and tighten as necessary.
4. Make sure the battery is fully charged. Charge or replace the battery as necessary.
5. Check the system fuse.
6. Check the fluid level as described in this chapter.
7. Use OMC Trim/Tilt In-Line Pressure Tester part No. 983977 to test hydraulic system. Attach the tester as follows to isolate specific components or circuits:

WARNING
Momentarily operate the trim/tilt motor in the UP direction, then the DOWN direction prior to loosening any fittings. Open the manual release valve one full turn to relieve any residual hydraulic pressure that may be present, then close the valve. To prevent personal injury, make sure suitable eye protection is worn and cover line fittings with a shop towel prior to loosening.

a. *Test trim-out/tilt-up side of the valve body and base of the hydraulic cylinder (isolate cylinder from gauge)*—Remove the oil line from the base of the cylinder. Connect the tester line between the fitting at the base of the cylinder and port "B" on the tester.

13

Connect the oil line removed from the base of cylinder to port "A" on the tester.

b. *Test trim-out/tilt-up side of the valve body and base of the hydraulic cylinder (isolate valve body from gauge)*—Remove the oil line from the base of the cylinder. Connect the tester line between the fitting at the base of the cylinder and port "A" on the tester. Connect the oil line removed from the base of the cylinder to port "B" on the tester.

c. *Test trim-in/tilt-down side of the valve body and top of the hydraulic cylinder (isolate cylinder from gauge)*—Remove the oil line from the top of the cylinder. Connect the tester line between the fitting at the top of the cylinder and port "B" on the tester. Connect the oil line removed from the top of the cylinder to port "A" on the tester.

d. *Test trim-in/tilt-down side of the valve body and the top of the hydraulic cylinder (isolate valve body from gauge)*—Remove the oil line from the top of the cylinder. Connect the tester line between the fitting at the top of the cylinder and port "A" on the tester. Connect the oil line removed from the top of the cylinder to port "B" on tester.

8. Open the shut-off valve in the tester (opposite side of port "B") one full turn counterclockwise.

9. Operate the unit UP and DOWN several cycles, then recheck the fluid level and add as necessary.

10. When the trim/tilt motor is operated in the direction to extend the cylinder (UP direction), and OMC Trim/Tilt In-Line Pressure Tester part No. 983977 is attached as outlined in Step 7a or Step 7b, the following pressures should be noted:

a. Pressure gauge should read approximately 250 psi (1724 kPa) as the trim/tilt cylinder is extending and approximately 1800 psi (12,411 kPa) as the unit stalls. The pressure gauge should not drop by more than 200 psi (1379 kPa) in 5 minutes from the stall reading when the trim/tilt motor is stopped. If leakage is noted, refer to Step 7a or 7b.

b. With the cylinder operated through a complete extended (UP) circuit, close the shut-off valve in the tester and watch the pressure gauge. The pressure gauge will show if leakage is present in the valve body if the pressure gauge is attached as outlined in Step 7a or in the hydraulic cylinder if the pressure gauge is attached as outlined in Step 7b.

11. When the trim/tilt motor is operated in the direction to retract the cylinder (DOWN direction) and OMC Trim/Tilt In-Line Pressure Tester pat No. 983977 is attached as outlined in Step 7c or Step 7d, the following pressures should be noted:

a. The pressure gauge should indicate approximately 800 psi (5516 kPa) as the trim/tilt cylinder is retracting and as the unit stalls. The gauge should not drop by more than 200 psi (1379 kPa) in 5 minutes from the stall reading when the trim/tilt motor is stopped. If leakage is noted, refer to Step 7c or 7d.

b. With the cylinder operated through a complete retracted (DOWN) circuit, close the shut-off valve and observe the pressure gauge. The gauge will show if leakage is present in the valve body if the gauge is attached as outlined in Step 7c or in the hydraulic cylinder if the gauge is attached as outlined in Step 7d.

12. If the system fails any part of Step 10 or Step 11, the problem is hydraulic. If the hydraulic systems checks out satisfactorily, the problem is in the electric system.

Trim and Tilt Switch Circuit Test

Refer to **Figure 5** for this procedure.

1. With the key switch ON, connect the voltmeter red test lead to point E1 in the trim/tilt junction box. Connect the black test lead to point G in the trim/tilt junction box. The meter should indicate battery voltage.

2. If the battery voltage is not shown in Step 1, move the red test lead to point J1 in the battery junction box. If battery voltage is noted, check the battery junction box 50 amp fuse. If the fuse is good, look for poor connections or an open circuit in the fuse holder and connecting wiring.

3. Move the red test lead to point E3 in the trim/tilt junction box. Move the trim/tilt switch to the DOWN position. If battery voltage is noted, move the red test lead to points E4 and E5. With the trim/tilt switch in the DOWN position, battery voltage should be present at each point. If voltage is noted, and the trim motor does not run, probe connector C2 at the pump motor. If voltage is shown at the connector and the motor does not run, test the motor as outlined in this chapter.

4. If no voltage is noted at point E3 in Step 3, check connector C1 between the trim/tilt junction box and trim/tilt switch. If the connector is good, check for an open circuit in the following:

   a. Green/orange wire between the trim/tilt switch and trim/tilt junction box.

   b. Trim/tilt switch between the green/orange and purple wires with the switch in the DOWN position.

5. Move the red test lead to point E6 in the trim/tilt junction box. Move the trim/tilt switch to the UP position. If battery voltage is noted, move the red test lead to points E7 and E8. With the trim/tilt switch in the UP position, there should be voltage at each point. If voltage is noted, and the trim motor does not run, probe connector C2 at the pump motor. If voltage is shown at the connector and the motor does not run, test the motor as described in this chapter.

6. If no voltage is noted at point E6 in Step 5, check connector C1 between the trim/tilt junction box and trim/tilt switch. If the connector is good, check for an open circuit in the following:

   a. Blue/orange wire between the trim/tilt switch and junction box.

   b. Trim/tilt switch between the blue/orange and purple wires with the switch in the UP position.

Trim Indicator Circuit Test

Refer to **Figure 5** for this procedure.

1. Turn the key switch ON.

2. Connect the voltmeter red test lead to point E9 on the indicator gauge. Connect the black test lead to the indicator G terminal. If battery voltage is noted, continue at Step 5.

3. If battery voltage is not noted in Step 2, move the red test lead to point E10 (accessory plug). If voltage is noted, an open circuit is present between the accessory plug and the trim indicator gauge.

4. If no voltage is noted in Step 3, move the red test lead to the accessory terminal on the key switch. If no voltage is noted at the accessory terminal, look for a bad fuse or an open in the key switch wiring. If the fuse and wiring are good, replace the switch.

5. Turn the key switch to OFF.

6. Disconnect the black/orange wire at the indicator gauge S terminal. With an ohmmeter on the low-ohm scale, connect the red test lead to the disconnected black/orange wire and the black test lead to the indicator gauge G terminal.

   a. With the outboard fully trimmed in (DOWN), the ohmmeter should indicate 82-88 ohms.

   b. With the outboard fully tilted UP, the ohmmeter should indicate 0-10 ohms.

7. If resistance is not as specified, check for an open circuit in the ground wire between the indicator gauge and the trim/tilt junction box or in the black/orange wire disconnected from the indicator gauge S terminal.

8. If the wiring is good, disconnect the black sending unit leads at the terminal strip in the trim/tilt junction box. Connect an ohmmeter between the disconnected sender leads and check the resistance of the sending unit. If not within

13

the specifications in Step 6, replace the sending unit (**Figure 6**).

Trim and Tilt Motor Amperage Test

This test evaluates the pump output pressure by determining the current requirements of the pump motor (**Figure 7**). Readings must be taken with the boat at rest.

1. Connect an ammeter between the positive battery terminal and the heavy red cable at the battery junction box.

2. Move the trim/tilt switch to the UP position and note the meter reading, then move the trim/tilt switch to the DOWN position and note the reading.

3. Compare the readings obtained in Step 2 to the specifications in **Table 1**.

   a. If the current draw is within specifications, the motor, hydraulic pump and relief valves are functioning properly.

   b. Low current draw indicates a malfunctioning pump, leaking valves, weak relief valves or leaking O-rings on the valve bodies.

   c. High current draw in either the UP or DOWN direction indicates a problem in the electric motor or hydraulic pump, or the relief valves are opening at too high pressure. With the motor separated from the hydraulic pump, perform a no-load current draw test as described in this chapter.

No-load Current Draw Test

1. Separate the electric motor (**Figure 7**) from the hydraulic pump.

2. Connect an ammeter in series with the motor and a fully charged battery. Connect the motor blue wire (UP) to the negative battery terminal and the motor green wire (DOWN) to the positive battery terminal. The motor shaft should rotate counterclockwise. Note the ammeter read-

ing. Reverse the motor leads and note the ammeter reading.

3. Ammeter should read a current draw of 7 amps at a minimum of 6700 rpm.

4. If the current draw is not as specified, repair or replace the motor.

System Removal/Installation

1. Disconnect the battery cables from the battery.

2. Remove the remote fluid reservoir from the mounting bracket and pour the fluid into a suitable container.

3. Disconnect the trim sender and electric motor wiring harnesses.

4. Rotate the manual release valve counterclockwise 2 full turns.

5. Use a lifting device or physically tilt the outboard motor outward until the motor tilt lock arms (**Figure 8**) can be engaged to secure the motor at the highest tilt position.

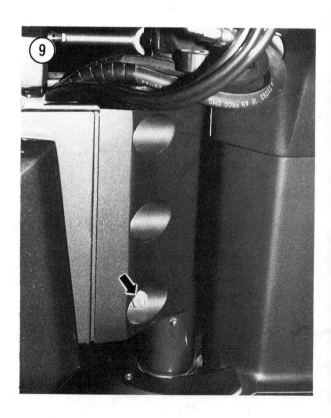

6. Mark the sending unit for reference during installation, then loosen the sending unit bracket mounting screws.

7. Loosen the cylinder support mounting screws, then slide the support up on the slotted holes and retighten the screws.

8. Place a sling around the midsection of the outboard motor and use a suitable hoist to support the assembly, thus relieving the load on the hydraulic cylinder.

9. Remove one screw from the hydraulic cylinder upper pin (**Figure 9**).

10. Use a suitable punch and mallet to drive the hydraulic cylinder upper pin from the swivel bracket.

11. With the outboard motor supported in the fully tilted UP position, release the tilt lock arms. Allow the outboard motor to lower until the tilt lock arms can be engaged in the lowest tilt lock position.

12. Remove the bushings from the hydraulic cylinder upper eyelet.

13. Remove the 4 screws securing the anchor bracket to the port and starboard transom bracket assembly. Pull the SelecTrim/Tilt assembly forward enough to allow the sending unit and electric motor wiring harnesses to be pulled through the lower transom cutout.

14. Withdraw the SelecTrim/Tilt assembly while slowly guiding the remote reservoir through the lower transom cutout.

15. Installation is the reverse of removal. Note the following during installation.

   a. Apply Scotch-Grip Rubber Adhesive 1300 to the anchor bracket gasket.

   b. The 2 disc locks for each of the 4 anchor plate mounting screws must be installed on the screws with the interlocking (teethed) side facing each other. Tighten the screws to 45-50 ft.-lb. (61-68 N·m).

   c. Tighten the screw retaining the hydraulic cylinder upper tilt pin to 18-20 ft.-lb. (24-27 N·m). See **Figure 9**.

   d. Apply terminal grease on the terminals in connector C2 (**Figure 5**). Apply terminal grease on the back side of the connector ends after assembling the connector.

   e. Refill the hydraulic system as outlined under *Hydraulic Pump Fluid Refill* in this chapter.

Table 1 CURRENT DRAW (AMPS) AND DURATION (UNDER LOAD CONDITIONS)

1.6 Sea Drive		
	Amps	**Time (seconds)**
Trimming up	12-14	11-14
Tilting up	15-17	12-16
Full tilt up (stall)	25-30	–
Tilting down	11-13	12-16
Trimming down	13-15	11-14
Full trim down (stall)	22-26	–
Trimmed in to full tilt up	–	24-29
Full tilted up to trim in	–	23-28
2.0, 3.0 & 4.0 Sea Drive		
	Amps	**Time (seconds)**
Trimming up	13-15	10-12
Tilting up	13-15	27-31
Tilting down	11-13	25-29
Trimming down	11-13	9-12
Trimmed in to full tilt up	–	38-44
Full tilted up to trim in	–	36-41

13

Chapter Fourteen

Jet Drives

Four jet drives were introduced in 1991. The jet drive models are based on the following outboard models:

a. *35 Jet*—2-cylinder loop charged models (40-50 hp).
b. *65 Jet and 80 Jet*—V4 cross flow models (85-115 hp).
c. *105 Jet*—1991 V6 cross flow models (150 hp).
d. *105 Jet*—1992-on 60° V6 models (150 hp).

Service on the power head and its related components and power trim and tilt assembly is the same as on propeller-driven models. Refer to the appropriate chapter and service section for the engine models or component serviced. Only service on the jet drive assembly is covered in this chapter.

MAINTENANCE

Outboard Mounting Height

A jet drive outboard must be mounted higher on the transom plate than an equivalent propeller-driven outboard motor. However, if the jet drive is mounted too high, air will be allowed to enter the jet drive resulting in cavitation and power loss. If the jet drive is mounted too low, excessive drag, water spray and loss in speed will result.

To set the initial height of the outboard motor, proceed as follows:

1. Place a straightedge against the boat bottom (not keel) and abut the end of the straightedge with the jet drive intake.

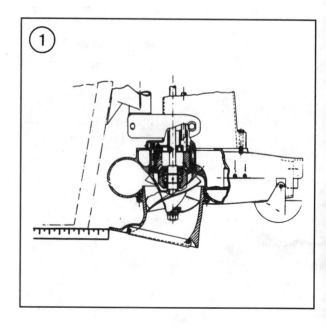

2. The fore edge of the water intake housing should align with the top edge of the straightedge (**Figure 1**).

3. Secure the outboard motor at the setting, then test run the boat.

4. If cavitation occurs (overrevving and loss of thrust), the outboard motor must be lowered 1/4 in. (6.35 mm) at a time until uniform operation is noted.

5. If uniform operation is noted with the initial setting, the outboard motor should be raised at 1/4 in. (6.35 mm) increments until cavitation is noted. Then lower the motor to the last uniform setting.

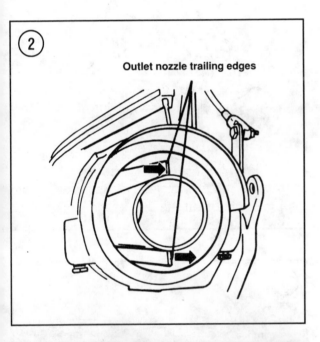

Outlet nozzle trailing edges

NOTE
The outboard motor should be in a vertical position when the boat is on plane. Adjust the motor trim setting as needed. If the outboard trim setting is altered, the outboard motor height must be checked and adjusted, if needed, as previously outlined.

Steering Torque

A minor adjustment to the trailing edge of the drive outlet nozzle may be made if the boat tends to pull in one direction when the boat and outboard are pointed in a straight-ahead direction. Should the boat tend to pull to the starboard side, bend the top and bottom trailing edge of the jet drive outlet nozzle 1/16 in. (1.6 mm) toward the starboard side of the jet drive. See **Figure 2**.

Bearing Lubrication

The jet drive bearing(s) should be lubricated after *each* operating period, after every 10 hours of operation and prior to storage. In addition, after every 50 hours of operation, additional grease should be pumped into the bearing(s) to purge any moisture. The bearing(s) is lubricated by first removing the vent hose on the side of the jet drive housing to expose the grease fitting. See **Figure 3**. Use a grease gun and inject OMC Wheel Bearing Grease into the fitting until grease exits from the end of the hose.

Note the color of the grease being expelled from the hose. During the break-in period some discoloration of the grease is normal. After the break-in period, if the grease starts to turn a dark or dirty gray, then the jet drive assembly should be disassembled as outlined under *Jet Drive* and the seals and bearing(s) inspected and replaced as necessary. If excessive moisture is expelled from the grease vent hose, then the jet drive should be disassembled and the seals replaced and the bearing(s) inspected and replaced as needed.

14

Directional Control

The boat's operational direction is controlled by a thrust gate via a cable and lever. When the directional control lever is placed in the full forward position, the thrust gate should completely uncover the jet drive housing's outlet nozzle opening and seat securely against the rubber pad on the jet drive pump housing. When the directional control lever is placed in full reverse position, the thrust gate should completely close off the pump housing's outlet nozzle opening. Neutral position is located midway between complete forward and complete reverse position.

Shift Cable Adjustment
(Shift Cam Models)

The directional control cable is properly adjusted if after placing the directional control lever in the full FORWARD position, the thrust gate *cannot* be moved into the NEUTRAL position by hand.

> *WARNING*
> *Shift cable adjustment must be correct or water pressure from the boat's forward movement can engage the thrust gate, causing REVERSE to engage unexpectedly.*

To adjust the shift cable, proceed as follows:
1. Place the remote control shift lever and the shift cam (**Figure 4**) in the NEUTRAL position. Adjust the shift cable trunnion to obtain this setting, then install the cable on its anchor and lock in place. Install the shift cable end on the shift cam stud. Install the washer and nut on the stud and finger tighten.
2. Shift the remote control shift lever into FORWARD.
3. When the roller (**Figure 4**) is in the FORWARD position, attempt to move the thrust gate upward (toward REVERSE). If the thrust gate can be moved upward, toward REVERSE posi-

tion, adjust the cable trunnion as necessary to prevent the gate from moving toward REVERSE.
4. After the correct adjustment is obtained, tighten the cable end retaining nut until it bottoms, then back the nut off 1/8 to 1/4 turn.

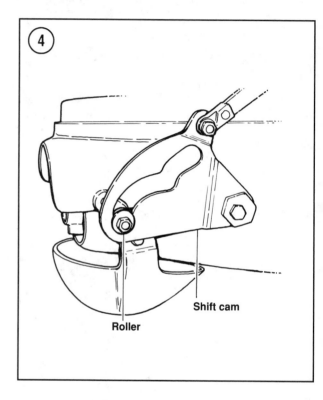

Shift cam

Roller

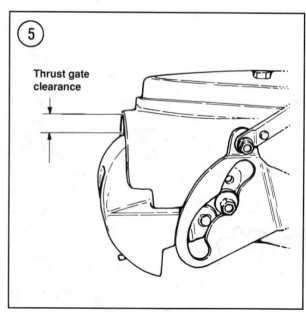

Thrust gate clearance

Thrust Gate Adjustment
(Shift Cam Models)

1. Place the remote control in the NEUTRAL position.

2. Hold the thrust gate up and check for the correct clearance between the thrust gate and water passage as shown in **Figure 5**. The clearance should be:

a. *35 Jet—9/16 in. (23.9 mm).*
b. *65, 80 and 105 Jet—15/32 in. (11.9 mm).*

3. If adjustment is necessary, loosen the lockscrew and turn the eccentric nut as necessary to obtain the correct adjustment. See **Figure 6**.

4. Check the shift cable adjustment. Adjust the cable as necessary.

Shift Cable Adjustment
(Shift Linkage Models)

The shift cable is properly adjusted if, after placing the remote control lever in the FORWARD position, the link between the thrust gate and the lower arm of the control cable pivot bracket are in alignment (**Figure 7**). The thrust gate should seat securely against the rubber pad on the jet drive pump housing.

> *WARNING*
> *Always use the lower hole of the thrust gate lever to attach the control linkage. See arrow,* **Figure 7**.

1. If adjustment is necessary, remove the shift cable from the shift lever and cable anchor.

2. Adjust the cable trunnion so, when reinstalled, the thrust gate is firmly seated against the rubber pad on the pump housing with the shift lever in the FORWARD position.

3. Reinstall the shift cable into its anchor and lock in place. Install the cable end retaining washer and locknut. Tighten the nut until bottomed, then back off 1/8 to 1/4 turn.

Impeller Clearance

If a loss of high speed performance and/or a higher than normal full throttle engine speed (not boat speed) is evident, check the clearance between the edge of the impeller and the water intake casing liner.

> *NOTE*
> *Impeller wear can occur quickly when operated in water with excessive silt, sand or gravel.*

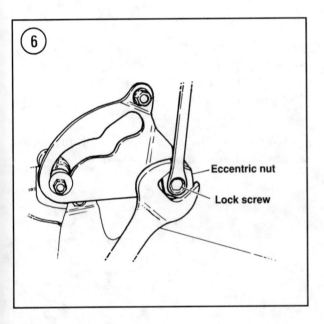

(6)

Eccentric nut

Lock screw

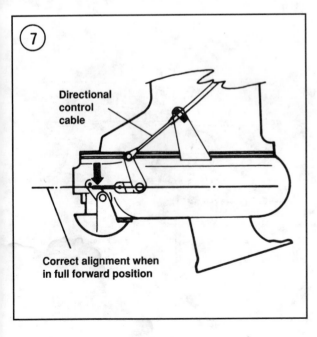

(7)

Directional control cable

Correct alignment when in full forward position

14

1. Disconnect the spark plug leads to prevent accidental starting.

2. Insert a selection of feeler gauge thicknesses through the clearance between the impeller blades and the intake liner. See **Figure 8**.

3. The impeller-to-liner clearance should be approximately 0.020-0.030 in. (0.5-0.8 mm).

4. If the clearance is not as specified, remove the 6 water intake housing mounting screws. Remove the intake housing.

5. Bend the tabs on the tab washer retaining the jet drive impeller nut to allow a suitable tool to be installed on the impeller nut. Remove the nut, tab washer, lower shims impeller, impeller key, impeller sleeve and upper shims. Note the number of lower and upper shims.

> *NOTE*
> *Lubricate the impeller shaft, impeller sleeve, and key with OMC Triple-Guard grease prior to reassembly.*

6. If clearance is excessive, remove shims as needed from below the impeller (lower shims) and position them above the impeller.

7. Install the impeller with the selected number of shims.

8. Install a new tab washer and impeller retaining nut on the drive shaft. Tighten the nut to 16-18 ft.-lb. (22-24 N•m). Do not bend the tabs on the tab washer at this time.

9. Apply OMC Gasket Sealing Compound to the threads of the intake housing retaining screws. Install the housing and screws. Tighten the screws finger tight.

10. Rotate the impeller to check for rubbing or binding.

11. Repeat Steps 2 and 3 to recheck impeller clearance. Readjust clearance as necessary.

12. After correct clearance is obtained, remove the intake housing screws and housing. Make sure the impeller nut is tightened to 16-18 ft.-lb. (22-24 N•m), then lock the nut in place with the tab washer.

13. Reinstall the intake housing. Make sure the housing is centered on the pump assembly and tighten the housing screws, in a crossing pattern, to 10-12 ft.-lb. (14-16 N•m).

Cooling System Cleaning

The cooling system can become plugged by sand and salt deposits if it is not flushed occasionally. Clean the cooling system after each use in saltwater.

1. Remove the plug and gasket from the port side of the jet drive pump housing to gain access to the flush passage. See **Figure 9**.

2. Install a suitable flushing adapter into the flush passage.

3. Connect a suitable freshwater supply to the adapter and turn on to full pressure.

> *CAUTION*
> *When the outboard motor is running, make sure a stream of water is noted being discharged from the motor's tell-tale outlet. If not, stop the motor immediately and correct the problem.*

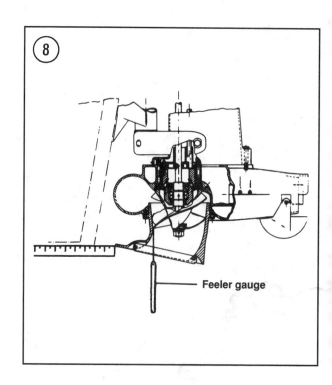

⑧

Feeler gauge

4. Start the motor and allow the freshwater to circulate for approximately 15 minutes.

5. Stop the motor, turn off the water supply and disconnect the water supply from the adapter. Remove the adapter and install the plug.

6. Using the hose, direct a freshwater supply into the intake passage housing area to flush the impeller and intake housing.

WATER PUMP

The water pump is mounted on top of the aluminum spacer on all models. The impeller is driven by a key which engages a groove in the drive shaft and a cutout in the impeller hub. As the drive shaft rotates, the impeller rotates with it. Water between the impeller blades and pump

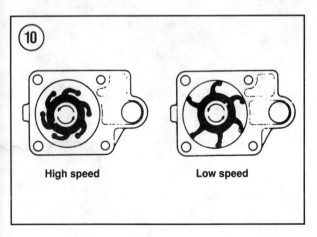

High speed   Low speed

housing is pumped up to the power head through the water tube.

The offset center of the pump housing causes the impeller vanes to flex during rotation. At low speeds, the pump acts as a positive displacement type; at high speeds, water resistance forces the vanes to flex inward and the pump becomes a centrifugal type. See **Figure 10**.

All gaskets should be replaced whenever the water pump is removed. Since proper water pump operation is critical to outboard operation, it is also a good idea to install a new impeller at the same time. To service the water pump, remove the jet drive assembly as described in this chapter and refer to the appropriate service section in Chapter Nine.

JET DRIVE

When removing the jet drive mounting fasteners, it is not uncommon to find that they are corroded. Such fasteners should be discarded and new ones installed. Apply OMC Gasket Sealing Compound to the threads of the mounting screws.

Removal

Refer to **Figure 11** or **Figure 12** for this procedure.

1. Disconnect the spark plug leads to prevent accidental starting.

2. Tilt the outboard to the fully UP position and engage the tilt lock lever.

3. Remove the shift cable from the shift cam or lever.

4. Remove the intake grate and the six intake housing mounting screws. Remove the intake housing. See **Figure 11** or **Figure 12**.

5. Bend the tabs on the impeller nut tab washer. Remove the impeller nut and tab washer. Discard the tab washer.

14

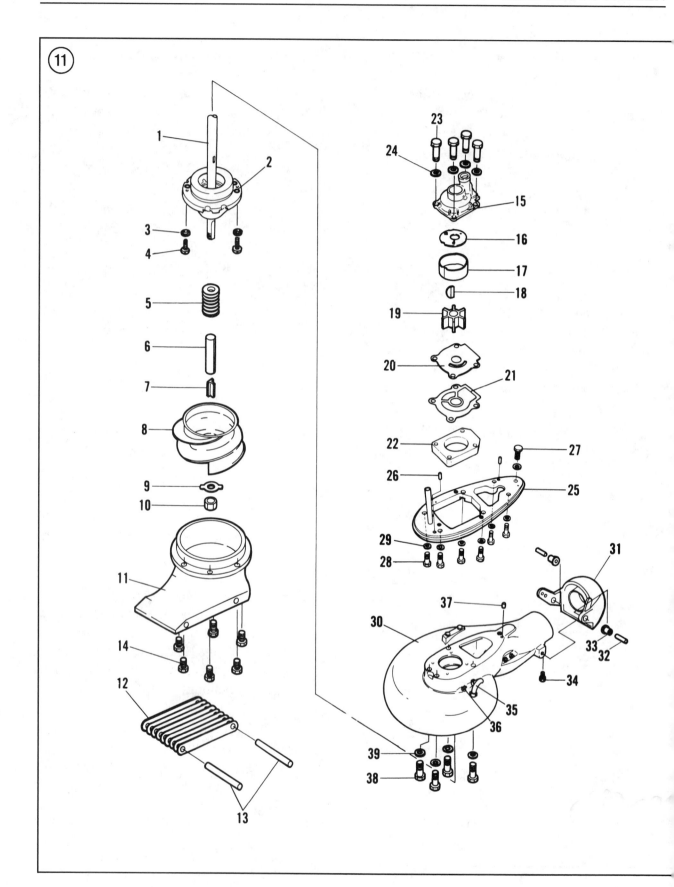

JET DRIVE ASSEMBLY
(35 JET)

1. Drive shaft and
   bearing housing assembly
2. O-ring
3. Lockwasher
4. Screw
5. Shims
6. Nylon sleeve
7. Impeller drive key
8. Impeller
9. Tab washer
10. Nut
11. Intake housing
12. Intake grill
13. Grill rods
14. Allen screws
15. Water pump housing
16. Plate
17. Pump insert
18. Impeller key
19. Impeller
20. Plate
21. Gasket
22. Water pump adapter
23. Bolts
24. Lockwashers
25. Adapter plate
26. Dowel pin
27. Bolts
28. Bolts
29. Lockwasher
30. Jet pump housing
31. Reverse gate
32. Pivot pin
33. Nylon sleeve
34. Bolt
35. Grease hose
36. Grease fitting
37. Dowel pin
38. Bolt
39. Lockwasher

NOTE
Note the number and location of impeller adjustment shims for reference during reassembly.

6. Remove the shims located below the impeller and note the number. Remove the impeller and the shims located above the impeller and note the number.

7. Slide the impeller sleeve and drive key off the drive shaft.

8. Remove the 4 screws located on the inside of the jet drive pump housing and adjacent to the bearing housing. Also remove the screw at the external bottom aft end of the intermediate housing which secures the jet drive pump housing to the adapter plate. Withdraw the jet drive assembly.

Installation

Refer to **Figure 11** or **Figure 12** for this procedure.

1. Install the fore and aft dowel pins in the jet drive housing.

2. Lubricate the drive shaft splines with OMC Triple-Guard grease. Wipe excess grease off the top of the drive shaft.

3. Apply OMC Gasket Sealing Compound to the threads of all mounting fasteners.

4. Install the jet drive assembly, making sure the drive shaft properly engages the crankshaft, the water tube enters the water pump and the lower exhaust housing does not slip out of place. Tighten the mounting screws to 18-20 ft.-lb. (14-16 N.m).

5. If the original bearing(s), bearing housing, jet drive pump housing, impeller and intake housing are being reinstalled, install the impeller shims in the same number and location from which removed. If any of the previously listed components are replaced, install all the adjustment shims below the impeller (next to retaining nut) and refer to *Impeller Clearance* in this chapter.

14

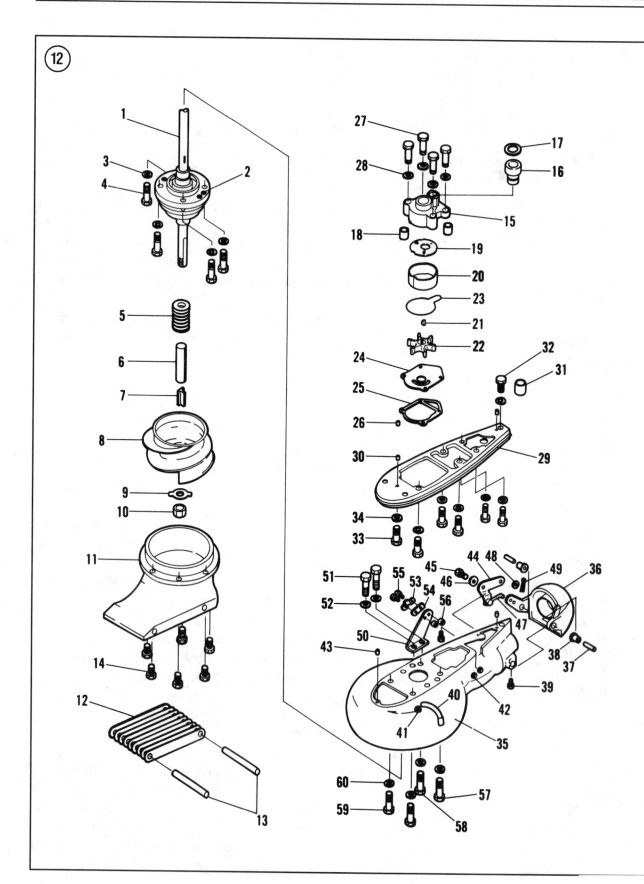

JET DRIVE ASSEMBLY
(65, 80 AND 105 JET)

1. Drive shaft and bearing
   housing assembly
2. O-ring
3. Lockwasher
4. Bolt
5. Shims
6. Nylon sleeve
7. Impeller drive key
8. Impeller
9. Tab washer
10. Nut
11. Intake housing
12. Intake grill
13. Grill rods
14. Bolts
15. Water pump housing
16. Brass water tube
    extension
17. O-ring
18. Water pump
    adapter
19. Plate
20. Pump insert
21. Impeller drive key
22. Impeller
23. Seal ring
24. Plate
25. Gasket
26. Dowel pin
27. Bolt
28. Lockwasher
29. Adapter plate
30. Dowel pin
31. Spacer
32. Bolt
33. Bolt
34. Lockwasher
35. Jet pump housing
36. Reverse gate
37. Pivot pin
38. Nylon sleeve
39. Bolt
40. Grease hose
41. Grease fitting
42. Clamp
43. Dowel pin
44. Shift arm
45. Bolt
46. Washer
47. Rod
48. Washer
49. Cotter pin
50. Bracket
51. Bolt
52. Washer
53. Clamp
54. Clamp plate
55. Bolt
56. Lockwasher
57. Bolt
58. Bolt
59. Bolt
60. Lockwasher

6. Lubricate the drive shaft and inner bore of the impeller with OMC Triple-Guard grease. Install the impeller sleeve into the jet drive impeller bore.

7. Install the adjustment shims above the impeller as noted during removal.

8. Slide the drive key and impeller onto the drive shaft.

9. Install the shims below the impeller.

10. Install a new tab washer, then the impeller nut on the drive shaft. Tighten the nut to 16-18 ft.-lb. (22-24 N·m). If impeller clearance is correctly adjusted, bend the tabs of the tab washer over to lock the impeller nut in place. Refer to *Impeller Clearance* in this chapter.

11. Apply OMC Gasket Sealing Compound to the threads of the intake housing fasteners.

12. Install the intake housing on the pump housing. Tighten the 6 intake housing screws in a crossing pattern to 10-12 ft.-lb. (14-16 N·m).

13. Install the shift cable and adjust as outlined under *Shift Cable Adjustment* in this chapter.

14. Complete the remaining installation by reversing the removal procedure.

BEARING HOUSING

Refer to **Figures 11-14** for this procedure.

1. Remove the jet drive assembly as outlined in this chapter.

2. Remove the water pump assembly. Refer to the appropriate service section in Chapter Nine.

3. Withdraw the aluminum spacer.

4. Remove the screws and washers securing the bearing housing to the jet drive housing. Withdraw the bearing housing assembly and drive shaft from the jet drive housing and place on a clean work bench.

5. Remove the snap ring from the bore in the top of the bearing housing.

CAUTION
Do not apply excessive heat to the bearing housing, as the grease seals may be damaged.

14

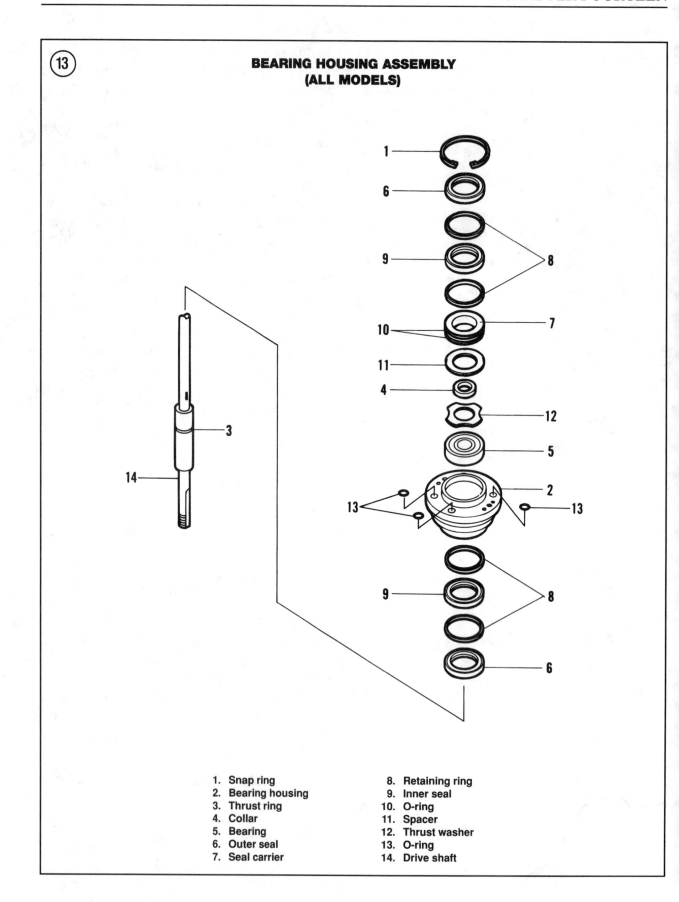

**BEARING HOUSING ASSEMBLY
(ALL MODELS)**

1. Snap ring
2. Bearing housing
3. Thrust ring
4. Collar
5. Bearing
6. Outer seal
7. Seal carrier
8. Retaining ring
9. Inner seal
10. O-ring
11. Spacer
12. Thrust washer
13. O-ring
14. Drive shaft

6. Apply heat to the bearing housing in increments. After each application of heat, strike the impeller end of the drive shaft against a wooden block. If the bearing housing has been heated to a sufficient temperature, the housing should slide down off the bearing(s). If not, apply additional heat to the bearing housing and reattempt removal of the bearing housing.

7. Withdraw the upper seal carrier and spacer from the drive shaft.

8. Press the bearing off the drive shaft.

9. Slide the thrust washer off the drive shaft.

10. Remove the collar and the thrust ring from the drive shaft, if needed.

11. Remove the grease seals and retaining rings from the bearing housing.

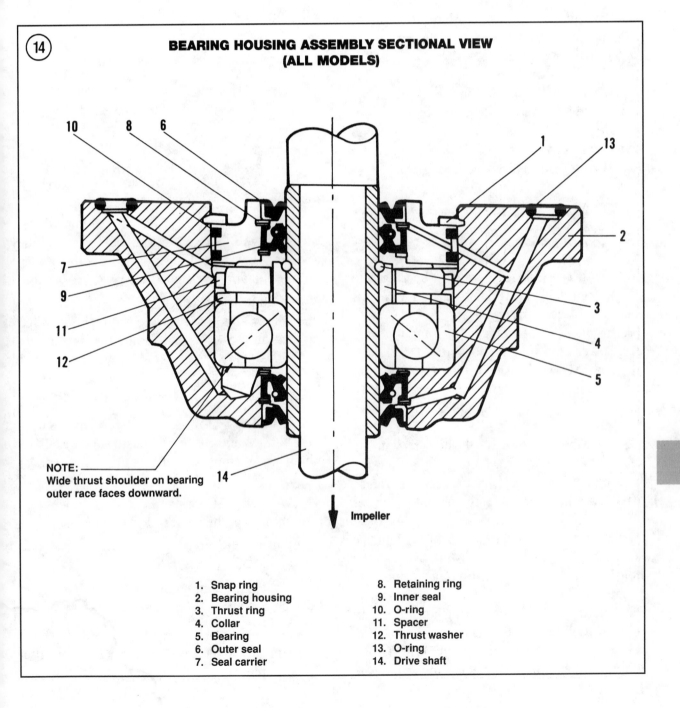

(14) **BEARING HOUSING ASSEMBLY SECTIONAL VIEW
(ALL MODELS)**

NOTE:
Wide thrust shoulder on bearing
outer race faces downward.

Impeller

1. Snap ring	8. Retaining ring
2. Bearing housing	9. Inner seal
3. Thrust ring	10. O-ring
4. Collar	11. Spacer
5. Bearing	12. Thrust washer
6. Outer seal	13. O-ring
7. Seal carrier	14. Drive shaft

14

12. Remove the grease seals and retaining rings from the upper seal carrier.

13. Clean and inspect the bearing housing, upper seal carrier and the drive shaft.

NOTE
Whenever the bearing is pressed from the drive shaft, it is recommended that the bearing be replaced.

14. Place the collar over the drive shaft with the grooved end of the collar facing the thrust ring on the shaft (**Figure 14**).

15A. *35 Jet*—Install the thrust washer onto the drive shaft with the gray teflon coated side facing toward the jet drive impeller.

15B. *All models*—Place the bearing on the shaft so the wide thrust shoulder on the bearing outer race is facing down as shown in **Figure 14**.

NOTE
Press only on the bearing inner race in Step 16 to prevent damage to the bearing.

16. Using a suitable tool, press the bearing onto the shaft until the thrust ring on the drive shaft is locked in place in the collar.

17. Install the inner seal retaining rings, one into each lower groove of the housing.

18. Apply OMC Gasket Sealing Compound to the outer diameter of the inner and outer seals. Lubricate the seal lips with OMC Triple-Guard grease.

19. Place the inner seal into the housing with the seal lip facing outward. Press the seal into the housing until seated against the retaining rings.

20. Install the outer retaining rings into the outer grooves of the housing.

21. Place the outer seal into the housing with the seal lips facing outward. Press the seal into the housing until seated against the outer retaining rings.

22. Thoroughly pack the bearing housing cavity with OMC Wheel Bearing grease.

23. Lubricate the 2 O-rings with OMC Triple-Guard grease. Install the O-rings into the grooves on the upper seal carrier. Lubricate the bearing housing bore to ease seal carrier installation.

24. Install the bearing housing onto the drive shaft and bearing assembly. Make sure the housing is properly aligned with the bearing. If the housing and bearing are properly aligned, only a small amount of pressure will be required to seat the bearing in the housing.

NOTE
A small amount of heat applied to the bearing housing will ease bearing and shaft assembly installation. Use caution not to overheat the housing as seal damage will result.

25A. *35 Jet*—Install the spacer over the collar and on top of the thrust washer.

25B. *65, 80 and 105 Jet*—Install the thrust washer with the gray teflon coating facing the bearing. Install the spacer over the collar and on top of the thrust washer.

26. Carefully press the upper seal carrier into the housing. Only light pressure should be required to seat the seal carrier if properly aligned with the housing.

27. Install the snap ring with the beveled side facing up.

28. Place new O-rings into position on the mating surface of the bearing housing and install the housing assembly into the jet drive pump housing.

29. Apply OMC Gasket Sealing Compound to the threads of the bearing housing fasteners.

30. Install the housing retaining screws and tighten to 60-84 in.-lb. (6.8-9.5 N•m).

31. Install the aluminum spacer on top of the jet drive housing.

32. Install the water pump. See Chapter Nine.

33. Install the jet drive assembly as outlined in this chapter.

INTAKE HOUSING LINER

Replacement

1. Remove the six intake housing mounting screws. Remove the intake housing. See **Figure 11** or **Figure 12**.

2. Identify the liner screws for reassembly in the same location, then remove the screws.

3. Tap the liner loose by inserting a long drift punch through the intake housing grate. Place the punch on the edge of the liner and tap with a hammer.

4. Withdraw the liner from the intake housing.

5. Install the new liner into the intake housing.

6. Align the liner screw holes with their respective intake housing holes. Tap the liner into place with a hammer if necessary.

7. Apply OMC Gasket Sealing Compound to the threads of the liner retaining screws.

8. Install the liner retaining screws and tighten securely.

9. Remove any burrs from the liner retaining screw area.

10. Apply OMC Gasket Sealing Compound to the threads of the intake housing fasteners.

11. Install the intake housing on the jet drive pump housing. Tighten the 6 fasteners in a crossing pattern to 10-12 ft.-lb. (14-16 N•m).

12. Refer to *Impeller Clearance* in this chapter.

14

Index

A

AC (alternating current)
  lighting coil. 50
Accumix oil injection 665-666
Anti-siphon devices 360
Anticorrosion maintenance 225-226

B

Battery 363-371
  charging system 50-58, 371-376
Bearing housing, jet drive 715-718
Breaker-point ignition testing
  1-cylinder models 63-65

C

Capacitor discharge ignition (CDI)
  1991-on 3 and 4 hp models 71-76
  troubleshooting 65
Carburetor 310-313
  2, 2.3 and 3.3 hp 313-316
  3 and 4 hp, 4 deluxe 316-321
  6-20 hp models 321-327
  Minlon, V4 and V6 loop
    charged models 342-351
  top feed, V4 and V6
    cross flow models 337-342
  TR and SV 25-70
    hp models 327-337
CD ignition 396-398
  all models except CD2U,
    3 and 4 hp and 60°
    V6 models 398-406
CD2 ignition system troubleshooting
  1992-on 35 Jet, 40 and 50 hp
    (except 48 hp) equipped with
    12 amp charging system 85-94
  1993-on 6-30 hp models 76-85
CD2U (under flywheel) ignition
  troubleshooting 65-71
CD2U ignition 392-396
CD3 ignition troubleshooting
  3-cylinder models 94-108

CD4 ignition system
  troubleshooting 108-116
  V4 loop charge models—
    120 and 140 hp; 2.0
    Sea Drive 116-129
CD6 ignition system troubleshooting
  1991-on V6 loop charge
    models—200 and 225 hp;
    3.0 Sea Drive 149-168
  1991 V6 cross flow models—
    105 Jet, 150 and 175 hp . . . 129-149
CD6 OIS ignition system
  troubleshooting, 60° 150
  and 175 hp models 168-179
CD8 ignition system
  troubleshooting, 1991-on
  V8 loop charged models—
  250 and 300 hp; 4.0
  Sea Drive models 179-198

E

Electric starting system 376
Electrical
  battery 363-371
  battery charging system 371-376
Engine 203-206
  flushing 226-227
  serial number 417
  temperature and overheating . 201-203
  timing and synchronization 243
Engine timing and synchronization
  1991 105 Jet, 150 and
    175 hp (90° V6 cross
    flow models) 288-290
  1991 and 1992
    60 and 70 hp, 3-cylinder
    models 263-270
  9.9 and 15 hp, 2-cylinder
    models 249-250
  1992-on 105 Jet, 1991-on
    150 and 175 hp
    (60° V6 models) 290-296

1993-on 200 and 225 hp (90°
  V6 loop charged models);
  4.0 Sea Drive, 250 and 300
  hp (90° V8 loop
  charged models) 301-304
1993-on 60 and 70 hp
  (3-cylinder models equipped
  with tiller handle) 270-274
1993-on 60 and 70 hp
  (3-cylinder models equipped
  with remote control) 274-277
1993-on 9.9 and 15 hp
  (2-cylinder models) 251-253
2.0 Sea Drive, 120 and
  140 hp (90° V4 loop
  charged models) 285-288
20, 25, 28 and 30 hp
  (2-cylinder models) 253-257
3 and 4 hp (2-cylinder
  models) 245-246
3.0 Sea Drive, 1991 and 1992
  200 and 225 hp (90° V6
  loop charged models) 296-301
35 Jet, 40, 48 and 50 hp
  (2-cylinder models) 257-263
4 deluxe models 246-247
6 and 8 hp (2-cylinder
  models) 247-249
65 Jet, 80 Jet, 1.6 Sea Drive
  and 85-115 hp (90° V4
  cross flow models) 278-284
required equipment 243-245

F

Fasteners and torque 418
Fastrak power trim/
  tilt system 653-661
  removal/installation 662-663
Flywheel 419-425
Fuel line and primer bulb 362
Fuel module and vapor separator
  60° V6 models 356-360
Fuel primer, manual 352-354

Fuel primer pump, electric
   V8 models 351-352
Fuel primer solenoid, electric. . . 354-356
Fuel pump. 307-310
Fuel system. 199-201
Fuel tank. 360-362

G

Gaskets and sealants. 418
Gearcase 556-622
   cleaning and inspection 567-569
   disassembly/reassembly 569-622
   removal/installation 556-567

I

Ignition
   CD 396-398
   CD, all models except CD2U,
     3 and 4 hp and 60°
     V6 models 398-406
   CD2U 392-396
   optical system, 60°
     V6 models 406-410
Ignition system 58-63, 390-391
   magneto breaker
     point service 391-392
Intake housing liner, jet drive. 719

J

Jet drive 711-715
   bearing housing 715-718
   intake housing liner 719
   maintenance 706-711
   water pump. 711

K

Key and neutral start switch. . . . 198-199

L

Leaf valves 523-530
Lubrication 215-220

M

Magneto breaker point ignition
   system service 391-392
Maintenance
   anticorrosion. 225-226

jet drives 706-711
Minlon carburetors, V4 and V6
   loop charged models. 342-351

N

Neutral start switch. 388-390

O

OMC variable ratio
   oiling (VRO) system. 666-672
Operating requirements 34
Optical ignition system, 60°
   V6 models. 406-410

P

Pinion gear depth, 40-70 hp,
   V4, V6 and V8 models 623-624
Power head
   crankshaft and connecting rod
     bearings cleaning and
     inspection, all models 478
   crankshaft reassembly
     and installation 498-510
   crankshaft cleaning and
     inspection 481-482
   cylinder block and crankcase
     cleaning and inspection
     all models 475-478
     general procedures 510-511
     reassembly 511-523
   disassembly. 443-475
   piston and connecting rod
     installation, all models except
     2.0- 2.3 and 3.3 hp 496-498
     reassembly 482-496
   piston cleaning and inspection
     all models 478-481
   removal/installation 425-442
Power trim/tilt assembly
   removal/installation
     40-50 hp 641-642
Power trim/tilt system
   40-50 hp 632-639
   conventional 642-650
   Fastrak. 653-661
   removal/installation
     conventional Trim/tilt. . . . 652-653
     Fastrak system 662-663
Pressure and vacuum test 624-625
Propeller 545-546

R

Rewind starter
   1991-92 9.9 and 15 hp 684-687
   2.0, 2.3 and 3.3 hp. 673-675
   20-30 hp 687-690
   3 and 4 (except 4 deluxe) hp. 675-678
   4 deluxe models 678-681
   40 hp 690-692
   6 and 8 hp; 1993-on 9.9
     and 15 hp. 681-684

S

Selectrim, 1.6 Sea Drive 693-700
Selectrim/tilt, 2.0, 3.0
   and 4.0 Sea Drives 700-705
Service precautions 543-545
Shift lever adjustment 625
Starter motor 376-388
Starting system 34-49
   electric. 376
Storage 220-224
Submersion, complete. 224-225

T

Thermostat 530-535
Top feed carburetor, V4 and
   V6 cross flow models 337-342
Touch-trim. 630-632
TR and SV carburetor
   25-70 hp models 327-337
Trim/tilt motor
   testing 640, 650-652, 661-662
Troubleshooting
   AC (alternating current)
     lighting coil. 50
   battery charging system 50-58
   breaker-point ignition testing
     1-cylinder models 63-65
   capacitor discharge
     ignition (CDI) 65
   capacitor discharge ignition
     system, 1991-on 3 and
     4 hp models. 71-76
   CD2 ignition system, 1992-on
     35 Jet, 40 and 50 hp (except
     48 hp) equipped with
     12 amp charging system 85-94
   CD2 ignition system, 1993-on
     6-30 hp models 76-85
   CD2U (under flywheel)
     ignition 65-71
   CD3 ignition system,
     3-cylinder models 94-108
   CD4 ignition system 108-116

15

Troubleshooting (continued)
   CD4 ignition system, V4 loop
      charge models—120 and
      140 hp; 2.0 Sea Drive..... 116-129
   CD6 ignition system, 1991
      V6 cross flow models—
      105 Jet, 150 and 175 hp ... 129-149
   CD6 ignition system, 1991-on
      V6 loop charge models—
      200 and 225 hp; 3.0
      Sea Drive 149-168

CD6 OIS ignition system, 60°
   150 and 175 hp models.... 168-179
CD8 ignition system, 1991-on
   V8 loop charged models—
   250 and 300 hp; 4.0 Sea
   Drive models........... 179-198
engine 203-206
engine temperature and
   overheating 201-203
fuel system 199-201
ignition system 58-63

key and neutral start switch . 198-199
operating requirements 34
starting system 34-49
Tune-up................... 227-239

W

Water pump............... 546-556
Water pump, jet drive 711

IGNITION SYSTEM
2.0, 2.3 AND 3.3 HP MODELS

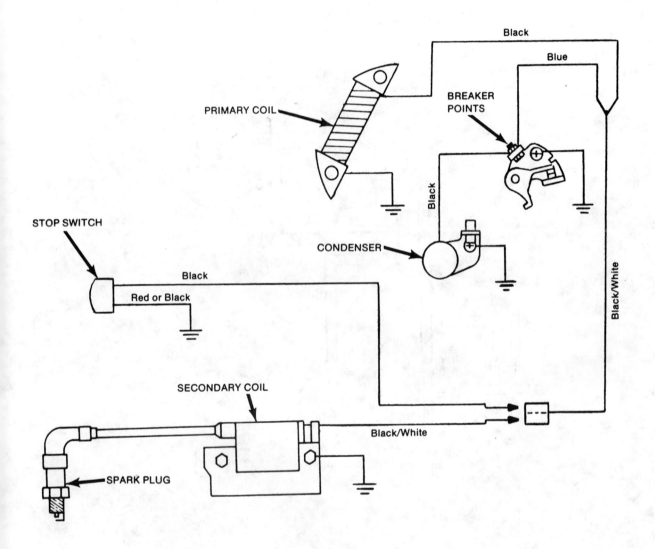

16

3 AND 4 HP

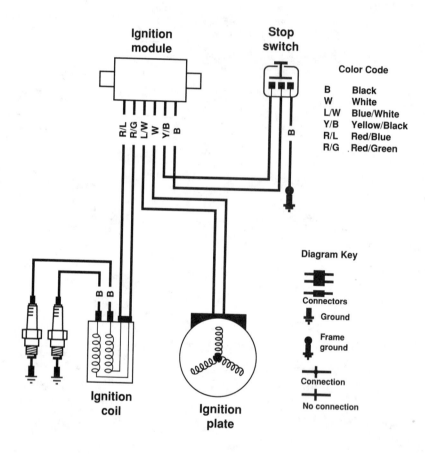

Ignition
module

Stop
switch

Color Code

B	Black
W	White
L/W	Blue/White
Y/B	Yellow/Black
R/L	Red/Blue
R/G	Red/Green

R/L R/G L/W W Y/B B

Diagram Key

Connectors

Ground

Frame
ground

Connection

No connection

Ignition
coil

Ignition
plate

UFI MODELS WITH MANUAL START AND
AC LIGHTING CONNECTOR

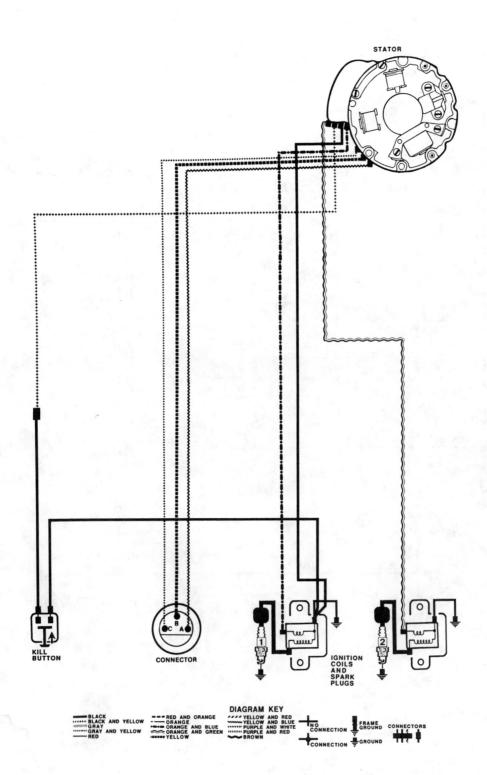

STATOR

KILL
BUTTON

CONNECTOR

IGNITION
COILS
AND
SPARK
PLUGS

16

DIAGRAM KEY

▬ BLACK	- - - RED AND ORANGE	⌁⌁⌁⌁ YELLOW AND RED
···· BLACK AND YELLOW	- · - ORANGE	⌇⌇⌇ YELLOW AND BLUE
▨ GRAY	·•· ORANGE AND BLUE	⦚⦚⦚ PURPLE AND WHITE
▤ GRAY AND YELLOW	≋≋ ORANGE AND GREEN	⦙⦙⦙ PURPLE AND RED
···· RED	▬ YELLOW	▬ BROWN

NO
CONNECTION

CONNECTION

FRAME
GROUND

GROUND

CONNECTORS

4 DELUXE — 8 HP WITH ALTERNATOR

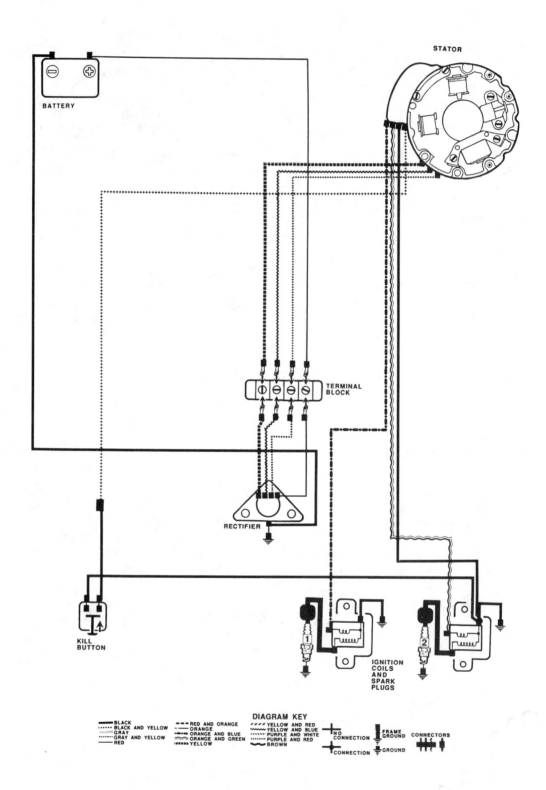

BATTERY

STATOR

TERMINAL BLOCK

RECTIFIER

KILL BUTTON

IGNITION COILS AND SPARK PLUGS

DIAGRAM KEY

BLACK
BLACK AND YELLOW
GRAY
GRAY AND YELLOW
RED

RED AND ORANGE
ORANGE
ORANGE AND BLUE
ORANGE AND GREEN
YELLOW

YELLOW AND RED
YELLOW AND BLUE
PURPLE AND WHITE
PURPLE AND RED
BROWN

NO CONNECTION
CONNECTION

FRAME GROUND
GROUND

CONNECTORS

6-15 HP ROPE START

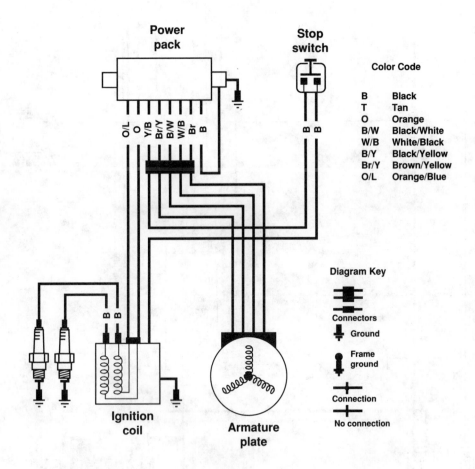

Power pack

Stop switch

Color Code

B	Black
T	Tan
O	Orange
B/W	Black/White
W/B	White/Black
B/Y	Black/Yellow
Br/Y	Brown/Yellow
O/L	Orange/Blue

O/L
O
Y/B
Br/Y
B/W
W/B
Br
B

Diagram Key

Connectors

Ground

Frame ground

Connection

No connection

B B

Ignition coil

Armature plate

16

1991-1992 9.9-15 HP REMOTE ELECTRIC START

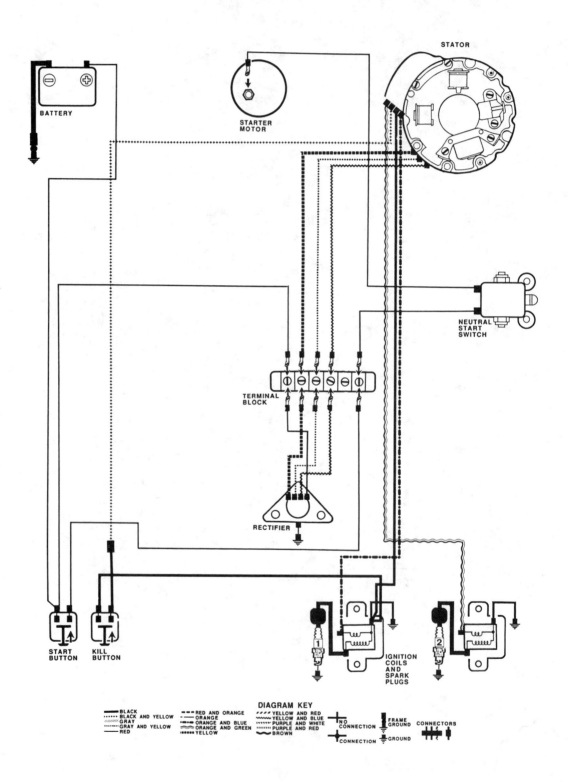

1993-ON 9.9 AND 15 HP ELECTRIC START

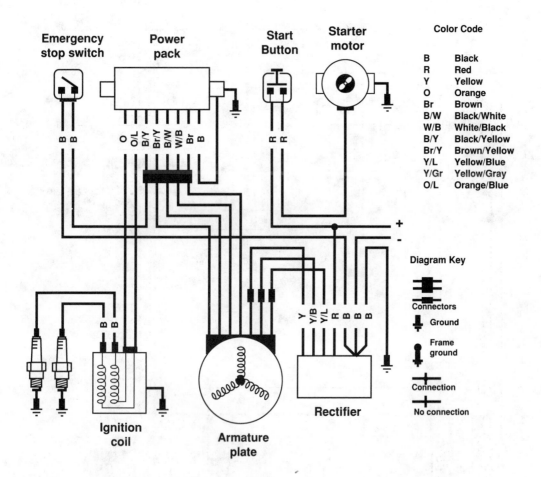

20-30 HP TILLER ELECTRIC

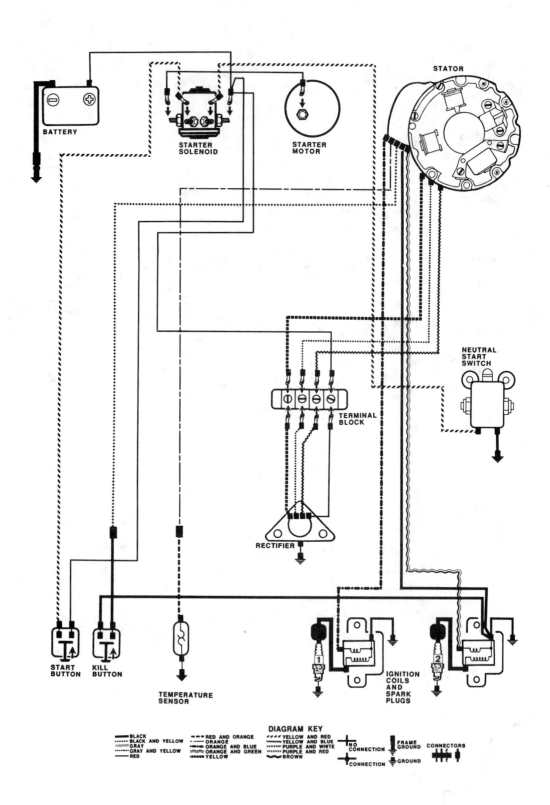

BATTERY

STARTER SOLENOID

STARTER MOTOR

STATOR

NEUTRAL START SWITCH

TERMINAL BLOCK

RECTIFIER

START BUTTON

KILL BUTTON

TEMPERATURE SENSOR

IGNITION COILS AND SPARK PLUGS

DIAGRAM KEY

BLACK	RED AND ORANGE	YELLOW AND RED
BLACK AND YELLOW	ORANGE	YELLOW AND BLUE
GRAY	ORANGE AND BLUE	PURPLE AND WHITE
GRAY AND YELLOW	ORANGE AND GREEN	PURPLE AND RED
RED	YELLOW	BROWN

NO CONNECTION

CONNECTION

FRAME GROUND

GROUND

CONNECTORS

20-30 HP REMOTE ELECTRIC START

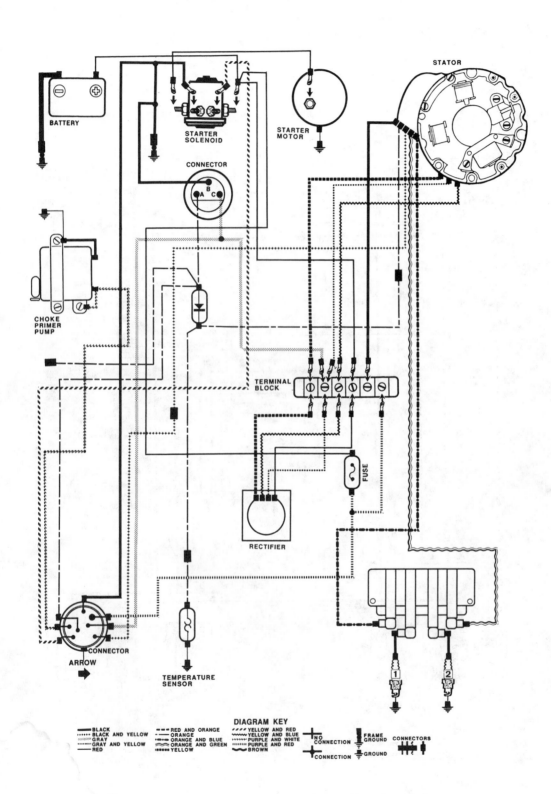

20-40 HP ROPE START

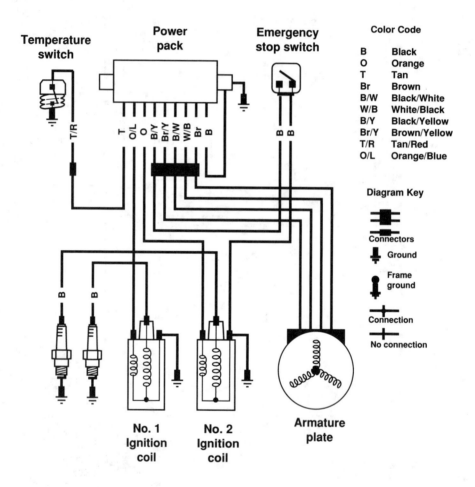

40-50 HP TILLER ELECTRIC

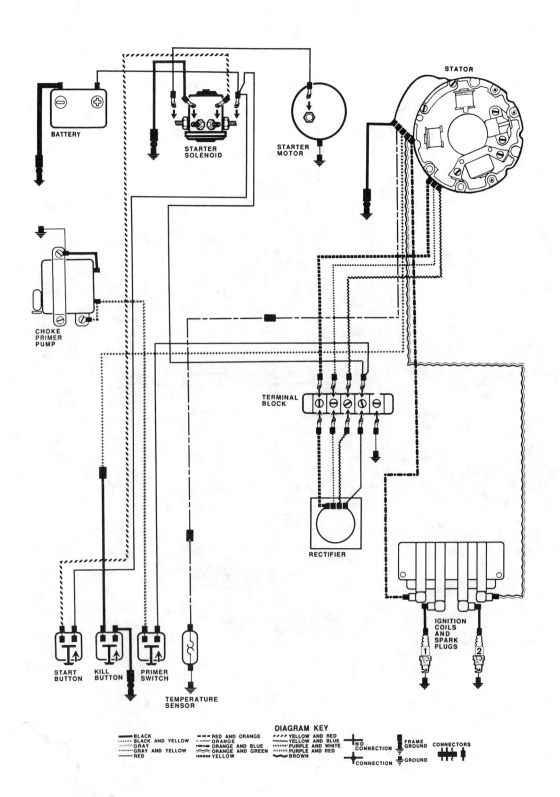

BATTERY

STARTER SOLENOID

STARTER MOTOR

STATOR

CHOKE PRIMER PUMP

TERMINAL BLOCK

RECTIFIER

IGNITION COILS AND SPARK PLUGS

START BUTTON

KILL BUTTON

PRIMER SWITCH

TEMPERATURE SENSOR

DIAGRAM KEY

BLACK
BLACK AND YELLOW
GRAY
GRAY AND YELLOW
RED
RED AND ORANGE
ORANGE
ORANGE AND BLUE
ORANGE AND GREEN
YELLOW
YELLOW AND RED
YELLOW AND BLUE
PURPLE AND WHITE
PURPLE AND RED
BROWN

NO CONNECTION
CONNECTION
FRAME GROUND
GROUND
CONNECTORS

16

40 AND 50 HP TILLER, POWER TRIM/TILT REMOTE

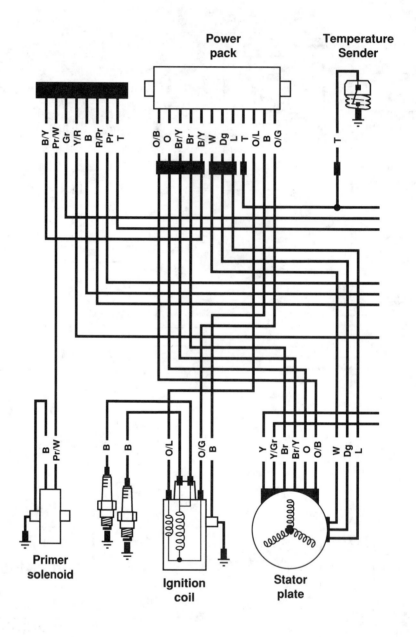

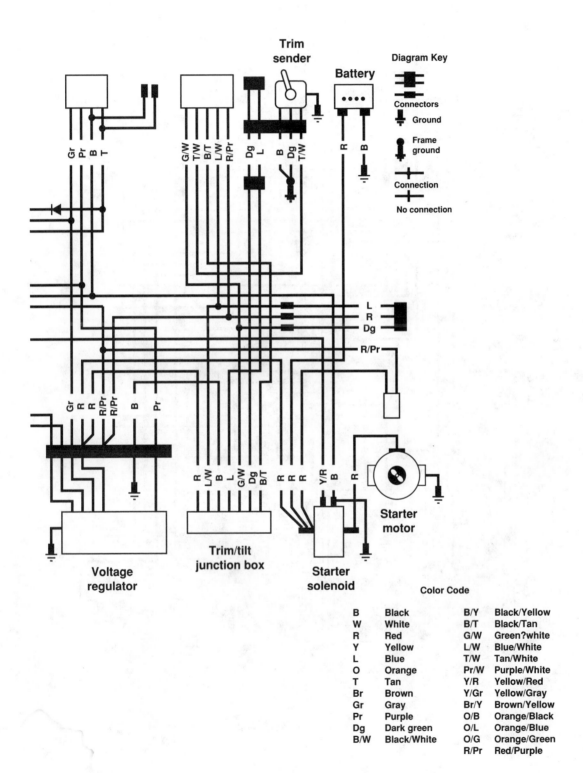

Trim sender

Battery

Diagram Key

Connectors

Ground

Frame ground

Connection

No connection

L
R
Dg

R/Pr

Starter motor

Voltage regulator

Trim/tilt junction box

Starter solenoid

Color Code

B	Black	B/Y	Black/Yellow
W	White	B/T	Black/Tan
R	Red	G/W	Green?white
Y	Yellow	L/W	Blue/White
L	Blue	T/W	Tan/White
O	Orange	Pr/W	Purple/White
T	Tan	Y/R	Yellow/Red
Br	Brown	Y/Gr	Yellow/Gray
Gr	Gray	Br/Y	Brown/Yellow
Pr	Purple	O/B	Orange/Black
Dg	Dark green	O/L	Orange/Blue
B/W	Black/White	O/G	Orange/Green
		R/Pr	Red/Purple

16

35 JET AND 40-50 HP REMOTE START

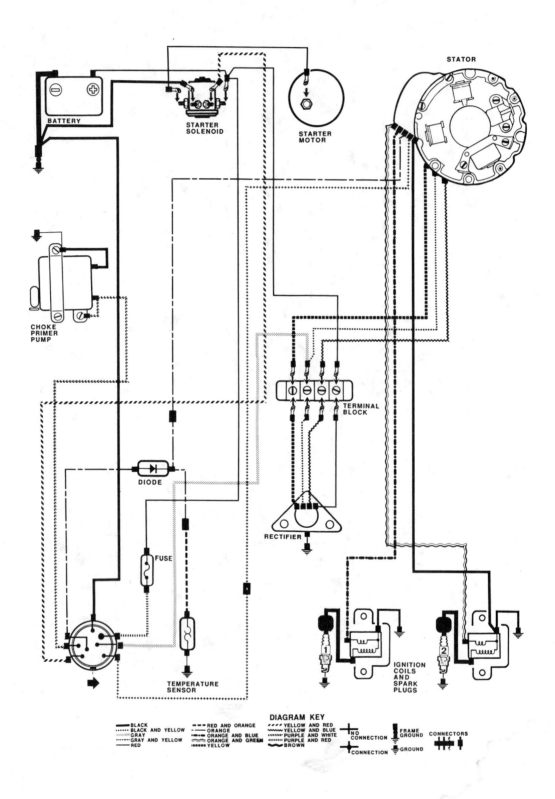

STATOR

BATTERY

STARTER
SOLENOID

STARTER
MOTOR

CHOKE
PRIMER
PUMP

TERMINAL
BLOCK

DIODE

RECTIFIER

FUSE

IGNITION
COILS
AND
SPARK
PLUGS

TEMPERATURE
SENSOR

DIAGRAM KEY

BLACK	RED AND ORANGE	YELLOW AND RED	NO CONNECTION
BLACK AND YELLOW	ORANGE	YELLOW AND BLUE	FRAME GROUND
GRAY	ORANGE AND BLUE	PURPLE AND WHITE	CONNECTORS
GRAY AND YELLOW	ORANGE AND GREEN	PURPLE AND RED	
RED	YELLOW	BROWN	CONNECTION GROUND

48 HP UFI

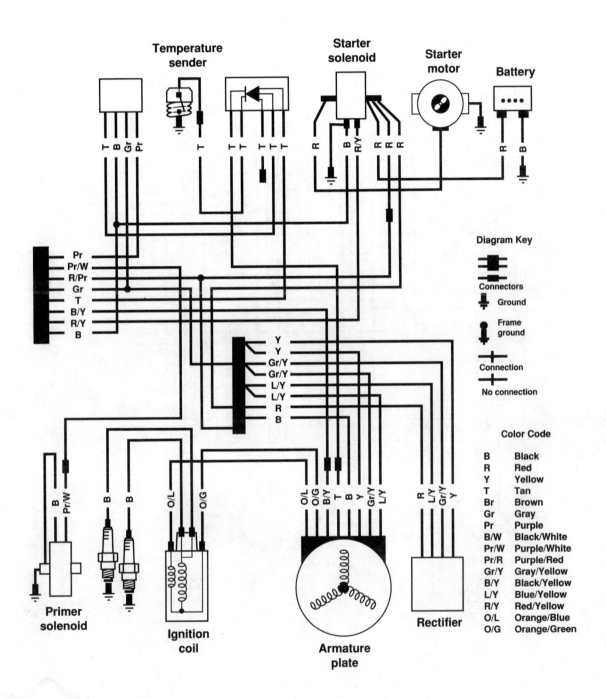

Diagram Key

Connectors

Ground

Frame ground

Connection

No connection

Color Code

B	Black
R	Red
Y	Yellow
T	Tan
Br	Brown
Gr	Gray
Pr	Purple
B/W	Black/White
Pr/W	Purple/White
Pr/R	Purple/Red
Gr/Y	Gray/Yellow
B/Y	Black/Yellow
L/Y	Blue/Yellow
R/Y	Red/Yellow
O/L	Orange/Blue
O/G	Orange/Green

Temperature sender

Starter solenoid

Starter motor

Battery

Primer solenoid

Ignition coil

Armature plate

Rectifier

16

40 AND 50 HP TILLER, POWER TRIM/TILT

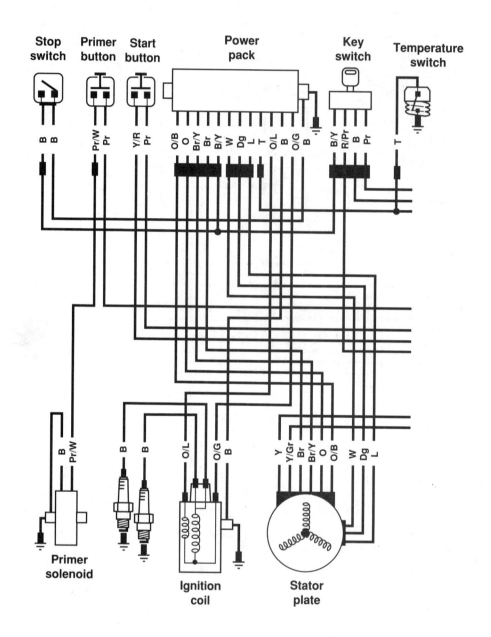

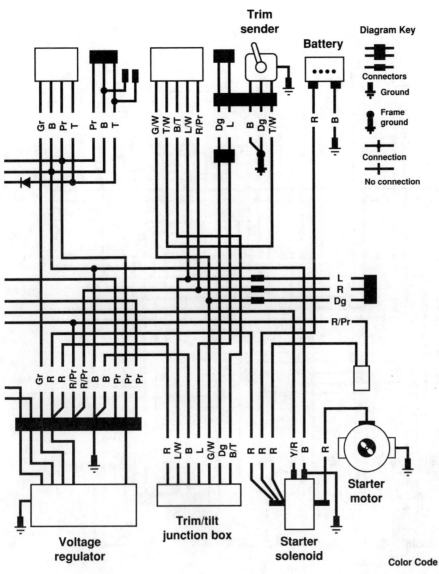

Trim sender

Battery

Diagram Key

Connectors

Ground

Frame ground

Connection

No connection

Voltage regulator

Trim/tilt junction box

Starter solenoid

Starter motor

Color Code

B	Black	B/Y	Black/Yellow
W	White	B/T	Black/Tan
R	Red	G/W	Green?white
Y	Yellow	L/W	Blue/White
L	Blue	T/W	Tan/White
O	Orange	Pr/W	Purple/White
T	Tan	Y/R	Yellow/Red
Br	Brown	Y/Gr	Yellow/Gray
Gr	Gray	Br/Y	Brown/Yellow
Pr	Purple	O/B	Orange/Black
Dg	Dark green	O/L	Orange/Blue
B/W	Black/White	O/G	Orange/Green
		R/Pr	Red/Purple

16

60 AND 70 HP TILLER, POWER TRIM/TILT

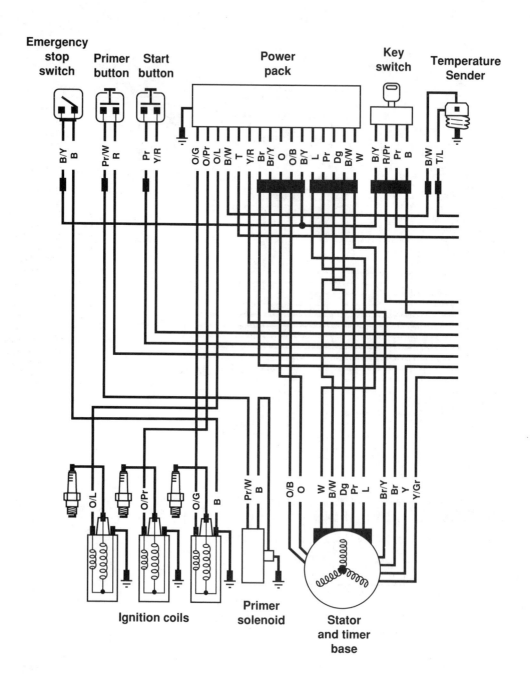

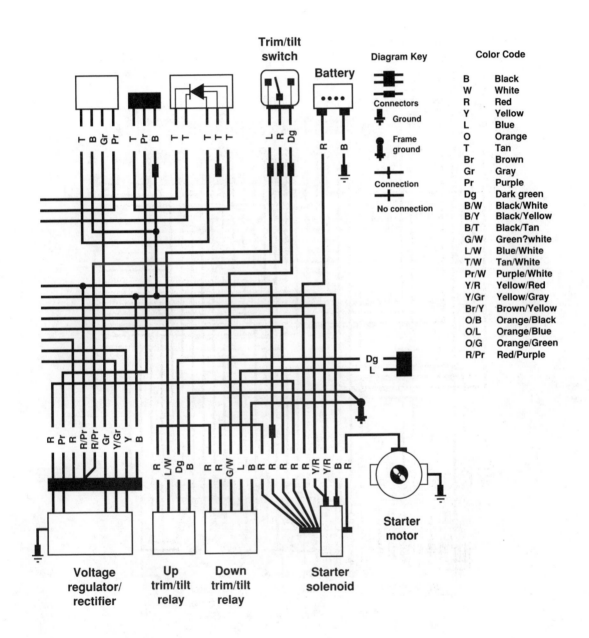

Trim/tilt switch

Battery

Diagram Key

Connectors

Ground

Frame ground

Connection

No connection

Color Code

B	Black
W	White
R	Red
Y	Yellow
L	Blue
O	Orange
T	Tan
Br	Brown
Gr	Gray
Pr	Purple
Dg	Dark green
B/W	Black/White
B/Y	Black/Yellow
B/T	Black/Tan
G/W	Green?white
L/W	Blue/White
T/W	Tan/White
Pr/W	Purple/White
Y/R	Yellow/Red
Y/Gr	Yellow/Gray
Br/Y	Brown/Yellow
O/B	Orange/Black
O/L	Orange/Blue
O/G	Orange/Green
R/Pr	Red/Purple

Voltage regulator/ rectifier

Up trim/tilt relay

Down trim/tilt relay

Starter solenoid

Starter motor

16

60 AND 70 HP REMOTE, POWER TRIM/TILT

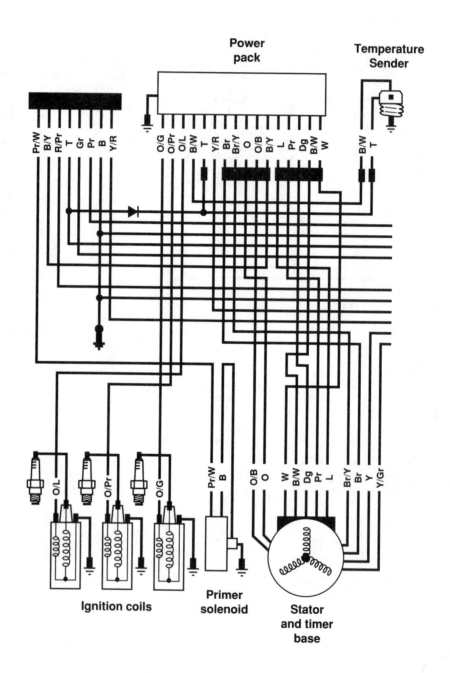

Power pack

Temperature Sender

Pr/W B/Y R/Pr T Gr Pr B Y/R

O/G O/Pr O/L B/W T Y/R Br Br/Y O O/B B/Y L Pr Dg B/W W

B/W T

O/L O/Pr O/G

Pr/W B

O/B O W B/W Dg Pr L Br/Y Br Y Y/Gr

Ignition coils

Primer solenoid

Stator and timer base

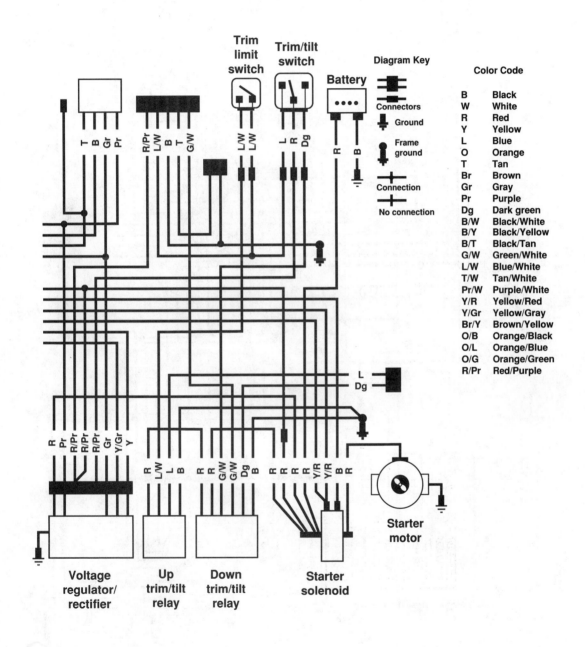

60-70 HP REMOTE START

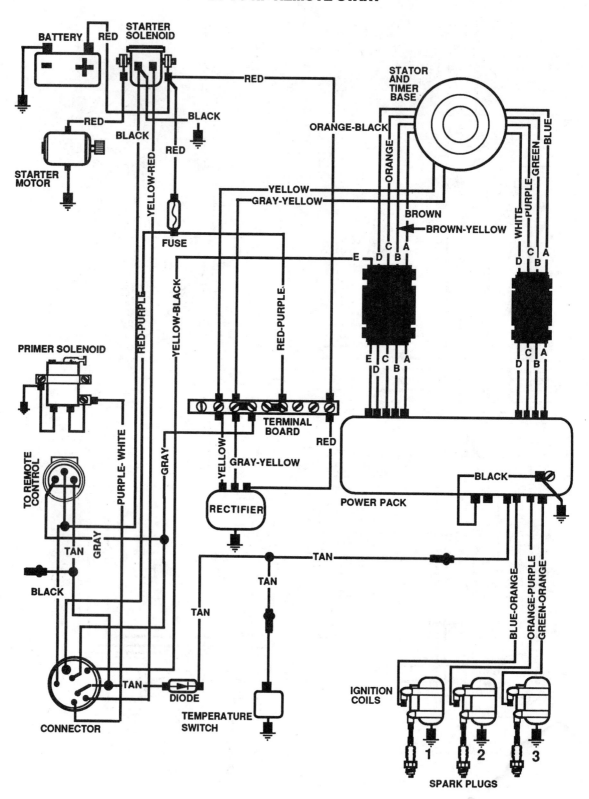

65 JET, 80 JET AND 85-115 HP

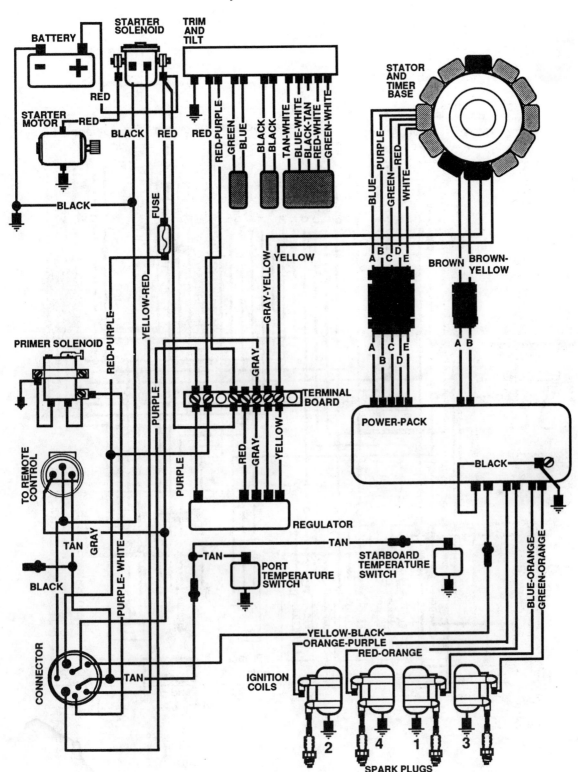

85 HP TILLER HANDLE

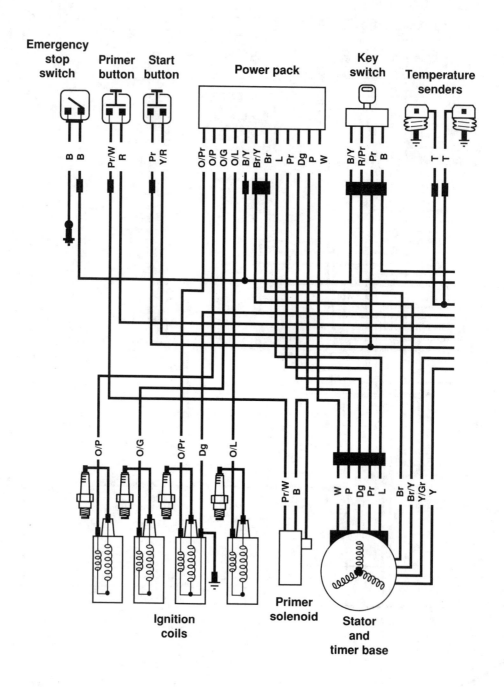

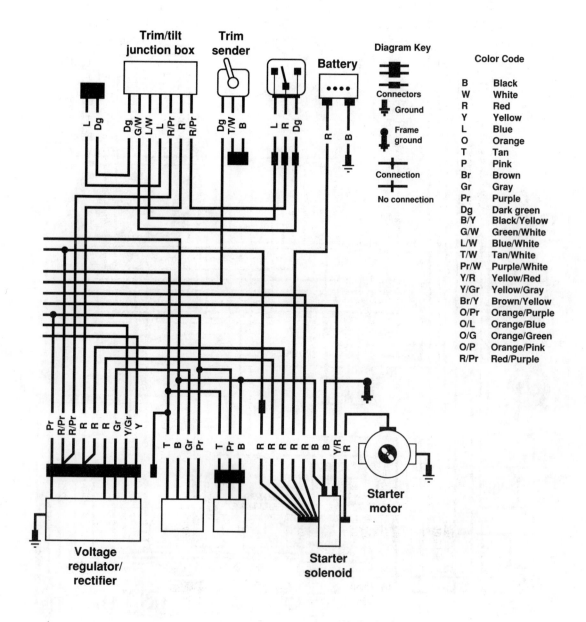

1991 V6 CROSS FLOW 150-175 HP (9 AMP)

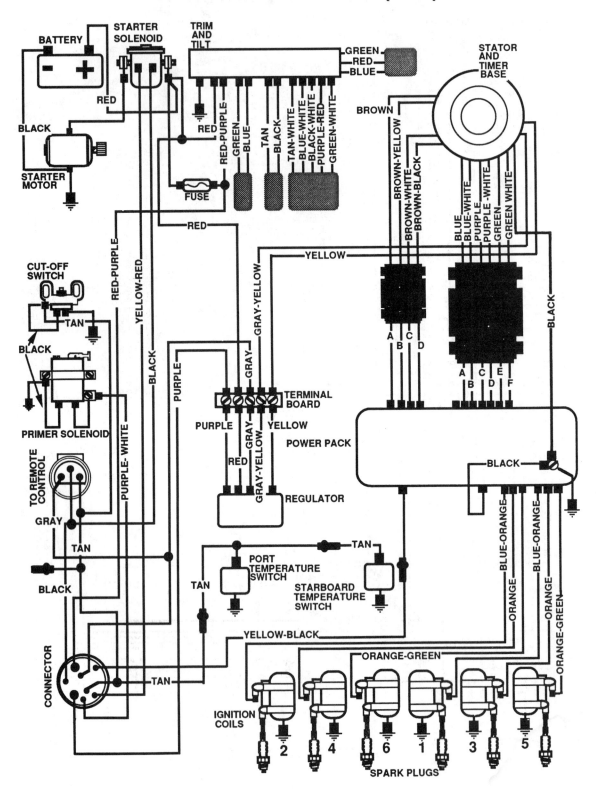

1991 V6 CROSS FLOW 150-175 HP (35 AMP)

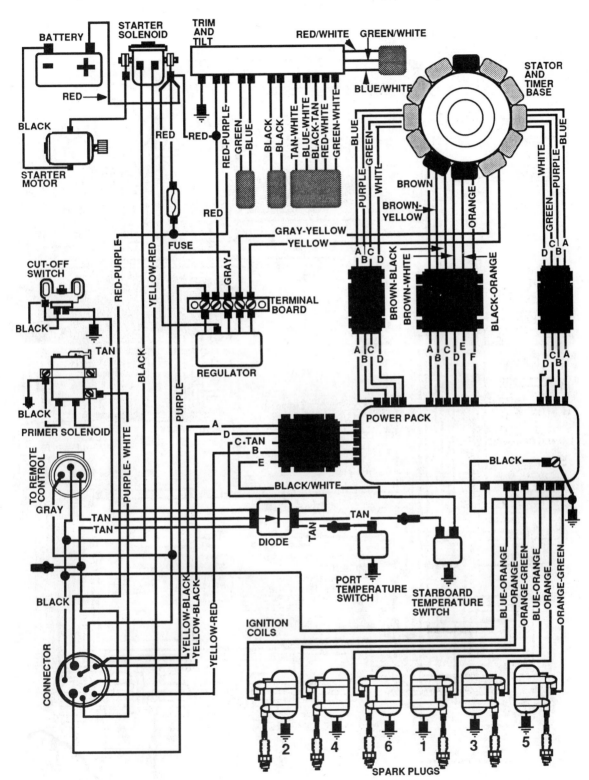

V4 LOOP CHARGED 120-140 HP

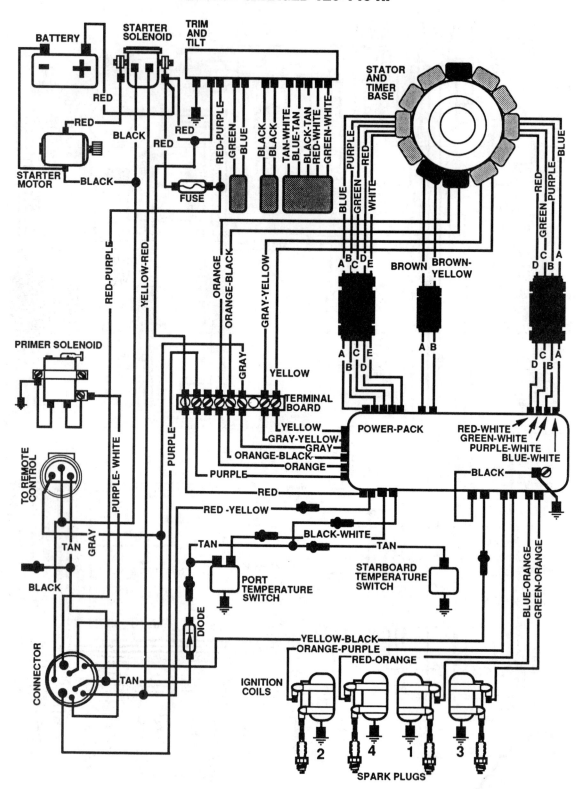

V6 LOOP CHARGED 200-225 HP

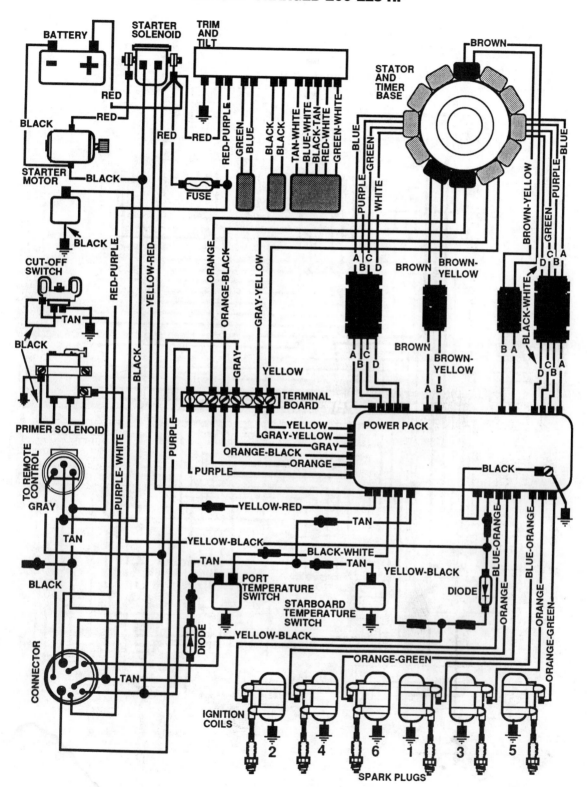

60° V6 150 AND 175 HP

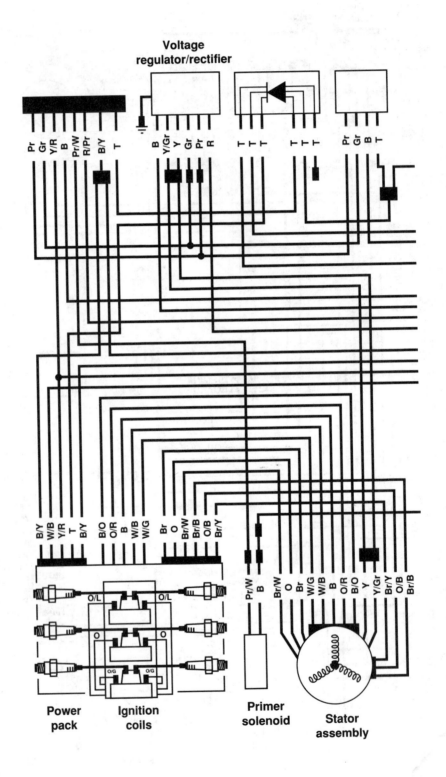

Power pack

Ignition coils

Primer solenoid

Stator assembly

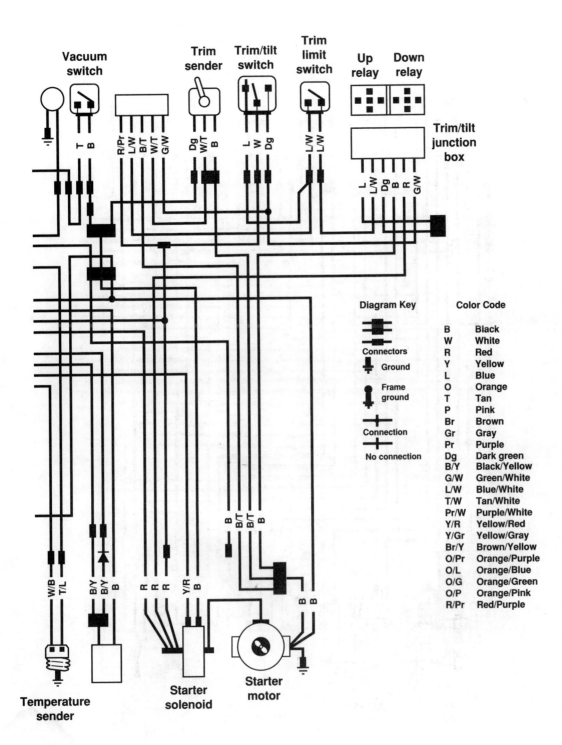

Diagram Key

Connectors

Ground

Frame ground

Connection

No connection

Color Code

B	Black
W	White
R	Red
Y	Yellow
L	Blue
O	Orange
T	Tan
P	Pink
Br	Brown
Gr	Gray
Pr	Purple
Dg	Dark green
B/Y	Black/Yellow
G/W	Green/White
L/W	Blue/White
T/W	Tan/White
Pr/W	Purple/White
Y/R	Yellow/Red
Y/Gr	Yellow/Gray
Br/Y	Brown/Yellow
O/Pr	Orange/Purple
O/L	Orange/Blue
O/G	Orange/Green
O/P	Orange/Pink
R/Pr	Red/Purple

Vacuum switch

Trim sender

Trim/tilt switch

Trim limit switch

Up relay

Down relay

Trim/tilt junction box

Temperature sender

Starter solenoid

Starter motor

16

V8 MODELS

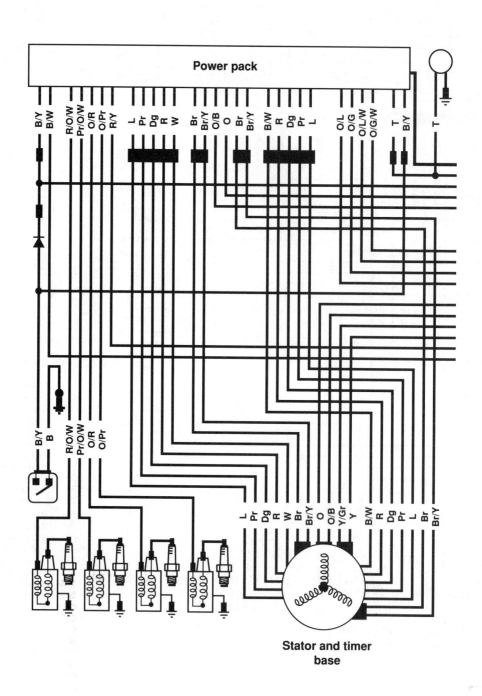

Stator and timer base

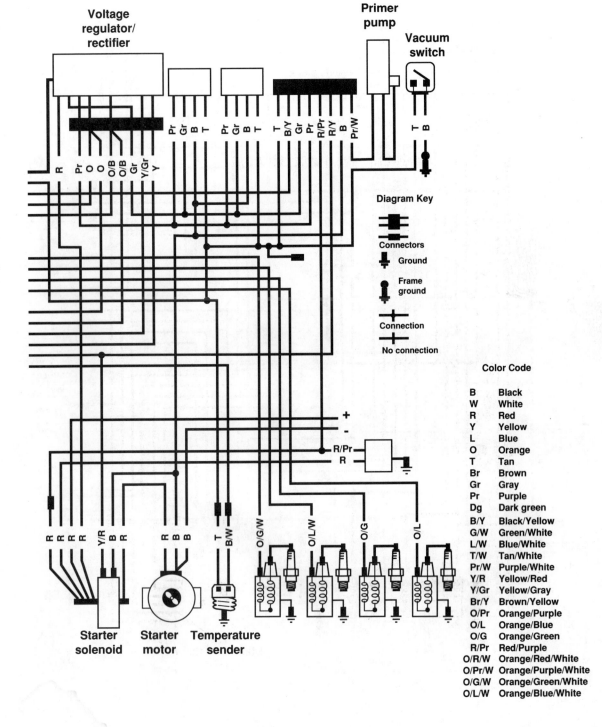

Voltage regulator/rectifier

Primer pump

Vacuum switch

Diagram Key

Connectors

Ground

Frame ground

Connection

No connection

Color Code

B	Black
W	White
R	Red
Y	Yellow
L	Blue
O	Orange
T	Tan
Br	Brown
Gr	Gray
Pr	Purple
Dg	Dark green
B/Y	Black/Yellow
G/W	Green/White
L/W	Blue/White
T/W	Tan/White
Pr/W	Purple/White
Y/R	Yellow/Red
Y/Gr	Yellow/Gray
Br/Y	Brown/Yellow
O/Pr	Orange/Purple
O/L	Orange/Blue
O/G	Orange/Green
R/Pr	Red/Purple
O/R/W	Orange/Red/White
O/Pr/W	Orange/Purple/White
O/G/W	Orange/Green/White
O/L/W	Orange/Blue/White

Starter solenoid

Starter motor

Temperature sender

16

CONVENTIONAL POWER TRIM/TILT

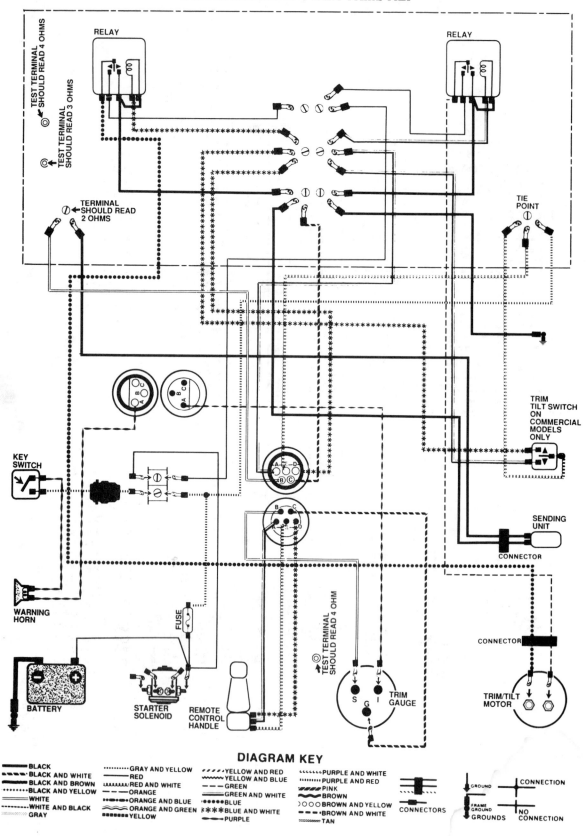

DIAGRAM KEY

BLACK	GRAY AND YELLOW	YELLOW AND RED	PURPLE AND WHITE	CONNECTION
BLACK AND WHITE	RED	YELLOW AND BLUE	PURPLE AND RED	
BLACK AND BROWN	RED AND WHITE	GREEN	PINK	
BLACK AND YELLOW	ORANGE	GREEN AND WHITE	BROWN	
WHITE	ORANGE AND BLUE	BLUE	BROWN AND YELLOW	
WHITE AND BLACK	ORANGE AND GREEN	BLUE AND WHITE	BROWN AND WHITE	
GRAY	YELLOW	PURPLE	TAN	CONNECTORS	GROUND / FRAME GROUND / GROUNDS / NO CONNECTION

FASTRAK POWER TRIM/TILT

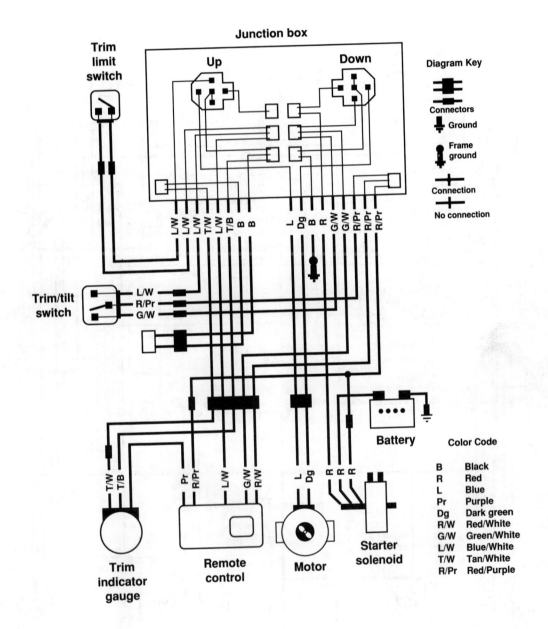

Junction box

Up   Down

Trim limit switch

Trim/tilt switch

Trim indicator gauge

Remote control

Motor

Starter solenoid

Battery

Diagram Key

Connectors

Ground

Frame ground

Connection

No connection

Color Code

B	Black
R	Red
L	Blue
Pr	Purple
Dg	Dark green
R/W	Red/White
G/W	Green/White
L/W	Blue/White
T/W	Tan/White
R/Pr	Red/Purple

16

SEA DRIVE SELECTRIM/TILT

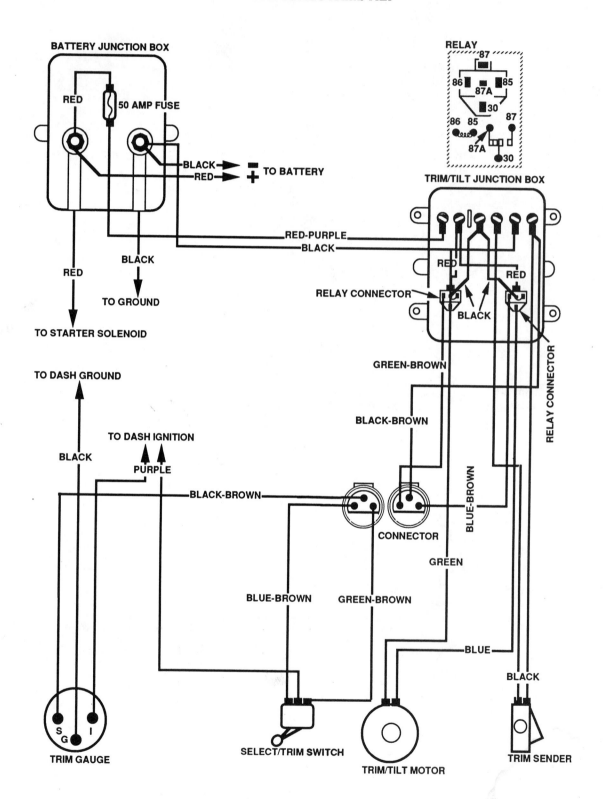

NOTES

MAINTENANCE LOG

Service Performed	Mileage Reading				
Oil change (example)	2,836	5,782	8,601		

← Barcode